# Literature
# Criticism from
# 1400 to 1800

# Guide to Gale Literary Criticism Series

| For criticism on | Consult these Gale series |
|---|---|
| Authors now living or who died after December 31, 1959 | *CONTEMPORARY LITERARY CRITICISM (CLC)* |
| Authors who died between 1900 and 1959 | *TWENTIETH-CENTURY LITERARY CRITICISM (TCLC)* |
| Authors who died between 1800 and 1899 | *NINETEENTH-CENTURY LITERATURE CRITICISM (NCLC)* |
| Authors who died between 1400 and 1799 | *LITERATURE CRITICISM FROM 1400 TO 1800 (LC)* <br><br> *SHAKESPEAREAN CRITICISM (SC)* |
| Authors who died before 1400 | *CLASSICAL AND MEDIEVAL LITERATURE CRITICISM (CMLC)* |
| Black writers of the past two hundred years | *BLACK LITERATURE CRITICISM (BLC)* |
| Authors of books for children and young adults | *CHILDREN'S LITERATURE REVIEW (CLR)* |
| Dramatists | *DRAMA CRITICISM (DC)* |
| Hispanic writers of the late nineteenth and twentieth centuries | *HISPANIC LITERATURE CRITICISM (HLC)* |
| Native North American writers and orators of the eighteenth, nineteenth, and twentieth centuries | *NATIVE NORTH AMERICAN LITERATURE (NNAL)* |
| Poets | *POETRY CRITICISM (PC)* |
| Short story writers | *SHORT STORY CRITICISM (SSC)* |
| Major authors from the Renaissance to the present | *WORLD LITERATURE CRITICISM, 1500 TO THE PRESENT (WLC)* |

ISSN 0740-2880

Volume 31

# Literature Criticism from 1400 to 1800

Criticism of the Works of Fifteenth- through
Eighteenth-Century Novelists, Poets, Playwrights,
Philosophers, and Other Creative Writers

**Jennifer Allison Brostrom,** Editor

**Jelena O. Krstovic´**
**Mary Onorato**
Associate Editors

**Gerald R. Barterian**
Assistant Editor

GALE

*an International Thomson Publishing company* I(T)P®

## STAFF

Jennifer Allison Brostrom, *Editor*

Dana Ramel Barnes, Denise Kasinec, Jelena O. Krstović, Michael Magoulias, Mary L. Onorato, *Associate Editors*

Gerald R. Barterian, Ondine Le Blanc, *Assistant Editors*

Susan M. Trosky, *Managing Editor*

Marlene S. Hurst, *Permissions Manager*
Margaret A. Chamberlain, Maria Franklin, *Permissions Specialists*
Susan Salas, Diane Cooper, Michele Lonoconus, Maureen Puhl, Shalice Shah,
Kimberly F. Smilay, Barbara A. Wallace, *Permissions Associates*
Sarah Chesney, Edna M. Hedblad, Margaret McAvoy-Amato, Tyra Y. Phillips,
Lori Schoenenberger, Rita Velázquez, *Permissions Assistants*

Victoria B. Cariappa, *Research Manager*
Tammy Nott, Tracie A. Richardson, *Research Associates*
Julia C. Daniel, Alicia Noel Biggers, Michelle Lee, Michele Pica, Cheryl Warnock, *Research Assistants*

Mary Beth Trimper, *Production Director*
Deborah Milliken, *Production Assistant*

C. J. Jonik, *Desktop Publisher*
Pamela A. Hayes, *Photography Coordinator*
Robert Duncan, *Scanner Operator*
Randy Bassett, *Image Database Supervisor*

This book is printed on acid-free paper that meets the minimum requirements of American National Standard for Information Sciences—Permanence Paper for Printed Library Materials, ANSI Z39.48-1984.

Library of Congress Catalog Card Number 94-29718
ISBN 0-8103-9276-3
ISSN 0740-2880
Printed in the United States of America

ITP™ Gale Research, an ITP Information/Reference Group Company.
ITP logo is a trademark under license.

10 9 8 7 6 5 4 3 2 1

# Contents

Preface   vii

Acknowledgments   xi

# Preface

*L*iterature Criticism from 1400 to 1800 (LC) presents criticism of world authors of the fifteenth through eighteenth centuries. The literature of this period reflects a turbulent time of radical change that saw the rise of modern European drama, the birth of the novel and personal essay forms, the emergence of newspapers and periodicals, and major achievements in poetry and philosophy. Many of these historical forces continue to influence modern art and society. *LC,* therefore, provides valuable insight into the art, life, thought, and cultural transformations that took place during these centuries.

## Scope of the Series

*LC* provides an introduction to the great poets, dramatists, novelists, essayists, and philosophers of the fifteenth through eighteenth centuries; and to the most significant interpretations of these authors' works. Because criticism of this literature spans nearly six hundred years, an overwhelming amount of scholarship confronts the student. *LC* therefore organizes this material into volumes addressing specific historical and cultural topics, for example, "Literature of the Spanish Golden Age," or "Literature and the New World." Every attempt is made to reprint the most noteworthy, relevant, and educationally valuable essays available.

Readers should note that there is a separate Gale reference series devoted exclusively to Shakespearean studies. Although belonging properly to the period covered in *LC,* William Shakespeare has inspired such a tremendous and ever-growing corpus of secondary material that the editors have deemed it best to give his works extensive coverage in a separate series, *Shakespearean Criticism.*

Each author entry in *LC* presents a survey of critical response to an author's oeuvre. Early criticism is offered to indicate initial responses, later selections document any rise or decline in literary reputations, and retrospective analyses provide students with modern views. The size of each author entry is a relative reflection of the scope of criticism available in English. Every attempt has been made to identify and include the seminal essays on each author's work and to include recent commentary providing modern perspectives.

The need for *LC* among students and teachers of literature and history was suggested by the proven usefulness of Gale's *Contemporary Literary Criticism (CLC), Twentieth-Century Literary Criticism (TCLC),* and *Nineteenth-Century Literature Criticism (NCLC),* which excerpt criticism of works by nineteenth- and twentieth-century authors. There is no duplication of critical material in any of these literary criticism series. Major authors may appear more than once in one or more of the series because of the great quantity of critical material available, and his or her relevance to a variety of thematic topics.

## Thematic Approach

Beginning with Volume 12, all the authors in each volume of *LC* are organized around such themes as specific literary or philosophical movements, writings surrounding important political and historical events, the philosophy and art associated with eras of cultural transformation, and the literature of specific social or ethnic groups. Each volume contains a topic entry providing a historical and literary overview, and several author entries, which examine major representatives of the featured period.

# Organization of the Book

Each entry consists of the following elements: author or thematic heading, introduction, list of principal works, annotated works of criticism (each preceded by a bibliographical citation), and a bibliography of further reading. Also, most author entries contain author portraits and other illustrations.

- The **Author Heading** consists of the author's full name, followed by birth and death dates. (If an author wrote consistently under a pseudonym, the pseudonym is used in the author heading, with the real name given in parentheses on the first line of the biographical and critical introduction.) Also located here are any name variations under which an author wrote, including transliterated forms for authors whose native languages use nonroman alphabets. Uncertain birth or death dates are indicated by question marks. Topic entries are preceded by a **Thematic Heading,** which simply states the subject of the entry.

- The **Introduction** to each entry provides social and historical background important to understanding the criticism, and an overview of the biography and career of the featured author.

- Most *LC* author entries include **Portraits** of the author. Many entries also contain illustrations of materials pertinent to an author's career, including author holographs, title pages, letters, or representations of important people, places, and events in an author's life.

- The **List of Principal Works** is ordered chronologically, by date of first book publication, identifying the genre of each work. In the case of foreign authors whose works have been translated into English, the title and date of the first English-language edition are given in brackets beneath the foreign-language listing. Unless otherwise indicated, dramas are dated by first performance, not first publication.

- **Criticism** is arranged chronologically in each author entry to provide a useful perspective on changes in critical evaluation over time. For the purpose of easy identification, the critic's name and the date of first composition or publication of the critical work are given at the beginning of each piece of criticism. Unsigned criticism is preceded by the title of the source in which it appeared. All titles by the author featured in the critical entry are printed in boldface type. Publication information (such as publisher names and book prices) and some parenthetical numerical references (such as footnotes or page and line references to specific editions of works) have been occasionally deleted to provide smoother reading of the text.

- Critical essays are prefaced by **Annotations** as an additional aid to students using *LC*. These explanatory notes may provide several types of useful information, including: the reputation of a critic, the importance of a work of criticism, the commentator's individual approach to literary criticism, the intent of the criticism, and the growth of critical controversy or changes in critical trends regarding an author's work. In some cases, these notes cross-reference the work of critics within the entry who agree or disagree with each other.

- A complete **Bibliographical Citation** of the original essay or book follows each piece of criticism.

- An annotated bibliography of **Further Reading** appears at the end of each entry and suggests resources for additional study. In some cases, significant essays for which the editors could not obtain reprint rights are included here.

# Cumulative Indexes

Each volume of *LC* includes a cumulative **Author Index** listing all the authors that have appeared in the following sources published by Gale: *Contemporary Literary Criticism, Twentieth-Century Literary Criticism, Nineteenth-Century Literature Criticism, Literature Criticism from 1400 to 1800,* and *Classical and Medieval Literature Criticism,* along with cross-references to the Gale series *Short Story Criticism, Poetry Criticism, Children's Literature Review, Authors in the News, Contemporary Authors, Contemporary Authors Autobiography Series, Contemporary Authors Bibliographical Series, Dictionary of Literary Biography, Concise Dictionary of Literary Biography, Something about the Author, Something about the Author Autobiography Series,* and *Yesterday's Authors of Books for Children.* Readers will welcome this cumulative author index as a useful tool for locating an author within the various series. The index, which includes authors' birth and death dates, is particularly valuable for those authors who are identified with a certain period but whose death dates cause them to be placed in another, or for those authors whose careers span two periods. For example, F. Scott Fitzgerald is found in *TCLC,* yet a writer often associated with him, Ernest Hemingway, is found in *CLC.*

Beginning with Volume 12, *LC* includes a cumulative **Topic Index** that lists all literary themes and topics treated in *LC, NCLC, TCLC,* and the *CLC* Yearbook. Each volume of *LC* also includes a cumulative **Nationality Index** in which authors' names are arranged alphabetically under their respective nationalities and followed by the numbers of the volumes in which they appear.

Each volume of *LC* also includes a cumulative **Title Index,** an alphabetical listing of all literary works discussed in the series. Each title listing includes the corresponding volume and page numbers where criticism may be located. Foreign-language titles that have been translated followed by the tiles of the translation—for example, *El ingenioso hidalgo Don Quixote de la Mancha (Don Quixote).* Page numbers following these translated titles refers to all pages on which any form of the titles, either foreign-language or translated, appear. Title of novels, dramas, nonfiction books, and poetry, short story, or essays collections are printed in italics, while individual poems, short stories, and essays are printed in roman type within quotation marks.

# A Note to the Reader

When writing papers, students who quote directly from any volume in the Literary Criticism Series may use the following general forms to footnote reprinted criticism. The first example pertains to material drawn from periodicals, the second to material reprinted from books.

T. S. Eliot, "John Donne," *The Nation and the Athenaeum,* 33 (9 June 1923), 321-32; excerpted and reprinted in *Literature Criticism from 1400 to 1800,* Vol. 10, ed. James E. Person, Jr. (Detroit: Gale Research, 1989), pp. 28-9.

Clara G. Stillman, *Samuel Butler: A Mid-Victorian Modern* (Viking Press, 1932); excerpted and reprinted in *Twentieth-Century Literary Criticism,* Vol. 33, ed. Paula Kepos (Detroit: Gale Research, 1989), pp. 43-5.

# Suggestions Are Welcome

Since the series began, features have been added to *LC* in response to various suggestions, including a nationality index, a Literary Criticism Series topic index, and thematic organization of entries.

Readers who wish to suggest new features, themes or authors to appear in future volumes, or who have other suggestions, are cordially invited to write to the editor.

# Acknowledgments

The editors wish to thank the copyright holders of the excerpted criticism included in this volume, and the permissions managers of many book and magazine publishing companies for assisting us in securing reprint rights. We are also grateful to the staffs of the Detroit Public Library, the Library of Congress, the University of Detroit Mercy Library, Wayne State University Purdy/Kresge Library Complex, and the University of Michigan Libraries for making their resources available to us. Following is a list of the copyright holders who have granted us permission to reprint material in this volume of **LC**. Every effort has been made to trace copyright, but if omissions have been made, please let us know.

## COPYRIGHTED EXCERPTS IN *LC,* VOLUME 31, WERE REPRINTED FROM THE FOLLOWING PERIODICALS:

**Comparative Literature Studies**, v. XIII, June, 1976. Copyright © 1976 by The Pennsylvania State University. Reproduced by permission of The Pennsylvania State University Press.—*Criticism,* v. XXXIV, Fall, 1992 for "Imperialist Beginnings: Richard Hakluyt and the Construction of Africa" by Emily C. Bartels. Copyright, 1992, Wayne State University Press. Reprinted by permission of the publisher and the author.—*Dispositio,* v. XI, 1986. © Department of Romance Languages, University of Michigan. Reprinted by permission of the publisher.—*English Literary Renaissance,* v. 20, Spring, 1990. Copyright © 1990 by English Literary Renaissance. Reprinted by permission of the publisher.—*The Guardian Weekly,* v. 135, December 28, 1986. Copyright © 1986 by Guardian Publications Ltd. Reprinted by permission of the publisher.—*The Hispanic American Historical Review,* v. 25, February, 1945. Copyright 1945, renewed 1972 by Duke University Press. Reprinted by permission of the publisher.—*The New York Review of Books,* v. XXII, May 15, 1975. Copyright © 1975 Nyrev, Inc. Reprinted with permission from The New York Review of Books.—*Novel: A Forum on Fiction,* v. 15, Spring, 1982. Copyright NOVEL Corp. © 1982. Reprinted with permission.—*Prose Studies,* v. 6, December, 1983. © Frank Cass & Co. Ltd. 1983. Reprinted by permission of Frank Cass & Co. Ltd.—*Representations,* v. 33, Winter, 1991 for " *Fierce and Unnatural Cruelty*: Cortés and the Conquest of Mexico" by Inga Clendinnen; v. 33, Winter, 1991 for "The Work of Gender in the Discourse of Discovery" by Louis Montrose. © 1991 by The Regents of the University of California. Both reprinted by permission of the publisher and the respective authors.—*Theological Studies,* v. 53, June, 1992. Reprinted by permission of the publisher.—*The Times Educational Supplement,* September 25, 1981. © The Times Supplements Limited 1981. Reproduced from The Times Educational Supplement by permission.—*The William and Mary Quarterly,* third series, v. XLI, April, 1984; v. XLIX, April, 1992. Copyright, 1984, 1992 by the Institute of Early American History and Culture. Both reprinted by permission of the Institute.

## COPYRIGHTED EXCERPTS IN *LC,* VOLUME 31, WERE REPRINTED FROM THE FOLLOWING BOOKS:

Anderson, Douglas. From *A House Divided: Domesticity and Community in American Literature*. Cambridge University Press, 1990. © Cambridge University Press 1990. Reprinted with the permission of the publisher and the author.—Bernal, Díaz. From *The Conquest of New Spain*. Translated by J. M. Cohen. Penguin Books, 1963. Copyright © J. M. Cohen, 1963. Renewed 1991 by Audrey Cohen. All rights reserved.—Edwards, Philip. From *Sir Walter Raleigh*. Longmans, Green and Co., 1953. Reprinted by permission of the publisher.—Elliott, J. H. From *The Old World and the New: 1492-1650*. Cambridge at the University Press, 1970. © Cambridge University Press 1970. Reprinted with the permission of the publisher and the author.—Enzensberger, Hans Magnus. From "Las Casas, or a Look Back into the Future," translated by Michael Roloff, in *The Devastation of the Indies: A Brief Account*. By Bartolomé de Las Casas, edited by Michael Roloff, translated by Herma Briffault. Seabury Press, 1974. English translations copyright © 1974 by The

xi

# The New World in Renaissance Literature

## INTRODUCTION

The revelation of America as a newly-discovered continent challenged fundamental aspects of the Renaissance worldview while introducing a new body of ideas and myths into European thought. Strongly influential in shaping perceptions of the New World were the published diaries and letters of such explorers as Sir Walter Raleigh and Hernán Cortés, which documented the course of exploration voyages and the characteristics of the new land and its inhabitants. The literary outgrowths of these popular writings included the expansion of travel literature, fictional genres including the imaginary voyage and the prose romance, and the imaginary societies depicted in Renaissance utopian literature.

Contemporary critics have noted that Renaissance exploration chronicles are characterized by the imposition of European images and values onto an unfamiliar world—explorers often recorded only what they expected to see, overlooking or severely altering features of the American landscape and Native American culture for which they had no familiar reference point. The Christian tradition, for example, contributed to the early conception of America as an Edenic land populated by "peaceful and innocent children", free from the corruption of material possessions and government. Conversely, as conflicts arose between Europeans and Natives, Indians were widely regarded as "children of Satan" who symbolized the dangerous implications of a world free of law or religion. The Renaissance idea of progress was also influential in depictions of the New World. Percy G. Adams commented: "Very early in the sixteenth century, the discovery of America became a symbol of discovery and invention in general as well as evidence to historians of the New World that their age had made advances over former ages." Such notions as manifest destiny, which have been formative in shaping the course of American history, find their roots in the earliest European colonization efforts and writings that promoted the myth of a European mandate from God to Christianize and profit from the New World.

---

## REPRESENTATIVE WORKS

Columbus, Christopher
  *Diario del primer viaje* [*Journal of the First Voyage*] 1492-1493

Cortés, Hernán
  *Cartas de relación de la conquista de Méjico* [*Letters from Mexico*] 1519-1526
Díaz del Castillo, Bernal
  *Historia Verdadera de la conquista de la Nueva España* 1632
Gómara, Franciso López
  *Historia General de las Indias* 1552
Hakluyt, Richard
  *The Principal Navigations, Voyages, Traffiques, and Discoveries of the English Nation* 1599
Harris, John
  *Navigantium atque Itinerantium Bibliotheca; or, a Compleat Collection of Voyages and Travels* 1705
Las Casas, Bartolomé de
  *Historia de Las Indias* [*History of the Indies*] c. 1527
  *Brevísima relación de la destrucción de las Indias* [*The Devastation of the Indies: A Brief Account*] 1552
Montaigne, Michel Eyquem de
  *Essais* [*Essays*] 1572-80
Raleigh, Sir Walter
  *The Discoverie of the Large, Rich and Bewtiful Empire of Guiana* 1596
Robertson, William
  *History of America* 1777
Waldseemüller, Martin
  *Cosmographiae Introductio* 1507
Winthrop, John
  *A Journal of the Transactions and Occurrences in the Settlement of Massachusetts and the Other New-England Colonies, from the Year 1630 to 1644* 1790

*Montaigne discusses the New World in his essays "Of Cannibals" and "Of Coaches."

## J. H. Elliott (essay date 1970)

SOURCE: "The Uncertain Impact," in *The Old World and the New: 1492-1650,* Cambridge at the University Press, 1970, pp. 1-27.

[*In the following essay, Elliott considers the impact of the New World on European thought during the Renaissance, and suggests that "tradition, experience, and expectation were the determinants of vision."*]

Nearly three hundred years after Columbus's first voyage of discovery, the Abbé Raynal, that eager inquirer

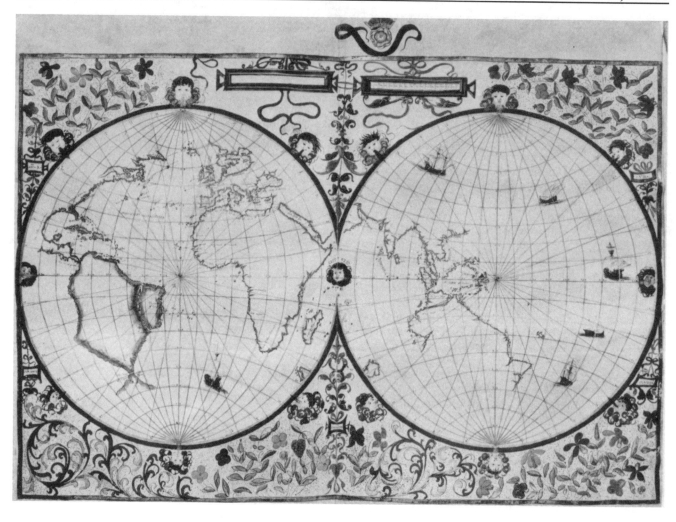

*A map of the world, from the atlas made by John Rotz for Henry VIII, 1542.*

after other men's truths, offered a prize for the essay which would best answer the following questions. Has the discovery of America been useful or harmful to mankind? If useful, how can its usefulness be enhanced? If harmful, how can the harm be diminished? Cornelius De Pauw had recently described the discovery of the New World [in *Recherches Philosophiques sur les Américains,* in *Œuvres Philosophiques*, 1794] as the most calamitous event in human history, and Raynal was taking no chances. 'No event', he had cautiously begun his vast and laborious *Philosophical and Political History of the Settlements and Trade of the Europeans in the East and West Indies* (1770), 'has been so interesting to mankind in general, and to the inhabitants of Europe in particular, as the discovery of the new world, and the passage to India by the Cape of Good Hope.' It took the robust Scottish forthrightness of Adam Smith [in *The Wealth of Nations,* 1776], whose view of the impact of the discoveries was generally favourable, to turn this non-committal passage into an *ex cathedra* historical pronouncement, 'the discovery

of America, and that of a passage to the East Indies by the Cape of Good Hope, are the two greatest and most important events recorded in the history of mankind'.

But in what, precisely, did their importance lie? As the candidates for Raynal's essay prize soon found out for themselves, this was by no means easy to decide. Of the eight essays which have survived, four took an optimistic view of the consequences of America's discovery, and dwelt at length on the resulting commercial advantages. But optimists and pessimists alike tended to wander uncertainly through three centuries of European history, anxiously searching for pieces of stray ammunition with which to bombard their predetermined targets. In the end, it was perhaps not surprising that standards were considered insufficiently high, and no prize was awarded.

Raynal's formulation of his questions no doubt tended to prompt philosophical speculation and dogmatic assertion, rather than rigorous historical inquiry. But this was less easily evaded in 1792, when the Académie Française asked competitors to examine the influence of America on the 'politics, commerce and customs of Europe'. It is difficult not to sympathize with the sentiments of the anonymous prize-winner. 'What a vast and inexhaustible subject', he sighed. 'The more one studies it, the more it grows.' Nevertheless, he succeeded in covering a great deal of ground in his eighty-six pages. As might have been expected, he was happier with America's political and economic influence on Europe than with its moral influence, which he regarded as pernicious. But he showed himself aware of the concealed danger in this enterprise—the danger of attributing all the major changes in modern European history to the discovery of America. He also made a genuine attempt, in language which may not sound totally unfamiliar to our own generation, to weigh up the profits and the losses of discovery and settlement. 'If those Europeans who devoted their lives to developing the resources of America had instead been employed in Europe in clearing forests, and building roads, bridges and canals, would not Europe have found in its own bosom the most important objects which it derives from the other world, or their equivalent? And what innumerable products would the soil of Europe not have yielded, if it had been brought to the degree of cultivation of which it is capable?'

In a field where there are so many variables, and where the qualitative and the quantitative are so inextricably interwoven, even the modern arts of econometric history cannot do much to help us assess the relative costs and benefits involved in the discovery and exploitation of America by Europe. Yet the impossibility of precise measurement should not be allowed to act as a deterrent to the study of a subject which has been regarded, at least since the late eighteenth century, as central to the history of Europe and the modern world.

For all the interest and importance of the theme, the historiography of the impact of America on Europe has enjoyed a distinctly chequered career. The eighteenth-century debate was conducted in terms which suggest that the participants were more concerned to confirm and defend their personal prejudices about the nature of man and society than to obtain a careful historical perspective on the contribution of the New World to Europe's economic and cultural development. It was not until Humboldt published his *Cosmos* in 1845 that the reactions of the first Europeans, and especially of the Spaniards, to the alien environment of America assumed their proper place in a great geographical and historical synthesis, which made some attempt to consider what the revelation of the New World had meant to the Old.

Nineteenth-century historiography did not show any great interest in pursuing Humboldt's more original lines of inquiry. The discovery and settlement of the

New World were incorporated into an essentially Europocentric conception of history, where they were depicted as part of that epic process by which the Renaissance European first became conscious of the world and of man, and then by degrees imposed his own dominion over the newly-discovered races of a newly-discovered world. In this particular story of European history—which was all too easily identified with universal history—there was a tendency to place the principal emphasis on the motives, methods and achievements of the explorers and conquerors. The impact of Europe on the world (which was regarded as a transforming, and ultimately beneficial, impact) seemed a subject of greater interest and concern than the impact of the world on Europe.

Twentieth-century European historiography has tended to pursue a similar theme, although from a very different standpoint. The retreat of European imperialism has led to a reassessment—often very harsh—of the European legacy. At the same time the development of anthropology and archaeology has led to a reassessment—sometimes very favourable—of the pre-European past of former colonial societies. Where European historians once wrote with the confidence born of an innate sense of European superiority, they now write burdened with the consciousness of European guilt.

It is no accident that some of the most important historical work of our own age—preoccupied as it is with the problem of European and non-European, of black and white—should have been devoted to the study of the social, demographic and psychological consequences for non-European societies of Europe's overseas expansion. Perhaps future generations will detect in our concern with these themes some affinity between the historians of the eighteenth and twentieth centuries. For Raynal and his friends were similarly consumed by guilt and by doubt. Their hesitancy in evaluating the consequences of the discovery and conquest of America sprang precisely from the dilemma involved in attempting to reconcile the record of economic and technical progress since the end of the fifteenth century with the record of the sufferings endured by the defeated societies. The very extent of their preoccupation with the great moral issue of their own times, the issue of slavery, helped to create a situation not without its parallels today. For if their preoccupation stimulated them to ask historical questions, it also tempted them to reply with unhistorical answers.

The Académie Française competition of 1792 shows that one of those questions concerned the impact of overseas expansion on Europe itself; and it is not surprising to find a renewed interest in this same question today. As Europe again becomes acutely aware of the ambivalence of its relationship to the outer world, so it also becomes aware of the possibility of seeing itself in a different perspective—as part of a universal community of mankind whose existence has exercised its own subtle and transforming influences on the history of Europe. The awareness is salutary, although it contains an element of narcissism, to which the eighteenth century self-indulgently succumbed. Moreover, where the relationship with America is concerned, this element is likely to be particularly well represented. For this has always been a *special* relationship, in the sense that America was peculiarly the artefact of Europe, as Asia and Africa were not. America and Europe were for ever inseparable, their destinies interlocked.

The part played by the American myth in the spiritual and intellectual development of Europe has now become a commonplace of historical study. In the early years of this century, the impressive work of Gabriel Chinard on America and the exotic dream in French literature [*L'Exotisme Américain dans la Littérature Française au XVIe Siècle,* 1911, and *L'Amérique et le Rêve Exotique dans la Littérature Française au XVIIe et au XVIIIe Siècle,* 1913] revealed in brilliant detail the fluctuating process by which an idealized New World helped to sustain the hopes and aspirations of the Old until the moment when Europe was ready to accept and act upon America's message of renovation and revolution. Chinard's work was complemented and amplified by Geoffrey Atkinson's study of French geographical literature and ideas [*Les Nouveaux Horizons de la Renaissance Française,* 1935], and, more recently, by Antonello Gerbi's massive survey of the eighteenth-century debate on America as a corrupt or an innocent world [*La Disputa del Nuoro Mondo*]. One further book stands out amidst the rapidly growing literature on Europe and the American dream—*The Invention of America,* by the distinguished Mexican philosophical historian, Edmundo O'Gorman, who has ingeniously argued that America was not discovered but invented by sixteenth-century Europeans.

Alongside these contributions to the study of the myth of America in European thought, an increasing amount of attention has been devoted, especially in the Hispanic world, to the writings of the Spanish chroniclers, missionaries and officials, as interpreters of the American scene. A vast amount of close textual study still remains to be undertaken, but enough has already been achieved to confirm the justice of Humboldt's slightly condescending verdict: 'If we carefully examine the original works of the earliest historians of the Conquista, we are astonished at finding in a Spanish author of the sixteenth century, the germs of so many important physical truths.' There are still great opportunities for research into the Spanish texts, as indeed into the general sixteenth-century literature of exploration and discovery. But the most rewarding results of this textual research are likely to come from intelligent attempts to set it into a wider context of information and ideas. The evidence of the texts can tell us much that we still need to know about non-European societies, by providing the essential material for 'ethnohistory', which sets the results of ethnographic study against European historical records. It can also tell us something of interest about European society—about the ideas, attitudes and preconceptions which made up the mental baggage of Early Modern Europeans on their travels through the world. What did they see or fail to see? Why did they react as they did? It is the attempt to suggest answers to some of these questions which makes Margaret Hodgen's recent history of *Early Anthropology in the Sixteenth and Seventeenth Centuries* such an important pioneering work.

This select company of books stands out, not only because of their intrinsic excellence, but also because of the particular line of approach adopted by their authors. All of them have sought, in some way, to relate the European response to the non-European world to the general history of European civilization and ideas. It is here that the most promising opportunities are to be found; and here, too, that there is most need for some kind of reassessment and synthesis. For the literature on the discovery and colonization of the New World is now enormous, but it is also in many respects fragmentary and disconnected, as if it formed a special field of historical study on its own.

[J. R. Hale, in *Renaissance Exploration,* 1968 said that] 'What is lacking in English is an attempt to tie in exploration with European history as a whole'. This lack provides some justification for an attempt to synthesize, in brief compass, the present state of thought about the impact made by the discovery and settlement of America on Early Modern Europe. Any such attempt must clearly lead into several different fields of inquiry, for America impinged on sixteenth- and early seventeenth-century Europe at innumerable points. Its discovery had important *intellectual* consequences, in that it brought Europeans into contact with new lands and peoples, and in so doing challenged a number of traditional European assumptions about geography, theology, history and the nature of man. America also constituted an *economic* challenge for Europe, in that it proved to be at once a source of supply for produce and for objects for which there existed a European demand, and a promising field for the extension of European business enterprise. Finally, the acquisition by European states of lands and resources in America was bound to have important *political* repercussions, in that it affected their mutual relations by bringing about changes in the balance of power.

Any examination of European history in the light of an external influence upon it, carries with it the temptation to find traces of this influence everywhere. But the absence of influence is often at least as revealing as its presence; and if some fields of thought are still curiously untouched by the experience of America, a hundred years or more after its discovery, this too can tell us something about the character of European civilization. From 1492 the New World was always present in European history, although its presence made itself felt in different ways at different times. It is for this reason that America and Europe should not be subjected to a historiographical divorce, however shadowy their partnership may often appear before the later seventeenth century. Properly, their histories should constitute a continuous interplay of two distinctive themes.

One theme is represented by the attempt of Europe to impose its own image, its own aspirations, and its own values, on a newly-discovered world, together with the consequences for that world of its actions. The other treats of the way in which a growing awareness of the character, the opportunities and the challenges represented by the New World of America helped to shape and transform an Old World which was itself striving to shape and transform the New. The first of these themes has traditionally received more emphasis than the second, although, ultimately, the two are equally important and should remain inseparable. But at this moment the second is in need of more historical attention than the first. From around 1650 the histories of Europe and America have been reasonably well integrated. But for the sixteenth and early seventeenth centuries, the significance of America for Europe still awaits a full assessment.

'It is a striking fact', wrote the Parisian lawyer, Etienne Pasquier, in the early 1560s, 'that our classical authors had no knowledge of all this America, which we call New Lands'. With these words he caught something of the importance of America for the Europe of his day. Here was a totally new phenomenon, quite outside the range of Europe's accumulated experience and of its normal expectation. Europeans knew something, however vaguely and inaccurately, about Africa and Asia. But about America and its inhabitants they knew nothing. It was this which differentiated the response of sixteenth-century Europeans to America from that of the fifteenth-century Portuguese to Africa. The nature of the Africans was known, at least in a general way. That of the Americans was not. The very fact of America's existence, and of its gradual revelation as an entity in its own right, rather than as an extension of Asia, constituted a challenge to a whole body of traditional assumptions, beliefs and attitudes. The sheer immensity of this challenge goes a long way towards explaining one of the most striking features of sixteenth-century intellectual history—the apparent slowness of Europe in making the mental adjustments required to incorporate America within its field of vision.

At first sight, the evidence for the existence of a time-lag between the discovery of America and Europe's assimilation of that discovery does not seem entirely clear cut. There is, after all, ample evidence of the excitement provoked in Europe by the news of Columbus's landfall. 'Raise your spirits . . . Hear about the new discovery!' wrote the Italian humanist Peter Martyr to the count of Tendilla and the archbishop of Granada on 13 September 1493 [in *Epistolario de Pedro Mártir de Anglería,*]. Christopher Columbus, he reported, 'has returned safe and sound. He says that he has found marvellous things, and he has produced gold as proof of the existence of mines in those regions.' And Martyr then went on to recount how Columbus had found men who went around naked, and lived content with what nature gave them. They had kings; they fought among each other with staves and bows and arrows; although they were naked, they competed for power, and they married. They worshipped the celestial bodies, but the exact nature of their religious beliefs was still unknown.

That Martyr's excitement was widely shared is indicated by the fact that Columbus's first letter was printed and published nine times in 1493 and had reached some twenty editions by 1500. The frequent printing of this letter and of the reports of later explorers and *conquistadores;* the fifteen editions of Francanzano Montalboddo's collection of voyages, the *Paesi Novamente Retrovati,* first published at Venice in 1507; the great mid-century compilation of voyages by Ramusio—all this testifies to the great curiosity and interest aroused in sixteenth-century Europe by the news of the discoveries.

Similarly, it is not difficult to find resounding affirmations by individual sixteenth-century writers of the magnitude and significance of the events which were unfolding before their eyes. Guicciardini lavished praise on the Spaniards and Portuguese, and especially on Columbus, for the skill and courage 'which has brought to our age the news of such great and unexpected things'. Juan Luis Vives, who was born in the year of America's discovery, wrote in 1531 in the dedication of his *De Disciplinis* to John III of Portugal: 'truly, the globe has been opened up to the human race'. Eight years later, in 1539, the Paduan philosopher Lazzaro Buonamico introduced a theme which would be elaborated upon in the 1570s by the French writer Louis Le Roy, and would become a commonplace of European historiography: 'Do not believe that there exists anything more honourable to our or the preceeding age than the invention of the printing press and the discovery of the new world; two things which I always thought could be compared, not only to Antiquity, but to immortality'. And in 1552 Gómara, in the dedication to Charles V of his *General History of the Indies,* wrote perhaps the most famous, and certainly the most succinct, of all assessments of the significance of 1492: 'The greatest event since the creation of the world (excluding the incarnation and death of Him who created it) is the discovery of the Indies.'

Yet against these signs of awareness must be set the no less striking signs of unawareness of the importance both of the discovery of America and of its discoverer. The historical reputation of Columbus is a subject which has not yet received all the attention it deserves; but the treatment of Columbus by sixteenth-century writers indicates something of the difficulty which they encountered in seeing his achievement in any sort of historical perspective. With one or two exceptions they showed little interest in his personality and career, and some of them could not even get his Christian name right. When he died in Valladolid, the city chronicle failed to record the fact. It seemed as though Columbus might be doomed to oblivion, partly perhaps because he failed to conform to the sixteenth-century canon of the hero-figure, and partly because the true significance of his achievement was itself so hard to grasp.

There were, however, always a few spirits, particularly in his native Italy, who were prepared to give Columbus his due. The determination of his son, Hernando, to perpetuate his memory, and the publication in Venice in 1571 of the famous biography [*Vida del Almiranta Don Cristóbal Colón*], helped to keep his name before the world. When Sir Francis Bacon included a statue of Columbus in the gallery in New Atlantis devoted to the statues of 'all principal inventors', his intended tribute to the discoverer of America was not in fact very original. In his *History of the New World,* published in 1565, the Italian Benzoni alleged that if Columbus had 'lived in the time of the Greeks or of the Romans, or of any other liberal nation, they would have erected a statue'. The same idea was expressed a few years earlier by another of Columbus's compatriots, Ramusio, who in turn probably lifted it from the *History of the Indies,* written by his Spanish friend, Gonzalo Fernández de Oviedo. Recalling famous statues of classical antiquity, Oviedo insisted that Columbus, 'the first discoverer and finder of these Indies', was even more worthy of commemoration. 'As a brave and wise sailor, and a courageous captain, he showed to us this New World, which is so full of gold that thousands of such statues could have been made out of the gold that is sent to Spain. But he is still more worthy of fame and glory for having brought the Catholic faith to these parts . . . .'

Gold and conversion—these were the two most immediate and obvious connotations of America, and those most likely to be associated with the name of its discoverer. It was only by slow degrees that Columbus began to acquire the status of a hero. He figured as the central protagonist in a number of Italian epic poems written in the last two decades of the sixteenth century, and in 1614 he at last appeared as the hero of a Spanish drama, with the publication of Lope de Vega's extraordinary play, *El Nuevo Mundo descubierto por Cristóbal Colón.* Lope shows a genuine historical appreciation of the significance of Columbus's achievement when he puts into the mouth of Ferdinand the Catholic a speech affirming the traditional cosmography of a tripartite globe, and scoffing at the possibility that there might exist a portion of the world still to be discovered. At the same time, his Columbus, as a dreamer mocked by the world, has already started on his career as the romantic hero who becomes the symbol of man's unquenchable spirit of discovery.

There were already intimations of this romanticization of Columbus during the sixteenth century. But more commonly he was set within the framework of a providential interpretation of history, which depicted him as a divinely appointed instrument for the spreading of the gospel—and even here he was likely to find himself relegated to second place by the more obviously heroic figure of Hernán Cortés. But not even the mass-conversion of hitherto unknown peoples was sufficient of itself to ensure a firm place for Columbus, or Cortés, or for the New World, in the European consciousness. In some circles—especially certain humanist and religious circles, and in the merchant communities of some of Europe's leading cities—the interest was intense, although partial, and often specialized, in character. But it seems that the European reading public displayed no overwhelming interest in the newly-discovered world of America.

The evidence for this assertion unfortunately lacks the firm statistical foundation which it should properly possess. At present, the most comprehensive information about sixteenth-century reading tastes comes from France, where Atkinson's survey of geographical literature indicates that between 1480 and 1609 four times as many books were devoted to the Turks and Asia as to America, and that the proportion of books on Asia actually increased in the final decade of his chosen period. For other parts of Europe, conclusions remain impressionistic. In England, there is little sign of literary interest before the 1550s, when the new Anglo-Spanish connection provided a belated stimulus. In Italy, the very considerable interest during the opening phase of the discoveries does not appear to have been maintained beyond the ending of active Italian participation around 1520; but a spate of translations of foreign accounts suggests that it revived sharply after 1550. Except for those with a professional interest in the subject, Spanish authors in the century following the discovery were strangely reticent about the New World. Until the publication in 1569 of the first part of Ercilla's *Araucana,* epic poems recounted the feats of Spanish arms in Italy and Africa, but ignored—to the chagrin of Bernal Díaz—the no less heroic feats of Spanish arms in the Indies. This neglect, in the nation where it is least to be expected, is not easily explained. It may be that neither *conquistadores* of relatively humble origins, nor their barbarian opponents, measured up to the high standards required of epic heroes.

But even if more statistical studies existed, it would not be easy to interpret their conclusions. This is a field in which the attempt to draw qualitative conclusions from quantitative data is more than usually dangerous. A recent investigation has uncovered at least sixty references to America in thirty-nine Polish books and manuscripts of the sixteenth and seventeenth centuries. The number is not unimpressive, but on closer inspection it transpires that the New World constantly reappears in a limited number of contexts—either as a symbol of the exotic, or as a testimonal to the achievements of the church triumphant—and that sixteenth-century Poles were not much interested in America. Conversely, it could be argued that the *qualitative* changes introduced into European thought by accounts of the New World and its peoples, far outweigh the quantity of information at the disposal of the reader. Montaigne was dependent on Gómara's *History of the Indies* for much of his information; but his reading of this one book, in the 1584 edition of the French translation, had profound consequences for his whole approach to the question of conquest and colonization.

In spite of this, it is difficult not to be impressed by the strange lacunae and the resounding silences in many places where references to the New World could reasonably be expected. How are we to explain the absence of any mention of the New World in so many memoirs and chronicles, including the memoirs of Charles V himself? How are we to explain the continuing determination, right up to the last two or three decades of the sixteenth century, to describe the world as if it were still the world as known to Strabo, Ptolemy and Pomponius Mela? How are we to explain the persistent reprinting by publishers, and the continuing use by schools, of classical cosmographies which were known to be outdated by the discoveries? How are we to explain that a man as widely read and as curious as Bodin should have made so little use of the considerable information available to him about the peoples of the New World in the writing of his political and social philosophy?

The reluctance of cosmographers or of social philosophers to incorporate into their work the new information made available to them by the discovery of America provides an example of the wider problem arising from the revelation of the New World to the Old. Whether it is a question of the geography of America, its flora and fauna, or the nature of its inhabitants, the same kind of pattern seems constantly to recur in the European response. It is as if, at a certain point, the mental shutters come down; as if, with so much to see and absorb and understand, the effort suddenly becomes too much for them, and Europeans retreat to the half-light of their traditional mental world.

There is nothing very novel about the form of this sixteenth-century response. Medieval Europe had found it supremely difficult to comprehend and come to terms with the phenomenon of Islam; and the story of the attempt at understanding is an intricate story of the interplay of prejudice, puzzlement and indifference, where there is no clear linear progression, but rather a series of advances and retreats. Nor is this a matter for surprise, for the attempt of one society to comprehend another inevitably forces it to reappraise itself. In his essay on 'Understanding a Primitive Society', Professor Peter Winch writes: 'Seriously to study another way of life is necessarily to seek to extend our own— not simply to bring the other way within the already existing boundaries of our own, because the point about the latter in their present form, is that they *ex hypothesi* exclude that other.' This process is bound to be an agonizing one, involving the jettisoning of many traditional preconceptions and inherited ideas. It is hardly surprising, then, if sixteenth-century Europeans either ignored the challenge or baulked at the attempt. There was, after all, an easier way out, neatly epitomized in 1528 by the Spanish humanist, Hernán Pérez de Oliva, when he wrote [in *Historia de la Invención de las Indias*] that Columbus set out on his second voyage 'to unite the world and give to those strange lands the form of our own'.

'Give to those strange lands the form of our own.' Here, surely, is revealed that innate sense of superiority which has always been the worst enemy of understanding. How can we expect a Europe so conscious of its own infallibility—of its unique status and position in God's providential design—even to make the effort to come to terms with a world other than its own? But this Europe was not the closed Europe of an 'age of ignorance'. Instead, it was Renaissance Europe—the Europe of 'the discovery of the world and of man'. If Renaissance ideas and attitudes played an important part—however elusive it may be to determine exactly *what* part—in prompting Europeans to set out on voyages of discovery and to extend their mental as well as their geographical horizons, might we not expect a new kind of readiness to respond to fresh information and fresh stimuli from a newly-discovered world?

The conclusion does not necessarily follow. In some respects the Renaissance involved, at least in its earlier stages, a closing rather than an opening of the mind. The veneration of antiquity became more slavish; authority staked fresh claims against experience. Both the boundaries and the content of traditional disciplines such as cosmography or social philosophy had been clearly determined by reference to the texts of classical antiquity, which acquired an extra degree of definitiveness when for the first time they were fixed on the printed page. Fresh information from alien sources was therefore liable to seem at worst incredible, at best irrelevant, when set against the accumulated knowledge of the centuries. Given this deference to authority, there was unlikely to be any undue precipitation, least of all in academic circles, to accept the New World into consciousness.

It is also possible that a society which is wrestling—as late medieval Christendom was wrestling—with great spiritual, intellectual and political problems, is too preoccupied with its internal upheavals to devote more than fitful attention to phenomena located on the periphery of its interests. It may be too much to expect such a society to make a further radical adjustment—and one which this time involves the assimilation of an entirely new range of alien experiences. Against this, however, it could be argued that a society which is in movement, and displays symptoms of dissatisfaction, is more likely to show itself capable of absorbing new impressions and experiences than a static society, satisfied with itself, and secure in the assurance of its own superiority.

The degree of success or failure in sixteenth-century Europe's response to the Indies can to some extent be measured by reference to another response in a not dissimilar situation—the response of the Chinese of the T'ang dynasty to the reconquered tropical southern lands of Nam-Viet, which has recently been examined by Professor Edward Schafer, in his remarkable book, *The Vermilion Bird*. His findings suggest that the difficulties confronting colonial officials of seventh-century China and of sixteenth-century Spain in assessing and describing an alien environment were by no means dissimilar, and that the nature of their response was much the same. The Chinese, like the Spaniards, observed and assiduously wrote down their observations, but they were, in Professor Schafer's words, the 'prisoners of their ecological lexicons'. Their minds and imaginations were preconditioned, so that they saw what they expected to see, and ignored or rejected those features of life in the southern lands for which they were mentally unprepared. They found (because they expected to find) the inhabitants barbarian and apelike, and the tropical landscape unalluring. No doubt the tendency to think in clichés is the eternal hallmark of the official mind; but it was only slowly that the unfamiliar environment widened the perceptions of some of the Chinese in the southern lands, and enriched their literature and thought.

There was no European equivalent to the poetically evocative response of the Chinese to their strange new world, but America ultimately extended Europe's mental horizons in other, and perhaps more important, ways. In both instances, however, there was the same initial uncertainty, and the same slowness to respond. Given the great mental adjustments to be made, the response of sixteenth-century Europe was perhaps, after all, not as slow as it sometimes appears to be. Nor was it by any means as slow as might have been anticipated from Christendom's record during the preceding millennium. Early Modern Europe showed itself quicker to

respond to the experience of the New World of America, than Medieval Europe to the experience of the world of Islam. This may suggest that the lessons taught by the Indies were more easily learnt, or that Europe at this moment was more ready to go to school. Probably it was a combination of both. No doubt it is possible to feel impatience at the slowness of the educational process—at the hesitations and the setbacks, and at the blind spots which still existed when the lessons were learnt. But there is also something rather moving about the groping of those sixteenth-century Europeans who sought to come to terms with the lands and peoples that had been so unexpectedly revealed to them on the far side of the Atlantic.

For the obstacles to the incorporation of the New World within Europe's intellectual horizon were formidable. There were obstacles of time and space, of inheritance, environment and language; and efforts would be required at many different levels before they were removed. At least four different processes were involved, each of which raised peculiar difficulties of its own. First of all there was the process of observation, as defined by Humboldt when he wrote: 'To see . . . is not to observe; that is, to compare and classify.' The second process was description—depicting the unfamiliar in such a way that it could be grasped by those who had not seen it. The third was dissemination—the diffusion of new information, new images and new ideas, so that they became part of the accepted stock of mental furniture. And the fourth was comprehension—the ability to come to terms with the unexpected and the unfamiliar, to see them as phenomena existing in their own right, and (hardest of all) to shift the accepted boundaries of thought in order to include them.

If one asks *what* Europeans saw on arriving on the far side of the Atlantic, and *how* they saw it, much will inevitably depend on the kind of Europeans involved. The range of vision is bound to be affected both by background, and by professional interests. Soldiers, clerics, merchants, and officials trained in the law—these are the classes of men on whom we are dependent for most of our first-hand observation of the New World and its inhabitants. Each class had its own bias and its own limitations; and it would be interesting to have a systematic survey of the extent and nature of the bias for each professional group, and of the way in which it was mitigated or altered, in individual cases, by a humanist education.

One Spanish official in the Indies who transcended many of the limitations of his class, and achieved an unusual degree of insight into Quechua society by dint of learning the language, was Juan de Betanzos. In the dedication to his History of the Incas, written in 1551, he spoke of the difficulties he had met in composing the work. There was such a quantity of conflicting information, and he was concerned to find 'how differently the *conquistadores* speak about these things, and how far removed they are from Indian practice. And this I believe to be due to the fact that at that time they were not so much concerned with finding things out as with subjecting and acquiring the land. It was also because, coming new to the Indians, they did not know how to ask questions and find things out, for they lacked knowledge of the language; while the Indians, for their part, were too frightened to give them a full account.'

The professional preoccupations of the *conquistadores,* and the difficulties of conducting any form of effective dialogue with the Indians, are more than enough to account for the deficiencies of their reports as descriptions of the New World and its inhabitants; and it is a piece of unusual good fortune that the conquest of Mexico should have thrown up two soldier-chroniclers as shrewd in their observation and as vivid in their powers of description as Cortés and Bernal Díaz. In Cortés's letters of relation it is possible to see at work the process of observation, in Humboldt's sense of the word, as he attempts to bring the exotic into the range of the familiar by writing of Aztec temples as mosques, or by comparing the marketplace of Tenochtitlán with that of Salamanca. But there are obvious limits to Cortés's capacity as an observer, particularly when it comes to depicting the extraordinary landscape through which his invading army marched.

This failure to describe and communicate the physical characteristics of the New World is not peculiar to Cortés. Admittedly, the failure is by no means complete. The Italian Verrazano conveys a clear impression of the thickly forested character of the North American coast; the French Calvinist minister, Jean de Léry, vividly describes the exotic flora and fauna of Brazil; the Englishman, Arthur Barlowe, conjures up the sights and smells of the trees and flowers on the first Roanoke voyage. Columbus himself shows at times a remarkable gift for realistic observation, although at other times the idealized landscape of the European imagination interposes itself between him and the American scene. But so often the physical appearance of the New World is either totally ignored or else described in the flattest and most conventional phraseology. This off-hand treatment of nature contrasts strikingly with the many precise and acute descriptions of the native inhabitants. It is as if the American landscape is seen as no more than a backcloth against which the strange and perennially fascinating peoples of the New World are dutifully grouped.

This apparent deficiency in naturalistic observation may reflect a lack of interest among sixteenth-century Europeans, and especially those of the Mediterranean world, in landscape and in nature. It may reflect, too, the strength of traditional literary conventions. The Spanish soldier of fortune, Alonso Enríquez de Guzmán, who embarked for the New World in 1534, firmly

announces in his autobiography [*Libro de la Vida y Costumbres de Don Alonso Enríquez de Guzmán*]: 'I will not tell you so much about what I saw as about what happened to me, because . . . this book is simply a book of my experiences.' Unfortunately he proves as good as his word.

Even where Europeans in the New World had the desire to look, and the eyes to see, there is no guarantee that the image which presented itself to them—whether of peoples or of places—necessarily accorded with the reality. Tradition, experience and expectation were the determinants of vision. Even a presumably sober official of the Spanish Crown, Alonso de Zuazo, manages to transmute Hispaniola in 1518 into an enchanted island where the fountains play and the streams are lined with gold, and where nature yields her fruits in marvellous abundance. Bernal Díaz, in many ways so down-to-earth and perceptive an observer, still looks at the conquest of Mexico through the haze of romances of chivalry. Verrazano brilliantly describes the Rhode Island Indians, with their dark hair, their bronzed colouring, their black and lively eyes. But were their faces really as 'gentle and noble as those of classical sculptures', or was this the reaction of a man with a Florentine humanist upbringing, who had already created for himself a mental image of the New World inspired by the Golden Age of antiquity?

It is hard to escape the impression that sixteenth-century Europeans, like the Chinese in the southern lands, all too often saw what they expected to see. This should not really be a cause for surprise or mockery, for it may well be that the human mind has an inherent need to fall back on the familiar object and the standard image, in order to come to terms with the shock of the unfamiliar. The real test comes later, with the capacity to abandon the life-belt which links the unknown to the known. Some Europeans, and especially those who spent a long time in the Indies, did successfully pass this test. Their own dawning realization of the wide divergence between the image and the reality, gradually forced them to abandon their standard images and their inherited preconceptions. For America was a *new* world and a *different* world; and it was this fact of difference which was overwhelmingly borne in upon those who came to know it. 'Everything is very different', wrote Fray Tomás de Mercado in his book of advice to the merchants of Seville; 'the talent of the natives, the disposition of the republic, the method of government and even the capacity to be governed'.

But how to convey this fact of difference, the uniqueness of America, to those who had not seen it? The problem of description reduced writers and chroniclers to despair. There was too much diversity, too many new things to be described, as Fernández de Oviedo constantly complained. 'Of all the things I have seen', he wrote of a bird of brilliant plumage, 'this is the one which has most left me without hope of being able to describe it in words.' Or again of a strange tree—'it needs to be painted by the hand of a Berruguete or some other excellent painter like him, or by Leonardo da Vinci or Andrea Mantegna, famous painters whom I knew in Italy'. But the sheer impossibility of the task itself represented a challenge which could extend the boundaries of perception. Forcing themselves to communicate something of their own delight in what they saw around them, the Spanish chroniclers of the Indies occasionally achieved a pen-picture of startling intimacy and brilliance. What could be more vivid than Las Casas's description [in *Apologética Historia Sumaria*] of himself reading matins 'in a breviary with tiny print' by the light of the Hispaniola fireflies?

Yet there are times when the chroniclers seem cruelly hampered by the inadequacies of their vocabulary; and it is particularly noticeable that the range of colours identifiable by sixteenth-century Europeans seems strictly limited. Again and again travellers express their astonishment at the greenness of America, but can get no further. Just occasionally, as with Sir Walter Raleigh in Guinea, the palette comes to life: 'We sawe birds of all colours, some carnation, some crimson, orenge tawny, purple, greene, watched [i.e. light blue], and of all other sorts both simple and mixt . . .' [*The Discoverie of the Large, Rich and Bewtiful Empyre of Guiana*, 1596]. Jean de Léry, too, can give some idea of the brilliance of plumage of the tropical birds of Brazil. But Léry possesses a quite unusual capacity for putting himself in the position of a European who has never crossed the Atlantic and is forced to envisage the New World from travellers' accounts. He instructs his readers [in his *Voyage fait en la Terre du Bresil*], for instance, how to conceive of a Brazilian savage. 'Imagine in your mind a naked, well-formed and well-proportionated man, with all the hair on his body plucked out . . . his lips and cheeks pierced by pointed bones or green stones, pendants hanging from his pierced ears, his body painted . . . his thighs and legs blackened with dye . . .' Yet even Léry admits defeat in the end. 'Their gestures and countenances are so different from ours, that I confess to my difficulty in representing them in words, or even in pictures. So, to enjoy the real pleasure of them, you will have to go and visit them in their country.'

Pictures, as Léry implied, could aid the imagination. Trained artists who accompanied expeditions to the Indies—like John White, on the Roanoke voyage of 1585, and Frans Post, who followed Prince John Maurice of Nassau to Brazil in 1637—might at least hope to capture something of the New World for those who had not seen it. But the problems of the artist resembled those of the chronicler. His European background and training were likely to determine the nature of his vision; and the techniques and the colour range with which he had familiarized himself at home were not

necessarily adequate to represent the new and often exotic scenes which he now set out to record. Frans Post, trained in the sober Dutch tradition, and carefully looking down the wrong end of his telescope to secure a concentrated field of vision, did manage to capture a fresh, if somewhat muted, image of the New World during his stay in Brazil. But once he was back in Europe, with its own tastes and expectations, the vision began to fade.

Even where the observer depicted a scene with some success, either in paint or in prose, there was no guarantee that his work would reach the European public in an accurate form, or in any form at all. The caprice of publishers and the obsession of governments with secrecy, meant that much information about the New World, which might have helped to broaden Europe's mental horizons, failed to find its way into print. Illustrations had to run further hazards peculiar to themselves. The European reader was hardly in a position to obtain a reliable picture of life among the Tupinambá savages of Brazil when the illustrations in his book included scenes of Turkish life, because the publisher happened to have them in stock. Nor was the technique of woodcuts sufficiently advanced, at least until the second half of the sixteenth century, to allow a very faithful reproduction of the original drawing. Above all, the existence of a middleman between the artist and his public could all too easily distort and transform the image he was commissioned to reproduce. Readers dependent on De Bry's famous engravings for their image of the American Indian could be forgiven for assuming that the forests of America were peopled by heroic nudes, whose perfectly proportioned bodies made them first cousins of the ancient Greeks and Romans.

In spite of all the problems involved in the dissemination of accurate information about America, the greatest problem of all, however, remained that of comprehension. The expectations of the European reader, and hence of the European traveller, were formed out of the accumulated images of a society which had been nurtured for generations on tales of the fantastic and the marvellous. When Columbus first set eyes on the inhabitants of the Indies, his immediate reaction was that they were not in any way monstrous or physically abnormal. It was a natural enough reaction for a man who still half belonged to the world of Mandeville.

The temptation was almost overpoweringly strong to see the newly-discovered lands in terms of the enchanted isles of medieval fantasy. But it was not only the fantastic that tended to obtrude itself between the European and reality. If the unfamiliar were to be approached as anything other than the extraordinary and the monstrous, then the approach must be conducted by reference to the most firmly established elements in Europe's cultural inheritance. Between them, therefore, the Christian and the classical traditions were likely to prove the obvious points of departure for any evaluation of the New World and its inhabitants.

In some respects, both of these traditions could assist Europeans in coming to terms with America. Each provided a possible norm or yardstick, other than those immediately to hand in Renaissance Europe, by which to judge the land and the peoples of the newly-discovered world. Some of the more obvious categories for classifying the inhabitants of the Antilles were clearly inapplicable. These people were not monstrous; and their hairlessness made it difficult to identify them with the wild men of the popular medieval tradition. Nor were they Negroes or Moors, the races best known to medieval Christendom. In these circumstances, it was natural for Europeans to look back into their own traditions, and seek to evaluate the puzzling world of the Indies by reference to the Garden of Eden or the Golden Age of antiquity.

The reverence of late medieval Europeans for their Christian and classical traditions had salutary consequences for their approach to the New World, in that it enabled them to set it into some kind of perspective in relation to themselves, and to examine it with a measure of tolerant interest. But against these possible advantages must be set certain obvious disadvantages, which in some ways made the task of assimilation appreciably harder. Fifteenth-century Christendom's own sense of self-dissatisfaction found expression in the longing for a return to a better state of things. The return might be to the lost Christian paradise, or to the Golden Age of the ancients, or to some elusive combination of both these imagined worlds. With the discovery of the Indies and their inhabitants, who went around naked and yet—in defiance of the Biblical tradition—mysteriously unashamed, it was all too easy to transpose the ideal world from a world remote in time to a world remote in space. Arcadia and Eden could now be located on the far shores of the Atlantic.

The process of transposition began from the very moment that Columbus first set eyes on the Caribbean Islands. The various connotations of paradise and the Golden Age were present from the first. Innocence, simplicity, fertility and abundance—all of them qualities for which Renaissance Europe hankered, and which seemed so unattainable—made their appearance in the reports of Columbus and Vespucci, and were eagerly seized upon by their enthusiastic readers. In particular, they struck an answering chord in two worlds, the religious and the humanist. Despairing of the corruption of Europe and its ways, it was natural that certain members of the religious orders should have seen an opportunity for reestablishing the primitive church of the apostles in a New World as yet uncorrupted by European vices. In the revivalist and apocalyptic tradition of the friars, the twin themes of the new world and the end of the world harmoniously blended in the great task of evangelizing the uncounted millions who knew nothing of the Faith.

The humanists, like the friars, projected onto America their disappointed dreams. In the *Decades* of Peter Martyr, the first popularizer of America and its myth, the Indies have already undergone their subtle transmutation. Here were a people who lived without weights and measures and 'pestiferous moneye, the seed of innumerable myscheves. So that if we shall not be ashamed to confesse the truthe, they seem to lyve in the goulden worlde of the which owlde wryters speake so much: wherein men lyved simplye and innocentlye without inforcement of lawes, without quarrelling Iudges and libelles, contente onely to satisfie nature, without further vexation for knowledge of thinges to come.'

It was an idyllic picture, and the humanists made the most of it, for it enabled them to express their deep dissatisfaction with European society, and to criticize it by implication. America and Europe became antitheses—the antitheses of innocence and corruption. And the corrupt was destroying the innocent. In his recently discovered *History of the Discovery of the Indies*, written in 1528, Pérez de Oliva makes the Indian *caciques* express their plight in speeches that might have been written for them by Livy. By emphasizing their fortitude and nobility of character, he effectively points the contrast between the innocence of the alleged barbarians, and the barbarism of their supposedly civilized conquerors. It was a device which was employed at almost the same moment by another Spanish humanist, who may also have been thinking of the horrors of the conquest—Antonio de Guevara in his famous story of the Danube peasant. As Sir Thomas More had already shown, the overseas discoveries could be used to suggest fundamental questions about the values and the standards of a civilization which was perhaps beyond reform.

But by treating the New World in this way, the humanists were closing the door to understanding an alien civilization. America was not as they imagined it; and even the most enthusiastic of them had to accept from an early stage that the inhabitants of this idyllic world could also be vicious and bellicose, and sometimes ate each other. This of itself was not necessarily sufficient to quench utopianism, for it was always possible to build Utopia on the far side of the Atlantic if it did not already exist. For a moment it seemed as if the dream of the friars and the humanists would find its realization in Vasco de Quiroga's villages of Santa Fe in Mexico. But the dream was a European dream, which had little to do with the American reality. As that reality came to impinge at an increasing number of points, so the dream began to fade.

**Hugh Honour on the lack of objectivity that characterized depictions of the New World by Renaissance artists:**

From the very beginning the American reality seems to have been too strange, too alien for most Europeans, and especially artists, to assimilate. . . .The study of antiquity and the sciences were interdependent in the Renaissance, and the widening horizons opened up by scientific and geographical discoveries were scanned through classical lenses. Just as botanists earnestly tried to identify plants from the New World with those mentioned by Dioscorides and Pliny, so artists strove to fit America into a classical scheme of things artistically. An extreme example of this is provided by Peter Paul Rubens in his evocation of Potosí, painted in 1635, with classical gods and goddesses completely overshadowing the monkeys and parrots and the Peruvians emerging from the silver mines. The European visions of both the classical past and of America were, of course, partly, perhaps largely, wish-fulfillment dreams. But the former was static, the latter constantly developing. And whereas Europeans tended to regard Antiquity as their parent, to be revered, America was their child—the inheritor and repository of their own virtues and vices, aspirations and fears.

*Hugh Honour  in an introduction to* The European Vision of America, *The Cleveland Museum of Art, 1975.*

## Percy G. Adams (essay date 1976)

SOURCE: "The Discovery of America and European Renaissance Literature," in *Comparative Literature Studies,* Vol. XIII, No. 2, June, 1976, pp. 100-15.

[*In the following essay, Adams discusses the treatment of the theme of the New World in several literary genres during the Renaissance.*]

There is great danger in talking about the "Renaissance," almost as much danger as there is in using other such terms—"Classicism," "Romanticism," "Baroque." Tags are neat but they are constricting and, ultimately, confusing. Haydn's fine study [*The Counter-Renaissance,* 1950] has suggested that to avoid a "doctrinaire approach" we can demonstrate the diversity of the period by speaking of a Renaissance and then of a Counter-Renaissance. But while two categories may be more acceptable than one, the thesis depends on leaving the so-called backward-looking "Classicists" in the "Renaissance" and placing the reforming "Romanticists" in the "Counter-Renaissance," Calvin and Machiavelli lying side by side in the counter camp. And so, having redefined by employing definitions that are themselves "doctrinaire" and, today, almost useless—witness Donald Greene on "Neo-Classicism"—

we are back to our problem. Fortunately, we need not define but can simply agree that we are concerned with the literature of Europe at a period in time extending from the discovery of the New World in the West to about the middle of the seventeenth century.

But we are to discuss not only the literature of the Renaissance; but also that New World in the West. And, no doubt, to define that World is even harder than to define the Renaissance—for many reasons. First, just as the Renaissance changed its countenance with time, so its knowledge of the Americas altered with every newly returned ship and every freshly written account, from the oft-published letters of Columbus and Vespucci to Raleigh and Van Noort, and from great collections such as Montalboddo's and Waldseemüller's in 1507 to Acosta and De Bry at the end of the sixteenth century. And, with changing information, maps were altered each decade; terrestrial globes replaced celestial globes; places and place names came and went, expanded or contracted.

Second, each part of Europe had its writers and its time for learning. The Italians and the Spanish, for example, were quick with their books while the English were notoriously late in sailing or publishing.

Third, the Spanish New World existed from Florida south; France ended in the late sixteenth century with its New World in Canada, while England only after 1580 cornered its Virginia and New England. Thus, because of different climatic conditions, kinds of people encountered, fur-seeking in Canada and gold-seeking in South America, the extended and heavy impact of Spanish culture on its possessions as opposed to a shorter and smaller impact in North America—because of many factors, then, each empire-seeking nation received its particular image with the use of the term "New World."

Fourth, since the Old World civilization and the New World peoples at first found it impossible to communicate with each other, not only, for example, do reports of the Conquistadores of South and North America conflict but they often show how the natives, out of fear, told not the truth but what the threatening Europeans wanted to hear.

Because, fifth, Europe brought much of its own image and bias with its soldiers and priests who crossed the Atlantic. Over and over it has been shown how Europe searched for, or found to its satisfaction, the Terrestrial Paradise, Atlantis, Ophir, even Prester John. And there were other marvels transplanted or invented, from interpretations of Indian religion to fantastic natural facts such as Pigafetta's Patagonian giants, David Ingram's elephants in North America,

*Painting by John White (1585) depicting native inhabitants of Virginia.*

or John Hawkins' Florida unicorn.

Sixth, the image of the New World was not only constantly changing and corrupted by its reporters, but various conflicting traditions grew up depending on whom one read—translators, for example, often blatantly altered facts that may or may not have been right to begin with. There was, for example, what Levin calls "the moral ambivalence of the golden lure" in the search for Paradise in the West, or the double myth about the indigenes of the Indies—one, that he was a Noble Savage, the other that he was sub-human and should be enslaved or exterminated. One example of intended mistranslation is the rendering of the Spanish physician Nicolás Monardes (1569-71) by John Frampton, who left the impression that all plants in the New World were health-giving and that henceforth there would be a cure for every physical ill; another is that of the zealous Hakluyt and his treatment of the account of De Soto's expedition as written by the Portuguese Gentleman of Elvas.

Seventh, and last, there were the Renaissance pictures of the people of the New World and there were the people themselves brought back to be displayed. Nearly every sixteenth-century collection or summary of voyages had certain illustrations—gigantic warriors bending Greek bows, nude nymphs, Europeanized landscapes. The eye-witness drawings by John White and Le Moyne were placed in De Bry in 1590 and thereafter became the bases for idealized pictures which gave the Indians the appearance and nature of ancient Greeks or Spartans. Such pictures did not always conform to the appearance of the real natives who were sometimes seen in Europe—almost every voyager to the New World treacherously captured one or more to bring back as slaves, to be presented to Frobisher's Henry VII or Ribaud's Queen, to be Europeanized, to dance on village greens on feast days, to die far from home.

It was, then, a changing, distorted, paradoxical New World which entered and affected Renaissance literature. To suggest the extent of that influence, let us look at two important literary themes and then sample the various literary genres.

Avoiding the Noble Savage, Paradise, and certain other themes so often and sometimes so beautifully handled by recent writers, let us turn first to the theme of the Cruelty of the Spaniards in the New World. From the earliest discoveries in the West Indies, greed for Western gold and condescension toward Indian "ignorance" of its value led to demands impossible to fulfill, bloody retaliations by the natives, and the rise of the extreme form of that "anti" image of the New World man as impossible to Christianize or civilize; that is, the judgment stated by Dr. Chanca on Columbus's second voyage, "their degradation is greater than that of any beast." But also, from the very beginning, there was a vigorous defense of the natives and an attack on their mistreatment by the Spaniards, all coming of course from Spain itself. After Montesinos' famous sermon of 1511 defending the Indians, the transplanted Italian Pietro Martire over and over asserted that certain of them "seeme to live in the goulden worlde," and he openly and shamefacedly condemned atrocities such as those of that butcher governor of Panama, Pedro Arias de Avila. When the debate grew heated over the nature of the Indians, with writers like Oviédo and Quevédo proving their sub-human nature by resorting to Aristotle, Bartolomé de las Casas came forward and, from about 1519 to his death, remained the chief spokesman against Spanish mistreatment. At least in theory his campaign won out, for in 1537 Pope Paul III's famous Bull made the Indians officially human, and in 1552-53 Las Casas was able to publish tracts which were not only inflammatory and exaggerated but which went all over Europe to give comfort and aid to Spain's political and religious enemies. In spite of the fact that saintly Spanish priests devoted their lives to the Americans, in spite of the fact that debates between Las Casas and Sepúlveda inspired "admirable laws," in spite of the fact that Spain led the way in exposing its own sins, the myth of Spanish cruelty in the New World became one of the strongest myths in history.

But that cruelty, of whatever amount, had been reported and other nations, especially England and France, adopted it with enthusiasm. As a theme in Renaissance literature, it is reflected best in the drama, which became so important in Europe only after Las Casas and his words were well known everywhere, and since England and Spain were rivals in producing good drama as well as good navigators, their plays expose the cruelty most often. The first to do so apparently came less than five years after Las Casas' fiery pamphlets in 1557 in Toledo. It was called *Las Cortes de la Muerte* (*The Assembly of Death*) and is a kind of morality play in which the body is a character, angels are personified, and the author laments Spanish lust for gold and the resulting cruel treatment of innocent Indians. Also in the morality tradition is Lope de Vega's well known *El Nuevo Mundo descubierto por Colón,* in which, along with Columbus and Indians, Providence, Idolatry, Religion, and the Devil argue as characters the rights and wrongs, the advantages and disadvantages of the discovery of America. But, as in a great number of his plays which deal with America, Lope's *El Nuevo Mundo* reflects his pride in Spanish conquests and colonizing achievements even as it laments the evil that went with the good, a fact true also of Tirso de Molina's patriotic trilogy about the Pizarros.

No English dramatists or poets, however, and there were many who dealt with the theme, found the good. Thomas Heywood in at least three plays, including *If*

*You Know Not Me, You Know no bodie* (1605), made the Spanish "tyrannous, cruel, lascivious," while Robert Greene in *Spanish Masquerado* (1589), inspired by the destruction of the Armada and finding evidence not only in Las Casas but in Castanheda's account of De Soto's expedition, showed the Spanish hunting Indians with dogs, cutting off their hands, tearing them with horses. It was a theme often found in England outside the drama, of course, as in John Donne's simile:

> And if they stand arm'd with seely honestie,
> With wishing prayers and neat integritie,
> Like Indians 'gainst Spanish hosts they be.

The best known of all English treatments of the theme is surely Davenant's "opera" *The Cruelty of the Spaniards in Peru* (1658), written two years after what is perhaps the most famous of all translations of Las Casas, that by Milton's nephew John Phillips. By Davenant's time, the cruelty of the Spaniards was being regularly contrasted with the kindness and humanity of the French, like Cartier and Champlain, or the good Protestant English, even after Puritan atrocities in New England and after the horrible aftermath of the 1622 massacre in Virginia. So Davenant not only has a spurious history of the Incas in his spectacle but concludes his conglomerate of speeches, songs, dances, and acrobatics with English soldiers heroically arriving to save the natives of Mexico from the villainous Cortés. By the time of Descartes and the Restoration of Charles II, then, such pieces of literature had helped advertise to Europe outside the Iberian peninsula the horrors of Spanish conquest and colonization.

A second theme, much more subtle, is that of the New World's possible influence on the doctrine of progress. In spite of the argument in J.B. Bury's seminal book leading to his thesis that the idea of progress really begins only with Descartes, the more one reads Renaissance writers the more one agrees with Hans Baron and others that Humanism did not slavishly follow the Greeks and Romans but, inspired by the ancient greats, took pride in its own accomplishments and looked forward to still greater ones. At any rate, the notion of progress is obviously closely linked with the Quarrel of the Ancients and Moderns and with the doctrine of Manifest Destiny, the former often considered late seventeenth-century, the other often considered distinctively American. It is provocative to see how the New World, discovered simultaneously with ancient thought and letters, gave gigantic impetus to this complex of theories found everywhere in literature.

Very early in the sixteenth century, the discovery of America became a symbol of discovery and invention in general as well as evidence to historians of the New World that their age had made advances over former ages. Pietro Martire (1533) is only one such early historian to point out that the ancients knew nothing, "as we do," of the New World. Another, Gómara (1552), expressed pride in the way Spain had "improved" her colonies and more than once announced that the moderns had gone beyond the Greeks and Romans; Granada (1582) pointed out that "in new lands there are discovered daily new animals with new abilities and properties, such as have never been known . . . ," a thesis supported by his predecessor, the physician Monardes, and even more vigorously by Monardes' translator, Frampton. The Inca Garcilaso (1609) not only defined three distinct stages of development in the history of his people but proudly asserted that the exploits of De Soto surpassed those of the ancients. With countless witnesses such as these, one can see why sixteenth-century geographers, philosophers, and readers scorned the ancient and once honored Ptolemy as each new map showed him ever more wrong or why they attacked Aristotle long before Bacon did.

The intellectual leaders of the sixteenth century knew and were impressed by America and what it meant. It would be easy to demonstrate that More, Erasmus, and other Humanists, as well as reformers like Luther, believed in progress, but it is appropriate here to start with that much admired friend of Erasmus and More, Juan Luis Vives. Close to great geographical as well as philosophical developments, the Spaniard Vives praised the giants of antiquity, but, he said, "they were men as we are, and were liable to be deceived and to err." Furthermore, the ancients, he asserted, knew that future ages would rise to heights they did not know, for they "judged it to be of the very essence of the human race that, daily, it should progress in arts, discipline, virtue and goodness." Even more influential throughout Europe was Jean Bodin, closely followed by his contemporary disciple Le Roy. Bodin, in more than one book, rejected all golden ages and the theory of man's degeneration and ended by showing that his age had not only invented gunpowder, the compass, and printing but also discovered new worlds and circumnavigated the globe. Preceded by thinkers like these and praising with so many of his immediate ancestors the geographical discoveries as well as the three wonderful inventions of the previous hundred years, Bacon developed out of Bruno the then striking theory that the moderns are the true ancients because they are the result of the aging of creativity and experience. And not only like the others was Bacon impressed with the opening up of a New World by means of the compass and gunpowder; he echoed Acosta in believing the Andes taller than any Old World mountains, praised Spain's farsighted activity in developing its dominions, pointed out that the Aztecs and Incas were examples of progress in America, and, exactly like Bruno and others, compared his own bent to intellectual discovery with the great discovery of Columbus.

With such New World historians and Old World thinkers to inspire them, belletristic writers of the Renaissance everywhere reflect the idea of progress and the worth of the moderns, some referring to the New World directly or to the theories of thinkers influenced by the New World. Even as Magellan was sailing through his Strait, Torres Naharro (1517) was comparing his new book to a ship setting sail to discover new worlds. Just as Du Bellay's famous *Défense* (1549) is nothing if not an illustration of a belief in progress, his friend Ronsard, who often turned to America for image and theme, believed with their friend Le Roy in some kind of forward movement in a designed world—"Toute chose à sa fin et tend à quelque bût" ("Hymne de l'été"). Across the Channel and a bit later, Spenser, like his teacher Ronsard, employed the New World in image and metaphor and believed in "a goal of perfection." But when, inconsistently, he argued in the "Mutabilitie" cantos that Nature had arranged all things neatly only to have Mutabilitie come along and destroy the order, his friend Hervey wrote that famous letter reprimanding him for such a philosophy because "Nature herself is changeable" and, Hervey said, because Jean Bodin was right in believing the present better than the past. One of the best examples of a great Renaissance creative writer's belief in progress is Ben Jonson, whose *Timber; or Discoveries* shows how closely he depended on the Vives passages we started with.

The entire subject needs another book-length study, one that would relate Progress and the Ancient-Modern debate to the theory of Manifest Destiny. For just as the Spanish believed they were the race chosen to improve, Christianize, and profit from the New World, as holy papal bulls even agreed, so French and English believed they were not just building empires in America but following a vision, carrying out a mandate from God or his earthly representative. Early in the sixteenth century, the Spanish Humanist Perez de Oliva saw a westward course of empire with Spain as God's agent. Edward Hayes, with Gilbert in Newfoundland, argued that "God had reserved" the New World north of Florida "to be reduced unto Christian civilitie by the English nation," a belief held later by many early colonizers of Virginia. Even John Donne, in spite of all his poems on the decay of man or of the loved one, preached that famous send-off sermon in 1622 in which he told the prospective colonists that they were leaving to make "this island . . . a bridge, a gallery to the new [World]." Such visions of a Passage to India, whether derived from good or evil or mixed motives, led smoothly to Jefferson's westward-looking eyes and Monroe's manifesto.

There are countless such themes given impetus by news out of the New World that could be traced through European literature, but let us also try the great literary genres, although we can pass over drama—late starting and already mentioned—and most lyric poetry, which, especially from the Pléaide to Dryden's "Ode to Charleton," has so many allusions to and metaphors depending on a knowledge of the New World. There are, however, two types of lyric poems uniquely related to America—the promotion poems like Drayton's famous Ode and the Bon Voyage or "puffing" poems such as those of Ronsard, de Baif, and Jodelle for Thévet's book on America, and Chapman's for Keymis on his expedition to Guiana. There is also a whole body of satirical literature inspired by new geographical discoveries, from Brant's *Narrenschiff* (1494) to the Elizabethan play *Eastward Ho!* to Bishop Hall's ridicule of lying travelers. Yet another genre is the dialogue or colloquy, important in university training and high on the best seller lists. Erasmus, easily the great name here, more than once turned to the New World for inspiration, as in "The Well-to-do Beggars," where the conversation dwells on cultural relativism by way of comparing naked Americans with clothed Europeans. There are other genres that need more attention, however.

One of these is the prose romance. The relation between the romance and the exploration of the New World is both complex and intriguing because the influence went west as well as east. Until the time of *Don Quixote,* Spain, even more than other countries, avidly read these romances and was inspired to seek the marvels described in them. The popularity of *Amadis* and *Palmerin* from 1508 on paralleled the popularity of the letters of Columbus and Vespucci or the *Decades* of Martire, and just as the romances told of giants, Amazons, dwarfs, Seven Cities, El Dorados, or fountains of youth, the "real" accounts brought back stories of giants, golden idols, and enchanted places *mas allá.* The educated Cortés read *Amadis* to his soldiers around the campfire, Spaniards were easily persuaded to join expeditions to an America that might be the ideal land for valorous action as well as rich treasure, and descriptions of Mexico City or Peru sent home to Spain often sounded like the literary romances themselves. Irving Leonard has told the story well, concentrating on early reports about islands of Amazons and on Caravajal's record of Orellana's voyage down the great river named for the women warriors he had to fight. In 1510 Montalvo published the fifth volume of his Amadis cycle, which was named *Sergas de Esplandián* and went through six Spanish editions during the century. In it is told the story of Calafia, queen of a race of Amazons who reside on a craggy island named "'California,'" celebrated for "its abundance of gold and jewels." All of this literature, but none more than *Esplandián,* had an incalculable influence on the exploits of Cortés and the Pizarros. For example, Cortés' fourth letter to the King tells how an expedition he sent out looking for Amazons and gold returned with the exciting news that ten days beyond their stopping point, the soldiers were told, there was an island rich in treasure and inhabited by women. This "island," or one like it, decorates most maps of the late sixteenth and seventeenth centuries, for not until after 1700 were cartographers finally convinced that lower California was a peninsula.

Closely related to the romance, especially in the Renaissance, is the epic, and while it has often been remarked that the great epics of the time looked back to Greece and Rome or were really romances in poetry like *Orlando Furioso* (1516), in one of these epics, *Gerusalemme Liberata* (1575), Tasso proudly announced the discovery of America by his countryman: "Un uom liguria," the gentle guide answered the wondering knight Ubaldo, "avrà ardimento / All' incognito corso esporsi in prima." That is to say, she went on, "Tu spiegherai, Colombo, a un novo polo / Lontano si le fortunate antenne, / Ch'a pena seguirà con gli occhi il volo/ La Fama ch'ha mille occhi e mille penne." And Tasso's friend Stigliane apparently thought of writing an epic to honor Columbus. Stigliane may have given up, but others did not, at least in England and Spain, for in those countries there were long poems inspired by the New World. None is as good, however, as Comoes' *Os Lusíadas* (1572) celebrating da Gama and Portugal. Of the many poems about America that have epic qualities, the best is undoubtedly Ercilla's *La Araucana,* published in three parts (1569, 1578, 1589) and written by a soldier-statesman who was in Peru for the wars he described in his poem. Ercilla, impressed not only by the Montesinos-Las Casas tradition but by his own experiences, treats the Araucanian Indians sympathetically in their heroic struggle against Spanish domination. In *ottava rima,* the poem provides local color, epic debates and a vision, much bloodshed, and reminiscences of scenes in Homer, Virgil, and Lucan. While Voltaire did not like its emphasis on war, neither did he approve of the *Iliad,* and he even found a speech by the cacique Colacola in Ercilla's second canto superior to anything in Homer. *La Araucana* may be the best epic in the Spanish language.

There is no English epic of the period, if we stop before Milton, unless we count *The Faerie Queene,* but there were long poems written in England dealing with America which come close. One was by a lad of eighteen at Exeter named William Kidley, who in 1624 used not only Richard Hawkins' own *Observations* but information collected from other sources to tell a patriotic tale of Britain's great exploits in the New World. A generation earlier, another young man, Stephen Parmenius, came to England from Hungary, bringing with him a fine classical education gained on the Continent. In England, he studied navigation at Oxford with Richard Hakluyt the younger, became enthusiastic about the colonizing ventures discussed all around

him, wrote a kind of épic published in 1582, the year of Hakluyt's first propagandistic collection, the *Divers Voyages,* and then, having convinced himself with his poem, sailed with Gilbert to Newfoundland and, like Gilbert, lost his life in the cold North Atlantic. The poem, in Latin hexameters, since Parmenius knew English most inadequately, has been retranslated (1972) in a splendid volume. Parmenius begins with fulsome praise of God, Queen Elizabeth, and Gilbert, considers the origins of the American Indians, most idealistically hopes to witness their conversion, longs to write *the* epic of "the rise of the new race," attacks Spain's cruelty and Europe's lust for gold, employs copious classical allusions, shows the influence of Virgil and Camoes, catalogues the exploits of British voyagers to the New World, and ends with a prayer to God, Elizabeth, and Britain that they will gently civilize the savages and join them with the English in a great expansionist and progressive movement. His is one of the most attractive poems about the New World, even though it has had no influence historically.

One of the chief influences in *belles lettres* that came with the discovery of America is the impetus given by that discovery to travel literature and pseudo-travel literature. Of course, the early Renaissance had its Marco Polos and Mandevilles to help, and then there was Pliny, whose unnatural natural history affected the best and worst of travel books until well after 1700; but after 1492 voyage literature not only became more popular with printing and with a New World to write about but it became better. The travel letters of two Italians, Columbus and Vespucci, for example, are both personal and objective, marvelous and yet realistic, a combination that would make such books more and more fascinating to European readers. Columbus could be objective in reporting his sailings and landings and troubles and yet insert a story of meeting a large Indian boat off Mexico filled with people dressed in dyed cotton, or Vespucci might tell of women warriors and a horrible cannibalistic orgy and record personal impressions of South America, where feathers were more valuable than precious metals. A Spaniard such as Alonso Enriquez de Guzmán, setting out for America in 1534, might have little on flora and fauna but much about his own experiences. A different kind of travel book, the letters of Cortés to his king, or Bernal Diaz's account of the conquest of Mexico, will often be as personal, but it will also become invaluable in every way to historians of Mexico and, at the same time, be as gripping as any novel. Such books will lead to others, to, for example, Ralegh's *Guiana,* which may be the best of real Renaissance travels, comparable to the best of the eighteenth and nineteenth centuries and a favorite, for example, of Defoe. By the end of the Renaissance, then, Europe had learned to write and read huge quantities of travel literature about the New World.

Close to the real travel book, so close in fact that often one cannot separate them, is the imaginary voyage, which, inspired in great part by the many actual travel accounts of the New World, grew to maturity in the Renaissance. These imaginary voyages could, in fact, pretend to be real, as did *La Vida de Marcos de Obregón,* by Vicente Espinel, who borrowed information and dates from Sarmiento's west-side visit to Magellan's Strait and then included what all readers agree is "geografia fantástica;" or an anonymous French ". . . lettre envoyée de la Nouvelle-France, par le sieur de Combes" (1609), which takes a fictional person to Canada by borrowing facts from Champlain and inventing others, carriages on wheels, for example. Or they could be completely plagiarized and intend to deceive, as in the case of Roberval's famous pilot Jean Alphonse and his *Cosmographie,* taken from a Spanish book of 1519 by Fernandez de Enciro. Or they could consist of marvelous adventures not all of which were intended to be taken as real, as the later books of *Pantagruel,* for example, which draw heavily on accounts of the New World, especially on those written by and told about Jacques Cartier, who lived in and sailed from Rabelais' Saint-Malo. Such pseudo-travel books would increase in number after the Renaissance and lead to many dozens in the eighteenth century.

And finally there are the Utopias. What can one say briefly? That after Plato, Utopias were normally celestial while, after America was discovered, they became earthly during the Renaissance, only to return often to outer space, or inner space, in the seventeenth and eighteenth centuries. That in the Renaissance, from More (1516) to Campanella (1623) and Bacon (1624, published later), Utopias were placed often in the West and employed facts gleaned from writers about America. More's Hythloday accompanied Vespucci, crossed South America with other travelers, and sailed west to Utopia, where, as with Martire's Indians, no one distinguished between *meum* and *tuum,* land is held in common, gold is despised, there is a plurality of religions, and, as with Vespucci, each home has behind it a beautiful garden open to all. Campanella, as Baudet says, "based much of his ideal state . . . on what he thought he knew of the Incas." And Bacon, who in the *Novum Organum* had thought the travels of the ancients "no more than suburban excursions" when compared with the voyages of Columbus and Magellan, in the *New Atlantis* often cites the New World historian Acosta as well as the Inca Garcilaso, shows a great interest in theories about ancient Atlantis as America, is one of the first important thinkers to ponder the question of the Jewish or other possible origins of human life in the New World, and of all the statues in his famous house of Salomon names one, that of Columbus, a fact that points not just to Benzoni, Ramusio, and Oviédo, all of whom had suggested that statues of Columbus be erected, but also to the long sixteenth-century tradition of using Columbus, as Lope

said, as a symbol for "man's unquenchable spirit of discovery."

It is perhaps this spirit of discovery, of experiment, of innovation, that is one of the marked characteristics of Renaissance *belles lettres*—from Erasmus and Luther, to Rabelais and the Pléaide, to the new drama, to Bruno and Bacon, just as it is of the early historians of America and of the daring sailors, greedy gold seekers, faithful or cruel government officials, and saintly priests who actually went to the New World. And perhaps as important for us to note now is that the influence of the New World on Renaissance literature is often no greater than the influence of that literature on the New World itself, its conquest and civilization. Not only, for example, did the literary themes of progress, science, Spanish cruelty, the earthly Paradise—all so indebted to Columbus, Magellan, and America—give back that influence to explorers and colonists in Virginia and South America, and not only did the chivalric romances receive encouragement from and yet aid exploration, but More's *Utopia,* which looked to the Western World and its European visitors, became a sort of second Bible to certain of those Spanish saints who hoped to Christianize the Indians. Las Casas tried to create Utopias, especially in Venezuela, but Vasco de Quiroga, a bishop and jurist, actually built communities in Mexico "pattern[ed] from the good republic proposed by Thomas More," its family and village plan, its elective system, its hospitals. It may be true, as Atkinson has shown for France, that in the sixteenth century western Europe published more books about the Old World than about the New, and certainly there were more love sonnets than embarkation odes, more plays about English Henrys and Richards than about Spanish Pizarros, but the New World, with its changing, challenging image, its cannibals and Noble Savages, its elusive waterways and treasures, its Aztecs and Incas, its villains and saints, its heroes and hopes—all this New World, without hundreds of years of written tradition, still attracted and inspired almost every writer, certainly every literary genre, after Columbus returned with his stirring news.

---

## UTOPIA VS. TERROR IN THE NEW WORLD

### Howard Mumford Jones (essay date 1964)

SOURCE: "The Anti-Image," in *O Strange New World: American Culture: the Formative Years,* The Viking Press, 1964, pp. 35-70.

[*In the following essay, Jones examines the opposing idealized and terrifying visions of the New World that characterized Renaissance thought.*]

The concept that the New World is the peculiar abode

of felicity lingered for centuries in the European imagination and, like the youth of America, is one of its oldest traditions. Virginia, wrote Michael Drayton in his famous poem of 1606, is earth's "onely paradise," and Goethe not long before his death declared: *"Amerika, du hast es besser/Als unser Continent, das Alte."* As for France, the studies of Gilbert Chinard have shown the connection between America and an exotic dream of difference and perfection. The vitality of the idea runs so deep and long, the traditional image can be adapted to humor, so that William Byrd's satirical "Journey to the Land of Eden" in 1733 and Martin Chuzzlewit's unfortunate real-estate speculation in the fever-ridden Eden of Dickens' novel are proof of the vigor of a concept that has a thousand aspects, . . . But the coin, to change the figure, has another side. Before we study its obverse, however, it is relevant to examine three or four famous philosophic evocations of the New World as the home of social perfection.

For example, Sir Thomas More located Utopia in the New World five years before Cortés discovered the great Aztec capital of Tenochtitlán. More's imagined Paradise he learned about from one Ralph Hythloday, first seen "with a blake sonne burned face, a longe bearde, and a cloke cast homely about his shoulders." He was a Portuguese learned in the tongues, a companion, it seems, of Amerigo Vespucci on his voyages. On the last of these Hythloday with twenty-two others, after much "intreataunce and . . . importune sute," was left behind in the country of "Gulike," which, I fear, does not appear on any map. From there with five companions he traversed the equatorial belt where there are only "greate and wyde desertes and wyldernesses," "intollerable heate," "wyld beastes and serpentes" and "people . . . no lesse sauage, wylde, and noysome then the verye beastes." But in the south temperate zone they came upon Utopia, the merits of which are now common knowledge. When at last they left that enchanting land, by "maruelous chaunce" they made their way to Taprobane (Ceylon) and Calicut (then a Portuguese station in India) and so to Europe. The two books that constitute the *Utopia* contrast the weakness and decay of Europe with the dream of a perfect society. Terror and cruelty, it will be observed, are confined to the torrid zone. Europe decays; America is promises. Nor was all this idle dreaming. The vogue of Erasmus and of Sir Thomas More in Renaissance Spain was great; and when Vasco de Quiroga went to New Spain as a judge (*oidor*) in 1530 he drew up a scheme for governing the Indians after the manner of the *Utopia*, which was seriously considered by the Council of the Indies.

But if More reported on the travels of Ralph Hythloday, Rabelais, in books iv and v of the chronicle of that hero's career, sent Pantagruel westward in order to consult the oracle of the bottle, a search that, as Chinard has shown, was strongly infiltrated with New World elements drawn from Peter Martyr and others; and the oracle of the bottle is not merely "Trinq," it is also, as the priestess announces, philosophical: "Down here, in these circumcentral regions, we place the supreme good, not in taking or receiving, but in giving and bestowing." This appeared about 1565.

More influential was Bacon's *The New Atlantis,* published posthumously in 1627, twenty years after Jamestown. This imaginary island lies in the South Seas somewhere west of Peru, a survivor from the catastrophe that overwhelmed Atlantis proper. *The New Atlantis* is a vision of a completely technological society, one in which wisdom and science are coterminous, an ideal to which many theorists would now like to push the United States. An interesting secondary element in Bacon's social paradise is his emphasis upon ceremony as essential to social harmony. Thus a formal family celebration in the book involves special robing, a throne, a canopy, a herald, emblematic grapes of gold, a scroll, and various other things. Nobody having stumbled upon Atlantean perfection in fact, Bacon is compelled to explain, through the Atlanteans, that America is younger a thousand years at least than the rest of the world. Imperfection has had at length to be reckoned with; and Bacon seems to regard the Indians as a race descending from some by-blow of Noah when he was repopulating the globe.

Utopianism *per se* is, indeed, not the whole of the story. A world coming fresh from the hand of the Creator must contain blessings for sick and weary mankind, and in 1569-1571 the Spanish physician Nicolas Monardes, born in Seville the year that Columbus's letter was first printed, a man much esteemed by his contemporaries, reported sufficient trial of plants, animals, medicinal stones, and other natural products in America to testify that a whole novel and miraculous pharmacopoeia was at last available to Europeans to heal them of their manifold diseases. This work falling into the hands of John Frampton, merchant, he "Englished" it in 1577 as *Joyfull Newes out of the Newe Founde World,* a book "treatyng of the singuler and rare vertues of certaine Hearbes, Trees, Oyles, Plantes, Stones, and Drugges of the Weste Indias" which yield "wonderfull cures of sundrie greate deseases that otherwise then by these remedies, thei were incurable." As one turns over Frampton's astonishing pages, there seems to be no reason why mankind should ever be sick again. Anime and copall, a gum called tacamahaca, another known as caranna, the oil of the fig tree of hell, bitumen, liquid amber, balsamo, guaiacan, the China root, "sarcaparaillia," the bloodstone, pepper, mechoacan, tobacco, and other New World discoveries will obviously end the ills that flesh is heir to. One drug is as good as another. Take, for example, sassafras, which "comforteth the Liver and the Stomacke and doth disopilate," is good for headaches, "griefes of the breast" and of the stomach, casts out "gravell and stones," provokes urine, "taketh awaie merveilouslie" the toothache, is excellent for gout and the "evill of the Joyntes," "maketh a man go to the stoole," and "dooeth great profite" in the evil of women. In short it is

> for all maner of deseases, without makyng exception of any. And beyng sicke of any maner of evill which commeth unto them [the Spaniards], sharpe, or large, hot, or colde, greevous or otherwise, they doe cure all with one maner of fashion, and they heale all with one maner of water, without makyng any difference, and the best is that all be healed, and of this they have so muche trust, that they feare not the evilles which are present, nor have any care of them that be to come, and so they have it for a universall remedy, for all maner of deseases.

Monardes, or Frampton for him, following the doctrine of correspondences, sometimes associates particular stones, plants, oils, or roots with particular diseases, but the general impression of *Joyfull Newes* is that most of the herbs and other flora tried by the Spaniards and reported by Monardes are good for anything. Monardes also recognizes the existence of the pox, various fevers, and other new and mysterious ailments originating in America, but these are of course curable by his wonder drugs. The American patent-medicine man selling his Indian remedies has a more ancient heritage than he knows.

By 1580, when the first edition of Montaigne's *Essays* appeared, which included the celebrated one "Of Cannibals," the problem of reconciling the unlovely aspects of New World life with the paradisiacal dream had become more acute. Like More but more credibly, Montaigne claims to have talked with a man who had been for ten or twelve years in the ill-fated French colony in Brazil founded by Villegaignon in 1557, but Montaigne has also read in Thevet, Jean de Léry, Benzoni, and other writers on discovery and settlement. Man, says Montaigne, should live according to nature, for nature's "purity" so shines forth as to put to shame our "vain and frivolous" performances. Among the Indians "the laws of nature still rule" uncorrupted by sophistication, and Montaigne admires the absence of laws, letters, labor, and the like burdens of humanity in that "very pleasant and temperate climate," where "the whole day is spent in dancing" and where even warfare is straightforward and simple.

But he must solve the problem of cannibalism, not to speak of that presented by polygamy, and it is amusing to watch the great Frenchman exercise his casuistry to get around these awkward practices. Of the two, polygamy is the more easily dealt with. "It is a remarkably beautiful thing about their marrages that the same jealousy our wives have to keep us from the affection and kindness of other women, theirs have to win this for them . . . they strive and scheme to have as many

companions as they can, since that is a sign of their husbands' valor."

Cannibalism is a thornier question. In one sense Montaigne frankly faces facts:

> After they have treated their prisoners well for a long time with all the hospitality they can think of, each man who has a prisoner calls a great assembly of his acquaintances. He ties a rope to one of the prisoner's arms, by the end of which he holds him, a few steps away, for fear of being hurt, and gives his dearest friend the other arm to hold in the same way; and these two, in the presence of the whole assembly, kill him with their swords. This done, they roast him and eat him in common and send some pieces to their absent friends.

But this custom, he says, is not, as with the ancient Scythians, a form of revenge, nor, as with the Portuguese, a form of torture. Who are we to reproach the cannibals? "I am heartily sorry that, judging their faults rightly, we should be so blind to our own." Montaigne tacitly changes the basis of his discourse to one of admiration for bravery, whether among the Indians, the Spartans, or the Hungarians. He abandons cannibalism to praise Indian poetry and the rationality of Indian comment on the French court.

In a subsequent essay, "Of Coaches," Montaigne recurs to the New World, emphasizes the brutality of its European conquerors, and argues: "I am much afraid that we shall have greatly hastened the decline and ruin of this new world by our contagion, and that we will have sold it our opinions and our arts very dear. It was an infant world; yet we have not whipped it and subjected it to our discipline by the advantage of our natural valor and strength, nor won it over by our justice and goodness, nor subjugated it by our magnanimity." Montaigne was a powerful force in building up the general concept of the delights of primitivism and the virtues of the noble savage; yet, being an honest man, he admits that the Earthly Paradise of the New World is somewhat less than perfection. Montaigne prepares us to examine the other side of the coin.

The association of the New World with unlimited riches is a commonplace in the history of ideas, but until one realizes how immediate, coarse, and brutal was the response of European greed to the prospect of boundless wealth, one cannot understand how quickly the radiant image became crossed with streaks of night. It may indeed be true that mere greed for gold will not suffice to explain the superhuman exploits of the conquerors, but it is also true that superhuman exploits would not have been undertaken without the dream of reward. The economic theory of the Renaissance could not think of wealth except in terms of a cash nexus binding man to man, a theory the more persuasive as rulers beheld the wealth of the Indies turning Charles

V into the master of Europe and doing mysterious things to prices. Gold, pearls, and precious stones were tangible, were concrete evidence of success, were proof that the New World was, if not the kingdom of Prester John, the empire of the Great Khan, or Asia heavy with the wealth of Ormuz and of Ind, then next door to it, or a passage toward it, or, better still, a richer and more wonderful land. The lust for gold conquered morality, judgment, humanitarianism, and religion. To watch the banausic greed for it corrupt idealism is like watching the inevitable march of a Greek tragedy.

Columbus, his associates, his crew, and his rivals were convinced that gold was at hand, or concealed, or in the next island. They could not conceive that the indifference of the Indians to what the Europeans thought of as tangible wealth was anything less than cunning or treachery. In the interior, says the admiral in his first letter, there are mines of metals—though he never saw them. The evidence? In exchange for a European strap a sailor received gold to the weight of two and a half *castellanos* (46 decigrams). When Columbus returned on his second voyage, the Indians continued to barter casual gold for straps, beads, pins, fragments of dishes, and plates, and Indian kings who sought him out wore facial masks of beaten gold and gold ornaments in their ears and nostrils. The Indian chief Guacamari, suspected of responsibility for the murder of Columbus's original colony on Hispaniola, tried to placate the admiral with a gift of eight and a half marks of gold, five or six hundred stones of various colors, and a cap with a jewel that the Indian seemed to value highly. Then as later, alas! the real source of gold was somewhere else—in this case in an island called Cayre, where there is much gold and "they go there with nails and tools to build their canoes, and . . . bring away as much gold as they please." An expedition to "Cibao" "found gold in more than fifty streams and rivers," "so many rivers, so filled with gold, that all of those who saw it and collected it, merely with their hands as specimens, came back so very delighted . . . that I feel diffidence in repeating what they say."

By the third voyage the inevitable had happened: the thirst for gold had led to the enslavement of the Indians and to double-dealing among the whites, as, for example, Bobadilla, who stole all of Columbus's gold without measuring it or weighing it, once he had the Columbus family in chains. The Lord comforted the admiral, however, by sending him a vision of the Nativity during the night at Veragua on his fourth voyage, showing that gold is everywhere, and an Indian took him up to a hilltop and explained that gold was all around him so that he saw "greater evidence of gold on the first two days than in Española [Hispaniola] in four years." Perhaps uneasily conscious that gold and Christianity do not always mix, Columbus appealed to the great example of Solomon: "Gold is most excellent. Gold constitutes treasure, and he who

possesses it may do what he will in the world, and may so attain as to bring souls to Paradise."

The Indians, as Peter Martyr observed, "know no difference between *meum* and *tuum*," but they learned to their sorrow that the white man's insatiable greed for property produced not happiness but treachery, enslavement, starvation, and death. The search for wealth became an obsession among the Europeans, sending Ponce de León, Hernando de Soto, Cabeça de Vaca, and scores of others on fruitless errands and often to miserable ends. Nothing is more characteristic than that Cabeça de Vaca, after his incredible sufferings in the New World, would neither affirm nor deny that there was gold in "Florida," an ambiguity that led many Spaniards to sell their possessions in order to join the ill-fated expedition of De Soto. Gold, it was thought, was everywhere. Fool's gold was solemnly loaded on Elizabethan ships and as solemnly assayed by London mineralogists—fool's gold or something like it. In the bleak Far North in 1577 Frobisher's historian, Dionysius Settle, could find no hurtful creeping beast "except some Spiders (which as many affirme, are signes of great store of gold)." As usual the natives made "signes of certaine people" living somewhere else "that weare bright plates of gold in their foreheads, and other places of their bodies." The mariners brought back some black stone. "And it fortuned a gentlewoman one of the adventurers wives to have a piece thereof, which by chance she threw and burned in the fire, so long, that at the length being taken forth, and quenched in a little vinegar, it glistered with a bright marquesset of golde. Whereupon the matter being called in some question, it was brought to certaine Goldfiners in London to make assay thereof, who gave out that it held golde, and that very richly for the quantity." Naturally the goldfiners "sought secretly to have a lease at her Majesties hands of those places, whereby to injoy the masse of so great a publike profit unto their owne private gaines."

Sir Humphrey Gilbert was so certain he would discover a gold mine in Newfoundland that he promised to ask no man for a penny toward financing his next expedition; and Sir George Peckham's "True Report" lists as probable products of the same territory gold, silver, copper, lead, tin, turquoise, ruby, pearl, marble, jasper, and crystal. Hariot in his *Briefe and True Report* on Ralegh's ill-fated colony tells of a man who gathered five thousand pearls from the Indians, "which for their likenesse and uniformity in roundnesse, orientnesse, and pidenesse of many excellent colors, with equality in greatnesse, were very faire and rare: and had therefore beene presented to her Majesty," but "through extremity of a storme," they were lost "in coming away from the countrey."

Laudonnière reported "good quantitie of Gold and Silver" among the savages of Florida, who "say that in the Mountaines of Appalatcy there are Mines of Copper, which I thinke to be Golde." Perhaps more momentous than even this delusive idea is the effect of lust for wealth upon European conduct in Florida:

> Golde and silver they [the Indians] want not: for at the Frenchmens first comming thither they had the same offered them for little or nothing, for they received for a hatchet two pound weight of golde, because they knew not the estimation thereof: but the souldiers being greedy of the same, did take it from them, giving them nothing for it: the which they perceiving, that both the Frenchmen did greatly esteeme it, and also did rigorously deale with them, by taking the same away from them, at last would not be knowen they had any more, neither durst they weare the same for feare of being taken away.

More commonly Indians were enslaved, tortured, or killed if they would not reveal the existence of gold they knew nothing about in fact.

These instances, though they illustrate the fixed idea of Renaissance man that gold, silver, precious stones, and pearls were easily to be found anywhere from the Arctic Circle to the Straits of Magellan, are not prerogative instances; for these we must turn to the incredible history of the Spaniards in Mexico and Peru. The pages of Prescott narrate a tale of gold and greed, blood and bravery, treachery and daring made so familiar by the literary skill of a great romantic historian, one need here merely recall a few familiar episodes. On receiving the first embassy from Montezuma, which brought, among other gifts, a wicker basket filled with gold ornaments, Cortés sent back a gilt helmet, asking that it be filled with gold, and told the ambassadors the Spaniards were troubled with a disease of the heart, for which gold was a specific remedy—one of the great ironical statements in the history of the New World. A second embassy brought Aztec "armor" embossed with gold, birds and animals in gold and silver, two circular plates, one of silver, one of gold, as large as carriage wheels, and much else. Far from placating the Spaniards, these gifts inflamed their cupidity, and the fateful invasion pushed forward. After they had entered Tenochtitlán the Spaniards broke into Montezuma's private treasury, a large hall filled with riches that included ingots of gold and silver and many precious jewels. Montezuma sought vainly to ransom himself and his empire by causing three great heaps of gold and golden objects to be piled before his conquerors, heaps so big that even after three days they were not turned into ingots. The predictable consequences followed: the common soldiers, charging their leaders with bad faith, came near mutiny over the division of the spoils, Montezuma was eventually killed, and his successor, Cuauhtémoc [Guatemozin], last of the Aztecs, refusing under torture to tell where there was more treasure except that it had been thrown into the water, was judicially murdered by the Spaniards. The

reconquest of the city and the failure to uncover more treasure stirred up the soldiers once more.

> The first ebullition of triumph was succeeded in the army by very different feelings, as they beheld the scanty spoil gleaned from the conquered city, and as they brooded over the inadequate compensation they were to receive for all their toils and sufferings. . . . Some murmured audibly against the general, and others against Guatemozin, who, they said, could reveal, if he chose, the place where the treasures were secreted. The white walls of the barracks were covered with epigrams and pasquinades levelled at Cortés, whom they accused of taking "one fifth of the booty as commander-in-chief, and another fifth as king."

Gómara reports a sentence worthy of an ancient Roman uttered by Cuauhtémoc while under torture, when a weaker victim complained: "And do you think I, then, am taking my pleasure in my bath?" Whatever the truth of the charges against Cortés, when he married upon his return to Spain, he gave his bride five invaluable emeralds cut by Aztec workmen, a gift that excited the greed and envy of the Queen of Spain. It is all like the curse of the Rhinegold.

The story of the conquest of Peru repeats in more lurid colors the story of the conquest of Mexico. The greed of Pizarro and his men was excited by glimpses of wealth caught on the coastal land, in Peru they seized the Inca Atahuallpa by treachery and simultaneously massacred some thousands of his attendants, the Inca, like Montezuma, sought to ransom himself and his people by filling a hall with gold, roving bands of Spaniards despoiled the Inca temples of their golden ornaments, the Inca was judicially murdered by the conqueror, civil war and conspiracy became commonplace, cruelty grew to be the daily experience of both Indian and Spaniard, and Pizarro and his attendants were eventually assassinated by Juan de Herrada and his followers. The epigraph from Lope de Vega's *El Nuevo Mundo* affixed by Prescott to the title page of the *History of the Conquest of Peru* could not be more ironically appropriate:

> *So color de religión*
> *Van a buscar plata y oro*
> *Del encubierto tesoro.*

The massacre of Atahuallpa's attendants followed upon the exclamation of a Christian priest to Pizarro: "Do you not see, that, while we stand here wasting our breath in talking with this dog, full of pride as he is, the fields are filling with Indians? Set on, at once; I absolve you."

One final document, too important as literature to be omitted, and we shall be done with this nightmare. This is Ralegh's *Discovery of Guiana* (1595), which, better than anything else in Elizabethan literature, represents the shimmering mirage of gold and glory through which the sixteenth century saw the New World. The fact that Ralegh is interested in making out the best possible case for himself increases our sense that gold was the obsession of the age. He actually found none, nor did a subsequent expedition, but he saw some of the "kind of white stone (wherin gold ingendred)" in "divers hils and rocks in every part of Guiana, wherein we traveiled." He reported that "al the rocks, mountains, al stones in ye plaines, woods, & by the rivers side are in effect throughshining, and seem marvelous rich" and were probably "El madre del oro" or at least "the scum of gold." He paraphrases from López de Gómara's *General History of the Indies* this description of the magnificence of Guaynacapa, ancestor of the supposed "emperor" of Guiana:

> All the vessels of his house, table and kitchin were of gold and silver, and the meanest of silver and copper for strength and hardnesse of metall. He had in his wardrobe hollow statues of gold which seemed giants, and the figures in proportion and bignesse of all the beasts, birds, trees, and hearbes, that the earth bringeth foorth: and of all the fishes that the sea or waters of his kingdome breedeth. He had also ropes, budgets, chestes and troughs of golde and silver, heapes of billets of gold, that seemed wood marked out to burne. Finally, there was nothing in his countrey, whereof he had not the counterfait in gold: Yea and they say The Ingas had a garden of pleasure in an yland neere Puna, where they went to recreat themselves, when they would take the aire of the Sea, which had all kinde of garden-hearbs, flowers and trees of golde and silver, an invention, and magnificence till then never seene.

Ralegh struggled up the mighty Orinoco toward the golden city of Manoa, but accident, ignorance, the season of the year, and the weariness of his men prevented him from reaching that fabulous capital. But Martínez, a solitary Spanish survivor of one of Ordas's wholesale executions, had seen it, learned the language of that place, and departed from it blind-folded. He christened the city El Dorado, and "As Berreo [Don Antonio de Berrio] informed mee,"

> Those Guianians, and also the borderers, and all other in that tract which I have seene, are marvellous great drunkards; in which vice, I thinke no nation can compare with them: and at the times of their solemne feasts, when the emperour caroweth with his captaines, tributaries, and governours, the maner is thus: All that pledge him are first stripped naked, and their bodies are anointed all over with a kind of white balsamum (by them called curca) of which there is great plenty. . . . When they are anointed all over, certeine servants of the emperour, having prepared golde made into fine powder, blow it thorow hollow canes upon their naked bodies, untill they be all shining from the foot to the head: and in

this sort they sit drinking by twenties, and hundreds, and continue in drunkennesse sometimes six or seven dayes together.

Ralegh never saw Manoa, but "whatsoever prince shall possesse it, that Prince shall be Lord of more golde, and of a more beautiful Empire, and of more Cities and people, then either the King of Spaine, or the great Turke." Guiana is the country of the future,

> the most eyther rich in golde, or in other marchandizes. The common souldier shall here fight for golde, and pay himselfe in steede of pence, with plates of half a foote broad, whereas he breaketh his bones in other warres for provant and penury. Those commanders and chieftaines that shoot at honour and abundance, shall finde there more rich and beautifull cities, more temples adorned with golden images, more sepulchres filled with treasure, then either Cortez found in Mexico or Pizarro in Peru. . . . Guiana is a countrey that hath yet her maydenhead, never sackt, turned, nor wrought . . . the graves have not bene opened for golde, the mines not broken with sledges, nor their Images puld downe out of their temples.

Alas! Ralegh had more influence upon literature than upon kings: within ten years he was a prisoner in the Tower, a final expedition proved a complete fiasco, and on October 29, 1618, he was beheaded. Fantastic as the dream of El Dorado may seem, let us not forget that in 1577 Sir Francis Drake, putting in at a Pacific coast port called Tarapaze, found on the seashore a sleeping Spaniard "who had lying by him 13. barres of silver, which weighed 4000. ducats Spanish; we tooke the silver, and left the man."

The consequences of this *idée fixe* were of first importance in altering the picture of an Earthly Paradise. Though it was not the sole cause, the hunt for gold was one of the principal causes for the enslavement of the Indians. On Hispaniola, for example, by the end of the fifteenth century anarchy was more common than order. The Indians, when they rebelled against their conquerors, were condemned to pay tribute in gold, and when they were unable to find gold they were condemned to slavery—unless, indeed, slavery had been a prior punishment for rebellion. The *hidalgo* was supposed to fight and govern, not to labor; wherefore the Indians had to labor for him, and their women serve as his harem. As the Indian was himself unaccustomed to toil, notably toil in the mines, the population rapidly declined. European madness led to suicide, to aborticide, to infanticide; and since, unfortunately for the subjugated race, the white man brought his own diseases with him, sickness took off thousands. [In a footnote, the critic adds: "Kidnaped Indians sometimes went on a hunger strike and starved to death and familial suicide among the Cuban Indians was notorious".] The population of Hispaniola has been

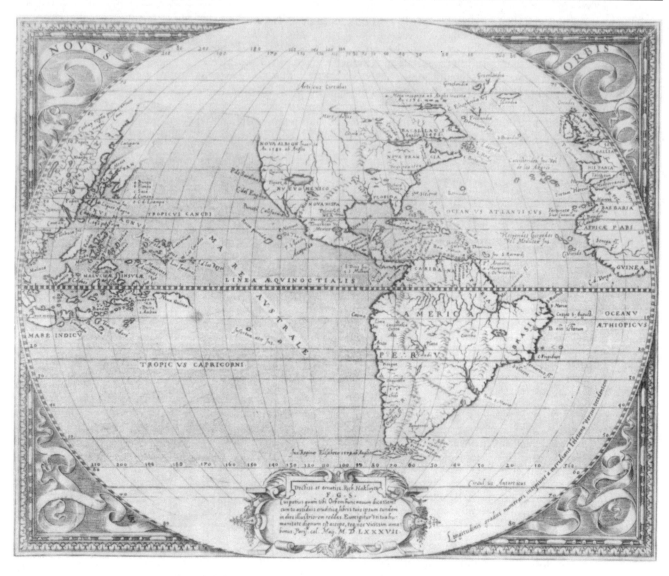

*A map of the New World from Hakluyt's edition of De Orbe Novo, 1587.*

estimated at a million in 1492; even if the figure is far too high, it is appalling to learn that the number of Indians living on that unhappy island had dropped to 14,000 by 1509. The Spanish court did what it could at long range to alleviate the lot of the Indians, and the great propaganda campaign of Montesinos and Las Casas finally ended the concept that the Indian was a natural slave. But the damage had been done.

Bloodshed, cruelty, and abuse could not last forever. The Anglo-Saxons remained alone in thinking that the only good Indian is a dead Indian, since the Spanish, the Portuguese, and the French, once the period of slaughter had waned, altered their philosophy and incorporated the Indians into their colonial cultures in greater or less degree. I have already said enough about the degrading effect of the lust for wealth upon the white conquerors. There is, apparently, something in-

herent in the extractive industries that awakens the baser emotions, as witness the California gold rush and that into the Yukon. But I suggest that the obsession with easy tangible wealth did more than cast a delusive mirage over the period of discovery and exploration. Its effects have never disappeared. The legendary Sicilian peasant who came to New York City only to be disappointed that the streets were not paved with gold is a symbolic cultural figure. Colonial promotion literature in France and England during the sixteenth and seventeenth centuries continually sounds the note of quick and rapid wealth, nor does this lure cease when, in the eighteenth century, it intermingles with the attractive picture of a radical republic. Greedy shipping interests had already begun to exploit the gullibility of simple men, as deluded immigrants swarmed aboard vessels that were sometimes no better than slave ships. These immigrants arrived in the New World in thousands of cases ill-equipped to survive—as ill-adapted to the New World as were the elder Shimerdas in *My Antonia* or the sodden proletariat pictured in *How the Other Half Lives, The Jungle,* or *Twenty Years at Hull House.* The tough-minded, of course, survived, and became the "New Americans."

If the discoverers, in Peter Martyr's words, "ruined and exhausted themselves by their own folly and civil strife, failing absolutely to rise to the greatness expected of men who accomplish such wonderful things"— a judgment at once understandable and premature— the natives of the New World proved to be something less than pastoral inhabitants of an Earthly Paradise. The contrast between the two sides of the shield was sometimes merely puzzling and sometimes horrifying. When Verrazano made his voyage along the Atlantic seaboard in 1524 he found the Indians of the Carolina coast friendly and good-looking. They showed, he said, "the greatest delight on beholding us, wondering at our dress, countenances, and complexion"; they were "of good proportions, of middle stature, a little above our own, broad across the breast, strong in the arms and well formed in the legs and other parts of the body." They lived in a plentiful and lovely country where "the air is salubrious, pure and temperate, and free from the extremes of both hot and cold" and the sea is "calm, not boisterous, and its waves are gentle." But when he got to Cape Cod or its vicinity all was changed. The vegetation was "indicative of a cold climate," and the people were "entirely different from the others we had seen . . . so rude and barbarous that we were unable by any signs we could make, to hold communication with them." Clad in skins, living by hunting and fishing, and raising no crops, the Indians were hostile. "No regard was paid to our courtesies; when we had nothing left to exchange with them, the men at our departure made the most brutal signs of disdain and contempt possible." And when the expedition tried to enter the interior, the Indians shot the white men with arrows and raised the most horrible cries.

But this contrast was comparatively mild. The Europeans also discovered cannibals. In the West Indies Columbus's men came across "a great quantity of men's bones and skulls hung up about the houses like vessels to hold things" and reported bestial habits of the Caribs that were far, far different from the bookish theoric Montaigne was to build on the cannibals. The Caribs raid other islands and treat their captives

with a cruelty which appears to be incredible, for they eat the male children whom they have from [captive women] and only rear those whom they have from their own women. As for the men whom they are able to take, they bring such as are alive to their houses to cut up for meat, and those who are dead they eat at once. They say that the flesh of a man is so good that there is nothing like it in the world, and it certainly seems to be so, for, from the bones which we found in their houses, they had gnawed everything that could be gnawed, so that nothing was left on them except what was too tough to be eaten. In one house there was a neck of a man found cooking in a pot. They castrate the boys whom they capture and employ them as servants until they are fully grown, and then when they wish to make a feast, they kill and eat them, for they say that the flesh of boys and women is not good to eat.

The Spaniards captured three such *castrati,* who had fled from the cannibals; four more *castrati* were captured by Vespucci.

Vespucci's men, if his letters are to be believed, were compelled to witness a practical demonstration in cannibalism. On his third voyage the mainland natives seemed to want to parley, and the voyagers in good faith set on shore a "very agile and valiant youth" to treat with them. Thereupon an Indian woman ran from the hill toward the shore, felled the young Christian with a club, and dragged his body up the hillside while the Indian warriors sent such a shower of arrows at the Europeans they could not rescue their shipmate. Other Indian women appeared, tore the young man to pieces, roasted him in the fire, and ate him before the eyes of his horrified companions. Vespucci also dwells upon the libidinousness of the Indian females, Indian promiscuity, treachery, and cannibalism—qualities scarcely offset by his belief that they live for 150 years and are rarely sick. All this was in South America. In the far north Dionysius Settle concluded that the inhabitants were "Anthropophagi, or devourers of mans flesh," "for that there is no flesh or fish which they find dead (smell it never so filthily) but they will eate it, as they finde it without any other dressing. A loathsome thing, either to the beholders or hearers." Loathsome, indeed, for as Peter Martyr is made to say in Richard Eden's colorful English, "There is no man able to behowlde them, but he shall feele his bowelles grate with a certen horroure, nature hath endewed them with soo terrible menacynge, and cruell aspecte." Ritualistic cannibalism was imitated by the *cimarróns,* escaped Negro slaves, who, when they could, "to feede their insatiable revenges," were "accustomed to rost and eate the hearts of all those Spaniards, whom at any time they could lay hand upon," and on occasion starving Spaniards also ate the flesh of the dead.

Equally appalling was human sacrifice, for example, that practiced by the Aztecs. There are many accounts, one of the most graphic being that by Gómara in his *Historia General de las Indias* (1552), which, despite attempts to suppress it, was widely disseminated in Spanish, Italian, French, and English, especially Part II, the *Conquista de México,* translated into English by Thomas Nichols as *The Conquest of the VV east India* (1578). The Nichols translation carries an even more authentic repulsion than does the Spanish original.

Elizabethans read of the great temple in Tenochtitlán with its two great altars, its twin hideous idols, its gutters of blood; and of

> other darke houses full of idols, greate & small, wrought of sundry mettals, they are all bathed and washed with bloud, and do shewe very blacke through theyr dayly sprinklyng and anoynting them with the same, when any man is sacrificed: yea and the walles are an inche thicke with bloud, and the grounde is a foote thicke of bloud, so that there is a diuelish stench. The Priests or Ministers goe dayly into those Oratories, and suffer none others but great personages to enter in. Yea and when any such goeth in, they are bounde to offer some man to be sacrificed, that those bloudy hangmen and ministers of the Diuell may washe their handes in bloud of those so sacrificed, and to sprinkle their house therewith.

The priest bound the victim face upward on a large sacrificial stone with convenient runnels, opened his living breast with a flint knife, tore out the heart, and, offering it to the idol, smeared the god with fresh blood. "This done, they pluckt of the skinnes of a certeine number of them, the which skinnes so many auntient persons put incontinent upon their naked bodies, al fresh & bloudy, as they wer fleane from the deade carcasses. . . . In *Mexico* the king him selfe did put on one of these skinnes, being of a principall captiue, and daunced among the other disguised persons, to exalte and honor the feast." I spare the reader other gory details but I must add that according to Gómara and Bernal Díaz del Castillo the victim was then cut up and eaten.

The torture of prisoners taken in Indian warfare was, Montaigne to the contrary notwithstanding, common practice before the Portuguese or any other Europeans taught torture to the aborigines. A single episode of such torture, drawn from the *Jesuit Relations,* ought to suffice:

> There is no cruelty comparable to that which they practice on their enemies. As soon as the captives are taken, they brutally tear off their nails with their teeth; I saw the fingers of these poor creatures, and was filled with pity, also I saw a large hole in the arm of one of them; I was told that it was a bite of the Savage who had captured him; the other had a part of a finger torn off, and I asked him if the fire had done that, as I thought it was a burn. He made a sign to show me that it had been taken off by the teeth. I noticed the same cruelty among the girls and women, when these poor prisoners were dancing; for, as they passed before the fire, the women blew and drove the flames over in their direction to burn them. When the hour comes to kill their captives, they are fastened to a stake; then the girls, as well as the men, apply hot and flaming brands to those portions of the body which are the

most sensitive, to the ribs, thighs, chest, and several other places. They raise the scalp from the head, and then throw burning sand upon the skull, or uncovered place. They pierce the arms at the wrists with sharp sticks, and pull the nerves out through these holes. In short, they make them suffer all that cruelty and the Devil can suggest. At last, as a final horror, they eat and devour them almost raw.

This, says one of the Jesuits cheerfully, is what some of us may look forward to.

So much for a Catholic martyr. In May 1782, near Muddy Creek, Pennsylvania, the Reverend John Corbley started to church with his wife and five children, suspecting no danger and, apparently, walking ahead of his family while he meditated deeply on his sermon. He was suddenly aroused by frightful shrieks as the Indians leaped on his family.

> My dear wife had a sucking child in her arms; this little infant they killed and scalped. They then struck my wife sundry times, but not getting her down, the Indian who had aimed to shoot me ran to her, shot her through the body, and scalped her. My little boy, an only son, about six years old, they sunk the hatchet into his brains, and thus dispatched him. A daughter, besides the infant, they also killed and scalped. My eldest daughter who is yet alive, was hid in a tree about twenty yards from the place where the rest were killed, and saw the whole proceedings. She, seeing the Indians all go off, as thought, got up and deliberately crept out of the hollow trunk; but one of them espying her, ran hastily up, knocked her down and scalped her; also her only surviving sister, on whose head they did not leave more than one inch round, either of flesh or skin, besides taking a piece out of her skull. She and the before-mentioned one are still miraculously preserved.

The whole ghastly operation took, he says, about ten minutes. The father fainted and was found and borne off by a friend who arrived after the massacre.

Not inexpert in torture, Europeans nevertheless felt there was something hellish and obscene about these animals that looked like men. Anything wicked could be postulated of them—lying, treachery, filthiness, greed, brutality, laziness, lasciviousness. Peter Martyr solemnly chronicles the tradition of a country called "Inzignanin," the original inhabitants of which had been visited by men who had tails a meter long. In the Arctic, Frobisher's crew captured a female "whom divers of our Saylers supposed to be eyther a devill, or a witch," so they plucked off her "buskins," found she was not cloven-footed, and "for her ougly hew and deformity we let her goe." One native of that region, being captured by a stratagem, for very choler and disdaine he bit his tongue in twaine," whereas others, to avoid being taken, committed suicide by jumping into the sea. At the other end of the globe Lopez Vaz, a Portuguese, reported that the natives of Tierra del Fuego were ten or eleven feet high. There were rumors of headless men with eyes in their breasts and of fierce Amazonian women. Obviously such creatures worshiped the devil, practiced every diabolical art, and were witches and wizards. Frobisher's crew were sure the Eskimos "are great inchanters, and use many charmes of witchcraft." John Davis found them filled with a "devilish nature." Henry Hawks wrote that the witchcraft of the Indians was such that when Europeans come near the seven golden cities of Cíbola, "they cast a mist upon them, so that they cannot see them." John Hawkins found them "no such kinde of people as wee tooke them to bee, but more devilish a thousand partes and are eaters and devourers of any man they can catch." Francis Drake, when he coasted along Brazil, watched the Indians making fires, "a sacrifice (as we learned) to the devils, about which they use conjurations, making heapes of sande and other ceremonies, that when any ship shall goe about to stay upon their coast . . . stormes and tempests may arise, to the casting away of ships and men." The chief god they worship, reported Captain John Smith, is the devil: "They say that they haue conference with him, and fashion themselves as neare to his shape as they can imagine." In this Protestant judgment Catholicism concurred. Wrote Father Joseph Jouvency: "They call some divinity, who is the author of evil, 'Manitou,' and fear him exceedingly. Beyond doubt it is the enemy of the human race, who extorts from some people divine honors and sacrifices." And Father Pierre Biard agreed:

> . . . all this region, though capable of the same prosperity as ours, nevertheless through Satan's malevolence, which reigns there, is only a horrible wilderness. . . .

> They are, I say, savage, haunting the woods, ignorant, lawless and rude: they are wanderers, with nothing to attach them to a place, neither homes nor relationship, neither possessions nor love of country; as a people they have bad habits, are extremely lazy, gluttonous, profane, treacherous, cruel in their revenge, and given up to all kinds of lewdness, men and women alike. . . .

The conflict of cultures was inevitable. When the white man tried to kidnap the Indian with the intent either of exhibiting him as a trophy, learning his language, or turning him into an interpreter, the Indian naturally grew suspicious and retaliated with whatever weapons he could command. When the Indian first roasted and ate a captured white man in order to acquire his knowledge or for ritualistic purposes sensible enough to the aborigine, the white man interpreted the act as the quintessence of diabolism. Against the superior military power and technological skill of the Europeans,

the Indian could oppose only cunning and his knowledge of the land. Renaissance man—and this is particularly true of the Renaissance Englishman—found it difficult to understand how human beings (if they were human) could live without visible government, religion, or morality, and he therefore tended to assume that Indian culture, like all the rest of the world, was somehow organized under a king or an emperor with whom one could deal legally in matters of war and peace and the sale of land. Obviously the Indian had no concept of what to the Europeans were the elements of civil society; and he could fight the white man only by what the white man thought of as the basest treachery. The Machiavellian qualities in the European power struggle in some degree prepared the discoverers and the early colonists for some amount of bad faith, but not for the Indian usage of bad faith. Neither party to a treaty could understand what the word meant to the other.

What could the Indians be, except children of the devil? On De Soto's expedition one Indian, visibly possessed by the devil, was subjected to exorcism by the friars. As late as 1666 George Alsop in *A Character of the Province of Maryland* not only seriously advanced the proposition that the "Susquehanok" Indians had no other deity but alleged that every four years a child was sacrificed to the devil, who in return permitted the Indians to talk to him by raising a great tempest; and Edward Johnson described their deity in some detail:

> It hath been a thing very frequent before the English came, for the Divell to appear unto them in a bodily shape, sometimes very ugly and terrible, and sometimes like a white boy, and chiefly in the most hideous woods and swamps . . . and since we came hither, they tell us of a very terrible beast for shape and bigness, that came into a wigwam toward the Northeast parts, remote from any English plantations, and took away six men at a time, who were never seen afterward.

Who but the offspring of Satan, theologians to the contrary notwithstanding, would destroy even their male children because of their dreams, or cast away their daughters at birth and cause them to be eaten by dogs? Or dispossess old women of such clothing as they had and shoot arrows at the pudenda? Or seize small children by the leg, throw them high in the air, and shoot them full of arrows before they reached the ground? Or kill a trusting New Englander, his Bible in his hand, rip him open, and put his Bible in his belly?

Cruelty begat cruelty, deceit was countered by deceit, and bad faith on the one side excused bad faith on the other. Although De Soto's expedition was, within reason, pacific in intention, the kidnaping of Indians by De Ayllón's expedition in 1521 had led to the massacre of some two hundred Spaniards by the Indians, and

De Soto found himself the heir of a hostile attitude he could do nothing to overcome. The story of his expedition is one long tale of ambush, treachery, and revenge. Thus, perhaps imitating Cortés and warned of the intention of the Chief Vitachuco to assassinate the Spanish leader, De Soto seized that Indian and thus set off a series of reprisals. Vitachuco and his fellow captives plotted against the Spaniards, and the chief attempted to strangle De Soto at high table, whereupon the captive Indians were massacred by the whites. The long struggle to overcome the Apalachee Indians, "gigantic in stature" and "very valiant and spirited" is a second chapter in the story, and the slaughter of both Indians and Spaniards at the burning of the Indian town of Mavila is a third—an episode that started an incipient mutiny in the remnants of De Soto's army. The Spaniards, working their way through difficult terrain, had to kidnap Indians for guides, the Indians retaliated by ambushing and assassinating the Spaniards, and the Spaniards countered on occasion by cutting off the hands and noses of Indians and sending them back to their villages as a warning. In the Pequot War of 1637, the burning and massacre of some hundreds of Indian men, women, and children trapped in the "fort" at Mystic, Connecticut—a massacre that continued until the English "grew weary"—drew no reproof from contemporary chroniclers but was on the contrary regarded as a signal proof of divine intervention. "The Lord," wrote Edward Johnson in his *Wonder-Working Providence* (1653), the first published history of Massachusetts, "was pleased to assist his people in this warre, and deliver them out of the Indians hands." As for the famous King Philip's War, which lasted two years, cost the lives of one-tenth of the adult males in the Massachusetts Bay Colony, and exposed two-thirds of the towns and villages to Indian raids, the contest was illustrated on the side of the Indians by the raping and scalping of women, the cutting off of fingers and feet of men, the skinning of white captives, the ripping open of the bellies of pregnant women, the cutting off of the penises of the males, and the wearing of the fingers of white men as bracelets or necklaces. Naturally the whites retaliated. When King Philip was finally shot, his head and hands were cut off and his body was quartered and hung on four trees. "The Providence of God wonderfully appeared" in this, wrote "R. H." in *The Warr in New-England Visibly Ended* (1677).

The discovery that the Earthly Paradise was inhabited by the offspring of Satan compelled Europeans to choose between two alternatives, neither of which proved successful. Either you converted the Indians into children of Christ or you exterminated them in a holy war. The Mediterranean peoples made more progress in converting the children of Satan, the British in exterminating them. The long history of American injustice to the red man springs from a profound and brutal misunderstanding that passed into literary tradition, for, as Roy Harvey Pearce has shown, the so-called Indian captivity narratives understandably passed from fact to fiction. They became exercises in emotion, not historical records. The Indian long remained a figure of terror, a child of hell, the evil being of *The Jibbenainosay* of Robert Montgomery Bird, the reason why Custer's massacre occurred and why Kentucky was known as a dark and bloody ground. If we put aside a few humanitarian successes like those of John Eliot and the Quakers, a handful of documents like Eleazar Wheelock's *Plain and Faithful Narrative of the Original Design, Rise, Progress and Present State of the Indian Charity-School at Lebanon* (1763) or William Smith's *Indian Songs of Peace: with a Proposal in a Prefatory Epistle, for Erecting Indian Schools* (New York, 1752)—and of course *Ramona and A Century of Dishonor*—it is clear that the Indian was not sentimentalized until he became relatively harmless. For most of North America throughout most of its history the Indian has been, like the rattlesnake, the alligator, and poison ivy, an inexplicable curse on Utopia. His tawny presence darkened the landscape, and his war whoop chilled the blood.

In 1493 the New World dawned on the European imagination as a few small, delectable islands, any one of which was understandable in terms of a *hortus inclusus,* the walls of which sheltered the Earthly Paradise, or a bower of bliss, or the garden of eternal youth and spring, from the dark wilderness of the world. By 1607 the New World had stretched to an endless and confusing coastline running from Greenland and Baffin Bay through Gargantuan twistings and turnings to the Strait of Magellan and Tierra del Fuego. In any circumstances such geographical extension would have rendered untenable the concept of an isle of youth, verdancy, sunshine, and perpetual spring. But something more troubling than the interminable extension of the land occurred. That something was the discovery of the terror of nature in the New World. In that vast region the extreme thing seemed to happen more often than not. It turned out to be a land of the incredible, the immeasurable, the unpredictable, and the horrifying.

For example, the Elizabethan who read Richard Eden's translation of Peter Martyr (1555) found the New World a strange jumble of phenomena, the abnormal being especially prominent. He might, it is true, get reconciled to white Indians, tortoises so thick they stayed the course of the ships, mountains whereof some were of bright blue or azurine color and others glistering white, peaks fifty miles high, the disappearance of the North Star, white and thick water, trees of such bigness that sixteen men joining hands together and standing in compass could scarcely embrace one of them, and so on, but what of the many furious seas running with a fall as if they were the streams of "floods," the whirlpools and shelves along the shore and in the ocean, with many other dangers and straits by reason of the multitude of islands, a river hastening with so swift and furious a course that by the violence and greatness thereof it drives back the ocean though the sea be rough and enforced with a contrary wind? There was, it was rumored, a gigantic lump somewhere in the middle of the earth, there were enormous tides and terrific lightning, there were men so huge that one of their feet was almost as long as two feet of a European, bats as big as doves, a monster which, coming out of the sea, carried away a sailor from the midst of his companions, a fish of such huge greatness that with a stroke of its tail it broke the rudder of a brigantine, another that carried off ten men, a curlew as large as a stork, apples that turned into worms, walking corpses, and a monster as big as an ox, armed with a long snout like that of an elephant and yet no elephant, of the color of an ox and yet no ox, with the "house" of a horse and yet no horse, with ears much like those of an elephant but not so open or so hanging down, yet much wider than the ears of other beasts. I assemble these details at random from a few pages of a single book. Let us go into more specific instances.

Even Columbus, that religious optimist, was occasionally appalled by the unbridled forces of nature. Consider this incident from his third voyage:

> And in the night, when it was already very late, being on the deck of the ship, I heard a very terrible roaring which came from the direction of the south towards the ship. And I stayed to watch, and I saw the sea from west to east rising, like a hill as high as the ship, and still it came towards me little by little. And above it, there came a wave which advanced, roaring with a very great noise with the same fury of roaring as that of the other currents, which, I have said, appeared to me as the waves of the sea breaking on the rocks. To this very day, I remember the fear that I had lest the wave should overwhelm the ship when it came upon her, and it passed by and reached the strait where it continued for a great while.

Things like this did not happen in the tidy Mediterranean.

Other Europeans suffered other experiences equally terrifying. While the Jesuit Father Biard went to visit some Malouins on the island of Emeneic in the Saint John River in French Canada, when he was about a league and a half from his destination, twilight ended, night came on, and the stars appeared, "when suddenly, toward the Northward, a part of the heavens became blood-red: and this light spreading, little by little, in vivid streaks and flashes, moved directly over the settlement of the Malouins and there stopped. The red glow was so brilliant that the whole river was tinged and made luminous by it. This apparition lasted some eight minutes, and as soon as it disappeared another

came of the same form, direction and appearance." The good father felt it was prophetic of something, he knew not what; the Indians said it meant war. "Everything was turned topsy-turvy; confusion, discord, rage, uproar reigned between our people and those of St. Malo. I do not doubt that a cursed band of furious and sanguinary spirits were hovering about all this night, expecting every hour and moment a horrible massacre of the few Christians who were there." Let modern man murmur something about the Aurora Borealis if he will; then let him think himself backward to an era when witchcraft was everywhere and Satan roamed a wilderness, seeking whom he might devour.

Or consider the white terror of the north. In the month of July 1497, Sebastian Cabot found monstrous heaps of ice swimming in the sea, amid continual daylight. During Martin Frobisher's first voyage a great island of ice fell apart, making a noise as if a great cliff had fallen into the ocean; during his second voyage, "in place of odoriferous and fragrant smels of sweete gums, & pleasant notes of musicall birdes, which other Countreys in more temperate Zones do yeeld, wee tasted the most boisterous Boreal blasts mixt with snow and haile, in the moneths of June and July"; and on his third he met "great Isles of yce lying on the seas, like mountaines," in "fogge and hidious mist" so thick the sailors in his little vessels could not see one another. Once

> the yce had so invironed us, that we could see neither land nor sea, as farre as we could kenne: so that we were faine to cut our cables to hang over boord for fenders, somewhat to ease the ships sides from the great and driry strokes of the yce: some with Capstan barres, some fending off with oares, some with planckes of two ynches thicke, which were broken immediately with the force of the yce, some going out upon the yce to beare it off with their shoulders from the ships. But the rigorousnes of the tempest was such, and the force of the yce so great, that not onely they burst and spoyled the . . . provision, but likewise so rased the sides of the ships, that it was pitifull to behold, and caused the hearts of many to faint.

In Warwick Sound "truely it was wonderfull to heare and see the rushing and noise that the tides do make in this place with so violent a force that even our ships lying a hull were turned sometimes round about even in a moment after the maner of a whirlepoole, and the noyse of the streame no lesse to be heard afarre off, then the waterfall of London Bridge." To Elizabethan ears this last comparison was not an anti-climax. When one considers that the largest vessels sent on these desperate seas were by our standards mere cockleshells, one's respect for the hardihood of the Tudor navy vastly increases.

The earth was likewise unpredictable. "In the far north there is great likelihood of Earthquakes or thunder: for that there are huge and monstrous mountaines, whose greatest substance are stones, and those stones so shaken with some extraordinarie meanes that one is separated from another, which is discordant from all other Quarries." The Jesuits attributed the extreme cold of Canada to the "wild and primitive condition of the land," which, because of the boundless forest, was never warmed by the sun, with the result that the snow and the water stagnated there "with no possibility of being consumed. Thus, from these lands nothing can arise except cold, gloomy, and mouldy vapors; and these are the fogs when the wind ceases, and are piercing cold when they are put in motion and blown into a fury."

In Middle America, at Darien, "when the slaves sprinkle the floor of the houses, toads spring into existence from the drops of water that fall from their hands, just as in other places I have seen drops of water changed into fleas," and the climate was so insalubrious that Spaniards returning from Panama "are as yellow as though they suffered from liver complaint." Why this affliction in the midst of plenty? For Peter Martyr also informed Pope Leo X that in Panama cabages, beets, lettuces, salads, and other garden stuff were ripe in ten days and that pumpkins and melons could be picked twenty-eight days after the seeds were sown. Such was the paradox of the New World.

The terrain of South America also had its fearsome aspects. So great was the fury of the current of the Orinoco that "if any boat but touch upon any tree or stake, it is impossible to save any one person therein" and "no halfe day passed, but the river began to rage and overflowe very fearefully, and the raines came downe in terrible showers, and gustes in great abundance." Ralegh, from whom this is taken, saw far off a mountain of crystal like a white church-tower, over which "there falleth . . . a mighty river which toucheth no part of the side of the mountaine, but rusheth over the toppe of it, and falleth to the ground with so terrible a noyse and clamor, as if a thousand great bels were knockt one against another. I thinke there is not in the world so strange an over-fall, nor so wonderfull to behold." Wonderful, indeed. Yet in that same strange continent a wind blows through the passes of the Andes "which is not very strong nor violent, but proceeds in such sort, that men fall downe dead, in a manner without feeling, or at the least, they loose their feete and hands: the which may seem fabulous, yet is it most true." This Jerome Costilla discovered, who lost his toes, "which fell off in passing the Desart of Chille, being perished with this ayre, and when he came to looke on them, they were dead . . . even as a rotten Apple falleth from the tree." Even weirder was the sight of the bodies of dead soldiers of Almagro's army lying "without any stinke or corruption" while a young boy kept alive in a cave nearby, feeding on dried horseflesh. "It is a strange thing, the quality of this cold ayre, which kils, and also preserves the dead bodies

without corruption."

And there were still different terrors:

> . . . the hot exhalations which engender in the inner concavities of the Earth, seeme to be the materiall substance of fire in the Volcans, whereby there kindleth another more grosse matter, and makes these shewes of flame and smoake that come forth. And these exhalations (finding no easie issue in the Earth) move it, to issue forth with great violence, whereby wee heare that horrible noise under the Earth, and likewise the shaking of the Earth, being stirred with this burning exhalation; Even as Gunpowder in mynes, having fire put to it breaks Rocks and Walls: and as the Chesnut laid into the fire, leapes and breakes with a noise, when as it casts forth the aire (which is contayned within the huske) by the force of the fire: Even so these Earthquakes doe most commonly happen in places neere the water or Sea. . . . There hath happened in Peru (the which is wonderfull, and worth to be noted) Earthquakes which have runne from Chille unto Quitto, and that is above a hundred leagues. . . . Upon the coast of Chille . . . there was so terrible an Earthquake, as it overturned whole Mountaines, and thereby stopped the course of Rivers which it converted into Lakes, it beat downe Townes, and slue a great number of people, causing the Sea to leave her place some leagues, so as the ships remayned on drie ground, farre from the ordinarie Roade, with many other heavie and horrible things.

Hispaniola developed sharks, a bitter-sweet lake, divine miracles, and diabolical tricks duly set forth in the Third Decade of Peter Martyr. Oviedo describes crows "whose breath stinketh in the morning, and is sweete in the afternoone: the excrement which they avoide is a living worme" and tells of "Caterpillers, which shine in the night fiftie or a hundred paces off, only from that part of the bodie whence the legges issue: others only have their head shining. I have seene some a spanne long very fearefull." The "crocodile" is again and again described, always in terms of loathing, as "a most fierce and cruell beast, although it be slow and heavie. Hee goes hunting and seekes his prey on the Land, what he takes alive, he drownes it in the water, yet doth he not eate it, but out of the water, for that his throate is of such fashion, as if there entred any water, he should easily be drowned. It is a wonderfull thing to see a combat betwixt a Caymant and a Tigre, whereof there are most cruell at the Indies." This particular "Caymant" carried off a young Indian child and "sodainely plunged into the Sea" with it.

Equally alarming was a "cunning and ferocious animal" whose habitat was, apparently, Venezuela:

> It is the size of a French dog and is very rarely seen. When twilight falls, it leaves its hiding-place in the woods and comes into the town, where it

prowls about houses, wailing loudly. Those who are ignorant of the animal's subtlety would believe a child was being beaten, and many inexperienced people were deceived into incautiously going to the place where the imaginary child was weeping. The wild beast, lying in wait, then springs upon the unfortunate creature, and in the twinkling of an eye tears him to bits.

Your only protection was to carry a burning torch and whirl it around, upon seeing which the animal flees. It is seldom seen in daylight.

And the sea, too, had its horrors. The Gilbert expedition, to choose only one instance, beheld in the ocean "a very lion to our seeming, in shape, hair and colour, not swimming after the maner of a beast by mooving of his feete, but rather sliding upon the water with his whole body (excepting the legs) in sight. [He passed by the little fleet] turning his head to and fro, yawning and gaping wide, with ougly demonstration of long teeth, and glaring eies . . . he sent forth a horrible voyce, roaring or bellowing as doeth a lion." Gilbert, seeing this monster, rejoiced "that he was to warre against such an enemie, if it were the devill." But the early accounts can furnish a whole menagerie, a weird aquarium of such fearful creatures.

It cannot be argued that these terrors were found everywhere except in the future United States. The Coronado expedition (1541) not only stumbled into the awe-inspiring spectacle of the Grand Cañon, but ran into "sandbanks of hot ashes which it was impossible to cross without being drowned," where "the ground . . . trembled like a sheet of paper . . . as if there were lakes underneath," so that "it seemed wonderful and like something infernal," and also into a hailstorm with hailstones as big as bowls or bigger, that fell thick as raindrops. The Narváez expedition started out numbering six hundred colonists and soldiers, of whom only four survived, and experienced terrific tempests during which "we heard much tumult and great clamor of voices, the sound of timbrels, flutes and tambourines as well as other instruments," and which lodged a boat in the treetops and disfigured some of the dead bodies so that they could not be recognized, but when the pitiful survivors in their crazy boats came to the mouth of the Mississippi, they were unable to make for land, so violent was the current, and suffered a wind that drove them further out to sea, not to speak of other gigantic calamities. De Soto found the same river so vast that "a man standing on the shore could not be told, whether he were a man or something else, from the other side," and the gigantic force of the current, flowing turbidly, brought down huge trees; and off the Texas coast the mosquitoes were so numerous that the sails, which were white, appeared black with these insects at daylight, and it was a question whether the men could survive their bites.

The details enumerated in these pages could be increased a thousandfold. I have not troubled to present what I have given in logical order or temporal sequence, preferring to suggest the illogical ways by which such things made their impression upon the European imagination. If the modern reader has acquired a feeling of a vague, rich jungle of repellent or terrifying things, animals, plants, and men, it is the impression he would have received, I suggest, had he been a literate European of the sixteenth or seventeenth century interested in reading about the new-found land. I suggest that this cloud of unpleasantness is one of the reasons why English colonial enterprise was so slow in getting under way. Between the cruelties of the Inquisition in Mexico—and on these one could read the reports of Job Hortop and David Ingram, in Hakluyt—and the cruelties of Satan and his savages, what room was there for the Englishman? Why should the Jacobean enterpriser bestir himself? Few expeditions returned any profit, many of them suffered disaster, and virtually all of them encountered something repellent in the way of climate, soil, wild beasts, wild Indians, or hostile whites. A powerful anti-image was formed.

Nor is the importance of this anti-image of the New World confined to the spacious days of great Elizabeth or those of her immediate successor. Modern literary theory, deeply influenced by the psychology of Freud and Jung, makes much play with the dark night of the American soul; and critics find such writers as Poe, Melville, Hawthorne, and Henry James more to their liking than they do writers like Franklin, Longfellow, Whittier, and Howells. This interesting revolution in taste springs from a sophisticated belief in myth, preferably primitive in tone. The myth-markers, however, do not go deep enough in time. If on the one hand the New World presented to the European Renaissance the possibility of that renewal of mankind that led the Jesuits to establish the almost perfect state in Paraguay and the Fourierists and their kind to create perfect commonwealths in Indiana, or on the Ohio or in the Middle West or in Texas, this obverse image, this other side of the coin, repelled and terrified, while it also fascinated, many minds. The unpredictable, the abnormal, the inhuman, the cruel, the savage, and the strange in terms of European experience were from the beginning part of the image of a land that was ours before we were the land's. The New World was filled with monsters animal and monsters human; it was a region of terrifying natural forces, of gigantic catastrophes, of unbearable heat and cold, an area where the laws of nature tidily governing Europe were transmogrified into something new and strange. Terror and gigantism have their attractions, psychologists say; and the Renaissance image of the New World was compounded of both positive and negative elements that attract and repel. We inherit the image, and its elements haunt us still.

## NEW WORLD EXPLORERS AND NATIVE AMERICANS

### J. H. Elliott (essay date 1975)

SOURCE: "The Great American Debate," in *The New York Review of Books,* Vol. XXII, No. 8, May 15, 1975, pp. 3-6.

[*In the following excerpt, Elliott discusses the debate surrounding exploration and colonization of America during the sixteenth and eighteenth centuries, which is the subject of Antonello Gerbi's critical study* The Dispute of the New World. *He then considers the "double vision" which "proved to be of critical importance for the evolution of European attitudes to the indigenous peoples of the Americas."*]

Anyone who is bothered by the marked absence of elephants from the woods and forests of America has only to turn to the pages of that great eighteenth-century naturalist, Buffon, to find the reason for this sad lacuna. Nature in America is less active, less varied, and less vigorous than in Europe because America is a new continent. Therefore the best it can manage in the line of pachyderms is the modest tapir. With time, perhaps, things may change—not that the tapir can ever hope to grow into an elephant, but at least those European breeds which, like the sheep and goat, have made the transatlantic crossing will no longer actually decrease in size in their new environment.

Buffon was a large man—a fact which may help to explain his predilection for the bigger animals as representing a higher level on the scale of creation. But within the large frame there dwelled a generous spirit, and when he moved from American quadrupeds to bipeds he treated the latter with relative moderation. The natives of America could not, of course, escape the general rule that governed the natural phenomena of the New World. "The savage is feeble and small in his organs of generation; he has neither body hair nor beard, and no ardour for the female of his kind. Although lighter than the European, on account of his habit of running more, he is nevertheless much less strong in body; . . . he lacks vivacity, and is lifeless in his soul."

But Buffon was ready enough to leave the question there. Not so, however, the abbé Cornelius de Pauw. In his *Recherches philosophiques sur les Américains* of 1768, this querulous dogmatist, suitably fortified by the rationalism of the eighteenth century at its most irrational, was unwilling to allow the human inhabitants of the New World the benefits of Buffon's doubts. For De Pauw the native American, so far from being

an immature animal or an overgrown child, was a degenerate being; and this was because De Pauw's America was not young but corrupt. In that debased environment only insects and reptiles prospered, and even these suffered from notable deficiencies, for "the American crocodiles and alligators have neither the impetuosity nor the fury of those of Africa."

Not surprisingly De Pauw's provocative assertions conjured up a storm of protest on both sides of the Atlantic. The virility of American men, the ardor of American women, the fecundity of American animals—all these became the subjects of furious and often erudite debate. Was America youthful or degenerate, innocent or corrupt? For the eccentric Lord Kames, South Carolina was the only exception to the general rule: "Europeans there die so fast that they have not time to degenerate." For Benjamin West, on the other hand, a Mohawk was comparable to the Apollo Belvedere, while Thomas Jefferson assembled a formidable array of statistics to refute the pernicious thesis of American degeneracy.

This great American debate, which long outlasted its eighteenth-century proponents, and indeed has continued into our own times, if in a somewhat debased and diluted form, is the subject of Antonello Gerbi's vast and fascinating book, *The Dispute of the New World.* A summary version of this first made its appearance in Spanish in 1943, but inflation then set in, and it re-emerged as an eight-hundred-page Italian volume in 1955. Now at last, updated and admirably translated by Dr. Jeremy Moyle, we have it in English; and none too soon, for this is a book which should be on the shelf of everyone who is curious not only about the European image of America but also about the history of man's attitude to man. Dr. Gerbi's study is a monument both to erudition and to fastidious wit; the outcome of years of reading and reflection by a historian of ideas who is at once playful and wise.

In method his book may have its defects, belonging as it does to the portmanteau school of intellectual history, which places comprehensiveness before selectivity. Indeed there are moments when the reader, plunged into yet another controversy between long-forgotten polemicists, is likely to feel that Dr. Gerbi has succumbed to Buffon's notion that perfection is directly correlated to size. But as a volume to be sampled rather than read at a sitting, and as a compendium of strange ideas and erudite digressions, *The Dispute of the New World* is a triumph. Even if Dr. Gerbi himself is almost painfully aware of the research still to be undertaken and of the books he has not read, he has succeeded in writing a book that will never have to be written again. The feat is sufficiently rare to deserve an accolade.

But why should anyone bother with these six hundred

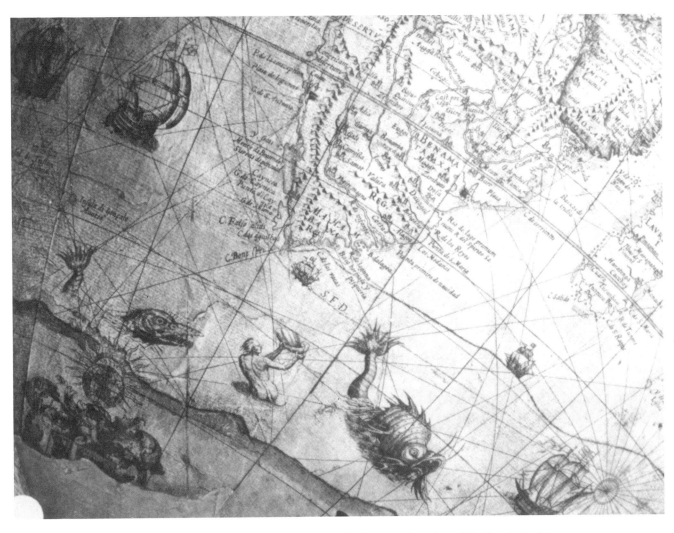

*Detail from the terrestrial globe of Emery Molyneux, 1592, depicting the course of Sir Francis Drake's voyage.*

tightly packed pages which set out to resurrect the often outrageous contributions of ill-informed dogmatists to a controversy that now appears as dead as the dodo? Apart from the insight they provide into some of the more startling vagaries of the human mind, there are at least two good reasons for taking the history of these often wild ideas more seriously than the ideas themselves. The first is the close relationship that existed, at some moments more than others, between attitudes and action. The second is the revelation of the degree to which Europe's vision of American reflected and still reflects its vision of itself.

Dr. Gerbi begins his study with Buffon and De Pauw, although he allows himself a number of backward glances as he follows the great debate. But these backward glances are themselves sufficient to indicate that, even if the thesis of the "weakness" or "immaturity" of the Americas first acquired a scientific formulation in the eighteenth century, it belonged to a general European discussion about the nature of the New World and its inhabitants which stretched right back to Columbus and the moment of discovery. Gerbi himself quotes a revealing remark by Queen Isabella, who, on being informed by Columbus that the trees in the Indies did not have deep roots, was moved to reply that "this land, where the trees are not firmly rooted, must produce men of little truthfulness and less constancy."

This remarkable regal pronouncement, which presumably derived from the environmental and climatic theories of classical antiquity, shows how Europeans tended from the beginning to see America with a double vision. On the one hand the New World was genuinely new—a veritable garden of Eden before the fall of man. Its inhabitants were innocent and uncorrupted beings, holding all things in common, and as yet unspoiled by the European vices of greed and litigation. On the other hand, the New World was a strange and treacherous world, whose trees had shallow roots, and whose peoples led primitive and barbarous lives, shamelessly exposing their nakedness, and eating reptiles and insects (or, still worse, each other).

This double vision proved to be of critical importance for the evolution of European attitudes to the indigenous peoples of the Americas. Arriving in the New World with their own stock of mental furniture and their inherited preconceptions, sixteenth- and seventeenth-century Europeans tended to see its inhabitants less as they were than as they expected them to be. And where reality did impinge, it often acted either to confirm prejudice or to encourage disappointment. If the native of the Americas was conceived of in advance as a noble savage, a closer acquaintance with the frequently shell-shocked victims of European conquest was liable to lead to disillusionment. If, on the other hand, the prior image was that of the ignoble savage, the very strangeness of native customs was liable to reinforce that image in culturally self-confident European minds. The image in turn provided a useful justification for European rule—as many settlers, and not least the promoters of the colonization of Virginia, were quick to grasp.

The Indians of North America must not be allowed to remain a "rude, barbarous and naked people," but must instead be brought to (English-style) "civilitie." This was the message that went forth from London in the 1620s, and provided a rationale for the efforts of the struggling colony. The story of these efforts has now been racily retold by Alden Vaughan in his *American Genesis,* which approaches them through a biographical account of Captain John Smith. Smith's career, both before and after his arrival in America, is a colorful one, and Vaughan makes the most of it; but perhaps its greatest interest lies in watching how a man who had dealt in his time with Transylvanians and Tartars turned his rough expertise on the North American Indians.

Perhaps because he came to the New World with fewer illusions than most of his compatriots, Smith proved a tough and resourceful colonist. He had a proper respect for the Indians' cunning and their warrior skills, but for him they were no more than dangerous adversaries, to be outwitted and subdued. He was impressed, as no Englishman could fail to be impressed, by the majestic figure of Powhatan, but showed not a trace of sympathetic understanding for the Indian way of life. The two worlds met in utter incomprehension when Smith attempted to get Powhatan to acknowledge his subjection to the English crown. "A foule trouble there was," wrote Smith, "to make him kneele to receive his Crowne, he neither knowing the majesty nor meaning of a Crowne, nor bending of the knee. . . ." What clearer indication of total barbarism?

The precariously stable relationship which Smith temporarily succeeded in establishing between the colonists and the Indians was a relationship based on fear; and, as such, a pattern for all too many of the relationships between the European and the non-European world. But, fortunately for the record, the story of Europe's overseas conquests is not exclusively defined by arrogance. Alongside the arrogance there has run a strain of guilt, which has consistently prevented the uncritical acceptance of what was done by Europeans in the name of civility and of Christianity. Against the cry of superiority has run the counter-cry of conscience, and nowhere was this cry more powerfully uttered than in the Hispanic world of the sixteenth century.

Ever since 1597, when the Mexican archbishop of Santo Domingo praised Bartolomé de Las Casas as "the apostle of the Indians," the great Spanish Dominican has stood as a symbol of Europe's uneasiness at its own colonial record. It is hardly surprising that the twentieth century, profoundly preoccupied with imperialism and the problems of decolonization, should have produced an immense concentration of studies on the words and works of Las Casas.

Here, after all, was one of the first Europeans to experience in his relations with non-Europeans that crisis of conscience that was to affect so many others down the course of the centuries. Arriving in Hispaniola in 1502 from his native Seville as a priest who was supposed to promote the Christianization of the natives, he soon became more interested in his agricultural and mining enterprises than in the religious instruction of his flock. But in 1514, after being denied absolution, he found his road to Damascus, and underwent a conversion experience which led him to join the Dominican order and devote his remaining fifty-two years to crusading on behalf of the oppressed Indians of America.

In letter and in person he pressed his case tirelessly at the court of Charles V and Philip II; he obtained permission to undertake a peaceful colonizing project, which proved a fiasco; he aroused the bitter hostility of the Spanish colonists, both as bishop of Chiapas and as a lobbyist in Spain, by his attempts to prevent the exploitation of the Indians and secure legislation to improve their well-being; and he produced some eighty writings—some of them extremely voluminous—to publicize his cause. The passionate commitment, the gift for publicity, the skill in exercising pressure on a vacillating government—all these make the great Dominican very much a figure for our times. If conquistadors like Cortés and Pizarro were the heroes of the imperialist Europe of the nineteenth century, Las Casas could hardly fail to be the hero of the anti-imperialist Europe of the twentieth. . . .

[Las Casas's] *In Defense of the Indians,* which has been translated from the surviving Latin manuscript into English by the Reverend Stafford Poole, is of the greatest historical interest because of the circumstances in which it was produced. In 1550, in one of the most remarkable episodes in the history of European colonization, the Emperor Charles V ordered that all conquests in the New World should be suspended until a verdict had been reached by a group of theologians and royal officials on the methods and merits of conquest. The case for and against the use of armed force against the indigenous peoples of America was put, respectively, by Juan Ginés de Sepúlveda and Bartolomé de Las Casas.

On the first day Sepúlveda spoke for three hours, summarizing his treatise, the *Demócrates Segundo,* which only found its way into print in the late nineteenth century. On the second day the seventy-six-year-old Las Casas characteristically launched into a public reading of every word of his monumental *In Defense of the Indians*—a process which went on for five days, no doubt to the exhaustion of the judges. These may be forgiven for asking one of their number to provide them with a summary, and it is this summary by De Soto that has had to stand as the expression of Las Casas's side of the argument until the present publication of the original treatise.

It must be confessed that anyone who picks up *In Defense of the Indians* in the hope of rapid enlightenment is likely to feel the deepest sympathy for the unfortunate judges. Las Casas never used one word where he could use three, and he batters away at his opponents with more vigor than finesse. And yet what a superb vindication of an oppressed people Las Casas managed to produce! Couched in the language of scholastic controversy, its method and its content inevitably seem alien and remote to the modern reader. But the message shines through, and now and again a vivid phrase comes ringing down the centuries. "Men want to be taught, not forced." "Has an Indian ever received a benefit from a Spaniard?"

At least to our eyes the moral victory lies with Las Casas. But to the judges the issue seems to have been less clear-cut. The debate apparently ended in a draw, and no formal verdict was ever returned. Some of the principles for which Las Casas had fought with such determination were, however, embodied in the ordinance promulgated by Philip II in 1573 to regulate new conquests. But it was one of the great tragedies of Hispanic colonization that theory and practice were always poles apart.

Although the debate was superficially concerned with the justice of military conquest, in reality it presented two opposing views of the native peoples of America. Sepúlveda, employing Aristotelian arguments, was attempting to justify European domination on the grounds of the natural inferiority of the Indian. Las Casas, operating within the same intellectual frame, was attempting to prove from his first-hand knowledge of the New World and its peoples that they were neither bestial nor barbarous. In the circumstances, it is not surprising that Sepúlveda should have been hailed as a hero by the colonists—or, for that matter, that Las Casas should at certain moments of his career have won the sympathetic attention of an emperor deeply concerned to prevent the establishment of a New World feudalism by the settler community. The ideas of both the great protagonists, however theoretical their presentation, were in fact intimately related to the problems of colonial rule and to the American reality.

This great Valladolid debate of the mid-sixteenth century was in reality the precursor of Dr. Gerbi's great debate of the mid-eighteenth century. In both debates the same themes recur-childishness and barbarism, degeneracy and innocence. The size and strength of the American Indian were as much matters of dispute for Las Casas and Sepúlveda as for Jefferson and De Pauw. And in both instances the debate was passionate because Europe, even more than America, was being put on trial. America, more than any other continent, was Europe's own creation. As such, it was bound to reflect in a very special way the hopes, the ambitions, and the disappointments of those who had created it. Had Europe made America, or destroyed it? Or a bit of both? With what justification, and to whose benefit, had it killed and colonized? Was Europe Captain John Smith, armed with all the self-righteousness of cultural and ethnic superiority? Or was it Bartolomé de Las Casas, deeply troubled by the awareness of a collective guilt? Or, again, was it after all perhaps a bit of both?

## Stephen Greenblatt (essay date 1991)

SOURCE: "Kidnapping Language," in *Marvelous Possessions: The Wonder of the New World,* The University of Chicago Press, 1991, pp. 86-118.

*[In the following essay—a version of which was originally presented at Oxford University and the University of Chicago in 1988—Greenblatt examines descriptions by several explorers of European interactions with Native Americans, and discusses the European approach to interpreting the gestures and signs of an alien culture.]*

On his third voyage to the New World, Columbus found himself anchored off the coast of an island he named Trinidad. A large canoe with twenty-four men, armed with bows and arrows and wooden shields, approached his ship. The sight impressed Columbus; the Indians, he writes, were 'well-proportioned and not negroes, but whiter than the others who have been seen in the Indies, and very graceful and with handsome bodies, and hair long and smooth, cut in the manner of Castile'. He noticed something else: 'They had their heads wrapped in scarves of cotton, worked elaborately and in colours, which, I believe, were *almaizares.*' *Almaizares* were veils or scarves worn by the Moors in Spain, most often as head coverings, and they resembled the East Indian turbans depicted in illuminations of Mandeville and Marco Polo. The natives of Trinidad made a further use of them as well: 'They wore another of these scarves round the body and covered themselves with them in place of drawers.'

As Tzvetan Todorov has shrewdly remarked, Columbus was less an intense observer than an intense reader of signs, and the details that he notes here as elsewhere are not attempts to record the world as it presented itself to his eyes but compilations of significant markers. The idea of discovery as entailing an act of sustained, highly particularized narrative representation of differences was quite alien to him; he had little or no interest in bringing back a rich, circumstantial description of the lands he had found. He had spent years before his embarkation in 1492 collecting signs, and this activity basically set the pattern of his observations thereafter.

Thus, for example, we find him noting in the margins of his books that in the Azores the sea had carried to shore the bodies of two dead men 'who seemed very broad in the face and of an appearance different from that of Christians'; or again that 'in Galway in Ireland, a man and a woman, of extraordinary appearance, have come to land on two tree trunks'; or again that 450 leagues west of Cape St Vincent a Portuguese pilot had hauled aboard his ship a 'piece of wood artificially worked, and, as he judged, not by means of an iron tool.' Columbus's log-book for the outbound voyage in 1492 suggests a kind of obsession with these signs, an obsession quite understandable under the circumstances:

> [September 17]: They saw much weed and very often and it was vegetation from rocks and it came from a westerly direction; they judged themselves to be near land. . . . [T]hey saw much more vegetation and what seemed to be river weed, in which they found a live crab that the Admiral kept; and he says that those were sure signs of land. . . . They saw many dolphins and the men of the *Niña* killed one. The Admiral says here that those signs were from the west where I hope that in mighty God in Whose hands are all victories that very soon He will give us land. (*Diario,* 33-5)

> [September 18]: There appeared in the north a large cloud mass, which is a sign of being near land. (*Diario,* 35)

> [September 19]: Some drizzles of rain came without wind, which is a sure sign of land. (*Diario,* 37)

> [September 20]: Two boobies came to the ship and later another, which is a sign of being near land.

(*Diario,* 37)

Three weeks later Columbus and his men are still noting the signs:

> [October 11]: They saw petrels and a green bulrush near the ship. The men of the caravel *Pinta* saw a cane and a stick and took on board another small stick that appeared to have been worked with iron, and a piece of cane, and other vegetation originating on land, and a small plank. The men of the caravel *Niña* also saw signs of land and a small stick loaded with barnacles. With these signs everyone breathed more easily and cheered up. (*Diario,* 57-9)

These signs, the last collected quite literally on the eve of the discovery, serve as confirmation and promise: confirmation of a theory, promise of the fulfillment of a desire. We can detect in each of the notations the trace of a pause, a caesura, that marks a tension between the visual and the verbal, seeing and reading. The visual seems inherently particularizing: *this* patch of seaweed, *that* bird; the verbal inherently generalizing and abstracting: seaweed and bird are written down as signs of a still invisible and featureless, but theoretically necessary, land. The tension does not disclose a stable or absolute difference here between vision as the particular and language as the general: not only are Columbus's observations known to us entirely through writing, but his act of writing them—and perhaps of seeing them in the first place—depends upon a structure of expectation and perception in which the word is at least as fully implicated as the eye. Still, the form of the journal entry characteristically registers first the material sighting and then its significance; the space between the two—what I have called the caesura—is the place of discovery where the explanatory power of writing repeatedly tames the opacity of the eye's objects by rendering them transparent signs.

That is, the sightings are important only in relation to what Columbus already knows and what he can write about them on the basis of that knowledge. If they fail in their promise, they will be demoted from the status of signs and not noticed any longer. It was, after all, the *known* world that Columbus had set out to discover, if by an unknown route: that was the point of reading Marco Polo and Mandeville. As Todorov writes, Columbus 'knows in advance what he will find; the concrete experience is there to illustrate a truth already possessed, not to be interrogated according to preestablished rules in order to seek the truth.'

The paradox of the meaningful—or perhaps we can simply say the full—sign is that it is empty in the sense of hollow or transparent: a glass through which Columbus looks to find what he expects to find, or, more accurately perhaps, a foreign word he expects to construe and to incorporate into his own language. In the late sixteenth century Richard Mulcaster wittily called this incorporation—the process of making the 'stranger denisons' of other tongues 'bond to the rules of our writing'—*enfranchisement*. The sign that Columbus cannot enfranchise, that is irreducibly strange or opaque, is *en route* to losing its status as a sign. For opacity here can only signal an obstacle standing in the way of the desired access to the known.

In a sense then the best voyage will be one in which one learns next to nothing; most of the signs will simply confirm what one already knows. Columbus wrote, to be sure, that 'the further one goes, the more one learns' (*andando más, más se sabe*). But the context in which he advances this perfectly banal proverb is revealing: he is arguing that the earth's surface has much more dry land than either the 'vulgar' or certain learned Greek and Arab geographers believe. Columbus's appeal to experience merely confirms the book of Esdras and a host of authorities who claim that 'of the seven parts of the world, six are uncovered and the one remaining is covered by water'. The experience is a sign that Columbus—and Petrus Comestor and Nicolaus of Lyra and St Augustine and St Ambrose and Cardinal Pedro de Aliaco and many others—were right all along. The important point is not that this view in fact turned out to be hopelessly wrong but that practical knowledge, the actual observations and recorded events, serve to confirm what Columbus already believes. If they do not, they are not made to serve as the bases for new, radically different hypotheses; they are for the most part simply demoted from signification. Only when these demotions become constant and when the pressure of articulating the known on the site of geographical or cultural difference becomes overwhelming does the representational system itself significantly change. And Columbus himself was strongly resistant to such change.

There is another sense too in which Columbus's reading of the signs tends to confirm what he already knows. In his log-book entry for October 12, 1492, he turns his attention to the naked bodies of the natives and tries to decipher what he sees:

> I saw some who had marks of wounds on their bodies and I made signs to them asking what they were; and they showed me how the people from other islands nearby came there and tried to take them, and how they defended themselves; and I believed and believe that they come here from *tierra firme* to take them captive [*por captivos*]. (*Diario*, 67)

This is, let us remember, the first day of contact between Europeans and natives, and we would do well to be skeptical about the exchange of signs that Columbus reports. I suppose that we are meant to imagine Columbus touching or pointing to the wounds and then miming the question 'why?' or 'who did this?'; the natives in return would gesture toward one of the other islands visible in the distance and then act out invasion, resistance, capture. But charades or pantomimes depend upon a shared gestural language that can take the place of speech; as anyone knows who has tried to ask the simplest of questions in a culture with a different gestural language, exchanges of the kind Columbus describes are fraught with difficulties. And Columbus, of course, takes a step beyond the exchange itself, declaring that he believes (*yo crey, e creo*) that the invaders do not come from the islands toward which the natives appear to be gesturing but from the mainland he has not yet seen and further that the purpose of these invasions is to take captives.

If we ask why he believes this on the basis of scars and a few gestures—why his discourse (anticipating much colonial discourse to follow) is a fantasmatic representation of authoritative certainty in the face of spectacular ignorance—the answer lies in part in his conviction that he is near the mainland of China. But beyond this conviction there is perhaps a deeper source of certainty: when he looks at the bodies of the natives, he sees their literal vulnerability (something that would have been largely hidden beneath the Europeans' armor). Immediately after he has recorded his belief that the inhabitants of the mainland come to take these natives as captives, he continues,

> They should be good and intelligent servants for I see that they say very quickly everything that is said to them; and I believe that they would become Christians very easily, for it seemed to me that they had no religion. Our Lord pleasing, at the time of my departure I will take six of them from here to Your Highnesses in order that they may learn to speak. No animals did I see on this island except parrots. (*Diario*, 67-9)

It is Columbus then who has come from the mainland and intends to take captives. The people he observes before him and whom he admires for skills similar to those of the parrots in the trees have almost no opacity. What he sees when he reads the signs and looks off toward China is himself.

Let us return now to Trinidad and to Columbus's attempt to read the signs. In search of the mainland, he encounters people who look different from the islanders he had been encountering; those have been naked and relatively dark-skinned; these are lighter in color and are wearing, if not clothes, then at least elaborately worked cotton scarves. The scarves must be read: they are, he says, *almaizares*, Moorish veils. This suggests to him that he is at last encountering not virtually transparent members of simple, backward tribes but a different civilization—closer to the culture of the East for which he had been so long searching—and he naturally wishes to make contact with them.

The Indians themselves appeared at first to share this desire. They shouted something to the Europeans which neither Columbus nor anyone else could understand; Columbus, for his part, ordered signs to be made that they should approach. But this initial attempt at communication was a failure; two hours passed, and the Indians kept their distance. Columbus ordered that pans and other bright objects be displayed, but though the Indians drew slightly closer, they did not come up to his ship where he waited eager, as he says, to have speech with them. He then had a remarkable idea: 'I caused to be brought up to the castle of the poop a tambourine, that they might play it, and some young men to dance, believing that they would draw near to see the festivity.' He hoped to coax the natives into contact not by addressing them or by offering objects—both of these time-honored expedients seemed to have failed—but by displaying an art form, staging a cultural event, representing a fiesta. The effect was immediate but not quite what he had in mind: 'As soon as they observed the playing and dancing, they all dropped their oars and laid hand on their bows and strung them, and each one of them took up his shield, and they began to shoot arrows.' The dancing that was for Columbus's culture a token of peace—one thinks of the graceful dancers in Lorenzetti's 'Buon Governo'—was evidently for the natives of Trinidad an unambiguous declaration of war. Columbus ordered the fiesta to stop and the cross-bows to fire: 'I never saw any more of them or of the other inhabitants of this island'.

This small fiasco may be taken as an introduction to a set of questions that greatly concerned both the Europeans and the natives of the New World: How does one read the signs of the other? How does one make signs to the other? How does one reconcile the desire for transparent signs with the opacity of an unknown culture? How does one move from mute wonder to communication? These questions will lead us from the display and interpretation of signs to the exchange of gifts and the bartering of goods, for the hand gestures and facial expressions and mutually incomprehensible speeches made at the first moments of contact almost immediately give way to the proffering of material objects: food, articles of clothing, crafted pieces of metal, stone or glass, animal skins. And barter and gift-giving in turn will lead us to the learning of language. The three modes of communication—mute signs, material exchange, and language—are in turn bound up in a larger question: how is it possible for one system of representation to establish contact with a different system? And this question will lead us to reflect on certain characteristics of the European system of representation in the early modern period—its mobility, its dependence on improvisation, and above all its paradoxical yoking of empty and full, worthless and valuable, counterfeit and real.

It is characteristic of Mandeville that he never registers the problem of cross-cultural communication. He claims to speak with Saracens, Jews, Armenians, Copts, Chaldeans, Indians, Tibetans, and the like with unmediated fluency. He acknowledges linguistic difference but only at the level of the alphabets that he reproduces in the spirit with which he records strange customs and beliefs. These alphabets—colorful, spectacularly inaccurate, and useless—are supremely unattached signifiers, material tokens of pretended travel and dispossession. But Mandeville's dialogues are only possible with imaginary others; in the early years of contact with the natives of the New World, voyagers frequently express frustration at the difficulty of understanding the other, and the sense of difficulty intensifies rather than lessens over time. 'Both parties were grieved that they did not understand one another,' writes Columbus in 1500, 'they in order to ask the others of our country, and our men in order to learn about their land'.

On his first voyage, provoked perhaps by the uniform nakedness of the peoples he encountered, Columbus had concluded that there was no substantial diversity of languages in the lands he had found; this apparent uniformity surprised and pleased him, for it would make the task of conversion much simpler: 'In all these islands, I saw no great diversity in the appearance of the people or in their manners and language. On the contrary, they all understand one another, which is a very curious thing, on account of which I hope that their highnesses will determine upon their conversion to our holy faith, towards which they are very inclined.' By the second voyage, he acknowledged that there was greater linguistic diversity than he had at first thought: 'It is the truth that, as among these people those of one island have little intercourse with those of another, in languages there is some difference between them'. And by the fourth voyage, the differences have multiplied and hardened into a serious obstacle: 'Of all these lands and of that which there is in them, owing to the lack of an interpreter, they could not learn very much. The villages, although they are very close together, have each a different language, and it is so much so that they do not understand one another any more than we understand the Arabs'.

The early discourse of the New World then is full of questions that cannot be asked or answers that cannot be understood. 'Due to the lack of language,' complains Verrazzano, 'we were unable to find out by signs or gestures how much religious faith these people we found possessed.' Canoes of Indians, Cartier writes, 'came after our long-boat dancing and showing many signs of joy, and of their desire to be friends, saying to us in their language: *Napou tou daman asurtat,* and other words, we did not understand. . . . And seeing that no matter how much we signed to them, they would not go back, we shot off over their heads two small cannon.' Dionise Settle writes glumly of the desolate northern islands to which the English had come, 'I have . . . left the names of the Countreys . . . untouched, for lacke of understanding the peoples language.' And Sir Richard Hawkins reports an encounter with two or three naked Indians who 'spake unto us, and made diverse signs; now pointing to the Harbour, out of which we were come; and then to the mouth of the Straites: but we understood nothing of their meaning. Yet they left us with many imaginations.' What the English did not imagine, until they thought about the encounter later, was that the Indians were probably warning them of an approaching storm, 'for they have great insight in the change of weather,' Hawkins notes, 'and besides have secret dealing with the Prince of Darknesse, who many times declareth unto them things to come.'

In the absence of a common language both Europeans and natives attempted, as we have seen several times now, to communicate with signs. Despite Columbus's experience off Trinidad, most of the early voyagers seem at least fitfully to share Augustine's conviction that there is 'a kind of universal language, consisting of expressions of the face and eyes, gestures and tones of voice, which can show whether a person means to ask for something and get it, or refuse it and have nothing to do with it.' Augustine is articulating assumptions that are bound up with the rhetorical culture of late antiquity. Quintillian had written of a 'law of gesture'—a *chironomia*—and sketched the range of bodily motions and expressions that could be used with powerful effect 'even without the aid of words.' For 'not only a movement of the hand, but even a nod, may express our meaning,' he observed, 'and such gestures are to the dumb instead of speech'. Quintillian took special note of the expressive power of dancing—a distant foreshadowing of Columbus's communicative experiment—but it was above all the hands that seemed to him eloquent, 'for other parts of the body assist the speaker, but these, I may almost say, speak themselves. . . . So that amidst the great diversity of tongues pervading all nations and people, the language of the hands appears to be a language common to all men'.

Certain Indian gestures—above all, perhaps, the tearful greeting widespread in South America and among some North American tribes—seemed irreducibly strange to most Europeans, but what is more striking is how confident the early voyagers were, despite their disappointments and frustrations, in their ability to make themselves understood and to comprehend unfamiliar signs. So, for example, Amadas and Barlowe report that on the first English voyage to Virginia in 1584 they made initial contact with a man who spoke 'of many things not understood by us.' Shortly thereafter they were greeted by an important personage—'the Kings brother'—who 'beckoned us to come and sit by

him, which we performed: and being set hee made all signes of joy and welcome, striking on his head and his breast and afterwardes on ours, to shewe wee were all one, smiling and making shewe the best he could of all love, and familiaritie.' He then 'made a long speech to us.' When the English responded by presenting gifts to the chief and to those around him, the chief gave in signs what the English construed as a brief lesson about the local social structure: 'presently he arose and tooke all from them and put it into his owne basket, making signes and tokens, that all things ought to bee delivered unto him, and the rest were but his servants, and followers.' That this 'nobleman's' smile denotes 'all love, and familiaritie' seems a barely plausible if exceedingly optimistic reading; that his gestures are intended to show that 'wee were all one' seems a more daring interpretive leap; that his way of receiving gifts discloses a set of social relationships (including a 'king,' 'servants, and followers') seems a rash presumption, dependent on the uncritical application of a European model.

Amadas and Barlowe have been sent by Sir Walter Ralegh to locate a promising territory for an English colony. Without understanding a word that has been said to them, they believe (or at least profess to believe) that the country they have 'discovered'—a country called 'Wingandacoa, and now by her Majestie Virginia'—is inhabited by 'people most gentle, loving, and faithfull, voide of all guile and treason, and such as live after the maner of the golden age'. Accordingly, all signs are read in the most favorable light, a light that discloses at once a reassuring confirmation of the familiar hierarchical social structure and a radical innocence. The gratifying consequence of this somewhat paradoxical combination of qualities is revealed by the favorable exchange rate: 'we exchanged our tinne dish for twentie skinnes, woorth twentie Crownes, or twentie Nobles: and a copper kettle for fiftie skins woorth fifty Crownes. They offered us good exchange for our hatchets, and axes, and for knives, and would have given any thing for swordes: but wee would not depart with any'. A lively interest in swords sits strangely with life in the manner of the Golden Age. But then it is already an odd Golden Age that has kings and servants. In Shakespeare's *Tempest* old Gonzalo is ridiculed for category confusions of this kind: 'The latter end of his commonwealth forgets the beginning'. It is not clear if such contradictions troubled Amadas and Barlowe—or if they even noticed them. There was little reason for them to construct a coherent, internally consistent account of Virginia; their report is a prospectus for potential investors in future voyages, and consequently they assemble an inventory of hopeful signs.

We should not underestimate the cynical calculation with which the early travel texts were often put together, but calculation cannot adequately explain the reckless optimism—epistemological as well as strategic—that they frequently express. It is not only rudimentary understanding that must be painstakingly learned but also an acknowledgment of opacity: Europeans found it extremely difficult to recognize just how difficult, distorted, and uneven were these first, tentative attempts at cross-cultural communication. As we have already seen in the case of Columbus, the great temptation was to assume transparency, to rush from wonder—the experience of stunned surprise—to possession or at least the illusion of possession. And hence the moments of blankness—'we could not understand . . . ,' 'we do not know . . . ,' 'we could not explain . . . ,'—are intertwined strangely with the confident assumption that there was no significant barrier to communication or appropriation: 'We passed through many and dissimilar tongues. Our Lord granted us favor with the people who spoke them for they always understood us, and we them. We questioned them, and received their answers by signs, just as if they spoke our language and we theirs.'

This assumption is fueled in part by a recurrent failure to comprehend the resistant cultural otherness of New World peoples. On the one hand, there is a tendency to imagine the Indians as virtual blanks—wild, unformed creatures, as naked in culture as they are in body. On the other hand, there is a tendency to imagine the Indians as virtual doubles, fully conversant with the language and culture of the Europeans. These tendencies seem like opposites, but they are in fact versions of one another, as we can glimpse in a remark by the chronicler Peter Martyr: 'For lyke as rased or vnpaynted tables, are apte to receaue what formes soo euer are fyrst drawne theron by the hande of the paynter, euen soo these naked and simple people, doo soone receaue the customes of owre Religion, and by conuersation with owre men, shake of[f] theyr fierce and natiue barbarousnes.' One moment the Indians have no culture; the next moment they have ours.

The assumption of cultural transparency was alluring but, as at least a few Europeans recognized, it was also dangerous and potentially unjust. Last Casas angrily attacks the pretense that complex negotiations could be conducted through interpreters who in reality 'communicate with a few phrases like "Gimme bread," "Gimme food," "Take this, gimme that," and otherwise carry on with gestures.' Narratives that represent Indians and Spaniards in sophisticated dialogue are, he suggests, most often intentional falsifications, designed to make the arbitrary and violent actions of the conquistadors appear more just than they actually were. No doubt Las Casas was right—the official reports bespeak a fathomless cynicism—but there also seems to have been a great deal of what we may call 'filling in the blanks.' The Europeans and the interpreters themselves translated such fragments as they understood or thought they understood into a coherent story, and they

came to believe that the story was what they had actually heard. It was all too easy to conclude that apparent incomprehension was willful non-compliance; there could be, and according to Las Casas there were, murderous results.

It is a source of mordant satisfaction—and a sign of the inescapable mutuality of language—that the assumption of cultural transparency was not limited to the Europeans and consequently that the danger was not limited to the natives. Consider the testimony of Hernando de Escalante Fontaneda who was shipwrecked in Florida and held captive by the Carlos (Calusa) Indians for some seventeen years. Escalante, who spoke four languages, occasionally served as interpreter for other shipwrecked Spaniards and helped to save their lives. 'For the natives who took them,' he reports in a 'memorial' transcribed around 1575, 'would order them to dance and sing; and as they were not understood, and the Indians themselves are very artful, (for the most so of any are the people of Florida,) they thought the Christians were obstinate, and unwilling to do so. And so they would kill them, and report to their cacique that for their craft and disobedience they had been slain, because they would not do as they were told.'

In a weird revision of the story with which we began, Spanish sailors are once again commanded to stage a fiesta, but now the command comes from their native captors in a language they do not understand. And, disastrously, the Spanish cannot communicate their failure to understand. Did such scenes actually take place? It is impossible to know—Escalante has a personal interest in emphasizing the importance of his unusual mastery of languages—but in his account at least the principal issue is a recognition of the existence of linguistic opacity. To survive, the Spanish must somehow prove that they cannot understand the words that are being spoken to them, and, in the face of their captors' presumption that they are both devious and disobedient, the proof requires some ingenuity. Hence Escalante describes a strange occasion in which he, in the company of a black captive, tried to demonstrate to a powerful cacique that it was language difference and not obstinacy that was the problem. The cacique is puzzled by the strange behavior of his captives and turns to Escalante for an explanation:

> 'Escalante, tell us the truth, for you well know that I like you much: When we require these, your companions, to dance and sing, and do other things, why are they so dissembling and obstinate that they will not? or is it that they do not fear death, or will not yield to a people unlike them in their customs? Answer me; and if you do not know the reason, ask it of those newly taken, who for their own fault are prisoners now, a people whom once we held to be gods come down from the sky.' And I, answering my lord and master, told him the truth: 'Sir, as I understand it, they are not contrary,

nor do they behave badly on purpose but it is because they cannot comprehend you, which they earnestly strive to do.' He said it was not true; that often he would command them to do things, and sometimes they would obey him, and at others they would not, however much they might be told. I said to him: 'With all that, my lord, they do not intentionally behave amiss, nor for perversity, but from not understanding. Speak to them, that I may be a witness, and likewise this your freedman.' And the cacique, laughing, said: 'Se-le-te-ga,' to the new comers; and they asked what it was he said to them. The negro, who was near to them, laughed, and said to the cacique: 'Master, I will tell you the truth; they have not understood, and they ask Escalante what it is you say, and he does not wish to tell them until you command him.' Then the cacique believed the truth, and said to me: 'Declare it to them, Escalante; for now do I really believe you.' I made known to them the meaning of Se-le-tega, which is, 'Run to the look-out, see if there be any people coming;' they of Florida abbreviate their words more than we. The cacique, discovering the truth, said to his vassals, that when they should find Christians thus cast away, and take them, they must require them to do nothing without giving notice, that one might go to them who should understand their language.

Escalante is recounting a kind of primal language lesson: not the learning of a new language but the acknowledgment of linguistic difference that must precede such learning. Without this acknowledgment, one's own language would seem as natural and inevitable as breathing, and in the face of strangers one would simply begin to speak (and, in the case of a chief, to issue commands). This, as Escalante conceives it, has been the problem in Florida: he depicts the cacique not as a malevolent brute but as a genially ignorant sovereign, a powerful liege lord accustomed to obedience. With Escalante's help, the cacique discovers the truth of difference—his Christian captives are not wicked but simply other—and he establishes regulations that ensure fair treatment. The language lesson then is the precondition for the invention of procedural justice.

Let us recall that Columbus took possession of the New World with a legal ritual performed in Spanish and that, after 1513, *conquistadores* were supposed to read to all newly encountered peoples the *Requerimiento,* a document in Spanish that informed these peoples of their rights and obligations as vassals of the king and queen of Spain. Prompt obedience, the text declares, will be rewarded; refusal or malicious delay will be harshly punished:

> And we protest that the deaths and losses which shall accrue from this are your fault, and not that of their Highnesses, or ours, nor of these cavaliers who come with us. And that we have said this to you and made this Requisition, we request the notary here present to give us his testimony in writing, and we ask the rest who are present that they should be witnesses of this Requisition.

A strange blend of ritual, cynicism, legal fiction, and perverse idealism, the *Requerimiento* contains at its core the conviction that there is no serious language barrier between the Indians and the Europeans. And to a thoughtful and informed observer like Las Casas, the dangerous absurdity of this conviction was fully apparent: Las Casas writes that he doesn't know 'whether to laugh or cry' at the *Requerimiento.*

From the perspective provided by Las Casas, Escalante's story would seem to be a sly, displaced critique of Spanish linguistic colonialism, a critique made possible by his long years living with the natives of Florida. The cacique's rule—that all requirements must be made in the language of the other—is set over against an injustice that began on October 12, 1492 and was given full institutional confirmation after 1513. And yet, though everything in Escalante's account would seem to call out for such a critique, it does not seem to have occurred to him. On the contrary, in his memorial he counsels the Spanish not to seek peace with the natives who are, he writes, 'very faithless.' Therefore, 'let the Indians be taken in hand gently, inviting them to peace; then putting them under deck, husbands and wives together, sell them among the Islands, and even upon Terra-Firma for money, as some old nobles of Spain buy vassals of the king. In this way, there could be management of them, and their number become thinned'. A process of mimetic doubling and projection—a representation of the natives as a displaced European self-representation—does not lead to identification with the other but to a ruthless will to possess.

The shipwrecked Spaniards, in Escalante's account, try to obey the commands of their captors, even without understanding them, but their efforts only make matters worse, for their moments of accidental or inspired compliance simply persuade the cacique that they are perversely obstinate at other moments. They are, in effect, discovering the limits of improvisation, the ability to insert the self in the sign systems of others. It is unusual to encounter an acknowledgment of its limits; more often the discourse of the New World celebrates the power not only to survive through improvisation but to profit hugely from the adroit manipulation of alien signs. Even the tearful greeting was not beyond imitation: Jean de Léry describes the Brazilian ceremony of welcome—'Then the women come and surround the bed, crouching with their buttocks against the ground and with both hands over their eyes; in this manner, weeping their welcome to the visitor, they will say a thousand things in his praise'—and he notes that the French accommodated themselves to it: 'If the newly arrived guest who is seated in the bed wants in turn to please them, he must assume the appropriate expression, and if he doesn't quite get to the point of tears (I have seen some of our nation, who, upon hearing the bleating of these women next to them, were such babies as to be reduced to tears themselves), at least when he answers them he must heave a few sighs and pretend to weep.' The untheatrical Calvinist Léry is made uneasy by the more flamboyant improvisers, weeping with their Brazilian hosts, but he grasps the essential principle: to 'assume the appropriate expression.' And this principle is repeatedly found as well among the natives.

Tzvetan Todorov has argued that the Indians were incapable of the improvisatory consciousness so marked in the Europeans, but the argument seems to me difficult to sustain in the face of the substantial evidence of the native mastery of European signs (a mastery confirmed even in the Europeans' contemptuous dismissal of the natives as 'parrots'). Such improvisation on the part of either Europeans or natives should not be construed as the equivalent of sympathetic understanding; it is rather what we can call appropriative mimesis, imitation in the interest of acquisition. As such it need not have entailed any grasp of the cultural reality of the other, only a willingness to make contact and to effect some kind of exchange. But the very existence of such exchanges—and they began in the very first moments of encounter, in situations of extraordinary cultural distance and mutual strangeness—is itself remarkable. We cannot make a universal principle out of this desire to possess a token of otherness, for there were peoples who resisted all contact and showed no interest in economic exchange, but it is sufficiently widespread to warrant a presumption about the behavior of most human beings (exactly the presumption that Columbus, setting out pots and pans on his deck, was displaying). And it is in these early exchanges that we can glimpse most clearly some of the founding acts of practical imagination in the European apprehension of the New World.

An early seventeenth-century report of an English expedition to New-foundland, under the leadership of the Bristol merchant John Guy, gives us an unusually detailed (and impressively modest) account of the tentative establishment of trading relations through the manipulation and interpretation of signs. In November, 1612, a small party of Englishmen came at night to a few uninhabited Beothuck Indian houses on a lake (the Indian inhabitants had gone to a nearby island): 'We fownd theare a copper kettle kepte very brighte, a furre gowne, some seale skinnes, ane old sayle, & a fishing reele. Order was taken that nothing should be diminished, & because the savages should know that some had bin theare, everything was removed out of his place, & broughte into one of the cabins, and laid orderlie one upon the other, & the kettle hanged over them, wheearin thear was put some bisket, & three or fower amber beades. This was done to beginne to winne them by fayre meanes.' 'To win them'—the purpose here is not military victory or the establishment of sovereign-

ty but the establishment of trading relations; what is to be won is confidence and trust. Accordingly, the English make explicit signs of their presence: it would presumably have been detected in any case, but by carefully moving the inhabitants' belongings and by leaving small gifts of food and beads, the English indicate both that they *wish* their presence known and that they come in friendship. Their act entails an imagining of the Beothuck response when they return to the village, a calculation of their probable interpretation of the signs—and the manifest fact that the intruders have so carefully imagined the villagers' response is implicitly one of the signs that they have left.

These initial gestures are rewarded:

> Presentlie two canoaes appeared, & one man alone comming towards us with a flag in his hand of a wolfskinne, shaking yt, & making a lowde noice, which we tooke to be for a parlie, wheareupon a white flag was put out & the barke & shallope rowed towards them: which the savages did not like of, & soe tooke them to theire canoaes againe, & weare goeing away. Wheareupon the barke wheared onto them & flourished the flag of truce, & came to anker, which pleased them, & then they stayed.

A key interpretive move is made when the English construe the wolfskin 'flag' and the loud noise as requests for a 'parley' (as opposed, for example, to construing them as a menace), and in a further act of interpretive sensitivity they grasp, after a small misstep, that they should not give the appearance of pursuit but rather come to anchor. At this point the two sides can actually make contact:

> Presentlie after, the shalloppe landed Mr. Whittington with the flag of truce, who went towards them. Then they rowed into the shoare with one canoa, thother standing aloofe of, & landed two men, one of them having the white skinne in his hand, & comming towards Mr. Whittington, the savage made a loude speeche, & shaked the skinne, which was awnsweared by Mr. Whittington in like manner & as the savage drew neere he threw downe the whitte skinne into the grownde. The like was done by Mr. Whittington. Wheareupon both the savages passed over a little water streame towards Mr. Whittington daunsing, leaping, & singing, & coming togeather, the foremost of them, presented unto him a chaine of leather full of small perwincle shelles, a spilting knife, & a feather that stucke in his heare. The other gave him ane arrow without a head, & the former was required with a linnen cap, & a hand towell, who put presentlie the linnen cap upon his head, and to the other he gave a knife. And after hand in hand they all three did sing, & daunce. Upon this one of our companie called Fraunces Tipton went a shoare, unto whom one of the savages came running: & gave him a chaine such as is before spoaken of, who was gratefied by Fraunces Tipton with a knife, & a small piece of

brasse. Then all fower togeather daunced, laughing,
& makeing signes of ioy, & gladnes, sometimes
strikeing the breastes of our companie & sometymes
theyre owne.

For a simple moment—two Indians and two Europeans imitating each other, exchanging small gifts and
dancing together on the shore—there is something like
a secular communion.

John Guy is principally interested in barter, and through
patience and cautious deduction—the essential elements
in the mode of 'silent trade' that is recorded as early
as Herodotus—he manages to effect some exchange.
The Indians go off but they leave some skins hanging
on poles; when these are left in place for several days,
the English conclude that they were goods intended
for trade:

> we remayned satisffied fullie that they weare broughte
> theather of purpose to barter with us, & that they
> would stand to our curtesie to leave for yt what we
> should thinke good. Because we weare not furnished
> with fit things for to trucke, we tooke onlie a beaver
> skinne, a sable skinne, & a bird skinne, leaving for
> them, a hatchet, a knife & fower needles threaded.
> Mr. Whittington had a paire of sezers which he
> lefte theare for a small beaver skinne, all the reste
> we theare untouched and came that nighte to the
> harbour that we weare in at our entring, which we
> call Flagstaffe Harbour, because we fownd theare
> the flagstaffe throwen by the savages away.

The English merchant's account is unusual for making
no great claims—no glimpse of vast riches, no promise
of easy conversion, no elaborate deductions about religious belief or social order. But for this reason his
account provides a useful elementary model—initial
contact, material exchange, and naming—for the hundreds and even thousands of more complex encounters
that have survived in the travel discourse of the period.
Consider, for example, the testimony of Jacques Cartier. When Cartier sees the Indians holding up furs on
sticks, he assumes that they are proposing to engage in
barter, though he does not immediately 'care to trust to
their signs.' On the next day he ventures to make some
signals in return—'we . . . made signs to them that we
wished them no harm'—and then sends two men on
shore 'to offer them some knives and other iron goods,
and a red cap to give to their chief.' The initial, tentative gestures then have materialized, as it were, into
gifts, and the gifts lead to further signs: 'The savages
showed a marvellously great pleasure in possessing
and obtaining these iron wares and other commodities,
dancing and going through many ceremonies, and
throwing salt water over their heads with their hands.'
And these signs of extreme joy lead in turn to what we
may call an extreme exchange: 'They bartered all they
had to such an extent that all went back naked without
anything on them'.

When the scene is repeated a few days later, with still
more intense manifestations of delight, Cartier ventures a further reading of the signs. The natives have
once again 'offered everything that they owned' so
that 'nothing was left to them but their naked bodies.'
From this the Frenchman concludes that 'they are people who would be easy to convert.' This conclusion
would seem to be based on their ease in the presence
of the Europeans and on their apparent willingness to
strip themselves bare, as if he saw them joyfully di-
vesting themselves of their beliefs as well as their
belongings. Cartier describes their evident delight as if
it were already an act of homage to the Christian god:
'Then they joined their hands together and raised them
to heaven, exhibiting many signs of joy.' As he looks
around the Gulf of St Lawrence on a warm July day,
Cartier draws similarly optimistic conclusions about
the land he has discovered: 'Their country is more
temperate than Spain and the finest it is possible to
see.' After taking inventory of its resources, he returns
to its inhabitants and pursues the reading of signs still
further: 'I am more than ever of opinion that these
people would be easy to convert to our holy faith.
They call a hatchet in their language, cochy, and a
knife, bacan. We named this bay, Chaleur Bay'.

These three sentences manifest the blank refusal of
logical connectives characteristic of much of early travel
writing, but there is a hidden logic: Cartier's reading
of the natives' response to barter has led him to the
conclusion that they would be easy to convert; the task
of conversion will necessitate the learning of their language, which here begins with the notation of their
words for two of the European articles in which they
take such delight; and the inscription of Indian words
in European letters is paradoxically a step toward the
renaming, the linguistic appropriation, of the land.
Perhaps we should call it the *misnaming* of the land,
since the conviction that Canada had the climate of the
Costa del Sol led to fatal blunders. (The inlet off the
Gaspee Peninsula is, however, still called Chaleur Bay.)

In Cartier, as in almost all early European accounts,
the language of the Indians is noted not in order to
register cultural specificity but in order to facilitate
barter, movement, and assimilation through conversion.
And though, as we have seen, the explorers often expressed frustration at their inability to understand the
natives, they did not, as a rule, make any serious attempt to overcome the language barrier by actually
learning Indian tongues. This is not only because explorers, by training and inclination, are not easily confused with linguists (or, more relevantly, with missionaries), but also because they had little practical interest
in immersing themselves in native culture and no desire to do so. To learn a language may be a step toward mastery, but to *study* a language is to place oneself in a situation of dependency, to submit. Moreover,
not understanding Indian speech allowed a certain

agreeable latitude in construing the signs of the other. 'When the Spaniards discovered this land,' writes Antonio de Ciudad Real in 1588, 'their leader asked the Indians how it was called; as they did not understand him, they said *uic athan,* which means, what do you say or what do you speak, that we do not understand you. And then the Spaniard ordered it set down that it be called *Yucatan.*' The Maya expression of incomprehension becomes the colonial name of the land that is wrested from them.

I have already quoted Verrazzano's admission that 'due to the lack of language, we were unable to find out by signs or gestures how much religious faith these people we found possess.' But the passage then continues:

> We think they have neither religion nor laws, that they do not know of a First Cause or Author, that they do not worship the sky, the stars, the sun, the moon, or other planets, nor do they even practice any kind of idolatry; we do not know whether they offer any sacrifices or other prayers, nor are there any temples or churches of prayer among their peoples. We consider that they have no religion and that they live in absolute freedom, and that everything they do proceeds from Ignorance; for they are very easily persuaded, and they imitated everything that they saw us Christians do with regard to divine worship, with the same fervor and enthusiasm that we had.

It is, of course, Verrazzano who is proceeding from an ignorance that he freely acknowledges, but this ignorance does not prevent him from constructing a promising model of the other. The model resembles that sketched by Columbus on the first day; it construes the Indian as a screen or a vacancy—a state of 'absolute freedom'—and imagines that this vacancy will be filled by imitation.

Such a conception of the Indians assimilates them in part to children, and we may relate this assimilation to the sense of infantilization that many people experience when they find themselves in a country where they do not speak the language. That this sense is not an exclusively modern one is confirmed by Mowbray's extravagant response in Shakespeare's *Richard II,* to his sentence of exile in France:

> I am too old to fawn upon a nurse,
> Too far in years to be a pupil now.

In the case of the New World voyagers, of course, what is striking is that, though they are on foreign shores, the Europeans do not feel themselves infantilized; it is rather the natives whom they see as children in relation to European languages.

It is perhaps because of this reversal that the European explorers and conquerors allow themselves on the whole to admire Indian facility in learning their tongues. We have already seen Columbus's comment on the Indians' ability to mimic. Similarly, the Earl of Cumberland reports that the natives of Dominica have 'great desire to understand the English tongue; for some of them will point to most parts of the body, and having told the name of it in the language of Dominica, he would not rest till he were told the name of it in English, which having once told he would repeate till he could either name it right, or at least till he thought it was right, and so commonly it should be, saving that to all words ending in a consonant they always set the second vowall, as for chinne, they say chin-ne, so making most of the monasillables, dissillables.' Or again John Brereton in 1602 writes that the Indians 'pronounce our Language with great facilitie; for one of them one day sitting by mee, upon occasion I spake smiling to him these words: how now, sirrha, are you so sawcy with my Tobacco? which words (without any further repetition) he suddenly spake so plaine and distinctly, as if hee had beene long Scholar in the Language.'

It is tempting to find in such moments of genial admiration relief from the miserable chronicles of colonial exploitation and violence, and those Europeans who regarded the Indians as able children certainly seem preferable to those who treated them as demonic beasts. But we must at least remark the eerie subtext of the exchange between John Brereton and his Indian interlocutor: the politics of domination and appropriation, the gross inequalities of economic, status, and power relations, are rehearsed—mimicked—in so reduced a form that the colonizer does not even notice them, any more perhaps than does the colonized, as he repeats the words, 'how now, sirrha, are you so sawcy with my Tobacco?'

The radically unequal distribution of power that lies at the heart of almost all language learning in the New World is most perfectly realized in the explorers' preferred method for dealing with the language problem, an expedient that maximizes rapidity of access and eschews an acknowledgment of the obstructive constraints of otherness. From the very first day in 1492, the principal means chosen by the Europeans to establish linguistic contact was kidnapping—or perhaps, after Mulcaster, we should call the act 'enfranchisement.' I have already cited Columbus's log-book entry, announcing his intention to seize several of the natives who have come to greet him and to take them back to Spain 'so that they can learn to speak.' On October 15, only three days after landfall, Columbus reports the escape of two of these captives: one seems to have jumped overboard and swum to shore, the other managed to flee in one of the native 'dugouts' that Columbus had earlier admired—they 'go marvelously,' he wrote on October 13th (*Diario,* 69). Now the marvel of the canoe's speed (for 'there were never ship's launch that could overtake it even if we had a big head start' [*Diario*, 81]) is disclosed as a strategic edge, one of the few technological advantages that the natives enjoy. Hence flight which Columbus sees as shameful—when the Spanish went in pursuit of the escapees, he writes, 'they all fled like chickens' (*Diario*, 81)—is in fact a form of politics, under the circumstances almost the only rational politics available to the natives.

Even Columbus seems to recognize that there is a strategic dimension to the flight of his captives, a dimension that requires a response beyond pursuit. Shortly after the escape an Indian paddles toward the ship in the hope of trading a ball of cotton and is seized by the Spanish sailors. Columbus writes that he sent for the Indian, gave him some small gifts—a red bonnet, small green glass beads, and two bells—and ordered that he be released:

> And later I saw, on land, at the time of the arrival of the other man—[the man] to whom I had given the things aforesaid and whose ball of cotton I had not wanted to take from him, although he wanted to give it to me—that all the others went up to him. He considered it a great marvel, and indeed it seemed to him that we were good people and that the other man who had fled had done us some harm and that for this we were taking him with us. And the reason that I behaved in this way toward him, ordering him set free and giving him the things mentioned, was in order that they would hold us in this esteem so that, when Your Highnesses some other time again send people here, the natives will receive them well. And everything that I gave him was not worth four *maravedís*. (*Diario*, 81-3)

We must recognize, I think, that this is largely a fantasy of astute improvisation: how could Columbus know what the man thought about the Spanish or about the captive who had escaped? But the fantasy is highly significant. It indicates that Columbus regards his gift-giving not only in terms of the politics of conversion but also in terms of the politics of empire. He wishes to make the escaped captive's story—that without warning the strangers seized him and took him from his island by force—seem a lie. Through unrequited generosity, Columbus wishes to create—he imagines that he has created—a sense of wonder in the natives that will put the escaped captive's story in doubt. And Columbus notes that this generosity is not even expensive: less than four *maravedís*'s worth. As early as October 15, 1492, then, wonder functions in Columbus as a strategy—here a strategy of deliberate deception, an opportunistic distortion of the awkward and potentially damaging reality of kidnapping natives to serve as interpreters.

On his second voyage, Columbus seized more natives—cannibals, as he thought, 'men and women and boys and girls.' He suggests to the Spanish king and queen that they be 'placed in charge of persons so that they may be able better to learn the language, employing them in forms of service, and ordering that gradually greater care be given to them than to other slaves, so that some may learn from others.' The crucial step, as he understands it, is to remove them as completely as possible from their own linguistic culture—if possible, by sending them to Castile or at the least by isolating them from one another on board ship. And in Castile too, he advises, it is important that they be isolated from their fellows: 'If they do not speak to each other or see each other until much later, they will learn more quickly there than here, and they will be better interpreters, although here there has been no failure to do what could be done.'

Columbus's ultimate hope is that Spanish language will, as it were, carry with it Spanish religion: 'there in Castile, learning the language, they will much more readily receive baptism and secure the welfare of their souls'. But this is the view of an explorer, not a missionary; the friars who came in the wake of the discovery and conquest painstakingly studied the native tongues, and, as Inga Clendinnen observes, they 'showed little enthusiasm for teaching their charges Spanish, for knowledge of Spanish would open the way to corrupting influences by challenging their own role as mediators between Spaniard and Indian. Discoverers like Columbus face an immediate need for interpreters, and the way in which he and almost every other European thinks to get them is through capture. The act is described with extraordinary frequency and casualness. An Indian was taken, notes Ponce de León, 'so that he might learn the language'. When his Indian ally Taignoagny asks Cartier to kidnap and take back to France one of his enemies, Cartier refuses, saying that the king, 'his master, had forbidden him to carry off to France any man or woman but only two or three boys to learn the language'. In the event, Cartier carries off the chief, Donnacona, and nine others. Charles V instructs Narváez in Florida that he is not to seize anyone 'except one or two people, no more, on each voyage of discovery, for interpreters, and other matters necessary to these voyages'. De Soto captures a hundred Indians and takes them:

> in chains with collars about their necks and they were used for carrying the baggage and grinding the maize and for other services which so fastened in this manner they could perform. . . . As soon as the women and young children were a hundred leagues from their land, having become unmindful, they were taken along unbound, and served in that way, and in a very short time learned the language of the Christians.

Indians who learned the language served as intermediaries, informants, and guides, but they could not always be counted upon to serve the colonists' interests.

For there was always the possibility—already glimpsed in the moment when the Indian simply repeats the Englishman's 'how now, sirrha, are you so sawcy with my Tobacco?'—that language learning will undermine the exploitative relation. At what point will the native, initiated into the European language and system of exchange, begin to realize that his people are being robbed? When will he counsel them to demand more for their goods and services? When will he cease to marvel and begin to curse? Cartier had seized two Indians, taken them to France, and then carried them back to Canada the next year to serve as interpreters. At first their presence was extremely useful, not only because they translated well but because they told their chief that they had been well treated in France. But it soon became clear to Cartier that his interpreters were not wedded to his own interests. When Indians came to the ships to exchange food for 'knives, awls, beads and other trinkets . . . we perceived,' the French recorder writes, 'that the two rogues whom we had brought with us, were telling them and giving them to understand that what we bartered to them was of no value, and that for what they brought us, they could as easily get hatchets as knives'. Thereafter, relations with the natives rapidly deteriorated.

The Europeans then queasily oscillate between the motives of exploitation and conversion: they have a simultaneous interest in preserving difference—hence maintaining the possibility of grossly unfair economic exchange—and in erasing difference—hence both Christianizing the natives and obtaining competent interpreters. They want the natives to be at once different and the same, others and brothers. Though far more difficult to come by, the most reliable interpreter, under these circumstances, was one of the Europeans' own, either an unfortunate who had been kidnapped by the Indians and then recovered or, much less frequently, someone of low status who had been deliberately left for months or years to live with the Indians. In the midst of a difficult voyage of De Soto, Juan Ortiz, a Spaniard who had been captured by the Indians and had learned their language, died, and his absence was sorely felt:

> After that, a youth who had been seized in Cutifachiqui and who now knew something of the language of the Christians, served as interpreter. so great a misfortune was the death of Juan Ortiz, with regard to the explorer trying to leave the land, that to learn from the Indians what he stated in four words, with the youth the whole day was needed; and most of the time he understood just the opposite of what was asked, so that many times it came about that the road they took one day, and at times, two or three days, they would return on, and they would wander about lost from one side of those woods to the other. (*New American World*, ii. 137)

Conversely, to have a reliable, resourceful interpreter

was an inestimable advantage; it is quite possible that Cortés would have failed to conquer the Aztec empire had he not had the astonishing services of the formidable Doña Marina.

. . . I want now to draw together the issues of representation, exchange, and captivity by looking at a single, rather marginal enterprise: the three attempts in the 1570s by Martin Frobisher to locate the Northwest Passage. The initial encounter between the English and the inhabitants of the large island they discovered (now known as Baffin Island) was marked by mutual caution: a single Eskimo came on board the English ship, the *Gabriel,* while a single Englishman ventured on land. The Eskimo made what appeared to be signs of 'great wondering at all things': the ship itself must have seemed unimaginably strange to him, and he was presented with some 'trifles' with which he seemed very pleased. (only the English food that he was given to taste appeared to leave him unimpressed.) After this brief mutual reconnaissance, the men were returned to their respective peoples, but Frobisher himself evidently remained suspicious. The natives made what the English construed as signs of friendship—'laying their head in their hands'—but the English refused to land more men. Instead they once again took an Eskimo on board and presented him with trifles, evidently pieces of cloth.

The repeated use of the term 'trifles' is worth remarking, since it signals not only the modest value of the English gifts, as they perceive them, but the entrancing prospect of a quick, easy profit. The European dream, endlessly reiterated in the literature of exploration, is of the grossly unequal gift exchange: I give you a glass bead and you give me a pearl worth half your tribe. The concept of relative economic value—the notion that a glass bead or hawk's bell would be a precious rarity in the New World—is alien to most Europeans; they think that the savages simply do not understand the natural worth of things and hence can be tricked into exchanging treasure for trifles, full signs for empty signs. Where they might then have imagined mutual gift-giving or, alternatively, a mutually satisfactory economic transaction, the Europeans instead tended to imagine an exchange of empty signs, of alluring counterfeits, for overwhelming abundance. Objects of little value provide access to objects of immense value; indeed the more worthless and hollow the trifle, the more value is gained in the exchange.

The inhabitants of the New World are particularly vulnerable, early voyagers report, to the allure of bright surfaces, as if their inward blankness compelled them to respond only to outward appearances. Europeans by contrast congratulate themselves for their greater perspicacity, but at the same time their accounts of the unequal exchanges frequently imply a sense of bad faith, a sense—reflected in the very term 'trifle'—that

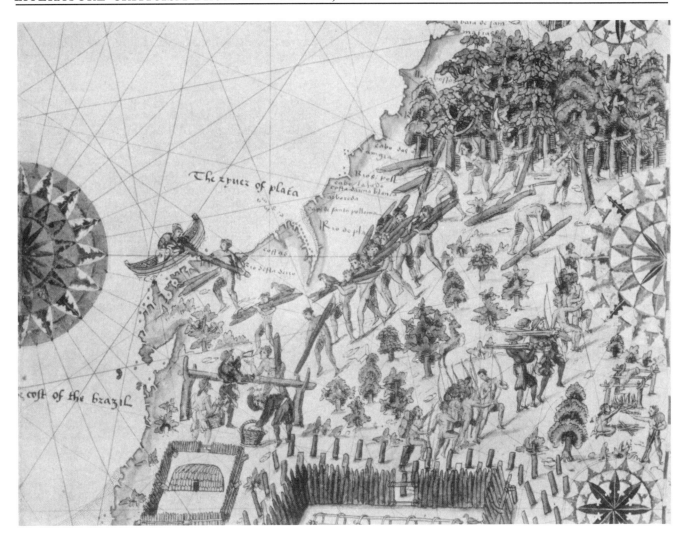

*Map of South America depicting the brazilwood trade, from the atlas of John Rotz, 1542.*

they are taking advantage of native innocence. Of course, this bad faith is part of the pleasure of the profitable transaction, but it is a distinctly uneasy pleasure, and the anxiety it aroused may be reflected in the frequency with which the early narratives associate unequal exchange with subsequent disaster.

The Eskimos did not wear gold ornaments, but they did have some objects of value: 'they exchanged coats of seales, and beares skinnes, and such like, with our men,' writes one of the participants in Frobisher's first voyage, 'and received belles, looking glasses, and other toyes, in recompense.' It was evidently the lure of such bargains that drew five English sailors who were carrying an Eskimo back to shore to attempt, against Frobisher's orders, to have some further 'traffic' with a group of the natives; the five were immediately seized and carried off. Now the usual situation—Europeans safely in possession of both natives and their valuables—was reversed, and the English feared the worst.

The fear, shaped by a powerful cultural fantasy operative in virtually all early encounters, was of cannibalism, a supposition strengthened by what the English had already seen of Eskimo eating habits: 'considering, also, their ravenesse and bloudy disposition in eating anye kinde of rawe flesh or carrion, howsoever stinking,' writes George Best, it seemed likely that the English prisoners would be viewed as quite good meat. The English later learned that the Eskimos, perhaps with a comparable opinion of English food, regarded the strangers as likely to be cannibals.

Frustrated in his attempts to recover his men, Frobisher determined at least, as Best puts it, 'to bring some token from thence of his being there'. The token was a native lured into English hands with trifles:

> for knowing well how they greatly delighted in our
> toyes, and specially in belles, he rang a pretie lowbel,
> making wise that he would give him the same that

would come and fetch it. And bycause they would not come within his daunger for feare, he flung one bell unto them, which of purpose he threw short, that it might fal into the sea and be lost. And to make them more greedie of the matter he range a lowder bell, so that in the ende one of them came neare the ship side to receive the bell, which, when he thought to take at the captaine's hand he was thereby taken himself; for the captain being redily provided, let the bel fal and cought the man fast, and plucked him with maine force boate and al into his bark out of the sea.

If Frobisher hoped to extract information from his prisoner about the kidnapped Englishmen, he was quickly disappointed: when the Eskimo found himself in captivity, Best writes, 'for very choller and disdain, he bit his tong in twayne within his mouth.' Nevertheless, he survived the voyage and made a sensation upon the *Gabriel*'s return to England, a living 'witnesse,' in Best's words, 'of the captaines farre and tedious travell towards the unknowne parts of the worlde, as did well appeare by this strange Infidel, whose like was never seen, red, nor harde of before, and whose language was neyther knowne nor understoode of anye'. The native was of particular interest to the public because his Tartar features were construed as a sign that Frobisher had indeed found the elusive passage to the East, but the display was soon cut short in the usual way by the captive's death. For reasons I do not understand it was first decided to embalm the corpse and send it back to the island, but the plan was abandoned. Instead Frobisher's partner and chief financial backer, Michael Lok, hired a Dutch engraver, William Cure, to make a death-mask and a Dutch painter, Cornelius Ketel, to make a series of portraits.

The Eskimo is taken as a 'token'—even without learning English, even with a language 'neyther knowne nor understoode of anye,' he is a valuable sign—and transformed into a 'witness' of otherness. When alive, he is displayed, with his boat, as a marvel, 'such a wonder onto the whole city and to the rest of the realm that heard of yt as seemed never to have happened the like great matter to any man's knowledge' [Lok]. When dead, he is first set to be transformed into a frozen image of himself and then, when this expedient fails, his appearance is registered in a set of pictorial images that supplement the verbal descriptions that are already in circulation. The captive then is caught up in a kind of representational machine that, at a minimum, produced the following images: numerous word 'pictures,' as Lok put it, 'in ink and paper,' the death-mask, two full-size portraits with boat and native dress (one painted for the queen and the other for the Muscovy Company), another depicting him in English dress, and yet another depicting him naked, along with two small pictures of his head.

The small pictures presumably direct attention specif-

ically to his Tartar-like features, but the full-size portraits appear to reflect a set of larger competing hypotheses about the meaning of Frobisher's savage. Depiction in native dress bespeaks an interest in the strangeness of distant peoples, in facial features, clothing, and tribal insignia that bear witness to difference, while the inclusion of the kayak suggests an interest in adaptive technology as well as appearance. In this representation the captive serves as a token of cultural otherness. The portrait in English dress by contrast appears to cancel difference and bears witness to the metamorphic power of clothing. It suggests that there is nothing ineradicable about the Eskimo's strangeness, that his savagery is an effect produced by appearances that can be altered. In this representation the captive serves as a token of assimilable otherness.

One portrait then implies an art that is the register of difference, a mimetic technique that enables its master to exchange trifles for treasure; the other portrait, converting the alien into a European, implies an art that is the register of equivalence, a mimetic technique that enables its master to transform others into brothers. Finally, the third portrait, the portrait of the Eskimo stripped of his clothing, suggests at once a resistant and absolute nakedness, specific, unique, and untranslatable *and* a bare, forked animality that is the common condition of all men and women. In this ambivalent representation the captive serves as an opaque, unreadable body and as a token of unaccommodated, universal humanity.

Frobisher had brought another kind of token back from his island, an ore sample that proved similarly open to competing interpretations. The first three assayers thought it worthless, but failure—an empty sign—was not acceptable, and an assayer was eventually found who declared that it was rich in gold. The report enabled Lok to raise enough capital to send Frobisher out on a second voyage, no longer principally to search for the Northwest Passage but to mine the ore and, if possible, to recover the five lost men. Frobisher was also instructed to bring back to England 'iii or iiii or 8 or tenne' of the natives, including some children, and he planned to take at least one captive immediately to serve as an interpreter. When uneasy gift and trading relations had once again been established with the natives, he saw his chance. After Frobisher presented some 'pinnes and pointes, and such trifles' to an Eskimo, 'one of the salvages for lacke of better marchandise, cutte off the tayle of his coate (which is a chiefe ornament among them) and gave it unto oure general for a present)'. At that moment of mutual exchange, the Englishman attempted to seize his prey; the native managed to resist, wounding Frobisher in the buttock, but he was eventually taken.

The English apparently never learned, or at least never bothered to record, their captive's name; he is called this 'straunge and newe praye,' 'our savage captive,' or simply one of the 'country people'. And he does not appear to have learned English or to have taught his captors his own language. But in a limited way he did serve as a useful interpreter and native informant. Best reports that in response to English questions asked in sign language, he denied that his people were anthropophagi: the bones that the English found were not, the captive indicated, the sign of a cannibal feast but the remains of a man slain by wolves. And when the English found a cache of objects—'sleddes, bridles, kettels of fishe skinnes, knives of bone, and such other like'—'our savage declared unto us the use of all those things' by acting out native practices: 'And taking in his hand one of those countrey brydels, he caughte one of our dogges, and hampred him handsomely therein, as we do our horses, and with a whip in his hande, he taught the dogge to drawe in a sledde as we doe horses in a coatche, setting himself thereuppon like a guide: so that we might see, they use dogges for that purpose, as we doe our horses'.

What does it mean for the Eskimo to perform his own culture as a kind of theatrical demonstration for the gaze of his captors? It means making the opaque signs of an alien world comprehensible, suggesting to the English certain parallels between what they regard as a strange, savage culture and their own. It means attempting to lay to rest his captors' worst fears, above all the fear of cannibalism, by emptying certain signs of their apparent meaning. It involves a co-operation that is also co-optation, since the co-operation has nothing reciprocal about it, and the captive remains just that, a prisoner on his own shores, miming his culture's survival skills for people who speak an unknown language, who come from an unknown place, who have already seized another of his tribe and who show no interest whatever in his own survival.

On one of the occasions on which the English had brought 'the savage captive' on shore 'to declare ye use of such things as we saw,' there was a strange occurrence. The native withdrew somewhat from the company of his captors—he was evidently not being held in close restraint—and, in Best's words, 'set up five small stickes round in a circle, one by another, with one smal bone placed just in ye middst of all'. The action was clearly purposive, but it was not an attempt to communicate, declare, or explain anything to the English. The man who first spotted it thought that it must be a charm or act of witchcraft—a possibility that was not for the English a quaint instance of native superstition, since sixteenth-century Europeans did not at all feel invulnerable to such charms. But after some discussion, the English came to the conclusion that the Eskimo was fashioning a symbolic representation, a sign, for his own people: 'ye best conjecture we could make thereof, was, that he would thereby his countreymen should understand y for our five men which they betrayed the last yeare (whom he sig-

nified by ye five sticks) he was taken and kept prisoner, which he signified by ye bone in ye midst.'

But how is this conjecture to be validated? How can the English know that they are not being bewitched or that the representation does not mean something else? After all, the sign is highly abstract; it does not readily suggest its own interpretation, and, if the sticks are indeed symbols of Englishmen, it certainly could as easily mean that the Eskimo is being held prisoner not in *exchange for* but more simply *by* a group of Englishmen. The English hypothesis is confirmed to their own satisfaction when the captive apparently confesses that he knows something about the five kidnapped Englishmen, though what he knows is by no means clear.

The 'confession,' or what the English imagined to be a confession, is not spontaneous; it is provoked by an English sign, a counter-representation, displayed to the native. Here is Best's account, following directly upon his conjecture about the meaning of the sticks and bone:

> For afterwardes, when we shewed him the picture of his countreyman, which ye last yeare was brought into England . . . he was upon the suddayne muche amazed thereat, and beholding advisedly the same with silence a good while, as though he would streyne courtesie whether shoulde begin ye speech (for he thoughte him no doubte a lively creature) at length, began to question with him, as with his companion, and finding him dumme and mute, seemed to suspect him, as one disdaynful, and would with a little help have growen into choller at the matter, until at last by feeling and handling, he founde him but a deceiving picture. And then with great noyse and cryes, ceased not wondering, thinking that we coulde make menne live or die at our pleasure.

> And thereuppon calling the matter to hys remembrance, he gave us plainely to understande by signes, that he had knowledge of the taking of our five men the last yeare, and confessing the manner of eche thing, numbred the five men upon his five fingers, and poynted unto a boate in our ship, which was like unto that wherein our men were betrayed: And when we made him signes that they were slaine and eaten, he earnestly denied, and made signes to the contrarie.

The Eskimo's initial response to the picture of his countryman, we are told, is governed by a code of manners—Best calls it 'courtesy'; as in the story of the tar baby, he becomes enraged when his companion remains 'dumb and mute.' He thinks that he is receiving a social affront, until he realizes 'by feeling and handling' that he is not dealing with a 'lively creature' but rather with a 'deceiving picture.' In an effort comparable to the English effort to understand the sticks and the bone, the captive then would appear to be moving from naïve literalism—mistaking the picture for a real person—toward a grasp of symbolic representation. And the crucial stage in this movement is a recognition of deceit, a perception of the counterfeiting or emptiness that is ambivalently interwined with the mimetic power of Western painting. This painting, unlike the non-naturalistic sticks and bones, looks like it will speak, but it remains 'dumb and mute.'

But just at the point in Best's account in which the native grasps that he is dealing with an empty sign, a trifle, a counterfeit, there is a shift in the opposite direction: from the disillusionment that comes with understanding that European representation is based upon empty signs to a radical subjection to the magical power revealed by the emptiness: 'And then with great noise and cryes, ceased not wondring, thinking that we could make men live or die at our pleasure.' The English have passed from the fear of native witchcraft to a conjectural understanding of native representation; the captive has passed from a sense of English representation to a conjectural fear of English witchcraft.

Why does the native move from credulity (the painting as living person) to disillusionment (the painting as counterfeit) to wonder (the English as magically powerful)? Two kinds of answers suggest themselves: the first is that the captive is constructing a conjecture about his experience. At first he thinks that the companion is alive, then he thinks that he has been turned into something 'dumb and mute'—that is, dead—then he concludes that the English have produced both of these experiences: hence they 'could make men live or die' at their pleasure. We cannot know, of course, if the Eskimo thought any such thing: what we are given are not his words—the English, you may recall, did not learn his language—but rather an English interpretation of the meaning of his 'noyse and cryes.' And when we grasp that we are dealing less with native experience than with English conjectures, we move to the second kind of answer: George Best is projecting onto the captive a characteristic English conception of their own powers of representation, and above all, of aesthetic representation. In this conception the artist is at once the bestower of life and the master of deception, art is that which resurrects the dead and art is a cunning counterfeit, the sign is full and the sign is empty. We sometimes treat these as alternative positions, but, as we have now seen again and again, they are inextricably bound together. In Renaissance English literature the paradox is perhaps most exquisitely realized in Prospero's double fantasy: art as absolute illusion ('the baseless fabric of this vision') and art as absolute power ('graves at my command / Have wak'd their sleepers, op'd and let 'em forth / By my so potent Art'). Best produces both fantasies, attributing them in immediate sequence to the savage who now knows that the painting is not his companion but a counterfeit

and hence a demonstration of the power of the English to give life or to kill.

According to Best, it is at the moment of this paradoxical recognition that the captive makes signs that 'plainely' show that he 'had knowledge of the taking of our five men'—that is, under the pressure of the painting, with its manifestation of English power, the Eskimo confesses his guilt and at the same time allays the wrost of the English suspicions, the fear that their kidnapped countrymen have been eaten. The reassuring confession is a tribute to the power of art, art that can, as Hamlet said of the theater, compel the guilty to proclaim their malefactions.

But if the English infuse into their strange encounter their powerful confidence in the system of symbolic representation that they carried with them, their dream of the executive power of signs, their fantasy of plenitude and control, they continue to be haunted by the sense of emptiness that is paradoxically bound up with the imagined potency of their art. For the empty results, frustrations, and hardships of the Frobisher voyages suggest how fragile this potency is, how much it depends upon wish-fulfillment, how tenuously it clings to the actual experiences of otherness. The great English artists of the Renaissance all grasp this terrible vulnerability: when they appropriate the imaginative energies of the New World discoveries, they carefully transform them into self-consciously fictive, deliberately ambivalent images of Noplace, Faery Land, and a mysterious island in a Virgilian ses.

In the trifling islands of art brutal power can be transformed into just authority, emptiness can be absorbed into desire, and loss can undergo a magical sea-change into infinite riches. But in the bleak tundra of Frobisher's island, craft and kidnapping, scanning the signs and scrabbling for gold, lead only to failure. The painting of a dead native cannot restore the lost Englishmen, imprisoned or buried somewhere in the cold, barren, nameless island; access to the Northwest Passage is blocked by ice; and instead of the spices and gold of Cathay, there is only the enigmatic black rock.

In the absence of any secure grasp of the native language or culture, the little that the English learn from their captive seems overwhelmed by all that they do not understand, and when they do not understand, they can only continue to entrap, kidnap, and project vain fantasies. Hence later in the second voyage they surprise and seize two women. One of them, Best writes, was old and ugly, and 'our men thought she had bin a divell or some witch, and therefore let her go'. The other was young and nursing a child whom the English had inadvertently wounded. They took these back to the ship and with great excitement brought the female and male captive together in what the English seem to have regarded as a theatrical spectacle: 'every man with silence desired to beholde the manner of their meeting and entertainment'. But the spectacle was incomprehensible: at first the captives were silent, then the woman turned away and began to sing, and then, when they were brought together again, the man 'with sterne and stayed countenance beganne to tell a long solemne tale.' The English, of course, could not understand any of it, and since the man and woman were strictly modest in each other's presence, there was little else to see. The reciprocal kidnapping has led then to an almost complete blankness.

On Frobisher's return, Queen Elizabeth finally gave the discovery a name, but it is one that encapsulates the whole problem of the voyage: she called the island 'Meta Incognita,' the unknown mark or boundary, the empty sign. The captives quickly died. The black rock still aroused enough hope, however, to fund yet a third voyage. This time the Eskimos altogether eluded capture, and the English worked in an eerie solitude to mine and load the ore. They had thought to leave some men behind, but the weather was miserable, and the plan was abandoned. Before they left, however, they built a house out of lime and stone. Frobisher thought perhaps that the structure, like the crosses and coats of arms left on other shores, would serve as a sign of English occupation and hence possession. In order 'to allure those brutish and uncivill people to courtesie,' writes Best, the house was filled with trifles: toys, bells, knives, pictures of men and women etched in lead, models of men on horseback, looking-glasses, whistles, and pipes. The Englishmen then built an oven, baked bread in it, closed the door and left the island.

There was no fourth voyage. The 1,296 tons of ore that Frobisher brought back from Meta Incognita was fool's gold.

---

## FURTHER READING

### Criticism

"Elizabethan Explorers." *The Church Quarterly Preview* XXXIII, No. LXV (October, 1891): 216-35.
> Offers a historical overview of the most influential exploration voyages and chronicles of the Elizabethan period.

Cressy, David. "Elizabethan America: 'God's Own Latitude?'" *History Today*, 36. (July 1986): 44-50.
> Provides an overview of "what the English wanted from America during the first Elizabethan period, and what they achieved."

Edwards, Philip, ed. *Last Voyages: Cavendish, Hudson, Ralegh: The Original Narratives.* Oxford: Clarendon Press, 1988, 268 p.
> Presents a modernized edition of *The Last Voyage of Thomas Cavendish, 1591-1593, The Last Voyage of Henry Hudson, 1610-1611,* and *The Last Voyage of Sir Walter Ralegh, 1617-1618.*

Ife, B. W. "Alexander in the New World." *Renaissance and Modern Studies* XXX. (1986): 35-44.
> Examines language and narrative structure in several accounts of Spanish discovery and conquest in the New World.

Iglesia, Ramón. "Bernal Díaz del Castillo's Criticisms of the *History of the Conquest of Mexico,* by Franciso López de Gómara." *The Hispanic American Historical Review* XX, No. 4 (November 1940):535-50.
> Argues that "the two pillars upon which rests the history of the Mexican conquest by the Spaniards" [the chronicles of Gómara and Díaz] are in fact "like sensitive thermometrical columns which vary continually" in response to the contemporary intellectual climate. Defends the relevance of Gómara's account of the Spanish conquest.

Parks, George Bruner. *Richard Hakluyt and the English Voyages,* edited by James A. Williamson. New York: American Geographical Society, 1928, 289 p.
> Discusses England's experience of "the sudden expansion of the world" during the Renaissance.

Sanford, Charles L. *The Quest for Paradise: Europe and the American Moral Imagination.* Urbana: University of Illinois Press, 1961, 282 p.
> Explores the influence of the "Edenic myth" on the development of American culture from the early years of colonization through the twentieth century.

Stout, Harry S. "Word and Order in Colonial New England." In *The Bible in America: Essays in Cultural History,* edited by Nathan O, pp. 19-38. Hatch and Mark A. Noll. New York and Oxford: Oxford University Press, 1982.
> Includes discussion of the Puritan movement in relation to New World settlement, and the application of "biblical doctrines to questions of a temporal and political nature" in America.

Wallace, Archer. "Religious Faith of Great Adventurers." In *The Religious Faith of Great Men,* pp. 3-15. Reprint. Freeport, NY: Books for Libraries Press, Inc., 1967.
> Attempts "to record, rather than to interpret, the religious thinking" of explorers including Columbus, Drake, Raleigh, and Shackelton.

# Hernán Cortés

## 1485-1547

(Variations on first name include Hernándo, Fernán, and Fernándo) Spanish conquistador and New World chronicler.

### INTRODUCTION

Cortés is chiefly known as the conqueror of the Aztec empire and the founder of colonial Mexico. His significance in American historiography has been largely informed by his correspondence, or, *Cartas de relación* (1519-1526) that he wrote to the Holy Roman Emperor Charles V (King Charles I of Spain) recounting various stages of the Mexican conquest. As a first-hand account of one part of the conquest of the Americas, these letters are a valuable resource not only for historical data, but also for what they reveal of the conquistador mentality.

### Biographical Information

Cortés was born in the Spanish town of Medellín in approximately 1484. His father, Martín Cortés de Monroy, was a minor aristocrat without titled lands who nonetheless provided his son with the opportunity, as part of the gentry, to participate in Spain's growing colonial enterprise. After studying law for two years at the University of Salamanca, Cortés abandoned his scholarly pursuits in 1504 and travelled to the Caribbean island of Hispaniola, where he worked as a notary. He accompanied Diego Velázquez in his conquest of Cuba in 1511 and served as his secretary for the next seven years. During this period he married Catalina Xuárez, who was related to Velázquez by marriage. In 1518, Velázquez put Cortés in charge of an expedition to explore the Mexican coast. Ignoring Velázquez's orders to confine his activities to exploration and trade, Cortés set out to conquer the powerful Aztec empire. After making an alliance with the Tlaxcalans, traditional enemies of the Aztecs, Cortés proceeded to the Aztec capital, Tenochtitlán, where he was received as an emissary of Charles V by the Aztec leader Montezuma II. Cortés took Montezuma prisoner and for some time was able to rule through him. During an Aztec uprising in 1520, however, Montezuma was slain, either by the Spanish or by his own people, and Cortés and his men were forced out of the city with heavy losses. After a protracted siege, during the course of which the city was virtually razed, Cortés finally defeated the Aztecs in 1521. The next year the emperor named him governor of Mexico, or

"new Spain." Following an abortive expedition into Honduras, Cortés was suspended from the office of governor in 1526. Two years later he returned to Spain to seek redress from the Emperor. Although the Emperor conferred on him the title of Marquis and confirmed his claim to the considerable wealth he had acquired in the New World, Cortés was not reappointed governor. He returned to Mexico that year, but never again exercised political power. In 1540 he retired to Spain, where he died in 1547.

### Major Works

Cortés's letters to Charles V provide a detailed account of his activities in Mexico from 1519 to 1526. Compilations of these *Cartas de relación* usually include five letters, although the first of these is actually a letter from the municipal council of Vera Cruz, the first city established by Cortés in Mexican territory, describing the foundation of the city and presenting the Spanish monarch with all the treasure (instead of the customary royal fifth) acquired thus far in the conquest. This letter is generally included in place of Cortés's own first letter, of which no copy exists. In fact, despite references to this first letter in Cortés's later correspondence, some scholars doubt its existence. The letter from the municipal council emphasizes Cortés's services to the crown and portrays Cortés's immediate superior, Governor Velázquez of Cuba, as a self-interested official who sought to restrict Cortés's activities to trade and exploration in order to enhance his own wealth and power at the expense of the Crown's interest in acquiring new territories. In the subsequent letters written by Cortés, the conquistador continued to describe and justify his actions while staking his claim to hold his authority directly from the king. The second letter describes events from the war against and alliance with the Tlaxcalans through the *noche triste* ("sad night") of July 10, 1520, during which Cortés lost over half his army during the flight from Tenochtitlán. The third letter records the siege and reconquest of the city, while the fourth letter describes Cortés's administration of the conquered territories. These four letters were published in Spain during Cortés's lifetime, helping to establish his reputation as one of the great conquistadors. His final letter, concerning his disastrous expedition to Honduras in 1526, reflects his experience of bureaucratic controls that greatly constricted his authority in New Spain, and differs markedly from the earlier letters in tone and content; it was not published until the nineteenth century.

## Critical Reception

Though he is assured a position in history as the conqueror of Mexico, Cortés's reputation is a subject of continuing debate. Until the twentieth century, Cortés's letters fulfilled their apparent purpose of perpetuating their author's fame and glory. However, changing attitudes towards colonialism during the course of the twentieth century have brought a reevaluation of Cortés's historical role, with many historians emphasizing his ruthless methods and his destruction of a flourishing civilization. This historical re-visioning has been accompanied by a focus on the letters as literary artifacts rather than as objective descriptions of the conquest of Mexico. Jonathan Loesberg (1983), for instance, looks at various rhetorical strategies employed by Cortés in his letters to establish his right to make decisions independent of his immediate superior, the governor of Cuba. Anthony Pagden (1971) also discusses ways in which Cortés seeks in his letters to reinforce both his authority and his reputation. In a similar vein, Stephanie Merrim (1986) examines how Cortés, in constructing his persona as narrator and agent in his *Letters,* seeks to present himself as a model subject and military leader in the service of the emperor. Inga Clendinnen (1991), on the other hand, finds in Cortés's letters indications of cultural miscommunica-

tions that contributed to the vulnerability of the Aztecs in the face of the Spanish invasion.

---

## PRINCIPAL WORKS

*Cartas de relación de la conquista de Méjico* [*Letters from Mexico*] (letters) 1519-1526

---

## CRITICISM

### The North American Review (essay date 1843)

SOURCE: *"Despatches of Hernando Cortés,"* in *The North American Review,* Vol. LVII, No. 121, October, 1843, pp. 459-90.

[*The following excerpt provides a detailed historical overview of Cortés's expedition to Mexico from 1518 to 1524, as well as extracts from Cortés's letters to the Emperor.*]

As the memoirs of a hero written by himself, the work before us possesses an interest of the same character with that of the Anabasis of Xenophon and the Commentaries of Cæsar; and though the Spanish leader may not claim the high literary rank which the Greek and Roman generals have attained as classical historians, we are not to conclude that Cortés has any occasion, even as an author, to deprecate criticism. The despatches possess the attractions of romance with the certainty of truth. Compared with his great rival in the conquest of American kingdoms, Cortés enjoyed advantages of which Pizarro was wholly destitute; and his origin, like that of the great hero of the nineteenth century, whom in many particulars he resembled, whilst it commanded for him the privilege of liberal instruction, was also such as required of him, if he aimed either at honors or wealth, to become the architect of his own fortunes.

In 1517, the first regular expedition that effected a landing on the Mexican coast was fitted out from Cuba. It was placed under the command of Cordova; and, as Bernal Diaz, who also accompanied Grijalva and Cortés, was with Cordova, and has left an account of all these enterprises, we possess regular details of the earliest attempts at colonization on the Spanish main.

The reception which the first adventurers met with exhibited a power of resistance, on the part of the natives, far beyond what was afterwards shown against Cortés. On landing on the coast of Yucatan, Cordova was surprised to find numerous warriors, who carried, besides their bows and arrows, lances and shields; and, though they were driven off by means of the musketry, the Spaniards met with a loss of fifteen men. At Potonchan, where they subsequently attempted to land, they were defeated, with the loss of fifty-seven men,—an event, however, which was in some degree explained by the fact, that the Indians were led by a Spaniard, who had been wrecked on the coast several years before, and had been made a cacique. It was in this voyage, that the Spaniards first saw those buildings of stone and lime, surrounded by fields of maize, which distinguished the habitations of the natives of the continent from those of the dwellers on the islands, and indicated the different character of the population.

Grijalva followed in the track of Cordova, routed the Indians in a pitched battle at the place where the latter was defeated, pursued his way along the coast, and, after touching at Tabasco, Guaxaca, and St. Juan de Ullua, proceeded as far as the river Panuco, where Tampico is now situated. The Spaniards were astonished at the high cultivation of the fields, and the beauty of the Indian edifices, and they gave such accounts to their countrymen as were calculated to stimulate them to new adventures. The Spanish expeditions of those times resembled private adventures far more than public undertakings. Each captain found provisions and sailors for himself, while the arms and some trifling necessaries were furnished by the government. So far was a permanent colonization from being their first object, that the instructions, in general, were to obtain as much gold as could be had in the least possible time.

These two expeditions had been fitted out under Velasquez, the governor of Cuba. This officer proposed to appropriate to himself both the glory and the profit to be derived from the discoveries effected under his auspices, while he avoided undergoing any of the hardships or dangers to which a personal participation in the enterprises might have subjected him. Though delighted with the result of Grijalva's voyage, of which he took care to obtain every advantage by the accounts which he transmitted to Castile, and in particular to his patron, the Bishop of Burgos, he became jealous of his lieutenant, and resolved to employ, for the expedition that he was about to fit out, a new commander. By the influence of his secretary and another officer, who are supposed to have stipulated for some advantages to themselves, Hernando Cortés was selected. . . .

Velasquez soon became dissatisfied with his selection, though it had been sanctioned by a formal agreement before a notary, on the 23rd of October, 1518, and a license had been obtained from the Royal Audience of Hispaniola, recognizing Cortés as the commander, and as jointly concerned with Velasquez in the outfit of the expedition. Cortés, however, being informed of the views of the governor, set sail from St. Jago de Cuba on the 18th of November, with three hundred Spaniards, in six vessels, and went to Trinidad, where he obtained another ship, and two hundred more men were enlisted. Thence he proceeded to the Havannah, where orders were received to arrest him; but we learn from Bernal Diaz, that he had already gained such power over the minds of men, that Pedro Barba, the lieutenant of Velasquez at that place, wrote, in answer to the governor, that if he attempted to obey the order, he was sure the town would be sacked, and Cortés would carry off all the inhabitants. Cortés himself, as if ignorant of what had occurred, wrote a letter, the day before he set sail, to Velasquez, vowing eternal friendship. He took his final departure with his fleet from Cuba, on the 18th of February, 1519. And, that religious enthusiasm might not be wanting, as an auxiliary to that avarice which was the impelling motive with most of his followers to embark in the expedition, Cortés carried out with him a standard with the motto, *"Amici, Crucem sequamur, et in hoc signo vincemus."*

The first land at which the expedition touched was the island of Cozumel, where the troops were mustered and were found to amount to five hundred and eight soldiers, and one hundred and nine mariners. There were thirteen musketeers, ten brass field-pieces, and thirty-two cross-bows. And this was the army that was to subdue a mighty empire!

The attention of the Spaniards, who at once commenced propagandism by destroying the idols, and erecting crosses and images of the Virgin Mary and of the saints, was attracted to the principal temple, which was built of stone, and contained a remarkable idol, so constructed that the priests entered it, and answered audibly the prayers and petitions addressed to it by the natives. But a more remarkable circumstance was the worship of a cross of stone, which the people adored as the god of rain, the origin of which cannot, it is said, be traced to the existence of Christianity among them at any former period. The remains of this temple were still to be seen, at the time of Mr. Stephens's late visit to Yucatan.

From Cozumel, the expedition proceeded to the river Tabasco, where Grijalva had been kindly received. Cortés, however, being refused admission to the city, which was situated a short distance up the river, had here his first engagement with the natives. In spite of the terror which the strange noise of the ordnance occasioned, they fought with desperation; but being pressed both on the side of the land and the water, they were driven out of the town. Cortés took up his quarters in the temple, "which afforded space enough to contain all the Spaniards, as it had a court and several large and elegant halls." After a further trial of Spanish prowess, the Indians, who began to regard their invaders as a superior race, begged for peace, and offered presents of gold wrought into various forms, resembling the human face, birds, and beasts. They also gave the invaders twenty female slaves, one of whom was Doña Marina, whom Father Clavigero calls the first Christian of the Mexican Empire. She was certainly the most celebrated woman in the story of the Conquest, and to her, scarcely less than to Cortés himself, is the success of the Spaniards attributed by the early annalists. She was a girl of great personal attractions and intelligence, the daughter of a cacique of Guasacualco, who had been sold into slavery. She retained a knowledge of her native tongue, which was that of Mexico, while she had acquired the Maya language, which was spoken at Tabasco. This latter was also known to Aguilar, a Spaniard, who was shipwrecked with the one to whom we have referred, as the leader of the Indians in the battle against Cordova; and thus early were full means of communication with the inhabitants, in all the regions visited by Cortés, obtained.

The female slaves were all baptized before they were allotted to the several leaders; and the same course was adopted, on like occasions, whenever similar presents were made by the Indian caciques, who often gave to the invaders their daughters and other dear relatives. Doña Marina, we are told, fell to the share of Puerto Carrero, but Cortés afterwards took her to himself, and had by her the son, who accompanied him to Algiers. She subsequently became the wife of a Spanish cavalier.

"In the expedition to Higunas, (Honduras,)" says Bernal Diaz, "when Cortés passed through Guasacualco, he summoned all the neighbouring chiefs to meet him; amongst others came the mother and half-brother of this lady. She had told me before, that she was of that province, and in truth she much resembled her mother, who immediately recognized her. Both the old lady and her son were terrified, thinking that they were sent for to be put to death; but Doña Marina dried their tears, saying that she forgave them; that, at the time they sent her from them, they were ignorant of what they did; and that she thanked God who had taken her from the worship of idols to the true Church, and was happier in having a son by her lord and master Cortés, and in being married to a cavalier like her husband, than if she had been sovereign of all the provinces of New Spain."

This statement does not seem to indicate, whatever may have been her other virtues, that very refined notions about chastity were entertained by the Mexican Saint. We ought not, however, to be severe in scrutinizing the actions of the Indian princess, who naturally looked to those by whom she was initiated in the Christian faith, for the rules of morality, by which to regulate her conduct; especially, as we learn from the very clever work on "Life in Mexico," as it now is, that indulgence is still granted, even among the de-

scendants of the conquerors, to females of the most exalted rank, whose womanly character is stained by the same transgressions, by which the Christian life of Doña Marina was unwittingly marked. . . .

Cortés proceeded from Tobasco by sea, along the coast, to St. Juan de Ullua, and, while in that neighbourhood, and about to select the site for a settlement, he received a delegation from Cempoal, a city containing sixty thousand inhabitants. The lord of this place had heard of the victory at Tabasco, and he now sent to ask the invaders to visit him, and to solicit an alliance, such as would enable him to throw off the yoke of the Mexicans. This invitation, so much in accordance with his own views, was gladly accepted by Cortés, and the troops marched into the city; but not being without apprehensions of treachery, they proceeded through the streets in the order of battle. They beheld with astonishment the beauty and extent of the city, far surpassing all that they had before seen in the New World.

> In the market-place of Cempoal, stood an immense building of stone and lime, with loop-holes and towers, the walls whitened with plaster, that glittered like silver as the sun shone upon them. At first, the Spaniards imagined these walls to be composed of solid silver, but this error was soon corrected. Within this palace was a long suite of apartments, in which the Spaniards fixed their quarters, planting the cannon at the doors for security, and keeping themselves in readiness in case of treachery. Their fears fortunately proved groundless; the cacique directed a splendid supper to be prepared for them, and convenient bedding. The next morning, the cacique waited upon Cortés, and made him many rare and valuable presents; amongst these were cotton garments in the Egyptian fashion, with a knot on the shoulder, and jewels of gold valued at two thousand ducats. This visit was returned by Cortés, on the following day, in a becoming manner. In his conversation, the cacique complained loudly of the oppression and tyranny of Montezuma, the Mexican ruler, who had but lately usurped the government of Cempoal; he also professed his willingness to join an alliance against him. At the same time, he extolled the riches and magnificence of the city of Mexico, planted in the midst of a great lake, and the splendor of the court of Montezuma.

The town of Vera Cruz, the first colony on the continent of North America, was first established about twelve miles from Cempoal, in the country of the Totonacs, a people who, like the Cempoallans, were anxious to throw off the Mexican yoke. Cortés took this occasion to dissolve all connexion with Velasquez, by resigning his command to the municipal authorities of Vera Cruz, whom, according to Gomara, he named himself, or who, as Bernal Diaz states, were elected in the manner customary in Spain. He was, at once, again invested with the authority of Captain-General and chief magistrate, though these arrangements were not made without difficulties being interposed by the partisans of Velasquez, who demanded that the expedition should return to Cuba.

While Cortés was engaged in laying out the new town, a deputation arrived from Montezuma, consisting of two of his nephews and a numerous retinue of nobles, bringing magnificent presents; and he determined to proceed at once to Mexico. Before setting out for the capital, he addressed to the Emperor, Charles the Fifth, his first despatch, of which no copy is extant; but from a reference to it in the second, we learn that it bore date on the 16th of July, 1519. Dr. Robertson tells us, in the preface to his "History of America," that having searched for it without success in Spain, it occurred to him that, as the Emperor was about setting out for Germany when the messengers from Cortés arrived in Europe, it might be in the imperial library at Vienna. Accordingly, through the British ambassador, he obtained an order that a copy should be sent to him. It was ascertained, however, that the document was not there; but an authentic copy of the letter of the magistrates of Vera Cruz, of which Bernal Diaz speaks, and which was transmitted to Charles the Fifth at the same time, was forwarded to Robertson, and is used in his history. . . .

Cortés sent to the Emperor, with his first despatch, all the gold and other valuable commodities, which he had been enabled to collect, having induced the soldiers to relinquish their share for the purpose. The enumeration of the articles, most of which were presents from Montezuma, is even now astonishing from the variety, elegance, and richness of the workmanship ascribed to them. The existence of books, the characters of which resembled Egyptian hieroglyphics, of which characters specimens, in columns of porphyry and basalt, are still to be seen in the Mexican States, attracted the attention of the Spanish *savans.* Four Mexican nobles and two native women were also sent to Europe.

But though the messengers, accompanied by the father of Cortés, who seems to have been a man of sufficient consideration to afford efficient aid to his son, were favorably received by the Emperor, the affairs of America were not yet deemed of so much importance as to command the attention of a sovereign, who was engrossed by the more dazzling pursuits of European ambition, or to induce him personally to arbitrate between Velasquez and Cortés. In the absence of Charles, Fonseca, Bishop of Burgos, the patron of Velasquez, and who for thirty years directed the affairs of Spanish America, was too powerful an enemy for Cortés to resist. It was not, indeed, till after the occurrence of the more brilliant events recorded in the two ensuing despatches that, by the influence of the Cardinal, afterwards Pope Adrian the Sixth, a reference was made to a special commission, composed of the grand Chancel-

lor and other eminent persons, which resulted in a triumphant verdict in favor of Cortés.

It was decided, that Velasquez had no other claim than for the money he had expended in the outfit of the expedition; but that by revoking the commission he had granted to Cortés, he had left him free to act as he should judge best for the royal service with the ships and men, which for the most part he had raised and equipped at his own expense and that of his friends. This decision was fully approved by the Emperor, and communicated to Cortés in a royal despatch, which contained likewise information of his appointment as Governor and Captain-General of New Spain, and the most flattering encomiums on his conduct. Other despatches were sent at the same time to Diego Velasquez and Francisco de Garay, censuring their past proceedings, and commanding them to desist from any future interference with the affairs of New Spain. These despatches were all dated the 22d of October, 1522. A more signal triumph could not have been achieved, which, while it gave additional lustre to the victorious career of Cortés, carried dismay to the minds of his great opponents, Fonseca and Velasquez, both of whom died not long after, in comparative disgrace.

The second despatch of Cortés is dated at Segura de la Frontera, on the 30th of October, 1520, and gives an account of his departure from Cempoal with fifteen horse and three hundred infantry, one hundred and fifty men and two horses being left at Vera Cruz. Cortés further says, that the whole province of Cempoal, with fifty thousand warriors and fifty towns and fortresses, was firm in its allegiance to his Majesty, the Cempoallans begging him to protect them against the mighty lord, who took their sons to be slain and offered as sacrifices to idols.

After describing how he had punished, as the necessity of the case and the service of his Majesty required, the delinquents who had been detected in the attempt to seize a brigantine, in order to send information to Velasquez that he had despatched a ship to the Emperor, Cortés gives, in a few words, an account of a measure which left to the Spaniards no alternative but to conquer or die.

Besides those who, from having been the servants and friends of Velasquez, wished to leave the country, there were others that entered into the same views, on beholding the great number and power of the people of the country, while the Spaniards were so few and inconsiderable. Believing, therefore, that if I left the ships there (at Vera Cruz) they would mutiny, and all be induced to depart, leaving me almost alone, and by this means the great service rendered to God and your Majesty be made of no avail; I determined, under the pretext that the ships were not seaworthy, to cause them to be stranded on the coast; thus taking away all hope of leaving the country, I pursued my route with greater feelings of security, having no fears that after our backs were turned, the people I had left at Vera Cruz would desert me.

Cortés also shows how he contrived, at this time, to rid himself of the expedition under Francisco de Garay, the Governor of Jamaica, who had manifested some disposition to interfere with his exclusive colonization of the coast.

The Spaniards were well received in the several provinces and towns through which they passed, which were very populous and all subject to Montezuma, or, as the name is invariably written by Cortés, Muteczuma. At Yztecmastitán, according to the despatch, the residence of the cacique was surrounded by a larger fortress than was to be found in half of Spain, and which was well defended by walls, barbacans, and moats, while his dominions were covered with inhabitants for three or four leagues without interruption. In this place Cortés remained three days, in order to await the return of messengers, Cempoallans, whom he had sent to the Tlascalans, a people, who, though their country was on all sides surrounded by the Mexicans, had never been conquered by them.

On reaching the frontiers of Tlascala, whither he went before the return of his embassy, Cortés met with a wall which was six miles long, of dry stone, nine feet high and twenty feet thick, surmounted throughout its whole extent by a breastwork a foot and a half thick. Soon after entering this territory, which possessed a population of 500,000, and had, as we have said, always successfully resisted the great Mexican empire, Cortés was engaged in several conflicts, in one of which, he says, that he was opposed to 149,000 men, who in four hours were so signally defeated as no longer to be able to annoy the Spanish camp. In none of these engagements did the invaders lose a single man, though they destroyed numerous towns and many thousand houses, besides killing and making prisoners large numbers of the natives. On one occasion, Cortés attacked, with one hundred foot and his small body of cavalry, a place which contained, according to his statement, 20,000 houses. The subjection of the province was, of course, soon effected, and the Captain-general of the Tlascalans came to the conqueror, and solicited, in the name of the caciques, that the troops of the state might be admitted into the service of his Majesty. This was a most important alliance for Cortés, and was probably essential to the success of his movement against Montezuma, in which expedition the Tlascalans accompanied him with all their forces, while they remained faithful to him on that reverse of fortune, which compelled him temporarily to abandon the city. . . .

In announcing the arrival of ambassadors from Mexico, and the discussions with them and the Tlascalans,

who were mutually intent on each other's destruction, Cortés instructs us in his policy, and indicates his reliance for success not less on those dissensions than on the small military force, with which he had begun his conquests.

> I was not a little pleased on seeing their want of harmony, as it seemed favorable to my designs, and would enable me to bring them more easily into subjection, according to the common saying *De Monte,* &c. I likewise applied to this case the authority of the Evangelist, who says, 'Every kingdom divided against itself shall be rendered desolate;' and I dissembled with both parties, expressed privately my acknowledgments to both for the advice they gave me, and giving each of them credit for more friendship towards me than I experienced from the other.

After a narrow escape at Cholula, from which the Spaniards were preserved by Doña Marina, who had learned from a native female the plan of the meditated attack, and which, as usual, Cortés contrived to turn to his own advantage, he entered the city of Temixtitan (Mexico), as a guest. Montezuma, whose whole policy had been vacillating in the extreme, made every effort to divert the Spaniards from visiting the capital, and offered for that purpose magnificent presents, the natural effect of which, however, was only to render stronger the inducements for conquest. . . .

The abilities of the Conqueror cannot be appreciated without a reference to the difficulties, in which he was involved by the continued hostility of Velasquez. In his wars with the natives, he enjoyed the superiority which European weapons afforded, and, while the Indians were unacquainted with gunpowder, they not unreasonably ascribed supernatural powers to those who could create, as it seemed, the thunder and lightning of heaven. But when, far in the interior of a foreign land, his handful of men were surrounded in a walled town by hundreds of thousands, whose first feelings of reverence and awe had been converted into implacable hatred, and whom daily intercourse and the means of observing the practice of all the European vices had taught that their invaders were mortal, he received intelligence of the arrival of a body of his countrymen, double the number of his own forces, and commanded by a rival, who enjoyed those advantages which the sanction of a regular authority confers, and which Cortés could with difficulty claim; when we learn that, from such embarrassments, he found means not only to extricate himself, but to turn the occurrence to his own advantage, and render it the source and foundation of new successes, we cannot fail to recognize in him an indomitable energy of character, and those resources adequate to every emergency, which are only to be found in men of the highest order of genius. Though Narvaez was invested with the authority of

Governor, derived from the same power that had given the original commission to Cortés, the latter determined at once to treat his rival as a usurper. With as large a force as he could collect, but which, after leaving five hundred men in garrison in Mexico, only amounted to seventy followers, or, including those added at Cholula, to two hundred and fifty, he proceeded to meet Narvaez at Cempoal. . . .

While these events were occurring at Cempoal, the Mexicans were not idle; but having confined the Spanish garrison to their quarters, they collected their forces with a view to the entire expulsion of the invaders. Though Cortés came back to the city with a greatly increased army, recruited from the followers of Narvaez, he was immediately attacked on entering the fortress, and was soon compelled, after repeated conflicts, during one of which Montezuma, still a prisoner in the hands of Cortés, was killed by his own people, to abandon it, and retreat to the province of Tlascala. Indeed, so determined were the Mexicans to expel the Spanish troops, that they made a deliberate calculation that they could afford to sacrifice twenty-five thousand natives to effect the destruction of one Spaniard. Nor was there only the ordinary desire to recover their liberty, that impelled them to this course. They were immediately stimulated to revenge, says Bernal Diaz, by the acts of Alvarado, who commanded in the absence of Cortés, and who fell upon the Mexicans, while they were holding a feast in honor of their gods, for which he had given consent.

Such were the disasters attendant on the precipitate retreat of Cortés, in which he lost during one night one hundred and fifty Spaniards and two thousand of his Indian auxiliaries, not to speak of forty-five horses, which, like elephants in the wars of antiquity, were then much more prized than any number of natives, that the anniversary of his departure has ever since been distinguished as the *noche triste* in the Spanish-Mexican calendar. And had not the Tlascalans, who, at that time, could hardly have been ignorant of the ultimate designs of the Spaniards, preferred the destruction of Mexico to their own independence, the fate of Cortés, in spite of all his former brilliant successes, would have been sealed. As it was, however, he was most kindly received on reaching the limits of their state, "and assured, that he might rely on their proving sure and fast friends to him, until death." Cortés availed himself of the hospitality of his generous allies, till his forces were sufficiently recruited to go in search of new victories; and this letter, after recounting several successes, and the subjugation of new provinces, concludes with an account of the preparations that he was making to obtain the command of the lakes, and to regain possession of Mexico.

The third Despatch, which is dated at the city of Cuyoacan, where the Spaniards established themselves during the rebuilding of the capital, commences with a narrative of the events which preceded the fall of Mexico. The termination of the war was effected only by the entire destruction of the most splendid city of the New World. The forces engaged in this affair were reviewed in the city of Tlascala, on the second day after Christmas, 1520, and found to consist of forty horse and five hundred foot. We shall give the speech of Cortés to his troops on this occasion, which is remarkable for the effrontery with which he asserts the justice of his cause, and for the apparent sincerity with which he brands, as rebels to his Catholic Majesty, those whom he had deprived of their national rights, and who were guilty of no other offence than that of having heaped largesses on their invaders, to be employed for their own destruction.

> I said, that they must know as well as myself, it was to promote the service of your sacred Majesty that we have established colonies in this country; and they also knew, that all the natives of it had acknowledged themselves your Majesty's vassals, and as such had for some time persevered in receiving good offices from us, and we the same from them; and that without any cause, the people of Culua, including those in the great city of Temixtitan, and all the other provinces subject to them, had not only rebelled against your Majesty, but even murdered several persons who were our kindred and friends, and had driven us entirely out of their land; and that they must likewise recollect what dangers and toils we had encountered, and at the same time be sensible of how great service it would be to God and your Catholic Majesty to endeavour to recover what had been lost, having on our part the justest cause and the best reasons for so doing, as we should both contend for the increase of our faith against a barbarous nation, and promote the service of your Majesty. Induced also by a regard to our own safety, and having the coöperation of many of the friendly natives, there were powerful causes to animate our hearts, and I therefore begged them to engage cheerfully in the enterprise, and take fresh courage.

The Spanish forces and munitions were somewhat augmented before they reached Mexico, so that on the 28th of April, 1521, they consisted of eighty-six horse, one hundred and eighteen archers and musketeers, seven hundred foot, armed with swords and bucklers, together with three heavy iron cannon, and fifteen small copper field-pieces. With these resources the investment of the city was made. For the attack, thirteen brigantines also had been built, and with them a great victory over the Indian canoes was achieved. We shall not attempt to give a detailed account of the several encounters between the Spaniards and their allies, amounting to forty thousand men on the one side, and the innumerable host of natives on the other, whom Cortés, "considering that they were rebels, and had discovered so strong a determination to defend themselves or perish," had no difficulty in satisfying his conscience that it was his duty to exterminate. One extract will show the commencement of the work of destruction.

> That they might become more sensible of their situation, I this day . . . set fire to those noble edifices in the great square, where on the former occasion, when they expelled us from the city, the Spanish troops and myself were quartered. These buildings were so extensive that a prince with more than six hundred persons in his family and domestic retinue would have found ample space for their accommodation. There were others adjacent to these, which, although somewhat smaller, were more gay and elegant, and served Muteczuma for aviaries, in which he had every variety of birds known in that country. Although it grieved me much, yet as it grieved the enemy more, I determined to burn these palaces; whereupon they manifested great sorrow, as well as their allies from the cities on the lake, because none of them had supposed we should be able to penetrate so far into the city. This struck them with terrible dismay.

The fighting was desperate, and the siege was continued for seventy-five days, during which the Spaniards met with several losses, and Cortés himself was often exposed to imminent hazard. On one occasion, about forty Spaniards, and more than one thousand of their Indian allies, were slain; but this was the last opportunity that the Mexicans had of rejoicing for a victory. This check induced the Spanish chief to adopt a plan, which brought about the utter destruction of the city. As he gained possession of the several streets, he resolved to destroy all the houses on both sides, so as to leave only open ground behind him, and to convert the canals and other openings from the lakes into firm land. The Mexicans resisted all overtures of peace, desiring death in preference. Cortés, on his side, was very anxious for an arrangement, that the inhabitants might not throw their treasure into the waters. His measures were at last successful, and the siege was concluded, and with it the Mexican empire. . . .

The Despatches continue the history of Mexico to the 15th of October, 1524; and the fourth is dated from Temixtitan (Mexico), after Cortés had received his appointment of Governor and Captain-general of New Spain. It points out the manner in which he disposed of Tapia, whom he induced voluntarily to retire, notwithstanding the royal commission which he had received, and of Garay, who had again landed in the country with a considerable force, but with whom Cortés effected his purpose by means of a proposed matrimonial alliance. It includes accounts of the exploration of the mining districts, of the rebuilding of the capital on a magnificent scale, for which the labor of the Indians was put in requisition, and of the course which was pursued in order to bring the whole country into subjection to the crown of Spain. Cortés also refers to the suppression of the rebellion at Panuco, and to the expedition to Honduras, on which occasion the unfortunate Guautimucin was hanged, to the attempts made for the discovery of the supposed strait connecting the two oceans, and to his early explorations of the South Sea, or Pacific ocean. It likewise contains several suggestions for the internal administration of the provinces, and for a religious establishment. . . .

## J. Bayard Morris (essay date 1928)

SOURCE: An introduction to *Hernándo Cortés: Five Letters 1519-1526,* translated by J. Bayard Morris, George Routledge & Sons, Ltd., 1928, pp. ix-xlvii.

[*In the following excerpt, Morris attempts to counter the charges of barbarism that have frequently been levelled against Cortés and briefly reviews the style and contents of the five* Cartas de relación.]

"Conquest" has always been held an ugly word: so much so that even conquerors themselves have been wary of it. The Norman William crossed the channel, as he announced, to assume a kingdom which was his by right of a rival's oath. Alaric the Goth led his barbarian mercenaries southward to the sack of Rome with the proclaimed intent of securing arrears of pay long overdue.

In like fashion the *conquistadores* of the New World might invent a hundred plausible reasons by which the white man was entitled to oust the native from the soil. They were bringing the benefits of a higher civilization: they were instituting orderly forms of government and administration of justice: above all they were spreading the true faith and guiding an erring flock into the fold. Such arguments have their weight, as they must always have: but they cannot obscure the main issue. The *conquistadores* were engaged primarily on the business of conquering. The war which Cortés waged in Mexico was essentially a war of conquest.

Between the Spaniards who conquered the New World and the buccaneering Englishmen of Elizabeth's reign who successfully robbed them of a large portion of its spoils there was indeed little to choose. The methods of Cortés in Mexico differed little from those adopted by the English in North America, in India and in New Zealand during the succeeding centuries. Moreover it would be untrue to suppose that sixteenth century Spain was entirely without its prophets to cry out upon the means taken to effect a conquest, which must appear to the more civilized minds of our day as iniquitous.

No voice was louder in denunciation than that of a Dominican Friar, Bartolomé de Las Casas. He had accompanied Ovando to Hayti in 1502, and spent the greater part of his life in the Islands and New Spain, refusing finally the wealthy archbishopric of Chiapa for the humble see of Cuzco where he died. His *Short Account of the Destruction of the Indies* was published at Seville in 1552. There is no hesitancy about the attack of this bishop militant.

"From that year of 1518," he says, "until today, which is now in the year 1542, has swelled up and come to a head all the wickedness, injustice, violence and tyranny which the Christians have done in the Indies. . . . I affirm it as very certain and approved that during these forty years (1502-1542) owing to the aforesaid tyrannies and infernal works of the Christians more than twelve million souls, men, women and children, have perished unjustly and tyrannically; and in truth I believe I should not be overstepping the mark in saying fifteen millions. . . ."

In questions of numbers, places, motives even, Las Casas often errs. But there can be no doubt as to the truth of many of the atrocities perpetrated in the Islands, and on the Mainland. They form an indictment against the Conquistadores as a whole which cannot be denied.

It would be easy to assume from this that the army by which the Conquest of Mexico was effected was an undisciplined array of freebooters in which every man was playing for his own hand: but it would be wrong. Cruelties and brutalities to natives on the part of individuals there might be: but the discipline was strict. Witness a few of the rules which Cortés had proclaimed to his men before setting out from Tlascala on the reconquest of Mexico.

*First:* Inasmuch as experience has shown us and we see each day with what solicitude the natives of these parts venerate their idols by which Our Lord God is highly displeased and the Devil greatly served; and whereas by removing them from such error and idolatry and bringing them to a knowledge of the true catholic faith, we shall not only be laying up eternal glory to our souls but also ensuring the aid of God in things temporal; therefore, I, Hernán Cortés, Captain-General and Chief Justiciar in New Spain, exhort and command all Spaniards in my company to hold as their principal end that of rooting out the aforesaid idolatries from the natives and bringing them to a knowledge of God and the true Catholic Faith. . . .

*Item:* Since by false swearing and blasphemies God is greatly displeased, . . . I order that no person of whatever condition shall dare to say "I don't believe in God," or "Damn it" (*Pese!*) or "God has no power": and the same to be understood of Our Lady and all the saints; under pain of the ordinary penalties and 15 *pesos* of gold.

*Item:* Since by gaming, blasphemies and many other indecencies are encouraged, I order that from now on no person play at cards or other games of chance, under penalty of losing all he has gained and twenty *pesos* of gold.

This rule to be relaxed on active service.

*Item:* No man to dare put hand to sword or dagger to strike another Spaniard, under penalty, for a gentleman of 100 *pesos,* and for a common soldier, 100 lashes.

*Item:* No captain to lodge in any other place than that assigned to him by the officer in command.

*Item:* No booty to be taken until the enemy is completely defeated.

*Item:* All booty to be brought immediately to me at the common store, under penalty of death and loss of all his goods.

It is plain that this was no rabble army, whose rank and file could not be kept in hand, and whose atrocities were therefore those of the nameless and irresponsible common soldiery. The atrocities were real enough and they were in general ordered by the leaders. But the impulse behind them was not so much one of terrorism (as Las Casas suggests): it was one of fear.

Fear, as it is probably the most primitive of all emotions, so it is the most potent to reduce men to the level of beasts.

The Aztec natives whom Cortés men had to contend against in New Spain were of very different stock from those whom they had hunted with greyhounds in Cuba. These "gentlesheep" (as Las Casas was pleased to call them) indulged in cannibalism and human sacrifices. Thousands upon thousands of native victims had thus met their deaths on the altars of Mexico and Yucatán: later, during the siege of the capital the Christians themselves were to see the naked bodies of their comrades, white amid the dusky hordes which surrounded them, being borne up for sacrifice to the high idol towers. That Spanish brutalities were dictated in large measure by fear becomes plain in many passages of the Letters.

The massacre of Cholula was obviously the work of men who were badly scared, and had good reason to be so. Albarado left in the capital while Cortés rides to oppose the further advance of Narváez acts not only as the coward but the bully. Very various reasons were given at the court-martial both by himself and those who were with him: "the priests in disobedience to Cortés's strict orders were preparing to make human sacrifices again." "Some of the natives had shouted that it would be the turn of the white men next." "An insurrection was being plotted," and so on. Through all his defence there shows plainly the figure of a man naturally headstrong and brutal whose nerves were very badly on edge.

Whatever deeds Cortés himself must finally be judged guilty of there is no doubt that he was habitually both more resolute and more cool-headed than any of his subordinates. A crowning example of this is given in an account of the spasmodic fighting with neighbouring tribes which followed the retreat from Mexico to Tlascala. . . .

> The city of Huaquechula has sent in chiefs with messages of submission. Moreover they brought the request that a small Spanish force should be sent there to assist them in capturing and putting to death a body of Mexican chieftains who had established themselves within the city and who were in communication with some thirty thousand of the enemy without. But the Spaniards, heard in a neighbouring town that the natives of Huaquechula were banded together with the Mexicans to entice them upon that pretext into the aforesaid city and there set upon them and kill them all. And as they were not wholly recovered from the fear that the natives of the capital had inspired in them, this news spread panic among them, and the Captain whom I had sent in command made such investigations as he thought proper, and placed under arrest all those chieftains from Huaquechula who were accompanying them: and so returned with them to Cholula, which is but four leagues from here, whence he sent them all back to me under a strong guard, together with the proofs which he had obtained. He wrote me, moreover, to say that his men were terror-stricken, and regarded the enterprise as one of extraordinary difficulty. I questioned the prisoners by means of the interpreters I had with me: and having used all diligence to discover the truth, it seemed to me that the Captain had not understood them aright. Thereupon, I ordered them to be freed, and satisfied them as to my trust in them as loyal vassals of your majesty.

Cortés accordingly set out and successfully concluded the expedition in person; "desiring," as he says, "to show no weakness nor fear before the natives, whether friends or enemies." Such were the actual difficulties of the Conqueror.

It is easy to see that had Cortés been anything less than himself, such blots on the history of the conquest as the massacre of Cholula and the torturing and final execution of Guatimucin, might well have been normal occurrences rather than isolated instances.

### THE LETTERS

Cortés's letters to the Emperor from Mexico are termed in Spanish *cartas-relaciones*—half letters, half despatches. They are not literary masterpieces. The vocabulary is very small. The same expressions, of time, place, action, are continually used, as in most documents of the official kind. Yet with a small vocabulary, his style is wordy and often involved. The one artistic effect of which he is a master is that of understatement: and it is a device which he employs unconsciously.

On the whole his prose is solid, never pedantic, controlled and forceful. Through it one perceives a man who of the two tools preferred the sword; yet on occasion could wield the pen in a fashion that was at least eminently workmanlike.

These five letters were all written from various cities in New Spain between the years 1519 and 1526. They vary greatly in length, the second, third and fourth being the longest, each containing in the original some 40,000 words, while the first and fourth run to 10,000 and 20,000 words respectively.

### "First Letter"

Cortés's first letter to the Emperor written in June or July 1519 has never been recovered. There is, however, little doubt about its contents. The Rica Villa of Vera Cruz had just been founded; and its Justiciary and Council lost no time in despatching a letter to Spain, to give, as they said, "a certain and true account of all that had been discovered in the two preceding years." The writer of this letter, it is clear, saw and perhaps copied in large part what Cortés himself was writing. It was this letter from Vera Cruz which was discovered in the Imperial Archives of Vienna during the last century.

The search revealed in addition what is now the **"Fifth Letter,"** which had previously been unknown.

In this **"First Letter"** the earliest discoveries of the mainland from 1517 onwards are sketched in a somewhat lengthy passage which has been abridged.

Diego de Velázquez, a year later . . . was obviously dissatisfied with what had been accomplished. He now set to work to fit out another expedition which should prove more advantageous to himself. It was for this expedition that he chose Cortés as leader.

The new Captain of men obviously showed a very different front to fortune than Grijalba, whose chances of success had been as rosy as his own. It is the man who makes the occasion.

At the end of the letter, the worthy Justiciary and Council of Vera Cruz endeavour at some length to justify their illegal proceeding in founding a settlement. It is not difficult to perceive the hand of Cortés here.

It will be noted that to commend further their action the citizens decided with Cortés to send the whole of the treasure (not merely the royal fifth) to the Emperor.

## "Second Letter"

"The first letter is the weakest, the second the most interesting; the third, the most dramatic," writes a French critic—M. Désiré Charnay. Actually the word "dramatic" may just as properly be applied to the second. There are passages of wonder and horror in this letter which might well belong to the Arabian Nights. The drama opens with the breaking-up of the boats; there follow the cautious but perilous advance into the heart of a hostile country, and the audacious capture of its monarch: the sky seems to have cleared, but suddenly the natives who have hitherto accepted the strangers as immortals to whom they owe allegiance, are violently disturbed by the arrival of rival "gods" in the shape of Pánfilo de Narváez with reinforcements from Velázquez. Open resistance succeeds and the climax is reached with the frenzied scenes of the *noche triste,* "the sorrowful night"—and the days of retreat that follow. Finally the remnants of the army arrive in Tlascala, and to their keen relief are well received by the natives.

The indomitable Cortés waits hardly till his wounds are healed before he is again in the field attacking neighbouring tribes who have been stirred up to rebel by the victorious Culuans. Despite all the fears of his men he is determined on reconquest: and already he embarks upon the task.

The Reconquest proper belongs to the **"Third Letter,"** and the account of certain preliminary operations which occurs at the end of the **"Second Letter"** has consequently been omitted.

## "Third Letter"

This letter may be split up into three portions: (*a*) the advance of Cortés into Culua and the capture and destruction of the various towns surrounding the great lakes; (*b*) the assault on the capital itself and its final submission: (*c*) various enterprises undertaken by the Conqueror to extend his power throughout Mexico, and the arrival of Cristóbal de Tapia from Spain, as agent of the Crown to examine the details of conquest.

The second portion describing the taking of Tenochtitlan is given in its entirely. The two other portions have been somewhat abridged.

Both this and the second letter were made public very soon after their arrival in Spain. A little German printer in Seville published the second on November 8th 1522 and the third on March 30 of the following year. They were almost immediately translated into Latin and Italian and sold in Germany and Italy.

## "Fourth Letter"

This letter is mainly concerned with affairs of organization. The visit of Garay, causing rebellion in Pánuco, and concluding with the Frenchman's death, is the most important incident. Elsewhere certain abbreviations have been made, particularly at the beginning where Cortés reports the progress of various expeditions.

Sandoval was sent east and succeeded in reaching the river Guasacualco and there founding the town of Espíritu Santo four miles from its mouth. Meanwhile messengers arrived from the ruler of Michoacan with presents and an offer to become a vassal of the great white Emperor. An officer proceeded to the province, and thence without orders further west to Coliman, where in spite of his forty horsemen and some hundred Spanish foot he suffered a defeat from the natives.

Albarado was sent south-east to Tututepec, where he succeeded in subduing the natives, holding the ruler of the province and his son captive. The inhabitants of Segura de la Frontera were ordered to proceed thither and found a new town of the same name. Albarado then returned to the capital. In his absence the town revolted and new *alcaldes* were set up. Cortés immediately despatched an officer, who returned with the ringleaders in chains.

The letter was published in Spain both at Toledo and Zaragoza in the year 1526.

## "Fifth Letter"

The expedition to Honduras started out with a long train of servants, butler, majordomo, treasurer, the keeper of the gold and silver plate, surgeon, numerous pages, falconers, even jugglers and tumblers, relates Bernardo Díaz del Castillo. A huge herd of swine accompanied the triumphant procession to provide fresh meat for the travellers.

But it was soon apparent that the journey was to be no picnic. At times the marshy ground rendered any advance at all impossible. Detours had to be made; bridges built; horses supported by bundles of rushes. Cortés was perhaps physically not quite the man that he had been. "I saw that he was much stouter," says Díaz de Castillo, "when we returned from the Higueras." Moreover, he relates, "he now formed a habit (which he had not had in Mexico) of always taking a short nap after the midday meal (failing which his food disagreed with him), and so no matter whether it rained or shone he would lie down under a tree . . . and would always sleep a little before recontinuing the march."

But the old spirit is there. He passes through the various river-villages and towns, most of whose inhabitants have fled, endures the bitterest extremes of hunger and toil, climbs the *sierras* on the eastern side, and finally arrives at Naco. There he finds remnants of treachery and desertion such as were but too common among the early settlers. The wretched survivors are rescued. Cortés conducts that singularly daring expedition up the river to obtain maize for his starving companions. He then proceeds further east and founds a successful settlement on the northern coast of Honduras.

Meanwhile he was being given out for dead in Mexico. He says little in the Letter of what happened in his absence. Two accounts were sent to the Emperor and the Council of the Indies respectively. The truth may be culled from both.

Cortés had left Alonso de Estrada (*tesorero*) and Rodrigo de Albórnoz (*contador*) in charge of the government. Hearing rumours of insurrection and misdemeanour he sent back two other officials from Tabasco with extensive powers. These were Gonzalo de Salazar (*factor*) and Per Almíndez Chirinos (*veedor*). They proved far more successful in securing obedience and were no less dishonest. Months passed and no news came from Cortés. Salazar and Chirinos, who now had the government in their own hands, proclaimed the Governor dead, and proceeded to raid his house and property. Rodrigo de Paz, whom Cortés had left as his steward and Chief Sheriff in New Spain, was arrested, accused of hoarding gold for his master which rightly belonged to the Emperor, twice put to the torture, and finally hanged after a trial farcical in its injustice. All Cortés's possessions, including slaves and cattle, were seized, and the two despots proceeded to govern Mexico unrestrained. The procurators of the various towns and country districts were required to subscribe to a document, drawn up of course by Salazar and Chirinos, begging the Emperor to confirm them in their offices.

Despotism, however, was not allowed to remain a monopoly of the two rulers. Ill-treatment of the native population grew rife, and Indian risings took place in all parts. On January 29th 1527 a courier at last arrived in Mexico with letters from the Governor.

At the news that he was still alive adherents hastened to rally to his cause. Estrada and Albórnoz were encouraged to make a stand. Within a few days Salazar was taken prisoner after an hour's fighting, and Chirinos was skulking in sanctuary.

Cortés returned at the beginning of June in 1526 to find the country more or less at peace. His triumphant route from Vera Cruz to the capital was lined with eager throngs of natives: they cried out "Malinche, Malinche": tears of joy streamed from their eyes. There could have been no more eloquent testimony to the misgovernment of the country during his long absence.

---

**Anthony Pagden on the tone and content of Cortés's Letters:**

All the "captains"—as they called themselves—of the Spanish crown were required by law to send regular reports (*relaciones*) on their activities, and most did; but none of these are anything more than perfunctory, usually disingenuous, accounts of services rendered. Cortés's letters are also disingenuous, but they are never perfunctory. They are far longer than the conventional *relación* and provided with a conscious, if often clumsy, narrative structure. They were also written in the form not, as was usual, of itemized accounts but of letters. Cortés spoke to his monarch respectfully but also directly and sometimes even threateningly as any great feudal lord would. It is unlikely that Charles V ever himself read any of these letters. During the 1520s he was engaged in more urgent matters than the internal affairs of what was then the least significant of his domains. But it was crucial to Cortés's ambitious enterprise for him to insist on the personal nature of his relationship with his king, since his success depended—as J. H. Elliott has indicated—on his ability to represent himself as a loyal, and frequently maligned and misrepresented, vassal. And in order to do this he had to describe his actions, and in particular the less obviously legitimate of them, in the context of his longer-term achievements and objectives. His letters, then, are, at one level, an exercise in legitimation.

*Anthony Pagden in the translator's introduction to* Letters From Mexico, *Yale University Press, 1986.*

---

## Jonathan Loesberg (essay date 1983)

SOURCE: "Narratives of Authority: Cortés, Gómara, Diaz," in *Prose Studies,* Vol. 6, No. 3, December, 1983, pp. 239-63.

[*In the following excerpt, Loesberg examines the rhetorical means by which Cortés, in his* Letters, *seeks to consolidate his authority and to justify his actions.*]

The one assumption which most disables an attempt to take seriously as literary texts such works as Cortés *Letters* and Diaz' *Conquest* is that which takes literariness as a matter of extrinsic, stylistic polish or, at best, as pertaining to certain formal qualities of a work which have no bearing on its political or historical status. Thus Diaz' translator, while he generally lauds Diaz' historicity, allows that "by his own confession, Diaz was a poor stylist," though "for all the roughness of his style, Bernal Diaz could sometimes be picturesque" [J.M. Cohen, 1963]. And, as if having read this passage, Cortés' translator opines that "with the exception of a number of well-turned remarks [Cortés] shows scarcely more literary skill than Bernal Diaz." It is precisely this separation between historical and literary value which disables us from seeing the literary shape of these works. In the case of Cortés, for instance, one cannot begin to understand the denseness of the narrative achievement until one places it in the context of the various conflicting demands of both his political situation as an unauthorized conquistador and his discursive situation as agent-historian. The conflict of Cortés' political situation may be summarized as one between his need to show himself as vitally important to the founding of a Mexican empire and his need to show himself as not powerful enough or ambitious enough to pose a threat to the Spanish throne. This situation was exacerbated by the fact that Cortés was only in the most narrowly legalistic sense not subject to the authority of Diego Velázquez. Velázquez had sent Cortés out on his expedition and had a commission from Charles V giving him power over the newly discovered territory. Thus Cortés' decision to explore further than his commission authorized and his subsequent battle with Velázquez' punitive expedition nearly constituted rebellion against the crown. Cortés could skirt these problems only by feigning ignorance of Velázquez' commission and having himself declared, through a legal loophole, the "chief justice captain and our leader" of the new territory, the founding of which had voided the authority of the instructions under which Velázquez had sent him out.

By arguing that he is essentially a better subject of the Crown than Velázquez, Cortés establishes his *prima facie* preferability as a conqueror. Accordingly, the First Letter, written by two of Cortés' soldiers, mentions Velázquez' greed constantly, even as it offers Charles gold as an incentive to commission Cortés. Thus the Letter urges

> that this land was very good and to judge by the samples of gold which the chieftains had brought, most wealthy also, and, moreover, that the chieftain and his Indians had shown us great goodwill: for these reasons, therefore, it seemed to us not fitting to Your Majesties' service to carry out the orders which Diego Velázquez had given to Hernando Cortés which were to trade for as much gold as possible and return with it to the island of Fernandina in order only that Diego Velázquez and the captain might enjoy it, and that it seemed to us better that a town with a court of justice be founded and inhabited in Your Royal Highness' Name.

In other words, because the land is wealthy and has a lot of gold, Cortés should not obey his original injunc-

tion to find gold and return with it; and in order to prevent Velázquez and Cortés from enjoying the gold to the detriment of Charles V, sole power should be given to Cortés. This logic only makes even minimal sense, of course, if one assumes that Cortés is a more reliable deputy than Velázquez.

Cortés himself has two, more powerful arguments however. The first is that he and only he is able to effect the conquest of New Spain. When he tells the King of his response to Panfile de Narváez' expedition, authorized by Velázquez to wrest control of the conquered territory from him, he explains that "when I saw the great harm which was being stirred up and how the country was in revolt because of Narváez, it seemed to me that if I went to where he was the country would, in great part, become calm, for the Indians would not dare to rebel once they had seen me." The interesting aspect of this situation is that it is a shadow play of Cortés' own conquest. Narváez is a shadow-Cortés, conquering where Cortés has conquered while Cortés is a shadow-Moctezuma, protecting the territory which is now his empire. But Cortés is a far more effective Moctezuma than the original even as Narváez is only a weak parody of Cortés. Cortés' mere appearance in a territory, going to where Narváez was, will quiet the populace. In other words, only Cortés can hold the land for Charles; and he holds it not only more effectively than Velázquez through Narváez, but even more effectively than Moctezuma himself.

Cortés' second argument involves directly his role as agent-historian. We can see its aspects by considering in conjunction two odd moments. In the first, the writers of the First Letter describe their investigation of an island:

> This island is small, and nowhere is any river or stream to be found, so that all the water which the Indians drink comes from wells. The land consists entirely of crags and rocks and forests; the only produce the Indians have is from beehives, and our deputies are conveying to Your Highness samples of the honey and beeswax from the hives for Your Inspection.

> Be it known to Your Majesties that the Captain urged the chieftains of that island to renounce their heathen religion; and when they asked him to give them a precept by which they might hence-forth live, he instructed them as best he could in the Catholic Faith.

This passage raises, I think, two questions. First, why does Cortés bother to send back samples of honey and beeswax? Surely that was not considered a valuable gift, worth taking up the place of gold. Second, why is the passage of description linked to that of proselytization? To get a closer fix on the first question, let us

*Depiction of Hernan Cortés by the Mexican painter Diego Rivera.*

juxtapose against this passage another in which Cortés offhandedly verifies a bit of information by saying, "all of which I later heard more fully from Mutezuma." The power of this seemingly subsidiary remark is that it suddenly spotlights Cortés' ability to be a first-hand gatherer of information. Only he can have his facts verified by Moctezuma himself. And this, of course, is where the sending of the honey and beeswax enters. Those are not presents of value, but tokens of Cortés' having been there on the scene. By seeing the beeswax and Moctezuma as incidents of finding information about the land, the linking of the proselytization immediately becomes clear as the exchange activity, the dissemination of information about religion. And we can now see the connection between Cortés' claim to be the proper choice for conquistador of the new lands and his claim to be the historian to be listened to (after all, Velázquez could write letters too). Just as he was the only one who could hold the land, he was also the only one who could supply reliable information about it and convey accurate information to it, simply because he was the only one who was on the scene, the only one who was witness to or supplier of any kind of information at all.

Both of these arguments for his political and narrative value, however, can also become arguments against those values, and in the same ways. The problem with Cortés' claim to be a shadow-Moctezuma, a reliable holder of the land, may be seen clearly in the light of J. H. Elliott's terse explanation, "it was the policy of the Castilian Crown, firmly laid down in the reign of Ferdinand and Isabella, that no subject should be permitted to grow overmighty." In other words, the very thing that made Cortés valuable, his power, also made him a threat. And the narrative situation is similar. Remember that the agent-historian, in his claim of first-hand factual knowledge always implicitly disallows his reader any valid judgement of his own, erasing the reader's authority. Thus what made Cortés a better choice of narrator than Velázquez, his physical participation and consequent special knowledge, for the very same reason tended to efface the audience to whom it was directed, Charles V.

But there is one more twist here. If Cortés' role as agent-historian seemed to give him too much power in one way, in another it did not give him nearly enough. To the extent that an agent-historian rests his authority on the knowledge of the facts, he is at the mercy of those facts. He does not claim to make his history but to report it. Thus even as the conquistador must react randomly, as best he may, in the face of the unknown, the narrator can only record and re-enact those reactions. He cannot control them. Such a situation is, of course, unstable, involving shifting judgements, shifting events. This formal instability is radically exacerbated, to say the least, by the fact that Cortés wrote his Second Letter after having lost Tenochtitlan but before having reconquered it. In the face of this instability, partly a result of events but partly built into the type of history he wrote, what remained of Cortés' claim to be powerful enough to win and control a new empire?

Cortés' handling of this problem in his Second and Third Letters entails a rhetorically brilliant manipulation of the possibilities of agent-narration. His first manoeuvre is to distance the narrator from the agent as sharply as possible in a history that still claims eyewitness knowledge as its authority. By stressing foreshadowing and design, Cortés, as much as he can, erases the possibility of contingency in the conquest he describes, thus creating what I will call here a narrative of control. The erasure of contingency, the insistence upon control, starts almost from the beginning of the Second Letter, when Cortés first mentions Moctezuma (although he writes as if he had referred to him in a prior letter):

> I also spoke of a great lord called Mutezuma, whom the natives of these lands had spoken to me about, and who, according to the number of days they said we would have to march, lived about ninety or a hundred leagues from the harbor where I

disembarked. And trusting in God's greatness and in the might of Your Highness's Royal name, I decided to go and see him wherever he might be. Indeed I remember that, with respect to the quest of this lord, I undertook more than I was able, for I assured Your Highness that I would take him alive in chains or make him subject to Your Majesty's Royal Crown.

This passage may not seem surprising until one remembers to place it in the context of other conquest narratives, which generally give some account of the relatively late discovery of Moctezuma's existence, the initial ignorance of his precise status and power, and the determination to go to see him which, by supplying a unified motivation and goal, hence-forth gives each history its individual plot design. Here there is neither discovery nor learning but an establishment by fiat of the goal of further activity and even a prediction of the extent to which the goal was effective: he did see Moctezuma, he did not manage to bring him back alive. Nor should the last admission of failure confuse us here. We must remember that Cortés did not have to mention an undertaking of which in fact he knew very well he had never informed Charles. The failure to fulfil the promise to capture Moctezuma was a failure of the agent Cortés. Nevertheless, the narrator's prediction here encompasses both the beginning and the end of the plot at once, replacing the agent's discoveries and surprises with the narrator's foreknowledge and control.

With seemingly astonishing daring, Cortés tests his replacement of agent with narrator by writing his narrative of control from a moment when control is lost. This may be less daring than necessity, though. Given that Cortés had not written before the *noche triste,* he could not wait until after the attempt at reconquest to write because obviously he could not know that of which he is concerned to assure Charles, that he would successfully retake the city. Moreover, since he had sent for aid, he needed to explain any reports Charles might get from elsewhere about the suddenly unstable situation. By writing precisely when all was up in the air, though, he could substitute his narrative's foreknowledge for actual event. To see how this substitution works, consider together these passages:

> Believing, therefore, that if the ships remained there would be a rebellion, and once all those who had resolved to go had gone I would be left almost alone, whereby all that in the name of God and Your Highness had been accomplished in this land would have been prevented, I devised a plan, according to which I declared the ships unfit to sail and grounded them; thus they lost all hope of escape and I proceeded in greater safety and with no fear that once my back was turned the people I had left in the town would betray me.

> . . . So Your Highness may be assured that if it

pleases Our Lord to favor Your Royal good fortune, all that was lost, or a great part of it, will shortly be regained, for each day many of the provinces and cities which had been subject to Mutezuma come and offer themselves as Your Majesty's vassals, for they see how those who do so are well received and favored by me, whereas those who do not are destroyed daily.

The first passage, noticeably does not describe the event of destroying the ships so much as the thinking behind devising a plan, making a plot. In a situation in which "what has been accomplished" could have been "prevented," Cortés through designing overcomes contingency. It is the narrative description of designing primarily, and the grounding only as a result of that designing, that creates the desired result. Cortés' prediction of success in the second passage has precisely the same narrative shape. It is foreknowledge based on reason and calculation. And the entire vector of the narrative encourages us to take design itself as effective because what the narrative foresees occurs.

In a narrative that insists on control rather than contingency, spatial facticity has entire priority over temporal event. Indeed Cortés emplots his narrative so that, as nearly as possible in a linear narrative, temporal sequence is erased. Here, for instance, is Cortés' account of his response to a group of Indians who wanted to join his forces although they had previously killed some Spaniards: "as they could not therefore excuse themselves from all blame, their punishment would be to return what belonged to us, and if they did so, although they deserved to die for having killed so many Christians, I would make peace with them because they begged me to do so." Despite the density of past event and future possibility that hovers behind this passage, it is more nearly, in Erich Auerbach's terms, a case of flat, foregrounded narrative, such as Homer's *Odyssey,* rather than layered and background narrative such as the *Bible*'s. A rather large complex of events is held together and resolved in a single moment through a series of logical connectives, "as," "therefore," "if," "although," and, unstated but implied, a "then" after "if" and a "nevertheless" after "although." The Indians' past crime and future punishment are all contained in a single proposition, present in space rather than extended through time. The meeting itself is a linguistic event parallel to this sentence since it is the event that signifies all these various resolutions, the return of Spanish property and the making of peace. The suggestion of the narrative as a whole is that the conquest exists almost as a single, externalizable, logical proposition rather than an unpredictable sequence of events.

Not surprisingly, in this form of emplotment, the Aztecs have very little interiority or psychological density. They are neither good nor bad but simply external objects that exist in relation to Cortés' various plots and designs. Here for instance is Cortés' first discovery of the Aztec empire's fragile political situation:

> When I saw the discord and animosity between these two peoples I was not a little pleased, for it seemed to further my purpose considerably; consequently I might have the opportunity of subduing them more quickly, for, as the saying goes, 'divided they fall.' . . . So I maneuvered one against the other and thanked each side for their warnings and told each that I held his friendship to be of more worth than the other's.

Cortés' political shrewdness has often been remarked upon nor do I mean to dispute it. But it is a shrewdness that runs in extremely narrow grooves. These Indians, although they are political enemies, are virtually undifferentiated within the narrative. Between "one" and "the other" or "each" and "the other's" there is only the slimmest grammatical and virtually no semantic differentiation. Here, as in all the other passages which describe Cortés' political machinations, the Indians are merely blank counters, objects whose only importance is their relationship to and within Cortés' designs.

The tactics of erasing sequence in favour of control and of subordinating all objects of plot to narrative design may alleviate the inherent instability in the narratives of agent-historians, but they would not seem designed to assuage the Crown's fear of conquistadors becoming overly powerful. But here is the telling effectiveness of Cortés' enhanced split between narrator and agent. Although the narrative voice is one of almost imperial authority and contol, the agent-Cortés consistently effaces himself, pictures himself as an institutional embodiment rather than an individual leader. One sees this most strikingly in Cortés' response to a message from Panfilo de Narváez:

> One of those clerics also told me that Diego Velázquez had empowered Narváez and the two clerics jointly to make this offer and any concessions I might wish. I replied that I saw no decree from Your Highness instructing me to deliver the land to them, and that, if indeed they brought one, they should present it before me and the municipal council of Vera Cruz in accordance with the practice in Spain.

It is easy to forget the political situation that makes this claim so absurd. Not only was Diego Velázquez the man who authorized Cortés' voyage but Cortés well knew that Velázquez already had imperial authorization for his activity. Vera Cruz, moreover, was the creation of Cortés that allowed him to have himself declared the Spanish captain in Mexico. Thus beneath the tip of this passage is an iceberg of rebellious, individual assertion. And yet Cortés manages to portray

his insubordination here as a responsiveness to rules and regulations. And, as we saw earlier, he attributes the imminent retaking of Tenochtitlan not only to his machinations but to those machinations as simply a grounding of Royal good fortune. By assigning all of his active powers to the controlling narrator, Cortés is able to portray his agent-self as an object of institutional and Royal will, an object of plot almost as much as the Indians are, one of the external facts upon which the narrative of control calls for its authority. Cortés maintains enough of the form of agent-histories to rest his authority upon his first-hand knowledge. Indeed he enhances the spatial quality of this appeal by as much as possible de-temporalizing his narrative. But, by opening a rift between agent and narrator, he also succeeds in making the form more politically palatable.

### Carlos Fuentes (essay date 1986)

SOURCE: "The Spanish Captain's Story," in *The Guardian Weekly,* Vol. 135, No. 26, December 28, 1986, p. 22.

[*In the following essay, Fuentes examines what he sees as the "democratic essence of Machiavellianism" that prompted the actions and writings of men like Cortés.*]

Hernan Cortes, the conqueror of Mexico, was seven years old when Columbus set foot in the New World. He came from a modest family in a modest town of barren Extremadura. At nineteen, he left home for the Indies. His Spanish inheritance was a vine and a beehive. In the New World, he conquered an empire nine times the size of Spain.

The letters sent by Cortes to Emperor Charles V between 1519 and 1526, in Anthony Pagden's definitive translation, tell the tale of this conquest with self-serving vigour, a dash of mythologising, and a subtle sense of legitimation. It all adds up to one of the most fascinating Machiavellian documents to come out of the Renaissance.

Machiavelli wrote *The Prince* in 1513, but it was only published after his death, in 1532. Cortes could not have read Machiavelli. But, as these letters prove, he was the best living proof that the Machiavellian idea was in the air of the sixteenth century.

A product of the enormous energy and movement of the Spanish war of Reconquest against the Moors, Cortes and his brethren represented the new men of an incipient middle class first liberated from feudalism by the shifting frontiers of the wars, the Christian repopulation of reconquered zones, and the rise of cities and towns rewarded with a modicum of municipal freedoms.

These events then prepared them to rise from anonymity to the challenge of the Renaissance enterprise of power as envisioned by Machiavelli. Power is truly deserved by those who by their courage and ability, and not by fortune or inheritance, are able to conquer it. Now everyone, if they know how to manipulate will and fortune, can be the Prince, instead of serving him.

Re-reading Pagden's translation, I am again struck by the democratic essence of Machiavellianism as acted out by men such as Cortes in the New World. Cortes writes to the King in order to put his conquests at the royal feet, but at the same time he is telling an extraordinary tale of how to acquire power in unprecedented, uncharted circumstances.

Akin to the models offered by Machiavelli, "little or nothing" in the life and enterprises of Cortes "can be attributed to fortune". As Machiavelli says of Agathocles, who rose to be king of Sicily, Cortes also " . . . achieved sovereignty, not by the favour of any one (but) by a thousand efforts and dangers," and he maintained it "with great courage and a great temerity".

Cortes came to Mexico, furthermore, as a "prophet armed". The Indians could hardly resist musket, cannon, and monstrous four-legged beasts. Even less could a culture based upon myth resist an invader who arrived in precise synchronisation with the announced return of the blond, bearded god Quetzalcoatl, the Plumed Serpent.

But Cortes did not know that he was, nor did he want to be, a prophet, much less a God. He wished to be what his ancestors could never have been: a prince, at least an *hidalgo*. To do this, he had to fight on three fronts: against the governor of Cuba, Velazquez, who had denied him the right to conquer and settle; against Montezuma, the Aztec emperor, who held sway over a vast and ominous land and its powerful armies; and against his own king, Charles V, who should be made to feel that these conquests were made in his name so that he would not hinder, but legitimise, Cortes's faraway actions in the New World.

Cortes defeated the authority of the governor of Cuba, by achieving success in Mexico—a highly improbably forecast when the Spanish captain destroyed his own ships in Veracruz and thus cut off his own retreat. The defeat of the Aztecs happened because Cortes employed to the hilt the combination of courage, audacity, and ability that Machiavelli called *virtu*: this prince of the New World intrigues, listens, and listens above all to the very human complaints of the tribes oppressed by Montezuma.

The Spanish captain united them all in what proved to be an invincible alliance against the Indian despot: the conquest of Mexico was more than the astonishing success of an army of less than 600 Europeans who cut off their retreat and confronted a theocratic empire. It was the victory of the other Indians, who assisted Cortes, against the Aztec overlord. It was the victory of the Indian world against itself.

Cortes defeated Montezuma because the Aztec emperor wanted to see in the Spanish captain a God, whereas Cortes refused to be a God and decided to be a man, and more than a man, a Renaissance Prince. But this was not to be allowed by the Spanish Crown; Cortes defeats Montezuma, but then he is defeated by Charles V. . . .

Cortes is the Prince who never was: this tale of melancholy courage is the stuff of the *Letters*. It is vastly relevant to the contemporary history of Latin America: Army, Church and State are our oldest institutions and here we witness their origin. Cortes, the military man, wished to legitimise his conquest by Christian evangelisation of the heathen and then offer it, *pro forma,* to a faraway sovereign, while proceeding to consolidate his own local power in Mexico.

The Church and the Crown were not going to permit this. Once the military phase of the conquest had been concluded, Cortes was named governor, then surrounded by a cloud of intriguing royal bureaucrats, finally shunted aside, accused of sundry crimes, and left to write pathetic letters to the King, asking for money to pay his sailors, while propagandising priests such as Las Casas furthered royal authority and further undermined the power of the conquistadores.

Two dates coincide here: The fall of Tenochtitlan, the Aztec capital, to Cortes, in 1521, and, that same year, the defeat of the revolution of the Castilian communities at the hands of Charles V. Thinking that he has triumphed in the New World, the conquistador has just been defeated in the Old World. He wanted to be a prince in the Indies because he had never been an *hidalgo* in Spain. He should have been a citizen first, both in the Old and in the New World.

His failure became ours. The vertical autocracy of Montezuma was substituted by the vertical autocracy of the Spanish Habsburgs. We are the defendants of both verticalities, and our stubborn struggles for democracy are all the more difficult, and perhaps, even admirable.

Machiavelli's *Prince* was first published in Spanish translation in 1552 and then included in the *Index Prohibitorum* by Cardinal Gaspar de Quiroga in 1584. But first, the Crown had ordered, in March of 1527, that there should be no further printings of the letters of Cortes. And in 1553, yet another royal decree was to forbid the export to the Indies of all histories of the Conquest. We were not allowed to know ourselves, so instead of histories we write novels.

Chroniclers such as Cortes, were not only our first historians but our first novelists. Out of their epic contradictions, new communities and finally new nations were born. Yet in Mexico there is no statue honouring Cortes: we have preferred to celebrate the defeated, forgetting that Cortes can be counted among them.

## Stephanie Merrim (essay date 1986)

SOURCE: "Ariadne's Thread: Auto-Biography, History, and Cortés' *Secunda Carta-Relación*," in *Disposi-tio*, Vol. XI, Nos. 28-29, 1986, pp. 57-83.

*[The following excerpt examines the importance of the intended audience in relation to the construction of the narrative "I" in Cortés's* Second Letter.*]*

In his mandate to Cortés to undertake the exploration of Tierra Firme, Governor of Cuba Diego Velázquez encharged his former secretary to submit a "muy complida e entera relación" of all that he saw, discovered and learned. This *relación* was to be relayed to Velázquez so that *he,* in turn, could "facer entera y verdadera relación al Rey nuestro Señor, y se lo envíe para que su Alteza lo vea." Cortés, for his part, pinpoints his 'original sin' against Velázquez—from which ultimately would issue the loss of the Mexican empire—as the fact that he sent the *relación* directly to the King rather than to Velázquez: "se habían movido con aquella armada y gente contra mí porque yo había enviado la relación y cosas desta tierra a vuestra majestad y no al dicho Diego Velázquez." From its inception, and in its very existence, we see, the *relación* represents a gambit for power.

This exchange and allegation gives us a sense, as well, of the legal and personal implications that writing, and his *relación,* held for Cortés. Writing, for Cortés, is fully tantamount to acting; not a substitute for action, it *is* action and a necessary complement to his own actions as a conqueror, which would remain incomplete and illegitimate until sanctioned by the King in his response to this dispatch. The verbal war enacted in the arena of the *"Segunda carta-relación,"* which Cortés writes in the throes of the reconquest of Mexico, figures as an extension of the original conquest and, to state the obvious, purports to redress through writing the seeming transgressions and tragic losses of the physical war. In securing the desired response from its interlocutor, the dispatch or autobiographical act—his bracketed off portion of history—would thus constitute a milestone and significant action in the *biography* of its writer. With his university education, legal training and years as secretary, Cortés was perhaps better prepared to wage the verbal than he was the physical battle. Indeed, as Beatriz Pastor has so comprehensively demonstrated, Cortés engages in a Machiavellian verbal war which fully partakes of the tactics, strategies and maneuvers characteristic of his leadership; the conqueror coordinates History with his story, and crafts a text whose every element is strategically conceived.

Supremely complex and self-conscious in its narrative as well as thematic aspects, Cortés' letter-*relación*-history-autobiography-apology-ethnography, etc., provides fertile grounds for our approach. Accepting the line of thought established by Pastor, we shall explore in schematic form the potential of the auto-bio-graphical model, its ability to separate and coordinate at least the most essential of the multiple layers and strands of Cortés' text.

*Carta:* letter, *grafía,* pragmatics.

*Relación:* legal case, *autos,* self-defense.

As does any letter with a greeting and signature, Cortés *"Carta-relación"* implicitly entails a contract between two parties. Hence, *autos,* the interests of the "I," are consistently figured in function of *grafía,* the interests of the other, the Crown. Cortés, this section will show, entirely equates his own interests with those of the Crown; indeed, only through the Crown can his own interests be served.

Cortés constructs his "I," in part, as that of a mere instrument and vassal serving the interests of the Crown; he empties his "self" of personal interests and motivations and fills his "I" with those he presumes to be of the other. The result is a theatrical and public, eminently contrived, textual *autos.* How to address the supreme authority, *Vuestra Alteza?* Textually, Cortés conceptualizes the Crown as a discrete set of functions and needs such as those laid out by Velázquez in detailing the points which Cortés' *relación* should cover. The conqueror will systematically address and satisfy these areas of inquiry.

The interests of the Crown (*grafía*), as equated to those of the *autos,* shapes Cortés' construction not only of his narrative "I," but also his characterization of the other figures who perform significant roles in the historical arena. These, in the case of the Second Letter, are invariably power-wielding figures, whose persons and power must verbally be molded or tamed in accordance with the interests of the *autos* and the *grafía.* The interrelation of *grafía-autos* thus involves *characterization,* of Moctezuma, Pánfilo de Narváez and Diego Velázquez.

In concrete terms, Cortés must:

a. Reassure the King of his loyalty to him.

b. Exalt his "I" by exalting his discoveries, achievements and triumphs, in a manner not threatening to the King.

c. Justify before the King his transgressions and failure—the imprisonment and death of the Aztec King; his actions regarding Velázquez and Narváez; the "Noche Triste" and loss of the Mexican empire—in order to attain the King's sanction of his power.

d. Effectively plead for aid from the Crown to achieve the reconquest of Mexico.

In what we now utilize as the **"First Letter of Relation"** ("De la justicia y regimiento de la rica Villa de la Vera Cruz"; 10 July 1519), Cortés attempted to legalize his renegade enterprise, which he had pulled out from under Diego Velázquez' grasp and control. During the interval between the First and Second letters, Cortés has both magnified his achievements by conquering Mexico *and* compounded his transgression by defeating Velázquez' envoy, Pánfilo de Narváez. The King, however, has yet to reply to Cortés' first communication. Given his pressing needs for food and reinforcements, we can see that both in legal and practical terms Cortés' entire enterprise rests on shaky grounds; the achievements of the "I" hinge, as we have said, on the response of the other.

In view of the magnitude of the events and Cortés' awareness of their import, one would expect this autohistorical discourse to assume the shape of a memoir (where *bios* = history). However, as it has been said [by Elizabeth Bruss, *Autobiographical Acts,* 1976], the writer with autobiographical impulses "may act to rebut his public character in the form of an apology or to sustain it in the form of . . . a memoir." Here, then, the weighty exigencies of the essential conjunction, *grafía-autos* shift the dominant of Cortés' text from memoir to apology.

The very act of writing to the King, we have seen, comprises an act of fealty. Throughout, it is Cortés' overriding intention to reaffirm his loyalty to the Crown and thus the propriety of his own actions. His autographic intentions lead to rhetorical formulations and invention.

—Cortés directly addresses the King at every step of the text ("vuestra alteza;" "vuestra sacra majestad"), maintaining constant functional and phatic contact with the receptor. The text is riddled with the marks of the *grafía*.

—Cortés ostentatiously complies with the formulae of epistolary address. The Letter's commentators have noted the marked contrast between the lexical and syntactical latinisms of the elaborate salutation and conclusion, and the "ritmo más castellano, más suelto" of the body of the letter.

—Cortés protests his loyalty to the Crown directly, through direct address, and indirectly, through the numerous speeches and harangues (*arengas*) both to his men and to the Indians reported through indirect discourse in the text. As Pastor notes, these speeches often draw on the medieval topoi of vassalage and service.

*Direct address/discourse:* "En esta gran ciudad estuve proveyendo las cosas que parecía que convenía al servicio de vuestra sacra majestad."

*Indirect discourse:* [calming the mutinous urges of his troops] "y yo les animaba diciéndoles que mirasen que eran vasallos de vuestra alteza, y que jamás en los españoles en ninguna parte hobo falta, y que estábamos in disposición de ganar para vuestra majestad los mayores reinos y señoríos que había en el mundo . . .".

—In an even more dramatic maneuver, Cortés repeatedly places fervent declarations of fealty [imagined, invented, or real?] in the mouths of the King's newest vassals, the Indians; speeches he nevertheless reports indirectly: [the entire Mexican *pueblo* swears loyalty to the King after Moctezuma addresses them] "y desde allí todos juntos y cada uno por sí prometían, y prometieron, de hacer y cumplir todo aquello que con el real nombre de vuestra majestad les fuese mandado, como buenos y leales vasallos lo deben hacer . . .". Subordinated to his voice and purposes, the many texts of the Indians' speeches form part of Cortés' text in every sense, for Cortés sets up a verbal empire for his monarch where not only he but his erstwhile adversaries, the Indians, are ruled by loyalty to the King.

(At least textually), immediately upon achieving the conquest of Tenochtitlán, Cortés takes inventory of his gains, and sends messengers in search of gold. Now, we recall that Velázquez had mandated Cortés to inform him about a wide range of matters: ethnographic, linguistic, botanical, religious, commercial, and so on. In writing to the King, whom he conceptualizes in terms of the Crown's *interests,* Cortés effectively interprets and prioritizes these various topics. Riches, commercially viable commodities, lands, and gold take first place and largely displace the other topics. Wherever possible, the exhaustive listing of these desired objects through a functional but chaotic enumeration displaces the "historical" narration as well; the momentous first encounter between Cortés and Moctezuma, for example, is depicted as essentially an exchange of precious objects (or worthless trinkets, on Cortés' part). The fact that the inventory—revealing to the King his new empire in all its splendor—performs a function crucial to the apology (in other words, "I,

Cortés, have conquered all of this for you, the King") perhaps explains the displacement.

—"La grandeza mexicana:" Exalting both his own achievement and the Crown's gain, "la grandeza mexicana" becomes the ruling criterion of Cortés' inventories and descriptions. Where other chroniclers insistently document similarities between the New World and *Spain,* in this section Cortés celebrates the almost Oriental pomp and grandeur of Mexico. He glories in the "unnatural" conjunction of civilization and barbarism which characterizes Moctezuma's court: "¿qué más grandeza puede ser que un señor bárbaro como éste tuviese contrahechos de oro y plata y piedras y plumas todas las cosas que debajo del cielo hay en su señorío . . .". That emotion and *admiratio* deriving from the novel of chivalry, to which other chroniclers would take recourse in expressing their *asombro* when faced with the marvels of the New World, Cortés reserves for the products of human artifice: [describing Tlaxcala, the first city encountered] "La ciudad es tan grande y de tanta admiración, que aunque mucho de lo que della podría decir deje, lo poco que diré creo es casi increíble." Clearly taking the Crown's interests into consideration, objects which could be priced but are priceless, incite Cortés' most fervent enthusiasm: [Moctezuma's jewels] "eran tales y tan maravillosas, que consideradas por su novedad y extrañeza no tenían precio, ni es de creer que alguno de todos los príncipes del mundo de quien se tiene noticia las pudiesen tener tales y de tal calidad." Though elsewhere Moctezuma will strategically be depicted as a weak and impotent monarch, in the inventory sections—serving another strategic aim—Cortés represents the Aztec monarch's riches and sovereignty as boundless.

—Writing the New World: Unlike the other chroniclers of the New World, Cortés' (self-stated) problems in writing the New World were far from epistemological. (We recall Bernal Díaz' quandary in *La verdadera historia de la conquista de la Nueva España* when faced with the verbal task: "porque hay mucho que ponderar en ellos que no sé cómo lo cuente: ver cosas nunca oídas, ni vistas ni aun soñadas como viamos." Rather, several times Cortés confesses his incapacity only to provide a sufficient register of the contents of Mexico: [to fully list the wonders of this New World] "sería menester mucho tiempo y ser muchos relatores muy expertos: no podré yo decir de cien partes una de las que dellas se podrían decir . . .".

Throughout the **"Second Letter of Relation,"** we have suggested, Cortés empties his "self" of interests to emphasize that he is not acting autonomously, but on behalf of the King and the interests of the Crown. Conceptually and verbally he sets up an unbroken continuum, Cortés-Crown: "En la otra relación, muy excelentísimo Príncipe, dije a vuestra majestad las ciudades y villas que hasta entonces a su real servicio se habían ofrecido y yo a él tenía sujetas y conquistadas." Aligning and equating his interests with the Crown's, Cortés justifies his apparent usurpation of power; any honor done him, for example, derives from Cortés' status as the Crown's intermediary: "y porque ellos tenían vergüenza en que yo estuviese tan mal aposentado, pues me dieron por su amigo y ellos y yo éramos vasallos de vuestra alteza . . . [they offered him food and lodging]." The topos of the selfless vassal who desires only to serve the King, Frankl notes, dates back to the era of transition in the late Middle Ages between feudalism to a centralized monarchy, a situation not dissimilar to that of Cortés in the New World.

—Again the actions of the Indians, textual reflectors of Cortés at key points, mirror those of the conqueror and reinforce his textual designs. For example, the Indians surrender to the Spaniards, "como si de *ab initio* hubieran conocido a vuestra sacra majestad por su rey y señor natural". In his remarkable speech to Cortés, Moctezuma articulates and inscribes his kingdom in the Cortés-Crown continuum: "vos sed cierto que os obedeceremos y ternemos por señor en lugar de ese gran señor que decís . . .". Moctezuma is ultimately shown to be so fully drawn into the continuum, now Moctezuma-Cortés-Crown, that he forsakes *his* personal interests and becomes, like, Cortés, a selfless servant of the Crown.

—In forging his own posture towards power, Cortés models himself on the King, as a just and benevolent monarch. He routinely pardons the Indians their transgressions and generously extends his protection to them: "Si leales vasallos de vuestra alteza fuesen, serían de mí, en su real nombre, muy favorecidos y ayudados . . .".

At the heart of his "fictionalization" of the conquest, Pastor astutely observes, lies Cortés' self-transformation from rebel to model leader, in the epic mold. Similar to the Cid, "[a]mbos expresan en los elementos concretos de su caracterización la suma de las cualidades objetivamente necesarias para realizar con éxito el proyecto . . ." [Pastor, *Discurso Narrativo,* 1983] in the **"Second Letter of Relation,"** Cortés thus endows himself with extraordinary personal valor and religious zeal. He is at once a man of peace and one capable of unerring action, the medieval hero—a servant of God and loyal vassal of the Crown. Cast in the epic mold, Cortés presents himself as infallible. Only when undermined by the traitors, Velázquez and Narváez, as we shall detail, is his infallibility foiled.

Cortés' characterization of the Aztec monarch responds profoundly to the *autos* and the *grafía:*

With regards to the *autos:* Cortés, model leader and avatar of the King, asserts his shining example over/

against the tarnished profiles of the other power-wielding figures of his textual empire (Moctezuma, Velázquez, Narváez). Textually, they will be denigrated and "eliminated."

With regards to the *grafía:* though he may be a pagan, Moctezuma remains an *Emperor,* Charles the Fifth's counterpart in the New World. Cortés' deposing of the Mexican emperor could all too easily be interpreted as a violation of the absolute rights of monarchy in general. In the Letter, Cortés' treatment of Moctezuma, the Aztec ruler's imprisonment and death, must thus be handled with extreme care, and Moctezuma shown to merit his fate. Cortés' Moctezuma is indeed, we will argue, that of the Divine Monarch who (in their first direct encounter, exposes himself as a mere flesh and blood mortal.

—Rather than his counterpart, Moctezuma emerges as the Spanish Emperor's *anti*-image: a tyrant and traitor. We first see Moctezuma through the eyes of the Cempoalan Indians, who welcome the Spaniards as an escape from tyranny: "Y me dijeron otras muchas quejas de él, y con esto han estado y están muy ciertos y leales en el servicio de vuestra alteza y creo lo estarán siempre por ser libres de la tiranía de aquél y porque de mí han sido siempre bien tratados y favorecios." In Cortés' eyes, Moctezuma proves himself unworthy of his absolute power because incapable of wielding it resolutely, with his equivocal actions towards the Spaniards. Even after Moctezuma has surrendered his kingdom and sworn loyalty to the Spanish Crown, he is suspected of collaborating with Narváez to overthrow Cortés, actions no longer merely equivocal but now overtly treacherous. Moctezuma, for reasons we now understand, plays a contradictory role in Cortés' textual scheme: at once a loyal vassal and, now, a traitor to the Crown.

—Similarly, Cortés' inventory of the refinements of the "barbarian's" court and pleasure palaces serves a dual purpose, pointing to Moctezuma's tragic flaw: his love of luxury and frivolity. The excessive indulgence that characterizes Moctezuma's court would contribute to his undoing. For, much as Nero fiddled while Rome burned, Cortés shows Moctezuma to be amusing himself and obliviously enjoying his pleasures during his confinement. Puerile and "effeminate" (as versus the "masculine" Spanish heroes), Moctezuma weeps before his people as he delivers them to the Spaniards. Clearly, W. H. Prescott's striking portrait of Moctezuma [in *History of the Conquest of Mexico,* 1959] as passive and melancholically self-indulgent but further elaborates the characterization already latent in Cortés' text.

[Cortés' representation of Narváez and Velázquez as usurpers is] doubtless the keypin of the letter, the rallying point towards which are geared all of Cortés'

contrivances. Victor Frankl and Beatriz Pastor have effectively drawn the lines of Cortés argumentation against Velázquez and Narváez, to wit: greed for material gain motivate them to seize Mexico for themselves and not for the Crown; where Cortés purportedly acts as a loyal vassal in the interests of the Crown, they act out of *self*-interest; traitors, Velázquez and Narváez incite the Indians and Moctezuma to rebellion against Cortés and thus against the Crown; obedience to Velázquez, himself guilty of flouting royal orders, thus comprises complicity with a traitor and—the final twist—rebellion against Velázquez' loyal service to the King. Let us now consider two aspects of the shape of Cortés' argument and its contextualization.

—Few passages bear fuller witness to Cortés' verbal craft than the brief lead-in to the news of Narváez' arrival. The narrative timing (if not Narváez') is perfectly tuned: Cortés has recounted the surrender of Moctezuma and, significantly, has just finished inventorying its rich contents. The listing style of the inventory dramatically cedes to an unusual spate of verbs, showing Cortés engaged in vital action in the King's service: "En esta ciudad estuve proveyendo las cosas que parecía que convenía al servicio de vuestra majestad, y pacificando y atraeyendo a él muchas provincias . . . y descubriendo minas, y sabiendo e inquiriendo muchos secretos de las tierras . . .". He confirms that Moctezuma and his people have gladly subjugated themselves to the Crown ("hacían todas las cosas que en el real nombre les mandaba . ."). The whole land is in peace ("estando toda quietud y sosiego en esta dicha ciudad,"); for the first time in this "chronicle" Cortés situates his narrative temporally, signalling the attainment of an important plateau. Eager to send a second *relación,* Cortés awaits the King's messengers and thus the monarch's em-powering reply to the first communication. Into this ideal configuration—the Old World's projections for the New telescoped into a single paragraph, with the precise admixture of loyalty, power and desire—intrudes Narváez: within the very sentence where Cortés promises to send "todas las cosas de oro y joyas que en ella había habido para vuestra alteza", comes the news that eighteen ships have landed near the San Martín mountains.

—Other aspects of Cortés' case against Narváez and Velázquez—here the *relación* fulfills its legal dimension—are far less subtle, and highly ironic. Narváez and Velázquez's transgressions essentially replay Cortés' own disobedience of the law in the aims of self-interest. Yet Cortés will assume the posture and voice of the Law to denounce the illegality of the interlopers' actions. (That Narváez has taken prisoner the representative of the *juez* in Hispaniola, Allyón, objectively sets the law on Cortés' side in pursuing the miscreants). Cortés repeatedly requests to see Narváez' authorization from the King and begs him to follow due process. Using legalistic language and argumentation, Cortés states that only when presented with such authorization can he be expected to comply with Narváez' demands: "Yo les respondí que no vía provisión de vuestra alteza por donde le debiese entregar la tierra, e que si alguna traía que la presentase ante mí y ante el cabildo de la Veracruz, según orden y costumbre de España, y que yo estaba presto de la obediencia y cumplir." Alternating with his legalistic tone, Cortés' invective against the traitors swells, reaching a fever pitch: "lo contrario haciendo, procedería contra ellos como contra traidores y aleves y malos vasallos que se rebelaban contra su rey y quieren usurpar sus reinos y señoríos, y darlas y aposesionar dellas a quien no pertenecían . . .".

In addition to the above, Cortés structures his self-defense on a simple equation: Cortés = peace and order / Narváez = violence and chaos. Narváez, we have seen, arrives in Mexico at the moment of Cortés' greatest plenitude and peace. Violence follows immediately upon his arrival as the Cempoala Indians rebel *not* against Cortés but, at least according to the author, against Narváez for inciting them to mutiny against the Crown. Cortés then departs for the coast *not* with the intentions of attacking Narváez, but to prevent further turbulence among the Indians. Cortés alleges that Narváez has drawn Moctezuma into his web of treachery, which definitely establishes all other power-wielding figures as traitors and leaves only Cortés as a true supporter of the Crown. And had he not intervened and restored order—the Spanish order—all that had been gained and depicted would have been lost: "E puede vuestra alteza ser muy cierto que si . . . salieran con su propósito, de hoy en veinte años no se tornara a ganar ni a pacificar la tierra que estaba ganada y pacificada."

—The equation takes on determining significance in the events leading up to the Noche Triste, the flight of the Spaniards from Tenochtitlán. As Cortés presents it, Narváez essentially entailed a threat to peace on two fronts, the coast *and* the city. Writing retrospectively Cortés attributes to himself the prevision that were he to leave for the coast to tend to one threat, the Aztecs of Tenochtitlán would mutiny: "con temor que salido yo de la dicha ciudad la gente se rebelase y perdiese tanta cantidad de oro y joyas y tal ciudad, mayormente que perdida aquella, era perdida toda la tierra." To forestall the realization of his "prophecy," Cortés shows himself taking every precaution to ensure the orderly functioning of Tenochtitlán in his absence. Moctezuma swears to maintain the *status quo*. That Pedro de Alvarado has been left in command is not mentioned. Indeed, the role of Alvarado and the Spaniards in the massacre of the Aztecs which resulted in the Noche Triste is *never mentioned*. Thus this, Cortés' only failure, must be attributed to his absence as occasioned by Narváez' presence, and to the chaos the latter reaps both directly and indirectly.

Increasing towards the end of the Letter, as the events narrated grow more dire and the need for self-justification more crucial, Cortés' depicts God as willing their positive outcome despite all odds. Where at other moments Cortés' overweening "I" assumes responsibility for *all* actions of the conquest, here he purposely disclaims responsibility, attributing his failures to Velázquez and Narváez, and his victories (against Narváez and in the Noche Triste) to divine intervention. Cortés reduces himself to the roles of (victim and) passive receptacle of divine favor as God, the Holy Spirit and the Virgin all collaborate in his enterprise.

The attribution of his victories to divine intervention is no mere rhetorical device in Cortés' Letter. As Pastor notes, "en el contexto de una ideología a caballo entre Edad Media y Renacimiento que reclama el origen divino de una monarquía que se apoya en la estrecha alianza entre el rey y Dios, la presentación de Dios como el aliado más fiel y constante de Cortés, y la de su empresa rebelde como acción favorecida y protegida repetidamente por la providencia, constituye la mejor forma posible de legitimación." Inscribing his enterprise in a providential framework exculpates Cortés *vis-à-vis* both Narváez and the Crown at the same time as it establishes an explicit link between King-God-Cortés that no monarch would renounce: "Y con la ayuda de Dios y de la real ventura de vuestra alteza, siempre los desbaratamos, y matamos muchos, sin que en toda la dicha guerra me matasen ni hiriesen ni un español."

—As the divine thus hovers closer within reach of the human plane—the structuring situation of romance—Cortés' narrative approaches the chivalric, i.e. the mode of representation of novels of chivalry. *The obstacles faced increasingly appear as superhuman, their surmounting as supernatural, miraculous.* Significantly, it is the battle against Narváez which marks Cortés' incursion into this medieval mode. Here, in contrast to his early frays with the Indians, Cortés formulaically commends himself to God and King before doing battle. The battle, which he notes took place on "el día de pascua de Espíritu Santo," was won with God's aid *within an hour* "sin muertes de hombres". Similarly, the only victory of the Noche Triste takes place in the temple which Cortés had earlier dedicated to the Virgin. Cortés emphasizes the miraculous nature of the victory: "Y crea vuestra sacra majestad que fue tanto ganalles esta torre, que si Dios no les quebrara las alas, bastaban veinte dellos para resistir la subida a mil hombres . . .".

Side by side with the chivalric mode in the final portions of the Letter, emerges a less formulaic and controlled style of writing, markedly different from the rest of the Letter and guaranteed to arouse the King's sympathy. In recounting the events of the Noche Triste and their aftermath in the "reconquest" now underway, Cortés' narrative assumes a heightened emotional tone, giving full bathetic vent to his own and his men's reactions to the terrifying developments, to their suffering, dangers confronted, and resulting tribulations. An increased use of similes, emphasizers and generalizations characterize this style. Further, in contrast to the logical and legalistic presentation of earlier matters, and revealing that presentation as a *style* in itself, here the Letter more often assumes the disjointed immediacy of a *chronicle,* with complex paragraphs, non sequiters, and a jumbled associative logic.

Is this a "zero-style?" True, the last ten pages of the Letter . . . are written simultaneously with the events of the "reconquest." Yet, given that the Letter ends with a plea for aid ("placerá a Nuestro Señor suplirá nuestras pocas fuerzas y enviará presto socorro," it would seem that his style responds to the final exigency of the *grafía-autos,* the petition. And this, in turn, explains the fact that the last portions of the Letter begin to resemble the narrative voice and choices of Bernal Díaz' *relación*—the chivalric topoi, the bathetic yet heroic tone, the subjective and associative cast. Both *petitioners* seek recompense and succor. Hence, the *grafía-autos* is not only the determining factor in both *relaciones,* but also determines similar textual characteristics.

*Grafía-Autos,* we have seen, largely involved matters of characterization and the narrative strategems of self-defense, which at times entailed recourse to a variety of discursive models (epistolary address, the epic, romances, and so on). The event-oriented *bios,* on the other hand, brings us more into the arena of history proper and historical discourse; thus the structural issues of Cortés' ordering, representation and selection of "historical" events, as well as the question of his referentiality (or "truth") will concern us here.

With regards to the latter issue, it is largely the historian's task to recreate the full historical scenario which Cortés purports to depict, and thus to establish the veracity of his account in absolute terms. We refer the reader, for example, to Eulalia Guzmán's *Relaciones de Hernán Cortés* [1958] for a meticulous—if tendentious—point by point critique of the "historicity" of Cortés' writings. While of necessity drawing on the larger historical picture, we leave such documentation largely to the historians and focus our attention on the *grafía(autos),* the *autos* understood here as a function of the *grafía:* on particular ways in which it motivates and shapes the historical narration of the *bios.*

In auto-historical discourse, we have said, the *bios* need not coincide absolutely with the history. In the case of the conqueror Cortés, however, "l'histoire c'est moi," in that the history *is* largely equated to his *bios,* construed broadly as the events which the individual has

experienced, influenced, or of which he has had knowledge.

The underlying equation of *bios* to history is but one of several structural manipulations responding to the *grafía/(autos).* We have already discussed Cortés' suppression of Alvarado and the other Spaniards' role in massacring the Indians, as well as the calculated narrative ordering of the events preceding Narváez' arrival. The negative space of the letter—what has strategically been left out, adjusted, distorted—demands to be charted. Interestingly, it might be said that Cortés presumed to control the negative as well as the positive space of the text, shaping them into doubles of sorts. Repeatedly taking recourse to the *brevitatis formulae* in his descriptions of Tenochtitlán (i.e. "no matter how much I have said, more of the same remains to be told"), Cortés would have the King believe what he has left out to be a mere extension of what he has included.

According to textual indications, this *relación* was drafted in at least two stages: Cortés states that he had already prepared a *relación* to send to the King by the time Narváez' ships arrived; the latter portion of the text appears to have been written in conjunction with the events of the "reconquest." Nonetheless, we find a surprising lack of synthetic comments, previewing or summarizing the events transpired. Nor does Cortés overtly reorder events in view of his retrospective insight. Instead, the broad scaffolding of the Letter remains faithful to a strictly chronological development.

Why? Cortés' adherence to the more primitive chronicle model, we would argue, comprises neither a "zero" style *or* structure. Rather, we surmise that the author purposefully suppresses the perspective of his overviewing "I" to best serve the interests of the *autos/grafía:* a chronological presentation lets events speak for themselves, and endows them with an almost ineluctable logic and causality. To heighten Narváez' treachery, then, it is greatly to Cortés' advantage both textually and personally to feign innocence.

Another important structuring pattern competes with the chronological. Throughout the Letter, Cortés depicts the Spaniards' confrontations with the Indians according to the following formula: the Spaniards do battle with the Indians, the Indians surrender, swear fealty to the Spanish King, and beg Cortés' pardon. Cortés emphatically establishes this pattern in the early portions of the Letter, a schematic itinerary of the episodes in which the Spaniards meet and defeat one group of Indians after another, as they consolidate their power before arriving in Tenochtitlán. The formula, so clearly a response to the Crown's interests, also frames the depiction of the confrontation between the two bands of Spaniards. In Cortés' rendering of his defeat of Narváez' troops, the latter's men not only accept defeat but see the error of their (and their leader's) ways: "prometidos ser obedientes a la justicia de vuestra majestad, diciendo que fasta allí habían sido engañados . . .".

—That this formulaic presentation of the historical events persists throughout the Letter establishes Cortés as infallible and at the same time imparts to the events of his conquest an inexorable, seemingly providential, rhythm of their own. The only rupture in the chain derives from Narváez' intervention which, in Cortés' account, determined the conqueror's loss of the Mexican empire. These events, which we have seen in detail, also occasion a less controlled, more immediate, discursive mode. Yet, significantly, the formulaic depiction of events reasserts itself in the very last pages of the Letter, as Cortés regains control and group after group of Indians come to offer their fealty to the King— which means that in terms of its representation of historical events the Letter has a circular development, the beginning and end being mirror images of each other. Significantly *and* strategically, for Cortés has received word of the arrival of yet another interloper, Francisco de Garay, and enjoins the King to intervene and thus to forestall a new disruption of the victorious chain of events.

Cortés' self-defense against Velázquez and Narváez entailed a carefully reasoned narrative strategem or essayistic argumentation, which presented the events from *his perspective* as well as according to his needs. Though obviously biased, such argumentation generally falls short of sheer fabrication. At other points, however, Cortés' rendering of the events exceeds the merely disingenuous to incur in patent falsification, through omission, misrepresentation or invention.

Events in the **"Second Letter-Relation"** involving Moctezuma are crucial both to the *grafía,* being an affront to the (Spanish) Emperor's conception of sovereignty, and to the *bios* as history, being milestones in the landscape of historical events. Further, Cortés directly exercised his thirst for power on the Aztec monarch, resulting in some of his more unpardonable actions. All of the above reasons begin to explain, perhaps, why Cortés' depiction of events involving Moctezuma has proved so highly suspect, ambiguous and problematical, challenged by other contradictory eyewitness reports both Indian and Spanish. Defiantly implausible as well, Cortés' accounts of, among others, the following events, have provoked heated controversies (again we refer the reader to Guzmán's edition of the Second Letter):

—Moctezuma's two astonishing speeches to Cortés on the occasion of their first encounter and during Moctezuma's imprisonment, identifying the Spaniard with Quetzalcóatl and ceding his empire outright to him on the basis of that identification.

—Moctezuma's docile acceptance of the Spanish King, of his own confinement and thus of Cortés' rule.

—Moctezuma's death: according to Cortés (but dramatically contradicted by other historians and chroniclers), Moctezuma *volunteers* to speak to his mutinous people: "dijo que le sacasen a las azoteas de la fortaleza, que él hablaría a los capitanes de aquella gente y les haría que cesase la guerra." There, on the parapet, he is immediately stoned by his people, resulting in his death three days later. Pastor well notes in this regard that for Moctezuma to have proposed the initiative makes his death a kind of suicide for which only he is responsible. Framed in a mere three clauses, Cortés' is the shortest account of Moctezuma's death to be found in any of the major chronicles. Moctezuma had ceased to fulfill his (militarily) strategic function ("y no sé lo que dél hicieron, salvo que no por eso cesó la guerra . . .") and thus ceases to exist for Cortés.

As this sampling of events indicates, Moctezuma has been victimized by Cortés in life and in death, in reality and textually. We have noted at more than one juncture the textual "victimization" of the Indians, how they are molded to Cortés' narrative designs. Here, Moctezuma acts as a ventriloquist, textually emptied of voice and power: at each step historical veracity ("truth") is replaced by textual verisimilitude in the sixteenth century sense of the word, that is, what indeed *did* happen is subordinated to what *should* have been happening (strictly) according to Cortés' terms of reference.

We have seen that Cortés goes to great lengths in constructing his textual "I" emptied of self-interests, an "I" configured as the locus of all matter of external forces, human and divine. Sixteenth century auto-historical discourse, we reiterate, does not obtain to self-discovery or contemplation. This does not necessarily mean, however, that a more intimate, less contrived or functional "I" will not, perhaps unwittingly, emerge from the text; indeed, this hidden "I" may run counter to and even undermine the constructed "I". Such is often the case with Cortés, aspects of whose other "I" betoken power, an egocentric power potentially threatening to the King and thus a threat as well to Cortés' own interests. As Pastor has noted, "[s]ucede que los mismos rasgos que caracterizan a Cortés como héroe renacentista y gobernante idóneo lo presentan como alguien potencialmente peligroso en un contexto político en el que el poder aparece fuertemente centralizada en la figura de un monarca absoluto."

Unlike Cortés' explicit and constructed "I" or *autos,* this other "I" which stands *apart* from the *grafía,* must be deduced. And it is largely the textual features of the narration of the *bios*-as-history which furnish the basis for such deductions. In other words, the *autos* shapes the narration and leaves its imprint, the tell-tale marks of the powerful "I," on it. These textual manifestations provide the outline of Cortés' inner world, revealing two essential dimensions of the conqueror: the mono-maniacal, all-controlling Cortés and Cortés as thinker-strategist.

Textually, Cortés places himself at the helm of the conquest, as the fulcrum on which rested the entire architecture of those events which yielded positive results. It is interesting that in the **"Second Letter"** no other single individual among Cortés' men emerges as having played an important role, either as advisor or leader; in the pantheon of power sit only Cortés, Moctezuma, King and God (and Narváez/Velázquez). Analogously, Cortés' "I" dominates the narration. No doubt the consistent use of the first person singular when clearly speaking for the actions of the entire group ("we") is one of the most striking features of Cortés' discourse, e.g. "Desde aquí anduve tres jornadas de despoblado y tierra inhabitable." Thematically and tex-tually Cortés' *relación* thus runs counter to Bernal Díaz' "democratization" of historiography, for Cortés dis-counts the advice of his troops—"E aunque todos los de mi compañia decían que me tornase porque era mala señal, todavía seguí mi camino, considerando que Dios es sobre Natura"—as well as textually suppressing their *nosotros*. In this regard, then, Cortés follows the tradi-tional "ruling class" histories, his focus limited to the power-wielding individuals and their actions.

—Others, and a third person narration, do enter Cortés' text, but largely through reported speech. As is not uncommon in sixteenth century drama, literature (with its predilection for dramatic dialogue) and historiogra-phy (Fernández de Oviedo's *Historia general y natu-ral de las Indias* being an excellent example), the important events in Cortés' dispatch tend not to be shown directly, but (re)told. That is to say, events are represented as and through speech acts. Now, Fernán-dez de Oviedo and, to a degree, Bernal Díaz, often convey events through direct discourse—rhetorical speeches, *arengas,* exhortations, and so on. Cortés, on the other hand, systematically utilizes *reported* speech (of his own and others' words), embedded indirect discourse, as his radical of historical presentation. For example:

> "Otro dia por la mañana . . . llegaron fasta diez o doce señores muy principales, según después supe, y entre ellos un gran señor [ . . . ] y llegados donde yo estaba, me dijeron que venían de parte de Muteczuma, su señor, y que los enviaba para que fuese conmigo, y que me rogaba que le perdonase porque no salía su persona a me ver y recibir, que la causa era el estar mal dispuesto; pero que ya su ciudad estaba cerca, que pues yo todavía determinaba ir a ella, que allá nos veríamos . . ."

We note from the example that this indirect reporting fully integrates and subordinates the speech acts of others into Cortés' own narrative: no quotation marks appear, the discourse retains the substance, but not the texture or contexture of the original statement. Those events in which Cortés did not directly intervene are narrated through such reported speech. Cortés may not have participated in them, but textually he appropri-ates them and all others in that they are subordinated to his analysis and voice. The narration, while multi-layered, remains a monologue.

—On two occasions, we recall, at least in principle Cortés cedes his voice to Moctezuma and "transcribes" his direct discourses to the Mexican people. Ironically, we have seen that these two speeches may well repre-sent the most manipulated discursive acts of the text. Still, at these two delicate moments Cortés ostensibly reneges authorial control, strategically suppressing his "I" as his best self-defense. So, too, at a handful of crucial moments, does Cortés bring his troops' point of view into the text to back up otherwise questionable decisions, as in deciding to flee from Tenochtitlán: "y por todos los de mi compañía fui requerido muchas veces que me saliese, y porque todos o los más estaban heridos, y tan mal que no podían pelear, acordé de lo hacer aquella noche". When Cortés makes textual room for others, it is in service of his own designs.

Commentators such as Manuel Alcalá [in *Cartas de relacion,* 1983] have readily cast Cortés in the mold of the Renaissance humanist, viewing his descriptions of Tenochtitlán as the product of a free-ranging thirst for knowledge. Nonetheless, this reader finds only one moment of truly disinterested scientific curiosity in the narrative: Cortés' exploration of the volcano, Popoc-atepetl ("y porque yo siempre he deseado de todas las cosas desta tierra poder hacer a vuestra alteza muy particular relación, quise desta, que me pareció algo maravilloso, saber el secreto"). At all other moments, at least in the text, Cortés' curiosity regarding the culture and world of the Indians, the Other, is clearly self-centered, limited to those aspects directly involv-ing his "I" and its/the Crown's interests. What appears to be disinterested curiosity or interest in the Other thus proves to be highly "interested," as evidenced by the following:

—The geography and demography of Mexico are por-trayed with an eye to military action: Cortés systemat-ically describes the location and composition of towns and cities in terms of how they might affect his mili-tary plans for conquest. For example, the extraordinary causeways of Tenochtitlán, the city in the water, first strike Cortés as military hazards rather than as marvels of the Indians' artifice.

—The majority of the information in the Letter regard-ing the social structure and culture of the Aztec capital enters the text through Cortés' inventory of Tenochtitlán. This essential ethnographic information, in other words, appears but indirectly. The reader must reconstruct the picture of Aztec society by piecing together the information gleaned from, but not purposely presented in, Cortés' lists.

—Cortés reserves his *asombro* for those things of most value to him. Other chroniclers would be awestruck and outraged by the Aztecs' religious practices, relating them (as do Bernal Díaz and Oviedo) in gory, even gothic, detail. Cortés with his pragmatic sense of "la grandeza mexicana" admires the height of the temple towers, the size of the idols, giving us a flat material sense of Aztec religious practices.

Be it with regard to their religious or other cultural practices, Cortés fails to probe beyond his immediate needs and concerns into the *why's* of these activities. He remains on the surface, a myopic and poor ethnographer. The **"Second Letter of Relation,"** with its founding image of the Aztec world, thus renders fuller testimony to its true subject, Cortés, than to its ostensible subject, Mexico.

For the reasons discussed above, . . . it behooves Cortés to frame his image according to the mold of the epic hero, man of action. Nonetheless, the predominating image of Cortés which emerges from the text is that of Cortés as a proto-Machiavellian leader, strategist and thinker. In other words, we encounter in Cortés the co-existence of the new and the old heroic ideals.

Given the enormous odds against the Spaniards, mental acts would have to prevail over the physical, *froda* (cunning) over *forza*. Cortés understood this and matched his considerable talents to the circumstances. His most crucial triumphant "actions" in the Second Letter are intellectual, and Cortés, hardly reticent in this regard, makes the reader party to his strategizing at every step. Early on, for example, we witness the crystallization of Cortés' divide and conquer philosophy: "vista la discordia y desconformidad de los unos y los otros, no hube poco placer, porque me pareció haber mucho a mi propósito, y que podría tener manera de más aína sujuzgarlos . . . *Omne regnun in seipsum divisum desolibatur*". The intricate cat and mouse game of deceptions and dissimulations which the Letter reveals Cortés to have played with Moctezuma no doubt fueled Tzvetan Todorov's portrait of the Spaniards' greater capacity to manipulate "signs" than their adversaries. While misguided in one respect—Moctezuma appears to have responded in kind to Cortés' manipulations—Todorov's reading accurately reflects the prominence Cortés' letter accords to his mental acts.

Force does have its place in the conquest and the Letter, but primarily as an aspect of Cortés' *froda* or as a last resort when strategizing fails. While the use of force is

intermittent, Cortés' mental machinations hold the conquest, and as we shall now discuss, the text, together.

Having implicitly defined the conquest as an intellectual achievement, Cortés presents himself as its author, its mastermind. Herein lies the most revealing autobiographical dimension of the letter, for Cortés makes the reader privy not to his emotional interiority but, we repeat, to the inner vaults of his intellectual self. More than anything else, the Second Letter is a map of Cortés' mental world as he processes the raw material of the conquest. Within the larger chronological framework, events are presented when and how they came to Cortés' attention. He reads the events, which appear as texts to be interpreted. On the basis of his analyses, Cortés takes action.

These cognitive processes are the key to the representation of each discrete historical event in the text, that is, to the text's microstructure. Verbs of cognition structure the paragraphs in that typically: Cortés SEES what is going on or receives information about events (hence the significance of reported speech, which translates events into *information*); Cortés REFLECTS on what he has perceived or learned, and DECIDES his course of action; Cortés ACTS, always successfully. For example:

> (deciding to leave Tenochtítlán to confront Narváez) "E como yo *vi* el gran daño que se comenzaba a revolver y como la tierra se levantaba a causa del dicho Narváez, *parecióme* que con ir yo donde estaba se apaciguaría mucho . . . y tambien porque *pensaba* dar orden con el dicho Narváez como tan gran mal como se comenzaba cesase. E así *me partí* aquel mismo día" [our emphasis].

The omnipresent cognitive pattern endows the text with an empirical cast, as well, importantly, as a legalistic one. Well practiced in legal thinking, Cortés imposes his logical powers on the unruly events, bringing them into the orderly sphere of mental acts.

Thus, Cortés' detached and insentient narration:

—Tends to represent events in terms of his reading of them and the success of his strategies. For this reason we find a very special "topography" in the text—not a physical topography of mountains scaled and valleys traversed, but a mental one, of challenges and responses. Throughout the narrative there abound plots and conspiracies which Cortés' astute mind perceives and foils, with the result that a rhythm of *engaño/desengaño* permeates the narration.

—Utterly dehumanizes the Indians, reducing them to pawns in his game. Cold as Cortés' textual treatment of Moctezuma may be, it is little compared to his frigid "objectification" of the masses of enemy Indians, whose murder and enslavement fulfill purely strategic needs: "y por fuerza de armas se tomaron, hice ciertos esclavos, de que se dió el quinto a los oficiales de vuestra majestad . . . por poner algún espanto a los de Culúa, y también hay tanta gente, que si no ficiese grande y cruel castigo en ellos, nunca se enmendarían jamás". Cortés' monomaniacal negation of the Other here reaches its chilling peak, providing definitive fodder for the *leyenda negra.*

—"Objectifies"—*cosifica*—the world of the Aztecs, transforming it into a consumer object denied autonomy and identity. This is most tellingly revealed on the last page of the Letter, and in the name with which Cortés baptizes Mexico: "Por lo que he visto y comprehendido cerca de la similitud que toda esta tierra tiene a España, así en la fertilidad como en la grandeza y fríos que en ella hace, y en otras muchas cosas que la equiparan a ella, me pareció que el más conviente nombre para esta dicha tierra era llamarse la *Nueva España* del mar Océano; y así, en nombre du vuestra majestad se le puso aqueste nombre."

## Inga Clendinnen (essay date 1991)

SOURCE: "'Fierce and Unnatural Cruelty': Cortés and the Conquest of Mexico," in *Representations,* Vol. 33, Winter, 1991, pp. 65-100.

[*In the following excerpt, Clendinnen exposes the miscommunications, arising from unbridgeable cultural differences between the Indians and the Spanish, that facilitated the conquest of Mexico.*]

The conquest of Mexico matters to us because it poses a painful question: How was it that a motley bunch of Spanish adventurers, never numbering much more than four hundred or so, was able to defeat an Amerindian military power on its home ground in the space of two years? What was it about Spaniards, or about Indians, that made so awesomely implausible a victory possible? The question has not lost its potency through time, and as the consequences of the victory continue to unfold has gained in poignancy. . . .

First, an overview of the major events. Analysts and participants alike agree that the Conquest falls into two phases. The first began with the Spanish landfall in April of 1519, and Cortés's assumption of independent command in defiance of the governor of Cuba, patron of Cortés and of the expedition; the Spaniards' march inland, in the company of coastal Indians recently conquered by the Mexicans, marked first by bloody battles and then by alliance with the independent province of Tlaxcala; their uncontested entry into the Mexican imperial city of Tenochtitlan-Tlatelolco, a magnificent lake-borne city of 200,000 or more inhabitants linked to the land by three great causeways; the

Spaniards' seizing of the Mexican ruler Moctezoma, and their uneasy rule through him for six months; the arrival on the coast of another and much larger Spanish force from Cuba under the command of Panfilo Narváez charged with the arrest of Cortés, its defeat and incorporation into Cortés's own force; a native "uprising" in Tenochtitlan, triggered in Cortés's absence by the Spaniards' massacre of unarmed warriors dancing in a temple festival; the expulsion of the Spanish forces, with great losses, at the end of June 1520 on the so-called "Noche Triste," and Moctezoma's death, probably at Spanish hands, immediately before that expulsion. End of the first phase. The second phase is much briefer in the telling, although about the same span in the living: a little over a year. The Spaniards retreated to friendly Tlaxcala to recover health and morale. They then renewed the attack, reducing the lesser lakeside cities, recruiting allies, not all of them voluntary, and placing Tenochtitlan under siege in May of 1521. The city fell to the combined forces of Cortés and an assortment of Indian "allies" in mid August 1521. End of the second phase.

Analysts of the conquest have concentrated on the first phase, drawn by the promising whiff of exoticism in Moctezoma's responses—allowing the Spaniards into his city, his docility in captivity—and by the sense that final outcomes were somehow imminent in that response, despite Moctezoma's removal from the stage in the midst of a Spanish rout a good year before the fall of the city, and despite the Spaniards' miserable situation in the darkest days before that fall, trapped out on the causeways, bereft of shelter and support, with the unreduced Mexicans before and their "allies" potential wolves behind. This dispiriting consensus as to Spanish invincibility and Indian vulnerability springs from the too eager acceptance of key documents, primarily Spanish but also Indian, as directly and adequately descriptive of actuality, rather than as the mythic constructs they largely are. Both the letters of Cortés and the main Indian account of the defeat of their city owe as much to the ordering impulse of imagination as to the devoted inscription of events as they occurred. Conscious manipulation, while it might well be present, is not the most interesting issue here, but rather the subtle, powerful, insidious human desire to craft a dramatically satisfying and coherent story out of fragmentary and ambiguous experience, or (the historian's temptation) out of the fragmentary and ambiguous "evidence" we happen to have to work with. . . .

The elegance of Cortés's literary craft is nicely indicated by his handling of a daunting problem of presentation. In his **"Second Letter,"** written in late October 1520 on the eve of the second thrust against Tenochtitlan, he had somehow to inform the king of the Spaniards' first astonishment at the splendor of the imperial city, the early coups, the period of perilous authority, the inflow of gold, the accumulation of magnificent riches—and the spectacular debacle of the expulsion, with the flounderings in the water, the panic, the loss of gold, horses, artillery, reputation, and altogether too many Spanish lives. Cortés's solution was a most devoted commitment to a strict narrative unfolding of events, so the city is wondered at; Moctezoma speaks, frowns; the marketplace throbs and hums; laden canoes glide through the canals; and so on to the dark denouement. And throughout he continues the construction of his persona as leader: endlessly flexible, yet unthinkingly loyal; endlessly resourceful, yet fastidious in legal niceties; magnificently daring in strategy and performance, yet imbued with a fine caution in calculating costs. . . .

Throughout the first phase of the Conquest we confidently "read" Cortés's intentions, assuming his perspective and so assuming his effectiveness. The Spanish commander briskly promises his king "to take [Moctezoma] alive in chains or make him subject to Your Majesty's Royal Crown." He continues: "With that purpose I set out from the town of Cempoalla, which I renamed Sevilla, on the sixteenth of August with fifteen horsemen and three hundred foot soldiers, as well equipped for war as the conditions permitted me to make them." There we have it: warlike intentions clear, native cities renamed as possessions in a new polity, an army on the move. Inured to the duplicitous language of diplomacy, we take Cortés's persistent swearing of friendship and the innocence of his intentions to Moctezoma's emissaries as transparent deceptions, and blame Moctezoma for not so recognizing them or, recognizing them, for failing to act. But Cortés declared he came as an ambassador, and as an ambassador he appears to have been received. Even had Moctezoma somehow divined the Spaniards' hostile intent, to attack without formal warning was not an option for a ruler of his magnificence. We read Moctezoma's conduct confidently, but here our confidence (like Cortés's) derives from ignorance. Cortés interpreted Moctezoma's first "gifts" as gestures of submission or naive attempts at bribery. But Moctezoma, like other Amerindian leaders, communicated at least as much by the splendor and status of his emissaries, their gestures and above all their gifts, as by the nuances of their most conventionalized speech. None of those nonverbal messages could Cortés read, nor is it clear that his chief Nahuatl interpreter, Doña Marina, a woman and a slave, would or could inform him of the protocols in which they were framed: these were the high and public affairs of men. Moctezoma's gifts were statements of dominance, superb gestures of wealth and liberality made the more glorious by the arrogant humility of their giving: statements to which the Spaniards lacked both the wit and the means to reply. (To the next flourish of gifts, carried by more than a hundred porters and including the famous "cartwheels" of gold and silver, Cortés's riposte was a cup

of Florentine glass and three holland shirts [Diaz, *Historia,* 1966]. The verbal exchanges for all of the first phase were not much less scrambled. And despite those reassuring inverted commas of direct reportage, all of those so-fluent speeches passed through a daisy chain of interpreters, with each step an abduction into a different meaning system, a struggle for some approximation of unfamiliar concepts. We cannot know at what point the shift from the Indian notion of "he who pays tribute," usually under duress so carrying no sense of obligation, to the Spanish one of "vassal," with its connotations of loyalty, was made, but we know the shift to be momentous. The identifiable confusions, which must be only a fraction of the whole, unsurprisingly ran both ways. For example, Cortés, intent on conveying innocent curiosity, honesty, and flattery, repeatedly informed the Mexican ambassadors that he wished to come to Tenochtitlan "to look upon Moctezoma's face." That determination addressed to a man whose mana was such that none could look upon his face save selected blood kin must have seemed marvelously mysterious, and very possibly sinister.

So the examples of miscommunication multiply. In this tangle of missed cues and mistaken messages, "control of communications" seems to have evaded both sides equally. There is also another casualty. Our most earnest interrogations of the surviving documents cannot make them satisfy our curiosity as to the meaning of Moctezoma's conduct. Historians are the camp followers of the imperialists: as always in this European-and-native kind of history, part of our problem is the disruption of "normal" practice effected by the breach through which we have entered. For Cortés, the acute deference shown Moctezoma's person established him as the supreme authority of city and empire, and he shaped his strategy accordingly. In fact we know neither the nature and extent of Moctezoma's authority within and beyond Tenochtitlan, nor even (given the exuberant discrepancies between the Cortés and Díaz accounts) the actual degree of coercion and physical control imposed on him during his captivity. From the fugitive glimpses we have of the attitudes of some of the other valley rulers, and of his own advisers, we can infer something of the complicated politics of the metropolis and the surrounding city-states, but we see too little to be able to decode the range of Moctezoma's normal authority, much less its particular fluctuations under the stress of foreign intrusion. Against this uncertain ground we cannot hope to catch the flickering indicators of possible individual idiosyncrasy. We may guess, as we watch the pragmatic responses of other Indian groups to the Spanish presence, that as *tlatoani* or "Great Speaker" of the dominant power in Mexico Moctezoma bore a special responsibility for classifying and countering the newcomers. From the time of his captivity we think we glimpse the disaffection of lesser and allied lords, and infer that disaffection sprang from his docility. We see him deposed

*An engraving from Herrera's* Decades *(1726), depicting Moteczuma's dream of the calamities to come during his reign.*

while he still lived, and denigrated in death: as Cortés probed into Tenochtitlan in his campaign to reduce the city, the defenders would ironically pretend to open a way for him, "saying, 'Come in, come in and enjoy yourselves!' or, at other times, 'Do you think there is now another Moctezoma to do what you wish?'" But I think we must resign ourselves to a heroic act of renunciation, acknowledging that much of Moctezoma's conduct must remain enigmatic. We cannot know how he categorized the newcomers, or what he intended by his apparently determined and certainly unpopular cooperation with his captors: whether to save his empire, his city, his position, or merely his own skin. It might be possible, with patience and time, to clear some of the drifting veils of myth and mistake that envelop the encounters of the first phase, or at least to chart our areas of ignorance more narrowly. But the conventional story of returning gods and unmanned autocrats, of an exotic world paralyzed by its encounter with Europe, for all its coherence and its just-so

inevitabilities, is in view of the evidence like Eliza's progression across the ice floes: a matter of momentary sinking balances linked by desperate forward leaps.

Of Cortés we know much more. He was unremarkable as a combat leader: personally brave, an indispensable quality in one who would lead Spaniards, he lacked the panache of his captain Alvarado and the solidity and coolness of Sandoval. He preferred talk to force with Spaniards or Indians, a preference no doubt designed to preserve numbers, but also indicative of a personal style. He knew whom to pay in flattery, whom in gold, and the men he bought usually stayed bought. He knew how to stage a theatrical event for maximum effect, as in the plays concocted to terrify Moctezoma's envoys—a stallion, snorting and plunging as he scented a mare in estrus; a cannon fired to blast a tree. When he did use force he had a flair for doing so theatrically, amplifying the effect: cutting off the hands of fifty or more Tlaxcalan emissaries freely admitted into the Spanish camp, then mutilated as "spies"; a mass killing at Cholula; the shackling of Moctezoma while "rebellious" chiefs were burned before his palace in Tenochtitlan. He was careful to count every Spanish life, yet capable of conceiving heroic strategies—to lay siege to a lake-girt city requiring the prefabrication of thirteen brigantines on the far side of the mountains, eight thousand carriers to transport the pieces, their reassembly in Texcoco, the digging of a canal and the deepening of the lake for their successful launching. And he was capable not only of the grand design but of the construction and maintenance of the precarious alliances, intimidations, and promised rewards necessary to implement it. In that extraordinary capacity to sustain a complex vision through the constant scanning and assessment of unstable factors, as in his passion and talent for control of self and others, Cortés was incomparable. (That concern for control might explain his inadequacies in combat: in the radically uncontrolled environment of battle, he had a tendency to lose his head.)

He was also distinguished by a peculiar recklessness in his faith. We know the Spaniards took trouble to maintain the signs of their faith even in the wilderness of Mexico; that bells marked the days with the obligatory prayers as they did in the villages of Spain; that the small supplies of wine and wafers for the Mass were cherished; that through the long nights in times of battle men stood patiently, waiting for the priests to hear their confessions, while the unofficial healer "Juan Catalan" moved softly about, signing the cross and muttering his prayers over stiffening wounds. We know their faith identified the idols and the dismembered bodies they found in the temples as the pitiless work of a familiar Devil. We know they drew comfort in the worst circumstances of individual and group disaster from the ample space for misfortune in Christian cosmology: while God sits securely in His heaven, all manner of things can be wrong with His world. Those miserable men held for sacrifice in Texcoco after the Spanish expulsion who left their forlorn messages scratched on a white wall ("Here the unhappy Juan Yuste was held prisoner") would through their misery be elevated to martyrdom.

Even against that ground Cortés's faith was notably ardent, especially in his aggressive reaction to public manifestations of the enemy religion. In Cempoalla, with the natives cowed, he destroyed the existing idols, whitewashed the existing shrine, washed the existing attendants and cut their hair, dressed them in white, and taught these hastily refurbished priests to offer flowers and candles before an image of the Virgin. There is an intriguing elision of signs here. While the pagan attendants might have been clad suitably clerically, in long black robes like soutanes, with some hooded "like Dominicans," they also had waist-long hair clotted with human blood, and stank of decaying

human flesh. Nonetheless he assessed them as "priests," and therefore fit to be entrusted with the Virgin's shrine. Then having preached the doctrine "as well as any priest today," in Díaz's loyal opinion (filtered though it was through the halting tongues of two interpreters), he left daily supervision of the priests to an old crippled soldier assigned as hermit to the new shrine and Cortés moved on.

The Cempoallan assault was less than politic, being achieved at the sword's point against the town on whose goodwill the little coastal fort of Vera Cruz would be most dependent. Cortés was not to be so reckless again, being restrained from too aggressive action by his chaplain and his captains, but throughout he appears to have been powerfully moved by a concern for the defense of the "honor" of the Christian god. It is worth remembering that for the entire process of the Conquest Cortés had no notion of the Spanish king's response to any of his actions. Only in September of 1523, more than two years after the fall of Tenochtitlan, and four and a half years after the Spanish landfall, did he finally learn that he had been appointed captain general of New Spain. It is difficult to imagine the effect of that prolonged visceral uncertainty, and (especially for a man of Cortés's temperament) of his crucial dependence on the machinations of men far away in Spain, quite beyond his control. Throughout the desperate vicissitudes of the campaign, as in the heroic isolation of his equivocal leadership, God was perhaps his least equivocal ally. That alliance required at best the removal of pagan idols and their replacement by Mary and the Cross, and at the least the Spaniards' public worship of their Christian images, the public statement of the principles of the Christian faith, and the public denunciation of human sacrifice, these statements and denunciations preferably being made in the Indians' most sacred places. Cortés's inability to let well alone in matters religious appears to have effected the final alienation of the Mexican priests, and their demand for the Spaniards' death or expulsion from their uneasy perch in Tenochtitlan. Cortés's claim of his early, total, and unresisted transformation of Mexican religious life through the destruction of their major idols was almost certainly a lie. (He had to suppress any mention of Alvarado's massacre of the warrior dancers in the main temple precinct as the precipitating factor in the Mexican "revolt" as too damaging to his story, for the Mexican celebrants would have been dancing under the serene gaze of the Virgin.) But the lie, like his accommodation to the cannibalism of his Tlaxcalan allies, was a strategic necessity impatiently borne. With victory all obligations would be discharged, and God's honor vindicated. That high sense of duty to his divine Lord and his courage in its pursuit must have impressed and comforted his men even as they strove to restrain him.

None of this undoubted flair makes Cortés the model

of calculation, rationality, and control he is so often taken to be. There can be some doubt as to the efficacy of his acts of terror. It is true that after the "mutilated spies" episode the Tlaxcalans sued for peace and alliance, but as I will argue, routine acts of war in the European style were probably at least as destructive of Indian confidence of their ability to predict Spanish behavior as the most deliberate shock tactics. The Spaniards' attack on the people of Cholula, the so-called "Cholula massacre," is a muddier affair. Cortés certainly knew the therapeutic effects of a good massacre on fighting men who have lived too long with fear, their sense of invincibility already badly dented by the Tlaxcalan clashes, and with the legendary warriors of Tenochtitlan, grown huge in imagination, still in prospect. As other leaders have discovered in other times, confidence returns when the invisible enemy is revealed as a screaming, bleeding, fleeing mass of humanity. But here Cortés was probably the unwitting agent of Tlaxcalan interests. Throughout the first phase honors in mutual manipulation between Spaniard and Indian would seem to be about even. The Cempoallan chief Cortés hoaxed into seizing Moctezoma's tax gatherers remained notably more afraid of Moctezoma in his far palace than of the hairy Spaniards at his elbow. Tricked into defiance of Moctezoma, he immediately tricked Cortés into leading four hundred Spaniards on a hot and futile march of fifteen miles in pursuit of phantom Mexican warriors in his own pursuit of a private feud, a deception that has been rather less remarked on. There are other indications that hint at extensive native manipulations, guile being admired among Indians as much as it was among Spaniards, and Spanish dependence on Indian informants and translators was total. But they are indications only, given the relative opacity and ignorance of the Spanish sources as to what the Indians were up to. Here I am not concerned to demonstrate the natives to have been as great deceivers as the Spaniards, but simply to suggest we have no serious grounds for claiming they were not.

Cortés's political situation was paradoxically made easier by his status as rebel. That saved him from the agonizing assessment of different courses of action: once gone from Cuba, in defiance of the governor, he could not turn back, save to certain dishonor and probable death. So we have the gambler's advance, with no secured lines back to the coast, no supplies, no reinforcements, the ships deliberately disabled on the beach to release the sailors for soldiering service and to persuade the faint-hearted against retreat. Beyond the beach lay Cuba, and an implacable enemy. The relentless march on Mexico impresses, until one asks just what Cortés intended once he had got there. We have the drive to the city, the seizing of Moctezoma—and then the agonizing wait by this unlikely Micawber for something to turn up, as the Spaniards, uncertainly tolerated guests, sat in the city, clutching the diminishing re-

source of Moctezoma's prestige as their only weapon. That "something" proved to be the Spanish punitive expedition, a couple of providential ships carrying gunpowder and a few reinforcements, and so a perilous way out of the impasse. Possibly Cortés had in mind a giant confidence trick: a slow process of securing and fortifying posts along the road to Vera Cruz and, then, with enough gold amassed, sending to the authorities in Hispaniola (bypassing Velázquez and Cuba) for ships, horses, and arms, which is the strategy he in fact followed after the retreat from Tenochtitlan. It is nonetheless difficult (save in Cortés's magisterial telling of it) to read the performance as rational.

It is always tempting to credit people of the past with unnaturally clear and purposeful policies: like Clifford Geertz's peasant, we see the bullet holes in the fence and proceed to draw the bull's-eyes around them. The temptation is maximized with a Cortés, a man of singular energy and decision, intent on projecting a self-image of formidable control of self and circumstance. Yet that control had its abrupt limits. His tense self-mastery, sustained in face of damaging action by others, could collapse into tears or sullen rage when any part of his own controlling analysis was exposed as flawed, as with his fury against Moctezoma for his "refusal" to quell the uprising in the city after Alvarado's attack on the unarmed dancers. He had banked all on Moctezoma being the absolute ruler he had taken him to be. He had seized him, threatened him, shackled him to establish his personal domination over him. But whatever its normal grounds and span, Moctezoma's capacity to command, which was his capacity to command deference, had begun to bleed away from his first encounter with Spaniards and their unmannerliness, as they gazed and gabbled at the sacred leader. It bled faster as they seized his person. Durán's account of Moctezoma pictured in native chronicles as emerging shackled from his first meeting with Cortés is "objectively" wrong, but from the Indian perspective right: the Great Speaker in the power of outsiders, casually and brutally handled, was the Great Speaker no longer. Forced to attempt to calm his inflamed people, Moctezoma knew he could effect nothing; that his desacralization had been accomplished, first and unwittingly by Cortés, then, presumably, by a ritual action concealed from us; and that a new Great Speaker had been chosen while the old still lived: a step unprecedented to my knowledge in Mexican history.

Cortés could not acknowledge Moctezoma's impotence. Retrospectively he was insistent that his policy had been sound and had been brought down only through the accident of the Mexican ruler's final unreliability. Certainly his persistence in its defense after its collapse in debacle points to a high personal investment: intelligence is no bar to self-deception. Nonetheless there must have been some relief at the explosive end to a deeply uncanny situation, where experience had offered no guide to action in a looking-glass world of yielding kings and arrogant underlings; of riddling speech, unreadable glances, opaque silences. The sudden collapse of the waiting game liberated him back into the world of decisions, calculated violence, the energetic practicalities of war—the heady fiction of a world malleable before individual will. . . .

We tend to have a *Lord of the Flies* view of battle: that in deadly combat the veils of "culture" are ripped away, and natural man confronts himself. But if combat is not quite as cultural as cricket, its brutalities are nonetheless rule-bound. Like cricket, it requires a sustained act of cooperation, with each side constructing the conditions in which both will operate, and so, where the struggle is between strangers, obliging a mutual "transmission of culture" of the shotgun variety. And because of its high intensities it promises to expose how one's own and other ways of acting and meaning are understood and responded to in crisis conditions, and what lessons about the other and about oneself can be learned in that intimate, involuntary, and most consequential communication.

The sources for the second phase are sufficiently solid. Given it is cultural assumptions we are after, equivocation in recollection and recording matter little. Cortés edits a debacle on the Tacuba causeway, where more than fifty Spaniards were taken alive through his own impetuosity, into a triumph of leadership in crisis; Díaz marvels at Spanish bravery under the tireless onslaughts of savages; both are agreed as to the vocabulary through which they understand, assess, and record battle behavior. Sahagún's informants, able to report only bitter hearsay and received myth on the obscure political struggles of the first phase, move to confident detail in their accounts of the struggle for the city, in which at least some of them appear to have fought, naming precise locations and particular warrior feats; revealing through both the structure and the descriptions of the accounts their principles of battle. Those glimpses can be matched against admittedly fragmentary chronicles to yield the general contours of Indian battle behavior.

Here the usual caveats of overidealization apply. If all social rules are fictions, made "real" through being contested, denied, evaded, and recast as well as obeyed, "rules of war," war being what it is, are honored most earnestly in the breach. But in the warrior societies of Central Mexico, where the battlefield held a central place in the imagination, with its protocols rehearsed and trained for in the ordinary routines of life, the gap between principle and practice was narrow. War, at least war as fought among the dominant peoples of Mexico, and at least ideally, was a sacred contest, the outcome unknown but preordained, revealing which city, which local deity, would rightfully dominate an-

other. Something like equal terms were therefore required: to prevail by mere numbers or by some piece of treachery would vitiate the significance of the contest. So important was this notion of fair testing that food and weapons were sent to the selected target city as part of the challenge, there being no virtue in defeating a weakened enemy. . . .

If war was a sacred duel between peoples, and so between the "tribal" gods of those peoples, battle was ideally a sacred duel between matched warriors: a contest in which the taking of a fitting captive for presentation to one's own deity was a precise measure of one's own valor, and one's own fate. One prepared for this individual combat by song, paint, and adornment with the sacred war regalia. (To go "always prepared for battle" in the Spanish style was unintelligible: a man carrying arms was only potentially a warrior.) The great warrior, scarred, painted, plumed, wearing the record of his victories in his regalia, erupting from concealment or looming suddenly through the rising dust, then screaming his war cry, could make lesser men flee by the pure terror of his presence: warriors were practiced in projecting ferocity. His rightful, destined opponent was he who could master panic to stand and fight. There were maneuverings to "surprise" the enemy, and a fascination with ambush, but only as a device to confront more dramatically; to strike from hiding was unthinkable. At the outset of battle Indian arrows and darts flew thickly, but to weaken and draw blood, not to pierce fatally. The obsidian-studded war club signaled warrior combat aims: the subduing of prestigious individual captives in single combat for presentation before the home deity.

In the desperation of the last stages of the battle for Tenochtitlan, the Mexican inhibition against battleground killing was somewhat reduced: Indian "allies" died, and Spaniards who could not be quickly subdued were killed, most often, as the Mexicans were careful to specify, and for reasons that will become clear, by having the backs of their heads beaten in. But the priority on the capture of significant antagonists remained. In other regards the Mexicans responded with flexibility to the challenges of siege warfare. They "read" Spanish tactics reasonably accurately: a Spanish assault on the freshwater aqueduct at Chapultepec was foreseen, and furiously, if fruitlessly, resisted. The brigantines, irresistible for their first appearance of the lake, were later lured into a carefully conceived ambush in which two were trapped. The horses' vulnerability to uneven ground, to attack from below, their panic under hails of missiles, were all exploited effectively. The Mexicans borrowed Spanish weapons: Spanish swords lashed to poles or Spanish lances to disable the horses; even Spanish crossbows, after captive crossbowmen had been forced to show them how the machines worked. It was their invention and tenacity that forced Cortés to the desperate remedy of leveling structures along the causeways and into the city to provide the Spaniards with the secure ground they needed to be effective. And they were alert to the possibilities of psychological warfare, capitalizing on the Spaniards' peculiar dread of death by sacrifice and of the cannibalizing of the corpse. On much they could be innovative. But on the most basic measure of man's worth, the taking alive of prestigious captives, they could not compromise.

That passion for captives meant that the moment when the opponent's nerve broke was helplessly compelling, an enemy in flight an irresistible lure. This pursuit reflex was sometimes exploited by native opponents as a slightly shabby trick. It provided Cortés with a standard tactic for a quick and sure crop of kills. Incurious as to the reason, he nonetheless noted and exploited Mexican unteachability: "Sometimes, as we were thus withdrawing and they pursued us so eagerly, the horsemen would pretend to be fleeing, and then suddenly would turn on them; we always took a dozen or so of the boldest. By these means and by the ambushes which we set for them, they were always much hurt; and certainly it was a remarkable sight for even when they well knew the harm they would receive from us as we withdrew, they still pursued us until we had left the city [Cortés, "Third Letter"]. That commitment bore heavily on outcomes. Had Indians been as uninhibited as Spaniards in their killing, the small Spanish group, with no secured source of replenishment, would soon have been whittled away. In battle after battle the Spaniards report the deaths of many Indians, with their own men suffering not fatalities but wounds, and fast-healing wounds at that: those flint and obsidian blades sliced clean. It preserved the life of Cortés: time and again the Spanish leader struggled in Indian hands, the prize in a disorderly tug of war, with men dying on each side in the furious struggle for possession, and each time the Spaniards prevailing. Were Cortés in our hands, we would knife him. Mexican warriors could not kill the enemy leader so casually: were he to die, it would be in the temple of Huitzilopochtli, and before his shrine.

If the measurable consequences of that insistence were obvious and damaging, there were others less obvious, but perhaps more significant. We have already noted the Spanish predilection for ambush as part of a wider preference for killing at least risk. Spaniards valued their crossbows and muskets for their capacity to pick off selected enemies well behind the line of engagement: as snipers, as we would say. The psychological demoralization attending those sudden, trivializing deaths of great men painted for war, but not yet engaged in combat, must have been formidable. (Were the victim actively engaged in battle, the matter was different. Then he died nobly; although pierced by a bolt or a ball from a distance, his blood flowed forth to feed the earth as a warrior's should.) But more than

Indian deaths and demoralization were effected through these transactions. To inflict such deaths—at a distance, without putting one's own life in play—developed a Mexican reading of the character of the Spanish warrior. . . .

There is in the *Florentine Codex* an exquisitely painful, detailed description of the Spaniards' attack on the unarmed warrior dancers at the temple festival, the slaughter that triggered the Mexican "uprising" of May 1520. The first victim was a drummer: his hands were severed, then his neck. The account continues: "Of some they slashed open their backs: then their entrails gushed out. Of some they cut their heads to pieces. . . . Some they struck on the shoulder; they split openings. They broke openings in their bodies." And so it goes on. How ought we interpret this? It was not, I think, recorded as a horror story, or only as a horror story. The account is sufficiently careful as to precise detail and sequence to suggest its construction close after the event, in an attempt to identify the pattern, and so to discover the sense, in the Spaniards' cuttings and slashings. (This was the first view the Mexicans had of Spanish swords at work.) The Mexicans had very precise rules about violent assaults on the body, as the range of their sacrificial rituals makes clear, but the notion of a "preemptive massacre" of warriors was not in their vocabulary.

Such baffling actions, much more than any deliberately riddling policy, worked to keep Indians off balance. To return to an early celebrated moment of mystification by Cortés, the display of the cannon to impress the Mexican envoys on the coast with the killing power of Spanish weapons: the men who carried the tale back reported the thunderous sound, the smoke, the fire, the foul smell—and that the shot had "dissolved" a mountain, and "pulverised" a tree. It is highly doubtful that the native watchers took the intended point of the display, that this was a weapon of war for use against human flesh. It was not a conceivable weapon for warriors. So it must have appeared (as it is in fact reported) as a gratuitous assault upon nature: a scrambled lesson indeed. Mexican warriors learned, with experience, not to leap and shout and display when faced with cannon fire and crossbows, but to weave and duck, as the shield canoes learned to zigzag to avoid the cannon shot from the brigantines, so that with time the carnage was less. But they also learned contempt for men who were prepared to kill indiscriminately, combatants and noncombatants alike, and at a secure distance, without putting their own lives in play. . . .

Spanish "difference" found its clearest expression in their final strategy for the reduction of the imperial city. Cortés had hoped to intimidate the Mexicans sufficiently by his steady reduction of the towns around the lake, by his histrionic acts of violence, and by the exemplary cruelty with which resistance was punished, to bring them to treat. Example-at-a-distance in that mosaic of rival cities could have no relevance for the Mexicans—if all others quailed, they would not—so the Spaniards resorted, as Díaz put it, to "a new kind of warfare." Siege was the quintessential European strategy: an economical design to exert maximum pressure on whole populations without active engagement, delivering control over people and place at least cost. If Cortés's own precarious position led him to increase that pressure by military sorties, his crucial weapon was want.

For the Mexicans, siege was the antithesis of war. They knew of encircling cities to persuade unwilling warriors to come out, and of destroying them too, when insult required it. They had sought to burn the Spaniards out of their quarters in Tenochtitlan, to force them to fight after their massacre of the warrior dancers. But the deliberate and systematic weakening of opposition before engagement, and the deliberate implication of noncombatants in the contest, had no part in their experience.

As the siege continued the signs of Mexican contempt multiplied. Mexican warriors continued to seek face-to-face combat with these most unsatisfactory opponents, who skulked and refused battle, who clung together in tight bands behind their cannon, who fled without shame. When elite warriors, swept in by canoe, at last had the chance to engage the Spaniards closely, the Spaniards "turned their backs, they fled," with the Mexicans in pursuit. They abandoned a cannon in one of their pell-mell flights, positioned with unconscious irony on the gladiatorial stone on which the greatest enemy warriors had given their final display of fighting prowess; the Mexicans worried and dragged it along to the canal and dropped it into the water. Indian warriors were careful, when they had to kill rather than capture Spaniards in battle, to deny them an honorable warrior's death, dispatching them by beating in the back of their heads, the death reserved for criminals in Tenochtitlan. And the Spaniards captured after the debacle on the Tacuba causeway were stripped of all their battle equipment, their armor, their clothing: only then, when they were naked, and reduced to "slaves," did the Mexicans kill them. . . .

There is something appealing to our sense of irony in the notion that the Spaniards' heroic deeds, as they saw them, were judged shameful by the Mexican warriors. But attitudes of losers have little historical resonance. Attitudes of victors do. Here I want to pursue an impression. Anyone who has worked on the history of Mexico—I suspect the case is the same for much of Latin America, but I cannot speak for that—is painfully impressed by the apparent incorrigibility of the division between the aboriginal inhabitants and the in-

comers, despite the domestic proximity of their lives, and by the chronic durability, whatever the form of government, whatever its public rhetoric, of systemic social injustice grounded in that division. In Mexico I am persuaded the terms of the relationship between the incoming and the indigenous peoples were set very early. A line of reforming sixteenth-century missionaries and upright judges were baffled as much as outraged by what they saw as the wantonness of Spanish maltreatment of Indians: cruelties indulged in the face of self-interest. Spaniards had been notoriously brutal in the Caribbean islands, where the indigenes were at too simple a level of social organization to survive Spanish endeavors to exploit them. Yet in their first encounters with the peoples of Mexico the Spaniards had declared themselves profoundly impressed. Cortés's co-venture with the Tlaxcalans seems to have involved genuine cooperation, a reasonably developed notion of mutuality, and (not to be sentimental) some affection between individuals.

Then something happened, a crucial break of sympathy. It is always difficult to argue that things could have been other than they turn out to be, expecially in the political maelstrom of post-Conquest Mexico. But despite the continuing deftness of his political maneuverings in the aftermath of the Conquest, I have a sense of Cortés relinquishing both his control over the shaping of Spanish-Indian relations and his naturally conservationist policies—a conservationism based in pragmatism rather than humanity, but effective for all that—earlier and more easily than his previous conduct would have us expect. His removal to Honduras in October 1524 was an extraordinary abdication of the official authority he had sought so long and had worn only for a year, and marked the end of his effective role in "New Spain." We tend to like our heroes, whether villains or saints or Machiavels, to be all of a piece: unchanging, untinctured emblems of whatever qualities we assign them, impervious to experience. But there are indicators in his writings as in his actions that Cortés was changed by his experience in Mexico, and that the change had to do with the obstinate, and to Spanish eyes profoundly "irrational," refusal or incapacity of the Mexicans to submit.

Cortés was sensitive to the physical beauty and social complexity of the great city of Tenochtitlan. It was the dream of the city that had fired his ambition, and provided the focus for all his actions. We must remember that Tenochtitlan was a marvel, eclipsing all other cities in Mesoamerica (and Europe) in size, elegance, order, and magnificence of spectacle. Cortés had contrived the complex, difficult strategy of the blockade, and pursued the mammoth task of implementing it, in order to preserve the city by demonstrating the futility of resistance. Then he watched the slow struggle back and forth along the causeways, as the defenders, careless of their own lives, took back by night what had been so painfully won by day. He moved his men onto the causeways, into physical misery and constant danger, and then was forced to undertake the systematic destruction of the structures along the causeways to secure the yards won, a perilous prolongation of a task already long enough.

So, with patience, access to the city was gained, and the noose of famine tightened. From that point victory was in Spanish (and our) terms inevitable. Yet still the resistance continued, taking advantage of every corner and rooftop. So the work of demolition went on. At last, from the top of a great pyramid Cortés could see that the Spaniards had won seven-eighths of what had once been the city, with the remaining people crammed into a corner where the houses were built out over the water. Starvation was so extreme that even roots and bark had been gnawed, with the survivors tottering shadows, but shadows who still resisted.

Cortés's frustration in being forced to destroy the city he had so much wanted to capture intact is manifest, as is his bewilderment at the tenacity of so futile a resistance: "As we had entered the city from our camp two or three days in succession, besides the three or four previous attacks, and had always been victorious, killing with crossbow, harquebus and field gun an infinite number of the enemy, we each day expected them to sue for peace, which we desired as much as our own salvation; but nothing we could do could induce them to it." After another largely unresisted thrust into the city, "We could not but be saddened by their determination to die."

He had no stomach to attack again. Instead he made a final resort to terror. Not to the terror of mass killings: that weapon had long lost its efficacy. He constructed a war-engine, an intimidatory piece of European technology that had the advantage of not requiring gunpowder: the marvelous catapult. It was a matter of some labor over three or four days, of lime and stone and wood, then the great cords, and the stones big as demijohns. It was aimed, as a native account bleakly recorded, to "stone the common folk." It failed to work, the stone dribbling feebly from the sling, so still the labor of forcing surrender remained.

Four days patient waiting, four days further into starvation, and the Spaniards entered the city again. Again they encountered ghostly figures, of women and gaunt children, and saw the warriors still stationed on the rooftops, but silent now, and unarmed, close-wrapped in their cloaks. And still the fruitless pretense at negotiation, the dumb, obdurate resistance.

Cortés attacked, killing "more than twelve thousand," as he estimated. Another meeting with some of the lords, and again they refused any terms save a swift death. Cortés exhausted his famous eloquence: "I said many things to persuade them to surrender but all to no avail, although we showed them more signs of peace than have ever been shown to a vanquished people for we, by the grace of our Lord, were now the victors." He released a captured noble, charging him to urge surrender: the only response was a sudden, desperate attack, and more Indians dead. He had a platform set up in the market square of Tlatelolco, ready for the ceremony of submission, with food prepared for the feast that should mark such a moment: still he clung to the European fiction of two rulers meeting in shared understanding for the transference of an empire. There was no response.

Two days more, and Cortés unleashed the allies. There followed a massacre, of men who no longer had arrows, javelins, or stones; of women and children stumbling and falling on the bodies of their own dead. Cortés thought forty thousand might have died or been taken on that day. The next day he had three heavy guns taken into the city. As he explained to his distant king, the enemy, being now "so massed together that they had no room to turn around, might crush us as we attacked, without actually fighting. I wished, therefore, to do them some harm with the guns, and so induce them to come out to meet us." He had also posted the brigantines to penetrate between the houses to the interior lake where the last of the Mexican canoes were clustered. With the firing of the guns the final action began. The city was now a stinking desolation of heaped and rotting bodies, of starving men, women, and children crawling among them or struggling in the water. Quauhtemoc was taken in his canoe, and at last brought before Cortés, to make his request for death, and the survivors began to file out, these once immaculate people "so thin, sallow, dirty and stinking that it was pitiful to see them."

Cortés had invoked one pragmatic reason for holding his hand in the taking of Tenochtitlan: if the Spaniards attempted to storm the city the Mexicans would throw all their riches into the water, or would be plundered by the allies, so some of the profit would be lost. His perturbation went, I think, very much deeper. His earlier battle narratives exemplify those splendid Caesarian simplicities identified by John Keegan [in *The Face of Battle,* 1977]: disjunctive movement, uniformity of behavior, simplified characterization, and simplified motivation. That style of high control, of magisterial grasp, falters when he must justify his own defeat on the causeway, which cost so many Spanish lives. It then recovers itself briefly, to fracture, finally and permanently, for the last stages of his account of the battle for Tenochtitlan. The soldierly narrative loses its fine onward drive as he deploys more and more detail to demonstrate the purposefulness of his own action, and frets more and more over native mood and intentions.

Cortés's strategy in the world had been to treat all men, Indians and Spaniards alike, as manipulable. That sturdy denial of the problem of otherness, usually so profitable, had here been proved bankrupt. He had also been forced into parodying his earlier and once successful strategies. His use of European equipment to terrify had produced the elaborate threat of the catapult, then its farcical failure. "Standard" battle procedures—terror-raiding of villages, exemplary massacres—took on an unfamiliar aspect when the end those means were designed to effect proved phantasmal, when killing did not lead to panic and pleas for terms, but a silent pressing on to death. Even the matter of firing a cannon must have taken on a new significance: to use cannon to clear a contended street or causeway or to disperse massed warriors was one thing: to use cannon to break up a huddled mass of exhausted human misery was very much another. It is possible that as he ran through his degraded routine of stratagems in those last days Cortés was brought to glimpse something of the Indian view of the nature and quality of the Spanish warrior.

His privilege as victor was to survey the surreal devastation of the city that had been the glittering prize and magnificent justification for his insubordination, and for the desperate struggles and sufferings over two long years, now reduced by perverse, obdurate resistance to befouled rubble, its once magnificent lords, its whole splendid hierarchy, to undifferentiated human wreckage. That resistance had been at once "irrational," yet chillingly deliberate.

He had seen, too, the phobic cruelty of the "allies," most especially the Tlaxcalans. He had known that cruelty before, and had used and profited from it. But on that last day of killing they had killed and killed amid a wailing of women and children so terrible "that there was not one man amongst us whose heart did not bleed at the sound."

Those luxurious killings are at odds with what I have claimed to be the protocols of Indian combat. Tlaxcalan warrior-to-warrior performance had been conventional enough: we glimpse them exchanging insults and dueling with Mexican warriors; quarreling over the place of danger while escorting the brigantines over the mountains. It is possible that they came to judge the inadequacies of Spanish battle performance with the leniency of increased knowledge, or (more plausibly) that they thought Spanish delicts none of their concern. During the conquest process they performed as co-ventures with the Spaniards, associates in no way subordinate and, given their greater investment, probably defining themselves as the senior partners in the association. It is in their attitude to Tenochtitlan and its inhabitants that their behavior appears anomalous. Cortés recalled that when he took the decision to raze the buildings of the city, a dauntingly laborious project,

the Tlaxcalans were jubilant. All non-Mexicans would have longed to plunder Tenochtitlan, had they dared, and all had scores to settle against Mexican arrogance. No victor would have left the city intact, built as it was as the testament of the Mexican right to rule. Nonetheless the Tlaxcalan taste for destruction was extravagant. Only the Tlaxcalans were relentless in their hatred of the Mexicans: other cities waited and watched through the long struggle for the causeways, "reading the signs" in the ebb and flow of what we would call the fortunes of battle, moving, deft as dancers, in and out of alliance. Only the Tlaxcalans sought neither loot nor captives as they surged into Tenochtitlan, but to kill. Where is the exemption of nonwarriors, the passion for personal captures, for the limited aims of tribute exaction, in those killings? Is this a liberation into ecstatic violence after a painfully protracted and frustrating struggle?

Licensed massacres are unhappily unremarkable, but there are more particular explanations. The Tlaxcalans had signaled their peculiar hatred of the Mexicans early: on the Spaniards' first departure for the Mexican city the Tlaxcalans, warning of chronic Mexican treachery, offered chillingly explicit advice: "In fighting the Mexicans, they said, we should kill all we could, leaving no one alive: neither the young, lest they should bear arms again, nor the old, lest they give counsel." Their long-term exclusion from the play of Mexican alliance politics, coupled with the massive power of the Mexicans, liberated them as underdogs from "normal" constraints. While other formidable Nahua-speaking cities and provinces were recruited into the empire, the Tlaxcalans were kept out. I have come to see their exclusion, their role as outsiders, not as an unfortunate quirk but a structural requirement, a necessary corollary, of the kind of empire it was. Asked whether he could defeat the Tlaxcalans if he so chose, Moctezoma was said to have replied that he could, but preferred to have an enemy against whom to test his warriors and to secure high-quality victims. I believe him. How else, with campaigns increasingly fought far afield, to make real the rhetoric, the high glamor, the authenticity of risk of warriordom? The overriding metaphor of Mexican life was contest, and the political fantasy of destined dominance required a plausible antagonist/victim. That essential role had devolved onto the Tlaxcalans. They made absolutely no obeisance to the Mexican view of themselves, and they were proximate enemies, penned like gamecocks in a coop—until the Spaniards came. Those wandering men without a city could not be pursued, subdued, or incorporated: they could only be destroyed, and that Cortés's conservationist talents and the Mexican cultural predilection for capturing significant enemies alive combined to preclude. The house of cards structure of the wider empire had been rendered unstable by their mere presence. Then they challenged the mutuality of interest bonding the valley city states, so opening Tenochtitlan to assault, and the Tlaxcalans took their chance to destroy people and city together.

Writing later of that day of killing, and what he saw his Indian "friends" do there, Cortés was brought to make one of his very rare general statements: "No race, however savage, has ever practiced such fierce and unnatural cruelty as the natives of these parts." "Unnatural" cruelty. Against nature. A heavily freighted term in early sixteenth-century Spain. He had described Moctezoma as a "barbarian lord" in his earlier letter, but he had done so in the course of an elaborate description of the Mexican city and its complex workings that demonstrated the Mexican ruler was a "barbarian" of a most rare and civilized kind. I think his view was changed by the experience of the siege. There he saw "fierce and unnatural cruelty," an unnatural indifference to suffering, an unnatural indifference to death: a terrifying, terminal demonstration of "otherness," and of its practical and cognitive unmanageability. Todorov has called Cortés a master in human communication. Here the master had found his limits.

In the aftermath of the fall of the city the Spaniards expressed their own cruelties. There was a phobic edge in some of the things done, especially against those men most obviously the custodians of the indigenous culture. There was a special death for priests like the Keeper of the Black House in Tenochtitlan, and other wise men who came from Texcoco of their own free will, bearing their painted books. They were torn apart by dogs.

I do not suggest that any special explanation is required for Spanish or any other conquerors' brutalities. All I would claim at the end is that in the long and terrible conversation of war, despite the apparent mutual intelligibility of move and counter-move, as in the trap and ambush game built around the brigantines, that final nontranslatability of the vocabulary of battle and its modes of termination divided Spaniard from Indian in new and decisive ways. If for Indian warriors the lesson that their opponents were barbarians was learned early, for Spaniards, and for Cortés, that lesson was learned most deeply only in the final stages, where the Mexicans revealed themselves as unamenable to "natural" reason, and so unamenable to the routines of management of one's fellow men. Once that sense of unassuageable otherness has been established, the outlook is bleak indeed.

## FURTHER READING

Alonso, Manuel Moreno. "The *Dialogue of the Dead* between Hernán Cortés and William Penn, and the Romantic Image of the Conquistador in England." *BHS* LXVI, No. 2 (April 1989): 141-54.

Examines the literary appropriation of the figure of Cortés in terms of changes in the way his character and actions were perceived in eighteenth-century England.

Ardura, Ernesto. "Hernán Cortez and the Mexican Iliad." *Américas* 18, No. 8 (August, 1966): 23-31.

Portrays Cortés as a hero of epic proportions in his pursuit of the conquest of Mexico.

Elliot, J. H. "Cortés, Velásquez and Charles V." In *Hernan Cortés: Letters from Mexico,* translated and edited by Anthony Pagden, pp. xi-xxxvii. New Haven and London: Yale University Press, 1986.

A historical overview of the circumstances surrounding Cortés's conquest of Mexico, focusing on the relationship between Cortés, the governor of Cuba, and the Spanish emperor.

Ott, Thomas O. Review of *Hernan Cortés: Letters from Mexico*, edited by A. R. Pagden. *History: Review of New Books* 15, No. 3 (May, June, July, August, 1987): 140.

Discusses the *Letters* as revealing the conquistador mentality with its complex combination of "God, sword, and greed."

Rabasa, José. "Dialogue as Conquest: Mapping Spaces for Counter-Discourse." *Cultural Critique*, No. 6 (Spring, 1987): 131-59.

A comparative study of Cortés's *Letters*, along with his "Map of Mexico City and the Gulf" and Sahagún's *Florentine Codex,* focusing on the power politics implicit in such acts of representation.

Valle, Rafael Heliodoro. "Adventurer or Apostle?" *Books Abroad* 16, No. 4 (October 1942): 377-79.

Examines the conflict between Indianistas and Hispanistas over the relative importance of Cortés's role in Mexican history.

Wagner, Henry R. *The Rise of Fernando Cortés*. Los Angeles: The Cortes Society, 1944, 564 p.

Brings together earlier sources on Cortés's life, and presents a detailed account of the conquest of Mexico and Cortés's achievements as an administrator and builder of cities.

# Bernal Díaz del Castillo

## 1496-1584

Spanish historian.

### INTRODUCTION

Although he identified himself primarily as a soldier, or *conquistador*, Bernal Díaz del Castillo has also claimed a place in world literature for his efforts as a historian. Díaz participated in the sixteenth-century expedition to Mexico led by explorer Hernán Cortés, which brought the powerful Aztec nation under Spanish control. Late in his life, chagrined by his disagreement with the chronicles of the conquest published by Francisco López de Gómara and Bartolomé de las Casas, among others, Díaz decided to record his recollection of the events, and completed *Historia verdadera de la Conquista de la Nueva España* [1632; *True History of the Conquest of New Spain*]. The "truth" Díaz emphasises in his title proceeds from his direct involvement in the history he describes—a status that distinguishes him from other historians, with the exception of Cortés. Unlike his commander, however, Díaz recorded events from the soldier's point of view, and it was this attention to evoking the specific and highly personal details of history that has contributed to the favorable reputation of his account.

### Biographical Information

Bernal Díaz was born in Medina del Campo, in Spain, and biographers place his uncertain date of birth anywhere from 1492 to 1496. Since his family, albeit of good reputation and possibly noble lineage, had only a modest income, Bernal set out to make his own fortune in 1514. He spent approximately three years with Spanish settlements in Panama and Cuba, before conceding that an advance in wealth would require more drastic measures. Consequently, he joined several expeditions to Central America, with the hope of acquiring riches either in gold or colonization of the land. After several luckless efforts with different commanders, Díaz joined the explorer Hernán Cortés, who was to become one of the most famous and infamous commanders in Spanish imperial history. The expedition encountered the Aztecs, a powerful nation ruled by the emperor Montezuma. What were, at first, peaceful relations, eventually degenerated into violence and spurred Cortés to amass an army that would quell the empire, reducing the Aztecs and many other Central American tribes to colonized peoples. Cortés's con-

quest would never have proceeded, as the *True History* consistently reminds its readers, without the forces he brought to Mexico. Once the Aztec empire was broken, Díaz and his comrades expected to make their homes in the new colony, filling government posts and directing the labor of local Indians, who were granted to colonial representatives in large groups called *encomiendas*. Díaz, however, felt less than adequately compensated for his service and—although provided with *encomiendas* in Guatemala after 1541—spent much of his later life suing the Spanish crown in an attempt to acquire more Indians.

Díaz's *True History of the Conquest of New Spain*, in its unedited form, is an extensive document that the impromptu historian began in 1552 and worked on for many years, allegedly spending entire days writing his memories. There are competing theories regarding the motivation that drove the former soldier's pen, but the greatest consensus conflates his historical project with his effort to be remunerated for his military services. In general, critics assume that Díaz began writing in or around 1552 with the aim of securing recognition for his own efforts and those of his comrades. Twelve years later, as he tells the story, he read for the first time the *Crónica de la Nueva España*, the history written by Cortés's chaplain, Francisco López de Gómara. This document and Cortés's letters present the conquest as Cortés's singular achievement, rarely mentioning the names of any of his captains. Díaz's own writing, in response, became all the more fervent and purposeful.

Díaz completed a first draft of the *True History* in 1568 and sent a manuscript to Spain in 1575, but it would not see publication until 1632, fifty years after his death in 1584. When Friar Alonso de Remón brought out the first edition in 1632, the book met with immediate popularity; readers embraced the old conquistador's memories, although they criticized the editor's abridgements and interpolations. Remón's faulty text went through many more printings before Genaro Garcia returned to Díaz's original manuscript to create a corrected edition in 1904. In the centuries since its first publication, the *True History* has seen many translations, including several into English, the latest of which is J. M. Cohen's abridged edition for Penguin in 1963.

## Major Work

Díaz's *True History* tells the story of Spain's conquest of Mexico. Unlike Cortés, Gómara, and Las Casas, however, Díaz emphasizes the details of a conquistador's everyday life; he also consistently draws the spotlight away from the general and shines it on the men who served him, remembering such minutia as their nicknames, habits, armor, and horses. Critics have catagorized the text as both a history and a memoir, because it adheres so closely to the author's life. In the Preliminary Note with which it opens, Díaz proclaims his intention to "describe quite plainly, as an honest eyewitness, without twisting the facts in any way." He begins with a brief history of his family and the circumstances that took him to the New World, then proceeds to the relation of his time in Cortés's command, which constitutes the great bulk of the history. We see the initially friendly, if cautious, relationship with Montezuma, followed by rising conflicts that lead to Cortés's abduction of Montezuma, the Mexican attack on Spanish soldiers known as La Noche Triste, and the seige that ultimately broke Mexico's strength and brought it under Spanish control. Díaz then relates the personal trajectories of his main characters, especially that of Cortés and himself. When editors abridge an edition for publication, it is often this dénoument that they cut, although they then sacrifice Díaz's emphasis on his fortunes after the conquest. Having established an estate and a family in Guatemala, the former soldier dedicated himself to securing their fortune. Both the growth of his family and his efforts on their behalf—

letters to the King in Spain, for example—figure prominently in the last part of the *True History*.

## Critical Reception

Despite the protests regarding Remón's errors in the first edition of the *True History*, the work met with immediate popularity among Spanish readers and brought its author considerable posthumous fame. His currency remained steady in the ensuing centuries, then experienced a peak in the nineteenth century during a resurgence of interest in Spanish colonial history. Several translations appeared in English, including Maurice Keatinge's in 1800 and John Ingram Lockhart's in 1844. Historians, many of whom considered Díaz vital to Mexican history, drew very liberally from the *True History*, creating texts that were amalgems of his work, that of other commentators, and the historian's. In these circumstances, writers invoked Díaz as part of a general discussion on the benefits and dangers of imperialism—questions central to the nineteenth century, since England and the United States were involved in their own imperialist enterprises. While many took issue with Díaz's justifications for conquest, most held his unembellished narrative style in high esteem, taking its simplicity for wholly reliable narration. Twentieth-century critics, on the other hand, while still very concerned with the study of imperialism, became more interested in the history's textuality. Discussions have focused on the *True History* as a literary document that drew upon certain literary conventions in order to make its unfamiliar world available to Spanish readers, and that contributing to the development of the novel. Consequently, the *True History*'s centrality as a historical document is now matched by its reputation as a work of literature.

---

## PRINCIPAL WORK

*Historia verdadera de la conquista de la Nueva España* [historical memoir] 1632
*Originally completed in 1575.

---

## PRINCIPAL ENGLISH TRANSLATIONS

*The True History of the Conquest of Mexico* (translated by Maurice Keatinge) 1800
*The Memoirs of the Conquistador Bernal Díaz del Castillo* (translated by John Ingram Lockhart) 1844
*The True History of the Conquest of New Spain* (translated by Alfred Percival Maudslay) 1908-1916
*The Bernal Díaz Chronicles: The True Story of the Conquest of Mexico* (translated by Albert E. Idell) 1956

*The Conquest of New Spain* (translated by J.M. Cohen) 1963

### *The Living Age* (essay date 1844)

SOURCE: A review of *The Memoirs of Bernal Díaz del Castillo,* in *The Living Age,* Vol. II, No. 13, August 10, 1844, pp. 232-41.

[*In the following excerpt from a review of John Lockhart's translation of Díaz's* Memoirs, *the critic condemns Cortés's cruelty, but finds honesty and eloquence in Díaz's account of the conquest.*]

Mr. Lockhart's translation [of Diaz's history] is one of those works for which we are indebted to that new and spreading interest awakened by the labors of Humboldt and his successors, in the field of Mexican antiquity. The magnificent remains of an extinct civilization brought to light, in various parts of the great American continent, have conferred an additional value on such descriptions of the ancient Aztec splendor as record the impressions of credible witnesses, when first it rose upon their astonished senses, like a bewildering dream. From the more polished pictures, and philosophic estimates, of historians like Robertson and Prescott, . . . it will interest many to turn to such direct testimonies as are furnished by the despatches of the Conquistador leader, Cortes, . . . or the quaint simple chronicling of this old soldier, a conquistador himself, and perhaps the most trustworthy amongst the narrators of the events of that conquest, so far as he had the capacity for discerning them. The strange, wild incidents of that extraordinary tale come out in all their freshness, in the curious details of Bernal Diaz; and the scenes of social magnificence, amid which they are laid, tell wonderfully in the rude sketching and unpremeditated cumulation of his pen. It is true, that the march itself, and the scenes through which it passed, have alike a different aspect to the reader of this day, from that which they wore to Bernal Diaz; but it is one of the strongest testimonies to the honesty of the old chronicler and the value of his chronicle, that the materials for this improved judgment are all, unconsciously, furnished by himself. The upright and earnest narrator had no wish either to suppress or color; and motives and meanings are avowed with a simplicity which is not the least amusing quality of his volumes. There is no concealing, for instance, that this extraordinary conquest originated in a mere vulgar desire for plunder; and was pursued (through dangers, and by deeds that make of the conquistadores a band of heroes, if men can be heroes who do great things from little motives) under the influence of the meanest of all passions—the love of gold. As gold, then, was the impelling spirit, so gold was the measure of the magnificence which they found. All things which appealed to their judgment was seen in its yellow atmosphere. The book of Bernal Diaz reads like "a golden legend"—the stream of his narrative flows on, like another Pactolus, amid all the varieties of its current, gold being ever at the bottom of the movement. The reader is in a perpetual El Dorado, where the spirit of gold is as active as at the marriage of Miss Kilmansegg. For gold, these heroes in the field became petty pilferers in quarters—from all around them and from each other. The only way to blind them was to throw *gold* "dust in their eyes." For the moral and political elements, which, in our day, are understood to be involved in the question of civilization, they had no apprehension—gold was *their* standard of value:—for the qualities of kindness, generosity, and forbearance which made the best part of Montezuma's greatness they had no discernment—their spirits, like their bodies, hung in chains of gold. The Mexican emperor was a great monarch, because his coffers were exhaustless,—and Mexico was a mighty empire, because its rivers ran gold.

As with the scenery of the narrative, so, also, with its incidents,—the spirit that reads them is a new one from that in which Bernal Diaz wrote. It is amusing to see the sort of undoubting faith with which Cortes and his companions are represented as wielding "the sword of the Lord and of Gideon,"—the easy unconsciousness with which the transparent mask of a religious purpose was worn, and the daring villanies that were perpetrated under its cover. In theology, certainly, Cortes was not strong. The sword of Gideon, in his hands, was far from being a sharp argument; and it was generally found that the aid of a more trenchant weapon was necessary to enforce its logic. The "stones and slings" of reasoning, wielded by him, rarely carried to their mark in the forehead of his opponent—whereupon he resorted to the more carnal instrument, which grew to be "like a weaver's beam." It was Cortes' easy and simple way, in township or in city, to enter into the high places of their immemorial gods—places surrounded by the sanctities of a superstition which was a part of their very natures,—and informing them, "o' the sudden," that their idols were impostors, to present them with an image of the Virgin Mary, which he requested might instantly take their place. For this they could rarely, at first, see any good reason; and we, in our day, are not greatly surprised at their dulness; but the conquistador was "seated on his horse;" the Spaniard would explain, to an assembled people, as propositions of the utmost simplicity, that he had come from a far country to oblige them, by the substitution of a prince called Don Carlos for their monarch Montezuma, and depose the gods Huitzilopochtli and Tetzcatlipuca, in favor of the Virgin. "We have already a master, and cannot help feeling astonished that you, who have but just arrived and know nothing of us, should, this instant, wish to impose a master on us;"—and "How can you ask us to abandon our gods, whom we have adored for so many years, and prayed and sacrificed to them?" were answers reasonably to be expected, "till further advice." The ordinary rejoinder, however, in such cases, was, that "a great number of these people were put to the sword, and some were burnt alive, to prove the deceitfulness of their false gods," and the sovereign rights of Don Carlos. Then, when the argument was complete, the conqueror would take tribute, in gold and women, from his gratified converts. The former of these articles, the *opimia spolia,* by an inherent virtue in itself, needed no form of purification, but passed at once from the coffers of the idolators into the pockets of the conquistadors, as a thing sacred enough for the *sacra fames* which it fed—but never satisfied. But the women Cortes in no case omitted to regenerate, by the rite of baptism, ere he distributed them, as concubines, among his soldiers!

All these things are, as we have said, set down by the quaint old soldier with the most delicious unreserve, in language picturesque from its very plainness, and in a manner as instructive as it is amusing. Much of the false after-philosophy with which the subject of the conquest has been surrounded, fades away in the inartificial page of the early chronicler. The lights of the theme are here tempered by all their shadows. The fancy which the later Spanish writers took captive with the swords of the conquistadores is here set free, and on the very field of their prowess. The weapon of honest Bernal Diaz struck on one side of the question only, but his pen shows both. It is Mr. Lockhart's opinion—and, for the translator of Bernal Diaz's book, a very strange one—that "the Spaniards were not the cruel monsters they have been generally described during those times. As far as the conquest of New Spain is concerned, they were *more humane than otherwise;* and if at times they used severity, we find that it was caused by the horrible and revolting abominations which were practised by the natives. We can scarcely imagine *kinder-hearted beings* than the first priests and monks who went out to New Spain." In so far as the translator makes a special application of this latter observation to the Father Olmedo, who went out with Cortes, we agree with him. The reader of Bernal Diaz's narrative yields an unresisting belief to all it tells; and there is proof of great prudence and moderation on the part of this father, for a priest following in the wake of a conquering and propagandist army. It is apparent that he often kept Cortes, over whom he had great influence, in check; but to Mr. Lockhart's view of the *humanities* exercised by the Spaniards generally in New Spain, we demur. We gather from Bernal Diaz that the conquest of that country was begun in cupidity, and pursued by a treachery so profligate, a hypocrisy so detestable, a butchery so cold-blooded and systematic, an ingratitude so foul and monstrous, that the more ferocious doings of Pizzaro, in Peru, were needed to redeem it from being, amid all its brilliancy, one of the most disgraceful pages in the world's history. With all his religious professions, however, and all his superstition, there is a shrewdness about this old writer which makes it very doubtful how far he suspected the worthlessness of some of the spells

with which he and his friends were conjuring. The spirit uppermost throughout his book, after the desire to tell the truth, is the wish to take so much of the entire fame of the conquest from Cortes as properly belongs to his brothers in arms; and the wounded feeling of the soldier, acting on a candid nature, helps him to a very clear appreciation of the qualities of his great leader. . . .

The honest annalist has told all—and told it well; and his narrative is made picturesque by many a figure, which gives it life and reality, . . . and many an allusion and self-reference which makes it touching. "Alas!" says Bernal Diaz, "now even, while I am writing this, the figure and powerful build of Christobal de Oli comes fresh to my memory, and my heart feels sore with grief." The amusing vanity of the old soldier, too, being never offensive, and based upon a long series of gallant services and sufferings, gives great piquancy to his gossip; and there is something genial about the man, which confers a pleasant flavor on all he says. Though wounded, both in his feelings and interests, by the neglect of Cortes, and eager to claim his share of that fame as a conquistador, which the latter sought to monopolize, he will let no man depreciate his chief. He loves to exhibit the conqueror as always foremost in action and readiest in resource. Through life, he never failed his illustrious leader; and, in this memoir, he becomes his apologist and panegyrist—though not an uncompromising one. "May the Almighty pardon his sins," he concludes, after a long summing up in his favor, "and mine also; and may he, also, grant me a happy death, for this is of more importance than all our conquests and victories over the Indians!"

*Our* summing up will be different from that of Bernal Diaz, because the figures that go to the account have another value in our day. If it were permitted us to praise evil, for the good it had done, then might the conqueror of Mexico be allowed to take his place among the truly great. It is impossible to read of the wholesale human sacrifices, and other abominations practised in New Spain, when Cortes found it, without feeling that, by whatever door it came in, the introduction of the improved civilization of the European world was a final gain and blessing. But the actor is not to be measured by this act—apart from his motives and his means. All are not great men who have done great things. It has been the long habit of history, while a poet or partisan, to deal much in hero-worship,—and history, become a philosopher, has much to rectify. It will have something to take from the fame of Cortes; and will find the testimony of Bernal Diaz useful for the purpose—far beyond what the chronicler intended.

## R. B. Cunninghame Graham (essay date 1915)

SOURCE:A preface to *Bernal Díaz del Castillo: Being Some Account of Him, Taken From His True His-*

*tory of the Conquest of New Spain,* Dodd, Mead & Company, 1915, pp. vii-xiv.

[*In the following excerpt, Graham suggests that Díaz's sincerity, attention to detail, and appreciation for the common soldier should make his* True History *the most favored account of the conquest.*]

In this, my little sketch, I am not much concerned with this or that edition; but chiefly with the man. What I discern in [Diaz] is steadfastness, sincerity, and in the main an absence of the gross superstitions that in his time blinded so many of his contemporaries, though he was ardent in his faith. His style is nervous, and though occasionally involved, remains after so many hundred years a well of pure Castilian, into which when you let down a bucket, it comes up, filled with good water, still sparkling, after the lapse of time.

Diaz had, as it were, a foot both in the camps of literature and arms. One was his natural place, the other he made for himself and filled it worthily.

To be a conqueror and an historian at the same time falls to the lot of few. Most conquerors (with some notable exceptions) have not been men of words.

Bernal Diaz del Castillo wielded both sword and pen, and after a long life of action he sat down to write in his old age. Although he loved and reverenced Cortés, his judgment was not blinded by his love, for no man saw another's faults more clearly; but as Don Quixote's madness did not abate an atom of the respect in which his squire held him, so it was with the soldier-chronicler and his general.

When fighting long was done, and he himself was Regidor of "this good town of Guatemala," oppressed with years, and with his limbs too stiff for any riding, but on a pacing mule, he chanced to come upon a history of the "Conquest of New Spain" that drove him furious.

He loved Cortés as perhaps few soldiers in the world have loved their generals, but to hear all the Conquest put down to his right arm, whilst he himself and all his comrades were quite forgotten and not named, stirred up the feelings of equality and pride, dear to all Spanish hearts. It was the braver of him, for he was poor, unlearned, and of all those who sailed from Cuba with Cortés, only five poor old men were left alive, crippled by debts and wounds.

Odds never daunted him his whole life long, either by land or sea, or if he fought with Christians or Infidels, and though his last adventure into literature was to the full as desperate, all things considered, as any he had yet encountered, he boldly plunged into it, and wrote a book unequalled in its kind in the whole world. Good

faith and a dry Spanish humour illumine every page.

After the fashion of the other conquerors of the New World he thought that he and all his fellows were instruments of God. This attitude persists most strongly in the human mind down to the present day.

Arrogance, cruelty, and pride of race, a lust of gold and a blind faith in their religion, together with an absolute contempt for that of other men, were the chief faults of all the Spanish conquerors; but in the main these faults are incidental to mankind, especially in those who find themselves placed, as they were, like gods amongst a weaker race of men. Who dare arise to-day in England or in France, in Spain or any other land and criticise them? Rather, it best becomes us to wonder at their exploits, forget their crimes and ask forgiveness for the sins of the same nature that we, the men of progress and of light, have fallen into, not having their excuse. They thought themselves the instruments of God, just as we think ourselves the instruments of progress, and it may be that both they and ourselves have been deceived about the estimate we put upon our deeds.

Cortés wrote well and picturesquely. Pedro de Alvarado in the two letters that remain to us of his, was clear and perspicacious, and neither of them coloured facts or canted, or seemed to think that anything he did was in the least unusual for gentlemen and Spaniards or for good Christians to do. Most of the conquerors who wrote were men in high position, well educated and obliged by their rank to deal rather with facts than with those little incidental things that preserve men and manners for us, and make the difference between a history and a chronicle.

Both Alvarado and Cortés wrote reports, which, as they dealt with stirring times and a new world, were interesting and strange; but Bernal Diaz writes of men round the camp fire, preserves their nicknames, tells of their weaknesses, and makes us see, not only them, but him himself, just as they sat and talked, cleaning their arms, or softening their wounds with grease taken from a dead Indian, "for medicines we had none." Withal, he was a man, honest and steadfast to his leaders, patient in hardships and a great lover of good horses, a taste befitting to a conqueror, for by the aid of horses "under God" was Mexico subdued. So much he loved them that he has set down the names and colours, qualities and faults of all the horses and the mares which came in the first fleet that sailed from Cuba with Cortés.

In a few lines he has embalmed the memory of Motilla, the best horse, as he says, either in the Indies or in Spain. We know Motilla as we know few living horses in the world, almost as well as the bright bay with three white stockings, and the long crinkly mane, turning his head towards Spinola, in the "Surrender of the town of Breda," under the clump of spears.

Here and there through his book are scattered passages that the whole world knows or should know, such as the fall of Mexico, with the sudden ceasing of the tumult that had gone on for ninety days, "so that we, the soldiers, all were deaf, as if we had been in a belfry with all the bells ringing, and they had all suddenly been stopped."

This and his description of Cortés, one of the most complete and most minute presentments of a man in any literature, together with his fine analysis of his own feelings when entering a fight, place the old soldier who "knew no Latin" as he says, in the first flight of natural writers . . . of those men who write, as it were, by nature, having been born free of the mystery, and not as is more usual, having bought their freedom at the price of toil. As to the man himself, he was undoubtedly brave and resourceful, weighty in council also, for on more than one occasion Cortés himself would have avoided losses and defeat, had he but followed his advice. He was not bloodthirsty, taking no delight in slaughter for itself, but at the same time looking on the killing of the Infidel as something necessary, but not to be indulged in as a sport. In fact, he had a sense of justice in his dealings with the Indians, and opposed all wanton cruelty. Of all the writers on the conquest, either of Mexico or of Peru, he stands the first in broad humanity, a quality which with his vigorous style and terse Castilian speech, make him a personal friend when you have read his book, just in the way that Sancho Panza and Don Quixote are our friends and not mere characters. . . .

## Arthur D. Howden Smith (essay date 1927)

SOURCE: An introduction to *The True History of the Conquest of Mexico,* by Bernal Díaz del Castillo, translated by Maurice Keatinge, Robert M. McBride & Company, 1927, pp. v-xv.

[*In this introduction to the second edition of Maurice Keatinge's translation of Díaz, Smith argues that Díaz described the "expedition to Mexico [as] essentially democratic," as opposed to Francisco López de Gómara's glorification of Cortés alone.*]

Stout, old Bernal Diaz del Castillo may have been a good soldier—he very ingenuously says that he was; he certainly was an excellent chronicler. Without his **Historia Verdadera de la Conquista de la Nueva España** we should know nothing of the more intimate aspects of one of the world's most dramatic episodes. We should have no sources of first-hand information on the day-to-day experiences of the men who waded through blood and agony to the greatest achievement

of militant Spain. We should have no picture, self-painted, of the veritable Conquistador, cruel, faithful, superstitious, lastful, generous, avaricious. We should have to rest our conception of the destruction of the Aztec Empire upon the three surviving letters of the four which Cortes wrote to Charles V: reports of a general who had placed himself in a difficult position politically, a creature of intrigue who was become the target for various intrigues launched by other colonial officers, jealous of his success, and who was therefore, compelled to twist and turn, to exaggerate, prevaricate, distort and dissemble, in his efforts to retain command of the expedition and satisfy the vaulting demands of his personal ambition.

Cortes, like all conquerors, was a confirmed egotist. His reports were designed to emphasize his value to his sovereign, and he was careful not to put forward his lieutenants lest one of them be selected to supplant him. What he deemed unfavorable to his own interests he suppressed; points which he considered advantageous he elaborated. Then, a few years after his death, appeared the formal history of the Conquest written by Gomara, who had been his chaplain and retained that post in the household of his son, Don Martin. Valuable as this work undoubtedly is, based on the statements and vanished papers of the first Marquis of the Valley, and probably checked by the oral traditions of other members of the family, it is marred by a sycophancy and untruthfulness which extort from Bernal Diaz the comment: "Where he has written eighty thousand, we should read one thousand."

Gomara's history evidently was the last straw to Bernal Diaz, who had nursed for years a very human resentment against the prevailing idea that the Conquest was the work of Cortes alone, the product of a superman's genius, although, apart from this, he retained for his old general an unblemished affection and admiration. So he sat himself down in the royal audencia of the city of Guatemala, in the year 1568—that is, some fifty years after the events of the Conquest—and addressed himself to the novel task of inscribing his recollections in accordance with this simple creed: "I say also that Cortes did everything that ought to be expected from a wise and valiant general, and that he owed his success, under God, to the stout and valiant captains, and to us brave soldiers, who broke the force of the enemy, and supported him by fighting in the manner we fought, and as I have related."

There spoke a Sixteenth Century democrat! In fact, it is impossible to read Bernal Diaz without perceiving that the expedition to Mexico was essentially democratic in its organization and methods of operation. Cortes, despite his commission from the Governor of Cuba, was really no more than the elected chief of his little army. He reported to a soldiers' council, was advised and criticized by his captains, treated his followers as brethren in adventure and was treated by them as one placed over them on suffrance. "Señors"—gentlemen—he called his men; and those of whom he was fondest or in whom he placed special trust were "Son Sandoval" and "Brother Bernal Diaz." Had he ever failed definitely, had a majority of his company lost confidence in him, he must have been deposed at once. He was respected and obeyed merely because he was able to prove that he was the one amongst them most fitted to command.

This feeling of military democracy was the inspiration of Spain's golden age, the key to the amazing exploits the Spaniards performed in the New World. While it burned, hot and clear, in the hearts of the young hidalgos and rugged peasantry of Castile, who formed the backbone of the American enterprises, the Spanish power flourished. When it commenced to flicker and die, under the dead weight of aristocratical and clerical inertia, the term of Spain's empire was set, notwithstanding several centuries should pass before the bulky edifice collapsed, rotted from porch to architrave by the arrogance and bigotry bred of democratic success.

To understand it you must cross the Atlantic and survey the Spain that produced Bernal Diaz, Alvarado, Martin Lopez, the shipman, and the rest of the three thousand, who, first and last, fought under Cortes' banner. For eight hundred years this Spain had battled to curb the Moors. War, unending war, was the national life. Generation succeeded generation in the struggle, which was waged bitterly, ferociously, with a recurrent rhythm as inevitable as fate. All men were soldiers. And partly because of this, partly because ages of contact with the Moors had infected the Spaniards with a measure of the tribal spirit their enemies had brought from Arabia, there developed a strong instinct for cooperative effort. Where all were soldiers all were equal under the sovereign. One hiladgo was as good as another hidalgo. In the swift forays of Moorish warfare individual initiative was at a premium, and the best man was nominated to lead.

It was a wonderful school for fighting-men, who, of necessity, must raise up fighting-men to take their places. The fathers of the Conquistadors, themselves Conquistadors, had only just crushed the last Moorish princes in El Andalus when the Genoese navigator, Cristóbal Colón, discovered, as he thought, an unknown part of Asia. For the first time in eight centuries Spain had no enemy in her midst—and her younger fighting-men, reared to the sword, possessing no other means of livelihood, found their occupation gone, their country exhausted and impoverished, unable to support itself by peaceful arts, thanks to the slaughter or expulsion of the Moorish farmers and artisans who had been the chief element in producing its wealth. Young Spain hailed this new land as a godsend. The dependent relatives of every noble family turned their faces restless-

ly toward the west; discontented farm lads and village wastrels hastened to enlist in the expeditions that fitted out for Hispaniola, Cuba, Jamaica and the mysterious Main.

Better a venture beyond the sunset, most of them felt, than service under the Great Captain, Gonzalo de Córdoba, in Italy, the only opportunity for military experience the period afforded at home. For your true daredevil could estimate quite justly the chance of fame or booty awaiting him in Europe; but the untrodden shores the caravels had coasted contained a kingdom, a province, a mountain of gold, for every lean-pursed youngster who took ship from Palos or Cadiz. So it was no accident that listed amongst Cortes' followers a Puertocarrero, a Ponce de Leon, a de Soto, scions of families that had been famous in all the wars of El Andalus. But—and mark this well!—a Puertocarerro, cousin to the Count of Medellin, was not counted superior to a Bernal Diaz, saving he had demonstrated himself braver or shrewder. Birthproud to an absurd degree, these emigrants were arrant democrats. Good blood entailed an increased obligation rather than a right to any peculiar privilege. And the readiness of Cortes to ignore this obligation, to take care that he profited immensely while his soldiers went unrewarded, was what galled Bernal Diaz. He leaves you in no doubt that according to his views Cortes failed to act as became an hidalgo and a great soldier.

But our Conquistador is entirely fair in his strictures on his leader. Praise balances blame. Indeed, the finest quality of this chronicle is the good temper with which controversial matters are discussed. Cortes the soldier, Cortes the politician, Cortes the man, each aspect of his general Bernal Diaz presents with scrupulous exactitude. He loves Cortes. He can both admire and condemn. Never once does he lose touch with the actuality of his subject, and in consequence he projects an extraordinarily plausible personality, full-rounded and appealing by reason of the very failings and frailties he assails, infinitely more persuading, more understandable, than the Cortes reflected in the three voluminous letters to Charles V. And for all the naïve superstition and medieval brutality constantly to the fore in his record, he manages to strike an odd note of modernity, with his spontaneous admiration for a brave enemy, his denunciation of the torturing and execution of Guatimoctzin, his rude conception of honor, his relentless endeavor to be equitable in his judgments.

Of the sources for the Conquest he is the soundest, and, I think, the most interesting. There is nothing polished or literary about him, but that constitutes his charm. You are meeting face to face a veritable Conquistador. His pages quiver with life, raw, angry, painful, appalling. Himself he strides forth of the type to meet you, a grizzled, ruddy-cheeked, rough-spoken ancient, curt in manner, opinionated, aggressive, narrowly religious, childishly vain, lion-hearted. You cannot help liking him and laughing at him and his swaggering boasts of the hundred and nineteen battles he had fought, his casual practice of dressing his wounds with strips of fat cut with his sword from a dead Indian's rump, his formal piety, his pungent estimates of human nature, his offhand references to the savage and lustful practices he took for granted, his persistent refusal to magnify exploits he regarded as too colossal to require exaggeration.

Even his limitations carry conviction. As [William] Prescott says:

> In reading his pages, we feel that whatever are the errors into which he has fallen, from oblivion of ancient transactions or from unconscious vanity— of which he had full measure—or from credulity, there is nowhere a wilful perversion of truth. Had he attempted it, indeed, his very simplicity would have betrayed him.

He is more often right than wrong, however, cautious in using figures and judicious in narrating incidents. For instance, where Cortes, eager to convince Charles of the merit of his services, claims 75,000 allies from Tlascala at the final siege of Tenochtitlan, Bernal Diaz tots them up to three xiquipuls, 24,000 men. And in describing the Aztecs' losses during the siege, he avoids quoting definite numbers, contenting himself with the remark that "I have read of the destruction of Jerusalem, but I cannot conceive that the mortality exceeded this of Mexico; for all the people from the distant provinces which belonged to this empire had concentrated themselves here, where they mostly died"—a statement which Prescott and others deride, although, if once you concede anything approaching the population the chroniclers assert for Aztec Mexico, it is conceivable that upwards of a million people collected in a municipal area which was likened to Venice, Cordova or Seville. Cortes writes to Charles that 40,000 were slain or taken in a single day, and says elsewhere that 50,000 died of disease and hunger.

Again, Cortes dismisses the sorry catastrophe of the Noche Triste in a sentence, and slides over the disastrous fighting which preceded it. He was not to blame for the plight in which he found himself after his return to Tenochtitlan, and it is difficult to see how he could have avoided the misfortunes incident to the retreat. But he seems to have been unwilling to admit in writing the losses he sustained. Bernal Diaz, on the other hand, dealing with the same events, tells the plain truth, which is distinctly to the credit of Cortes, who, after losing eight hundred and fifty out of thirteen hundred and ten men, all his cannon, all his arquebusses, all his gunpowder, most of his crossbows and most of his horses, was yet able to extricate himself

---

**Díaz recounts Montezuma's first appearance before the Spanish Soldiers:**

When we came near to Mexico, at a place where there were some other small towers, the great Montezuma descended from his litter, and these other great Caciques supported him beneath a marvellously rich canopy of green feathers, decorated with gold work, silver, pearls, and chalchihuites, which hung from a sort of border. It was a marvellous sight. The great Montezuma was magnificently clad, in their fashion, and wore sandals of a kind for which their name is cotaras, the soles of which are of gold and the upper parts ornamented with precious stones. And the four lords who supported him were richly clad also in garments that seem to have been kept ready for them on the road so that they could accompany their master. For they had not worn clothes like this when they came out to receive us. There were four other great Caciques who carried the canopy above their heads, and many more lords who walked before the great Montezuma, sweeping the ground on which he was to tread, and laying down cloaks so that his feet should not touch the earth. Not one of these chieftains dared to look him in the face.

*Bernal Díaz, in* The Conquest of New Spain, *translated by J.M. Cohen, Penguin Books, 1963.*

---

from the Aztec hordes and with cold steel win his most notable battle at Otumba, while his men were still bleeding from the wounds they had received in slashing their escape across the broken causeways.

A marvelous story! And Bernal Diaz conveys it to you adequately because he is so artlessly sincere as to trench upon the preserves of art. Where will you find a more sympathetic sketch of a commander than he gives of Cortes? And in reading of the fight with Narvaez, in Cempoal, you sense and see, with startling authenticity, the steaming tropic darkness, the intermittent showers and moonshine and the cocuyo beetles that flickered over the ranks and made Cortes' enemies believe a stalwart array of musketeers were tramping up the street between the white-walled palaces and temples. When he tells of Donna Marina's meeting with the mother who had sold her into slavery he unconsciously limns a portrait of himself, no less vivid than the impression he conveys of the character of the extraordinary woman, who was for a time Cortes' mistress and wrought more for the conqueror than either of the colorless wives he found in Cuba and Old Spain. Consider, too, the conclusion of his description of the invaders' first arrival on the outskirts of the Aztec capital: "When I beheld the scenes that were around me, I thought within myself that this was the garden of the world! But all is destroyed, and that which was a lake is now a tract of fields of Indian corn, and so entirely altered that the natives themselves could hardly know it."

He was not insensible to the tragedy implicit in his comrades' achievements, this rough, gruff, old Conquistador.

Once in a while, in his frank, ingenuous way, he thrusts a torch into the blurred medley of Indian mishaps and rivalries that smoothed the Spaniards' path, as when he remarks innocently how, after Cortes was driven from Tenochtitlan, in the summer of 1520, and retired to Tlascala to recuperate, the smallpox became so prevalent that "many of the great lords of the natives died of it," including the Aztec Emperor Coadlavaca, who had succeeded Montezuma, and Maxicatzin, one of the princes of the Tlascalans, the Spaniards' allies. He speaks of this outbreak of smallpox solely because it required Cortes to settle several disputes over the succession to lordships. Perhaps he was ignorant of the fact that the Indians had never been exposed to the disease previously, and that its ordinary virulence was increased a thousand fold amongst such unsalted barbarians. Certainly, he seems to have had no appreciation of the influence the scourge must have exerted in the Spaniards' favor. But with our presentday knowledge we may be justified in surmising that it very possibly furnished the last fillip necessary to reduce the offensive strength of the Aztecs to a point which rendered hopeless their fight for freedom. It is no reflection upon the generalship of Cortes or upon the sturdy valor of his troops to say that they succeeded as much through the divisions and calamities of their foes as through their own endeavors.

The Spaniards, as Bernal Diaz makes evident, were not so efficiently equipped as we moderns usually suppose. Very few possessed armor; three fourths of them were contented with a pike or sword and buckler. The captains had morions, and usually, a breastplate or half-armor. Here and there you might find a fellow with a leathern jack. Of the five hundred and eight soldiers who sailed with Cortes, sixteen fought on horseback, with sword and lance; thirteen owned arquebusses and thirty-two were crossbowmen, a number of these latter being Italians, a race at that time as noted for skill with the arbalest as the English yeomanry were with the longbow. A certain number, unspecified, were detailed to serve the artillery, an arm with which Cortes was unusually well-supplied; he had originally ten brass field-pieces, very small ones, of course, and four falconets, weapons not much larger than blunderbusses. So much for "the iron conquerors" of poem and story! It was pikemen and sworders, shoulder to shoulder, using the point, who won the victory—with the very substantial aid of Indian allies, who hated the Aztecs worse than the white invaders.

One of the things I like about Bernal Diaz is that he conveys the psychology of the man in the ranks. In the letters of Cortes there is no note of individual and mass effort, no inkling of the fears and misgivings of the soldiers. They are formal narrations of victory, centering skilfully around the personality of the leader. Cortes writes of triumphs gained by Cortes and his army; Bernal Diaz describes how the army Cortes commanded won its battles and surmounted its obstacles, specifying with meticulous accuracy the performance of any soldier of outstanding fame. His memory for details is so extraordinary that some sceptics have doubted its value, even questioned his existence, for the reason that his name does not appear amongst the four hundred and forty-four signatures to the letter addressed to Charles V by the officers and soldiers of the army, petitioning the Emperor to continue Cortes in command. The answer to this is that the army's letter was drafted at the time, in the fall of 1520, when he was sick—in his own words, "being ill of a fever, and throwing up blood at the mouth."

As to the question of his memory, it should be recalled that he was a very old man when he wrote his history. He says that he left his birthplace, Medina del Campo of Old Castile, in 1514, when he probably was not more than eighteen. This would make him seventy-two at the commencement of his chronicle, and seventy-six at its conclusion "on this twenty sixth day of February, in the year of our Lord, one thousand five hundred and seventy two." Throughout the years since the Conquest he must have devoted much consideration to the epochal events of his youth. The Conquistadors were all marked men, a class apart, about whom rapidly developed a legendary interest, to whom all classes looked up with a reverence almost superstitious. Wherever they went they were urged to recount their reminiscences.

For half a century, Bernal Diaz had talked and thought of the stupendous period which witnessed the destruction of the Indian empire. Whenever he encountered a fellow Conquistador they would sit and patch their memories together, and all folk within reach, great and humble, would gather to listen to them. By 1568, when he started to write, there were but five men alive of those who had sailed from Cuba in the original expedition—"and we are very old, and bowed down with infirmities, and very poor, and with a heavy charge of sons to provide for, and of daughters to marry off, and grandchildren to maintain, and little rent to do it withal! and thus we pass our lives, in pain, in labor and in sorrow."

He regarded himself as the spokesman of his dead comrades. No one else had told their story. Except for Martin Lopez, a man named Granado and two he does not name, the other Conquistadors were gone, and the record of their deeds buried with them. So he set himself, with the patient determination of an old man immersed in his subject, to whom time was become no more than a shadow crouched at his shoulder, to write out all that had occurred as he had happened to see it or hear of it, distributing praise and blame with an even hand in the perspective of the years. The result is the most attractive historical document of its kind in any European language, as absorbing today as it was when, having passed the scrutiny of the Council of the Indies and the clerical authorities, it was first published in 1632, long, long after our Conquistador had been interred in some forgotten cemetery of Guatamala City. . . .

---

**William Prescott notes Diaz's perspective on conquest**

A good criterion of the moral sense of the actors in these events [of the conquest] is afforded by the reflections of Bernal Díaz, made some fifty years, it will be remembered, after the events themselves, when the fire of youth had become extinct, and the eye, glancing back through the vista of half a century, might be supposed to be unclouded by the passions and prejudices which throw their mist over the present. "Now that I am an old man," says the veteran, "I often entertain myself with calling to mind the heroical deeds of early days, till they are as fresh as the events of yesterday. I think of the seizure of the Indian monarch, his confinement in irons, and the execution of his officers, till all these things seem actually passing before me. And, as I ponder on our exploits, I feel that it was not of ourselves that we performed them, but that it was the providence of God which guided us. Much food is there here for meditation!" There is so, indeed, and for a meditation not unpleasing, as we reflect on the advance, in speculative morality, at least, which the nineteenth century has made over the sixteenth. But should not the consciousness of this teach us charity? Should it not make us the more distrustful of applying the standard of the present to measure the actions of the past?

*William H. Prescott, in* The History of the Conquest of Mexico, 1843

---

**Ramón Iglesia (essay dates 1935 and 1940)**

SOURCE: "Two Studies on the Same Subject," in *Columbus, Cortés, and Other Essays,* edited and translated by Lesley Byrd Simpson, University of California Press, 1969, pp. 34-63.

[*In the following piece, Iglesia has combined two essays from different points in his career. In the first, he praises the democratic principle Díaz promotes; in the second, which followed Iglesia's own military experience, he suggests that Díaz too harshly criticizes Gómara's* History of the Conquest of Mexico.]

I am aware that it is not quite the thing for a historian to talk about himself; but I cannot avoid it, nor do I wish to do so. Before the Spanish Civil War I was preparing a critical edition of the *True History of the Conquest of New Spain* by Bernal Díaz del Castillo. Having been invited to read a paper before the XXVI Congress of Americanists at Seville, in 1935, I was obliged to summarize pretty drastically—as one is always forced to do—my notions about some aspects of Spanish historiography, especially the work of Bernal Díaz. That summary comprises the first of the two studies presented below. In it I accept as true the story of the conquest as given by Bernal, that is, that it was the men of Cortés' company, and not Cortés himself, who carry its whole weight and who take the initiative and responsibility in its most critical moments. Cortés is only one man among many.

If the Civil War had not intervened, the prologue that I planned to write for my edition of Bernal, of which the study I mentioned is only a sketch, would have been conceived and oriented in similar terms. But the war broke out, I was caught up in it, and so acquired a direct and living experience of military problems, an experience that all the history books in the world could not have given me. I saw at first hand what war is, a touchstone for all human values, because in war we are always under the pressure of death, which in ordinary times is kept out of sight. I saw the part played by commanders who knew how to obey and die, and I saw the deep need of hierarchy and discipline in an army, something that we had been forgetting, or perhaps scorning, in our civilized, liberal, and individualized society. And this is what made me review my whole concept of a number of historical problems, including the work of Bernal Díaz. After the war I reread his book and studied more carefully than before the text of Gómara. I compared the two and derived conclusions that will be found in the second of the studies offered below. In them, although I do not accept the exclusive importance that Gómara gives to Cortés, I recognize now that Cortés' part in the conquest was much more significant than Bernal allows.

Would I have experienced this change in my point of view if the Civil War had not affected my life so tremendously? Surely not. For this reason it occurred to me that the simultaneous publication of the two studies might be of interest to those trusting believers who think that the simple accumulation of data in a straight line is the best approach to historical knowledge. This may give them something to think about, for what occurred with me was not a simple accumulation of data, *but a change in my point of view,* brought about, not by reading and reflection, but by a living experience, an *Erlebnis.* One and the same person—if it is allowable to say that I am the same person I was before the war—this person, studying the same theme, using the same method, can derive different and even opposite conclusions if his life has suffered a change. Is this not a theme worthy of the attention of the scientific historians? I believe it is. . . .

Is it possible, then, as we have been told lately, for the historian to put aside his personality completely? If it is not possible, to what extent can or should his personality and the feeling of his time and circumstances affect his vision of the past? What complex of ideas and sentiments does the historian use, consciously or unconsciously, to analyze the facts and select and interpret them, now that the need for selection, interpretation, and synthesis is so urgently recognized? Will not this subjective element upset the unity and cohesion of the historical knowledge that was acquired with such a deal of effort? I submit these pressing questions to awaken the positivist historians and interrupt their endless siesta of publishing documents. If it is true that such questions complicate horribly the mission of the historian, it is also true that his work risks sterility if he does not try to answer them honestly and straightforwardly.

### I. Bernal Díaz del Castillo and Popularism in Spanish Historiography (1935):

Of all disciplines, history is the one that most closely approaches life. To this indestructible relationship history owes her weakness and her strength. It makes her norms variable and her trustworthiness doubtful. At the same time it gives her universality, significance, and sobriety.

These words of Huizinga very likely have general application, but I consider them more applicable to Spain than to any other country. In Spain history is so intimately linked with life that our most valuable historical works were written, so to speak, on the wire edge of events, works that sprang from a direct knowledge of those events, from living with them.

It frequently happens that a Spanish scholar, composing a history of a lofty and scientific kind based upon documents and reading, fails in his purpose. It will suffice, for example, to recall what happened with the official history of the Indies. On the other hand, any witness of, or actor in, significant events commonly has among us Spaniards a capacity and a plastic power of description, a directness of style and accuracy of detail, which I do not believe are equalled in the historical works of other nations. . . .

While in Spain erudite historians are wreaking havoc, writing extravagant accounts of the life of *El Gran Capitán,* Latin screeds on the life of Cisneros, a vast lot of sketches about Charles V, and collecting documents about him, the unlettered Spaniard of the Indies, with his delight in contemplating never-before-seen

wonders and in performing fantastic exploits, overflows his banks in a boundless flood. His subject is no longer the heroic deed of kings and nobles, but those of any captain or soldier in an expedition of conquest, thereby lowering the social level of author and subject. Fernández de Oviedo makes it clear that he is concerned with a typically Spanish trait:

This is a rare and precious gift of nature, not to be seen so fully and generously conceded in any other nation as in the Spanish people, because in Italy, France, and most of the countries of the world, only the nobles are especially trained in, or naturally inclined to war, for of the common people and those engaged in the mechanical arts and agriculture, and plebeians, few are those in foreign nations who take up arms or have any desire to do so. But in our Spain it seems that all are commonly born to, and principally dedicated to, arms and their exercise. And so true is this that everything else is merely accessory, and they willingly abandon it in favor of a military life. And this is the reason why, although they are few in number, the Spanish conquistadors have always accomplished in those parts what the men of other nations have failed to do.

It is a foreigner, Friederici, who tells us that there is no other country with so large a number of soldier-chroniclers as our own. It is characteristic of them that they despise book learning, even though they tend to display, ingenuously and frequently, the little that they do possess. Gonzalo Fernández de Oviedo offers a prime example of this attitude, informing us at every step that erudition and elegance of style are worthless unless the author has lived through the events he describes. His target is Peter Martyr, the court chronicler, who wrote his *Décadas de Orbe Novo* without leaving Spain, "Especially since the said authors relate what they please, not as actors, like our Spaniards, but as mere armchair spectators." "I did not gather my materials from the two thousand volumes I might have read . . . , but got everything I have written here from the two thousand travails and hardships and perils I underwent in the past twenty-two years and more, in which I witnessed and experienced these things in my own person." Outbursts like these are frequent in the pages of Oviedo.

If, deep down, Oviedo feared that his culture was insufficient, even more fearful was Captain Bernal Díaz del Castillo, one of the fighting men who distinguished themselves in the conquest of Mexico. He tells us himself that he abandoned his writing when the chronicle of Gómara, the chaplain of Cortés, came to his hands. Nevertheless, and happily for us, he took up his task again when he became convinced of the misstatements made by the priestly panegyrist of his chief. Bernal Díaz has the same attitude toward Gómara that Oviedo has toward Peter Martyr. Even so, although his book possesses unique and marvelous qualities, posterity has not done justice to its merits, but rather has accepted the adverse judgment of Antonio de Solís, the eighteenth-century chronicler, who, buttressed behind his excellent prose, has given us the classical version of the Spanish conquest of Mexico. Solís says of Bernal's work:

> Today it is accepted as true history, owing to the very slovenliness and unadorned simplicity of its style, which has the effect of establishing its verisimilitude and convincing some readers of the writer's sincerity. But, although he is favored by the fact that he has witnessed the events he wrote about, it is evident from his work that he is not so free of prejudice as to keep it out of his pages. He shows himself to be as satisfied with his simplicity as he is querulous about his own fortunes. In his lines his envy and ambition are undisguised, and often his illtempered feelings turn into complaints of Cortés, the principal character of his history, whose designs he tries to fathom, for the purpose of belittling and amending his counsels, frequently asserting as fact, not what his commander had ordered and planned, but the grumblings of the soldiers, in whose republic there is as much of mob spirit as there is in any other, all republics being equally endangered if those who were born to obey are allowed to express their opinions.

Historians, in their evaluation of the chronicle of Bernal, usually follow the lead of Solís. All of them speak of his crudity of style, his arrogance, and the animosity toward Cortés he shows in his chronicle. All of which is inexact. It would be difficult to surpass Bernal's style in its descriptive force and grace of narration. He has a feeling for effective detail, aided by an astonishing memory. When Alonso de Grado, a captain who had fallen foul of Cortés, spends two days in the stocks, Bernal tells us of it, and adds: "I remember that the wood of the stocks smelled something like garlic or onions." In his desire to attain the greatest credibility he does not think it beneath him to relate the smallest details. He never forgets to count the steps of the temples. "And then we descended the steps, and, since there were a hundred and fourteen of them, and since come of our soldiers were sick with the buboes or humors, their thighs hurt when they climbed down." Nor did the heaps of skulls escape his attention.

> I remember that in a square, where there were certain shrines, a great many rows of skulls were piled up in such wise that they could be counted, for they were regularly arranged, and it seems that there were more than a hundred thousand of them. In another part of the square there were so many rows of shinbones and bones of dead men that they could not be counted.

It is not in relating the minute details, however vigorous and savory they may be, that Bernal is the great

artist, but in his wider pictures, where his pen retains its precision and strength. He describes the reversals in a combat with as much care as he gives to the fight in the great market of Mexico, or to the life that Moctezuma led. Here is a scene chosen at random:

> And after these exchanges they told us in sign language that we should go with them to their village, and we wondered whether we should go or not, and we decided to go, but cautiously. And they took us to some very large houses, which were shrines for their idols, well constructed of stone and lime, and on the walls many figures of serpents and great snakes were painted, and other pictures of ugly idols; and around them, beyond the idols, on something resembling an altar, there were objects like crosses, all painted, at which we were astonished, as by something never-before-seen or heard of. And it seems that at that time they had sacrificed some Indians to their idols, to induce them to give them victory over us, and many Indian women were laughing and enjoying themselves, apparently very peaceably. But so many Indians were assembling that we feared we might be in for a row like the one we had at Cotoche. And while they were standing around in this fashion, many other Indians came up, dressed in very ragged blankets, carrying dry reeds, which they deposited on a flat place. And after them came two companies of Indian bowmen, with lances and shields and stones, clad in cotton armor, in formation, each company with its captain, and they took their stand a little apart from us. And then at that moment ten Indians emerged from another house, which was also a shrine for their idols, wearing long white blankets that came down to their feet, their hair very long and tangled and matted with blood, so matted that it could not be separated with a comb, but would have to be cut. These last were their priests, who in New Spain are commonly called *papas,* which is what I shall call them from now on. And these papas brought pots of incense, somewhat like resin, which they call *copal,* and with earthen braziers full of burning coals they began to perfume us, and told us in sign language to leave their country before the wood they had there should catch fire and be consumed; otherwise, they would make war on us and kill us. And then they ordered the reeds to be ignited, and the papas left us without another word. And those in the companies who were in fighting trim began to whistle and sound their conches and rattles.

After reading passages like the above, it is hard to understand the verdict of a historian of the stature of [William] Prescott: "The literary merits of the book are slight, as one might expect, given the class of the author." Prescott also speaks of the vulgar vanity of Bernal, who erupts in truly comic ostentation on every page of his book. The great North American historian must have had a strange notion of human nature if, according to him, exploits like the conquest of Mexico would fail to arouse pride in those who participate in

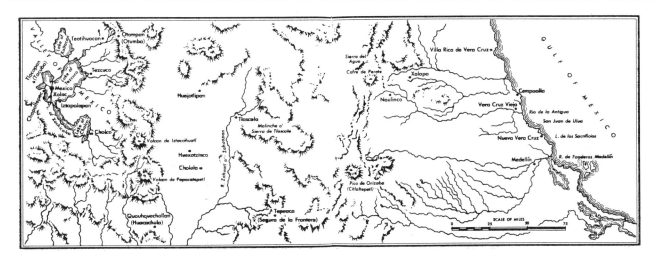

*A map of Mexico adapted from Prescott's history.*

them. The conquistadors were fully aware of the historic significance of their acts, and remarks like the following are frequent in Bernal:

> In reply to what you say, gentlemen, that no famous Roman captain ever did such great deeds as we did, I say you speak truly. And now and henceforth, with the help of God, histories will give them greater importance than they gave to those of former times. Since the beginning of the world what men have dared to invade, with four hundred soldiers, and we were even fewer, a strong city like Mexico, which is as large as Venice, more than 1500 leagues from our Castile, and seize such a great lord and execute his captains in his presence?

If the reader doubts the active participation of our chronicler in the great enterprise, he should read the final chapters of the book, especially the astonishing "List of the battles and skirmishes in which I took part." A man with such exploits to his credit could well afford to talk about them without being accused of vulgar vanity. "And among the stout conquistadors my companions, many of whom were very brave, I was counted as one and the oldest of all. And I say again that I, I, and I, and I repeat it many times, was the oldest of them and have served His Majesty as a very good soldier."

The attitude of Bernal toward Cortés, and the relationship between the soldiers and their commander, poses an extremely delicate question, nothing less than the relationship between an individual genius and the masses. Solís, with his aristocratic bias, answers it bluntly in his words quoted above. Nevertheless, expeditions of conquest may well convince us that he is wrong, that those who participated in them played a very different part from that of the common soldier of our day, and that they were consulted in the most se-

rious decisions. This reduces the singular and outstanding greatness of the leader and makes the mass a principal actor in the epic; it is the mass itself that is endowed with extraordinary and unique qualities. In Bernal's pages this breath of the mass is always throbbing strongly in the urge toward a common goal:

> And this is where the chronicler Gómara tells us that when Cortés ordered the ships scuttled, he did not dare to let the soldiers know that he intended to go to Mexico and seek out the great Moctezuma. But this is not so. Does he imagine that we Spaniards are such as would hesitate to march on to war and riches? And while we were in that *villa* [of Vera Cruz] and had nothing to do but finish the building of the fort, most of us soldiers told Cortés to let it go as it was, since it was now ready for timbering, and we also told him that, now that we had spent more than three months in that country, it would be a good thing to go and find out what kind of person the great Moctezuma was, and to seek booty and adventure.

According to Bernal, Cortés would call together a council of his captains and distinguished soldiers whenever a matter of importance had to be decided: "Our captain resolved to call a meeting of certain captains and a few soldiers who he knew were favorable to him, because they were as intelligent as brave, and because he never did anything without first getting our opinion about it." This should not surprise us, if we bear in mind that when expeditions were planned, the soldiers themselves had a voice in the election of their leader. "And all of us soldiers there present said that Juan de Grijalba should be in charge, since he was a good captain and there was no fault in his person or in his ability to command." Vargas Machuca confirms this state of affairs in his *Milicia y descripción de las*

*Indias:*

> The soldier must accept this obligation, he being under the orders of his chief, although this is a duty that the soldiers of the Indies observe very badly, in the arrogant belief that they know as much as their chiefs and that they, being experienced, have no need of anyone to tell them what to do, and, convinced of this, they fall into a thousand errors for which they should be punished.

Bernal never displays malice toward Cortés. "No captain was ever obeyed with as much respect and promptness as Cortés," he tells us, and he adds that he will call Cortés only by his name, with no other title, because the name of Cortés by itself is above all panegyrics.

> And, since our captain was bold and daring, I shall omit from here on such epithets as valorous, or brave, nor shall I refer to him as the Marqués del Valle, but only as Hernán Cortés, because the unadorned name of Cortés was held in as much esteem and respect, in all the Indies as well as in Spain, as was the name of Alexander of Macedonia, or, among the Romans, that of Julius Caesar, or Pompey and Scipio, or Hannibal among the Carthaginians, or Gonzalo Hernández [de Córdoba] in our Castile. And the valiant Cortés himself did not wish to be known by those lofty titles, but only by his name.

What Bernal gives us is a living portrait of Cortés, a man of flesh and blood, not a character in an academic tragedy. In Bernal's pages, Cortés, without lessening his heroic stature, purges himself, and laughs and jests with the Indians. He does not use lofty speech, but an ordinary and popular one. "And Cortés said he could not rest, because siestas are not for the lame goat, and that he wanted to be with his men in person." "And Cortés answered them half angrily, saying that it was better to die bravely than in dishonor." Nor will Bernal fail to tell us that, in the division of the spoils, Cortés and his captains took the lion's share, especially when the captive native women were distributed, leaving for the soldiers only the old and ugly. The ponderous Solís apparently had this kind of thing in mind when he wrote: "[That he would not] waste his time in insignificant details, which either soil the page with indecencies, or fill it with what is least worthy, thus adding more to the thickness of the book than to its merit."

I don't believe that today this opinion is shared by anyone. The greatness of a history rests precisely on the fact that its personages are men, not gods. And Solís, who has Cortés wear the buskin of tragedy, must have known that the footgear worn by the chief, as well as by the soldiers, was the alpargata.

The greatest significance of the work of our chronicler is for America, especially for Mexico and Guatemala.

The Mexican historian Carlos Pereyra has written pages warm with admiration for the work of Bernal. But it is also a Mexican, Genaro García, the editor of Bernal's chronicle, who levels a new charge against our author. He says of Bernal that he depresses the Indians and exalts the Spaniards more than he should, "To make a contrast, or, perhaps, to weaken somewhat the interest that the Indians might awaken in the reader." That García is mistaken is apparent from a careful reading of Bernal's pages. Our chronicler greatly admires the warlike virtues of the Mexicans. He speaks with immense respect and affection of Moctezuma and his qualities of a great lord. He loves the Indians of his encomienda and is happy to hear that they will become good Christians.

The conduct of the conquistadores [of Mexico] was more humane than that of any colonial force of our day, as is well proved by the punitive expedition of Gonzalo de Sandoval against a subject town of Texcoco:

> In that town a great deal of blood was found splashed on the walls, blood of the Spaniards they had killed, with which they had sprinkled their idols. Also there were two faces they had flayed, the skins of which were dressed like glove leather, complete with beards, and placed as an offering on one of their altars. There were also the skins of four horses, tanned and very well preserved, with hair and shoes, hanging as an offering to their idols in the main temple. And there were many garments of the Spaniards they had killed and offered to the same idols. And on a wall of the house where the Spaniards had been held captive, these words were written in charcoal: 'Here the luckless Juan Yuste was imprisoned, with many others of his company.' This Juan Yuste was one of the horsemen killed there, one of the persons of quality that Narváez had brought. All of this filled Sandoval and his men with pity, but there was nothing to be done about it except to treat the people of the town with kindness, for they had not waited, but fled, taking their wives and children with them. And some of the women they had captured were weeping for their husbands and fathers. And Sandoval, seeing this, set them free, with four nobles he had taken, together with their wives, and sent them to summon the people of the town, and they all came and begged forgiveness.

I have already spoken of the process of democratization in the chronicles, a process that concerns content rather than style. There is more popularism and a more direct style in the early royal chronicles than in those of the fifteenth-century nobles. The tendency toward elegance that had blended harmoniously with popularism in Pero López de Ayala—less in Alonso de Palencia—breaks openly with popularism beginning with the Renaissance days of the Catholic Monarchs. By that time the conflict between the vulgar and the learned had become irreducible in historiography. And while the so-called mob opens the way in its own fashion in the splendid flowering of the chronicles of the Indies, which reached its height in the work of Bernal, the learned scholars of the Peninsula lose themselves in collecting materials and polishing their prose. Only direct contact with living events will enliven chronicles such as those of Hurtado de Mendoza and Mármol Carvajal, who wrote of the war with the Moriscos of Granada. This preoccupation with form, which is so pronounced in these two authors, in the seventeenth century will go to the extreme of abandoning the writing of history altogether, in favor of treatises on how history should be written, and discussions of qualities that the historian should possess—Cabrera de Córdoba, for example, and Fray Jerónimo de San José. The baroque school will distort the facts in its quest of interpretations and moral sentences. Scholars of the stature of Nicolás Antonio will introduce the niceties of the seventeenth century. But popular historiography will not raise its head again, for it is buried in America along with the soldiers who wrote it.

### II. Bernal Díaz del Castillo's Criticism of López de Gomara's History of the Conquest of Mexico (1940):

According to Prescott, the two pillars upon which rests the history of the conquest of Mexico by the Spaniards are the chronicles of Gómara and Bernal Díaz del Castillo. To me, however, these two pillars, with their inimitable symmetry, are not pillars as much as sensitive barometers that register continual changes in the prevailing climate of opinion.

At the moment we are witnessing a rise in the stock of Bernal Díaz, and he seems definitely to have passed Gómara, who has little hope of regaining his lost ground. I myself, in the XXVI Congress of Americanists held in Seville in 1935, broke a lance in support of Bernal, whose chronicle I was then editing. I repeated the criticisms of Gómara then in fashion, calling him a panegyrist of Cortés, a servile adulator, and heaven knows what else.

The trouble with me was that I had not read Gómara with sufficient attention. I do not suggest that all those who shared my attitude in 1935 feel the same way. No indeed. But the fact is, that having read Gómara more carefully, and compared his work with that of Bernal Díaz, I have formed opinions quite at variance with those I then held, so much so that the present essay turns out to be a lance broken in defense of Gómara, or at least an effort to establish a balance between the two, which today has veered strongly toward Bernal Díaz.

It is well known—and here I accept the current version, for which see the following essay—that Bernal

Díaz, then an old man, undertook to write the history of the conquest. He had already completed several chapters when Gómara's book came to his hands. Upon reading it his first feeling was one of discouragement. He thought that his own narrative could never compete with that of the secular priest, and he was on the point of giving it up; but he continued his reading and discovered, according to his account, that Gómara's work was so full of falsifications that he felt encouraged to proceed with his own work, for the purpose of disproving them.

> I shall use my pen as a good pilot swings his lead, to discover the shoals that he suspects lie ahead of him—which is what I shall do with the errors of the chroniclers, not all the mistakes, to be sure, for if I should note them all the cost of gathering the gleanings would be greater than that of the harvest itself.

Today, generally speaking, Bernal Díaz' opinion is accepted. His ***History of the Conquest*** is the "true" one, as he entitled it—which seems to imply that Gómara's is not, a matter to which I wish briefly to call the reader's attention.

I shall preface my remarks with an observation, to wit, that I do not believe in historical impartiality, in the sense given to it by positivistic historiography, that is, the existence of a definite and unique truth that can be established. When I studied chemistry as an undergraduate—and I make this plea because I am not up on the present state of the question—we were taught that there existed a certain number of elements over and above those that could be identified in a body supposed to be unique. In like fashion what I understand by historical truth might be explained. Beyond a doubt events occurred in a certain way, in a unique way; but to establish them, as in the analysis of elements, we cannot go beyond the viewpoint of those who witnessed them, lived with them, and observed them. The narrator's viewpoint is the simple element of our investigation. When the actors in the events are various, or the witnesses, we can gather together their viewpoints in homogeneous groups; but if there is disagreement among them, there will be a new factor in our selection, which will be, whether we like it or not, our own viewpoint as conditioned by, or limited by, a series of factors as complicated as those we are examining. Contrary to the view that is commonly accepted, I do not believe that observing historical events from a greater distance gives us a clearer picture of them.

A typical illustration of what I am saying occurs in the history of the conquest of America by the Spaniards. Depending on who is doing the writing, and his race and beliefs, opinions clash fiercely, and pens carry on the quarrel as they write. In the Congress of Americanists just mentioned, there was one session in which the members almost came to blows in the discussion of the person and works of Father Las Casas. "What a deplorable spectacle!" said some. "What an inevitable spectacle!" I thought, for if life consists of strife and conflict, the account of such strife and conflict, that is, history, must be impassioned and biassed. We may consider ourselves lucky if passion is kept within noble bounds and if the account of events is not deliberately falsified; but what we can never avoid is that the account of the events studied will vary according to the viewpoint of those who witness and analyze them.

I'm afraid that this introduction is getting to be too long, but I think it is necessary if we are clearly to see what I am driving at. When we admit the relativity and contingency of historical knowledge we gain a greater freedom of movement, a greater validity in our conclusions, since we recognize *a priori* its limitations.

Let us, then, face directly the problem raised by the historiography of the conquest of Mexico and by an appreciation of the two basic texts. In the name of so-called historical impartiality, today the work of Bernal Díaz is preferred to that of Gómara. Why? Is Bernal really more sincere and less impassioned than Gómara in his narrative? I propose to demonstrate that he is not. Is this preference owing to literary and stylistic excellence? Again, no, because, although Bernal's work is evidently unique in its freshness and spontaneity, it is also evident that Gómara's is one of the most beautiful products of the Spanish language. Well, then, why this preference? Why is it that Bernal's book is frequently reprinted, while Gómara's, which had an unprecedented success at the time it appeared, is now rare and is read by few—outside the specialists, of course—in Spain or Mexico.

This preference is owing to what I have already said about viewpoint, that is, to that fact that in the pages of Bernal, despite his protestations of loyalty to and admiration for Cortés, there runs a barely concealed resentment and a furious urge to belittle his merits, while in Gómara the conqueror is glorified. Bernal's viewpoint, indeed, coincides with that of an epoch which strives to bring everything down to a common level, an epoch which looks with suspicion upon men of genius, especially in the field of political and military affairs. Please understand that I am not anti-democratic—if I were I shouldn't be here. What I am doing is to point out certain tendencies of democratic thought which in the terrain of historical investigation have led us to assume attitudes that are patently demagogic. I haven't the slightest doubt that the conquest of America was carried out by common men, who played an outstanding part in it; but what these same masses do when they lack superior leaders to give them ideals and guide their energies may be seen in the conquest of the West Indies, in the civil wars of Peru, and in a whole series of episodes that we

needn't go into here.

Cortés, with all his defects—and he wouldn't have been human if he hadn't had them—was a superior man, although Bernal refuses to admit it, that is, the exceptional character of Cortés personality. For Bernal, Cortés was a good captain and nothing more, a type that abounded among the Spaniards of those days. For Gómara, Cortés was a genius. Today's historians look with approval upon the testimony of Bernal, for the same reason that makes them solemnly repeat any gossip of any servant girl in Cortés *residencia* unfavorable to the conqueror—all this, of course, in the name of historical impartiality.

Things would be clearer, perhaps, if we should recognize that Bernal Díaz is just as biassed as Gómara, but that their viewpoints are opposed, which is apparent when they assess the work of Cortés. Gómara, chaplain of the Marqués del Valle and closely associated with him during his sojourn in Spain, writes a life of Cortés and is paid for it. Bernal, on the other hand, a common soldier who would have remained anonymous but for his own testimony, resents Cortés because the latter quite unabashedly uses the first person singular and passes over the merits of his companions. Bernal attacks him head on:

> And I say this, that when Cortés first wrote to His Majesty his pen dripped with pearls and gold, all in praise of himself, without a word of praise for our brave soldiers. To my knowledge, he makes no mention of Francisco Hernández de Córdoba, or of Grijalba, but speaks of himself alone, taking the credit for everything, the discovery and the honor. And he even said at the time that all this were better left unsaid and not transmitted to His Majesty; but there must have been someone who told him that our King and Lord would certainly be informed of what was going on.

According to Bernal Díaz, Cortés falsified the truth for his own ends, in order to win concessions from the Emperor, and ignored the rest of his men completely. When Cortés was in Spain, "He did not take the trouble to solicit anything for us which might have been to our profit, but only for himself." This is a pretty startling accusation coming from the mouth of Bernal, who was not precisely a model of disinterestedness, and had few scruples himself about falsifying the truth. He continually bemoans his poverty and neglect—this contrary to the documentary evidence we have concerning the closing years of his life, when his lamentations become loudest.

> And I say this, with sadness in my heart, because I am poor and very old, with an unmarried daughter on my hands, some of my sons grown up and bearded, and others still to be reared, and I cannot go to Castile to tell His Majesty things necessary to his royal service, or to beg well-deserved favors for myself.

If we compare Bernal's statement with the evidence supplied by the documents mentioned, we shall see the need of picking our way very carefully among them. He is afflicted with the same unrestrained greed that afflicts all his companions, and he does not disguise it, but makes the quest for booty one of the motives of the conquest:

> They died that cruel death [that is, sacrificed by the Aztec priests during the retreat of the Noche Triste] in the service of God and His Majesty, to spread light among those who dwelt in darkness, and also to gain riches, which all of us in common came to seek.

Bernal's attitude is that of a resentful man. He reproaches Cortés always for taking the lion's share of the booty of the conquest. Nor does he allow his own name to remain obscure in his narrative. Since his part in the conquest is secondary, he has to raise the level of all the men and depress that of Cortés, in order to place himself in the foreground, for it was not only the thirst for riches that motivated Bernal, but the thirst for glory, typical of the men of the Renaissance. At the end of his book he includes a brief dialogue, not fully realized, between himself and "the good and illustrious Fame," in which he does not conceal his resentment at all. "Fame cries loudly, saying that it would be just and reasonable for us to enjoy a good income. She asks where our palaces and mansions are, and what coats of arms do we carve on them different from the others, as a memorial to our heroic deeds of arms." Fame also asks where are the tombs of the conquerors, and Bernal answers:

> They are in the bellies of the Indians, who devoured our legs and things and arms and fleshy parts, burying the rest, except the intestines, which they tossed to the tigers and serpents and falcons, which were kept at the time for show in the great houses. These were their sepulchres and there their coats of arms.

Greed, thirst for glory, and resentment join hands at the end of the dialogue:

> In reply to my request the most virtuous Fame answers and says she will grant it most willingly, for she says she is astonished that we do not have the best allotments of Indians in the country, since we conquered it, and since His Majesty has commanded that they be given us, just as they were given to the Marqués del Valle, although it is understood that they will be not so great, but moderate.

If Cortés deprives his companions of their just reward, Gómara removes their last hope of getting it, for he makes no mention of their deeds. Hence Bernal in-cludes the two of them in his reproaches. He frequently repeats that if Gómara wrote as he did, praising only Cortés and failing to mention the deeds of the other captains and soldiers, it was because "his palm had been greased and he had been paid for it." Gómara's account is false, but the real falsifier is Cortés. "He [Gómara] is far from the truth in what he writes, but in my opinion it is not his fault but that of his informer."

According to Bernal, Cortés is as much to blame for falsifying the truth as Gómara is for relating what he has not witnessed. In all wars the scorn of the fighting men for those in the rear is typical, as is their indignation when the latter describe military actions in which they have not participated. Bernal, in his soldiers pride, continually scolds Gómora for so doing. His "I am not surprised that he is wrong in what he says, for he knows it only at second hand," and his "He was badly informed" are sharply contrasted with the precision of his own recollections: "As I write this I can see everything before my eyes as if it happened only yesterday." A certain licentiate, to whom Bernal showed his manuscript, "and who was very rhetorical and had a great opinion of himself," reproaches Bernal for using the first person so much. Bernal replies that only one who had been in a war was fit to talk about it; "But one who had not been in a war, who hadn't seen it or understood it, how could he talk about it? While we were fighting could the clouds or the birds passing overhead have informed him? Or should he not take the word of the captains and soldiers who were there?"

This for Gómara, who, to Bernal's despair, possessed a style that lent great luster to his narrative. Bernal affects to give it no importance, but he has misgivings: "And whoever reads his history will believe it to be true, such is the eloquence of his style, although it is quite contrary to what really happened." "And let the reader disregard his rhetoric and polish, which is evidently more pleasing than this coarseness of mine." That this modesty of Bernal's is false, and that he was not as indifferent to literary grace as he pretended, is apparent in the dialogue he had with the licentiate, who said of his manuscript "that it is written in our popular speech of Old Castile, which these days is held to be the most pleasing, for it does not indulge in pretty sayings or gilded phrases, such as are employed by some writers, but is plain and open, which is the foundation of all good speech."

Gómara, who was not in the conquest, Gómara, who possesses literary talent, is, to cap it all, a secular priest. And Bernal shares the opinion of Cortés himself and that of so many other conquistadores concerning the part played by the secular clergy in the Indies. All the respect and veneration he has for the friars turns into strictures on the secular clergy. One need not delve very deeply into his book to unearth such remarks as these:

> I wish to bring this to mind so that the curious reader, as well as the priests who now have charge of administering the holy sacraments and doctrine to the natives of these parts, may see how that soldier who stole two chickens in a peaceful village almost lost his life for it, and see how the Indians should be treated and not stripped of their goods.

> And the Indians treated the secular priests with equal courtesy, but after they came to know them better and had seen some of them, nay, all, and how greedy they were, and how they commit excesses in the villages, they turn away from them and will not have them for priests, but only Franciscans and Dominicans; and it is of no avail for the poor Indians to appeal to the bishop, for he will not listen to them. Oh, what I could say about this business, but it will have to remain in the inkwell!

In view of this cargo of phobias he has against Gómara, it is not to be expected that the pilot's lead he spoke of should function with any precision. In fact, most of Bernal's commentaries are nothing but violent outbursts, such as: "Neither in the beginning, nor the middle, nor the end do they [Cortés and Gómara] relate what truly happened in New Spain." "They lie in everything they write, so why should I bother to correct each individual lie, which would be only a waste of paper and ink? Be damned to him and his style!" "And if everything he writes in his other chronicles of Spain are in the same vein, why, I say, damn them also for old wives' tales and lies, however beautiful his style!"

All this is of interest as an index to a state of mind which we cannot ignore if we wish to assess at their true value the valid criticisms that Bernal levels at Gómara. The purpose of my study is not to make an exhaustive confrontation of the two, which would be useful, but out of place here. I wish simply to call attention to the problem.

Well, then, what exactly are the objections that Bernal makes to Gómara's account? On many occasions Bernal remarks at the end of his chapters: "This is what happened, not what is told by the chronicler Gómara." "This is where the chronicler Gómara repeats many things of which he was given a false account." And so on. But Bernal's own narrative becomes suspect as we compare the two texts. Let us examine in both authors the account of Cortés' preparations for his enterprise, or his meeting with Jerónimo de Aguilar, or his interview with the emissaries of Moctezuma at San Juan de Ulúa. I frankly confess that I see no essential difference between them which would justify Bernal's strictures. Bernal, who possessed a great sense of detail and a memory of astounding fidelity, was doubtless

able to note discrepancies that escape our attention, but his commentary is always out of proportion. His boasted skill in heaving the lead is not good enough, as is proved by two episodes that I should like to emphasize.

In his desire to contradict Gómara, Bernal not only disagrees with him in his relation of fundamentally identical events, but he makes Gómara say things that Gómara did not say anywhere, as when he speaks of the Spaniards' stay in Cempoal. According to Bernal Díaz:

> This is the place where the chronicler Gómara says Cortés spent many days, and where he plotted the rebellion and alliance against Moctezuma. But Gómara was ill-informed, because, as I have said, we left there the following morning. And I shall tell later on just where the rebellion was planned, and why.

Well, in Gómara's account there is no mention that the alliance against Moctezuma was made in Cempoal. What Gómara does say is that the cacique of Cempoal, "the fat cacique," complained to Cortés of the dreadful slavery they were suffering, which is just what Bernal says, and that the rebellion and alliance against the Aztec monarch was plotted later on at Quiahuiztlán, as Bernal also says.

The same thing occurs at the occupation of Cingapancinga. Bernal states: "And this affair at Cingapancinga was the first military exploit of Cortés in New Spain, and it was very useful to us, not, as the chronicler Gómara says, that we killed and seized and destroyed so many thousands of men in the action at Cingapancinga." Now, Gómara says nothing at all about the fight, for the simple reason that there was no fight, since the natives offered no resistance and the forces of Moctezuma had abandoned the place. "And Cortés [says Gómara] begged the soldiers and guards not to harm the inhabitants, but to let them go free, although without arms and banners—which was a novel thing to the Indians." The killing of thousands of Indians does not appear anywhere in Gómara, but only in Bernal's head in his frantic anxiety to discredit the other.

Up to this point Bernal's criticisms are not justified, but they have another aspect that deserves more careful consideration, that is, his objection to Gómara's account of the part played by Cortés. Here, beyond a doubt, Gómara's pen ran away with him. His book would have gained in stature if he had entitled it *The Life of Hernán Cortés,* instead of *The Conquest of Mexico,* for he concentrates his attention exclusively upon the Extremaduran hero and always credits him with every kind of exploit, which justifies this indignant outburst of Bernal:

Cortés never said or did a thing without first consulting with us and obtaining our agreement, even though the chronicler Gómara says: 'Cortés did this, went there, and returned from yonder.' And he says many other things that won't hold water, for, even if Cortés had been made of iron, as Gómara tells us in his history, he could not have been everywhere at once.

We must admit that Bernal is right in this, as he is right in his detailed knowledge of events. For example, it was not Cortés who entered the Alvarado River, but Alvarado himself, who penetrated that country for the first time shortly after the landing of the Spaniards. All this is very well, but what we cannot accept is Bernal's constant use of the first person plural: "We agreed, we ordered, we acted," which reduces Cortés to nothing but a tool in the hands of his captains. "It seems that God gave us soldiers such favor and good counsel so that we might advise Cortés in the things he did so well." "And let us say that all of us who were there unanimously encouraged Cortés and told him to take care of himself." However onesided Gómara's vision is when he ignores the companions of Cortés, I think it is more acceptable than that of Bernal, who portrays a Cortés ruled by the opinions of a junta.

I regret that I have no exact knowledge of the organization of the military hierarchy in those days. What we now call a general staff did not, of course, then exist, with its specific duty of preparing the decisions of the commander. But then, as now and always, the decision, with or without previous advice, was the responsibility of the chief and not that of his subordinates. Bernal contradicts himself here, for when he describes the character of Cortés he insists that Cortés was a very stubborn man.

> And he was very stubborn, especially in matters pertaining to war, for, no matter what advice and arguments we gave him about things he had not considered in the combats and forays forays he ordered us to undertake, as when we marched around the lake or attacked the rocks that are now called Los Peñoles del Marqués and told him that we ought not to climb up to the rocks and forts until we had them surrounded, because of the many stones that came bounding down from the forts and knocked us off and because it was impossible for us to defend ourselves because of the speed and violence with which they came, and it would mean risking the lives of all of us, since we lacked the strength, knowledge, and skill [for it], nevertheless he stubbornly insisted, against the advice of all of us, and we had to undertake the ascent. And we were in great danger, and eight soldiers died there, and all the rest of us were bruised and wounded, and we accomplished nothing worthy of mention mention until we changed our plan.

*A Native American image shows Montezuma receiving Cortés.*

All this against Cortés, but it runs counter to the allegation that Cortés was pulled this way and that by the opinions of his captains. Exactly the contrary must have been true, that is, that Cortés was so able and had such address in explaining his plans to his men that they came to believe that they had made them. In this regard Orozco Berra, when speaking of the seizure of Moctezuma, makes a very just observation: "The general had made his plan, but, as he always did, pretended to accept the opinions of others, so as not to be saddled with the sole responsibility if the question should arise."

This is the truth, and Bernal's attempt to twist it is in vain. At the time the ships were destroyed, Bernal himself admits that it was Cortés idea.

> And, as I understood it, Cortés himself had already planned it when we proposed it to him; but he wanted it to appear as coming from us, because in the event that he should be asked to pay for the ships, he could say that he did it on our advice, and that we should all share in the cost.

Bernal is very indignant with Gómara for stating that the conqueror kept his plan under the greatest secrecy, and he gives us to understand that the soldiers knew of it.

> This is where the chronicler Gómara tells us that when Cortés ordered the ships scuttled he did not dare let the soldiers know about it who wished to go on to Mexico and seek out the great Moctezuma. But it did not happen as he says. Does he imagine that we Spaniards are such as would hesitate to march forward to war and riches?

This appreciation of the courage (and the greed) of the Spaniards is all very well, and it's a pity that Bernal should once again contradict himself. When he describes the reactions of the soldiers who want Cortés to give up the enterprise, he has them say: "It would be a good thing if we had all those ships we scuttled, or at least two of them, to use in case of need, if the need should arise; but he, without telling us about it, or about anything at all, on the advice of someone who knew nothing of the risk, ordered them all scuttled."

Really, this famous impartiality and this tested veracity of Bernal Díaz confuses things terribly. If the soldiers knew that the ships were to be destroyed, why do they complain that they had not been told of it? Lying, friend Bernal, requires a good memory. It would have been better for you to content yourself with saying that Cortés at times had followed the advice of some of his captains, but without implying that it was they and the soldiers who decided everything, as if Cortés did not exist. War is not decided by committees and votes, as Bernal would have us believe when he tells of the celebrated meeting of the Spaniards at Cholula, when they thought they were going to be attacked by the natives.

> That very night Cortés asked our advice about what we should do, because he had very outstanding men of good counsel, and, as commonly happens in such matters, some said it would be well to veer off and go by way of Huejotzingo; others, that we should make peace in any way we could; still others of us gave it as our opinion that if we allowed those treacherous acts to go unpunished, we should be inviting worse trouble everywhere, and, since we were in that large town [Cholula] and had plenty of supplies, we should fight them there, where we could punish them more severely than in the open country, and that we should at once warn the Tlaxcalans who were there. And this last advice was approved by all.

Cortés says not a word. Apparently Bernal fails to note that Cortés is the one who makes the decisions at critical moments, as he did at the forking of the roads leading to Mexico. "Cortés then said we should take the road that had been obstructed." But this is the exception. Bernal's Cortés is as dense as his companions are in Gómara's account; but where Gómara omits, Bernal deforms.

A final example, the accounts of the seizure of Moctezuma. In Bernal's narrative he tells us who composed the junta of Cortés, the junta which is the conqueror's advisory and executive organ, without which Cortés does not take a step. Naturally, Bernal himself is a member of it: "Four of our captains, all told, and some twelve soldiers whom he trusted, and I was one of these." It is they and not Cortés who thought up the plan to seize Moctezuma, and it is they who work out

the smallest details of the daring exploit. Cortés—such an irresolute man, of course—does not clearly see how they can arrest Moctezuma when he is surrounded by his warriors.

> And our captains, who were Juan Velázquez de León, and Diego de Ordaz, and Gonzalo de Sandoval, and Pedro de Alvarado [told him] that if Moctezuma should make a disturbance or shout when he was informed that they were going to arrest him, he should answer for it in his person, and that if Cortés did not wish to carry it out immediately, he should give them permission to do so.

I doubt that there is a better commentary on the effrontery of Bernal, which, as we are beginning to see, was in no sense inferior to that of Gómara, than the paragraph in the second *Letter* of Cortés, referring to the lost first *Letter*: "And I remember, with respect to the search for this lord, that I offered to do much more than was possible for me to do, because I assured Your Majesty that I would have him either a prisoner, or dead, or subject to the royal crown of Your Majesty." That is to say, the idea of seizing the sovereign had been conceived by Cortés from the moment he learned of his existence.

With regard to the statements of Bernal concerning the group of captains—the matter of the soldiers seems more difficult now—whom Cortés consulted before taking important decisions, this we may admit, but not that this group was the center of the conquest, the inspiration and encouragement of Cortés, as Bernal informs us. In any event, the criticism I have noted do not justify the burial, the oblivion, and discredit of Gómara. It should be borne in mind that Bernal does not refute Gómara's account in the large, but only in the violent attacks mentioned above. He admits without demur Gómara's description of the main episodes of the conquest: the war with Tlaxcala, the massacre at Cholula, the entrance into Mexico, the fight with Narváez, the escape from the capital, the march to Honduras. And please don't tell me that this is because Bernal tells us that he will never mention Gómara again, for he does so a little after describing the entrance into Mexico: "And since I am sick of noting how far the chronicler Gómara strays from what really happened, I shall not mention it again." But this is beyond Bernal's power and he returns to the attack whenever he finds, or thinks he finds, an excuse for it, as, for example, when he comments of "Alvarado's Leap": "I say that at the time no soldier stopped to see whether he leaped much or little, because we had enought to do to save our own lives."

Before closing, I should like to make an observation which I offer to the attention of some patient student. Let him give more thought to a comparison of the texts of Bernal and Gómara, and perhaps he will find that Gómara gives valuable assistance to Bernal, helping him to give tone to his work, to organize his chapters, and the like. This is a suggestion that I cannot fully defend at the moment, but I believe that Gómara not only stimulated Bernal, but provided him with a model to follow in his narrative. This by itself would be to the credit of Gómara, an author who deserves our attention on many counts. By all means let Bernal be edited and studied—no one could be less suspect than I in so saying, since I spent almost four years working on an edition of his book, which the Civil War prevented me from completing. But don't let a passion for Bernal and the oblivion of Gómara be the fruit of resentment, because Gómara's work, like that of Cortés, can be disputed as much as you like, but it can never be ignored.

---

**Montezuma and Cortes's first conversation, as documented by Diaz:**

If on other occasions [Montezuma] had sent to forbid our entrance into his city, it was not of his own free will [he said], but because his vassals were afraid. For they told him we shot out flashes of lightning, and killed many Indians with our horses, and that we were angry *Teules,* and other such childish stories. But now that he had seen us, he knew that we were of flesh and blood and very intelligent, also very brave. . . .

We all thanked him heartily for his signal good will, and Montezuma replied with a laugh, because in his princely manner he spoke very gaily: 'Malinche, I know that these people of Tlaxcala with whom you are so friendly have told you that I am a sort of god or *Teule,* and keep nothing in any of my houses that is not made of silver and gold and precious stones. But I know very well that you are too intelligent to believe this and will take it as a joke. See now, Malinche, my body is made of flesh and blood like yours, and my houses and palaces are of stone, wood, and plaster. It is true that I am a great king, and have inherited the riches of my ancestors, but the lies and nonsense you have heard of us are not true. You must take them as a joke, as I take the story of your thunders and lightnings.'

Cortes answered also with a laugh that enemies always speak evil and tell lies about the people they hate, but he knew he could not hope to find a more magnificent prince in that land, and there was good reason why his fame should have reached our Emperor.

While this conversation was going on, Montezuma quietly sent one of his nephews, a great *Cacique,* to order his stewards to bring certain pieces of gold, which had apparently been set aside as a gift for Cortes. . . worth in all more than a thousand pesos, and he gave it all cheerfully, like a great and valiant prince.

*Bernal Diaz, in* The Conquest of New Spain,
*translated by J.M. Cohen,*
*Penguin Books, 1963.*

---

**Henry R. Wagner (essay date 1945)**

SOURCE: "Three Studies on the Same Subject: Bernal Diaz del Castillo," in *The Hispanic American Historical Review,* Vol. 25, No. 1, February, 1945, pp. 155-90.

[*The following is an excerpt from Wagner's exhaustive analysis of Díaz's accuracy, in which he concludes that the author made many errors.*]

What's in a name? Much more than is implied in the question. In fact, speaking in terms of mass psychology, everything is in a name. Only remember the power of a successful slogan in a political campaign. Remember "Rum, Romanism, and Rebellion." A few centuries ago "True Accounts" and "True Relations" were eagerly swallowed by an always gullible public. Perhaps they were true: the term did not imply that others, falsified, were to be contradicted by the "True" ones. The titles of these sometimes lurid accounts of murders, hangings, shipwrecks or other such calamities were simply catchwords, not to delude the public but simply to entertain it.

When Bernal Díaz del Castillo set out to write a history of the conquest of Mexico, I am sure he had just such a title for it in mind, but that during the course of compiling the work, he struck upon the happy idea of calling it an ***Historia verdadera,*** in contradistinction to what he repeatedly tells us was a false one, the *Conquista de Nueva España,* by Francisco López de Gómara. From the day Díaz' work was printed in 1632 to the present a ***True History*** it has been to almost innumerable writers on the subject. Only one, to my knowledge, has outrightly called it in question; the rest have accepted it for what Díaz called it, without questioning the accuracy of its title. If some other writer agreed with Díaz, good; if he disagreed, so much the worse for him. And yet those who followed him blindly occasionally called attention to some patent error.

The salient facts of the conquest can be divided into three classes: First, those concerning which all competent authorities agree; second, those concerning which they do not agree but which can be substantiated from contemporary sources; and third, those concerning which there is neither agreement nor means of substantiation. The last almost always are found in only one writer and the facts in Díaz del Castillo's work especially fit into this class. In his case these add picturesqueness to his narrative and make it interesting reading. Many of Francisco Cervantes de Salazar's facts also belong to this class. There is every reason to believe both these writers used their imaginations too freely. Cervantes de Salazar was not an eyewitness of the events which he chronicled. When he did not follow López de Gómara he used what he called *memoriales,* written by old conquistadores, or oral evidence obtained from them. Little or no proof can be adduced to substantiate these accounts; in fact, in some cases we have Cortés' direct contemporary evidence that Cervantes' informants were stressing their own services too strongly. That Díaz del Castillo generally employed similar practices stands out in almost every page of his work; they, too, recounted his own services. Baltasar Dorantes de Carranza in his *Sumaria relación* tells us that as time went on all the conquistadores became *hidalgos* and many claimed the honor who only came after the conquest. The truth is apparent in the *relaciones de servicios* which were written by many of Cortés' men during the next half century following the conquest. The figures of their companions faded from their memories; only their own remained. This trait is noticeable in the petitions of the men who sought from the emperor grants of coats of arms. Each one seems to have been the most important man of the conquest.

Such is the *hoja de servicios* of Díaz, as, following Luis González Obregón, I prefer to call his work. It is true that he did not forget his companions; he extolled their prowess and passed lightly over their vices. But it was always *I, I.* One cannot imagine how Cortés could have conquered the country without Díaz by his side to advise him and to fight for him.

An exception was made above to the worshippers of Díaz, a now almost unknown writer on the conquest, Robert Anderson Wilson. Wilson did not believe that Díaz wrote the **True History**. He had other peculiar ideas, but on the whole he compiled a reasonably accurate account of the conquest, considering the few authorities he had at hand. Wilson, who had been in Mexico twice, was very observant; and many of his remarks are well worth consideration. He was intensely anti-Catholic, and to this attitude was largely due his opinion of Díaz' work. We now know, of course, that Díaz del Castillo signed his name to his book; but in 1859, when Wilson wrote, the manuscript was still concealed in Guatemala. When it passed to the National Archives of that country I do not know, but it was probably there in 1859. The mere fact that Díaz' name is signed to it does not prove that he wrote it; but the presumption that he did so may be accepted without quibbling.

It is with some trepidation that I discuss the merits of Díaz' work; for many writers, especially in recent times, have considered it the most reliable source for the history of the conquest of Mexico. Prescott, for example, says that "the two pillars on which the story of the conquest mainly rests are the chronicles of Gómara and Bernal Díaz," and in fact he based his own history largely on these two works. . . .

None of the editors of Díaz' work appears to have analyzed its contents adequately, and this task I shall undertake. Díaz del Castillo remained in Mexico until the latter part of 1539. After recounting the story of the conquest and his journey with Cortés to Honduras, he tells briefly the events of the rule of Luis Ponce de León and Licenciado Marcos de Aguilar, which he did not witness in whole. He discusses the preparations for Cortés' journey to Spain, his banishment from Mexico City by Estrada, and his stay in Spain. He then devotes a chapter to the first and second audiencias; and since he was then present in Mexico City, he gives us many interesting details about their proceedings, including some notices of the various suits brought against Cortés and the latter's various adventures on the South Sea after his return. Like most of Díaz' dates, when he gave any, those here mentioned are usually erroneous. Díaz concludes this part of the narrative with an account of the *fiesta* in Mexico in 1538 to celebrate the truce contracted for ten years in Aguas Muertas between the kings of France and Spain. He then tells of Cortés' and his own visit to Spain in 1539. He ends his narrative with some account of the Coronado expedition, the death of Alvarado and the death of Cortés. Then follow his summary of Cortés' character, his account of the followers of Cortés with some general observations, and the story of his own visit to Spain in 1550. At the end is a chapter dealing with the history of Mexico and Guatemala after 1540. This part of the manuscript is badly mutilated. The conquest proper, to August 13, 1521, occupies all of the first volume of García's text and 136 pages of the second. Díaz' account of the siege of Tenochtitlán is the most important part of the **Historia** because he was in the city with Cortés; and while he did not accompany some of the numerous forays of Cortés, Sandoval and others, still he could have heard about them at the time. Aside from his roster of the conquistadores the rest of the book contains little that cannot be gathered elsewhere with more certainty.

I cannot subscribe to the theory that Díaz wrote his book to combat the errors in López de Gómara's *Conquista de Mexico*. It is much more like an autobiography than a history, and I believe that the first part was written long before he went to Guatemala to live. If this theory be correct it naturally follows that he revised his work much later, as indeed he claims. He first mentions seeing Gómara's, Illescas', and Giovio's accounts while he was writing his book. He enlarges on this theme later by telling how, while copying his work clearly, he showed it to two *licenciados,* who took two days to read it. He told them not to make any changes in it because all he wrote was true. They replied that it was written in good Castilian and marveled at his memory, but thought it would have been more appropriate if some one else had recounted his own feats and that he should call as witnesses other chroniclers to justify his statements about what he had not himself seen. He then refers to the letters written by Cortés and Mendoza in 1539 and states that he carried *probanzas* of his services which he presented with them before the Council of the Indies. When we examine the letter of Cortés we find that he states that Díaz carried with him a *relación.*

As one who has seen hundreds of such *relaciones* I may explain their nature and the necessity for presenting them. A *relación de servicios* was an *ex parte* statement of his services by the claimant, usually declaring that he had served at his own expense and had not been rewarded. "Rewarded" as a rule meant suitably so. It is not known just when it became obligatory for an applicant for a high position to file a *relación de servicios* with certifications from those under whom he had served, but in Díaz' time most, if not all such *relaciones* were filed in connection with requests for encomiendas of Indians. For just this reason Díaz del Castillo prepared his. Inasmuch as he filed with it his letters of recommendation from Cortés and Mendoza, it is probable that he also submitted other letters. Díaz' *probanza* is extant and has been printed. It is not a *relación de servicios,* but was presented to show the encomiendas which had been granted to him and how they had been taken away. A *probanza* or *información* was another *ex parte* proceeding, taken under oath. Witnesses were called and an interrogatory was presented to them to bring out the points the party wished to prove. A *probanza* was carried out under oath to clarify facts which it was desirable to set forth in perpetuity, and that is exactly what Díaz del Castillo calls this document; but he used the plural, intimating that he presented more than one.

Thus we see that as early as 1539 Díaz had written down in some form his complaints about his loss of encomiendas and very proabably he had also presented a *relación* of his services, as stated by Cortés in his letter of 1539. Since Díaz had been endeavoring to obtain redress from the audiences and from Mendoza it is likely that he had filed with them similar documents much earlier. I believe, therefore, that he had written his reminiscences in this form long before 1539 and that these documents, of which he said he kept copies, formed the basis of the ***Historia verdadera.*** In this way one may account for his remarkable "memory" of the events of the conquest. Díaz may have had another aid. In explaining how he was able to remember so much of what happened forty years earlier, and after speaking of his presentation of his documents before the Council of the Indies in 1540, he remarked that it was easy to remember his companions because there were altogether only 550, all of whom knew each other. He spoke especially about those who were killed, wounded, or missing. Later Díaz discusses this question, which seemed to worry him a great deal, in these words: "Let us make here a comparison. Let us assume that a valorous captain sets out from Castile to war against the Moors and Turks with 20,000 soldiers. After fixing his camp he sends captains with men to differ-

ent places. After the battle they return to the camp and give an account of those killed, wounded, or prisoners. So when we went with Cortés together, in the battles we knew who had been killed or wounded and of those sent to other provinces." If this means anything, it means that Cortés set down lists of his losses after the battles and by inference Díaz saw them. Perhaps he copied them.

Díaz then speaks of later information, about 1551, after his return from Spain. He says that the conquistadores in Mexico agreed to send *procuradores* to Spain and wrote to him in Guatemala. He mentions the authors of the letters, Juan de Limpias Carbajal, Andrés de Tapia and Pedro Moreno Medrano, who furnished him with the names of the persons who had joined in the agreement. He says he showed these letters to the conquistadores in Guatemala. From this letter he no doubt obtained information about those still alive, and these may be the men he says he corresponded with to obtain information about events he had forgotten. One of the obsessions of Díaz was that he was the oldest conquistador then living among only five of Cortés' companions and eleven of those of Narváez still alive. In making the first statement he probably meant that he was the only one alive who had been on all three expeditions. Of the list of the thirty-one members of the Hernández de Córdoba expedition I have found only six who took part in the Grijalva expedition, but there were no doubt others. All but one of these came with Cortés as well. I do not think any of them was alive at the time Díaz wrote but there were a number of Cortés' men still living. It should be noted, of course, that we do not know the names of all those who accompanied Hernández de Córdoba or Grijalva. The only one Díaz mentions as still alive is Martín López, but there were others, such as Diego de Coría, who lived long after Díaz. In view of Díaz' absence from Mexico since 1541, it is not to be wondered at that he could not keep track of all his old associates. He seems to have had the habit of stating that a man had been killed by the Indians when he did not know anything about him. He was probably right in most cases; and he may have had, as suggested above, more information on the subject than we now have available from other sources.

If Díaz' book had any object beyond that of recounting his own adventures, it was to enter a vigorous protest against the failure of Cortés, and afterward especially of Gómara, to give due credit to the soldiers who had accompanied Cortés, of whom naturally he was one. Except for two passages, there is no good evidence in Díaz' work that he ever saw the printed letters of Cortés. After speaking of Cortés' soldiers Díaz continues: "This says Bernal Díaz del Castillo, the author of this account: If Cortés had written this the first time that he gave an account of the affairs of New Spain it would have been well, but on that occasion when he wrote he took all the honor and glory of the conquest to himself and gave no account of us. . . ." This I take to have been a direct reference to the second letter of Cortés. Again, writing of the Honduras expedition, Díaz says he afterward saw a printed account of it.

The book contains a curious mixture of the most extravagant praise of Cortés with criticisms of him, sometimes even bitter. Díaz frequently mentions the failure of Cortés to acknowledge the services of his companions, and he is also very critical of Cortés' division of the loot, especially of good-looking women. The habit of the officers of taking all of these was one of Díaz' chief complaints. His numerous criticisms of Gómara are to a large extent based on the same neglect attributed to Cortés in not allotting a due share of the glory to the common soldiers. If one takes the trouble to compare his statements of the alleged errors of Gómara with the actual facts, most of the differences are of the most trivial character. Many of such statements were taken from Cortés' letters and in such cases I prefer to accept Cortés' testimony to that of Díaz. It is possible that in this roundabout method, Díaz was criticizing his commander. In many cases it is impossible to say which author is right since we have no contemporary evidence with which to compare them. In other cases we do have such evidence in the *residencia* documents, and there we find Díaz mistaken. It is probably due to the reverential attitude of Díaz' editors in recent years that none of them has made any attempt to check up the facts in his account. It is true that it has only been in the last hundred years that we have had any contemporary documents with which to compare it, except Cortés' own letters, and many of these have only been printed within the last fifty years. With trifling exceptions, all the biographers of Cortés have used only secondary sources. None has thoroughly examined the contemporary evidence. If so, numberless errors committed by Díaz del Castillo would have been found.

It appears from Díaz' rather numerous references to Cortés' letters, and especially to one in print, that he had seen them and perhaps had made use of them. He tells us that he read some of them before they were sent. He especially refers to one which he says filled twenty-one pages and declared that he also read it before it was dispatched. From the statement that in this letter Cortés asked a license of the emperor to go to Cuba to seize Velásquez, it must have been the one of 1524, since that is the only one in which this is mentioned. Díaz, however, is writing of an earlier period, and it may be that the letter he saw is now lost. He speaks as if Ávila took it in 1522, for he says that Ávila and Quiñones left Veracruz on December 20 of that year. There is some evidence that Cortés sent by Rivera, who also left in 1522, another letter, written after May 20. This letter of Cortés is now lost. The one of 1520 is briefly mentioned, and elsewhere Díaz

referred to other letters of Cortés without saying he had read them. At the time of writing the letter of 1522 sent by Rivera, Díaz says most of the conquistadores wrote a joint letter with Cortés, Fray Melgarejo, and Alderete, lauding Cortés. Cortés, in his letter of October 15, 1524, says that he sent a letter to the king by Rivera relating what had happened after his second letter was dispatched. By the second letter he probably meant that of May, 1522, now usually known as the third. Rivera arrived at Seville shortly before November 8, 1522, and consequently he could hardly have left Veracruz after August. Therefore, Díaz is mistaken in saying he departed on December 20. Alderete left with Ávila and died on the voyage after sailing from Veracruz. Díaz appears to have been very badly mixed.

A very strange statement occurs about an expedition with Mazariegos during the Honduras campaign. Díaz says: "I would not write thus . . . in order not to appear to be bragging about this, but it was known in all the camp and I even saw it afterward in print in some letters and relations which Cortés wrote." This passage carries with it some interesting implications. Cortés wrote a *relación,* now lost, from Truxillo in 1525. It is what I call the *Quinta.* After his return to Mexico in 1526 he wrote another, which I call the *Sexta.* No evidence exists that either of these was published at the time, the *Sexta* only having been printed some one hundred years ago. In this *relación* Cortés makes no mention of this incident, but he might have done so in the *Quinta,* which probably gave a more detailed account of his journey to Honduras. The statement also occurs in the Remón text, and seems to prove that the *Quinta relación* was certainly printed, perhaps in 1526, before the edict to burn Cortés' books was carried into effect. If so, however, there is no indication that Gómara saw it.

That Díaz at times copied Gómara has frequently occurred to me. There are several passages in his book that look very much like it, although the language has been changed so that a palpable plagiarism cannot be proved. When Díaz' memory was at fault or he was writing of some event in which he had not himself taken part, the temptation to use a narrative he had in his hands must have been very great. Still, we must take into consideration that when two writers are describing the same event, their narratives may read much alike. Díaz knew, or claimed to know, that Cortés had given Gómara much information; and he further must have recognized Cortés' own letters, which are embodied in Gómara's book. Since Cortés was writing almost contemporaneously with the occurrences he was describing, Díaz often must have sought to refresh his memory from his letters when available. In some cases he inferentially denies the truth of some of Cortés' own statements which Gómara copied, and some of these concern events at which Díaz confesses he was not present. One case of considerable importance may be cited. Díaz says that Cortés sent Olid from Tepeaca to Huaquechula with most of the horsemen and cross-bowmen, some three hundred in all. Among these were many of Narváez' men, who became frightened and refused to proceed. Olid wrote about the situation to Cortés, who became angry and used some hard words in his answer. Thereupon Olid ordered his men to go forward. Gómara said that Olid did not understand the interpreters and came back from Huejotzingo and that Cortés himself went with the force. Gómara further stated that the trouble arose in Huejotzingo, but Díaz denies that the force ever went near that place. Now, Cortés himself tells us the whole story. He says that the force he sent went to Cholula and thence through the province of Huejotzingo. His captain (Olid) took the chiefs of Huejotzingo prisoners and returned to Cholula, whence he sent them to Cortés with a letter in which he said his men were much frightened at the prospects. With all possible haste, Cortés himself set out, arriving the same day at Cholula. He then went to Huejotzingo, where the chiefs had been imprisoned, and released them. Cortés then led the force and attacked Huaquechula and continued with it to the end of that particular campaign. Gómara simply copied Cortés' story almost word for word, only adding the names of the captains which Cortés had neglected to give. Who shall we say was right? Surely, Cortés had no object in giving a false account of the occurrence.

Another erroneous statement is made by Díaz about the order of Cortés to build some brigantines to return to Spain, after Montezuma had ordered him to leave the country. Gómara says that he sent some men to cut timber for building them but told them to delay the work as much as possible. What happened he does not say, but Díaz alleges that one of the men, Martín López, told him secretly that they worked as hard as possible and had three vessels set up in the shipyard. Cortés in his letter does not mention this incident. Díaz admits that he did not know what took place between Cortés and López. López himself afterward described this shipbuilding enterprise and spoke only of one ship.

Díaz states that the reason the conquistadores did not receive just remuneration was that they did not know how to get it. They finally discovered that it was necessary to go to Spain, as Cortés, Alvarado, Montejo, and others had done. They accordingly sent a memorial to Spain to beg that henceforth whenever encomiendas became vacant these should be given to them in perpetuity. When the first audiencia came to Mexico Díaz says it had orders to take from such persons as had great encomiendas part of them and to put them into a pool from which the true conquistadores should receive the best towns. The reason why the audiencia did not do this was the bad advice given it by the *factor,* Gonzalo de Salazar, who told them that if they obeyed the conquistadores and *pobladores* would find

themselves with Indians in perpetuity. Consequently they would not have so much respect for the audiencia, which would not be able to take away Indians or grant them to those who wanted them and which thus would have less power and less riches. Truly, he says, Nuño de Guzmán, when towns became vacant, gave the Indians in deposit to conquistadores. This seems somewhat contradictory. Nevertheless, it is a fact that Díaz thought that Nuño de Guzmán and the two *oidores* had treated the conquistadores fairly well.

On examining the instructions given this audiencia I find that they contain a clause permitting the audiencia to make a perpetual *repartimiento* of Indians, according to the quality of the persons and their services, but apparently there was a string attached to this power. The audiencia was to furnish to the crown a report of what had been done in this respect so that an order could be given for the convenience of the royal service and the gratification of the settlers and conquistadores. These instructions were dated April 5, 1528.

Díaz, who was no fool, had some good ideas about governing the country. He was of course in favor of perpetual encomiendas. He suggested that Mexico be divided into five parts, one for the king, another for the church and hospitals, and the other three for Cortés and the other conquistadores, in accordance with their respective merits, quality, and service. This, he said, should have been agreeable to the emperor, since the conquest had cost him nothing.

It is in the accounts that Díaz gives of his own participation in affairs that we discern the essential vanity of the man. More especially is this noticeable in his everlasting claims to have been called into the councils of war which Cortés held from time to time. The only such council of war that he ever could have attended was one where the whole army took part. In a number of cases he tells us who composed these councils. They were the principal men in the army—and himself. In view of Díaz' subordinate position, such stories are simply incredible. I can hardly doubt that Cortés felt kindly disposed toward him, for he was a young man and probably had some attractive traits. He was a willing fighter, no doubt, and a loyal soldier. On several occasions he mentions advice which Cortés gave him personally but which he never seems to have accepted. Probably he thought he knew better than the boss, or it is possible that he disliked Cortés, despite the glorified man which he made him out to be. There is a vein of this running all through the book.

While Díaz' work is far from being a "True History" as he called it, it is still the most interesting account of the conquest that we have; and this no doubt accounts for its popularity. The author relates innumerable incidents of which no record can be found elsewhere. Whether they are true or not makes no difference: they are interesting and frequently spicy. Occasionally Díaz makes a statement of some importance. Lacking any other contemporary evidence for it, we have to accept it for what it is worth. The book is badly arranged— in fact, there is little or no arrangement to it. In the middle of some description the author wanders off to tell us about something which happened many years later or to inject an opinion of his own. This, to be sure, was more or less the habit of such contemporary chroniclers as Gonzalo Fernández de Oviedo and Bartolomé de las Casas, and perhaps Díaz should not be criticized too much. Withal, these characteristics would make it much better to call his book *The Reminiscences of Bernal Díaz del Castillo.*

The most satisfactory part of the book is the account of the capture of Tenochtitlán, a fact from which we can draw several useful conclusions. First, it appears that the final result was not due to the valor of the Spaniards, the tactics employed by Cortés, nor the aid of the Lord as so often claimed by him, but to the persistent preoccupation of the Mexicans with capturing for sacrificial purposes the Spaniards and especially their leaders. Several times Cortés himself, who could have been killed, only escaped capture by a miracle. Second, the Indian allies were more of a hindrance than a help. Díaz tells us that on several occasions it was necessary to remove them from the causeways because they interfered with the fighting. After Cortés' defeat they deserted for the most part, leaving only some 170 with the three divisions of the army. Their chief use was later in demolishing buildings and filling up the canals. Third, there was the change in tactics due to the advice of Ixtlilxochitl to use the brigantines at night to prevent food and water from entering the city. This good advice, Díaz says, Cortés adopted and was so pleased that he embraced the Texcocan chief and promised to give him towns. This plan turned out to be so successful that hunger and thirst finally led to the defeat of the Mexicans.

Díaz was continually complaining of his poverty, and in 1551 he received a license in Spain to take with him free of import duty goods to the value of five hundred pesos and six jackasses. A cedula was also issued to the audiencia in Guatemala to allow Díaz to have two armed guards, since he had enemies. Licenciado Zorita also tells us he had a good encomienda. One of his encomiendas was, no doubt, Zacatepeque, which he obtained as a result of a cedula. Licenciado Cerrato, the president of the audiencia, appointed him as a *visitador,* since he had experience in that type of work under the bishop of Santo Domingo.

The *probanza* of 1539 is remarkable for the paucity of questions about Cortés' early campaign. Not a word is said of the fighting in Tlaxcala, nor about the *Noche Triste* and the subsequent Tepeaca campaign. Díaz merely had the witnesses asked about the foray of Cortés around the lake and the conquest of the city. To all this brevity and omission of important services which Díaz in his book claimed to have performed there is one striking exception. In Question No. 5 the witnesses were to be asked if they knew that Díaz accompanied Cortés on his first *entrada* to Cimpancinga, which was left as well pacified as the country around Cempoalla. This exception is singular, to say the least, for the campaign to Cimpancinga was much like that of the "Noble Duke of York, he had 10,000 men; he marched them up a hill one day and marched them down again. There is some question whether any fighting at all took place.

A possible solution to the problem might be that, while Díaz came with Cortés, he remained in Veracruz until the spring of 1521. The letter of recommendation of Cortés is framed in very general terms that Díaz came with him and served in the conquest of the city. No doubt Cortés wrote any number of such letters for different persons and perhaps signed many which the petitioners had written themselves.

There are two important questions:

First, did Díaz come with Cortés? Hernández said he knew it because he was present. Vázquez made the same statement. Villanueva came with Narváez and found Díaz with Cortés. Marín confirmed the question.

Second, was Díaz at the *entrada* of Cimpancinga? Hernández thought he remembered that Díaz was there, because he must have been. Vázquez believed so but was uncertain because some remained in the port. Villanueva said it must have been true since Díaz had come with Cortés. Marín believed so. The testimony of Marín on this part of Díaz services was the least valuable for Díaz. He began by asserting that he had known Díaz for seventeen or eighteen years and was uncertain about everything before the conquest. In fact he only gave doubtful assent to Díaz' questions until the one about the tour around the lake and the conquest. All the witnesses, however, stated that Díaz came with Cortés. The implication of Marín's statement about Cimpancinga is that Díaz was not there.

On the whole the evidence produced in this *probanza* that Díaz came with Cortés is unconvincing. Even Cortés' letter fails to prove it. Any one twenty years after the conquest could have made a general statement that he knew that Díaz had come with Cortés, because, in the first place, he was likely to be a hand-picked witness, expected to answer the question in the affirmative; and secondly, because after that lapse of time any man present at the conquest could be claimed as a *primer conquistador,* which by then included all those who had taken part in the conquest.

Coupled with this uncertainty are the numerous errors

in Díaz' *Historia verdadera,* especially concerning the events during the journey to Veracruz and from Cempoalla to the Tlaxcala country. The internal evidence that Díaz was not then present is startling, if not entirely convincing. Díaz' memory, or that of those who gave him the information, was very bad. This part of the book must have been written about 1550 rather than in 1566 or 1568 as usually assumed. Of course, all this account was written by Díaz in the first person, but that does not necessarily mean that he was present. It might easily have been but a part of his scheme to give credibility to his narrative. He did not, however, derive his knowledge about this part of the campaign from Gómara's *Conquista.* But he could easily have obtained it from old comrades when in Mexico City in 1538 or 1539, or even earlier, in 1529.

---

**Julie Greer Johnson characterizes the presence of women in Díaz's text:**

Viewing the extraordinary events of his early manhood after the passage of many years, Bernal Díaz creatively merges reality and fantasy in his history and thus links the exciting advent of the Modern Age with the time honored element of Medieval literature. The bizarre, somnambular dimension of an era of exploration made this combination of fact and fiction a natural, harmonious one as his artistic interpretation of several female participants in the conquest demonstrates.

The best example of Díaz' use of literary technique to delineate the character and personality of prominent women of the conquest may be seen in his portrayal of Indian women. As a part of the strange yet fascinating American setting, these women were surrounded by an aura of magic which inspired this sixteenth-century chronicler to enchance their roles historically and to fashion them in the image of paragons of Spanish literature. This flare for invention is absent form his descriptions of Spanish women, although these passages are generally well written and contain more precise, historically accurate information.

*Julie Greer Johnson, "Bernal Díaz and the Women of the Conquest," in* Hispanofila, *1984.*

---

## Stephen Gilman (essay date 1961)

SOURCE: "Bernal Díaz del Castillo and 'Amadís de Gaula'," *Studia Philologica: Homenaje Ofrecido a Dámaso Alonso,* Vol. 2, 1961, pp. 99-114.

[*Whereas earlier commentators have praised the realism of Díaz's descriptions, Gilman posits that the style of* The True History of the Conquest of New Spain *derives from Romances of Chivalry. In the following essay, he traces the influence of the* Amadís de Gaula, *arguing that Díaz adapts the familiar style of the ro-*

*mance in order to describe an unfamiliar world.*]
One of the fascinations of the *Historia verdadera de la conquista de la Nueva España* for the lover of Spanish literature is to encounter here and there along the slow broad current of the narrative familiar islands of style and literary reference. Here is a chronicle of the extreme and the unknown—extremities of superhuman and inhuman behavior in an *orbis novus* where unknown nations worship unknown gods with unknown words. How could mediaeval Castilian, a still primarily oral language of inrooted immediacy, be used to tell about such things? Each chronicler of the Indies had to find his own answers to this central question, and if López de Gómara chose the phrasing of oratory and an heroic decorum, Bernal Díaz preferred to approximate the unknown and the extreme to his own day by day living of them. Experience and words are to be as one. This is what he means by adjective so often repeated, "verdadera". It is a promise to bring the story into his own language—"llanamente"—rather than to fabricate a style of forced extremities. But, aside from the inverted pride of this choice (a pride central to the enormous creative and mnemonic effort) what does it do to Bernal Díaz' style? It is not necessary to ask if the choice is really possible, for the *Historia verdadera* is there before us, a witness to itself. The important question, it seems to me, is a different one: what happens to a language so self-consciously familiar, so determinedly recognizeable, when it must deal with "la conquista de la Nueva España" and all that is therein involved and implied? Many things, of course, happen: distortions of words, uncertainties of terminology, monotonies of phrasing—the inevitable graying and blurring of the marvel. Yet, at the same time, there is also a wonderful self-enrichment as Bernal Díaz' Castilian, faced with this ultimate challenge, explores itself and all that it has been capable of signifying. Just as in the *Martín Fierro,* it is not so much a question of saying something new, as of the language using a new world to know itself and exploit itself profoundly. Hence, those familiar islands of style so refreshingly and expressively recreated amid the flow of exotic happening, islands which constitute a kind of primordial anthology of Spanish letters.

Here we shall be primarily concerned with Bernal Díaz' best known source of style and reference, the *Amadís de Gaula* and the Romances of Chivalry of which it is the paladin. Nevertheless, since Bernal Díaz' way with the *Amadís* can only be understood in terms of the larger problem of how to tell the new with old words, it is better to begin by establishing a context. Let us, therefore, examine briefly some of the other literary reminiscences offering themselves momentarily as solutions to the narrative dilemma. A recurrent device—perhaps less a reminiscence than the independent result of a parallel situation—is the emergence of the chronicler almost as a personage of his chronicle. Like the poets of the "cuaderna vía", Bernal Díaz in his own voice continually directs the course of events: "Dejemos esto y digamos cómo el capitán les dió muy buena respuesta . . ." or again, a page further on, "No sé yo para qué lo traigo tanto a la memoria sino que, en las cosas de la guerra, por fuerza hemos de hacer relación dello". On one occasion we are even more touchingly reminded of the voice of Berceo complaining of the gathering darkness. Here the aged writer contrasts the frailty of his 84 years with the agility of the conquistador he had been:

> Y un día . . . vimos venir por la playa cinco indios . . . y con alegres rostros nos hicieron reverencia a su manera, y por señas nos dijeron que los llevásemos al real. Yo dije a mi compañero que se quedase . . . e yo iría con ellos, que en aquella sazón no me pesaban los pies como agora que soy viejo.

Here Bernal Díaz not only displays an age-old "integralismo" but also uses it as Berceo had used it (to borrow for a second time words from Castro) "para garantizar la autenticidad de lo narrado". Past and present experience are here and elsewhere kept in balance, in order that they may reinforce each other, in order that the marvellous may be credible. As we read of wonders long past, the voiced presence of the chronicler directing his story and recalling his youth insures our belief. This naiveté has a hidden function.

A different way of achieving the same end is the approximation of remembered experience, not with the writer's present, but with the eternal realm of proverbs. [Gilman adds, "Bernal Díaz' great and characteristically Spanish talent was for the continual humanization and vivification of his prose, whether by self-reference, by voiced proverbs with all their oral implication, or by the other means here suggested".] For Bernal Díaz can and does wield the condensed wisdom of the language with as much malice as Fernando de Rojas or Cervantes. Here, he is engaged in explaining how Cortés was urged by his men to disregard the instructions of the governor of Cuba, Diego Velásquez, and to set out as a conquistador on his own:

> Por manera que Cortés lo aceptó, y aunque se hecía mucho de rogar y, como dice el refrán, tú me lo ruegas y yo me lo quiero, y fué con condición que le hiciésemos justicia mayor y capitán general. . . .

There is something here of rough military humor, but the ultimate purpose is not merely to be funny. Rather, by inserting the proverb with such apparent carelessness, Bernal Díaz presents Cortés' self-interest and Macchiavellian *virtú* for our immediate recognition. The suggested role of an ostensibly reluctant girl surrounded by eager suitors and the naively self-centered eagerness of the second dative ("yo *me* lo quiero") surpass mere verisimilitude of motive and behavior in favor of direct intuition. The flesh and blood authenticity of this otherwise incredible hero is not only

"guaranteed" but made almost palpable.

Of a more literary nature and perhaps more self-consciously composed are moments in which echoes from 15th century biography and *La Celestina* are clearly audible. It is as if the chronicler had paused to grasp in his memory a profile, a situation, a relationship. The flow of happening comes to a halt, and, there, within a frame of familiar style, we find, for example, the Emperor Montezuma:

> Era el gran Montezuma de edad de hasta cuarenta años y de buena estatura e bien proporcionado e cenceño, e pocas carnes, y la color ni muy moreno, sino propia color e matiz de indio, y traía los cabellos no muy largos, sino cuanto le cubrían las orejas, e pocas barbas prietas e bien puestas e ralas, y el rostro algo largo y alegre, e los ojos de buena manera, e mostraba en su persona en el mirar, por un cabo amor e cuando era menester graveded; era muy polido e limpio, bañábase cada día una vez a la tarde. . . .

Montezuma up to this moment of first meeting has been a distant, mysterious figure, the goal of perilous journeying: "nuestra demanda y apellido fué ver al Montezuma". But now he is brought close up. He is made known feature by feature, expression by expression, habit by habit, as Bernal Díaz adapts for his own purposes the descriptive techniques of a Pérez de Guzmán or a Pulgar. It is not so much a matter of a source or an influence (notions far too crude for such tenuous reminiscence) as of using a ready-made style with built-in expectations and connotations to achieve a well-timed metamorphosis, the metamorphosis of Montezuma from legend to person. A sense of narrative variation and of timing is one of the charms of the *Historia verdadera*.

An immensely difficult problem for Bernal Díaz must have been the conversations of the Indians among themselves. From his own experience he was acutely aware of the alien quality not only of their words but of the very nature of their interpersonal relationships. But, at the same time, neither he nor any one else in his century possessed narrative tools capable of dealing with a culture different at the root. Bernal Díaz' solution is always faithfulness to his own point of view, but when what he has to say makes this impossible, instead of inventing rhetorical orations, he tries as well as he can to imagine on his own terms what might have been said. And he does so with due hesitancy and apology: "les hizo Maseecasi . . . un razonamiento, casi que fué desta manera según después se entendió, aunque no las palabras formales: 'Hermanos y amigos nuestros . . .'". On at least one occasion, however, the nature of the conversation inspires him to give a Celestinesque turn to his rendition. It is night; the conquistadores are encamped in Cholula on their way to the capital; the air is clouded with suspicion; an old Indian woman hoping to arrange an advantageous marriage for her son with doña Marina, draws her apart and hints at a conspiracy within the town; doña Marina answers trying to draw her out:

> ¡Oh, madre, qué mucho tengo que agradeceros! Eso que decís, yo me fuera agora con vos, pero no tengo aquí de quien me fiar mis mantas y joyas de oro, ques mucho; por vuestra vida, madre, que aguardéis un poco vos y vuestro hijo, y esta noche nos iremos que ahora ya veis que estos teules están velando, y sentirnos han.

The fact of doña Marina's dissimulation as well as the old woman's crafty desire to find a rich wife for her son has evidently reminded Bernal Díaz of feminine conversation in *La Celestina*. He recreates the style of its dialogue, however, not only because of its decorum but also (just as for the biographical profile of Montezuma) to hold the situation still for our better recognition. The atmosphere of uncertainty and intrigue which surrounded the Spaniards in the unknown city is rendered by calculated stylistic artificiality. Surely, as Bernal Díaz knew, neither doña Marina nor the old woman spoke in this way, but as Bernal Díaz also knew, his problem was not just to translate words. He had to find ways to translate not just meaning but the vital situation, itself.

The "romancero" is another source for reference and style, but it is used in a somewhat different way. On at least two occasions, ballad fragments are repeated, not by Bernal Díaz, but by the other companions of Cortés who are brought back to life and speech on his pages. And on both occasions the inference is that the ballad is somehow tiresome, impertinent in its oral over-familiarity. These verses are so well known that there is something of Cervantine irony in their rapprochement to the new reality of America. Menéndez Pidal [in *Los romances de América*] describes the first instance in this way:

> Navegando Harnán Cortés, en 1519, la costa de Méjico, para ir a San Juan de Ulúa, los que ya conocían la tierra iban mostrándole la Rambla, las muy altas sierras nevadas, el río de Albarado donde entró Pedro de Albarado, el río de Banderas . . . , la isla de Sacrificios, donde hallaron los altares y los indios sacrificados cuando lo de Grijalva; y así se entretenían, hasta que arribaron a San Juan. A alguien le parecían impertinentes aquellos recuerdos pasados y tan perder el tiempo como recitar el romance de Calaínos. "Acuérdome—dice Bernal Díaz del Castillo—que llegó un caballero que se decía Alonso Hernández Puertocarrero, y dijo a Cortés: 'Paréceme, señor, que os han venido diciendo estos caballeros que han venido otras dos veces a esta tierra:
>
> > Cata Francia, Montesinos, cata París la ciudad,

cata las aguas del Duero do van a dar a la mar;

> yo digo que miréis las tierras ricas, y sabeos bien gobernar'. Luego Cortés bien entendió a qué fin fueron aquellas palabras dichas y respondió:
>
> > 'Dénos Dios ventura en armas como al paladín Roldán,
>
> que en lo demás, teniendo a vuestra merced y a otros caballeros por señores, bien me sabré entender'".

Yet, at the same time that the ballad seems to bring a slight smile to the lips of the speakers, it also manages to touch the center of Bernal Díaz' dilemma: confrontation with a reality that is new and overwhelming. The only other traditional ballad so remembered is that recited two decades before by Sempronio (with comparable irony) as the saddest song he knew:

> Mira Nero de Tarpeya a Roma cómo se ardía.

Again the ballad chosen describes the act of looking at something extraordinary or marvellous—and so helps to communicate the vital situation of the conquistador.

Thus it is that Cortés' soldiers actually invent a new ballad to portray him beholding México for the first time since "la noche triste":

> . . . digamos como Cortés y todos nosotros estábamos mirando desde Tacuba el gran cu de Huichilobos y el Tatelulco y los aposentos donde solíamos estar, y mirábamos toda la ciudad y los puentes y calzadas por donde salimos huyendo; y en este instante sospiró Cortés con una muy gran tristeza, muy mayor que la que antes traía, por los hombres que le mataron antes que en el alto cu subiese, y desde entonces dijeron un cantar o romance:
>
> > En Tacuba está Cortés con su escuadrón esforzado,
> > triste estaba y muy penoso, triste y con gran cuidado,
> > una mano en la mejilla y la otra en el costado. . . .

Here the elements of stopped motion and of pictorial presence are emphatic. The fragment—although introduced in a different way—has exactly the same narrative function as the reminiscence of a past style. If a pen portrait is guided by the tradition of the *Generaciones y semblanzas* and a scene of nocturnal whispering and intrigue is held together with Celestinesque dialogue, certain moments of sheer visual confrontation are caught for us through the "romancero". The difference, however, is that the ballad is presented as the association of someone directly involved in the experience—an association recalled by Bernal Díaz for his own purposes: communication.

Of all the literary references in the *Historia verdadera,* readers in our time have been most charmed by those from the Romances of Chivalry, particularly the *Amadís de Gaula.* Unlike López de Gómara who, according to Ramón Iglesia [in *Cronistas e Historiadores*], deplored "las creencias fabulosas de los conquistadores", Bernal Díaz lived within such "creencias", within the realm of adventure, and reference to *Amadís* leads the reader into it along with him. The blind [William] Prescott [in his *History of the Conquest of Mexico*, 1845] sees for us all when with entranced exclamation he comments on one passage:

> All round the margin, and occasionally far in the lake, they beheld little towns and villages, which, half concealed by the foliage, and gathered in white clusters around the shore, looked in the distance like companies of white swans riding quietly on the waves. A scene so new and wonderful filled their rude hearts with amazement. It seemed like enchantment; and they could find nothing to compare it with, but the magical pictures in the "Amadís de Gaula". Few pictures, indeed, in that or any other legend of chivalry, could surpass the realities of their own experience. The life of the adventurer in the New World was romance put into action. What wonder, then, if the Spaniard of that day, feeding his imagination with dreams of enchantment at home, and with its realities abroad, should have displayed a Quixotic enthusiasm,—a romantic exaltation of character, not to be comprehended by the colder spirits of other lands!

Prescott, the "cold spirited" fireside Romantic, is not alone in his enthusiasm. A writer of antithetical sensibility to his, Alfonso Reyes, uses the same passage from Bernal Díaz as an epigraph to his exquisitely etched *Visión de Anáhuac.* And along with these two, Irving Leonard, Anderson Imbert, Américo Castro, and many others have been stimulated by the same rapprochement of fictional to historical adventure to relive the past. According to Fernando Benítez [in *La ruta de Hernan Cortes*], even Bernal Díaz himself returned over the bridge of this chivalresque comparison to "la primera impresión, la imborrable":

> El veterano que se ha lanzado a la búsqueda del tiempo perdido, recuerda cincuenta años después, en su modesta casa de Guatemala, la imagen de la ciudad reflejándose en sus lagos. Los templos, los palacios, el pardo caserío, han surgido nuevamente de las aguas. El antiguo soldado no traza esta vez el cuadro de Tenochtitlán con tres o cuatro certeros brochazos realistas, según ha sido su costumbre en Cempoala, Tlaxcala o Cholula. Bernal, ahora, apunta una sugerencia rara en él: el sueño y Amadís de Gaula. Es decir, dos sueños.

Admitting the fascination, the almost Quixotic incitement to the imagination, of the *Amadís de Gaula* encountered in such circumstances, it is misleading to emphasize it so uniquely. Let us for our part try to see it in the context of the whole—that is to say, of the continuing narrative problem which led to other varieties of literary and stylistic reminiscence. Bernal Díaz' recourse to the *Amadís* is clearly an effort to approximate the known to the unknown, the new world to familiar language and experience. As such it is comparable to the use of proverbs, to the insertion of ballad fragments, and to the other examples here assembled. So understood, we may expect to find the Romances of Chivalry referred to in two distinct ways: first, like the ballads, as the spontaneous associations of the conquistadores, themselves (associations used, as it were, later by the chronicler for his own ends); and, second, like *La Celestina,* as a model for style at certain crucial moments. That is to say, we expect to find in the *Amadís* something more than a call to adventure; we expect to find its function within the narrative.

Examples of the second variety—the unacknowledged use of chivalresque style—abound. Bernal Díaz, the chronicler, with great frequency in his description depends on that naive use of the superlative so characteristic of the Romances of Chivalry:

> . . . en lo más alto de todo el cu estaba otra concavidad muy ricamente labrada la madera della, y estaba otro bulto como de medio hombre y medio lagarto, todo lleno de piedras ricas y la mitad dél enmantado. Este decían que el cuerpo dél estaba lleno de todas las semillas que había en toda la tierra, y decían que era el dios de las sementeras y frutas; no se me acuerda el nombre, y todo estaba lleno de sangre, así paredes como altar, y era tanto el hedor que no víamos la hora de salirnos afuera. Y allí tenía un atambor muy grande en demasía, que cuando le tañían el sonido dél era tan triste y de tal manera como dicen estrumento de los infiernos, y más de dos leguas de allí se oía; decían que los cueros de aquel atambor eran de sierpes muy grandes. E en aquella placeta tenían tantas cosas muy diabólicas de ver, de bocinas y trompetillas y navajones, y muchos corazones de indios que habían quemado, con que sahumaron a aquellos sus ídolos, y todo cuajado de sangre.

Here the breakdown of the whole into successive declarations of experience and the augmentation of each declaration to the maximum ("muy ricamente labrada", "todo lleno de piedras ricas", "tambor muy grande en demasía", "tanto el hedor que . . .", "el sonido tan triste", etc.) has the unique purpose of stimulating wonder. Just as in the *Amadís* and so many of its successors, the reader must banish all sophistication and enter the adventure. His experience as a reader of Romances is called upon, in order that he may assimilate in his imagination the explicit wonder of what is told. Because he is used to this style, he knows already how to convert the superlatives and explanations into a feeling of his own. The style of the *Amadís,* in other words, is one more means of stopping the past and sharing the new world. And precisely because the **Historia verdadera** is not a novel, because it is so authentically "verdadera", these primitive novelistic techniques for converting a narrative into an experience are all the more effective. A style which in its native habitat, Romances of Chivalry, has been flat and unconvincing to every generation of readers since Cervantes is here deeply moving. It is a way of letting us do what we want to do: to hear for ourselves with wondering dread the rolling of the serpent drum.

---

**Bernal Díaz' recourse to the *Amadís* is clearly an effort to approximate the known to the unknown, the new world to familiar language and experience.**

*—Stephen Gilman*

---

Despite the extreme importance of the style of the *Amadís* to Bernal Díaz' description, it is the first variety of literary reference—through the spontaneous associations of the conquistadores themselves—that so teased the imaginations of Prescott, Alfonso Reyes, and the others. All of them refer to one climatic passage, surely the best known in the entire **Historia Verdadera,** that which recalls the last day of journeying to México and the first view of the city in the lake:

> Y acabada la plática, luego nos partimos, e como habían venido aquellos caciques que dicho tengo, traían mucha gente consigo y de otros muchos pueblos que están en aquella comarca, que salían a vernos. Todos los caminos estaban llenos dellas (que no podíamos andar, y los mismos caciques decían a sus vasallos que hiciesen lugar, e que mirasen que éramos teules, que si no hacían lugar nos enojaríamos con ellos. Y por estas palabras que les decían nos desembarazaron el camino e fuimos a dormir a otro pueblo que está poblado en la laguna, que me parece que se dice Mezquiqui, que después se puso nombre Venezuela, y tenía tantas torres y grandes cues que blanqueaban, y el cacique dél e principales nos hicieron mucha honra, y dieron a Cortés un presente de oro e mantas ricas, que valdría el oro cuatrocientos pesos; y nuestro Cortés les dió muchas gracias por ello. Allí se les declaró cosas tocantes a nuestra santa fe, como hacíamos en todos los pueblos por donde veníamos, y, según paresció, aquellos de aquel pueblo estaban muy mal con Montezuma, de muchos agravios que les había hecho, y se quejaron dél. Y Cortés les dijo que pronto se remediaría, y que agora llegaríamos a

Méjico, si Dios fuese servido, y entendería en todo). Y otro día por la mañana llegamos a la calzada ancha y vamos camino de Estapalapa. Y desque vimos tantas ciudades y villas pobladas en el agua, y en tierra firme otras grandes poblazones, y aquella calzada tan derecha y por nivel cómo iba a Méjico, nos quedamos admirados, y decíamos *que parescía a las cosas de encantamiento que cuentan en el libro de Amadís, por las grandes torres y cues y edificios que tenían dentro en el agua,* y todos de calicanto, y aún algunos de nuestros soldados decían que si aquello que vían, si era entre sueños, y no es de maravillar que yo lo escriba aquí desta manera, porque hay mucho que ponderar en ello que no sé cómo lo cuente: ver cosas nunca oídas, ni vistas, ni aun soñadas, como víamos.

I have given such lengthy context to the reminiscence of the *Amadís* (including in parentheses sentences crossed out by Bernal Díaz, himself) for three reasons. In the first place, we are helped thereby to appreciate the two-fold nature of the gathering marvel. Not only do stout Cortés and all his men gaze in wild surmise at the city, but they, themselves, as wizard-like "teules", are objects of wonder. They feel encased in wonder—almost as if they themselves were characters in a Romance of Chivalry being read by an Indian public. In the second place, we are reminded of the continuing chivalresque vocation and rationalization which comes to the surface in the explicit reference. The conquistadores remember the *Amadís* because, as has often been pointed out, their impetus and vocation—Castro would say, their "incitación"—are of the same stuff as Don Quijote's. In the words of Ramón Iglesia, "la sombra de los libros de caballería se proyecta sobre la empresa de los conquistadores". Finally, and most important of all, we are led to notice the approximation of the *Amadís* reference to the problem of language: "porque hay mucho que ponderar en ello que no sé cómo lo cuente: ver cosas nunca oídas, ni vistas, ni aun soñadas, como víamos". The *Amadís,* in other words, like Menéndez Pidal's snatches of balladry, is something more than a spontaneous association of those who first saw the extraordinary scene. For the aged chronicler it was a convenient way of telling the reader about it, a kind of literary shorthand. On this point we must be both precise and repetitive. Not only does the reference express (particularly to latter-day readers) the breathless wonder of first encounter; not only does it reflect a sense of self as knight-errant; but also it is a way of solving the problem of communication. That is to say, it is a way of helping the reader to see what was seen.

What, then, was it that they saw? The actual things seen are listed by Bernal Díaz in the sentences surrounding the *Amadís* invocation: "ciudades y villas pobladas en el agua", "aquella calzada tan derecha y por nivel cómo iba a Méjico", "grandes torres y cues y edificios que tenían dentro en el agua, y todos de calicanto". This bare naming is, of course, insufficient for the narrator's purpose. All these things must be gathered into a scene, held for a moment before the reader in terms of some sort of familiar composition. And in the *Amadís de Gaula,* remembered by his comrades, Bernal Díaz found exactly what he needed:

> Y al tercer día . . . partieron de allí, y fueron su camino y al quinto día halláronse cerca de un castillo muy fuerte que estaba sobre un agua salada y el castillo había nombre Bradoid, y era el más hermoso que había en toda aquella tierra y era asentado en una alta peña y de la una parte corría aquel agua y de la otra había un gran tremedal, y de la parte del agua no se podía entrar sino por barca y de contra el tremedal había una calzada tan ancha que podía ir una carreta y otra venir, mas a la entrada del tremedal había una puente estrecha y era echadiza y cuando la alzaban quedaba el agua muy honda, y a la entrada de la puente estaban dos olmos altos y el gigante y Galaor vieron debajo de ellos dos doncellas y un escudero. . . .

The *Amadis* in those days was not, as it is for us, a more or less unread text, a mere title suggestive of chivalric ideals and hazy adventures. It was rather, as it was for its most celebrated reader, intensely perused and intensely present, sharply visual. Hence, its suitability to this particular moment. The first long-awaited sight of lake, and city—after the unsatisfactory descriptions of the Tlaxcalans and the distant glimpse that Diego de Ordaz and his comrades had of it from the summit of Popocatepetl—is the apogee of marvel and so of memory, visual memory: "agora que lo estoy escribiendo se me representa todo delante de mis ojos como si ayer fuera cuando esto pasó." How fitting that the vividly familiar scene from *amadís* (familiar because oft-read and oft-imagined) should serve to shape and to communicate the vivid alienness of the scene that emerges from Bernal Díaz' memory! In a passage in which the problem of communication comes to climax, Bernal Díaz' talent for timing and literary reference meets the challenge. Here as elsewhere, the new and old have merged to a single image.

Thus, in a very real way, this one passage from the **Historia verdadera**—a passage fascinating to generations of vicarious adventurers—is representative of all of American literature. The New World must be given in translation; yet in the very act of translation there can be linguistic salvation, recreation of the old in such a way that it means more than it ever meant before. Language and tradition, both English and Spanish, are submitted in America to the proof of adventure. As for Bernal Díaz, it was his honor to have achieved this adventure of the pen with even more glory than that of the sword so long before. Once the *Amadís* had enabled him to hold forever on paper the first marvel of discovery, he goes on with undiminished literary command to translate for us his experience of the whole of the city: plazas, buildings, canals, commerce, palaces,

gardens, and all the rest. The chivalresque superlative can carry it all over; indeed, it learns to carry more than any writer of an authentic "libro de caballerías" ever thought to ask of it. The final view, strangely comparable to that of Valencia seen by Jimena and her daughters from the Alcázar, is given when Cortés and his men follow Montezuma up the great temple pyramid. Seen from above rather than from afar, the resonance of Urganda la desconocida and the castle of Bradoid is nonetheless still audible. For Bernal Díaz goes on translating an architecture alien in shape and function into the turrets and crenelations of medieval fancy. Yet, unlike the castle-inns of don Quijote, there is here neither humorous misrepresentation nor wilful failure to portray Aztec reality. Instead, I would maintain, the view from the temple is one of the most moving and authentically communicative passages ever written in Spanish:

> Y luego [Montezuma] le tomó [a Cortés] por la mano y le dijo que mirase su gran ciudad y todas las más ciudades que había dentro en el agua, e otros muchos pueblos alrededor de la misma laguna en tierra, y que si no había visto muy bien su gran plaza, que desde allí la podría ver muy mejor, e ansí lo estuvimos mirando, porque desde aquel grande y maldito templo estaba tan alto que todo lo señoreaba muy bien; y de allí vimos las tres calzadas que entran en Méjico, ques la de istapalapa, que fué por la que entramos cuatro días hacía, y la de Tacuba, que fué por donde después salimos huyendo la noche de nuestro gran desbarate, cuando Cuedlavaca, nuevo señor, nos echó de la ciudad, como adelante diremos, y la de Tepeaquilla. Y víamos el aguq dulce que venía de Chapultepec, de que se proveía la ciudad, y en aquellas tres calzadas, las puentes que tenían hechas de trecho a trecho, por donde entraba y salía el agua de la laguna de una parte a otra; e víamos en aquella gran laguna tanta multitud de canoas, unas que venían con bastimentos e otras que volvían con cargas y mercaderías; e víamos que cada casa de aquella gran ciudad, y de todas las más ciudades questaban pobladas en el agua, de casa a casa no se pasaba sino por unas puentes levadizas que tenían hechas de madera, o en canoas; *y víamos en aquellas ciudades cues e adoratorios a manera de torres e fortalezas, e todas blanqueando, que era cosa de admiración, y las casas de azoteas, y en las calzadas otras torrecillas e adoratorios que eran como fortalezas.* Y después de bien mirado y considerado todo lo que habíamos visto, tornamos a ver la gran plaza y la multitud de gente que en ella había, unos comprando y otros vendiendo, que solamente el rumor y zumbido de las voces y palabras que allí había sonaba más que de una legua. . . .

**Anthony J. Cascardi (essay date 1982)**

SOURCE: "Chronicle Toward Novel: Bernal Díaz' History of the Conquest of Mexico," in *Novel: A Fo-*

*rum on Fiction,* Vol. 15, No. 3, Spring, 1982, pp. 197-212.

[*In the following essay, Cascardi describes Díaz's* True History *as a hybrid text that combines autobiography and fiction, and that anticipates the emergence of the novel.*]

For readers who felt themselves estranged from modern fiction by the very title of John Barth's essay "The Literature of Exhaustion," these have been years both for recouping losses and for gathering new forces. Barth himself inaugurated the decade with a sequel to the 1967 piece, this one bearing a far more encouraging title: "The Literature of Replenishment." It is true that there have been assessments of modern fiction as penetrating as Barth's first *Atlantic* article, but it must be said that few could match his title. Walter Benjamin's essay on Leskov years earlier may have been more prophetic (given the equivocal workings of prophecies), Harry Levin's prognosis in the concluding pages of *The Gates of Horn* a more measured and equilibrated judgment of the future of modern fiction, but one would have to look outside the domains of literature and literary criticism, perhaps to Ortega y Gasset's *La deshumanización del arte* (1927), to find a title as misleading as that which Barth chose in 1967. The companion piece runs no risk of alienating writers, critics, or readers; its title makes us all feel vigorous and well. Yet the more one scrutinizes the two essays, the more apparent it becomes that already in the 1960s works such as García Márque *Cien años de soledad* and Barth's own *The Sot-Weed Factor* were engaged in a return to origins for replenishing strength much more than they were the resigned reprisals of worn and tired beginnings. The replenishment of which Barth writes is firmly rooted in the beginnings of the novel in pre—novelistic prose genres. Barth's *Chimera* itself drew heavily on the *Thousand and One Nights* and on the Cervantine arabesques of interwoven tellers and tales. With his more recent *Letters* (1979), the epistolary novel (if one may still use the word after Proust and Joyce), one of the many forms from which the modern novel took its first nourishment, has also been rejuvenated.

It is one of these pre-novelistic forms, the chronicle, and one specific example of the chronicle, which is my subject here: Bernal Díaz del Castillo's **Historia verdadera de la conquista de la Nueva España**. What is it that makes Bernal's chronicle such a unique text within the larger novelistic tradition? What is it that ultimately sets it apart? If the work is indeed a chronicle, then of what sort? The answers to these questions, I think, are of broad significance to modern readers; and while I can only intimate the full extent of those implications here, I trust that a re-evaluation of any work whose roots are intertwined with those of the novel is an enterprise that will interest readers of a fiction whose putative exhaustion and vigorous replenishment alike are bound to those same roots.

**James Fitzmaurice-Kelly describes Díaz's style:**

Diaz del Castillo, who had served under Cortés, wrote in extreme old age at Guatemala, but he wrote about what he knew at first hand. He was most interested in horses: he stops very often to say that 'so and so rode a chestnut horse, another a grey.' But he abounds in interesting details: he tells about the first dances in the New World and describes how the soldiers of Cortés capped their chief's quotations from the *romances*. And then he will break off suddenly to say that Lopez de Gómara says such and such things, 'which,' adds the indignant old soldier, 'are all lies—*mas todo es mentiras.*' As against Lopez de Gómara, Diaz del Castillo's authority holds good. He has not indeed the qualities of the philosophic historian; but he writes with ease and fluency. The everyday details that he gives, though perhaps beneath the dignity of the muse of history, add to the savour of his work.

*James Fitzmaurice-Kelly, in* A New History of Spanish Literature, *Oxford University Press, 1926.*

To continue our scrutiny of titles, let us consider the nature of the "truth" announced in the history of the conquest of Mexico as Bernal writes it. Like Don Quixote after him, Bernal has his models to follow, his justice to be done, his own truths to inscribe in the world. Yet the truth he seeks to sustain is not that of the knight errant, nor is it solely factual. Rather, his truth is a function of a vital perspective on the events he narrates. The mere concatenation of events was itself no new achievement in the ***Historia verdadera***; indeed, this level of organization had already been provided in López de Gómara's *Historia de las Indias,* one of Bernal's principal models. Yet it is at the same time Gómara's work that Bernal sets out to rewrite; for in contrast to the "official" history as told from the perspective of the mounted knight, Bernal narrates "true" history: the Conquest not merely as told by but as lived by a soldier, by one who knew the mud of the trenches and who suffered thirst on the parched Mexican terrain. These two interdependent coordinates of Bernal's chronicle are already evident in his title: his truth is corrective truth (the very word order in Spanish, ***Historia verdadera,*** suggests this much); and it is a truth that depends on the lived experiences of the chronicler. Following convention, Bernal insists that his is an eyewitness account of the Conquest, but it is really much more: it is the account of a vital witness, of one whose life and chronicle were, in effect, co-terminous.

As a form of vital verbal truth, Bernal's chronicle is

naturally *sui generis*. But it defines itself within and against the forms of fiction of his day, most notably the romances of chivalry. The romance shares a relationship not only with the books of history but with the emergent novel. The complementarities are evident in the first true novel. Don Quixote sets out to re-enact the deeds of the heroes of romances, and finds his illusions struck down by the world of prosaic fact. In the process, however, Cervantes has mined one major vein of the novelistic tradition: that of critical realism. And as Sancho and the world of down-to-earth reality become tinged with the hues of romance, Cervantes strikes a second vein of the novelistic tradition: that of idealism. As Harry Levin showed so masterfully in *The Gates of Horn,* realism in the novel is the consistent conflation of these two veins, a synthesis: "the imposition of reality upon romance, the transposition of reality into romance." Yet in the *Historia verdadera* Bernal Díaz did not draw on the romances of chivalry as Cervantes did. These romances appear rather at crucial moments, as literary and stylistic resources to aid in describing the marvelous but not fantastic realities of the New World within the bounds of contemporary literary awareness. For Bernal, it is Gómara's history that serves some of the same purposes that the romances did for Cervantes: both are texts to be rewritten. But Bernal competes with Gómara for the privilege of truth and authority. He writes not only as Cervantes did, with the pen, but also as Don Quixote did, with his life. The *Historia verdadera* itself becomes Bernal's romance, for he is as much a part of it, and it a part of him, as the romances were for the aberrant *hidalgo* of La Mancha. A Don Quixote, a Madame Bovary, a Pierre Menard *avant la lettre,* Bernal is a man who has conjoined vital and verbal experience. Unlike the authors of those fictions, he does so without recourse to parody or irony: his is a project neither ingenuous nor trivial, for it is as serious as the meaning of lived experience itself.

Quoting Pascal, Harry Levin characterized the stylistic corollary of the synthesis mentioned above in these terms: "'True eloquence makes fun of eloquence.' True literature, we might conclude, deprecates the literary." Here again we find the rubric of Bernal's singularity. For the final truth of his *Historia* is a function of the interlacing of his personal style with the truth and fact of vital experience. If his narrative style finds a quotient of its truth in the *sermo humilis,* it was Gómara's heroic rhetoric which, in Bernal's view, ceaselessly undermined the validity of that "official" account of the Conquest. Bernal's eloquence does not run to parody or satire, and thus he remains apart from the tradition which, for the novel, was begun with the *Quixote* and which shows its full vigor in the parodies of John Barth. In Gómara's history, Bernal finds a firmly established written basis for his own text, and it is from the interaction of that official history and Bernal's life that the "eloquence" of the *Historia verdad-*

*era* is born. Yet Gómara's text is more than a negative example for Bernal. It is not only representative of the "official" and therefore false version of the Conquest; it is at the same time his model, and it is this model and ones like it which Bernal takes as the concordance of his truth. If Gómara's text in itself lacked validity, and had the elevated style to prove just that, it remained nonetheless an indelible point of reference for Bernal, capable of corroborating the validity of his own account. Yet where the demands of truth are greatest, where language confronts the radically unfamiliar spectacles of the New World, neither the eloquent *sermo humilis* nor the official style of Gómara could suffice to render that truth credible.

If it is indeed true that truth is stranger than fiction, then that proverbial dictum pertains with uncanny accuracy to what are among the most memorable passages of the *Historia verdadera.* For precisely where Bernal faces the marvels of the New World—such as the view of the city in the lake—he turns not to the polished rhetoric of a Gómara but to the romances of chivalry and the popular ballads. These are his primary aids in describing a world both marvelously new and intimately familiar in terms of the awareness of contemporary readers. Bernal had lived these experiences; indeed, he had lived them in and through the language of the ballads and the romances of chivalry; both stylistically and in overt allusion they bridge the gap between the *sarmo humilis* and the rhetorical prose of Gómara, and they do this in moments where neither style could portray vital experience. In the words of Stephen Gilman, "Bernal goes on translating an architecture alien in shape and function into the turrets and crenelations of medieval fancy."

If in Bernal's relationship to Gómara's history and to the *libros de caballerías* there is always some degree of approximation or divergence, no such conditions pertain as regards his own spontaneous style throughout most of the narrative passages of the *Historia.* For in the realm where truth and experience are one, style is inseparable from either of those terms. Just as Don Quixote is eponymous for Cervantes' novel, so too is there an indivisibility between Bernal Díaz del Castillo and his *Historia verdadera,* and this unity is everywhere evident in terms of style. With but a change of context, Gilman's central statement about the *Historia verdadera* could be applied to the *Quixote:* "Experience and words are to be as one". If Don Quixote dedicates himself to the reassuring proposition that resemblances and signs have *not* dissolved their alliance, Bernal needs no such a priori limitation in writing the Historia. When, in the verbal process of composing his history, limiting conditions did intervene, Bernal drew from them an even deeper relationship between his written history and the events of his own life. As the text has come down to us, the *Historia verdadera* is the unfinished account of the Conquest of

Mexico—the events of Bernal's young manhood—as told by Bernal when he is well into his eighty-fourth year. In the half-century interim, however, we cannot imagine that Bernal remained silent about the Conquest; certain inconsistencies and contradictions in the text which have puzzled scholars are evidence of this. On the contrary: the text of his account is formed from the slow decay of the impressions that accompany actual experience, and from their simultaneous reconstruction in the memory, through numerous retellings. There is much evidence of an oral style in the written prose of the *Historia verdadera,* yet to relate this solely to the demands of any particular level of style is to ignore the process of its composition. World and existence, telling and living, are one.

Ortega y Gasset's well-known statement about approximating literature and life from the philosopher's point of view could well apply directly to the *Historia verdadera.* Each man is the novelist of himself, Ortega proposed, and for Bernal that process of self-creation is manifestly evident in the attraction that events fifty years old have maintained through the process of their continued oral and written narration. If on one score Bernal resembles Cervantes' character, on another he resembles the novelist himself—although for this comparison one would fare better with James Joyce or Marcel Proust as the paradigm than with Cervantes. George D. Painter suggested that Proust's novel is in fact more a creative autobiography than a fiction. If the assertion that autobiography and fiction are one turns out to be too large for Proust, and untrue for Cervantes, it does contain a kernel of truth that applies to the *Historia verdadera:* word and experience are conjoined not simply in the past but in the narration itself; narration prolongs past experience as a part of present life.

The proximity of literature and life is perhaps best revealed not by an examination of the correspondences between the two, but by a consideration of what it is that separates them. For it is precisely the passage of time and the transfiguration of experience into memories that at once marks the disjunction and imposes the need to reconstitute experience in narrative form. Somewhat paradoxically, it is the awareness of the distance between literature and life that in many novelists has brought their closest approximation. Proust knew himself well enough, and knew the craft of writing well enough, to comment [in *Contre Sainte-Beuve, Suivi de nouveaux mélanges*] that "A book is the product of another self than the one we display in our habits. . . . If we would try to comprehend it, we can do so by seeking to re-create it in ourself to the very depth of our being." In Proust, this attempt takes the form of a *recherche du temps perdu,* and with it comes a poignant realization of the gulf that separates memory and experience, literature and life; in the double meaning of Proust's title, that search is also time wasted. In-

deed, the spaces between those terms can be filled with more than a thousand pages and never be exhausted. At the same time the parameters of human life remain so intransigent that they heighten an awareness of life's coexistent possibilities and limitations. Walter Benjamin wrote of Proust [in *Illuminations*] that "he is filled with the insight that none of us has time to live the true dramas of the life that we are destined for. This is what ages us—this and nothing else." Bernal Díaz grew old elaborating the *Historia verdadera,* and sensed that his destiny was with the past. Carlos Fuentes once remarked [in a lecture et Harvard University, 21 April 1980] in this regard that the *Historia verdadera* was Bernal's failed epic: as Bernal tells of the exploits and hardships of the Conquistadors he once again places destiny before him; on every page of his chronicle Bernal seeks that destiny, and it eludes him, precisely because it is past. Such is the cruelty of memory.

Of all the distances traversed in Bernal's account of the Conquest, of all the hours spent in preparation for the sieges, of all the battles won, of all the time and human energy wasted, none was as great in magnitude as the space which separated past and present for Bernal, and however close he may have been to his memories of the Conquest he could never revive experience in pristine form. His memory was prodigious, to be sure, and through it the smallest details in the *Historia verdadera* seem to have retained much of the original force of experience. Yet the magnetic attraction that these details have for him is an attraction galvanized through memory: only because they are no longer a part of him is he drawn to them so strongly. And perhaps because Bernal's memory was so active, building the *Historia verdadera* by a process of slow accretion over roughly half a century, any tragedy, and melancholy associated with the Conquest, such as that of the "Noche Triste" told in Chapter 145, is not that of memory or of time but of the events themselves. Bernal was sustained by his memories all his life, and he was released from them only in death; his memories so prevaded his life that they left him little time to reflect on the years that had passed since the Conquest. Blind and deaf at the time of his death, he left the chronicle of his memories as the sufficient legacy of his life: "porque soy viejo de más de ochenta y cuatro años y he perdido la vista y el oír, y por mi ventura no tengo otra riqueza que dejar a mis hijos y descendientes, salvo esta mi verdadera y notable relación" ("I am now an old man, over eighty-four years of age, and have lost both sight and hearing; and unfortunately I have gained no wealth to leave to my children and descendants, except this true account, which is the most remarkable one").

To speak of the narrative structure of the *Historia verdadera* is to speak of memory—at once Bernal's greatest ally and his most formidable foe. Yet he was so close to his memories that he himself may not have been aware of either fact. If his memory first made possible the very existence of his chronicle, it also determined its formation in crucial ways, among the most important of which is his seeming inability to omit details. It is true that for what he considers reasons of style Bernal recognizes the tedium that extensive description can impose, but even in those numerous cases where he claims to be abbreviating his account, he is compelled all the same to make note of what he omits. It is as if the writing of the *Historia verdadera* consisted of Bernal's installment payments toward the treasure or his life—for he gained no wealth from his participation in the Conquest. At the same time, he pays a debt to a most demanding creditor: out of duty, he inscribes in the register of memory even those events he purports to omit. If it is true that the modern novel begins with the *Quixote,* then it could also be said that the novel was born from the dialectics of remembrance and forgetting. The two are equally important; the novelist must select. Cervantes knew this as well as anyone after him: "En un lugar de la Mancha, *de cuyo nombre no quiero acordarme . . .*" ("In a place in La Mancha, *whose name I do not wish to remember*"). Proust, of course, faced this dialectic from the opposite perspective. Unlike Bernal, who saw no need to forget, and who could not help his own memory, Proust plumbs the depths of memory and comes to invent a new mechanism of remembrance. As he explored the caverns of his memory, Proust was brought to realize the insufficiency of memory when measured against the experience of vital perceptions. Samuel Beckett writes [in *Proust*] that "Proust had a bad memory" and goes on to say that

> the man with a good memory does not remember anything because he does not forget anything. His memory is uniform, a creature of routine, at once a condition and a function of his impeccable habit, an instrument of reference instead of an instrument of discovery. The paean of his memory: 'I remember as well as I remember yesterday . . .' is also its epitaph, and gives the precise expression of its value. He cannot *remember* yesterday any more than he can remember tomorrow. He can contemplate yesterday hung out to dry with the wettest August bank holiday on record a little farther down the clothes-line. Because his memory is a clothes-line and the image of his past dirty linen redeemed and the infallibly complacent servant of his reminiscent needs.

This too is the memory of Borges' Funes, an archive so complete that it can only be described, as Borges describes it, as a garbage heap. Bernal similarly lacks the gift of great selective talent; he can seem to forget nothing. But his powers of remembrance were so large that, more like Cervantes' fictional character than the narrator of the *Quixote,* he was able to reunite memory with experience as one; in situations as fortuitous as

those in which Proust's Marcel encounters the magic of teacup and cake, he was able to superimpose the past on the present as if nothing had ever dissociated the two.

---

**Rolena Adorno on Diaz's justification of the conquest :**

Bernal's very real, very deep ire against Gómara was in part a product of the conquistador's frustration at the harm that the written histories did the conquistador/ encomendero's cause. Thus, when Bernal harangued against Gómara and others for not having been present at the conquest, his real complaint was not that they could not "get their facts straight," but that they could not share the conquistadors' point of view nor write about them in an appropriately sympathetic manner. That is why, in Bernal's view, they presented accounts— be they accurate or inaccurate in detail—which missed the mark ("no aciertan") because their narratives did not capture the perspective, or therefore reflect the interests, of the veterans who had fought the war. Examining Las Casas's activism, we can better understand additional dimensions of Bernal's criticism of Gómara and, at the same time, raise the issue of the generally overlooked importance of Las Casas—indeed of the whole conquest debates of the 1540's and 1550's—to Bernal's literary vocation and production.

. . . [The] just war debate was not a generalized and self-evident background to Bernal's literary activity but rather the very platform on which it unfolded.

*Rolena Adorno, "Discourses on Colonialism: Bernal Díaz, Las Casas, and the Twentieth-Century Reader," in* MLN, *1988.*

---

The novel, it has been said, is in its very formlessness a literary approximation to the flow of human life, and in Bernal's chronicle the life of the past flows, or overflows, from one chapter to the next with no sense that life, aligned to the written word, can be limited by the strictures of narration. When Bernal ends a given chapter, his ending is more often than not also a first sally into the chapter to follow. Inertia is alien to his prose, which carries forth with its own weight; as he relates the past he endows it with the momentum of present experience. Like the "phantom chapters" of the *Quixote* on which Raymond Willis has written, the 214 divisions of the *Historia verdadera* seem to impose their arbitrary junctures transparently on a flow whose force they cannot stop or adequately measure. The *Historia verdadera* reads not unlike the novels of Proust or Joyce in this regard—as one continuous novel, one extended phrase, punctuated and bound only by the printer's conventions. The structure of Bernal's chronicle is determined by the nearly infinite and seemingly formless space of memory, and by the interpolation of over fifty years of life between the Conquest and his death.

The detailed patterns of this prose appear like the designs faintly sketched on the underside of a tapestry, not because they have faded with time but because in the approximation of word and experience any pattern is likely to seem somewhat vague or out of place. By attenuating the grandiose design and resplendent colors of the prose of the official chronicle of the Conquest, Bernal has been able to let writing and experience coalesce. The thread of the narrative is, in its overall plan, that of a linear progression; yet all the twists and turns and detours along the way weave a text that is far from simple in its exposition. The digressions of Bernal's prose are, in fact, so compelling that the principal strand of the narrative is often of diminished importance. Bernal is drawn to digress by the force of his own vital truth and by the momentum of his own writing. As he pulls himself back to return to the duty of his chronicle, to register the events of history which the official text had sanctioned as significant, the tension between the truth of personal writing and that of history officially conceived marks Bernal's prose as with the creases of a fabric drawn taut between two equally tenacious poles. If Bernal does fulfill a duty to official truth, his own writing at the same time obeys the kinetic laws of vital experience.

Here is where Bernal's oral style is most in evidence—in the digressions and interpolations, in the details that bring us, the readers, face to face with the people and events that Gómara only lets us see from afar. Time and again Bernal reminds himself that there is a chronicle demanding to be written, and in so doing he reveals that the digressions from this chronicle hold at least as much significance as the events canonized as important: "quiero volver a mi materia" ("I want to return to my subject"); "volvamos a nuestro cuento" ("let us get back to the story"); "tornemos a nuestra relación" ("let us return to our account"); "dejemos esto y pasemos adelante" ("let us leave this and move along"). As Bernal enters or exits from a digression, then, his prose becomes self-conscious. His own writing becomes his guiding point of view; it speaks of its own action, fully aware of what it wants to do. If, as Robert Alter convincingly suggests [in *Partial Magic: The Novel as a Self-Conscious Genre*, 1975] the tradition of the modern novel is to a large degree the tradition of a self-conscious genre—that is to say of a novel which recognizes its own novelistic status—then Bernal's self-conscious prose is a forthright sally into that very world.

Yet whereas the novel, in the tradition of Cervantes, Fielding, and Sterne, uses interpolation as a means to expose the artifice of narration itself, Bernal's digressions offer evidence of a more personal self-awareness. When Bernal recalls the details of the magnificent life of Montezuma—his eating habits, the human sacrifices, the rare birds and trees of his Court, the tapestries of his palace—he works tirelessly to keep his prose on a rectilinear course. He cannot; his interest in all this is so great that his prose encircles itself innumerable times; it seeks a place simply to begin: "Digo que había tanto quescribir, cada cosa por sí, que yo no sé por dónde encomenzar, sino que estábamos admirados del gran concierto e abasto que en todo tenía, y más digo, que se me había olvidado, que es bien tornallo a recitar, y es que le servían a Montezuma, estando a la mesa cuando comía, como dicho tengo, otras dos mujeres" ("I should say that there was so much to describe, each thing by itself, that I don't know where to begin, except to say that we were amazed at the great order and abundance of everything, and I should also say, since I had forgotten to and since it is worthwhile to go back and say it, that when Montezuma was eating at table, two other ladies served him"). In a passage that opposes the truth of vital (and dynamic) narration to the established truth of official history, and that asserts, in the end, the supremacy of the former, Bernal rewrites the myth that Cortés intentionally grounded his ships:

> *Pues otra cosa peor dicen: que Cortés mandó secretamente barrenar los navíos; no es ansí, porque por consejo de todos los más soldados y mío mandó dar con ellos al través, a ojos vistos . . . Dejemos esta plática y volveré a mi materia, que, después de bien mirado todo lo que aquí he dicho, que es todo burla lo que escriben acerca de lo acaescido en la Nueva España, torne a proseguir mi relación, porque la verdadera policía e agradecido componer es decir verdad en lo que he escrito. Y mirando esto acordé de seguir mi intento con el ornato y pláticas que verán para que salga a luz, y hallarán las conquistas de la Nueva España claramente como se han de ver. Quiero volver con la pluma en la mano, como el buen piloto que lleva la sonda descubriendo bajos por la mar adelante cuando siente que los hay; . . .*

What is worse, they say that Cortés secretly ordered the ships grounded; that is not so, for on my advice and on the advice of all the other soldiers he ordered them turned around, plain for all to see. . . . Let us leave this matter and get back to the subject, for when all that I have written here is carefully considered—for what they have written about what has happened in New Spain is false—I would turn to continue my account, because good rearing and pleasing form is to tell the truth in what I have written. And seeing this I decided to go on with my project, with the ornamentation and speeches necessary for it to come to light; and they will find the conquests of New Spain clearly told, as they must be. I shall use my pen as a good pilot heaving the lead, in order to discover the shoals that he suspects lie ahead of him; . . .

Rather than insist that what we know to be fiction is really fact, Bernal asserts the veracity of his history in opposition to what we thought to be in fact truth, and to his vital history he allies his personal narrative style. The digressions and details toward which his prose is pulled are as much a part of history as the meeting between Cortés and Montezuma, or any of the military encounters between the Spaniards and the Aztecs.

Gómara, it is true, directed his *Historia de las Indias* to the reader seeking a plain and simple account of the Conquest; its organization, he says, is methodical, its chapters brief, its sentences clear and short. Yet the polished eloquence, particularly of the second part of his history (the *Historia de la conquista de México*) betrays a good measure of the topical humility behind those claims. Precisely because Bernal chose and used the *sermo humilis,* however, he is able to narrate with equal success both the momentous events of the Conquest and the less ponderous, although no less pertinent, details of personal reminiscence that might otherwise find no place in the annals of history. In certain ways, the close-up perspectives that Bernal gives us— he will recall the number of steps of a temple, or the smell of the wood of the stocks—suggest the pictorial art of the Middle Ages, an art which knew no unifying perspective or point of view. Bernal's perspective is guided entirely by his own vision, which shifts with the gaze of his memory, and which brings all that it sees into the foreground. At the same time, however, even in Bernal's narrative digressions, his close-ups lend a sense of human presence to his account—a sense not to be found in medieval art. As Cortés and Montezuma meet, for instance, Bernal lets us see the facial expressions of them both—the smiles, the gravity, the perturbation. He describes the Aztec ruler in corporeal terms which in turn bespeak his character:

> *Era el gran Montezuma de edad de hasta cuarenta años y de buena estatura e bien proporcionado, e cenceño, e pocas carnes, y la color ni muy moreno, sino propia color e matiz de indio, y traia los cabellos no muy largos, sino cuanto le cubrían las orejas, e pocas barbas prietas e bien puestas e ralas, y el rostro algo largo e alegre, e los ojos de buena manera, e mostraba en su persona, en el mirar, por un cabo amor e cuando era menester gravedad; . . .*

The great Montezuma was about forty years old, of good height and well proportioned, slender and spare of flesh, not very swarthy, but of the natural color and shade of an Indian. He did not wear his hair long, but just so as to cover his ears; his scanty black beard was well shaped and thin. His face was somewhat long, but cheerful, and he had good eyes and showed in his appearance and manner both kindness and, when necessary, gravity; . . .

The meeting of Cortés and Montezuma is one of the most impressive moments of the entire chronicle, not so much for the pomp and anticipation surrounding the event as for the purely personal terms in which the two men discover each other. The Spaniards, who originally thought the people of the New World to be a lost tribe of Israel, and the Indians, who thought the Europeans to be gods and their descendants, here embrace as men of flesh and blood. "'Señor Malinche,'"—begins Montezuma—" 'véis aquí mi cuerpo de hueso y de carne como los vuestros, mis casas y palacios de piedra e madera e cal; de señor, yo gran rey sí soy, y tener riquezas de mis antecesores sí tengo, mas no las locuras e mentiras que de mí os han dicho, ansí que también lo ternéis por burla, como yo tengo de vuestros truenos y relámpagos.' E Cortés le respondió también riendo, e dijo que los contrarios enemigos siempre dicen cosas malas e sin verdad de los que quieren mal" ("'Señor Malinche, my body is of flesh and bone like yours, my houses and palaces of stone and wood and lime; that I am a great king and inherit the riches of my ancestors is true, but not all the nonsense and lies that they have told you about me, although of course you treated it as a joke, as I did your thunder and lightning.' Cortés answered him, also laughing, and said that opponents and enemies always say evil and false things of those whom they hate"). This moment of disillusionment is a great one indeed, powerful enough to have stirred the deadpan with of a modern satirist like Donald Barthelme. When Bernal lets us see behind all the regal trappings and superstitious beliefs, however, he is not uncovering a vacuum that pretense veils; rather, he strips Cortés and Montezuma so that we might see, along with them, the solid human stuff common to them both.

E. M. Forster wrote [in *Aspects of the Novel*, 1972] that "since the novelist is himself a human being [like his characters], there is an affinity between him and his subject matter which is absent in many other forms of art." Out of context, the statement may seem naive; yet it illuminates the human affinity that Bernal is able to find among all the participants of the Conquest, friend and foe alike. Thus the "shelteredlessness" which Lukács finds to be central to man's condition in the novel pertains with only the most minor reservations to the ***Historia verdadera***. Exposure to the elements is a basic condition of life, as Bernal tells it, and only those who have experienced the extreme harshness of the elements can, in his view, appreciate the ordeal of the Conquest. He writes of thirst: "Digo que tanta sed pasamos, que las lenguas y bocas teníamos hechas grietas de la secura, pues otra cosa ninguna para refrigerios no lo había.!Oh qué cosa tan trabajosa es ir a descubrier tierras nuevas, y de la manera que nosotros nos aventuramos! No se puede ponderar, sino los que han pasado por aquestos excesivos trabajos" ("So great was our thirst that our mouths and tongues were cracked from dryness, and there was nothing to give us relief. Oh! what hardships one endures when discovering new lands in the way we set out to do; no one can appreciate the excessive hardships who has not suffered them as we did". With no less immediacy, he writes of the cold winds of the plains: "Antes que amanesciese con dos horas comenzamos a caminar, y hacía un viento tan fró aquella mañana, que venía de la sierra nevada, que nos hacía temblar o tiritar, y bien lo sintieron los caballos que llevábamos, porque dos dellos se atorton-aron e estaban temblando" ("We started our march two hours before dawn, and there was such a cold wind that morning blowing down from the snowy mountains that it made us shiver and shake, and the horses we had with us felt it keenly, for two of them were seized with colic and were trembling all over".) The shared experience between man and beast is not at all gratu-itous in Bernal: his intense focus on the human world was bound to turn towards the purely corporeal as-pects of human existence, and these were best ren-dered in terms of the animal world. Whatever impres-sion of human greatness that is to be gained from his chronicle must come from beneath, so to speak, from the flesh-and-bones effort and the immediate physical rewards derived therefrom. When he recalls, for in-stance, what it was like to carry supplies like pack animals, he exalts the work of the Conquest, not its splendor: ". . . no podíamos sufrir la carga, cuanto más muchas sobrecargas, y que andábamos peores que bestias, porque a las bestias desque han hecho sus jornadas les quitan las albardas y les dan de comer, y reposan, y que nosotros de día y de noche siempre andábamos cargados de armas y calzados" (". . . we could not bear the burden, and even more many over-burdens, and we went along worse than beasts, be-cause once they have done their day's work their packs are removed and they are given food, and they rest; but we spent day and night always loaded down with arms and footgear".) If the Conquistador is a great man, it is because his work is of such magnitude that he must suffer greater hardship than the beasts of bur-den.

For Bernal, style is a form of intensified, nearly cor-poreal, self-awareness. Through style he experienced himself as a temporal being, subject to the emotional development that comes with the years, and to the infirmities of the senses that cannot resist the passage of time. Style and writing, writing and the process of life, are for Bernal one and the same, and his style is thus rarely fixed: it evolves, it matures, just as he does, in the process of textual elaboration. A *Bildungsroman* in the literal sense of the word, Bernal's chronicle is both an extended lesson in writing and a course in self-discovery. Gradually, Bernal grows more at ease with the demands of narration; with each chapter, his pen conforms more easily to the contour of his hand; his grasp becomes ever more certain, his stylus ever more supple under his grip. With the passage of nar-rative time, Bernal grows as a narrator and distances himself from the lived events to which he was at first bound. In the antepenultimate chapter he includes a report of the various skirmishes and battles in which

he was involved; here, events succeed one another in summary form, with little or no elaboration. They are pure "chronicle," one might say, for they list with resolute impartiality the principal events of the Con-quest in which Bernal took part. As his style matures, and as he himself ages during the course of the narra-tion, Bernal weans himself away from the action of his narration. Finally, he can begin to look back on it as part of the past: "Como acabé de sacar en limpio esta mi relación . . ." ("As I finished making a fair copy of my account . . ."), begins Chapter 212. In the penul-timate chapter he responds to the inquiries of certain religious inquisitors; his perspective is finally "offi-cially" guided:

> Y entonces el mesmo presidente, juntamente con la Real Audiencia, me enviaron provisión a mí y al beneficiado y por mí nombrado, para ser visitadores generales de dos villas, que eran Guazacualco y Tabasco, y nos enviaron la instrucción de qué manera habían de ser nuestras visitas y en cuántos pesos podíamos condenar en la sentencias que diésemos, que fue hasta cincuenta mil maravedís, y por delitos y muertes y otras cosas atroces lo remitiésemos a la misma Audiencia Real. Y también nos enviaron provisión para hacer la descripción de las tierras de los pueblos de las dos villas, lo cual visitamos lo mejor que podimos, y les enviamos el traslado de los procesos y descripción de las provincias y relación de todo lo que habíamos hecho.

> And then the president himself, together with the Royal Audience, ordered me and the beneficiary I have mentioned to be general inspectors of two towns, Guazacualco and Tabasco, and they sent us instructions on how our visits were to be conducted and the limit on the fines we could impose, which was fifty thousand *maravedís,* except for crimes and killings and other heinous things which we were to refer to the Royal Audience itself. And they also ordered us to describe the lands and the two towns, which we inspected as best we could, and we sent them the transcripts of the trials and of the description of the provinces and an account of all that we had done.

If for the major portion of the ***Historia verdadera*** Bernal's narrative follows closely the meandering paths of remembered experience, it is only in the final chap-ters—and, of course, in the "nota preliminar," written last—that his point of view is sufficiently independent of the narrative to confer any specific organization on it. As Bernal matures, and as his style is gradually submitted to a number of controls, a fixed point of view gradually emerges. In the final chapters, the dom-inant action of Bernal's chronicle is no longer deter-mined exclusively by a continuously shifting aware-ness. As in the passage above, his point of view is finally imposed from without; in this case, it is a per-spective measured against official standards. The nar-rative soon trails off; we are only two chapters from the conclusion of the work, but Bernal begins to construct a narrative governed and directed by a stable point of view. The final chapters of the *Historia verdadera* offer a glimpse of this novelistic form of narration in Bernal's critical evaluation of social conditions in the New World and in his narrative self-judgment.

Recall that the pseudo autobiography of Lazarillo de Tormes, by contrast, begins with a distanced point of view: Lázaro relates from an adult perspective all that his feigned epistolary correspondent might need to know in order to understand the remarkable *caso,* the *ménage à trois,* in which Lázaro finds himself at the conclusion of the last chapter. The point of view is here imposed by the caso and by the fictional "audience," and the narration pretends to give a full account of Lázaro's life according to these exigencies. As a supremely caustic ironist, however, the author of the *Lazarillo* could not help also distancing himself from those demands; he has his own bitterly critical purpose in relating the "full account" of Lázaro's life.

In Chapter 212 of the *Historia verdadera* Bernal acquiesces to the request of two *licenciados* who wish to examine his chronicle: "[M]e rogaron dos licenciados que se la emprestase por dos días por saber muy para extenso las cosas que pasamos en las conquistas de Méjico y Nueva España y ver en qué diferían lo que tienen escrito los coronistas Gómara y el dotor Illescas acerca de los heroicos hechos y hazañas que hecimos en compañía del valeroso marqués Cortés, e yo les presté un borrador" ("[T]wo scholars asked me to lend them my account for two days in order to learn extensively of what happened during the conquests of Mexico and New Spain and to see in what ways it differed from that which the chroniclers Gómara and Dr. Illescas had written about the heroic deeds and the great feats that we did in company of the valiant Marquis Cortés; and I lent them a draft".) Like Lázaro, he underscores that his account is an extensive one; he too claims that it holds exclusive rights to the truth. Here and in the brisk enumeration of events in the penultimate chapter, Bernal aligns his text to a publicly sanctioned standard of judgment. Even though he maligns one of the *licenciados* ("era muy retórico y tal presunción tenía de sí mismo"; "he was very rhetorical and presumptuous", it is by virtue of their demands that Bernal becomes distanced from his own text and sees it as receding into the past. If experience and writing had once been mediated only by the imperceptible workings of memory, now they are also mediated by the recollection of the written text: Bernal refers not only to what he has done, but to what he has written of actions. He defends his humble style against the rhetorical demands of the scholars, he pits his chronicle against the works of Gómara and Illescas, but now his defense is a defense of what he has written, not only of what he is writing. In this way, Bernal uses the

conventions of official history in order to establish a point of view *vis-à-vis* his own work. He adopts the form of the chronicle, the encyclopedic format, the repeated claims to truth, in order to situate himself in relation to the book he has written. Thus the whole of the *Historia verdadera* is Bernal's effort to construct a point of view appropriate to himself.

In arguing for the novelistic tendencies of the *Historia verdadera,* I do not mean to say that questions of perspective, judgment, point of view, and narrative self-awareness are unique to the novel. On the contrary: they are crucial in historical narrative as well. Yet this is not so quickly recognized. [In *Metahistory: The Historical Imagination in Nineteenth-Century Europe,* 1973] Hayden White showed the extensive degree to which the work of the great nineteenth-century European historians conforms to distinctive literary patterns. But much of the Renaissance has been overlooked. In a certain way, Bernal anticipates the insights of contemporary antipositivist historians who claim that there is no such thing as objective, impartial history. Ramón Iglesia looked at the *Historia verdadera* [in *Columbus, Cortés, and other Essays*] through his experience of the Spanish Civil War and saw the question as implicit in Bernal's work: can or should the historian dissociate his personal point of view from the history he is writing?

This question is vexing, and crucial to any distinction of the novelistic and historiographical aspects of the *Historia verdadera.* To some extent, every historian must be as is Bernal, involved and interested in his own writing. Américo Castro said [in *An Idea of History,* 1977] of history in general that "human phenomena do not of their own accord find their proper place in the past. Rather, they are situated by the observer along a temporal perspective that begins at the yesterday of his personal experience and stretches back into the depths of time. The historian—or the chronicler—in addition to the task of dating, feels his facts to be near or far, close or remote." As historian, Bernal feels his facts to be extremely near, too near perhaps; he remembers today as well as he remembers yesterday. Through his own writing, the depths of time are coincident with his remembered experience. But because his memory is so personal he has no sense of collective future, no sense of time beyond his own life. For this reason, the work is no history at all.

Bernal's consistently personal stylistic involvement deprives his work of pertinence to a whole collection of people, to the sum of interests which may gather in a people over time. This confirms the novelistic penchant over the "historical" nature of his book. Bernal recognizes the importance of the past, but he cannot escape its memory; he seems blind to the future. The vital dimension of his work is an effective way of creating and giving meaning to present experience in

**Díaz describes the misery in Mexico City following the conquest:**

Now to speak of the dead bodies and heads that were in the houses where Guatemoc had taken refuge. I solemnly swear that all the houses and stockades in the lake were full of heads and corpses. I do not know how to describe it but it was the same in the streets and courts of Tlatelolco. We could not walk without treading on the bodies and heads of dead Indians. I have read about the destruction of Jerusalem, but I do not think the mortality was greater there than here in Mexico, where most of the warriors who had crowded in from all the provinces and subject towns had died. As I have said, the dry land and the stockades were piled with corpses. Indeed, the stench was so bad that no one could endure it, and for that reason each of us captains returned to his camp after Guatemoc's capture; even Cortes was ill from the odours which assailed his nostrils and from headache during those days in Tlatelolco. . . .

As there was such a stench in the city, Guatemoc asked Cortes' permission for all the Mexican forces who remained there to go out to the neighbouring towns, and they were promptly told to do so. For three whole days and nights they never ceased streaming out, and all three causeways were crowded with men, women, and children so thin, sallow, dirty, and stinking that it was pitiful to see them. Once the city was free from them Cortes went out to inspect it. We found the houses full of corpses, and some poor Mexicans still in them who could not move away. Their excretions were the sort of filth that thin swine pass which have been fed on nothing but grass. The city looked as if it had been ploughed up. The roots of any edible greenery had been dug out, boiled, and eaten, and they had even cooked the bark of some of the trees.

*Bernal Díaz, in* The Conquest of New Spain,
*translated by J.M. Cohen, Penguin Books, 1963.*

terms of the past, but it does not allow for projection into the future. When Castro spoke of the historical dimension of human community, he implied that the historian's narrative must give evidence of its value *for* the future, of his concern not only to remember the past but to shape the coming world. Bernal's failure in this regard removes his work from the strictly historical sphere of narrative prose. As I have tried to show, the work exhibits striking novelistic tendencies. Bernal wrote the ***Historia verdadera*** at a moment when the modern novel was just beginning to find its own possibilities in the resources of the existing factual and fictional genres. Not long after Bernal's death Cervantes published the first part of the *Quixote* (1605). Cervantes' parodic use of the historiographer's conventions, his teasing references to the work of an Arab historian, are well

known. Cervantes called his work an "historia" (story, history). The word itself registers the ambiguities which are evident in Bernal's ***Historia verdadera***.

---

## FURTHER READING

### Biography and History

Cerwin, Herbert. *Bernal Díaz: Historian of the Conquest.* Norman: University of Oklahoma Press, 1963, 239 p.

    The major biography of Díaz in English.

Grauer, Ben. "How Bernal Díaz's 'True History' Was Reborn." In *Bouillabaisse for Bibliophiles*, edited by William Targ, pp. 229-48. Metuchen, NJ: Scarecrow Reprint Corporation, 1968.

    Relates Grauer's ultimately successful efforts to rescue Díaz's Guatemala manuscript from decay.

Wagner, Henry. "Three Studies on the Same Subject: The Family of Bernal Díaz del Castillo" and "Notes on Writings By and About Bernal Díaz del Castillo." *Hispanic American Historical Review* 25, No. 1 (February 1945): 191-211.

    The first essay carefully traces the history of the family Díaz raised in Guatemala; the second annotates lesser known documents by and about Díaz.

### Criticism

Arocena, Luis A. "Bernal Díaz del Castillo." In *Latin American Writers*, Vol. I, edited by Carlos A. Solé and Maria Isabel Abreu, pp. 17-21. New York: Charles Scribner's Sons, 1989.

    Praises the *True History* for its documentation of the conquest and its portrait of a typical conquistador's social perspective.

Boruchoff, David A. "Beyond Utopia and Paradise: Cortés, Bernal Díaz and the Rhetoric of Consecration." *MLN* 106, No. 2 (March 1991): 330-69.

    Asserts that Díaz both drew on and undermined literary convention, thus creating an innovative text to describe an unknown world.

Brody, Robert. "Bernal's Strategies." *Hispanic Review* 55, No. 3 (Summer 1987): 323-36.

    Argues with earlier suggestions that Díaz's history embodies an argument for growing political democracy; asserts, instead, that Díaz pled only for his own deserts.

Iglesia, Ramón. "Introduction to the Study of Bernal Díaz del Castillo and his *True History*." In his *Columbus, Cortés, and Other Essays*, pp. 64-77. Berkeley and Los Angeles: University of California

Press, 1969.

Iglesia's most critical discussion of Díaz, in which he calls the historian "discontented and litigious" and "peevish and resentful."

Johnson, Julie Greer. "Bernal Díaz and the Women of the Conquest." *Hispanofila* 28, No. 82 (September 1984): 67-77.

Focuses analysis on Díaz's portrayal of women, concluding that he depicts doña Marina—the Indian woman who acted as an interpreter for Cortés—as a conventional literary heroine.

# Richard Hakluyt

## c. 1552-1616

English editor, geographer, and translator.

## INTRODUCTION

As a translator and editor, Hakluyt played an important role in the dissemination of navigational and topographical information which encouraged English explorers to set out on voyages of discovery and conquest during the sixteenth century. His *Voyages* (1598-1600) constitutes a unique record of European exploration that provides insight into Elizabethan thought preceding England's colonial expansion. A founding member of the Virginia Company, Hakluyt was also instrumental in the establishment of a permanent English colony in North America.

## Biographical Information

Hakluyt was born in London, the second of five children, to Margery and Richard Hakluyt of Herefordshire. At the age of five, following the death of his father, Hakluyt was taken in by his cousin and guardian—also named Richard Hakluyt—then a student in the Middle Temple, and later a lawyer much involved in international exploration and mercantilism. The elder Hakluyt first sparked his younger cousin's interest in geography by showing him a map, then drawing the young scholar's attention to the 23rd and 24th verses of the 107th Psalm of the Bible, which states: "They that go down to the sea in ships, that do business in great waters; these see the works of the Lord, and his wonders in the deep" (King James translation). Subsequently, a dual interest in exploration and religion was to characterize Hakluyt's entire career as both geographer and cleric. Following his schooling at Westminster, Hakluyt was admitted to Christ Church College, Oxford University, where he was a contemporary of Sir Walter Raleigh and Sir Philip Sidney. He received his B.A. 1574 and an M.A. in 1577; he was ordained in 1580, and in 1583 he was appointed chaplain to Sir Edward Stafford, the English ambassador to Paris. In Paris, Hakluyt became familiar with French, Spanish, Italian, and Portuguese narratives of exploration, and while translating the voyage narratives of Antonio Galvano and Ferdinando de Soto, he became determined to promote English exploratory seafaring. In 1582 he published his first collection of voyage narratives, *Divers Voyages Touching the Discouerie of America* (1582), and followed this with *A Discourse on Western Planting* (1584). Hakluyt's career as a cleric sustained his scholarship, and his literary endeavors brought royal preferment in the form of clerical appointments. Elizabeth's pleasure with Hakluyt's *Discourse on Western Planting* resulted in his appointment as a prebendary of Bristol, a major port city, in 1584. In 1590, following the publication of his most important work, *The Principall Navigations, Voiages and Discoveries of the English Nation* (1589), he was granted the rectory of Witheringsett-cum-Brockford, in Suffolk. Here he prepared a new enlarged edition of the *Principall Navigations*, and worked with Raleigh to publicize and encourage investment in the Virginia Company. In 1602 Hakluyt received a prebend at Westminster, and the following year he was appointed Archdeacon. During the last four years of his life, Hakluyt was rector of Gedney, Lincolnshire. He died on November 23, 1616.

## Major Works

Hakluyt's *Divers Voyages Touching the Discouerie of America* presented legal argument for England's claim on American land, accounts by Giovanni da Verrazano and Giovanni Battista Ramusio with maps by John Lok describing the east coast of North America, and practical advice for potential explorers. His next work, *A Discourse on Western Planting* (1584) gained the attention of Queen Elizabeth I. Designed to persuade the Queen to support American colonization, it was intended as a private court document with the title, "A Particular Discourse Concerning the Great Necessity and Manifold Commodities That Are Likely to Grow to This Realm of England by the Western Discoveries Lately Attempted." Finally published in 1877, it provides the most direct evidence of Hakluyt's own thoughts on the links between economics and geography, and the likely material benefits of English colonization of North America.

Hakluyt is best known as the editor of *The Principall Navigations, Voiages and Discoveries of the English Nation* (1589; enlarged edition, 1598-1600). The enlarged edition of this work, reprinted in 1908 as *Hakluyt's Voyages*, included such new exploration chronicles as the voyages of Sir John Hawkins, Sir Humphrey Gilbert, Martin Frobisher, and Sir Francis Drake. Blending the romance and wonder of travel with the sparse, restrained style of the sailor witness, *Hakluyt's Voyages* was Hakluyt's *magnum opus,* and remains his most celebrated work. Although Hakluyt's motives were strongly patriotic, he also acknowledged and translated many foreign narratives, including René de Laudonnière's *A Notable Historie Containing Foure Voyages Made by Certayne French Captaynes unto Florida* (1587), Antonio Galvano's *The Discouerie of the World from Their First Originall unto the Yeere of Our Lord 1555* (1601), and Ferdinando de Soto's *Virginia Richly Valued, by the Description of the Maine Land of Florida, her Next Neighbour* (1609).

## Critical Reception

Hakluyt's industrious and painstaking scholarship brought him substantial royal favor, the friendship of Raleigh and Sidney, and the patronage of Sir Francis Walsingham, Elizabeth I's secretary of state. While *Hakluyt's Voyages* was used as both a practical guide by explorers and as a spur to motivate the next generation of adventurers, Hakluyt also contributed a significant literary influence: Shakespeare's *Othello*, *Twelfth Night*, and *The Tempest* all make reference to *Hakluyt's Voyages*, as does Milton's *Paradise Lost*. Hakluyt's reputation as an editor grew markedly after his death, when readers were disappointed with the comparatively lackluster editing of his successor and literary executor Samuel Purchas. In the eighteenth century, the practical value of *Hakluyt's Voyages* diminished as English geographical knowledge became more refined, but the literary quality of his endeavors found new favor. His reputation received a considerable boost in 1846 with the founding of The Hakluyt Society, which has continued to publish accounts of exploratory travel. In the modern era, critics such as Clennell Wilkinson have found the appeal of *Hakluyt's Voyages* to lie in the documentary flavor of its "true stories." Virginia Woolf emphasized the influence of Hakluyt's editions on the English language, and detected in *Hakluyt's Voyages* a new, self-conscious literary mode. More recently, the descriptive language of Hakluyt's narratives has been analyzed from a postcolonial perspective, with critics such as Emily C. Bartels providing a re-assessment of the Elizabethan colonial mind.

---

## PRINCIPAL WORKS

*Divers Voyages Touching the Discouerie of America, and the ilands adiacent vnto the same, made first of all by our Englishmen, and afterwards by the Frenchmen and Britons* (travel essays) 1582

*A Notable Historie Containing Foure Voyages Made by Certayne French Captaynes unto Florida* [translator] (travel essay) 1587

*De orbe novo Petri Martyris Anglerii Mediolanensis*

[editor] (travel essay) 1587

*The Principall Navigations, Voiages and Discoveries of the English Nation, Made by Sea or over-land, to the remote and farthest distant quarters of the Earth, at Any Time within the compasse of these 1500 yeeres* (travel essays) 1589; revised and enlarged, 1598-1600; also published as *Hakluyt's Voyages* 1908

*The Discoveries of the World from Their First Originall unto to Yeere of Our Lord 1555* [editor and translator] (travel essays) 1601

*Virginia Richly Valued, by the Description of the Maine Land of Florida, Her Next Neighbour* [translator] (travel essay)

*A Discourse on Western Planting, Written in the Year 1584* (essay) 1877

---

## CRITICISM

### Virginia Woolf (essay date 1925)

SOURCE: "The Elizabethan Lumber Room," in *Collected Essays, Vol. I.* Harourt, Brace & Company, 1966, pp. 46-53.

[*Virginia Woolf (1882-1941) was an influential modern British novelist and essayist associated with the Bloomsbury Group. In the following review essay, originally published in* The Common Reader *(1925), Woolf detects Hakluyt's influence on the English language, arguing that the "extravagance" and "hyperbole" of Elizabethan literature stems from the Elizabethan passion for discovery that was promoted by Hakluyt's publications.*]

These magnificent volumes [*Hakluyt's Voyages*] are not often, perhaps, read through. Part of their charm consists in the fact that Hakluyt is not so much a book as a great bundle of commodities loosely tied together, an emporium, a lumber room strewn with ancient sacks, obsolete nautical instruments, huge bales of wool, and little bags of rubies and emeralds. One is for ever untying this packet here, sampling that heap over there, wiping the dust off some vast map of the world, and sitting down in semi-darkness to snuff the strange smells of silks and leathers and ambergris, while outside tumble the huge waves of the uncharted Elizabethan sea.

For this jumble of seeds, silks, unicorns' horns, elephants' teeth, wool, common stones, turbans, and bars of gold, these odds and ends of priceless value and complete worthlessness, were the fruit of innumerable voyages, traffics, and discoveries to unknown lands in the reign of Queen Elizabeth. The expeditions were manned by 'apt young men' from the West country, and financed in part by the great Queen herself. The ships, says Froude, were no bigger than modern yachts. There in the river by Greenwich the fleet lay gathered, close to the Palace. 'The Privy council looked out of the windows of the court . . . the ships thereupon discharge their ordance . . . and the mariners they shouted in such sort that the sky rang again with the noise thereof'. Then, as the ships swung down the tide, one sailor after another walked the hatches, climbed the shrouds, stood upon the mainyards to wave his friends a last farewell. Many would come back no more. For directly England and the coast of France were beneath the horizon the ships sailed into the unfamiliar; the air had its voices, the sea its lions and serpents, its evaporations of fire and tumultuous whirlpools. But God too was very close; the clouds but sparely hid the divinity Himself; the limbs of Satan were almost visible. Familiarly the English sailors pitted their God against the God of the Turks, who 'can speake never a word for dulnes, much lesse can he helpe them in such an extremitie. . . . But howsoever their God behaved himself, our God showed himself a God indeed. . . .' God was as near by sea as by land, said Sir Humfrey Gilbert, riding through the storm. Suddenly one light disappeared; Sir Humfrey Gilbert had gone beneath the waves; when morning came, they sought his ship in vain. Sir Hugh Willoughby sailed to discover the North-West Passage and made no return. The Earl of Cumberland's men, hung up by adverse winds off the coast of Cornwall for a fortnight, licked the muddy water off the deck in agony. And sometimes a ragged and worn-out man came knocking at the door of an English country house and claimed to be the boy who had left it years ago to sail the seas. 'Sir William his father, and my lady his mother knew him not to be their son, until they found a secret mark, which was a wart upon one of his knees.' But he had with him a black stone, veined with gold, or an ivory tusk, or a silver ingot, and urged on the village youth with talk of gold strewn over the land as stones are strewn in the fields of England. One expedition might fail, but what if the passage to the fabled land of uncounted riches lay only a little farther up the coast? What if the known world was only the prelude to some more splendid panorama? When, after the long voyage, the ships dropped anchor in the great river of the Plate and the men went exploring through the undulating lands, startling grazing herds of deer, seeing the limbs of savages between the trees, they filled their pockets with pebbles that might be emeralds or sand that might be gold; or sometimes, rounding a headland, they saw, far off, a string of savages slowly descending to the beach bearing on their heads and linking their shoulders together with heavy burdens for the Spanish King.

These are the fine stories used effectively all through the West country to decoy 'the apt young men' lounging by the harbour-side to leave their nets and fish for gold. But the voyagers were sober merchants into the bargain, citizens with the good of English trade and the welfare of English work-people at heart. The captains are reminded how necessary it is to find a market abroad for English wool; to discover the herb from which blue dyes are made; above all to make inquiry as to the methods of producing oil, since all attempts to make it from radish seed have failed. They are reminded of the misery of the English poor, whose crimes, brought about by poverty, make them 'daily consumed by the gallows'. They are reminded how the soil of England had been enriched by the discoveries of travellers in the past; how Dr. Linaker brought seeds of the damask rose and tulipas, and how beasts and plants and herbs, 'without which our life were to be said barborous', have all come to England gradually from abroad. In search of markets and of goods, of the immortal fame success would bring them, the apt young men set sail for the North, and were left, a little company of isolated Englishmen surrounded by snow and the huts of savages, to make what bargains they could and pick up what knowledge they might before the ships returned in the summer to fetch them home again. There they endured, an isolated company, burning on the rim of the dark. One of them, carrying a charter from his company in London, went inland as far as Moscow, and there saw the Emperor 'sitting in his chair of estate with his crown on his head, and a staff of goldsmiths' work in his left hand'. All the ceremony that he saw is carefully written out, and the sight upon which the English merchant first set eyes has the brilliancy of a Roman vase dug up and stood for a moment in the sun, until, exposed to the air, seen by millions of eyes, it dulls and crumbles away. There, all these centuries, on the outskirts of the world, the glories of Moscow, the glories of Constantinople have flowered unseen. The Englishman was bravely dressed for the occasion, led 'three fair mastiffs in coats of red cloth', and carried a letter from Elizabeth 'the paper whereof did smell most fragrantly of camphor and ambergris, and the ink of perfect musk'. And sometimes, since trophies from the amazing new world were eagerly awaited at home, together with unicorns' horns and lumps of ambergris and the fine stories of the engendering of whales and 'debates' of elephants and dragons whose blood, mixed, congealed into vermilion, a living sample would be sent, a live savage caught somewhere off the coast of Labrador, taken to England, and shown about like a wild beast. Next year they brought him back, and took a woman savage on board to keep him company. When they saw each other they blushed; they blushed profoundly, but the sailors, thought they noted it, knew not why. Later the two savages set up house together on board ship, she attending to his wants, he nursing her in sickness. But, as the sailors noted again, the savages lived together in perfect chastity.

All this, the new words, the new ideas, the waves, the

savages, the adventures, found their way naturally into the plays which were being acted on the banks of the Thames. There was an audience quick to seize upon the coloured and the high-sounding; to associate those

> frigates bottom'd with rich Sethin planks, Topt with the lofty firs of Lebanon,

with the adventures of their own sons and brothers abroad. The Verneys, for example, had a wild boy who had gone as pirate, turned Turk, and died out there, sending back to Claydon to be kept as relics of him some silk, a turban, and a pilgrim's staff. A gulf lay between the spartan domestic housecraft of the Paston women and the refined tastes of the Elizabethan Court ladies, who, grown old, says Harrison, spent their time reading histories, or 'writing volumes of their own, or translating of other men's into our English and Latin tongue', while the younger ladies played the lute and the citharne and spent their leisure in the enjoyment of music. Thus, with singing and with music, springs into existence the characteristic Elizabethan extravagance; the dolphins and lavoltas of Greene; the hyperbole, more surprising in a writer so terse and muscular, of Ben Jonson. Thus we find the whole of Elizabethan literature strewn with gold and silver; with talk of Guiana's rarities, and references to that America—'O my America! my new-found-land'—which was not merely a land on the map, but symbolized the unknown territories of the soul. So, over the water, the imagination of Montaigne brooded in fascination upon savages, cannibals, society, and government.

But the mention of Montaigne suggests that though the influence of the sea and the voyages, of the lumber room crammed with sea beasts and horns and ivory and old maps and nautical instruments, helped to inspire the greatest age of English poetry, its effects were by no means so beneficial upon English prose. Rhyme and metre helped the poets to keep the tumult of their perceptions in order. But the prose writer, without these restrictions, accumulated clauses, petered out in interminable catalogues, tripped and stumbled over the convolutions of his own rich draperies. How little Elizabethan prose was fit for its office, how exquisitely French prose was already adapted, can be seen by comparing a passage from Sidney's *Defense of Poesie* with one from Montaigne's Essays.

> He beginneth not with obscure definitions, which must blur the margent with interpretations, and load the memory with doubtfulness: but he cometh to you with words set in delightful proportion, either accompanied with, or prepared for the well enchanting Skill of Music, and with a tale (forsooth) he cometh unto you, with a tale which holdeth children from play, and old men from the Chimney corner; and pretending no more, doth intend the winning of the mind from wickedness to virtue; even as the child is often brought to take most wholesome

things by hiding them in such other as have a pleasant taste: which if one should begin to tell them the nature of the *Aloës* or *Rhubarbarum* they should receive, would sooner take their physic at their ears than at their mouth, so is it in men (most of which are childish in the best things, till they be cradled in their graves) glad they will be to hear the tales of Hercules. . . .

And so it runs on for seventy-six words more. Sidney's prose is an uninterrupted monologue, with sudden flashes of felicity and splendid phrases, which lends itself to lamentations and moralities, to long accumulations and catalogues, but is never quick, never colloquial, unable to grasp a thought closely and firmly, or to adapt itself flexibly and exactly to the chops and changes of the mind. Compared with this, Montaigne is master of an instrument which knows its own powers and limitations, and is capable of insinuating itself into crannies and crevices which poetry can never reach; capable of cadences different but no less beautiful; of subtleties and intensities which Elizabethan prose entirely ignores. He is considering the way in which certain of the ancients met death:

> . . . ils l'ont faicte couler et glisser parmy la lascheté de leurs occupations accoustumées entre des garses et bons compaignons; nul propos de consolation, nulle mention de testament, nulle affectation ambitieuse de constance, nul discours de leur condition future; mais entre les jeux, les festins, facecies, entretiens communs et populaires, et la musique, et des vers amoureux.

An age seems to separate Sidney from Montaigne. The English compared with the French are as boys compared with men.

But the Elizabethan prose writers, if they have the formlessness of youth, have, too, its freshness and audacity. In the same essay Sidney shapes language, masterfully and easily, to his liking; freely and naturally reaches his hand for a metaphor. To bring this prose to perfection (and Dryden's prose is very near perfection) only the discipline of the stage was necessary and the growth of self-consciousness. It is in the plays, and especially in the comic passages of the plays, that the finest Elizabethan prose is to be found. The stage was the nursery where prose learnt to find its feet. For on the stage people had to meet, to quip and crank, to suffer interruptions, to talk of ordinary things.

> *Cler.* A pox of her autumnal face, her pieced beauty! there's no man can be admitted till she be ready now-a-days, till she has painted, and perfumed, and washed, and scoured, but the boy here; and him she wipes her oiled lips upon, like a sponge. I have made a song (I pray thee hear it) on the subject.

[Page *sings.*

Still to be neat, still to be drest, &c.

*True.* And I am clearly on the other side: I love a good dressing before any beauty o' the world. O, a woman is then like a delicate garden; nor is there one kind of it; she may vary every hour; take often counsel of her glass, and choose the best. If she have good ears, show them; good hair, lay it out; good legs, wear short clothes; a good hand, discover it often: practise any art to mend breath, cleanse teeth, repair eyebrows; paint and profess it.

So the talk runs in Ben Jonson's *Silent Woman,* knocked into shape by interruptions, sharpened by collisions, and never allowed to settle into stagnancy or swell into turbidity. But the publicity of the stage and the perpetual presence of a second person were hostile to that growing consciousness of one's self, that brooding in solitude over the mysteries of the soul, which, as the years went by, sought expression and found a champion in the sublime genius of Sir Thomas Browne. His immense egotism has paved the way for all psychological novelists, autobiographers, confession-mongers, and dealers in the curious shades of our private life. He it was who first turned from the contacts of men with men to their lonely life within. 'The world that I regard is myself; it is the microcosm of my own frame that I cast mine eye on; for the other I use it but like my globe, and turn it round sometimes for my recreation.' All was mystery and darkness as the first explorer walked the catacombs swinging his lanthorn. 'I feel sometimes a hell within myself; Lucifer keeps his court in my breast; Legion is revived in me.' In these solitudes there were no guides and no companions. 'I am in the dark to all the world, and my nearest friends behold me but in a cloud.' The strangest thoughts and imaginings have play with him as he goes about his work, outwardly the most sober of mankind and esteemed the greatest physician in Norwich. He has wished for death. He has doubted all things. What if we are asleep in this world and the conceits of life are as mere dreams? The tavern music, the Ave Mary bell, the broken pot that the workman has dug out of the field—at the sight and sound of them he stops dead, as if transfixed by the astonishing vista that opens before his imagination. "We carry with us the wonders we seek without us; there is all Africa and her prodigies in us.' A halo of wonder encircles everything that he sees; he turns his light gradually upon the flowers and insects and grasses at his feet so as to disturb nothing in the mysterious processes of their existence. With the same awe, mixed with a sublime complacency, he records the discovery of his own qualities and attainments. He was charitable and brave and averse from nothing. He was full of feeling for other and merciless upon himself. 'For my conversation, it is like the sun's, with all men, and with a friendly aspect to good and bad.' He knows six languages, the laws, the customs and policies of several states, the names of all the constellations and most of the plants of his country, and yet, so sweeping is his imagination, so large the horizon in which he sees this little figure walking that 'methinks I do not know so many as when I did but know a hundred, and had scarcely ever simpled further than Cheapside'.

He is the first of the autobiographers. Swooping and soaring at the highest altitudes, he stoops suddenly with loving particularity upon the details of his own body. His height was moderate, he tells us, his eyes large and luminous; his skin dark but constantly suffused with blushes. He dressed very plainly. He seldom laughed. He collected coins, kept maggots in boxes, dissected the lungs of frogs, braved the stench of the spermaceti whale, tolerated Jews, had a good word for the deformity of the toad, and combined a scientific and sceptical attitude towards most things with an unfortunate belief in witches. In short, as we say when we cannot help laughing at the oddities of people we admire most, he was a character, and the first to make us feel that the most sublime speculations of the human imagination are issued from a particular man, whom we can love. In the midst of the solemnities of the Urn Burial we smile when he remarks that afflictions induce callosities. The smile broadens to laughter as we mouth out the splendid pomposities, the astonishing conjectures of the *Religio Medici.* Whatever he writes is stamped with his own idiosyncrasy, and we first become conscious of impurities which hereafter stain literature with so many freakish colours that, however hard we try, it is difficult to be certain whether we are looking at a man or his writing. Now we are in the presence of sublime imagination; now rambling through one of the finest lumber rooms in the world— a chamber stuffed from floor to ceiling with ivory, old iron, broken pots, urns, unicorns' horns, and magic glasses full of emerald lights and blue mystery.

## Clennell Wilkinson (essay date 1927)

SOURCE: "Hakluyt," in *The London Mercury,* Vol. XVII, No. 97, November, 1927, pp. 62-9.

[*In the following laudatory essay, Wilkinson provides an overview of Hakluyt's life and work and considers his qualities as an editor. Wilkinson suggests that the strength of* The Principal Voyages *lies in Hakluyt's artless editing and his skill at finding the romance in true stories.*]

I think it was Mr. Hilaire Belloc who once divided funny stories into two classes—those which are funny simply because they are funny, and those which are funny because they are true. He might have gone further and applied his theory to stories of all sorts. Even then he would not have reached the central fact, which is that true stories have a particular quality, a manner and charm of their own, which distinguishes them from all others. "Truth is stranger than fiction," we say; and certainly its strangeness, its delightful unexpectedness, is one of the characteristics that mark it off most decisively from the manufactured climaxes of a modern novel. But it would be better to say simply that truth is *different* from fiction—that it is not only stranger, but, in its own way, more beautiful, more moving, stronger, deeper, touching some chord in us that fiction can never reach. For we all can recognize a true story. We can recognize its *style*—what we call the "ring of truth." It is almost as though all true stories were written by the same author—which, indeed, when you come to think of it, they are. "This story, gentlemen, happens to be true," is an introduction which immediately arrests the attention of any audience. They turn eagerly towards you, as though you had mentioned the name of some favourite popular writer. It is obviously not a love of truth for truth's sake that moves them, but just a love of true stories—or of this particular style in story-telling of which the vogue, in contrast with the changing fashions of fiction, began at the beginning and will last to the end. There is no need to labour the point: we shall have to return to it later. It is very apposite to our subject, because in Richard Hakluyt's *Principal Navigations, Voyages, Traffiques and Discoveries of the English Nation* we have probably the finest collection of true stories ever published in any language. . . .

Hakluyt himself was in Mr. Masefield's words, an "almost perfect editor," and therefore the less his work is edited by us the better. It must often have been tempting to pause and explain. Hakluyt's place-names, for instance, are sometimes different from those in modern use; especially in Russia and the East it is difficult to follow his itineraries without the aid of a good historical atlas. . . . Most people who read Hakluyt read him for the fun of the thing, and do not want to be interrupted. Nothing is further from their thoughts than any of those practical, patriotic or scholarly motives by which Hakluyt himself professes to have been inspired.

Indeed, we may take leave to doubt even that profession, though it comes from one of the most truthful persons that ever lived. We may question whether Hakluyt knew his own heart. When he assures Sir Francis Walsingham and the rest, in his Epistle Dedicatorie, that the reason why he undertook this work (which was really his life's work) was partly to bring more money into the Royal exchaquer and partly to offer a cure for the unemployment problem, we may agree respectfully that these considerations no doubt sustained and strengthened his resolve; but we do not for a moment suppose that they were his real motives. They were good cards to play at the time. The Queen

always wanted money, and the unemployment problem, originally created by the suppression of the monasteries, had been rendered more acute by the inauguration of a period of European peace—or, at any rate, a reduction in the number of wars. The situation, indeed, was not unlike that with which we are trying to deal to-day. In a letter to Sir Walter Ralegh, written in 1587, advocating the colonisation of Florida, Hakluyt says:

> Seeing therefore we are so farre from want of people, that retyring daily home out of the Lowe Countreys they go idle up and downe in swarms for lack of honest intertainment, I see no fitter place to employ some part of the better sort of them trained up thus long in service, than in the inward partes of the firme of Virginia against such stubborne Savages as shal refuse obedience to her Majestie. And doubtlesse many of our men will bee glad and faine to accept this condition, when as by the reading of this present treatie they shall understand the fertilitie and riches of the regions confining so neare upon yours [Sir Walter's colony of Virginia], the great commodities and goodnesse whereof you have bin contented to suffer to come to light.

He could hardly have put it lower. But we know him better: we know that he is not stating his motives, but is simply advancing topical arguments in explanation of the appearance of his book, in defence of that passion for travel literature which was already in him. For it is a curious fact that, while we have so miserably little knowledge of Hakluyt's life, we can trace the birth of this romantic passion of his almost down to the very day and hour. He has told us all about it himself. Hakluyt was born of a good Welsh family (not Dutch, as his name might suggest), either in or near London, about the year 1553. On reaching a suitable age, he was sent as a Queen's scholar to Westminster, "that fruitfull nurserie," as he gratefully calls it; and it was while he was there that the incident occurred which was to have such a powerful influence upon the rest of his life—and incidentally to supply us, his descendants, with one of the prettiest little pictures of daily life in Elizabethan London that we possess. "It was my happe," one day, he tells Walsingham, "to visit the chamber of Mr. Richard Hakluyt my cosin, a Gentleman of the Middle Temple." Now this elder Richard was a man of parts. He was evidently a barrister of some distinction, for our own Richard Hakluyt goes on to remark that he was "well knowen unto you"—that is, to Mr. Secretary Walsingham; but his practice was not so large as to preclude a certain dalliance with subjects outside the range of the law. He happened on this occasion to be in—otherwise we should certainly never have heard of him. Moreover, there chanced to lie upon his table, or his "boord," certain "books of Cosmographie," together with "an universall Mappe," or map of the world—it is impossible to guess which, for so many were being produced

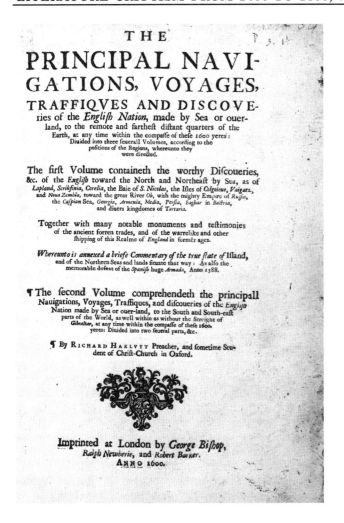

THE

# PRINCIPAL NAVI-
# GATIONS, VOYAGES,

TRAFFIQVES AND DISCOVE-
ries of the *Engliſh Nation*, made by Sea or ouer-
land, to the remote and fartheſt diſtant quarters of the
Earth, at any time within the compaſſe of theſe *1600* yeres:
Diuided into three ſeuerall Volumes, according to the
poſitions of the Regions, whereunto they
were directed.

The firſt Volume containeth the worthy Diſcoueries,
&c. of the *Engliſh* toward the North and Northeaſt by Sea, as of
*Lapland, Scrikfinia, Corelia,* the Baie of *S. Nicolas,* the Iſles of *Colgoieue, Vaigatz,*
and *Noua Zembla,* toward the great River *Ob,* with the mighty Empire of *Ruſſia,*
the *Caſpian* Sea, *Georgia, Armenia, Media, Perſia, Baghar* in *Baſtria,*
and diuers kingdomes of *Tartaria.*

Together with many notable monuments and teſtimonies
of the ancient forren trades, and of the warrelike and other
ſhipping of this Realme of *England* in former ages.

*Whereunto is annexed a briefe Commentary of the true ſtate of* Iſland,
and of the Northren Seas and lands ſituate that way : As alſo the
memorable defeat of the *Spaniſh* huge Armada, Anno *1588.*

¶ The ſecond Volume comprehendeth the principall
Nauigations, Voyages, Traffiques, and diſcoueries of the *Engliſh*
Nation made by Sea or ouer-land, to the South and South-eaſt
parts of the World, as well within as without the Streight of
*Gibraltar,* at any time within the compaſſe of theſe *1600.*
yeres: Diuided into two ſeuerall parts, &c.

¶ By R ICHARD H AKLUYT Preacher, and ſometime Student of Chriſt-Church in Oxford.

Imprinted at London by *George Biſhop,*
*Ralph Newberie,* and *Robert Barker.*
A NN O *1600.*

*Title page of the* Principal Navigations.

at that time. Seeing his young cousin "somewhat curious in the view thereof," the elder Richard played up nobly. He explained to the lad all the advances that had lately been made in the study of geography—a subject probably not included in the Westminster curriculum. Warming to his task, he even took "his wand" and pointed out with it all the "known Seas, Gulfs, Bayes, Straights, Capes, Rivers, Empires, Kingdomes, Dukedomes, and Territories of each part" with appropriate remarks upon their commercial possibilities. And after they had pored over the map together for some time, "he brought me to the Bible," and, turning to the 107th psalm, read out the well-known passage about those who go down to the sea in ships. It was a gesture worthy of an Elizabethan, and it was a decisive moment in the carrer of Richard Hakluyt, the younger. We may hazard the guess that the elder Richard felt more than sufficiently rewarded by a glance at his young cousin's face. He little knew what he had done for himself. Thus is immortality conferred. It should be a lesson for all of us who have inquisitive young relatives at Westminster. Twenty-five years later Hak-

luyt wrote:

which words of the Prophet together with my cousins discourse (things of high and rare delight to my yong nature) tooke in me so deepe an impression, that I constantly resolved, if ever I were preferred to the University, where better time, and more convenient place might be ministered for these studies, I would by God's assistance prosecute that knowledge and kinde of literature, the doores whereof (after a sort) were so happily opened before me.

So the great idea was born. A few years later Hakluyt went up to Christ Church, where we know almost nothing of his career; but in 1577, after taking his M.A., he began at Oxford the first public lectures in geography that "shewed both the old imperfectly composed and the new lately reformed mappes, globes, spheares and other instruments of his art." What is known of the rest of his life can be very briefly stated. In 1583 he was appointed chaplain to the English Ambassador in Paris, with instructions from Walsingham to keep a careful eye on the doings of France and Spain, and to make "diligent inquiries of such things as might yield any light unto our western discoverie in America." He lived in France for five years. He was a good French scholar—though not so fluent a speaker, he tells us, as his friend, Sir Walter Ralegh—and no doubt he used his time well. We know that he published several works, mostly concerned with travel, and had the honour of presenting one of them to Queen Elizabeth during a visit to London. But it was not until 1589, the year following his final return to England, that his *magnum opus,* **The Principal Navigations, etc.,**" familiarly known to us as **Hakluyt's Voyages,** saw the light. By that time he had been made a prebendary of Bristol, in recognition of his work in France, and in 1590 he was instituted to the rectory of Witheringsett-cum-Brockford, in Suffolk, where he lived until 1602, largely engaged in his favourite "kinde of literature." In 1602 he probably moved to London, where he was presently made archdeacon of Westminster; and in 1612 he took the living of Gedney, in Lincolnshire, where four years later he died, aged sixty-three. He died just too soon. He left behind him sufficient MSS to have formed another volume of his famous **Voyages,** but on his death this mass of material fell into the hands of Samuel Purchas, who published the greater part of it in his *Pilgrims* (1625), but completely ruined it by bad editing—clumsy cuts and abridgments, and unnecessary annotations. It is one of the little ironies of literary history that the most reverent, restrained and self-effacing of editors should himself have been so roughly treated.

What, then, was Hakluyt's method? It is not a subject which he would dream of discussing himself. Our ignorance of his career would seem to him quite natural; an editor, he plainly indicates, should be a shadowy figure in the background, one whose personality has been allowed to merge itself in the work as a whole. We get glimpses here and there. For instance, explaining the arrangement of his collection, in one of his dedications—how he has begun with narratives of Eastern travel and then moved over to the West—he mentions incidentally that such a mass of material is only to be got together after "huge toile" and "with small profit to insue," so that he now wonders at himself that he was able to do it. It involved, he says in another preface, "great charges and infinite cares," "many watchings, toiles and travels, and wearying out of my weake body." In the course of his description of "the voyage of M. Hore and divers other gentlemen, to Newfoundland, and Cape Briton, in the yere 1536," he remarks that "Richard Hakluyt of Oxford" rode two hundred miles across England to interview the only living survivor of this voyage, one Master Buts, and obtain the true account from him. In some respects Master Buts's story is one of the least satisfactory in the book; it lacks colour, and even the air of truth, and our editor might have thought himself but poorly rewarded for his trouble were it not for the report of a remarkable oration by the captain of the ship in which he appealed to his starving company not to fall into the horrible sin of cannibalism. It is plain that Hakluyt was prepared to test every story, by personal inquiry if necessary. We should have liked his own account of that two hundred mile ride. Those were the days when, as Fynes Moryson tells us, England was famous for having the best inns in the world (it sounds almost impossible); we should have liked to have heard how Richard Hakluyt fared in them. We should have liked a description of the whole journey and of the people he met, somewhat in the manner of Froissart's well-known account of his ride across France to the court of the Count of Foix. We might even have sacrificed Master Buts's voyage for it. But it would be idle to expect anything of the kind from Hakluyt: he was far too conscientious, too impersonal an editor. He *was* an editor, however, not a mere compiler. There is a justness in the arrangement and length of the stories which betrays the wise use of a blue pencil. There is a similarity in the information supplied by a large proportion (though not all) of the contributors, which suggests that Hakluyt may have sought to lessen his "huge toile" by the use of a fixed *questionnaire*. Moreover he has, in some vague way, not easy to define, impressed his own personality upon the whole collection and given it a unity apart from the subject matter. It is not the style—for that, as we have seen, is the style of all true stories. It is not the mere diction, for that is of the time. It is something more elusive; but it is there, and I should be surprised if any reader of the *Voyages* had failed to notice it.

One more fact about this extraordinary man, before we turn to the voyages themselves. It is that he never apparently attempted nor desired to visit any of the countries which he dreamed and wrote about, and praised so earnestly all his life. He represented Virginia as a land flowing with milk and honey, but he himself was content to settle down at Witheringsett-cum-Brockford, in Suffolk. He had dedicated his life to "that knowledge and kinde of literature,"—in fact to travel literature, not to travel. Perhaps, tucked away somewhere at the back of his mind, there may have been the fear of disillusionment.

Confronted now by this magnificent array of narratives, what adequate praise can any man give to them, except to repeat stupidly that there is nothing like them anywhere else in the world? They range from Ralegh's admirably cool yet sympathetic account of the last fight of Sir Richard Grenville (he could admire, you feel, while he could not quite understand) to the story of how that equally great traveller, Anthony Jenkinson, narrowly escaped with his life from the hands of Cossack brigands on the borders of Persia—from the classic description of the defeat of the Armada to the daily journal of some half-educated sailorman. Yet they are all alike in every essential quality. They all have the same keen flavour of the truth. They never mention scenery, for instance, except incidentally. All they seem to be trying to tell you is that there is money to be made out of the "treyne oil" and furs of the grey Murman coast, gold to be found in rivers of El Dorado, oysters hanging in clusters on the West Indian trees (Ralegh was one of the most faithful believers in these oyster trees, as he was in El Dorado, in the Amazons and in the one-eyed tribes). They paint the skies blue and set the palm trees swaying in the breeze by pure accident, as it were. It is not the art that conceals art, but the art that is totally unaware of its own existence. "This," you say to yourself, "is where a stylist like Ralegh will fail: Ralegh unfortunately can write"—and indeed he can, much better than Hakluyt. But no such disaster occurs. Ralegh's dedications, of which there are many (the extent of Hakluyt's debt to him is not, perhaps, generally recognized) are written each in the manner of a set piece, in that wonderfully musical prose of which he was master. But as soon as he settles down to the narrative of a voyage, he becomes as simple and convincing as Jenkinson. A true story should be allowed to tell itself. The possession of an individual style in the narrator is a defect—an intrusion. It fogs and spoils the story, as popular actor-managers so often spoil Shakespeare. No such charge can be brought against Ralegh. It is difficult to quote from his narrations; but here is one of his rare descriptive passages, with an amusingly businesslike twist to its tail:

> I never saw a more beautiful countrey, nor more lively prospects, hils so raised here and there over the valleys, the river winding into divers branches, the playnes adjoining without bush or stubble, all faire greene grasse, the ground of hard sand easie to march on, for horse or foote, the deere crossing in every path, the birdes towards the evening singing on every tree with a thousand severall tunes, cranes

and herons of white, crimson, and carnation, pearching on the rivers side, the aire freshe with a gentle Easterly winde, and every stone that we stouped to take up promised either golde or silver by his complexion.

Which is not a bad summary of the general attitude of Elizabethan explorers towards the "new countries." We are apt to forget the astonishing range of Hakluyt's collection. He promises us "voyages," by land and sea, but he gives us infinitely more. For example, in these volumes are included some of the most moving stories of captivity ever written. Miles Phillips's stolid, tight-lipped account of his appalling sufferings at the hands of the Inquisition in Mexico is something to be remembered—he seems to be setting his teeth as he writes. The night before the day appointed for judgment upon the English captives, "they came to the prison where we were, with certaine officers of that holy hellish house, bringing with them certaine fooles coats which they had prepared for us, being called in their language S. Benitos, which coats were made of yellow cotton and red crosses upon them, both before and behind." And in the morning, after breakfast, "we set foorth of the prison, every man alone in his yellow coat, and a rope about his necke, and a great greene Waxe candle in his hand un-lighted," and so marched through the crowded market place of Mexico City to the scaffold, where they were made to sit down and hear judgment pronounced upon them, John Gray, John Brown, James Collier and the rest of these Englishmen, "some to have 200 stripes on horseback, and some 100, and condemned for slaves to the gallies, some for six years, some for 8 and some for 10." "Which being done, and it now drawing toward night, George Riverly, Peter Momfrie, and Cornelius the Irishman, were called and had their judgment to be burnt to ashes, and so were presently led away to the place of execution in the market place but a little from the scaffold, where they were quickly burnt and consumed." Miles Phillips himself was sent to serve as a slave in a monastery, from which he eventually escaped. Nowhere do we realise more clearly than in the pages of Hakluyt the bitter hatred inspired by these "devildoms of Spain." Cruelty, indeed, was the prevailing vice of the brilliant sixteenth century—a thing quite shocking and inexplicable to this present age. An Englishman, Lionel Plumtree, travelling in the Middle East, could record with evident satisfaction that certain "Cassaks" who had made a piratical attack upon his ship, being captured by the local authorities, "were put to most cruell torments, according to their deserts."

Thus does Hakluyt, setting out with no other intention than to interest us in foreign parts, reflect most vividly the Europe of his day, in all its weakness and its strength. The lighter side is pleasantly prominent: we may discover little touches of unconscious humour on almost every page. In the course of John Davis's first

voyage for the discovery of the North-west Passage, he landed a party with instructions to "allure" the natives to them. Their idea of doing this was to "make a great noise," causing "our Musicians to play, ourselves dancing." Apparently the natives were highly pleased by this lively demonstration, which nowadays would be considered extremely bad for the white man's prestige. We get some curious sidelights upon their idea of a suitable diet for the tropics. Every man was allowed several gallons of beer a day, and one of the principal reasons for the abandonment of Frobisher's last voyage was the fact that his casks were running dry. "All the way homeward they drank nothing but water," says the chronicler plaintively.

But it is impossible to indicate the greatness of Hakluyt by a series of disconnected quotations. It is not a question of this passage or that, but of the cumulative effect of the whole. Indeed you cannot find anywhere in the *Voyages* a passage that can fairly be called "typical." His book is as varied in pattern as life itself. One moment you are drifting in a canoe down a South American river with painted savages shooting at you from the banks; the next you are one of a huddled group of sheepskin-clad merchants on a snow-swept plateau in the Middle East, calling upon your comrades for one last charge against the Turkish brigands who gallop round and round, like vultures circling round a corpse. One moment you are the half-naked slave of some Algerian bey; the next you ride dignified, in furs and velvet, in the train of an English Ambassador to the Muscovite Tsar. Always you jot down notes about the trade openings for English goods, the commercial possibilities of the country. This Master Richard Hakluyt of Oxford, who has asked for a record of your experiences, is particularly insistent upon that (yet his eye lights up strangely as you recount some adventure by the way). You are traders of course, nothing else— plain English merchants from Norwich and Bideford and Rye. Never will you acknowledge that craving that is within you to find out everything, to know and experience everything, to hug all the New World to you—roses and thorns alike—in one eager, fierce embrace. You do not pause for self-analysis. You are of the sixteenth century, when the world was suddenly young again, and the morning stars sang together— perhaps for the last time.

All this Hakluyt has faithfully transcribed for us. He succeeded because he had the right idea. He could not fail. He knew that the truth was sufficient for his purpose—that no one who really wanted to know what Englishmen had done in the past would begin by reading *The Charge of the Light Brigade,* or would turn to Tennyson's *Revenge* for the best account of the death of Grenville. He set himself patiently to dig for and disinter the romantic truth itself. And if we could follow his method today, if we could hunt down every adventurous voyager by land or sea and make him tell his story simply, in his own words, then—allowing for all the disadvantages of our greater geographical knowledge, our decayed prose style, and the effect upon the narrators of our meretricious "education"—there can be no reasonable doubt that we should again produce a book which future generations would hail as one of the greatest of our time. It would not be too big a book. In attempting to estimate Hakluyt's achievement we must remember not only what he included but what he left out. He must have had a fine sense of discrimination. And it may be added that his contemporaries showed an equally fine discrimination (which their descendants have not always succeeded in imitating) when they accorded Hakluyt the honour of a burial in Westminster Abbey.

## James A. Williamson (essay date 1928)

SOURCE: An introduction to *Richard Hakluyt and the English Voyages,* by George Bruner Parks, edited by James A. Williamson, American Geographical Society, 1928, pp. xi-xvii.

[*In the following excerpt, Williamson places Hakluyt's* English Voyages *in a historical context. Williamson considers Hakluyt the major historian of Elizabethan colonial expansion, and finds in his work crucial evidence of the "ideas and outlook of the Elizabethans."*]

The Elizabethan age was not spacious, as we are sometimes told, but narrow and needy. It was a time of industrious study of man and nature as well as of books, and its adventures were undertaken not from swashbuckling zest but because good men found their country in a tight place and staked their lives and fortunes to redeem it. It was a time of more loss than profit, of more misery than glory. Drake's record has deceived many; he was an exception, not a type. He was supremely fortunate, but few of those who followed him came home rich; most of them left their bones in the tropics. Sir Humphrey Gilbert did hard and varied service and made nothing by it. Sir John Hawkins deserves to live less for his slaving than for his prosaic battle with corruption in the Navy Office. Sir Francis Walsingham, a chronic invalid, toiled for the state, lived frugally, and died in debt. And as a type of the merchant-patriot we may take old Michael Lok, who made a modest fortune in European trade, staked every penny on the Arctic passage to Cathay, was bankrupt and imprisoned, spent his declining years in exile, and is last seen at eighty, still writing and scheming for the discovery which would profit his country but hardly himself. If we probe beneath the incidents and seek out the motives we find no absent-minded empire-building but a reasoned, cooperative effort which left no means untried to attain a definite goal. The way of these men was hard, and their reward small. Posterity can see that they were successful beyond their dreams,

but they themselves closed their eyes on failure; the success revealed itself slowly after they were dead. Richard Hakluyt's epic is no paean of victory but a tribute to service and suffering; his heroes are not "glorious" but "worthy." That is the best word he can bestow upon them.

The Elizabethan field has still its harvest to be reaped; and the Hakluyts, as their works are revealed in these pages, may point the way to it. That way is not chiefly to retail exciting incidents, although they have their illustrative uses, but to study history and to think.

From it there emerges the truth about Elizabethan efforts, and much more besides. For the sixteenth century is but the first chapter of the modern drama, itself preceded by a medieval prologue. In four centuries European man has attained to world power, power not only over other races of men but also over seas, deserts, jungles, and mountains, the obstacles of nature which have in previous ages circumscribed the actions of the most gifted peoples. He has not done this by superior intelligence, nor is it at all certain that he owes his success very largely to superior ethics. That and other circumstances are debatable; but at least it is clear that an indispensable factor in the process has been the series of reactions set up by the European world travelers of the sixteenth century. Discovery led to trade and to the plunder of helpless peoples possessed of mineral wealth. Stores of gold, silver, and gems became available as currency; great trading operations concentrated much of this wealth in a few hands; and before the close of that first century there were great capitalists on the Continent and smaller ones in England controlling a fund of fluid wealth ready to be directed to enterprise which promised further advance of the same sort. This prominence of the new kind of wealth was the most significant product of the age of discovery. Wealth in the form of landed estates had been real enough but not available for the promotion of mercantile undertakings; wealth represented by a strong room filled with bullion was a dynamic force, a concentration of power capable of being exerted in any direction.

There followed the seventeenth century, of colonization and the oceanic trading monopolies, systematically designed for the acquisition of more fluid capital. England, France, and Holland challenged and surpassed Portugal and Spain, who had been first in the field but had allowed their methods to become stereotyped and lifeless. Collateral developments aided mercantile efficiency. National law in strongly governed states rendered wealth secure. International law began to take shape and acquire validity. Religious inhibitions on the free use of capital grew obsolete. Joint stock, the sale of shares, insurance, paper substitutes for coin, all invented by medieval Italians for their Mediterranean trade, attained a world-wide vogue. Communication became more rapid, and the multiplication of printed books stored and transmitted a fluid capital of experience comparable to that of gold. The energizing force flowed into ever new veins, industry subdivided and specialized, comfort became more general, and untrammelled thought grew more ingenious in ministering to it. Social Europe in the age of Louis XIV was a different world from the Europe of the Emperor Sigismund and the Hundred Years' War—a tract of prosperity compared with a waste of brutish misery; and the story was yet at its beginning.

In the eighteenth century the colonies grew up and became nations; the thirteen English colonies of America at least did so, whilst those of Spain and Portugal developed in the same direction, and the little nucleus of Frenchmen on the St. Lawrence had multiplied to 70,000 when they came under the British flag. The multiplication of the American stock, even more than its political development, was the outstanding world phenomenon of this century. In 1700 the thirteen colonies contained about 200,000 people; every twenty years or so the numbers doubled; and by 1800 the population of the United States was over 5,000,000. These people were still almost exclusively agricultural. They imported nearly all their cloth, ironware, pottery, and luxury manufactures; and the reaction of this great new market upon the industries of Europe was immense. Central and South America added their demands. The West Indies of England, France, and Spain employed great numbers of slaves, enriched planters and traders, and called in their turn for manufactures in exchange for their products. In the East the process was different, but its effects were the same. Where the seventeenth century had witnessed trading posts in India, the eighteenth saw its conquest and the fuller exploitation of its market for manufactured goods. The Dutch extended their hold upon the islands of Asia, and all the sea powers reached farther still to tap the commerce of China. France, in spite of disastrous wars and more disastrous finance, expanded her trade abroad and her industries at home and, if she had reformed instead of destroying her institutions, might have taken the lead in the industrial transformation that has produced the world of today. That, as it fell out, became the destiny of England. Her ocean trade was as great as that of France; and her home population, which had to feed it, was only one-third as numerous. Thus demand necessitated a new kind of supply, mass production for distant markets, scope for the inventions of an alert people, and the application of a now enormous capital to the new organization.

A hundred years ago the world entered an unprecedented phase. "Modern history" began with the Renaissance; but, unless we are to apply the term to two very dissimilar periods, we must reckon that it ended with Napoleon. The age that then commenced awaits a name, and only its tendencies are as yet discernible;

its main characteristics have still, perhaps, to show themselves. In one aspect it is but an intensification of the earlier process; more transoceanic settlement of Europeans, more tropical dependencies, more mass manufacture, more raw materials, much more fluid capital. But in another sense it is different. In the seventeenth century, even in the eighteenth, few men were conscious of change. There was a slow beneficent movement, but environment remained substantially unaltered. In the present period a man who lives out his years is born in one world and dies in another. The old, even the middle-aged, are strangers in an unfamiliar scene. The pace has many times multiplied in proportion to the duration of life, and one of its consequences has been the mental and moral unrest of the modern world. This rapid development is agreed to be, in the main, beneficial. Yet it has disquieting features. The question is not whether the advance of scientific organization is in itself desirable, but whether it may not be outrunning the capacity of man to adapt himself to it. With the statement of the question this survey reaches the limits of history and may fitly be brought to a close.

Such has been the working of the forces brought to birth by those old students, speculators, and men of action of the Renaissance. Apart from its intrinsic interest it calls for study, for it is only by knowing the past and realizing how it has produced the present that we can hope to control our own surroundings. Fertile scholarship is working towards a synthesis soundly based upon a multitude of special studies in which history, geography, and economic science bear the leading parts. That is only a statement of what the Elizabethans aimed at in their attempt to solve the problems of their time. . . .

The history of Elizabethan expansion is to a great extent the work of Richard Hakluyt, to a greater extent perhaps than the record of any other large movement can be ascribed to the labors of any one historian. He preserved a mass of material that would otherwise have perished, and he handled it with an enthusiasm and common sense which have made his work live through the centuries in a manner that its mere content would not have ensured. To appreciate that point we need only compare the collection of Samuel Purchas, similar in topics and greater in bulk, yet dull and repellent to the reader and not exploited even by scholars with the assiduity bestowed upon the *English Voyages*. Purchas arranged a museum; Hakluyt gathered the materials of a history and dealt so cunningly with them that they became a history whilst retaining their guise of raw materials—a double achievement which no modern editor has had the art to imitate.

The value of the *English Voyages* to compilers of narrative has long been known. It has perhaps been overestimated, for the riches of the book seem to excuse one for neglecting to look elsewhere. It is too easy to assume that Hakluyt is complete and that further research is needless. That, however, is not true; Hakluyt is no more complete than any contemporary historian can be. Political hindrances, personal jealousies, the reticence of men about their past, an honorable respect for such scruples, some inevitable falsity of perspective have all led to suppressions. The last of these errors is certainly the least conspicuous; in the main, Hakluyt's perspective from the sixteenth century is that which the twentieth century is rediscovering, and conscious omissions form the chief reason why research has need to dig under and around him. The reality of that need requires emphasis, and we may be sure that Hakluyt himself would today be the first to recommend it.

His work, which will be shown to consist of much more than the **English Voyages,** has another value, which has not been so well understood; it helps to reveal the ideas and outlook of the Elizabethans. The ideas governed the actions and can be understood by reading the textbooks of the time, by studying its propaganda and its personal relationships, and by scrutinizing its deeds before their proper background, the historical and geographical knowledge of their doers. Hakluyt did much to synthetize this knowledge for his own generation; but his contribution and that of others have been too little regarded by later interpreters, with unfortunate results to the presentation of history.

One may in fact be bold to say that the commonly accepted story of Elizabethan expansion is vitiated by false traditions concocted partly by those whose study has been too shallow and still more by those who have viewed too narrow a field. Instead of a reasoned unity we have too often a series of episodes, brilliant but disconnected, annals and not history. The brilliance conceals the defect. The details are so interesting— Drake's plunder, Gilbert's heroism, the flamboyance of Raleigh, the greatest costume actor in any age—that general readers and popular writers have asked for nothing more, have taken for granted that the Elizabethans were romantic and unaccountable, and have forgotten that the actions of large groups of men need a sober explanation and, for the performers, undoubtedly had one. So we have as a usual conception that Drake in his Pacific raid was nothing but a glorious pirate, that Hawkins was a mere slave trader and therefore disreputable, that Raleigh alone begot a colonial empire, that the East India Company was founded because pepper was dear, that the mass of English merchants and seamen were of no importance and need not be mentioned, and that Hakluyt was a literary man fired with romance, whose studies served for delight and nothing more.

Such things, it is true, are not expressly stated in learned works, but they are sometimes implied in them; for the

romantic tradition has created such an atmosphere that even those who have read the truth in the records have allowed their vision to be fogged. In more popular writings the error holds full sway, for romance is a better seller than reality; and one-sided books continue to appear, overdrawing first Drake then Raleigh (they are the favorites) and exhibiting the special illusion of biographers, that their hero alone did everything notable in his age. A more general theme is no less constant: that England's greatness was due to persons of poor character, scape-graces and ne'er-do-wells, a reckless, improvident, almost imbecile crew, and that Providence admired their boyish hardihood and brought to nought the subtlety of their rivals. That is a deception arising from an English habit of self-depreciation, first practiced by the Puritans as a pious reaction against the wordly self-confidence of their predecessors and remaining as a permanent strand in the national character. Cromwell, we may remember, going into action at the head of the best-trained army an English field had ever seen, ascribed the victory of "a company of poor ignorant men"—fifty per cent more numerous than their opponents—to divine intervention alone. Modern romancers have seized upon the paradox whilst varying its terms. For the modest Puritan they have substituted the legendary younger son with his company of tatterdemalions, and they have obscured the truth that it was by organization and not improvidence that great leaders accomplished great deeds. A war-drilled generation knows better, but literary convention is apt to lag behind experience.

A different approach discovers a truer story. It is symptomatic of the methods so commonly applied in the past to the study of Elizabethan expansion that the life and work of Richard Hakluyt, the clergyman, and of his cousin, Richard Hakluyt, the lawyer, have never before been fully examined. The record of their careers is barren of adventure and almost of incident and offers no attraction to the romantic biographer. Yet . . . it is an important record to the historian and one that gives him an established body of contemporary doctrine to which he may relate the diverse undertakings of the time; or, to use a metaphor, provides a backbone to which a dismembered skeleton may be articulated. More than this, it shows the doctrine in course of development, from the medieval ignorance of the age of discovery to the clear-cut aims with which the seventeenth century set forth on its career of oversea construction. In this process the elder Hakluyt (the lawyer) is virtually a newly discovered agent. We have had hitherto a very dim conception of him, but his function as an accumulator and exchanger of information is here established, to the strengthening of the argument that a conscious design inspired the actions of his age. His younger cousin had been more celebrated but always for only a portion of his work, and he too stands forth in a new guise as an unwearied agent in almost all the propaganda of the movement towards expansion. His unselfishness and breadth of mind have hitherto been guessed at rather than fully proved; and the revelation of his often anonymous contributions to the cause, both in labor and in money, places his fame upon a secure foundation. . . .

**James A. Williamson (essay date 1946)**

SOURCE: "Richard Hakluyt," in *Richard Hakluyt & His Successors: A Volume Issued to Commemorate the Centenary of the Hakluyt Society,* edited by Edward Lynam, The Hakluyt Society, 1946, pp. 9-46.

[*In the following excerpt, Williamson describes the conditions that prompted English maritime expansion and considers Hakluyt's role as a publicist and "master mind" behind Elizabethan colonial enterprise.*]

That Hakluyt was consciously a publicist and a historian as well as a geographer may be seen from his own words. In his dedication of a publication to Raleigh in 1587 he remarks that 'geography is the eye of history', in a context which leaves no doubt that history is the primary motive and geography the accessory. Eleven years later he repeats the idea in his preface to the first volume of the enlarged *Principal Navigations*. Having spoken of his labour to bring to light the ancient deeds and to preserve the recent exploits of the English nation 'for the honour and benefit of this commonwealth wherein I live and breathe', he says that he has used the aids of geography and chronology, 'the sun and the moon, the right eye and the left, of all history'. In the dedication of the same volume to Lord Howard of the Armada, he describes how, having 'waded on still farther and farther in the sweet study of the history of cosmography, I began at length to conceive that with diligent observation something might be gathered which might commend our nation for their high courage and singular activity in the search and discovery of the most unknown quarters of the world'. His fullest account of his own development occurs in the 1589 dedication to Sir Francis Walsingham of the earlier edition of his greatest work. He begins with the well-known account of his introduction to geography by his cousin, Hakluyt the lawyer, and of his resolution, while yet a schoolboy, to pursue the subject. He did so, he says, with unflagging zest, and in due course it led him to seek acquaintance with sea-captains, merchants and mariners, to learn of their discoveries and appreciate their motives. Then in 1583 he went for five years to the English embassy in Paris, where he talked with Frenchmen and Portuguese who could satisfy his curiosity. While there he found that the record of English deeds was small in comparison with that of the Portuguese, Spaniards and Frenchmen, and that his countrymen were contemned for want of enterprise and failure to seize their opportunities. He thought the reproach unjust and determined to remove it by publishing to

the world a great history of English achievements beyond the sea. So, from a geographer studying for intellectual pleasure he had become a historian of patriotic inspiration. He was already, as we know from other evidence—the *Divers Voyages* of 1582, and the *Western Planting* of 1584—a publicist and a counsellor for present and future national enterprise across the ocean. That was a natural growth from his geographical knowledge and his patriotism.

---

**Michael Kraus stresses Hakluyt's important role in England's colonial expansion:**

English activity in colonial expansion had been slow in starting, but once interest was aroused in lands beyond the seas it was vigorous in its growth. A knowledge of important events was expected of the cultivated individual, for one of the marks of a well-read man was his familiarity with the facts of history. . . . The greatness of England and the spread of her power overseas were celebrated in numerous histories written in Tudor and Stuart days. The English bourgeoisie experienced a very rapid development in the sixteenth century, and to the need for broader economic opportunities perceived by a rising capitalist class was joined a swelling national confidence in England's imperial destiny. . . . The expansion of England was in large part, says [Hakluyt's] biographer, due in fact to the stimulus given it by his publications. Perhaps no historian again wielded so much power over a nation's destiny until the nineteenth century, when the German writers helped create Bismarck's empire, and Captain Alfred T. Mahan stimulated a naval race among the great powers.

*Michael Kraus in an introduction to* A History of American History, *Farrar & Rinehart, Inc., 1937.*

---

The Elizabethan period called for work of this kind, and would have been poorer and less successful without it. It was with good reason that the Elizabethan writers, and notably Hakluyt, spoke always with reverence of Henry VIII for his leadership and of Henry VII for his wisdom. The first two Tudors restored national prosperity, and maintained it, by vindicating the rule of law and by claiming for England her place as one of the great powers of Europe. In their time trade flourished and wealth increased. A bad interval followed, dating from Henry VIII's last war with France and Scotland, and continuing into the early years of Elizabeth. English merchants lost their hold on foreign markets, the government of Edward VI was corrupt and partisan, Mary led the country to a French war in which England suffered clear defeat, the Navy was no longer adequate to prevent invasion, and unemployment spread poverty through the land. Over all this anxiety loomed the unsolved religious problem, whereby it seemed that, whether England became officially Catholic or Protestant, the conflict was so bitter and the rivals so evenly matched that civil war and perhaps even conquest by a foreign power were hardly to be averted. The economic difficulty underlay all else, the decline of the old trades with neighbouring Europe, in which England had prospered under the Henries. The remedy was sought some time before the reign of Elizabeth began, and in one aspect it may be said that the Elizabethan expansion dates from the foundation of the Muscovy Company in 1552, with its ambition of founding a new trade with Asia and its achievement of founding one with Russia. Unincorporated adventures were at the same time trading with Barbary and Guinea, and a flood of energy was released which never slackened until the British oceanic interest was permanently established.

Knowledge, guidance and inspiration were needed to direct advance and preserve determination through disappointments. They were supplied by many minds and from many angles. Just as Drake was not the only great seaman of his time, nor Shakespeare the only dramatist, so Hakluyt was not the only creator of the public pride in maritime achievement nor supplier of the facts upon which it rested. Each of these three in his own sphere was the greatest example of a widespread talent, its exponent, its moulder and its crown. Drake and Shakespeare were of quality supreme; and if that height cannot be claimed for Hakluyt, he had at least the genius that consists in taking pains.

The public interest with which he was concerned was first the revival and then the advancement of national greatness by means of trade. For a long half-century before his time Spain and Portugal had been expanding in the outer continents, while England had grown rich in Europe. With the mid-Tudor depression England awoke to the truth that in the great newly discovered world lay her future also. The effort was to be primarily and mainly by sea, although enterprise deep in the heart of Asia also played its part. Oceanic trade being the aim, discovery with a view to trade came into the plan. The Muscovy Company was so named only after the event; its style at the outset was 'The Merchants Adventurers for the Discovery of New Trades', and its operations were to be in isles and continents unknown. It did, in fact, open a new trade with Asia when its servant Anthony Jenkinson reached Persia by way of Russia, having first been into central Asia as far as Bokhara. With most of the Elizabethan projectors Asia in its many aspects was the ultimate goal. Some hoped to reach its eastern coasts by discovering the North-West Passage round North America or by using the South-West Passage through Magellan's Straits. Some thought to sell English cloth in its northern regions by discovering the North-East Passage round the Siberian coast and then passing on to China and Japan. Others desired to follow the Portuguese round the Cape of Good Hope to India and southern Asia; and others again to reach that end through the Levant and the Turkish dominions.

Hakluyt's publications aided most of the Asiatic approaches, but he had other views as well. North America as a stepping stone to Asia appealed to him, and for its own sake it appealed more strongly still. It was there, indeed, that his heart's desire really lay. He was the most forceful advocate of the colonial school of thought, which looked for social betterment not only through the expansion of trade but by the founding of new homes for the hungry and destitute in the vacant lands across the sea. For that purpose North America was the obvious scene of effort; and the more their minds dwelt upon it the more Hakluyt and his friends could discern rich and varied possibilities. They dreamed of farmlands, timber, vineyards, fisheries, trading posts to exchange their manufactures for furs and skins, naval bases to bridle the Spanish treasure route, all to constitute a new English nation freed from the overcrowded poverty that depressed them at home.

The growth of sea power was inseparable from these proposals, for voyages created sea power. The point of view of sea power was different from ours to-day. None doubted, indeed, that the defence of the realm rested on it. The difference was in the emphasis placed on its ingredients. Where we are accustomed to count battleships and cruisers in assessing the state of the national defence, the Elizabethans counted seamen and merchant shipping. In the numbers of skilled seamen consisted the safety of the nation. It was not thought possible to improvise the crews of fighting ships out of landsmen when the need should arise. The men must be already existing, a class apart, bred from boyhood to the sea, irreplaceable if lost. So, throughout the Tudor period, public opinion and state policy insisted that English seamen must find extensive employment in all sorts of trades, in voyages long and short; and anyone who established a new sea trade, such as that to the Levant or the Newfoundland fishery, was reckoned a promoter of wealth and a defender of his country. Sea power and material gain were the two main aspects of the mercantile policy. None can say whether the primary motive was to create wealth in order to support sea power, or to create sea power in order to defend the wealth. Public thought made no distinction. The two were one.

Hakluyt therefore worked for the increase of seamen. There must be new trades to employ more of them, discovery to create openings for new trades, scientific navigation to preserve their lives from shipwreck. He did not go to sea himself, and so never realized the truth that appealed to John Hawkins, that disease killed infinitely more men than accident, and that hygiene could save more than navigation. But Hawkins was almost alone in perceiving that. His fellow-captains until the days of Cook accepted pestilence as inevitable in conditions which they made no attempt to change. With reservation of that blind spot we may credit Hakluyt with promoting the increase of seamen by all available means. The ships themselves followed as a matter of course, the merchantmen, the private men-of-war, the Royal Navy. There was less talk about the ships, for they were easier to come by than the men. The arguments on the policy, design and tonnage of the fighting Navy, which in our days have been vigorously carried on in the public press, were conducted in secret by the Crown and its Ministers and the officers of the Navy Board. Hakluyt and the publicists had nothing to say on the subject. Richard Hawkins discussed the design of ships-of-war in his *Observations,* written in the last year of Elizabeth's reign, and he then kept the book in cold storage for twenty years before printing it. It was a matter solely for the experts, and there was no public opinion to express or satisfy. The lack of emphasis on the Royal Navy was largely due to the fact that in the public mind all ships were fighting ships. All the fleets mobilized for war in the Tudor period and long before it consisted of a majority of privately owned vessels and a minority of those belonging to the Crown; and it was popularly supposed that, even as late as the Armada campaign, the fighting was done by the whole shipping of the nation. Only the seamen knew that by 1588 it was an obsolete conception, and that the Queen's ships bore the brunt, while the merchantmen were merely auxiliaries. There was, indeed, an intermediate class that was capable of serious fighting, the men-of-war privately owned for oceanic adventure by such men as Hawkins, Drake, Raleigh and Leicester, whose purposes were combatant rather than mercantile, and the well-armed fleet of the Levant Company, which had to fight its way through a Mediterranean swarming with Catholic and Mahometan enemies. Hakluyt's propaganda emphasized the value of these enterprises, and he devoted special attention to publicizing the Levant trade and to the value of a colonial trade in creating large merchantmen.

Was the public appreciation of all these issues spontaneous, or did it need rousing? The answer is that it was much more sluggish than would have been adequate to the Elizabethan achievement without the work of Hakluyt. Public opinion was of different sorts according to the topic. On sentimental and religious issues, such as Henry VIII's divorce of Catherine of Aragon or his overthrow of the papal jurisdiction, it was very widespread, 'jangled in every alehouse'; and in the contest between Catholics and Protestants in Elizabeth's reign there must have been few men who did not form views of their own. The commercial policy of the early Tudor sovereigns had a large body of support from the more intelligent elements in both town and country. The merchants collected and exported the cloth and the raw wool which were England's leading exports,

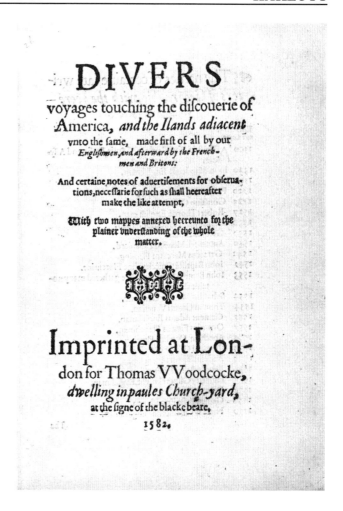

*Title page of* Divers Voyages *(1582).*

but the countryside produced it. Almost every Parliament of the Tudor period enacted detailed legislation on the cloth trade, of which many of the Members had an intimate knowledge. But public opinion was unanimous on the mercantile policy as applied to the old commerce with Spain, Flanders and Germany, and there was little need for the persuasions of the publicist.

The creation of an oceanic interest, on the other hand, and the promotion of discovery in unknown regions, were in a different category, with a natural appeal only to a small minority. It is remarkable how few traces the American discoveries of the Cabots and the seamen of Bristol have left in the literary record. Chronicles and histories and informative books were produced in the early sixteenth century, but they almost ignore the ocean and its interests, as they could not have done had there been any sustained public appreciation of the subject. Henry VIII failed in his desultory attempts to encourage oceanic enterprise, not so much from lack of purpose on his own part as because his subjects, even of the sea-trading classes, were indifferent or hostile. Representative merchants of London condemned a royal proposal for a transatlantic trading company in 1521 on the ground that it would excite Spanish jealousy and imperil London's business nearer home. There were a few enthusiasts such as John Rastell (More's brother-in-law) and the Thorne family, merchants of Bristol, but they failed to elicit any public response. With the exception of a few pages in a little book by Rastell there was no work printed in England on discovery and extra-European projects until the sixteenth century had run half its course.

The mid-Tudor depression changed the conditions by diminishing the wealth gained in the old European trades. Unemployment and beggary threatened the social order, and in the search for remedies the thinking public were compelled to extend their vision. The City of London, which had turned its face against Henry's oceanic plan of 1521, subscribed with ardour in 1552 to the Duke of Northumberland's joint-stock company for the finding of the North-East Passage. The departure next year of its first expedition under Willoughby and Chancellor was a public occasion in London, and almost suddenly discovery became popular. That year Richard Eden published his *Treatise of the New India,* a translation dedicated to Northumberland. The patron was unfortunately executed a few weeks later by the incoming Queen Mary, but Eden squared his position in his next book, a translation of Peter Martyr's *Decades of the New World,* with some trowel-laid flattery of King Philip, the new Queen's new husband. Eden's work gave the English public its first history of the discovery of America. Much of it had been written half a century earlier, but it was all new to English readers. He also included something quite up-to-the-minute, in narratives of two pioneer voyages to the Gold Coast and other parts of West Africa, led respectively by Thomas Wyndham and John Lok in 1553-4 and 1554-5. Eden was interested in the romance of adventure and strange lands, and revelled in describing the habits and appearance of the African 'oliphant', whose tusks formed part of the booty of the new adventurers. His books satisfied a new market of readers ready to be interested; but he had not gone as far as to formulate any scheme for English empire-building. His oracle was the aged Sebastian Cabot, lately returned to England to organize its undertakings after thirty-five years in Spanish service; and Cabot was a secretive man not given to enunciating his plans.

The publicity of the Elizabethan age, with its three aspects of geography, history and incitement to enterprise, was now launched, slightly before the accession of the Queen herself. Clement Adams, a disciple of the new movement, had already engraved a world-map of which copies adorned the royal galleries and the houses of London merchants, and he seems also to have published an account of the first north-eastern voyage, which had opened the new trade with Moscow by way of the White Sea. Manuals of navigation by Eden and others followed, and then, in the fifteen-sixties, three or four published works on Florida, which had become topical through the foundation and overthrow of a French colony whose Huguenot promoters had English connections. The Florida affair was the first occasion of any manifestation by the English government of interest in America since the middle years of Henry VIII; but the plans miscarried and Spain asserted her claim to the coast. The voyages of John Hawkins with manufactures from England and slaves from Africa for sale to Spanish America were at first kept as secret as possible. The last of them, however, in 1567-9, resulted in the famous treachery and fight against odds at San Juan de Ulua. It inflamed the seamen of England against Spain and invigorated the combative Protestantism of the new English generation, and called for an authoritative public statement. Hawkins furnished it in a *True Declaration* published in 1569.

So far we have taken account only of the published work of Hakluyt's predecessors. There was also a good deal of unpublished speculation circulated in manuscript or by oral discussion. Dr John Dee, known to the Queen and received at court, was persistent in impressing on the great men his views on the approach to Asia by any of the ocean routes. Sir Richard Grenville and a group of west-country magnates sought sanction for a voyage through the Straits of Magellan to discover Terra Australis Incognita, the continent thought to border the South Pacific. Hawkins and Drake, disillusioned of trading with the Spanish empire, looked for revenge by capturing its treasure fleets.

Published historico-geographical work grew important again in the late seventies with the new public interest in Frobisher's north-western discoveries. It was then that Gilbert's *Discourse* on the North-West Passage came into print. Next year (1577) Richard Willes published his *History of Travel in the West and East Indies,* covering Eden's old ground in the west and providing much information new to England on the east. Thomas Nicholas, a merchant who had been maltreated by the Inquisition in the Canary Islands, brought out a translation of a Spanish account of China, and a history of Cortez in Mexico. John Frampton, another merchant who had been racked in the Inquisition at Seville, printed in English a Spanish account of the natural products of America; another volume, of sinister significance to his enemies, describing the ports and havens of the West Indies; and yet a third on Asia, no less a work than the first English translation of the *Travels of Marco Polo.* Several books and pamphlets also appeared on Frobisher's voyages.

Altogether, the public interest in oceanic expansion had been stimulated by 1580 to an unprecedented height. This new literature created a branch of practical learning that was as yet sporadic and uncoordinated and gave rather a view of great possibilities than a plan for their realization. The subject was founded, but it awaited a master mind to drive its lessons home.


## W. Nelson Francis (essay date 1955)

SOURCE: "Hakluyt's *Voyages*: An Epic of Discovery," in *The William and Mary Quarterly,* third series, Vol. XII, No. 3, July, 1955, pp. 447-55.

[*In the following essay, Francis notes the commercial and patriotic origins of English seafaring in the late sixteenth century. Providing a brief sketch of a typical voyage from* The Principal Voyages, *Francis praises Hakluyt's restrained editorial style and his industrious scholarship.*]

In an age when tales of strange voyages are reasserting their age-old fascination, when any strange craft from Heyerdahl's primitive balsa raft to Beebe's super-scientific bathysphere is almost sure to produce a best seller, an older classic of the literature of discovery deserves to be known. I call it an epic, though it was not primarily intended as a work of literature at all; most of its many authors were blunt men of action, to whom the pen was an unwieldy instrument at best. Yet in one sense my title is not a misnomer, since the book possesses to a high degree many of the qualities which distinguish the great epics—in its setting, which is the oceans of the world, from the arctic ice north of Russia to the islands of the South Seas; in its recurring tales of conflict between man and man and between man and the elemental forces of nature; and in its theme, the turning outward of England from insularity to empire, and the growing resolve of Englishmen to make up by courageous and often unscrupulous action for their tardiness in accepting the challenge of the new-found lands across the sea.

The book deserves to be known by its full, mouth-filling Elizabethan title: ***The Principal Navigations, Voiages, Traffiques and Discoveries of the English Nation, made by Sea or over-land, to the remote and farthest distant quarters of the Earth, at any time within the compasse of these 1500 yeeres. . . . By Richard Hakluyt.***" Less leisurely ages have shortened this title to ***"Hakluyt's Voyages"***—a misleading abbreviation, since Hakluyt is the author of very few of the accounts he edited, and himself never took a longer voyage than across the English Channel. The first edition appeared in 1589. Coming as it did on the heels of the great maritime victory over the Spanish Armada, it had a success which encouraged its compiler to expand it from one to three large folio volumes, which appeared in successive years from 1598 to 1600. Even in the somewhat cut-down Everyman's Library edition it fills eight volumes, about 3,200 ordinary pages. To read it through is a task recommended only to those plodders who like books that offer a real trial of endur-

ance. But for the ordinary reader it is one of the best browsing-books in the world's literature.

In the rather grandiose title already quoted, Hakluyt claimed to cover 1,500 years of English seafaring history. But largely because of shortage of material, the story of the first fourteen centuries occupies but a small part of his first volume. After their first venturesome migration from their Continental home across the North Sea, the Anglo-Saxons almost entirely gave up seafaring: they realized on a racial scale the fondest hope of every sailor—to "swallow the anchor" and settle down on a farm. During the centuries when their Scandinavian cousins were pushing their frail open boats ever westward, from Iceland to Greenland and from Greenland to Vineland, the Anglo-Saxons were alternately fighting among themselves, living in insular peace and complacency, or attempting to repel others of those same Scandinavians who preferred marauding to exploration. Nor, in spite of their Viking ancestry, did the Norman conquerors encourage maritime enterprise. During the four and a half centuries from William the Conqueror to Henry VIII, the English kings were chiefly concerned with extending, holding, or regaining the extensive lands in France to which they laid claim by feudal right. Military operations demanded no more naval support than was needed to transport troops across the Channel. And although England engaged in foreign trade, a large part of it was conducted in ships of other nations. It was not until the rediscovery of the New World at the end of the fifteenth century that Englishmen began to go to sea in any numbers, and to write the accounts of their voyages which fill up Hakluyt's big volumes.

Even at that, they were late. After three centuries during which England has been virtually undisputed mistress of the seas, it is hard for us to understand the almost total lack of interest which she showed toward the discoveries which aroused the Mediterranean world to a fever of excitement. Except for the abortive voyage of the Cabots—themselves Italians, be it noted—she did nothing at all for sixty years, and she did not establish a permanent settlement for over a hundred. Viewed from the opposite historical perspective, however, this apathy seems natural enough. With no nautical tradition and, in Henry VIII, a monarch whose interests were marital rather than maritime, England was not ready for a career of discovery and colonization. Other nations had the ships and the men with the skill and courage to sail them; occasionally also they had rulers, like the Portuguese Prince Henry the Navigator, who were willing and able to give both financial support and enthusiastic appreciation to their explorers. By the time the English awoke, the Portuguese had for generations been following Vasco da Gama's trail around the Cape of Good Hope eastward to the Indies, and the Spanish had established their empire on its ultimately insecure golden foundation in the western lands discovered by the Italian Columbus. Even the Pope had blessed the Spanish-Portuguese monopoly, dividing the world between the two empires by his famous line 370 leagues west of Cape Verde. The plums had been picked; there was nothing for the English to do but to rob those who had picked them or to climb higher in the tree in search of some that had been overlooked.

Ultimately they tried both, the latter first. Or to abandon the figure, they began to search for new routes and new lands which they could exploit without trespassing on Spanish or Portuguese territory. Since the routes to the southeast and southwest were taken, this meant sailing north. The first Englishman to point clearly to the northerly routes was a certain Robert Thorne, a London merchant who had lived for many years in Seville, where was located the Spanish academy of navigation. Hakluyt prints the letter Thorne wrote to Henry VIII in 1527, and a tremendously interesting letter it is. He sent a map along with it, on which he demonstrated that the northeast route around Norway and the northwest route around Newfoundland were both shorter ways to get to the rich lands of Cathay than the Portuguese route around Africa. As to the hardships of arctic sailing, he finds them overrated; in fact, he finds an advantage to outweigh them in the perpetual daylight of the arctic summer:

> Shippes may passe and have in them perpetuall clerenesse of the day without any darkenesse of the night: which thing is a great commoditie for the navigants, to see at all times round about them, as well the safeguards as dangers.

He concludes with a declaration of faith that might well serve as a motto for the intrepid explorers of a generation later:

> For as all judge [there is no vacuum in Nature]: so I judge, there is no land unhabitable, nor Sea innavigable.

But Robert Thorne's clarion call to the realization of England's manifest destiny in the arctic went unheeded for twenty-six years. The King continued to waste many hundred times the cost of a voyage of exploration in fruitless wars with France, the only outcome of which was national bankruptcy. Nor did matters improve under his saintly but young and sickly son, Edward VI. In fact, by the middle of the century England had declined to the position of an insignificant insular state, almost beneath the notice of the proud and wealthy Spanish empire. It was not until the last year of Edward's reign, 1553, that the sad state of English trade led to the first attempt to carry out Thorne's suggestions about new routes and new lands to the north.

As the account in Hakluyt (written by a certain Clement Adams) makes very clear, the motive for this pioneer voyage was purely commercial. The merchants of London, so Adams tells us, became worried over the shrinking markets for English goods abroad and the growing demand for foreign goods at home; they were facing what the economists call an unfavorable trade balance. The remedy was obvious—in fact, it had been obvious for forty years, though few had seen it. As Adams puts it:

> For seeing that the wealth of the Spaniards and Portingales, by the discoverie and search of newe trades and Countreys was marveilously increased, supposing the same to be a course and meane for them also to obtain the like, they thereupon resolved upon a newe and strange Navigation.

They called into council Sebastian Cabot, veteran of his father's voyage of sixty years earlier, and with his help quickly reached a decision:

> It was at last concluded that three shippes should be prepared and furnished out, for the search and discoverie of the Northerne part of the world, to open a way and passage to our men for travaile to newe and unknowen kingdomes.

A stock company was formed; the ships were built and stocked with provisions for eighteen months; and Sir Hugh Willoughby was chosen Admiral of the fleet, with "one Richard Chanceler, a man of great estimation for many good partes of wit in him," as his lieutenant. The only mention which the chronicler makes of the ordinary seamen occurs in his report of a speech made by Sir Henry Sidney (father of the famous Philip) to his fellow stockholders, in which he contrasts the easy life which they will live at home with the hardships and difficulties faced by Willoughby and Chanceler, not the least of which would be the labor of keeping "the ignorant and unruly Mariners in good order and obedience."

There is the picture complete—a pattern of preparation for a voyage repeated again and again in Hakluyt's pages. The indispensable foundation for the whole is supplied by the backers, shrewd London merchants, ready to risk a little capital but by no means their precious lives on dangerous voyages. Then there are the ships—small, but sturdily built and able to go anywhere that skillful and cautious mariners would take them; the provisions—usually not enough and often scandalously bad (Chanceler found before he left England that some of his food had rotted and the barrels of wine had leaked); the leadership—often divided between gentlemen-adventurers and professional sailors, with frequent conflict between headlong foolhardiness and pride of rank on the one hand and overprudence and professional jealousy on the other; and finally the crews—ruffians from the London streets, unruly and undisciplined, suspicious of their leaders, capable equally of superhuman labor and endurance or craven fear and surly indolence, after the manner of sailors in all times and places.

There is room here only to sketch the actual voyage of Willoughby and Chanceler—an excellent one with which to begin one's browsing in Hakluyt. After a rousing send-off, the ships slipped out of the Thames and turned northward. Their goal was to find a northeast passage to Cathay and the Indies; their route was one which events of World War II made familiar—the convoy route from England around the North Cape to northern Russia. On the way a storm separated them, but they went on, each thinking the other was lost. Waiting for Willoughby at their appointed rendezvous, a Norwegian trading-post just beyond the North Cape, Chanceler encountered some Scottish merchants who tried to get him to turn back. His answer strikes a note repeated again and again in the later voyages: the combination of dauntless courage with flamboyant utterance which in any age but the Elizabethan would be bombastic:

> But hee holding nothing so ignominious and reprochfull, as inconstancie and levitie of minde, and perswading himselfe that a man of valour coulde not commit a more dishonourable part then for feare of danger to avoyde and shunne great attempts, was nothing at all changed or discouraged with the speeches and words of the Scots, remaining stedfast and immutable in his first resolution: determining either to bring that to passe which was intended, or els to die the death.

He went on, skirting the Murman coast and finally arriving in the White Sea. Here he left his ship where the port of Archangel now is and made the 1500-mile overland journey by sledge to Moscow and the court of the Tsar. What he found there is another story, well worth looking into Hakluyt to discover. Meanwhile Willoughby had sailed across the Barents Sea to Nova Zembla and back to a deserted harbor in Lapland. Here later voyagers found his ship frozen in the ice, her crew to the last man dead of starvation and cold.

I have dwelt at some length on this particular voyage, partly because it was one of the first, and partly because it was so typical—in its commercial motive, its account of hardships suffered and difficulties overcome, and its partial tragedy—of so many others to come. There are seven and a half more volumes of Hakluyt's collection, of whose contents I can give only a hint. Their real riches the browser must uncover for himself. First comes the series of voyages which followed this pioneer attempt—trading voyages to Moscow and exploring voyages farther and farther eastward, encountering only ice and more ice instead of the balmy spice-laden air of the Indies. Among them is the amazing overland journey of Anthony Jenkinson, from Archangel on the White Sea to Bokhara in Persia. Then the interest swings away from the northeast toward the northwest, partly under the influence of an eloquent essay by Sir Humphrey Gilbert, proving to his own satisfaction at least the existence of a clear and open passage around Newfoundland to China, Japan, and the spice islands. Here are met the greatest explorers of them all—men like Martin Frobisher, first to land on Baffin Land, who just missed finding the passage through to Hudson's Bay; and John Davis, the finest English sailor and navigator of the century, whose name is perpetuated in Davis Strait, between Greenland and Baffin Land. Again follow frustration and failure to bring home the rich profits in gold and oriental goods which the merchants at home expected. Again the interest shifts, this time away from exploration altogether and toward out-and-out piracy. The reader who looks beneath the surface of the stories will see England as a "have-not" nation, at first tentatively and then boldly plundering the complacent "haves," Portugal and Spain. Here are encountered the true swashbuckling Elizabethan adventurers—Sir John Hawkins, forcing the West Indian Spaniards at point of gun to buy his African slaves; and the great Drake himself, triumphantly circumnavigating the earth, his ship so full of Spanish plunder that he would only take the gold and jewels, not bothering with the silver. Finally come the first fumbling and inept beginnings of the art of colonizing, in which the English were eventually to lead the world. The reader who browses on through to the end will be rewarded by finding the accounts of the first English settlements in North America, with their tragic and mysterious end. Fortunately for the unity of Hakluyt's book, its appearance coincided with an epoch in the history of England's relations with the New World. After 1600 the men who sailed westward were of a different type. They were no longer adventures hired to go out and bring back gold and riches or to singe the Spaniard's beard; now they were settlers, cutting off home ties and resolving to begin a new life in the new lands. Their story is no longer part of the epic of exploration; it is instead a part of our own colonial history.

In attempting to convey the sweep and scale of this book, I have called it an epic. That is really an erroneous term. An epic is the creation of an artist; Hakluyt's *Voyages* is the labor of a scholar. In fact, it belongs to the very select group of works of painstaking and monumental scholarship which have gained and held an audience outside of scholarly circles—the group which also includes Gibbon's *Decline and Fall of the Roman Empire,* Boswell's *Life of Johnson,* and Frazer's *Golden Bough.* Meticulous accuracy, scholarly skepticism, and infinite industry are the qualities that went into the composition of Hakluyt's work. In one of the great poems inspired by the voyagers, the

"Ode to the Virginian Voyage," the poet Drayton apostrophizes its author as "Industrious Hakluyt," and that I am sure is the epithet which he would himself have chosen. At one time he took a painful journey of two hundred miles on horseback to exchange a few words with the only survivor of one of the early voyages to Labrador. Yet he never allowed his passion for inclusiveness to overwhelm his keen critical judgment. Every account that went into his collection he checked for authenticity by every resource at his command. In an age that loved tales of wonder, stories of

> the Cannibals that each other eat, The Anthropophagi, and men whose heads
>
> Do grow beneath their shoulders,

Hakluyt refused to make his book a collection of the tall tales of travelers. In spite of the great bulk of his book, he rejected more than he printed.

Like all true scholars, Hakluyt let his work speak for itself, without intruding his own personality. But in the one place where it is the scholar's privilege to speak in his own person—his prefaces and dedications—he gives us some insight into the feelings that led him to neglect his official and easy occupation of country clergyman for the arduous and exacting labors of geographical scholarship. The first impulse, he tells us, came while he was a mere schoolboy, visiting the study of his namesake and cousin, also a geographer. His own words are classic:

> I do remember that being a youth, and one of her Majesties scholars at Westminster that fruitfull nurserie, it was my happe to visit the chamber of M. Richard Hakluyt my cosin, a Gentleman of the Middle Temple, . . . at a time when I found lying open upon his boord certeine bookes of Cosmographie, with an universall Mappe: he seeing me somewhat curious in the view therof, began to instruct my ignorance. . . . He pointed with his wand to all the knowen Seas, Gulfs, Bayes, Straights, Capes, Rivers, Empires, Kingdomes, Dukedomes, and Territories of ech part, with declaration also of their speciall commodities, & particular wants. . . . From the Mappe he brought me to the Bible, and turning to the 107 Psalme, directed mee to the 23 & 24 verses, where I read, that they which go downe to the sea in ships, and occupy by the great waters, they see the works of the Lord, and his woonders in the deepe.

With such imaginative stimulation, most ordinary boys would simply want to go to sea. But Hakluyt showed his scholarly temperament from the start: he went to the University, where he studied geography and navigation and read every account of travel he could lay his hands on, learning four modern languages, in addition to Latin and Greek, for the purpose. Before he left Oxford he was lecturing on geography and cosmography, the most learned man in England in these

subjects. He took orders in the church merely as a means of livelihood, and embarked immediately on the tremendous task of collecting the scattered accounts of all the English voyages.

I ought not to conclude without a word of warning. He who must have his adventure spiced with hysterical journalism will not like this book. To those whom a diet of radio serials has made addicts of the ominous voice and the synthetic sound-effect, Hakluyt will be boring. But for members of the increasingly small group of those who are still able to perceive in an unemotional printed account the real thrills and dangers that lie beneath the surface understatement, here is a treasure. Let me illustrate briefly what I mean. In October of 1580, an expedition headed by Arthur Pet and Charles Jackman, the last to attempt the northeast passage, was returning to England after penetrating farther east than any of their predecessors. As they came down the Norwegian coast, they met head winds and storms, and put into a fjord to await better weather. The account goes on:

> The 7 day [of October] we set saile; for from the first of this moneth untill this 7 day, we had very foule weather, but specially the fourth day when the wind was so great, that our cables brake with the very storme, and I do not thinke that it is possible that any more wind then that was should blow: for after the breaking of our cable, we did drive a league, before our ankers would take any hold: but God be thanked the storme began to slacke, otherwise we had bene in ill case.

Now breaking cables and dragging anchors are the things which the mariner fears and hates more than anything, because they betray him when he has a right to feel secure. The anchor is the universal symbol of security; when it fails, the last support of faith and guarantee of rest is gone. Yet with cables broken and auxiliary anchors dragging, this matter-of-fact chronicler says that if the storm had not abated, they *would have been* in ill case!

He then, who likes the characteristic understatements of true men of action—the calmly matter-of-fact accounts of incredible hardships and heroic daring written by men unskilled in the facititious devices and tricks of the higher journalism—who, in short, likes to exercise his imagination rather than have it belabored from without, will find this his book. Let him get the eight volumes, equip himself with an atlas—or better yet, a globe—and settle down to browse. He will not be disappointed.

**Christopher Hill (essay date 1965)**

SOURCE: "Ralegh—Science, History, and Politics,"

in *Intellectual Origins of the English Revolution,* Oxford at the Clarendon Press, 1965, pp. 154-62.

[*Hill is an important Marxist historian whose work focuses on the English Civil War. In the following excerpt, Hill considers Hakluyt's work as publicist and foreign policy propagandist for Sir Walter Ralegh.*]

Ralegh's foreign policy was not his private affair, but was the policy of a whole group, whose main publicists were the two Richard Hakluyts. Ralegh was intimately connected with them. The younger Hakluyt's **Discourse of Western Planting** was written in 1584 'at the request and direction of Ralegh', to whom most of Hakluyt's works were dedicated. The policy of the Hakluyts was at once patriotic and imperialist. England had got left behind in the grab for the New World by Spain and Portugal, whose empires were menacingly united in 1580. After a rapid expansion of English cloth exports in the first half of the sixteenth century, relative stagnation followed. Unemployment created social, political, and national dangers, as Ralegh and many other observers noted. But the younger Hakluyt was shrewd enough to realize that England's over-population was only relative. The colonization of North America would not only get rid of England's immediate surplus population: it would also provide raw materials for home industries, and so prepare for a long-term solution. The object of economic policy should be to make England self-sufficient, an exporter of highly finished manufactured goods. North America would yield dye-stuffs for the clothing industry, the naval stores for which England was dependent on Baltic supplies, and timber to relieve England's fuel shortage. The reduction of the Indians 'to civility, both in manners and garments' would provide a new market. Given an economically self-sufficient Empire, England need not bother about capturing markets in Europe.

But England's road was blocked by Spain, on whose empire, in Bacon's phrase, 'the sun never sets'. Spain closed the whole American continent to English settlers, English goods, and English religion. So this policy, as Sidney and Hakluyt saw, involved war with Spain. Colonization was thus strategically vital. Occupation of North America could command the Newfoundland fishing banks and the Spanish homeward route from the Indies. 'Traffic followeth conquest.' But with this base in the New World, war against Spain could be made to pay for itself: 'we must not look to maintain war upon the revenues of England', Ralegh warned Cecil in 1595. Privateering could enrich individual merchants and gentlemen: gold and silver could be diverted from Spain to England. Such a war had religious as well as patriotic overtones. Foxe had traced the sufferings and struggles of God's people down to the Marian martyrs: Hakluyt's book also started with the beginning of the Christian epoch; but his Englishmen have passed over to the offensive against Antichrist, bringing the Gospel to parts of the world which had never yet heard it. If the worst came to the worst—and this illustrates the anxieties still felt by Elizabethan Englishmen, which we are too apt to forget because we know the end of the story—'a place of safety might there be found, if change of religion or civil wars should happen in this realm'

War against Spain was necessary, the Hakluyts thought, not only to preserve England's national independence, but also to bring salvation to millions of American Indians, who had within living memory been subjugated to popery and Spanish cruelty. Puritan ministers, dangerously unemployed and restless at home, could be sent abroad to convert the heathen. 'God hath reserved' North America 'to be reduced unto Christian civility by the English nation'. Because of Spanish cruelty the Indians—'a poor and harmless people created of God'—would offer willing allies against Spain, as Ralegh often found. Ralegh's imperial policy envisaged the export of English arts and English women to Peru, the arming and training of the Indians, who were to be used to establish Peruvian independence of Spain, under allegiance to England. Ralegh's good treatment of the Indians at Trinidad in 1595 was remembered in 1605 and 1626, when they 'did unanimously own the protection of the English' against Spain. In Guiana 'he left so good and so great a name behind him . . . that the English have often been obliged to remember him with honour'. Most of his contemporaries', Professor Quinn [in *Ralegh and the British Empire* (1947)] sums up, 'regarded the Spanish empire as something to be robbed: Ralegh thought of it as something to be replaced by an English empire. He therefore considered seriously the problems of English rule over a native population.' This underlines the tragedy that Ralegh could interest James only in robbery.

Hakluyt and Ralegh, then, put forward a national policy which offered something to all sections of the community. From the unemployed to Puritan ministers anxious to extend true religion, from City merchants to discontented younger sons of the landed class, all, it seemed, had something to gain.

In 1596 Ralegh's devoted adherent Lawrence Kemyis, a Balliol geographer and mathematician who like Wright had thrown up his fellowship to go to sea, published a *Relation of the Second Voyage to Guiana*. To this George Chapman, member of Ralegh's circle and friend of Hariot, prefixed a poem. Chapman urged 'patrician spirits', 'that know death lives where power lies unused' no longer to

be content like horse to hold
A threadbare beaten way to home affairs.

They should

scorn to let your bodies choke your souls
In the rude breath and prison'd life of beasts.
You that herein renounce the course of earth
And lift your eyes for guidance to the stars,
That live not for yourselves, but to possess
Your honour'd country of a general store;
In pity of the spoil rude self-love makes
Of those whose lives and years one aim doth feed,
One soil doth nourish, and one strength combine;
You that are blest with sense of all things noble,
In this attempt your complete worths redouble.

Once Elizabeth blessed

with her wonted graces
Th'industrious knight, the soul of this exploit
[Ralegh]

she would create

A golden world in this our iron age. . . .
A world of savages fall tame before them,
Storing their theft-free treasuries with gold;
And there doth plenty crown their wealthy fields,
There Learning eats no more his thriftless books,
Nor Valour, estridge-like, his iron arms. . . .
There makes society adamantine chains,
And joins their hearts with wealth whom wealth
  disjoin'd.

Hakluyt and Ralegh, like Bacon, synthesized and gave organized form to the thinking of large numbers of less articulate Englishmen. John Hawkins saw himself as the successor of Foxe's martyrs when he was frustrated in his attempt to sell bootleg negro slaves in Spanish America. Martin Frobisher prayed in 1577 for a safe return to England so that his discoveries 'might redound to the more honour of [God's] holy name, and *consequently* to the advancement of our commonwealth'. Lawrence Kemyis thought it had 'pleased God of his infinite goodness, in his will and purpose to appoint and reserve this empire [of Guiana] for us'. Hakluyt was the spokesman of this newly self-conscious nationalism.

A full-scale policy of imperial conquest could not be carried out without government support, without a powerful navy. In 1577 Ralegh's friend John Dee, who appears to have originated the phrase 'the British Empire', had advocated a standing royal navy to police the seas against pirates, and so protect merchants and the fishing industry. Under James and Charles this became a crying need, when the Algiers pirates mastered up-to-date techniques of navigation. But, apart from Mansell's abortive expedition of 1620-1, it was not until the sixteen-fifties that Blake's fleet bombarded Algiers and Cormwell's troops captured Jamaica and Dunkirk. For two generations the advocates of the Hakluyt-Ralegh policy laboured to convince govern-

ments of its desirability and feasibility: but in vain. Elizabeth 'did all by halves', as Ralegh said. 'Neither James I nor Charles I . . . ever sent a ship across the Atlantic.' There were serious limits to the effectiveness of colonization by private enterprise, as the early colonists found to their cost.

After the defeat of the Armada had first shaken the fixed belief of Englishmen in the omnipotence of Spain, a massive propaganda campaign was undertaken to convince a sufficient number of influential people that England's destiny lay in grandiose exploits across the ocean. The younger Hakluyt decided to embark on his *magnum opus,* a careful collection and publication of facts on Baconian lines, a few months after the Armada's defeat had opened up dazzling new prospects. Hariot's *Brief and True Report* on Virginia appeared in 1588; Ralegh's *Discovery of Guiana* in 1591; and Hakluyt's **Voyages,** reprinting both of them, rounded off the campaign. In merchant circles, at least, it was very successful. The East India Company supplied as reading matter to its ships the Bible, Foxe's *Acts and Monuments,* Perkins's *Works,* and Hakluyt. The combination is significant. Hakluyt acted as Ralegh's publicity agent in the campaign, and seems deliberately to have worked to get books dedicated to Ralegh, often dictating the content of the dedication so as to stress Ralegh's international reputation.

Throughout the *History of the World* the over-riding importance of exhorting his readers against Spain is never far from Ralegh's mind. Spanish America would be as easy to conquer as Syria under the sons of Aram. Xerxes reminded Ralegh of Philip II. Alexander's tactics against Bessus led Ralegh to urge future invaders of Guiana or the West Indies always to 'burn down the grass and sedge to the east of them'. The wars between Rome and Carthage gave rise to a long digression on sea power and naval strategy, and to warnings against the dangers of trading with Spain. A discussion of tyranny prompted the improbable reflection that under a king like James 'it is likely, by God's blessing, that a land shall flourish with increase of trade in countries before unknown; that civility and religion shall be propagated into barbarous and heathen countries; and that the happiness of his subjects shall cause the nations far removed to wish him their sovereign'. In the 'Conclusion to the whole work' Ralegh noted that Spanish power was the greatest that had been seen in western Europe since the fall of the Roman Empire; still this power could easily and cheaply be restrained if England, France, and the Netherlands went over to the offensive. 'The obedience even of the Turk is easy and a liberty in respect of the slavery and tyranny of Spain', Ralegh had written in 1591.

For Hakluyt and Ralegh an alliance with the Netherlands was the necessary concomitant of their anti-Spanish policy. For this there were ideological reasons ('after my duty to mine own sovereign', wrote Ralegh, 'and the love of my country, I honour them most'). The Netherlands also provided a model of economic behaviour. But a Dutch alliance was also a practical necessity, even if the Dutch proved ungrateful competitors. For 'this long calm' after the peace of 1604 'will shortly break out in some terrible tempest', as it did in the year of Ralegh's execution. Yet Ralegh's interest in the shipping industry led him to advocate its encouragement and something very like a Navigation Act against Dutch competition. Like many English merchants, Ralegh was ambivalent in his attitude towards the Netherlands. Dutch merchants monopolized the carrying trade, and insisted on continuing to trade with Spain even in time of war. Ralegh 'was the first which made public the growth by sea of the Dutch, and the riches they derived from their fishing upon the coasts of England and Scotland, and the consequences which would necessarily follow, not only to the loss of the King's sovereignty of the British seas, but to the trade and navigation of England otherwise'. The cry was taken up by Tobias Gentleman and other pamphleteers, and echoed by Hakewill. But James 'stopped his ears to Sir Walter's advice concerning the Dutch fishing' and only opened them when Ralegh promised him gold from Guiana. To the Dutch alliance Ralegh came to add an alliance with the Palatinate and the maintenance of the Protestant interest in France and Switzerland—an object dear to Oliver Cromwell's heart.

Neither Elizabeth, James, nor Charles had any use for this foreign policy. They regarded the Dutch as rebels and Spain as the greatest monarchy in Christendom, with whom it would be folly for England to engage in war *à l'outrance*. Nor had any of them much sympathy with the commercial or religious ideals which underlay Hakluyt's and Ralegh's schemes. But to many merchants and ministers, and to a large group in every House of Commons, the policy was very attractive. From 1612 the Virginia Company tried to carry it out. Hakluyt, a founder-member, may have organized the Company's propaganda campaign. Bacon, Coke, Fulke Greville, Viscount Lisle, Hariot, and Briggs were members, together with Theodore Gulston, Thomas Winston, and Sir Oliver Cromwell, uncle of the Protector. All the great London livery companies subscribed.

A list of the motives of the Virginia Adventurers, drafted in 1612, is a summary of Hakluyt's policy: (i) convert the Indians; (ii) export surplus population, 'the rank multitude'; (iii) supply England with naval stores and (iv) minerals; (v) provide a base for Atlantic shipping and (vi) explorations to reveal a northwest passage to the Far East. The Virginia Company was supported by a propaganda campaign conducted by ministers (mainly Puritan). Thus William Crashawe spoke in 1613 of a work so honourable to God, our religion, our King and our country; so comfortable to the souls

of the poor savages, and so profitable to the Adventurers . . . as the like . . . hath not been attempted in the Christian world these many ages'. Propaganda against Spain and for American colonization was continued by Samuel Purchas, whose *Pilgrimage* ran to four editions between 1613 and 1626, and together with his *Hakluytus Posthumus* had a great influence.

---

**David Freeman Hawke on the unusual nature of Hakluyt's contribution to the exploration voyages:**

There is something preposterous about a mild, retiring preacher emerging out of Elizabethan England as one of the giants of the age. Indeed, Hakluyt's whole life skirts the absurd. He knew more about the New World than any other man of the day, yet he never saw it. Salty phrases dot his writings—"it is high time for us to weigh our anchor, to hoist up our sails"—yet he knew nothing firsthand about a sailor's life. He produced the greatest collection of sea tales ever assembled in the English language without once having ventured upon the ocean. In a hyperbolic age, he had a passion for truth, and once he rode two hundred miles to check the facts about an early and insignificant expedition to America—Master Hore's in 1536—from a lone survivor. He was a visionary and romantic who gave sound advice to businessmen prepared to invest in risky projects overseas. He was a scholar who mingled with ease among courtiers and statesmen and with equal ease among sailors in the rowdy taverns of the port towns where he collected accounts of their latest adventures.

*David Freeman Hawke, in an introduction to* Hakluyt's Voyages to the New World, *edited by David Freeman Hawke, The Bobbs-Merrill Company, Inc., 1972.*

---

**David B. Quinn and Alison M. Quinn (essay date 1973)**

SOURCE: An introduction to *Virginia Voyages from Hakluyt,* edited by David B. Quinn and Alison M. Quinn, Oxford University Press, London, 1973, pp. vii-xvii.

[*In the following essay, the critics provide an overview of Hakluyt's career and chronicle his involvement, along with that of Grenville and Ralegh, in the discovery and settlement of North America.*]

Richard Hakluyt led a relatively long, assured, and peaceful life from 1552 to 1616. He studied, taught, and lectured at Christ Church from 1570 to 1583: he acted as chaplain to the English ambassador in Paris from 1583 to 1588, though with long home leaves, and enjoyed thereafter a pleasing plurality of benefices, canonries at Westminster and Bristol, livings at Wetheringsett and Gedney, a chaplaincy at the Savoy. Once he had passed through the discipline of his university training and had reinforced it with a wide range of modern languages, he devoted himself almost wholly to geographical and historical studies. These were not confined to libraries and to correspondence or personal contacts with English and continental scholars, but involved a considerable amount of research and field-work of a less conventional sort.

In 1568 when he was still a schoolboy at Westminster School, he was inspired by a visit to his elder cousin, Richard Hakluyt of the Inner Temple, to take up the study of geography and, in particular, that of the new discoveries outside Europe which had taken place in the previous century. His cousin, giving more time to this, one feels, than to law, had built up an impressive range of correspondence with men as far afield as Mexico and Goa, was busy assembling documents on economic and trading conditions outside Europe and was exploiting his knowledge by placing it at the disposal of merchants who were interested in opening up new channels of trade. The younger Hakluyt, during the next ten years, while he was completing his formal education (he graduated B.A. in 1573 and M.A. in 1577), followed his cousin's example in the study of the expanded world picture which presented itself at this time to young Englishmen (as it had earlier to Europeans), but gradually developed a personal approach or rather a series of personal approaches to its problems.

He was keenly interested in descriptions of foreign lands and of travel to and in them by sea and land: he rapidly appreciated that a great deal of the attraction in the literature of discovery lay in being able to capture the authentic voice of the traveller. The traveller's descriptions of what he saw, experienced, of what he felt even, formed a vital part in the understanding which the scholar and the reader could gain from sharing, through him, in the process of discovery. This led Hakluyt to despise the historical compendia, such as those of Sebastian Münster and André Thevet, into which the records of the discoveries and the new empires were being assimilated. His first and inevitable approach to the narratives of overseas exploration was, not surprisingly for one of his academic training, a literary one. He looked for effective narratives which were already in print. He found a great variety in Ramusio's *Navigationi et viaggi,* arranged in order on a regional basis, and as he learnt Italian and got his friend (and probably tutor) John Florio to translate some of them, he gradually established his own criteria as a collector and interpreter of travel materials. Though he remained willing to read and collect records of travel by anyone at any time or place he came to concentrate on two reasonably distinguishable categories of material. His first was that by non-English writers on areas which he thought Englishmen ought to travel to, trade with, perhaps even settle in; his second was that writ-

ten by Englishmen in any circumstances involving travel outside the British Isles. These were categories at once shifting and didactic, shifting because the grounds on which such actions might appear advisable changed as the result of external forces and the expanding range of his own interests; didactic because it assumed that Hakluyt knew or thought he knew what English travellers, merchants, would-be colonists should do. This latter confidence sprang initially from his cousin's expertise in advising merchants on possible channels of trade; it was fostered and canalized by meeting men who had firm beliefs, even obsessions, about their own objectives as explorers or settlers and who proved willing to consult and employ him to further their particular ends. Hakluyt thus found himself not only collecting but selecting travel literature, picking out those narratives which would best illustrate the region which interested him or which those who consulted him wished at once to promote, explore, and exploit. Precisely what fixed his attention so particularly on North America is not wholly clear: it may partly have been the result of his own selective intelligence working on the available material: it was largely the effect of being involved in a small but expanding group of persons, centering on his cousin and on John Dee, who had begun seriously to discuss prospects of North American exploration and who were being stirred into action by the restless insistence of Sir Humphrey Gilbert.

England's earliest continuous interest in North America was in the Newfoundland inshore fishery. This had grown up without corporate or governmental sponsorship but as an economic asset it was vulnerable to international pressures and so was bound, as tension with Spain grew, to involve at least the concern of government. A more temporary interest had been Florida (then understood as the coast-line of the three most southerly states in the present-day south-eastern United States). Aroused by French activity shortly after 1560, it had faded out, it seemed, in the early 1570s. It had subsequently been replaced by much higher latitudes, in the North-west Passage speculations and adventures between 1574 and 1578, culminating when the Baffin Island gold-search, into which it had been diverted, was proved a fiasco and brought discredit on north-west venturing. Before this lost its glamour, a new phase of interest developed farther south, in the mainland to the south of Newfoundland and to the north of whatever posts the Spaniards had been able to maintain in Florida. Gilbert's patent of June 1578 gave him potential authority in an undefined area, which his supporters knew to be this part of North America. The elder Hakluyt wrote notes to show how the more northerly parts of it might be both exploited commercially and settled; John Dee presented a map to the Queen and attempted to convince her that England had good prior title by discovery to North America. It was into this activity that the younger Richard Hakluyt was drawn. The precise date is not known. It is most likely to have been in 1579, after Gilbert returned unsuccessful from his first poorly planned and executed voyage of reconnaissance. His function was to add both propaganda and information to the publicity for the western ventures. It is characteristic of him that he should have done so by presenting documents of travel, carefully translated, edited from manuscript or reprinted, rather than lengthy appeals to national pride or even to commercial cupidity: narrative as specific as possible, and hard facts as reliable as he could find them, were his stock in trade. Thus he set John Florio to work to translate Cartier texts from Ramusio in support of a detached (and unsuccessful) branch of the Gilbert enterprises and these duly appeared in 1580 as *A shorte and briefe narration of the two nauigations and discoueries to the Northweast partes called Newe Fraunce.* His next was a more ambitious one in which he (with some help from a young Hungarian scholar, Stephen Parmenius) put together a collection of English, French, and Spanish documents on what was known of eastern North America and which could prove at the same time useful to English explorers and also informative and stimulating to readers who were potential investors in the enterprises. *Diuers voyages touching the discouerie of America, and the ilands adiacent vnto the same, made first of all by our Englishmen, and afterwards by the Frenchmen and Britons* appeared in May 1582, and played its part in getting Gilbert on his way, though not until June 1583. Hakluyt was now launched as an adviser, as an editor, and as a man who had lent a somewhat new note to the publication of English travel collections (though it had already been sounded rather mutely by Richard Eden and Richard Willes), that of the forceful direct narrative by a leading participant in an exploring voyage, even if his leading narrative (Verrazzano's) had come to him from Ramusio and the other, Ribault's, had already been printed in 1563 but forgotten.

The years 1583 to 1588 were the busiest in Hakluyt's quiet life. In Paris between September 1583 and July 1584, he read and digested a large number of Spanish and Italian works on the New World, sought out manuscripts of French American ventures, talked to the royal cosmographer André Thevet and the botanist Pierre Pena, visited merchants and pilots in Paris, Rouen, and elsewhere. The main focus of his activity was directed to eastern North America. Successively, Gilbert, Sir George Peckham, and Christopher Carleill during this period of time failed to mount any effective expedition to explore the North American coastline, to find new trades in its waters and amongst its indigenous peoples, or to lay any foundations for English transatlantic settlement. This last had come to Hakluyt to represent the greatest good; Englishmen still had a chance to step in and conquer where Spaniards and French hesitated. There was, moreover, one last leader left in the field, Walter Ralegh. Gaining in March 1584 the patent

relinquished by his dead half-brother, he had sent out in April a reconnaissance under Amadas and Barlowe, on the long route by way of the West Indies, to find a harbour and a possible place for settlement to the north of Spanish Florida, whose northernmost outpost was in modern South Carolina. Apprised of this voyage by Sir Francis Walsingham (who was himself deeply interested in the venture) and by Ralegh, Hakluyt was brought back to England by July to give his advice on both broader and narrower implications of the American enterprise. Between July and early October Hakluyt completed his longest sustained piece of argument, 'The particular discourse'—labelled by successive editors as *'Discourse on Western Planting'* and *'Discourse of Western Planting'*. Its purpose was to spell out why and how England should establish herself in North America. It appeals to history, to rivalry with imperial and Catholic Spain, to geography (climate and ease of access), to commerce at sea, on land, and by means of English colonies, to settlement for English men and women who might be regarded as surplus to the needs of their own land. North America could make England rich; could make her powerful as well. The discourse was basically an appeal to Queen Elizabeth to lend at least some of the resources of the state to the American enterprise. Both Walsingham and Ralegh hoped for something from the Queen when Hakluyt laid it in her hands on 3 October 1584, before he went back to his Paris post. The Queen in the end provided a few crumbs, but little comfort for the 1585 venture. But the discourse was intended as ammunition for the promoters of further expeditions as well. Though confidential and unpublished, a few copies were circulated in influential hands, and much detailed advice was culled from it for the planning of the next American voyage.

Though Hakluyt stayed long enough in England to hear of the discovery by Amadas and Barlowe of the Carolina Outer Banks and the forest-ringed sounds which lay behind them, he was nevertheless away from England during the preparations for the voyage which was to plant the first tentative English colony on American soil and which represented thus the coming to fruition of his fondest hopes. The Queen agreed that the new land called, it was thought, Wingandacoia should be named for her hardest-held attribute, Virginia. She knighted Walter Ralegh, made him governor of Virginia with a seal of his own but without permission himself to attend the establishment of the settlement. The last honour was reserved for Sir Richard Grenville; but the Queen gave the expedition powder, a ship and loaned some of her soldiers, including Ralph Lane, who was at this time serving in Ireland but was now to be first commander of the small colonial garrison in Virginia. A garrison was duly placed on Roanoke Island, inside the Outer Banks, in July. Exploration was to be undertaken inland and to the north; Thomas Harriot was to survey and John White to record graphically the resources, human, animal, and vegetable, of the hot summery coastlands. Grenville came back in triumph in October, having taken a rich Spanish prize on his return voyage—an action which was now the highest patriotism since a sea war between England and Spain had begun in May while he was absent. Hakluyt was in England in the early summer of 1585 and again in 1586, hanging on there into July and possibly August. He thus learnt both of the establishment of the first colony and of its end. For Lane, lacking supplies and reinforcements, came back with Drake, who had called in at the Outer Banks after his successful raid on the West Indies. He was thus primed on the resources of North America and on the problems which its indigenous peoples and its character presented. He stressed that the colonizing programme should be renewed, but farther north on Chesapeake Bay where an exploring party had reported more fertile land and deeper harbours and channels accessible from the ocean. He also interviewed with Harriot a rescued Frenchman and a Spanish prisoner on the geography of the American coastland and hinterland to the south of Virginia.

Hitherto Ralegh's ventures had been given no direct printed publicity; now it was decided that Hakluyt should publish all the contingent materials he could in order to provide some comparison between what the English were doing and the French and Spaniards had done. Ralegh commissioned Harriot and White to prepare the notes and drawings they had as the basis for a comprehensive report on the area explored 1585-6 (though some had been lost and they were consequently not fully comprehensive). Harriot was also given the task of compiling a chronicle of successive voyages and would therefore have been entrusted with a growing body of documentary material. Hakluyt, once back in Paris, employed a young friend Martin Basanier to put in print the manuscript of René de Laudonnière's *L'histoire notable de la Floride,* which he had obtained from Thevet, with a flattering dedication to Ralegh for emulating and surpassing the French Florida ventures. He himself obtained a copy of Mendoza's *China* (Madrid, 1586) which had an interesting narrative of the expedition of Antonio de Espejo in western North America in 1583, which he excerpted and published immediately in Paris, following it up by Basanier's French translation. Preparations were made to have both Laudonnière and Mendoza translated into English and published in London later.

Meantime, Sir Richard Grenville, who had gone out too late with supplies and reinforcements for the first Virginia colony, had left only a handful of men to maintain an English presence on Roanoke Island, and came home in December not unduly optimistic. Many of the settlers of 1585-6 had also given Virginia a bad press; not only were there no gold, jewels, or exotic commodities, but the Indians had been hostile, and there seemed little hope of establishing a flourishing colony.

Hakluyt's intensive publicity in Paris was not seconded in England. It would appear that Harriot's report on the resources of Virginia was ready in February 1587 but was held back. Laudonnière, it is true, appeared in translation and with a propagandist dedication to Ralegh which provided an advertisement for future Virginia voyages. Ralegh, deprived of subscribers by the tales Lane's men told, held back any major venture in 1587. Instead he sponsored an autonomous venture under John White, this time as governor and not simply artist, to establish the City of Ralegh on the shore of Chesapeake Bay. White's colonists were mainly persons and families of small resources who backed his beliefs and those of Harriot and some others of the first colonists, that Virginia was indeed a place for farmers to prosper, even if there was no Peru or Mexico to open up its mines for them.

White sailed in April: his colonists established themselves not on Chesapeake Bay but on the old site at Roanoke Island—from which the 1586 party left by Grenville had disappeared—but they sent him back to England to make sure that their location was known and that supplies were rapidly sent. As his daughter, son-in-law, and grand-daughter were among those left behind he was not likely to relax his efforts to return. He did not get back until November, by which time Hakluyt had returned to Paris. During what was probably a short visit to England in October he had had news from an earlier vessel of the safe arrival of the colonists. He incorporated this good news in his dedication to his translation of Laudonnière. But this was the last good news that was to be received from Virginia for a considerable time.

Though he did not send White away at once with aid, Ralegh changed his mind again about Virginia. He decided to launch with sufficient backing a new large Virginia venture to be under the command of Sir Richard Grenville. The squadron was preparing early in 1588 at Bideford when Harriot's *A briefe and true report* was at last released as publicity for Virginia and for a further enterprise. But fate—or Spain—intervened. The departure of the Spanish Armada was now believed to be imminent. Every ship was needed in the Channel and so the Virginia venture was called off. Grenville's squadron was incorporated in Drake's fleet at Plymouth. After hard pressing White got two small vessels in which to go, with a few planters and supplies, to the aid of the Virginia settlers. He set out in May but the piratical activity of his seamen and of the other ships they met drove them home, robbed and helpless, so that contact with the Roanoke Island settlement was lost. Hakluyt had been in England between January and March while prospects still were bright. During a further visit from May to July he learnt of the severe setback which first Ralegh and then White

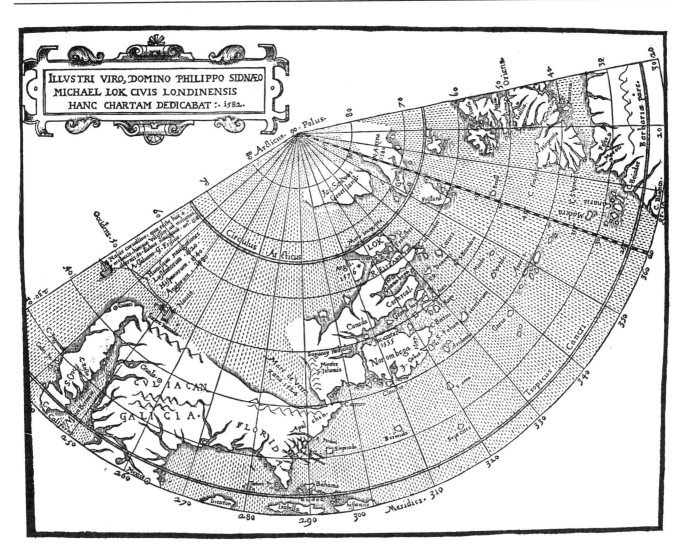

*Map of North America by Michael Lok, from Hakluyt's* Divers Voyages, *1582.*

had suffered. There was little he, in Paris, or anyone in England could do until the clash with Spain was over. Already, too, his activities had turned in another direction: in Paris in 1587 he had edited his first scholarly work—a Latin edition, the first since 1530, of all eight decades of the new world by Peter Martyr (*De orbe novo . . . decades octo*). On his visit to England he had met Theodor de Bry, the Frankfurt entrepreneur, to whom he had conveyed the news of the existence, first, of a series of fine Indian drawings by John White (to which Harriot was compiling what was in effect a commentary), and second, a second series of drawings of Florida Indian scenes made by Jacques le Moyne de Morgues in 1564-5 and now recopied at Ralegh's instance and expense. De Bry went back with a collection of White drawings, doubtless to White's financial benefit, and so the germ was planted of the great project to publish an illustrated series of volumes, with texts in various languages, on America.

Hakluyt's tour of duty in France ended in 1588. Later in the year he conveyed the ambassador's wife to London and settled there. Early in 1589 he was engaged in trying to see what could be salvaged from the Virginia venture. Ralegh encouraged the formation of a sort of holding company of London merchants and interested persons who would try to find backing for a further attempt to supply or rescue the Roanoke colonists. Hakluyt was named as one of nineteen grantees on 7 March 1589. But nothing was done: shipping was still held back from all but damaging anti-Spanish ventures: money too must have been short: for the time being Virginia like its settlers was in limbo.

It was in this period of inaction so far as North America was concerned that Hakluyt's major work which had been claiming his attention for many years, finally took shape. It appears probable that, at the time (1581-2) he was completing **Divers voyages,** he was struck by how little was known or was available about English enterprises to North America or indeed about English travel, discovery, and commerce outside the rather narrow bounds of European trade and journeyings. His elder cousin had much interest of his own on conditions in India, Mexico, and elsewhere. Thus the younger man obtained, possibly before he went to France in 1583, more probably on one or more of his visits in later years, information on these areas. Moreover, Hakluyt had many personal contacts with leading members of the Muscovy and Levant Companies who let him see and probably lent him records of their ventures. He had the assistance of Sir Francis Walsingham and Lord Burghley in getting access to government papers. He worked through many older chronicles and books on Portuguese and Spanish overseas enterprises for gleanings on English activity overseas. He gathered up what had already appeared in print in English. He requested journals and documents from captains and seamen returned from overseas voyages—he was, for example, on close terms, with Hawkins, Frobisher, Drake, and Cavendish, all of whom gave him materials. Gradually, a body of narrative material, with linking documents, began to take shape in his hands as the first framework of a general collection on the English voyages. What we cannot assess is how rapidly the collection grew, though each of his visits from Paris must have been occupied, partly, in assembling its constituents. By the time of his final return in 1588 the bulk of the materials was already in his possession.

He wished above all else to present as much as possible on North America. To the few items he had in 1582 he added only rather garbled accounts of voyages by John and Sebastian Cabot, by John Rut in 1527, and by Richard Hore in 1536. From Hawkins he got John Sparke's account of the English visit to Florida in 1565. From Edward Hayes and Richard Clarke he obtained full accounts of Sir Humphrey Gilbert's last voyage, to which he added various propagandist tracts of the years 1582-4; but he was determined to bring together as much as he could on the recent Virginia voyages.

In the end he did well so far as bulk is concerned, and also in the quality of the material; but it is highly probable that what he was to print on the ventures of 1584-6 came to him from Ralegh by way of Thomas Harriot and that it had been to some extent predigested while in their hands. Arthur Barlowe's narrative of the 1584 voyage was not a simple journal but a journal rewritten, perhaps by Ralegh, possibly by Harriot, to fit the propaganda needs of the last months of 1584 and the first of 1585. The journal of the 1585 voyage was similarly trimmed to highlight some and to suppress other episodes in the voyage. Lane's narrative of the 1585 colony, too, had almost certainly had some passages deleted or pruned. Moreover, Walsingham had

received letters from the participants in the 1585 voyages, Lane and Grenville among them, which he did not pass on to Hakluyt to print, perhaps because there were in them reflections on certain persons engaged on the voyage. There was certainly some suppression and some consequent distortion in the picture which these narratives presented of the two expeditions and the first settlement, but there is no reason to consider that everything, or almost everything, contained in them was not first hand and authentic. There was gain too in their pruning: Ralegh certainly had a better ear for a good phrase, for a vivid paragraph, for the contrast between significant detail and stark outline, which gives, for example, the so-called *Tiger* journal of the 1585 voyage so much of its effect. We cannot be sure that the subeditor was Ralegh rather than Harriot, but it was certainly one or the other. To balance narrative with analysis Hakluyt had permission to reprint Harriot's *A briefe and true report,* with its discussion of settlement problems and analysis of natural resources and aboriginal society. There is no reason to consider that Hakluyt was in any way dissatisfied with what he obtained.

For Grenville's 1586 voyage Hakluyt was unlucky. There is reason to think Grenville kept his own journal of the 1585 voyage, though this did not reach Hakluyt. It is highly probable that he kept one also in 1586 and that others were kept as well, but Hakluyt could not lay hands on any and so he collected such scanty information as he could and wrote his own brief second-hand narrative. John White kept journals of the 1587 and 1588 voyages and these he passed on, probably directly, to Hakluyt. Hakluyt seems to have presented them in full with the possible excision of entries where little took place on the long transatlantic passages. They were plain and unadorned but effective, even poignant, documents of a lost colony. Later in the production of the book Hakluyt added the grant of 7 March 1589 to which he was a party to signify that all intention of relieving the Roanoke settlers had not been given up. The voyage collection, now at last given the title *The principall navigations voiages and discoueries of the English nation,* was put through the press efficiently, though with some signs of pressure towards the end, in the closing months of 1589. Whether it appeared in December 1589 or in January (or even February) 1590 we cannot tell.

To Hakluyt the narratives of the Virginia voyages from 1584 onwards represented a vital element in his record of English enterprise in North America. He considered them as historical documents, no doubt, but he also thought of them as guides and an inspiration to future transatlantic explorers and planters. When he came in the 1590s to assemble his voyage collections on a much larger scale there was not much he could add to what had been already published. He suppressed White's narration of the abortive voyage in 1588, cut the almost equally abortive assignment of 1589, as both had been wholly superseded. He added another, characteristic, narrative by John White of the voyage to Roanoke Island which he had eventually been able to make in 1590. Though in this White told much less than the full story of the outward voyage, his picture of the search on Roanoke Island for the lost colonists is an intricate and effective one. The latest document was a covering letter sent with the 1590 narrative from Ireland, to which White had retired, discouraged, unable to find either the backers or the will to cross the Atlantic to Roanoke Island for a sixth time. In the collections which Hakluyt made towards a final edition in the years after 1600 there was apparently nothing more on the Virginia voyages—at least Samuel Purchas makes no mention of any in his *Pilgrimes,* for which he used so much of Hakluyt's later collections, and which had come to him in Hakluyt's last years and after his death in 1616.

### Peter Vansittart (essay date 1981)

SOURCE: "Hakluyt's Emporium," in *The Times Educational Supplement,* No. 3404, September 25, 1981, p. 25.

[*In the following review essay, Vansittart provides a vivid sampling of Hakluyt's narratives of discovery, and considers their place in the English literary tradition.*]

Geographer, linguist, historian, Richard Hakluyt was also Archdeacon of Westminster, diplomat, and busy advocate of Elizabethan sea-power, overseas trade, colonial enterprise. Often considered chiefly as a maritime narrative . . . [**Hakluyt's Voyages**] is an anthology of both land and sea travels, from eye-witnesses of most varied classes, ranks, occupations, involving Raleigh (as author), Humphrey Gilbert, Hawkins, Frobisher, Drake, and other names lesser but scarcely ignoble. Heroes, rakes, profiteers, zealots, desperadoes, all were space-invaders and, encountering so many strange peoples in different cultural stratas, they were also time-travellers. Their assignments ring like antique gongs: Muscovy, Cathay, Bohara, Ormuz, Kazan, Astrakhan, Alexandria. They describe Persia, Goa, Venice, Jerusalem, India, penetrate Newfoundland, venture the Straits of Magellan and dare the Horn. Gilbert, significantly, spent two years preparing an expedition to find the North West Passage, yet failed, fatally.

The missives are primarily business reports involving the prospects of exchanging cloth, ornaments, general goods, for silks, jewels, spices, gold, together with reports of native conditions and Spanish hostility. But they are also sustained adventure tales with prodigious wealth of detail, bizarre, unexpected, horrifying or

severely factual, inducing a vivid sense of small, precarious vessels and caravans daring, with so much temerity, uncharted hazards—whirlpools, rocks, tempest, disease, cannibals, lice as big as beans, arbitrary fines, imprisonment, torture by capricious rulers, Moslem or pagan, and their extortionate officials: condemnation to galleys, mines, the stake, and circumcision.

Famished sailors ate each other in Newfoundland, and, at sea plotted mutiny, or were agonized into respectful protest. "We have thought good to show unto you, being our Master, our whole minds and griefs in writing." But Raleigh himself cannot resist marvellous digressions, "though impertinent in some sort to my purpose", fascinated by reports of warlike Amazons at Tobago, men with eyes in their shoulders and mouths in their breasts, and an Arawakan drink powdered with the bones of great lords. Such incidentals have won many readers. "Babylon is from hence fifteen days' journey, whereas by true report be great store of dates." Carious human touches abound. "We had aboard us a French-man, a trumpeteer, who, being sick and lying on his bed, took his trumpet notwithstanding, and sounded till he could sound no more, and so died." Then, "Divers women have such exceeding long breasts that some of them will lay the same upon the ground and lie down by them."

In Florida, a Frenchman saw a snake with three heads and four feet, unicorns fought lions, and, more plausibly, "a friar, who, taking upon him to persuade the people to subjection, was by them taken, and his skin cruelly pulled over his ears, and his flesh eaten." Samoyed cannibals revered swordswallowing shamans. Ivan the Terrible's courtiers lengthened their hair when out of favour, his singers "delighted our ears little or nothing," and, from future husbands, his female subjects received love-tokens that included a whip for their own chastisement. We glimpse Ivan, the Great Mogul Akbar, the Inquisition terrorizing gentle Mexicans, Russian Lenten insobrieties and the exchange of dyed Easter eggs, Biman women doing the hard outdoor work and the men keeping house: fine town planning at Pegu whose inhabitants blackened their teeth to distinguish them from dogs.

Tartars used hawks to slay wild horses. "Art or science have they none, but live most idly, sitting round in great companies in the fields, devising and talking most vainly." Venetian women wore shoes "very nearly half a yard from the ground." Cambaians kept hospitals for lame dogs, cats, birds, and fed ants with meat. Royal Javanese wives when widowed were expected to undergo mass-suicide. Ralph Fitch had recognizable English disdain for an Indian prophet: "They took him for a holy man, but sure he was a lazy lubber." There are fearful accounts of storm, shipwreck, abstruse deaths, usually with notable absence of whining and self-pity, more often a stoic acceptance, or even rejoicing, concerning the inevitability and wisdom of God's purposes.

All this confirms Virginia Woolf's verdict on Hakluyt's collections: "Part of their charm consists in the fact that Hakluyt is not so much a book as a great bundle of commodities loosely lied together, an emporium, a lumber room strewn with ancient sacks, obsolete naval instruments, huge bales of wool and little bags of rubies and emeralds."

Yet there are sober matters of history and anthropology quite outside the lumber room. Robert Gainish, a sea-captain, reports satyrs and headless men, but quotes Pliny, Aristotle, Josephus, Philostratus, Gemma Frisius, Soline, Diodurus Siculus, an interesting comment on Tudor education. Contacts with indigenous peoples suggest less innate violence than general greed and fear, by no means obsolete. Hawkins used *the Jesus* as a slaver! Spanish cruelty, prolonged and systematic, still astonishes and perturbs; like the Nazis in Russia, Philip's men forfeited much initia, goodwill by mass-extermination and bigotry. There emerges an accusing sense of missed opportunities. Europeans might have harmonized huge territories had their projects been less impelled by nationalism and religion, sometimes more intolerable even than the extremes of private profit. Inescapable is the universal relativity of religions, political notions, morals, values. The ubiquitous nakedness seldom seems erotic to these Elizabethan explorers, merely fellow humans seen in perspective, like the cow described by a modern child as "an animal with legs all the way down to the ground." There was not only savagery but aimiable curiosity and resonably honest bargaining.

Virginia Woolf disliked the effect of these exotic discoveries on English prose style, but, here at least, the style is remarkably even: plain, without the extravagances of many coeval poets, critics, literary men. It is surely part of a prose tradition direct, sometimes moralizing and sententious but usually precise and hard-hitting, stretching from King Alfred through Bunyan, Defoe, Cobbett, to Russell, Priestley, Orwell.

## Emily C. Bartels (essay date 1992)

SOURCE: "Imperialist Beginnings: Richard Hakluyt and the Construction of Africa," in *Criticism*, Vol. XXXIV, No. 4, Fall, 1992, pp. 517-38.

[*In the following essay, Bartels provides a close textual analysis of the accounts of voyages to Africa in* The Principal Navigations. *With particular reference to descriptions of Moors and Negroes, Bartels detects and discusses an implicit "strategy of representation" in the narratives and in Hakluyt's editorial policy.*]

In 1589, when Richard Hakluyt produced his first edition of the ***Principal Navigations,*** England was a long way from securing an empire or articulating an imperialist policy. Despite some forty years of cross-cultural exploration and trade, its efforts paled in comparison to those particularly of the Spanish, French, and Portuguese, who dominated the trade in Asia, Africa, and the Americas. While the state patented such companies as the Muscovy (1552) and Levant (1581), which staked claims to trading rights in specific regions and along certain routes, these enterprises and other, colonialist projects such as Ralegh's Virginia settlement were financed primarily by enterprising merchants and entrepreneurial nobles. Only in Ireland, whose "restless population" was pressing all too closely upon the borders, did Elizabeth support settlement, and then only to a limited degree.

As Kenneth Andrews has argued, [in *Trade, Plander, and settlement Maritime enterprise and the geneses of the British Empire, 1480-1630*] a major impediment to the development of empire was, ironically, what prompted that development in the first place—the pressing need for economic capital. Faced with a serious depression in the 1550s, England began to look to overseas markets for immediate profit. Though later these markets would be pursued as a means of long-term relief (of developing an expanded cloth trade, for example, or providing jobs for emigrants abroad and the unemployed at home), initially they provided a source, literally and figuratively, of gold. While money was necessary for empire-building, the preoccupation with profit took precedence over and attention from other endeavors critical for that project, such as the enhancement of sea power, foreign settlement and governance, and the development of a unified imperialist agenda. Resultingly, as Andrews has suggested, England's expansionism was disunified and divided. In the West, where other European powers had major strongholds, English efforts took on an aggressive edge, leading to the literal colonization of America but aimed at a more figurative colonization of the Iberian trade. In the East, where English footing was more secure, the impulse was to keep the peace and to develop commerce without conflict (and colonization). Though, as Andrews acknowledges, these two projects inevitably intersected, they nonetheless defined two distinct modes of imperialism: one militant and acquisitive, and so impacting most forcefully on England's international position; and the other, peaceful and mercantilic, and so primarily affecting commerce.

It was the propagandists of these endeavors who pulled the two impulses together and who, more than any other forces, laid the ideological foundation for empire. For despite and because of the state's preoccupation with material profit and because of their dependence upon noble patrons, they were forced, regardless of their own motivations, to voice a sort of "economic nationalism," to represent expansionism as vital for "the country's good" in broad economic and political terms. Richard Hakluyt's ***Principal Navigations*** was the most popular and influential of this propaganda during the Elizabethan period and for several decades after. In his dedicatory epistle to his leading patron, Sir Francis Walsingham, Hakluyt defines himself as an authority on Europe's cross-cultural exploits and offers his collection as a defense against charges that England was "sluggish" and neglectful in such endeavors. Drawing upon travel accounts of those involved in overseas voyages and documents of merchants, trading companies, adventurers, statesmen, and the state, he sets out to prove to the (European) world that the English, "in compassing the vaste globe of the earth more then once, have excelled all the nations and people of the earth". Although he insists in his preface "to the favourable Reader" that he is not concerned with "any action perfourmed neere home, nor in any part of Europe," his subject is as much Europe and England's place within it as it is non-European worlds (as his subsequent derogation of the "monstrous Spanish army" suggests).

Though as a clergyman, Hakluyt had much to gain in preferments from the court in speaking up thus for England, historians have generally accepted his nationalism as sincere, particularly because of his long career as an advocate for the wide-ranging benefits of expansionism and his relentless efforts to rally seamen, merchants, adventurers, intellectuals, noblemen, and the monarch collectively around the cause. Opinion has been divided, however, about where his primary concern lay, whether in the nation's economic status or in its international politics and position. In the ***Principal Navigations*** at the least, both are equally important, not as signs of Hakluyt's priorities (which are finally impossible to recover), but as indications of the bifurcated impulses which defined England's efforts overseas. Although, in an important new study of English nationalism, [*Forms of Nationhood: The Elizabethan Writing of England*] Richard Helgerson assigns Hakluyt a predominantly economic motive, a desire to valorize commercialism as an honorable national aim, he also contends that to do so the ***Navigations*** had to bridge the gap between the economic interests of the merchants and the imperialist interests of the gentry, "superimposing the ideological and economic asymmetries of his culture to represent and to enforce a coupling of classes in an enterprise he defined as national." Wherever his primary interest lay, Hakluyt had to bring profit and power together as Helgerson suggests, in order to unify and promote overseas efforts—and with them English imperialism.

Africa provided a particularly useful subject for such a project and stands out within the ***Navigations*** as unique. For "the dark continent" was a place half-way between East and West, peopled with both the familiar figure of the Moor, who had been a part of England's crosscultural contact with the East for centuries, and the unfamiliar figure of the Negro, who, in his newness, nakedness, and incivility, resembled the Indian to the West. While England's interventions in Africa were, as in the East, mercantilic rather than colonialistic, they were as aggressively aimed against other European powers as those in the New World. Hakluyt capitalizes on these differences in his representations, producing an Africa which is at once familiar and unfamiliar, civil and savage, full of promise and full of threat.

Christopher Miller, a leading scholar of "Africanist discourse," has uncovered [in *Blank Darkness: Africanist Discourse in French*] a similar double vision in French texts of the nineteenth century, arguing that this ambiguity exposes Europe's longstanding ambivalence about Africa, itself, and the possibility of "maintaining an identity in discourse." In looking diachronically rather than synchronically at the earlier stages of that discourse, however, his study overlooks critical historical forces which suggest a different discursive shape. In the case of early modern England, in the context of a nascent imperialism, and in the hands of a propagandist such as Hakluyt, the possibility of maintaining an identity in discourse was called crucially into play. The contradictions within Hakluyt's Africanist vision emerge not as an expression of ambivalence, but as a means of erasing the ambivalence surrounding England's expansionist endeavors. For by both obscuring and exposing differences within "the dark continent," Hakluyt displays the difference between England and Africa, "proving" England's superiority not only over Africa, but also, more importantly (to England), over the European and non-European powers vying for the same imperial space. What results amidst the difference is an English nation which is not ambivalent and not obscure, a nation whose standards of civility are stable and clear and whose expansionism is as vital as it is just.

A major problem complicating our understanding of the Renaisance conception of Africa has been that the identity it gains in texts such as Hakluyt's seems inconsistent and confused. Not only are the native peoples identified by broad categories (Africans, Negroes, Moors, Black Moors, "Ethiopes," and even Indians), but also how these categories are constituted and differentiated is neither stable nor clear. In Hakluyt, the term "Moor," for example, sometimes designates color (black), sometimes religion (Moslem), sometimes region (Mauritania), sometimes all of the above, and sometimes none. In the case of religion, Moors are sometimes accused of being "infidels" (a term often, but not exclusively, equated with Moslems), sometimes represented as devout followers of God, albeit a Moslem one, and sometimes associated with no religion at all. The most sustained treatment of their religion comes in a report of China, in which Mohammedanism becomes little more than an absurd and trivializing abstinence from pork. Yet this kind of reductive clarity seems possible only here, in representations of China; in Africa the terms are not so clear.

Designations of skin color prove equally slippery. Though Moors are often characterized as black, they and their blackness come in vague and various shades. In one account we hear of "Moores of tawnie colour and good stature," whose king dressed "in a gowne of crimosine Sattin pinked after the Moorish fashion downe to the knee." Ironically, it is not race but fashion which is distinguished as "Moorish," presented here as if common knowledge (though mentioned nowhere else in Hakluyt). Elsewhere Richard Eden, who narrates two of the most prominent accounts of Africa, describes the king of Benin as "a blacke Moore (although not so blacke as the rest)." With the color difference appearing so vague, the "great reverence" the Moors show their king defines them instead. Eden singles it out for didactic display, as a lesson to Christian readers who, if they "would give as much to our Savior Christ . . . should remoove from our heads many plagues which we daily deserve for our contempt and impietie." Yet reverence is an equally unreliable measure of "Moorishness." In other accounts we hear of M. Christopher Lyster, who was "long detained in miserable servitude" in Barbary by "the cruel hands of the Moores," and of the "great store of men of warre, being Moores" residing in the East Indies.

It is not just what constitutes each group that is unclear, however, but also how these groups differ from one other—how Moors differ from black Moors, "Ethiopes" from Moors, Negroes from "Ethiopes," and so on. Eden interrupts his report of a voyage to Guinea to "speake somewhat of the countrey and people." "It is to be understood," he explains,

> that the people which now inhabite the regions . . . of Guinea, and the middle parts of Africa, as Libya the inner, and Nubia, with divers other great & large regions about the same, were in old time called Aethipes and Nigritae, which we now call Moores, Moorens, or Negroes, a people of beastly living, without a God, lawe, religion, or common wealth, and so scorched and vexed with the heat of the sunne, that in many places they curse it when it riseth.

From this description, it is unclear whether Ethiopes and Nigritae and the terms (Moors and Negroes) that replace them are synonymous, or whether all or just Negroes comprise a single race of people who are black (scorched by the sun), savage, and irreligious. To make matters worse, Eden subsequently distinguishes the Nigritae as a sub-group of Ethiopians, noting that "the

Ethiopians called the Nigritae occupy a great part of Africa." His assertion not only calls admittedly obsolete terms back into currency for no apparent reason; it also obscures their relation to, and the difference between, Moors and Negroes. What fascinates Eden most about this region is that on one side of its border, the Nigritis River, "the inhabitants are of high stature and black, and on the other side, of browne or tawnie colour, and low stature." For him, the visible differentiation of peoples is "marveilous and very strange"—and for us, notably absent throughout.

Scholars faced with these inconsistencies have generally taken them at face value, as a problem rather than a strategy of representation, as a sign that Renaissance ideas of African races and religions were poorly formed at best. Consequently, they have tried to sort out the "facts," to locate a consistent conception that predominated despite the contradictions. Othello has been a prime target of such investigations, with critics attempting to decide which cultural conceptions of the Moor Shakespeare would have drawn upon and whether he intended his Moor to be black or tawny, and so, more or less malign. Such determinations seem, however, to miss the point, for they overlook the context in which and the conditions under which the vision of Africa was produced and discount the possibility that the resulting discrepancies *defined* as well as problematized that vision and were finally more strategic than accidental.

While we might attribute those discrepancies to the collection's multiple authorship, Hakluyt's decision to reproduce only one-fourth of the available accounts of voyages to Africa, to exclude a dubious account by David Ingram which appeared in his earlier *Divers Voyages* (1582), and to present the fantastical tales of *Mandeville's Travels* only in Latin in his first edition reminds us that he selected the resulting vision. The first edition bears the clear imprint of his "economic nationalism," for after a first printing (and perhaps under the pressure of the Muscovy Company) Hakluyt deleted an account of Russia which showed the narrator in "an undignified light" and threatened to destabilize further dealings with the Tsar. The "personality" of the *Navigations* is especially evident in contrast with the heavily religious collection Samuel Purchas produced after Hakluyt's death and from his unpublished materials.

Tellingly, too, the accounts Hakluyt does include are riddled with internal inconsistencies. Part of the problem there as well is multiple authorship, for Hakluyt's narrators mix knowledge gained from "actual" experience with that acquired (and not always acknowledged) from other, predominantly classical or medieval texts. Although Eden declares the Ethiopians a godless race, he then (as he notes, following Gemma Phrysius) locates among them "certaine Christians under the dominion of the great Emperour of Aethiopia, called Prester John," a quasi-mythological figure "discovered" repeatedly in the heart of Africa from the twelfth to the seventeenth centuries. Too, after presenting an allegedly unadulterated account of a voyage, "so well observed by . . . experience," told by "an expert Pilot," Eden offers his own description of Africa, including a catalogue of exotics such as the Anthropophagi, Blemines, and Satyrs, which appeared in almost every classical, medieval, and contemporary depiction of Africa available to the Renaissance. Rather than gesturing towards a new-found reality, these inclusions seem instead to evoke a narrative tradition whose object was the marvelous rather than the real. Despite the resulting inconsistencies, to recite inherited "truths" was to validate the narrator's authority, to expose his comforting (though textual) familiarity with a threateningly unfamiliar subject.

Indeed, part of the point was to retain the unfamiliarity of the native subject and so to create a critical boundary between Africa and England. In classifying the African people as Africans, Negroes, and Moors, Hakluyt's narrators strategically obscure their individuality and amplify their alterity. Homogenization is an almost inevitable hazard of ethnographic study, which must to some degree universalize in order to describe. Yet here the categories are amorphous as well as broad, and the confusion between them allows the negative associations coupled to any one group to be spread categorically across the continent. Because we are told in some places but not in others that Moors are black or Moslem, two usually incriminating marks of difference, any reference to Moors conjures up the possibility that they might be either or both. And because other African groups are not always distinguished from Moors, they are subject to the same assumptions. We are encouraged to expect the worse, to expect Moors and "Ethiopes" of unstated color and unstated faith to exhibit an inherent blackness of soul. Consequently, potentially objectifiable distinctions based on such aspects as religion, race, and region lose their meanings. Not to be Moslem in Africa is as incriminating as to be Moslem, to be "tawny" as incriminating as to be black, and to live on one side of the river the same as to live on the other. The impression that persists is one of undifferentiated darkness.

When the narrators do move in to give specifics, their efforts are geared not towards disclosing ethnographic knowledge but towards uncovering the possibility and legitimacy of profiting from cross-cultural contact. What counts as a measure of identity beyond the group names is their trading behavior, as evaluated by the English. Natives who are resistant to negotiations become "wilde and idle"; those who are willing or eager become "goodlier men," "more gentle in nature," and, significantly, more like "us." The latter are given language, like "ours," which consists almost exclusively of terms of exchange—"golde," "basons," "much, or great store," "graines ynough," "hennes ynough," "give me a knife," "give me bread," "put foorth, or emptie," "hold your peace," "I thanke you," "ye lye." In familiarizing the natives thus and denying their alterity, the narrators prove them fit subjects for negotiations and use them as signposts for areas of lucrative trade.

More prominent, however, is the assertion of the Africans' difference, or rather, culpable and curious differentness, which proves them fit subjects for exploitation. Depictions of "goodlier" natives are less frequent and less detailed than those of the "wilde and idle" sort, whose resistance needs to be exposed and explained. When it is explained, as Peter Hulme has suggested in the case of Caribbean encounters, it is always to the advantage of the English. When the Africans refuse to bargain after being cheated, or having their towns burned or citizens kidnapped, like the Indians they are presented as savage, irrational, or erratic and the English blameless. Even in the face of the most flagrant exploitation, they remain the offenders. William Towerson (after Eden the most prominent contributor to Hakluyt's Africanist vision) writes of one Negro leader who, following prolonged but unsuccessful bargaining, insisted on paying only "one Angell, and twelve graines for four elles" of cloth. When the English offered instead three "elles" "of some rotten cloth," he refused, and Towerson turns his resistance into a sign of stubbornness, noting that the English threatened to "go away, as indeed we could have done, rather then have given that measure, although the cloth was ill, seeing we were so neere to the places, which are judged to be better for sale." Set next to places "better for sale," the Negro is criticized for expecting "that measure," which was first suggested by the English for rotten cloth and which he, in fact, refused.

Even when the natives are not found culpable, they appear, nonetheless, incriminatingly curious. Throughout the narratives, we are repeatedly reminded that they have *a* particular—and particularly odd—"manner." For example, Towerson notes that a group of Negroes in Guinea, hesitant to trade, first "required a reward" as, he explains, "the most part of them will doe." Two days later, after some goods had been exchanged, they asked the British to "tary" while they spread their newly gained cloth on the shore, an action Towerson dismisses as being "as their manner is." When further interactions were interrupted by a native who came running from the town and whom the rest of the Negroes followed into the woods, Towerson is ready to suspect "some knavery." Only after announcing his suspicion—after we are made to see the native "manner" as erratic—does he explain that the Portuguese were advancing.

Just as these repeated references to what "their manner

is" create subjects who are collectively and categorically unlike "us," so too do the summary characterizations of the groups, such as Eden's description of Moors and Negroes as "a people of beastly living, without a God, lawe, religion, or common wealth" who habitually curse the scorching sun. In their eccentricity and succinctness, these generalizations match and blend in with those describing the inhabitants inherited from earlier sources, such as the Troglodytes, who "dwel in caves and dennes," eat snake meat, and chatter and grin rather than talk, the Garamantes, "whose women are common: for they contract no matrimonie, neither have respect to chastitie," or the Anthropophagi, who "are accustomed to eat mans flesh." Just as these exotic depictions serve to validate the narrators' authority, so too do the characterizations of native groups and native manners work to validate English intervention, to create subjects whose only individuality is incriminatingly curious. While both kinds of representations pretend to expose ethnographic knowledge, both strategically distort or obscure it in the service of idelogical profit, blurring identifying differences within Africa to produce a "dark continent" whose clearest feature is its difference from England.

Despite the obfuscation of internal cultural differences, Hakluyt's narratives do make an important distinction between the two most prominent groups, the Negroes and the Moors. Both are part of a composite African subject, who is inconsistently invested with an incriminating race and religion, who is civil when he trades and savage when he doesn't, but they are placed at opposite ends of a spectrum of civility—Negroes at the lowest, Moors at the highest. While this difference lends an air of inclusiveness and hence objectivity to the whole, it ultimately serves to reaffirm the relative inferiority of the African subjects. For in the manner and matter of presentation, the narratives undermine the differences they "discover," making Africa a place where degrees of civilization no longer mean anything, and where the people, even at their most civilized best, are always, already unlike "us."

Despite their inconsistencies, Hakluyt's narratives characterize Negroes as primitive, incomprehensible, and uncivilized, even if civil. Though their leaders are assigned English titles such as "king" or "captain," the only time a Negro is singled out by name is in the case of "George our Negro," whom the voyagers had taken to England, "schooled," and brought back to Africa as their liaison. Also, physical descriptions are called in to attest to the Negroes' primitivism. We hear, for example, of Negroes who are "mighty big men," wearing nothing but loin cloths made of bark, whose heads are "painted with divers colours," whose skin is "raced with divers workes, in maner of a leather Jerkin." Although women rarely figure in Hakluyt, it seems no coincidence that, when they appear in Africa, they appear in Negro communities and serve to dehumanize the native population. Towerson describes them and their relation to and difference from certain Negro men by "their breastes, which in the most part be very foule and long, hanging down low like the udder of a goate." To reinforce the point, he later returns to the women, remarking that some "have such exceeding long breasts, that some of them wil lay the same upon the ground and lie down by them."

(This strategy is paralleled and the same image evoked, interestingly, in one of Hakluyt's accounts of the Indians, who are also primitivized via physical details. In describing Indian women, one narrator records that they disdain to give birth when they are young, for fear that they will develop "hanging breasts which they account to be great deforming in them." In turning from maternity to deformity, the narrator defines Indian mothers through what seem abnormalities—both the hanging breasts and the women's disdain—in much the same way as Towerson characterizes Negro women by their "exceeding long breasts.")

Just as the elaboration of such physical details portrays Negroes as curiously primitive, so does the omission of speculation about their customs, the description of which, after representations of their trading practices, provides the most sustained images of the natives. Negro rituals are presented out of context, not as a validation or even a recognition of alternative cultural codes, but as curiosities. Towerson writes of one Negro "king" who insisted that his European visitors come to him three times before he would receive their gifts. This done, the Negroes carried out "certaine ceremonies," upheld "both here and in all the countrey," that involved burying some portions of drink, pouring other portions on piles of palm leaves, and "doing great reverence in all places to the same Palme trees." Afterwards, the king drank while his people cried "Abaan, Abaan, with certaine other words, like as they cry commonly in Flanders, upon the Twelfe night." Towerson ignores the possible religious or political import of the ritual, and, even when he asserts its resemblance to the familiar (European) tradition of Twelfth Night, he centers only on "certaine . . . words," abstracted for the ceremony and noted because of their sound rather than their sense.

Granted, the appearance and behavior of the Negroes may have seemed strange to the outsiders, whose interaction with the native people was seriously limited. Yet instead of acknowledging or confronting reactions of surprise, wonder, or fear, or admitting a lack of comprehension, the narrators record strange sights and events as characterizing matters-of-fact which incriminate rather than differentiate the people. Through this almost emotionless reporting, the gap in understanding between cultures is rewritten as a gap within the "other" culture, which thus appears incomprehensible rather than not comprehended, uncivilized rather than civilized in a different (non-European) way.

Moreover, although, as the above descriptions attest, Negroes are not always represented as "savages," their actions are repeatedly implicated as threateningly unpredictable and potentially hostile, especially when the English might be faulted for aggression. For example, we hear of Negroes, originally defined as "civill," who, following a common negotiating practice, willingly agreed to leave three of their men in the English ships as an act of good faith. Two of them suddenly "made themselves sicke" and got leave to go ashore, while the third jumped ship. Meanwhile, the Negroes on shore "laied hands" on the English "with great violence, and tore all their apparell from their backes" and shot poisonous arrows at others. Only after we see the natives (and favorable impressions of them) as violently untrustworthy do we hear that three weeks before an English ship "had taken three of their people," whom the Negroes intended to rescue by taking and exchanging English hostages. While this information modifies our impression of native hostility, it does not erase it. Placed as an afterthought at the end of the episode, it assumes a secondary importance inessential to the course of events and the characterization of the natives. Even when outside authorities seem to be in control, Negroes are assigned an incriminating agency. In one instance we hear of Negroes in "Mowre" who stopped negotiations with the English after someone from the nearby castle "caused" them to depart. When the English came ashore to see what was happening, the Negroes "cast stones at them, & would not suffer them to come up to their towne." Ignoring the complicating factor of the castle authorities, the narrator centers instead on the Negroes' aggression.

African Moors appear, in contrast, as notably more civilized and more familiar. While most depictions of Negroes highlight erratic if not hostile behavior, the most detailed accounts of Moors, despite occasional references to their "cruel hands," center on their emperors, who are given important names, positions, and voices. Unlike Negro "kings," Moorish leaders reside within luxurious courts and are surrounded by attendants, fine goods, and entertainments, which sometimes include English dogs and English music. Edmund Hogan writes of one emperor, Mully Abdelmelech, who enjoyed "baiting buls with his English dogges" and who, after receiving a lute, asked that English musicians be sent to him. As this account suggests, Moors are comprehensible: they not only listen to "our" music; with no mention of the language barrier, they also seem to speak "our" language. Their interactions with the English, for whom they act as hosts and with whom they engage in sustained communication, are far more extensive than those of the Negroes, who usually appear for trade negotiations and disappear immediately after.

In part the difference between the representations of the two groups may derive from the fact that Moors were textually and actually more familiar to the English than were Negroes. Sometimes Orientalized, the image of the Moor was connected to a long history of contact with the East, which seemed a more knowable Other than Africa. During the Elizabethan period, too, Moors appeared prominently at court as ambassadors and diplomats. In addition, "blackmoores" were visible enough by 1596 that Queen Elizabeth proclaimed there were "allready to manie" in the realm and seized an opportunity to exchange several for English hostages held in Spain and Portugal.

Yet within Hakluyt, familiarity is contingent upon civility: Moors are like "us" because they are civil—which means, as with "goodlier" Negroes, civil to "us." Hakluyt includes within the collection correspondence between the Queen and various Moorish leaders, displaying the latter as literate, articulate, and diplomatic *and* protective of English needs. We hear Muley Hamet (Abdelmelech's successor), in a "well and truely translated" edict, vowing to protect the English merchants within his "stately palaces" and insisting that

> our princely counsaile wil defend them by the favor of God, from any thing that may impeach or hurt them . . . and that, which way soever they shall travile, no man shall take them captives in these our kingdomes, ports, and places which belong unto us . . . and that no man shall hinder them by laying violent hand upon them, and shall not give occasion that they may be grieved in any sort by the favour and assistance of God.

In responding, the Queen seconds this impression by at once praising the Emperor's civility and linking it to his cooperation with the English. Complementing "the great affection and good wil" he has shown, she insists that she therefore "could not omit to magnifie [him], according to [his] desert." She does, however, omit to fully meet his demands for "certaine things."

Hakluyt's narratives (and the queen) even call in the Moslem religion to familiarize and civilize the Moors. Though Moslems were sometimes represented as infidels, when Elizabeth needed to strengthen her alliance with the Turks (also Moslems), she turned to their leaders as allies "against all the Idolaters and false professors of the Name of CHRIST dwelling among the Christians." When she writes to Muley Hamet, she suggests a similar compatibility, expressing her desires that "Our Lord keepe and preserve" his "high and mightie person." Muley Hamet himself calls on "the Name of the pitifull and the mercifull God," sometimes identified as Moslem and sometimes not. Too, while it is unclear whether Abdelmelech was a Moslem (we know only that he was *called* "the Christian king"), Hogan praises him for "liv[ing] greatly in the feare of God, being well exercised in the Scriptures, as well in the olde Testament as also in the New." Once again the praise points back to England, to the fact that the Emperor "beareth a greater affection to our Nation then to others because of our religion, which forbiddeth worhip of Idols." Though Hogan ascribes the Moors' "affection to our Nation" to shared religious beliefs, his praise of the Moors' faith seems to derive from rather than inspire that "affection." Either way, such references to religion familiarize and "civilize" Moors, setting them notably apart from Negroes, who are found practicing either nothing or the idolatry condemned, as these accounts stress, by Christianity and Islam alike.

Moors appear then as subjects whose customs and beliefs are more knowable and whose civility, particularly since it is put down in writing, is more sure. "Goodlier" Negroes may allow profitable exchange, but the brevity of reports of successful bargaining and the preponderance of accounts of disaster remind us that their willingness or ability to interact is as limited as their hospitality is unreliable. Despite these important differences, however, Hakluyt also enforces the similarity of the two groups, aligning the most civilized with the most savage in one disenfranchised whole. Although Negroes stand out as dangerously unknowable, there are comparable gaps in the portrayal of Moors. Neither Negroes nor Moors are given any families, any social codes or values which might validate their alterity, or any communal or personal existence outside their confrontations with the Europeans. Further, both groups are denied claims to their lands and resources. While Moors appear as the titular heads of kingdoms, they are expected to allow the English safe passage through their territories and are denied civility (or fragmented into "cruel hands") if they create impediments. In matters of land and resources, civilized Moors must be not merely cooperative but also willing to sacrifice Africa's well-being for England's, to defend the English merchants "from any thing that may impeach or hurt them," even if it costs African lives or "lackes." Negroes are given even less claim to their lands and resources, and seem to pop up arbitrarily from regions identified primarily by the temporal and geographic measures of the voyagers' positions. Nor do Negroes seem to have any claims to themselves. Not only do the narrators record English kidnappings with matter-of-fact nonchalance; instead of mentioning (potentially angry) Negro reactions to these events, they emphasize how "very glad the Negroes were when their countrymen were returned and how they received "our Negroes" with "all the friendship they could."

Importantly too, behavioral distinctions also break down. While Negroes are represented as naive and unreasoning, Moors, despite their superior civility, are made to seem calculating and unreasonable and the

"subtile" dealings of both little different. Like Negroes, Moors are shown to resist English advances, though with subtle rather than violent tactics. Hogan displays Abdelmelech as untrustworthy by highlighting his manipulative and punitive use of delay, as I have argued elsewhere. Creating an incriminating link between punishment and delay, he records Abdelmelech's expressed intentions to punish the Spanish ambassador (whom he dislikes) by forcing him to "attend twentie dayes after he hath done his message." And when we hear that the Moor made Hogan wait several days to be received and then curtailed interactions because of a "sore leg," which he exercised vigorously nonetheless, we can only be suspicious. Too, when Hogan mentions leaving only with part of what he requested, he leaves us with an impression of the Moor as cunning and uncooperative. Our trust is shaken further as he undermines Abdelmelech's promise to let English musicians live in his country "according to their law and conscience" by insisting that the Spanish and Portuguese who greeted him were there "more by the kings commandement then of any good wils of themselves: for some of them although they speake me faire hung downe their heads like dogs."

What results from this and similar instances are Moors whose calculated resistance emerges from a familiar cover of civility to match the irrational and unpredictable hostility of Negroes. Despite the varying levels of civility between the two, we are encouraged to expect a variance within both, to expect "goodlier" Negroes to become "wilde" and hospitable Moors to become "cruel." There seems finally little difference between Abdelmelech's evasive ploys and the Negroes' sudden jump from the English ships, and what difference there is one of subtlety—one which means everything and nothing. What does make a difference is that in Africa civility and savagery inevitably collide, proving the inhabitants unpredictably Other and unmistakably unlike "us."

By distorting and collapsing intracultural and amplifying intercultural differences and by figuratively dispossessing the Africans of their land, Hakluyt's narrators not only exonerate English exploitation in trade negotiations; they also beg for more extensive intervention, which would truly "civilize" uncivilized natives. They beg, that is, for an imperialist, if not colonialist, agenda whose goal would extend beyond immediate profit to a broader moral and political domination. Yet the subject at issue is not just Africa, not just the dominated, but also the dominators. For Hakluyt's Africa provides an incriminating reflection of two of England's major competitors for empire, the Portuguese and Turks. Aligning each with a different native group (Portuguese with Negroes, Turks with Moors), the narratives prove them finally as indistinguishable, unreliable, and uncivilized as the Africans. The point is not just to show the natives' vulnerability and need for outside intervention, but to distinguish *English* intervention as superior to that of others, to condemn "their" imperialism while condoning "ours."

Throughout the **Navigations,** representations of Negroes implicate the Portuguese and exonerate the English. Negroes were literally objects of exchange between the two European powers, but it is their ideological rather than material value that is most important even within those accounts which treat them as commodities. One narrator uses a trade in which the English gave the Portuguese five Negroes for forty chests of sugar to denigrate—by emphasizing the smallness of the chests—both the value of the Negroes and the integrity of the Portuguese. When Negroes are treated as subjects, they fill a similar function. For example, while both European groups kidnapped and enslaved Negroes, native reactions are used to differentiate between their practices. Towerson writes of one Negro who complained to the English that "the Portugals are bad men, and that they made them slaves if they could take them, and would put yrons upon their legges." When the Negro then asked the English to account for the men whom they kidnapped, Towerson explains: "We made him answere that they were in England well used, and were there kept till they could speake the language, and then they should be brought againe to be a helpe to Englishmen in this Countrey." He validates this excuse by remarking that the Negro (implicitly, satisfied) "spake no more of that matter." Elsewhere too, while "our Negroes" appear willing to accept, if not embrace, captivity under the English, those enslaved or "befriended" by the Portuguese are shown protesting actively or acquiescing out of fear.

Further, Negro responses not only attest to Portuguese incivility; their hostility is suggestively ascribed to the Portuguese. At times the narrators present the relation between the two peoples as domination and sympathetically excuse Negro resistance on the grounds that "their subjection is so great to the Portugales." At other times, however, who is dominating ceases to matter and the offenses of both peoples are conflated. When the Negroes would not come forth at "Don Johns towne," Towerson writes, the English concluded that "the Portugals were in the towne." Pursuing the natives nonetheless, with no better success, the English then took "twelve goats and fourteene hennes" in punishment, "without doing any further hurt." Towerson does not state whether the Portuguese were actually present, though he was there and would have known. We hear only that the "towne," whether inhabited by Negroes and Portuguese or just Negroes, was punished as if both people were equally culpable and distinctions between them moot.

Towerson interweaves this incident and that of an accompanying ship of English who (presumably at the same time) encountered the stone-throwing Negroes at Mowre. Though the Negroes at Mowre appear self-motivated, the interweaving of the two events obscures how distant or distinct the two communities were and whether the Portuguese were, in fact, present in both. That Towerson makes no attempts to clarify this presence suggests that it ultimately does not matter: the Negroes' seemingly autonomous aggression and commissioned resistance are equally incriminating to them and to the Portuguese, who are merged as a single subject. Towerson again shows an inattention to differences between the two when he reports elsewhere that the English "heard two calievers shot off upon the shore, which we judged to be either by the Portugales or by the Negroes of the Portugales." Thus, though the Portuguese were imperializing outsiders like the English and, ironically, the narrators of some of Hakluyt's accounts, they are nonetheless blurred into the African landscape and aligned with the most uncivilized natives and the most hostile actions. Either by condemning or "becoming" the Portuguese, Negroes evidence the otherness not only of Africa but, more importantly, of a European competitor who posed a greater threat to English interests.

On the other end of the spectrum, Turks, an even greater competitor, are implicated by the figure of the Moor. Though Elizabeth attempted to ally herself with the Turks, their imperialism was viewed as a serious threat to England's national security. Because of their awesome power and reputation as barbaric aggressors, in order to pave the way for English imperialism promoters had to distinguish it from Turkish efforts—and in a way which did not endanger necessary alliances. African Moors, who had neither the power nor the desire for empire and whose closeness to Negroes "proved" their incivility, provided that way.

Representations of Turks and Moors, like those of Indians and Negroes, share general characterizing features. In Hakluyt Turks, like Moors, figure predominantly as emperors, with exotic names and titles and comparable, though more luxurious, courts. They too are displayed in correspondences with the Queen as literate and cooperative, granting the Crown's petitions for the safe passage, and they too are Moslems who, in allying themselves with England, reveal their reverence for "the most mighty & most holy God, . . . worshipped and feared with all purenesse of minde, and reverence of speech." At the same time, however, their civility is made to seem as uncertain and unreliable as that of Moors. In one account detailing the English's hospitable reception at the court of the "Great Turk," the narrator keeps his and our eye on the myriad of well-equipped guards standing alertly by. Elsewhere and more explicitly, Turkish leaders are accused of multiple deceptions—most vehemently, perhaps not coincidentally, in an account of a Turkish "king" in Africa.

In that account, Turks and Moors are notably confused and Turkish identity made a matter of religion (as Moorish identity sometimes was). Though the episode takes place in Barbary, a region associated with Moors, it is unclear whether the "king" was a Moor or a Turk. We are told only that Moors were the "husbandmen of the countrey," that the king was subject to the Great Turk and to his janissaries, and that he was served by both Turks and Moors. Both possibilities are kept in play during a lengthy account and excoriation of his false promises, and it is only when the king demands that his visitors "turne Turke" that we learn he was a Turk himself. Even then, what that means is clouded by his characterization as "an infidell that hath not the feare of God before his eyes." To be a Turk is to be a Moslem infidel. As several references to those who have "turned Turk" suggest, Turks are made as well as born—and significantly, of the stuff that Moors are made on.

In an odd turn of narrative, Hakluyt himself recounts an alleged interaction, reported by Moors, in which the Portuguese told the Moors that the English were "cruell people and men-eaters." Admitting no similarity between the narrative fashioning he records and that which he deploys, Hakluyt declares it "spitefull dealing," ironically even as he uses the event to criticize the Portuguese and the Moors, who are guilty of self-serving representation, if not misrepresentation. For us, however, this incident offers a telling reflection of how easily the tables can be, and were, turned to indict an Other—and an Other's imperialism. Just as the Portuguese cannibalize the English to set the Moors against them, and just as the Moors expose the Portuguese to set the English against them, so too does Hakluyt incriminate the Portuguese and the Moors to set the English against both. That European as well as African subjects are included in that "both" reminds us too that Hakluyt's vision of Africa is one which knows no geographical bounds, either within "the dark continent" or between it and Europe, America, and the East.

Despite the narrators' ostensible intention to "speake somewhat of the countrey and people," Hakluyt's Africa is continually pressed into abstraction. To retrieve from it a definitive image of a "black man" or Moor is to obscure the obfuscation crucial to it. Rather than helping us (and Renaissance society) understand the racial and cultural differences of figures such as Othello, the *Navigations* prevents us (and them) from doing so, creating instead an impression of undifferentiated otherness. When we compare Hakluyt's vision to that of other Africanist texts, we should consider not what cultural knowledge they extract from it but how they negotiate its darkness, how they attempt to clarify or amplify its alienating uncertainties, and to what ends. For Renaissance representations of Africa were as full of difference as Africa itself, and in attempting to understand them, we must first discern what difference

the difference inscribed on and erased from Africa finally makes. In Hakluyt's *Principal Navigations,* Africa's value lies not merely in its promise of immediate material profit but more importantly in its reflection of England's power and right to power across the globe. Helgerson has argued that as England launched into overseas activities, Hakluyt had "to reinvent both England and the world to make them fit for one another." And this is surely true in the case of Africa. For, indeed, Hakluyt invents an Africa which at once begs for outside intervention and incriminates the "wrong" outsiders for intervening, and an England which can successfully negotiate between the two.

---

## FURTHER READING

**Criticism**

Review of *The Principal Navigations,* by Richard Hakluyt. *The Athenaeum,* No. 3979 (30 January 1904): 137-8.

> Review of two volumes of *The Principal Navigations* which finds in Hakluyt's literary style an echo of Robert Burton's *The Anatomy of Melancholy.*

Jones, John Winter. Introduction to *Divers Voyages Touching the Discovery of America and the Islands Adjacent.* London: The Hakluyt Society, MDCCCL, 171 p.

> A wide-ranging introduction to Hakluyt's first major work. Addresses the French exploration of Florida, includes Hakluyt letters, dedicatory epistles, and the latin text of Royal patents for discovery.

Froude, James Anthony. "England's Forgotten Worthies." In *Short Studies on Great Subjects,* pp. 32-77. London: Dent, 1964.

> Generally unfavorable review of The Hakluyt Society's edition of Hakluyt's *Voyages.* Froude nonetheless praises the English voyagers whose narratives constitute "the Prose Epic of the modern English nation."

Cawley, Robert Ralston. "Warner and the Voyagers." *Modern Philology* XX, No. 2 (November 1922): 113-47.

> A close textual study which traces the influence of Hakluyt's *The Principal Navigations* in William Warner's historical poem *Albion's England.*

Kerr, Willis Holmes. "The Treatment of Drake's Circumnavigation in Hakluyt's *Voyages,* 1589." *The Papers of the Bibliographical Society of America* 34 (Fourth quarter, 1940): 281-302.

> Detailed bibliographical analysis of the 1589 edition of *The Principal Navigations* which addresses the omission of the account of Drake's circumnavigation.

Trevor-Roper, H.R. "The Homer of Herefordshire." *The New Statesman* LVI, No. 1437 (27 September 1958): 419-20.

Provides a brief overview of Hakluyt's career, and suggests that the *Discourse of Western Planting* (1584) is Hakluyt's "most significant" writing.

Quinn, David B. "Richard Hakluyt, Editor." In *Richard Hakluyt, Editor: A Study Introductory to the facsimile edition of Divers Voyages (1582).* Amsterdam: Theatrum Orbis Terrarum Ltd. 1967, 87 p.

Considers the role of *Divers Voyages* as propaganda for the colonization of North America, and assesses Hakluyt's work as a translator and editor of voyage narratives.

Shawcross, John T. "The Bee-Simile Once More." *Milton Quarterly* 15, No. 2 (May 1981): 44-7.

Takes Milton's use of a bee simile in *Paradise Lost* as evidence that the poet was influenced by Hakluyt's *The Principal Navigations*.

Morris, Jan. "Hakluyt for Beginners." *Encounter* LIX, No. 3-4 (September-October 1982): 43-5.

Review of *Hakluyt's Voyages* which considers the wide variety of voyage narratives and the national character of the voyagers.

Quinn, David B. "Early Accounts of the Famous Voyage." In *Sir Francis Drake and the Famous Voyage, 1577-1580*, edited by Norman J.W. Thrower, pp. 33-48. Berkeley: University of California Press, 1984.

Discusses Hakluyt's part in the publishing history of the narrative of Sir Francis Drake's circumnavigation.

---

**For further information on Hakluyt's career and works, see the following volume published by Gale Research: *Dictionary of Literary Biography*, Volume 136.**

---

# Bartolomé de Las Casas

## 1474-1566

Spanish historian and polemicist.

### INTRODUCTION

Often characterized by modern historians as the "Defender and Apostle to the Indians," Bartolomé de Las Casas is known for exposing and condemning the violent practices of Spanish colonizers of the New World against native Americans. Marked by emotionally charged language and often exaggerated statistics, Las Casas's works caused him to be harshly criticized in his own lifetime as a threat to Spanish rule in America. Though more than four hundred years have passed since his death, the works of this controversial Dominican friar continue to elicit strong reactions from both detractors and defenders.

### Biographical Information

Bartolomé de Las Casas was born to an aristocratic family in Seville in 1474. He studied theology and law at the University of Salamanca before accompanying Columbus on his third voyage to America in 1498. In 1511 Las Casas went to Santo Domingo to join the priesthood; a year later, he participated in the colonization of Cuba. The torture, enslavement, and generally inhumane treatment of the Indians that he witnessed during Cuba's colonization compelled him to defend them against further mistreatment, and in 1521, by the decree of the Holy Roman Emperor Charles V (who was also king Charles I of Spain), Las Casas was granted an opportunity to plan and implement a system of non-violent colonization and Christian indoctrination in the district of Cumaná in Venezuela, but the experiment failed. Disheartened, he joined the Dominicans in 1523 and for several years refrained from any direct involvement in Spain's colonial policies. During this period of profound introspection, he began to write his first extensive works, the *Historia de las Indias* (*History of the Indies*; 1875) and the *Apologética historia sumaria* (*Summary Apologetical History*; 1951). In the 1530s Las Casas began once again to take an active role with regard to Spanish policies, travelling to Venezuela, Perú, New Granada, Darién and Guatemala to observe colonial practices. Assuming that the royal family and governing councils in Spain were unaware of the violent acts that conquistadors committed in their names, Las Casas drafted and circulated among them many treatises, proclamations, and petitions calling for the reform of Spain's coloni-

zation practices. Named Bishop of Chiapas in Mexico in 1543, Las Casas remained in this position until he returned to Spain in 1549. In Spain, he began writing his *Apología* (*In Defense of the Indians;* 1552). This became the basis of his argument against Juan Gines de Sepúlveda, an Aristotelian scholar who argued at the council of Valladolid in 1550-51 for the continued violent means of New World conquest on the grounds that there is a natural inequality among human beings. Las Casas actively campaigned for more humane treatment of Native Americans until his death in Madrid in 1566.

### Major Works

Las Casas began writing his first comprehensive work, *Historia de las Indias*, around 1527. This polemical work outlines Europe's New World conquests from 1492 to 1520 and attempts to portray Native Americans as culturally different from, but equal to Europeans. At the same time, Las Casas started his *Apologética historia sumaria*, which recognized the legitimacy of Native American societies and argued that they would best respond to non-violent means of Christian indoctrination. Many of Las Casas's subsequent works consist largely of excerpts from these two histories. His most famous, the *Brevísima relación de la destrucción de las Indias* (*The Devastation of the Indies: A Brief Account*, 1552), was his only work published before his death. Written in 1542 and published ten years later in Seville without the consent of the Royal Council, the *Brief Account* was Las Casas's most acrimonious assault on Spanish colonial policies. It was officially banned in Spain by the Holy Tribunal of Zaragoza in 1660, but new editions appeared periodically throughout Europe.

**Critical Reception**

During his lifetime, many Spanish nationalists and governmental officials characterized Las Casas as a traitor and a fanatic who should be publically reprimanded and whose writings should be banned. Despite the negative reception in his homeland, Las Casas's influence had enduring political repercussions. His defense at Valladolid influenced Philip II's 1573 ordinance regulating the use of armed force during new conquests. His *Brief Account* was used as a source of anti-Spanish propaganda by the English at the end of the sixteenth century, and later by other countries including the Netherlands, Italy, Germany, France, and the United States. In 1898, prior to the Spanish-American War, a translation of the *Brief Account* (entitled *An Historical and True Account of the Cruel Massacre and Slaughter of 20,000,000 People in the West Indies by the Spaniards*) was published in New York in an effort to arouse negative sentiments against Spaniards in Cuba. Some modern Spanish historians still characterize Las Casas as delusional and dangerous, but many others contend that his often exaggerated testimony and somewhat dubious statistics do not significantly lessen the value of either his analyses or his humanitarian principles.

## PRINCIPAL WORKS

*Brevísima relación de la destrucción de las Indias* [*The Devastation of the Indies: A Brief Account*] (polemical history) 1552
*Apología* [*In Defense of the Indians*] (speech) c.1552
*\*Historia de las Indias* [*History of the Indies*] (history) c.1527
\*\**Apologética historia sumaria cuanto a las cualidades, dispución, descripción, cielo y suelo destas tierras, y condiciones naturales, policías, repúblicas, manera de vivir e costumbres de las gentes destas Indias occidentales y meridionales cuyo imperio soberano pertence a los Reyes de Castilla* [*Summary Apolo-*

*getical History of the Qualities, Disposition, Description, Sky, and Soil of These Lands, And, Natural Conditions, Politics, Republics, Way of Living and Customs of These Western and Southern Indies Whose Sovereign Empire Belongs to the Kings of Castile*] (history) c.1527-1551

\*Las Casas began writing this work circa 1527. The manuscript was published in 1875.

\*\*Las Casas began writing this work circa 1527 and completed it circa 1551. A version was published in 1951.

## CRITICISM

### Sir Arthur Helps (essay date 1867)

SOURCE: A preface to *The Life of Las Casas: "The Apostle of the Indies,"* George Bell and Sons, 1890, pp. v-xv.

[*In the following excerpt, from a biography originally published in 1867, Helps presents a laudatory characterization of Las Casas as a historian, philanthropist, and a highly original thinker.*]

The life of Las Casas appears to me one of the most interesting, indeed I may say the most interesting, of all those that I have ever studied; and I think it is more than the natural prejudice of a writer for his hero, that inclines me to look upon him as one of the most remarkable personages that has ever appeared in history. It is well known that he has ever been put in the foremost rank of philanthropists; but he had other qualifications which were also extraordinary. He was not a mere philanthropist, possessed only with one idea. He had one of those large minds which take an interest in everything. As an historian, a man of letters, a colonist, a missionary, a theologian, an active ruler in the Church, a man of business, and an observer of natural history and science, he holds a very high position amongst the notable men of his own age. The ways, the customs, the religion, the policy, the laws, of the new people whom he saw, the new animals, the new trees, the new herbs, were all observed and chronicled by him.

In an age eminently superstitious, he was entirely devoid of superstition. At a period when the most extravagant ideas as to the divine rights of kings prevailed, he took occasion to remind kings themselves to their faces, that they are only permitted to govern for the good of the people; and dared to upbraid Philip the Second for his neglect of Spanish and Indian affairs, through busying himself with Flemish, English, and French policy.

At a period when brute force was universally appealed to in all matters, but more especially in those that pertained to religion, he contended before Juntas and Royal Councils that missionary enterprise is a thing that should stand independent of all military support; that a missionary should go forth with his life in his hand, relying only on the protection that God will vouchsafe him, and depending neither upon civil nor military assistance. In fact his works would, even in the present day, form the best manual extant for missionaries.

He had certainly great advantages: he lived in most stirring times; he was associated with the greatest personages of his day; and he had the privilege of taking part in the discovery and colonization of a new world.

Eloquent, devoted, charitable, fervent, sometimes too fervent, yet very skilful in managing men, he will doubtless remind the reader of his prototype, Saint Paul; and it was very fitting that he should have been called, as he was, the "Apostle of the Indies."

Nothwithstanding our experience, largely confirmed by history, of the ingenuity often manifested in neglecting to confer honour upon those who most deserve it, one cannot help wondering that the Romish Church never thought of enrolling Las Casas as a saint, amongst such fellow-labourers as Saint Charles of Borromeo, or Saint Francis of Assisi.

His life is very interesting, if only from this circumstance, that, perhaps more than any man of his time, he rose to great heights of power and influence, and then, to use a phrase of his own, fell sheer down "into terrible abysses." His spirit, however, almost always rose indomitable; and the "abysses" did not long retain him as their captive.

Among his singular advantages must be mentioned his great physical powers, and tenacity of life. I do not remember that he ever mentions being ill. He exceeded in his journeyings his renowned master and friend, Charles the Fifth, and he lived fully as laborious a life as did that monarch.

When Charles, a youth of sixteen, came to the throne, Las Casas was a man of about forty, of great power and influence. He soon won the young king's attachment; during the whole of whose active life he worked vigorously with him at Indian affairs; and when, broken in health and in spirit, Charles retired to San Yuste, Las Casas was in full vigour, and had his way with Philip the Second, not, however, without the aid of the Imperial recluse. For almost the last business which Charles attended to was one in which the dying monarch gave his warm support to his friend Las Casas.

With Charles's grandfather, Ferdinand the Catholic, Las

Casas had also worked at Indian affairs; and, with his usual sincerity, had not failed to inform that king of many truths which concerned his soul and the welfare of his kingdom.

Columbus, Cardinal Ximenes, Cortes, Pizarro, Vasco Nuñez, Gattinara the great Flemish statesman, were all known to Las Casas: in fact, he saw generations of notable men—statesmen, monarchs, inventors, discoverers, and conquerors—rise, flourish, and die; and he had continually to recommence his arduous conflict with new statesmen, new conquerors, and new kings. He survived Ferdinand fifty years, Charles the Fifth eight years, Columbus sixty years, Cortes nineteen years, Ximenes forty-nine years, Pizarro twenty-five years, and Gattinara thirty-seven years.

> **Eloquent, devoted, charitable, fervent, sometimes too fervent, yet very skilful in managing men, he will doubtless remind the reader of his prototype, Saint Paul; and it was very fitting that he should have been called, as he was, the "Apostle of the Indies."**
>
> —*Sir Arthur Helps*

He was twenty-eight years old when he commenced his first voyage to the Indies; and he was still in full vigour, not failing in sight, hearing, or intellect, when, at ninety-two years of age, he contended before Philip the Second's ministers in favour of the Guatemalans having Courts of Justice of their own. Having left the pleasant climate of Valladolid, doubtless excited by the cause he was urging, and denying himself the rest he required, he was unable to bear up against that treacherous air of Madrid, of which the proverb justly says, "though it will not blow out a candle, it will yet kill a man," and so, was cut off, prematurely, as I always feel, in the ninety-second year of his age.

His powers, like those of a great statesman of our own time, decidedly improved as he grew older. He became, I believe, a better writer, a more eloquent speaker, and a much wider and more tolerant thinker towards the end of his life. His best treatise (in my judgment) [On Peru] was written when he was ninety years of age, and is even now, when its topics have been worn somewhat threadbare, a most interesting work.

To show that I have not exaggerated his great natural powers as well as his learning, I need only refer to his celebrated controversy with Sepulveda. This Sepulveda was then the greatest scholar in Spain, and was backed, moreover, by other learned men; but Las Casas was quite a match for them all. In argument he was decidedly superior. Texts, quotations, conclusions of

Councils, opinions of fathers and schoolmen were showered down upon him. He met them all with weapons readily produced from the same armouries, and showed that he too had not in vain studied his Saint Thomas Aquinas and his Aristotle. His great opponent, Sepulveda, in a private letter describing the controversy, speaks of Las Casas as "most subtle, most vigilant, and most fluent, compared with whom the Ulysses of Homer was inert and stuttering." Las Casas, at the time of the controversy, was seventy-six years of age.

The reader of this introduction will perhaps think that if Las Casas is such a man as I have described, and his life is of such exceeding interest, it is strange that, comparatively speaking, so little has been heard about him. This, however, can be easily explained. His life can only be fully portrayed after reference to books, manuscripts, and official documents of the greatest rarity, not within the reach even of scholars, until recent years. The government of Spain has of late years thrown open to all students, in the most unreserved manner, its literary treasures, and afforded every facility for their study. In modern times, too, the Americans have take great pains to investigate the early records of America, and have always been remarkably generous, in the use they have allowed to be made of the documents which they have rescued and brought together.

There are few men to whom, up to the present time, the words which Shakespeare makes Mark Antony say of Caesar, would more apply than to Las Casas:—

> The evil that men do lives after them,
> The good is oft interred with their bones.

At one inauspicious moment of his life he advised a course which has ever since been the one blot upon his well-earned fame, and too often has this advice been the only thing which, when the name of Las Casas has been mentioned, has occurred to men's minds respecting him. He certainly did advise that negroes should be brought to the New World. I think, however, I have amply shown in the "Spanish Conquest" that he was not the first to give this advice, and that it had long before been largely acted upon. It is also to be remembered, that this advice, to introduce negroes, was but a very small part of his general scheme. Had that been carried into effect as a whole, it would have afforded the most efficient protection for negroes, Indians, and for all those who were to be subject to the Spanish Colonial Empire.

However, Las Casas makes no such defence for himself, but thus frankly owns his great error, saying, in his history, "This advice, that licence should be given to bring negro slaves to these lands, the Clerigo Casas first gave, not considering the injustice with which the Portuguese take them and make them slaves; which

advice, after he had apprehended the nature of the thing, he would not have given for all he had in the world. For he always held that they had been made slaves unjustly, and tyrannically; for the same reason holds good of them as of the Indians."

This one error must not be allowed to overshadow the long and noble career of one, who never, as far as I am aware, on any other occasion, yielded to worldly policy; who, for nearly sixty years, held fast to a grand cause, never growing weary of it; and who confronted great statesmen, potent churchmen, and mighty kings, with perfect fearlessness, in defence of an injured, a calumniated, and down-trodden race,—a race totally unable to protect themselves from the advance of a pseudo-civilization which destroyed as much as it civilized.

## Lewis Hanke (essay date 1953)

SOURCE: "Bartolomé de Las Casas and the Spanish Empire in America: Four Centuries of Misunderstanding," in *Proceedings of the American Philosophical Society,* Vol. 97, No. 1, February, 1953, pp. 26-30.

[*In the following excerpt, Hanke, an American professor of Latin American history, briefly reviews the ongoing controversies surrounding the reputation of Las Casas.*]

When Ferdinand Cortez and his little band of Spaniards fought their way in 1519 from the tropical shores of the coast of Mexico up to the high plateau and first saw stretched below them the great Aztec capital Tenochtitlán, gleaming on its lake under the morning sun, they experienced one of the truly dramatic moments in the history of America. Fortunately we have the words of a reporter worthy of the scene, the foot soldier Bernal Diaz del Castillo, whose *True History of the Conquest of New Spain* is one of the classics of the western world. He wrote:

> Gazing on such wonderful sights we did not know what to say or whether what appeared before us was real; for on the one hand there were great cities and in the lake ever so many more, and the lake itself was crowded with canoes, and in the causeway were many bridges at intervals, and in front of us stood the great City of Mexico, and we . . . we did not even number four hundred soldiers.

Today, studying the copious records of the conquest of America, we may be struck with a kindred astonishment that a few members of this same Spanish nation, confronting multitudes of their own countrymen, dared to maintain that the truly Christian method of peaceful persuasion was the only permissible way to achieve the high purpose of that conquest. Most of these soldiers of God who insisted that the cross, not the sword, should be the prime instrument of conquest, were friars, and, of these, the one who has come to symbolize the movement was the Dominican Bartolomé de Las Casas. His efforts, in a brutal period, to protect the Indians from cruel treatment and exploitation by his fellow countrymen, and his insistence that the newly discovered natives were human beings who should be Christianized by peaceful means alone, astonish us today. And if Las Casas were able to see the tremendous influence his writings have exerted in the world during the last four hundred years, he would probably be as surprised as was Bernal Diaz del Castillo standing on the hill overlooking Mexico City with Cortez and his handful of *conquistadores*.

The four-hundredth anniversary of the printing in Seville of the first books by Las Casas affords us an opportunity to consider anew the historic influence and contemporary significance of this hotly disputed figure in the history of that great procession of events which sixteenth-century Spaniards considered the most wondrous since the coming of Christ—the discovery, conquest, and colonization of America. His contemporaries considered Las Casas variously to be a saintly leader, a dangerous fanatic, or a sincere fool. Even today his memory is kept green by active disputation; arguments over his reliability have broadened out until the reputation of this one man has become inextricably bound up with judgments on the Spanish colonial régime as a whole.

Unfavorable judgments are still being made, at least in English-speaking lands, on what Spaniards called "the great enterprise of the Indies." Did not the late Judge Alan Goldsborough, in sentencing the Puerto Rican Oscar Collazo to death for his share in the attempt on the life of President Truman, indulge in gratuitous references to the iniquities of the Spanish colonial system? And when the *New York Times* on May 14, 1951, editorialized on the four-hundredth anniversary of the University of San Marcos in Lima, Peru, did it not consider the establishment of such a famous educational institution a "spark of civilization in the horrors of Spanish treachery, greed, and oppression"?

Las Casas was largely responsible for creating this dark picture of Spanish action in America, yet his life is not particularly well known. We do not know where he is buried and the total amount of information on the man Las Casas is pitifully small. No contemporary wrote down a description of his physical appearance and no painter recorded it. Las Casas apparently felt no urge to write an autobiography and we have to depend largely upon his historical and polemical writings, which are magnificently full of his public controversies, to provide the basis for our knowledge today about his place in history.

We know that he was born in Seville in 1474, and may have studied at the University of Salamanca before going to the New World in 1502, where his father and uncle had gone before him. He became a priest, but this did not prevent him from participating in the conquest of Cuba and receiving Indians and land as a reward. In 1514 he experienced a radical change of heart, came to feel that the Indians had been unjustly treated by his countrymen, and determined to dedicate the remainder of his days to their defense.

He became the renowned champion of the Indians, and for half a century was one of the dominating figures of the most exciting and glorious age Spain has ever known. In the years between his great awakening in 1514 in Cuba and his death at Madrid in 1566 at the age of ninety-two, he was successively reformer at the court in Spain, unsuccessful colonizer in Venezuela, obstructor of wars he considered unjust in Nicaragua, fighter on behalf of justice for the Indians in bitter debates among the ecclesiastics in Mexico, promoter of the plan to conquer and Christianize, by peaceful means alone, the Indians in Guatemala, successful agitator before the Spanish court on behalf of many laws to protect the American natives, and Bishop of Chiapa in southern Mexico. After his final return to Spain in 1547 at the age of seventy-three, he served as attorney-at-large for the Indians during the last two decades of his life, during which he also produced and published some of his most important works.

Of those writings of Las Casas published in his own lifetime, the tract that most immediately inflamed the minds of Spaniards was the *Very Brief Account of the Destruction of the Indies*. This unbridled denunciation of Spanish cruelty and oppression toward the Indians, full of horrifying statistics on the number of Indians killed and other harsh accusations, was printed in 1552 in Seville. The bellowing noises Las Casas made as he conducted his furious assaults on many of the greatest leaders of the conquest did not predispose men, either then or later, to appreciate or to look closely into the footnote citations or learned arguments that he developed in eight other treatises and printed at about the same time and the same place. Many translations of the *Very Brief Account* were brought out in English, Dutch, French, German, Italian, and Latin and powerfully influenced the world to believe that Spaniards are inherently cruel, as evidenced by their treatment of the American Indians. The famous De Bry drawings used to illustrate many of these translations, depicting gleeful Spaniards hunting Indians with mastiffs and butchering even women and children in many unpleasant ways, spread far and wide the charges of Las Casas even to those who could not read. His writings, and the political use made of them by several countries, ushered in the modern age of propaganda.

Englishmen above all used Las Casas translations as

siduously in their political disputes with Spain, and the legend of Spanish cruelty was carried to the English colonies in North America. Even before the Pilgrims left Holland the gruesome pictures which illustrated the Dutch editions of Las Casas, according to William Bradford in his famous *History of Plimmoth Plantation,* served to "deter the Leyden congregation from adventuring within the reach of so cruel and murderous fanatics." Such Puritan leaders as Cotton Mather had familiarized themselves with the story of Spanish enormities as delineated by Las Casas in the many editions brought out in England whenever patriotism or political objectives required that the specter of a cruel and tyrannical Spain be evoked. John Phillips, the translator of the 1656 edition, seems to have had more imagination than his predecessors, for he entitled it *The Tears of the Indians: Being an Historical and true Account of the Cruel Massacres and Slaughters of above Twenty Millions of innocent People . . . Written in Spanish by Casaus, an Eyewitness of those things*.

The words of the translator of the 1699 version reflected well the aims of those who brought Las Casas to the attention of the English-speaking world. In the preface the translator says:

> This Bishop writes with such an Air of Honesty. Sincerity, and Charity, as would very well have become one of a better Religion than that in which he had the unhappiness to be educated. It may well surprise the Reader to hear a Spanish Prelat declaim so loudly against Persecution, and plead so freely for Liberty of Conscience in a Country subjugated to the Inquisition. To hear him in his dispute against Doctor Sepulveda, deny all methods of violence for the propagation of the Truth, as more suitable [*sic*] to the Maxims of Mahometism than the Principles of Christianity: to hear him assert the Natural Right of all Mankind to Liberty and Property, and inveigh against all Usurpation and Tyranny in the smartest Terms, is enough to move any one's Wonder, and Pity too.

The last English translation, or rather publication based upon Las Casas, since the translators were no more faithful to the original text than are some of our propagandists today, appeared in New York in 1898. It was designed to incite Americans against the Spaniards in Cuba and was entitled *An Historical and True Account of the Cruel Massacre and Slaughter of 20,000,000 People in the West Indies by the Spaniards*. This last known version in English had one subtle propaganda twist which no previous editor had thought of. Although a number of the famous horrible illustrations were reproduced, one page in the book was left blank because, explained the editor, the illustration originally planned to go there was simply too frightful to include. As the historian Albert Bushnell Hart pointed out, "The belief that the Spaniards were inherently cruel

to all the natives and harsh to their own people had great effect in bringing on the Spanish-American war and the annexation of the Philippines."

The most notable effect of the Las Casas treatises of 1552 and their many translations was felt in Spain itself. Up until about 1700 many Spaniards considered him one of their national glories who may have made mistakes but was still a great man. After 1700 the tenderness of Spain to foreign criticism became more noticeable and some Spaniards found it impossible to bring themselves to believe that a Spanish Dominican, and a bishop at that, could have written such terrible accusations against his own people. The veritable rash of reprints of the *Very Brief Account of the Destruction of the Indies* that broke out during the tumultuous period of the wars for Spanish-American independence between 1810 and 1830 turned Spaniards even more against Las Casas. Editions—all in Spanish—appeared in London, Bogotá, Puebla, Philadelphia, Paris, Guadalajara, and Mexico City. It is a tremendous irony of history that the writings of this single sixteenth-century Spaniard, addressing his own people in an effort to shock them into turning aside from their ungodliness, came to be published in so many lands and so many languages that they served to crystallize for centuries hostility against Spain. A further irony is that this Christian man of peace who emphasized the love of God and insisted on kindness toward the Indians aroused in Spaniards so much animosity and bitterness. Las Casas exalted all the peaceful virtues in his writings, but his whole life was an attack—a fierce and uncompromising attack—on whatever he conceived to be bad for the Indians.

Not only did his exaggerations deform the reality of Spanish action in America; they also fixed in many Spaniards' minds a false, or at least incomplete, concept of Las Casas and blinded them to his virtues. The praise, sometimes excessive, that has been bestowed upon him by his Dominican brothers and others who have termed him "a true servant of God" has been withheld by many and in recent years he has even been called a pre-Marxist who preached the class struggle. His sanity has been questioned, and once his work was described as "the wretched and frenzied piety of the anarchical Father Las Casas." A Spanish bibliographer, in assessing opinion on Las Casas today, considers his writings "dangerously eloquent," while a Mexican scholar describes him as "an admirable devil-possessed person, whose egalitarian concept of humanity was dangerously modern."

Other voices have been raised in Spain, in America, and elsewhere to defend and to explain Las Casas. The popularity of Las Casas is unmistakable in some parts of Spanish America. Guatemala recently struck off a special postage stamp in his honor and used his likeness on its one-centavo coins; statues of him have been erected in Mexico in years past. Some taxi-drivers in Mexico City know about Las Casas, and an interesting essay could be written on the popularity of Las Casas in Spanish America. The anonymous writer who urged that a statue of Las Casas be placed at some strategic spot in the New World, such as the Isthmus of Panama, exemplified the wide-spread devotion to him in Spanish America. And the bitterness which still exists in America against the Spanish *conquistadores* may be gauged by the fact that Mexican public opinion has never permitted a statue to Cortez in the land he conquered for Spain.

The tumult and the shouting that accompanied Las Casas throughout his life have lasted until today. Historical perspective was long ago lost, and a set of clichés substituted. Few Spaniards or non-Spaniards bothered to learn more about Las Casas than that he exaggerated the number of Indians killed. Just as in the case of our own William Lloyd Garrison, men have hesitated between the views that he was a high-minded idealist of heroic accomplishments and that he was an impractical fanatic who accomplished some few good works in a most disagreeable way. The great and well-nigh insuperable problem faced by every student of Las Casas, then, is how to prevent the heat he generates from scorching the judgment of those who study his life. It is not difficult to understand why four centuries of misunderstanding have resulted.

During the last fifty years, however, scholars have been increasingly pointing out that Las Casas was much more than a propagandist. He was also a historian, whose *History of the Indies* remains one of the basic documents of the discovery and early conquest of America. He has come to be recognized as a political theorist of importance, and as one of the first anthropologists of America. Likewise his contributions in the fields of geography, philosophy, and theology are being studied today. Although sixteenth-century Spain was a land of eminent scholars and bold thinkers, few of his contemporaries were more independent in their judgments, more learned in upholding their opinions, or more universal in their range of interests than Las Casas.

Today, as the world gropes to find some honest basis for an enduring peace among peoples of diverse cultures, it is not the multiplicity of his intellectual interests nor the single-minded devotion of this friar to the Indians which excites our respect and sympathy as much as his attitude toward non-Spaniards and non-Christians. For Las Casas rejected the popular view that the Indians discovered in Spain's onward rush through the lands of the New World were beasts, nor did he subscribe to the theory that they were slaves by nature, according to the Aristotelian view, or child-like creatures with such limited understanding that they were to be treated as perpetual minors. Las Casas, on the contrary, insisted that the civilization of the strange beings

brought to the notice of the world by the discovery of America not only deserved study but also respect. He advanced the idea that Indians of the New World compared very favorably with the peoples of ancient times and maintained that the Maya temples in Yucatan were not less worthy of admiration than the pyramids in Egypt, thus anticipating the conclusions of twentieth-century archaeologists. Most startling of all his views, at least to the proud Spaniards of his day who dominated the European world, was the statement that in some respects Indians were superior to Spaniards.

Other Spaniards at the time of the conquest held that all these new peoples were an inferior type of humanity which should be submitted to the rule of Spaniards. One of the greatest jurists and thinkers of the time, Juan Ginés de Sepúlveda, felt no hesitation in pronouncing Indians to be not quite men, above monkeys to be sure, but unworthy of being considered in the same class with Spaniards.

Las Casas pitted all of his enormous vitality, wide learning, and skill in debate against these views. He passionately urged that the Indians, though different from Spaniards in color, customs, and religion, were human beings capable of becoming Christians, with the right to enjoy their property, political liberty, and human dignity, and that they should be incorporated into the Spanish and Christian civilization rather than enslaved or destroyed. One more step was thus taken along the road of justice for all races in a world of many races. For though Las Casas started out as a defender of Indians only, he came to oppose Negro slavery as well "for the same reasons," and to work for "the liberty of all the people of the world."

He believed, with a profound conviction, that peoples everywhere might be civilized if only peaceful Christian methods were employed, and that "no nation exists today, or could exist, no matter how barbarous, fierce, or depraved its customs, which may not be attracted and converted to all political virtues, and to all the humanity of domestic, political and rational men." Even the wandering, half-naked savages of the coast of Florida are rational men who may be taught. They are merely in that rude state in which all other people existed before receiving instruction. We see here the first emphatic statement after the invention of printing of that "self-evident truth" proclaimed by the Declaration of Independence and immortalized by Abraham Lincoln in the Gettysburg Address "That all men are created equal."

What greater fruit could the discovery of America and of her many diverse peoples have borne than the conclusion of Las Casas: "All the people of the world are men"? To me it is clear that this belief of Las Casas, or hypothesis if you will, will survive the centuries and will come to be recognized as one of Spain's greatest contributions to the world.

Herein lies the present-day and, indeed, the enduring significance of this friar for modern men. Do not the principles he advocated for the relations between peoples of the New World have a more universal application; indeed, does he not have a special and urgent meaning for the whole world today? May we not more properly describe him, as did Manuel José Quintana over a century ago, as "an honor not only to Spain, but to America and to the whole world"? The Chilean Nobel poet, Gabriela Mistral, expresses it simply: "Las Casas is an honor to mankind."

## Hans Magnus Enzensberger (essay date 1966)

SOURCE: "Las Casas, or a Look Back into the Future," translated by Michael Roloff, in *The Devastation of the Indies: A Brief Account* by Bartolomé de Las Casas, edited by Michael Roloff, translated by Herma Briffault, The Seabury Press, 1974, pp. 3-34.

[*In the excerpt below, originally published in 1966, Enzensberger describes Spanish attempts to discredit Las Casas and praises his analysis of the workings of colonialism.*]

"The Indies [that is: the West Indian Islands and the coasts of Central and South America] were discovered in the year one thousand four hundred and ninety-two. In the following year a great many Spaniards went there with the intention of settling the land. Thus, forty-nine years have passed since the first settlers penetrated the land, the first so-claimed being the large and most happy isle called Hispaniola, which is six hundred leagues in circumference. Around it in all directions are many other islands, some very big, others very small, and all of them were, as we saw with our own eyes, densely populated with native peoples called Indians. This large island was perhaps the most densely populated place in the world . . . And all the land so far discovered is a beehive of people; it is as though God had crowded into these lands the great majority of mankind.

"And of all the infinite universe of humanity, these people are the most guileless, the most devoid of wickedness and duplicity, the most obedient and faithful to their native masters and to the Spanish Christians whom they serve. They are by nature the most humble, patient, and peaceable, holding no grudges, free from embroilments, neither excitable nor quarrelsome. These people are the most devoid of rancors, hatreds, or desire for vengeance of any people in the world. And because they are so weak and complaisant, they are less able to endure heavy labor and soon die of no matter what malady . . .

"Yet into this sheepfold, into this land of meek outcasts there came some Spaniards who immediately behaved like ravening beasts, wolves, tigers or lions that had been starved for many days. And Spaniards have behaved in no other way during the past forty years, down to the present time, for they are still acting like ravening beasts, killing, terrorizing, afflicting, torturing, and destroying the native peoples, doing all this with the strangest and most varied new methods of cruelty, never seen or heard of before . . .

"We can estimate very surely and truthfully that in the forty years that have passed, with the infernal actions of the Christians, there have been unjustly slain more than twelve million men, women and children. In truth, I believe without trying to deceive myself that the number of the slain is more like fifteen million . . .

"Their reason for killing and destroying such an infinite number of souls is that the Christians have an ultimate aim, which is to acquire gold, and to swell themselves with riches in a very brief time and thus rise to a high estate disproportionate to their merits. It should be kept in mind that their insatiable greed and ambition, the greatest ever seen in the world, is the cause of their villainies. And also, those lands are so rich and felicitous, the native peoples so meek and patient, so easy to subject, and that our Spaniards have no more consideration for them than beasts. And I say this from my own knowledge of the acts I witnessed. But I should not say 'than beasts' for, thanks be to God, they have treated beasts with some respect; I should say instead like excrement on the public squares."

So begins the ***Brief Account of the Devastation of the Indies,*** which Fray Bartolomé de Las Casas wrote in 1542.

Whether it is true what this book says, whether its author should be believed—this question has produced a quarrel that has been smoldering, burning and flaming up for four hundred years. This quarrel has been waged by scholars and their tracts and dissertations, their investigations and commentaries could fill an entire library. Even in our day a generation of specialists in Spain, Mexico, South America and the United States is poring over the faded prints, letters and manuscripts from the pen of the Dominican monk from Seville. Yet the quarrel about Las Casas is not an academic one: what is under dispute is genocide, committed on twenty million people.

Since such a state of affairs does not sit well with the preferred contemplative stance of historical writing without anger and prejudice, it is scarcely surprising that the colleagues from the monk's fraternity, the theologians, historians and legal scholars have dropped all niceties in their choice of weapons. Where they

*A page from* A Brief Account.

lacked arguments they reached for rusty knives. They are, as we shall see, in use even today. The *Brief Account* had scarcely been published when the Court historian of Charles V, the famous Dr. Juan Ginés de Sepúlveda, produced a pamphlet *Against the premature, scandalous and heretical assertions which Fray Bartolomé de las Casas has made in his book about the conquest of the Indies, which he has had printed without permission of the authorities.* The very title signals with the fence posts of the Inquisition. Later Las Casas was called a traitor and a Lutheran. In 1562 the Council of the City of México petitioned the King that Las Casas' writings had caused such an uproar that they had had to convene a commission of legal scholars and theologians to draw up an expert opinion against this "impudent frater and his teachings"; the King ought to reprimand Las Casas publically and prohibit his books. A few years later the viceroy of Perú wrote: "The books of this fanatic and malicious bishop endanger the Spanish rule in America." He too demanded a royal prohibition; he too commissioned a refutation: for the official historians the fight against

Las Casas turns into a flourishing business. The assessor, a man by the name of Pedro Sarmiento de Gamboa, has the following to say: "The devil has made a cunning chess move by making this deluded churchman his tool." In 1659 the censor of the Inquisition office in Aragón rules that "this book reports of very horrifying and cruel actions, incomparable in the history of other nations, and ascribes them to Spanish soldiers and colonizers who the Spanish King sent forth. In my opinion such reports are an insult to Spain. They must therefore be suppressed." Thereupon the Holy Tribunal of Zaragoza finally issued a prohibition of the book in 1660. Yet new editions keep appearing: in 1748 the Seville Chamber of Commerce has a Latin translation confiscated, and even in 1784 the Spanish ambassador to France demands a confiscation of a reprint.

Since the seventeenth century Las Casas' opponents have developed an even more elegant method to extirpate him. The historian Juán Meléndez, a Dominican, simply declared at that time that the *Brief Account* was a forgery; noted authorities, whom he asked, had informed him that the book was written by a Frenchman and had been translated into Spanish with a forged title; something which should surprise no one: as the Spanish enjoyed the greatest fame as proclaimers of truth, the forgers had no choice but to camouflage their lies in this manner. Even in 1910 a Spanish historian seriously maintained that the *Brief Account,* to the best of human judgment, was not by Las Casas.

The reputation of the accused was not notably improved by this astonishing acquittal. Recent historians who write in Spanish have characterized him in the following words: "mentally ill" (1927); "a pigheaded anarchist" (1930); "a preacher of Marxism" (1937); "a dangerous demagogue" (1944); "a leveller possessed by the devil" (1946); "delusionary in his conceptions, boundless and inopportune in his expression" (1947); and the most respected Spanish historian of the twentieth century, Ramón Menéndez Pidal, in 1963 in Madrid, at age ninety-three, published an extensive book, which sought to exorcise the spirit of Las Casas once and for all. The American Lewis Hanke, who has devoted his life to the study of the *Conquista,* remarks about this work of exorcism:

> Don Ramon passionately denies that Las Casas was an honorable man. He calls him a megalomaniac paranoid. In his retrospective look at the conquista Don Ramon scarcely detects a single dead Indian through his colored glasses: instead he sees a scene of well-being and of cultural progress for which America has to thank the Spaniards.

Only the unparalleled success which the *Brief Account* has had makes these tenacious and furious polemics comprehensible. Las Casas wrote a great deal: largescale chronicles, theological and legal disputations, petitions and tractatuses. To this day there is no complete edition of his works. The scientifically most significant of them were first published in 1877 and 1909. Their long submersion in darkness has obvious reasons. The *Brief Account,* true to its title, is nothing but a concise synopsis of the investigations and experiences which Las Casas elaborates in greater detail elsewhere. It was meant for a single reader: his Catholic Majesty, Charles I of Spain, as Charles V Emperor of the Holy Roman Empire. Yet the *Brief Account*'s appearance in book form, at a time when printing was just beginning to flourish, acquainted all of Europe with it. Its original publication in 1552 in Seville was followed by translations into all the important languages of the time: Paris 1579; London 1583; Amsterdam 1607; Venice 1630 were the first foreign places of publication, followed by Barcelona, Brussels, Lyon, Frankfurt, and later by Philadelphia, New York, Havana, Buenos Aires, Lima, São Paula, México and Santiago de Chile.

The book's sensational effect provides an early example of the power of the press. The *Brief Account* reached one of its climaxes during the rivalry between Spain and England at the turn of the sixteenth century. A second wave of translations was brought on by the French Enlightenment. The third flood of reprints occurred between 1810 and 1830 in Latin America: at that time the *Brief Account* won direct influence on the leaders of the wars of independence against the Spanish colonial power; Simón Bolívar valued Las Casas, and the fact that he himself was a descendant of the conquistadors did not prevent him from making the book serve his revolutionary intentions. Las Casas had to serve as the chief witness against the Spanish even during the Spanish-American War in 1899, which secured control over the Caribbean area and rule over the Philippines for the United States.

The *Brief Account* was not spared by the tumult of power-political interests. Time and again Spain's opponents used Las Casas, often in a pharisaical manner, and so it is not surprising that the Hispanic world to this day discusses the book from a perspective which seems foolish to us: namely, whether or not it "sullies" the honor of Spain. Las Casas has become the exponent of the so-called Black Legend. *Leyenda negra* as the Spanish historians with a terminological trick call every conception of the conquest of South America which does not sing the official song of praise: as though what disparages the "honor of Spain" had been seized, willy-nilly, out of the blue.

This whole polemic is antiquated and superfluous. Spain's honor does not interest us. The French enlightener Jean François Marmontel, in his work on the destruction of the Inca Empire, referring to Las Casas, already stated in 1777 what there is to be said on this subject: "All nations have their robbers and fanatics, their times of barbarousness, their attack of rabies." The question of national character is not on the agenda. The extermination of the European Jews by the Germans, the Stalinist deportations, the extinction of Dresden and Nagasaki, the French terror in Algeria, the Americans in South East Asia have demonstrated even to the most obtuse that all peoples are capable of everything: and while the *Brief Account of the Devastation of the Indies* is being published once more in a new English translation the last of the Indians in Brazil are being inexorably exterminated.

The historians of the nineteenth century tried tenaciously, at times desperately, to invalidate Las Casas, and not alone out of chauvinism or cowardice, but because the events he describes would have destroyed their historical picture. They believed in the mission of Christianity or in the "values" of European civilization and what transpired during their own time in the Congo, in Indonesia, in India and China they would have regarded as impossible as the genocide Las Casas describes.

We have no such doubts. The news we receive on TV each day would suffice to disabuse us of them. The actuality of the book is monstrous, has a penetratingly contemporaneous smell to it. Of course our way of reading it is not devoid of an element of deception. Every historical analogy is ambiguous: for whoever rejects this analogy history becomes a pile of insignificant data; for whoever accepts it at face value, leveling the specific differences, it becomes aimless repetition, and he draws the false conclusion that it has always been this way, and the tacit consequence that, therefore, it will always remain so too. No, Las Casas was not our contemporary. His report treats of colonialism in its earliest stage; that is, the stage of robbery pure and simple, of unconcealed plundering. The complicated system of exploitation of international raw materials was as yet unknown at his time. Trade relations did not play a role during the Spanish conquista, nor the spread of a superior material civilization; no "development policy" of whatever kind served it as justification—only a veneer of Christianity that proposed to convert the heathen, inasmuch as they survived the Christians' arrival. In its primal state colonialism could do without the fiction of partnership, of bilateral trade. It did not offer anything, it took what it found: slaves, gold, anything it pleased. Its investments were confined to the indispensable essentials of every colonial exploitation: to armed power, administration and the fleet. For these reasons the Spanish conquerors could also ignore the dialectic of enslavement which Sartre describes in a few sentences:

That is what is so annoying about slavery: if you tame a member of our species, you diminish his or her profitability; and as little as you provide him or her with, a human being as a workhorse is always going to cost more than he or she earns. That is why the colonial masters are forced to stop their breaking-in process halfway. The result: neither human being nor animal, but native . . . Poor colonial masters: that constitutes his dilemma. He should really kill those whom he robs. But that is just what he cannot do, because he also has to exploit them. He cannot transform the massacre into genocide or the enslavement to the point of brutalization, and that is why he must necessarily lose control.

Such a dilemma only occurs when the colonialists set themselves long-term objectives, when they begin to calculate the profitability of their venture. Such a rational procedure of exploitation was unknown in the sixteenth century. The conquista did not know double bookkeeping, not even the tally of the simplest statistics; the continent's depopulation did not trouble it.

Las Casas' opponents did not hesitate to make him responsible, as it were, for the irrationality of the genocide. There is no trusting his figures it was and still is said; they betray a medieval relationship to arithmetic. South and Central America never held 12, 15 or 20 million inhabitants during the time of the conquest; as in the reports of the crusaders the word "million" simply means many people. Such an approach has something repulsive about it from the very outset. It would like to prove Las Casas a liar but let the murders go scot-free because they only killed 8, 5 or 3 million Indians instead of 20 million. That is the way the *National Zeitung* protects the German fascists, claiming that not 6 million Jews were killed but at most 5.

Aside from the moral insanity manifested by such sophistry, it is also factually wrong. Two American scholars who have investigated the demographic conditions in old México in recent years reached the conclusion that in the 30 years between Cortez's landing and the writing of the *Brief Account* the population of Central México dwindled from 25 to roughly 6 million. That means that the conquista alone must have had 19 million victims in México alone; Las Casas names only 4. Even if mindful of the virus illnesses, of malaria, of the famine and forced labor, that is of the indirect causes of the depopulation, one reaches the conclusion that Las Casas was probably rather too careful with his figures.

Let us leave these examples of arithmetic aside. Las Casas spent more than forty years in the American colonies. What he reports are to a large part observations and firsthand experiences. The witness's life testifies to their authenticity. Where it contradicts the reports of other witnesses the historical investigator must engage in lengthy comparisons. We are not engaged in anything of the kind. What is decisive for today's reader of the *Brief Account* are two critieria that academic investigators usually ignore; that is, first

of all, the inner cohesiveness of the book, its eye for detail, its care in sketching the episode. Las Casas rarely spends much time with abstract thesis, and he not only describes the most horrible cruelties but also shows the grinding everyday life; he shows us, if the abbreviation be permitted not only the torture instrument but also the fight for the daily crust of bread.

A second, external, criterion of Las Casas' credibility is the precision of his view of the structure of colonial rule. Since these structures still exist today his statements are verifiable. For this one does not need to be a Hispanic scholar, a visit to South Africa will suffice.

If one tests the *Brief Account* from this perspective one notices first of all its author's economic acuity. The cleric Las Casas did not confine himself to theological observations, he analyzes the basic structure and exposes the technique of colonial exploitation whose first step is the recruitment of forced labor. For this purpose there existed the so-called *encomienda* system. *Encomienda* means as much as recommendation. A random number of Indians was distributed by the local commanders to the individual Spanish landowners and "recommended" to them for the reason that they required this protection for their prompt conversion. In reality the status of these protégés was that of serfs: they were totally at the mercy of their new masters, and received no wages or upkeep for the work that their protector (*encomendero*) asked them to do.

The economy of the colonializers concentrated on two forms of business which dominate the economy of many South American nations to this day: mining and plantations. But whereas the North American concerns now extract tin, copper, lead and vanadium, the conquistadors were interested in one metal only: gold.

Contact with the motherland during the time of the conquista was expensive, time-consuming and dangerous; exploitation of the overseas possessions thus had to confine itself to the most valuable commodities. That explains a further specialty of the colonializers: the pearl fishing in the Caribbean of which Las Casas provides an unforgettable description.

> The pearl fishers dive into the sea at a depth of five fathoms, and do this from sunrise to sunset, and remain for many minutes without breathing, tearing the oysters out of their rocky beds where the pearls are formed. . . . It is impossible to continue for long diving into the cold water and holding the breath for minutes at a time, repeating this hour after hour, day after day; the continual cold penetrates them, constricts the chest, and they die spitting blood, or weakened by diarrhea. The hair of these pearl divers, naturally black, is as if burnished by the saltpeter in the water, and hangs down their back making them look like sea wolves or monsters of another species.

That is not a hearsay report: only someone who has seen the burnished hair and the encrusted shoulders with his own eyes speaks like that. This description by Las Casas led, incidentally, to a royal prohibition of pearl fishing—one of the few, and shortlived, victories which fell the valiant bishop's way.

Another enterprise which Las Casas had in mind could only develop when one region after the other had been depopulated: the slave trade. After the Indians had been cut down by the millions, and tormented to death, the colonializers noted with astonishment and even with a certain regret that they were running out of labor power. At this moment the savage became a commodity and the deportations became a profitable business in which the military and officials, who formed primitive corporations, engaged on their own account.

> The colonized world is a divided world. The dividing line, the border is marked by barracks and police stations. The rightful and institutional interlocutor of the colonized, the spokesman of the colonial masters and the repressive regime is the cop or the soldier . . . The agent of power employs the language of pure power. He does not conceal his sovereignty, he exhibits it . . . The colonial master is an exhibitionist. His need for security makes him remind the colonized, with a loud voice: "I am master."

These sentences are from a modern phenomenology of colonial rule. Frantz Fanon developed them in the first chapter of his book *The Wretched of the Earth* (1961). Las Casas' observations, made four hundred years earlier, coincide with them exactly. Even the manifestly senseless cruelties, even the *conquistadores'* terroristic arbitrariness had its psychological function in that it demonstratively cut the New World in two. Proof of the fact that the Indians were not human beings was provided by the Spaniards anew every day when they acted as if they were not dealing with human beings: "But I should not say `than beasts' for, thanks be to God, they have treated beasts with some respect; I should say instead like excrement on the public squares." . . .

But the blind terror with which the colonial masters demonstrate who they are and that the colonized are nothing leads to a new dilemma. It assures the colonizers of their identity while simultaneously endangering their ideology. Once they become afraid of the colonized their terror robs them of their justification which they would not like to relinquish. For the colonial master not only wants to have power, he also wants to be in the right: to the point of nausea he keeps asserting that he has a mission, that he serves God and the King, is spreading the Christian teachings and the values of civilization; in one word, that he basically has something higher in mind. He cannot do without a good conscience. But this means that he must hide the terror

which he practices so ostentatiously and must deny his own demonstration. Something peculiarly schizophrenic, an absurd formalism thus is attached to all colonial undertakings. Of this too, the *Brief Account* provides an excellent example:

> And because of the pernicious blindness that has always afflicted those who have ruled in the Indies, nothing was done to *incline* the Indians to embrace the one true Faith, they were rounded up and in large numbers *forced* to do so. Inasmuch as the conversion of the Indians to Christianity was stated to be the principal aim of the Spanish conquerors, they have dissimulated the fact that only with blood and fire have the Indians been brought to embrace the Faith and to swear obedience to the kings of Castile or by threats of being slain or taken into captivity. As if the Son of God who died for each one of them would have countenanced such a thing! For He commanded His Apostles: "Go ye to all the people" (*Euntes docete omnes gentes*). Christ Jesus would have made no such demands of these peaceable infidels who cultivate the soil of their native lands. Yet they are told they must embrace the Christian Faith immediately, without hearing any sermon preached and without any indoctrination. They are told to subject themselves to a King they have never heard of nor seen and are told this by the King's messengers who are such despicable and cruel tyrants that deprive them of their liberty, their possessions, their wives and children. This is not only absurd but worthy of scorn.

> This wretch of a Governor thus gave such instructions in order to justify his and their presence in the Indies, they themselves being absurd, irrational, and unjust when he sent the thieves under his command to attack and rob a settlement of Indians where he had heard there was a store of gold, telling them to go at night when the inhabitants were securely in their houses and that, when half a league away from the settlement, they should read in a loud voice his order: "Caciques and Indians of this land, hark ye! We notify you that there is but one God and one Pope and one King of Castile who is the lord of these lands. Give heed and show obedience!" Etc., etc. "And if not, be warned that we will wage war against you and will slay you or take you into captivity." Etc., etc.

The sentence that not the murderer but the victim is guilty becomes the dominant maxim under colonial rule. The "native" is the potential criminal per se who must be held in check, a traitor who threatens the order of the state: "Those who did not rush forth at once," Las Casas says, "to entrust themselves into the hands of such ruthless, gruesome and beastial men were called rebels and insurgents who wanted to escape the service of His Majesty."

But this guilty verdict is the very thing that helps the colonized to perceive their situation. For it leads to its own fulfillment: fiction becomes reality, the raped resort to violence. Las Casas describes several instances where it came to armed actions of resistance, even to small guerillas. He calls the Indian attacks where "a considerable number of Christians" lost their lives a "just and holy war" whose "justifiable causes will be acknowledged by every man who loves justice and reason." Without hesitating, in three sweeping sentences which have been left unscarred by the centuries, Las Casas thinks his thoughts to their conclusion:

> And those wretches, those Spaniards, blinded by greed, think they have the God-given right to perpetrate all these cruelties and cannot see that the Indians have cause, have abundant causes, to attack them and by force of arms if they had weapons, to throw them out of their lands, this under all the laws, natural, human, and divine. And they cannot see the injustice of their acts, the iniquity of the injuries and inexpiable sins they have committed against the Indians, and they renew their wars, thinking and saying that the victories they have had against the Indians, laying waste the lands, have all been approved by God and they praise Him, like the thieves of whom the prophet Zechariah speaks: "Feed the flock of the slaughter; whose possessors slay them, and hold themselves not guilty: and they that sell them say, Blessed be the Lord; for I am rich."

The book that Las Casas left behind is a scandal. In its original sense the word scandal means as much as trap. The scholars who warn us of him have entangled themselves in that old *skandalon*. They do not sense that their quarrel is only a distant echo of a huge conflict. The storm in the water glass of their profession points to other storms. The ruffle in the historical consciousness indicates enormous tremors in historical reality. The process which began with the *Conquista* is not yet over. It continues in South America, Africa and Asia. It does not behoove us to speak the verdict about the monk from Seville. Perhaps he has spoken ours. . . .

Bartolomé de las Casas was not a radical. He did not preach revolution. His loyalty to the Church and to the crown are undisputed. He fought for the equal rights of the Indians as subjects of an authority which he acknowledged. A radical transformation of the social order was as unthinkable for him as for his contemporaries: he wanted to bring the one that existed to the point where it would redeem its ideology. Every social order contains a utopia with which it decorates itself and which it simultaneously distorts. Las Casas did not guess that this promise, which was also contrary to the idea of the state of his time, can only be fulfilled at the price of revolution, partially, occasionally, as long and insofar as a new form of domination does not encapsulate and negate it again.

Yet utopian thoughts were not alien to Las Casas. He

was the contemporary of Thomas More and of Machiavelli, of Rabelais and of Giovanni Botero. In 1521 he tried nothing less than the founding of his own Nova Atlantis. The undertaking shows the unity of theory and practice which characterizes all his work. It ended catastrophically.

At his audience with Charles V Las Casas suggested to the emperor, as proof that his principles withstood the test of practice, to found a model colony of "the plough and the word." The emperor decreed the district of Cumaná in Venezuela to him with the proviso that "no Spanish subject may enter this territory with arms." Las Casas recruited a group of farmers, outfitted an unarmed expedition and started to build his colony. Attacks by Spanish soldiers and by slave dealers into the peaceful territory, uprisings by embittered Indians, whiskey smuggling and acts of violence destroyed the colony in a short time. None of the defeats which he suffered hurt Las Casas more deeply than this one.

The proof of the experiment has not been exhausted to this day. There is no peaceful colonialism. Colonial rule cannot be founded on the plough and the word but only on the sword and the fire. Every "alliance for progress" needs its "gorillas," every "peaceful penetration" is dependent on its bomber commando, and every "reasonable reformer" such as General Lansdale finds his Marshal Ky.

Bartolomé de las Casas was not a reformer. The new colonialism which today rules the poor world cannot invoke his name. In the decisive question of force Las Casas never wavered; the suppressed people lead, in his words, "This fight is occurring before our very eyes." The regime of the wealthy over the poor, which Las Casas was the first to describe, has not ended. The ***Brief Account*** is a look back into our own future.

## Lewis Hanke (essay date 1974)

SOURCE: "Analysis of Las Casas's Treatise," in *All Mankind is One: A Study of the Disputation Between Bartolomé de Las Casas and Juan Gines de Sepúlveda in 1550 on the Intellectual and Religious Capacity of the American Indians,* Northern Illinois University Press, 1974, pp. 73-112.

[*In the excerpt below, Hanke details Las Casas's refutation of Sepúlveda's arguments at the council of Valladolid in 1550-51.*]

The main lines of the argument Las Casas developed at Valladolid in his presentation to the Council of the Fourteen in August 1550 have been known ever since 1552, when he published a résumé by Domingo de Soto of both his own views and those of Sepúlveda. Soto, the Dominican theologian who was a member of the Council appointed to hear the controversy, and who had been commissioned by his colleagues to prepare a summary of both arguments, never mentioned the second part, the Spanish *apología*. He remarked, however, that Las Casas had once said more than was necessary on a certain point and, at another time, had been "as copious and diffuse as the years of this business," especially in his response to Sepúlveda's charge that the Indians were barbarians and therefore slaves by nature, "to which he did not respond in any one place, but in all his writings may be found his arguments on this topic which may be reduced to two or three main points" (an accurate and perceptive description of Las Casas's writings). At another point Soto stated:

> The bishop described at length the history of the Indians, showing that although some of their customs were not particularly civil, they were not however barbarians on this account but rather a settled people with great cities, laws, arts, and government who punished unnatural and other crimes with the death penalty. They definitely had sufficient civilization that they should not be warred against as barbarians.

As Las Casas stated to Prince Philip in the dedicatory letter of the *Defense*, he was responding point by point to the doctrine presented by Supúlveda in his manuscript *Apología*, which was a résumé of *Democrates Alter*. (It will be recalled that Las Casas complained that several copies of this manuscript were circulating in Spain in the years immediately preceding the Valladolid dispute.) He had to use a summary of this treatise because no copy of the complete text was available to him at the time he was marshaling his hundreds of citations for the *Defense*, which was written, he informed Philip, "at the cost of much sweat and sleepless nights." Las Casas's purpose was a comprehensive demolition of Sepúlveda, "wrong both in law and in fact," and a demonstration of how he "has distorted the teachings of philosophers and theologians, falsified the words of Sacred Scripture, of divine and human laws, and how no less destructively he has quoted statements of Pope Alexander VI to favor the success of his wicked cause. Finally, the true title by which the Kings of Spain hold their rule over the New World will be shown."

Thus did Las Casas, at almost eighty years of age, and after half a century of experience in America, explain how he came to "unsheathe the sword [pen] for the defense of the truth" in one of his most significant writings on the history of Spain in America and on the nature of the Indians. Although the manuscript embodying Las Casas's attack was already bulky, he requested Philip to command Sepúlveda to give him a copy of the complete Latin work so that he could refute his falsehoods even more thoroughly.

Before we enter into the story of this argument it may be useful to have a closer view of the complicated and controversial subject: Is war lawful as a means for spreading Christianity in America? This question has two aspects.

First, its legality: Is war against the Indians ever just, in itself, as a means of attracting them to the true religion? Sepúlveda had expounded his views on this theoretical issue in his Latin treatise *Democrates Alter* and in the summary of this treatise, which Las Casas had read. Las Casas presented his position in the *Defense*, whose text is the basis for this study.

Second, its factual basis: Are the Indians really in such a state of inferiority and barbarism in relation to the rest of the civilized people that this fact alone justifies such war, according to natural law, as a means of liberating them from such inferiority and barbarism? Sepúlveda invoked the testimony of the royal historian Gonzalo Fernández de Oviedo y Valdés in his *Historia general y natural de las Indias*, which had rendered a very unfavorable opinion on Indian capacity and character. To prove the contrary, Las Casas devoted a large part of his *Defense* to expounding his very favorable view of the Indians and to attacking Oviedo tooth and nail. Moreover, he composed the second part of his *Defense*, in Spanish, to demonstrate the truth of his contention that the Indians are not "irrational or natural slaves or unfit for government."

Las Casas divided the Latin part of his argument, the *Defense*, into two well-defined sections. In the first he replied to the four reasons Sepúlveda adduced in favor of waging war against the Indians, and in the second he commented on the "authorities" Sepúlveda cited to substantiate his position.

The imposition of a scholastic organization of thought on the torrential prose of Las Casas does not give the reader a true understanding of the rare combination of passion and erudition that marks the *Defense*. Sarcasm, learning, indignation, and memorable phrases are to be found throughout this treatise, which probably presents a more comprehensive view of Las Casas's thought than any other. Certainly he referred to it so frequently in his printed 1552 treatises as to indicate that he looked upon it as the most detailed exposition of his views. The present analysis, however, will not attempt to tell all; the *Defense* is such a rich and varied combination of his fundamental doctrine and his experiences in the New World that it will doubtless be studied as long as the world maintains its interest in the history of Spain in America and in that procession of remarkable events called the expansion of Europe.

*The First Section: Las Casas's Response to Sepúlveda's "Four Reasons for Justifying War Against the Indians in Order to Convert Them":*

Las Casas made it clear at the beginning of the **Defense** that his principal concern was to attack those who condemned "*en masse* so many thousands of people" for faults that most of them did not have. "What man of sound mind will approve a war against men who are harmless, ignorant, gentle, temperate, unarmed, and destitute of every human defense?" He then announced that he would prove Sepúlveda and his followers were wrong in law, a subject he had treated "at greater length elsewhere and in general," and wrong in fact.

> For the Creator of every being has not so despised these peoples of the New World that he willed them to lack reason and made them like brute animals, so that they should be called barbarians, savages, wild men, and brutes, as they [i.e., the *Sepúlvedistas*] think or imagine. On the contrary, they are of such gentleness and decency that they are, more than the other nations of the entire world, supremely fitted and prepared to abandon the worship of idols and to accept, province by province and people by people, the word of God and the preaching of the truth.

Then Las Casas plunged into such a detailed rebuttal of each reason, with so many subsidiary arguments, that at times the reader is almost lost in his torrent of words and in the multiplicity of his learned references. A notable characteristic of the disputation at Valladolid was the way in which both Las Casas and Sepúlveda drew upon the immense reservoir of doctrine and example that was represented in the Bible, the writings of Church fathers, and other authorities and events of the past as recorded by historians. Each contestant tried to demonstrate that his opponent misunderstood, and at times twisted, the words of these authorities and the experience of the past to fit his own argument.

*Rebuttal of Sepúlveda's First Argument: "Indians Are Barbarous":*

To Sepúlveda's argument that the inhabitants of the New World were in such a state of barbarism that force was required to liberate them from this condition, Las Casas replied that one cannot generalize about "barbarians" in such a loose and broad way. He examined Aristotle's statements on barbarism and found several different kinds:

1. *Those who are barbarians because of their savage behavior.* Las Casas replied that, even those who live in the most highly developed states, such as Greeks and Latins, can be called barbarians if their behavior is sufficiently savage. However, the Spaniards, in their treatment of the Indians, "have surpassed all other barbarians" in the savagery of their behavior.

2. *Those who are barbarians because they have no written language in which to express themselves.* Such

persons are barbarians in only a restricted sense, Las Casas said, and do not fall into the class that Aristotle described as pertaining to natural slaves. Spanish missionaries, before and after Las Casas, emphasized the beauty and intricacy of the Indian languages, and the Dominican friar Domingo de Santo Tomás published a grammar of the Peruvian Indians' language to prove their rationality.

3. *Those who are barbarians in the correct sense of the term.* These, Las Casas argued, are the only ones who may properly be placed in Aristotle's category of natural slaves. They are truly barbarians

> either because of their evil and wicked character or the barrenness of the region in which they live. . . . They lack the reasoning and way of life suited to human beings. . . . They have no laws which they fear or by which all their affairs are regulated . . . they lead a life very much that of brute animals. . . . Barbarians of this kind (or better, wild men) are rarely found in any part of the world and are few in number when compared with the rest of mankind.

Such men are freaks of nature, "for since God's love of mankind is so great and it is His will to save all men, it is in accord with His wisdom that in the whole universe, which is perfect in all its parts, His wisdom should shine more and more in the most perfect thing: rational nature." To find a large part of the people of the world barbaric in this sense would mean a frustration of God's plan, according to Las Casas, who explained that he had discussed this more fully in his treatise **The Only Method of Attracting All People to the True Faith,** in which he proved that "it would be impossible to find one whole race, nation, region, or country anywhere in the world that is slow-witted, moronic, foolish, or stupid, or even not having for the most part sufficient natural knowledge and ability to rule and govern itself." Even such barbarians should be attracted to the Christian faith by peaceful means; nevertheless, the Indians are not this kind of barbarian, but fall within the second class.

Then Las Casas launched into a description of those barbarians who are "not irrational or natural slaves or unfit for government." They have "kingdoms, royal dignities, jurisdiction, and good laws and there is among them lawful government." Then followed such an optimistic description of Indian culture that one is not surprised that he promised to spell out his views on Indian achievements in greater detail in the second part of the **Defense.** This argument sounds very much like the parallel one developed in the **Apologetic History.**

Las Casas was reacting, of course, to Sepúlveda's harsh estimate of Indian capacity, for Sepúlveda described them thus:

In prudence, talent, virtue, and humanity they are as inferior to the Spaniards as children to adults, women to men, as the wild and cruel to the most meek, as the prodigiously intemperate to the continent and temperate, that I have almost said, as monkeys to men.

Several versions of Sepúlveda's treatise, one of which may have been the text that was available to Las Casas while he was preparing his argument at Valladolid, included the "monkeys to men" phrase in this denunciation of Indian character; however, the most complete and apparently latest version of the text of the treatise prepared by Sepúlveda omits this phrase.

In the definitive text of this treatise (prepared by Losada) Sepúlveda softened his position somewhat, but still had a very low opinion of the Indians' capacity and felt that Spaniards were supremely superior:

Now compare their gifts of prudence, talent, magnanimity, temperance, humanity, and religion with those little men (*homunculos*) in whom you will scarcely find traces of humanity; who not only lack culture but do not even know how to write, who keep no records of their history except certain obscure and vague reminiscences of some things put down in certain pictures, and who do not have written laws but only barbarous institutions and customs. But if you deal with the virtues, if you look for temperance or meekness, what can you expect from men who were involved in every kind of intemperance and wicked lust and who used to eat human flesh? And don't think that before the arrival of the Christians they were living in quiet and the Saturnian peace of the poets. On the contrary they were making war continuously and ferociously against each other with such rage that they considered their victory worthless if they did not satisfy their monstrous hunger with the flesh of their enemies, an inhumanity which in them is so much more monstrous since they are so distant from the unconquered and wild Scythians, who also fed on human flesh, for these Indians are so cowardly and timid, that they scarcely withstand the appearance of our soldiers and often many thousands of them have given ground, fleeing like women before a very few Spaniards, who did not even number a hundred.

Sepúlveda then said that Cortez, whom he greatly admired, had decisively demonstrated the greatness of Spaniards in his conquest of Mexico: "Can there be a greater or stronger testimony how some men surpass others in talent, industry, strength of mind, and valor? Or that such peoples are slaves by nature?" And then Sepúlveda seems to reply to those who, like Dürer, praised the artistic skill of the Indians:

But even though some of them show a talent for certain handicrafts, this is not an argument in favor of a more human skill, since we see that some small animals, both birds and spiders, make things which no human industry can imitate completely.

Even the relatively advanced Mexican Indians fell far short of an acceptable standard:

Nothing shows more of the crudity, barbarism, and native slavery of these men than making known their institutions. For homes, some manner of community living, and commerce—which natural necessity demands—what do these prove except that they are not bears or monkeys and that they are not completely devoid of reason? . . . Shall we doubt that those peoples, so uncivilized, so barbarous, so wicked, contaminated with so many evils and wicked religious practices, have been justly subjugated by an excellent, pious, and most just king, such as was Ferdinand and the Caesar Charles is now, and by a most civilized nation that is outstanding in every kind of virtue?

Sepúlveda never abandoned the view that Indian culture was vastly inferior to that of Spaniards. Some years after the Valladolid meeting, in a political treatise dedicated to Philip II, he returned to this favorite theme in referring to the justification of wars against the Indians:

The greatest philosophers declare that such wars may be undertaken by a very civilized nation against uncivilized people who are more barbarous than can be imagined, for they are absolutely lacking in any knowledge of letters, do not know the use of money, generally go about naked, even the women, and carry burdens on their shoulders and backs just like beasts for great distances.

The proof of their savage life, similar to that of beasts, may be seen in the execrable and prodigious sacrifices of human victims to their devils; it may also be seen in their eating of human flesh, their burial alive of the living widows of important persons, and in other crimes condemned by natural law, whose description offends the ears and horrifies the spirit of civilized people. They on the contrary do these terrible things in public and consider them pious acts. The protection of innocent persons from such injurious acts may alone give us the right, already granted by God and nature, to wage war against these barbarians to submit them to Spanish rule.

Then he listed the great benefits Spain had conferred on the Indians, in much the same way as the standard ordinance of 1573, and asked: "With what behavior, with what gifts will these people repay such varied and such immortal benefits?"

Las Casas attacked this opinion of Indian culture by charging that Sepúlveda depended for his knowledge of these matters on Oviedo, whom Las Casas considered "a deadly enemy of mankind" and utterly wrong on Indian capacity. Las Casas reproached his adversary for missing the truth by failing to consult reliable ecclesiastics and such writers as Paulus Jovius, whose histories gave a more balanced view. Las Casas could not resist pointing out his own long experience, and Oviedo's evident self-interest: "The testimony of such a person as myself, who has spent so many years in America, on the character of the Indians nullifies any allegation founded solely on the testimony of Fernández de Oviedo who had a preconceived attitude against the Indians because he held Indians as slaves."

Las Casas made a final point against the use of force in Spanish treatment of the Indians. Even if it were granted—as it was not—that they had no keenness of mind or artistic ability, they still would not be obliged "to submit themselves to those who are more intelligent . . . even if such submission could lead to [their] great advantage." Here it is evident that Las Casas was aware of Sepúlveda's contention that the Conquest conferred great benefits on the Indians.

Turning to the fourth category, adduced from Holy Scripture, *that those people who are not Christians may be called barbarians and clearly the Indians are barbarians in this sense,* Las Casas recapitulated his analysis of the four classes of barbarians and said that they may be reduced to two large categories, as follows. *Those improperly termed barbarians* comprise the first, second, and fourth classes—together with the Indians—but even Christians are barbarians (of the first class) if they manifest savage customs, and *those properly termed barbarians* comprise only the third class, from which Indians are definitely excluded. Las Casas concluded his exposition of barbarism by observing that Sepúlveda either did not understand or chose not to understand these distinctions with respect to the different classes of barbarians. As if to underline the connection between the *Defense* and the *Apologética Historia,* Las Casas put a long statement on the various kinds of barbarians, based upon the argument in the *Defense,* at the end of the *Apologética Historia.*

*Rebuttal of Sepúlveda's Second Argument: "Indians Commit Crimes Against Natural Law":*

To Sepúlveda's contention that war against the Indians may be justified as punishment for the crimes they commit against natural law, with their idolatry and sacrifice of human beings to their gods, Las Casas responded with the following syllogism: All punishment presupposes jurisdiction over the person receiving it, but Spaniards enjoy no jurisdiction over Indians, and hence they cannot punish them.

In the course of his exhaustive study of the nature of jurisdiction Las Casas made a notable statement for a mid-sixteenth-century Spanish Christian. He held that Jews, Moslems, or idolaters who live in a Christian kingdom are under the temporal jurisdiction of the Christian prince, but *not* with respect to spiritual matters (a view that was shared by Vitoria and Vera Cruz). Perhaps Las Casas was following the doctrine he had been familiar with as a young man. As Richard Konetzke [1958] has emphasized, kings in medieval Spain permitted full freedom of worship to their subjects, and as late as 1492 the Catholic Kings Ferdinand and Isabella assured the subjugated Moorish people, after the conquest at Granada, that they could remain in the country and that they would be guaranteed the free exercise of their Islamic religion, their property, and their customs. But in the years after the voyages of Columbus the Crown's authority had steadily tightened, and the modern state which aspires to gain strength by wiping out dissension was well advanced in Spain after 1551, when Las Casas was putting the text of his *Defense* in final shape. Moreover, Las Casas stated that Jews, Moslems, and idolaters who do not live in a Christian kingdom are not under the jurisdiction of the Church, nor any Christian prince, no matter how their crimes may violate natural law. Heretics, however, can be punished if they fail to observe "the obedience promised to God and the Catholic Church in baptism."

Las Casas cited authority after authority to prove his contention that unbelievers do not come under the competence of the Church. Thus the Church cannot punish pagans who worship idols merely because of their idolatry. Nor is it the business of the Church to punish the unbelief of the idolaters, which Las Casas explained in this way:

> The worshipers of idols, at least in the case of the Indians, about whom this disputation has been undertaken, have never heard the teaching of Christian truth even through hearsay; so they sin less than the Jews or Saracens, for ignorance excuses to some small extent. On this basis we see that the Church does not punish the blindness of the Jews or those who practice the Mohammedan superstition, even if the Jews or Saracens dwell in cities within Christian territories. This is so obvious that it does not need any proof. Rome, the bastion of the Christian religion, has Jews, as also do Germany and Bohemia. And Spain formerly had Saracens, who were commonly called Mudejars, whom we saw with our own eyes.
>
> Therefore, since the Church does not punish the unbelief of the Jews even if they live within the territories of the Christian religion, much less will it punish idolaters who inhabit an immense portion of the earth, which was unheard of in previous centuries, who have never been subjects of either the Church or her members, and who have not even known what the Church is.

The conclusion to this detailed exposition is clear: "There is no crime so horrible, whether it be idolatry or sodomy or some other kind, as to demand that the gospel be preached for the first time in any other way than that established by Christ, that is, in a spirit of brotherly love, offering forgiveness of sins and exhorting men to repentance."

The many examples Las Casas introduced into his text after what must have been a wide-ranging search during those "sleepless nights" of study all pointed to one conclusion: "No pagan can be punished by the Church, and much less by Christian rulers, for a crime or a superstition, no matter how abominable, or a crime, no matter how serious, as long as he commits it . . . within the borders of the territory of his own masters and his own unbelief." Not that Las Casas admitted many "abominations"; rather, he dedicated much space to an exegesis of Pope Paul III's bull *Sublimis Deus* of 1537, which had played such a prominent part in the long struggle, described above, over Indian capacity. Although Las Casas analyzed the declaration in the light of fundamental and unshakable principles, he did not fail to apply them to the Indians. The methods of force and terror used to preach the faith to them had been "contrived by the devil in order to prevent the salvation of men and the spread of the true religion. And, in truth, this is . . . what they did in treating the Indians as though they were wild and brute animals so that they might exploit them as if they were beasts of burden."

*Rebuttal of Sepúlveda's Third Argument: "Indians Oppress and Kill Innocent Persons"*:

War against the Indians, Sepúlveda argued, may be justified because the Indians oppress innocent persons and kill them in order to sacrifice them to their gods or to eat their bodies, therefore armed intervention against the Indians would prevent an act contrary to natural law, to which all are subject. Here Las Casas entered into the most complicated and subtle questions in the whole treatise, as may be seen from the large amount of space he gave to this argument. Both adversaries, and such eminent authorities of their time as Francisco de Vitoria, accepted the basic premise. Las Casas, however, strove mightily to demonstrate that the Indians did not commit such acts, and that, if they *did* worship idols or engage in human sacrifices to their gods, these acts could be justified.

The methods by which Las Casas and Sepúlveda invoked the Bible to support their respective positions are worthy of more extended treatment than can be given here. Suffice it to say that Las Casas twitted his opponent:

> He has not diligently searched the scriptures, or surely has not sufficiently understood how to apply them, because in this era of grace and mercy he seeks to apply those rigid precepts of the Old Law that were given for special circumstances and thereby he opens up the way for tyrants and plunderers to cruel invasion, oppression, spoliation, and harsh enslavement of harmless nations.

What God, centuries ago, commanded the Jews to do to the Egyptians and Canaanites should not be applied to Indians of the New World. Later Las Casas stated that "not all of God's judgments are examples for us." The prophet Elisha cursed forty-two boys who mocked him, calling him a "baldhead," for which they were torn to pieces by bears. If men were to imitate such judgments, "we would commit a vast number of most unjust and serious sins and thousands of absurdities would follow."

Las Casas also denounced as an absurd argument Sepúlveda's invocation of Saint Cyprian because this Church father approved the killing of those who, having heard and embraced the truth of the gospel, returned to idolatry. The Indians, obviously, did not fall into this category. Thus we see the importance of Oviedo's view, had it been accepted, that the Indians had once received the faith and had then reverted to their previous idolatry.

To illustrate his position that the Indians could not justly be punished, because no outside power held jurisdiction over them, Las Casas set forth his ideas in some detail on the conditions under which the Church or Christian princes might have jurisdiction over infidels: (1) when infidels are in fact subjects of the Church or some Christian prince, (2) when the Church or a Christian prince is able to change their potential jurisdiction (*en hábito*) over infidels to actual jurisdiction (*a acto*). Six examples of condition two were given, and Las Casas found that the Indians fit into none of the six cases. But special twists to the argumentation on two of the six circumstances merit attention—the fourth and the sixth.

The fourth circumstance occurs when pagans make obstacles *per se,* and not *per accidens,* for Christian preachers. Las Casas had to admit that missionaries had been killed in the New World, but not because they were preachers *per se* but because the Indians tried to defend themselves from the bad treatment of the accompanying soldiers who waged war against them. His previous treatise, **The Only Method of Preaching the True Faith,** had concentrated on this theme alone, and its doctrine was given in résumé: "What does the gospel have to do with firearms? What does the herald of the gospel have to do with armed thieves?"

The Church has an obligation to preach the gospel to all nations, but Las Casas declared (and illustrated his doctrine with four examples) that it does not follow from this that Christians can force unbelievers to hear the gospel. The conclusion will be no surprise to those familiar with other Las Casas treatises, particularly *The Only Method of Preaching the True Faith:*

> From the foregoing it is evident that war must not be waged against the Indians under the pretext that they should hear the preaching of Christ's teaching, even if they may have killed preachers, since they do not kill the preachers as preachers or Christians as Christians, but as their most cruel public enemies, in order that they may not be oppressed or murdered by them. Therefore let those who, under the pretext of spreading the faith, invade, steal, and keep the possessions of others by force of arms—let them fear God, who punishes perverse endeavors.

The final case brought forward by Las Casas holds unusual interest, for he invoked Erasmus to support his position—probably one of the few times that the sage of Rotterdam was so cited before a royal council in Spain. In this instance Las Casas referred to the doctrine of Alberto Pío, Prince of Carpi, who advanced the idea that the Church may wage war against infidels who maliciously impede the spread of the gospel. Las Casas agreed with this, especially with respect to the Turks, a point on which he was at one with Sepúlveda, who had dedicated a book to Charles V in which he advocated war against the Turks as soon as possible. Las Casas, we know, felt just as strongly as his opponent on this point.

Opposition to the anti-Moslem crusades was considered in Catholic Europe to be a Lutheran error, and one of Sepúlveda's objectives at Valladolid may have been to make the Leopoldo of his treatise, the character who questions the justice of war against the Indians, a quasi-Lutheran, inasmuch as Luther attacked the campaigns against Turkey in his *Resolutiones*. If so, Sepúlveda failed, as Las Casas seems never to have been touched by the Inquisition, despite his strong advocacy of several unpopular doctrines. At any rate, he always held that just war could be levied against the Turks and the Saracens; however, Indians were in an entirely different category, he wrote: they could not be justly warred against because their resistance was purely defensive in the face of conquistador attacks. In adopting this position Las Casas knew very well that the Prince of Carpi had been Sepúlveda's protector when the latter had first arrived in Rome as a young man, and that Sepúlveda had published his *Antapologia* in 1532 to take the part of his protector when the Prince of Carpi was feuding with Erasmus. Las Casas evidently considered Erasmus a Christian thinker in this matter:

> Erasmus never dreamed of what Carpi cites against him. In fact [he] very explicitly teaches the Catholic opinion in his commentary on the psalm "Give to

the Lord, you sons of God," as well as in many other passages in his writings. Possibly Carpi was seeking glory by attacking Erasmus, to whom our Sepúlveda, in putting together his little book, did not devote much attention, contrary to rumor.

The sixth circumstance occurs when infidels injuriously oppress innocent persons, and specifically by sacrificing them or eating their bodies. Here again Las Casas coincided in principle with Sepúlveda and Francisco de Vitoria in upholding the traditional doctrine of the Church, that all men are obliged to aid the innocent who is in danger of being killed unjustly. But does this doctrine apply to the Indians? Yes, said Sepúlveda, while Vitoria agreed less definitely, and Las Casas argued that such an application must be "the lesser evil." For example, one must refrain from war, and even tolerate the death of a few innocent infants or persons discovered to be killed for sacrifice and cannibalism, if in trying to prevent such deaths one should "move against an immense multitude of persons, including the innocent, and destroy whole kingdoms, and implant a hatred for the Christian religion in their souls, so that they will never want to hear the name or teaching of Christ for all eternity. All this is surely contrary to the purpose intended by God and our mother the Church." Even though some wicked persons would escape punishment, this would be the lesser evil. "Would he be a very good doctor who cuts off the hand to heal the finger?"

When Las Casas got down to cases, he must have had in mind the post-1514 experiences of Oviedo and other Spaniards when they tried to read the requirement to Indians:

> Let us put the case that the Spaniards discover that the Indians or other pagans sacrifice human victims or eat them. Let us say, further, that the Spaniards are so upright and good-living that nothing motivates them except the rescue of the innocent and the correction of the guilty. Will it be just for them to invade and punish them without any warning? You will say "No, rather, they shall send messengers to warn them to stop these crimes." Now I ask you, dear reader, what language will the messengers speak so as to be understood by the Indians? Latin, Greek, Spanish, Arabic? The Indians know none of these languages. Perhaps we imagine that the soldiers are so holy that Christ will grant them the gift of tongues so that they will be understood by the Indians? Then what deadline will they be given to come to their senses and give up their crimes? They will need a long time to understand what is said to them, and also the authority and the reasons why they should stop sacrificing human beings, so that it will be clear that evils of this type are contrary to the natural law.

> Further, within the deadline set for them, no matter what its length, they will certainly not be bound by

the warning given them, nor should they be punished for stubbornness, since a warning does not bind until the deadline has run out. Likewise, no law, constitution, or precept is binding on anyone unless the words of the language in which it is proposed are clearly understood, as the learned jurists say. . . .

Now, I ask, what will the soldiers do during the time allowed the Indians to come to their senses? Perhaps, like the forty monks Saint Gregory sent to convert the English, they will spend their time in fasting and prayer so that the Lord will be pleased to open the eyes of the Indians to receive the truth and give up such crimes. Or, rather, will not the soldiers hope with all their hearts that the Indians will become so blind that they will neither see nor hear? And then the soldiers will have the excuse they want for robbing them and taking them captive. Anyone who would foolishly and very unrealistically expect soldiers to follow the first course knows nothing about the military mind.

Human sacrifice required much explanation. Las Casas held that the Indians were "in probable error" for such actions, but added: "Strabo reminds us that our own Spanish people, who reproach the poor Indian peoples for human sacrifice, used to sacrifice captives and their horses." Ancient customs are hard to eradicate: "There is no greater or more arduous step than for a man to abandon the religion which he has once embraced." Las Casas concluded that proving the sinfulness of human sacrifice to those who practice it is very difficult, a basic question to which he applied four "principles":

1. No nation is so barbarous that it does not have at least some confused knowledge about God.

2. By a natural inclination men are led to worship God according to their capacities and in their own ways. We must offer Him whatever we have—our wealth, energies, life, and our very soul—for His service.

3. There is no better way to worship God than by sacrifice.

4. Offering sacrifice to the true God or to the one thought to be God comes from the natural law, while the things to be offered to God are a matter of human law and positive legislation.

From these principles one may adduce that Las Casas recognized the good faith of the pagan in his religion, even if it were idolatrous, and justified the pagan's human sacrifice as a natural act because he was offering his most valuable possession, his life, to the God he considered the true one. Neither Sepúlveda nor Vitoria, nor indeed few theologians then or later, adopted a similar view. Thus Las Casas respected, perhaps

more than any of his contemporaries, the beliefs, rites, and customs of the Indians as appropriate and proper for them, but in the minds of many of his contemporaries he must have seemed to be teaching something very close to heresy, although the Inquisition never called him to account. For him, the religious beliefs of the Indians were valid—for them at that time—and in no wise indicated atheism. He even considered them more truly religious than those Spaniards who tried to attract Indians to their civilization and their religion by "fire and sword": "If Christians use violent methods to impose their will on the Indians, it would be better for them to maintain their own religion; indeed, in such a case the pagan Indians would be those on the right path and Christians should learn from them how to conduct themselves."

He closed his argument on human sacrifice with these words:

> Thus it is clear that it is not possible, quickly and in a few words, to make clear to unbelievers, especially ours, that sacrificing men to God is unnatural. On that account, we are left with the evident conclusion that knowledge that the natives sacrifice men to their gods, or even eat human flesh, is not a just cause for waging war on any kingdom. And again, this longstanding practice of theirs cannot be suddenly uprooted. And so these entirely guiltless Indians are not to be blamed because they do not come to their senses at the first words of a preacher of the gospel. For they do not understand the preacher. Nor are they bound to abandon at once their ancestral religion, for they do not understand that it is better to do so. Nor is human sacrifice— even of the innocent, when it is done for the welfare of the entire state—so contrary to natural reason that it must be immediately detested as something contrary to the dictates of nature. For this error can owe its origin to a plausible proof developed by human reasoning.

> The preceding arguments prove that those who willingly allow themselves to be sacrificed, and all the common people in general, and the ministers who sacrifice them to the gods by command of their rulers and priests labor under an excusable, invincible ignorance and that their error should be judged leniently, even if we were to suppose that there is some judge with authority to punish these sins. If they offend God by these sacrifices, he alone will punish this sin of human sacrifice.

As Las Casas stated over and over again during the course of his disquisition on sacrifice: "It is not altogether detestable to sacrifice human beings to God from the fact that God commanded Abraham to sacrifice to Him his only son."

Anyone who is familiar with the genuine horror produced in the Spaniards by human sacrifice, from foot soldiers to priests, as evidenced in the many chronicles of the Conquest, must reckon the attitude of Las Casas to such ceremonial sacrifices—especially in Mexico—as one of the most remarkable of all his doctrines. It was, moreover, a doctrine to which he was firmly committed, as may be seen from his even more extensive treatment of it in the *Apologética Historia,* in which he used the same authorities and examples to reach the same conclusions on the justification for human sacrifice by the American Indians. Toward the end of his long life, in a letter to his fellow Dominicans in Chiapa, he proudly referred to the arguments he presented against Sepúlveda in Valladolid: "In this controversy I maintained and proved many conclusions which no one before me dared to treat or write about." And the only specific doctrine he mentioned was his defense of human sacrifice by the Indians.

*Rebuttal of Sepúlveda's Fourth Argument: "War May Be Waged Against Infidels in Order to Prepare the Way for Preaching the Faith":*

In this section Las Casas argued against Sepúlveda's use of the parable of the wedding feast, when the Lord commanded his servants to go into the highways and byways and "force them to come in." He had treated this subject in other writings, but in refuting Sepúlveda he used language reminiscent of his bitter attacks on the Conquest in his *Very Brief Account of the Destruction of the Indies:*

> At this point I would like Sepúlveda and his associates to produce some passage from sacred literature where the gospel parable is explained as he explains it; that is, that the gospel (which is the good and joyful news) and the forgiveness of sins should be proclaimed with arms and bombardments, by subjecting a nation with armed militia and pursuing it with the force of war. What do joyful tidings have to do with wounds, captivities, massacres, conflagrations, the destruction of cities, and the common evils of war? They will go to hell rather than learn the advantages of the gospel. And what will be told by the fugitives who seek out the provinces of other peoples out of fear of the Spaniards, with their heads split, their hands ampu- tated, their intestines torn open? What will they think about the God of the Christians? They will certainly think that [the Spaniards] are sons of the devil, not the children of God and the messengers of peace. Would those who interpret that parable in this way, if they were pagans, want the truth to be announced to them after their homes had been destroyed, their children imprisoned, their wives raped, their cities devastated, their maidens deflowered, and their provinces laid waste? Would they want to come to Christ's sheepfold with so many evils, so many tears, so many horrible massacres, such savage fear and heartbreaking calamity? Does not Paul say, "Treat each other in the same friendly way as Christ treated you"?

Sepúlveda's fourth argument also provided Las Casas with an opportunity to deliver one of his fundamental statements on the nature of man, based on one of his favorite authorities, Saint John Chrysostom:

> Just as there is no natural difference in the creation of men, so there is no difference in the call to salvation of all of them, whether they are barbarous or wise, since God's grace can correct the minds of barbarians so that they have a reasonable understanding. He changed the heart of Nebuchadnezzar to an animal mind and then brought his animal mind to a human understanding. He can change all persons, I say, whether they are good or bad: the good lest they perish, the bad so that they will be without excuse.

Therefore Las Casas concluded that "since the nature of men is the same and all are called by Christ in the same way, and they would not want to be called in any other way."

The wedding parable was then explained in familiar terms, after which Las Casas turned to Sepúlveda's use of Constantine the Great's wars against unbelievers so that once subjected to his rule, "he might remove idolatry and the faith might be introduced more freely." Historical data was produced on the Goths and the barbarian Irish to show "how great an opportunity is given to pagans to blaspheme Christ if war is waged against them and how great a hatred for Christian religion is implanted in the hearts of pagans by war.... Pagans, therefore, must be treated most gently and with all charity." If not, the results will be disastrous:

> Now if Christians unsettle everything by wars, burnings, fury, rashness, fierceness, sedition, plunder, and insurrection, where is meekness? Where is moderation? Where are the holy deeds that should move the hearts of pagans to glorify God? Where is the blameless and inoffensive way of life? Where is humanity? Finally, where is the meek and gentle spirit of Christ? Where is the imitation of Christ and Paul? Indeed, thinking about this pitiful calamity of our brothers so torments me that I cannot overcome my amazement that a learned man, a priest, an older person, and a theologian should offer deadly poisons of this type to the world from his unsettled mind. Moreover, I do not think that anyone who fails to see that these matters are clearer than the noonday sun is truly Christian and free from the vice of greed.

Christ did not arm his disciples and authorize the use of force to teach the truths of Christianity: "How does it agree with the example of Christ to spear unknowing Indians before the gospel is preached to them and to terrify in the extreme a totally innocent people by a display of arrogance and the fury of war or to drive them to death or to flight?" Preaching the faith by massacres and terror was an Islamic practice that must not be emulated by Christians.

Las Casas aimed to meet, and defeat, every one of his adversary's arguments. . . .

**Carl F. Starkloff, S. J. (essay date 1992)**

SOURCE: "Aboriginal Cultures and the Christ," in *Theological Studies,* Vol. 53, No. 2, June, 1992, pp. 288-312.

[*In the following excerpt, Starkloff presents Las Casas as a model for a "culturally sensitive" approach to promoting Christian faith.*]

Our model for a cultural Christology for mission among aboriginal peoples originates historically in the campaign of the great apologist for the Amerindians, Bartolomé de las Casas (1474-1566). There has been so much discussion of him, especially during the recent controversies over the Columbus quincentennial, that there would hardly seem to be anything more to say. But his political and theological writings do indeed help open the way to a Christology for aboriginal cultures.

Las Casas's life is becoming better known with contemporary historical writing, but it may be helpful here to mention the high points of that long and dramatic life. Las Casas came to "the new world" about one decade after Columbus's first voyage; he came in the role of a cleric not yet ordained to the priesthood, and as a recipient of a grant of land known as *encomienda,* which was a kind of fiefdom taken from aboriginal ownership and awarded to colonists, leaving the resident Indians bound to that land. After his ordination (probably the first in the "new world"), he continued his land ownership and served as chaplain to the *encomenderos.*

However, the abuses, indeed atrocities, being committed by the colonists did not go undenounced. There was a sizeable group of scholars and missionaries, most of them Dominicans, who preached against this evil. Las Casas does not seem to have been touched by that preaching for some time, even when he was denied the sacraments by a Dominican. However, there was obviously something taking place within him, because in 1515 he began to criticize Spanish practices and to try to effect humane changes in the *encomienda* system. But these actions very quickly proved insufficient for him, as he became convinced of the inherently evil nature of the system.

In 1522 Las Casas entered the Dominicans, where he was to remain virtually cloistered for five years. When he emerged, profoundly changed not only spiritually but intellectually, he undertook a campaign for colonial reform that lasted through nearly forty years of astounding labors until his death in Vallodolid at the age of ninety-two. This campaign included a brief tenure as Bishop of Chiapas, during which time he engaged in many encounters with the conquistadores which often put him in danger of death. He made eight trips across the Atlantic to plead his case in the Spanish court. His most famous trip was his final one, undertaken in order to do theological battle with Juan Ginés de Sepulveda, the most prominent ideologue of the conquistadors; he did not exactly "win" this debate, but he succeeded in preventing any acceptance of Sepulveda's theories among respected scholars or political leaders. He was highly regarded in his lifetime by both King Charles V and King Philip II.

The present article is not intended as a history of the work of Las Casas; my intention here is to present him as a theological exemplar whose theory and praxis might serve as models for a culturally sensitive Christology. As Lewis Hanke points out, Las Casas was a largely self-taught theologian, deeply influenced by the Dominicans after he entered the order at the age of forty-eight. During his "cloistered" years, Las Casas acquired a training grounded in the Salamanca School as represented, for example, by Francisco Vitoria and Dimingo de Soto. Typical of this school was the conviction that "thought and action must be so intimately fused that they cannot be separated, and that spiritual truths must be made manifest in the world about us."

Historian Juan Friede, an expert on Las Casas, has penetrated to the heart of the problem of cultural oppression. Beneath the horrifying accounts of the conquistadores' atrocities, beneath the greed and outright sadistic cruelty of so many oppressive colonials, Friede places his finger on the phenomenon of cultural blindness and of forced acculturation. Paulo Friere was to deal with the same problem later under the name of "cultural invasion."

Regarding Las Casas's epic warfare against this kind of oppression, Friede and Keen have written [in *Bartolomé de Las Casas in History: Toward an Understanding of His Work,* 1971]: "His teachings concerning the unity of mankind, the principle of self-determination, and the right of men to the satisfaction of their elementary material needs have acquired a new relevancy, a new *actualidad.*" Another historian says of him: "His life is a magnificent lesson and example of the conduct (the honesty, study, and valor) that should guide the actions of the Christian intellectual confronting a hostile political environment."

The work of Las Casas is especially pertinent to the present essay, because he sought finally to free the Amerindians from foreign control and restore them to their own leaders—a principle of indigeneity, the violation of which creates the most subtle kind of oppression. Las Casas himself had to evolve into this position; as one of his biographers writes, he underwent an initial conversion from calloused slaveholder and *encomendero* to a benevolent local despot seeking to create a paternalistic utopia inspired by his reading of Thomas More. It was the failure of this project that led Las Casas into a second conversion, his entry into the Dominicans and the eventual undertaking of his passionate life's work: to completely obliterate the *encomiendas*. Finally, he saw that nothing less than a radical turn to indigenous leadership could reverse the process of oppression.

It is to this later Las Casas that we look for our model of a culture-transforming Christology. This radical reformer not only sought to rescue theology from the clutches of an arid late medieval scholasticism and return it to a sophisticated interpretation based on Scripture, patristics, and authentic scholasticism, but also called it out from the halls of the university into the struggles of the world. The translator of his famous *Defense* writes that Las Casas thus helped to enact a four-fold reform of theology, renewing it from the Bible, from earlier and especially patristic theologians, from canon law and Roman civil law, and even from Aristotle—where "the Philosopher" was compatible with Christian morality.

Narrowing down the scope of this dramatic and complex period of history, our focus here will be on three aspects of Las Casas's thought and praxis: (1) his re-emphasis on the person and witness of Jesus Christ, over against Aristotle, as the final court of appeals on human rights and dignity; (2) his interpretation of local aboriginal life and attitudes, remarkable for its time, over against such academic theorizing about them as the work of his antagonist Sepulveda; and (3) his sense for the integrity and slow pace of change of cultures, likewise remarkable for its time, grounded in a respect for the "natural" rights of human beings regardless of religious or moral condition.

### Jesus, God's Witness against Exploitation

Although it is probably safe to assume that the vast majority of conquistadores cared little for ideological debate, they nonetheless welcomed the writings of Sepulveda, which justified making war on the Indians and enslaving them. Being an Aristotelian and humanist, Sepulveda appealed especially to Aristotle's teaching on natural hierarchies of humanity and on the justification for the superior enslaving the inferior [in his *Politics*]. While even Las Casas, being a true son of Aquinas, hesitated to dismiss Aristotle completely, and even used him at other points of his argument, on this matter he was uncompromising: wherever Aristotle opposed the deep personalistic love of Jesus for all, Las Casas simply exclaimed, "Goodbye, Aristotle! From Christ, the eternal truth, we have the command, 'You

must love your neighbor as yourself.'"

Las Casas's Christology can be divided into two types: first, a kind of social-gospel Christology that asks simply, "What would Jesus do and what did Jesus teach in these cases?" This is the Las Casas who refuses to allow Aristotelianism to override authentic Christian moral theology. His *Defense* is filled with such examples. While we cannot here discuss in detail Las Casas's exegetical work, it is pertinent to mention his refutation of Sepulveda's use of the parable of the feast in Luke 14:15-24. One of Sepulveda's major arguments for justifying war on the Indians lay in the words of the householder who sent out his servants to find guests for the feast: "Force them to come in." Las Casas simply returned to the patristic distinctions in hermeneutics, citing the above case as one of figurative interpretation signifying peaceful forms of persuasion. Sepulveda employed so many arguments favoring forced conversion of the Indians that one quotation from Las Casas is appropriate: "They should be ashamed who think to spread the gospel by the mailed fist." He frequently employs a form of contemplative interpretation, calling his readers to imagine, almost in an Ignatian manner, the gentle persuasion of Jesus in contrast to the violence permitted by Sepulveda.

Other statements which exemplify his thought are the following: "Christ wanted love to be called his single commandment" (citing Col 3:17), and "Christ seeks souls, not property. He who alone is the immortal king of kings thirsts not for riches, not for ease and pleasures, but for the salvation of mankind, for which, fastened to the cross, he offered his life." In sum, for Las Casas, only in imitating the example and teaching of Christ and the Apostles will pagans be able to acknowledge, of their own free will, the way of truth and the worship of the one true God.

The second dimension of Las Casas's Christology is more subtle, and in a sense ironic. While he rejects Aristotle as the final arbiter of Christian ethics, nonetheless, as a good Thomist, he embraces the Thomist distinction between nature and supernature. However, far from espousing a distinction-of-planes theory, such as has been eschewed by Gutiérrez [in *A Theology of Liberation: History, Politics and Salvation,* 1973] Las Casas's point was that all humankind is gifted by God with the "same" nature, regardless of religious affiliation or even regardless of moral condition. Thus, for example, he wrote of the Indians, "They are our brothers, redeemed by Christ's most precious blood, no less than the wisest and most learned men in the whole world," and for this reason, St. Paul could write that he had a duty to Greeks and barbarians as much as to the Jews (Rom 1:14-15). It is the same Christ for all. In his famous speech before King Charles V, Las Casas said:

If the blood of one man (Abel) never ceased crying to God, until it was avenged, what shall not the blood of the thousands do, who, having perished by our tyranny and oppression, now cry to God: *vindica sanguinem nostrum Deus noster*. By the blood of Jesus Christ, and by the stigmata of St. Francis, I beg and beseech your majesty to put a stop to that torrent of crime and murdering of people, in order that the anger of God may not fall upon us all.

Las Casas continues the scholastic teaching that the pope has no jurisdiction over pagans, and he argues in the *Defense* that the Church has *dominium* over people only after they have made a free faith-choice and accepted baptism. In other words, we see here a Christology that is not only "kenotic" as relating to earthly rule, but one that respects the goodness of nature (and therefore, of culture). While there is indeed only one graced order, Christ loves the "nature" even of those who have not explicitly espoused that order.

### Las Casas, Interpreter of Aboriginal Life

Las Casas possessed the gift for "listening to a culture," even though his friendly interpreters admit that he probably exaggerated the virtues of aboriginal peoples for the sake of argument. He was able to do what so many missionaries (as well as anthropologists) have failed to do: to understand the Indians as persons rather than as conglomerate groups. Pagden points out [in *The Fall of Natural Man*, 1982] how, in contrast to blanket categorizing of aboriginals as "barbarians," Las Casas could grasp the truth that all peoples and persons are unique.

As a true pastor, Las Casas the bishop made a sharp distinction between those who "blaspheme" and those Indians who spoke out in anger against the mistreatment and atrocities perpetrated in the name of expansion and even of missionary activity. The colonists, as well as many missionaries apparently, simply assumed that the gospel was self-evident and *"ex opere operato,"* in a false understanding of that phrase. Therefore conversions should be forced, and the "heathen" were inexcusable whenever they resisted. Colonists also seized upon biblical condemnations of human sacrifice to justify their attacks on Indians. Against all of this, Las Casas challenged the Spaniards to conceive how their gross mistreatment of the Indians could possibly create conditions in which the gospel could be accepted in faith and freedom.

It was in this context that Las Casas constructed his famous defense of the Indians against the charge of human sacrifice. He argued that according to natural law sacrifice is the highest form of worship. It was not self-evident, he argued, that such worship should not extend even to the killing of human beings. That is, human sacrifice might conceivably be offered in good conscience. In such cases, he offered a contextualized version of the just-war theory to the effect that any war which cannot prevent the evils it inflicts on innocent victims, should be stopped, and no attention paid to the wrongs the war would attempt to right. In all of this, Las Casas contrasts the gentleness of Christ with the violence of the colonists.

### Las Casas, Culture, and Natural Human Rights

Las Casas had a keen sense of the integrity of cultures as grounded in natural human rights and he appreciated the slow pace of change of cultures. His Christology can be seen as one that deeply respected culture as a "natural right." As we have seen, his common-sense Christianity clearly perceived the absurdity of expecting rapid conversion and change, especially when promoted by "the mailed fist." He anticipated the age of dialogue when he wrote, "Does the Indian who has never heard the name of Christ believe any less, at least in a human way, that his religion is true, than the Christian does of his religion?"

[Angel Losada in Friede and Keen's *Bartolomé de Las Casas in History,* 1971] calls Las Casas a forerunner of the doctrine of pluralism, especially in his willingness to tolerate human sacrifice in order to avoid the greater evil of a war of conquest that would destroy thousands. He worked toward gradual transformation, based on good example and preaching. Another writer sees Las Casas as a true Catholic reformer reflecting the best in Luther and Calvin, "an early, shining, though incomplete application of the principles that should govern missionary work among non-Christian peoples."

Again we note Las Casas's concern to protect the rights of unbelievers. Christology thus respects these rights in both Christian and non-Christian. As Pagden illustrates, Las Casas held that all communities founded on civic virtues and values can achieve a state of "active happiness." There is a delicate balancing of "nature and grace" here that is a forerunner of later thinkers like Ripalda, Rahner, and de Lubac.

This is not to overlook the fact that Las Casas was indeed a very evangelical missionary. What he saw, however, that few of his age seemed to see, was that there are "successive creative epochs" and historical phases, and all societies and cultures must pass through them to the final phase, each being at a different stage. . . .

## Rolena Adorno (essay date 1992)

SOURCE: "The Discursive Encounter of Spain and America: The Authority of Eyewitness Testimony in the Writing of History," in *The William and Mary Quarterly,* third series, Vol. XLIX, No. 2, April, 1992, pp. 210-28.

*[Adorno is a Professor of Romance Languages at Princeton University. In the following excerpt, she describes Las Casas's use of Alvar Núñez Cabeza De Vaca's account of the 1527 Spanish expedition to Florida as a source of information for his own* Apologética historia sumaria.]

The eyewitness account, Cabeza de Vaca's *relación* of the 1527 expedition to Florida, was published twice during the reign of Charles V. It appeared before royal attempts to control publications on the Indies and again during the time when the rights to the rewards of the conquests became a topic of heated controversy. The success of Cabeza de Vaca's writing can be explained by the fact that it took a counter-conquest position. That is, Cabeza de Vaca advocated peaceful conversion of the natives and demonstrated that good treatment of the Indians produced results that served both the well-being of native populations and the economic interests of Spaniards.

Las Casas was one of Cabeza de Vaca's most remarkable readers, and an exceedingly careful one. In his **Apologética historia sumaria,** he cited extensively Cabeza de Vaca's account of the peoples and customs of Florida. Cabeza de Vaca had been a member (royal treasurer, in fact) of the Narváez expedition, five hundred men strong, sent to conquer Florida in 1527. The territory of Florida extended around the rim of the Gulf of Mexico, all the way from the peninsula of contemporary Florida to the recently settled province of Pánuco (near present-day Tampico) in Mexico. Suffering shipwreck, hunger, and the hostility of native groups, only Cabeza de Vaca and three fellow expeditionaries survived. In search of civilization the four traversed the lands from the Gulf coast of Texas south to the Río Grande, then west across northern Mexico to the Gulf of California, and ultimately south and southeast to Mexico-Tenochtitlán, where they arrived in July 1536.

Given their inability to speak most native languages (Cabeza de Vaca claimed to have learned six), problems of interpretation in face-to-face encounters were compounded when Cabeza de Vaca tried to interpret the experience in the remarkable narration he prepared for Charles V. He told of his band's arrival, after years spent with nomadic and semisedentary groups, at a settlement that practiced agriculture, where the inhabitants cultivated squash and beans, hunted bison in the north, and slaughtered livestock for food. At Christmastime 1535, the four survivors discovered for the first time evidence of other Europeans—a native who was wearing around his neck as ornaments a buckle from a sword belt and a horseshoe nail. In contrast to the marauding horsemen in search of natives to enslave, the unarmed Cabeza de Vaca and his companions came in peace. He recounted how they sought to resettle the lands abandoned by the natives, who had been terrorized by the other Spaniards.

Cabeza de Vaca's account came to be one of Las Casas's many sources for the **Apologética historia sumaria,** which compilations of information about writers who made use of Cabeza de Vaca's *relación* have often overlooked. Las Casas employed Cabeza de Vaca's work in two ways: as a source of information on native customs and as an authority on peaceful colonization. Las Casas described the purpose of his **Apologética** to "investigate, conclude, and prove with evidence that all [the peoples of the world], speaking *a toto genere,* although some more and others a bit less but none exempt, enjoy the benefit of very good subtle and natural intellects and most capable understanding and are likewise all prudent and endowed naturally with the three types of prudence described by Aristotle." In particular, he sought to demonstrate the "universal propensity and natural inclination of humanity to seek its maker and first cause," discussing the utility of religion and setting forth the principles that characterized societies that were especially religious.

When in chapter 124 of the **Apologética** Las Casas introduced the subject of the peoples of Florida, which he called a "great and long land" containing "immense nations," he made two points: European explorers discovered neither idolatry nor sacrifices there, and "the one who knew most about it was Alvar Núñez Cabeza de Vaca, a gentleman born in Jerez de la Frontera." Anyone familiar with Las Casas's penchant for suppressing the names of men he did not admire ("*un cierto capitán.*" "*un cierto recinoy procurador*") understands the honor thus bestowed, and it is confirmed by the extent of his borrowings, for Las Casas appropriated and synthesized a great deal of information from Cabeza de Vaca's *relación* in his chapters 206 and 207 on the customs of the Indians of Florida.

At the end of chapter 206, Las Casas explains that he had taken the customs he described from Cabeza de Vaca's account and that they came from many groups, not all customs pertaining to each group. His impressively careful reading of Cabeza de Vaca is borne out by his observation that all of the groups about whose customs Cabeza de Vaca wrote were near the coast of the "*mar del Norte*" and neighboring areas but not very far inland. Scholarship on Cabeza de Vaca's route of travel and locations of long stays confirms the correctness of Las Casas's assessment. While Cabeza de Vaca identified groups with great specificity when possible, Las Casas simply referred to them as "*algunas naciones de aquellas tierras*" and tended to combine them.

In order to appreciate Las Casas's ethnic descriptions in chapter 206, we must look first at chapter 207, in

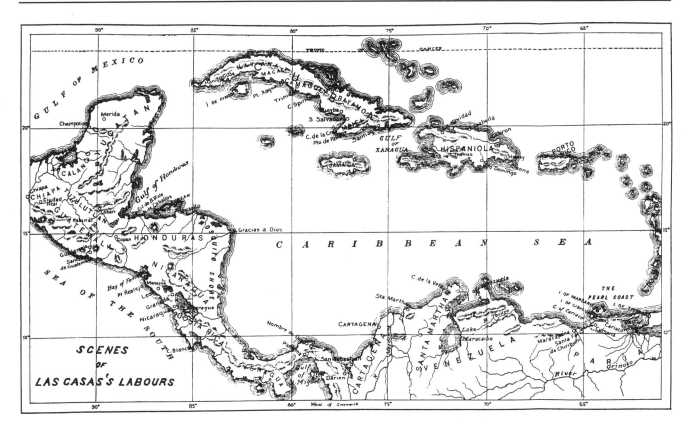

*Map of Las Casas's travels.*

which Las Casas sums up these peoples as *"barbarísi-mas gentes,"* with the purpose of arguing that they represented the first stage of human development through which all civilized peoples had passed and that they could be brought to civil order and Christianity at least as easily as the ancient Greeks, because they were rational men with the same "qualities, dispositions, and natural human inclinations that were shared naturally and universally by all men." Then he presented, from among peoples more and less ancient, a series of counterparts to the "Floridian" customs described in chapter 206. These included the consumption of wild fruits and reptiles and other "vile and abominable things," the killing of infant daughters in order to avoid marrying them to members of enemy nations, the ceaseless labors of women at the hearth and in the field, homosexual marriages, drunkenness, and thievery.

This chapter, in which Las Casas declared that "it is proven that many ancient peoples had customs as barbarous and more so than those of the Indians," provides the key to the way Las Casas read and reinscribed Cabeza de Vaca's account. His hopping from one of Cabeza de Vaca's clusters of description to another, as well as his reordering of the discussion, was done in order to set forth certain notorious customs and then destigmatize them with equally and more

shocking historical examples. In other words, he used examples of scandalous customs from Cabeza de Vaca in chapter 206 in order to undermine them in chapter 207. But this does not fully describe his strategy. At the same time, in chapter 206, he interspersed these reprehensible practices with others that, as described by Cabeza de Vaca, were exemplary in a positive sense.

The laudable customs and traits of the Floridians were, in order of appearance, monogamy (except among shamans, whose polygamy was accepted and whose wives lived together in harmony), gift giving by a bridegroom to his future in-laws while refraining from personal contact with them after marriage, divorce by mutual agreement of childless couples and its prohibition among those with children, great affection for children and year-long mourning for their death, certain curative practices of the natives found to be effective by the Spaniards, solemn mourning customs, sexual abstinence during pregnancy and for two years after giving birth, breastfeeding to the child's age of twelve years due to nutritional need, and the retirement of women from usual chores while menstruating. To this he added descriptions of great physical stamina, high spirits, ritualized greetings and gift giving, great skill in war, great ability to suffer physical hardship, the use of women as mediators to settle disputes between warring groups, and other means of settling disputes without resorting to arms. Appreciating Cabeza de Vaca's firsthand experience as an invaluable source, Las Casas was able to make some of his most subtle and potentially most effective arguments in favor of the "foundations and principles and natural inclinations toward the sciences and virtues" that these "very barbarous people" possessed and shared with the rest of humanity.

Here we see—the more clearly for having reconstructed the compositional process—Las Casas's remarkable achievement. Through exhaustive comparisons of cultural descriptions, he argued that observable behavior was not a sound basis for judging one society as inferior or superior to another. He added, for those who nevertheless insisted on making judgments on this basis, that he could provide as many examples of admirable behavior among the "barbarian" groups of the Indies as among the civil orders of Europeans and the ancients. Cabeza de Vaca had provided Las Casas with a cornucopia of information that he could exploit and then make irrelevant.

Las Casas also drew from Cabeza de Vaca an authoritative elucidation of Amerindian readiness to receive Christianity that undergirded his model of peaceful colonization. Las Casas's pragmatic goal of bringing Amerindian peoples into the Christian fold is never far from the surface of his academic study. The argument that the Amerindians were worthy of Christ and capable of leading virtuous lives was essential to the *Apologética,* and it was the explicit program of Las Casas's first major work, *Del unico modo de atraer a la gente a la verdadera religion* (circa 1534).

On this score, it is evident that Las Casas carefully pondered Cabeza de Vaca's experience, as reported in Mexico in 1536 and at court in 1537. The former's peaceful conversion experiment in Verapaz from 1537 to 1550 followed the writing of *Del único modo*. Las Casas's sensitive readings of Cabeza de Vaca in the *Apologética* attest both to the importance he ascribed to Cabeza de Vaca's experience and to its potential impact in orienting future missionary efforts.

That Las Casas saw powerful consequences issuing from Cabeza de Vaca's testimony is manifested by the frequency with which he cited that testimony on crucial topics: the absence of such obstacles to the faith as idolatry and sacrifice, the intuitive worship of the Judeo-Christian god under another name and the aptitude for conversion, the good treatment received by the unarmed Spaniards from the peoples of Jalisco. Las Casas's readings of Cabeza de Vaca on these issues transformed the latter's interpretation of his historical experience into a theoretical argument about the spiritual worth of all peoples; utilizing the empirical in the service of the theoretical, he constructed the theoretical with pragmatic consequences in view. Here

we examine briefly this other use Las Casas made of Cabeza de Vaca's text, not as a source of ethnographic information but as an authority on the natives' readiness to receive Christianity.

Although overlooked until recently, the efforts made by Cabeza de Vaca and his companions to resettle the native populations of Nueva Galicia (northwestern Mexico) became the outstanding lesson of his book. The use that Las Casas made of Cabeza de Vaca highlights this original purpose. Most significant, Las Casas began his treatment of Cabeza de Vaca's experience with the latter's most comprehensive and impassioned statement to his king. Starting at the climax of Cabeza de Vaca's account in order to begin his own discussion of the inhabitants of Florida, Las Casas confirmed and further empowered Cabeza de Vaca's words. Las Casas declared:

> This [gentleman], having lived and walked through those lands nine continuous years, in the report that he gave to the Emperor about them, says these words, nearly at the end: "God our Lord in His infinite mercy grant that in the days of Your Majesty, and under your power and authority, these peoples come to be, truly and with their complete will, subject to the true Lord who created and redeemed them, which we take it for very certain to happen thus, and that Your Majesty is to be one to put this into effect, which will not be difficult to do, because two thousand leagues that we walked over the land and over sea in the boats, and ten other months when, after leaving our captivity, without stopping we traversed the land, we found neither sacrifices nor idolatry." These are his words.

The immediate context for Cabeza de Vaca's remarks was his description of the resettlement of war-ravaged Nueva Galicia, the conquest of which by Nuño de Guzmán in 1530-1531 was detailed in Las Casas's *Brevísima relación*. Cabeza de Vaca did not discuss that conquest per se, but his account of coming upon the first signs of Christians, at the Rio Yaqui, is immediately followed by a description of devastated lands and peoples; settlements had been burned, men, women, and children carried off into slavery, agricultural lands abandoned. The Cabeza de Vaca party's reunion with their countrymen produced a dispute with one of Guzmán's lieutenants, Diego de Alcaraz, who was capturing Indians for sale as slaves. Subsequently, the governor Melchior Díaz enlisted the four newcomers in efforts to resettle the inhabitants of Culiacán. After baptizing the children of the lords, instructing the people to build churches and adorn them with crosses, and securing a promise from the *alcalde* that there would be no more slaving, they left Culiacán and went further south to the settlement of San Miguel. There Indians were waiting to inform them that natives had resettled; two weeks later, Alcaraz arrived and made the same report. At this point in his narrative Cabeza de Vaca addressed the emperor with the words that Las Casas repeated verbatim, as quoted above. Las Casas then carefully reiterated how, once united with Spaniards in the territory of "the kingdoms of Jalisco," Cabeza de Vaca had conversed with the natives of this area and discovered that they worshiped "a man who was in the sky" whom they called Aguar and to whom they attributed the "creation of the world and everything in it." Here Las Casas took advantage of Cabeza de Vaca's interpretation of the shared identity of the Indian and Christian deities. Las Casas told how Cabeza de Vaca had assured the natives that Christians worshiped that same deity, that the Christians called him God, and that the natives should do as well, to which the natives agreed. Thus Las Casas was able to make one of his central arguments about the ancient, intuitive knowledge that the Indians had of the Judeo-Christian god by relying on Cabeza de Vaca's account. He concluded: "Great and very great is the propinquity, aptitude, and disposition that those peoples have to come to the knowledge of their and our true Lord." He suggested that every true lover of God would relish the opportunity to serve in the evangelization of those "starving and ignorant and well-disposed peoples." In this light, the reasons for Las Casas's praise of Cabeza de Vaca are clear: both Cabeza de Vaca's knowledge based on firsthand observation and his experience of peaceful colonization made him an exemplar of Las Casas's ideals. The information provided by Cabeza de Vaca's interpretation of his experience with the natives of Florida became for Las Casas not only eyewitness testimony but also moral authority, which he put to the service of his own far-reaching philosophical arguments.

*Conclusion: From Testimony to Authority:*

The literary practices examined here were never a matter of simple textual citation, for the need to insist upon or to graft on precedents of experience preserved through interpretations fixed in writing yielded both productive and subversive results. Many times it led the protagonists of history to take pen in hand on finding their role in historic events ignored or distorted in the writings of others. Thus Bernal Díaz recalled his decades-past experience in light of the way professional historians had appropriated it and given it new meanings, as he sought to recover those that had been lost. Yet in recovering his own experiences he colored them according to his current self-interest. When he took issue with Gómara and Las Casas, it was to dismiss their accounts, undermining them in his own "true history" of the conquest. When Alvar Núñez Cabeza de Vaca wrote his final report to the emperor on his years of travail in North America (although quite close in time to the events recorded), he did it with the knowledge of the conquest of New Spain and New Galicia. His original account of his experience was already mediated by the reports he had heard of those

events. There is no doubt that he was truly moved by what he had heard and seen in Nueva Galicia and that his literary effort was motivated by a vision of compassion and justice much broader than the narrow needs of his own failed conquest experience.

When Las Casas appropriated Cabeza de Vaca's convictions and observations into his own, he too performed acts of reinscription that served purposes consonant with his long-held views on the Amerindians and the best ways to evangelize them. In Las Casas's myriad verbatim borrowings from Cabeza de Vaca, the latter's authority is cited again and again, although not always in the ways we are accustomed to seeing it in modern scholarship. More than exploiting an author's work, this type of textual borrowing reconstitutes it, either as evidence to be displayed or as testimony to be refuted in the second author's work.

In the case of the chronicles of the Indies, this practice had two sources. One is the model of erudite written histories; the other is the written proceedings that accompanied and constituted the work of the Royal Council of the Indies and the Audiencias. Authority and the notions of evidence and testimony are pertinent to both the historiographic and the juridical traditions. Erudite works such as Gómara's history and Las Casas's *Apologética* are exemplary and novel because they draw the traditions together, relying on ancient authority and contemporary eyewitness testimony. The discursive encounter of Spain and America was characterized by this conjunction of history and law, the confluence of historical authority and juridical testimony. In that fluid zone there was room for movement, and distinctions blurred. Thus, even though in his prologue to the *Historia de las Indias* Las Casas had roundly eliminated from the noble realm of the historian's art all but the most learned, reserving the domain preferably for priests, we find that in the *Apologética historia sumaria* he privileged not only the testimony but also the authority of one who would have been so categorically excluded. By 1632, the publication of Bernal Díaz del Castillo's *Historia verdadera de la conquista de la Nueva España* revealed that the old dichotomy between testimony (*de re*) and authority (*de dicto*) was breaking down. A century of writing on the Indies had shifted the boundaries of the discursive encounters and made possible the incorporation of authors undreamed of a hundred years earlier.

**Gustavo Gutiérrez (essay date 1992)**

SOURCE: A foreword, translated by Robert R. Barr, to *Witness: Writings of Bartolomé de Las Casas,* edited and translated by George Sanderlin, Orbis Books, 1992, pp. xi-xxii.

[*Gutiérrez is a Peruvian priest who works with the*

*poor in Lima and who is considered one of Latin America's foremost liberation theologians. In this excerpt, he describes the theological grounds for Las Casas's argument opposing the use of armed force against the indigenous peoples of the New World.*]

For a full nineteen years, the inhabitants of the so-called West Indies had suffered occupation, mistreatment, exploitation, and death at the hands of those who, from their European viewpoint, considered themselves the discoverers of these lands. The newcomers dealt with the Indians, says Las Casas, "as if they had been good-for-nothing animals," since they only sought to "grow rich on the blood of those poor wretches." This induced the Dominican religious of Hispaniola to combine "rights with facts" ("el derecho con el hecho")—to combine their reflection with a knowledge of the situation, and to confront the oppression they saw there with the "law of Christ."

The Dominican friars delegated to one of their number, Antón Montesino, the task of making this denunciation, which he performed in his sermon for the Fourth Sunday of Advent, 1511. Let us reproduce here the passage that Fray Bartolomé cites verbatim from that sermon:

> You are all in mortal sin, and live and die in it, because of the cruelty and tyranny you practice among these innocent peoples. Tell me, by what right or justice do you hold these Indians in such a cruel and horrible servitude? . . . And what care do you take that they should be instructed in religion, so that they may know their God and creator, may be baptized, may hear Mass, and may keep Sunday and feast days?

The friars go even further, with Montesino as their spokesperson. To these denunciations they add the foundation of what was to yield a distinct characteristic. The Indians are persons. Consequently they have all of the rights of persons. "Are these not human beings?" Then they recall the demand of the gospel: "Are you not bound to love them as you love yourselves? Don't you understand this?" They were enunciating something radically required of any Christian: an acceptance of the equality of persons, including Spaniards and Indians, before God ("as yourselves"), and then—over and above the demands of justice, which were being so perfidiously violated—leaping to the categories of love, which knows no juridical or philosophical limits. This evangelical perspective, it seems to me, is the key to an understanding of the challenge issued by the Dominicans.

Thus was posed, as clearly as could be, a central question, and one that will be debated long and passionately. Who is the Indian? Who, for the Europeans, in the dweller of the so-called New World? Actually, the matter divides into two great questions: Who are the Indians from the viewpoint of their human condition? And who are the Indians, considered from a religious perspective? Answers will vary. Among them, the most original and most evangelical is that of Bartolomé de Las Casas.

### Human Condition of the Indian

Ever since they began having contact with the Indians, Europeans arriving here regarded them as inferior beings. We find this attitude in the descriptions written by Christopher Columbus himself, only to worsen with the passing years, as the Indians were treated more and more callously. Soon, theories would be formulated concerning their human condition. As Las Casas puts it, it was their treatment in practice as "irrational beasts" that was the "cause of the doubt in the minds of persons who had never seen them as to whether they were human beings or animals." Two clear, opposite positions now took shape.

### Two Classes of Human Beings

As the sixteenth century opens, we find an important theologian in Paris among the first to speak of the inferiority of the American person. We refer to the Scotsman John Major, who cites Aristotle in support of his ideas. In an attempt to justify the European conquest of the Indies, Major writes:

> The first persons to occupy those lands may by right govern the tribes that inhabit them. In Books I, III, and IV of the *Politics,* the Philosopher states that there can be no doubt that some are by nature slaves and others free, that this is inescapably to the advantage of some, and that it is just that some should command and others obey, and that in [the matter of] dominion, which is as it were connatural, one must command, and therefore dominate, and another obey.

The battle lines were drawn. Some are born to slaveholding, others to slavery. It is all a matter of nature. Accordingly, Europeans may licitly exercise dominion over the inhabitants of the Indies. And not only may they do so, but they must—for the very benefit of these lesser beings. Philosophy and theology, then, find themselves in the service of European imperialism. Let us not imagine that we are dealing with an isolated position. The ideas expounded by Major in Paris will be in evidence in Burgos, too, when—due to the protest of the Hispaniola Dominicans—the first laws of the Indies will be discussed in 1512. Spanish theologians of note will maintain the same theses as their Scots colleague.

Let us limit ourselves to a consideration of the most vehement and best known representative of this line of thinking: Ginés de Sepúlveda. Here we have a most bitter adversary of Las Casas, and one with whom the latter maintained a heated polemic in Valladolid until 1550. Sepúlveda was a leading authority on, and translator of, Aristotle, and like Major, appealed to "the Philosopher" as one of his sources. The Spanish humanist explains:

> With perfect right do the Spanish exercise their dominion over these barbarians of the New World and outlying isles, who in prudence, natural disposition, and every manner of virtue and human sentiment are as inferior to Spaniards as children to adults, women to men, cruel and inhuman persons to the extremely meek, or the exceedingly intemperate to the continent and moderate—in a word, as monkeys to men.

Those born to be slaves must be subjected to those destined to dominate. This will be one of the justifying reasons for the wars against the Indians. The purpose of these wars is regarded as the guarantee that they are waged "with rectitude, justice, and piety, and that, while affording some utility to the people that conquer, they provide a much greater benefit to the barbarians that are conquered." The Indians gain in humanity by being subjugated to the Europeans, even by means of war.

To be sure, these expressions and notions shock us. But we must at least give them credit for honesty. There are still persons today whose discourse is egalitarian enough, but whose practice demonstrates a similar contempt for non-European races and cultures.

### All Human Beings Are Equal

Las Casas is a fierce champion of the equality of all human beings. It is something of which he is deeply convinced, and he refers to it over and over again. One of his most important works, the ***Apologética Histórica,*** is devoted to demonstrating the integrally human condition of the Indians. He tells us of the social, cultural, artistic, and ethical achievements of the native populations. The guiding thread in this description—which is one of the most important sources of our knowledge of the old civilizations of the Indies—is expounded in passages like this one:

> All the nations of the world are made up of human beings, and of each and every human being there is one definition and one only: that they are rational. [This means that] all have their understanding and will and their free choice, inasmuch as they are fashioned to the image and likeness of God. . . . All have the natural principles or germinal capacity to understand and to learn, and to know the sciences and things that they know not.

There are not two classes of human beings, then. Rather, all of us have been made to the image and likeness of God. We all have reason, will, and free choice. We are all fundamentally equal. To this forthright declaration of human equality, Las Casas adds a no-less-determined defense of freedom. He writes, in one of his treatises:

> From their very origin, all rational creatures are born free—inasmuch as, in one equal nature, God has not made us slaves of one another but has granted to all an identical [freedom of] choice. Therefore one rational creature is not subordinate to another, as, for example, one human being to another, seeing that freedom is a right present in human beings necessarily and *per se,* in virtue of the very principle of the rational creature. Therefore it [freedom] is a natural right.

The thesis is clear. The Spanish Dominican takes a position diametrically opposed to the one we have examined in the foregoing section, which is that some persons must of necessity be subject to others. According to Las Casas, Europeans and Indians share one and the same human nature. Consequently he rejects the claim that wars may be legitimately waged for the purpose of gaining dominion over the Indian nations. Instead, he demands respect for the cultures, customs, and even religions of the native peoples.

Being free and equal, the Indians have a right to the ownership of goods. Those are in grievous error, then, who think that they may be deprived of such. For the same reason, the native political authorities that govern these lands are legitimate, and therefore ought to be respected by all. The Indies are not a "no man's land." Indeed, Europeans may not remain on this continent unless the Indians accept that presence. In two bold tractates, Las Casas postulates: "No subjection, no servitude, no task may be imposed on the people to be burdened with the same unless that people give its free consent to such imposition." The popular will must prevail even over that of the rulers of a given society: "The kings, princes, elders, and high functionaries who have imposed taxes and tribute have done so by virtue of the free consent of the people, and all of their authority, power, and jurisdiction has come to them through the popular will." Las Casas' forthright defense of democracy has its roots in certain currents of medieval thought, as well as in his personal experience as a member of the Dominican Order.

His conviction of the equality of all human beings, and his vigorous proclamation of the Indians' right to be free, are the twin pillars of Las Casas' philosophical anthropology. One of Bartolomé's strengths is that he is not afraid to go wherever his theology and his conscience may dictate. How simple. And yet how difficult for so many.

*Salvation in Christ*

The conquest and colonization of the Indies was quickly presented in Europe as a missionary endeavor. The salvation of the new infidels, through their incorporation into the church, was to be the primary motive advanced to justify the European presence on this continent. The proclamation of salvation in Jesus Christ constitutes Las Casas' great concern, as well, and thus is the basic reason for his own missionary effort. Naturally this involves the question of the religious status of those who will receive the gospel message. Here again, two great responses present themselves.

*Infidels and Idolaters*

From the outset, missionaries to the Indies had wondered: To what class of infidel did the inhabitants of these lands belong? Were they hearing the gospel for the first time? Had the gospel been preached before, so that therefore they must have rejected it? What was the difference between them and the Muslims—the infidels to whom the Spaniards were most accustomed? One thing was sure: they were infidels. Furthermore they were idolaters: not only had they not received faith in Christ, they worshiped false gods to boot. Here, as well as with regard to the precise nature of this idolatry, various opinions prevailed.

The subject was not merely theoretical. While some of the responses given to these conundrums were exotic ones, all were laden with practical consequences in terms of how the Indians were to be treated. The most important concerned the licitness and legitimacy of wars of conquest as a means of evangelization, along with the ensuing domination. Many were the theologians (Ginés de Sepúlveda among them), and even missioners, who saw no other way of Christianizing these peoples whom they regarded as inferior, recalcitrant, and unteachable.

Bartolomé, for his part, regarded it as scandalous and sacrilegious to preach the gospel by means of death-dealing wars and exploitation. In his first book, he propounds a thesis that he will spend the rest of his life defending:

> The one and only method of teaching men the true religion was established by Divine Providence for the whole world, and for all times, that is, by persuading the understanding through reasons, and by gently attracting or exhorting the will. This method should be common to all men throughout the world, without any distinction made for sects, errors, or corrupt customs.

The manner of evangelization Las Casas proposes is an expression of respect for the freedom of the Indians—in this case, freedom of religion. War is radically contrary to the spirit and letter of the message of Jesus.

On the point of respect for the religious customs of the Indians, Las Casas holds a very firm position. Let us see, for example, the most difficult and delicate situation that he had to face: that of the human sacrifice and cannibalism that had been discovered among some Indian nations. Sixteenth-century Europeans were speechless with horror. Our Dominican friar makes a daring effort to understand this behavior from within the Indians' religious world. His reasoning is as follows. Any religious person seeks to offer God the most valuable thing in his or her possession. But surely human life is the most precious thing we have. Consequently, says Las Casas—generating chills, of course, in his hearers and readers—"unless some human or divine positive law forbids them to do so, and in the absence of grace or doctrine, as human beings they are obliged to offer to the true God, or to the one they consider to be the true God, human sacrifices."

Obviously there is no question of approving such sacrifices. Las Casas rejects them out of hand. He is only attempting to understand why certain Indian peoples went so far as to perform them. One of the great efforts of our friar was to see things from within the Indian world. Here, the result is a profound respect for the religious customs of the Indians, and for their religious freedom.

*Scourged Christs*

For Las Casas, salvation in Christ is strictly bound up with the establishment of social justice. The bond is so important for him that it leads him, on two important points, to invert the hierarchy of problems traditionally posed by missionaries. Fray Bartolomé regards the main question as that of the salvation of the Spaniards themselves, and not only that of the infidel Indians. Those who claim to be Christians must cease from their robbery and exploitation of the Indians, else they will surely be condemned: "for it is impossible that anyone be saved without observing justice." In other words, the salvation of the "faithful" is at greater risk than that of the "infidels." This is at the root of the task Las Casas takes upon himself with regard to the "faithful."

Furthermore, with prophetic insight, he sees in the Indians more the evangelical "poor" than infidels. And so he writes to Charles V of Spain that if the evangelization of the Indians means "their death and total destruction, as has been the case until now, it would not be unsuitable that Your Majesty should cease to be their lord, and that they had never been Christians." That is, an "infidel, but living, Indian" is of greater value than a "Christian, but dead, Indian." Here, on the basis of the gospel, Bartolomé calls into question the whole religious and social order being imposed in the Indies. Las Casas so energetically defends the value of human life, including physical life, because for him physical life, too, is a precious gift of God.

We must not think, however, that Las Casas sees in the Indian only the poor—those favorite persons of the God of the Reign. Surely this was his primary intuition. But he gradually perceives the injustices that victimize blacks (many of them Muslims), *guanches* (inhabitants of the Canary Islands), and even the Spanish poor.

However, there can be no doubt that his great concern was for the fate of the vast majority of the inhabitants of these lands, the Indies, whom he saw dying in wars, oppression, and illness. The root of his strong position, and the basis of its full meaning, lies in his fertile christological outlook.

From the very outset of his battle, Las Casas had gained a clear awareness that the oppression of the Indian is contrary to the "intention of Jesus Christ and of the whole of Scripture." What God wishes is rather the "liberation of the oppressed." This conviction was deeply rooted in our Dominican missioner, and it constituted a driving force in the struggle he was to wage for the rest of his life. The poor are God's favorite persons because, says Las Casas, "of the least and most forgotten, God has an altogether fresh and vivid memory." This preference, then, ought to be a norm of life for the Christian. And reminding us that those who exploit and murder the Indian do so "first and foremost for gold," Bartolomé excoriates the perpetrators of this evil, saying, "Christ did not come into the world to die for gold." On the contrary, it will be gold, money, ambition for wealth, and capital that will put Christ to death, by murdering the Indians, the poor. On one of his most profound, most beautiful, and most evangelical pages, the Dominican friar will identify the "Indian oppressed" with Christ himself.

In his *History of the Indies,* Las Casas tells us of his effort, shortly after his conversion, to "come to the rescue of this wretched folk, and stay their perishing." It was now that he embarked on the difficult and questionable enterprise of a peaceful colonization in the territory of today's Venezuela. To this purpose, he paid the King money in exchange for the concession of lands and other considerations.

These negotiations scandalized someone who thought very highly of the cleric Las Casas, who favored his admirer with an explanation. The reply in question constitutes one of the most impressive passages of his entire work. *"I leave in the Indies,"* he says, *"Jesus Christ,* our God, scourged and afflicted and beaten and crucified *not once, but thousands of times,* when the Spaniards devastate and destroy its peoples."

Hence Bartolomé's conviction that, if you love Christ, you will do your best to free the Indians, and to prevent their being "deprived of life before their time" through the regime of the *encomienda,* or royal bestowal of lands and their inhabitants on the colonists. Indeed, Las Casas identifies the Indians with Christ. Thus he manifests an acute sense of the poor, and of the concrete, material, temporal life of the poor. To despoil them, exploit them, kill them, is to "blaspheme the name of Christ."

There are echos of this biblical notion (cf. Rom. 2:24) in another work of Fray Bartolomé de Las Casas. Writing on the subject of the bond between love for God and love for neighbor, Las Casas explicitly cites Matthew 25, the Parable of the Last Judgment. "God takes as done to himself," he observes, "the deeds done in ministry discharged on behalf of his servant." What is done to or for the poor reaches beyond them, to God present in them. A few pages further on, he cites Augustine's trenchant question: "If, then, that one must go to eternal fire to whom Christ says, 'I was naked and you did not clothe me,' what will be the lot of the one to whom he says, 'I was clothed and you stripped me naked'?" Because this is what is actually happening in the Indies. There, not only are the naked not clothed, but the poor are wretchedly, violently stripped even of what they have. They are despoiled of what is theirs by right. The poor, and, in them, Christ himself, are plundered.

This outlook is obviously beyond the grasp of those who regard the Indians as a naturally inferior race, like Las Casas' great adversary Ginés de Sepúlveda (or his sophisticated followers today). Nor indeed is it available to those who see in these natives only the depositories of rights formally equal to those of everyone else, but who fail to look beyond, like Francisco de Vitoria. We reach this pinnacle of spirituality only if, like Bartolomé de Las Casas, we perceive the Indians as the poor of the gospel.

And here we plumb to the core of Las Casas' theological thought. Yes, the dwellers of the Indies are persons, equal to Europeans, human beings with all of the rights thereunto appertaining. But more than this, for Las Casas they are "our brothers and sisters, and Christ has given his life for them" to the point of identifying himself with these "Indian oppressed." Las Casas had the perspicacity, and the daring, to see the Indian as more than an infidel, more than a non-Christian. He looked more closely, and saw someone poor, in the gospel sense. His life and work can only be understood from a point of departure in this germinal intuition. . . .

**Anthony Pagden (essay date 1992)**

SOURCE: An introduction to *A Short Account of the*

*Destruction of the Indies* by Bartolomé de Las Casas, edited and translated by Nigel Griffin, Penguin Books, 1992, pp. xiii-xli.

[*In the following excerpt, Pagden details the historical importance of Las Casas's life and works.*]

The **Short Account of the Destruction of the Indies** was the first and the most bitter protest against the excesses of European colonization in the Americas, and its author, Bartolomé de Las Casas, 'Defender and Apostle to the Indians', the most controversial figure in the long and troubled history of Spain's American empire. In the four hundred years since his death he has been given many roles to play: the voice of a European Christian conscience raised against the casual slaughter of thousands of 'barbarians' in a remote, barely imaginable quarter of the globe; the creator of the 'Black Legend', a distorted Protestant-inspired record of Spanish atrocities and cruelties which was to darken every attempt to exonerate Spanish imperial ventures from the sixteenth to the eighteenth centuries; the distant, unwitting father of Spanish-American independence, 'that friend of humanity', in the words of 'The Liberator' Simón Bolívar, 'who with such fervour and determination denounced to his government and his contemporaries the most horrific acts of that sanguineous frenzy'; and the equally unwitting progenitor of today's Liberation Theology. In Latin America he is still ubiquitous. Even in Spain, despite murmurings of protest from the Catholic reactionaries of the late nineteenth century, he has been hailed as the 'authentic expression of the true Spanish conscience', in an attempt to explain away the destruction of the 'Indian' peoples as a passing aberration in the nation's history. And for many, both in Spain and beyond, his presence seems, somehow, to redeem the inescapable complicity of all Europe in the Spanish conquests. The Abbé Guillaume Raynal, author, together with Diderot, of the *Philosophical and Political History of the Two Indies,* the fiercest and the most widely read condemnation of European colonialism to be written during the Enlightenment, looked forward to a more generous age when 'these unfortunate lands which have been destroyed will be repopulated and acquire laws, customs, justice and liberty'. And he imagined a statue of Las Casas, 'in which you will be shown standing between the American and the Spaniard, holding out your breast to the dagger of the latter to save the life of the former. And on the base such words as these should be inscribed: IN A CENTURY OF FEROCITY, LAS CASAS, WHOM YOU SEE BEFORE YOU, WAS A BENEVOLENT MAN'. There are now, throughout the Americas, dozens of such statues.

Some of Las Casas's many identities have been devised to serve political and moral interests he would not have shared and may not even have understood. The 'Black Legend' was largely an instrument of Anglo-Dutch propaganda, and he would have been horrified at the uses to which the despised Protestant heretics had put his work. Independence from Spain was something he never contemplated even for the Indians, let alone the descendants of the conquistadores themselves. Liberation Theology's implicit claim that the 'poor of Christ' possess a privileged understanding of the human condition comes close to his self-consciously prophetic, apostolic vision of the new American Church. Nevertheless, he would never have accepted any kind of revolt against the power of either the Church or the State. His attacks on the behaviour of the conquistadores, on the agents of the Crown, even on members of the clergy were relentless and uncompromising. But he was never once during his lifetime formally accused of heterodoxy, nor ever suspected of treason. Only his fiercest enemy, Juan Ginés de Sepúlveda . . . suggested that his writings were heretical and a threat to the interests of the Spanish monarchy. Las Casas, in fact, regarded all rebels as disrupters of 'the common reason of man.' Like many radicals, he was, in all respects but one, the staunchest of conservatives. Self-educated, his massive if erratic learning was directed only against those who argued that the conquest of America had conferred upon the Castilian Crown rights to the goods or the labour of the native inhabitants of the Americas.

Las Casas's understanding of the historical and eschatological significance of the discovery and conquest of America contrasted an early vision of peaceful settlement with the rapacious horrors of the conquests which followed. Columbus, whose diary he preserved and edited, had, in Las Casas's view, been chosen by God for his learning and virtue to bring the Gospel to the New World. It was for this, he wrote, 'that he was called Christopher, that is to say *Christum ferens*, which means carrier or bearer of Christ'. It was the Spanish settlers, men precisely like Las Casas as he had once been, who had transformed a trading and evangelizing mission not unlike that practised by the Portuguese along the coast of Malacca into genocidal colonization. Twice, once in Cumaná on the Venezuelan coast between 1520 and 1521, and then again between 1545 and 1560, in the optimistically named Verapaz ('True Peace'), a region in modern Honduras, Las Casas attempted to create peaceful settlements of the kind which the missionaries might have been able to build if the Spanish colonists had not got there first: settlements of priests and honest farmers. Both experiments failed. The priests at Cumaná and the 'simple labourers' whom Las Casas had fetched from Castile for the purpose were massacred after a slaving raid on the area by Guayquerí Indians, who could not be expected to distinguish between one Spaniard and the next. . . Verapaz lasted longer, but it, too, collapsed under pressure from Spanish settlers and from the often less than peaceable ambitions of the 'honest farmers' themselves.

But for all his insistence that the Crown had seriously

mismanaged its colonies and that the behaviour of the colonists had 'given reason for the name of Christ to be loathed and abominated by countless people', Las Casas never once denied, as many of his fellow-Dominicans effectively did, that the Spanish Crown was the legitimate ruler of the Americas and he persisted until his death in the belief that the indigenous peoples had, in ignorance but in good faith, voluntarily surrendered their natural sovereignty to the King of Spain. In a tract entitled *Comprobatory Treatise on the Imperial Sovereignty and Universal Jurisdiction which the Kings of Castile Have over these Indies,* printed in the same year as the *Short Account,* and probably in an attempt to deflect official criticism from it, Las Casas set out to 'silence those who say that, because I detest and severely abominate all that has happened in the Indies—as I do, and intend to do as long as I live—I thereby somehow impugn and detract from the aforesaid title'. The argument which ran through this and so many of his other quasi-legal works was simple: the kings of Spain are the legitimate rulers of the Americas; but they are so because—and *only* because—in 1493 Pope Alexander VI 'donated' to the Catholic monarchs Ferdinand and Isabella sovereignty over all the newfound lands in the Atlantic which had not already been occupied by some other Christian prince.

There were many (many of them close associates of Las Casas) who denied that the papal claim to 'plenitude of power' over the entire world, and with it the right to give away the lands of pagan princes, was a valid one. Las Casas never questioned it. It was, as he said time and again, the only possible legitimation of the Spanish presence in the Americas. But although the papal grant might confer sovereignty over the New World upon the Catholic monarchs, it did not confer property rights over the persons or lands of its inhabitants. These, he insisted, remained theirs by natural right. Nor did it entirely deprive the native rulers of their political authority. As Las Casas stated explicit in the very last work he wrote, *On Royal Power,* the 'kings' and 'princes' of the Americas enjoyed the same status as the nobility in Naples and Milan, both of which also formed part of the Spanish Empire at this time. Furthermore, Alexander VI had charged the Catholic monarchs to 'induce the peoples who live in such islands and lands to receive the Catholic religion, save that you never inflict upon them hardships and dangers'. The Indians were not chattels or goods; they were subjects of the Castilian Crown—'our subjects and our vassals', as Queen Isabella herself had phrased it. For the Spaniards to treat them like animals was thus against God's laws, the laws of nature, and a violation of the laws of Castile. It was also an abomination in God's eyes: a denial of the humanity which all men, whatever their beliefs or cultural preferences, shared. Las Casas was even prepared to argue, both in the *Short Account* and later and at greater length in *On Royal Power,* that the Indians now had sufficient

cause, 'under natural, divine, and Roman law', for *them* to wage a 'just war' against the Spaniards.

Las Casas's entire life was dedicated to demonstrating the truth of these claims, first to his king, then to the royal administration—the Council of the Indies—and then to the world at large. As he stated in the preamble to his will, 'I have had no other interests but this: to liberate [the Indians] from the violent deaths which they have suffered and suffer . . . through compassion at seeing so many multitudes of people who are rational, docile, humble, gentle and simple, who are so well equipped to receive our Holy Catholic Faith and every moral doctrine and who are endowed with such good customs, as God is my witness.' In pursuit of these ends Las Casas wrote a vast number of works. The bulk of these consisted of detailed and endlessly reiterated proposals for legal and institutional reform. They included, however, in addition to the *Short Account,* two further descriptive works: a massive *History of the Indies* and an equally immense work of comparative ethnology, significantly entitled *Apologetic History of the Indies.*

The *History of the Indies* contains most of the material to be found in the *Short Account*. It was, said Las Casas, 'a book of the greatest and ultimate necessity', and it had been written to demonstrate that there was no people on earth, no matter how seemingly 'barbarous' their condition, that could be denied membership of the 'Christian family'. The *History* can be read, partly as a narrative, much of it first-hand, of the discovery and conquest of the Indies, partly as a record of the Spaniards' subsequent bloody exploits, and partly as an autobiographical account of the passage of its author from ignorance to enlightenment. In 1559, however, Las Casas forbade the printing, or even the criculation of the manuscript, until forty years after his death. Then, he said, it might be printed 'if it is thought to be convenient for the good of the Indians and of Spain'. But by 1590 Spain's position was too perilous for it to be conceivable that any further condemnation of its agents could be thought to be 'for its good' and the text was not published until 1875. . . .

The *Short Account* is, as Las Casas claims, an epitome, suitably re-worded for a popular audience, of the records of Spanish brutality given in the *History,* together with some gory details of its own. The purposes of the two works were, as he made clear in the prologue to the *History,* identical. Both were true and unembellished records of what had been seen by him and by those he knew. Unlike the *History,* however, the *Short Account* is, by implication at least, a *relación*—the name given to the official report, witnessed and authenticated by a notary, which every royal officer in the Indies was expected to provide of his activities. Hernán Cortés's massively over-extended letters to Charles V were described by their author as 'letters of account' (*cartas de relación*), thus suggesting that, despite their narrative structure and epistolary form, their *content* possessed all the accuracy of a legal document. Las Casas's title was intended to convey the same impression. The aims of Cortés and Las Casas could not have been more different, but their rhetorical strategies were, unsurprisingly perhaps since both men inhabited the same political and literary culture, very similar. Like Cortés's *Letters,* the **Short Account,** in its final printed form, was meant in the first instance for a royal reader, in this case the future Philip II, before whom it would have been unthinkable to lie. Like Cortés's *Letters* it was intended not merely to inform but to persuade. It was in the most immediate, most transparent sense of the word, an exercise in propaganda. Many of the stories which Las Casas told may, indeed, have literally been true. Some of them, the numbing round of killings, beatings, rapes and enslavements, certainly were. But others, such as the story of the Spaniard who stopped the mouths of the prisoners he was torturing with wooden bungs so as not to disturb his commander's siesta, have classical antecedents and constitute part of a recognizable rhetorical strategy for arousing wonder in the reader. The same is true of Las Casas's figures. These begin as precise accounts—the population of the Mexican town of Cholula, for instance, is given as 'some thirty thousand inhabitants'—balanced estimates—'at a conservative estimate . . . more than twelve million souls, women and children among them'—and then slide, as the work reaches its conclusion, into the indeterminacy of 'teeming millions'. A lot of energy, most of it wasted, has been spent on verifying (or falsifying) the number of the dead given in the **Short Account.** But, quite apart from the fact that *all* such figures in the sixteenth century were, of necessity, very approximate, Las Casas's figures, always rounded up to the nearest thousand, were not offered as a factual record. As with the Roman historian Flavius Josephus's account of the destruction of Jerusalem by Titus, which Las Casas cites at length in the prologue to the **History** (and as, indeed, with Cortés's own account of the size of the native armies he had to face), the inflation of numbers was meant only to impress upon the reader the literal magnitude of thc event.

Like Cortés's *Letters,* Las Casas's **Short Account** also constituted a petition. But whereas Cortés's was a petition for honours, Las Casas's was a petition for justice. His motive for writing the work was, as it was with the **History,** 'the very great and final need to make known to all Spain the true account and truthful understanding of what I have seen take place in this Indian Ocean'. He was, he claimed, the only reliable witness to what had occurred in the Americas 'wherever Christians have set foot', for only he had been willing to break the 'conspiracy of silence about what has really been happening'. 'It has become the custom', he complained, 'to falsify the reports sent back to Spain about the damaging nature of Spanish actions in the New World.' Those few who, like himself, were prepared to risk official disapproval and, more dangerous still, the fury of the settlers, found that their 'reliable eye-witness accounts' were 'totally discounted' by indifferent royal auditors who returned statements which were at best 'hazy and unspecific' and were always more concerned with any financial loss to the Crown than they were with the ceaseless haemorrhage of human life. Only his own **Short Account** was true, not only because it did not fudge the facts but because it alone dealt with the one feature of the Spanish settlement of America which mattered: 'the massacres of innocent people'. These were, he claimed, of such magnitude that not only did they 'silence all talk of other wonders of the world', they also threatened to destroy the existing world order, 'to bring a collapse of civilization and to presage the end of the world'. Little wonder, then, that when Las Casas told his story to those he met in Spain, they 'listened open-mouthed to his every word'.

Las Casas's task, as he saw it, was to bear witness. He was, he asserted again and again, a recorder, an historian in the proper, ancient sense of that term. In the prologue to the **History**—a long, somewhat disjointed essay on the identity and purpose of the historian's task—he stated that the majority of the historians of antiquity had written either out of the desire to demonstrate their eloquence, or out of a need to glorify their rulers. (So, too, Las Casas implied, had all the other historians of the Indies, in particular Fernández de Oviedo.) Those who escaped this fate fell into two categories. There were some, like the Greek Diodorus Siculus who, because they had been present at all that they described, had been able, as Diodorus put it, to provide 'the reader, through such a presentation of events, with the most excellent kind of experience'. And then there were those, like Josephus, the historian of another race (the Jews) who had been destroyed by a rapacious imperial power, who had written 'to bear witness to great and noteworthy deeds for the benefit of many': great and noteworthy deeds which the official record would prefer to have silently forgotten or presented as something other than what they were. In Las Casas's writings the two objectives were merged. He wrote to reveal the truth of what had been hidden and, like Diodorus ('more like a holy theologian than a damned pagan philosopher'), he, too, had 'been there'; he, too, could transmute the narrative of what he had seen into a mode of experience.

Las Casas's claim for these two aspects of his works can be repeatedly found in nearly all of them. In part this was, as we have seen, a claim to be the only one willing to speak out about matters others would prefer to leave hidden. In part, however, it marked the beginning of a divide, which was to characterize most subsequent writings about the Americas, between those who had and those who had not been there. In the mid-sixteenth century, this distinction was far less obviously significant than it would be today. In the intellectual world to which Las Casas belonged it was believed that the nature of the universe and of man could be known only through a body of authoritative texts—the Bible, the writings of the Church Fathers and a select number of ancient authors—and through commentaries on those texts. The gathering of empirical data was only of secondary importance and, by and large, had to be fitted into a framework already established by the texts. When America was discovered every attempt was made to find a place for it in classical and biblical schemes of classification. Unknown plants, such as tobacco, were given a place in a natural history which derived from the work of Dioscorides, a first-century Greek physician. The religion of the Indians was treated as a corrupt or preverted form of Christianity or, in some cases, of Judaism. Even the continent itself was located, as best it could, within the Ptolemaic world picture which, of course, allowed for the existence of only three continents and one ocean.

For those who had been to America, however, the very newness of the New World was not something which could be so casually overlooked. The missionaries, in particular, were often acutely aware of the distance, geographical and conceptual, they had had to travel. In a dialogue written in 1551 by the Franciscan Pedro de Quiroga for the instruction of his fellow-missionaries, the principal speaker, Barchilón, warns his friend Justino who has just arrived from Spain: 'Have no dealings with the things of this land until you understand them, because they are strange affairs and a strange language which only experience will reveal to you.' Quiroga, like Las Casas, knew that in America nothing was ever quite what it seemed, particularly if you went expecting it to be not very different from Europe. You had, as Barchilón implied, to learn how to speak again as you had as a child, through direct and immediate contact with the things of the world. Until and unless you had mastered this new speech America would remain a massive, frequently threatening presence which could all too easily overwhelm the imagination.

A similar sense of the weight of the new is proclaimed in the very first sentence of the *Short Account*. The discovery and subsequent Spanish occupation, Las Casas cautions his readers, will seem 'quite incredible to anyone who has not experienced it at first hand'. This is a familiar plea to the reader's trust. But a sense of the distances which separated the impact of the unmediated experience from what could only be known through language was a feature of all the early chronicles of the Indies. Oviedo declared that he would need a Leonardo da Vinci or a Mantegna or a Berruguete—'famous painters,' he added, flaunting his European culture, 'whom I met in Italy'—to render accurately the flora of Hispaniola. Alonso de Zuazo, a judge on

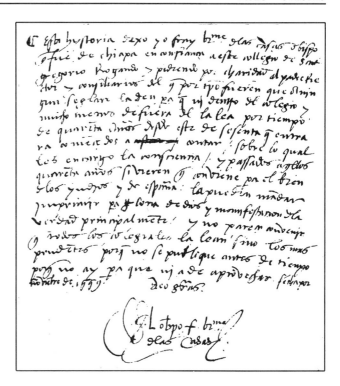

*Directions given by Las Casas for the publication of his work.*

the island of Cuba, abandoned his attempt to described the goods on sale in the market in Mexico City because, he explained, 'you will not gain thereby any understanding of the quality of the fruit, for such cannot be understood without the senses of sight, smell, and taste'. As Michel de Certeau has observed of such claims, 'only the appeal to the senses . . . and a link to the body . . . seem capable of bringing closer and guaranteeing, in a single but indisputable fashion, the real that is lost in language'. It was precisely the 'real that is lost in language' which Las Casas, in both the *Short Account* and the *History,* attempted so painfully to transcribe.

History of the kind Las Casas wrote was the crucial exception to the notion of a text-bound science. Las Casas specifically repudiated textual knowledge. 'I am,' he told Charles V's minister, the Seigneur de Chièvres, 'the oldest of those who went over to the Indies and, in the many years that I have been there and in which I have seen with my eyes, I have not read histories which could be lies but instead I have experienced.' The narratives which the *History* provides are 'true' precisely because they are the record of things which the historian himself has seen. The Greek word *historein,* said Las Casas, quoting the great seventh-century encyclopaedist, St Isidore of Seville, 'means "see" or "know" ', and, among the ancients, only those who had witnessed, or who had seen with their own eyes what they recounted, wrote history. We know those things which we have seen with our own eyes better than those which we know by hearsay. The true historian is a witness. 'Only I,' Las Casas told the Council of the Indies, who have been 'an eye-witness for all the years since they [the Americas] were discovered', who have 'wandered through these Indies since very nearly the year 1500', could be trusted to 'know what I write'. The eye, which offers direct access to the world of experience, takes priority over the ear and, because what it sees is both transparent and innocent, the witness it bears is exempt from interpretation. But, of course, the witness's experience had to be transmuted *into* text. The only science which provided any guidelines as to how to do *that* was the law and it is, therefore, unsurprising that much of the rhetoric, and some of the compositional strategies of Las Casas's writings, are so clearly indebted to forensic practice. As with the record of any judicial procedure, the process of transmuting direct testimony into language must, inevitably, result in a text which is uneven and, in Las Casas's word, 'uncured'. The very roughness of the historian's prose thus becomes evidence of the directness of his speech. The appeal to precisely those features of the text which, in any other circumstances, would have reduced its value in the reader's eyes becomes what in the elaborate language of sixteenth-century rhetoric was known as 'capturing the good will of the reader' (*captatio benevolentiae*). The 'poverty of vocabulary and humility of the style' of the *History* is, said Las Casas, proof of both accuracy and sincerity. Here, his Italian translator claimed of the *Short Account,* is a work 'which looks only at the simple naked truth—at the facts—without caring for method or for eloquence of any kind'.

Like most instances of *captatio benevolentiae,* however, these assertions are very largely false. Las Casas, it is true, was not an elegant prose stylist. And many of his writings were, indeed, 'uncured'. But both the *Short Account* and the *History,* intended as they were for large general audiences, were carefully composed to make the 'simple naked truth' not merely evident but also compelling. Nor is it, of course, the case that Las Casas was present at all the events he describes. He witnessed the conquest of Cuba and was present on the mainland of Venezuela and parts of Mexico. But he never set foot in the areas of the largest, most devastating conquests, Central Mexico and Peru. When dealing with these areas then, he substitutes another's eyes for his own. 'I was told', 'I heard it from one who was there', 'he told me so', and similar phrases are used to punctuate the narrative. Sometimes, too, he incorporates entire documents into the texts. The Franciscan Marcos de Niza's account of the killing of the Inca Atahualpa, for instance, is in effect a deposition, a sworn testimony written precisely by one who had 'first-hand experience of these people' and was thus able to bear 'true witness'. So, too, is the letter of 1541 from the bishop of Santa Marta to the King.

But Las Casas, and those of his associates like Marcos de Niza, was not only *there*. He was there with a purpose, to bear witness to that to which 'no chronicle could ever do justice, nor any reader respond to save with horror and disbelief', and to bring it back home to Spain. For forty-two years, he says at the end of the *Short Account,* 'these matters have been constantly before my eyes and on my mind'. Before he had gone to America and returned, the Spaniards had known nothing of the lands their fellow-nationals were in the process of destroying. 'I can swear before God,' he wrote in 1535, 'that, until I went to this royal court, even in the time when the Catholic king Don Ferdinand was still alive, no one knew what thing the Indies were, nor of their greatness, their opulence, their prosperity'—nor, he added, 'of the destruction which had been wrought in them'.

The *Short Account* was intended to alert the King's moral imagination in the hope that the Crown might act to save the Americas before it was too late. But it had another overt purpose. 'My deep love of Castile,' he wrote at the very end of the work, 'has also been a spur, for I do not wish to see my country destroyed as a divine punishment for sins against the honour of God and the true Faith'. So far, God had confined himself to sinking Spanish treasure ships and fomenting civil war in judgement on 'the great iniquities committed by the Spanish'. But Las Casas remained certain until his death that God had more terrible punishments in store for Spain, if the Spaniards continued with the wanton destruction of His people. 'I believe,' he stated in his will, 'that because of these impious and ignominious deeds, so unjust, tyrannical and barbarously done in the Indies and against the Indians, God must certainly envelop Spain with his fury and his anger'. The use of the term 'destruction' in the title of the *Short Account* was an implicit reference to an earlier 'destruction' of Spain, the Arab invasion of 711. And, in case Las Casas's readers were in any doubt about the association between the Muslim destruction of Spain and the Christian destruction of America, Las Casas spelled it out in a list of solutions to the Indian 'problem' known as *Among the Remedies,* printed at the same time and in some versions in the same volume as the *Short Account.* 'Spain,' he wrote, 'was destroyed once by Moors . . . and it is rather to be believed that this was because of the sins of all the people and of the harm and evil they had done to their neighbours. And now we have heard many say, "Pray to God that He does not destroy Spain for the many evils which we have heard are committed in the Indies".' And, he went on, if such persons, unlearned and inexperienced, can say that, 'it must be no small warning nor small threat from God'. Las Casas's prophetic claims played upon fears which were already widespread in Spain, as the Turkish presence in the Mediterranean increased year by year. For many, and in particular for one of such an apocalyptic cast of mind as Las Casas, God's displeasure could be the only cause of the repeated successes of the Ottoman fleet and of such instances of internal unrest as the revolts of the towns (*comuneros*) of Castile against Charles V in 1520-21. Even Spain's current financial crisis, he believed, could be seen as a portent of impending retribution.

Las Casas's explicit association between Arab conqueror and Spanish conquistadores also reversed a common stereotype. As he himself records, the conquistadores had frequently compared their activities to those of the Christian heroes of the Reconquest of Spain from the Arabs. New arrivals in the Americas often had masses said on landing for the soul of that legendary hero of the Reconquest, El Cid, thus symbolically stating their own intentions to re-enact in another place what had come to be thought of as the defining event of the Spanish past. In Las Casas's eyes these men, in the accounts they gave of their deeds, drew not only upon false analogies, they also distorted language itself. In their own estimation, they were conquistadores, conquerors. 'But this term "conquest",' wrote Las Casas in a memorandum of 1542, 'is tyrannical, Mohammedan, abusive, improper, and infernal.' A 'conquest', he went on, can be conducted only against 'Moors from Africa, Turks and heretics who seize our lands, persecute Christians and work for the destruction of our faith'. You can only speak to the woefully under-informed of 'conquering' peoples so gentle that they would flee rather than fight, whose wars were 'no more deadly than our jousting, or than many European children's games' and whose arms—even those of the Inca—were 'a joke'. 'Conquest' belonged with those other terms with which the conquistadores decorated the accounts they gave of their own deeds—with 'victories' which designated only massacres, 'uprising' which described the Indians' terrified attempts to escape their persecutors, and 'rebellions' which denoted legitimate resistance against 'the forces of plague and carnage'.

For Las Casas, these 'men of blood', far from being Christian knights, or the heroes of the ballads and chivalric romances which seem to have been their favourite reading, were themselves 'Moorish barbarians'. All men, as he had told Sepúlveda in 1551, no matter what their cultural origins, became barbarians when driven to perform 'cruel, inhuman, wild, and merciless acts'. In America the world had been reversed. In America, it was the Europeans, 'anaesthetized to human suffering by their own greed and ambition', who were the savages, and the Indians, whose culture was poor, whose technology was nonexistent and who had very few, if any, of the arts and sciences which for all Europeans marked the inevitable stages towards true civility, who were 'civilized'. . . .

The ***Short Account*** was written in protest at a moment when it still seemed possible to reverse the damage Spanish colonization had done, when it still, to Las Casas at least, seemed possible that his 'earthly paradise' might be transformed into the image of the primitive Apostolic Church. But he was already too late. By the time this book was published the destruction of the Indies was virtually complete. The Indians, their culture all but eradicated or forgotten, were already faced with the need either to become a lowly, marginalized part of the European colonial system or, as they continue to do in increasing numbers, to perish altogether.

**Martin E. Marty (essay date 1992)**

SOURCE: A foreword to *In Defense of the Indians*, edited and translated by Stafford Poole, Northern Illinois University Press, 1992, pp. xiii-xvii.

[*In the excerpt below, Marty discusses the experience of the modern reader encountering Las Casas's writings.*]

Half a millennium after the event, historians and the general public have learned to say not that Columbus *discovered* America but that with his voyages he *encountered* a world that was new to Europeans. It also should long ago have been noticed that Columbus never really did "discover" the Native Americans whom he called Indians. The adventurer brought stereotypes into which these people had to fit: we Europeans, he deduced, might both "save" them and "enslave" them.

Bartolome de Las Casas, a Dominican priest, might more properly have been described all along as the one who *discovered* these Americans. Now we might also change that to say he *encountered* them. Las Casas smashed his own stereotypes and came to know these as the "others" who were not simply objects for salvation, certainly not subjects for slavery, nor mere pagans or heathen, enemies or permanent strangers. They were full fellow human beings, possessing valid traditions, dignity, and rights.

Not every one in his day thought so. For decades Las Casas, officially named to be the protector of the Indians, pleaded their case in two hemispheres. He did so at risk to reputation and even life, but he never tired. The priest denounced slaveholders in America and defended their slaves in Spain. Las Casas created trouble for conquistadores while he spoke up for their conquered victims—most of whom were dying as a result of imported European diseases against which they had no immunity, the Europeans' cruel disregard for Native American life, or formal and constant warfare against them.

The slaveholders and killers had their defenders in high

places, especially among those who profited from slavery, whether in America or Spain. The most notable advocate was Juan Gines de Sepulveda, a Cordoban theologian, who . . . argued on Aristotelian grounds that war against the Native Americans was just. Why? Because they were inferior to the Spaniards, just as children were to adults, women to men, and even as apes were to humans. Almost sixty years after Columbus's first encounters and fifty after Las Casas first sailed to America, Sepulveda and Las Casas squared off in the face of distinguished theologians at the Council of Valladolid. . . .

[The] genre of the **Defense** can be offputting, unless and until one lets the book's character work its effects on the modern consciousness. The vehemence of his *ad hominem* argument and the emotional language used seem more appropriate for stagy television programs rather than a literary and legal search for truth. The reader must understand that, for Las Casas, profound and vital truths were at stake in his debates. (And he was right.) Stating these truths demanded acts of passion, and they were forthcoming. . . . Las Casas circles around and then spirals back to revisit Sepulvedan arguments he has already successfully demolished. The empathic reader sees that at once. When I read Las Casas's explosive and repetitive passages, however, I learned not to be put off but to be enthralled: they have a kind of ritual, incantatory power that does not take away from the argument but reinforces it. Indeed, thinking of the paragraphs as musical themes a composer keeps developing is an appropriate way to be drawn into the still compelling case of the old Dominican.

Along with the overwhelming argument, the over-defense of the Indians, and the overkill of Sepulveda (who may not have felt a thing!), there are other alienating features. Not only is the world of Las Casas past and thus foreign; it issues from a world view few will share today. I would like to think that not a single reader would approve his defense of the natives on the grounds that they were not Catholic heretics, against whom war would be just. Also, one hopes that even the most ardent Catholic missionaries have a hard time endorsing the thought world of Las Casas and his kind. These late medieval figures pictured the struggle for Indian souls to be desperate: policies that cut short the life of the unredeemed or that drove the Indian into hostility against Spain and Christianity threatened to send precious souls to eternal fires of hell. Sepulveda seemed not to care; the Indians were pagan, savage, apelike, worthy of death and hell. Las Casas, in return, fairly shrieks: the natives are citizens, capable of nobility, often to be admired and never to be killed or enslaved. Failure to understand the cosmic backdrop of the issues will mean keeping Las Casas only at a distance, when he belongs up close in a world where "rights" remain at stake even where "mission" often

fades.

Third, get ready not only for a world that is distant because it is past and because it exposes a cosmic backdrop that is hard to recover today, but also for a world that sets before us a very imperfect human being. Don't get me wrong. While not eligible to be a *Lascasista,* whether on linguistic, cultural, or religious grounds, I am in the company of those who regard him as heroic and in a way saintly.

To certify credentials: eight years before the Columbus quincentennial that brought Las Casas to the fore once again, I began my own history, titled *Pilgrims in Their Own Land: 500 Years of Religion in America,* not with Virginians and Puritans of 1607 and 1620/1630, as historians of my kind used to do, but with a chapter on "The Conqueror Versus the Missionary." In it is a picture of Las Casas that we captioned as if it were a *Who's Who* entry: "Known as the Protector of the Indians, Bartolome de Las Casas (1474-1566) never set foot on what is today the United States. Paradoxically, he is remembered widely as the first great figure to speak up for the rights of minorities in the New World, even though he played a brief part in legitimizing black slavery. His portrayals of Spanish cruelties in the Americas gave rise to a 'Black Legend' about Spaniards, which the English happily exploited to show themselves in a more favorable light."

---

**Balance is the last and least thing Las Casas sought. He was for justice, truth, and the rights of the Indians, and would stay around as long as it took to make his point.**

*—Martin E. Marty*

---

Such a portrait caption was a protection against contemporaries who expect our ancestors to be as virtuous, indeed as perfect as we—we of the generations of genocides and Holocaust, prejudices and racisms and two World Wars. It was also an anticipation of a Lascasian reference I must reenter into the record:

> Las Casas did the Indians no favor when he over-advertised their virtues; it would be unwise to misrepresent him here. A man of his own day, a day that took human slavery for granted, he made a tragic proposal back in 1516—one that had enormous consequences. While outlining his communal system [he was also the hemisphere's pioneer European utopian experimenter] for the New World he added a fatal line: "If necessary white and black slaves can be brought from Castile." Two years later he shortened this proposal simply to "Negro slaves." Like other early protectors of the Indians, Las Casas thought them superior to black

Africans, but because he was already the voice of conscience to thoughtful people in church and court, his word meant more than the word of others. In 1518 Charles V first authorized the purchase of slaves for use in the Indies. Years later Las Casas vehemently reversed his stand. In his *Historia* he, almost alone in his time, said that "the same law applies equally to the Negro as to the Indians," but by then it was too late to do much good.

Reprinting that paragraph serves as a reminder that even the most ardent *Lascasista* has to qualify claims for his heroism or sainthood. At our house whenever, yes whenever—for the occasions are frequent—one reads an honest biography, there comes a moment when that reader gasps or gulps or sighs. His or her mate then is trained to ask, by now by instinct, "What was *his* [or *her*] cosmic flaw?" Las Casas had a cosmic flaw, or at least offered a cosmically flawed proposal in 1518, and the reader of this *Defense* centuries later has to reckon with it in any effort to create a balance sheet on the author.

Balance is the last and least thing Las Casas sought. He was for justice, truth, and the rights of the Indians, and would stay around as long as it took to make his point. He would shout as loud as he thought necessary. He would cry not in sentimentality but in rage and sympathy as often as the tears would naturally well up, and he would plead even at the expense of his own dignity. And while writing at white heat, he could also keep cool enough to cite classic theologians and philosophers who were as vivid to his hearers at Valladolid and his readers everywhere as most of them are obscure . . . to most of us in our time. . . .

Las Casas, as I mentioned above, "came back" during the Columbus quincentennial of 1992. This time, much of the public who are of European descent, eager to repent for the sins of foreparents five centuries ago, sometimes ready to make some redress, and willing to make Columbus and the Spaniards their own verbal victims mindlessly wrote off all Europeans of five centuries ago as dehumanizers who plotted genocide and were almost apelike exploiters. Those of our contemporaries who stayed around long enough to do their own examining found that matters were then, as they always are, more complicated than stereotypers let them be. There were countervoices among the explorers, among them some missionaries, all of whose assumptions none of us share but some of whose expressions all of us might share.

Among them, as the stock of Columbus has turned bearish, that of Las Casas has gone bullish. He strikes many as worthy of investment: investment of time and energy, of a second look for some, and a first look for many. If *In Defense of the Indians* is the text that serves as that first look, its readers have chosen well.

By letting us move around firsthand in an alien world, those who make it available have also exposed to view a profound and impassioned soul who helps make some issues of the 500-year-old events seem current, still demanding, still urgent.

**David M. Traboulay (essay date 1994)**

SOURCE: "Bartolomé de Las Casas and the Issues of the Great Debate of 1550-1551," in *Columbus and Las Casas: The Conquest and Christianization of America, 1492-1566,* University Press of America, Inc., 1994, pp. 167-89.

[*In the following excerpt, Traboulay examines Las Casas's arguments in favor of the rights of native Americans and the reception of his ideas in Europe and the colonies.*]

In late 1550, an assembly of jurists and four theologians met with the council of the Indies in Valladolid at the request of the king to hear the opposing views of Bartolome de Las Casas and the noted Spanish Aristotelian scholar, Gines de Sepulveda, on the conquest of America. This debate encapsulated the often conflicting Spanish responses to the conquest. Sepulveda himself never came to America, but relied for his information on historians like Oviedo who had taken a dim view of Indian rights. In light of the tense political situation in Peru and Mexico following the New Laws of 1542, Sepulveda became the darling of the colonists for his support of a militant imperialism in America. For the advocates of the rights of native Americans, Las Casas's defense was one of the splendid moments of their struggle. For Las Casas himself, it represented the maturation of his reflections on the consequences of the clash between European and American civilizations. He was seventy-six years old. Although he remained in contact with his friends in America and was still active in Spain in support of Indian causes, he had left America for good in 1547.

News about the uproar caused by his *Confesionario,* twelve rules for confessors, urging the denial of absolution to colonists who held encomiendas and Indian slaves until they made restitution to the Indians, had already reached Spain. No sooner had Las Casas arrived in Spain in 1547 than he learned that the emperor saw the *Confesionario* as implying criticism of the Crown's role in the colonization of America and demanded an explanation in writing. Las Casas then hurriedly composed his *Thirty Propositions* in which he argued that the purpose of Europe's mission in the new world was to preach the message of Christianity to its peoples. Using the familiar argument of pope Innocent IV, he stated that the pope had "the authority and power of Jesus Christ . . . over all human beings, Christians and non-Christians, insofar as he determined what is necessary to guide and direct them to the end of eternal life and remove obstacles to it." The bulls of donation of Alexander VI were intended to coopt the Iberian monarchs in the project of "expanding and protecting the faith, the Christian religion, and converting the infidels." For Las Casas, the principal reward of the Crown would be in advancing the spiritual purpose of the Spanish presence in America, not in its material and commercial ambition.

Native rulers, he insisted, could not be deprived of their sovereignty. They preserved the right to lordship, dignity, and royal preeminence in accordance with "natural law and the law of nations." In his mind, those who opposed this view have encouraged unspeakable theft, violence, and tyranny. Idolatry did not constitute a just cause for seizing the property of native lords or their subjects. After all, the gospel had not been previously preached to them. They should therefore not be punished except those who "with malice prevent the preaching of the faith." Native rulers were expected to recognize the Spanish Crown as universal lords and sovereigns after they freely chose to become Christian. They could not be punished, if they chose not to convert. The colonists did not have a just cause to make war against "the innocent natives who were secure and peaceful in their own lands and homes." Armed conquests had no basis in law and "were, are, and will be unjust, iniquitous, tyrannical, and condemned by every law from the time of the discovery of the Indies till today." As for the labor systems, he felt that the devil himself could not have invented a more effective way to destroy the world of native Americans than the encomienda and the repartimiento which forced the Indians to work for Spaniards in the mines and as carriers over two hundred leagues. He reminded the king that he had the responsibility of "protecting native laws and customs which were just, changing those which were not, and helping them overcome the defects in their system of governing."

The New Laws of 1542 and the refusal of missionaries to grant absolution to the colonists unless they made restitution to wronged Indians made the political climate charged with emotion. The king's sensitivity to Las Casas's criticism of the Spanish conquest was mild compared to the storm that threatened from the treatise, *Democrates Secundus,* by Gines de Sepulveda. An Aristotelian scholar who had written several works of history and literature, Sepulveda had written the *Democrates Secundus* probably in 1544 to defend the Crown's military conquests in America. His political views were already well-known. In 1529 he had exhorted the emperor Charles V to undertake a crusade against the Turks; he had supported the militant position of his patron Alberto Pio, prince of Carpi, against the pacifism of Erasmus. After receiving initial support for the publication of *Democrates Secundus* from the council of Castile, the book was sent in 1547/48 to

a commission of theologians at the universities of Salamanca and Alcala who condemned it. Sepulveda was certain that Las Casas was behind the decision. He sent a summary of the book to the papal court where it was published in the form of an *Apologia.* All copies of this work were ordered to be burned in Spain. Las Casas in turn wrote his own *Apologia* to counter Sepulveda's justification of Spanish military conquests. Las Casas's *Confesionario* on the one hand, and Sepulveda's *Democrates Secundus* on the other, riveted the minds of those who were interested in America and caused the emperor to convene a meeting of theologians and jurists in Valladolid and have them decide the merits of the two views of the conquest of America. In 1550 and 1551, Las Casas and Sepulveda presented their arguments. After Sepulveda summarized the main points of his thesis, Las Casas read from his *Apologia* for several days. Although both claimed victory in the debate, no formal decision was taken by the commission.

Though a former student of Pomponazzi at the Spanish college in Bologna, Sepulveda was hardly an enlightened humanist. Anthony Pagden [in *The Fall of Natural Man,* 1982] described his mind as "rigidly orthodox and highly chauvinistic." He agreed that conversion of native Americans to Christianity was an important purpose of the encounter, but he felt that military conquest was appropriate because it facilitated the task of conversion. Dispossession of Indian sovereignty and property was justified because Indians were cultural barbarians and must submit to their European cultural superiors. To support his argument, he borrowed heavily from Aristotle's notion of natural slavery as well as Augustine's definition of slavery as punishment for sin. Native idolatry, human sacrifice, and cannibalism were in his mind the evidence to support his position. The use of Aristotle's notion of natural slavery to justify war against the Indians had a long history. Until Vitoria, Las Casas, and the Salamancan theologians constructed arguments against it, theologians like John Major and Palacios Rubios made significant use of it in elaborating their views of the Spanish conquest. Sepulveda's use of this argument demonstrated its persistence and significance for those who supported militant imperialism. The tone of Sepulveda's work was extremely deprecating to native Americans. Part of the reason was his dogmatic, ideological mind. One could see this in his earlier defense of Alberto Pio against the pacifist views of Erasmus; but, resentment against him arose because he chose to write his work in the form of a dialogue rather than in the scholastic manner. The polarities of civilized and barbarian were used for good literary effect, but were not in the process nuanced. For him, Indians had weak minds and practiced barbarous customs. They were capable of improvement through Christian and European rule and customs; they could as natural slaves even become friends of their civilized rulers. While their talents might improve beyond those of monkeys or bears, their mental limitations could not transcend those of bees or spiders. Indians were not human beings in his opinion; they had only the appearance of men. He contrasted the courage, magnanimity, and civilized virtues of Spaniards with the savagery of native Americans who rejected civilized life. For him, Hernan Cortes was noble and courageous; Moctezuma, cowardly. He articulated this moral polarity between civilized Europeans and barbarous Indians to serve his argument that Spanish masters were morally and politically justified in ruling over native Americans. This notion of natural slavery placed limits on the usefulness of the concept of civilization for human development. How different was Vitoria's view of the alleged savagery of native Americans. Vitoria stated that the description of some of the native cultures of America resembled the cultural level of peasants in Europe. It was culture, not natural slavery, that was responsible for the diversity and strangeness of Indian customs.

Las Casas's defense of native Americans and their cultures rested on the *Apologia* from which he read and his *Apologetica historia,* completed after 1551. Las Casas had hoped that these works would have a wider audience than the commission at Valladolid. His purpose was to demonstrate by argument and the evidence of his experience that Indian peoples were members of the human community and that their pre-conquest societies were true civil societies, in spite of the differences of their customs. As Anthony Pagden has pointed out, Las Casas's work was original because he sought to prove that "beneath the glaring cultural differences between the races of men there existed the same set of social and moral imperatives."

Las Casas accepted Sepulveda's paradigm for determining human development. Civil society and Christianity were the keys to cultural transformation and the realization of human potential. He argued that the splendid cities of the Aztecs and Incas were eloquent witnesses of Indian civil society before the Spanish conquest. But he defined civil society more broadly. Where groups of families came together and built houses, there existed true civil society. This intellectual move was of course calculated to include all Indian societies, even those in the Caribbean and Florida, in his definition of civil society. Conversion to Christianity was important for native development, but their societies were already sufficiently developed that their consent was necessary. They could therefore be converted only by peaceful means.

This philosophy of conversion was enunciated in his first major work on the Indies, the *De Unico Vocationis Modo*. Completed between 1538 and 1539 while in Mexico to attend a conference on ecclesiastical reform, it included pope Paul III's papal bull, *Sublimis Deus,* which claimed that native Americans were rational and endowed with liberty and free will. Conversion by peace and kindness was advocated by Las Casas from his early years as a Dominican friar. That was essentially the spirit behind his failed colonizing attempt in Cumana in 1521, although Spanish soldiers were a part of that project. Critics like Oviedo never stopped chiding him with biting sarcasm about the Cumana experiment. The *De Unico Vocationis Modo* was inspired, however, by a significant success. Las Casas proposed that a small contingent of friars alone and unaccompanied by soldiers be allowed to bring the Indians of an unconquered region of Guatemala, Tuzulutlan, under Spanish rule peacefully and to preach the gospel to them. The Franciscan, Jacobo de Tastera, had already had success with a similar project in the Yucatan. On May 2, 1537, the project began. Some verses of poetry covering Christian doctrine were composed in Quiche and set to music and given to four Christian Indian merchants to memorize. They recited the verses and sang before the cacique of Tuzulutlan for eight days, answering questions as well. The cacique invited the friars to come to his town, built a church, and himself converted to Christianity. It was with confidence, then, that Las Casas would assert his method of evangelization, a method that had a certain resonance with the thirteenth-century Majorcan, Ramon Llull: "One and only one is the method that Divine Providence instituted in all the world and at all times to teach men the true religion, namely, that which persuades the understanding with reason and gently attracts the will, and this is common to all men without any difference."

Angel Losada reminded us that Las Casas was not a pacifist. He felt that war was sometimes a necessary evil, especially some wars against Muslims and heretics. Las Casas did not dismiss lightly Sepulveda's reasons for arguing that Spain's wars in America were just. In a sense, the center of the controversy was fixed on the Aristotelian distinction between civilized and barbarian peoples and the presumed rights of the former to rule over the latter. War against the natives was justified if they refused to accept Spanish imperial rule, according to this line of argument. Las Casas found this argument unacceptable. He argued that Sepulveda's definition of barbarian was too simple. There were many definitions of barbarian. If the term barbarian was used for non-Christians, then the Indians were barbarians. But in no way were they cruel or inhumane and incapable of self-government which was the definition offered by Sepulveda. He insisted that native Americans did not belong to the class of barbarians that Aristotle recommended be hunted and brought forcefully to civilized life. Peaceful means was the only legitimate way. Indeed, Indian arts and crafts and their ability to learn the European liberal arts constituted proof that Indians were rational and capable of governing themselves.

Las Casas's argument against conquest and dispossession on the grounds of idolatry, human sacrifice, and cannibalism showed a skilful mind at home in history, law, and theology. Military intervention could take place, he argued, only if the occupying power had jurisdiction over that territory. But neither the pope nor Christian rulers possessed universal political jurisdiction. In his mind, freedom, not force, was the more defensible Christian approach to religious differences. Citing the examples of Christian practices towards Muslims and Jews in Europe, Las Casas showed that although Jewish and Muslim minorities were under the political jurisdiction of Christian rulers in Europe, they could not be punished for their religious rituals. The infidelity of Jews and Muslims was more serious than that of American Indians because Jews and Muslims had been exposed to Christian teachings. Yet, Las Casas emphasized that they possessed rights against forced labor and oppression. Was intervention not justified to save innocent victims from ritual sacrifice? Las Casas accepted the principle that human beings were responsible for other human beings and were obligated to come to the assistance of the innocent against suffering and death. But he defended all the same the native American case as different. For one thing, he contended that the wars of conquest in America had caused greater human destruction than ritual human sacrifice. The lesser evil was in the circumstance more appropriate than the destruction of kingdoms and cities. Correction or reform was the objective of punishment. It would have been more useful to pardon their past practice of human sacrifice. After all, he reminded his audience, the ancient Spaniards, Greeks, and Romans practiced ritual human sacrifice. In addition, Abraham's offer to sacrifice his son demonstrated the significance of the idea of sacrifice to divine worship. The appeal to abandon human sacrifice like all religious conversion should be made by rational teaching and persuasion, not by force.

In an interesting twist to the question of ritual human sacrifice, Las Casas argued that it demonstrated a deep religious devotion on the part of native Americans. Indians had some knowledge of God and loved God more than themselves: "They offered to their Gods their most precious and beloved of possessions, namely, the sacrifice of their children." Those societies which "ordained by law and custom that human sacrifice be offered to their Gods at certain times . . . had a more noble concept and esteem of their Gods." Human sacrifice was not opposed to natural reason; it was an error rooted in natural reason itself. Indians could not be expected to abandon the religion of their ancestors until they were persuaded by peaceful means of a better alternative. Las Casas concluded: "If such sacrifices offend God, it is for God alone to punish this sin, and not for men." For Las Casas, then, the conditions essential for the mission to civilize and Christianize America were respect for the culture and beliefs of native Americans and that they should be allowed to choose freely to accept or reject Christianity.

The acrimony of this debate was caused in large part by the chain of events arising from the reform legislation of 1542. In the hearing before the council of the Indies in 1541, Las Casas gave an oral presentation of his *Very Brief Relation of the Destruction of the West Indies*. Not one to mince his words or to compromise, he accused the Spanish colonists of exterminating the Indians in region after region of the Americas. He framed his argument by establishing a dualism between evil Spaniards and good Indians. From the perspective of Las Casas, the stakes were too high to have faith in quiet diplomacy. The catastrophe that befell the natives of the Caribbean and the terror practiced in Mexico and Peru left Las Casas no alternative but to paint the colonization of America in black and white. In his mind, the social consequences of the search for riches were ruining the mission to Christianize the native people. He placed hope in convincing the king to issue laws to protect them. He found the peoples of America "patient," "humble," and "peaceful." They possessed a lively intelligence and were willing "to receive our holy catholic faith and to be endowed with virtuous customs." Into this flock of peaceful native people came the Spaniards like "hungry wolves, tigers, and cruel lions . . . for forty years they have torn them to bits, killed them, caused them anguish, affliction, and torment, and destroyed them." As evidence, Las Casas drew attention to the fact that only 200 natives of Española remained and that the population of Puerto Rico and Jamaica were similarly ravaged and destroyed: "We should realize the truth that in forty years some twelve million souls of men, women, and children have died unjustly and tyrannically at the hands of the Christians." The cause of this destruction, he felt, was the insatiable thirst and ambition for gold. Initially, the Indians thought that the Spaniards had come from heaven until they were subjected to vexations of every kind.

In his *Entre Los Remedios,* Las Casas proposed solutions to create a more humane order in America. The eighth remedy was considered the most significant in that it exercised a major influence on the New Laws of 1542. Las Casas argued that America should be integrated into the Spanish kingdom and all its peoples be incorporated as free subjects and vassals of the Spanish Crown. He warned that they should not be entrusted to individual Spaniards. America and its people should be under the jurisdiction of the Crown. " . . . not now, nor ever in perpetuity can they be taken or alienated from the Crown, nor given to anyone as vassals in encomienda or as feudal vassals." Insisting that the immediate abolition of the encomienda become a principle that all future monarchs should swear to uphold, Las Casas gave twenty reasons to support his point of view. He reminded the king that the purpose of the Spanish presence in the new world was to convert the Indians to Christianity: "As the purpose of the rule of Your Majesty over these peoples is no other than the preaching and establishment of the faith among them, and their conversion and knowledge of Christ . . . Your Majesty is obliged to remove all the obstacles in the way of this project." He then went on to show that the encomienda had hindered this purpose. He reminded the king that queen Isabella herself had ordered Columbus in 1499 to return the Indian slaves he had brought to Spain, exclaiming angrily: "What power does the Admiral have to give my vassals to anyone."

It seemed to him that the objectives of the missionaries were at odds with those of the colonists. Control over the native people was important to the world of the colonists because the labor of the native people was indispensable for the acquisition of wealth. But such a world, Las Casas argued, inspired only fear on the part of the Indians. Missionaries were witnesses of this and were resented by the colonists as "disturbing their temporal interests." The encomienda did not create a viable society because husbands were separated from their wives and fathers from their children to work far from their communities. If this system was conceived as a way of teaching the Indian civilization, he was convinced that it was a failure. The colonists were more like an enemy than teachers. Their efforts to uplift those under their care were nothing but "pretentious, false, and deceitful." Indians did not need teachers in civil affairs; they needed people to preach the tenets of Christianity and to provide responsible government for free communities and people. The burden of serving the Crown and the colonists in addition to their native lords was overwhelming and unbearable: "All the peoples and communities of the [New] World are free. They do not lose their freedom when they observe Your Majesty as their universal lord. Even if before they suffered defects to their republics, it was incumbent upon Your Majesty to remedy these defects so that they would enjoy a better quality of liberty . . . there is no power on earth which sanctions making the condition of the free worse and less free; only blame. The key of justice does not err; Liberty is the most precious and highest of all the temporal goods of this world." In the actual functioning of the encomienda, the condition of the Indians had changed from freedom to slavery. Indian towns were destroyed and their peoples made into abject slaves, reduced to "pure beasts," crushed "like salt in water," in a world where their consent and free will played no part.

He was of the opinion that the initial allocation of native people in Española lacked any authorization from the Crown. The encomienda, therefore, exceeded the terms of the agreement in establishing the colony on Española. When governor Ovando came to Espanola in 1502, he was instructed to treat the Indians as "free human beings with much love, affection, charity, and justice." In order to satisfy the wishes of those who came with him, he distributed Indians among them. He defended this practice by informing the Crown that the native people did not want to communicate with Spaniards and that this practice was necessary to encourage contact. Las Casas insisted that this report was a blatant lie. Relations between the native people and the Spaniards had actually improved before Ovando arrived. He confessed that there were even marital relations between Spaniards and Indians. To the historical argument that the institution of the encomienda was established against the orders of the Crown was added a more philosophical line to which Las Casas would repeatedly return. The encomienda was illegal because it did not receive the "consent of all those peoples who were not called, heard, or defended . . . as required by natural, divine, canon, and imperial law." He warned the king that unless the encomienda were abolished and the Indians taken from the control of the colonists, they would perish shortly and the vast lands of the new world would be empty of the native inhabitants. The private allocation of Indians to individual colonists worked against the interests of the Crown. He insisted that if the native people were treated as free vassals of the Crown, the new world would bring prosperity to Spain. The death, suffering, and demoralization of the Indians that resulted from the encomienda brought neither riches nor glory. If the Indians were placed under royal jurisdiction, they would feel great joy and consolation, knowing that they would no longer be "condemned to perish, and that life and happiness would come to them."

The abolition of the encomienda would give Spain the opportunity to atone for the destructiveness of the conquest of America. The whole world should know that the "money, gold, and wealth taken from the Indies were robbed, usurped, and seized violently and unjustly from the native owners." Las Casas concluded this treatise by repeating the warning that unless the tyrannical institution of the encomienda were abolished, all the Indies would in a few days be barren and depopulated like Española and other islands of the Caribbean. Then "God will send horrible punishments and perhaps will destroy all of Spain."

Contemporary historians agreed that the New Laws issued in 1542 reforming Spanish policies in America were inspired largely by Las Casas. Future Indian slavery was forbidden and existing slaves were to be freed unless their owners could show legitimate title. Indians could not be used as carriers. As for Indians held in encomienda, all public officials were to transfer immediately their Indians to the jurisdiction of the Crown. The encomiendas of private colonists who could not show legal title were also revoked. More significantly, the encomienda was to be gradually suppressed. No new ones were to be granted and, on the death of existing owners, their encomiendas were to be transferred to the Crown. There were other important measures. Explorers had to have a license for future discoveries. Religious had to be taken along and, above all, the native people were to be treated with respect. Las Casas complained about the policy of gradual abolition, but these laws were nevertheless impressive. The problem lay in putting them into effect. The resentment on the part of the colonists was deep. There were protests, riots, and open rebellion. Delegations of colonists and their sympathizers hurried to Spain to protest the New Laws. In the meantime, Las Casas was consecrated bishop of Chiapas in 1544 with the expectation of carrying out a more humane kind of encounter between Spaniards and native Americans with the assistance of the spirit of the New Laws. On his way to Central America to take up his post, he learned that the New Laws were not put into practice and that there was a movement, backed by some religious, to have the laws revoked. When he reached Chiapas and urged the colonists to free their Indian slaves, Las Casas was harassed and subjected to abuse. There were also threats to his life. It was the rebellion in Peru, however, that convinced the king that the New Laws threatened the survival of his empire in America. The viceroy of Peru, Nuñez Vela, was unable to enforce the laws; Gonzalo Pizarro refused to recognize him and considered himself king of Peru. Bowing to pressure, the emperor revoked the law dealing with the inheritance of the encomiendas on Oct. 20, 1549. In early 1546, Las Casas had decided to give up the office of bishop. The anger of the colonists that was directed at him made his work as bishop ineffective. He journeyed to Mexico to participate in a conference of bishops to discuss doctrinal matters. When this was over, he convened a meeting of Franciscans, Dominicans, and Augustinians to discuss the vexing problem of Indian slavery.

In his treatise on Indian slavery, Las Casas argued that all Indian slaves were held unjustly. The temper of that age had permitted slavery provided that the slaves were captives in a just war. His argument was built on the premises that, first, the wars against the native Indians were not just and, second, that the Crown did not issue any authorization permitting slavery. Reiterating once more that the native Americans were different from Turks and Moors in that the Indians had no history of causing injury to Christians or taking their lands, he implied that the objective of reconquest, legitimate in the cases of Spain and Jerusalem, was invalid in America. Spanish presence in America was legitimate only in its mission to evangelize the native Americans. No divine or human law permitted war to advance this cause. As for the reason of the defense of innocent Indian victims against ritual human sacrifice, Las Casas contended that it was not worth much comment because "our Spaniards never went to war for this purpose, but to kill, despoil, and rob the innocent; to usurp their lands, their homes, their states, and their

dominion." While Las Casas built his argument within the framework of the medieval European canon and civil law tradition, his use of concrete and extreme language to narrate his story and illustrate his analysis was designed to persuade the authorities of the reality of the human destructiveness in the Americas.

To an extent, the debate over the European encounter with America was conducted in too theoretical a manner. Early in the sixteenth century, the question of Spain's right to dominion over America was raised, especially after Montesions and the Dominicans had voiced criticism of Spanish policies. The first responses of John Major, Matias de Paz, and Palacios Rubios were conceived broadly within the context and traditions of Europe. The injunction called the *Requerimiento* which the king asked Palacios Rubios to draw up and which had to be read to the native people prior to intervention was meant to convince Europeans that the Spanish conquest was based on legal principles. For Las Casas, the reading of the injunction that "God chose S. Peter as leader of mankind . . . to establish his seat in all parts of the world and rule all people, whether Christians, Moors, Jews, Gentiles or any other sect" was nothing but hypocrisy. The proclamation that the pope had granted the Spanish Crown dominion over America and that, unless they complied, war would be waged against them was unjust and detestable. Las Casas exonerated Palacios Rubios whom he described as favoring the Indian cause. He saw instead the influence of the opinion of Hostiensis that non-Christians had no right to dominion. James Muldoon has argued persuasively [in *The Americas,* 1980] that the *Requerimiento* was inspired more by the views of Innocent IV than Hostiensis. The injunction was conceived to counteract possible charges by other European countries that the Spanish conquest was based on the views of John Wyclif that dominion depended on Christian grace which was condemned at the council of Constance in 1414. What the *Requerimiento* said in effect was that native American communities possessed real dominion, but that native dominion could be superseded by the right of evangelization. One might add that this was the theoretical framework that influenced the Salamancan theologians and jurists. The example of the *Requerimiento* highlights the difficulty of evaluating the sincerity of the laws that were passed to ameliorate Indian exploitation. The significance of the efforts of Las Casas and his supporters was to make the intellectual debate in Europe respond to the actual conditions of colonial life in America.

Wars against native Americans were unjust also because they were not authorized by the Crown. Indeed, Spanish colonists made little effort to put into practice laws and decrees that were passed to protect the welfare of the Indians. It was therefore illegal to make slaves of Indian captives. When the labor supply became scarce, some colonists would sail with two or three ships to the islands of Española, Puerto Rico, and Cuba, and also to the mainland. They would attack Indian villages at night in order to seize captives. They would pack three to four hundred people in one ship with the hope of selling them as slaves. Other colonies arbitrarily demanded Indian labor and products. Slaves were sometimes branded and chained. Las Casas remarked that he had seen this with his own eyes. Whole regions were depopulated by the kidnapping of Indians as slaves. What Las Casas described was, from the perspective of the Indians, a state that practiced terror. Indian slavery was but one form of terror. To the question whether slavery practiced by native Americans was milder than Spanish slavery, Las Casas maintained that there was no equivalence between Indian and European slavery. Slavery practiced by Indians was "a light burden"; it connoted a person who had a greater obligation to help and serve. An Indian who was a slave of other Indians was little different from a master's son because "he had his home, his herd, his wife, and children, and enjoyed liberty as other free subjects." Where Indian practices went beyond the boundaries of justice, Las Casas urged them to remember that it was the Christian practice to preserve good native laws and customs and extirpate evil ones. In this general thesis on slavery, he exhorted his audience to be mindful that liberty was the most precious and worthy possession after life itself. It must be pointed out that when Las Casas wrote this denunciation of slavery, he had not yet condemned African slavery. In fact, his slave, Juanillo, often accompanied him to ferry him across rivers. It was after the anti-slavery conference in Mexico in 1546 that he confessed that African slavery was as unjust and cruel as Indian slavery.

Las Casas drew several conclusions from his argument condemning all Indian slavery as unjust. He urged the king to free all Indians held as slaves by Spaniards; bishops were obliged to plead before the Crown and council of the Indies to free Indian slaves from tyranny and oppression and "if necessary, to risk their lives." Finally, he asked Franciscan, Dominican, and Augustinian religious to refuse to absolve any Spaniard who held Indian slaves unless he was examined by the Audiencia in accordance with the New Laws.

At the second conference of the friars in Mexico, Las Casas presented his *Confesionario*. As bishop of Chiapas, he had already put into practice several of the measures he recommended. His refusal to absolve slaveowners was already well-known. This formulary for confession was meant to apply to conquistador, encomendero, slaveholders, and merchants who were engaged in selling arms. The central theme was the imperative of restitution before absolution could be given. The antagonism of the colonists to Las Casas was not surprising. On his deathbed or healthy, the penitent had to execute a legal document in the presence of a public notary empowering the confessor to free all Indian slaves, if he had any, and to distribute all his property to the Indians he had exploited or their survivors. After all, Las Casas contended, he had brought nothing from Spain. All that he had accumulated in America was through the labor of the Indians. No property was to be granted to the conquistador's heirs. Even if he had one hundred legitimate children, they were not to receive one cent. To add to his humiliation, he had to acknowledge that he had participated in "such and such conquests or wars against Indians in these Indies, and that he was an accomplice in the robbery, violence, death, and captivity of Indians as well as the destruction of many of their towns and villages." Even colonists who were not conquistadors but who had Indians allocated to them had to restore whatever they had taken as tribute and services to the surviving Indians, their heirs, or the villages where they lived. It is worthwhile underscoring the two principles that he insisted on. First, he urged freedom for all who were enslaved or exploited; second, restitution and compensation had to be given to the victims. Manuscript copies of this work circulated in America and Spain. Sepulveda had no hesitation in labeling the work "scandalous and diabolical."

Did these rules have any impact? Guillermo Lohmann Villena has presented evidence that in Peru the Lascasian teaching on restitution did produce fruit. The publication of several of his works in 1552 circulated the ideas of Las Casas. In addition, his friends and supporters, especially Fray Tomas de San Martin and Fray Domingo de Santo Tomas in Peru, had nurtured the spiritual climate of Peru by their sermons on the need for restitution. Tomas de San Martin had written a stinging criticism of the encomienda to the king in 1551, and in 1553 wrote a manual on confession for conquistadors and encomenderos. He wrote this work in Seville at the same time that Las Casas was there. It is possible to see the hand of Las Casas in this work. For San Martin, the conquistadors obtained their wealth unjustly and both biblical and canon law traditions had counselled restitution of ill-gotten goods as the price of moral reintegration. Encomenderos came in for a more realistic approach in that they were entitled to receive tribute with an easy conscience provided that they treated their Indians humanely and followed the required rules governing the use of Indian services. Fray Domingo de Santo Tomas, professor of theology at the university of San Marcos in 1553 and successor to Tomas de San Martin as bishop of Charcas, similarly identified with Las Casas in his actions and ideas. When he visited Spain between 1555 and 1561, he kept up a correspondence with Las Casas. The archbishop of Lima, Jeronymo de Loaysa, also corresponded with Las Casas. The Lascasian vision therefore found fertile soil in Peru. Another reason why some conquistadors observed the rule of restitution was, Guillermo Lohmann Villena pointed out, that the Spanish colonists were not the monolithic, greedy, and cruel exploiters as Las Casas painted them. To be sure, they were thirsty for wealth. But some were moved by the suffering of the Indians. The picture of the conquistador Francisco Pizarro that we get from his will (1537) showed a man who set aside funds "to rescue Christian captives from the Turks, to pay a cleric to teach Indians, and to offer masses for the soul of Indians who died in the campaigns."

In a document witnessed by Fray Domingo de Santo Tomas in 1563, Nicholas de Ribera declared that "I have taken account and searched my conscience and consulted with theologians and experts in moral questions. I confess that I owe the Indians of my encomienda a debt and I am responsible for paying eight thousand gold pesos . . . I ask that they be paid from my property." It seemed that Las Casas's censure of the wealth of the colonists and their treatment of the Indians troubled the consciences of the conquistadors and clerics. With the passing of the first conquistadors, the admonitions of Las Casas lost their force only to revive again in the 1560s. The right of the encomenderos to receive tribute became once more an important issue. Las Casas's doctrine of restitution was for a time an effective instrument in regulating the greed of the colonists.

When Las Casas sailed for Spain in 1547, his writings and political activity were already well known. His uncompromising moral stance, the harshness of his rhetoric, and the severity of his solutions did not endear him to conservatives like Sepulveda. That was why the debate at Valladolid did not illuminate the question or lead to the possibility of a compromise. The manichaean shape of the arguments of both Las Casas and Sepulveda made discourse difficult. Yet, in 1550 most of the contemporaries of Las Casas were recording the destruction of the Indies and the astounding deaths of the native people. The chronicles and histories concluded that the search for gold and wealth was the overriding motivation. It is difficult to dispute Las Casas's narrative. His analysis of the human catastrophe was not unreasonable. He made an excellent case for attributing the causes of destruction to the nature of the conquests and the establishment of forced labor systems. The number of deaths was too enormous and Indian suffering too moving to permit him to be tender with conquistadors and encomenderos. He had hoped that only by a brutal analysis could be expect a more humane policy. The defense of the dignity of native Americans was an important struggle; so too were his concern and projects for Indian cultural and social development. The abolition of forced labor systems was the prerequisite for both causes.

Although he never returned to America, Las Casas became the representative of Indian reform at the court of Spain. He corresponded frequently with his friends like Tomas de San Martin and Domingo de Santo Tomas in Peru, or Alonso de la Vera Cruz and Alonso de Zorita in Mexico. Whenever he learned that there were moves to reimpose the encomienda, he was quick to organize his political network to block these measures. This was not an easy time for Phillip II who found the treasury with scarce resources at his accession to the Spanish throne in 1556. He decided to grant encomiendas in perpetuity as a way of raising new funds. Las Casas immediately presented a petition showing that more funds could be raised if the king freed the Indians and restored native rulers. This was not accepted, of course. But it effectively blocked Philip's initial policy until the royal commission decided to allow perpetual encomiendas only for the first conquistadors, one lifetime for some colonists, and others to revert permanently to the Crown. Due to Las Casas's life-long struggle, royal legislation was able to control the arbitrariness of the encomenderos. In some cases, as under the administration of judge Zorita, Indian tribute was actually lowered.

Yet, the Indians did not benefit a great deal from these changes. Phillip II's desperate need for greater financial revenue led generally to increased taxation. The dramatic decline in Indian population should have lowered the tax burden for Indian communities. But, despite protective legislation, tax rolls were padded. Some Indian communities that had been exempt from tribute, lost this status. That was why Las Casas continued to criticize the encomienda with no less vigor than when he first raised the issue in 1515. Consider, for example, the memorandum he sent to the council of the Indies in 1562; "For days upon days, years upon years we have overlooked the two kinds of tyranny by which we have destroyed countless republics; one called conquest when we first entered . . . The other was and is tyrannical government . . . to which they gave the name repartimiento or encomienda." The conclusion of this work summed up well Las Casas's perspective on the encounter between Europeans and native Americans: "First, all the wars which were called conquests were and are unjust. Second, we seized unjustly all the kingdoms and governments of the Indies. Third, encomiendas or repartimientos of Indians are cruel, in themselves evil, and therefore tyrannical. Fourth, all who grant them or receive them are in mortal sin. If they do not give them up, they will not be saved. Fifth, the king . . . cannot justify the wars and theft against the native people . . . any more than the Turks can justify their wars and plunder against Christian towns. Sixth, all the gold, silver, pearls, and other riches which have come to Spain . . . have been stolen. Seventh, unless they make restitution . . . they will not be saved. Eighth, the native peoples of the Indies . . . have the right to make a just war against us and to drive us from the face of the earth. This right will last until the day of judgement." These were the issues he fought for throughout his long life. The doctrine of restitution became more urgent in his later years. In his very last work, a petition to pope Pius V, he asked the pope to excommunicate anyone who said that the war against the Indians was just only because of their idolatry. He urged the pontiff to demand that those bishops, friars, and clergy who have enriched themselves and lived magnificently "make restitution of all the gold, silver, and precious stones they have acquired."

During his retirement, he completed his major work, *The History of the Indies*. Although the narrative ended in the early 1520s, it presented a story of the conquest of the Caribbean that was coherent, comprehensible, and sad. He minimized the effects of diseases on the decline of the native population, to be sure. But, the weight of the evidence for his argument that the Spaniards were responsible for the destruction of the Indians was massive. It was the experience of the cruelties of the Caribbean encounter that influenced his later political activity and writings. Criticism of the colonists remained unrelieved by any distinctions. A general condemnation of Spaniards seemed unwarranted. Was he not favored at court? Was his influence among the theologians and jurists at the universities of Spain not profound? In America, he must have been aware that he was respected by most of the religious. It was true that the outstanding Franciscan missionary, Fray Toribio de Motolinia, had written a harsh letter about him to Charles V in 1555, but that was in response to Las Casas's criticism of the practice of mass baptisms of native Americans. Franciscans like bishop Zumarraga and Jacobo de Tastera were keen supporters of his missionary methods. The tone of bitterness in his works would suggest that his efforts were solitary and attended by failure. But that conclusion would miss the major significance of his work which was that he created a reform movement which confronted the advocates of militant imperialism in Spain and America. Wherever and whenever the burdens of the labor system and Indian servitude became overwhelming, Las Casas and his supporters challenged the system. Anton de Montesinos and Pedro de Cardoba in the Caribbean, Tomas de San Martin and Domingo de Santo Tomas in Peru, Jacobo de Tastera in Central America, Alonso de la Vera Cruz and Alonso de Zorita in Mexico, Marcos de Niza in the borderlands, and Francisco de Vitoria in Spain were among those who respected Las Casas and supported the cause of Indian rights and peaceful conversion. Las Casas could not be unaware how deep an influence he had. The plan of judge Zorita and the Franciscan Jacinto de San Francisco to pacity and convert the nomadic tribes to the north of Mexico was inspired by Las Casas's successful experiment in Tuzulutlan, Guatemala. Zorita corresponded frequently with Las Casas. Indeed, it was Las Casas and the Franciscan Alonso Maldonado de Buendia who presented Zorita's plan to the council of the Indies in 1562. The council was still committed to conquest as the means of pacification and offered faint support. They approved it provided that financial support came out of Zorita's

pocket. The plan did not get off the ground then, but when the policy of "war by fire and blood" proved a failure, Zorita's Lascasian plan was later put into effect with some success and would inspire the creation of the mission system during the later Spanish expansion on the American continent.

Another consequence of the reform movement was the struggle to transfer the sixteenth century European system of justice to America, to give it teeth, and to direct colonial society in a more humane way. The use of legal and theological arguments in the debates over treatment of the native peoples seemed at times tiresome and irrelevant. But the intellectual context of Spain and Europe determined the forms of the debate. The European legal system, largely the legacy of the theological culture of the middle ages, was nevertheless an impressive achievement. If the obsession with legality was one aspect of this culture, a relatively broad area of freedom of expression was the other. The issue was to make the system of justice effective. The actions of the conquistadors during the initial conquests of the Caribbean, Mexico, the Yucatan, and Peru made one wonder whether they were constrained by any form of justice. As Vitoria had remarked, there were so many stories of massacres that it would be more appropriate to speak of power than justice.

The observations of Las Casas, Ramon Pane, and Bernardino de Sahagun, among others, showed that native American communities had effective systems of justice of their own. It would certainly have been appropriate and useful had they been allowed to contribute to the system of justice created in America. The insistence of Las Casas, Vera Cruz, and Zorita on the natural rights and liberty of the native communities was meant to preserve many of the features of Indian justice. As Spanish America was drawn more tightly into an imperial system, this part of Las Casas's movement came to an end. In any case, the logic of medieval Christianity with its dogma of superiority over all other religions made it unlikely that it would allow a different system of justice to operate alongside its own. The missionary orders were prepared to allow some aspects of the indigenous cultures to thrive, but not native religions. Like Europeans of that time, native American justice and morality sprang from their religious beliefs. It was easy to see the physical cruelty and death that resulted from slavery, the encomienda, and diseases; few were aware, however, of the cultural death that the native people suffered when their religion was deliberately destroyed.

A clear illustration of the enduring significance of the questions of the Spanish right of conquest and the natural rights of the native people was the Spanish right of conquest of the Philippines in 1571 by Miguel de Legaspi. The Augustinian friars, led by Andres de Urdaneta, condemned the conquest as unjust. They argued that the two conditions for a just war, authorization from the king and native aggression, did not exist. Phillip II had specifically enjoined Legaspi to secure the friendship of the native communities by peaceful means. The issue of Spanish dominion remained unsettled. The Augustinians and Jesuits came to support Spanish rule over the Philippines on the basis of the papal grants. For the Dominicans, however, as was their history in America, that principle alone was not satisfactory. Under the first bishop, Domingo Salazar (1581), and Miguel de Benavides, the third archbishop of Manila, the Dominicans did not accept the political sovereignty of Spain. They argued that the Spanish Crown was only an instrument of the spiritual power of the pope. The remaining way open for legitimate jurisdiction was the free consent of the natives. This was possible, Benavides stressed, if missionaries were sent to convert the natives by peaceful means. In 1597 Phillip II issued a decree offering restitution of tribute unjustly taken from the native people of the Philippines who were not Christian. The decree asked that the people voluntarily consent to submit to the Crown of Spain.

Consent of the governed, authorization from a duly constituted ruler, protection of the innocent, and the right of evangelization became principles governing the relations between Christian Spain and the non-Christian worlds in the sixteenth century. They represented an early formulation of principles of international relations. Sixteenth-century Spanish political thought resonated with these ideas. It must be remembered, however, that these principles in all likelihood stemmed from the thirteenth century works of Aquinas, Roman Llull Ramon Penyafort, and pope Innocent IV, on the one hand, and the expansion of Western Europe on the other. By the middle of the seventeenth century, the question of the Spanish right to conquest was no longer important. Juan de Solorzano y Pereira (1575-1654) published in 1629 and 1639 his volumes on Spain's right to America entitled *Disputatio de Indiarum iure*. It was a detailed account and analysis of those who questioned Spain's conquest of the Indies. Solorzano did not share their judgment. For him, Spain's conquest was justified. Spain had come to have jurisdiction over America by virtue of the papal donation; its dominion was achieved through subsequent occupation. His argument was derived from Roman law and was similarly used to justify ancient Roman conquests. What Solorzano's argument suggested was that the Spanish conquest of America was already consolidated and was not any longer problematical. The theory of natural rights had given way to legal rights obtained by a sufficiently long period of occupation. Solorzano's interests lay more in preserving the legitimacy of the Spanish monarchy's rule over the empire and the civilized legislation it inspired to govern the Americas than in articulating the rights of native peoples.

The central significance of Las Casas was his awareness of the human destructiveness that was taking place and his struggle to put a stop to it. Although he might have exaggerated the responsibility of human beings in the deaths of the native Americans and ignored the role of epidemics, the catastrophic decline of the native population was undeniable and was the context that shaped his sensibility and his politics. He had come to know, love, and sympathize with the native people. He obviously felt that a radical attack on the colonial system could reverse the genocide that was taking place.

Las Casas's writings criticizing the Spanish colonists were used by Spain's enemies as propaganda in the sixteenth-century conflicts between Protestant England and Catholic Spain, and in the struggle of the Protestant Dutch to become independent of Spain. The first English edition of *The Very Brief Relation of the Destruction of the West Indies* was published in 1583 in London; in 1578, the first Dutch edition. Of greater political consequences were the Latin (1598) and German (1599) editions of the same work published and illustrated in Frankfurt by Jean Theodore and Jean Israel de Bry. These editions carried the message of Spain's cruelty throughout Europe. The Spanish conquest, not Las Casas's struggle for justice, was emphasized in these editions. Conquest, not the struggle for justice, came to define the Spanish legacy in America, at least for the English-speaking world. If the European discovery of America became a major source of interest and inspiration in the first part of the sixteenth century, the schism within Christian Europe that resulted from the Protestant and Catholic reformations created ideological tensions and political conflicts in Europe and America. The political context in Europe explained in part the popularity of Las Casas's works. His critique of Spanish policies and defense of the rights of native Americans might make it appear that his struggle was against Spanish imperial civilization. But that would be to misunderstand him and his work. Placing his hopes for changes in policy on the Spanish monarchy, he remained close to the center of power at court throughout his political life. Through the efforts of his friends and sympathizers at the major universities of Spain, he was able to bring his deas and causes into the mainstream of Spanish intellectual and political life. The distinction between Las Casas and Spanish civilization in America is questionable. Las Casas's struggle for justice for native Americans in the sixteenth century was also the Spanish struggle for justice. It was equally true, however, that, despite the laws and rules that were won to protect native Americans, their condition did not appreciably improve nor their near extinction significantly come to an end. The self-interest of the powerful colonists in America and the growing sense of the importance of American resources to the Spanish Empire were the dynamics that proved stronger than the laws to control these interests.

## FURTHER READING

### Biography

MacNutt, Francis Augustus. Preface to *Bartholomew De Las Casas: His Life, His Apostolate, and His Writings*, pp. v-xxiii. New York: G.P. Putnam's Sons, 1909.

A biographical account of Las Casas and his candid criticisms of Spanish maltreatment of American natives.

Magner, James A. "Bartolomé De Las Casas: Protector of the Indians, Bishop of Chiapas." In his *Men of Mexico*, pp. 62-90. Milwaukee: The Bruce Publishing Company, 1942.

A comprehensive biography which details Las Casas's role as historian and philanthropist.

### Criticism

Baptiste, Victor N. *Bartolomé de Las Casas and Thomas More's Utopia*. Culver City: Labyrinthos, 1990, 76 p.

A comparative study of the connections and similarities between Las Casas's *Memorial de Remedios para las Indias* and Thomas More's *Utopia*.

Comas, Juan. "Historical Reality and the Detractors of Father Las Casas." In *Bartolomé de Las Casas in History: Toward an Understanding of the Man and His Work*, edited by Juan Friede and Benjamin Keen, pp. 487-537. DeKalb: Northern Illinois University Press, 1971.

A comprehensive defense designed to "provide documentary proof against the avalanche of falsehoods designed to tarnish the great name of Las Casas."

Elliott, J.H. *The New York Review of Books* XV, No. 4 (November 1970): 30-2.

Review of Sir Arthur Helps's *The Life of Las Casas*, first published in 1867.

Gutiérrez, Gustavo. "And They Said They Would See It . . ." In his *Las Casas: In Search of the Poor of Jesus Christ*, pp. 455-60. Maryknoll: Orbis Books, 1992.

Gutiérrez applauds Las Casas's anti-violent position regarding the conversion of native Americans to Christianity.

Keen, Benjamin. "Approaches to Las Casas, 1535-1970." An introduction to *Bartolomé de Las Casas in History: Toward an Understanding of the Man and His Work*, edited by Juan Friede and Benjamin Keen, pp. 3-63. DeKalb: Northern Illinois University Press, 1971.

A thorough overview of the intentions and international reception of Las Casas and his writings.

# Sir Walter Raleigh

## 1554-1618

(Also spelled Ralegh) English courtier, poet, prose writer.

### INTRODUCTION

Few of Elizabeth I's courtiers symbolized the Elizabethan era as comprehensively as did Sir Walter Raleigh. His flamboyant style, adventureous spirit, outspoken political views, and boundless ambition have come to represent the Renaissance ideals of exploration and learning. As well as having been a man of action, Raleigh has become recognized in modern times as a highly accomplished literary stylist and technician in both verse and prose. Raleigh's *History of the World* (1614), an unfinished chronicle undertaken while Raleigh was imprisoned, was a standard reference in England and the American colonies for a century after its publication and influenced political and religious thought throughout the seventeenth century. His poem *The Ocean to Cynthia* (1592?), undiscovered until the 1870s, established in modern times the poetic ability praised by his contemporaries, among them Spenser. Some critics have compared Raleigh's poetry with that of Donne and Sidney, and have discovered in his verse an anticipation of the seventeenth century metaphysical style.

### Biographical Information

Raleigh was born c. 1554 in Hayes, Devonshire, England, into a family of moderate prosperity. Although not of the nobility, Raleigh's family had ties to Elizabeth's court through marriage. Raleigh's early education is not documented, although his lifelong anti-Catholic stance, while in keeping with Elizabeth's policies, is attributed to a strict Protestant upbringing. As a teenager, Raleigh was in France during the Civil Wars, where he fought for the Huguenot forces. Upon his return to England, Raleigh studied at Oriel College, Oxford, from 1572 to 1574. He left without taking a degree and enrolled in one of the four Inns of Court which, according to Steven May, were social clubs as well as law schools, "and thus the proper addresses for gentlemen in search of patronage and career openings at court or in the state at large." Raleigh's earliest poetry, a series of commendatory verses for George Gascoigne's *The Steele Glas* (1576) dates from this period. In 1578, Raleigh took part in his half-brother Sir Humphrey Gilbert's expedition on the

*Falcon* in search of the Northwest Passage. The journey was derailed by privateering and piracy; the *Falcon* was defeated by the Spanish off Cape Verde, giving Raleigh his first naval military experience. In 1580, Raleigh was appointed head of an infantry company in the Irish Wars and quickly distinguished himself in battle. Upon his return to England in 1581, Raleigh's military successes, including the capture of important enemy documents, as well as influential patronages, led to a meteoric rise in Elizabeth's favor. Legend has it that Raleigh first caught the Queen's attention by covering a muddy patch in her path with his cloak, but it was more likely his knowledge of Irish affairs, his eloquence and learning, and high recommendations from other important courtiers that quickly established Raleigh as a favorite of the Queen. Elizabeth granted him many important posts and privileges, including the patent for licensing wine sales, a monopoly that brought Raleigh much wealth and influence. For the next two decades, Raleigh held a position of power and influence in the political life of England, and in 1584 he was elected to Parliament. In 1587 he gained official standing in Court as captain of the Queen's Guard, an important post for its intimate access to the Queen. Raleigh was one of the first to realize that England's hope for domination over Spain lay in the establishment of a lucrative colonial empire. He sponsored England's first voyages to the New World, sending colonists to Virginia in 1585 and 1587, and popularized his efforts in England through the introduction of tobacco to court circles. Although the colonists of 1585 came home safely aboard Francis Drake's ship, the latter colonists at Roanoke mysteriously disappeared. Raleigh never abandoned the lost colony and sent rescue ships to Virginia as late as 1602. These efforts at exploration were interrupted by the threat from the Spanish Armada in 1588. Although Raleigh's role in Spain's defeat was apparently conducted from shore, the warship he designed for the campaign was chosen as the flagship for the great battle. In 1589 a minor rift with Elizabeth, caused by mounting rivalry between several of her privileged courtiers, led Raleigh to travel to Ireland, where he formed a close friendship with Edmund Spenser. Immediately recognizing the significance of the *Faerie Queene*, Raleigh brought Spenser back to court to present the work to Elizabeth. In addition, Raleigh wrote several dedicatory sonnets to the work. During his period of greatest influence, Raleigh wrote and published essays on important political questions and historical events, including treatises on war, relations with Spain, and an account of the 1596 battle with the Spanish at Cadiz. Raleigh probably wrote most of his verse during this time, all of which was privately circulated, reflecting his relationship as a privileged courtier and suitor to the Queen.

Raleigh's confident, often swaggering court persona and his many successes over his rivals led to conflicts with other powerful courtiers, among them the Earl of Essex. Due to these rivalries, Raleigh's position in Elizabeth's favor began to erode in the late 1580s and early 1590s, culminating in the revelation in 1592 of Raleigh's secret marriage to Elizabeth Throckmorton, an attendant of the Queen. The couple was immediately imprisoned in the Tower of London, and Raleigh expressed his sense of loss and anger about the incident in his most important surviving poem, *The Ocean to Cynthia*. By 1593, the Queen's need for Raleigh's services to halt Spanish piracy led to his release from the Tower. Raleigh paid Elizabeth his portion of the booty from the ship to secure his freedom, thus beginning a slow climb back into her favor. He returned to Parliament and eventually regained his post as Captain of the Guard, although the intimate royal access he had once enjoyed was never fully restored. In an attempt to gain favor as well as satisfy his restless spirit, Raleigh undertook an expedition to Guiana, publishing an account of the wealth and potential of the area in 1596. Upon the Queen's death in 1603, Raleigh's fortunes became increasingly precarious. James I distrusted Raleigh because of Raleigh's role in Essex's execu-

tion and because of their conflicting views towards Spain and Catholicism. Acrimony between the King and Raleigh led to a charge of conspiracy with Spain against James I. Although Raleigh conducted himself with characteristic wit and aplomb during his defense, his trial for treason was a foregone conclusion for political reasons. Raleigh was imprisoned in the Tower for treason in 1603. He spent most of the rest of his life imprisoned in the Tower, which became for him a very productive intellectual time. Raleigh pursued his interests in politics, geography, religion, and philosophy, and produced several influential prose works, including his ambitious *The History of the World*. Written as a tribute to his patron Prince Henry, the incomplete work was published in 1614 and contained influential passages on the danger of incompetent rulers. In an attempt to restore his court status, Raleigh convinced the King to release him for an ill-fated return expedition to Guiana in 1617 in order to obtain the riches he failed to find on his first voyage. The expedition was a failure, resulting in the death of his son and the humiliation of his forces. Upon his return, Raleigh wrote an "Apology" for his second Guiana trip and attempted to flee to France, but he was intercepted, arrested, and informed of his imminent execution. Raleigh was beheaded for treason on October 29, 1618, displaying at his death a courage, calm and fortitude that earned him immediate martyrdom among his contemporaries and symbolized his legendary, extraordinary career for subsequent generations.

**Major Works**

Raleigh's two great surviving works, *The Ocean to Cynthia* and *The History of the World*, represent his embodiment as the quintessential Renaissance gentleman scholar, learned and ambitious. Raleigh followed the Elizabethan convention among courtiers of circulating his poetry in private, unpublished form. As a result, much of his poetry was lost, and his renown as a writer was limited to the *History* until the discovery of four fragments of *The Ocean to Cynthia* in 1870 in Lord Salisbury's library at Hatfield. Prior to the discovery of the Hatfield manuscript, Raleigh's non-dedicatory poetry could be found published only in scattered anthologies, notably *The Phoenix Nest* (1593) and *Britton's Bowre of Delight* (1591). Spenser provided scholars with evidence of the existence of Raleigh's long Cynthia poem in his *Colin Clouts Come Home Againe*, a recollection of his first meeting with Raleigh in Ireland in which he refers to the poem, and again in a reference to the work in the *Faerie Queen*. The Hatfield fragments appear to be portions of a much larger poem, entitled "The 21th: and last booke of the Ocean to Scinthia", and "The end of the 22 Boock, entreatinge of Sorrow." The former is over 500 lines, while the latter breaks off after 20 lines. The enigmatic titles of the fragments led scholars to believe that an immense and ambitious epic poem in twenty-two parts had once existed. However, recent scholarship has doubted the existence of such a work, crediting Raleigh with using the titles to suggest an epic scope to please the Queen. As in all of Raleigh's court poetry, *The Ocean to Cynthia* is addressed to the Queen and reflects his standing in her favor at the time. There is evidence that Raleigh and Elizabeth exchanged original poetry as a means of communication and as a method of sweetening the perpetual courtship the Queen demanded from her courtiers. Poems dating from Raleigh's early days at court are written in the Petrarchan model from the point of view of an adoring lover, to which the Queen sometimes responded with verses of her own. It is not surprising, then, that poetry was the method Raleigh chose in his attempt to appease the Queen after her discovery of his secret marriage. *The Ocean to Cynthia* was written to please the Queen, but it is also an expression of frustration and anger at Raleigh's imprisonment, a courtier's plea of mercy to his Queen, a rejected suitor's plea to his object of love. Among his prose works, Raleigh's Guiana essays, his several discourses on Parliament and relations with Spain, and his essay offering worldly advice to his son (1603) were influential both in private circulation and published form. However, the popularity of *The History of the World* overshadowed Raleigh's other accomplishments as a writer and poet for nearly a century after its publication in 1614. Characteristically ambitious in scope, Raleigh intended to cover all of history from the Creation to his own time, but the work was never finished, breaking off after the 2nd century B.C. Although historically discredited after the seventeenth century, the work endured as a standard text for a hundred years after its publication and is thought to be among the first attempts at a comprehensive worldwide historical study. The "Preface" to the work, also referred to as "A Premonition to Princes" was celebrated for its lucid warning against the danger of tyrants. The *History*'s closing paragraph, beginning "O eloquent, just, and mighty Death!" is still regarded as a superb example of Raleigh's ability to blend his technical skills of language and learning into expressive, enduring poetic constructions.

## Critical Reception

Prior to the discovery of the Hatfield fragments, scholars were preoccupied with establishing a definitive body of work directly attributed to Raleigh. Poems in several different notable anthologies were wrongly identified as Raleigh's. It is only in the twentieth century that controversies surrounding authorship have begun to settle. Raleigh's poetry and prose writings in general have been viewed primarily as examples of Elizabethan patronage literature, with an emphasis on the works' relationship to Elizabeth, James I, and Prince Henry. Other critics have studied Raleigh's philosophical and poetic impact on Spenser and the *Faerie*

*Queene*. Late twentieth century criticism has moved to examine Raleigh's contributions to Elizabethan literary forms apart from the traditional client-patron model, focussing on the language and structure of his important works both as prime examples of the literature of his time and as precursors to later trends in metaphysical styles. Critics have also argued over the relative completeness of his *History* and *The Ocean to Cynthia* and the works' effectiveness as self-contained texts. The study of Raleigh's important writings, particularly his complex *The Ocean to Cynthia*, remains open to students of his work as scholars continue to be challenged to identify and interpret Raleigh's ambitious oeuvre.

## PRINCIPAL WORKS

*A Report of the Truth of the Fight about the Iles of Acores, this last Sommer. Betwixt the Reuenge, one of her Maiesties Shippes, And an Armada of the King of Spaine* (essay) 1591
*The Ocean to Cynthia* (poetry) 1592?
*The Discoverie of the Large, Rich and Bewtiful Empire of Guiana* (travel essay) 1596
*A Relation of Cadiz Action, in the Year 1596* (essay) 1596‡
*Of a War with Spain and our Protecting the Netherlands* (essay) 1602
*Sir Walter Raleighs Instrvctions to his Sonne and to Posterity* (prose) 1603-05†
*The History of the World* (history) 1614
*The Prerogative of Parliaments in England* (essay) 1615*
*Sir Walter Raleigh's Sceptick* (essay) 1651
*Three Discourses of Sir Walter Ralegh* (prose) 1702
*The Works of Sir Walter Ralegh* 2 Vols. (essays, letters, poetry) 1751
*The Works of Sir Walter Ralegh* 8 Vols. (essays, letters, poetry) 1829
*The Poems of Sir Walter Ralegh*, edited by Agnes M. C. Latham (poetry) 1929

*First published in 1628.

†First published in 1632.

‡First published in 1700.

## CRITICISM

### Ernest A. Strathmann (essay date 1951)

SOURCE: "Of Human Knowledge," in *Sir Walter Ralegh: A Study in Elizabethan Skepticism*, Columbia University Press, 1951, pp. 219-53.

[*In the essay below, Strathmann places Raleigh's thought in the context of Greek, Roman, and Renaissance scepticism:"we find in [Raleigh's] utterances and writings support for his modest reputation in the seventeenth century as a philosophic sceptic."*]

"But for myself, I shall never be persuaded that god hath shut up all light of learning within the lantern of Aristotle's brains."

*History,* Preface, sig. D2ᵛ

Strict philosophical skepticism is far more rare in the history of human thought than is its popular counterpart. The varied manifestations of what is popularly called "skepticism" have in common a tendency to challenge received opinions or the dicta of established authority and to submit them to the tests of reason and experience. Often it is the dogmatism of religion or the weight of social custom that is challenged, and then skepticism in common usage is identified with rebellion against a church or refusal to accept the mores of a time or place as inherently right. It has been necessary to elaborate upon Ralegh's religious beliefs because many of his contemporaries and some of his modern readers and critics have labeled him, wrongly, a religious skeptic. The results are much the same for skepticism directed toward custom: although indifferent to popular opinion during much of his lifetime and not intolerant of divergences from English or European standards, Ralegh is not given in his writings, as Montaigne is, to reflections on the vagaries and conflicts of human conduct. Nevertheless, even putting aside these dominant popular meanings of skepticism as directed against religion and custom, we find in Ralegh's utterances and writings support for his modest reputation in the seventeenth century as a philosophic skeptic.

Naturally one does not expect to find a systematic philosophy in the work of a man whose studies were, in part, his recreation. Like most men known as skeptics—Montaigne, for example—Ralegh is selective and not always consistent in the application of his doubts. Nevertheless, there is real value in turning first to the relationships between his ideas and the formal skepticism of Greek philosophy. Pyrrhonic skepticism accounts for Ralegh's one direct essay on the subject, **The Skeptic,** in effect an incomplete translation; the ancient skeptical writings, either in originals or more commonly in translations and adaptations, provided the Elizabethan with the tools of skeptical thought; and by Academic skepticism—the formal system which his own loose methodology most closely approximates—one can measure the causal, less consistently skeptical, modes of Ralegh's thought. Usually, however, Ralegh's questioning of authority assumes less technical forms: his distrust of authority stemming from Aristotle or the schoolmen; or his consideration of the problem of historical method. The evidence here is not limited to

generalized pronouncements. Both as man of action and as historian Ralegh was frequently confronted with problems which called for decision, and it is therefore possible to check his practice, sometimes credulous, against his skeptical theory.

Skepticism of a more thoroughgoing kind than the world has known since was important in Greek and Roman thought for five centuries. During that time it was the philosophy of two schools, one of which was consistently skeptical to the point of rejecting the name of "school" or "sect" as suggestive of dogmatism. Skepticism as a distinct philosophy, not as an element in several early Greek philosophies, began with Pyrrho of Elis in the fourth century B.C., found a home in the New Academy under Arcesilaus, and was invigorated by late disciples of Pyrrho, who regarded Academic skepticism as tending toward dogmatism. Pyrrho himself seems to have been interested chiefly in the ethical aspects of skepticism rather than its application to the problems of knowledge. For studies of the modern period, the most useful distinction of the early skeptical philosophies is between Academic skepticism, which was speculative, and the revived and formalized Pyrrhonism of Alexandria and Rome, which was empiric. This distinction is emphasized in the opening lines of our most comprehensive account of Pyrrhonism (and the source of Ralegh's essay), the *Pyrrhonean Hypotyposes,* or *Outlines of Pyrrhonism,* compiled by Sextus Empiricus about A.D. 200 [all references to *Outlines of Pyrrhonism* are to the Loeb edition, translated by R. B. Bury, Book I]. Sextus begins by classifying three approaches to philosophical problems:

> The natural result of any investigation is that the investigators either discover the object of search or deny that it is discoverable and confess it to be inapprehensible or persist in their search. So, too, with regard to the objects investigated by philosophy, this is probably why some have claimed to have discovered the truth, others have asserted that it cannot be apprehended, while others again go on inquiring.

Those who believe they have found the truth are dogmatists (for example, Aristotle, Epicurus, the Stoics); the Academics consider the truth inapprehensible; the Skeptics keep on searching for the truth. Near the end of Book I, Sextus compares skepticism with other philosophies, somewhat at length with the Academic.

> Furthermore, as regards the End (or aim of life) we differ from the New Academy; for whereas the men who profess to conform to its doctrine use probability as the guide of life, we live in an undogmatic way by following the laws, customs, and natural affections.

Herein lies an important difference between the two

main skeptical philosophies, recognized also by later historians, who do not, however, follow Sextus in his identification of skepticism with Pyrrhonism alone. The Pyrrhonists, says Sextus, regard sense impressions as equally probable or improbable; the Academics find some impressions probable and others improbable. The distinction which he makes is an important one. Arcesilaus had based his theory of ethics on what appears reasonable, and the Academy under Carneades developed a theory of probabilities which classified sense impressions in such a way as to make possible a relative assent, even though objective knowledge was deemed impossible. The Pyrrhonists did not deny that the truth could be known; their argument was that it was not yet known, that they suspended judgment and continued the search. Both philosophies were based upon the inability of the senses alone to inform us of the true nature of what is perceived, and both evolved, with the differences indicated, into logical complexities which do not bear upon Ralegh's less subtle reflections.

So many connotations have clustered about the term "skepticism" in modern times that it is desirable, before turning to *The Skeptic,* to note some of the principal tenets and characteristics of the Pyrrhonism from which it derives. As the system evolved, it was defined in a number of tropes ("a manner of thought, or form of argument, or standpoint of judgment"): first ten, then five, and finally two [Mary P. Patrick, in *Sextus Empiricus and Greek Scepticism,* 1899]. The purpose of the tropes is to demonstrate that phenomena, or appearances, are so involved in relativity and change that they offer no satisfactory foundation for knowledge. The ten tropes from which Ralegh takes his essay are, except for the tenth, concerned with the unreliability of sense perception, either because of physical differences in the observers or because of external differences. The Pyrrhonists did not doubt the appearances, but whether the reality corresponds to the appearance; indeed, their criterion *is* the appearance:

> For since this lies in feeling and involuntary affection, it is not open to question. Consequently, no one, I suppose, disputes that the underlying object has this or that appearance; the point in dispute is whether the object is in reality such as it appears to be.

Contrary to the jeers of scoffers, these skeptics did not deny sensation, did not pretend that in freezing weather they felt no cold, although Pyrrho himself was credited with indifference to extreme discomfort. They argued not that they were immune to feelings but that their refusal to consider one state better than another made suffering more easily endured. Their aim was peace of mind (*ataraxia*), which they thought could be best attained by suspending judgment in investigations and ceasing to fret over the difficulty of knowing, "for

the man who opines that anything is by nature good or bad is for ever being disquieted." Unlike later and less formal skepticism, Pyrrhonism was conservative in its tendencies. Since we do not know what is true, or which of two things is better, we must accept the reports of our senses as a practical guide in life and we must conform to the religion and morality of the society in which we live. "Adhering, then, to appearances we live in accordance with the normal rules of life. undogmatically, seeing that we cannot remain wholly inactive." The method by which the Pyrrhonists arrived at this *modus vivendi* was by opposing the testimony of one sense to that of another sense, or the testimony of one sense under certain conditions to the testimony of the same sense under other conditions, or one argument to another argument. (As we shall see, this method of opposing arguments to each other is one element in Pyrrhonism which left a durable impress upon Ralegh's thought.) In time the skeptical attitude came to be summarized in certain phrases: "I know nothing"; and "no more" (that is, no more one thing than another).

This limited summary, largely of the first book of the *Outlines of Pyrrhonism,* may give some idea of the context of Ralegh's skeptical essay and, in general, may provide the background needed to interpret his less formal adaptations of skeptical thought and method. *The Skeptic* is a translation, with some condensations, omissions, and a few changes, of the first three Pyrrhonic tropes and part of the seventh. Its heading— "The skeptic doth neither affirm, neither deny any position; but doubteth of it, and opposeth his reasons against that which is affirmed or denied, to justify his not consenting"—is adequately explained as a brief statement of the skeptic position; the phrasing, however, has parallels in the *Outlines,* Book I, Chapter XXIII: "Of the Expression 'I Determine Nothing.'" In the present state of our bibliographical information, all that we know about the essay is that it was first published in 1651 under the title *Sir Walter Ralegh's Skeptic; or, Speculations.* Following it in the same volume are two other works which also have proved to be in large part translations: *Causes of the Magnificency and Opulency of Cities,* and the *Seat of Government.* A few letters, poems, and Ralegh's speech on the scaffold complete the book. After this first edition *The Skeptic* was frequently reprinted as part of the volume entitled *Remains,* and [T. N.] Brushfield reports [in his *A Bibliography of Sir Walter Ralegh,* 1908] a copy of the essay, with the position of some paragraphs altered, in the Lansdowne Manuscripts.

In his short treatise, which occupies only eight and one half pages in the *Works,* Ralegh gives a fairly complete version of the First Mode, but as he progresses his cuts and changes become more drastic. The skeptic's "first reason ariseth from the consideration of the great difference amongst living creatures, both in the matter and manner of their generation, and the several constitutions of their bodies." If the instruments of sense are changed, their perceptions change: things appear pale to a man with jaundice, distorted to one who rubs his eyes. Everyone knows what oddities appear in convex or concave mirrors. Why, then, is it not reasonable to assume that diverse animals, with eyes shaped quite differently, see objects in a variety of ways? The same argument applies to the other senses. One can report the appearance of things, but not "what they are in their own nature." Nor is it just for man to prefer his judgment of things perceived to that of other animals.

> They are living creatures as well as I: why then should I condemn their conceit and phantasy concerning any thing, more than they may mine? They may be in the truth and I in error, as well as I in truth and they err.

The argument that man's imagination is superior is rejected by citing instances of the intelligence of dogs; and if speech (a dubious accomplishment at best) is to be considered, animals too can communicate with each other.

Moving on to the Second Mode, even if we concede the superiority of man's judgment over that of animals, men differ greatly among themselves in their faculties. One man's meat is another man's poison. Nor can we find a guide to the true nature of things in opinion:

> . . . for either we must believe what all men say of it, or what some men only say of it. To believe what all men say of one and the same thing is not possible; for then we shall believe contrarieties; for some men say that the very thing is pleasant which others say is displeasant.

If we are to believe only some men, which of the philosophers, each praised by his own school, shall we follow? The Third Mode concerns the contradictory reports of the several senses upon the same objects; as, "Honey seemeth to the tongue sweet, but unpleasant to the eye; so ointment doth recreate the smell, but it offendeth the taste." When we see how the perception of a man who is born blind and deaf are limited, so that he will conclude that an object has only those qualities which are apparent to his other senses, how can we be sure that objects under our observation do not have more qualities than we can perceive with our own five senses? Shifting abruptly to the Seventh Mode, Raleigh concludes the summary (in the form in which it has come down to us) with a short paragraph on the differences in the appearances of things under different circumstances; for example, "Sands being separated appear rough to the touch, but in a great heap soft."

When we go outside the Ralegh bibliography for information on the translations of Sextus Empiricus the results are tantalizing and inconclusive. Thomas Nashe, in his Preface to Sidney's *Astrophel and Stella* (1591), refers to the works of Sextus Empiricus as "lately translated into English, for the benefit of unlearned writers." Then, in *Summer's Last Will and Testament* (probably performed in 1592; published 1600), Nashe versified an extended borrowing from Sextus which makes up seventy lines of a long speech by Orion. This is one of the better-known passages from the *Outlines of Pyrrhonism,* describing the reasoning powers and special abilities of dogs. Further, a very similar version of the praise of dogs occurs ten years after the first appearance of *Summer's Last Will* in a work attributed to Samuel Rowlands, *Greene's Ghost Haunting Cony-catchers* (1602). The late R. B. McKerrow made a comparative study of the passages in Nashe and Rowlands and of the corresponding Latin version in the edition by Henri Étienne in 1562, but without reference to Ralegh's **The Skeptic**. Dr. McKerrow considered it unlikely that Nashe followed either the original Greek or the Latin of Étienne; he found that Rowlands' version was more complete than that of Nashe and that he kept the order of Sextus; and he noted that Nashe and Rowlands have one passage (*Summer's Last Will,* lines 692-97) which is not in Sextus. He considered several possible explanations of the relationships between the versions by Nashe and Rowlands, and inclined to the belief that both were using an English translation. However, he left the question open because the translation, which should be dated about 1590, is not known today.

Does Ralegh's **The Skeptic** derive from the lost translation? Is it possible that Ralegh himself was the translator of 1590? Dr. McKerrow cites two "errors," in other references to Sextus by Nashe, which may serve as clues. Nashe's version reads "ashes" where the original calls for "asses," and so does Ralegh's; but, unfortunately for a suggestive lead, so does the first full-length English translation of the *Outlines of Pyrrhonism* known to me: that by Thomas Stanley in *The History of Philosophy* (1659). The second error by Nashe (a reading of "bones" for "beans") occurs in a passage which is omitted entirely from Ralegh's **The Skeptic** and which Stanley translates correctly. The fact that Nashe, Ralegh, and Stanley agree on the first error suggests that it originates in the sixteenth-century Greek or Latin text, neither of which have I seen. The passage on the intelligence of dogs is greatly condensed in **The Skeptic,** so that comparison with the extended versions by Nashe and Rowlands is of little avail. In short, the relationship of **The Skeptic** to the English translation of 1590 cannot be determined on the basis of the meagre evidence now available; for Ralegh's essay, as for the immediate origin of the passages used by Nashe and Rowlands, the question is still open.

The passages used by Nashe and Rowlands, the reference to a translation extant in 1591, and miscellaneous allusions and borrowings show that the Pyrrhonic philosophy was not unfamiliar to the Elizabethans. Two editions of the Latin translation of Sextus Empiricus by Henri Étienne were available; and the conveninent summaries and anecdotes by Diogenes Laertius were somewhat more detailed for Pyrrhonism than for other philosophies. The skeptical point of view was presented also in works which, although less systematic than the *Outlines of Pyrrhonism,* show their indebtedness to Sextus Empiricus. Such a book is Henry Cornelius Agrippa's *Of the Vanity and Uncertainty of Arts and Sciences* [translated by James Sanford, 1569], which falls short of "pure" skepticism in method but nevertheless is a compendium of skeptical arguments, sometimes stated in the phrasing of the *Outlines of Pyrrhonism.* Agrippa's book is uncertain in intent, and there is some justification for the translator's assertion, in his preface to the reader, that Agrippa attacks not learning and reason but their abuses. He protests the tyranny of authority, and exalts ignorant piety over the false learning of men. . . . Best known today of all sixteenth-century Pyrrhonists, of course, is Montaigne, who at one stage of his reading was so powerfully impressed by the skeptical tropes that he had some of them inscribed on the beams of his study. Indeed, Montaigne's indebtedness to Sextus Empiricus has misled one scholar [A. H. Upham, in his *The French Influence of English Literature*] into finding in the *Essais* the source of Ralegh's *The Skeptic.*

Before we turn to more general evidences of Ralegh's skepticism, it would be well to draw together a few conclusions about *The Skeptic,* warranted by this survey of its background and of the content of the document itself. Clearly, in this brief exercise Ralegh is not an innovator; he is exercising his intellectual curiosity in a field which in the sixteenth century had already aroused speculative interest. His essay is limited to those parts of the *Outlines of Pyrrhonism* concerned with the unreliability of sensory knowledge; if, as seems probable, he read further in that work, he could have found in a later chapter ammunition for his own attack on the "principles". One point about the essay that cannot be overstressed is its isolation. There is no comment, such as enlivens some of the borrowed passages in the *History;* most significantly, there is no relationship whatever between this exercise—well described in the first edition as "speculations"—and Ralegh's discourses on religion. When skeptical arguments are applied to religion, as they are occasionally in the Preface to the *History,* they are used in defense of faith, in the manner of the Christian apologists, not to discredit it. Finally, as we have seen many times over in quotations from the *History,* Ralegh subordinates reason to faith and to scriptural authority; but in that he considers reason a dependable guide to trustworthy conclusions he is not a good Pyrrhonist. There are exceptions, it is true, in notable passages in the *History* which exalt experience over reason; but the evidence of the *History* is overwhelmingly on the side of a method which argues from reason and probability. In that, and in his most definite statement of method, Ralegh inclines toward the skepticism of the Academy rather than that of Pyrrho.

A bridge between Ralegh's brief exercise in formal skepticism and his less systematic challenges of intellectual authority is found in a strongly worded passage in the Preface of the *History.* The context is an attack upon Aristotle's denial of the Creation in time, a doctrine of faith which is "too weighty a work for Aristotle's rotten ground to bear up." Despite its length, the passage merits quotation in full, for it offers the best single explanation of Ralegh's philosophy and also suggests, in the context of Elizabethan scholarship, the reasons for the easy misinterpretation of his position.

> And it is no less strange that those men which are desirous of knowledge (seeing Aristotle hath failed in this main point [that is, in denying the creation] and taught little other than terms in the rest) have so retrenched their minds from the following and overtaking of truth, and so absolutely subjected themselves to the law of those philosophical principles, as all contrary kind of teaching, in the search of causes, they have condemned either for fantastical or curious. But doth it follow that the positions of heathen philosophers are undoubted grounds and principles indeed, because so called? Or that *ipsi dixerunt* doth make them to be such? Certainly no. But this is true: That where natural reason hath built anything so strong against itself as the same reason can hardly assail it, much less batter it down, the same in every question of nature and finite power may be approved for a fundamental law of human knowledge. For, saith Charron in his book *Of Wisdom,* "Tour proposition humaine a autant d'authorité que l'autre, si la raison n'on fait la difference; Every human proposition hath equal authority, if reason make not the difference," the rest being but the fables of principles. But hereof how shall the upright and unpartial judgment of man give a sentence, where opposition and examination are not admitted to give in evidence? And to this purpose it was well said of Lactantius, . . . "They neglect their own wisdom, who without any judgment approve the invention of those that forewent them, and suffer themselves, after the manner of beasts, to be led by them." By the advantage of which sloth and dullness, ignorance is now become so powerful a tyrant as it hath set true philosophy, physic, and divinity in a pillory, and written over the first, *Contra negantem principia;* over the second, *Vertus specifica;* and over the third, *Ecclesia Romana.*

> But for myself, I shall never be persuaded that God hath shut up all light of learning within the lantern of Aristotle's brains; or that it was ever

said unto him, as unto Esdras, "Ascendam in corde tuo lucernam intellectus"; that God hath given invention but to the heathen; and that they only have invaded nature, and found the strength and bottom thereof; the same nature having consumed all her store and left nothing of price to after-ages. That these and these be the causes of these and these effects, time hath taught us, and not reason; and so hath experience, without art. The cheese-wife knoweth it as well as the philosopher that sour rennet doth coagulate her milk into a curd. But if we ask a reason of this cause, why the sourness doth it? whereby it doth it? and the manner how? I think that there is nothing to be found in vulgar philosophy to satisfy and many other like vulgar questions.

The passage concludes with remarks, already quoted, on the presumption of many, who, while ignorant of very simple things in nature, will attempt to "examine the art of God in creating the world."

This key statement illustrates the application of some traditional skeptical arguments to two major obstacles to independent investigation: the domination of the "principles" and the authority of Aristotle. Both problems have appeared with some frequency in [previous discussions]; the "principles" figured especially in Christian arguments that divinity, like other sciences, was entitled to proceed from accepted premises, and it was on the issue of "principles" that Ralegh and Ironside disagreed. A third idea in the passage, the occasional defeats of reason by experience, is here secondary to the central issue of freedom of investigation. Although Ralegh's statement is marked by the characteristic vigor of his style, the ideas are not novel; indeed, the interest of the quotation lies partly in the evidence it offers on the transmission of skeptical ideas.

Take, for example, Ralegh's approving quotation from [Peter] Charron, which reads in its context:

> There have been some in our time [marginal note: Copernicus, Paracelsus] that have changed and quite altered the principles and rules of our ancients and best professors in astronomy, physic, geometry, in nature, and the motion of the winds. Every human proposition hath as much authority as another, if reason make not the difference. Truth dependeth not upon the authority and testimony of man: there are no principles in man if Divinity have not revealed them; all the rest is but a dream and smoke.

Charron's book *Of Wisdom* [translated by Samson Lennard, 1612] is largely a systematization of Montaigne's "essais," and the lines which Ralegh approved come from the famous *Apology for Raimond Sebond:*

> For every science has its presupposed principles by which human judgment is hemmed in on all sides.

If you happen to drive against this barrier where the principal error lies, they have instantly this saying in their mouths: that there is no disputing with persons who deny first principles.

Now, there can be no first principles for men, if they are not revealed to them by Divinity; of all the rest—the beginning, the middle, and the end—there is nothing but dream and vapor. Against those who argue by presupposition we must presuppose the opposite of the very axiom which is in dispute. For every human presupposition and every enunciation has as much authority as any other, if the reason does not distinguish between them. Therefore they are all to be put into the balance, and first the general axioms and those which tyrannize over us.

The ultimate source of this denial of the authoritative principle is the *Outlines of Pyrrhonism,* a work which made a far more profound impression upon Montaigne than it ever did upon Ralegh. There is no record that Ralegh scratched the skeptical tropes on the beams of *his* Tower. According to Sextus Empiricus, "The main basic principle of the Skeptic system is that of opposing to every proposition an equal proposition; for we believe that as a consequence of this we end by ceasing to dogmatize." And most pertinent is the chapter entitled "Of the Phrase 'To Every Argument an Equal Argument is Opposed'":

> So whenever I say "To every argument an equal argument is opposed," what I am virtually saying is "To every argument investigated by me which establishes a point dogmatically, it seems to me there is opposed another argument, establishing a point dogmatically, which is equal to the first in respect of credibility and incredibility"; so that the utterance of the phrase is not a piece of dogmatism, but the announcement of a human state of mind which is apparent to the person experiencing it.

In such a roundabout fashion, although he knew the *Outlines of Pyrrhonism,* did Ralegh sometimes derive his skeptical arguments. Likewise some phrases and the point of view of the extended quotation from his Preface are in harmony with the opening pages of Agrippa's *Of the Vanity and Uncertainty of Arts and Sciences:*

> For every science hath in it some certain principles, which must be believed and cannot by any means be declared: which if any will obstinately deny, the philosophers have not wherewith to dispute against him, and immediately they will say, that there is no disputation against him which denieth the principles. . . .

In the same context, Agrippa quotes as an example of slavish obedience to intellectual authority the Pythagoreans' "Ipse Dixit," spoken of their master. Since Ralegh makes no reference in this passage to

Agrippa—as he does to Charron—these particular verbal similarities are interesting chiefly as showing how early in the Elizabethan period skeptical ideas found popular expression.

Turning from questions of the derivation and currency of these ideas to an analysis of Ralegh's meaning, we find his first proposition—that philosophical principles are not exempt from liberty of examination—limited to matters which can be encompassed by the legitimate activity of the human intellect: " . . . where natural reason hath built anything so strong against itself as the same reason can hardly assail it, much less batter it down, the same *in every question of nature and finite power* may be approved for a fundamental law of human knowledge." The exception, here italicized, is of the utmost importance, for it concedes to the supernatural and to Infinite Power an area of operation in which "natural reason" must yield to revelation. Over and over again, in *The History of the World,* Ralegh has deferred first to Scripture, and then to reason and probability. But "in every question of nature and finite power" the reason is helpless if it is to be held spellbound by the "fables of principles." Ignorance, too dull and slothful to reexamine his inherited knowledge, has become a tyrant who pillories true philosophy, physic, and divinity: true philosophy, with the common retort of the schools, "contra negantem principia"; true physic, by labeling it "vertus specifica"; and true divinity, by calling it the Roman Church.

This attack upon the tyranny of the "principles," even though it has a counterpart in Pyrrhonic arguments, differs in language and objectives from that negative system. At this point, as commonly in the *History,* Ralegh appeals to reason, which the true Skeptic distrusts. As for objectives, he clearly believes in the possibility of extending the bounds of knowledge, once so-called laws are submitted to "opposition and examination." This applies especially to his emphasis on the need for independent research in natural philosophy. . . . But apart from science, Ralegh's point of view inclines to the Academic skeptical position, which sees as possible at least a relative truth. When he relies upon "reason and the most probable circumstances thereon depending," or "nature, reason, policy, and necessity," or "reason and probable conjecture," he is using neither the language nor the method of a Pyrrhonist. For Ralegh, as for many another "skeptic," skepticism is not a system, not a philosophy of life, but a weapon for an attack upon dogmatism.

One possible inconsistency in Ralegh's attitude toward the "principles" must be noted. In a discussion of the extent to which the laws of Moses are authoritative for other peoples, he draws an analogy between the debt of political institutions to Moses, the lawgiver appointed by God, and the debts of the "sciences" to metaphysics:

Wherefore that acknowledgment which other sciences yield unto the metaphysics, that from thence are drawn propositions able to prove the principles of sciences which out of the sciences themselves cannot be proved, may justly be granted by all other politic institutions to that of Moses; and so much the more justly by how much the subject of the metaphysics, which is *Ens quatenus Ens,* being as it is being, is infinitely inferior to the *Ens Entium,* the being of beings, the only good, the fountain of truth, whose fear is the beginning of wisdom.

Although Ralegh is here citing the principles merely for a rhetorical comparison and is not passing judgment upon them, the figure of speech is in an entirely different vein from the forthright approval of the skeptical pronouncement out of Charron.

The rejection of the principles as eternally valid led naturally to the denial of the authority of Aristotle, the second major point in the quotation from Ralegh's preface. The declaration of intellectual independence quoted at the head of this [essay] is comparable to Bacon's "knowledge derived from Aristotle, and exempted from liberty of examination, will not rise again higher than the knowledge of Aristotle." But neither Bacon in 1605 nor Ralegh in 1614 was an innovator in this particular phase of intellectual history; it is especially true of Ralegh that his share in the overthrow of Aristotle's authority lies largely in the authority of his own name and the magic of his pen. For Bacon, of course, the story is different and of greater significance in the history of thought; but he, too, is a late recruit in the attack upon Aristotle, however sweeping and influential his plans for the advancement of learning.

Aristotle enjoyed a paradoxical reputation in the sixteenth century. On the one hand he was considered the apostle of the atheistic doctrine that the world was eternal (the context, be it remembered, of the extract from the *History* now under discussion); on the other hand, much of his philosophy had become identified with Catholic teaching to the point that, in some quarters, an attack on Aristotle was itself construed as irreligious. A striking example of such an attitude is found in the scene in Marlowe's *Massacre at Paris,* wherein Ramus, a victim of the St. Bartholomew's slaughter, is taunted by the Duke of Guise for challenging the logic of Aristotle. Opposition to the authority of Aristotle took many forms, ranging from the deferential attitude of critics who respected his great learning, but insisted on recognition of the advancement of knowledge through discoveries in astronomy, geography, and natural philosophy, to impatient denunciations of the tortuous methods of the Aristotelians. Aristotle's system of logic had been criticized with such effect by Ramus that the "new" logic was widely accepted among Protestants; and in the experimental sciences there had been, throughout the sixteenth century and especially in the latter half, a firm insistence on the need for testing old "facts" and on the possibility of new knowledge.

Consequently, when Ralegh denies to the ancients the exclusive possession of nature's secrets he is joining a progressive party, not founding one. Nevertheless, academic devotion to Aristotle continued strong, and the encounter with Ironside, who argued from logical principles and the authority of Aristotle, is an example of it from Ralegh's own experience. He had no reason to assume that the spirit of free inquiry, even in the restricted area which he assigned to it, had won the day. It must be remembered, too, that in scientific studies academic conservatism was only one obstacle, no longer as formidable as it had once been; in his discussion of natural magic and miracles, . . . Ralegh is more concerned with superstitious prejudice than with the barriers raised by a system of logic and by ancient authority. His own attitude toward Aristotle is usually denunciatory, especially where his opposition has religious support. Thus he adds a skeptical judgment to a statement from Aristotle on the soul, and dismisses certain opinions of the Aristotelians on natural magic as "brabblings." He finds most of the Schoolmen

> . . . rather curious in the nature of terms, and more subtle in distinguishing upon the parts of doctrine already laid down, than discoverers of anything hidden, either in philosophy or divinity; of whom it may be truly said . . . "Nothing is more odious to true wisdom than too acute sharpness."

And in the same vein,

> But this I dare avow of those Schoolmen, that though they were exceeding witty, yet they better teach all their followers to shift than to resolve by their distinctions.

If we bring to the support of this brief summary of Renaissance opinion on Aristotle a few specific references we may perhaps see Ralegh's position in better perspective. In his notes on Augustine's *City of God* [1610] Ludovicus Vives comments that Plato was long preeminent over Aristotle until mercenary ends brought about the decline of learning; then Aristotle's logic and physics drove out not only Plato but better works of Aristotle. Because they do not understand Plato and because he teaches no tricks of disputation, the Schoolmen have nothing to do with him. A marginal note, presumably by the translator or a late editor, enforces the point: "This is no good doctrine in the Louvainists' opinion, for it is left out as distasteful to the schoolmen, though not to direct truth." Again, Vives reproves Aquinas and others for defining matters of divine nature "according to Aristotle's positions, drawing themselves into such labyrinths of natural questions that you would rather say they were Athenian sophisters

than Christian divines." A marginal note adds: "No word of this in the Louvain copy." Here we have the mark of a broad, but of course not always consistent, division: the Protestants leaning upon the teachings of Plato and Augustine, the Catholics following Aristotle and Aquinas.

Skepticism in general about the authority of Aristotle, without immediate religious bias though concerned with the relationship of reason and faith, is found in Montaigne's *Apology for Raimond Sebond*. In a passage immediately preceding the comment on the principles, quoted above as Charron's source, Montaigne observes that

> . . . the opinions of men are adopted in conformity with ancient beliefs, upon authority and trust, as if they were religion and law. What is commonly believed about it is accepted as if by rote. This truth, with its whole structure and equipment of arguments and proofs, is received as though it were a firm and solid body which is not to be shaken, not to be subjected to judgment. On the contrary, everyone, as best he may, cements and fortifies this belief with the utmost power of his reason, which is a supple and pliable instrument, and adaptable to every shape. And thus the world comes to be filled and stuffed with inanities and falsehoods.

> The reason why men raise so few doubts is that they never put common impressions to the test. . . . The god of scholastic learning is Aristotle; it is an impiety to dispute his decrees, as it was to dispute those of Lycurgus at Sparta. His doctrine, which is perhaps as false as any other, is by us treated as magisterial law. I do not know why I should not as readily accept either the Ideas of Plato, or the Atoms of Epicurus [Montaigne continues with a list of major philosophies]. . . . And yet all this [the opinion of Aristotle on the principles of natural things] no man must dare to disturb except for an exercise in logic. Nothing therein is discussed with a view to raising doubts, but only to defend the founder of the school against objections from without. His authority is the mark beyond which it is not permitted to inquire.

Even apart from the similarity due to Ralegh's borrowing from the disciple of Montaigne, the historian and the essayist are on common ground in their scorn of the blind acceptance of authority. Montaigne is far more vigorous than Ralegh in his denunciation of the pretensions of reason, but neither man holds consistently to that skeptical position.

These illustrations, which could be extended indefinitely, may be brought to a close by two quotations so dated that the publication of the **History** falls midway between them. Addressing Ralegh as a patron in 1596, John Hester [in *A Hundred and Fourteen Experiments of Paracelsus,* 1596] makes a plea for freedom of research outside the province of divinity, which rightly requires obedience and belief.

> [All other faculties] tending to government or ornament of a life natural so carry a privilege of more liberty in search, and large scope in practise, that to rest content with the inventions of other is as odious to the learned as it is for frank hearts to feed on other men's trenchers, or fine wits to be set to tell the clock while grosser heads are better employed.

Although he does not name Aristotle, Hester's plea clearly merits a place among the many statements challenging the prerogatives of authority. More explicit is a statement published almost twenty years after the *History* by a clergyman who admires the great learning of Aristotle but emphasizes the limits imposed upon his observations, for example by his restricted knowledge of geography. In an essay addressed "To the venerable artists and younger students in divinity in the famous University of Cambridge" [appended to Thomas James, *The Strange and Dangerous Voyage*, 1633], William Watts discusses the problem of harmonizing the remarkable discoveries in North America with Aristotle's rules. "Of this one thing am I confident," he tells the students, "that you are all so rational and ingenuous as to prefer truth before authority: *amicus Plato, amicus Aristoteles*, but *magis amica veritas*." The same God who gave Aristotle his good parts has also raised up many other excellent spirits, and it would be a discouragement of invention and observation to submit all their work to Aristotle's authority. "Let it not then be thought unequal to examine the first cogitations of the old philosophy by the second thoughts of our more modern artists." In that way we may expect the same improvement in "physics" that we have already made in geography, mathematics, and mechanics. Watts names and praises famous scholars who have already stood against the authority of Aristotle. The date of Watts's essay indicates that if Ralegh were not the first to assail the dragon Error neither, in the first years of the seventeenth century, was he tilting at windmills.

The third point in Ralegh's skeptical pronouncement is the praise of experience over reason—as he puts it, "time hath taught us, and not reason; and so hath experience, without art." At first glance this disparagement of reason and learning has the appearance of true skepticism; but in its full context the few sentences on this theme are a transition to the main point of a very long paragraph: the presumption of man, helpless to explain some of the simplest phenomena of nature but confident in determining the secrets of God. Here again skepticism is enlisted in the cause of religion. But the disparagement of reason is not wholly inconsistent with setting up natural reason, a few sentences earlier, as a better guide to knowledge than docile acceptance of the principles. The praise of reason emphasizes man's powers; the disparagement of reason emphasizes the limitations upon those powers. The first passage concerns the exercise of "natural reason," assisted by "opposition and examination"; reason in the second passage seems to be akin to ratiocination. Elsewhere in the *History* Ralegh illustrates, from one of the great lessons of geographical discovery, the value of experience over "contemplation." While agreeing that the terrestrial paradise was not located "under the equinoctial," Ralegh dismisses the ancient argument, in its day a "reasonable conjecture," against such a location: that the extreme heat of the tropics would be unbearable.

> ... yet now we find that, if there be any place upon the earth of that nature, beauty, and delight that Paradise had, the same must be found within that supposed uninhabitable burnt zone, or within the tropics and nearest to the line itself. For hereof experience hath informed reason, and Time hath made those things apparent which were hidden and could not by any contemplation be discovered.

Thus the errors in the maps of geographers, who mark the unknown regions of the earth according to hearsay, are "many times controlled by following experience and found contrary to truth."

Ralegh's concise statement of his skeptical position in the Preface to the *History* is not isolated like *The Skeptic*, but incorporated in his major work. The value of this passage lies in its concentration on a few major issues, by which we may define Ralegh's place among his contemporaries. We find him an advocate of ideas neither entirely new nor yet firmly established. The "principles" were still valid in argument; the authority of Aristotle still weighty; reason still the acknowledged means for determining truth on the basis of facts already known. Ralegh's skeptical opinions on such matters were understood and shared by many men of letters and of science in his day, but they were open to misunderstanding in the confusion of an age which sometimes identified the teachings of Aristotle with Christianity. To understand the operative limits of Ralegh's skepticism, however, we must turn from the compact selection from the Preface to a sampling of his working methods in handling the varied problems which attracted his interest.

Something of the temper of Ralegh's mind has already been disclosed in a review of his opinions on religion, ethics, and science; for example, in his efforts to find the most probable and reasonable explanations of Scriptural problems, his avoidance of dogmatism in painstaking attempts to solve problems of chronology, and his defense of natural magic and of freedom in experimentation. There remains the broad question to which suggestive but partial answers have been given [earlier]: to what extent is Ralegh the historian, or Ralegh the empire-builder, governed by the skeptical attitude displayed in the Preface? The question may be answered, apart from what has already been said about his practices and beliefs, by a specific consideration of his historical method and of some of his credulities.

The dominant idea of **The History of the World** is that all human affairs are under God's providence, sometimes inscrutable but always operative. The purpose of the historian is didactic, but he is free to explain, if he can, the agency of second causes in performing God's will. In the exposition of second causes, Ralegh's virtue lies less in careful sifting of evidence than in fair warning to the reader of the uncertain state of the question in hand. His method varies: where he is greatly interested, as in problems of chronology and geography, he proceeds carefully and judiciously; where he is not interested, or where he finds the evidence scanty and entangled in conjecture, he is likely to become impatient and hack at knots indiscriminately.

A good starting point for a review of Ralegh's method is a section entitled "A digression wherein is maintained the liberty of using conjecture in histories." After some highly speculative discourse on the parentage of Joash and his relationship to Athaliah, Ralegh observes:

> In handling of which matter, the more I consider the nature of this history and the diversity between it and others, the less, methinks, I need to suspect mine own presumption, as deserving blame for curiosity in matter of doubt or boldness in liberty of conjecture. For all histories do give us information of human counsels and events, as far forth as the knowledge and faith of the writers can afford; but of God's will, by which all things are ordered, they speak only at random and many times falsely.

The merit of the history of the kings of Israel and Judah is that it refers

> all unto the will of God, I mean to his revealed will; from which, that his hidden purposes do not very, this story by many great examples gives most notable proof. True it is that the concurrence of second causes with their effects is in these books nothing largely described, nor perhaps exactly in any of those histories that are in these points most copious. For it was well noted by that worthy gentleman, Sir Philip Sidney, that historians do borrow of poets not only much of their ornament but somewhat of their substance. Informations are often false, records not always true, and notorious actions commonly insufficient to discover the passions which did set them first on foot.

Although the historian may be excused "when finding apparent cause enough of things done [he] forbeareth to make further search," nevertheless the motivation of great events is often to be found in seeming trifles. "For the wisest of men are not without their vanities which, requiring and finding mutual toleration, work more closely and earnestly than right reason either needs or can." Since it is the "end and scope of all history to teach by example of times past such wisdom as may guide our desires and actions," it is no wonder that the chronicles of the kings of Judah and Israel, written by men divinely inspired, should be concerned with teaching us the way to true felicity rather than with elaborating upon second causes. Yet one may lawfully gather such information from pagan histories or other circumstances as long as he does not "derogate from the first causes by ascribing to the second more than was due."

> Such, or little different, is the business which I have now in hand, wherein I cannot believe that any man of judgment will tax me as either fabulous or presumptuous. For he doth not fain that rehearseth probabilities as bare conjectures; neither doth he deprave the text that seeketh to illustrate and make good in human reason those things which authority alone, without further circumstance, ought to have confirmed in every man's belief. And this may suffice in defense of the liberty which I have used in conjectures, and may hereafter use, when occasion shall require, as neither unlawful nor misbeseeming an historian.

A like tolerance toward historical invention is shown in dealing with periods barren of records. If the stories of Annius are to be regarded as always untrustworthy, how is it that information not available in any other source turns up in histories by "painful and judicious writers"? Concurrent history supports the particular fact in question, the duration of the reign of Phul, an Assyrian king; "yet all of them took it from Annius." It is a just punishment for his falsehoods that Annius is doubted when he speaks truth; although, Ralegh notes slily,

> for our own sakes we make use of his boldness, taking his words for good, whereas (nothing else being offered) we are unwilling ourselves to be authors of new, though not unprobable, conjectures. Herein we shall have this commodity, that we may without blushing alter a little to help our own opinions and lay the blame upon Annius, against whom we shall be sure to find friends that will take our part.

To enforce his argument in support of the historian's liberty to construct the most plausible story he can out of meagre resources, Ralegh turns to analogy and anecdote.

> I neither do reprehend the boldness of Torniellus in conjecturing, nor the modesty of Scaliger and Sethus Calvisius in forbearing to set down as warrantable,

such things as depend only upon likelihood. For things whereof the perfect knowledge is taken away from us by antiquity must be described in history as geographers in their maps describe those countries whereof as yet there is made no true discovery; that is, either by leaving some part blank or by inserting the land of pigmies, rocks of loadstone, with headlands, bays, great rivers, and other particularities agreeable to common report, though many times controlled by following experience and found contrary to truth. Yet indeed the ignorance growing from distance of place allows not such liberty to a describer as that which ariseth from the remediless oblivion of consuming time.

The errors in geography can be corrected. Neither climate nor danger will restrain the daring seaman; he will go where he will, and return to damn the fictions of the cartographer. Ralegh recalls that he once asked a distinguished prisoner, Don Pedro de Sarmiento, whether an island in the Straits of Magellan had not hindered his attempts to plant a Spanish colony there.

> . . . he told me merrily that it was to be called the Painter's Wife's Island; saying that, whilst the fellow drew that map, his wife, sitting by, desired him to put in one country for her, that she in imagination might have an island of her own. But in filling up the blanks of old histories we need not be so scrupulous. For it is not to be feared that time should run backward and, by restoring the things themselves to knowledge, make our conjectures appear ridiculous. What if some good copy of an ancient author could be found, showing (if we have it not already) the perfect truth of these uncertainties? Would it be more shame to have believed, in the meanwhile, Annius or Torniellus than to have believed nothing? . . . Let it suffice that, in regard of authority, I had rather trust Scaliger or Torniellus than Annius; yet him than them, if his assertion be more probable and more agreeable to approved histories than their conjecture. . . .

Thus Ralegh, content to discriminate for his readers fact and conjecture, regards a plausible story as better than none.

An attitude so tolerant of speculation hardly qualifies as "skeptical"; but many of his other comments on historical guess-work are more in the vein of the Preface. In the very chapter which contains the digression on liberty of conjecture, he declines to extend the discussion of the alternate names of Joash:

> . . . yet because I find no other warrant hereof than a bare possibility, I will not presume to build an opinion upon the weak foundation of mine own conjecture, but leave all to the consideration of such as have more ability to judge and leisure to consider of this point.

The heading of another section carries the warning, "A private conjecture of the author." Concerning the Roman wars in Spain he concludes, "I am weary of rehearsing so many particularities whereof I can believe so few. But since we can find no better certainties, we must content ourselves with these." The *History* abounds in "asides" such as these, some of the best in the comments on chronology already quoted.

The questioning of Aristotle and the Schoolmen extends to other forms of intellectual authority outside the requirements of religious faith. These challenges in the *History* read like variations on a theme. Disagreement may be respectful, as toward the church fathers:

> And it is true that many of the Fathers were far wide from the understanding of this place. I speak it not that I myself dare presume to censure them, for I reverence both their learning and their piety, and yet not bound to follow them any further than they are guided by truth; for they were men, *Et humanum est errar.*

On the other hand, Annius, who is accepted in the absence of other authority when his yarns are plausible, receives a wry dismissal when they are not: "The obscurity of the history gives leave to Annius of saying what he list. I, that love not to use such liberty, will forbear to determine anything herein." Even more tart is the comment on the learned Goropius Becanus: "But as he had an inventive brain, so there never lived any man that believed better thereof and of himself.' Perhaps the best single pronouncement on the proper attitude toward authority is what Ralegh says of his own opinions on the location of the terrestrial paradise: " . . . this is the reward that I look for, that my labors may but receive an allowance suspended, until such time as this description of mine be reproved by a better."

Naturally, Ralegh encountered in the course of his historical work many problems not reduced to such simple terms as the acceptance or rejection of authority. Novelty for its own sake does not interest him; he is inclined to suspect the motives of too eager a pursuit of originality.

> As for those that with so much cunning forsake the general opinion when it favoreth not such exposition as they bring out of a good mind to help where the need is not over-great, I had rather commend their diligence than follow their example.

Such wrongheaded independence may serve to introduce and propagate error.

> There is no error which hath not some slippery and bad foundation, or some appearance of probability resembling truth, which, when men who study to be

singular find out (straining reason according to their fancies), they then publish to the world matter of contention and jangling; not doubting but in the variable deformity of men's minds to find some partakers or sectators, the better by their help to nurse and cherish such weak babes as their own inventions have begotten.

Ralegh is critical of those who "prefer the commentator before the author; and to uphold a sentence giving testimony to one clause do carelessly overthrow the history itself, which thereby they sought to have maintained." Sometimes he records the process of change in his own opinions. For example, "following the common belief and good authority," he had once thought reverently of the Sibylline oracles; but he was well on the way to abandoning that credulity "when that learned and excellent work of Master Casaubon upon the *Annals* of Cardinal Baronius did altogether free me from mine error." In like fashion, the legend of Simon Magus probably originated in a false conjecture.

Such conjectures, being entertained without examination, find credit by tradition, whereby also, many times, their fashion is amended and made more historical than was conceived by the author.

In actual practice, when he is weighing the truth or falsehood in the many stories which crowd the pages of the *History,* Ralegh shows the same mixture of hardheaded practicality and easy gullibility which contribute to the fascination of the Elizabethan Period. He records omens seriously, yet he can remark ironically, concerning a Roman disaster at sea, that the Romans "knew better how to fight than how to navigate, and never found any foul weather in the entrails of their beasts, their soothsayers being all land prophets." Heathen oracles and prophecies he distrusts as devised after the event; but, in keeping with his reverence for Holy Writ, he denounces Porphyry bitterly for applying the same argument to the prophecies of Daniel. Spanish stories of help in battle from the Virgin and angels he dismisses as "Romish miracles"; but he accepts as "certainly true" that the mass desertion of the dogs belonging to a French army clearly presaged its ensuing defeat. Reports of unusual natural phenomena he is usually inclined to accept; in one instance he calls upon hearsay, authority, and a none too closely reasoned personal experience to support a reference to a fountain.

that at midnight is as hot as boiling water and at noon as cold as any ice, to which I cannot but give credit, because I have heard of some other wells of like nature, and because it is reported by Saint Augustine, by Diodore, Herodotus, Pliny, Mela, Solinus, Arianus, Curtius, and others; and indeed our Baths in England are much warmer in the night than in the day.

Like his contemporaries, he has exaggerated ideas of the height of mountains, the highest of which, he affirms, does not rise above thirty miles. The vitality of the men of old is attested by the fact that "Galen did ordinarily let blood six pound weight, whereas we (for the most part) stop at six ounces."

The most notorious of the credulities charged against Ralegh is found in *The Discovery of Guiana*. Trusting to hearsay, Ralegh avows his belief in the existence of a race of monstrous men.

. . . on that branch [of the river] which is called Caora are a nation of people whose heads appear not above their shoulders, which, though it may be thought a mere fable, yet for mine own part I am resolved it is true, because every child in the provinces of Arromaia and Canuri affirm the same. They are called Ewaipanoma; they are reported to have their eyes in their shoulders and their mouths in the middle of their breasts, and that a long train of hair groweth backward between their shoulders. [Ralegh cites confirmations by the son of the chieftain, Topiawari, and continues] . . . but it was not my chance to hear of them till I was come away, and if I had but spoken one word of it while I was there I might have brought one of them with me to put the matter out of doubt. Such a nation was written of by Mandeville, whose reports were held for fables many years, and yet since the East Indies were discovered we find his relations true of such things as heretofore were held incredible. Whether it be true or no the matter is not great, neither can there be any profit in the imagination; for mine own part I saw them not, but I am resolved that so many people did not all combine or forethink to make the report.

As Mr. Harlow notes, the legend was persistent among the Indians, and this loose-jointed passage is not quite as droll as it appears to a better-informed posterity. In a sense, this is a premature application of Ralegh's faith in the correction of reason by experience, decidedly faulty because "for mine own part I saw them not" and neither the affirmations of "every child" nor the assurances of a chieftain's son are impressive evidence. Also, the story appears in a propagandist work in which Ralegh is throwing together every possible argument to enlist official support for occupying Guiana. He dangles the lures of gold, of other rich resources, and of advantage against Spain. If the marvelous will help, in it goes; though he is careful to note that the accuracy of the tale does not affect his main purpose.

In the *History* Ralegh disavows such a reliance on hearsay, as of "no authority or credit." And for a marvel similar to that which entertained the readers of *The Discovery of Guiana* he has rational explanations to offer. The legendary Arimaspi who fought the griffins for their gold were called one-eyed "by reason that they used to wear a vizard of defense with one sight in the middle to serve both eyes, and not that they had by nature any such defect." The fable, he explains, can be moralized to mean:

> That if those men which fight against so many dangerous passages for gold or other riches of this world had their perfect senses and were not deprived of half their eyesight (at least of the eye of right reason and understanding) they would content themselves with a quiet and moderate estate, and not subject themselves to famine, corrupt air, violent heat, and cold, and to all sorts of miserable diseases.

Thirdly, although the griffins are feigned, it might in a sense be truly said that in America wild animals defend the mines of gold and alligators guard precious pearls—simply because gold and pearls are found in dangerous places, not because they are valued by the denizens of those regions. "And though the alegartos know not the pearl, yet they find savor in the flesh and blood of the Indians whom they devour." All this rationalizing is preceded by a blunt rejection of fables about the Arimaspi and the Cyclops: "But (for mine own opinion) I believe none of them."

Ralegh does not link his discussion of the Arimaspi with his own tale about the "Ewaipanoma"; but in another, and not dissimilar, instance, he does use the *History* to support a story in the *Discovery*. He devotes an entire section, two pages in length, to what the historians, including Spaniards and Portuguese reporting on discoveries in South America and Africa, have had to say about the Amazons; and concludes:

> I have produced these authorities in part to justify mine own relation of these Amazons, because that which was delivered me for truth by an ancient Casique of Guiana, how upon the river of Papamena (since the Spanish discoveries called Amazons) that these women still live and govern, was held for a vain and unprobable report.

On this story, of course, Ralegh finds himself in better company than in his account of the telescoped Ewaipanoma. The measure of his success or failure in judging such tales is not simply by his belief or disbelief, nor according to later verification or exposure; but by his adherence to his own standards of evidence. He can thrust aside the Arimaspi; he can muster help against the Amazons; but when he encounters the marvelous Ewaipanoma he falls victim to his own propaganda.

**Philip Edwards (essay date 1953)**

SOURCE: "The Prose," in *Sir Walter Ralegh*, Longmans, Green and Co, 1953, pp. 127-71.

[*In the following essay, Edwards examines the nature of Raleigh's prose works, focusing in particular on his treatment of military and naval engagements, his reflective writings, and his conception of historiography.*]

The profuseness and variety of Ralegh's prose writings are formidable. As a naval commander, he sends an excited account of a great battle to a friend; for his son he inscribes some rather heavy-handed paternal advice; he translates excerpts from a Sceptic philosopher; he extols the virtues of Guiana as a colony; he composes a treatise on the art of war at sea; from the Tower he gives a monarch advice on the disposing of his children in marriage, writes a tract on parliamentary government, and over the long years sets forth his sombre philosophy of history in his story of man from his beginnings to the days of the Roman Empire. The reader may well be daunted by such diversity of material, much of it written for occasions and purposes that have now no interest, much of it fragmentary, and some of it, alas, very dull. The prose is not very accessible, either, to the general reader: the last edition of the Works was in 1829, and the selections from the prose that are available suffer from the disadvantages of all anthologies. The purpose of this [essay] is to sort out for the reader, with the help of liberal quotation, what is important and valuable among the mass of Ralegh's writings in prose.

I shall not exhibit strings of passages as particularly fine specimens of English prose-style: a collocation of eloquent paragraphs set down for the reader to admire would be as useless as the detached 'beauties' of Shakespeare. In prose as in verse, it is vain to consider style as a thing in itself. Form depends on function, and how good the form, or style, of a passage is, cannot be judged until we take the whole work into account, examine its aim and intention and see what part the passage plays in fulfilling that aim. I shall concern myself with what Ralegh has to say and how effectively he says it.

In the first place, Ralegh's prose must be divided into two kinds: the prose of action, and the prose of reflection. Within these two divisions will be found many different types of writing, answering the needs of particular works, but this first separation is fundamental

### The Prose of Action

The prose of action comprises accounts of actions or exploits in which Ralegh took part or had a particular interest. This type of literature is one we know well enough today, but Ralegh's reasons for writing were generally very different from the reasons of those who today publish stories of personal adventure and unusual excitements. Ralegh never thought of the writing-up of his actions as a 'literary' endeavour or an attempt to make capital from the public's desire for vicarious adventure—nor did he undertake exploits in order to write books about them. Some of his 'prose of action', for example, is embedded in his historical writing, where it serves for illustration and comparison; accounts of his last fatal expedition were written as memoranda or private letters in his own justification; the **Discovery of Guiana** was written to enlist approval and support for a colonial scheme.

The earliest piece is Ralegh's first published work in prose and concerns an action in which he took no part: *A Report of the Truth of the Fight about the Isles of Azores this last Summer, Betwixt the Revenge, one of Her Majesty's Ships, and an Armada of the King of Spain* (1591). To appreciate how good this account of Grenville's heroic foolhardiness is, the reader should turn, after sampling it, to the ballad which Ralegh's account inspired Tennyson to write on the subject. Tennyson, substituting a rather jaunty bravado for the spirit that moves Ralegh, and writing up the story in verse, loses the ready appeal which Ralegh's direct and unadorned relation has. Ralegh's heart and style go together; both heart and style are a little uneasy in Tennyson, and they are out of step. Ralegh knows that the tale of Grenville's astonishing 'greatness of heart' in defying impossible odds is so impressive that the deeds are best left to speak for themselves, with as little elaboration and indirection as possible.

The spirit behind the work is, like the style, simple and without subtlety. Ralegh is moved by admiring wonder at a course of action quite impolitic and inexpedient, foredoomed to failure, which, because it humiliated an arrogant and evil enemy, deserved to be called not folly but heroism. Ralegh loves Grenville's courage and resolution 'never to submit or yield' in a cause sanctified as a good cause. The love and wonder make his account glow with enthusiasm. 'The other course had been the better', he says—to have got out of the way when the Spanish fleet bore up—'notwithstanding, out of the greatness of his mind, he could not be persuaded.' Ralegh tells quickly and vividly how the little English fleet was caught at anchor and unready, the ships' companies halved by disease and many men ashore; how Grenville in the *Revenge* 'utterly refusing to turn from the enemy' sailed into the midst of the two Spanish squadrons; how he was laid aboard by ship after ship in turn, but fought them all off, inflicting heavy losses, through the afternoon and night until he himself was wounded and his ship had become a hulk, and all that flesh and blood could do to resist had been done. . . .

The celebration of Grenville's pertinacity and courage was only a part of Ralegh's purpose in writing his narrative; the pamphlet is also designed as a blow in the anti-Spanish campaign, in support of Ralegh's policy of aggression. So the action of the *Revenge* is set within an account of recent happenings in the war and is accompanied by general reflections on the Spanish menace. Ralegh reminds his readers with some satisfaction of the fate of Spanish imperialist designs in 1588, when the invincible Armada was 'driven with squibs from their anchors and chased out of the sight of England'. Grenville's fight is a moral victory in the cause so near to Ralegh's heart. But his hostility to Spain as he here expresses it is not a jingoistic and truculent one. The emphasis is everywhere on defence against being engulfed by a cruel and irreligious imperialism rather than on attack against a rival power. Ralegh's indignation at the barbarities practised by the Spaniards in the Indies and Peru, under the cloak of spreading faith amongst the heathen, rings with a sincere and genuine tone.

The other naval action of which Ralegh has left an account is the engagement at Cadiz (seen by Ralegh as revenge for the *Revenge*). . . . The account, not published in his lifetime, is given in a letter to an unnamed friend and is born of an entirely different spirit from the account of the *Revenge;* the difference is reflected in the markedly different style. There is a boyish exuberance about it all, like the zest of a fighter-pilot; the description of how Essex called out 'Entramos' and 'cast his hat into the sea for joy' is typical of the mood of the whole. The mood has its dangers: it may descend into a cocksure bravado, an unjustified contempt for the enemy and a delight in battle for its own sake. The only time Ralegh actually oversteps the mark is at the very end when his lust for loot and his spite at not being able to satisfy that lust are very apparent. In general, one is more impressed by the very real daring and skill that lie behind the racy narrative.

The letter wonderfully conveys Ralegh's excitement. Take the unusually vivid images, for example: 'They hoped to have stumbled the leading ship', 'I was first saluted by the fort called Philip', 'I bestowed a benediction amongst them', 'I laid out a warp by the side of the *Philip* to shake hands with her', 'The Flemings . . . used merciless slaughter till they were by myself and afterwards by my Lord Admiral beaten off'. The sheer energy of the account is remarkable. The sense of immediacy and participation is brought to the reader far more vividly than in most eye-witness narratives, yet Ralegh is no war-correspondent but a leading participant, fully and hotly engaged in the business of the battle and concerned in his report only to tell his correspondent just what happened. Here is an extract from the extraordinary description of the final plight of the Spanish Galleons:

> They all let slip and ran aground, tumbling into the sea heaps of soldiers, so thick as if coals had been poured out of a sack, in many ports at once—some drowned and some sticking in the mud. The *Philip* and the *St. Thomas* burned themselves; the *St.*

*Matthew* and the *St. Andrew* were recovered by our boats ere they could get out to fire them. The spectacle was very lamentable on their side, for many drowned themselves; many, half-burned, leapt into the water; very many hanging by the ropes' ends by the ships' side under the water even to the lips; many, swimming with grievous wounds, strucken under water and put out of their pain; and, withal, so huge a fire, and such tearing of the ordnance in the great *Philip* and the rest when the fire came to them, as if any man had a desire to see Hell itself, it was there most lively figured.

In such a passage, we can see that the thrill of the romance and glory of war is not the whole of Ralegh's attitude and that the utter disenchantment with war which finds expression in *The History of the World* and the *Discourse of the Cause of War* is perhaps born of a very real and personal knowledge of the suffering to the unoffending that is brought by the ambitious schemes of contending States.

Other naval and military adventures of his own, or that he heard from the lips of participants, are scattered about the *History,* where they are used for comment of various kinds—the assault on Fayal during the Islands Voyage (V, I, ix) illustrating the theory that it is easier to assault a coast than to defend it. These accounts are too fragmentary, however, to be discussed on their own.

There is no doubt that much of the appeal of Ralegh's 'prose of action' for the modern reader is that it gives us an easy entry into the heart of that unique world of Elizabethan maritime adventure—the Armada, Drake, the North-West passage, Hakluyt. Whether or no it is true that the sea is in the Englishman's blood, *writings* about the sea are: he thrills all the more to discovery, exploration and sea-battles when he has not to endure the hard-lying and scanty fare that inevitably attend them. Ralegh is a superb dispenser of Elizabethan adventure, and that without striving for effect. The plain statement of facts which opens his *Discovery of Guiana* captures the glamour of voyaging to far-off and little-known lands in a way an historical novelist might well envy:

> On Thursday the 6 of February in the year 1595, we departed England, and the Sunday following had sight of the north cape of Spain, the wind for the most part continuing prosperous; we passed in sight of the Burlings and the Rock, and so onwards for the Canaries, and fell with Fuerte Ventura the 17 of the same month, where we spent two or three days and relieved our companies with some fresh meat. From thence we coasted by the Gran Canaria, and so to Tenerife, and stayed there for the *Lion's Whelp,* your Lordship's ship, and for Captain Amyas Preston and the rest; but when after 7 or 8 days we found them not, we departed and directed our course for Trinidado with mine own ship and a small barque of Captain Cross's only (for we had before lost sight

> of a small gallego on the coast of Spain which came with us from Plymouth). We arrived at Trinidado the 22 of March, casting anchor at Point Curiapan, which the Spaniards call Punto de Gallo, which is situate in 8 degrees or thereabouts; we abode there 4 or 5 days, and in all that time we came not to the speech of any Indian or Spaniard: on the coast we saw a fire, as we sailed from the point Carao towards Curiapan, but for fear of the Spaniards, none durst come to speak with us.

. . . . .

Although it is true, and Ralegh excuses himself for it, that he has 'neither studied phrase, form nor fashion', *The Discovery of Guiana* is not simply a straightforward journal of events. He wanted to advertise the virtues of Guiana as a colony, and blended with direct description are passages of deliberate eloquence painting as attractive a picture as possible to the English reader who might have capital for investment. The 'earthly-paradise' passages . . . are very skilfully done and are a tribute to Ralegh's art rather than to the unconscious poetry in the soul of an explorer. However, the work stands by the freshness and vividness of its reporting rather than by Ralegh's powers of persuasion; it is in fact because it is a travel book without the literary vices of most travel books that it is so fine a literary work. The images have the spontaneity of a gay fancy: 'flowers and trees of that variety as were sufficient to make ten volumes of herbals'; along the river where tribes lived in tree-houses his boat grounded 'and stuck so fast as we thought that even there our discovery had ended and we must have left sixty of our men to have inhabited like rooks upon trees with those nations'; the marvellous crystal mountain was like 'a white church tower of exceeding height' and the torrent that dashed down it 'falleth to the ground with a terrible noise and clamour, as if a thousand great bells were knocked one against another'.

It is pathetic indeed to turn from the optimistic and eager narrative of the promise of Guiana to the wretchedness of Ralegh's various accounts of the utter failure of the 1618 expedition. . . . Here is different prose indeed; at times strained, hectic and disordered, but at times of great nobility, when Ralegh's spirit rises in passion against the injustice he has received or when, in the simplest words, despair records despair. . . . The **"Apology"** for his voyage is of course not at all in the same category with other 'prose of action' since it is less an account than an argument in self-justification. Though the language stutters at times with indignation and bitterness, it has its own distinction: Ralegh was almost incapable of writing badly. Is it so strange, he writes, that he should have failed in his enterprise 'being but a private man and drawing after me the chains and fetters wherewith I had been thirteen years tied in the Tower'? The long-drawn-out cadences carry the sense onwards though syntax is lost in the eagerness with which he writes:

> A strange fancy had it been in me to have persuaded my son, whom I have lost, and to have persuaded my wife to have adventured the eight thousand pounds which His Majesty gave them for Sherborne, and when that was spent to persuade her to sell her house at Mitcham, in hope of enriching them by the mines of Guiana, if I myself had not seen them with my own eyes; for being old and sickly, thirteen years in prison and not used to the air, to travail and to watching, it being ten to one that I should ever have returned, and of which by reason of my violent sickness and the long continuance thereof no man had any hope, what madness would have made me undertake this journey, but the assurance of the mine?

### The Prose of Reflection

The miscellaneous works of 'reflection' are an arid field: they do not increase our respect for Ralegh as a writer or a thinker though they show the breadth of his interests. The political writings are tedious, derivative and inconsistent. ***The Prince or Maxims of State*** and ***The Cabinet Council*** (the manuscript of which came into the hands of Milton, who published it) cannot be considered as original writings, so heavily do they rely on other authors, and as both the matter and the manner are uninteresting they may be left to the specialist in Renaissance political theory and the influence of Machiavelli on English thought. A more lively piece of political theory is ***The Prerogative of Parliaments in England,*** written during Ralegh's last years in the Tower and addressed to the King. Framed as a dialogue between a Counsellor of State and a Justice of the Peace, its retailing of constitutional history is enlivened by the disagreement of the protagonists and sharpened by the contemporary references and anecdotes which Ralegh intersperses. Ralegh has been attacked for being too much on the side of absolute monarchy, and Stebbing quite rightly defends him on the grounds that a Tudor courtier could not help looking at the monarchy with different eyes from those of the Long Parliament. He points out that Ralegh's tract was actually written to persuade the King to call a Parliament, and was far too much to the 'left' in tone for the pleasure of James's court. It is the Justice of the Peace who is given the better of the argument all along, as he defends the acts of Parliament throughout its history, sticks up for its rights and assures his opponent that Crown and Parliament are each other's helpmeets rather than antagonists. A note of adulation and deference to the King and his rights it would be extraordinary not to find in a work of persuasion addressed to His Majesty: Ralegh's candid opinion of monarchs can be seen in ***The History of the World*** where tact and diplomacy do not inhibit him as they do here—as when for example the Justice warns the Counsellor not to 'dig out of the dust the long-buried mem-

ory of the subjects' former contentions with the King'. 'What mean you by that?' asks the Counsellor. 'I will tell your Lordship when I dare', comes the answer. It is worth mentioning in passing that this work shows a far greater understanding of the dynamics of social and political change than all the pieces Ralegh translated from Italian theorists: 'The wisdom of our own age is the foolishness of another: the time present ought not to be referred to the policy that was but the policy that was to the time present: so that the power of the nobility being now withered and the power of the people in the flower, the care to content them would not be neglected.'

The style of the work calls for little comment: there is considerable variety, from the colloquial exchanges like this, on Richard II:

> Yet you see he was deposed by Parliament.

> As well may your Lordship say he was knocked on the head by Parliament,

to such heavy Old Testament rhythms as in:

> Nay, my Lord, so many other goodly manors have passed from His Majesty as the very heart of the kingdom mourneth to remember it, and the eyes of the kingdom shed tears continually at the beholding it: Yea, the soul of the kingdom is heavy unto death with the consideration thereof.

Other advice that the King received from his temerarious prisoner related to the proposed double match of Prince Henry and his sister with a princess and prince of the House of Savoy. Though Ralegh is always deferential when he speaks directly to James, the tone of the whole is very much man-to-man, and some of the implications are not exactly discreet, as, for example, when he speaks in disgust of the callousness of Kings in using their children as pawns in political chess. Both tracts—Ralegh wrote one opposing each of the two suggested marriages—are readable and convincing. Ralegh demonstrates the impolicy and uselessness of any alliance with Savoy, and hostility to Spain is the leit-motiv of his song—'It is the Spaniard that is to be feared: the Spaniard, who layeth his pretences and practices with a long hand.'

The way in which Ralegh tenders advice to his monarch is very unlike the way in which he lectures his own family. We could wish on the whole that Ralegh had not written his ***Instructions to his Son and to Posterity***. Here is a Polonius indeed (but a really strong-minded Polonius, whose advice is decidedly instruction) laying down the law on friendship, marriage, conduct, servants, economy, drink. The trouble with the instruction given is not that it is always faulty or over-prudent, but that the motivating spirit is worldly, politic and calculating. The very first chapter, on the choice of friends, is unpleasant in its cunning and its eyeing of the main chance. Friendships are never to be struck up with those who are poorer or inferior in rank because those friends will pursue the relationship for mercenary ends only, but 'let thy love be to the best so long as they do well; but take heed that thou love God, thy country, thy Prince and thine own estate before all others.' Or again, 'Take also special care that thou never trust any friend or servant with any matter that may endanger thy estate.'

The almost fanatic concern for the preservation of one's estate inspires all along the more repellent axioms. The words about the settlement one ought to make for one's wife are so remarkable that they should be given in full:

> Let her have equal part of thy estate whilst thou livest, if thou find her sparing and honest, but what thou givest after thy death, remember that thou givest it to a stranger, and most times to an enemy; for he that shall marry thy wife will despise thee, thy memory and thine, and shall possess the quiet of thy labours, the fruit which thou hast planted, enjoy thy love and spend with joy and ease what thou hast spared and gotten with joy and travail. Yet always remember that thou leave not thy wife to be a shame unto thee after thou art dead, but that she may live according to thy estate . . . But howsoever it be, or whatsoever thou find, leave thy wife no more than of necessity thou must, but only during her widowhood, for if she love again, let her not enjoy her second love in the same bed wherein she loved thee, nor fly to future pleasures with those feathers which Death hath pulled from thy wings, but leave thy estate to thy house and children in which thou livest upon earth whilst it lasteth.

The strange absence of any note of charity, love, liberality or selflessness is again impressive in a warning against borrowing and lending and standing surety. Take care, he says, 'that thou suffer not thyself to be wounded for other men's faults and scourged for other men's offences—which is, the surety for another, for thereby millions of men have been beggared and destroyed, paying the rockoning of other men's riot . . . If thou smart, smart for thine own sins, and, above all things, be not made an ass to carry the burdens of other men: if any friend desire thee to be his surety, give him a part of what thou hast to spare. If he press thee further, he is not thy friend at all.'

The end and aim of all the advice is self-interest. To see love of God conjoined with love of one's own estate, tempts us to think that the persuasion to godliness is but perfunctory and that Mammon is the real object of worship. And nowhere is there even lip-service paid to the other great commandment to love one's neighbour as oneself. But although the worldly wis-

dom of the homilies is suffocating, it is to be remembered that these injunctions are hardly intended by Ralegh to lay bare his 'philosophy of life'. Like some of Bacon's essays they have a limited end and narrow sphere of operation: they are specially designed as a guide to social behaviour in a particular social environment. In addition, it cannot be denied that a good deal of the advice is at least prudent and sensible and right-minded (though never great-hearted). The 'great care to be had in the choosing of a wife' has its moments as an essay in prose on the theme of 'conceit begotten by the eyes'. Even here, however, selfishness creeps in: he advises his son to take more care that his wife loves him 'rather than thyself besotted on her', but 'be not sour or stern to thy wife, for cruelty engendreth no other thing than hatred.'

It would be interesting to know how the *Instructions* were complied; they often seem to bear the stamp of a man who has just been stung by a disappointment or a piece of treachery and in his immediate mortification makes a note in his commonplace book to warn others. 'If thou trust any servant with thy purse, be sure thou take his account before thou sleep.' It would also be interesting to know the date of composition, and whether the style was at all influenced by Bacon's *Essays*. 'Speaking much, also, is a sign of vanity; for he that is lavish in words is a niggard in deeds . . . He that cannot refrain from much speaking is like a city without walls and less pains in the world a man cannot take, than to hold his tongue.' But the style in general has the tone of the Hebrew prophet: some quotation from the chapter on 'what inconveniences happen to such as delight in wine' may serve to illustrate this and conclude the discussion of the work:

> A drunkard will never shake off the delight of beastliness, for the longer it possesseth a man, the more he will delight in it, and the older he groweth, the more he shall be subject to it, for it dulleth the spirits and destroyeth the body as ivy doth the old tree and as the worm that engendreth in the kernel of the nut.

> Take heed, therefore, that such a cureless canker pass not thy youth, nor such a beastly infection thy old age, for then shall all thy life be but as the life of a beast and, after thy death, thou shalt only leave a shameful infamy to thy posterity, who shall study to forget that such a one was their father.

The difficulty with many of Ralegh's miscellaneous writings is that they hardly seem to be self-contained or completed works, or that they have perhaps been put together to serve some special purpose we know nothing about. *The Sceptic* is a translation from Sextus Empiricus, and we can only glean from other writings of Ralegh how far it is to be taken as representing his own views. The *Treatise on the Soul* one can hardly discuss at all without more knowledge. Strathmann, who calls it 'a summary of conventional beliefs', is not entirely certain of its authenticity; he suggests it may be rather an abstract of another work than an independent essay. It is certainly difficult to know what should have induced Ralegh to compose it, if he did. The modern reader who perseveres with the little treatise may feel the same impatience with the discussion that Ralegh himself felt with Ironside's attempts to define the nature of the soul.

No such lack of individuality marks a piece of a very different kind indeed, an essay on war, probably only in draft form or perhaps a fragment of a larger projected work, first printed in 1650 with the title *A Discourse of the Original and Fundamental Cause of Natural, Customary, Arbitrary, Voluntary and Necessary War*. This was probably written after *The History of the World;* Ralegh reflects on what must, after all his researches, have seemed the usual trade and occupation of mankind. Though ill-balanced as a whole, the essay is most powerfully written, and the attitude to war should be contrasted with that implied in the letter on the Cadiz action. It never enters Ralegh's head that war at any time is glorious; the farthest he goes in justifying it at all is to admit that it may be *necessary* to repel an invader and that it may be *legitimate* to occupy by force sparsely-inhabited regions—though he points out that there is no clear division between a harmless occupation and the abominable war of invasion which carries in its train the extermination of a native population. On the causes of war, Ralegh speaks often in terms a modern can understand—discontent and unemployment at home will often make a ruler find a pretext for a war, and so will a heavy increase of population and the consequent need for *lebensraum*. But the chief cause of the chief kind of war (arbitrary war) is, of course, ambition:

> To speak in general: whosoever hath dominion absolute over some one, authority less absolute over many more, will seek to draw those that are not wholly his own into entire subjection. It fares with politic bodies as with physical: each would convert all into their own proper substance, and cast forth as excrements what will not be changed.

Ralegh has the Elizabethan horror of civil war—'a greater plague cannot come upon a people'. Although he cannot share the Tudor belief in the divinity of monarchy, believing as he does that laws are man-made and can, theoretically, be changed by the will of man, he does argue that since human nature is imperfect, all human government is imperfect, and that it is far, far better to acquiesce in obedience to the established government than to institute chaos and anarchy by setting out to introduce another form of government by means of civil war. In any case, civil dissension never proceeds from principles or high motives: the perpetual restlessness of mankind is used by the avarice, ambition and vengefulness of the few. Liberty is but a word in the mouth in time of civil war: 'The common people of England have suffered the same fate as other nations: they have been drawn with heat and fury to shed one another's blood for such a liberty as their leaders never intended they should have.' This thought leads Ralegh on to a great passage of pity for all who die in war ignorant of the base and selfish ends they have given their lives to promote:

> What deluded wretches, then, have a great part of mankind been, who have either yielded themselves to be slain in causes which, if truly known, their heart would abhor, or been the bloody executioners of other men's ambition! 'Tis a hard fate to be slain for what a man should never willingly fight, yet few soldiers have laid themselves down in the bed of honour under better circumstances.

Whether one agrees with Ralegh's attitude or not, the intellectual power of his work must be recognised; the insoluble puzzle is to know how the author could also be the author of *Instructions to his Son* and the compiler of *Maxims of State*.

We shall leave aside the multitude of short tracts which show the insatiable curiosity of Ralegh's mind, discourses on the invention of ships, on war with Spain, orders to be observed by commanders of his fleet, observations touching trade and commerce with the Hollander, and turn now to the great history of the world.

### *The Composition of The History of the World*

Of his temerity in setting out, an ageing prisoner, to write a history of the world that should be no mere sketch or popular account, but a comprehensive record of all ages past, Ralegh was himself fully aware. 'In whom had there been no other defect (who am all defect) than the time of the day, it were enough: the day of a tempestuous life, drawn on to the very evening ere I began.' Had he started the work in his youth and freedom, 'I might yet well have doubted that the darkness of age and death would have covered over both it and me long before the performance'. An undertaking so preposterously difficult in the circumstances, none but a Ralegh would have had the daring to consider or the self-confidence to embark upon. It is Virginia and Guiana in the world of learning; not the diligence and the energy even of a Ralegh could carry the colossal project to completion. When the task was begun it is impossible to say: the plan must have been maturing in his mind for years, certainly before the 1607 (or 1608) often conjectured as a starting-point. Some hint that the first volume was nearing its conclusion in 1611 is given by an entry in the Stationers' Register of that year, but it was not until 1614 that there appeared a

*Title page of Raleigh's* The History of the World *(1614).*

folio without title-page, giving in 1,000,000 words the story of mankind from the Creation to Rome in the second century B.C. That Ralegh intended, and indeed had 'hewn out', a second and third volume, he tells us himself at the close of the first, adding that many discouragements 'persuaded his silence', including the death of the young Prince Henry, to whom the work had been directed. The work was well received by all save King James, who found his prisoner 'too saucy in censuring princes', and through the century it achieved a real eminence of favour, especially with the republicans: Cromwell recommended it, Milton used it. Ralegh's bibliographer, T. N. Brushfield, gives a list of eleven editions published before the turn of the century. But fashions in history change: there seem to be only three editions between 1687 and the present day; the last edition was 1829. Matthew Arnold made a disparaging comparison of Ralegh's method with that of Thucydides. There are, however, some signs that the work is more charitably received than it was in the last century, though it must be confessed that no one would dream of turning to it as an authority. It is, frankly, not the history that really interests *us;* but that it is more than an empty monument of English prose, I shall try to demonstrate in the succeeding pages.

There has been some sharpness in the arguments on how much Ralegh was indebted to others in composing the ***History***. It is not to be expected that such a work could have been written by the most learned historian (which Ralegh was not) without consultations with others any more than without using other men's books. Ben Jonson (in his cups) claimed that 'the best wits in England were employed for making of his History' and that he himself 'had written a piece to him of the Punic War which he [Ralegh] altered and set in his book'. What sounds in Jonson's mouth like the immoral employment of other men's brains is presumably only a rather extended use of any scholar's practice of asking for information and clarification among his acquaintances. For Ralegh, the physical difficulty of seeing all the works he wished to consult must have been great, and he must have been forced to rely upon learned friends more than he would have done had he had freedom of movement. Traditionally, among his helpers are named Dr. Robert Burhill (for 'Mosaic and Oriental antiquities'), Harriot and the two other 'magi' of Ralegh's fellow-prisoner Northumberland, and Sir John Hoskyns. Ralegh indicates in the Preface the sort of consultation he practised, when he acknowledges his ignorance of Hebrew and says that occasionally he has 'borrowed the interpretation of some of my learned friends.'

Rather more perturbing evidence of reliance on others has been found in the first chapter, in the account and explanation of the Creation. That much of Ralegh's philosophy as revealed here is conventional and familiar is immaterial: we have learned to expect from Ralegh the rephrasing of traditional and time-honoured thought. But it appears that the extremely learned citations of authorities gathered at the foot of these early pages are sometimes dust in the eyes of the reader. Dr. Arnold Williams has explained [in *Studies in Philology*, xxxiv, 1937] how anyone who wished to gather all the opinions expressed by theologians on the first three chapters of Genesis would find them most conveniently collected for him in many commentaries. Such a commentary was that of Benedict Pererius, *Commentariorum et Disputionum in Genesin*. Ralegh hardly mentions Pererius in his footnotes, but Dr. Williams shows that the impressive review of the schoolmen and church-fathers is not based on original reading but is simply taken out of Pererius's commentary, even to the point of fairly close translation in the text itself. Once, indeed, Ralegh slips in translation. 'Beroaldus affirmeth that *bdela* in Hebrew signifieth "pearl": so doth Eugubinus; and Jerome calls it "oleaster".' Unfortunately, in Pererius's Latin text, Jerome Oleaster is the name of another authority who supports the interpretation that *bdela* means 'pearl'. This discovery of Ralegh's reliance on ready-made commentaries does not mean that he has surrendered his own interpretations and his liberty of conjecture. But before we congratulate Ralegh on the wide reading he undertook for his ***History,*** we must remember such short cuts as these which he ingeniously and silently took.

### *The Purpose of History*

In composing a history of the world, Ralegh gives very much more than a record of events. To begin with, 'history' is an all-embracing term: almost every known branch of learning is used or discussed in the work—philosophy, theology, comparative religion, ethics, geography, astronomy and astrology, political theory, biblical criticism, and the art of war. This is so, not because, as an historian, Ralegh likes to indulge in asides or in a little trespass outside his province, or even that his work must take cognisance of the fruits of research in other branches of knowledge. There is simply no segmentation of these different learnings; Ralegh's study is Man, and all aspects of that study are as one. An account of Man which concentrated on political history or social history would have seemed false and partial history. Ralegh begins his ***History*** at the Creation not merely because he must begin at the beginning, but because he cannot separate history from metaphysics, and the history of man is meaningless unless prefaced with a conception of the nature of man, his relation with God and the purpose of his being on earth at all. Like the ideal epic poem, Ralegh's ***History*** was to expound 'all ye know and all ye need to know'; it is indeed an interpretation of man, explained in terms of his history.

Again, the notion of history as a faithful presentation of the events of the past for the reader to find what interpretation and derive what profit he can from them was quite foreign to Renaissance ideas. No historian considered an accumulation of accurate facts as his objective. The 'ending end of all earthly learning', said Sir Philip Sidney, is 'virtuous action'. Knowledge for knowledge sake was meaningless; knowledge was for the betterment of the individual and society, and the scholar had to make clear the present and immediate value of his researches. History was understood to be a study of the past undertaken in order to throw light on the events of the present—and what had no contemporary application was not worth the recording. From a study of history, Puttenham the rhetorician said, a man learns 'what is the best course to be taken in all his actions and advices in this world'. Ralegh is at one with his age in considering history to be justified only in so far as it serves to instruct men how to behave in the sight of their fellow-men and in the sight of God. His great Preface is called by a modern scholar [L. B. Campbell] the 'fullest and most inspired expression' of 'the great tradition' of the Renaissance view of the use of history.

History, Ralegh explains, multiplies almost infinitely the experience available to any one man in his lifetime; history 'hath given us life in our understanding', we behold plainly our long dead ancestors living again and by the example of their fortunes and follies learn what, in our own lives or our own society, is meet to be followed and pursued. 'We may gather out of history a policy no less wise than eternal, by the comparison and application of other men's fore-passed miseries with our own like errors and ill-deservings.' In the body of the *History* we find scattered such observations as that the 'end and scope of all history [is] to teach by examples of time past such wisdom as may guide our desires and actions' (II, 21, vi).

The doctrine that history must always convey its lesson to modern times can be seen on the pragmatic level in the realm of social conduct and of state 'policy'. Ralegh always draws the moral of the story. Darius fights the invader Alexander instead of breaking his fury by delaying tactics (IV, 2, iii). 'The invaded', comments Ralegh, 'ought evermore to fight upon the advantage of time and place. Because we read histories to inform our understanding by the examples therein found, we will give some instances of those that have perished by adventuring in their own countries to charge an invading army . . .' Asides like this are everywhere to be seen. Opening the *History* quite at random, one finds that the life of the king Amazia gives rise to a very interesting little essay on the uselessness of a regime of severity to cover weakness in the personality of the ruler. A section on the strife of the Carthaginians with their mercenaries is followed by a long section of general reflection on a tyranny and its consequences. Every effect noted in the *History* is given a cause—'Such was the recompense of his treachery . . .'

Every incident is searched for its bearing on matters of general interest. What Ralegh gathers from the story of Samson is amusing enough (II, 15, i). The first comment is on Samson's mother being forbidden strong drink during her pregnancy: 'it seemeth that many women of this age have not read, or at least will not believe this precept; the most part forbearing not drinks; . . . filling themselves with all sorts of wines and with artificial drinks far more forcible: by reason whereof, so many wretched feeble bodies are born into the world, and the races of the able and strong men in effect decayed.'

But although this kind of moralising, in things both of little and great importance in worldly action, is rooted in Ralegh's method, and although it gives a constant alertness to all he says, for not an action is noted unless it can be made to bear fruit, yet it is but dallying beside the main purpose of the *History*. Ralegh's phrase was 'a policy no less wise than eternal' and that which really inspires him is not worldly wisdom but the desire to show how human history, which is a record of God's providence and His judgments on the deeds of humankind, provides constant lessons to all who study it, princes and private men, how to frame their lives in a manner acceptable to God. For Ralegh, God is with mankind from the beginning to the end of Time, punishing and rewarding and bringing to pass in every least action. So that in writing history, we teach by the examples of the rise and fall of great men and great nations 'for what virtue and piety God made prosperous and for what vice and deformity he made wretched'. 'God's judgments upon the greater and the greatest have been left to posterity, first, by those happy hands which the Holy Ghost hath guided [in the Old Testament], and secondly by their virtue who have gathered the acts and ends of men mighty and remarkable in the world [historians].' Since God's judgments do not vary, what his providence and justice allotted to past ages and different empires he will allot to our own day and age. 'We find that God is everywhere the same God.'

> The judgments of God are for ever unchangeable; neither is he wearied by the long process of time and won to give his blessing in one age to that which he hath cursed in another. Wherefore those that are wise, or whose wisdom, if it be not great, yet is true and well grounded, will be able to discern the bitter fruits of irreligious policy, as well among those examples that are found in ages removed far from the present as in those of latter times.

To prove how the examples of past times act as a warning to men of the present to avoid incurring the wrath of God, Ralegh in his Preface runs rapidly—and devastatingly—through the lives of the kings of England pointing out their viciousness and the harvest they reaped.

Such then is the purpose and intention Ralegh had in compiling a history of the world. Not to present only an accurate record of the main events of the past, but to give a picture of man, his nature and development, for the purpose of inculcating in his readers the wisdom they needed so to guide their steps in this world as to achieve God's blessing. This aim Ralegh shares with all his contemporaries who dealt with the past, whether it be Shakespeare in his historical plays or Holinshed in his Chronicles. . . .

### Chronology and Miracles

The modern reader will find the contents-list of ***The History of the World*** exceedingly odd. The problems of chronology presented by Genesis and the Old Testament have ceased to worry us; the life-spans of the patriarchs, the location of Paradise, the kind of wood used for the Ark, are no longer of vital concern to the serious historian. The space given to the retelling of Hebrew history would seem less disproportionate had Ralegh carried his work on to later volumes, but even so, the attention he gives it shows that the various epochs had a quite different value for Ralegh than for us and that he had a loyalty to the Old Testament as an historical record which a later age has rejected. Fidelity to the Bible is the cause of most of the strangeness of the appearance of the ***History*** and also the cause of most of Ralegh's difficulties in arranging his account of human affairs.

In the first place, there is 'that never resolved question and labyrinth of times'. Within the Old Testament there was a host of difficulties in establishing the proper dating of the events described, and then there was the problem of dovetailing into it the pagan records of antiquity. The difficulties of chronology that faced the Renaissance historian and the solutions which Ralegh put forward have been fully analysed by E. R. Strathmann: the enormous concern Ralegh had about the problems is evident in almost every chapter of the ***History*** and in the formidable chronological table in which Ralegh sets out his synchronisation of the various records available to him. Professor Strathmann has high praise for Ralegh's 'studious industry', and if we may tend to regret that so much diligence and time had to be spent in attempting to reconcile the irreconcilable, we can at least admire the seriousness and sobriety of Ralegh's methods. Cardinal with Ralegh is the truth of the Bible: to reconcile the Bible with itself he is prepared to spend all the endeavours of reason. Where in the end it is not possible to square differences and disagreements, as in the question of the length of time between the Flood and the birth of Abraham, it is not the Bible, but man's imperfect understanding that is to be blamed. Ralegh has not reached his confidence in the inviolability of the Scriptures without great struggle; like Sir Thomas Browne, he has fought the battle of Lepanto within himself. But having determined that, in spite of apparent inconsistencies and absurdities, the Bible presents an accurate record of history, he is prepared to go to infinite pains to explain as reasonable what may seem dark to human understanding. Chapter Seven of the first book, an account of the Flood, is one of profound interest as an example of Ralegh's method. He takes in every account of the great floods of antiquity, assesses with scrupulous care the evidence on the various problems associated with the story—his witnesses ranging from Galileo to soothsayers he has spoken with in America. The whole exposition is a remarkable example of Ralegh's 'use of new learning to bolster old belief', to use Professor Strathmann's phrase.

The details of Ralegh's chronological struggles need not concern us: his acceptance, for example, of Egyptian records but his denial that they can be taken at their face value as appearing to prove 'men before Adam'. But there are other difficulties the solving of which provides a good deal that is of interest to the modern reader, like the relation of ancient non-biblical legends and early history to the Old Testament. His attitude to pagan legends in general is that they are dark expressions of truths to be found in the Scriptures:

> Now as Cain was the first Jupiter, and from whom also the Ethnicks had the invention of sacrifice: so were Jubal, Tubal and Tubalcain (inventors of pastorage, smithscraft and music) the same which were called by the ancient profane writers Mercurius, Vulcan and Apollo . . .

Although the muddle is sometimes appalling, when Moses, Prometheus, Hercules, Hermes Trismegistus and Aesculapius are all thrown together and their achievements rationally discussed, one has to admire Ralegh for his earnestness within the framework of his assumptions. And his conviction, in dealing with Greek legends, that 'most fables and poetical fictions were occasioned by some ancient truth, which either by ambiguity of speech or some allusion they did maimedly and darkly express' anticipates modern reconstructions of the historicity of the legendary heroes of Greece and Crete—even though his own rationalising of Minos or Oedipus may not provide food for more than amusement.

As with chronology and pre-history, so with miracles: the testimony of Scripture must not be impeached, but must be supported by every effort of reason. This is not to say that Ralegh tries to explain away miracles by a naturalistic interpretation—quite the reverse. The passage of the Israelites across the Red Sea (II, 3, viii) is discussed with an awe-inspiring fund of information, geographical and scientific, to prove that the rolling back of the waters could have come about in no other way but by the direct hand of God.

But in spite of our admiration for the intellectual energy Ralegh shows, it is undoubtedly a relief to turn from his attempts to use the Old Testament as a basis for the early history of mankind and make it yield a reasonable account (wrestlings which Ralegh's faith demanded and which ours does not) to the less debatable ground of Greek and Roman history. There the settling of problems which by their nature cannot be settled, no longer hinders the unrolling of Ralegh's map of human achievement.

. . . . .

### The Style of the 'History'

The greatest writing in the **History** is in the passages of general reflection we have been quoting from. Even though the quotations are not so full as they should be to give the proper flavour of Ralegh's prose, their length will indicate how Ralegh achieves his effects not by the single pregnant of illuminating phrase, but by the onward surge of a paragraph. His prose is like the sea whose majesty is not in single waves but in the piling up of wave upon wave against the shore. Long and intricate sentences and balanced clauses build up passage after passage of solemnity and dignity. The rhythm is never staccato, but is sometimes kept moving and flowing almost for a whole folio page before it sinks to rest. One example will serve to show the architecture of his prose; in the following passage he is talking of the seven ages of man and has come to describe the last, which is compared to Saturn:

> wherein our days are sad and overcast, and in which we find by dear and lamentable experience and by the loss which can never be repaired, that of all our vain passions and affections past, the sorrow only abideth. Our attendants are sicknesses and variable infirmities, and by how much the more we are accompanied with plenty, by so much the more greedily is our end desired, whom when Time hath made unsociable to others, we become a burthen to ourselves, being of no other use than to hold the riches we have from our successors. In this time it is, when (as aforesaid) we for the most part, and never before, prepare for our eternal habitation, which we pass on unto with many sighs, groans and sad thoughts, and in the end by the workmanship of death finish the sorrowful business of a wretched life, towards which we always travel both sleeping and waking: neither have those beloved companions of honour and riches any power at all to hold us any one day, by the glorious promise of entertainments; but by what crooked path soever we walk, the same leadeth on directly to the house of death, whose doors lie open at all hours and to all persons. For this tide of man's life, after it once turneth and declineth, ever runneth with a perpetual ebb and falling stream, but never floweth again; our leaf once fallen, springeth no more, neither doth the sun or the summer adorn us again with the garments of new leaves and flowers. (I, 2, v).

Though the imagery is often formal and conventional and too little varied, metaphorical writing often brings great power. When he talks of the blindness of the Greeks to their danger from Philip, he writes: "Indeed it was not in their philosophy to consider that all great alterations are stormlike, sudden and violent, and that then it is overlate to repair the decayed and broken banks when great rivers are once swollen, fast-running and enraged."

It must be said that Ralegh's narrative style, though never dull, is not the most brilliant. Not that there is not vividness: the story of Alexander moves in alert fashion, enlivened by sudden sallies of the historic present. Indeed, the chapter on Alexander is probably the very best in the work; for narrative, description, reflection and interpretation, it is a typical example of Ralegh's methods and an outstanding example of his style. He seems to have absorbed and assimilated his material and to be writing from himself. Elsewhere, Ralegh seems unable to make the actions of the past live with the vividness he had given in his younger years to the accounts of actions in which he had himself taken part. But it is a saving grace of the **History** that both matter and manner are made fresh and insistent by the constant introduction of contemporary events. These intercalations show how alive Ralegh's own imagination was and how much history was for him what he claimed it to be—a comment from the past on the sort of actions and experiences undergone by modern man. There can be nothing dead in history to a man for whom every least incident stirs his memory and brings out a parallel incident from his own experience. And the reader's imagination also is kept alert by being constantly reminded of the unfailing relevance of history. Ralegh never fails to write interestingly when he dips into the rich store-house of his experience, and the style of the **History** is kept abundantly alive by his asides. He relates the smoking out of the enemy from the caves of Languedoc during the French civil wars, his landing at Fayal, the assault on Cadiz. Sometimes it is just an anecdote: Alexander's intolerance of an insult recalls Sir John Perrot's famous scoff at Elizabeth, which more than anything else caused his ruin; the furnishing of the dark corridors of history by conjecture he compares to the inventiveness of map-makers, and relates the story of Don Pedro de Sarmiento, Ralegh's prisoner, who put an island in a map to please his wife. Towards the end of the work, when Ralegh has presumably realized that he will never extend his history to modern times, there is a far greater introduction of parallels and illustrations, not only from Ralegh's experience, but from the whole of modern history. It is very important to remember that the dipping into his own memory and the drawing of parallels ancient and modern are not tokens of a meandering, conversational attitude to history, but evidence of the way in which Ralegh's whole mind was engaged on what he was writing. Nothing was

*Engraving of Sir Walter Raleigh by Simon Passe which appeared in the third edition of* History of the World.

foreign, nothing separate and useless. Like the poet that he was, his whole experience, in seemingly distinct spheres, stood alert and at call to furnish an illustration or provide a comment.

*Video meliora proboque; deteriora sequor.* One would think, as Ralegh drives home the shining moral of his **History,** that all the lusting after the rewards of men and the battling for might and empire are but the building of Babel, impious strivings that cannot buy lasting satisfaction in this life and forbid all hope of salvation—one would think that he had achieved in himself that patience and wisdom and understanding, that clear-eyed rejection of the world with its storms and strains and false values, which came to King Lear as he went prisonwards:

> so we'll live
> And pray, and sing, and tell old tales, and laugh
> At gilded butterflies and hear (poor rogues)
> Talk of court-news, and we'll talk with them too—
> Who loses and who wins, who's in, who's out,
> And take upon's the mystery of things
> As if we were God's spies. And we'll wear

> out,
> In a wall'd prison, packs and sects of great ones,
> That ebb and flow by the moon.

Upon such sacrifices the gods indeed throw incense. But Ralegh was still to give the most frightening confirmation of his own vision of unteachable man, who will not, because he cannot, renounce his affection for what the world has to offer. Two years after the publication of the **History of the World** Ralegh wins his freedom to prosecute his mad endeavour in Guiana, to win back those things his words had constantly and insistently declared to be a nothingness: honour, position and wealth. He denied his own better knowledge in coveting those things, and the utter and wretched failure of his mission is really the final word and seal upon his historian's survey of the futility of ambition.

> When is it that we examine this great account? Never while we have one vanity left us to spend; we plead for titles till our breath fail us, dig for riches whiles our strength enableth us, exercise malice while we can revenge, and then, when Time hath beaten from us both youth, pleasure and health, and that nature itself hateth the house of old age, we remember with Job that we must go the way from whence we shall not return, and that our bed is made ready for us in the dark . . .

> But what examples have ever moved us? What persuasions reformed us? Or what threatenings made us afraid? We behold other men's tragedies played before us; we hear what is promised and threatened; but the world's bright glory hath put out the eyes of our minds, and these betraying lights (with which we only see) do neither look up towards termless joys nor down towards endless sorrows, till we neither know nor can look for anything else at the world's hands.

## Christopher Hill (lecture date 1962)

SOURCE: "Ralegh—Science, History, and Politics," in *Intellectual Origins of the English Revolution,* 1965. Reprint by Oxford at the Clarendon Press, 1980, pp. 131-224.

*[In the following excerpt, taken from an expanded version of a lecture originally delivered at Oxford University in 1962, Hill provides an overview of Ralegh's social, political, and intellectual background, focusing in particular on the courtier's literary and scientific pursuits and his involvement in foreign policy during the reigns of Elizabeth I and James I.]*

Sir Walter Ralegh was born in 1554, so he was not fifty when Elizabeth died and his career as a royal favourite came to an end. But Ralegh had been no mere courtier. He founded the first English colony in America, in Virginia, though it failed to survive. He wrote *The Discovery of Guiana,* a first-rate travel book as well as a classic of empire. But within a year of James I's accession the great proponent of anti-Spanish policies was condemned to death on a highly dubious charge of conspiring with Spain. He was imprisoned in the Tower, where he wrote the *History of the World*. In 1616 he was released to sail to Guiana, whence he promised to bring back gold for the King without fighting the Spaniards. He brought no gold, and he did fight the Spaniards: in 1618 he was executed, at the demand of the Spanish ambassador, Gondomar.

At first sight Ralegh would seem an unsuitable Parliamentarian and Puritan hero: the unpopular favourite at Queen Elizabeth's court, with the reputation of an atheist; the man who was made to blush in the Parliament of 1601 when his monopoly of playing cards was attacked, and whose 'sharp speech' in defence of his office as Lord Warden of the Stannaries caused a 'great silence' in the House. But 'the country hath constantly a blessing for those for whom the court hath a curse'; to be publicly tried and executed for treason was a sure way to popularity under the old monarchy, a posthumous popularity that the Earl of Essex shared with Ralegh. And his two trials dramatized Ralegh's anti-Spanish position.

There are many other reasons why Ralegh's name carried weight with the seventeenth-century revolutionaries. If we ask ourselves what were the main changes which the political revolutions of the century brought about, I suppose we should say (i) a decline in the power of the crown *vis-à-vis* Parliament; (ii) the adoption of an aggressive imperialist foreign policy; (iii) an extension of economic liberalism; (iv) the redistribution of taxation; (v) the beginnings of religious toleration; and I should like to add (vi) the triumph of modern science. To all these changes Ralegh contributed significantly. Let us look at each of them in turn, starting with science.

In her work, *Leicester, Patron of Letters,* Miss Rosenberg has established Ralegh as the heir of Leicester's patronage. After what she modestly described as a fairly thorough survey of the field, she concluded that 'the writers and scientists associated with the patriotic cause of establishing England's empire in the western world dedicated their works by common consent to its acknowledged leader Sir Walter Ralegh and to those openly associated with his plans for exploring and colonizing America'. I shall return to this 'clearly defined propaganda campaign' later. At the moment I wish only to draw attention to Ralegh's inheritance of Leicester's influence. Ralegh, we are told, hired Thomas Churchyard to write a play in the cause of Leicester's foreign policy.

Ralegh was in many ways the heir of Sir Philip Sidney and his group, as well as of Sidney's uncle Leicester—not least in his patronage of science. Sidney and his friend Sir Edward Dyer (Leicester's secretary) at one time took lessons in chemistry from John Dee. Before and after Sidney's death Dyer acted as patron to Dee, as well as to Thomas Digges, Humphrey Cole the instrument-maker, and John Frampton, the merchant who had been racked in the Spanish Inquisition and who was a translator of scientific books and a propagandist for overseas expansion. The younger Hakluyt had been a protégé of Dyer and the Sidney group: his *Divers Voyages* of 1582 was dedicated to Sidney. Michael Lok dedicated to Sidney his map designed to show English priority in the exploration of North America. Timothy Bright, the inventor of shorthand, dedicated more than one of his books to Sidney, with whom in 1572 he had taken refuge from the Massacre of St. Bartholomew in the English Embassy. Bright was the author of a popular treatise on melancholy in which he compared the human mind to a clock or a windmill: Shakespeare and Robert Burton both probably studied this treatise. Bright was also a supporter of chemical medicine, and published an abridgement of Foxe's *Acts and Monuments,* dedicated to Sir Francis Walsingham.

Bright was an enthusiastic Ramist, as were most members of the Sidney group. De Banos's life of his master was dedicated to Sidney in 1576 because of Ramus's affection and respect for him. Sidney's tutor, Nathaniel Baxter, was a supporter of Cartwright, a translator of Calvin, and commentator on Ramus, whom he venerated. His commentary on Ramus's *Dialectics* contained a foreword to Fulke Greville. Sidney paid for the education of Abraham Fraunce, who became a noted Cambridge Ramist and Puritan. Fraunce dedicated several unpublished Ramist treatises to 'his very good master and patron Mr. Philip Sidney'. William Temple, the most important English Ramist, dedicated his edition of Ramus's *Dialectics* to Sidney in 1584, and in consequence became his secretary. Milton's Preface to the *Art of Logic* cites Sidney for the view (which Milton shared) that Ramus was the best writer on the subject. Sidney, in recommending arithmetic and geometry to his brother Robert in 1580, added that Ciceronianism was the worst abuse of Oxford men, 'qui dum verba sectantur, res ipsas negligunt'. 'All is but lip-wisdom, which wants experience', cried Musidorus in *Arcadia.* And Fulke Greville observed that

> Sciences from Nature should be drawn
> As arts from practice, never out of books.

Sidney's friend Daniel Rogers wrote a poem *In Indignissimum Petri Rami fatum* on Ramus's death in the Massacre of St. Bartholomew. When Bruno visited England in 1582 he found the scholastic atmosphere of

Oxford uncongenial: he hastened to London to enjoy the company of Sidney and Greville. Bruno dedicated two of his books to Sidney. 'Why turn to vain fancies', he asked, 'when there is experience itself to teach us?' The Sidney group was almost unique in England in welcoming Buchanan's criticisms of the Ancients in his *Rerum Scoticorum Historia.*

Ralegh was a friend of Sidney's, whom he quoted in *The History of the World,* and on whom he wrote a noble epitaph: his cousin and intimate friend, Sir Arthur Gorges, wrote two. Ralegh took over some of Sidney's patronage, notably that of Hakluyt. *The Faerie Queene,* which began under Sidney's patronage, was published with Ralegh's. Michael Lok translated *The Mexican History in Pictures* (1591) for Ralegh, at Hakluyt's instance. Richard Carew, a Cambridge contemporary and friend of Sidney's, dedicated his *Survey of Cornwall* to Ralegh in 1602. When Sidney's father, Sir Henry, died in 1586, Ralegh took over the patronage of John Hooker's *Irish Historie.* Sidney, devout Protestant though he was, was little more backward than Ralegh in plundering the Church.

The Sidney circle shared Ralegh's hostility to Spain and desire for a Dutch alliance, as well as 'that heroical design of invading and possessing America'. Fulke Greville's *Life of Sidney* was one of the most powerful expressions of this policy. Greville attributed to Sidney the view (shared by Ralegh) that the Spanish empire by its cruelty had flouted divine law and so was doomed. Greville, both in his own person and in Sidney's, spoke, like Ralegh, of the importance of freedom for the commercial classes, and especially for free access to the Spanish empire; and in favour of the yeomanry. Many of Greville's ideas, as has often been pointed out, anticipate or echo those of his friend Bacon: but his political speculations are much more daring. His scepticism compares with that of George Gascoigne and Ralegh. The *Life of Sidney* was first published in 1652, under the Commonwealth.

There are links between the political thought of the Sidney group and Ralegh, as well as in attitudes towards foreign policy. The Sidney circle admired the political theory of George Buchanan, and Greville showed lasting traces of his influence, as well as of that of his friend Duplessis-Mornay. So did Ralegh. Like Ralegh, Greville accepted the fact of rebellion, though both were anxious to deny it as a right. There are passages in the *Life of Sidney* which are closely parallel to *The Prerogative of Parliaments.*

Most interesting of all is the literary connexion. The Sidney group has been described as the workshop of the New Poetry; it is remarkable how often and how closely Ralegh's name is associated with them. Both in printed and manuscript collections his poems occur alongside those of Sidney, Greville, and Dyer; and his name is mentioned together with theirs in the main contemporary works of criticism. Between Spenser and Ralegh the links are obviously close, of ideas as well as in politics. The Preface and Conclusion to Ralegh's *History* seem to echo the Mutability Cantos. And Nature's reply to Mutabilitie in these cantos, it has been argued, anticipates the position which Hakewill took up against Goodman in denying the decay of the world. Change for Spenser is the fate of everything, and this change is both cyclical and not cyclical. All things

> By their change their being do dilate,
> And turning to themselves at length again
> Do work their own perfection so by fate:
> Then over them Change doth not rule and
>      reign,
> But they reign over Change, and do their
>      states maintain.

It is not without reason that Marvell (or whoever wrote *Britannia and Rawleigh*) quoted Spenser as well as Ralegh.

We first hear of Ralegh as a literary figure when he contributed a laudatory poem to George Gascoigne's *The Steel Glass* in 1576. Gascoigne was a friend and associate of Ralegh's half-brother, Sir Humphrey Gilbert. He was also one of the early translators of the classics who had suffered persecution. In *The Steel Glass* Ralegh no doubt approved of Gascoigne's social attitudes in criticizing officials, soldiers, lawyers, and exalting Piers Plowman: but it is notable too that the poem is written in blank verse, which Gascoigne himself claimed in his preface was a more exalted form, more effective for satire. Now we know that Sidney himself in the *Defence of Poesie* opposed 'the tinkling sound of rhyme, barely accompanied with reason'; and it appears to have been a settled conviction of his group, shared by Dyer and the puritanically-minded Thomas Drant.

A line of poets could be traced from Sidney and Spenser through Sylvester and Browne to Wither—not, admittedly, of a rising quality, but of a consistent political attitude. We might find that Milton bore more relation to this group than has been realized. We might also with profit reflect more, as Edward Thompson suggested, on the influence of Ralegh's prose on Milton's writings.

After the deaths of Sidney and Leicester, Ralegh continued their patronage of scientists and navigators. He helped Dee. Ralegh and Humphrey Gilbert planned to found a teaching and research academy in London, which would bring modern and practical subjects to royal wards and other sons of nobles and gentlemen—mathematics, cosmography, astronomy, naval and military training, navigation, shipbuilding, engineering, medicine, cartography, languages, and above all history. The teaching would be in English. The object of the academy was to teach 'matters of action meet for present practice': the doctor of physic would lecture alternately on physic and surgery. Elizabeth, however, was as unwilling to finance this academy as James I was to finance Bacon's schemes. As with many similar projects which lacked the capital backing of a merchant prince like Gresham, nothing came of it. Bacon, however, expected Ralegh's support for a scientific college. Ralegh's relative and ally Sir Arthur Gorges translated Bacon's *De Sapientia Veterum* into English, and his *Essays* into French, both in 1619.

. . . . .

Thomas Hariot, one of the greatest astronomers and mathematicians of his day, is another link between Ralegh and the Sidney circle. Hariot was successively mathematics tutor to Philip Sidney's younger brother Robert, to Ralegh, and to his son. As Viscount Lisle Robert Sidney was Hariot's executor when he died in 1621. Ralegh fully appreciated the importance of mathematics and astronomy for the art of navigation. In his lessons to Sir Walter and his sea-captains Hariot always contrived to 'link theory and practice, not without almost incredible results'. The words are Hakluyt's [in *Virginia Richly Valued*, 1609]. Hariot remained a protégé of Ralegh's—some said a deistic or atheistic influence on him. In fact there is no doubt of Hariot's faith, which he told his doctor was threefold—'in God Almighty, in medicine as being ordained by Him', and in 'the doctor as his minister'. 'I have learnt of you', one of Hariot's correspondents told him, 'to settle and submit my desires to the will of God.'

Ralegh, who made each of his voyages a scientific expedition, in 1585 sent Hariot as surveyor to Virginia with Sir Richard Grenville's expedition. Hariot's *Brief and True Report of the New Found Land of Virginia* (1588) was much admired by Hakluyt, who reprinted it. It is one of the earliest examples of a largescale economic and statistical survey, including 'marketable commodities' as well as a very sympathetic account of native religion and customs. (Hariot learnt the Indians' language and preached to them.) The first edition was illustrated by John White, another of Ralegh's protégés. The edition of 1590 included engravings of Picts, which showed that they had been as savage as the natives of Virginia: a notable contribution to historical imagination, which was used by Vico. Hariot was later an adviser to the Virginia Company. He acted as agent for Ralegh during the latter's absence at sea. He was one of Ralegh's constant associates during his imprisonment in the Tower, and the 'true and loving friend' of Sir Arthur Gorges.

Hariot was in close and friendly touch with Dee and Hakluyt, knew Gilbert and his work, corresponded with

Kepler on optics, and was using the telescope for astronomical purposes at about the same time as Galileo. Hariot produced telescopes for sale in the last twelve years of his life (1609-21). He first observed what we know as Halley's Comet, and is said to have predicted seven of the nine comets he saw. Hariot determined specific gravities by weighing in air and in water, though he did not publish his results. He was also 'one of the founders of algebra as we know the science today', and made advances towards its application to geometry. He believed in the existence of a North-Western Passage, and like Briggs wrote a treatise to prove it. He was held in the highest esteem by Briggs and by the early members of the Royal Society. Wallis thought that Hariot laid 'the foundation . . . without which that whole superstructure of Descartes (I doubt) had never been'. Descartes, we now know, had in fact read Hariot's *Artis Analyticae Praxis,* published posthumously in 1631. The Royal Society conducted a diligent but unsuccessful search for Hariot's papers in 1662-3. Some of them have been discovered recently, and historians of mathematics are astonished at the way in which 'deep Hariots mind, In which there is no dross but all's refined' had apparently solved some of the most complicated problems in navigational mathematics a whole generation before Napier, Briggs, and Gunter. But his tables, instruments, and rules for making charts were reserved for the use of Ralegh and his associates.

Hariot clearly felt constrained by the censorship, felt 'stuck in the mud'. In 1598 his friend George Chapman suggested that Hariot's writings could not be published 'now error's night chokes earth with mists', 'this scornful . . . world . . . her stings and quills darting at worths divine.'

Hariot leads us to consider the connexions between Ralegh and Henry Percy, ninth Earl of Northumberland, 'the wizard Earl'. They had been intimate since at least 1586, and political associates from about 1600. Northumberland, Essex's brother-in-law, protested vigorously against Ralegh's condemnation in 1603. But after Gunpowder Plot the Earl himself was sentenced to a fine of £11,000 and perpetual imprisonment for misprision of treason, on evidence not much stronger than that which had led to Ralegh's conviction. In the early fifteen-nineties, when Ralegh was in disgrace, a number of his followers, including Hariot and Robert Hues, passed from his service to Northumberland's, though Ralegh retained their close friendship. About this time George Peele apostrophized Northumberland

That artisans and scholars dost embrace
And clothest Mathesis in rich ornaments,
That admirable mathematic skill,
Familiar with the stars and zodiac.

Hariot drew a pension of £80, later £100, from

Northumberland from 1589 to 1621. Whilst the Earl was in the Tower, Hariot seems to have acted as supervisor of his affairs and tutor to his children. He was Librarian at Sion, Northumberland's house, and had a laboratory there. It seems to have been Hariot who first roused the Earl's interest in mathematics and astronomy. Northumberland was also interested in anatomy, medicine, geography, and cosmography: he had books by Napier, William Gilbert, Kepler, Tycho Brahe, Bruno, and Hakluyt in his library, and many others on chemistry, mathematics, and medicine. He advised his son to study—*inter alia*—arithmetic, geometry, the doctrine of motion, optics, astronomy, the doctrines of generation and corruption (alchemy and/or biology?), cosmography, and navigation.

Around Ralegh and Northumberland we can distinguish a literary and scientific group. This consisted of the Earl's 'three Magi'—Hariot, Robert Hues, and Walter Warner—together with the poet, mathematician, and Hermeticist, Matthew Roydon, a former friend of Sidney's, who may have written *Willobie His Avisa* as a defence of the Ralegh group, and George Chapman, who dedicated books to Ralegh and Bacon. Chapman spoke warmly of Hariot and Hues in the Preface to his translation of Homer. Hues had been an undergraduate at Brasenose College and then went to sea. He dedicated the first (Latin) edition of his *Treatise on Globes* to Ralegh in 1592. The dedication attacked the 'great ignorance' of the Ancients, and pleaded for more mathematical knowledge among navigators. Praised by Hakewill, it remained the standard work throughout the seventeenth century. There were thirteen editions before 1663. Hues was one of Ralegh's executors. He also acted as tutor to Northumberland's eldest son, the later Parliamentarian, and received a pension of £40 from the Earl. He is said to have had connexions with Gresham College. Warner, pensioner of Northumberland's, friend of Hakluyt and Gorges, continued Briggs's work on logarithms, and claimed to have given Harvey the idea which led to his discovery of the circulation of the blood. He was later alleged to have taught Thomas Hobbes all the mathematics he knew: Hobbes certainly had mathematical manuscripts of Warner's in his possession in 1634.

To these we must add Marlowe until his death in 1593—Marlowe who was once described as Ralegh's 'man', who 'read the atheist lecture to Ralegh and others', whose *Passionate Shepherd* Ralegh answered, whose *Hero and Leander* Chapman completed. Marlowe held discussions on Biblical criticism and comparative religion with Hariot, Warner, and Roydon, of a kind which scandalized the government's informers and helped to create the legend of Ralegh's 'school of atheism'. Marlowe is interesting for our purposes because he was very much aware of the potential political implications of the new science. This is the subject of *Doctor Faustus:* but the theme was also touched upon by Tamburlaine when he said

> Our souls, whose faculties can comprehend
> The wondrous architecture of the world,
> And measure every wandering planet's course,
> Still climbing after knowledge infinite,
> And always moving as the restless spheres,
> Will us to wear ourselves and never rest,
> Until we reach the ripest fruit of all,
> The perfect bliss and sole felicity,
> The sweet fruition of an earthly crown.

The very personal individualism of Tamburlaine's conclusion would not be shared by all those who appreciated his statement of the problem created by the new lust for knowledge and power over things. And Marlowe's own interest in the republican Lucan suggests that he too may have had more general ideas.

Giacopo Castelvetro, a radical Italian Protestant refugee, was probably in Northumberland's service from 1597 to 1607: he had previously been a protégé of Ralegh's. He published books on medicine and cryptography, and seems to have helped Hakluyt in his propaganda campaign on behalf of overseas exploration. In Italy Castelvetro was in trouble with the Inquisition as a relapsed Calvinist heretic, who believed in nothing; in England he was regarded as an Arian. Northumberland also gave a pension of £40 to the mathematician and astronomer Nathaniel Torporley (1564-1632), literary executor under Hariot's will. Among the other 'Atlantes of the mathematical world' who frequented Northumberland's household was Thomas Allen of Gloucester Hall, friend of Dee and Hariot, whom the Earl of Leicester had consulted as an astrologer.

In some ways the most interesting member of the group was Nicholas Hill, the first Modern to defend actively the atomic theories of Democritus and Epicurus. Hill was an intimate acquaintance of Ralegh's, and was in Northumberland's service. He helped the Earl with his alchemical and astrological experiments. Although Hill rejected all aristocratic patronage on principle, he dedicated his *Philosophia Epicurea* to the Earl's eldest son. Hariot appears to have considered atomism a plausible hypothesis, basing himself on Gilbert. Hill accepted the idea of a heliocentric and infinite universe, and of a plurality of worlds. He was discussed by Robert Burton, quoted by Wilkins, and looks forward to Hobbes and Locke in his mechanist philosophy. Hill is often described as a papist, apparently on the authority of John Aubrey. A Catholic who chose to live much of his life at Rotterdam, and whose books were published at Geneva, must have been something of an oddity. I suspect Hill was no more a Catholic than his patron the Earl of Northumberland. Finally, Richard Liburne, father of the future Leveller leader, was probably serving in the Earl's household when he married in 1599...

. . . . .

Ralegh, 'whose reading made him skilled in all the seas', was praised as early as 1586 as a patron of the sciences connected with navigation and exploration. He had a detailed knowledge of scientific and technological developments as they affected navigation, at a time when such a knowledge was regarded as lower-class and 'mechanical' rather than respectable and 'martial'. He was noted for his own experiments and innovations in shipbuilding, and appreciated the importance of having the most up-to-date style of pump in order to reduce dampness on board ship. He was a pioneer in naval medicine, dietetics, and hygiene. His orders for his voyage of 1617, stressing cleanliness, absence of litter between decks, and the precautions to be taken by landing parties in eating fruit, fish, and hogs, were well ahead of contemporary practice. He tried, though unsuccessfully, to discover from the Guianan Indians their remedy for the wounds made by poisoned arrows. The apothecary John Hester, whose running battle with the surgeons and physicians helped to establish Paracelsanism in England, dedicated *A Hundred and Foureteene Experiments of Paracelsus* to Ralegh in the early fifteen-eighties: in it Hester pleaded for liberty of research. The surgeon John Gerarde dedicated his *Herbal* to Ralegh in 1597. He may have been a subscriber to Ralegh's 1589 scheme for planting Virginia, as Thomas Hood certainly was.

During his imprisonment in the Tower Ralegh (like Northumberland) conducted chemical and medical experiments with the aid of the Puritan Lady Apsley, Lucy Hutchinson's mother. Bacon recorded this activity in his private notebook as a good omen for the future reception of his own philosophy of works. Among other things, Ralegh tried to distil fresh from salt water, to find ways of keeping meat fresh at sea, and to devise remedies against scurvy. He supplied medicines to many of his friends. His 'cordial' cured Queen Anne, and was cited in 1664 to prove 'the great advantages that the modern pharmacy carrieth legitimately above the ancient, by reason that it is enlightened with the glorious light of chemistry'. It was still used by Robert Boyle to cure fevers, and in 1712 Swift discussed it with Stella. Boyle's father, the great Earl of Cork, used to recommend his friend Ralegh's remedy for the spleen and the gravel.

In his *History* Ralegh praised Galileo, as Milton did in *Paradise Lost*. Ralegh accepted diurnal rotation of the earth, and owned a copy of Copernicus as well as of Machiavelli. Ralegh's opposition to the 'verbal doctrine' of Aristotle must have delighted Bacon, as his refusal to defer to the authority of the early Christian Fathers would delight Milton. Despite occasional professions of belief in the decay of the world, Ralegh

normally spoke up for the Moderns against the Ancients. The whole emphasis of the *History,* after a few preliminary genuflections, is on law as against chance. Even Ralegh's interest in magic links up with his interest in chemistry and medicine. Magic is 'the wisdom of Nature'. Referring specifically to 'the chemists', Ralegh said: 'The third kind of magic containeth the whole philosophy of nature; not the brabblings of the Aristoteleans, but that which bringeth to light the inmost virtues, and draweth them out of nature's hidden bosom to human use.' Magic he defined as 'the investigation of those virtues and hidden properties which God hath given to his creatures, and how fitly to apply things that work to things that suffer'. Magic, like science for Bacon, could be used for 'the help and comfort of mankind'. Bacon had thought that there was a core of physical knowledge in alchemy, magic, and astrology, which was worthy of scientific investigation. Sir Thomas Browne also believed that 'traditional magic' proceeded upon 'principles of nature'; 'at first a great part of philosophy was witchcraft'. Boyle later attempted the investigation which Bacon had proposed.

There is as yet no agreement among historians about the exact contribution of alchemy to the origins of scientific thinking. Paracelsus had boasted that natural magic and alchemy were 'firmly based on experience, . . . by which all arts should be proved'. For our purposes it is notable that Recorde, Dee, Thomas Digges, Gilbert, John Woodall, Napier, Matthew Roydon, and Nicholas Hill, as well as Copernicus, Bruno, and Kepler, were interested in magic; and that John Hester, the leading English exponent of Paracelsus's doctrine, had links with Ralegh. Dee defined 'archemistrie' as 'scientia experimentalis'. There was certainly an underground alchemical tradition which had long been handed on verbally: Richard Bostock in 1585 argued that Paracelsus was no more the inventor of chemistry than Wyclif, Luther, and Calvin were the inventors of the Gospel when they restored religion to its primitive purity. So long as Scotus and Aquinas were 'maintained, defended and privileged by princes and potentates, it was hard for truth to show his face abroad openly'. A reformation was as necessary in science now as it had formerly been in religion, to overthrow Aristotle, Galen, 'and other heathen and their followers', and allow 'the chemical doctrine agreeing with God's word, experience, and nature' to 'come into the schools and cities', relying on 'due trial by labour and work of fire and other requisite experiments'. Dee's Preface, as Professor [Hiram] Haydn pointed out [in *The Counter-Renaissance*], was in the Paracelsan alchemical tradition: it looked back as well as forwards. Marlowe's Faustus, the magician *par excellence,* defended Ramus against Aristotle as well as Paracelsus against Galen. In science, as in religion, the sixteenth century saw the break-through to respectability of ideas which had long seethed underground among the craftsmen. It is noteworthy how often the intellectual spokesmen of the plebeian religious radical movements were men with a medical background—from Paracelsus and Servetus to Chamberlen and Culpeper. The combination of chemistry with magic and radical religious convictions was repeated by John Webster in the sixteen-fifties: he quoted Dee's Preface.

We should beware of thinking that, because in the long run science shed alchemy and astrology, therefore every scientist who took these subjects seriously was a charlatan. Recorde, Dee, Digges, Napier, Copernicus, Kepler, Bacon are not so lightly to be dismissed. 'In those dark times', said Aubrey apropos Thomas Allen, 'astrologer, mathematician, and conjurer were accounted the same things.' So cool and level-headed asceptic as John Selden was at once a supporter of the new astronomy and a great admirer of Robert Fludd the Rosicrucian, who thought chemistry was the search for God. Selden himself used often to dive into the books of alchemists, astrologers, and soothsayers. If Ralegh believed in sympathetic medicines—and the evidence is dubious—so did Bacon and Fellows of the Royal Society, including Sir Kenelm Digby and John Locke, much later in the seventeenth century. What is interesting for us is Ralegh's defence of the alchemical tradition, which from Paracelsus to Webster, was more than once associated with religious and political radicalism.

. . . . .

'As theory, Ralegh's political writings have no importance whatsoever. He thought of nothing new.' Mr. Stapleton's first sentence does not seem to me to be proved by the second. It is true that Ralegh was not a Bodin, Hobbes, or a Harrington. It is that the *Cabinet Council*, the *Maxims of State,* and other works attributed to him are compilations with commentary, not original works. But these very compilations introduced some of the ideas of writers like Machiavelli and Bodin under the respectable shadow of Ralegh's name: and in the *Prerogative of Parliaments* he put forward a programme which opponents of the court in the sixteen-twenties found useful. Without claiming too much for the originality of Ralegh's political ideas, we may see some importance in the fact that they were collected together and systematized by the victim of Spain and James I.

We need not take too seriously the story, which Aubrey repeats, that Ralegh advocated a republic in 1663. But it is significant that during the years 1600-28 three English translations of Lucan—regarded as the republican poet *par excellent*—were published. The first was by Marlowe, a member of Ralegh's circle. The second was by Ralegh's cousin and close associate, Sir Arthur Gorges, with a congratulatory sonnet by Ralegh. The third was by Tom May, the future historian of the Long Parliament and the friend of the republican Henry Marten. Republican opinions were attributed to Ralegh in Marvell's *Britannia and Rawleigh* (if it is Marvell's); in 1683 there was a eulogistic biography of Shaftesbury called *Rawleigh Redivivus*—not Hampden or Pym or Vane or Cromwell, but Ralegh.

Ralegh's political thought ruthlessly emphasizes expediency, utility, in a way that anticipates Hobbes. In civil wars 'all former compacts and agreements for securing of liberty and property are dissolved, and become void: for flying to arms is a state of war, which is the mere state of nature, of men out of community, where all have an equal right to all things: and I shall enjoy my life, my subsistence, or whatever is dear to me no longer than he that has more cunning, or is stronger than I, will give me leave'. 'That any particular government is now *Jure Divino* is hard to affirm, and of no great use to mankind. For let the government of any country where I am a subject be by divine institution or by compact, I am equally bound to observe its laws and endeavour its prosperity.' James would not like that very much. The very title of *The Prerogative of Parliaments* must have sounded like a manifesto to the king who exalted his own royal prerogative, who thought that Parliament's liberties were derived from him by grace, and who considered that Ralegh's **History** had been 'too saucy in censuring princes'.

But it is difficult to extract a consistent political philosophy from Ralegh's writings. His account in the **History** of the origin of political society appears to derive from Buchanan, Sidney's favourite. Yet Ralegh also declared that the sovereign, the prince, is exempt from human laws; elsewhere he advocates an ultimate right of resistance, 'since no prince can shew a patriarchal right, and a community is under conditions'. In particular 'the common people of England' have often been persuaded to fight 'for such a liberty as their leaders never intended they should have'—hence their reputation abroad for 'a turbulent and disquiet spirit'. But the greatest liberty is good government, and this England has, at least potentially. Ralegh never suggested that monarchy was more acceptable to God. He had no use for theories of paternal government derived from God's grant to Adam of 'dominion over . . . every living thing that moveth upon the earth'. The rule of a king, on the contrary, is the rule of one freeman over others. In the Preface to the **History** Ralegh distinguished between a 'Turk-like' monarchy, such as Philip II tried to establish over the Netherlands, and the absolute monarchies of England and France. Asiatic despotism, with the consequent 'general want of liberty among the people', makes a foreign conquest 'easy and sure'. Whereas it was traditional to regard Nimrod as a subverter of liberty, Ralegh collected authorities who regarded him as a colonizer rather than a tyrant. Nimrod was a *de facto* ruler, elevated for sound Hobbist reasons, which Ralegh is at pains to make clear. With his accustomed slide from first to second causes, Ralegh argued that God first made men see the necessity of kingship, which he had ordained by his eternal providence; but '(speaking humanly), the beginning of empire may be ascribed to reason and necessity'; laws were soon established 'for direction and restraint of royal power'.

Ralegh in fact had a very Harringtonian view of the evolution of the English constitution. He approvingly quoted Bacon for the view that 'monarchs need not fear any curbing of their absoluteness by mighty subjects, as long as by wisdom they keep the hearts of the people. . . . Every sheriff and constable being sooner able to use the multitude, in the king's behalf, than any overweening rebel, how mighty soever, can against him. Ralegh was still thinking in traditional Tudor terms, of feudal revolt as the greatest danger, and of the middling sort as the natural supporters of sovereignty. He had after all helped to suppress Essex's revolt in 1601. Most of the laws of England, like Magna Carta, are Acts of Parliament, 'to the obedience of which all men are therefore bound, because they are acts of choice and self-desire'.

It is only when we come to *The Prerogative of Parliaments* that we see how far Ralegh would have limited kingly power. With an appearance of great objectivity, the Justice in Ralegh's dialogue makes out a case for political opposition to the crown—even violent opposition—in every historical instance which the Councillor brings forward. Ralegh's argument urges the King to abandon those councillors—including, though he is too wise even to hint this, the Spanish ambassador—who advise him to dispense with Parliaments. Ralegh's aim is to convince James that Parliament *cannot* be wished out of existence, because those whom it represents cannot be wished out of existence. Therefore the King would be prudent and well advised to co-operate with Parliament. For, Ralegh says in a Carlylean passage, 'that policy hath never yet prevailed (though it hath served for a short season) where the counterfeit hath been sold for the natural, and the outward show and formality for the substance'. 'Shall the head yield to the feet? certainly it ought, when they are grieved', as they are, for example, by monopolies, impositions, arbitrary imprisonment, and refusal of free speech in Parliament. The remedy for the financial difficulties of the Crown 'doth chiefly consist in the love of the people', which 'is lost by nothing more than by the defence of others in wrongdoing—the only motives of mischances that ever came to kings of this land since the Conquest'.

The tone is mild and persuasive, but the implied threat is clear. When the J.P. (who represents Ralegh's point of view in the dialogue) mentioned digging 'out of the dust the long buried memory of the subjects' former contentions with the king', the Councillor asked sharp-

ly 'What mean you by that?' 'I will tell your Lordship, when I dare', was the reply. 'To say that his Majesty knows and cares not, that, my Lord, were but to despair all his faithful subjects.' 'It cannot be called a dishonour, for the King is to believe the general Council of the kingdom, and to prefer it before his affection.' James will do himself no good by kicking against the pricks: even kings are subject to historical necessity. This doctrine would not be unacceptable to Parliamentarians who could not counter the traditional royal arguments, but felt that they had a stronger case than they could establish in terms of mere legalism.

Ralegh's condemnation in 1603 was, among other things, part of the price paid for the Spanish peace of 1604. For, though Ralegh was accused of plotting with Spain, in fact he was leader of the bellicose anti-Spanish party, and many of the judges who condemned him soon accepted Spanish pensions. In 1618, it was generally held, Ralegh was betrayed to execution by the Spanish faction, 'then absolute at court'; he was 'sacrificed to advance the matrimonial treaty' with Spain, said Howell. In this case popular legend was entirely justified, except that it underestimated the complicity of James I, who was personally responsible for betraying to Spain all the details of Ralegh's Guiana expedition of 1617, so ensuring its failure and Ralegh's execution. Of the relation of his execution to James's foreign policy there can be no doubt. Secretary Winwood, Ralegh's backer, whose son supported Parliament in the civil war, died towards the end of 1617; and for the next seven years James pursued a pro-Spanish policy with as much vigour as he was capable of. But, as a contemporary shrewdly observed in 1618, Ralegh's 'death will do more harm to the faction that procured it than ever he did in his life'.

Ralegh's foreign policy was not his private affair, but was the policy of a whole group, whose main publicists were the two Richard Hakluyts. Ralegh was intimately connected with them. The younger Hakluyt's *Discourse of Western Planting* was written in 1584 'at the request and direction of Ralegh', to whom most of Hakluyt's works were dedicated. The policy of the Hakluyts was at once patriotic and imperialist. England had got left behind in the grab for the New World by Spain and Portugal, whose empires were menacingly united in 1580. After a rapid expansion of English cloth exports in the first half of the sixteenth century, relative stagnation followed. Unemployment created social, political, and national dangers, as Ralegh and many other observers noted. But the younger Hakluyt was shrewd enough to realize that England's overpopulation was only relative. The colonization of North America would not only get rid of England's immediate surplus population: it would also provide raw materials for home industries, and so prepare for a long-term solution. The object of economic policy should be to make England self-sufficient, an exporter of highly finished manufactured goods. North America would yield dye-stuffs for the clothing industry, the naval stores for which England was dependent on Baltic supplies, and timber to relieve England's fuel shortage. The reduction of the Indians 'to civility, both in manners and garments' would provide a new market. Given an economically self-sufficient Empire, England need not bother about capturing markets in Europe.

But England's road was blocked by Spain, on whose empire, in Bacon's phrase, 'the sun never sets'. Spain closed the whole American continent to English settlers, English goods, and English religion. So this policy, as Sidney and Hakluyt saw, involved war with Spain. Colonization was thus strategically vital. Occupation of North America could command the Newfoundland fishing banks and the Spanish homeward route from the Indies. 'Traffic followeth conquest.' But with this base in the New World, war against Spain could be made to pay for itself: 'we must not look to maintain war upon the revenues of England', Ralegh warned Cecil in 1595. Privateering could enrich individual merchants and gentlemen: gold and silver could be diverted from Spain to England. Such a war had religious as well as patriotic overtones. Foxe had traced the sufferings and struggles of God's people down to the Marian martyrs: Hakluyt's book also started with the beginning of the Christian epoch; but his Englishmen have passed over to the offensive against Antichrist, bringing the Gospel to parts of the world which had never yet heard it. If the worst came to the worst— and this illustrates the anxieties still felt by Elizabethan Englishmen, which we are too apt to forget because we know the end of the story—'a place of safety might there be found, if change of religion or civil wars should happen in this realm'.

War against Spain was necessary, the Hakluyts thought, not only to preserve England's national independence, but also to bring salvation to millions of American Indians, who had within living memory been subjugated to popery and Spanish cruelty. Puritan ministers, dangerously unemployed and restless at home, could be sent abroad to convert the heathen. 'God hath reserved' North America 'to be reduced unto Christian civility by the English nation'. Because of Spanish cruelty the Indians—'a poor and harmless people created of God'—would offer willing allies against Spain, as Ralegh often found. Ralegh's imperial policy envisaged the export of English arts and English women to Peru, the arming and training of the Indians, who were to be used to establish Peruvian independence of Spain, under allegiance to England. Ralegh's good treatment of the Indians at Trinidad in 1595 was remembered in 1605 and 1626, when they 'did unanimously own the protection of the English' against Spain. In Guiana 'he left so good and so great a name behind him . . . that the English have often been obliged to remember him with honour'. 'Most of his contemporaries', Professor

Quinn sums up, 'regarded the Spanish empire as something to be robbed: Ralegh thought of it as something to be replaced by an English empire. He therefore considered seriously the problems of English rule over a native population.' This underlines the tragedy that Ralegh could interest James only in robbery.

Hakluyt and Ralegh, then, put forward a national policy which offered something to all sections of the community. From the unemployed to Puritan ministers anxious to extend true religion, from City merchants to discontented younger sons of the landed class, all, it seemed, had something to gain.

In 1596 Ralegh's devoted adherent Lawrence Kemyis, a Balliol geographer and mathematician who like Wright had thrown up his fellowship to go to sea, published a *Relation of the Second Voyage to Guiana*. To this George Chapman, member of Ralegh's circle and friend of Hariot, prefixed a poem. Chapman urged 'patrician spirits', 'that know death lives where power lies unused' no longer to

> be content like horse to hold
> A threadbare beaten way to home affairs.

They should

> scorn to let your bodies choke your souls
> In the rude breath and prison'd life of beasts.
> You that herein renounce the course of earth
> And lift your eyes for guidance to the stars,
> That live not for yourselves, but to possess
> Your honour'd country of a general store;
> In pity of the spoil rude self-love makes
> Of those whose lives and years one aim doth
>     feed,
> One soil doth nourish, and one strength
>     combine;
> You that are blest with sense of all things
>     noble,
> In this attempt your complete worths redouble.

Once Elizabeth blessed

> with her wonted graces
> Th'industrious knight, the soul of this exploit
> [Ralegh]

she would create

> A golden world in this our iron age. . . .
> A world of savages fall tame before them,
> Storing their theft-free treasuries with gold;
> And there doth plenty crown their wealthy
>     fields,
> There Learning eats no more his thriftless
>     books,
> Nor Valour, estridge-like, his iron arms. . . .

> There makes society adamantine chains,
> And joins their hearts with wealth whom
>     wealth disjoin'd.

Hakluyt and Ralegh, like Bacon, synthesized and gave organized form to the thinking of large numbers of less articulate Englishmen. John Hawkins saw himself as the successor of Foxe's martyrs when he was frustrated in his attempt to sell bootleg negro slaves in Spanish America. Martin Frobisher prayed in 1577 for a safe return to England so that his discoveries 'might redound to the more honour of [God's] holy name, and *consequently* to the advancement of our commonwealth'. Lawrence Kemyis thought it had 'pleased God of his infinite goodness, in his will and purpose to appoint and reserve this empire [of Guiana] for us'. Hakluyt was the spokesman of this newly self-conscious nationalism.

A full-scale policy of imperial conquest could not be carried out without government support, without a powerful navy. In 1577 Ralegh's friend John Dee, who appears to have originated the phrase 'the British Empire', had advocated a standing royal navy to police the seas against pirates, and so protect merchants and the fishing industry. Under James and Charles this became a crying need, when the Algiers pirates mastered up-to-date techniques of navigation. But, apart from Mansell's abortive expedition of 1620-1, it was not until the sixteen-fifties that Blake's fleet bombarded Algiers and Cromwell's troops captured Jamaica and Dunkirk. For two generations the advocates of the Hakluyt-Ralegh policy laboured to convince governments of its desirability and feasibility: but in vain. Elizabeth 'did all by halves', as Ralegh said. 'Neither James I nor Charles I . . . ever sent a ship across the Atlantic.' There were serious limits to the effectiveness of colonization by private enterprise, as the early colonists found to their cost.

After the defeat of the Armada had first shaken the fixed belief of Englishmen in the omnipotence of Spain, a massive propaganda campaign was undertaken to convince a sufficient number of influential people that England's destiny lay in grandiose exploits across the ocean. The younger Hakluyt decided to embark on his *magnum opus*, a careful collection and publication of facts on Baconian lines, few months after the Armada's defeat had opened up dazzling new prospects. Hariot's *Brief and True Report* on Virginia appeared in 1588; Ralegh's *Discovery of Guiana* in 1591; and Hakluyt's *Voyages*, reprinting both of them, rounded off the campaign. In merchant circles, at least, it was very successful. The East India Company supplied as reading matter to its ships the Bible, Foxe's *Acts and Monuments*, Perkins's *Works*, and Hakluyt. The combination is significant. Hakluyt acted as Ralegh's publicity agent in the campaign, and seems deliberately to have worked to get books dedicated to Ralegh, often dictating the content of the dedication so as to stress Ralegh's international reputation.

Throughout the *History of the World* the over-riding importance of exhorting his readers against Spain is never far from Ralegh's mind. Spanish America would be as easy to conquer as Syria under the sons of Aram. Xerxes reminded Ralegh of Philip II. Alexander's tactics against Bessus led Ralegh to urge future invaders of Guiana or the West Indies always to 'burn down the grass and sedge to the east of them'. The wars between Rome and Carthage gave rise to a long digression on sea power and naval strategy, and to warnings against the dangers of trading with Spain. A discussion of tyranny prompted the improbable reflection that under a king like James 'it is likely, by God's blessing, that a land shall flourish with increase of trade in countries before unknown; that civility and religion shall be propagated into barbarous and heathen countries; and that the happiness of his subjects shall cause the nations far removed to wish him their sovereign'. In the 'Conclusion to the whole work' Ralegh noted that Spanish power was the greatest that had been seen in western Europe since the fall of the Roman Empire; still this power could easily and cheaply be restrained if England, France, and the Netherlands went over to the offensive. 'The obedience even of the Turk is easy and a liberty in respect of the slavery and tyranny of Spain', Ralegh had written in 1591.

For Hakluyt and Ralegh an alliance with the Netherlands was the necessary concomitant of their anti-Spanish policy. For this there were ideological reasons ('after my duty to mine own sovereign', wrote Ralegh, 'and the love of my country, I honour them most'). The Netherlands also provided a model of economic behaviour. But a Dutch alliance was also a practical necessity, even if the Dutch proved ungrateful competitors. For 'this long calm' after the peace of 1604 'will shortly break out in some terrible tempest', as it did in the year of Ralegh's execution. Yet Ralegh's interest in the shipping industry led him to advocate its encouragement and something very like a Navigation Act against Dutch competition. Like many English merchants, Ralegh was ambivalent in his attitude towards the Netherlands. Dutch merchants monopolized the carrying trade, and insisted on continuing to trade with Spain even in time of war. Ralegh 'was the first which made public the growth by sea of the Dutch, and the riches they derived from their fishing upon the coasts of England and Scotland, and the consequences which would necessarily follow, not only to the loss of the King's sovereignty of the British seas, but to the trade and navigation of England otherwise'. The cry was taken up by Tobias Gentleman and other pamphleteers, and echoed by Hakewill. But James 'stopped his ears to Sir Walter's advice concerning the Dutch fishing' and only opened them when Ralegh promised him gold from Guiana. To the Dutch alliance Ralegh came to add an alliance with the Palatinate and the maintenance of the Protestant interest in France and Switzerland—an object dear to Oliver Cromwell's heart.

Neither Elizabeth, James, nor Charles had any use for this foreign policy. They regarded the Dutch as rebels and Spain as the greatest monarchy in Christendom, with whom it would be folly for England to engage in war *à l'outrance*. Nor had any of them much sympathy with the commercial or religious ideals which underlay Hakluyt's and Ralegh's schemes. But to many merchants and ministers, and to a large group in every House of Commons, the policy was very attractive. From 1612 the Virginia Company tried to carry it out. Hakluyt, a founder-member, may have organized the Company's propaganda campaign. Bacon, Coke, Fulke Greville, Viscount Lisle, Hariot, and Briggs were members, together with Theodore Gulston, Thomas Winston, and Sir Oliver Cromwell, uncle of the Protector. All the great London livery companies subscribed.

A list of the motives of the Virginia Adventurers, drafted in 1612, is a summary of Hakluyt's policy: (i) convert the Indians; (ii) export surplus population, 'the rank multitude'; (iii) supply England with naval stores and (iv) minerals; (v) provide a base for Atlantic shipping and (vi) explorations to reveal a north-west passage to the Far East. The Virginia Company was supported by a propaganda campaign conducted by ministers (mainly Puritan). Thus William Crashawe spoke in 1613 of 'a work so honourable to God, our religion, our King and our country; so comfortable to the souls of the poor savages, and so profitable to the Adventurers . . . as the like . . . hath not been attempted in the Christian world these many ages'. Propaganda against Spain and for American colonization was continued by Samuel Purchas, whose *Pilgrimage* ran to four editions between 1613 and 1626, and together with his *Hakluytus Posthumus* had a great influence.

Sir Edwin Sandys, who was Treasurer of the Virginia Company in 1619-20, consciously aimed at carrying out Hakluyt's policy. He was a friend of Selden's and a leading opposition figure in the House of Commons. In the Parliament of 1614 he supported Sir Roger Owen's view that all kings had originally been elected, 'with reciprocal conditions between king and people'. A king by conquest might be forcibly overthrown. Sandys introduced secret balloting at the Company's elections, a procedure which Charles I was to forbid to all companies, but which the Pilgrim Fathers and the Royal Society alike used in elections. In the 1621 Parliament Sandys said 'Let us not palliate with the King, but with the people', and even went so far as to ask 'What is the bill of the Sabbath . . . to a man in want?' In 1620 James intervened to force Sandys's replacement as Treasurer of the Virginia Company: 'Choose the devil if you will, but not Sir Edwin

Sandys.' Gondomar asserted that the Company 'was but a seminary to a seditious Parliament'. But Sandys remained a force until the Company was dissolved in 1624. He attacked Gondomar as an enemy of the Company in the 1624 Parliament, where 'there was above one hundred Parliament men that were of the Virginia Company'. Sandys, son of a Marian exile, was a patron of the Pilgrim Fathers. His *Europae Speculum* was often associated with Ralegh's **History** as a source of general information.

There is thus clear continuity of the imperial theme in cementing the alliance between merchants and a section of the gentry. A paper of 1623, 'Reasons showing the benefit of planting in New England', in addition to the conventional themes of converting the heathen, finding cloth markets, exporting the unemployed, providing work for those of the poor who remained in England, added that 'if he be a gentleman, or person of more eminency who hath no great stock to continue his reputation here at home', and if he could raise £100 or £200 capital, by emigrating he would 'not only be able to live without scorn of his maligners but in a plentiful and worthy manner'.

Ralegh's associate, the third Earl of Cumberland, had attempted in 1598-9 to capture Porto Rico as a base against Spain. This looks forward to Pym's Providence Island Company and Cromwell's Western Design, linked by the voyages of Captain William Jackson in 1642-5. Jackson, who had the backing both of the Providence Island Company and of Maurice Thompson, later Cromwell's leading financier, seized Jamaica in 1643 and so (Jackson echoes Ralegh's words) 'the veil is now drawn aside, and their weakness detected by a handful of men, furnished and set out upon the expense of one private man'. What could not the English state do? Cromwell soon showed.

For the continuity of policy we have to look from Hakluyt and Ralegh through the Virginia and Providence Island Companies and Captain Jackson, on to Hugh Peter, who in 1645 told the Lord Mayor and Aldermen of London, the two Houses of Parliament, and the divines of the Westminster Assembly, that England had a double interest: first the maintenance of the Protestant cause on the Continent; secondly war with Spain for the West Indies. When Cromwell resumed Ralegh's policy, he found that his problem was exactly that which Ralegh had explained to James: 'how to free your people from the Inquisition of Spain, enlarge their trades, and be secured not to have your ships stayed in his ports at his pleasure'. The manifesto which Milton drafted in 1655 to justify war on Spain dwelt, as Ralegh would have done, on Spanish ill-treatment of the Indians as crying for retribution. After the Restoration Sprat in his *History of the Royal Society* again echoed Ralegh (and Bacon) when he said: 'the English greatness will never be supported or increased in this age by any other wars but those at sea': though now he spoke from experience, not speculatively.

## C. A. Patrides (essay date 1971)

SOURCE: An introduction to *The History of the World* by Sir Walter Raleigh, edited by C. A. Patrides, 1614. Reprint by Temple University Press, 1971, pp. 1-39.

[*In the essay below, Patrides analyzes the Christian historiographical method that informs Raleigh's* The History of the World.]

**The History of the World** has been termed 'the first serious attempt in England, and one of the first in modern Europe, at a history the scope of which should be universal in both time and space' [by Newman T. Reed, in *Northwestern University Summaries of Dissertations* II, 1934]. In fact, however, its general framework is not in the least original; it belongs to the tradition of Christian historiography which reaches its terminal point some fifty years later in *Paradise Lost*. Ralegh's prose work and Milton's poem are the two greatest formulations in English of the mode of thinking which over the centuries interpreted history as a progressive manifestation of the divine purpose in a linear movement extending from the creation to the Last Judgement. The interpretation originated with the great prophets who looked on history as the arena wherein God acts in judgement or in mercy. Once extended by St Paul and accepted by the early apologists, the theory was further developed by Eusebius of Caesarea who argued that the Christian faith was established even before the creation of the world. But the most influential formulation was ventured by St Augustine who in *De civitate Dei* maintained that all events are inexorably progressing towards their final consummation in God. Subsequent commentators were even more insistently bent on imposing order on historical events, and often co-ordinated history in terms of Four Monarchies or Six Ages. The links forged through the centuries involve any number of works written or compiled, but the principal performances remain the *Historia sacra* of Paulus Orosius, the *Historia ecclesiastica gentis anglorum* of St Bede, the *Chronica* of Otto of Freising, the colossal *Speculum historiale* of Vincent of Beauvais, and the composite *Flores historiarum* of Roger of Wendover which was continued along drastically original lines in the *Chronica maiora* of Matthew Paris. The advent of Protestantism did not terminate the tradition; quite the contrary, since Luther himself provided an outline of historical events in terms of the Six Ages, Melanchthon lent his assistance to a similar performance by Johann Carion, Sleidanus wrote the enormously popular *De quatuor summis imperiis,* and a legion of minor writers promptly fell in step. In England, Ralegh's own

endeavour had been preceded by attempts like Holinshed's *Chronicles* (1577), Lodowick Lloyd's *The Consent of Time* (1590), John More's *Table from the Beginning of the World* (1593), William Perkins's *Specimen digesti* (1598), and Anthony Munday's *Briefe Chronicle* (1611), and was to be followed by works like Henry Isaacson's *Saturni ephemerides* (1633), James Ussher's *Annals* (1650-54), William Howell's *Institution of General History* (1661), and Robert Baillie's *Operis historici* (1668). The common denominator of these works is their linear conception of history from the creation, and their insistent proclamation that history is a record of divine mercies and judgements.

Ralegh's celebrated Preface to **The History of the World** is a lucid testimony to his espousal of the commonly-accepted providential theory of history. Known in time as 'A Premonition to Princes', the Preface asserts that *'Events are always seated in the inaccessible Light of Gods high Providence'*. The quoted statement is not Ralegh's; it is borrowed from Sir William Sanderson's restatement of Ralegh's thesis in 1656, precisely because Sanderson was favourably disposed to Ralegh the historian even while he was militantly opposed to Ralegh the political figure. 'The Scales of Gods Providence', continued the impressed Sanderson [in *A Compleat History of the Lives and Reigns of Mary Queen of Scotland, and of her Son and Successor, James*], 'are never at rest, always moving; now up, now down; to humble, and to exalt.' He went on:

> Reade but the story of some Centuries of our *Christian* world, abreviated in the *Preface* of Sir *Walter Ralegh's* History: How long was it, that wickedness had leave to lord it? With what strength of policy, the Tyrants of each time, sold themselves to settle the work of sin? And though in the period of that portion of time (compared with everlasting) and of our neighbour-affairs, (with the succeeds of the vast Universe) In these (I say) he religiously observes (perchance in some) the most notorious impieties punished and revenged . . .

Significantly, while Ralegh during the trial of 1603 was censured for his alleged 'heathenish, blasphemous, atheistical, and profane opinions', in 1618 he was assured by Sir Edward Montague, the Lord Chief Justice [as quoted by David Jardine in *Criminal Trials,* 1832]: 'Your faith hath heretofore been questioned, but I am satisfied you are a good Christian, for your book, which is an admirable work, doth testify as much'.

But if both friends and enemies understood the general import of Ralegh's work and responded with enthusiasm, King James, as we have seen, thought that Ralegh had been 'too sawcie in censuring princes'. The royal displeasure may appear singularly odd since Ralegh had simply restated widely-accepted assumptions. But however enthusiastic the common reception of the 'lessons' repeatedly drawn from history, monarchs were always concerned lest the fondness for 'parallelism' should lead to treasonous equations of the past with the present. Their concern was not imaginary. Thomas Heywood in 1612 explicitly observed [in *An Apology for Actors*] that 'If wee present a forreigne History, the subiect is so intended, that in the liues of *Romans, Grecians,* or others, either the vertues of our Country-men are extolled, or their vices reproued'. We have indeed ample evidence to substantiate the inclination of the Elizabethans and Jacobeans to discern contemporary references in works of history no less than in dramatic literature. Under the circumstances it is not surprising that both Elizabeth and James restricted the activities of historians considerably, and sometimes decisively. Hardly unaware of these developments, Ralegh in his Preface piously disclaimed any interest in reproaching the present through the past, but wittily proceeded to leave the question wide open:

> It is enough for me (being in that state I am) to write of the eldest times: wherein also why may it not be said, that in speaking of the past, I point at the present, and taxe the vices of those that are yet lyuing, in their persons that are long since dead; and haue it laid to my charge. But this I cannot helpe, though innocent. And certainely if there be any, that finding themselues spotted like the Tigers of old time, shall finde fault with me for painting them ouer a new; they shall therein accuse themselues iustly, and me falsly.

The reaction of one spotted tiger we know! King James suppressed Ralegh's work not only because it was said to censure princes but especially because it appeared to be a veiled denunciation of his reign. Part of the 'evidence' consisted of Ralegh's several comparisons of the early seventeenth century with the expired glories of the Elizabethan age. But even more crucial was his unremitting series of 'parallels'—some intentional, some accidentally relevant—for instance the portrait of the irresolute King Rehoboam who was 'transported by his familiars and fauourites', and especially the account of the great Queen Semiramis and her incompetent successor Ninias ('esteemed no man of war at all, but altogether feminine, and subjected to ease and delicacy'). King James knew well enough whom Ninias was supposed to represent!

The providential theory of history espoused in the Preface to *The History of the World* extends well into the work itself. But Ralegh's concern is not merely to affirm that history is a record of divine judgements. His principal aim is to assert the unity of historical events by an emphasis on the order pervading their entire course since the creation of the world. True, the fundamental assumptions of the Christian faith do not appear to concern him; his vision is obviously not Christocentric, and the Last Judgement—so common an element in other universal histories—is not accommodated within his scheme. One is tempted to conclude that Ralegh was not 'orthodox' but (as we have been told often enough) a thoroughgoing sceptic, perhaps even an 'atheist', and at any rate not 'a religious person'.

Ralegh's reputed 'atheism' need not detain us long since it is refuted in chapter after chapter of *The History of the World*. At the same time, however, some readers are still of the opinion that 'it cannot be urged that Ralegh was in any profound sense a religious person'; his religion was rather 'a habit of thought than an ecstatic union with the Deity', 'there was so much more of speculation than of faith in his attitude'. But must one subordinate reason to faith, or experience ecstasy, before he can be called religious? The student of Ralegh's thought is constantly subjected to similarly odd assumptions which yield equally odd conclusions. He is justly alarmed by the sharply divergent views propounded in recent years. Should he accept one historian's opposition between 'orthodoxy' and 'scepticism'? Should he assent to the emphasis which a scholar places on orthodoxy at the expense of the sceptical strain? Should he agree with another historian who pursues Ralegh's 'scepticism' all too relentlessly? Threatened as we are by ever more exaggerated readings of the inquiring mind of Ralegh, we would be well advised to remember the relative nature of the terms at our disposal. 'His scepticism', we have been wisely reminded [by F. Smith Fussner in *The Historical Revolution*, 1962], 'was academic—and, by Montaigne's standards, shallow.

'Orthodoxy' is likewise relative. *The History of the World,* judged in the light of Christian theology, can only be found wanting; but judged in the light of Christian historiography—its natural milieu—it will be discovered to conform to the patterns of thought already established by tradition. Ralegh's vision may not extend to the end of history but there was adequate precedent in the equally restricted conception of Eusebius. The Last Judgement must in any case be regarded as inevitable once we are given the pattern of history's linear progress so strenuously insisted upon by Ralegh, and especially the division of history into Four Monarchies which he so firmly asserts in the final pages. By the same token, *The History of the World* while not Christocentric is resolutely *theo*centric—precisely the burden of the traditional universal history! However, it would be foolish to deny that Ralegh's silences on Christ or the Last Judgement are in themselves most eloquent. Indeed, it was noted at the time of his execution that 'he spake not one word of Christ, but of the great and incomprehensible God', which a wit promptly saw as evidence that Ralegh was 'an a-christ, not an atheist'. This is as much as to say that Ralegh was by nature non-devotional. His place in the manifestation of the religious impulse in seventeenth-century England is not with Herbert or Crashaw but with Milton or the Cambridge Platonists. So far indeed, he is entirely 'modern'.

But was Ralegh 'modern' in the historiographical sense as well? Matthew Arnold thought him, on the contrary, quite 'ancient', which is to say obsolete, largely because he accepted the Bible as an authority of unquestionable validity. If we are also shocked by Ralegh's uncritical attitude to the Bible, it should be held in mind that his behaviour is fully representative of his age. Well aware that 'divine testimonies doe not perswade all naturall men to those things, to which their owne reason cannot reach', he was also convinced that 'both the truth and antiquitie of the bookes of God finde no companions equall, either in age or authority'. Ralegh may often permit his Icarian reason to rise into perilous domains but in the end circumscribes it within the bounds of Scriptural authority.

Equally representative of his age is the attitude he displays towards authorities other than the Bible. Like most historians of his own day, he invokes authorities to establish the consensus of opinion; and where he finds them in disagreement, he simply selects the interpretation most suitable to his particular purposes. In this respect the first four chapters of *The History of the World* are of fundamental importance, for Ralegh's treatment of the vast commentaries on Genesis sets the tone of the entire work as he moves through them without pausing to consider their relative merits. His attitude to individual writers is similarly uncritical. Marsilio Ficino, for instance, is repeatedly cited as an authority on morality and religion, but we may well doubt whether Ralegh was even aware of his importance as a Platonist.

But this is not to say that *The History of the World* is merely a composite work based on an uncritical accumulation of authorities. The evidence on hand supports neither Aubrey's belief [in *Brief Lives*, edited by O. L. Dick, second edition, 1950] that Ralegh had simply 'compiled' his work, nor Ben Jonson's claim that 'The best wits of England were Employed for making of his historie'. Ralegh was by nature 'an undefatigable reader': even before his imprisonment, we are told, he never embarked on the high seas but 'he carried always a Trunke of Bookes along with him'. Once in prison he naturally depended on the assistance of friends and acquaintances for the provision of 'old books, or any manuscrips, wherin I cann read any of our written antiquites'. The research and the writing were almost entirely his own. The research itself yielded no mean contributions in several spheres. The translation of his raw material into the prose of his great *History* demonstrates how disinclined he was slavishly to imitate the sources consulted, for the information available to him was constantly modified and adapted to the purposes of his overall design. The celebrated digression on 'conjectures' is in this respect not irrelevant. . . .

Ralegh's apparent credulity is repeatedly qualified even through mere phrases, witness the opening clause of the following sentence:

> if we may beleeue *Herodotus,* the Armie of *Xerxes,* being reviewed at *Thermopylæ,* consisted of fiue millions, two hundred eightie three thousand two hundred twenty men—(III vi 2)

—besides, adds Ralegh dismissively, 'besides Laundresses, Harlots, and Horses . . .'.

But the total control which Ralegh exercised over *The History of the World* is nowhere more clearly evident than in the unity he imposed on its various parts.

*The History of the World* was never completed. Ralegh wrote and published only Part One whose narrative ends abruptly in 168 B.C., with a page or two added on the rising Roman Empire; and despite reports that he had also written a second part which he then destroyed, we may rest assured that the work was simply abandoned. But critics are generally agreed that Ralegh's *History* is as unaffected by its incompleteness as is *The Faerie Queene.*

Yet *The History of the World* would appear to lack unity. David Hume [in his *History of England,* 1868] was perhaps the first—though certainly not the last—to differentiate sharply between the 'Jewish and Rabbinical learning' in Books I-II, and 'the Greek and Roman story' of Books III-V. The distinction is now widely accepted as self-evident: nearly all scholars respond to Ralegh's work much the same way that Henry James reacted to George Eliot's *Daniel Deronda* ('all the Jewish burden of the story tended to weary me'). The most crucial argument involves the claim that in the *History* 'the theological system which dominates the first part is much less in evidence in the second'. 'Ralegh's providential interpretation of events is commonest', we are told, 'when he is following the Bible'; but 'when he follows secular sources, he is more apt to offer human causes'. 'His precepts looked back', writes another scholar, 'his practice looked forward. In precept he stressed the role of God as a cause, but in practice he pursued the secondary causes of accident and motive.' Lately, it has even been suggested [by Christopher Hill, in *Intellectual Origins of the English Revolution,* 1965] that Ralegh was 'on the side of the Moderns against the Ancients':

> Ralegh's importance is that he employed a secular and critical approach to the study of world history which was in very large part a study of Biblical history; and that he did this in English, in a work which was a best-seller. So he contributed, perhaps more than has been recognized, to that segregation of the spiritual from the secular which was the achievement of the seventeenth century.

So much for the claims of our scholars. Let's now look at Ralegh's work.

The precise way that Books I-II could be said to prepare for 'the Greek and Roman story' in Books III-V will be suggested later; here we may usefully remind ourselves that the opening books contain something more than 'Jewish and Rabbinical learning'. They also contain a host of mythological references and any number of quotations from authors of every age to the Renaissance. These references and quotations jointly testify to one 'truth' in particular, that within the historical process mankind forms an interdependent entity, a spiritual unity. Ralegh details his conviction in divers ways. There is the premeditated fusion of pagan myths and Christian verities until the suggestiveness of the first yields to the certainty of the second. There is the patient exposition of the series of events which led from the creation of Adam to the rise of individual tribes and finally nations. There are the incessant reminders that the history of nations is coeval. In the following quotations—all of which are opening sentences of sections in Book II—Ralegh's immediate interest is to co-ordinate his chronological framework but he simultaneously endeavours to consolidate the various families of men into a unity:

> And in this age of the World, and while *Moses* yet liued, *Deucalion* raigned in *Thessalie, Crotopus* then ruling the *Argiues* . . . (II vi 5)

> Neare the beginning of *Salomons* raigne, *Agelaus* the third of the *Heraclidæ* in *Corinth; Labotes* in *Lacedæmon;* and soone after *Syluius Alba* the fourth of the *Syluij,* swaied those Kingdomes: *Laoesthethes* then gouerning *Assyria: Agastus* and *Archippus* the second and third Princes after *Codrus,* ruling the *Athenians. . . .* (II xviii 6)

> The first yeare of *Manasses* was the last of *Romulus.* . . . (II xxvii 6)

> There liued with *Ioas, Mezades* and *Diognetus* in *Athens: Eudemus* and *Aristomides* in *Corinth:* about which time *Agrippa Syluius,* and after him *Syluius Alladius,* were Kings of the *Albans* in *Italie. Ocrazapeo,* commonly called *Anacyndaraxes,* the thirtie seuenth King succeeding vnto *Ophratanes,* began his raigne ouer the *Assyrians,* about the eighteenth yeare of *Ioas,* which lasted fortie two yeares. In the sixteenth of *Ioas, Cephrenes,* the fourth from *Sesac,* succeeded vnto *Cheops* in the Kingdome of *Ægypt,* and held it fiftie yeares. . . . (II xxii 6)

When all is said, however, the cardinal way Ralegh asserts the unity of mankind is through the providential theory of history.

The theory of providential causation espoused in ***The History of the World*** is not a conclusion which Ralegh

attained late in life. In 1591—which is to say over twenty years before the publication of the *History*—he had related the engagement between the *Revenge* and the Spanish fleet in purely secular terms, but in the end ascribed the final destruction of the enemy to the intercession of God:

> Thus it hath pleased God to fight for vs, & to defend the iustice of our cause, against the ambicious & bloody pretenses of the Spaniard, who seeking to deuour all nations, are themselues deuoured. A manifest testimonie how uniust & displeasing, their attempts are in the sight of God, who hath pleased to witnes by the successe of their affaires his mislike of their bloudy and iniurious designes, purposed & practised against all Christian Princes, ouer whom they seeke vnlawfull and vngodly rule and Empery.

This astonishing claim is certainly not warranted by Ralegh's rousing narrative of mere men at war. It therefore surprises, perhaps even it shocks—yet one may well ask whether Ralegh had not actually intended the reader to be surprised, even to be shocked. The theory of providential causation is after all not a readily apparent 'fact'; it is a mystery which defies comprehension. 'We oft doubt', says the Chorus in *Samson Agonistes,* 'What th' unsearchable dispose / Of highest wisdom brings about'; 'Oft he seems to hide his face, / But unexpectedly returns'. It may well be, I suggest, that Ralegh's assertion of divine intervention in the fight between the *Revenge* and the Spanish fleet is not in the least gratuitous; he meant it because he planned it. Significantly, the role played by purely 'human causes' is not denied; it is simply placed within the larger context of supernatural causation.

But we prefer explicit assertions, whether of God's total subordination of the created order to his omnipotent purposes, or man's unobstructed pursuit of his own destiny. We incline favourably to the deployment of terms like pre-destination or free will, oblivious of the fact that these are not merely philosophical concepts but states of experience beyond definition. It is not as if we have not been warned against over-simplifications in Christian theology and in all great literature! The classical concept of *moira* is instructive, for we could mistake it for 'fate', perhaps even for pre-destination: the Delphic oracle spoke, *therefore* Oedipus acted as he did. But a man forewarned of his destiny who nevertheless thoughtlessly kills an elderly man and foolishly marries a woman twice his age without ever pausing to reflect on the past, is surely 'fated' so long as we take 'fate' to mean the destiny of man as it has been predicted by the gods but is enforced by the individual himself. Christian thinkers arrived at an identical balance. St Paul exhorted the faithful to 'work out *your own* salvation with fear and trembling; for *it is* God which worketh in you both to will and to do of his good pleasure' (Phil. 2:12 f.). In the Johannine

Apocalypse the Lamb is reported as saying, 'Behold, I stand at the door, and knock: *if* any man hear my voice, *and* open the door, I *will* come in to him, and will sup with him, and he with me' (Rev. 3:20). The same balance controls St Augustine's brilliant 'inconsistency' in upholding man's free will at one moment and denying it the next, no sooner asserting that our salvation is both 'from the will of man and from the mercy of God' than adding that 'the whole process is credited to God, who both prepareth the will to receive divine aid and aideth the will which has been thus prepared'. During the controversies ushered in by the Reformation the balance was upset, as Protestants charged that Catholics made free will 'the absolute Lord of its own actions', and Catholics charged that Protestants 'leaue vs as a stone or blocke to be moued by God onely'. But the principal thinkers of that turbulent era never really abandoned the traditional 'inconsistency' of the Bible and St Augustine. There was Luther, beguiled into dazzling contradictions as he defended the folly of his God against the wisdom of Erasmus. There was even Arminius, widely maligned as *Pelagius redivivus,* who unhesitatingly asserted that God's grace 'goes before, accompanies, and follows', 'excites, assists, operates' whatever we do. There was Hugo Grotius, never in doubt that man possesses free will ('not an errour of *Pelagius,* but Catholick sense'), yet as convinced that grace does not depend on man's free will because 'Grace worketh how far, and how much it pleaseth'. Similarly, John Donne was assured not only that the will of man is 'but Gods agent', but also that 'neither God nor man determine mans will . . . but they condetermine it'. The same 'inconsistency' appears in Shakespeare's plays, manifesting itself at one end of the pendulum's swing in Cassius' statement that the fault is not in our stars but in ourselves, and in the other in Florizel's words in *The Winter's Tale* that we are 'the slaves of chance'. Yet occasionally the pendulum stands still over statements like Hamlet's:

> There's a divinity that shapes our ends,
> Rough-hew them how we will.
>
> (v ii 10-11)

Hamlet's 'fate' is the universal concept of *moira* which attributes primacy to God yet senses that somehow man's faculties and godlike reason must hew—perhaps only rough-hew—his own destiny. Human experience confirms that the course of our lives must be attributed to 'human causes', but it confirms also belief in supernatural causation, even in the unexpected intervention of God 'to fight for vs'—as Ralegh said of the destruction of the Spanish—'& to defend the iustice of our cause'.

Ralegh's account of the fight of the *Revenge* in 1591 asserts providential causation abruptly, unexpectedly, well past the half-way mark of the narrative. Another work, the popular **Instructions to his Son,** has a different strategy: the worldly wisdom of its early sections may appear to be 'coldly prudential', even 'calculating', but it terminates in the firm proclamation of the final chapter, 'Let God be thy protector and director in all thy Actions'. In Ralegh's words,

> Serve God, let him be the Author of all thy actions, commend al thy endevours to him that must either wither or prosper them, please him with praire, lest if he frowne, he confound all thy fortunes and labors like drops of Rayne on the sandy grounde.

**The History of the World** deploys an entirely different strategy again. The providential control of history is asserted neither at the half-way mark nor at the end; it is on the contrary proclaimed with appropriate magniloquence at the outset, in both the Preface and the opening lines of the main text. . . . The tactic carries a number of implications which do not appear to have been appreciated fully.

The Preface and the opening chapters jointly maintain several things at once. They assert providential causation in a particular way, by means of precise 'examples'. But the examples are *not* drawn from biblical history; on the contrary they are first drawn from the history of England, France and Spain—what we persist in calling 'secular' history—and only thereafter confirmed through any number of analogous precedents culled from the Scriptures. In other words, Ralegh serves notice at the very outset of **The History of the World** that historical events since the creation are indivisible; they may *not* be sundered into 'sacred' and 'secular' history, not even when in pursuit of man's behaviour in history the emphasis appears to be placed on 'the secondary causes of accident and motive'. The point is of fundamental importance since it constitutes the first step in Ralegh's attempts to educate the reader.

The second step is taken almost at the same time. Once Ralegh in the Preface has surveyed the history of England and other nations, he advances to the opening chapters, which cumulatively invoke the Bible as their principal authority. A multitude of other authorities are also cited, but they are consistently cited with approval only where they endorse the claims of the Bible. Ralegh's method is displayed not only in the opening chapters, however, but throughout the better part of Books I and II. As we are made constantly aware of his ambition to look on events from both the human and the divine standpoints, so we are also invited to observe his consistent allocation of primacy to God. In his own words on a particular occasion,

> though (speaking humanely) the beginning of Empire may be ascribed to reason and necessitie; yet it was God himself that first kindled this light in the minds of men. . . .

The statement could be made to appear merely gratuitous so long as we are prepared to ignore either the emphasis placed earlier on the omnipotence of God, or the insistence on the subservience of the created order to its Creator, or the intricate balance maintained between divine foreknowledge and man's free will. All other events are similarly qualified. Details set forth in nominally secular terms ('speaking humanly') are sooner or later qualified by Ralegh's metaphysical claims. Lest the reader tends to overlook the sacred framework, Ralegh intervenes with either an immediate judgement or an evaluation which concludes the given chapter. Immediate judgements abound. While reciting the deeds of Abimelech, for instance, Ralegh pauses to promote a specific event into a general principle:

> All other passions and affections by which the soules of men are tormented, are by their contraries oftentimes resisted or qualified. But ambition, which begetteth euery vice, and is it selfe the childe and darling of *Satan,* looketh only towards the ends by it selfe set downe, forgetting nothing (how fearefull and inhumane soeuer) which may serue it: remembring nothing, whatsoeuer iustice, pietie, right or religion can offer and alleadge on the contrary. . . . (II xiii 7)

Again, the reign of King Amaziah affords Ralegh the opportunity to castigate a particular form of pride—'a foolish and a wretched pride, wherwith men being transported, can ill endure to ascribe vnto God the honour of those actions, in which it hath pleased him to vse their owne industrie, courage, or foresight'—and to commend the 'heroism' involved in acknowledging God's assistance:

> so farre from weaknesse is the nature of such thanksgiuing, that it may well be called the height of magnanimitie; no vertue being so truly heroicall, as that by which the spirit of a man aduanceth it selfe with confidence of acceptation, vnto the loue of God. (II xxxii 8)

The narration of 'the Greek and Roman story' is similarly oriented. In the battle of Salamis—a nominally 'secular' event . . . Ralegh's metaphysical claims are advanced during the evaluation of the character of Xerxes at the end of the same chapter. . . . The Persian defeat, it is implicitly asserted, was the direct result of the tyrannical rule of Xerxes—which is to say that God once again deployed secondary causes as instruments of his justice, in this instance the Greeks to defeat the Persians. It is not without significance that as much is maintained in the prolonged chapters devoted to the rise of the Athenian Empire, its destruction by Sparta, and the subordination of all the Greeks to the Macedonians. The common denominator of all these phases of Greek history is the usurpation of sovereignty by force and the consequent divine punishment. Just as Athens deprived her colonies of their freedom, so Sparta imposed her tyrannical authority on Athens—and so, in turn, both were overcome by the Macedonians:

> two people [who] deserued best the plague of tyrannie, hauing first giuen occasion thereunto, by their great ambition, which wearied and weakened all the Countrie by perpetuall Warre. (III viii I)

Here the alert reader recalls numerous formulations of the same general principle in the 'Jewish' books, for instance:

> Neither was it *Ierusalem* alone that hath so oftentimes beene beaten downe and made desolate, but all the great Cities of the world haue with their inhabitants, in seuerall times and ages, suffered the same shipwracke. And it hath beene Gods iust will, to the end that others might take warning, if they would, not onely to punish the impietie of men, by famine, by the sword, by fire, and by slauerie; but hee hath reuenged himselfe of the very places they possest; of the wals and buildings, yea of the soyle and the beasts that fedde thereon. (II xii 3)

Much later, in Ralegh's account of Alexander the Great, we read again of 'the infinite spirit of the *Vniuersall,* piercing, mouing, and gouerning all thinges'. Finally, a few pages from the end, the advent of the Roman Empire is prefaced with the ominous remark,

> Now began the *Romans* to swell with the pride of their fortune; and to looke tyrannically vpon those that had beene vnmannerly toward them before. . . .

***The History of the World*** is constructed as a series of interlocked parallel movements orchestrated by God but performed by man himself.

Ralegh's own exposition, then, appears not to support the alleged severance of his work into two disconnected parts. The reader who reaches 'the Greek and Roman story' in Book III is already sufficiently educated to read a nominally secular history in the terms dictated by Ralegh. For by then the method has been demonstrated repeatedly; the principal authority has been proclaimed in no uncertain terms; secular sources have been made to bow before the Bible; the sacred framework of universal history has been firmly established; and 'human causes' have been relentlessly subordinated to providential causation.

Ralegh himself [as F. P. Wilson in *Elizabethan and Jacobean* and M. C. Bradbrook in *The School of Night* point out] was able to survive in the midst of apparent 'contradictions', for he possessed that distinctly Renaissance gift which was a 'capacity to live and think upon many different levels'. But realistic as he was, he knew that the reader—however well 'trained' to read history *sub specie aeternitatis*—was all too often bound to extricate secular events from their divine context. Hence the warning in the Preface that it is a 'monstrous' impiety to confound God and Nature—primary and secondary causes—or the insistence that God intervenes not as a *deus ex machina* but 'by the *medium* of mens affections, and naturall appetites'. Hence also the constant reminders of providential causation in the last three Books, and hence too the emphasis so often placed on the inadequacy of explaining human affairs through a consideration of secondary causes only. True, the burden of Ralegh's observations frequently appears to be on the pragmatic at the expense of the moral; worse, Machiavelli often seems to rear his head, as in the long digression on tyranny. But the reader who is mindful of the framework erected in Books I and II will observe that the pragmatic is circumscribed by the moral, even as he will conclude that the long shadow cast by Machiavelli cannot by itself achieve Ralegh's conversion into a representative of 'free inquiry'. Upon consideration even the numerous 'digressions' will emerge as indispensable amendments to Ralegh's central design. I am aware of the claim that

> Some of his digressions, such as those on the location of the earthly paradise, or on free will and destination, are academic discussions apart from the general movement of the *History*. His most significant digressions are those dealing with political theory; they show, however, the same confusion which has been noted in the whole plan for the work.

But even a minimum of reflection will establish that Ralegh's 'digressions' are as relevant to *The History of the World* as Milton's are to *Lycidas*. The digression on the location of Eden, for instance, is intended not so much to demonstrate the range of Ralegh's scholarship as to teach a method of approach to contradictory sources. The digression on free will and predestination is of capital importance in a work which has already proposed to explore the conduct of man within a sacred context, thereby to exhibit (as Milton phrased it on a parallel occasion) 'supernal Grace contending / With sinfulness of Man' [*Paradise Lost,* XI 359-360]. The digressions of political theory, finally, should hardly surprise us in a work of history. It were indeed very odd had they been missing!

Ralegh's method in *The History of the World* is not dissimilar to the method of his friend Spenser in *The Faerie Queene* or of Milton in *Paradise Lost*. Their scope is of equally epic proportions, and equally encyclopaedic; their aim is alike to teach by example ('so much more profitable and gratious'); and their assumptions are ultimately grounded upon the Scriptures and built with the materials of tradition. Moreover, each attempted to train his reader responsibly to study 'the whole book of sanctity and vir-

tue'.

Ralegh's style is sometimes said to possess 'a dignity and majesty unequalled save in the writings of the greatest masters of the English language'. Normally, however, praise is reserved for his 'fitful splendor', for those 'occasional pieces of gorgeous prose' which like the famous peroration on Death dispose many readers to use phrases such as 'the most beautiful passage of prose' in English literature. But the praise of isolated passages is as meaningless as the claim that Ralegh's prose is 'unequalled'. Far more enlightening, I should think, are the attempts to contrast the style of Ralegh's letters with the 'formal prose' of *The History of the World,* or to compare the clarity of his prose with the practice of his contemporaries [as in "Sir Walter Ralegh's Prose," in *The Times Literary Supplement*, January 31, 1935]:

> no Elizabethan is less affected, or freer from intolerable divagations and toilsome 'Asiatic' circumlocutions. Ralegh's final judgement on Epaminondas has often been praised. It is unsurpassed for conciseness, is epigrammatic without being false, packed without being obscure. . . .

Even more instructive, however, is the demonstration of the unity which links the divers 'pieces of gorgeous prose'.

We have already noted that the unity of Ralegh's subject is centred on the providential theory of history, even as the unity of his method is the gradual education of the reader to recognise the constant presence of God within the historical process. Concurrently, however, there is a unity of style—subdued where he discusses the information provided by his sources, solemn where he ponders questions of general principle, assured where he proclaims the authority of the Bible, spirited where he describes the clash of mighty armies, eloquent where he recites the achievements of great men, vehement where he portrays evil in action, serene where he posits the intervention of God. The unity of Ralegh's style must be attributed, I think, to his successful modulation of an infinitely varied tone. Different subjects have different cadences, and in each case, once the cumulative effect is achieved, the measure alters in accord with the new theme. Thus Jupiter's wondrous sexual exploits are boomed forth through an overwhelming roll-call of the women he 'rauished, betrayed, stole away, and tooke by strong hand':

> *Niobe, Laodemia,* and *Alcema* the wife of Amphitryon, by whom he had *Pelasgus, Sarpedon, Argus,* and *Hercules:* by *Taygete* he had *Taygetus,* of whom the mountaine *Taygetus* tooke name, with another sonne called *Saon,* of whom *Sauona:* by *Antiope* he had *Amphion* and *Zetus:* by *Laeda, Castor & Pollux, Helen & Clytemmestra:* by *Danaë Perseus:* by *Iordana Deucalion:* by *Charme* (the

daughter of *Eubulus*) *Britomartis*, by *Protogenia* he had *Athlius* the father of *Endymion*. . . . (I vi 5)

—and so on. We are of course reminded of Milton, not only in the similarity of their magniloquent voices but in the equally implicit moral judgement.

The influence of Ralegh on Milton is beyond dispute. As we have been told repeatedly, Milton even adapted Ralegh's wording on two occasions. One is Ralegh's prefatory sonnet to *The Faerie Queene* ('Methought I saw the graue where Laura lay') which was obviously recollected by Milton in Sonnet XXIII ('Methought I saw my late espoused saint'). The other occasion involves the exotic lines of *Paradise Lost* on

Rich *Mexico* the seat of *Mo[n]tezume*,
And *Cusco* in *Peru*, the richer seat
Of *Atabalipa*, and yet unspoil'd
*Guiana*, whose great Citie *Geryons* Sons
Call *El Dorado:*

(XI 407-11)

which echo Ralegh's similarly evocative lines on

that mighty, rich, and beawtifull Empire of *Guiana*, and of that great and Golden City, which the Spaniards call *El Dorado*, and the naturals *Manoa*, which Citie was conquered, reedified, and inlarged by a younger sonne of *Guianacapa* Emperor of *Peru*, at such time as *Francisco Pazaro* and others conquered the said Empire, from his two elder brethren *Guascar*, and *Atabalipa*, both them contending for the same, the one being fauoured by the *Oreiones* of *Cuzco*, the other by the people of *Caximalca*. . . .

Milton's debt to Ralegh extends also to **The History of the World,** possibly in the kinship which may be said to exist between Milton's Satan and Ralegh's Xerxes but especially in the description of the Indian figtree whose leaves are plucked by Milton's Adam and Eve to cover their nakedness:

The Figtree, not that kind for Fruit renownd,
But such as at this day to *Indians* known
In *Malabar* or *Decan* spreads her Armes
Braunching so broad and long, that in the ground
The bended Twigs take root, and Daughters grow
About the Mother Tree, a Pillard shade
High overarcht, and echoing Walks between;
There oft the *Indian* Herdsman shunning heate
Shelters in coole, and tends his pasturing Herds
At Loopholes cut through thickest shade: Those
  Leaves
They gatherd, broad as *Amazonian* Targe,
And with what skill they had, together sowd. . . .

(IX 1101-12)

Details apart, however, Ralegh's influence on Milton

can best be measured in terms of the remarkable tonal range of **The History of the World** which finds its finest counterpart in the equally polyphonic music of *Paradise Lost.* Milton responded to Ralegh because he discerned in him an artist who, like himself, had achieved a style answerable to his great argument.

Milton's contemporaries responded no less enthusiastically. Most readers of the **History** were attracted by Ralegh's espousal of the traditional theory of history—witness in particular the decision of Alexander Ross, a rather fierce guardian of orthodoxy, to attempt both its abridgement and its continuation. But even authorities on historiography praised Ralegh's achievement, for example the scholar Diggory Wheare, whose statement in 1623 [in his *The Method and Order of Reading . . . Histories*] coincides with the verdict of his century. 'Of al modern Writers', said Wheare, 'Sir *Walter Rawleigh* our Country-man deserves the first place.'

The response of republicans was additionally conditioned by their view of Ralegh as a martyr of Stuart tyranny. But Cromwell himself extolled the **History** primarily because it orders divers elements into an impressively unified structure. As he advised his son [in *The Writings and Speeches of Oliver Cromwell,* 1939], 'Recreate yourself with Sir Walter Raughleye's History: it's a body of history, and will add much more to your understanding than fragments of story'. Cromwell had no difficulty, it appears, to wind his way through Ralegh's 'many cunning passages, contrived corridors / And issues . . .'

### Stephen J. Greenblatt (essay date 1973)

SOURCE: "Ralegh's Court Poetry," in *Sir Walter Ralegh: The Renaissance Man and His Roles,* Yale University Press, 1973, pp. 57-98.

*[In the following analysis of Raleigh's court poetry, which focuses on* The Ocean to Cynthia, *Greenblatt examines the ways in which the poetry was shaped by Raleigh's relationship with Queen Elizabeth I and his desire to forge a successful career for himself at court.]*

*My soul the stage of fancy's tragedy*

Most of Ralegh's poems were intimately linked with his place in the court and, in particular, with his "fantastic courtship" of the queen. As it was considered slightly improper for a gentleman to appear in print, he chose to publish very little. Quite apart from the social stigma, the general public was an undesirable audience, for things that could be safely said in the poems of a favorite to the queen were liable to be grossly misunderstood by readers unfamiliar with the language of the court. Consequently, though his reputation as a

*The Ark Ralegh, built to Ralegh's specifications and at his expense.*

poet was widespread, Ralegh's verses circulated in manuscript and were probably known firsthand by only a select few. Yet it is misleading to conclude, as Agnes Latham does [in *The Poems of Sir Walter Ralegh*], that Ralegh's poetry "was no part of his public character, but something essentially intimate and private". Public and private are perplexing terms here, for Ralegh's relationship with the queen, the subject and occasion for most of his poems, was his chief occupation and career for many years. This career was a constant, demanding theatrical performance, the kind of performance we do not usually associate with the "intimate and private." Like his letters, Ralegh's poetry displays the power of self-dramatization, not a rich and complex inner life. The poetry was both an outgrowth of that power and an important means of creating the finished product: the marvelous image he presented to the court and especially to the queen. Of course, his poems may have had private echoes and hidden meanings—as we have already seen in the epitaph "Even such is tyme"—but such meanings were always embedded in public utterances. His poems then cannot be read as confessions, moments when the favorite put

down his mask and spoke out in his own true voice. It is unlikely that there was such a "true voice," for, like the queen, Ralegh was an actor who was thoroughly committed to the role he had fashioned for himself.

In the elaborate and subtle performance that Ralegh and the queen played together, poetry had an important function from the start. Thomas Fuller, who was the first to relate in print the famous story about the cloak laid in the mud for the queen to walk on [in *The History of the Worthies of England*], adds that Captain Ralegh later inscribed on a window which Elizabeth was sure to pass:

Fain would I climb, yet fear I to fall;

under which Elizabeth wrote:

If thy heart fails thee, climb not at all

Whether or not these stories are in themselves true, they undoubtedly reflect two means of Ralegh's swift rise to favor: the perfect theatrical gesture and the display of courtly wit in poetry.

The kind of poetic dialogue Fuller describes always sounded a bit far-fetched until the recent discovery of an authentic poetic exchange between Ralegh and the queen [**"Fortune hathe taken away my love"**; "Ah silly pugge wert thou so sore afraid"]. Ralegh mourns the loss of his mistress' love in the grand language of poetic despair: he is dead to all joys, he only lives to woe, he searches the heaven and the earth for his lost love. There is something vast and heroic in his sorrow. His love has not simply left him for another; she has been conquered by Fortune, the blind goddess who rules on earth and has no regard for man's virtue. But Ralegh himself is defiantly superior to that great power: "though fortune conquer thee; / no fortune base nor frayle shall alter mee." To this the queen replies: "Ah silly pugge wert thou so sore afraid, / mourne not (my Wat) nor be thou so dismaid." The drop in tone is sharp and immediate. From heroic love and despair, we descend to reassuring but demeaning pleasantries; from the address to "my soules heaven above . . . my worldes joy," we shift to the easy, almost proprietary familiarity of "silly pugge . . . my Wat." The queen assures Ralegh of her good will and encourages him to be confident, but her poem is, on the whole, rather careful and restrained. The central concern is less her regard for Ralegh than her own mastery of Fortune: "never thinke fortune can beare the sway, / if vertue watche & will her not obay." The queen can and must be sovereign over all things, even Fortune. As for Ralegh's protestations of despair, the queen treats them with a light, gentle mockery:

> Dead to all joyes & living unto woe.
> Slaine quite by her that nere gave wiseman
>   blowe
> Revive again & live without all drede.

Elizabeth manages both to play the game of poetic love and to remain aloof from it, to indulge herself without commitment and to participate without danger. Ralegh, however, must assert his total involvement.

In *The Queen and the Poet,* Walter Oakeshott attempts to link each of Ralegh's poems to a particular moment in his career at court. Oakeshott argues that the poems "were written for special occasions, the occasion most often being to please, or pacify, the Queen," and he succeeds in exploding the notion that poetry for Ralegh was merely a pleasant pastime. Unfortunately, both the chronology of the poetry and the history of Ralegh's relationship with the queen are riddled with uncertainties. Moreover, even if the poems could be dated with perfect accuracy and linked precisely with the vicissitudes of Ralegh's career as favorite, a great part of their significance would lie beyond their immediate utility on a particular occasion. For though each poem may have been written to serve the needs of his

career, the mark of Ralegh's best poetry is its transcendence of the local and immediate, its capacity to fuse intense personal feeling with a larger vision, its power to transform the self.

Ralegh's self-fashioning is paradoxical: it bends art to the service of life—advancing his career, justifying his actions, enhancing his reputation—and it transforms life into art, leading ever further from the career toward symbolic characterization and transcendent meaning. It exists in time and in spite of time; it addresses a specific historical audience and yet turns inward, cryptically mirroring the self; it reflects the world and creates its own world. Ralegh's career generated constant pressure to create images of the self, but, conversely, there were moments when his whole experience of life seemed caught up in symbolic meanings that had their own generative power. Thus Ralegh's polished performance at his execution was intended at once to create a heroic image of himself, countering the charges against him, and to transform the local and particular crisis in his life into the universal struggle of the individual against Time and Death. Similarly, he contrived, largely through his poetry to the queen, both to fashion a self-enhancing courtly identity and to transform his troubled personal relations with Elizabeth into a powerful symbolic nexus of love, time, and mortality.

Consideration of Ralegh's court poetry in recent years has been dominated by the suggestion that Ralegh was the author of a vast lost poem portraying himself as the Shepherd of the Ocean and the queen as Cynthia. This notion was engendered chiefly by the discovery in the last century of a manuscript in Ralegh's own hand, preserved in the Cecil archives at Hatfield House, containing what appear by their titles to be fragments of a far larger poem: **"The 21th: and last booke of the Ocean to Scinthia"** and **"The end of the 22 Boock, entreatings of Sorrow."** The latter breaks off in midphrase after some twenty lines, but the former—though it too shows signs of incompleteness—is a substantial work over 500 lines long.

Further evidence that Ralegh had planned and at least partially written a great poem to the queen has been seen in Spenser's tributes to the poetry of his friend and patron. The two had met in Ireland during the summer of 1589 when Ralegh had left the court in some slight disfavor. Spenser recalls this meeting in *Colin Clouts Come Home Againe,* describing a visit from the "Shepheard of the Ocean" whose song

> was all a lamentable lay,
> Of great unkindnesse, and of usage hard,
> Of *Cynthia,* the Ladie of the Sea,
> Which from her presence faultlesse him
>   debard.
> And ever and anon with singulf[s] rife,

He cryed out, to make his undersong
Ah my loves queene, and goddesse of my life,
Who shall me pittie, when thou doest me
    wrong?

[164-71]

It is unlikely that this lament was identical with the poems to Cynthia in the Hatfield House manuscript, which have no "undersong" and which probably date from the much more serious disgrace in 1592. But perhaps Spenser heard earlier portions of the *Ocean to Cynthia* which were subsequently lost or destroyed. It would be to these too that he refers in *The Faerie Queene,* praising

that sweet verse, with Nectar sprinckeled,
In which a gracious servant pictured
His *Cynthia,* his heavens fairest light.
[*F. Q.,* III, Proem, iv]

Likewise, in a dedicatory sonnet to Ralegh, Spenser compares his own "unsavory" verses to "the streames, that like a golden showre/Flow from thy fruitfull head, of thy loves praise":

Yet till that thou thy Poeme wilt make
    knowne
Let thy faire Cinthias praises bee thus rudely
    showne.

Finally, in the famous letter to Ralegh in which he expounds "his whole intention" in *The Faerie Queene,* Spenser points to a specific parallel between his great epic and Ralegh's "excellent conceipt":

In that Faery Queene I mean glory in my generall intention, but in my particular I conceive the most excellent and glorious person of our soveraine the Queene, and her kingdome in Faery land. And yet in some places els, I doe otherwise shadow her. For considering she beareth two persons, the one of a most royall Queene or Empresse, the other of a most vertuous and beautifull Lady, this latter part in some places I doe expresse in Belphoebe, fashioning her name according to your owne excellent conceipt of Cynthia, (Phoebe and Cynthia being both names of Diana).

As if to confirm this parallel, Ralegh twice refers to "Belphoebe" in the 21st Book of *Ocean to Cynthia:*

Bellphebes course is now observde no more,
That faire resemblance weareth out of date.
[271-72]

A Queen shee was to mee, no more Belphebe,
A Lion then, no more a milke white Dove.
[327-28]

The conceit of Belphoebe, like a once powerful met-
aphor that has become a cliché, "weareth out of date." Elizabeth has changed from mistress to sovereign, breaking the bonds of love.

It is tempting then to credit Ralegh with a lost poetic masterpiece, like the fabled "second volume" of *The History of the World* which his seventeenth-century admirers imagined he had thrown into the fire in despair. But that great poem may well be as chimerical as the completion of the *History.* Regarded soberly, Spenser's praises are little more than expressions of gratitude to the powerful patron who had introduced him to the court and helped to incline the queen in favor of his poem with two commendatory sonnets. They flatteringly hint at more, but Spenser's tributes actually tell us only that Ralegh addressed the queen as Cynthia in some of his poems and that these poems involved both praise and complaint.

As for those tantalizing fragments, the 21st and 22nd Books of the *Ocean to Cynthia,* the 21st Book is 522 lines long—this would suggest, assuming books of equal length, a complete poem of almost 12,000 lines! It is difficult to imagine Ralegh even having the time to write so much, let alone the inclination or inventiveness. Ralegh may simply have used the grandiose titles to create the aura of an immensely long poem, suggesting to the queen—and to himself, perhaps—an almost boundless suffering immortalized in verse. He need not have had the slightest intention of continuing the poem, for what really mattered was the vague impression of epic scope and grandeur. This picture of Ralegh, the illusionist, accords with the Ralegh we have seen in his letters and at his execution—the self-dramatizer, the manipulator of appearances.

While the possibility of a lost great work cannot be ruled out entirely, and while there were almost certainly some small losses, there is little likelihood that Ralegh ever wrote the vast poem implied by those titles. Far more plausible is Agnes Latham's suggestion that "*Cynthia* was a cumulative poem written over a period of years, and that the 'lamentable lay' which Spenser heard, and which was provoked by the events of 1589, was no more than the latest installment." This basic theory is followed by Philip Edwards, Walter Oakeshott and, most recently, Pierre Lefranc [in *Sir Walter Raleigh, Ecrivain*] to whom the four poems in the Hatfield House manuscript and another autograph poem unearthed recently suggest not a single, unified account of the relations between Ralegh and the queen but a cycle of heterogeneous pieces written at different moments of his career.

Lefranc includes in this cycle a group of Ralegh's poems published anonymously in *The Phoenix Nest* (1593). Arrested in 1592 upon the queen's discovery of his secret marriage, Ralegh released, according to Lefranc, a number of poems intended for the cycle. H took great precautions to keep definite proof of his authorship from the general public, but the queen and perhaps a few others would have understood that the release of these poems constituted an intentional indiscretion and a warning. The silent agreement between Ralegh and the queen regarding the secrecy of the cycle had been broken, and a threat was thereby implied that the rest of these private poems might someday be aired before the public.

Such a theory may be attractive in the light of Ralegh's daring and his power to manipulate men and appearances, but it is highly implausible, for he would not have been foolish enough to imagine that he could frighten the queen in this way. Elizabeth could not be threatened by verses or by anything else. Those who published things offensive to her quickly learned to repent of their folly, like John Stubbs and his publisher who both lost their right hands for opposing in print the Alençon marriage scheme. Ralegh may have intended certain of the poems in *The Phoenix Nest* as complaints of a rejected favorite, he may have intended them to move the queen's compassion or even remorse, but he could hardly have meant them as threats.

Lefranc's idea of a threat arises in part from his notion of the secrecy of the supposed cycle. He imagines that the very "conceit" of the queen as Cynthia was the intimate possession of Ralegh and Elizabeth, and that consequently, even the allusions in Spenser were the result of "private indiscretions." There does not appear to be any evidence for this theory apart from the fact that the unfinished poems in the Hatfield House manuscript were never published and apparently never circulated during Ralegh's lifetime. This in itself is hardly enough to warrant the notion of a great secret enterprise, planned and partially executed over a number of years, zealously kept from the eyes of all but the chosen few. There is no reason to believe that some poems were written independently and later "attached" to the cycle, as Lefranc would have it, or that Ralegh released to the general public poems which were originally written for the cycle, or indeed that Ralegh ever thought of his poems as part of a cycle. In fact, the only value of the term "cycle" here is to emphasize the powerful shaping imagination that lay behind this body of diverse poems, the imagination that seized upon a troubled relationship and transformed it into a work of art with its own set of meanings and coherences. The poems were evidently written for specific occasions, but they are all caught up in the overarching self-fashioning of Ralegh's life.

At the center of the poems to Elizabeth is the shifting image of the lady—the queen, Cynthia, the mistress—and the changing voice of the poet—chanting the praises of a goddess, crying out against the coldness of his beloved and the misery of age, bewailing his isolation and loneliness, attempting to understand how the same

love could be both the emblem of eternity and the embodiment of mutability. In his best poems, Ralegh does not present a complete unit of feeling or thought, a fixed image, a single tone, but attempts, rather, to render in verse the very process of shifting from one unit to another and his own futile efforts to stabilize the image and the voice. In the minor poems printed in *The Phoenix Nest,* however, the poles of belief and emotion are each given concise, individual expression.

At one extreme is the queen as goddess and the poet as worshiper:

> Praisd be Dianas faire and harmles light,
> Praisd be the dewes, wherwith she moists the
>    ground;
> Praisd be hir beames, the glorie of the night,
> Praisd be hir powre, by which all powres
>    abound.
>
> Praisd be hir Nimphs, with whom she decks
>    the woods,
> Praisd be hir knights, in whom true honor
>    lives,
> Praisd be that force, by which she moves the
>    floods,
> Let that Diana shine, which all these gives.
>
> In heaven Queene she is among the spheares,
> In ay she Mistres like makes all things pure,
> Eternitie in hir oft chaunge she beares,
> She beautie is, by hir the faire endure.
>
> Time weares hir not, she doth his chariot
>    guide,
> Mortalitie belowe hir orbe is plaste,
> By hir the vertue of the starrs downe slide,
> In hir is vertues perfect image cast.
>
>> A knowledge pure it is hir worth to kno,
>> With Circes let them dwell that thinke not
>> so.
>>                                    [*Poems*]

Elizabeth is transformed almost completely beyond human personality, appearing as an image of static, timeless perfection to the mortal who speaks, or rather chants, her praises. This is not simply a tactful love poem which aims at praising the "real" person of the queen figured forth as Diana; it does not establish a coherent set of simple equivalences, like a code, where each attribute of Diana stands for a praiseworthy quality of the queen. There are such equivalences—Diana's nymphs and knights and perhaps "hir powre, by which all powres abound"—but these are intertwined with attributes which have no simple correspondences—Diana's "faire and harmles light," "the dewes, wherwith she moists the ground," "hir beames, the glorie of the night." The presence of the latter indicates that the poet does not encourage us to look *through* his image to the substantial reality behind it— the reality of the aging Elizabeth—but to know and pay tribute to the qualities that inhere in the figure of Diana into whom the queen has been transformed: perfect beauty and virtue, supreme power, and, above all, the mastery of time and mutability. Ralegh's Diana is above the realm of flux, deceptive appearance, sinister transformation, the realm evoked by the reference to Circe. And she is also above mere human relationships; it is enough simply to have the pure knowledge of her worth. Insofar as the poem celebrates Elizabeth at all, it celebrates her in her role, the ideal of perfection to which she was wedded at the moment of her consecration. "In hir is vertues perfect image cast"— the sculpture metaphor suggests that the praise is for the wonderful work of art into which the queen has been transformed.

The poem which pays tribute to this transformation is itself highly artificial. The anaphora in the first seven lines, the overall absence of syntactical tension or complexity, the perfect containment of the verse within the shell of its own metrical pattern create the mythic time suited to the ritual of praise for Diana's static, self-contained virtue. The work seems to reflect the strong Elizabethan sense of the interrelation of poetry and music, the delight in formal patterns of sound and feeling. Elsewhere in Ralegh's poetry, there is emphasis on the divided and tormented self. In **"Praisd be Dianas faire and harmles light,"** however, the poet is not a fully realized character but an anonymous voice. These verses do not address the reader as an individual moral agent, but speak for a whole community, banishing all who disagree:

> A knowledge pure it is hir worth to kno,
> With Circes let them dwell that thinke not so.

Poetry such as this, with its emphasis on fluency rather than complex syntax, on generalized patterns of feeling rather than on individual sensibility, affirms man's place in a harmonious, orderly universe where isolation and uniqueness are impossible. The sense of a reassuring correspondence between the order of the cosmos and the order of man is nicely caught in Ralegh's carefully patterned lines, with their play on the meanings of "virtue":

> By hir the vertue of the starrs downe slide,
> In hir is vertues perfect image cast.

"The vertue of the starrs" (i.e., astrological influence) works upon the world of man through the mediation of the sphere of the goddess Diana who is the perfect image of moral virtue. This correspondence accords very well with the notion of the queen's "two persons" which Spenser expressed in his letter to Ralegh: "a most royall Queene or Empresse" by whom, as God's anointed representative on earth, the divine will is expressed on earth, and "a most vertuous and beautifull Lady."

**"Praisd be Dianas faire and harmles light"** presents the queen as goddess. Elsewhere in *The Phoenix Nest* Ralegh portrays her as the beautiful and gracious lady of innumerable Renaissance love lyrics:

> Those eies which set my fancie on a fire,
> Those crisped haires, which hold my hart in chains,
> Those daintie hands, which conquer'd my desire,
> That wit, which of my thoughts doth hold the rains.
>
> Those eies for cleernes doe the starrs surpas,
> Those haires obscure the brightnes of the Sunne,
> Those hands more white, than ever Ivorie was,
> That wit even to the skies hath glorie woon.
>
> O eies that pearce our harts without remorse,
> O haires of right that weares a roiall crowne,
> O hands that conquer more than Caesars force,
> O wit that turns huge kingdoms upside downe.
>
> > Then Love be Judge, what hart may thee withstand:
> > Such eies, such haire, such wit, and such a hand.
>
> > > [*Poems*]

Obviously, such flattering verses must have pleased the aging queen and enabled Ralegh to sustain the elaborate fiction of courtship. They also enabled him to display the graceful wit and facility expected of the accomplished gentleman. Castiglione, for example, had advised that the courtier be practiced "in writing verse and prose, especially in our own vernacular; for, besides the personal satisfaction he will take in this, in this way he will never want for pleasant entertainment with the ladies, who are usually fond of such things."

But this kind of poem (of which Ralegh undoubtedly wrote many) had, I believe, a function beyond flattery, self-display, and light entertainment. Like **"Praisd be Dianas faire and harmles light,"** such verses provided—primarily for Ralegh himself—a deep reassurance. Anonymous, superficial, static, and utterly conventional, they evoke a world of shared values, a world in which the individual is almost indistinguishable from the society at large. Even when they speak of the "defeat" of the lover whose heart is held in chains, they bear witness to a public, comprehensible world:

> Sought by the world, and hath the world disdain'd

Is she, my hart, for whom thou doost endure,
Unto whose grace, sith Kings have not
    obtaind,
Sweete is thy choise, though losse of life be
    sowre:
        Yet to the man, whose youth such pains
            must prove,
        No better end, than that which comes by
            Love.

                            [*Poems*]

The familiar rhythms and banal diction underscore the consoling sense of community.

There is no stamp of a single, unique consciousness on these passionless love poems. **"Those eies which set my fancie on a fire,"** for example, is ascribed to Ralegh only because it appears at the heart of the so-called "Ralegh group" in *The Phoenix Nest*; it might otherwise be attributed to virtually any contributor to that anthology or to any other in the period. Only one poem in the group, **"Farewell to the Court,"** creates the sense of an individual:

Like truthles dreames, so are my joyes
    expired.
And past returne, are all my dandled daies:
My love misled, and fancie quite retired,
Of all which past, the sorow only staies.

My lost delights now cleane from sight of
    land,
Have left me all alone in unknowne waies:
My minde to woe, my life in fortunes hand,
Of all which past, the sorow only staies.

As in a countery strange without companion,
I onely waile the wrong of deaths delaies,
Whose sweete spring spent, whose sommer
    well nie don,
Of all which past, the sorow only staies.

        Whom care forewarnes, ere age and
            winter colde,
        To haste me hence, to find my fortunes
            folde.

                            [*Poems*]

This lyric seems to have occupied a special place in Ralegh's consciousness. In ***Ocean to Cynthia***, he recalls it as a premonition of his present suffering:

Twelve yeares intire I wasted in this warr,
Twelve yeares of my most happy younger
    dayes,
Butt I in them, and they now wasted ar,
Of all which past the sorrow only stayes.
So wrate I once, and my mishapp fortolde.
                            [120-24]

"Farewell to the Court" would seem then to refer to an earlier and less serious disgrace in Ralegh's career than the disaster of 1592, probably to the mysterious trouble in the summer of 1589 which led to his brief exile from the court. Indeed, Lefranc suggests that the shores which have disappeared behind the horizon are those of England and the "countrey strange" is Ireland. But the landscape is more psychological than literal: it is not the coasts of England but "My lost delights" that are "now cleane from sight of land," and if Ireland was the origin for the "countrey strange," it has been transformed by the poet's imagination into a metaphor expressing his sense of isolation and of the distance that separates him from the joys of his past. Cut off from the timelessness of the goddess and the shared time of the community, the voice of the poet conveys a feeling of personal time, a sense of the past and of the ongoing process of aging, which sets it apart from Ralegh's other poems in *The Phoenix Nest*.

**"Praisd be Dianas faire and harmles light"** and **"Farewell to the Court"** represent opposite poles in Ralegh's imaginative transformation of his relationship with the queen: the one with its virtually anonymous speaker, its tone of ritual adoration, its sense of timelessness, and, of course, its transcendent goddess, and the other with its personal voice, its tone of sorrow and regret, its deep rootedness in time, and its almost total absorption in the poet's emotions. As Ralegh matured poetically, he did not move from one pole to the other, from an impersonal, hieratic style and subject matter to an intensely individual and resonant verse, but rather discovered ways of bringing them together. One splendid reconciliation of this kind is the famous Walsingham ballad (*Poems*).

C. S. Lewis remarked sourly of this poem [in *English Literature in the Sixteenth Century*] that "it has no unity of style at all." This is true enough, but it is precisely in the mingling and manipulation of diverse styles that Ralegh achieves his effects. The opening:

    As you came from the holy land
        Of Walsinghame
    Mett you not with my true love
        By the way as you came?

is very much in the manner of the old ballad upon which Ralegh's poem is based, the ballad which perhaps began:

    As I went to Walsingham
    To the shrine with speede.

Likewise, the fifth and sixth lines:

    How shall I know your trew love
    That have mett many one

strongly resemble the version Ophelia sings in her distraction:

> How should I your true-love know
>     From another one?
>                         [*Hamlet,* IV, V, 23-24]

But in the third stanza, Ralegh begins to move away from the diction and imagery of the popular ballad (Ophelia's "By his cockle hat and staff / And his sandal shoon") toward the style and thematic concerns of his own sophisticated court poetry. The mistress with her divine form and angelic face recalls the beautiful lady of **"Those eies which set my fancie on a fire"** and, still more, the goddess, set above time and mutability, of **"Praisd be Dianas faire and harmles light."** It is because of these associations—timeless perfection, divine grace, heavenly beauty—that the fifth stanza is so poignant and powerful:

> She hath lefte me here all alone,
>     All allone as unknowne,
> Who somtymes did me lead with her selfe,
>     And me lovde as her owne.

Breaking through both the simple accents of the ballad and the ritual adoration of the court poem is the personal note of suffering and anguish, the voice of **"Farewell to the Court"**:

> My lost delights now cleane from sight of
>     land,
> Have left me all alone in unknowne waies.

The voice of despair and loneliness expresses above all a sense of time, of aging:

> I have lovde her all my youth,
>     Butt now ould, as you see,
> Love lykes not the fallyng frute
>     From the wythered tree.

Of course, as the image suggests, growing old is natural and inevitable, and yet there is a lingering sense of betrayal and disillusionment, not only in the fickleness of love but in the triumph of time. The image describes not a process of maturation and ripening, but a death—the tree itself is withered.

Up to this point, the seventh stanza, the dialogue form has been merely a convenience, a conventional device of the ballad to move the poem along:

> How shall I know your trew love
>
> Such an one did I meet, good Sir
>
> Whats the cause that she leaves you alone.

Tension has existed not between the two speakers, the abandoned lover and the pilgrim, but between the conventional form and content with its basic anonymity and the personal voice of suffering in the fifth and seventh stanzas. But in the concluding stanzas the dialogue form is realized and made to carry the full weight of the argument. In response to the lover's bitter sense of age and betrayal, the pilgrim criticizes love as a "careless chylld," both careless of the pain he causes others and free from the care, the suffering of love:

> Know that love is a careless chylld
>     And forgets promyse paste,
> He is blynd, he is deaff when he lyste
>     And in faythe never faste.
>
> His desyre is a dureless contente
>     And a trustless joye
> He is wonn with a world of despayre
>     And is lost with a toye.

By subtle modulations of rhythm, sound, and alliteration, Ralegh manages to convey the uneasiness and instability of passion and the deflating, trivializing fickleness of childish love.

The suffering individual, however, is not satisfied with this view of love. He identifies the "chyldysh desyres/ And conceytes" with the love of womankind, and then, looking inward, he perceives a love which is above time and mutability:

> Butt true Love is a durable fyre
>     In the mynde ever burnynge;
> Never sycke, never ould, never dead,
>     From itt selfe never turnynge.

Once again, part of the power of these intense lines is derived from the sharp contrast with the style of the preceding stanzas. There is an effect of surprise, a sudden rush of energy as the haunting, personal note breaks through the anonymous moralizing that has gone before.

The contrast of styles is linked with the opposition of two kinds of love, symbolized by a blind and faithless child (who is also sometimes deaf, according to Ralegh) and by "a durable fyre / In the mynde ever burnynge." The child is, of course, the blind Cupid of Renaissance mythology, and the opposition is related to a major theme in the iconology of the period. To the modern reader, the blindness of Cupid alludes only to the irrationality of amorous choices, but for the mythographers and artists of the Renaissance it had darker associations. According to Erwin Panofsky [in *Studies in Iconology*], "Blind Cupid started his career in rather terrifying company: he belonged to Night, Synagogue, Infidelity, Death and Fortune. . . ." The figure represented a love that was *morally* blind, an illici sensuality that was a slave to time and tainted by death. By Ralegh's day, these overtones of evil had been largely dissipated by the frequent use of the figure in different contexts, many of them trivial or neutral. Yet the overtones remained as a potential, to be evoked, as Panofsky observes, "wherever a lower, purely sensual and profane form of love was deliberately contrasted with a higher, more spiritual and sacred one, whether marital, or 'Platonic,' or Christian." Just such a contrast is made in the Walsingham poem, though it is tempered by the simplicity of the ballad framework and by a certain minimal tact. The contrast—between a faithless love that abandons the aging lover and seeks after novelty and a true love that never changes—is a version of the rivalry between "Amor profano" and "Amor sacro." The former love is confined by the body and hence by time—"Love lykes not the fallyng frute / From the wythered tree"—while the latter is a fire which forever burns in the mind. That fire is related ultimately to "the most holy fire of true divine love" of which Bembo speaks so ecstatically in *The Courtier* as the fulfillment of all the strivings of man's soul. This is the very heart of the Neoplatonic system of Ficino and Pico, the *amor divinus* which "possesses itself of the highest faculty in man, i.e. the Mind or intellect, and impels it to contemplate the intelligible splendour of divine beauty." In Ralegh's poetry, however, the essential content of that system—the religious vision—has disappeared. What remains is the fire which burns in the mind, the love which leads beyond the self, beyond time, beyond mortality, and this love is focused not upon God but upon the queen. Yet though his royal mistress is invested with all the titles of divinity, though she is as fair as the heavens and possesses a divine form and an angelic face, still she is human and subject to weakness and inconstancy. The divine love of the poet is betrayed by the very symbol of perfection, constancy, and hope, and the result of this betrayal is intense anguish. This anguish is felt in **"Farewell to the Court,"** in the sonnet **"My boddy in the walls captived,"** . . . and in the Walsingham ballad. But it receives its ultimate expression in Ralegh's masterpiece, **"The 21th: and last booke of the Ocean to Scinthia."**

From an obscure, powerless gentleman of slender means, a young soldier who had come to the court with neither extraordinary qualifications nor influential friends, Ralegh had risen by the mid-1580s to a place, as he himself put it, "to be beleved not inferrior to any man, to plesure or displesure the greatest; and my oppinion is so receved and beleved as I can anger the best of them" (*Letters*). He had all those things which made the favorites of the queen so virulently hated by the people—lucrative monopolies, large royal grants of land and money, an influential and highly conspicuous place in the court. In 1587 he was named Captain of the Queen's Guard, a position requiring his constant attendance upon his royal mistress. This prox-

imity was of enormous importance to him, for although he became involved in many projects, including privateering and the Virginia Company, although he served as Member of Parliament for Devon, patronized poets, historians, and scientists, his career always remained dependent upon the queen's favor.

Relying on this personal relationship, Ralegh made little or no attempt to align himself with a strong party. His contempt for the "rascal multitude" was notorious, and his relations with the great nobles, who considered him an upstart, were always strained. Newsletters, court circulars, polemical pamphlets, ballads, all were full of stories of his intolerable pride and insolence. There was wild talk about the extravagance of his dress—jewels in his shoes worth 6,600 gold pieces, a suit adorned with £60,000 worth of precious gems. And indeed the magnificence of his clothing is borne out by portraits of this period such as the lovely miniature by Nicholas Hilliard, depicting Ralegh in a jewel-studded cap and a collar edged with beautiful lace. . . . Likewise, in a painting dated 1588, Ralegh wears a large pearl earring and is resplendently dressed in an embroidered doublet and fur-collared cloak virtually covered with pearls. In the upper lefthand corner of the painting, above his motto "Amore et Virtue," there is a small crescent moon, a symbol of Cynthia or Diana. As this symbol suggests, the splendid adornments were not only arrogant displays of wealth, they were signs of Ralegh's favor and part of the elaborate, slightly exotic image with which he captivated his royal mistress.

In the spring and summer of 1592 Ralegh was at the summit of his career. In May, the queen remitted to him a debt of £5,000, and in June she gave him the beautiful Sherborne estate which she had wrested for that purpose from the Bishop and Chapter of Salisbury. Even more important, perhaps, for a man who desired to hold sway over others, that spring Ralegh was given his first naval command—an expedition against the Spanish fleet. But all during that period of unmatched honor and prosperity, there were dark rumors circulating. On March 10, 1592, Ralegh wrote to Cecil.

> I mean not to cume away, as they say I will, for feare of a marriage, and I know not what. If any such thing weare, I would have imparted it unto yourself before any man livinge; and, therefore, I pray believe it not, and I beseich yow to suppress, what you can, any such mallicious report. For I protest before God, ther is none, on the face of the yearth, that I would be fastned unto. [*Letters*]

We may indeed believe that at that moment there was no one on earth that Ralegh would willingly have been fastened to, but, as we saw in his speech on the scaffold, Ralegh's protestations to God were not to be trusted.

There *was* a marriage, to Elizabeth Throckmorton, one of the queen's maids of honor. Even if the "love" between the aging queen and her favorite had been tacitly understood by both to be an elaborate game (which is not at all clear), there was nonetheless a terrible betrayal involved. After a rather mysterious delay during which there may have been unsuccessful efforts to patch things up, Ralegh and his wife were imprisoned in the Tower.

It was in this crisis, in the shock and frustration and anguish of imprisonment that *Ocean to Cynthia* was born. Probably, confession and apologies were called for, but Ralegh turned instead to the abandoned lover's gestures of despair: theatricalism was always closer to his nature than contribution. . . .

*Ocean to Cynthia* is, on one level, only another such performance, in which Ralegh presents himself as a distracted lover cruelly abandoned by his mistress. Indeed, a reasonably accurate summary of the poem can be lifted directly from [Sir Arthur] Gorges' letter: "when she went away he might see his death before his eyes, with many such like conceits." The actual circumstances of his disgrace were, of course, an impediment to this role, but Ralegh's tactic is simply to dismiss his feelings toward his wife as a regrettable but passing error, while ardently proclaiming his everlasting love for the queen:

> But thow my weery sowle and hevy thought
> Made by her love a burden to my beinge,
> Dust know my error never was forthought
> Or ever could proceed from sence of Lovinge.
> Of other cause if then it had proceedinge
> I leve th'excuse syth Judgment hath bynn
>    geven;
> The lymes devided, sundred and a bleedinge
> Cannot cumplayne the sentence was unyevunn.
>
> [336-43]

"Her love," that is, Ralegh's love for the queen, weighs heavily upon his mind and soul in his disgrace. His "error" was only a superficial affair, not really affecting him at all except as it brought about the anger of the queen. Indeed that passing fancy, that "frayle effect of mortall livinge" (445), was so insignificant in itself that the queen's reaction, as the brutal image of quartering suggests, was harsh, hasty, and unjust. The offender is transformed into the pitiable victim. In lines which echo the eighth, ninth, and tenth stanzas of the Walsingham ballad, Ralegh boldly turns the tables upon the queen:

> Such is of weemens love the carefull charge,
> Helde, and mayntaynde with multetude of
>    woes,
> Of longe arections such the suddayne fall.
> Onn houre deverts, onn instant overthrowes

> For which our lives, for which our fortunes
>    thrale.
>
> [228-32]

This approach is maintained as well in Ralegh's letters of this period—the pathetic appeal that is at the same time a reproach:

> There were no divinety, but by reason of compassion; for revenges are brutish and mortall. All those times past,—the loves, the sythes, the sorrows, the desires, can they not way down one frail misfortune?
>
> [*Letters*]

and the sense of exaggerated, unjust punishment:

> I only desire thatt I may be stayd no on[e] houre from all the extremetye that ether lawe or presedent can avowe. And, if that bee to[o] litle, would God it weare withall concluded that I might feed the lions, as I go by, to save labor. For the torment of the mind cannot be greater. . . .
>
> [*Letters*]

Ralegh carries the criticism of the queen's fickleness and her tyranny so far in *Ocean to Cynthia* that the basic assumption that he wrote the poem to mollify the queen and excuse himself is called into question. As with the *"Appologie* **for the ill successe of his enterprise to** *Guiana,"* what begins as an expression of contrition becomes something quite different as he composes it. The manuscript of *Ocean to Cynthia* is in Ralegh's best hand, "comparable with that in which he addressed King James after his disgrace in 1603" (*Poems*), but it is clearly unfinished and was apparently abandoned. It would seem that at some point—possibly as late as the very draft we possess—Ralegh realized that what he had written could only enrage the queen still further. This uneasy realization seems to be the meaning of that difficult little poem, **"If Synthia be a Queene, a princes, and supreame,"** which accompanies the 21st and 22nd Books in the Hatfield House manuscript. If Elizabeth no longer loves him, if she is a queen and not Belphoebe, then the verses he has written must not be shown to her ("Keipe thes amonge the rest, or say it was a dreame"). For without the predisposition to like them for his sake, she will only loathe them and disdain him the more. And neither her disdain nor his despair has any need to be augmented—he has experienced an excess of both.

*Ocean to Cynthia* then was probably never shown to the queen. Addressed, despite its title, not to Cynthia but to the poet himself, it probes the hidden frustration and resentment of a man who, as Elizabeth's "silly pug," had played the rapt worshiper for over ten years. There is no warrant, however, to dismiss the expressions of love in *Ocean to Cynthia* as mere cynical flattery. Ralegh's courtship of the queen was for those years the chief focus of all his intellectual and emotional energies, the central core from which his far-ranging activities derived their meaning. His secret marriage emphasizes the quality of acting in that courtship, but it does not prove Ralegh a mere hypocrite; there is ample evidence of his power to believe in his own fictions, to commit himself to the role he played. Moreover, commitment to the role of the queen's lover was reinforced by Elizabeth's extraordinary personal qualities, by the very practice of idealization over many years in a court where everyone professed himself a worshiper, and by the whole national cult of Eliza, which was constantly reiterated in pageants and festivals, formal ceremonies and popular ballads, royal progresses and religious services.

Most important, Ralegh's courtship of the queen helped to shape his entire imaginative world and to determine his sense of himself. When he was at the height of his favor, there was an imaginative synthesis of private and public, for Elizabeth was at once mistress and ruler, and Ralegh was both lover and subject. In the role which he played with such conviction, his most intense personal feelings were bound up with his service to the state, his life as a citizen. The world of his imagination was a Golden Age world in which the subjective, individual will and the objective, civic will were one. Ralegh did not need to have a full sense of individuality, for his mistress was the symbol of the nation, the anointed minister of God's will. The absence of full self-consciousness is reflected in the highly generalized voice of early poems like **"Praisd be Dianas faire and harmles light"** and **"Those eies which set my fancie on a fire,"** the voice that merges so easily with hundreds of others just like it. His poetic imagination participates in the shared emotional life of the entire nation rather than seeking forms which individualize and discriminate.

With Elizabeth's displeasure and Ralegh's disgrace, the synthesis of the individual and the community begins to disintegrate. The community breaks into rival factions, vying for the queen's favor:

> The tokens hunge onn brest, and kyndly
>     worne
> Ar now elcewhere disposde, or helde for
>     toyes;
> And thos which then our Jelosye removed,
> And others for our sakes then valued deere.
> The one forgot, the rest ar deere beloved,
> When all of ours douth strange or vilde
>     apeere.
>
> [263-68]

And the queen herself is now an ambiguous figure, shifting from an abstract symbol of perfection, "Th'Idea remayninge of thos golden ages" (348), to a fickle and cruel woman. This ambiguity casts shadows upon the past, even, paradoxically, as the past is being idealized:

> Such force her angellike aparance had
> To master distance, tyme, or crueltye,
> Such art to greve, and after to make gladd,
> Such feare in love, such love in majestye.
> My weery lymes, her memory imblamed,
> My darkest wayes her eyes make cleare as
>     day.
> What stormes so great but Cinthias beames
>     apeased?
> What rage so feirce that love could not allay?
> Twelve yeares intire I wasted in this warr,
> Twelve yeares of my most happy younger
>     dayes,
> Butt I in them, and they now wasted ar,
> Of all which past the sorrow only stayes.
> So wrate I once, and my mishapp fortolde.
>
> [112-24]

Ralegh's verse manages to retain the significance of both sides of the exploding image, to convey a complex attitude that stops short of corrosive sarcasm, even in a moment of sardonic perception like "Such art to greve, and after to make gladd." The ageless goddess, the principle of harmony, purity, and love, is glimpsed for a moment in a vision of the past and then gives way abruptly to the personal anguish of "Twelve yeares intire I wasted in this warr." All of the latent tensions in Cynthia's love, her "art to greve" as well as to gladden, are suddenly crystallized in the single word "warr": the long courtship is now seen as a destructive and futile struggle. The poet's memory, pictured a few lines above as a healing force, bitterly re-evaluates the past. His imagination, which had once kept his beloved continually present—"Farr *off* or nire, in waking or in dreames" (110)—now dwells upon its own premonitions of grief:

> Of all which past the sorrow only stayes.
> So wrate I once, and my mishapp fortolde.

Resentment and adoration continue to struggle and alternate throughout ***Ocean to Cynthia,*** but underlying both is the poet's loneliness: the loneliness of disfavor and imprisonment and, beyond these, the loneliness of the individual who has come to a full awareness of himself for the first time. With the breakdown of the synthesis of the objective and subjective will, the individual is thrown back upon himself, without the support of the community, nation, or any of those complex means that man has developed to escape from isolation. His new self-awareness is above all a sense of time and mortality against which he is defenseless. Cynthia's love had sheltered him, for she was above time—"Time weares hir not, she doth his chariot guide"—but now he is an isolated, mortal individual on the threshold of oblivion:

> But as a boddy violently slayne
> Retayneath warmth although the spirrit be
>    gonn,
> And by a poure in nature moves agayne
> Till it be layd below the fatall stone;
> Or as the yearth yeven in cold winter dayes
> Left for a tyme by her life gevinge soonn,
> Douth by the poure remayninge of his rayes
> Produce sume green, though not as it hath
>    dunn;
> Or as a wheele forst by the fallinge streame,
> Although the course be turnde sume other way
> Douth for a tyme go rounde upon the beame
> Till wantinge strength to move, it stands att
>    stay;
> So my forsaken hart, my withered mind.
> Widdow of all the joyes it once possest,
> My hopes cleane out of sight, with forced
>    wind
> To kyngdomes strange, to lands farr off
>    addrest.
> Alone, forsaken, frindless onn the shore
> With many wounds, with deaths cold pangs
>    inebrased.
> Writes in the dust as onn that could no more
> Whom love, and tyme, and fortune had
>    defaced,
> Of things so great, so longe, so manefolde
> With meanes so weake, the sowle yeven then
>    departing
> The weale, the wo, the passages of olde
> And worlds of thoughts discribde by onn last
>    sythinge:
> As if when after Phebus is dessended
> And leves a light mich like the past dayes
>    dawninge,
> And every toyle and labor wholy ended
> Each livinge creature draweth to his restinge
> Wee should beginn by such a partinge light
> To write the story of all ages past
> And end the same before th'aprochinge night.
>                             [73-103]

At the heart of this rich and suggestive passage is the anguish of radical isolation: "Alone, forsaken, frindless onn the shore." The "shore" refers both to the land of exile, exile from all hopes and joys and from the lady who was their source, and to the kingdom of death. The poet's bitter loneliness arises not simply from his disgrace but from a new and tragic awareness of mortality, a sense of isolation from any transcendent force or any movement toward the renewal of life.

The tragic sense darkens everything, from the memories of Cynthia, to the sterile, empty landscape, to the very act of writing. Indeed, poetry itself—the circumstances of its composition, the nature of its forms and images, its stylistic level—is one of the crucial symbols of the poet's tragic condition. If Cynthia's love was his very life and that love has ended, then his writing can be only the twitching of a corpse, his creative energy no more significant than the meaningless growth of plants in winter or the motion of a water wheel winding down. Or, if he still has some remnant of life, the poet is like a shipwrecked and dying sailor scratching his last words in the dust; with the first storm they will vanish. Moreover, in the little time that remains to him, he cannot begin to compass the complexity of his theme; he can never record the "worlds of thoughts" within him.

*Ocean to Cynthia* registers a mind in disorder, a sensibility which has lost its coherence:

> Lost in the mudd of thos hygh flowinge
>    streames
> Which through more fayrer feilds ther courses
>    bend,
> Slayne with sealf thoughts, amasde in fearfull
>    dreams,
> Woes without date, discumforts without end,
> From frutfull trees I gather withred leves
> And glean the broken eares with misers hands,
> Who sumetyme did injoy the waighty sheves
> I seeke faire floures amidd the brinish sand.
>                             [17-24]

The "withred leves" and "broken eares" which symbolize the collapse of his career and the misery of his existence are also the blighted fragments of poetry which he has managed to glean from his bitter experience. Fuller and richer forms, "faire floures" of rhetoric and emotion, are no longer possible, because the poet's imagination was utterly bound up with the love of the mistress who has now forsaken him:

> Oh hopefull love my object, and invention,
> Oh, trew desire the spurr of my consayte,
> Oh, worthiest spirrit, my minds impulsion,
> Oh, eyes transpersant, my affections bayte,
> Oh, princely forme, my fancies adamande,
> Devine consayte, my paynes acceptance,
> Oh, all in onn, oh heaven on yearth
>    transparant,
> The seat of joyes, and loves abundance!
> Out of that mass of mirakells, my Muse,
> Gathered thos floures, to her pure sences
>    pleasinge.
>                             [37-46]

His love was his inspiration: "the spurr of my consayte . . . my minds impulsion." Without this creative force, the kind of poetry he once wrote ("thos floures, to her pure sences pleasinge") is no longer possible. That poetry was part of an imaginative world now irrevocably lost:

All in the shade yeven in the faire soon
  dayes
Under thos healthless trees I sytt alone,
Wher joyfull byrdds singe neather lovely
  layes
Nor Phillomen recounts her direfull mone.
No feedinge flockes, no sheapherds
  cumpunye
That might renew my dollorus consayte,
While happy then, while love and fantasye
Confinde my thoughts onn that faire flock to
  waite;
No pleasinge streames fast to the ocean
  wendinge
The messengers sumetymes of my great woe,
But all onn yearth as from the colde stormes
  bendinge
Shrinck from my thoughts in hygh heavens
  and below.

[25-36]

The "sheapherds cumpunye" recalls the meeting pictured by Spenser in *Colin Clouts Come Home Againe*
where, by the banks of a pleasing stream, the Shepherd
of the Ocean sang his "lamentable lay" to Colin. Sorrows in this pastoral world are shared and transformed
into flowing, musical verse, poetry which pleases and
reassures even in expressing "great woe." For Ralegh,
the pastoral represents a human condition anterior to a
full consciousness of time, death, and individuality. It
is set against the silent, dead world in which the poet
now lives, the wasteland in which there is neither shared
joy nor shared sorrow, but only aching loneliness and
the total isolation of the self:

But all onn yearth as from the colde stormes
  bendinge
Shrinck from my thoughts in hygh heavens
  and below.

The mind reaches out to make contact with the world,
but the world shrinks back.

For the new human condition of radical isolation, there
must be a new kind of poetry. In the very first lines of
*Ocean to Cynthia,* Ralegh confronts the problem of
style:

Sufficeth it to yow my joyes interred,
In simpell wordes that I my woes cumplayne,
Yow that then died when first my fancy erred,
Joyes under dust that never live agayne.
If to the livinge weare my muse adressed,
Or did my minde her own spirrit still inhold,
Weare not my livinge passion so repressed,
As to the dead, the dead did thes unfold,
Sume sweeter wordes, sume more becumming
  vers,
Should wittness my myshapp in hygher kynd,

But my loves wounds, my fancy in the hearse,
The Idea but restinge, of a wasted minde,
The blossumes fallen, the sapp gon from the
  tree,
The broken monuments of my great desires,
From thes so lost what may th'affections bee,
What heat in Cynders of extinguisht fiers?

[1-16]

Poetic style and emotion are all but inseparable. A
phrase like "The broken monuments of my great desires" which refers to the poet's frustration and despair
also suggests the nature of the verse: the complex
syntax, logical discontinuities, sudden shifts of imagery and leaps in time. C. S. Lewis has observed of
*Ocean to Cynthia* that "as often happens in the work
of an amateur, what is unfinished is more impressive,
certainly more exciting, than what is finished," but the
poem's merits are not adventitious. Ralegh may have
intended to rework certain verses, but there is no evidence whatever that he would have altered its basic
character. On the contrary, the continual references to
things broken, fragmented, withered, and distorted, to
words scratched in the dust by a dying man, to an
immense history begun too late ever to be finished
indicate that Ralegh was remarkably aware of what he
was doing. *Ocean to Cynthia* is not only about the
death of love but about the death of a whole imaginative world sustained by that love.

The poet of *Ocean to Cynthia* has no firm ground
anywhere—his mistress' love, the natural world around
him, his poetic style, his very identity, all are subject
to instability and uncertainty. Even the names "Ocean"
and "Cynthia" seem strangely ambiguous and inconclusive. By themselves they are splendid and suggestive images for the relationship of subject and queen:
the ocean eternally drawn by the moon but never reaching her, the moon constantly changing and yet always
reaffirming herself; the ocean restless and immensely
powerful, the moon cold, distant, and beautiful. But
Ralegh does not weave his poem around these images
or draw out their latent meaning. On the contrary, the
queen is at one moment the moon and at the next the
sun (see 104-19) and Ralegh, the "Ocean," is alternately drowning in destructive floods (see 132-42) and
dying of fierce thirst (see 237-40, 478-80). Identity is
at all times too problematical in this poem for names
to denote anything clearly: the self and the beloved
continually shift in and out of focus, continually assume new qualities that modify or contradict the old.
If the names "Ocean" and "Cynthia" do have any constant meaning in the work as a whole, it lies only in
the suggestion of uncertainty and flux which they both
convey.

Similarly, the recurrent images in the poem—fire, water,
natural fertility—constantly promise a coherent and
logical path through the tangle of shifting emotions, a

resolution which they just as constantly fail to deliver. The imagery is tantalizingly interwoven in subtle and complex patterns, but, as in a kaleidoscope, the pieces fall into new and entirely different configurations as soon as they are perceived. The constant shifting from a world of dust to a world of mud and raging waters, from "th'Arabien sande" (478) to the "trobled ocean" (484), from the fire of destruction to the vestal fire of love, from the waters of redemption to the waters of death, finally leaves the reader with a sense of disorientation and bewilderment.

The instability of the imagery reflects the turbulent flux of the poet's emotions. The praise of the goddess becomes anguish at the waste of twelve long years in a bitter war; the beautiful, sweet face untouched by time is transformed into the cruel mask of an executioner; love itself turns into a curse bringing despair and death. Adoration and harsh reproach follow so quickly upon each other that at last they are indistinguishable:

> And like as that immortall pour douth seat
> An element of waters to allay
> The fiery soonn beames that on yearth do
> 　　beate
> And temper by cold night the heat of day,
> So hath perfection, which begatt her minde,
> Added therto a change of fantasye
> And left her the affections of her kynde
> Yet free from evry yevill but crueltye.
>
> 　　　　　　　　　　　　[205-12]

As God placed "an element of waters" (Genesis 1:7) between the earth and the sun for the protection of living things, so perfection has added inconstancy to Cynthia's nature! We await a resolution, a decisive turn to bitter irony or to love, but none is forthcoming. Instead, the mind of the poet constantly revolves upon itself, spiralling ever deeper into isolation.

Although in their constant shifts and reorientations, Ralegh's images become riddling and elusive, individually they are quite simple and public. With a few exceptions, they are drawn from the most conventional stockpile of the period: falling fruit, dust, fire, ice, blood, streams, grazing flocks, shepherd's pipes, sun, moon, and ocean. [Philip Edwards] has even suggested that Ralegh "is a plain man's poet; his fancy lingers by the experiences of everyday life, the permanent, the factual." But the very universality and simplicity of the images only heightens the sense of the poet's powerful shaping fancy:

> Such is agayne the labor of my minde
> Whose shroude by sorrow woven now to end
> Hath seene that ever shininge soonn declynde
> So many yeares that so could not dissende
> But that the eyes of my minde helde her

> beames
> In every part transferd by loves swift thought;
> Farr off or nire, in wakinge or in dreames,
> Imagination stronge their luster brought.
>
> 　　　　　　　　　　　　[104-11]

The relation between the poet's imagination and the world is deliberately rendered complex and ambiguous, for the mind both perceives and half creates. The drama of the poem takes place not in the realm of "the permanent, the factual," but in the poet's troubled consciousness, in his shifting perceptions of the world.

Ralegh's method in *Ocean to Cynthia* is highly personal, but it is not completely without parallel in the period. For example, in Sidney's famous "Ye Goteheard Gods," the conventional meanings of the sestina's terminal words are broken down in the successive stanzas. The mountains, valleys, and forests that begin as the properties of pastoral poetry and everyday life gradually become the landscape of the imagination, changing with the emotional moods of the speakers. One use of a word never completely cancels another—the effect is cumulative, inclusive, even where meanings are contradictory. William Empson [in his *Seven Types of Ambiguity*] has followed the metamorphoses of each of the key words through the poem. For example,

> *Mountains* are the haunts of Pan for lust and Diana for chastity, to both of these the lovers appeal; they suggest being shut in, or banishment; impossibility and importance, or difficulty and achievement; greatness that may be envied or may be felt as your own (so as to make you feel helpless, or feel powerful); they give you the peace, or the despair, of the grave; they are the distant things behind which the sun rises and sets, the too near things which shut in your valley; deserted wastes, and the ample pastures to which you drive up the cattle for the summer.

The images of *Ocean to Cynthia* have a similar ambiguity: thus, fire suggests the joyous ardor of love and the torments of hell; the searing pain of memory or the means of obliterating the past; the impulse to poetic creation or the destroyer of poetry; the pure, ethereal essence of beauty and the humble means used by the ploughman to destroy the stubble in his fields. In both poems there is no final determination of meaning, no veil to be lifted or essence to be revealed, but only ceaseless turns and returns.

Yet despite these resemblances, "Ye Gote-heard Gods" and *Ocean to Cynthia* are radically different. Sidney's Strephon and Klaius are like the speakers of Ralegh's early poems—virtually anonymous voices, undifferentiated from each other and from the hundreds of other figures just like them. They are not so much characters as convenient devices in the service of the formal structure to which Sidney faithfully and brilliantly adheres. Even at the climax of passion, the emotions never threaten to upset the exquisite balance and order of the form:

> *Strephon.* I wish to fire the trees of all these
>     forrests;
> I give the Sunne a last farewell each evening;
> I curse the fidling finders out of Musicke;
> With envie I doo hate the loftie mountaines;
> And with despite despise the humble vallies;
> I doo detest night, evening, day, and morning.
>
> *Klaius.* Curse to my selfe my prayer is, the
>     morning;
> My fire is more, then can be made with
>     forrests;
> My state more base, then are the basest
>     vallies;
> I wish no evenings more to see, each evening;
> Shamed I hate my selfe in sight of
>     mountaines;
> And stoppe mine ears, lest I growe mad with
>     Musicke.
>
>                                        [49-60]

For all the despair and violence, there is no straining against the structure. In **Ocean to Cynthia,** on the contrary, the speaker's powerful and individual sense of time constantly erupts into the poem, displaying itself in the explosions and slackenings of meter, the strained or broken syntax, the leaps in logic and meaning. There are traces of control, faded memories of Ralegh's former manner: a penchant for latinate syntax, the frequent use of repetition and parallelism, a division into quatrains (masked in the original manuscript by the absence of regular stanza divisions). But these barely suffice to keep the poem from anarchy. As if reacting to a verse that relies on form almost at the expense of consciousness, Ralegh writes a poem that relies on consciousness almost at the expense of form. **Ocean to Cynthia** seems to occupy that strange interior space between a sensation and the expression of that sensation in words, forever arrested at the moment of coming into being.

The order of Ralegh's poem comes not from quatrains or rhyme or syntax, nor from the principles of duration and repetition that govern poetry as musical expression, nor from the progressive development of images, but from an inner principle of continuity, a core of the self that resists the constant pull toward chaos. This principle—which Ralegh calls "love"—holds together not only the poem but the poet's very mind:

> But in my minde so is her love inclosde
> And is therof not only the best parte
> But into it the essence is disposde . . .
> Oh love (the more my wo) to it thow art

> Yeven as the moysture in each plant that
>     growes,
> Yeven as the soonn unto the frosen ground,
> Yeven as the sweetness, to th'incarnate rose,
> Yeven as the Center in each perfait rounde,
> As water to the fyshe, to men as ayre,
> As heat to fier, as light unto the soonn.
> Oh love it is but vayne, to say thow weare,
> Ages, and tymes, cannot thy poure outrun. . . .
> Thow are the sowle of that unhappy minde
> Which beinge by nature made an Idell thought
> Begon yeven then to take immortall kynde
> When first her vertues in thy spirrights
>     wrought. . . .
> From thee therefore that mover cannot move
> Because it is becume thy cause of beinge.
>                                        [426-43]

This love, then, has all but displaced God in Ralegh's world; the unmoved mover, it grants the poet's soul immortality. And yet, even as Ralegh speaks of his soul's essence and the essence of his poem, his statement calls forth a counterstatement:

> Yet as the eayre in deip caves under ground
> Is strongly drawne when violent heat hath rent
> Great clefts therin, till moysture do abound,
> And then the same imprisoned, and uppent,
> Breakes out in yearthquakes teringe all
>     asunder,
> So in the Center of my cloven hart,
> My hart, to whom her bewties wear such
>     wounder,
> Lyes the sharpe poysoned heade of that loves
>     dart,
> Which till all breake and all desolve to dust
> Thence drawne it cannot bee, or therin
>     knowne.
> Ther, mixt with my hart bludd, the fretting
>     rust
> The better part hath eaten, and outgrown. . . .
>                                        [450-61]

The love which was the element of unity, coherence, and immortality is now pictured as an explosive, destructive force hidden at the core of the self, poisoning and corroding the vital energies until at last it is violently released in the total annihilation of being.

And then, almost abruptly, the poet's will to continue questioning, probing, complaining gives way: "Butt stay my thoughts, make end, geve fortune way" (474). There has been no resolution; there is no reason to close but the exhaustion reflected in the attenuated rhythm: "Thus home I draw, as deaths longe night drawes onn" (509). Yet even here, on the threshold of death, the poet cannot completely free himself from thoughts of the past. In an extraordinary passage, the dream of love bursts once again into the verse:

On Sestus shore, Leanders late resorte,
Hero hath left no lampe to Guyde her love;
Thow lookest for light in vayne, and stormes
　arise;
Shee sleaps thy death that erst thy danger
　syth-ed
Strive then no more, bow down thy weery
　eyes,
Eyes, which to all thes woes thy hart have
　guided.
Shee is gonn, Shee is lost! Shee is found,
　shee is ever faire!
Sorrow drawes weakly, wher love drawes not
　too.
Woes cries, sound nothing, butt only in loves
　eare.
Do then by Diinge, what life cannot do. . . .
　　　　　　　　　　　　[487-96]

The sudden outburst, "Shee is found, shee is ever faire!"
is a momentary gasp of hope, a split-second vision of
the kind of poem Ralegh would like to have written: a
poem in celebration of renewed love. The vision van-
ishes as abruptly as it came, and the poet returns to the
slow process of dying.

Again and again *Ocean to Cynthia* frustrates the reader's desire for order, tempting him with patterns and
forms which suddenly are interrupted or dissolve or
veer away from his grasp. At the close of the 21st
Book, there is one last such experience:

My steapps are backwarde, gasinge on my
　loss
My minds affection, and my sowles sole love,
Not mixte with fancies chafe, or fortunes
　dross.
To God I leve it, who first gave it me,
And I her gave, and she returned agayne,
As it was herrs. So lett his mercies bee,
Of my last cumforts, the essentiall meane.
　　But be it so, or not, th'effects, ar past.
　　Her love hath end; my woe must ever
　　last.
　　　　　　　　　　　　[514-22]

Finally after all his suffering and anxious isolation, the
poet, like Petrarch at the end of the *Canzoniere,* turns
to God and prays for his mercy and comfort. The reader feels relief, a sense of homecoming—and then the
final couplet shatters this last movement toward transcendence. The "it" in that detached and indifferent
phrase "But be it so, or not" is nothing less than God's
mercy. The poet's suffering overpowers God Himself,
and the 21st Book ends not on a note of divine consolation but with an expression of private grief.

Yet the final outcome is not as significant as the process of the poem, its constant fluctuation of feeling.

Cut off from the traditional principles of stability in
his world and in himself, the poet undergoes a prolonged crisis of identity; conflicting images of the self
and the beloved present themselves on the stage of his
consciousness for a moment and then retire. The shat-
tered poet of *Ocean to Cynthia* resembles Richard II
in Pomfret Castle, who endlessly shuffles in his mind
a set of symbols that constantly shift their meaning:

Thus play I in one person many people,
And none contented. Sometimes am I a king:
Then treasons make me wish myself a beggar,
And so I am. Then crushing penury
Persuades me I was better when a king:
Then am I king'd again; and by and by
Think that I am unking'd by Bolingbroke,
And straight am nothing.
　　　　　　　　　　　　[v, v, 31-38]

As in Shakespeare's play, the tragedy in Ralegh's poem
begins with something external—a fall from power,
the destruction of a social role—and then moves deeper and deeper into the self. Ralegh sets out to write the
conventional "complaint" of the abandoned lover, the
part into which he cast himself after his disgrace. But
the old style, with its timeworn formulas, strict formal
controls, and a clear sense of identity, could not represent the isolation and the turbulent flux of his consciousness. And so Ralegh moves on his own, falter-
ingly, brilliantly, toward a new mode of self-representation. The theatricalism remains, but the stage has been
internalized: "My sowle the stage of fancies tragedye"
(144). The critical issue is no longer the fall from high
estate, but the tragedy of the imagination.

Once again, *Ocean to Cynthia* resembles *Richard II.*
Shut up in his dark cell, the deposed king struggles to
comprehend the disintegration of his life:

I have been studying how I may compare
This prison where I live unto the world;
And, for because the world is populous,
And here is not a creature but myself,
I cannot do it. Yet I'll hammer it out.
My brain I'll prove the female to my soul,
My soul the father; and these two beget
A generation of still-breeding thoughts;
And these same thoughts people this little
　world,
In humours like the people of this world,
For no thought is contented.
　　　　　　　　　　　　[v, v, 1-11]

Isolated from the community of men and from his own
past, Richard's mind turns to the fashioning of metaphors—to the creation of poetry—as his only means of
reestablishing a coherent relation between himself and
the world. In the past, such creation came easily to
him. Sustained by the ceremonies of kingship, by the

stable role that he had inherited, he had effortlessly spun a complex web of metaphors. But now, his isolation has profoundly altered the nature of poetic creation. He must "hammer out" his metaphors, grapple with his "still-breeding thoughts," and create a new kind of poetry-in-process. If ultimately he fails to achieve any lasting coherence, he at least attains a heroic stature in the attempt.

Similarities between Shakespeare's play and *Ocean to Cynthia* are not the result of literary influence but of a common mood of doubt, a shared vision of the self and the universe as problematic and crisis-torn. Like *Richard II*, Ralegh's poem manages to capture that mysterious moment when the old fabric is undone and the new only beginning to be woven. It affords a precious glimpse of a dark and largely uncharted process: change in man's consciousness of himself. Such change is notoriously difficult to follow, because it almost never occurs as a cataclysm, but consists rather of a series of small, diverse, and exceedingly numerous alterations, like the movement of vast land masses that only rarely is violent enough to be felt as an earthquake. Thus historians clearly perceive a major alteration in consciousness between the Middle Ages and the Renaissance but cannot pin down the boundaries or even agree on the critical events. But in Ralegh's life and verse this slow change seems to be violently compressed. It is as if he entered history with a slightly archaic consciousness and had suddenly to catch up.

The 21st Book of *Ocean to Cynthia* is followed in the Hatfield House manuscript by a brief fragment in tercets entitled **"The end of the bookes, of the Oceans love to Scinthia, and the beginninge of the 22 Boock, entreatinge of Sorrow"** (*Poems*). The first nine lines are very much in the spirit of the preceding book: a declaration of grief by one in the evening and winter of his life, one whose times, "runn out in others happines, / Bring unto thos new joyes, and new borne dayes" (8-9). But the remaining lines turn—with a characteristic syntactical jolt—in a new direction:

So could shee not, if shee weare not the
  soonn,
Which sees the birth, and buriall, of all elce,
And holds that poure, with which shee first
  begunn;
Levinge each withered boddy to be torne
By fortune, and by tymes tempestius,
Which by her vertu, once faire frute have
  borne,
Knowinge shee cann renew, and cann create
Green from the grounde, and floures, yeven
  out of stone,
By vertu lastinge over tyme and date,
Levinge us only woe, which like the moss,
Havinge cumpassion of unburied bones
Cleaves to mischance, and unrepayred loss.

For tender stalkes—

                        [10-22]

The sense of isolation and mortality is undiminished, but there is a new note of resignation, of near acceptance. In a few lines, Ralegh sketches the last act of his tragedy, passing from anguish to a recognition of the larger movement in which his personal destiny had played only a minute part. He perceives a power which is at once in time and above it, a power which brings all things to fruition, leaves them to die, and passes on undiminished. He cannot share in this eternal process, for he views it from the time-bound perspective of the suffering individual, of the "withered boddy" and of "unrepayred loss." But there is a new sense of objectivity in the fragment, an objectivity in the contemplation of his own wretchedness that gives the closing image of the moss its strange air of detachment. It is as if Ralegh had passed *through* extreme self-consciousness to a state which more nearly resembles the consciousness of his early poems.

The fragment's return to the spirit of the past was prophetic. When a fleet he and others had financed brought back a fabulously rich Portuguese carrack, the *Madre de Dios,* Ralegh was released from the Tower. In time, he was partially reconciled with the queen and even reinstated as a favorite. But the relations between them were never what they once had been; the intimacy and intensity were gone. The only poem to the queen which survives from these last years of her reign is the lyric **"Now we have present made,"** an epilogue to Cynthia. Oakeshott discovered an autograph copy on the flyleaf of a notebook in which Ralegh assembled material for *The History of the World,* in other words, a notebook which Ralegh had with him during the years in the Tower from 1603 to 1616. As the lyric was probably written in 1602, it appears that after Elizabeth's death and Ralegh's imprisonment—after the collapse of his entire world—he copied out for himself a poem that he had written a few years earlier which recalled far happier days. Even when the poem was originally composed, shortly before the queen's death, it recreated an earlier mode of vision, a recollection of a time before the bitterness of the Essex rebellion and the melancholy of the closing years of the reign.

The lyric may have been, as Oakeshott suggests, the epilogue to an entertainment held in the queen's honor, which would help to explain the opening lines. But there is also a suggestion in the first stanza of a broader retrospect encompassing the many images in which Elizabeth had been figured over the years:

Now we have present made
To Cynthia, Phoebe Flora.
Diana, and Aurora.
Bewty that cannot vade.

The unpleasant memories of the queen's fickleness and vindictiveness have been purged away. She is once more a goddess, almost completely divorced from human nature:

> A floure of loves own planting
> A patern keipt by nature
> For bewty, forme, and stature
> When shee would frame a darlinge.

Those lines almost certainly recall earlier verses, now lost, to which Ralegh also alludes in *Ocean to Cynthia:*

> that natures wonder, Vertues choyse,
> The only parragonn of tymes begettinge
> Devin in wordes, angellical in voyse;
> That springe of joyes, that floure of loves own
>     setting [ . . . ]
> Such didsst thow her longe since discribe.
>
> [344-47, 351]

Again and again in this final poem to the queen, Ralegh reaches back into the past, giving form to the underlying unity of all the poems of his long courtship. "Time conquering all she mast'reth / By beinge alwaye new" (11-12) recalls both the fragment of the 22nd Book and **"Praisd be Dianas faire and harmles light"**; the "elementall fire / Whose food and flame consumes not" (13-14) is like both the "vestall fier that burnes, but never wasteth" of the 21st Book (189) and the "durable fyre / In the mynde ever burnynge" of the Walsingham ballad; the image of the quill drawn from an angel's wing recalls the second of Ralegh's introductory sonnets to *The Faerie Queene*. The anguished sense of isolation and mortality which gave *Ocean to Cynthia* its power is missing. Yet this too has left its traces in the poem's closing moments:

> But loves and woes expenc
> Sorrow can only write.
>
> [31-32]

**"Now we have present made"** is Ralegh's epilogue to his entire poetic self-dramatization.

## Marion Campbell (essay date 1990)

SOURCE: "Inscribing Imperfection: Sir Walter Ralegh and the Elizabethan Court," in *English Literary Renaissance,* Vol. 20, No. 2, Spring, 1990, pp. 233-53.

*[In the following essay, Campbell analyzes the structure and historical context of Raleigh's "The Ocean to Cynthia," arguing that the work is "a poem consumed with loss" for Raleigh's failure to remain in favor with Queen Elizabeth I.]*

The poem by Sir Walter Ralegh known as **"The Ocean to Scinthia"** has long provided a puzzle for critics, who acknowledge its emotional power and intellectual complexity, but feel uneasy about its clearly unfinished state. In twentieth-century criticism the poem has been largely ignored, or patronized, or else appropriated for an alien aesthetic; Donald Davice, for example, writing in 1960 [in *Elizabethan Poetry*], constructs it as a proto-modernist fragment, a daring prolepsis of the work of Eliot and Pound. In what follows I shall place **"The Ocean to Scinthia"** in a different critical formation, and argue that a knowledge of its original social context is a condition of its readability.

The temptation to make a narrative of Ralegh's life is not easily resisted; the episode we are concerned with has the shape of a tragedy. In 1592 Walter Ralegh, lowly-born, self-made courtier and favorite of Queen Elizabeth, is at the height of his power and fortune. He is Captain of the Queen's Guard (a position of special influence because it gives him constant and direct access to the Queen), and has received numerous grants of money, monopolies, and land, most recently the large and prosperous estate of Sherbourne. He is extravagant in behavior, splendid in dress, devoted to the Queen but feared and hated by the rest of the court and the populace at large for his damnable pride and ambition. With a turn of the wheel of fortune in the summer of 1592, he is sent to the Tower on Elizabeth's orders. While in prison he acts out the following scene, described by Arthur Gorges in a letter to Robert Cecil:

> I cannot chuse but aduertyse you of a straunge Tregedye y$^t$ this d[ay] had lyke to haue fallen owte betweene the Captayne of the Guarde, and the Lyuetennaunt of the Ordenaunce; If I had not by greate chaunce cum*m*en a[tt] the very instant to haue turned it into a Com*m*edye. For vppon the re[port] of hyr Ma:$^{ts}$ beings att S:$^r$ George Caryes; S:$^r$ W. Rawly hauing gazed an[d] syghed a longe tyme att hys study wyndow; fro*m* whence he mygh[t] discerne the Barges and boates aboute y$^e$ blackfryars stayers; soodayn[ly] he brake owte into a greate distemper, and sware y$^t$ hys Enymyes hadd of purpose brought hyr Ma:$^{tie}$ thethar, to breake hys gaule [in] sounder w$^t$ Tantalus Torment; that when shee wentt a way he myght see hys deathe before hys Eyes; w$^t$ many such lyke conc[eyts.] And as a mann transported w$^t$ passion; he sware to S:$^r$ George Care[w] that he wolde disguyse hymeselfe; and gett into a payer of Oares to Ease hys mynde butt w$^t$ a syght of the Queene; or els he p*r*otest[ed] his harte wolde breake. But the trusty Iaylor wold non of y$^t$ for displeasing the hygher powers, as he sayde w$^{ch}$ he more respect[ed] then the feading of hys humor; and so flatly refused to p*er*mitt hym[e]. But in conclusion vppon this disspute they fell flatt owt to collor[yq] outragius wordes; w$^t$ stryuing and struggling att y$^e$ doores, y$^t$ al[l] lamenes was forgotten; and in the fury of the conflyct, y$^e$ Iaylor [he] had hys newe perwygg torne of hys crowne. / And ye[t heare] the battle ended not, for att laste

they had gotten ow[te theyr daggers;] w^ch when I sawe I played the styckler betwene theme, and [so] purchased such a rapp on the knockles, y^t I wysht bothe theyr [pates] broken; and so w^t much a doo, they stayed theyr brawle [to see] my bloodyed fyngers . . . I feare S:^r W. Rawly; wyll shortely growe [to be] Orlando furioso; If the bryght Angelyca *per*seuer agaynst [hyme] a l[y]tt[le] lon[ger.]

This scene provides an emblem of Ralegh's relationship to the Queen. It is a nicely shaped account of a dramatic performance, with Ralegh in the central role. Gorges presents it as a tragedy that turns into a comedy, as his own intervention prevents any violent outcome and reconciles the antagonists in a farcical resolution, featuring the comic props of torn periwigs, broken pates, and bloody knuckles. It is staged in a room in the Tower, the scene of Ralegh's imprisonment, but with a window that looks out on the Thames, where the court life from which Ralegh is excluded continues as usual: a view of the royal barge on the river was apparently the inspiration for this performance. Its audience is ostensibly Arthur Gorges, but as he himself makes clear in a postscript to the letter ("I could wyshe hyr Ma:^tie knewe"), the real audience is the Queen. The absence of Elizabeth necessitates the performance but also renders it futile, which is why the theatrical presentation has to be reported, re-presented in the form of a letter. Ralegh's act is structured as a drama, but the rhetoric of its passion is Petrarchan. The Petrarchan lover's mistress is always absent, and the only access he has to her is by sight or (more problematically) by literary self-presentation. Ralegh here plays the role of the melancholic and choleric lover, gazing and sighing and breaking into sudden rage at his mistress' proximity but inaccessibility. Instead of the sweet death of passion that the lover desires, he suffers the death of deprivation, absence, and loss: "when shee wentt a way he myght see hys deathe before hys Eyes." In his premediated disguise he imitates those literal disguises which Ovidian lovers willingly assume in order to get access to their mistresses, as well as the psychological disguise or transformation that a Petrarchan lover involuntarily undergoes through the power of desire. What breaks the tension of the scene is not sexual release but violent words and actions ("att laste they had gotten ow[te theyr daggers]"). The dagger is directed against the jailer, who is the surrogate for the woman who has captivated him. Gorges concludes his description by providing the literary source or analogue for Ralegh's performance: he has been playing the role of Ariosto's Orlando *furioso,* driven mad by his unrequited love for the fair Angelica. Paradoxically, what the self-consciously literary language and Petrarchan conceits draw attention to here is a set of literal, not figurative meanings. Ralegh is "imprisoned" not by his love for an inaccessible woman but by the walls of the Tower of London; the death

figured by the Queen's absence and withdrawal of favor might well be effected by execution; his only chance of reprieve is to convince Elizabeth that his faithfulness as a lover guarantees his loyalty as a subject; his only mode of access to the Queen is through such indirect, coded connivances as this dramatic performance and its verbal report.

My second text is a letter of about the same date (July 1592), again sent to Robert Cecil, this time written by Ralegh himself. Ralegh is still in the Tower and the Queen is about to leave court on one of her regular Progresses:

> My heart was never broken till this day, that I hear the Queen goes away so far of,—whom I have followed so many years with so great love and desire, in so many journey, and am now left behind her, in a dark prison all alone. While she was yet nire at hand, that I might hear of her once in two or three dayes, my sorrows were the less: but even now my heart is cast into the depth of all misery. I that was wont to behold her riding like *Alexander,* hunting like *Diana,* walking like *Venus,* the gentle wind blowing her fair hair about her pure cheeks, like a nymph; sometime siting in the shade like a Goddess; sometime singing like an angell; sometimes playing like *Orpheus.*

The implicit audience for this letter is once again the Queen, and the text is written around her absence. Ralegh plays the part of the abandoned, heartbroken lover while Elizabeth is cast as a series of historical and mythological figures of power—Alexander, Diana, Venus, Orpheus, nymph, angel, goddess. Her power is vested in her sovereignty, her chastity, her beauty, her artistry, and her divinity. These comparisons are the common currency of praise in the cult of Elizabeth, and Ralegh's participation in that cult is not to be seen as any less sincere because it is so conventional. Nor is his love for the Queen to be read as simply metaphorical; as he says, "All wounds have skares, but that of fantasie." The proof that his love wound is more than a fiction is the scar of his imprisonment. In any case, the letter subordinates flattery of the other to pity for the self, and expresses more compliant than contrition: "All those times past,—the loves, the sythes, the sorrows, the desires, can they not way down one frail misfortune? Cannot one dropp of gall be hidden in so great heaps of sweetness? I may then conclude, *Spes et fortuna, valete.* She is gone, in whom I trusted, and of me hath not one thought of mercy, nor any respect of that that was. Do with me now, therefore, what you list. I am more weary of life then they are desirous I should perish; which if it had been for her, as it is by her, I had been too happily born." The letter dramatizes—melodramatically and self-indulgently—Ralegh's sense of lost identity now that he can no longer claim any relationship with the Queen. Even that last desperate act of self-assertion of an abandoned lover—to die for his mistress—is impossible: Ralegh may perish *by* the Queen, but not *for* her. He subscribes himself "Your's, not worthy any name or title, W.R.," where the initials stand as ciphers for an empty self waiting to be filled by the restoration of the Queen's favor. Furthermore, the doubling of "name or title" suggests that Ralegh is primarily concerned with a social identity: loss of the Queen's favor brings not just psychological but also social and financial devastation. This letter, like the dramatic performance discussed earlier, is a coded bid for the restoration of royal patronage.

Such letters provide a context in which to read Ralegh's longest and most enigmatic poem, **"The Ocean to Scinthia."** The poem shares with the letters a Petrarchan vocabulary of thwarted love, broken faith, and unrewarded service. It too focuses on the experience of love as loss by contrasting past and present, and its mode is self-consciously literary and theatrical. Like the two letters to Cecil, it was, I believe, the product of Ralegh's imprisonment in the Tower in 1592. This is the date suggested by Ralegh's twentieth-century editor Agnes Latham, and accepted by most modern commentators, although there is no reliable contemporary evidence for the dating of any of Ralegh's poems. Even if the poem was not written when Ralegh was literally in the Tower, however, it is explicable only in terms of that experience, for it requires the physical imprisonment of its author by a female monarch in the role of Petrarchan mistress. It represents Ralegh's exclusion from a social system which confers identity upon the poet and significant on his poem.

**"The Ocean to Scinthia"** takes the form of a lover's lament for a lost mistress. The "Shepherd of the Ocean" is the whimsical pastoral title given by Spenser to Ralegh in *Colin Clouts Come Home Againe,* a piece of wit based on Ralegh's prowess as a sea captain and on Elizabeth's pronunciation of his given name "Walter" as "Water," in mockery of his broad West-Country accent. The mythological conceit of the Queen as Cynthia, chaste goddess of the moon, seems to have been especially associated with Ralegh: in the prefatory letter to *The Faerie Queene* Spenser commends Ralegh on his "excellent conceipt of Cynthia," and the most famous miniature of Ralegh shows him as Elizabeth's courtier in an elaborate costume encrusted with pearls (the Queen's sign of virginity), with a crescent moon of pearls in the top left-hand corner. **"The Ocean to Scinthia"** alludes not only to the story of the mortal shepherd Endymion who fell in love with the moon goddess, but also to the moon's attractive power over the waters of the ocean. Although the title leads one to expect a poem addressed "to Scinthia," Ralegh begins by talking to a personified aspect of himself ("my ioyes interred")

> Sufficeth it to yow my ioyes interred.
> in simpell wordes that I my woes cumplayne,

> you that then died when first my fancy erred.
> ioyes vnder dust that never live agayne:
> If to the liuinge weare my muse adressed.
> or did my minde her own spirrit still inhold.
> weare not my livinge passion so repressed,
> as to the dead, the dead did thes vnfold,
> svme sweeter wordes, svme more becuming
>     vers,
> should wittness my myshapp in hygher kynd.
> but my loues wounds, my fancy in the hearse
> the Idea but restinge, of a wasted minde.
> the blossvmes fallen, the sapp gon from the
>     tree.
> the broken monuments of my great desires,
> from thes so lost what may th' affections bee,
> what heat in Cynders of extinguisht fiers?
>
>                                         (ll. 1-16)

The introspective or self-referential nature of the complaint is thus established at the outset: Cynthia is not accessible to Ralegh even as the recipient of his verse, and he himself is his only audience. Subject merges into object, by a confusion of pronouns which suggests both self-division and enforced solipsism. "Loss," "death," and "woe" are words echoed throughout the poem. The decorum of grief is foregrounded immediately in the "simpell wordes" we are promised and delivered, and the "hygher kynd" that is eschewed. The verse is elaborately patterned, the syntax complex; rhythm and rhyme fall regularly here, although even these ordering principles are dislocated as the poem proceeds. The poem is figured as a dead shell of verse, like the poet's faculties deprived of the animating force of love. The prodigality and confusion of imagery constitute traces of a lost structure of meaning: what remains is experienced as decay, ruin, and fragmentation.

"The broken monuments of my great desires" epitomizes a poem long taken to be unfinished. The poem's confusing syntax seems to support such a reading, for the grammatical logic by which it achieves its effects is not always clear. Its long and syntactically complicated sentences offer the appearance, and sometimes the actuality, of syntactical irresolution. Clauses accumulate without being subordinated to a finite verb; the writing relies heavily on parallelism and repetition, and defeats readers in search of syntactical clarity and regularity. This effect is replicated by the use of extended similes which, like epic similes, are frequently digressive and seem to obscure rather than clarify their referents. Far from being cumulative, such chains of similes collapse back on themselves instead of developing climactically. The poem we are reading represents itself as the unnatural and futile product of an obsessive need to write, even when meaning is no longer attainable. Both the need to write and the futility of doing so are asserted in the confusions of the text.

The mismatch between what the title promises and what the poem performs is a further sign of a purpose imperfectly executed or fundamentally misconceived. The moon's control over the waters of the ocean is not replicated as an ordering principle in the poem, nor does Ralegh use the mythological associations of Cynthia to develop a sustaining fiction or narrative structure. His poem neither tells the story of the Ocean's love to Cynthia nor exhibits any sign of narrative progression. It conspicuously avoids such principles of order. The same is true of Ralegh's use of two other conventions which could have functioned as structuring devices, pastoralism and Petrarchism. The poem begins by recalling the pastoral fellowship (celebrated in Spenser's *Colin Clouts Come Home Againe*) from which Ralegh has been excluded:

> No feedinge flockes, no sheapherds cumpunye
> that might renew my dollorus consayte
> while happy then, while loue and fantasye
> confinde my thoughts onn that faire flock to
>     waite.
>
> (ll. 29-32)

Love, of course, is a central preoccupation in the pastoral world, and unrequited love a common theme of shepherds' songs. Exclusion from natural consolations designates the alienating power of Cynthia's rejection, emphasized in the preceding stanzas by the picture of a pastoral world intact but inaccessible to him alone. These pastoral references return perfunctorily at the end of the poem, as attempts are made to present old age and imminent death in traditional pastoral terms as an incorporation into the landscape. But in place of resignation and extinction we find the continuing agony of loss: "My steapps are backwarde, gasinge on my loss, / my minds affection, and my sowles sole love" (ll. 514-15). The inefficacy of the pastoral conventions signifies an ordered world from which the poet is excluded. The crypto-presence of the Petrarchan convention is equally obvious. The mistress who holds complete sway over her lover's body, heart, and soul is the source of his poetic inspiration. Traditional Petrarchan oxymora are mobilized: "Such heat in Ize, such fier in frost remaynde" (l. 69). Cynthia is presented inevitably as perfect in her beauty and virtue. Along with an inaccessible mistress and a desperate lover, the cast of the poem also included successful rivals. Collectively, these Petrarchan commonplaces gesture toward a system which has lost its power to sustain hopes or explain existence.

Lacking a future, Ralegh turns to the past in a poem remarkable for its inclusion of quotations from or allusions to his own earlier verse. Self-quotation—the recycling of words given a radically new meaning in a different context—is a feature of Ralegh's career, notably in his appropriation and rewriting of the final stanza of one of his love poems ("Nature that washt her hands in milke") as his own epitaph in verses reputedly inscribed in his Bible on the night before his execution. Such bizarre juxtapositions of context constitute the textuality of "**The Ocean to Scinthia**":

> Twelue yeares intire I wasted in this warr
> twelue yeares of my most happy younger
>     dayes,
> butt I in them, and they now wasted ar
> of all which past the sorrow only stayes,
> So wrate I once and my mishapp fortolde
> my minde still feelinge sorrowful success
> yeven as before a storme the marbell colde
> douth by moyste teares tempestious tymes
>     express.
>
> (ll. 120-27)

Here Ralegh himself draws attention to the quotation as a prolepsis of what he is suffering now. It is as though the earlier text, itself concerned with the passing of joy and the continuing of sorrow, were scripting both the poem he is writing and the situation it describes. The quotation erupts into the poem, fracturing its surface and drawing attention to its own textuality. Never quite sure of the source of the words we are reading, we are made forcibly aware that this is not a seamless text but one cobbled together from bits and pieces of earlier writing. Quotation is thus annexed into the rhetoric of fragmentation.

"**The Ocean to Scinthia**," in short, appears unfinished in such formal respects as meter, rhyme, and stanza form. Its syntax is frequently ambiguous, and the relationship between its literal and metaphorical levels is unstable. It exhibits no discernible structure, narrative or otherwise. It reads like a highly introspective poem which continually gestures toward a public world from which it has been excluded. Furthermore, it keeps on foregrounding its own origins and thematizing its irresolutions. The poem's enigmatic title can be taken as a particularly interesting example of this self-consciousness. Its full title in the one surviving manuscript copy is "**The 21th: and last booke of the Ocean to Scinthia**"; it is followed by an even more fragmentary poem entitled "**The end of boockes, of the Oceans love to Scinthia, and the beginninge of the 22 Boock, entreatinge of Sorrow.**" Ralegh's poetic reputation over the last hundred years has been shadowed by the myth of his lost masterpiece, *Cynthia,* imagined by critics to have been an immense cycle poem in twenty-two books, celebrating the poet's love for his Queen. The reputation of the Cynthia poems now available has been compromised by this belief that they are merely small fragments of a lost whole. In the absence of any tangible evidence for the existence, let alone the nature, of a vast *Cynthia* poem in twenty-two books; and faced with the confessed failure of modern critics to imagine how such a project might be conceived, let alone sustained; and given the further problem that the manuscript titles seem to bear little relation to the substance of the poems, we must take seriously the contention that the titles represent a rhetorical strategy designed precisely to highlight their fragmentariness, and to point up ironically the disparity between their ambition and their achivement. Consequently, I want to argue that the poem which calls itself **"The 21th . . . booke of the Ocean to Scinthia"** is presented as radically incomplete, addressed to an absent Queen whose presence alone would complete it.

I now want to return to the scene of Ralegh's imprisonment, which is the enabling context for the texts I have been discussing. First it is important to take account of an element not yet mentioned—namely, the reason for his disgrace. In March 1591/1592, in the face of growing rumors at court, Ralegh wrote to Cecil: "I mean not to cume away, as they say I will, for feare of a marriage, and I know not what." But shortly after, it was revealed that the Queen's favorite courtier had indeed secretly committed marriage with Elizabeth Throckmorton, one of the Queen's Maids of Honor. For this offense they were both arrested and sent to the Tower. There are a number of puzzles here. Why was marriage a transgressive act at the Elizabethan court, and more importantly, how are we to understand the relationship between Ralegh's role as Petrarchan lover to Queen Elizabeth and as real-life husband to Elizabeth Throckmorton? Elizabeth's hostility to the marriage of her courtiers and favorites is well known, and political explanations of this have recently begun to displace those historical and "psychological" interpretations which focus on the Queen's neurotic jealousy. Elizabeth kept close watch over court marriages in order to protect the bloodlines of her aristocracy and thus control the exercise of power through the inheritance of wealth and title. The marriage of the Earl of Hertford and Lady Catherine Grey, for example, which took place without Elizabeth's permission, was perceived as a direct threat to her authority, since any child they had would be a potential heir to the throne. The couple were imprisoned in the Tower and their marriage annulled in order to render their children illegitimate and thus unable to inherit the crown. In this instance the political issues are clear, but less so in the case of Elizabeth's opposition to the marriages of three of her favorites, all supposedly suitors to the Queen herself: Leicester and Lettice Knollys, Ralegh and Elizabeth Throckmorton, and Essex and Frances Walsingham, the widow of Sir Philip Sidney. The notion of "courtship" cannot have been simply an inert trope for "courtiership"; otherwise the furor surrounding these marriages would not have been so great, nor so costly for the men and women involved. Ralegh's marriage posed no political threat to Elizabeth, but it angered her nevertheless because it occurred without her permission and against her will; it was an assumption of personal autonomy that she was not prepared to allow her courtiers. More significantly, it violated the code of patron-

age whereby the courtier sued for the favor of his royal mistress and was rewarded not with sexual "grace," but with money and position. Elizabeth construed Ralegh's marriage as unfitting him for this role. He, on the other hand, attempted first to deny it and then to pass it off as an inconsequential error—in **"The Ocean to Scinthia"** he claims that his "error never was forthought / or ever could proceed from sence of lovinge" (ll. 338-39). But if Ralegh tried to claim that his marriage belonged to a different order of reality from his relationship with the Queen, she by contrast seemed to insist that the boundaries between fiction and reality were not so easily drawn, and that the strength of the patronage system consisted precisely in the impossibility of distinguishing between the code and the encoded. Ralegh was certainly playing a role as Elizabeth's lover, but in order to sustain it he had to forgo marriage to the Queen or anyone else. It is significant that what Elizabeth denies Ralegh is not sex—for his self-conscious, aggressive virility was a crucial aspect of his image at court—but the sanctioned and stable form of marriage. Marriage was too strong a closure: the distance between monarch and subject, like that between lady and lover, had to be kept open by desire. The fiction had to be realizable although it would never be realized. Ralegh's premature closure of that gap by his marriage removed him from a social system that operated under the dictates of desire. The dynamics of the court situation require one to keep active both terms of the metaphor that connects love and ambition, sex and power.

This crossing of codes can be illustrated by a recapitulation of the events surrounding Ralegh's imprisonment in 1592. Ralegh presents himself as the Queen's suitor and, after winning her grace, receives money and land; he is rewarded, that is, in terms of the code of patronage, not love. His position at court remains completely dependent on Elizabeth's personal favor; he is unable to establish any independent power base, and therefore he cannot afford to alienate the Queen's affections. He makes a marriage that serves no political alliance, but is merely the satisfaction of a private desire; yet his attempt to keep the marriage secret indicates that he recognizes its political implications. Elizabeth responds as a betrayed mistress, but exacts a public penalty for a crime construed politically as treason, a crime against the person of the monarch. From the Tower, Ralegh attempts to exonerate himself in a series of texts in which he adopts once again the role of Petrarchan lover. This strategy is completely ineffectual, however, because through his marriage Ralegh himself has ruptured the system of symbolic exchange on which the love game was based. The affair is finally resolved not at the symbolic but at the economic level. Ralegh is released five weeks after being imprisoned because only he can stop his sailors from looting a Portuguese treasure ship captured by his fleet. He supervises the distribution of profits from the ship, but his own share of an immensely profitable venture is a mere two thousand pounds from an investment of thirty-four thousand. By contrast, Elizabeth (who as usual had invested very little) received eighty thousand pounds. In other words, Ralegh purchased his freedom not with verse but with hard cash. He was not received at court for another five years, and he never regained his full influence there. As [Leonard] Tennenhouse concludes [in "Sir Walter Ralegh and the Literature of Clientage," in *Patronage in the Renaissance,* ed. Guy Fitch Lytle and Stephen Orgel, 1981]: "For transgressing the rules upon which his social status, political power, and economic well-being rested, Ralegh was in effect punished with the equivalent of a heavy fine, exile from Court, and a greatly weakened political position."

Power relations in the Elizabethan court were enormously complicated by the fact that the monarch at the center of a phallocratic structure had a female body. This fractured the homology between the "natural" hierarchical relationship of male and female and the hierarchy of prince and subject. The contradiction was partly negotiated by a doctrine based on medieval political theology and encoded in Elizabethan law in 1561, the doctrine of the Queen's two bodies. The *corpus naturale* was fallible and mortal, but the *corpus politicum* was unerring and immortal. Unlike the modern state, which is defined territorially with power vested in neither the ruler nor the ruled, the Elizabethan body politic was contained within the natural body of the Queen. Even though her body natural was female, the power symbolized by her body politic was decidedly male. This necessitated a change in Tudor somatic symbolism to insure a privileging of the female body. Henry VIII's state power had been expressed in images of personal virility, the "manhood" necessary both to protect his nation and to engender an heir for it. Elizabeth was intent on fostering a much more exact identification of her body with the body of the realm. With its inviolable frontiers, moral purity, and unchanging physical state, virginity became the connecting link between the natural and political bodies. The Queen's marriage prospects were the most significant political issue for decades of Elizabeth's reign, as her counselors feared first that as a woman she was too weak to rule without a husband, and then that her failure to produce a natural heir would plunge the country into a crisis of succession. Her femininity was constructed consistently as a lack. Elizabeth, by contrast, presented her virginity as the single most important guarantee of her country's safety, a personal virtue that was simultaneously a political asset.

The iconography of much Elizabethan portraiture presents the Queen's body as identical in limits and sanctity to the land of England. The Armada victory was established and celebrated as the defense of the Queen's body against violation by the hated Spanish king. This is the theme of the Queen's famous address to her troops preparing the defense against the Armada: "I know I have the body but of a weak and feeble woman; but I have the heart and stomach of a king, and of a king of England too; and think foul scorn that Parma or Spain, or any Prince of Europe should dare to invade the borders of my realm; to which rather than any dishonour shall grow by me, I myself will take up arms." Here Elizabeth acknowledges the vulnerability of her female body at the same time as she proclaims its defense by her body politic. The two are seen not as grotesquely disjunctive in the mingling of male and female, but as mutually defining as the relationship between realm and sovereign. At the level of the body natural Elizabeth admits that her female parts are inferior to (because constitutionally weaker and less perfect than) those of the male; this is the dominant construction of gender at this period, and one that Elizabeth cannot challenge. However, at the level of the symbolic body (the body politic, which is the domain of political power), her female body, with all the signs of its femininity intact, assumes masculine powers at the expense of a group of symbolically feminized male subjects. In this way Elizabeth preserves the hierarchies of gender, but still exercises the full rights of phallocratic dominion.

Elizabeth manipulated this symbolism successfully throughout her reign, but for her male courtiers it remained a source of anxiety. In this context, the strategies of Petrarchan representation were discovered to be particularly useful. "Petrarchism," as Louis Montrose reminds us [in *Literary Theory / Renaissance Texts,* ed. Patricia Parker and David Quint, 1986], "is one of the discourses in which a recognizably modern mode of subjectivity—an introspective egocentricity founded upon the frustration and sublimation of material desires—is first articulated and actively cultivated." Furthermore, it requires to be understood as a gendered discourse: the subjectivity so fashioned is distinctively masculine. The main elements of the Petrarchan dynamic are an actively desiring male subject and a passive female object. The project of the Petrarchan lover is self-construction, and this is achieved by the shaping and reshaping of the feminine Other whose body is the body of the text, subjected to masculine control. In content Petrarchan lyric poetry presents an all-powerful woman who as chaste, beloved, and beautiful goddess, or inspiring muse, seems to control the abject male, frustrating his "natural" desires and dictating his verse. Structurally, however, the power relations are reversed, because the woman is in fact controlled, indeed created, by the self-creating male subject. Such poetry reasserts in the realm of the symbolic those patriarchal prerogatives that an individual male feels himself unable to exercise in the social world.

At the Elizabethan court Petrarchism was the favored mode of address to the Queen. Its usefulness is immediately apparent: it offered a sanctioned literary code for articulating and perhaps turning to advantage an anomalous political situation—namely, the sovereignty of a woman in a phallocratic order. The role of the Petrarchan mistress was particularly amenable to Elizabeth's project of self-fashioning, for it provided those elements of purity, inaccessibility, and desirability that she was so adept at manipulating. She used the codes of Petrarchism to claim her femininity as a source of power. But as we have seen, those codes were double-edged: the male courtier who adopted them was able to take advantage not only of their strategies of praise and protestations of subjection, but also of their covert self-assertion in the structural privileging of the male subject over the female object. The demystification of the Queen's sovereignty as erotic attraction, and the translation of the body of the state into a female body, make that body available not only for veneration but also for violation. As Montrose points out, "erotic conventions structure Elizabethan relations of power in ways advantageous to the writing subject." It is no accident, therefore, that male poets preferred to represent the Queen as "Belphoebe," chaste goddess and Petrarchan mistress, rather than as Gloriana, the sovereign Queen. Spenser appears to offer Elizabeth a choice of roles: "But either Gloriana let her chuse, / Or in *Belphoebe* fashioned to bee: / In th'one her rule, in th'other her rare chastitee" (*Faerie Queene* III, Proem V). But while Belphoebe is a character inside *The Faerie Queene,* fashioned by Spenser himself, Gloriana remains outside its representative strategies, as the goal which the poem desires but never achieves, except in a projected ending where the powers of Gloriana are transfigured into those of God himself. No other Elizabethan poem rivals Spenser's in attempting to represent the sovereign power of Elizabeth. Instead, the Queen tends to be figured forth in countless Petrarchan and pastoral guises, where she provides the subject of the verse by becoming the object of the poet's self-presentation. The lines from the Proem to Book III of *The Faerie Queene* quoted above occur in the context of a complimentary allusion to Ralegh, which is echoed in a line from **"The Ocean to Scinthia"**: "a Queen shee was to mee, no more Belphebe" (l. 327). Ralegh's marriage, and Queen Elizabeth's reaction to it, deny him access to the strategies of Petrarchan representation by which alone he can approach his sovereign. He can manipulate her as Belphoebe, but as Queen she is literally inaccessible to him. The signs of her absolute royal power are his imprisonment and his loss of social identity: in the Tower, he says [in **"My boddy in the walls captived"**], "I alone / speake to dead walls, butt thos heare not my mone." He becomes silent not because he cannot speak but because he is not heard. Only as Belphoebe (or her alternative image, Cynthia) does Elizabeth provide an audience for Ralegh's verse; he cannot address her as Queen.

This is why **"The Ocean to Scinthia"** is addressed to the poet's dead joys, and why it obsessively recycles fragments of his past in a vain attempt to construct for himself a present. It is also why the poem remains incomplete; it cannot form a finished, perfected piece of work without the audience of the Queen. **"The Ocean to Scinthia"** is frequently taken to be a classic of introspection, one of the earliest English Renaissance texts to portray the isolated speaking voice of an individualized poet. But I think that this is a romantic misreading of a poem which demonstrates the ego's incapacity to fashion itself inside poetic discourse without social sanction. Two elements of that formulation—self-fashioning within a work of art—are brilliantly identified in Stephen Greenblatt's pioneering study of Ralegh [*Sir Walter Ralegh: The Renaissance Man and His Roles,* 1973], where the metaphor of theatricality is used to demonstrate the intimate connection between Ralegh's "life" and "art," and to illuminate the "roles" that he adopts on the "stage" of the Elizabethan court. Greenblatt argues convincingly that Ralegh's "dramatic sense of life" meant that he lived out a series of roles—splendid courtier, brave adventurer, betrayed lover, wise and witty writer, patient and sardonic prisoner, heroic martyr—in which reality and fiction were evenly mixed and mutually sustaining: "Ralegh's self-fashioning is paradoxical: it bends art to the service of life—advancing his career, justifying his actions, enhancing his reputation—and it transforms life into art, leading even further from the career toward symbolic characterization and transcendent meaning." In making the dichotomy between art and life so exact, however, Greenblatt allows too neatly for the translation of one into the other, and consequently underplays the informing significance of social context. Any move toward "transcendent meaning" in Ralegh's art is blocked by the intransigences of the real-life situation that scripts it. Art does not—cannot—provide compensation in a private world for any deprivation or loss suffered publicly: it merely repeats that loss in a different mode. Ralegh's identity is socially fashioned—that is the point of describing it in terms of role-playing—and poetry provides one of the forums for that fashioning. But both "life" and "poem" are products of a social process. The imbrications of art and life are troped convincingly by Greenblatt as role-playing, but a major consequence of that metaphor, that every performance implies an audience and therefore a context, is underestimated. So, although his study goes a long way towards freeing **"The Ocean to Scinthia"** from largely formalist readings, it effectively preserves the aesthetic as a shaping category separate from the social. My contention, on the contrary, is that while these categories are theoretically separable (and have indeed been separated by all critics of Ralegh's life and works), Ralegh's dilemma was the impossibility of maintaining that distinction in the Elizabethan court. Ralegh's identity as courtier, lover, and poet depends on Elizabeth's playing the role of

Queen, mistress, and reader: those identities are the product of a relationship, and are neither self-generating nor self-sustaining. Ralegh's social identity is eradicated when he is disgraced, just as his very existence is threatened by the Queen's displeasure. The letters and poems he directs to the Queen attempt to reassert his identity by reestablishing a relationship with her through Petrarchan discourse. But because Elizabeth believes the Petrarchan role is betrayed by his marriage, she refuses to respond in any mode but that of Queen, exacting a fine and imposing a banishment. The poetry remains inert because it is ineffectual. **"The Ocean to Scinthia"** cannot provide the ground for a renewed self-fashioning because it is denied the feminine Other, which it requires for the construction of a masculine self, and because it no longer participates in the social system which would confer meaning upon it.

**"The Ocean to Scinthia,"** then, is a poem consumed with loss, and in particular with the loss of the woman who provided the principle of intelligibility for Ralegh's life and art. Words fail to "knit up" that loss, because Elizabeth is the enabling cultural presence in Ralegh's world. With her loss the poet loses access to that whole system of signification centered on the Queen, and he is doomed to meaninglessness. The poem mimes in language a desire that cannot link up with its object, with the result that words remain signs without significance. Critics have tended to read this poem as depicting the exhaustion of a whole order of symbolism, and as an attempt to establish a new site of transcendent value in the self. But I believe on the contrary that the deepest source of the despair it articulates is that the symbolic order is intact but inaccessible to Ralegh. The poem demonstrates over and over again that the natural and social worlds—together with the values they symbolize, encoded in the material forms of language and poetry—survive, but the poet cannot make use of them. The poem is preoccupied with ending; but because it cannot achieve its goal (an end outside the text), it remains unfinished, trapped in the repetition of its gestures of impotence:

> Butt stay my thoughts, make end, geue fortvne
> way
> harshe is the voice of woe and sorrows sovnde
> cumplaynts cure not, and teares do butt allay
> greifs for a tyme, which after more abovnde
> to seeke for moysture in th' arbien sande
> is butt a losse of labor, and of rest
> the lincks which tyme did break of harty bands
> words cannot knytt, or waylings make a new,
> seeke not the soonn in clovdes, when it is sett . . .
> On highest mountaynes wher thos Sedars grew
> agaynst whose bancks, the trobled ocean bett
> and weare the markes to finde thy hoped port
> into a soyle farr of them sealves remove
> on Sestus shore Leanders late resorte
> Hero hath left no lampe to Guyde her love
> Thow lookest for light in vayne, and stormes arise

> Shee sleaps thy death that erst thy danger syth-ed
> strive then no more bow down thy weery eyes
> eyes, which to all thes woes thy hart have guided
> Shee is gonn, Shee is lost, Shee is fovnd, shee is
>   ever faire,
> Sorrow drawes weakly, wher love drawes not too
> woes cries, sound nothinge, butt only in loves eare
> Do then by Diinge, what life cannot doo . . .
>
>                                           (ll. 474-96)

Here the poet understands that sorrow, the substance of his song, simply multiplies itself, increasing rather than purging grief. Words are empty ciphers which cannot restore lost love or make present the absent mistress. Once the light of Hero's love is extinguished, Leander is doomed to drown: "Shee sleaps thy death that erst thy danger syth-ed" (l. 490). The final lines here make clear the dangers of that destabilizing of subjectivity which the poet has been forced to experience: there is no referent for these random perceptions. For Ralegh the Queen is "lost," although she remains "ever faire" in the Elizabethan court from which he is excluded. Even his sorrow, the only mode of self-determination left to him, is meaningless without the love to which it refers. The elaborate chiasmus of the last line shows the deadlock he has reached: the outcome of his sorrow is simple extinction, the loss of all social, psychological, and physical identity. But the poem cannot stop even at such an apparently definite point of no return. It struggles on for a further twenty-six lines, invoking conventional pastoral and religious consolations only to find them totally irrelevant: "But be it soo, or not, th' effects, ar past, / her love hath end. my woe must ever last" (ll. 521-22). The strong couplet ending reinforces the bleak statement here: because Cynthia's love is ended, the Ocean's woe is everlasting. And like the sea from which he takes his name, the poet's identity is unfixed and boundless, his poem an unstructured and meaningless fragment. In terms of the signifying system of the poem itself, Cynthia, its principle of intelligibility, is absent, because in the public world the poet strives to imitate, the Queen is cut off irrevocably from the poet. Moreover, Ralegh cannot exist separately from that social world, for its significance as well as its perfectibility remain a function of the relationship between the Queen and her court. Excised from that relationship, Ralegh discovers that he means nothing, and that the only thing he can inscribe in his writing is imperfection. So the poem passes into oblivion, and waits for some three hundred years before being rediscovered as a historical and poetic curiosity.

In conclusion, I want to return to some lines from **"The Ocean to Scinthia"**:

> as if when after phebus is dessended
> and leues a light mich like the past dayes
>   dawninge,

and every toyle and labor wholy ended
each livinge creature draweth to his restinge
wee should beginn by such a partinge light
to write the story of all ages past
and end the same before th'aprochinge night.

(ll. 97-103)

Inside the lyric mode of **"The Ocean to Scinthia"** Ralegh contemplates the possibility of writing his life not as Petrarchan drama but as universal history. It was an opportunity he was to be given after the death of Elizabeth by the accession of a male monarch whose literary interests were defined in the public forms of history, philosophy, and divinity. In July 1603 Ralegh was again arrested and sent to the Tower on a charge of treason, although this time the monarch was James I, and Ralegh was implicated in a direct rather than a symbolic plot on the King's life. He was put on trial, and although the evidence against him was flimsy and almost certainly fabricated, and in spite of his brilliant self-defense, he was found guilty and sentenced to death. At the last moment he was reprieved, but remained in the Tower for the next thirteen years.

These circumstances repeat in a grimmer mode those of his earlier period of imprisonment under Elizabeth, and again Ralegh turns to writing in an effort to establish his innocence and buy his freedom. Once more, however, the text proves useless and remains incomplete. The literary task Ralegh undertakes in 1604 is the one foreshadowed in **"The Ocean to Scinthia,"** the writing of "the story of all ages past" as an act of assertion against the gathering darkness. But as the lines indicate, the project is inconceivable except as a gesture of hopeless defiance, and its failure, its imperfection, is part of its script. Ralegh's **History of the World** was addressed not to King James, whose personal hatred and mistrust of Ralegh was one of the major reasons for his downfall, but to James's heir Prince Henry. Henry's enlightened literary and scientific interests, his manifest Protestantism, and his financial generosity made his court an attractive alternative source of patronage in the early years of James's reign. Henry showed Ralegh great favor, interceding for him with the King and protecting his financial interests; Ralegh in turn dedicated **The History of the World** to Henry. Prince Henry's death in November 1612 meant the end of Ralegh's hopes of freedom, the loss of his estate at Sherbourne which Henry was holding in his name, and the failure of his text. Deprived of its intended audience, the **History,** like **"The Ocean to Scinthia,"** became meaningless. Leonard Tennenhouse has shown persuasively how the narrative strategies of the **History** are decentered by Henry's death: Ralegh loses interest in his story and does not continue it beyond 167 B.C., thus excluding all mention of Christ. This is an astonishing omission in a self-styled providential history, since Christ's incarnation should have provided the central demonstration of God's control over human affairs. Book V of Ralegh's history proceeds mechanically in its cataloguing of events, and regains force and direction only in its final paragraphs on the power of death:

> O eloquent, just and mightie Death! whom none could aduise, thou hast perswaded; what none hath dared, thou hast done; and whom all the world hath flattered, thou only hast cast out of the world and despised: thou hast drawne together all the farre stretched greatnesse, all the pride, crueltie, and ambition of man, and couered it all ouer with these two narrow words, *Hic iacet.*

> Lastly, whereas this Booke, by the title it hath, calles it selfe, The first part of the *Generall Historie* of the *World,* implying a *Second,* and *Third* Volume; which I also intended, and haue hewen out; besides many other discouragements, perswading my silence; it hath pleased God to take that glorious *Prince* out of the world, to whom they were directed; whose vnspeakable and neuer enough lamented losse, hath taught mee to say with Iob, *Versa est in Luctum Cithara mea, et Organum meum in vocem flentium.*

Here Ralegh explicitly links the incompletion of his text to the absence of his patron. This suggests that the social context determines both the literary strategies of the author as well as the reading practices of its contemporary audience. When the **History** was published in 1614, King James ordered all copies to be seized, thus justifying Ralegh's fear that without a patron his text would be literally unreadable. When Ralegh was released from the Tower in 1617 (having regained the patronage of the King by his plan to discover the fabulous wealth of El Dorado), James permitted and profited from the reprinting of the **History.** Even a brief recounting of these events suggests that literary texts could not *create* patronage relationships, although they themselves could be radically altered or disabled by changes in existing patronage systems. Such texts, in other words, are not autonomous but produced in the social world by relations of power and desire. The fate of Ralegh's vast and unfinished **History of the World** provides support for the argument that it was social determinants rather than textual inadequacies which prevented **"The Ocean to Scinthia"** from achieving closure.

## Louis Montrose (essay date 1991)

SOURCE: "The Work of Gender in the Discourse of Discovery," in *Representations,* No. 33, Winter, 1991, pp. 1-41.

[*In the following essay, Montrose examines the cultural background of Raleigh's* The Discoverie of Guiana *(1596), focusing specifically on the presence of such opposing values in the work as European and Indian, English and Spanish, culture and nature, and male and female.*]

Early modern Europe's construction of its collective Other in "the New World"—its construction of the "savage" or the "Indian"—was accomplished by the symbolic and material destruction of the indigenous peoples of the Western Hemisphere, in systematic attempts to destroy their bodies and their wills, to suppress their cultures and to efface their histories. This process of protocolonialist "othering" also engages, interacts with, and mediates between two distinctive Elizabethan discourses: one, articulating the relationship between Englishmen and Spaniards; the other, articulating the relationship between the woman monarch and her masculine subjects. The latter discourse is inflected by the anomalous status of Queen Elizabeth—who is at once a *ruler,* in whose name the discoveries of her masculine subjects are authorized and performed; and also a *woman,* whose political relationship to those subjects is itself frequently articulated in the discourses of gender and sexuality. The paradoxes and contradictions implicit in each of these discourses are foregrounded when they are brought together in a conjuncture with the discourse of discovery. Within the intertwined and unstable terms of collective national and gender identity, I focus upon an individual Englishman and Elizabethan subject—Sir Walter Ralegh—whose production of these discourses in his writings and performances is marked by the idiosyncrasies of his personal history and circumstances.

The writings of critics, too, are necessarily subject to historical and idiosyncratic marking. I remain uncomfortably aware that the trajectory of this essay courts the danger of reproducing what it purports to analyze: namely, the appropriation and effacement of the experience of both native Americans and women by the dominant discourse of European patriarchy. It is necessary, I believe, not only to resist such a dominant discourse but also to resist too rigid an understanding of its dominance. In other words, it is necessary to anatomize these elements of heterogeneity and instability, permeability and contradiction, that perpetually forestall ideological closure. Thus, while I have no illusion that I have wholly resisted complicity in the operations of that dominant discourse, my attempt has been to locate and discover a few of the places of stress where its operations may be critically observed.

By the 1570s, allegorical personifications of America as a female nude with feathered headdress had begun to appear in engravings and paintings, on maps and title pages, throughout Western Europe. Perhaps the most resonant of such images is Jan van der Straet's drawing of Vespucci's discovery of America, widely disseminated in print in the late sixteenth century by means of Theodor Galle's engraving. . . . Here a naked woman, crowned with feathers, upraises herself from her hammock to meet the gaze of the armored and robed man who has just come ashore; she extends her right arm toward him, apparently in a gesture of wonder—or, perhaps, of apprehension. Standing with his feet firmly planted upon the ground, Vespucci observes the personified and feminized space that will bear his name. This recumbent figure, now discovered and roused from her torpor, is about to be hailed, claimed, and possessed as *America.* As the motto included in Galle's engraving puts it, "Americen Americus retexit, & Semel vocavit inde semper excitam"—"Americus rediscovers America; he called her once and thenceforth she was always awake." This theme is discreetly amplified by the presence of a sloth, which regards the scene of awakening from its own shaded spot upon the tree behind America. Vespucci carries with him the variously empowering ideological and technological instruments of civilization, exploration, and conquest: a cruciform staff with a banner bearing the Southern Cross, a navigational astrolabe, and a sword—the mutually reinforcing emblems of belief, empirical knowledge, and violence. At the left, behind Vespucci, the prows of the ships that facilitate the expansion of European hegemony enter the pictorial space of the New World; on the right, behind America, representatives of the indigenous fauna are displayed as if emerging from an American interior at once natural and strange.

Close to the picture's vanishing point—in the distance, yet at the center—a group of naked savages, potential subjects of the civilizing process, are preparing a cannibal feast. A severed human haunch is being cooked over the fire; another, already spitted, awaits its turn. America's body pose is partially mirrored by both the apparently female figure who turns the spit and the clearly female figure who cradles an infant as she awaits the feast. Most strikingly, the form of the severed human leg and haunch turning upon the spit precisely inverts and miniaturizes America's own. In terms of the pictorial space, this scene of cannibalism is perspectively distanced, pushed into the background; in terms of the pictorial surface, however, it is placed at the center of the visual field, between the mutual gazes of Americus and America, and directly above the latter's outstretched arm.

I think it possible that the represented scene alludes to an incident reported to have taken place during the third of Vespucci's alleged four voyages, and recounted in his famous letter of 1504. I quote from the mid-sixteenth-century English translation by Richard Eden:

> At the length they broughte certayne women, which shewed them selves familier towarde the Spaniardes: Whereupon they sent forth a young man, beyng very strong and quicke, at whom as the women wondered, and stode gasinge on him and feling his apparell:

there came sodeynly a woman downe from a mountayne, bringing with her secretly a great stake, with which she gave him such a stroke behynde, that he fell dead on the earth. The other wommene foorthwith toke him by the legges, and drewe him to the mountayne, whyle in the mean tyme the men of the countreye came foorth with bowes and arrowes, and shot at oure men. . . . The women also which had slayne the yong man, cut him in pieces even in the sight of the Spaniardes, shewinge them the pieces, and rosting them at a greate fyre.

The elements of savagery, deceit, and cannibalism central to the emergent European discourse on the inhabitants of the New World are already in place in this very early example. Of particular significance here is the blending of these basic ingredients of protocolonialist ideology with a crude and anxious misogynistic fantasy, a powerful conjunction of the savage and the feminine.

This conjunction is reinforced in another, equally striking Vespuccian anecdote. Vespucci presents a different account of his third voyage in his other extant letter, this one dated 1503 and addressed to Lorenzo Piero Francesco de Medici. Like the previous letter, this one was in wide European circulation in printed translations within a few years of its date. Here Vespucci's marvelous ethnography includes the following observation:

> Another custom among them is sufficiently shameful, and beyond all human credibility. Their women, being very libidinous, make the penis of their husbands swell to such a size as to appear deformed; and this is accomplished by a certain artifice, being the bite of some poisonous animal, and by reason of this many lose their virile organ and remain eunuchs.

> (*Letters*)

The oral fantasy of female insatiability and male dismemberment realized in the other letter as a cannibalistic confrontation of alien cultures is here translated into a precise genital and domestic form. Because the husband's sexual organ is under the control of his wife and is wholly subject to her ambiguous desires, the very enhancement of his virility becomes the means of his emasculation.

In the light of Vespucci's anecdotes, the compositional centrality of van der Straet's apparently incidental background scene takes on new significance: it is at the center of the composition in more ways than one, for it may be construed as generating or necessitating the compensatory foreground scene that symbolically contains or displaces it. In van der Straet's visualization of discovery as the advance of civilization, what is closer to the horizon is also closer to the point of origin: it is where we have come from—a prior epi-

sode in the history of contacts between Europeans and native Americans, and an earlier episode in the history of human society; and it is now what we must control—a cultural moment that is to be put firmly, decisively, behind us. In the formal relationship of proportion and inversion existing between America's leg and what I suppose to be that of the dismembered Spanish youth, I find a figure for the dynamic of gender and power in which the collective imagination of early modern Europe articulates its confrontation with alien cultures. The supposed sexual guile and deceit that enable the native women to murder, dismember, and eat a European man are in a relationship of opposition and inversion to the vaunted masculine knowledge and power with which the erect and armored Vespucci will master the prone and naked America. Thus, the interplay between the forground and background scenes of the van der Straet-Galle composition gives iconic form to the oscillation characterizing Europe's ideological encounter with the New World: an oscillation between fascination and repulsion, likeness and strangeness, desires to destroy and to assimilate the Other; an oscillation between the confirmation and the subversion of familiar values, beliefs, and perceptual norms.

Michel de Certeau reproduces the engraving of Vespucci's discovery of America as the frontispiece of his book *The Writing of History*. As he explains in his preface, to him this image is emblematic of the inception of a distinctively modern discursive practice of historical and cultural knowledge; this historiography subjects its ostensible subject to its own purportedly objective discipline; it ruptures the continuum "between a subject and an object of the operation, between a *will to write* and a *written body* (or a body to be written)." For de Certeau, the history of this modern writing of history begins in the sixteenth century with "the 'ethnographical' organization of writing in its relation with 'primitive,' 'savage,' 'traditional,' or 'popular' orality that it establishes as its other." Thus, for him, the tableau of Vespucci and America is

> an inaugural scene. . . . The conqueror will write the body of the other and trace there his own history. From her he will make a historied body—a blazon—of his labors and phantasms. . . .

> What is really initiated here is a colonization of the body by the discourse of power. This is *writing that conquers*. It will use the New World as if it were a blank, "savage" page on which Western desire will be written.

"America" awakens to discover herself written into a story that is not of her own making, to find herself a figure in another's dream. When called by Vespucci, she is interpellated within a European history that identifies itself simply as History, single and inexorable; this history can only misrecognize America's history as sleep and mere oblivion. In 1974, when a speaker at the first Indian Congress of South America declared, "Today, at the hour of our awakening, we must be our own historians," he spoke as if in a long suppressed response to the ironic awakening of van der Straet's *America*, her awakening to the effacement of her own past and future.

Although applied here to a graphic representation that is iconic rather than verbal, de Certeau's reflections suggestively raise and conjoin issues that I wish to pursue in relation to Sir Walter Ralegh's ***The Discoverie of the large, rich, and beautifull Empire of Guiana*** (1596) and some other Elizabethan examples of "writing that conquers." These issues include consideration of the writing subject's textualization of the body of the Other, neither as mere description nor as genuine encounter but rather as an act of symbolic violence, mastery, and self-empowerment; and the tendency of such discursive representation to assume a narrative form, to manifest itself as "a historied body"—in particular, as a mode of symbolic action whose agent is gendered masculine and whose object is gendered feminine. Rather than reduce such issues to the abstract, closed, and static terms of a binary opposition—whether between European and Indian, Culture and Nature, Self and Other, or, indeed, Male and Female—I shall endeavor to discriminate among various sources, manifestations, and consequences of what de Certeau generalizes as the "Western desire" that is written upon the putatively "blank page" of the New World, and to do so by specifying the ideological configurations of gender and social estate, as well as national, religious, and/or ethnic identities, that are brought into play during any particular process of textualization.

An "inaugural scene" of Elizabethan New World colonialism is textualized in Arthur Barlowe's report to Ralegh. Fortuitously, it was on the fourth of July in 1584 that "the first voyage made to . . . America" at the "charge, and direction" of Ralegh "arrived upon the coast, which we supposed to be a continent, and firme lande." Barlowe relates the Englishmen's discovery of America; having found the mouth of a river,

> we entred, though not without some difficultie . . . and after thankes given to God for our safe arrival thither, we manned our boates, and went to viewe the land . . . and to take possession of the same, in the right of the Queenes most excellent Majestie, as rightfull Queene, and Princesse of the same: and after delivered the same over to your use, according to her Majesties grant, and letters patents, under her Highnes great Seale. (94)

The letters patent issued to Ralegh on 25 March 1584 had granted

> to our trusty and welbeloved servaunte Walter

Raleighe Esquier and to his heyres and assignes for ever free liberty and licence from tyme to tyme and at all tymes for ever hereafter to discover search fynde out and viewe such remote heathen and barbarous landes Contries and territories not actually possessed of any Christian Prynce and inhabited by Christian people . . . and the same to have holde occupy and enjoye to him his heyres and assignes for ever. (82)

Barlowe does not perceive the natives to be barbarous but, on the contrary, "in their behaviour as mannerly, and civill, as any of Europe" (98-99). Nevertheless, unbeknownst to these heathens, not merely their alien religious practices but their very freedom from prior colonization, their unpossessed condition, has *in principle* sanctioned their dispossession even before Ralegh's expedition sets sail from England to discover them.

Barlowe writes that, having first taken legal and ritual possession in the queen's name, "Wee viewed the lande about us. . . . I thinke in all the world the like aboundance is not to be founde" (94-95). This abundant country is called, by the "very handsome, and goodly people" who already inhabit it, "Wingandacoa, (and nowe by her Majestie, Virginia)" (98-99). William Camden soon records that Virginia is "so named in honour of Queen Elizabeth, a virgin." Significantly, the naming of "Virginia" was "the first such imperious act sanctioned by an English monarch." Having authorized her subjects' acts of discovery and symbolic possession, the English monarch assumes the privilege of naming the land anew, and naming it for herself and for the gender-specific virtue she has so long and so successfully employed as a means of self-empowerment. Queen Elizabeth participates in an emergent colonialist discourse that works to justify and, symbolically, to effect the expropriation of what it discovers. Typically, this discourse denies the natural right of possession to indigenous peoples by confirming them to be heathens, savages, and/or foragers who neither cultivate the land nor conceptualize it as real property; or it may symbolically efface the very existence of those indigenous peoples from the places its speakers intend to exploit. What was Wingandacoa is now rendered a blank page upon which to write Virginia. Thus, the Virgin Queen verbally reconstitutes the land as a feminine place unknown to man, and, by doing so, she also symbolically effaces the indigenous society that already physically and culturally inhabits and possesses that land. In this royal renaming, considerations of gender difference interact with those of ethnic difference; the discursive power of the inviolate female body serves an emergent imperialist project of exploration, conquest, and settlement.

Although England's first American colony was claimed in her name and named in her honor, Queen Elizabeth herself demonstrated little enthusiasm or material support for the various colonizing ventures that ignited the energy, imagination, and desire of many of her restive masculine subjects. Preeminent among those subjects was Walter Ralegh. Ralegh's tireless promotion of exploration and colonization was driven not only by intellectual curiosity, and by a patriotic devotion to the creation of an overseas empire that would strengthen England against Spain both economically and strategically; it was driven also by his extraordinary personal ambition. In his social origins, Ralegh was the youngest son of a modest though well-connected West Country gentry family. Thus, he was wholly dependent upon the queen's personal favor not only for the rapid and spectacular rise of his fortunes but also for their perpetuation; in the most tangible and precarious way, Ralegh was Elizabeth's creature. The strategy by which he gained and attempted to maintain the royal favor was systematically to exploit the affective ambiguity of the royal cult; to fuse in his conduct and in his discourse the courtship of the queen's patronage and the courtship of her person.

Observing Elizabeth's open display of intimacy with Ralegh during the Christmas festivities at court in 1584, a German traveler recorded that "it was said that she loved this gentleman now in preference to all others; and that may be well believed, for two years ago he was scarcely able to keep a single servant, and now she has bestowed so much upon him, that he is able to keep five hundred servants." In surveying the leading courtiers attending upon the queen at this event, Lupold von Wedel had already noted the earl of Leicester, "with whom, as they say, the queen for a long time has had illicit intercourse," and Sir Christopher Hatton, "the captain of the guard, whom the queen is said to have loved after Lester" (263). Such opinions—which seem to have been offered readily to von Wedel by his native English informants, and which he duly noted in his diary—suggest that many at court did not regard the queen's perpetual virginity as a literal truth. This is not to suggest that they therefore necessarily regarded it as a mere fraud—although there is surviving testimony that at least a few of the queen's subjects thought precisely that. Many at court may have regarded the royal cult as a necessary and effective, collectively sustained political fiction, as a mystery of state quite distinct from the question of whether or not Elizabeth Tudor was a woman who had yet her maidenhead. Whatever the precise nature and degree of Ralegh's intimacy with Queen Elizabeth, in 1587 he succeeded Hatton as Captain of the Guard; in both physical and symbolic terms, he now officially protected, and controlled access to, the queen's body. However, whatever honors, offices, patents, and leases the queen might grant to her favorite, without clear title to great manorial lands he had no secure source of income and status, and no hope of founding and sustaining his own lineage. What the royal patent for Virginia and the subsequent commission for Guiana gave to Ralegh was

the prospect of possessing vast riches and vast lands, a prospect that would never be available to him at home in England.

Although, in the later 1580s, Ralegh was displaced as the queen's preeminent favorite by the earl of Essex, he nevertheless continued to enjoy considerable royal confidence and favor. In 1592, however, Queen Elizabeth learned of Ralegh's secret marriage to her namesake, Elizabeth Throgmorton, one of the young ladies attendant at court, and of the birth of their first child. Both offenders were imprisoned in the Tower for several months, and Ralegh continued in disgrace and away from the court for some time longer. In the extravagant and fragmentary complaint, *The Ocean to Cynthia,* Ralegh wrote of the queen as his royally cruel mistress: "No other poure [power] effectinge wo, or bliss, / Shee gave, shee tooke, shee wounded, shee apeased." Perhaps it cannot be decided, finally, whether to attribute the queen's anger toward Ralegh (and toward other noblemen and courtiers in his circumstances) to the sexual jealousy of a mistress, betrayed by her lover; to the moral outrage of a virgin and the guardian of virgins, victimized by men's lasciviousness; or to the political perturbation of a militarily and fiscally weak ruler, whose attempts to maintain an absolute command over her courtiers' alliances and their attentions had been flagrantly flouted. Indeed, the various and conflicting recorded perceptions and attitudes of Elizabethan subjects strongly suggest that such undecidability is itself the historically relevant point; that it is, in fact, a structural feature of the Elizabethan political system. A strategic ambiguity that might be manifested as paradox, equivocation, or contradiction, it was of potential if limited utility both to the monarch and to her (masculine) subjects. For the latter, however—as Ralegh's case demonstrates—it also carried considerable potential liabilities.

The issuance in 1594 of a royal commission allowing Ralegh to maraud the Spanish Caribbean may be interpreted as a gesture of returning favor. Thus authorized, in 1595 he set sail for Guiana, about which he had been gathering reconnaissance and speculation for several years. By the beginning of the new decade, the focus of Ralegh's interest in the New World had begun to shift southward, to the Caribbean and the Orinoco basin. This was part of a larger strategy to confront England's mighty adversary directly at sea and on land, in both the old world and the new. In the public self-presentations of the *Discoverie,* Ralegh maintains that his aims are wholly patriotic and untainted by mercenary considerations. The goal is the destruction of Spain's economic and geopolitical hegemony in Europe and the Americas. England will be able to counter Spain's power if Englishmen can discover and conquer an indigenous American empire rivaling in riches those plundered by the Spanish in Mexico and Peru. The imperial strategy presented to the queen and her councillors is that the extortion of gold from the (mythical) Empire of Guiana, either by tribute or by conquest, will load her shaky exchequer with more than enough resources to "defend all enemies abroad, and defray all expences at home" (430); it will make England prosperous and invincible. Despite his repeated representations of himself as un-self-interested, Ralegh's writings reveal him to be preoccupied with the prospect of enormous personal wealth and power, for which the unprecedented successes of Cortés and Pizarro now provided models. Ralegh's expedition traveled several hundred miles of the Orinoco basin, encountered numerous indigenous social groups, and conducted a few raids on Spanish outposts. They failed, however, to find the anticipated empire of El Dorado, the Inga of Manoa, or his fabled riches. Indeed, the tangible returns from the voyage were so negligible that some of Ralegh's more skeptical fellow countrymen raised doubts as to whether it had actually taken place. It was both to justify the recently concluded expedition and to promote further interest, support, and investment that in 1596 Ralegh published *The Discoverie of Guiana*.

We may regard with a certain skepticism the claim that Queen Elizabeth's virtues inspired virtuous conduct in her subjects; however, there is no doubting that the courtly politics of chastity bore acutely upon the commander of the Guiana voyage. An anonymous letter concerning the circumstances of Ralegh's disgrace in 1592 can provide us with a thematic link between that episode and the discourse of his *Discoverie* in 1596:

> S.W.R., as it seemeth, have been too inward with one of Her Majesty's maids. . . . S.W.R. will lose, it is thought, all his places and preferments at Court, with the Queen's favour; such will be the end of his speedy rising. . . . All is alarm and confusion at this discovery of the discoverer, and not indeed of a new continent, but of a new incontinent.

Although of uncertain provenance and authenticity, this wittily scurrilous text does help to foreground and contextualize the *Discoverie*'s recurrent references to Ralegh's restraint of himself and his subordinates, his repudiation of concupiscence and his strategic tempering/temporizing of his announced quest for wealth and power.

In his dedicatory epistle to Lord Howard and Sir Robert Cecil, Ralegh represents both the conduct of his discovery and the account in which he discovers it as intended to mollify the queen's displeasure and to regain her favor:

> As my errors were great, so they have yeelded very grievous effects. . . . I did therefore even in the winter of my life, undertake these travels . . . that thereby, if it were possible, I might recover but the

moderation of excesse, & the least tast of the greatest plenty formerly possessed. . . . To appease so powrful displeasure, I would not doubt but for one yeere more to hold fast my soule in my teeth, till it were performed. (339)

Indeed, Ralegh goes so far as to suggest that the narrative of his exploit should be read as a penitential journey, an act of fleshly purgation undertaken to expiate the incontinent lapse in his devotion to the queen:

> I have bene accompanyed with many sorrowes, with labour, hunger, heat, sickenes, & perill. . . . [They] were much mistaken, who would have perswaded, that I was too easefull and sensuall to undertake a journey of so great travell. But, if what I have done, receive the gracious construction of a painefull pilgrimage, and purchase the least remission, I shall thinke all too litle. (339-40)

Read in the context of Ralegh's fall from grace, the *Discoverie* operates on the model of book 2 of Edmund Spenser's *Faerie Queene* (1590), as a compensatory "Legend of Sir Walter, or of Temperance." The hero of this exemplary autobiographical narrative of restrained desired and deferred gratification eschews both Avarice and Lust, both Mammon and Acrasia:

> If it had not bin in respect of her highnes future honor & riches, [I] could have laid hands on & ransomed many of the kings & Casiqui of the country, & have had a reasonable proportion of gold for their redemption: but I have chosen rather to beare the burden of poverty, then reproach, & rather to endure a second travel and the chances therof, then to have defaced an enterprise of so great assurance, untill I knew whether it pleased God to put a disposition in her princely and royal heart either to folow or foreslow the same. (342-43)

> I neither know nor beleeve, that any of our company one or other, by violence or otherwise, ever knew any of their women. . . . I suffered not any man . . . so much as to offer to touch any of their wives or daughters: which course so contrary to the Spaniards . . . drewe them to admire her Majestie, whose commaundement I tolde them it was. (391)

In short, Ralegh's discovery of a new continent discovers him to be newly continent. As if to redress his conduct with Elizabeth Throgmorton, in these and a number of other passages Ralegh pointedly defers the desired consummation with Guiana until a royal blessing has been secured. Nevertheless, it is the prospect of that consummation that drives the narrative.

Himself a man from a society in which women—with one extraordinary exception—are politically invisible, Ralegh is predisposed to characterize the indigenous societies of the New World as if they are exclusively masculine. The Tivitivas, for example, "are a very goodly people and very valiant, and have the most manly speech and most deliberate that ever I heard, of what nation soever" (382-83). Ralegh admires these alien nations for their collective virility. Nevertheless, at a higher level of abstraction and under stronger rhetorical pressure, these apparently masculine societies—societies from which women have already been verbally effaced—are themselves rendered invisible by a metonymic substitution of place for persons, a substitution of the land for its inhabitants. This land which is substituted for its manly inhabitants is itself gendered feminine and sexed as a virgin female body:

> To conclude, Guiana is a countrey that hath yet her maydenhead, never sackt, turned, nor wrought, the face of the earth hath not bene torne, nor the vertue and salt of the soyle spent by manurance, the graves have not bene opened for golde, the mines not broken with sledges, nor their Images puld downe out of their temples. It hath never bene entred by any armie of strength, and never conquered or possessed by any christian Prince. (428)

In this concluding exhortation of his masculine readership, Ralegh's description of Guiana by means of negatives conveys a proleptically elegiac sympathy for this unspoiled world at the same time that it arouses excitement at the prospect of despoiling it. His metaphor of Guiana's maidenhead activates the bawdy Elizabethan pun on *countrey,* thus inflaming the similitude of the land and a woman's body, of colonization and sexual mastery. By subsuming and effacing the admired societies of Amerindian men in the metaphorically feminine Other of the land, the English intent to subjugate the indigenous peoples of Guiana can be "naturalized" as the male's mastery of the female. The ideology of gender hierarchy sanctions the Englishmen's collective longing to prove and aggrandize themselves upon the feminine body of the New World, and, at the same time, the emergent hierarchical discourse of colonial exploitation and domination reciprocally confirms that ideology's hegemonic force.

Queen Elizabeth names the eastern seaboard of North America, in her own honor, *Virginia.* When her "trusty and welbeloved servaunt Walter Raleighe" describes the northeast interior of South America as a virgin, the rhetorical motive is not an homage to the queen but rather a provocation to her masculine subjects: "Guiana is a countrey that hath *yet* her maydenhead" (428; italics mine). There exists an intimate relationship between the figurations of these two places, as there does between Elizabeth and Ralegh themselves: it is as if the queen's naming of Virginia elicits Ralegh's metaphor of Guiana's fragile maidenhead. Addressing Ralegh in a dedicatory epistle to his edition of Peter Martyr's *De orbe novo* (1587), Richard Hakluyt imag-

ines "your Elizabeth's Virginia" as Ralegh's bride, her depths as yet unprobed for their hidden riches. Hakluyt takes imaginative liberties in Latin; however, it is difficult to imagine that Ralegh himself, in a printed address to the queen's subjects, would be so impolitic as to represent the plantation of Virginia in the same terms that he uses to represent the conquest of Guiana. If he cannot write explicitly of Virginia's rape, this is because the queen and her courtier share a common discourse of discovery, grounded in a territorial conception of the female body.

As de Certeau suggests in his discussion of van der Straet's icon, the "historied" and gendered body of America calls attention to the affinity between the *discovery* and the *blazon,* two Renaissance rhetorical forms that organize and control their subjects—respectively, the body of the land and the body of the lady—by means of display, inventory, and anatomy. As Nancy Vickers has remarked [in *Shakespeare and the Question of Theory,* 1985], "The blazon's inventory of fragmented and reified parts [is] a strategy in some senses inherent to any descriptive project. Typically, in both the blazon and the discovery, the dynamics of this descriptive situation are gendered in a triangulated relationship: a masculine writer shares with his readers the verbal construction/observation of a woman or a feminized object or matter; in doing so, he constructs a masculine subject position for his readers to occupy and share." In *The Arte of English Poesie,* George Puttenham exemplifies "your figure of *Icon,* or resemblance by imagerie and portrait," first by citing "Sir Philip Sidney in the description of his mistresse excellently well handled," and then by piecemeal quotation from one of his own *Partheniades:*

> written of our sovereign Lady, wherein we resemble every part of her body to some naturall thing of excellent perfection in his kind, as of her forehead, browes and haire. . . . And of her lips. . . . And of her eyes. . . . And of her breasts. . . . And all the rest that followeth.

Puttenham's *Partheniades* were conceived and presented as a New Year's gift, as a rhetorical instrument for ingratiating himself with the queen and eliciting some reciprocal benefit. Thus, subsequently, he can display in print an example of how he has, by figure, "excellently well handled" his sovereign. When an Elizabethan subject devises a blazon of his royal mistress, he gives an explicitly political charge to a poetic figure already marked by the politics of gender.

Queen Elizabeth might not only be figured in an erotic blazon but might also be troped in the similitude of land and body. In her special case, however, the representational strategies of the trope might well serve to aggrandize the sovereign rather than to subordinate the woman. Her own naming of Virginia for herself is a variation on such a strategy; another, from one of her speeches, will be discussed below. Here I want to consider the "Ditchley" portrait of Queen Elizabeth (ca. 1592), by Marcus Gheeraerts the Younger. . . . This striking painting, the largest known portrait of the queen, represents her standing, like some great goddess or glorified Virgin Mary, with her feet upon the globe and her head amidst the heavens. The cosmic background divides into sunlight and storm; according to the now fragmentary sonnet inscribed on the canvas, these signify, respectively, the heavenly glory and divine power of which the queen is the earthly mirror. She stands upon a cartographic image of Britain, deriving from Christopher Saxton's collection of printed maps. Like Saxton's 1583 map, the painting divides England into counties, each separately colored, and marks principal towns and rivers. Much of the monarch's island nation is enclosed by the hem of her gown, a compositional feature perhaps recalling the iconography of the *Madonna della misericordia*. This representation of Queen Elizabeth as standing upon her land and sheltering it under her skirts suggests a mystical identification of the inviolate female body of the monarch *with* the unbreached body of her land, at the same time that it affirms her distinctive role as the motherly protectress of her people. But the painting also asserts, in spectacular fashion, the other aspect of Elizabeth's androgynous personal symbolism—her kingly rule; it affirms her power *over* her land and *over* its inhabitants. The cartographic image transforms the *land* into a *state;* and by the division of the land into administrative units, its inhabitants are marked as the monarch's political and juridical subjects. It is against such official figurations of the relationship between the woman ruler and her masculine subjects that Ralegh's figuration of his own and his fellows' relationship to Guiana resonates as a belligerent though displaced gesture of resistance.

Ralegh's "discoverie" is both a text and an event; and the declaration in its title that this doubled discovery has been "performed in the yeere 1595 by Sir Walter Ralegh" compounds the difficulty in keeping them distinct: the text is also an event, and the event, a text. In his prefatory addresses to his powerful friends and patrons, Lord Howard and Sir Robert Cecil, and "To the Reader," Ralegh specifically cites and seeks to defend himself against charges that he had in fact "hidden in Cornewall" instead of sailing to Guiana; that he had planned to sell his services to none other than King Philip (339) instead of returning to England; that the few putative gold samples brought back from Guiana were actually worthless marcasite or, if genuine, had been bought in Barbary and then transported *to* Guiana (343-46). The only evidence Ralegh can adduce for his having physically performed his discovery is contained in the text itself, which purports to be a record of the event. The performance of Ralegh's discovery becomes socially accessible and meaningful

only as a writing performance, as *ethnography*—only, that is, when it has been textualized as his ***Discoverie***. However, the status of the ***Discoverie*** as an historical record is always vulnerable to subversion by its status as rhetorical invention. Thus, in his attempt to represent his ***Discoverie*** as the transparent record of his discovery, Ralegh must seek to deprecate its style: he humbly prays "that your honors will excuse such errors, as without the defense of art, overrun every part of the following discourse, in which I have neither studied phrase, forme nor fashion" (343). Ralegh's continuous attempts to document his experience in his narrative and his continuous attempts to ground his narrative in the objective reality of his experience can only prove mutually defeating.

Ralegh can claim no more than to be the first *Englishman* to explore parts of the Orinoco basin, and to discover those parts to *English* readers. His text cannot and makes no attempt to erase the footprints of the Spaniards who have preceded him everywhere he goes, and who have either knowingly or unknowingly provided almost all of the practical information as well as the fantasies that have generated the motives and underwritten the execution of his project. Over the course of more than three decades, more than two dozen groups of Spanish adventurers had explored the Amazon and Orinoco basins in search of El Dorado. Ralegh rehearses some of these undertakings in his ***Discoverie;*** he cites and quotes from Spanish books on the New World, both in Spanish and in English translation; he uses information gained from discussions with his captive, Don Antonio de Berreo, the governor of Trinidad; and he appends to his text relevant Spanish documents that had been intercepted at sea. The notable lack of success of the prior Spanish undertakings in the region, despite their enormous scope, might well have discouraged further attempts. Ralegh, however, manages to construe the Spanish failures hopefully, as a sign of special providence: "It seemeth to mee that this empire is reserved for her Majesty and the English nation, by reason of the hard successe which all these and other Spanyards found in attempting the same" (362).

Spanish tales are the sources repeatedly invoked by Ralegh in his strained and circumstantial attempts to substantiate his own claims for the existence of "the great and golden citie of Manoa," which was said to have been founded somewhere in Guiana by the Incas after the fall of Peru. His descriptions of the wondrous riches of El Dorado are merely extrapolated from the Spanish narratives of Peru that he cites (see esp. 355-58). What is perhaps his most artfully circumspect and obfuscating position occurs near the end of the ***Discoverie:***

> Because I have not my selfe seene the cities of Inga, I cannot avow on my credit what I have heard, although it be very likely, that the Emperour Inga

hath built and erected as magnificent palaces in Guiana, as his ancestors did in Peru, which were for their riches and rareness most marvellous and exceeding all in Europe, and I thinke of the world, China excepted, which also the Spaniards (which I had) assured me to be true. (424-25)

Ralegh's final position concerning the existence of Manoa ultimately relies upon assurances from the rivals and enemies who are temporarily within his power; furthermore, whatever their credibility, the precise subject of these Spanish assurances is rendered conspicuously obscure and ambiguous by Ralegh's syntax. In effect, the very Spaniards whom Ralegh's text repeatedly represents as the cruel and deceitful foes of Englishmen and Indians alike are also the authorities upon whose knowledge and experience Ralegh has pursued his own discovery.

The *Discoverie* is haunted by a subversive irony, one that it nowhere explicitly confronts but does frequently if obliquely register, such as when the writer anxiously strives to authenticate his narrative. This epistemological and ideological destabilization arises from Ralegh's repeated need to ground his own credibility upon the credibility of the very people whom he wishes to discredit. One of the central ways in which Ralegh attempts to obfuscate this predicament of dependency upon and identification with the enemy is through an absolute distinction of the Englishmen's sexual conduct in the New World from that of the Spaniards. The rhetorical operations of gender performed in the *Discoverie* are considerably more complicated than the familiar trope of the feminine land might at first suggest. This complication is in part related to the pervasive Spanish presence in Ralegh's text and in the country it purports to discover.

The priority of Iberian claims to much of the New World could be discredited by English and other Northern European and Protestant writers by an insistence upon the necessity for effective, material occupation rather than merely symbolic discovery and possession. Regarding Guiana, in particular, English concerns about the validity of rival and prior Spanish claims were partially addressed by English arguments against both the moral and the strategic wisdom of conquest, and in favor of an alliance with the "Inga" or emperor of Manoa, or a persuasion of indigenous peoples to embrace English overlordship. By the persistent rehearsal of Spanish atrocities against the Indians, the English also tried to turn Spanish precedence to their own advantage. Ralegh could assure himself and his English readers that God had reserved Guiana for England's dominion; and at the same time, both to himself and to the Indians of Guiana, he could represent his own imperialistic venture as a holy and humanitarian war of liberation against Spanish oppression. For example, Ralegh relates that in his conversation with

the chieftain Topiawari,

> I made him knowe the cause of my comming thither, whose servant I was, and that the Queenes pleasure was, I should undertake the voyage for their defence, and to deliver them from the tyrannie of the Spaniards, dilating at large . . . her Majesties greatnesse, her justice, her charitie to all oppressed nations. (399)

The "oppressed nations" of the New World are to be liberated from the Spanish tyrant so that they may be more benignly and effectively subjected to the English savior.

Ralegh's ironic discovery of the Spaniards' prior discoveries drives home to his English readers the embarrassment of England's cultural and imperial *belatedness*. Many Elizabethan writers voice a nagging concern that—in military, commercial, and/or artistic terms—the English are a backward and peripheral nation. This concern is usually manifested as an anxious and impatient patriotism. For example, in *A Relation of the Second Voyage to Guiana,* Laurence Keymis writes that

> it were a dull conceite of strange weaknes in our selves, to distrust our own power so much, or at least, our owne hearts and courages; as valewing the Spanish nation to be omnipotent; or yeelding that the poore Portugal hath that mastering spirit and conquering industrie, above us.

Keymis was Ralegh's lieutenant, and performed this "second Discoverie" (441) in 1596, under Ralegh's instructions; his written account was printed in the same year. As this passage from Keymis clearly suggests, a belligerent and chauvinistic national consciousness is almost invariably expressed in the terms and values of a collective national character that is culturally encoded as masculine. Such encoding leads all too predictably to imagery such as Ralegh's, which figures England and Spain as manly rivals in a contest to deflower the new found lands: at the beginning of his *Discoverie,* Ralegh invites his readers to "consider of the actions of . . . Charles the 5. who had the maidenhead of Peru, and . . . the affaires of the Spanish king now living" (346); at the end, he invites them to consider that "Guiana is a countrey that hath yet her maydenhead" (428). In order to represent Ralegh's discovery of Guiana iconically, we might triangulate the scenario of van der Straet's drawing: upon coming ashore, the Englishman discovers America in the arms of a Spaniard.

The ubiquitous figure of the Spaniard is an unstable signifier in the text of Ralegh's *Discoverie:* he is, at once, an authority to be followed, a villain to be punished, and a rival to be bested. For the Englishmen in the New World, the Spaniards are proximate figures of Otherness: in being Catholic, Latin, and Mediterranean they are spiritually, linguistically, ethnically, and ecologically alien. At the same time, however, England and Spain are intertwined with each other in an encompassing European system of economic, social, and political structures and forces; and they share an ambient Christian and classical cultural, moral, and intellectual tradition. The sign of the Spaniard in English discovery texts simultaneously mediates and complicates any simple antinomy of European Self and American Other.

We can begin to observe how gender and sexual conduct are figured into this complex textual play of otherness by juxtaposing two passages from Keymis's *Relation*. Near the end of his narrative, Keymis asks his English readers, rhetorically:

> Is it not meere wretchednesse in us, to spend our time, breake our sleepe, and waste our braines, in contriving a cavilling false title to defraude a neighbour of halfe an acre of lande: whereas here whole shires of fruitfull rich grounds, lying now waste for want of people, do prostitute themselves unto us, like a faire and beautiful woman, in the pride and floure of desired yeeres. (487)

Here the already familiar similitude of the earth and the female body—"fruitfull rich grounds" and "a faire and beautifull woman"—is activated through a peculiarly dissonant and degraded fantasy of *self-prostitution*. It is as if the writer's imagination of the New World has taken corruption from his already disconcerting representation of the old one: we are exhorted to repudiate our homegrown and familiar greed and fraudulence, not because they are immoral but because they are paltry; they must be reconceived on a grander scale, in the large, rich, and beautiful empire of Guiana.

In an earlier passage, Keymis writes of the Indians' present predicament, that

> for the plentie of golde that is in this countrey, beeing nowe knowen and discovered, there is no possibilitie for them to keepe it: on the one side they coulde feele not greater miserie, nor feare more extremitie, then they were sure to finde, if the Spaniardes prevayled, who perforce doe take all things from them, using them as their slaves, to runne, to rowe, to bee their guides, to cary their burthens, and that which is worst of all, to bee content, for safetie of their lives, to leave their women, if a Spaniard chance but to set his eye on any of them to fancie her: on the otherside they could hope for, nor desire no better state and usage, then her Majesties gracious government, and Princely vertues doe promise, and assure unto them. (472)

The Indians who are the collective subject of this passage are exclusively the Indian *men;* "their women" are the (male) Indians' most valued and most intimate possessions, serving to define and to make manifest their own freedom and masculinity. One of the most conspicuous ways in which the Spaniards assert their enslavement of native American men is precisely by their casual use of the bodies of native American women. In Keymis's representation of the Spaniards, the rape of the Indians' lands and the rape of "their women" go hand in hand. In the case of Englishmen, however, masculine sexual aggression against the bodies of native women has been wholly displaced into the exploitation of the feminized new found land. Indeed, the Englishment's vaunted sexual self-restraint serves to legitimate their exploitation of the land. Furthermore, such masculine desires for possession have been subjected to a form of reversal, in that Keymis's discourse renders Englishmen not as territorial aggressors but rather as passive beneficiaries of the animated land's own desire to be possessed: "Fruitfull rich grounds, lying now waste for want of people, do prostitute themselves unto us, like a faire and beautiful woman." The sexual conduct of European men in the New World is sometimes explained away as the unbridled expression of an essential male lustfulness. It might be more useful to understand it as an ideologically meaningful (and overdetermined) act of violence. This violence is impelled by, enacts, and thus reciprocally confirms the imperatives of appropriation, possession, and domination that characterize the colonialist project in general, imperatives that are themselves discursively figured in gendered violence.

The topic of sexual conduct can become a point of convergence for a multiplicity of discourses—among them, gender, ethnicity, nationality, and social estate. I write of "ethnicity" and "social estate" rather than "race" and "class" because, in the Elizabethan context, some of the contemporary assumptions implicit in the terms "race" and "class" do not seem to be either adequate or appropriate. For example, concerning "class": not only different categories of social rank but also different systems of social categorization and stratification sometimes overlapped, contradicted, or excluded one another. And concerning "race": prejudicial early English perceptions of native Americans—unlike contemporaneous perceptions of Africans—were not given a physical basis in their appearance and skin color but were based exclusively upon their supposed savagery. Furthermore, issues of "class" and "race" might be conflated. The statuses of "Indians" and "the meaner sort" of English people were sometimes analogized: Indians were said to be like English rogues and vagabonds, and unruly English forest dwellers like Indians.

A particularly instructive convergence of Elizabethan discourses of sex, gender, ethnicity, nationality, and social rank is provided in the following extended passage from Ralegh's *Discoverie,* a part of which I have already quoted:

> [The Arwacas] feared that wee would have eaten them, or otherwise have put them to some cruel death (for the Spaniards, to the end that none of the people in the passage towards Guiana or Guiana it selfe might come to speach with us, perswaded all the nations, that we were man-eaters, and Canibals) but when the poore men and women had seen us, and that wee gave them meate, and to every one something or other, which was rare and strange to them, they beganne to conceive the deceit and purpose of the spaniards, who indeed (as they confessed) tooke from them both their wives and daughters dayly, and used them for the satisfying of their owne lusts, especially such as they tooke in this maner by strength. But I protest before the Majestie of the living God, that I neither know nor beleeve, that any of our company one or other, by violence or otherwise, ever knew any of their women, and yet we saw many hundreds, and had many in our power, and of those very yong, and excellently favoured, which came among us without deceite, starke naked.
>
> Nothing got us more love amongst them then this usage: for I suffered not any man to take from any of the nations so much as a Pina, or a Potato roote, without giving them contentment, nor any man so much as to offer to touch any of their wives or daughters: which course so contrary to the Spaniards (who tyrannize over them in all things) drewe them to admire her Majestie, whose commaundement I tolde them it was, and also wonderfully to honour our nation.
>
> But I confesse it was a very impatient worke to keepe the meaner sort from spoyle and stealing, when we came to their houses: which because in all I coulde not prevent, I caused my Indian interpreter at every place when wee departed, to know of the losse or wrong done, and if ought were stolen or taken by violence, either the same was restored, and the partie punished in their sight, or else was payed for to their uttermost demand. (390-91)

By a fine irony that Ralegh fails to appreciate, the spectral New World cannibals who so horrified and fascinated sixteenth-century European writers and readers appear to the equally horrified Arwacas to be Englishmen. The English unmask the Spanish deception by reversal: they offer to feed meat to the Indians rather than to eat them. (This is also a reversal in another sense, since perhaps the most commonly recorded initial gesture of friendship made toward Europeans by New World peoples was to offer food.) Ralegh purports to have learned from the Indians that the Spaniards have misrepresented the English as anthropophagi: through this heavily mediated pattern of assertion

and denial, Ralegh's text voices the Englishmen's own consuming desire to consume the Indians' land and goods; it registers a fleeting intimation that the "man-eaters, and Canibals" of the New World are actually a projection—and, by this means, a legitimation—of the Europeans' own predatory intentions toward their hosts.

Whereas the English bestow gifts upon the Indians, the Spaniards take from them, using Indian women "for the satisfying of their owne lusts." Although, for purposes of contrast to the Spaniards, it would have been necessary only to reaffirm the absence of sexual violence from English behavior, Ralegh insists that to the best of his knowledge none in his company, "by violence, *or otherwise,* ever knew any of their women" (italics mine). And he goes out of his way to suggest that this chaste conduct has been heroically maintained against the great temptations posed to the male concupiscible appetite by the young, well-favored, and naked women whom the Englishmen have held in their power. Ralegh is at pains to inhibit any culturally inscribed predisposition in his (masculine) readers that would identify the naked maidens in his text as conventional allegorical personifications of Lasciviousness and Indolence—such as those which populate the exotic pleasure gradens of Spenser's Legend of Temperance. Although he credits reports that the Amazons are both violent and lustful, the women whom he claims to have actually encountered in Guiana Ralegh represents as neither deceitful nor predatory—such attributes tend to be reserved for the Spanish men. However, in this passage and elsewhere, his contrary emphasis upon feminine innocence and vulnerability, upon the potential victimization of women, simultaneously disempowers them and legitimates their condition of dependency. It also reduces them to functioning as the collective instrument for making comparisons among *men.* It is crucial to Ralegh's text that what is at issue is not masculine sexual prowess but, on the contrary, the ability of European men to govern their concupiscible appetites. In *The Book named The Governor,* Sir Thomas Elyot writes that

> continence . . . is specially in refraining or forbearing the act of carnal pleasure, whereunto a man is fervently moved, or is at liberty to have it. Which undoubtedly is a thing not only difficult, but also wonderful in a man noble or of great authority, but as in such one as it happeneth to be, needs must be reputed much virtue and wisdom, and to be supposed that his mind is invincible.

Ralegh's concern with sexual conduct is not inscribed within an autonomous discourse about human, masculine, or personal sexuality; rather, it is the somatic focus of concerns that are fundamentally ethical, social, and political. "We saw many hundreds, and had many in our power": it is precisely their refusal to abuse their own position of mastery over the Indians that is the measure of the Englishmen's collective self-mastery, that provides proof of the ascendancy of (what Sir Philip Sidney would call) their erected wits over their infected wills. And this self-mastery might not only help them to distinguish themselves as *Men* from *Women*, to whom unruliness and lasciviousness were traditionally ascribed; it might also help them to distinguish themselves as *Englishmen* from the lustful and un-self-governable Spaniards. Here misogynistic sentiments subserve anti-Spanish ones, in a project aimed at mastering native Americans.

However, having made this moral distinction among men exclusively upon the ground of national difference, Ralegh goes on to say that he had to exercise vigilant control over the inherent tendency toward lawlessness among "the meaner sort" within his own company. He now shifts categories so as to mark hierarchical social differences among the Englishmen themselves. Now, within the restricted domain of Englishness, "the meaner sort" have become structurally equivalent to Spaniards—just as, in other Elizabethan and Jacobean ideological contexts, they are negatively represented as analogous to Indians. If gentlemen have the capacity and the duty to govern themselves, they also have the prerogative and the obligation to govern their social inferiors, who are incapable of self-government. To quote Elyot once more,

> To him that is a governor of a public weal belongeth a double governance, that is to say, an interior or inward governance, and an exterior or outward governance. The first is of his affects and passions, which do inhabit within his soul, and be subjects to reason. The second is of his children, his servants, and other subjects to his authority. (183)

Although it is "worke to keepe the meaner sort from spoyling and stealing," the perceived necessity that the gentleman undertake this burdensome duty defines and legitimates the hierarchical ordering of society; and by actually undertaking it, he reciprocally confirms the congruence of his status with his virtue.

The rhetorical shifting and swerving of Ralegh's text invite some scrutiny. In the first paragraph of the long passage quoted above, Ralegh represents the Englishmen as antithetical to the Spaniards, on the basis of their disinterested generosity toward the Indians: "Wee gave them meate, and to every one something or other, which was rare and strange to them"; in the second paragraph, we are circumstantially informed that although Ralegh forbade his men "so much as to offer to touch any of their wives or daughters," he did permit them to take other forms of Indian property, as long as reparation was made; in the third paragraph, we learn that Indian property was in fact being "stolen or taken by violence" by some of these same gift-giving Englishmen, though not without punishment by their

commander. If English virtue becomes a little soiled in the working, an occasion is nevertheless provided to demonstrate containment of the poorer sort's petty thievery by the moral rectitude and judicial vigilance of their betters. Yet it is precisely by an emphatic insistence upon both triviality and scrupulosity—"I suffered not any man to take from any of the nations so much as a Pina, or a Potato roote"—that this discourse obfuscates the magnitude of the theft being contemplated and prepared by Ralegh himself, which encompasses nothing less than the entire land and everything in it.

The circuitous movement of Ralegh's discourse at once admires the Indians for their innocent trust and displaces onto the Spaniards the implicit betrayal of that trust which is at the heart of the English enterprise. However, the ***Discoverie*** also represents the Spaniards as brutally direct in their intentions toward the Indians. What Ralegh seems to be evading—and what his text nevertheless intermittently discovers—is a recognition that the most massive deception of the Indians is being perpetrated by Ralegh himself. And although evaded, this self-compromising perception may be surfacing obliquely in Ralegh's emphatic characterization of the Indian maidens who were held in his power as being "without deceit, starke naked": here the insidious erotic provocations of female nudity have been transformed into an emblematic, exemplary—and, perhaps, an obscurely self-admonitory—honesty. An appropriate gloss on Ralegh's naked maidens is provided by the emblem of the Graces in Spenser's Legend of Courtesy:

> Therefore they alwaies smoothly seeme to
>   smile,
> That we likewise should mylde and gentle
>   be,
> And also naked are, that without guile
> Or false dissemblaunce all them plaine may
>   see,
> Simple and true, from covert malice free.
>           (*Faerie Queene,* 6.10.24)

At several points in the text of the ***Discoverie,*** Ralegh discovers his systematic and strategic duplicity toward the Indians, thereby inviting his readers' admiration and complicity. For example, he explains to his readers that

> I did not in any sort make my desire for gold knowen, because I had neither time, nor power to have a greater quantity. I gave among them manie more peeces of g d, then I received, of the new money of 20 shil gs with her Majesties picture to wear, with pron se that they would become her servants then forth. (415)

To his readers, Ralegh once again represents himself as a masterful strategist, simultaneously covetous and generous, cynical and patriotic. The Indians' very acceptance of Ralegh's dissembled gifts betokens their uncomprehending entry into the circulations of England's nascent imperial economy—an economy to be fueled, in the future, by their own gold. This passage also allows us to observe something of the subtlety and guilefulness of Ralegh's rhetoric of address to his readers. He gains the confidence of his fellow countrymen by sharing with them what he claims to have withheld from the Indians; yet what he actually shares with them is another set of equivocations and excuses for his having returned empty-handed. As occurs repeatedly in the *Discoverie,* what Ralegh claims to be a deeply considered policy of restraint collapses into a series of circumstantial impediments and uncertainties. We may begin to wonder if Ralegh's representation of his duplicity toward the Indians is not a screen for his duplicity toward his readers, and perhaps toward himself.

Surely the most remarkable disruption of ideological consistency on the surface of Ralegh's text occurs just a paragraph earlier than this last example, in the course of yet another explanation/excuse for his failure to have plundered the (nonexistent) domain of the Inga of Manoa:

> I thought it were evill counsell to have attempted it at that time, although the desire of gold will answere many objections: but it would have bin in mine opinion an utter overthrow to the enterprize, if the same should be hereafter by her Majestie attempted: for then (whereas now they have heard we were enemies to the Spaniards & were sent by her Majesty to relieve them) they would as good cheap have joyned with the Spaniards at our returne, as to have yeelded unto us, when they had proved that we came both for one errant, and that both sought but to sacke & spoile them, but as yet our desire of gold, or our purpose of invasion is not knowen unto them of the empire. (413-14)

At this point of ideological contradiction, the elaborate system of moral difference between the Englishman and the Spaniard is momentarily ruptured; the deep structural opposition that has in large part generated the narrative of the *Discoverie* threatens to collapse. This contradiction might be perceived from at least two perspectives. From one perspective, we apprehend the dissonance between two simultaneously held codes of value: on the one hand, the text's invocation of the normative moral beliefs and judgments nominally shared by its readers; and on the other, its solicitation of their complicity in and admiration for their fellow countryman's cunning and morally equivocal statecraft. From another perspective, we experience a brief eruption into discourse of the subliminal counter-awareness that English desires in the New World are fundamentally identical to Spanish ones, that *we* are really very much like *them*. This awareness is registered in

the striking phrase, "We came both for one errant": Here the unusual form of the noun *errand* not only suggests a task, and a journey by which to accomplish it, but also intimates that the journey is wayward and the enterprise corrupt. That this passage may, even today, generate an intolerable ideological dissonance is perhaps indicated by its complete and unacknowledged effacement from the most readily available current edition of the *Discoverie*.

Ralegh exhorts his English readers to liberate the Indians from Spanish exploitation and oppression; at the same time, he incites them to plunder Guiana for themselves. The ideological coherence of the *Discoveries* is destabilized by a fundamental contradiction in its hortatory aims, a moral contradiction between charity and avarice. In this intolerable situation, in which the Other is always threatening to collapse into the Same, feminine figures must be textually deployed in an attempt to keep Spaniards and Englishmen apart. Thus, distinctions between Man and Woman, and between European and Indian, may both qualify and be qualified by the pervasive textual operation of distinctions between Englishmen and Spaniards that are made on the basis of national identity, cultural and religious values, and social behavior. It is precisely by constructing and reiterating a moral opposition between Spanish lust and tyranny, on the one hand, and English continence and justice, on the other—an opposition epitomized in the contrasting conduct of Spanish and English men toward Indian women—that the discourses of Englishmen such as Ralegh and Keymis obscure the fundamental *identity* of English and Spanish interests in Guiana: "For the plentie of golde that is in this countrey, being nowe knowen and discovered, there is no possibilitie for [the Indians] to keepe it" (Keymis, 472); "We came both for one errant . . . both sought but to sacke & spoile them" (Ralegh, 414). Greed is here the common denominator of "Western desire."

Ralegh frequently writes respectfully and admiringly of the native Americans whom he purports to have encountered during his discovery. They are worthy to be the prospective allies and tributary peoples of the Empress Elizabeth. I think it important to acknowledge such sympathetic representations of various indigenous individuals and groups, while at the same time remaining aware that the very condition of sympathy may be enabled by prior processes of projection and appropriation that efface the differences and assimilate the virtues of the Indians to European norms. Furthermore, such instances of apparently enlightened familiarization cannot be considered in isolation from Ralegh's projection of radical and hostile Otherness elsewhere. This projection operates in two general directions, toward the foreground and toward the margins of the known world; and it also operates in two discourses, which might be called the discourses of morality and of wonder. In the discourse of morality, as I have already suggested, this Otherness is constituted in the proximate, ubiquitous, and tangible Spaniards. In the discourse of wonder, Otherness is figured in the spectacular myth of El Dorado, the Inga of Manoa (356-61), who is frequently represented as an imperial oppressor of Ralegh's tribal allies; and also in those residual Herodotean and Mandevillean curiosities such as anthropophagi, acephali, and Amazons, who haunt the margins of Ralegh's text and of whom he writes only circumspectly and at second hand. Unsurprisingly, from this latter catalogue of marvels it is the Amazons who most arouse Ralegh's interest.

Ralegh discovers the Amazons to his readers more than once during the meandering discourse of his journey. Although these occurrences may appear to be incidental to the *Discoverie's* narrative, they have an integral place in its textual ideo-logic of gender and power. The matriarchal, gynocratic Amazons are the radical Other figured but not fully contained by the collective imagination of European patriarchy. Sixteenth-century travel narratives often recreate the ancient Amazons of Scythia in South America or in Africa. Almost invariably, the Amazons are relocated just beyond the receding geographical boundary of *terra incognita,* in the enduring European mental space reserved for aliens. The notion of a separatist and intensely territorial nation of women warriors might be seen as a momentous transformation of the trope identifying the land with the female body. Implicit in the conceptual shift from *the land as woman* to *a land of women* is the possibility of representing women as collective social agents. Predictably, such a disturbing notion produces a complex and at best morally ambiguous masculine representation of feminine agency. In any event, such women as the Amazons are not merely assimilable to the landscape; nor are they assimilable to the goods and chattels possessed by the men of their group. Unlike the other indigenous societies described by Ralegh, in the case of the Amazons it is the women who are synonymous with the political nation; indeed, Amazon men are literally non-existent. And as a particular (and particularly extreme) construction of the feminine gender, the Amazons enter into complex and multiple articulations, not only with the textual figurations of masculinity in the *Discoverie* but also with its other significant feminine representations: the women among the native American people encountered by Ralegh, who are victimized by the Spaniards, and the queen of England, to whom Ralegh himself is subject.

It is a discussion about the circulation of gold and other commodities among the peoples situated between the Orinoco and the Amazon that provides the immediate occasion for Ralegh's lengthy digression on the remarkable tribe for whom the latter river has been named:

> [I] was very desirous to understand the truth of those warlike women, because of some it is beleeved, of others not. And though I digresse from my purpose, yet I will set downe that which hath bene delivered me for trueth of those women. . . . The memories of the like women are very ancient aswell in Africa as in Asia. . . . In many histories they are verified to have bene, and in divers ages and provinces: but they which are not far from Guiana doe accompany with men but once in a yere, and for the time of one moneth, which I gather by their relation to be in April: and at that time all kings of the borders assemble, and queenes of the Amazones; and after the queenes have chosen, the rest cast lots for their Valentines. . . . If they conceive, and be delivered of a sonne, they returne him to the father; if of a daughter they nourish it, and reteine it: and as many as have daughters send unto the begetters a present; all being desirous to increase their owne sex and kind: but that they cut off the right dug of the brest, I doe not finde to be true. It was farther tolde me, that if in these warres they tooke any prisoners that they used to accompany with those also at what time soever, but in the end for certeine they put them to death: for they are sayd to be very cruell and bloodthirsty, especially to such as offer to invade their territories. (366-67)

This Amazonian anticulture precisely inverts European norms of political authority, sexual license, marriage and child-rearing practices, and inheritance rules. Such conceptual precision suggests that it was not merely the antiquity and wide diffusion of the idea of the Amazons that compelled Ralegh and his contemporaries to entertain seriously the possibility of their existence. Elizabethan perception and speculation were structured by the cognitive operations of hierarchy and inversion, analogy and antithesis. By the logic of these operations, a conceptual space for reversal and negation was constructed within the world picture of a patriarchal society. Among those figures which might occupy this space were the Amazons. Since they didn't exist, it proved necessary to invent them—or, in the case of the New World, to reinvent them.

Ralegh's ethnography of the Amazons divides into two antithetical parts, each largely defined by their collective conduct toward alien men: the first is focused upon the Amazons' orderly, periodic, and eminently civilized ritual cohabitation with men of neighboring tribes. Because it is performed for purposes of procreation—in order to ensure the perpetuation of "their owne sex and kind"—this apparently remote Amazonian practice is not without relevance to the always sensitive Elizabethan succession question. It may be that Ralegh was obliquely criticizing the queen's earlier refusal to marry and her ongoing refusal to designate a successor. In any case, the relevant point is that the centrality that had been given to such matters of state from the very inception of Elizabeth's reign predisposed Englishmen to take a keen interest in the ways in which other actual or imagined societies might structure the processes of political succession and social reproduction. Taking place at the margins of the Amazons' territory, on the boundary between matriarchal and patriarchal societies, this sexual rite serves to mark the feminine and masculine genders as mutually exclusive and, simultaneously, to mediate their radical difference through sexual intercourse. The second, strongly contrasted part of the digression is a brief but sensational account of the impulsive and random mixing of violence and lust in the Amazons' conduct toward their masculine captives. This latter mode of Amazonian behavior—an irascible and concupiscible distemper provoked by attempts "to invade their territories," to violate their body politic—inverts and doubles the violent and lustful conduct frequently associated with the masculine Spanish invaders. In Ralegh's narrative of the Amazons' response to invasion, sexual conduct takes the form of reciprocal aggression between the genders rather than a practice of either procreative of abstinent virtue. Construed as a struggle between women and men for the control and disposition of their own and of each other's bodies, the sexual is here synonymous with the political. Gender and rule, sex and power: these are the concerns that preoccupy Ralegh in his desire "to understand the truth of those warlike women"; we might expect such concerns to be of more than incidental interest to a gentleman who is subject to a woman monarch.

Although Amazonian figures might at first seem suited to strategies for praising a woman ruler, they are not conspicuous among the many encomiastic mirrors of Queen Elizabeth produced by her own subjects. The one notable exception, the heroic Amazon Queen Penthesilea, may have been acceptable and appropriate precisely because she sacrificed herself not for the Amazonian cause but for the cause of patriarchal Troy, the mythical place of origin of the Britons. Otherwise, the sexual and parental practices habitually associated with the Amazons must have rendered them, at best, an equivocal means for representing the Virgin Queen. She herself seems to have been too politic, and too ladylike, to have pursued the Amazonian image very far. However, she could transform it to suit her purposes. If report speaks true of her, she did so most notably when she visited Tilbury in 1588, in order to review and to rally the troops that had been mustered in expectation of a Spanish invasion. According to the subsequent recollection of Thomas Heywood, among others, on that momentous occasion the Queen of England was "habited like an *Amazonian* Queene, Buskind and plumed, having a golden Truncheon, Gantlet, and Gorget, Arms sufficient to expresse her high and magnanimous spirit." The theme of her speech was by then familiar to her audience:

> Let Tyrants fear, I have always so behaved my self,
> that under God I have placed my chiefest strength,
> and safeguard in the loyal hearts and good will of

my subjects. . . . I know I have the bodie, but of a weak and feeble woman, but I have the heart and Stomach of a King, and of a King of *England* too.

Elizabeth's strategy of self-empowerment involves a delicate balance of contrary gestures. On the one hand, she dwells upon the feminine fralty of her body natural and the masculine strength of her body politic—a strength deriving from the love of her people, the virtue of her lineage, and the will of her God. In other words, she moderates the anomalous martial spectacle of feminine sovereignty by representing herself as the handmaiden of a greater, collective, and patriarchal will. On the other hand, she subsumes the gesture of womanly self-deprecation within an assertion of the unique power that inheres in her by virtue of her office and nation. Her feminine honor, the chastity invested in a body that is vulnerable to invasion and pollution, is made secure by the kingly honor invested in her body politic. She adds, defiantly:

> I . . . think foul scorn that *Parma* or *Spain,* or any Prince of Europe should dare to invade the borders of my Realm, to which rather then any dishonour shall grow by me, I my self will take up arms, I my self will be your General, Judge, and Rewarder of everie one of your virtues in the field.

Queen Elizabeth's putative speech presents the threat of invasion in the most intimate and violent of metaphors, as the attempt by a foreign prince to rape her. Like the iconic effect of the Ditchley portrait, the rhetorical force of this speech is partly due to Elizabeth's identification of corporeal with geopolitical boundaries, to her subtle application of the land/body trope to herself: she identifies her virginal female body with the clearly bounded body of her island realm, threatened with violation by the masculine Spanish land and sea forces personified in King Philip and the duke of Parma. Such an illegitimate sexual union would contaminate the blood of the lineage and dishonor not only the royal house but the whole commonwealth. The Roman matron Lucretia submitted to and was ritually polluted by sexual violation, and her suicide was required in order to cleanse the social body. In contrast, the royal English virgin will defend and preserve both herself and her state. If Queen Elizabeth at Tilbury resembles the Amazons in her martial stance, she differs from them in leading an army of men. By insisting, however impractically, that she herself will be the leader of her army, the queen implies that she will not be merely the passive object of male power—even if the intended use of that power is to protect her against the aggression of others. Thus, Elizabeth's own gendered, metaphorical discourse anticipates Ralegh's: England is a country that has yet her maidenhead—and Ralegh's virgin queen, not wholly unlike his Amazons, will prove herself a virago toward those who offer to invade her territories.

In the wake of the Armada's failure, Ralegh can tell all the tribes he encounters in the New World that the queen will protect them as she has protected herself, her own people, and the Protestant cause in Europe:

> I made them understand that I was the servant of a Queene, who was the great Casique of the North, and a virgine . . . that shee was an enemie to the Castellani in respect of their tyrannie and oppression, and that she delivered all such nations about her, as were by them oppressed, and having freed all the coast of the Northren world from their servitude, had sent mee to free them also, and withall to defend the countrey of Guiana from their invasion and conquest. (353-54)

However, at the very end of his narrative, in a characteristically shameless display of his duplicity, Ralegh invites Elizabeth to betray the Indians' trust; in effect, he exhorts her to emulate "the Castellani in respect of their tyrannie and oppression" by undertaking her own conquest of Guiana:

> For whatsoever Prince shall possesse it, shall be greatest, and if the king of Spaine enjoy it, he will become unresistable. Her Majestie hereby shall confirme and strengthen the opinions of all nations, as touching her great and princely actions. And where the South border of Guiana reacheth to the Dominion and Empire of the Amazones, those women shall hereby heare the name of a virgin, which is not onely able to defend her owne territories and her neighbours, but also to invade and conquer so great Empires and so farre removed. (431)

Ralegh seems to insinuate that Elizabethan imperial designs upon the Empire of Guiana might be extended to the Empire of the Amazons. Ralegh's rhetorical tactic for convincing the queen to advance his colonial enterprise is apparently to associate her ambiguously with the Amazons, and then to offer her a means by which to distinguish herself from them. It is precisely by her pursuit of a policy of invasion and conquest that, in Ralegh's terms, "a virgin" may disassociate herself from "those women." He insinuates that a woman who has the prerogative of a sovereign, who is authorized to be out of place, can best justify her authority by putting other women in their places. He seeks to persuade the queen not merely to emulate the Amazons' vigilant territoriality but to overgo them by emulating the Spaniards' rampant invasiveness. In effect, by appropriating the royal tropes of feminine self-empowerment such as those employed in Elizabeth's Tilbury speech, Ralegh endorses a martial and heroic—a manly and kingly—image of feminine authority. But he does so precisely in order to bend the royal will to his own designs. Suffice to say that Her Majesty was unyielding.

Ralegh's exhortation of Queen Elizabeth to overgo the Amazons by offensive warfare, and to outmaneuver

King Philip of Spain by possessing Guiana, is immediately preceded by an exhortation of his masculine readership, who are potential volunteers and investment partners for the conquest and settlement of Guiana. Employing a gender-specific rhetorical strategy distinct from that addressed to the queen, Ralegh elaborates a geography of Elizabethan masculine desire, discovering that "there is a way found to answer every mans longing" (342). The object of this overdetermined desire encompasses identity and security, knowledge, wealth, and power. It seeks to know, master, and possess a feminized space—or, in the language of Ralegh's Virginia patent, "to discover search fynde out and view . . . to have holde occupy and enjoye"; it is a desire that is most vividly realized as the prospect of deflowering a virgin. In his prefatory address "To the Reader," he bids Englishmen to "consider of the actions of both Charles the 5. who had the maidenhead of Peru, and the abundant treasures of Atabalipa, together with the affaires of the Spanish king now living" (346); and, at the end, he exhorts them to emulate King Philip's father by taking Guiana's maidenhead just as he had taken Peru's. In urging these English gentlemen to emulate the rapacious and spectacularly successful Spanish imperialism that now threatens England's very existence, Ralegh holds out to them the prospect of rewards graded to their various statuses:

> The common souldier shall here fight for golde, and pay himselfe in steede of pence, with plates of halfe a foote broad, whereas he breaketh his bones in other warres for provant and penury. Those commanders and chieftaines that shoot at honour and abundance shall finde there . . . rich and beautiful cities . . . temples adorned with golden images . . . sepulchres filled with treasure. (425)

As is common in the promotional literature for Elizabethan colonizing ventures, Ralegh envisions exploration, trade, and settlement abroad as an escape valve for the frustrations of disaffected or marginalized groups, and as a solution to endemic socioeconomic problems at home: "Her Majestie may in this enterprize employ all those souldiers and gentlemen that are younger brethren, and all captaines and chieftaines that want employment" (430). Thus, the potentially riotous malcontents among her majesty's masculine subjects may displace their thwarted ambitions into the conquest of virgin lands. Himself a younger brother, a soldier, and a gentleman in need of advancement, Ralegh might well be considered a special case of the general social problem that he here seeks to redress to his own inestimable advantage.

Together with his company, and his readers, Ralegh encounters in the New World the presence of England's implacable Spanish foe—the specular figure of desiring European Man. Thus recontextualized in the body of Guiana and in the body of Ralegh's book, the Englishman's relationship to the Spaniard manifests itself as a disturbing oscillation between identity and difference, between the acknowledgment and the obfuscation of their common longing. Ralegh can reassure his English gentleman readers that, although "Charles the 5 . . . had the maidenhead of Peru," there remain in the New World other countries that have yet their maidenheads. It is not the English monarch but rather her masculine subjects who are exhorted to emulate the king of Spain. Whether as the virgin protectress of the Indians or as their Amazonian conqueror, Queen Elizabeth cannot comfortably be analogized to Charles V; she cannot take maidenheads. As I have tried to show, the conjunctures, exchanges, and contradictions between the categories of gender and nation could be employed to produce moral distinctions between Englishmen and Spaniards. But they could also dispose English subjects to identify with Spaniards and with the king of Spain himself on the basis of their manly rivalry for possession of the feminized land. In the face of a tangible Spanish threat to what were perceived to be the mutual interests and shared identity of English men and women of all estates, Queen Elizabeth's Tilbury speech may have been relatively successful at producing an identification of the collective social body with the feminine body of the monarch. However, for its masculine Elizabethan readers, the violent rhetoric of Ralegh's *Discoverie* generates identifications with the agency of England's masculine enemies; and in this very process of identification and emulation, these Englishmen will necessarily be alienated from their own sovereign, who cannot occupy the position of the agent in such a gendered and sexed discourse.

The final sentence of the *Discoverie,* following immediately upon Ralegh's exhortation to the queen to overgo the Amazons, balances against its initial deferential gestures an ultimate assertion of the subject's resolve: "I trust . . . that he which is King of all Kings and Lord of Lords, will put it into her heart which is Ladie of Ladies to possesse it, if not, I will judge those men worthy to be kings thereof, that by her grace and leave will undertake it of themselves" (431). Ralegh has good reason to doubt that the queen will be moved to action by his own imperial vision. The requisite phrase, "by her grace and leave," does little to qualify the assertion of a strong, collective, and defiant response by the queen's masculine subjects to her anticipated lack of enthusiasm. Invoking the aid of an emphatically masculine God, Ralegh employs the epithet "Lord of Lords" to figure superlative authority and potency; in contrast, his epithet for his monarch, "Ladie of Ladies," figures superlative feminine gentility. The *Discoverie*'s final clause—"I will judge those men worthy to be kings thereof, that by her grace and leave will undertake it of themselves"—envisions the queen's most manly subjects, like so many Tamburlaines, seizing the opportunity to repudiate their unworthy subjection and to make

themselves kings by their deeds. Nor does Ralegh's perfunctory gesture of deference to the queen neutralize his bold, final symbolic act, in which he arrogates the authority to judge who is worthy to be a king. It seems to me that this closing period of Ralegh's *Discoverie* manifests a considerable strain between two Elizabethan subject positions and two different notions of the "subject": a strain between the subject's courtship of and deference to his queen, and his contrary impulse to assert his own masculine virtue and to put his sovereign in her place as a woman. Nevertheless— and the point cannot be made too strongly—however clever and rhetorically skillful the arguments and insinuations of Ralegh's text, they exerted no discernible power over the queen's policies. Whatever personal predispositions or pragmatic military, diplomatic, and fiscal considerations may have governed Elizabeth's refusal to endorse Ralegh's grandiose scheme, she was also, in effect, resisting his attempts discursively to construct and delimit her gender identity and her sovereignty, to influence her fantasy and to control her will.

Ralegh emphasizes that the Englishmen "had many" of the Indian women "in [their] power" (391); and he represents territorial conquest as the enforced defloration and possession of a female body. Such forms of discursive intimidation and violence may be identified as the compensatory tactics of a masculine Elizabethan subject who is engaged with his monarch in a gendered struggle for mastery and agency, authority and will. If we widen our perspective, however, Queen Elizabeth herself may be understood to be a feminine subject who had been engaged since the very beginning of her reign in compensatory tactics of her own. Elizabeth's political genius was to appropriate and maintain a space for feminine authority within the dominant masculine and patriarchal structures of Tudor society. However, to the extent that such tactics became a successful strategy of power, they also tapped the alternating current of misogyny in her ostensibly adoring and obedient masculine subjects. Such attitudes of hostility, distrust, and contempt were expressed toward women and toward the category of Woman; and they were also expressed toward the sovereign, often indirectly or equivocally but also occasionally with remarkable bluntness. Thus, to formulate Ralegh's practices in terms of "compensatory tactics" may be merely to reobjectify Woman as the threatening Other of the masculine subject: his own gendered violence has now been rendered understandable—perhaps even sympathetic. In other words, unintentionally and unreflectively, such a formulation may be complicit in the very tactics that it describes.

Many who have not read Ralegh's *Discoverie* may, nevertheless, be familiar with the phrase, "Guiana is a countrey that hath yet her maydenhead." It has been cited and quoted frequently in studies of English Renaissance culture, and has been made the subject of discourses ranging from ideological analysis to prurient anecdote. Our contemporary discourses about rape emphasize its character as an act of rage, rather than an act of desire. Some would therefore deny it the status of a specifically sexual crime; others argue compellingly that, to the contrary, rape is always a socially sexed crime that must be contextualized within a larger system of gender politics. Whether the action is physical or metaphorical, whether its object is a woman, a man, or a "countrey," that object is always positioned as feminine. These emphases are certainly relevant to Ralegh's notorious metaphor—and, equally, to the ways in which we critically re-present it. My immediate concern has been with the historically and textually specific work performed by this metaphor in Ralegh's *Discoverie,* and with its articulation among other rhetorical/ideological elements in the collective Elizabethan discourse of discovery. The female body maps an important sector of the Elizabethan cultural unconscious; it constitutes a veritable matrix for the forms of Elizabethan desire and fear. The feminized topographical and textual spaces of the new found land; the heroic, fecund, and rapacious Amazons; the young, well-favored, and naked maidens of Guiana; the pure and dangerous, politic and natural bodies of the Queen of England: it is through the symbolic display and manipulation of these feminine representations—in discursive acts of violence or adoration, or of violent adoration—that "every mans longing" is given a local habitation and a name.

The subject of Ralegh's *Discoverie* is a masculine subject, one who is textually defined not in terms of his subjective experience of sexuality but rather by means of a complex process of social positioning. The narrative and descriptive movements of Elizabethan texts construct multiple—and potentially contradictory—subject positions for writers and readers by means of continually shifting and recombined sets of oppositional or differential terms, terms that are culture-specific in their content and resonance. The project of Ralegh's prose tract, as of Spenser's heroic poem, is (in the words of Spenser's Letter to Ralegh, appended to *The Faerie Queene* in 1590), "to fashion a gentleman or noble person in vertuous and gentle discipline." In both texts, this fashioning is produced in a conjunction of identifications and distinctions that are made in terms of gender, nation, religion, social estate, and condition of civility or savagery (which we might call ethos). The system of Aristotelian ethics that provides a foreconceit for Spenser's Legend of Temperance also provides the conceptual framework within which Ralegh thinks his own daily actions and interactions. But whereas Spenser's polysemous allegorical fiction works explicitly toward a general system of moral virtue, Ralegh's ostensibly factual narrative inscribes elements of such ideological schemata into its intended representations of particular persons and events.

I have suggested some of the ways in which, through the construction/observation of his narrative and descriptive objects, the writing subject obtains coordinates for the constant if often subliminal process by which he locates his shifting position in moral and social space. Ralegh's observations of the Spaniards, of the warriors of Guiana and "their women," of the Amazons, and of "the meaner sort" of Englishmen all work interdependently so as to exemplify in Ralegh himself the ethical and political congruence of the temperate man and the governor, the national and social congruence of the Englishman and the gentleman. At the same time that the persona of the author is dialectically fashioned in relationship to the personae narrated and described in his text, he is also so fashioned in relationship to the readers whom he defines by addressing them in his text. In the case of Ralegh's *Discoverie,* as I have already suggested, these gender- and status-specific objects of address include Queen Elizabeth herself, who is obliquely addressed and directly discussed throughout the text; Lord Howard ("Knight of the Garter, Baron and Councellor, and of the Admirals of England the most renowmed"), and Sir Robert Cecil ("Councellor in her Highness Privie Councels")—two of the most powerful men in England, to whom the *Discoverie* is directly addressed; and a general readership of Elizabethan masculine subjects—gentlemen, soldiers, potential investors, and colonists—who are directly addressed in an initial epistle and at the close of the work.

However distinctive in detail, Ralegh's individual relationship to Queen Elizabeth was shaped by a cultural contradiction that he shared with all members of his nation, gender, and social estate: namely, the expectation that he manifest loyalty and obedience to his sovereign at the same time that he exercised masculine authority over women. His relationship to Howard and Cecil was also conditioned by a cultural contradiction, one specific to men of the social elite and the political nation: namely, that while mastery of oneself and one's social inferiors was central to the ideology of the gentleman, the extreme degree of stratification in Elizabethan society meant that most relationships between gentlemen were also hierarchical, and required elaborate if often subtle forms of deference toward social superiors. (At the very beginning of the *Discoverie,* Ralegh addresses Howard and Cecil as his patrons and protectors, giving them their full titles as quoted above, but he compensates for this requisite positioning of himself as a dependent by also addressing them intimately as his friends and, in Howard's case, as his kinsman.) In his strategies of address, Ralegh must make his appeal in terms of the interests, desires, and national identity he has in common with general readership, but without compromising the position of distinction and superiority that is the basis of his claim to authority over them. A dissonance that is intermittently registered throughout the text of the *Discoverie* is powerfully foregrounded and heightened when, in the rhetorical violence that governs his final address to these readers, Ralegh abandons his previous claim and responsibility to govern their appetites. This dissonance between Ralegh's representation of his own conduct as temperate and judicious and his incitement of others to conduct that is passionate and rapacious has a multiple and contradictory ideological import that lies beyond the controlling intentions of the writing subject: it simultaneously affirms and subverts—and thus, ultimately, destabilizes—the identification of the *masculine* subject with the authority of his *feminine* sovereign; it destabilizes the moral distinction of the *virtuous* Englishman from the *degenerate* Spaniard, and of the *reasonable* gentleman from the *sensual* commoner; and it destabilizes the legitimacy of *civil* European attempts to possess *savage* America. Although Ralegh declares triumphantly that "there is a way found to answer every mans longing," the textual operations of the ***Discoverie*** discover the way to be errant and the answer equivocal.

---

## FURTHER READING

### Bibliography

Mills, Jerry Leath. *Sir Walter Ralegh: A Reference Guide*, edited by James Harner. Boston: G. K. Hall & Co., 1986, 116 p.

    A bibliography of Ralegh's writings, including a listing of critical writing on his works.

*Sir Walter Ralegh, An Annotated Bibliography*, compiled by Christopher M. Armitage. Chapel Hill: The University of North Carolina Press, 1987, 236 p.

    A complete bibliography of Ralegh's works as well as works about him.

### Biography

Adamson, J. H. and Folland, H. F. *The Shepherd of the Ocean: An Account of Sir Walter Ralegh and his Times*. Boston: Gambit, 1969, 464 p.

    A complete study of Ralegh's life and career.

Cunningham, Karen. "'A Spanish heart in an English body': the Ralegh treason trial and the poetics of proof." *The Journal of Medieval and Renaissance Studies*, Vol. 22, No. 3, Fall, 1992, pp. 327-51.

    Discusses Ralegh's treason trial in the context of legal and cultural history.

May, Steven W. *Sir Walter Ralegh*, edited by Arthur F. Kinney. Boston: Twayne Publishers, 1989, 164 p.

    Provides a comprehensive overview of Ralegh's life and works.

Quinn, David Beers. *Set Fair for Roanoke: Voyages and Colonies, 1584-1606*. Chapel Hill: The University of North Carolina Press, 1985, 467 p.

    Published for America's Four Hundredth Anniversary Committee. Studies the founding and demise of Roanoke, including Raleigh's role in the venture.

Wallace, Willard M. *Sir Walter Raleigh*. New Jersey: Princeton University Press, 1959, 334 p.

    Discusses Raleigh's early experiences, his career as poet and adventurer, and his later years of declining power.

### Criticism

Beer, Anna. "'Knowinge shee cann renew': Sir Walter Ralegh in Praise of the Virgin Queen." *Criticism*, Vol. XXXIV, No. 4, Fall, 1992, pp. 497-515.

    Discusses the form of *The Ocean to Cynthia* and challenges the notion of the poem's incompleteness.

Bowers, R. H. "Raleigh's Last Speech: The 'Elms' Document." *The Review of English Studies*, Vol. II, New Series, No. 7, July, 1951, pp. 209-16.

    Discusses the surviving transcripts of Raleigh's final words on the scaffold and presents the text of his speech.

Brooke, Tucker. "Sir Walter Ralegh as Poet and Philosopher." In his *Essays on Shakespeare and Other Elizabethans*, pp. 121-44. New Jersey: Yale University Press, 1948. Reprint by Archon Books, 1969.

    Surveys Raleigh's life, poetry, and philosophical beliefs.

Creighton, Louise. "Sir Walter Ralegh." In *The Cambridge History of English Literature*, edited by A. W. Ward and A. R. Waller, Vol. IV, pp. 59-76. New York: G. P. Putnam's Sons, 1910.

    Provides overview of Raleigh's prose writings.

Davie, Donald. "A Reading of *The Ocean's Love to Cynthia*." In *Elizabethan Poetry*, edited by John Russell Brown and Bernard Harris, pp. 71-89. London: Edward Arnold Publishers, 1960.

    Examination of Raleigh's poem as an expression of his ambivalence at being excluded from Renaissance society during his period of disfavor.

Horner, Joyce. "The Large Landscape: A Study of Certain Images in Ralegh." *Essays in Criticism*, Vol. V, No. 3, July, 1955, pp. 197-213.

    Explores imagery in Raleigh's major works, emphasizing the role of nature and the sea.

Johnson, Michael L. "Some Problems of Unity in Sir Walter Ralegh's *The Ocean's Love to Cynthia*." *Studies in English Literature*, Vol. XIV, No. 1, Winter, 1974, pp. 17-30.

Discusses the consistency and success of the poem's metaphorical and thematic structure.

Luciani, Vincent. "Ralegh's *Discourse of War* and Machiavelli's *Discorsi*." *Modern Philology*, Vol. XLVI, No. 2, November, 1948, pp. 122-31.
  Examines the influence of Machiavelli on Raleigh's work.

Michel-Michot, Paulette. "Sir Walter Raleigh as a Source for the Character of Iago." *English Studies*, Vol. 2, No. 1, February, 1969, pp. 85-89.
  Discusses similarities between Raleigh's court persona and Shakespeare's Iago.

Oakeshott, Walter. *The Queen and the Poet*. London: Faber and Faber, 1960, 232 p.
  Examines several aspects of Raleigh's work, including his relationship with Elizabeth I. Includes *The Poems to Cynthia*.

Racin, John. "Sir Walter Ralegh as Historian: An Analysis of *The History of the World*." In *Elizabethan and Renaissance Studies*, edited by Dr. James Hogg, pp. 147-76. Austria: Institut für Anglistik und Amerikanistik Universität Salzburg, 1974.
  Comprehensive discussion of Raleigh's *The History of the World*, including the philosophical and theologic elements of the work.

Sackton, Alexander. "The Rhetoric of Literary Praise in the Poetry of Raleigh and Chapman." *Texas Studies in Literature and Language*, Vol. XVIII, No. 3, Fall, 1976, pp. 409-21.
  Discusses Raleigh's two poems in praise of Spenser's *Faerie Queene*.

Sprott, S. E. "Ralegh's 'Sceptic' and the Elizabethan Translation of Sextus Empiricus." *Philological Quarterly*, Vol. XLII, No. 2, April, 1963, pp. 166-75.
  Compares and contrasts the surviving manuscript versions of Raleigh's essay.

Ure, Peter. "The Poetry of Sir Walter Ralegh." In his *Elizabethan and Jacobean Drama*, edited by J. C. Maxwell, pp. 237-47. Liverpool: Liverpool University Press, 1974.
  Overview of Raleigh's court poetry.

Williams, Edith Whitehurst. "The Anglo-Saxon Theme of Exile in Renaissance Lyrics: A Perspective on Two Sonnets of Sir Walter Ralegh." *ELH*, Vol. 42, No. 2, Summer, 1975, pp. 171-88.
  Examines Raleigh's sonnets in the context of Old English Lyric.

# John Winthrop

## 1588-1649

English-born political thinker, historian, and journal writer.

## INTRODUCTION

The first and most influential governor of the Massachusetts Bay Colony, Winthrop is primarily remembered for his *A Journal of the Transactions and Occurrences in the Settlement of Massachusetts and the Other New-England Colonies, from the Year 1630 to 1644*, in which he chronicled the daily life, tribulations, and important events in the colony. Along with his writings on theology, the Antinomian controversy, and treaties with Native Americans, Winthrop's *Journal* constitutes one of the seminal records of the everyday life of early settlers in America. Critics also consider Winthrop a primary architect of American Puritanism. In his sermon "A Modell of Christian Charitie," delivered on board the ship *Arbella* in 1630 while he was on his way to America, Winthrop introduced two concepts that proved extremely influential in shaping colonial thinking and policy: the "City on a Hill," or the idea that the righteousness and material success of the Puritan colony would serve as an example to others, and the concept of adivine covenant binding the community together through shared responsibility.

## Biography

Winthrop was the son of the lord of the manor at Groton in Suffolk, England. He enrolled at Trinity College, Cambridge, when he was fourteen years old; while a student, he fell gravely ill and underwent a religious conversion, becoming identified with the Puritan group within the Church of England. Winthrop's essay entitled "Experiencia," written in 1607-13 and the only surviving record of this time of his life, deals with his religious experience and documents that he had made "a new Covenant with the Lorde." Winthrop soon left Trinity and in 1605 married Mary Forth. He studied law in London at the Inns of Court, and records identify him as a justice of the peace in Suffolk in 1617. Around this same period Winthrop assumed supervision of the manor from his father, and was also facing tragedy in his personal life: his wife had died in 1615, and Winthrop's second wife, Thomasine Clopton, died a year after they married, in 1617. Now married to his third wife, Margaret Tyndal, and finding it difficult to support his many children because of a regional economic crisis, Winthrop received a government post as a common attorney in the Court of Wards and Liveries in London. It was also about this time that Winthrop officially joined the Puritans, a militant subgroup of the Church of England which was frequently in conflict with the high Anglicanism of King Charles I. Unwilling to continue to make the compromises needed to placate government and church authorities in England, some Puritans organized the New England Company in 1628, intending to relocate to America; they reorganized in 1629, became chartered as the Massachusetts Bay Company, and elected Winthrop governor. He served terms from 1629 to 1633, 1637 to 1640, 1642 to 1644, and from 1646 until his death in 1649. As governor, Winthrop was often summoned to mediate between warring parties, contend with conflicts relating to jurisdiction, settle conflicts with the Indians, and decide questions of economics. Along with other colonial leaders, Winthrop sought to apply Puritan philosophy to the practical affairs of the Bay Colony, advocating broad participation by members of the community, a mixture of democracy and aristocracy, the growth of churches, and experiments in wages and prices designed to keep citizens from preying upon each other. Anyone dissenting from their consensual orthodoxy was obliged to leave, for Winthrop and his magistrates were determined to shelter their model society from any civil or religious influence that might adversely affect it. Winthrop died in 1649, in the midst of his political career and still engaged in writing his journal.

**Major Works**

Winthrop's first and, as many scholars have asserted, most significant legacy to New England was the sermon "A Modell of Christian Charitie," in which he explained to his fellow immigrants the magnitude of the task they were undertaking. They were chosen by God to perform a role and would be watched by all other people, Winthrop maintained; as in the biblical City upon a Hill, everyone would be interpreting their success or failure in America as a sign of God's pleasure or displeasure with them. By virtue of sailing to New England they had entered into a covenant with God involving each person in the community. If they adhered strictly to the divine will, they would be rewarded with prosperity, security, and success; and those evidences of God's favor would inspire England and other nations to emulate the New England way. If they settled for less than perfection in themselves and in those around them, they would suffer God's wrath. Like "A Modell of Christian Charitie," Winthrop's *Journal* was an effort to discern the divine pattern in the events of daily life in the colony and to justify the role New Englanders believed themselves called to play. Written as a diary and never revised, the *Journal* remained unpublished long after Winthrop's death, though colonial historians drew upon the work as a source of information. In 1790 Jonathan Trumbull, Governor of Connecticut, copied the first two of the three *Journal* notebooks and submitted them to Noah Webster for printing. Critics agree that Winthrop's *Journal* provides the fullest eyewitness rendering of the first two decades of Massachusetts colonial history: Winthrop provides a rich record of events, explicates political and religious points of view held by the colonists, and presents anecdotes that illustrate the Puritans' notion of themselves as fulfilling a divine mission. He reported on all matters impersonally, usually only identifying himself as "the governour," and only occasionally stating his own opinions. Winthrop also wrote two other historical works, the only ones published during his lifetime. *Antinomians and Familists condemned by the synod of elders in New-England: with the proceedings of the magistrates against them, and their apology for the same* is a collection of materials related to the Anne Hutchinson controversy of the 1630s. Hutchinson and her followers dissented from the teachings of Puritan ministers who emphasized salvation through good works rather than through God's

grace; following a trial in which Winthrop defended the right of the community to protect itself from dissenters, she was banished from the colony. Winthrop's *A Declaration of Former Passages and Proceedings Betwixt the English and the Narrowgansets with Their Confederates, Wherein the Grounds of Justice of the Ensuing Warre are Opened and Cleared* explores in pamphlet form the conflict between the colonists and the Rhode Island Indians and outlines Winthrop's fears concerning the future.

**Critical Reception**

Winthrop was revered by his contemporaries and later New Englanders as an inspired spiritual leader and wise politician. Cotton Mather, in his *Magnalia Christi Americana; or, The Ecclesiastical History of New England* (1702), extolled Winthrop's integrity and sagacity, comparing him to the biblical Nehemiah. In the twentieth century, critics have explored various aspects of Winthrop's thought, for example his economic ideas, political philosophy (particularly his concept of the social covenant and the rights and responsibilities of individuals within it), and his complex role as both admirer and prosecutor in the trial of Anne Hutchinson. Some have criticized Winthrop as a narrow-minded and authoritarian leader who sought a homogenous society at the price of personal liberty. Winthrop's *Journal* continues to attract scholarly attention, with commentators focusing on stylistic and structural elements, narrative tone and perspective, and the interplay between history and spiritual autobiography in the work. Lee Schweninger, summarizing Winthrop's overall contribution to American literature, has written, "He was able to preserve for future generations both the actual historical record of the building of Boston in New England and his vision of a city on a hill, not only as a model but as an emblem, a symbol of the potential of humanity."

---

**PRINCIPAL WORKS**

*Antinomians and Familists condemned by the synod of elders in New-England: with the proceedings of the magistrates against them, and their apology for the same* (prose) 1644; also published as *A Short Story of the rise, reign, and ruin of the Antinomians, Familist & libertines,* 1644

*A Declaration of Former Passages and Proceedings Betwixt the English and the Narrowgansets, with Their Confederates, Wherein the Grounds and Justice of the Ensuing Warre are Opened and Cleared* (prose) 1645

*A Journal of the Transactions and Occurrences in the Settlement of Massachusetts and the Other New-England Colonies, from the Year 1630 to 1644* (journal) 1790; also published as *The History of New*

*England from 1630 to 1649,* 1825-26, rev. ed. 1853

*Winthrop Papers.* 5 vols. (prose, journal, history, letters) 1929-47

---

## CRITICISM

### John Winthrop (sermon date 1630)

SOURCE: A sermon delivered in 1630, in *Life and Letters of John Winthrop, Vol. II,* second edition, by Robert C. Winthrop, Little, Brown, and Company, 1866, pp. 18-20.

[*In the following excerpt from his famous sermon "A Modell of Christian Charity," delivered on board the ship Arbella in 1630, Winthrop outlines the nature of the covenant forged between the colonists and God.*]

Thus stands the case between God and us. We are entered into a Covenant with Him for this work. We have taken out a commission. The Lord hath given us leave to draw our own articles. We have professed to enterprise these and those ends, upon these and those accounts. We have hereupon besought of Him favor and blessing. Now if the Lord shall please to hear us, and bring us in peace to the place we desire, then hath he ratified this Covenant and sealed our Commission, and will expect a strict performance of the articles contained in it; but if we shall neglect the observation of these articles which are the ends we have propounded, and, dissembling with our God, shall fall to embrace this present world and prosecute our carnal intentions, seeking great things for ourselves and our posterity, the Lord will surely break out in wrath against us; be revenged of such a (sinful) people, and make us know the price of the breach of such a Covenant.

Now the only way to avoid this shipwreck, and to provide for our posterity, is to follow the counsel of Micah, *to do justly, to love mercy, to walk humbly with our God.* For this end, we must be knit together, in this work, as one man. We must entertain each other in brotherly affection. We must be willing to abridge ourselves of our superfluities, for the supply of other's necessities. We must uphold a familiar commerce together in all meekness, gentleness, patience, and liberality. We must delight in each other; make other's condition our own; rejoice together, mourn together, labor and suffer together, always having before our eyes our commission and community in the work, as members of the same body. So shall we *keep the unity of the spirit in the bond of peace.* The Lord will be our God, and delight to dwell among us, as his own people, and will command a blessing upon us in all our ways. So that we shall see much more of his wisdom, power, goodness and truth, than formerly we have been

acquainted with. We shall find that the God of Israel is among us, when ten of us shall be able to resist a thousand of our enemies; when he shall make us a praise and a glory, that men shall say of succeeding plantations, 'the Lord make it likely that of *New England.*' For we must consider that we shall be as a City upon a hill. The eyes of all people are upon us. Soe that if we shall deal falsely with our God in this work we have undertaken, and so cause him to withdraw his present help from us, we shall be made a story and a by-word throughout the world. We shall open the mouths of enemies to speak evil of the ways of God, and all professors for God's sake. We shall shame the faces of many of God's worthy servants, and cause their prayers to be turned into curses upon us till we be consumed out of the good land whither we are a-going.

I shall shut up this discourse with that exhortation of Moses, that faithful servant of the Lord, in his last farewell to Israel (Deut. 30).

> Beloved, there is now set before us life and good, Death and evil, in that we are commanded this day to love the Lord our God, and to love one another, to walk in his ways and to keep his Commandments and his Ordinance and his Laws, and the articles of our Covenant with him, that we may live and be multiplied, and that the Lord our God may bless us in the land whither we go to possess it. But if our hearts shall turn away, so that we will not obey, but shall be seduced, and worship and serve other Gods, our pleasure and profits, and serve them; it is propounded unto us this day, we shall surely perish out of the good land whither we pass over this vast sea to possess it;

Therefore let us choose life that we, and our seed may live, by obeying His voice and cleaving to Him, for He is our life and our prosperity.

### Cotton Mather (essay date 1702)

SOURCE: "Nehemias Americanus: The Life of John Winthrop, Esq., Governour of the Massachuset Colony," in *Magnalia Christi Americana; or, The Ecclesiastical History of New-England, Vol. I,* Silas Andrus and Son, 1855, pp. 118-31.

[*Mather was a renowned American clergyman and scholar who was associated with the Salem witchcraft trials, but later repudiated them. His works include* Wonders of the Invisible World *(1693),* Essays to Do Good *(1710), and* Ratio Disciplinae *(1726). In the following excerpt from his best-known work, first published in 1702, Mather praises the wisdom, integrity, and sagacity Winthrop exhibited in his role as governor of "our American Jerusalem."*]

Let Greece boast of her patient Lycurgus, the lawgiver, by whom diligence, temperance, fortitude and wit were made the fashions of a therefore long-lasting and renowned commonwealth: let Rome tell of her devout Numa, the lawgiver, by whom the most famous commonwealth saw peace triumphing over extinguished war and cruel plunders; and murders giving place to the more mollifying exercises of his religion. Our New-England shall tell and boast of her Winthrop, a lawgiver as patient as Lycurgus, but not admitting any of his criminal disorders; as devout as Numa, but not liable to any of *his* heathenish madnesses; a governour in whom the excellencies of Christianity made a most improving addition unto the virtues, wherein even without *those* he would have made a *parallel* for the great men of Greece, or of Rome, which the pen of a Plutarch has eternized.

A stock of *heroes* by right should afford nothing but what is *heroical;* and nothing but an extream degeneracy would make any thing less to be expected from a stock of Winthrops. Mr. Adam Winthrop, the son of a worthy gentleman wearing the same name, was himself a worthy, a discreet, and a learned gentleman, particularly eminent for skill in the law, nor without remark for love to the gospel, under the reign of King Henry VIII., and brother to a memorable favourer of the reformed religion in the days of Queen Mary, into whose hands the famous martyr Philpot committed his papers, which afterwards made no inconsiderable part of our *martyr-books.* This Mr. Adam Winthrop had a son of the same name also, and of the same endowments and imployments with his father; and this third Adam Winthrop was the father of that renowned John Winthrop, who was the father of New-England, and the founder of *a colony,* which, upon many accounts, like *him* that founded it, may challenge the first place among the English glories of America. Our John Winthrop, thus born at the mansion-house of his ancestors, at Groton in Suffolk, on June 12, 1587, enjoyed afterwards an agreeable education. But though he would rather have devoted himself unto the study of Mr. John Calvin, than of Sir Edward Cook; nevertheless, the accomplishments of a lawyer were those wherewith Heaven made his chief opportunities to be serviceable.

Being made, at the unusually early age of *eighteen,* a justice of peace, his virtues began to fall under a more general observation; and he not only so bound himself to the behaviour of a Christian, as to become exemplary for a conformity to the laws of Christianity in his own conversation, but also discovered a more than ordinary measure of those qualities which adorn an officer of humane society. His justice was impartial, and used the ballance to weigh not the cash, but the *case* of those who were before him: *prosopolatria* [respect of persons] he reckoned as bad as *idolatria:* his wisdom did exquisitely temper things according to the *art of governing,* which is a business of more contriv-

ance than the *seven arts* of the schools; *over* still went before *terminer* in all his administrations: his courage made him *dare to do right,* and fitted him to stand among the lions that have sometimes been the supporters of the throne: all which virtues he rendred the more illustrious, by emblazoning them with the constant liberality and hospitality of a gentleman. This made him the *terror* of the wicked, and the *delight* of the sober, the *envy* of the many, but the *hope* of those who had any hopeful design in hand for the common good of the nation and the interests of religion.

Accordingly when the noble design of carrying a colony of chosen people into an American wilderness, was by some eminent persons undertaken, *this* eminent person was, by the consent of all, chosen for the Moses, who must be the leader of so great an undertaking: and indeed nothing but a *Mosaic spirit* could have carried him through the temptations, to which either his farewel to his own land, or his travel in a strange land, must needs expose a gentleman of his education. Wherefore having sold a fair estate of six or seven hundred a year, he transported himself with the effects of it into New-England in the year 1630, where he spent it upon the service of a famous plantation, founded and formed for the seat of the most *reformed Christianity:* and continued there, conflicting with temptations of all sorts, as many years as the *nodes* of the *moon* take to dispatch a revolution. Those persons were never concerned in a new plantation, who know not that the unavoidable difficulties of such a thing will call for all the prudence and patience of a mortal man to encounter therewithal; and they must be very insensible of the influence, which the *just wrath* of Heaven has permitted the *devils* to have upon this world, if they do not think that the difficulties of a new plantation, devoted unto the evangelical worship of our Lord Jesus Christ, must be yet more than ordinary. How prudently, how patiently, and with how much resignation to our Lord Jesus Christ, our brave Winthrop waded through these difficulties, let posterity consider with admiration. And know, that as the picture of this their governour was, after his death, hung up with honour in the state-house of his country, so the wisdom, courage, and holy zeal of his life, were an example well-worthy to be copied by all that shall succeed him in government.

Were he now to be considered only as a Christian, we might therein propose him as greatly imitable. He was a very religious man; and as he strictly kept his *heart,* so he kept his *house,* under the laws of piety; there he was every day constant in holy duties, both morning and evening, and on the Lord's days, and lectures; though he wrote not after the preacher, yet such was his attention, and such his retention in hearing, that he repeated unto his family the sermons which he had heard in the congregation. But it is chiefly as a governour that he is now to be considered. Being the governour over the considerablest part of New-England, he maintained the figure and honour of his place with the spirit of a true gentleman; but yet with such obliging condescention to the circumstances of the colony, that when a certain troublesome and malicious calumniator, well known in those times, printed his libellous nick-names upon the chief persons here, the worst nickname he could find for the governour, was *John Temper-well;* and when the calumnies of that ill man caused the Arch-bishop to summon one Mr. Cleaves before the King, in hopes to get some accusation from him against the country, Mr. Cleaves gave such an account of the governour's laudable carriage in all respects, and the serious devotion wherewith prayers were both publickly and privately made for his Majesty, that the King expressed himself most highly *pleased* therewithal, only *sorry* that so worthy a person should be no better accommodated than with the hardships of America. He was, indeed, a governour, who had most exactly studied that book which, pretending to teach politicks, did only contain *three leaves,* and but *one word* in each of those leaves, which word was, MODERATION. Hence, though he were a zealous enemy to all vice, yet his practice was according to his judgment thus expressed: "In the infancy of plantations, justice should be administered with more lenity than in a settled state; because people are more apt then to transgress; partly out of ignorance of new laws and orders, partly out of oppression of business, and other straits. [LENTO GRADU] (by slow degrees) was the old rule; and if the strings of a new instrument be wound up unto their heighth, they will quickly crack." But when some leading and learned men took offence at his conduct in this matter, and upon a conference gave it in as their opinion, "That a stricter discipline was to be used in the beginning of a plantation, than after its being with more age established and confirmed," the governour being readier to see *his own* errors than *other men's,* professed his purpose to endeavour their satisfaction with less of *lenity* in his administrations. At that conference there were drawn up several other articles to be observed between the governour and the rest of the magistrates, which were of this import: "That the magistrates, as far as might be, should aforehand ripen their consultations, to produce that unanimity in their publick votes, which might make them liker to the voice of God; that if differences fell out among them in their publick meetings, they should speak only to the case, without any reflection, with all due modesty, and but by way of question; or desire the deferring of the cause to further time; and after sentence to imitate privately no dislike; that they should be more familiar, friendly and open unto each other, and more frequent in their visitations, and not any way expose each other's infirmities, but seek the honour of each other, and all the Court; that one magistrate shall not cross the proceedings of another, without first advising with him; and that they should in all their appearances abroad, be so circumstanced as to prevent all contempt of authority;

and that they should support and strengthen all under officers. All of which articles were observed by no man more than by the governour himself.

But whilst he thus did, as our New-English Nehemiah, the part of a *ruler* in managing the public affairs of our American Jerusalem, when there were Tobijahs and Sanballats enough to vex him, and give him the experiment of Luther's observation, *Omnis qui regit est tanquam signum, in quod omnia jacula, Satan et Mundus dirigunt* [A man in authority is a target, at which Satan and the world launch all their darts.]; he made himself still an exacter *parallel* unto that governour of Israel, by doing the part of a neighbour among the distressed people of the new plantation. To teach them the frugality necessary for those times, he abridged himself of a thousand comfortable things, which he had allowed himself elsewhere: his *habit* was not that *soft raiment,* which would have been disagreeable to a wilderness; his table was not covered with the superfluities that would have invited unto sensualities: water was commonly his own drink, though he gave wine to others. But at the same time his liberality unto the needy was even beyond measure generous; and therein he was continually causing "the blessing of him that was ready to perish to come upon him, and the heart of the widow and the orphan to sing for joy:" but none more than those of deceased Ministers, whom he always treated with a very singular compassion; among the instances whereof we still enjoy with us the worthy and now aged son of that reverend Higginson, whose death left his family in a wide world soon after his arrival here, publickly acknowledging the charitable Winthrop for his *foster-father.* It was oftentimes no small trial unto his faith, to think how a table for the people should be furnished when they first came into the wilderness! and for very many of the people his own good works were needful, and accordingly employed for the answering of his faith. Indeed, for a while the governour was the Joseph, unto whom the whole body of the people repaired when their corn failed them; and he continued relieving of them with his open-handed bounties, as long as he had any stock to do it with; and a lively *faith* to *see* the return of the "bread after many days," and not starve in the days that were to pass till that return should be seen, carried him chearfully through those expences.

Once it was observable that, on February 5, 1630, when he was distributing the last handful of the meal in the barrel unto a poor man distressed by the "wolf at the door," at that instant they spied a ship arrived at the harbour's mouth, laden with provisions for them all. Yea, the governour sometimes made his own *private purse* to be the *publick:* not by *sucking* into it, but by *squeezing* out of it; for when the publick treasure had nothing in it, he did himself defray the charges of the publick. And having learned that lesson of our Lord, "that it is better to give than to receive," he did, at the general court, when he was a third time chosen governour, make a speech unto this purpose: "That he had received gratuities from divers towns, which he accepted with much comfort and content; and he had likewise received civilities from particular persons, which he could not refuse without incivility in himself: nevertheless, he took them with a trembling heart, in regard of God's word, and the conscience of his own infirmities; and therefore he desired them that they would not hereafter take it ill if he refused such presents for the time to come." 'Twas his custom also to send some of his family upon errands unto the houses of the poor, about their *meal time,* on purpose to *spy* whether they *wanted;* and if it were found that they wanted, he would make *that* the opportunity of sending supplies unto them. And there was one passage of his charity that was perhaps a little unusual: in an hard and long winter, when wood was very scarce at Boston, a man gave him a private information that a needy person in the neighbourhood stole wood sometimes from *his* pile; whereupon the governour in a seeming anger did reply, "Does he so? I'll take a course with him; go, call that man to me; I'll warrant you I'll cure him of stealing." When the man came, the governour considering that if he had stolen, it was more out of necessity than disposition, said unto him, "Friend, it is a severe winter, and I doubt you are but meanly provided for wood; wherefore I would have you supply your self at my wood-pile till this cold season be over." And he then merrily asked his friends, "Whether he had not effectually cured this man of stealing his wood?"

One would have imagined that so good a man could have had no enemies, if we had not had a daily and woful experience to convince us that goodness it self will make enemies. . . . The governour had by his unspotted integrity procured himself a great reputation among the people; and then the crime of popularity was laid unto his charge by such, who were willing to deliver him from the danger of having *all men speak well of him.* Yea, there were persons eminent both for figure and for number, unto whom it was almost *essential* to *dislike* every thing that came from *him;* and yet *he* always maintained an amicable correspondence with them; as believing that they acted according to their judgment and conscience, or that their eyes were held by some temptation in the worst of all their oppositions. Indeed, his right works were so many, that they exposed him unto the envy of his neighbours; and of such *power* was that *envy,* that sometimes he could not *stand before it;* but it was by *not standing* that he most effectually *withstood* it all. Great attempts were sometimes made among the freemen to get him left out from his place in the government upon little pretences, lest by the too frequent choice of one man, the government should cease to be by *choice;* and with a particular aim at him, sermons were preached at the anniversary Court of election, to disswade the freemen from

chusing one man twice together. This was the reward of his *extraordinary serviceableness!* But when these attempts *did* succeed, as they sometimes did, his profound humility appeared in that equality of mind, wherewith he applied himself chearfully to serve the country in whatever station their votes had alloted for him. And one year when the votes came to be numbered, there were found six less for Mr. Winthrop than for another gentleman who then stood in competition: but several other persons regularly tendring their votes before the election was published, were, upon a very frivolous objection, refused by some of the magistrates that were afraid lest the election should at last fall upon Mr. Winthrop: which, though it was well perceived, yet such was the self-denial of this patriot, that he would not permit any notice to be taken of the injury. But these trials were nothing in comparison of those harsher and harder treats, which he sometimes had from the frowardness of not a few in the days of their paroxysms; and from the faction of some against him, not much unlike that of the Piazzi in Florence against the family of the Medices: all of which he at last conquered by conforming to the famous Judge's motto, *Prudens qui Patiens* [He is prudent who is patient.]. The oracles of God have said, "Envy is rottenness to the bones"; and Gulielmus Parisiensis applies it unto rulers, who are as it were the *bones* of the societies which they belong unto: "Envy," says he, "is often found among them, and it is rottenness unto them." Our Winthrop encountred this *envy* from others, but conquered it, by being free from it himself.

Were it not for the sake of introducing the exemplary skill of this wise man, *at giving soft answers,* one would not chuse to relate those instances of wrath which he had sometimes to encounter with; but he was for his gentleness, his forbearance, and longanimity, a pattern so worthy to be written *after,* that something must here be written *of* it. He seemed indeed never to speak any other language than that of Theodosius: "If any man speak evil of the governour, if it be through lightness, 'tis to be contemned; if it be through madness, 'tis to be pitied; if it be through injury, 'tis to be remitted." Behold, reader, the "meekness of wisdom" notably exemplified! There was a time when he received a very sharp letter from a gentleman who was a member of the Court, but he delivered back the letter unto the messengers that brought it, with such a Christian speech as this: "I am not willing to keep such a matter of provocation by me! Afterwards the same gentleman was compelled by the scarcity of provisions to send unto him that he would sell him some of his cattle; whereupon the governour prayed him to accept what he had sent for as a *token* of his good will; but the gentleman returned him this answer: "Sir, your overcoming of yourself hath overcome me:" and afterwards gave demonstration of it. The French have a saying, That *Un honesté homme, est un homme mesle!*—a *good* man is a *mixt* man; and there hardly ever was a more sensible *mixture* of those two things, *resolution* and *condescention,* than in this good man. There was a time when the court of election being, for fear of tumult, held at Cambridge, May 17, 1637, the sectarian part of the country, who had the year before gotten a governour more unto their mind, had a project now to have confounded the election, by demanding that the court would consider a petition then tendered before their proceeding thereunto. Mr. Winthrop saw that this was only a trick to throw all into confusion, by putting off the choice of the governour and assistents until the *day* should be over; and therefore he did, with a strenuous resolution, procure a disappointment unto that mischievous and ruinous contrivance. Nevertheless, Mr. Winthrop himself being by the voice of the freemen in this exigence chosen the governour, and all of the other party left out, that ill-affected party discovered the *dirt* and *mire,* which remained with them, after the *storm* was over; particularly the serjeants, whose office 'twas to attend the governour, laid down their halberts; but such was the condescention of this governour, as to take no present notice of this anger and contempt, but only order some of his own servants to take the halberts; and when the country manifested their deep resentments of the affront thus offered him, *he* prayed them to overlook it. But it was not long before a compensation was made for these things by the *doubled respects* which were from all parts paid unto him. Again, there was a time when the suppression of an *antinomian* and *familistical* faction, which extreamly threatned the ruin of the country, was generally thought much owing unto this renowned man; and therefore when the friends of that faction could not wreak their displeasure on him with any *politick* vexations, they set themselves to do it by *ecclesiastical* ones. Accordingly when a sentence of banishment was passed on the ringleaders of those disturbances, who

> —*Maria et Terras, Cœlumque profundum,*
> *Quippe ferant Rapidi, secum vertantque per*
>   *Auras;*

> [Rack sea and land and sky with mingled
>   wrath,
> In the wild tumult of their stormy path.]

many at the church of Boston, who were then that way too much inclined, most earnestly solicited the elders of that church, whereof the governour was a member, to call him forth as an *offender,* for passing of that sentence. The elders were unwilling to do any such thing; but the governour understanding the ferment among the people took that occasion to make a speech in the congregation to this effect:

"BRETHREN: Understanding that some of you have desired that I should answer for an *offence* lately taken among you; had I been called upon so to do,

I would, first, have advised with the ministers of the country, whether the *church* had power to call in question the *civil court;* and I would, secondly, have advised with the rest of the *court,* whether I might discover their counsels unto the *church.* But though I know that the reverend elders of this church, and some others, do very well apprehend that the *church* cannot enquire into the proceedings of the *court;* yet, for the satisfaction of the weaker, who do not apprehend it, I will declare my mind concerning it. If the church have any such power, they have it from the Lord Jesus Christ; but the Lord Jesus Christ hath disclaimed it, not only by *practice,* but also by *precept,* which we have in his gospel, Matt. xx. 25, 26. It is true, indeed, that *magistrates,* as they are *church-members,* are accountable unto the *church* for their failings; but that is when they are out of their calling. When Uzziah would go offer incense in the *temple,* the officers of the church called him to an account, and withstood him; but when Asa put the prophet in prison, the officers of the church did not call *him* to an account for *that.* If the *magistrate* shall in a *private way* wrong any man, the church may call him to an sccount for it; but if he be in pursuance of a course of *justice,* though the thing that he does be *unjust,* yet he is not accountable for it before the church. As for my self, I did nothing in the causes of any of the brethren but by the advice of the elders of the church. Moreover, in the *oath* which I have taken there is this clause: 'In all cases wherein you are to give your vote, you shall do as in your judgment and conscience you shall see to be just, and for the publick good.' And I am satisfied, it is most for the glory of God, and the publick good, that there has been such a sentence passed; yea, those brethren are so divided from the rest of the country in their opinions and practices, that it cannot stand with the *publick peace* for them to continue with us; Abraham saw that Hagar and Ishmael must be sent away."

By such a speech he marvellously convinced, satisfied and mollified the uneasie brethren of the church; *Sic cunctus Pelagi cecidit Fragor*—[To silence sunk the thunder of the wave]. And after a little patient waiting, the *differences* all so wore away, that the church, meerly as a token of respect unto the governour when he had newly met with some *losses* in his estate, sent him a present of several hundreds of pounds. Once more there was a time when some active spirits among the deputies of the colony, by their endeavours not only to make themselves a Court of Judicature, but also to take away the *negative* by which the magistrates might check their votes, had like by over-driving to have run the whole government into something too *democratical.* And if there were a town in Spain undermined by *coneys,* another town in Thrace destroyed by *moles,* a third in Greece ranversed by *frogs,* a fourth in Germany subverted by *rats;* I must on this occasion add, that there was a country in America like to be confounded by a *swine.* A certain *stray sow* being found, was claimed by two several persons with a claim so equally maintained on both sides, that after six or seven years' *hunting* the business from one court unto another, it was brought at last into the General Court, where the final determination was, "that it was impossible to proceed unto any judgment in the case." However, in the debate of this matter, the *negative* of the *upper-house* upon the *lower* in that Court was brought upon the stage; and agitated with so hot a zeal, that a *little more, and all had been in the fire*. In these agitations, the governour was informed that an offence had been taken by some eminent persons at certain passages in a discourse by him written thereabout; whereupon, with his usual *condescendency*, when he next came into the General Court, he made a speech of this import:

> I understand that some have taken offence at something that I have lately written; which offence I desire to remove now, and begin this year in a reconciled state with you all. As for the *matter* of my writing, I had the concurrence of my brethren; it is a point of judgment which is not at my own disposing. I have examined it over and over again by such light as God has given me, from the rules of religion, reason and custom; and I see no cause to retract any thing of it: wherefore I must enjoy my liberty in that, as you do your selves. But for the *manner*, this, and all that was blame-worthy in it, was wholly my own; and whatsoever I might alledge for my own justification therein before men, I wave it, as now setting my self before another Judgment seat. However, what I wrote was upon great provocation, and to vindicate my self and others from great aspersion; yet that was no sufficient warrant for me to allow any distemper of spirit in my self; and I doubt I have been too prodigal of my brethren's reputation; I might have maintained my cause without casting any blemish upon others, when I made that my conclusion, 'And now let religion and sound reason give judgment in the case;' it looked as if I arrogated too much unto my self, and too little to others. And when I made that profession, 'That I would maintain what I wrote before all the world,' though such words might modestly be spoken, yet I perceive an unbeseeming *pride* of my own heart breathing in them. For these failings, I ask pardon of God and man.

*Sic ait, et dicto citius Tumida Æquora placat,*
*Collectasque fugat Nubes, Solemque reducit.*

[He speaks—but ere the word is said,
Each mounting billow droops its head,
And brightening clouds one moment stay
To pioneer returning day.]

This acknowledging disposition in the governour made them all acknowledge, that he was truly "a man of an excellent spirit." In fine, the victories of an Alexander, an Hannibal, or a Cæsar over *other* men, were not so glorious as the victories of this great man over *himself*,

which also at last proved victories over other men.

But the stormiest of all the *trials* that ever befel this gentleman, was in the year 1645, when he was, in *title*, no more than Deputy-governour of the colony. If the famous Cato were forty-four times called into judgment, but as often acquitted; let it not be wondred, and if our famous Winthrop were one time so. There hapning certain seditious and mutinous practices in the town of Hingham, the Deputy-governour, as legally as prudently, interposed his authority for the checking of them: whereupon there followed such an *enchantment* upon the minds of the deputies in the General Court, that upon a scandalous petition of the delinquents unto them, wherein a pretended invasion made upon the liberties of the people was complained of, the Deputy-governour was most irregularly called forth unto an ignominious *hearing* before them in a vast assembly; whereto with a *sagacious humilitude* he consented, although he shewed them how he might have refused it. The result of that hearing was, that notwithstanding the touchy jealousie of the people about their liberties lay at the bottom of all this prosecution, yet Mr. Winthrop was publicly acquitted, and the offenders were severally fined and censured. But Mr. Winthrop then resuming the place of Deputy-governour on the bench, saw cause to speak unto the *root of the matter* after this manner:

> "I shall now speak any thing about the past proceedings of this Court, or the persons therein concerned. Only I bless God that I see an issue of this troublesome affair. I am well satisfied that I was publickly *accused*, and that I am now publickly *acquitted*. But though I am justified before men, yet it may be the Lord hath seen so much amiss in my administrations, as calls me to be humbled; and indeed for me to have been thus charged by men, is it self a matter of humiliation, whereof I desire to make a right use before the Lord. If Miriam's father spit in her face, she is to be ashamed. But give me leave, before you go, to say something that may rectifie the *opinions* of many people, from whence the distempers have risen that have lately prevailed upon the body of this people. The questions that have troubled the country have been about the *authority of the magistracy*, and the *liberty of the people*. It is *you* who have called *us* unto this office; but being thus called, we have our authority from God; it is the ordinance of God, and it hath the image of God stamped upon it; and the contempt of it has been vindicated by God with terrible examples of his vengeance. I entreat you to consider, that when you chuse magistrates, you take them from among your selves, 'men subject unto like passions with your selves.' If you see our infirmities, reflect on *your own*, and you will not be so severe censurers of *ours*. We count him a good servant who breaks not his covenant: the covenant between us and you, is the oath you have taken of us, which is to this purpose, 'that we shall govern you, and judge your causes, according to God's laws, and our own,

according to our best skill.' As for our skill, you must run the hazard of it; and if there be an error, not in the will, but only in skill, it becomes you to bear it. Nor would I have you to mistake in the point of your own *liberty*. There is a liberty of corrupt nature, which is affected both by men and beasts, to do what they list; and this liberty is inconsistent with authority, impatient of all restraint; by this liberty, *Sumus Omnes Deteriores* [we are all the worse for it]; 'tis the grand enemy of *truth* and *peace,* and all the ordinances of God are bent against it. But there is a civil, a moral, a federal liberty, which is the proper end and object of authority; it is a liberty for that only which is *just* and *good;* for this liberty you are to stand with the hazard of your very lives; and whatsoever crosses it is not authority, but a distemper thereof. This liberty is maintained in a way of subjection to authority; and the authority set over you will in all administrations for your good be quietly submitted unto, by all but such as have a disposition to shake off the yoke, and lose their true liberty, by their murmuring at the honour and power of authority.

The spell that was upon the eyes of the people being thus dissolved, their distorted and enraged notions of things all vanished; and the people would not afterwards entrust the helm of the weather-beaten bark in any other hands but Mr. Winthrop's until he died.

Indeed, such was the *mixture* of distant qualities in him, as to make a most admirable temper; and his having a certain greatness of soul, which rendered him grave, generous, courageous, resolved, well-applied, and every way a *gentleman* in his demeanour, did not hinder him from taking sometimes the old Roman's way to avoid confusions, namely, *Cedendo* [by yielding the point]; or from discouraging some things which are agreeable enough to most that wear the name of *gentlemen*. Hereof I will give no instances, but only *oppose* two passages of his life.

In the year 1632, the governour, with his pastor, Mr. Wilson, and some other gentlemen, to settle a good understanding between the two colonies, travelled as far as Plymouth, more than forty miles, through an howling wilderness, no better accommodated in those early days than the princes that in Solomon's time saw "servants on horseback," or than *genus* and *species* in the old epigram, "going on foot." The difficulty of the *walk,* was abundantly compensated by the honourable, *first* reception, and *then* dismission, which they found from the rulers of Plymouth; and by the good correspondence thus established between the new colonies, who were like the floating bottels wearing this motto: *Si Collidimur Frangimur,* [If we come into collision, we break]. But there were at this time in Plymouth two ministers, leavened so far with the humours of the rigid separation, that they insisted vehemently upon the unlawfulness of calling any unregenerate man by the name of "good-man such an one," until by their indis-

creet urging of this whimsey, the place began to be disquieted. The wiser people being troubled at these trifles, they took the opportunity of Governour Winthrop's being there, to have the thing publickly propounded in the congregation; who in answer thereunto, distinguished between a *theological* and a *moral* goodness; adding, that when Juries were first used in England, it was usual for the crier, after the names of persons fit for that service were called over, to bid them all, "Attend, good men and true;" whence it grew to be a *civil custom* in the English nation, for neighbours living by one another, to call one another "good man such an one;" and it was pity now to make a stir about a civil custom, so innocently introduced. And that speech of Mr. Winthrop's put a lasting stop to the little, idle, whimsical conceits, then beginning to grow obstreperous. Nevertheless, there was one civil custom used *in* (and in few *but*) the English nation, which this gentleman did endeavour to abolish in this country; and that was, *the usage of drinking to one another.* For although by drinking to one another, no more is meant than an act of courtesie, when one going to drink, does invite another to do so too, for the same ends with himself; nevertheless the governour (not altogether unlike to Cleomenes, of whom 'tis reported by Plutarch, . . . *Nolenti poculum nunquam præbuit,*) [Never urged the reluctant to drink] considered the *impertinency* and *insignificancy* of this usage, as to any of *those ends* that are usually pretended for it; and that indeed it ordinarily served for *no ends* at all, but only to provoke persons unto *unseasonable* and perhaps *unreasonable* drinking, and at last produce that abominable *health-drinking,* which the fathers of old so severely rebuked in the Pagans, and which the Papists themselves do condemn, when their casuists pronounce it, *Peccatum mortale, provocare ad Æquales Calices, et Nefas Respondere* [It is a deadly sin to challenge another to a drinking match, and it is impious to accept such challenges]. Wherefore in his own most hospitable house he left it off; not out of any silly or stingy fancy, but meerly that by his *example* a greater temperance, with liberty of drinking, might be recommended, and sundry inconveniences in drinking avoided; and his example accordingly began to be much followed by the sober people in this country, as it now also begins among persons of the highest rank in the English nation it self; until an order of court came to be made against that ceremony in drinking, and then, the *old wont* violently returned, with a *Nitimur in Vetitum* [A bias towards the forbidden indulgence].

Many were the afflictions of this righteous man! He lost much of his estate in a ship, and in an house, quickly after his coming to New-England, besides the prodigious expence of it in the difficulties of his first coming hither. Afterwards his assiduous application unto the publick affairs, (wherein *Ipse se non habuit, postquam Respublica eum Gubernatorem habere cœpit)* [He no longer belonged to himself, after the Republic had once made him her Chief Magistrate] made him so much to neglect his own private interests, that an unjust steward ran him £2,500 in debt before he was aware; for the payment whereof he was forced, many years before his decease, to sell the most of what he had left unto him in the country. Albeit, by the observable blessings of God upon the posterity of this liberal man, his children all of them came to fair estates, and lived in good fashion and credit. Moreover, he successively buried three wives; the first of which was the daughter and heiress of Mr. Forth, of Much-Stambridge in Essex, by whom he had "wisdom with an inheritance;" and an excellent son. The second was the daughter of Mr. William Clopton, of London, who died with her child, within a very little while. The third was the daughter of the truly worshipful Sir John Tyndal, who made it her whole care to please, first God, and then her husband; and by whom he had four sons, which survived and honoured their father. And unto all these, the addition of the *distempers,* ever now and then raised in the country, procured unto him a very singular share of trouble; yea, so hard was the measure which he found even among pious men, in the temptations of a wilderness, that when the thunder and lightning had smitten a wind-mill whereof he was owner, some had such things in their heads as publickly to reproach this charitablest of men as if the voice of the Almighty had rebuked, I know not what oppression, which they judged him guilty of; which things I would not have mentioned, but that the instances may fortifie the expectations of my *best* readers for such afflictions.

He that had been for his attainments, as they said of the blessed Macarius . . . (*an old man, while a young one,*) and that had in his *young* days met with many of those *ill* days, whereof he could say, he had "little pleasure in them;" now found *old age* in its infirmities advancing *earlier* upon him, than it came upon his much longer-lived progenitors. While he was yet seven years off of that which we call "the grand climacterical," he felt the approaches of his dissolution; and finding he could say,

> *Non Habitus, non ipse Color, non Gressus*
> *Euntis,*
> *Non Species Eadem, quæ fuit ante, manet;*

> [I am not what I was in form or face,
> In healthful colour or in vigorous pace.]

He then wrote this account of himself: "Age now comes upon me, and infirmities therewithal, which makes me apprehend, that the time of my departure out of this world is not far off. However, our times are all in the Lord's hand, so as we need not trouble our thoughts how long or short they may be, but how we may be found faithful when we are called for." But at last when *that year* came, he took a cold which turned into a feaver, whereof he lay sick about a month, and in

that sickness, as it hath been observed, that there was allowed unto the serpent the "bruising of the hell;" and accordingly at the *heel* or the *close* of our lives the *old serpent* will be nibbling more than ever in our lives before; and when the devil sees that we shall shortly be, "where the wicked cease from troubling," that *wicked one* will trouble us more than ever; so this eminent saint now underwent sharp conflicts with the tempter, whose *wrath* grew *great,* as the *time* to exert it grew *short;* and he was buffeted with the disconsolate thoughts of black and sore *desertions,* wherein he could use that sad representation of his own condition:

> *Nuper eram Judex; Jam Judicor; Ante*
> *Tribunal*
> *Subsistens paveo; Judicor ipse modo.*

> [I once judged others, but now trembling
> stand
> Before a dread tribunal, to BE judged.]

But it was not long before those clouds were dispelled, and he enjoyed in his holy soul the great consolations of God! While he thus lay ripening for heaven, he did out of obedience unto the *ordinance* of our Lord, send for the elders of the church to pray with him; yea, they and the whole church *fasted* as well as *prayed* for him; and in that *fast* the venerable Cotton preached on Psal. xxxv. 13, 14: "When they were sick, I humbled my self with fasting; I behaved my self as though he had been my friend or brother; I bowed down heavily, as one that mourned for his mother:" from whence I find him raising that observation, "The sickness of one that is to us as a friend, a brother, a mother, is a just occasion of deep humbling our souls with fasting and prayer;" and making this application:

> Upon this occasion we are now to attend this duty for a governour, who has been to us as a friend in his *counsel* for all things, and help for our bodies by *physick,* for our estates by *law,* and of whom there was no fear of his becoming an *enemy,* like the friends of David: a governour who has been unto us as a brother; not usurping authority over the church; often speaking his advice, and often contradicted, even by young men, and some of low degree; yet not replying, but offering satisfaction also when any supposed offences have arisen; a governour who has been unto us as a mother, parent-like distributing his goods to brethren and neighbours at his first coming; and *gently* bearing our infirmities without taking notice of them.

*Such* a governour, after he had been more than ten several times by the people chosen their governour, was New-England now to lose; who having, like Jacob, first left his council and blessing with his children gathered about his bed-side; and, like David, "served his generation by the will of God," he "gave up the ghost," and fell asleep on March 26, 1649. Having, like the dying Emperour Valentinian, this above all his other *victories* for his triumphs, *His overcoming of himself.*

The words of Josephus about Nehemiah, the governour of Israel, we will now use upon this governour of New-England, as his

EPITAPH.

. . . VIP FUIT INDOLE BONUS, AC JUSTUS:
ET POPULARIUM GLORLE AMANTISSIMUS:
QUIBUS ETERNUM RELIQUIT MONUMENTUM,
*Novanglorum* MŒNIA.

[He was by nature a man, at once benevolent and just: most zealous for the honour of his countrymen; and to them he left an imperishable monument— the walls of Jerusalem.]

## Edgar A. J. Johnson (essay date 1930)

SOURCE: "Economic Ideas of John Winthrop," in *The New England Quarterly,* Vol. III, April, 1930, pp. 235-50.

[*In the following essay, Johnson provides a detailed examination of Winthrop's ideas regarding wealth. He notes that Winthrop's ideas, though not original, are significant because they accurately reflect Puritan ideology.*]

How important a role a philosophy plays in men's actions and lives can actually never be determined. A philosophy is never a prime mover, but often an influence so omnipresent and persistent that it becomes worth while to investigate the thoughts as well as the deeds of great men. For this reason, it seems worth while to examine the economic thoughts of John Winthrop. He held definite views about wealth, production, value, communism, colonization, and kindred subjects. He was well equipped in theory before he set out on one of the greatest economic missions of modern times.

There is indeed little that is original in Winthrop's economic thought. But originality is a gift which the gods give reluctantly; and to be great is not necessarily to be original. Winthrop reflected the current beliefs of his age reasonably well. He was not a political economist, but a political and religious leader; and as such, we would not expect him to have more than a reasonable acquaintance with economic speculation. As a devout Christian, economics to him was concerned with what should exist, and with proper relations between citizens of a Christian commonwealth. This is as much as to say Winthrop's ideas were mediaeval, transmitted to him chiefly through English ecclesiastical sources.

Like his mediaeval predecessors, Winthrop accepted the idea of a blissful state of primitive communism which was presumed to have existed when men (in a state of innocency) had all in common. "The first right to the earth," wrote Winthrop, "was naturall when men held the earth in common every man soweing, and feeding where he pleased." But the fall of man brought an end to this ideal communism (the period analogous to the golden age of the ancient Greeks), and man in his corruption acquired an insatiable acquisitive propensity. "Adam in his first estate," said Winthrop, "was a perfect modell of mankinde," and love was the sole principle of human relations. "But Adam rente himselfe from his Creator" and, as a consequence, "rent all his posterity allsoe one from another." As a result of this moral degradation, "every man is borne with this principle in him to love and seeke himselfe onely, and thus a man continueth till Christ comes and takes possession of the soule and infuseth another principle, love to God and our brother."

Possessed with an economic motive, man seeks wealth. What should be the attitude of the Christian toward this search? That intemperance in the pursuit of riches injures public morals, was clear to Winthrop. It may have been more than a political consideration which led him to castigate Thomas Dudley for building an unnecessarily elaborate house for himself and thereby setting a bad example for the community. For the pursuit of wealth for ostentation's sake was not the mediaeval view which Winthrop had inherited. Wealth was conceived to be a manifestation of God's bounty and God's benevolence, entrusted to men who must husband it as stewards. The Gospel law, according to Winthrop, not only sanctions, but expects men to accumulate wealth. The reader must not be misled. The accumulation of wealth was not idealized as an end. It was lawful and necessary to lay up riches, but not indefinitely, or for their own sake. Nay, the Christian must "lay upp as Joseph did to have ready uppon such occasions, as the Lord, (whose stewards wee are of them) shall call for them from us." Wealth, then, was a gift from a benevolent God, the acquisition of which was necessary for the individual and for the state. The desire for wealth was the result of man's fall from grace and his relinquishment of primitive communism. But even corruptible men must be God's stewards and therefore husband wealth for the glory of God.

Although God's bounty was the first cause of wealth, it was not the sole cause. Man himself was not passive; wealth was the result of labor. This theory had found frequent expression in the mediaeval philosophy, and Winthrop tersely and accurately states the ecclesiastical theory when he says that "whatsoever wee stand in need of is treasured in the earth, by the Creator and is to be fetched thence by the sweat of our

Browes." Labor, therefore, was a second, but an indispensable, factor of production made mandatory under the Gospel, and was equivalent to appropriation of a divine bounty. Idleness could not be countenanced in the Christian Commonwealth, because not only would it impair mankind morally, but arrest the very production of necessary wealth.

The product of labor, Winthrop understood, varied as between various countries, and was partly the result of the density of population. In England, for example, where the land "growes weary of her Inhabitants," Winthrop believed that the "labor and cost to recover or keep somtymes a Acre or two of land" would be as great as that which in America would "procure them many hundred as good or better." Moreover, differential returns would appear between different occupations within the same country, and as a historian Winthrop recorded that the profitableness of agriculture led to a scarcity of wage earners and an increase of those who chose to live "by planting and other employments of their own."

It is indeed America's good fortune that Winthrop forsook his philosophical writings and became an historian. But for those who are interested in Winthrop himself, it is most unfortunate, because as a writer of history he became primarily a chronicler. Thus his readers lose sight of the patient philosopher who sought the aid of theology and natural law as a guide to conduct. In consequence, one must infer much of what Winthrop thought about many economic problems. Take, for example, the theory of value. If Winthrop were thoroughly mediaeval he would have accepted the doctrine of just price. Whether he did or not, we do not know. He records facts in his history which prove the prevalence of the doctrine in Massachusetts Bay. But his conversion was too complete: the philosopher bows to the historian. Even so, we should be grateful, for it is Winthrop's history which gives us the charming account of John Cotton and of his whole-hearted acceptance of the mediaeval theory of just price.

Robert Keayne, a prominent merchant of Boston, was haled before the Great and General Court charged with notoriously oppressing the buyers of his merchandise. The House of Deputies found him guilty and set his fine at £200 (a huge sum for colonial days), but the magistrates were disposed to be more lenient. They urged that there was no law which limited profits; that it was common practice in other countries to buy cheap and sell dear; that Keayne was not the only offender; that the law of God provided for no punishment except double restitution; and, lastly, that perfectly equitable prices could not be determined. Encouraged by the doubt thrown upon the existence of a just price by these arguments educed in his behalf, Keayne sought to make excuses for his conduct when he was summoned before the church of Boston and the austere

John Cotton. He argued that the cause of his oppressive trading was, first, ignorance of the true price of some wares; and, secondly, a reliance upon false principles of trade, such as, "if a man lost in one commoditie, he might help himself in the price of another."

There was no hesitation on Cotton's part in a situation which the Puritan law-giver could not disregard: oppression of the public by a merchant; doubts as to the existence of such a thing as just price; and, lastly, admission by the defendant and sinner that he had been misled by "false principle." Lest others should fall into similar iniquity, the learned Cotton set forth the ecclesiastical position concerning value and price "in his public exercise the next lecture day." Following the method of Thomas Aquinas, he first enumerated the reason which induced men to sell goods at oppressive prices. Then over against these false principles he set his art of economics, the rules for trading consistent with the Christian life.

Against the first false principle, "that a man might sell as dear as he can, and buy as cheap as he can," he set the Christian's first "rule for trading," in which the mediaeval theory of just price was epitomized. "A man may not sell above the current price, *i.e.*, such a price as is usual in the time and place, and as another (who knows the worth of the commodity) would give for it, if he had occasion to use it; as that is called current money, which every man will take." Here is the familiar mediaeval doctrine that a just price is the amount which an intelligent, uncoerced buyer, thoroughly conversant with the value of a certain commodity, would give for it. The second false principle, "if a man lose by casualty of sea, etc. in some of his commodities, he may raise the price of the rest," Cotton found to be incompatible with Christian conduct and irreconcilable with the Christian idea of providence. "Where a man loseth by casualty of sea," declared Boston's great divine, "it is a loss cast upon himself by providence." Was it not plain that if a man could "ease himself of it by casting it upon another" he could thereby thwart God's intention and arrogantly "seem to provide against all providences?" Only in one case could prices be raised; only when there was a scarcity of the commodity in question, for then it was "the hand of God upon the commodity, and not the person." But might not one mildly ask just how to discover when the hand of God was raised against the person and when against the commodity? A shipwreck, for example, must evidently be the hand of God raised against a particular merchant and could not justify an increase in his retail mark-up for other goods. But a drought or a hail storm would presumably be the hand of God upon wheat or barley and justified an advance. How happy is he who knows the cause of things!

But what if the unwary merchant bought too dear? Could he not recoup from his customers? Cotton's answer was terse: "A man may not ask any more for his commodity than his selling price, as Ephron to Abraham, *the land is worth thus much*." Given the hand of God for or against a commodity, there *is* a price which is the *just* price. Yet surely the merchant ought to be allowed to take advantage of his skill or ability, for these are the talents which God gave him. The unbending Cotton would yield no quarter to this worldly argument. Commodities have a value which can be determined by the fiction of the intelligent, uncoerced buyer; and "when a man loseth in his commodity for want of skill, etc. he must look at it as his own fault or cross, and therefore must not lay it upon another."

That Cotton accepted the mediaeval doctrine of just price is indisputable, for not only did he make this unmistakable pronouncement in the case of the unhappy Mr. Keayne but he also incorporated the doctrine in his proposed Mosaic code of laws for Massachusetts Bay. But what of Winthrop? What theory of value did he accept? Unfortunately we do not know. He took pains to record carefully the details of Keayne's trial and humiliation; but unfortunately, his historical method is too perfect. Sometimes one wishes the impartial observer would lapse occasionally into partiality. It is only on the subject of wages and of interest that Winthrop is explicit. Like the mediaeval writers and the English mercantilists, he complains about the rise of wages, the consequence of which, he explained, was that all who had goods to sell raised their prices. But one can not be certain whether he meant that the rise of wages led to a rise in prices because of increased cost of production, or whether it was the increased amount of purchasing power in the hands of the wage earners, which made it possible for sellers to obtain higher prices. The General Court sought to deal with the difficulty by regulating wages. This was in 1633. Winthrop does not comment on the wisdom of this policy, but ten years later he frankly admitted the futility of attempting to stop a rise in wages when a country provided abundant opportunity for wage earners to become planters. He nevertheless believed, as did the mercantilists, that high wages tend to demoralize laborers. The consequences of high remuneration, said he, were two-fold: "1. Many spent much time idly etc. because they could get as much in four days as would keep them a week. 2. They spent much in tobacco and strong waters etc. which was a greate waste to the commonwealth." But may it not be just the reverse, as Adam Smith cogently said: the "excessive application during four days of the week" is the "real cause of the idleness of the other three, so much and so loudly complained of"?

The justification of taking interest on loans, or "usury," was so generally accepted in Europe by Winthrop's time that one can readily understand why his views would differ from those of mediaeval writers. Yet Winthrop saw the question primarily as a moral one, and in his mind, the taker of interest must exercise careful judgment lest he offend the divine law. He admitted the necessity and the justice of interest, provided there be no oppression of the poor and necessitous. "What rule must wee observe in lending?" asks an imaginary questioner of Winthrop. That depends, he answers, upon whether the borrower "hath present or probable or possible means of repayeing thee." If he has neither, the Christian should not lend at all. He should give! On the other hand, if the borrower has the ability to repay, then the Christian may "looke at him not as an Act of mercy, but by way of Commerce." Lending, in brief, was to be confined to those who were able and competent to repay. It involved a legitimate interest charge, and should be governed by the rules of justice. But lending was to be carefully distinguished from giving or forgiving. The poor should be objects of mercy and no interest ought to be taken from those who were deserving of charity. "If any of thy brethern be poore," wrote Winthrop, quoting Deuteronomy XV, 7, "thou shalt lend him sufficient." Indeed this is not lending, but giving, and the Christian must give to the poor man "according to his necessity." Or, if a loan has already been made, "whether thou didst lend by way of Commerce or in mercy, if he hath noething to pay," the Christian must forgive the debt. The only exception which Winthrop would allow was that of a pledge given for a loan. But even here, the law of love should modify the contract where the borrower was necessitous.

So much has been written about Puritan individualism that it may seem unnecessary to touch upon this issue; nevertheless, let us make inquiry to see what Winthrop's views actually were. Was he a defender of individualism, or was there some place for communism in his economic philosophy? It has already been shown that he accepted the time-honored theory of a state of primitive communism and of its termination when mankind degenerated from that degree of ethical perfection which could have made earthly communism possible. For with man's fall from grace, came self-love. Till man is raised from his fallen estate, he argued, pure communism, originally intended by the Creator, is impossible; and in its place God has sanctioned another plan of social organization, a system of private property—and inequality.

As the **"Modell of Christian Charity"** begins, "God Almightie in his most holy and wise providence, hath soe disposed of the condition of mankinde, as in all times some must be rich, some poore, some highe and eminent in power and dignitie; others meane and in subjection." To him, as to his mediaeval predecessors, inequality of wealth was no chance phenomenon: it was a trust relationship with the author of all riches. The divine scheme, moreover, was not mere favoritism but a purposeful partition. It revealed the glory of God's wisdom "in the variety and difference of the creatures"; it served also the function of "moderating and restraining" the avaricious natures of men, "soe that the riche and mighty should not eate upp the poore, nor the poore and dispised rise upp against their superiours and shake off theire yoake." Inequality, in brief, should teach mercy and justice to the favored; resignation to the poor. But Aristotle had set forth as a principle that where only two classes exist in society, the state can never have tranquillity, since one class can not obey and can only rule despotically, while the other can not rule and must be ruled like slaves. Winthrop, on the contrary, believed that the very existence of inequality would lead to the moral improvement of society by a distribution of duties. For each must realize that he has "need of other, and from hence they might be all knitt more nearly together in the Bonds of brotherly affection." For it must be remembered that "noe man is made more honourable than another or more wealthy etc. out of any perticuler and singuler respect to himselfe, but for the glory of his Creator and the common good of the Creature, Man."

Winthrop not only believed that property was theologically justified, but also he believed that property was sanctioned by natural law. "God hath given to the sonnes of men a double right to the earth," he wrote in his **"Conclusions,"** "a natural right and a civil right." The first right to land was a natural right, the right of all men to use the fruits of the earth. But to this was added a civil right, whereby rights to particular parcels of property arose from the performance of certain arts of improvement. This part of Winthrop's philosophy was what we designate today as the "labor theory of property." Hugo Grotius had earlier set forth the same doctrine, and upon this theory Winthrop justified the taking up of land in America by the Massachusetts Bay Company. The natural right to the earth existed when men held all land in common. But men improved land "by enclosing and peculiar manurance and this in time gave them a Civill right." To encroach upon land so improved would be theft, but to take up land still held under the natural right was compatible with Christian conduct. And since the American Indians "inclose noe land neither have any setled habitation nor any tame cattle to improve their land by," Winthrop could find no reason why the Massachusetts Bay Company could not lawfully plant in New England.

But in spite of Winthrop's profound respect for property, and in spite of his acceptance of the mediaeval notion of economic classes, he found room in his philosophy for some exceptions. These exceptions proceeded from the Christian doctrines of charity. Pure communism, he believed, could obtain only in a society of ideal men. But a circumstantial communism might become necessary, and to a discussion of this, Winthrop turns in his **"Modell."** First, he sets forth a theory of social relations. Originally man's relations

with his fellow-man were determined by the law of nature. This required that every man should help his fellow-man "in every want or distresse," and "that hee performe this out of the same affection which makes him carefull of his owne goods." The law of nature could have application only in "the estate of innocency." When that blissful period had ended, the law of nature was supplanted by "the lawe of the Gospell" whose obligations upon men are not constant and immutable but vary between "seasons and occasions." Indeed, there are times, said Winthrop, "when a Christian must sell all and give to the poore, as they did in the Apostles times." There are other times when Christians "must give beyond their ability, as they of Macedonia," and "likewise community of perills" calls for extraordinary liberality. The sharing of goods under the "Gospell law" was a requirement of God, although the extent of this enforced communism was dependent upon circumstances. For example, all sharing of goods, Winthrop carefully pointed out, must be subsequent to the provision for one's own family of the "probable meanes of comfortable subsistence." In short, "the Gospel law" requires always circumstantial communism, while a "community of perill" might require almost complete sharing of goods. But what constituted a "community of perill"? Winthrop cites the case of the Primitive Church as an illustration when the early Christians "sold all, had all in Common, neither did any man say that which he possessed was his owne." In like fashion, the return from captivity, with the danger of enemies common to all, demanded a greater sharing of goods than ordinarily was necessary. We see, therefore, that Winthrop's theory of communism converges with his theory of the origin of wealth. The duties of lending, giving, forgiving, and sharing were the consequences of the divine distribution of private property. "The care of the publique must oversway all private respects," wrote Winthrop, and "particular Estates cannott subsist in the ruine of the publique." Private property must be limited by enforced circumstantial communism on occasions of danger; and by public interest, love, and Christian charity at all times. And this is exactly what mediaeval scholars had written.

Finally, there remains to be seen what Winthrop thought about colonization; for his philosophy is of importance only because he attempted to apply it as the leader of a great colonial movement. Colonization to him should be a means to "improve our lives to doe more service to the Lord." There had been "great and fundamental errors" committed in previous projects of colonization, but the most important error was that "their maine end was carnall and not Religious." With true optimism Winthrop prophesied in 1629 that the economic, political, and religious problems of England would profoundly affect the type of prospective colonists. The "ill condition of the tymes," he wrote, are "likely to furnish those plantations with better members then usually have undertaken that worke in former tymes."

---

**Miller on Winthrop's "A Model of Christian Charity" Sermon (1630):**

We wonder whether, once Southampton and Land's End had sunk beneath the eastern horizon, once he had turned his face irrevocably westward, Winthrop suddenly realized that he was sailing not toward another island but a continent, and that once there the problem would be to keep the people fixed in the mold of the Cambridge Agreement, to prevent them from following the lure of real estate into a dispersion that would quickly alter their character. . . . He seems apprehensive that old sanctions will not work; he wants all the company to swear an oath, to confirm their act of will. This band have entered into a covenant with God. . . . Therefore this society, unlike any in Europe, will be rewarded by divine providence to the extent that it fulfills the covenant. Likewise it will be afflicted with plagues, fires, disasters, to the extent that it fails. Profound though he was, Winthrop probably did not entirely realize how novel, how radical, was his sermon. . . . What in reality he was telling the proto-Americans was that they could not just blunder along like ordinary people, seeking wealth and opportunity for their children. Every citizen of this new society would have to know, completely understand, reckon every day with, the enunciated terms on which it was brought into being, according to which it would survive or perish. This duty of conscious realization lay as heavy upon the humblest, the least educated, the most stupid, as upon the highest, the most learned, the cleverest.

*Perry Miller, in* Nature's Nation, *The Belknap Press, 1967.*

---

Colonization to Winthrop was an honorable work and a Christian duty. For God had commanded the sons of Adam to multiply and replenish the earth. Indeed it was only on this condition that the earth had been given to men. Unused land, or land held by natural law, was lawfully seizable. For as long as any vacant land exists, God's commandment to subdue the earth is yet unfulfilled. Colonization was therefore a duty to God. But in addition, colonization was also a duty to one's fellowman. For why should men in crowded countries make life difficult for their fellows while they "suffer a whole Continent as fruitful and convenient for the use of man to lie in waste"? Self-interest, coupled with a feeling of charity, should impel colonization.

Finally, colonization would provide a means whereby men of certain convictions could regulate economic matters in accordance with the moral law. In England, "all arts and trades are carried on in that deceiptful and unrighteous course, as it is almost impossible for a good and upright man to maintain his charge and live comfortable in them." Winthrop believed that social reconstruction was necessary, and was possible only in

a colony. To achieve this goal, however, the colony must be recruited selectively. No men inimical to these ideals should be included. But those who would labor and fear God, those who would subscribe to a philosophy of wealth essentially like that which has just been described; these were acceptable material. Artisans, rather than gentlemen, should therefore be the raw material of colonies, free men in minds and bodies! As Francis Bacon in the essay "Of Plantations," so Winthrop insisted that a successful colony could not be formed from criminals. He purposed to learn from the mistakes of previous American plantations, one of which he conceived to be the use of "unfitt instruments—a multitude of rude and misgoverned persons, the very scumme of the people."

Such was the economic philosophy of Winthrop. It is a fair example of the economic ideas of the American Puritans. Wealth and wealth-getting were not despised. The Puritan was not truly ascetic. Nor did he idealize wealth-getting as it is the fashion to believe to-day. He attempted to impose the social philosophy of the mediaeval schoolmen on a pioneer community where the temptation to a life of material acquisition was limited only by the opportunity. Herein is another evidence of the immense gulf that separates the Puritan ideals of 1630 from the current social philosophy of New England (and America) in 1930.

## Stanley Gray (essay date 1930)

SOURCE: "The Political Thought of John Winthrop," in *The New England Quarterly*, Vol. III, October, 1930, pp. 681-705.

[*Below, Gray presents an overview of Winthrop's political philosophy, stressing his reliance on the idea of the social convenant.*]

> God Almightie in his most holy and wise providence hath soe disposed of the Condicion of mankinde, as in all times some must be rich some poore, some highe and eminent in power and dignitie; others meane and in subieccion.

In this opening sentence of **"A Modell of Christian Charity"** John Winthrop reveals the bases of his political thought. The over-ruling sovereignty of God, the natural character of the inequality of men, and, most important, the benevolent implications which he drew from that inequality, are here set forth as the background of the ideas we are to examine. God has ordered "all these differences for the preservation and good of the whole"; to "manifest the work of his Spirit" in restraining the wicked, and in "exercising his graces"—"mercy, gentleness, temperance" in the "greate ones"—"faithe, patience, obedience" in the "poore and inferior sorte." We shall not understand

Winthrop and his political thought unless we remember always that much of what seems arbitrary and ungentle in this man was conditioned in his mind by a never-failing sense of the Christian duty of the "greate ones"; a duty enforced by an awful sanction.

John Winthrop was born into the English squirearchy. From the time of his majority he was accustomed to magisterial authority, and the damp of a lingering feudalism yet permeated the custom of the manor of Groton. He emigrated before democratic ideas had impinged on the aristocratic tradition, while the cloud of civil war and the gruesome scene at Whitehall were unseen, unthinkable. That excessive paternalism which has ever ruled the English countryside was strong in his nature. He had been a model of "mercy, gentleness, temperance" to his own tenants, and had firmly insisted on their "patience, obedience, etc." in return. He could imagine no other order sanctioned by the word of God.

. . . . .

The compact theory, with its roots in the Middle Ages, refurbished in time of need by the politico-religious minorities of the sixteenth century, was a familiar concept by the opening of the great century of English colonization. We need not wait for the word-battle preceding the Revolution to find American writers talking in terms of the social contract. The Revolutionary thinkers were merely drawing through Locke upon the thought of a much earlier time. Hence it is not surprising to find Winthrop asserting that

> it is clearly agreed, by all, that the care of safety and welfare was the original cause or occasion of commonweales and of many familyes subjecting themselves to rulers and laws; for no man hath lawfull power over another, but by birth or consent.

Young Henry Vane dissented, on this occasion. Such a definition, he said, might do for commonweales in general; but Massachusetts was a Christian commonwealth, her government resting on a patent from the King. To which Winthrop answered:

> When I describe a commonwealth in general, . . . the churches or christians which are in it, fall not into consideration . . . for it may be a true body politicke, though there be neither church nor christian in it. The like may be sayd for the forme of government, whether it be by patent or otherwise yet it is a government. . . . My intent was to prove the proprietye and priviledges of a common weale which may also belong to such government among Turkes and Pagans. . . .

Note the secular character of this conception of the state. No medieval thinker from Augustine on would have agreed to this rejection of Christianity as an indispensable basis of the commonwealth.

Winthrop, then, like the political thinkers of eighteenth-century America, based his state upon contract. Unlike them, he drew no democratic corollaries from this basis. We have already seen the aristocratic tinge in his thought. It crops up again and again in his writings. There has remained to us the draft of a proposed bill to remedy "Common Grevances," which Winthrop and his friends drew up evidently to present to Parliament in 1624. Only a part of the paper is in Winthrop's hand, but we may reasonably take the whole document as an expression of the opinions of Winthrop himself. The section just before his pen took up the work proposes stringent laws to limit hawking privileges, and on this ground:

> The difference betweene principalitie and popularie that alwaies have byn such, that from the lawe of nature order and antiquitie, a perpetuall precedencie and dominacion hath been in the one, and an invyolable lawe of conformitie and submission hath byn in thother.

In 1634 Boston elected seven men to divide the remaining lands of the town. Some prominent men were passed over, and Winthrop was barely elected; "the rest," he tells us, were "of an inferior sort." The Governor refused to serve with colleagues, and a new election was held. This time the people remembered their bounden duty to their leaders. And later, when the New England colonies confederated, the province of Sir Ferdinando Gorges was not invited to join. A village there lately "had made a taylor their mayor."

This disparity between the ranks of men is not to be regretted as a flaw in unperfected society, thinks Winthrop. It is a result of Divine beneficence. "Heerin would the Lord our God have his excellent wisdome and power appeare, that he makes (not the disparitye onely but) even the contrarietye of parts, in many bodyes, to be the meanes of the upholding and usefullnesse thereof." One is reminded of Aristotle's criticism of the unity of Plato's *Republic*. Winthrop owned, and presented to Harvard, the *Works* of Jacques Le Fevre, who wrote a paraphrase of the *Politics* of Aristotle. But we do not know that Winthrop ever read Le Fevre's paraphrase, and his opinion in this case is obviously founded on Christian theology.

Was this inequality of men, this disparity between the ranks of society, to remain a social fact only, or should it be translated into political terms? What class should govern, and what form should the government take?

There is no evidence that Winthrop ever questioned monarchy as a valid form of government. He left England ten years before republicanism came into existence. Deputy-Governor Dudley once refused to sign a petition of Massachusetts to the King, on the ground, said Winthrop, "that we gave the king the title of sacred majesty, which is the most proper title of princes, being the Lord's anointed. . . ." Charles Stuart lost some of his "anointed" character for the colonists as the Civil War progressed, but we must not assume that this altered Winthrop's opinion as to monarchy in general. He died shortly after the King was executed, and we have no means of knowing what his opinion of that event was, or might have been.

Winthrop condemned democracy in strong terms. The Reformation, for him, implied neither religious toleration nor political democracy. An oft-quoted passage shows not only his repugnance to democracy, but his preference for a "mixt Aristocratie":

> Now if we should change from a mixt Aristocratie to a meere Democratie: first we should have no warrant *in scripture* for it. . . . A Democratie is, among most Civill nations, accounted the meanest and worst of all formes of Government . . . and Historyes doe recorde, that it hath been allwayes of least continuance and fullest of troubles.

Yet if Massachusetts was a mixed aristocracy, it was a broad one. Actual power came from the freemen, and no important official had legal authority except by virtue of election by them. Even though the number of freemen may have been only one in four or five of the adult males by 1670, as Palfrey computes, this was large enough to exclude the colony from the category of aristocracy. If we except the standing council, which existed but three years, there was no formally aristocratic element in the government. Winthrop apparently thought that the extensive power of the magistrates, and the fact that the best men were chosen, provided the element of aristocracy, which was diluted or "mixt" by the limited powers of the deputies. But this was to confuse powers with the source of those powers. The mistake does not, however, invalidate the conclusion that Winthrop himself preferred aristocracy.

In the few months before October, 1630, a few men ruled the colony with no check whatever. Even by 1634 there had been grudgingly admitted into the franchise not more than two hundred freemen. Winthrop's desire to keep the governing class as small as possible is shown by his answer to the freemen who demanded their full rights under the charter. The freemen are too numerous to make or execute laws; they may appoint a committee to revise the laws if summoned by the governor, and to consent to taxation. Winthrop's wish was disregarded, and the freemen came into their full rights shortly after this incident; but we have seen enough to realize that the good governor himself would have been heartily glad to keep government always in the hands of a few trusted men. Between 1636 and 1639 there existed in the colony a standing council, elected for life: Winthrop, Dudley, and Endecott. When it was abolished upon the deputies' protest, the order

of repeal was drawn up so that no condemnation of the institution was implied. The whole tone of Winthop's narrative proves that he held the standing council to be a useful and permissible organ, and that he resented the demand for its abrogation.

The evolution of a trading corporation into a commonwealth forced the Massachusetts leaders to allow a considerable number of the people more power than their judgment or desire dictated. They made the best of the situation by binding the people to as narrow limits as they could. Although the colony enjoyed representative government, many of the rights which we should consider essential to liberty were absent. Free speech was denied in principle as well as in fact. "It is licentiousnesse, and not liberty, when a man may speake what he list," wrote Winthrop. When we learn that the statement refers to the case of a man who was punished for censuring the General Court while a member thereof, and during the regular session, we wonder what real value debates in that body could have had. Winthrop castigated Coddington and others who signed a petition in favor of the unfortunate John Wheelwright. The petition seems mild enough now, but all the disclaimers of presumption and disrespect could not save the signers from Winthrop's reproof that—

> you invite the body of the people to join with you in your seditious attempt against the Court . . . against the rule of the Apostle, who requires every soul to be subject to the higher powers, and every Christian man to study to be quiet, and to meddle with his own business.

Furthermore, Winthrop abhorred what we regard as the very essence of a system based on an elected legislature.

> Sedition doth properly signifie a going aside to make a party, and is rightly described by the Poet . . . *In magno populo cum sæpe coorta est seditio sævitque animis*, etc. . . . Tully saith, *Seditionem, esse dissensionem omnium inter se, cum eunt alii in aliud*, when the people dissent in opinion and go several wayes. Isidore saith, *Seditiosus est, qui dissentionem animorum facit et discordias gignit.*

Such a definition of sedition rules out any organized political opposition—a thing unknown anywhere, to be sure, in 1637. Further, it makes impossible any concerted effort to unseat those in power. The voter could vote as he pleased, but he must do it respectfully, he must not publicly persuade others to vote as he voted, and he must not criticize those in office.

It is well to remember that free speech, the right of petition, and the right of organized opposition were the fruits, not the precursors of the seventeenth century; and we must not blame Winthrop because he was not in advance of current thought. Nevertheless it must be said that by denying these rights to the people, and by maintaining a close alliance with the ministry, the leaders of Massachusetts Bay were able to set up an aristocracy in fact. These leaders were not unscrupulous men avid of power, but sincere zealots of aristocratic birth and training who honestly believed that it was for the good of the people to keep power in the hands of those best fitted to exercise it.

Winthrop's theory of the proper relation of leaders to people is brought out admirably in his famous definition of liberty.

> There is a twofold liberty, natural . . . and civil or federal. The first is common to man with beasts and other creatures. . . . This is that great enemy of truth and peace . . . which all the ordinances of God are bent against. . . . [Civil liberty] is the proper end and object of authority, and cannot subsist without it; and it is a liberty to that only which is good, just, and honest. . . . This liberty is maintained and exercised in a way of subjection to authority.

This definition has been widely praised. Lately Mr. Edwin D. Mead has said of it: "If there were anywhere in the English world in the 1630's a nobler definition of liberty true and false than that in Winthrop's 'Little Speech' I do not know where to find it." This is indeed a conception of liberty perfectly familiar to "the English world in the 1630's"; but it is nothing more. Without the aura of Winthrop it would be distasteful to most modern readers. Whether we like the definition or not, it is good to know what precisely we are praising or blaming. For, since the day when Winthrop soothed the ruffled deputies with the charm of his rich Biblical prose, the expansive thought of the eighteenth century has changed many of the world's ideas, and none more than that of liberty. Just what "liberty" does mean in the twentieth century, it would be rash to say. Many would agree with Soame Jenyns, a placeman of 1765, that liberty "is a phrase of so various a signification, having within these few years been used as a synonymous term for blasphemy, bawdy, treason, libels, strong beer, and cyder, that I shall not presume to define its meaning." Broadly speaking, most of us start by thinking of liberty as an uncontrolled right to do anything, and then pare it down to suit the exigencies of society, as we conceive them. When we are through, however, we have a great deal left; and so enduring has been the idea of inalienable natural rights that old-fashioned people are rash enough to believe that we have more left than we have given up. "Liberty" needs no document to justify itself; "authority" (at least in theory) must substantiate every claim to infringe it.

A study of Winthrop's ideas indicates at once the opposite character of his conception. The man *in* society does not start with rights. He subjects himself to

the government of others when he enters the compact, and "liberties" which he possesses thereafter are the result of grant from those in authority. The large, indefinite "right" in the body politic is "authority." There is, properly speaking, no "liberty"; there are only "liberties"—definite privileges, usually enrolled in an imposing document and provable in court. This use of the word "liberty" occurs often in Winthrop's works. It would be strange if we should find any other use of it, for then indeed would Winthrop have been ahead of his times. One might be given the "freedom" of a town, a town might possess the "liberty" of holding a market on Wednesdays, but few, besides some despised sectaries, gave any broader meaning to these terms in the early seventeenth century. In Massachusetts Bay the "liberty" of the freeman was restricted to the election of officers and a share in making laws. The definition of what was "good, just, and honest" was the province of the magistrates, and in some cases of the General Court, to determine. When they rejected free speech, the right of petition, and the right to oppose the government, they were neither ahead of nor behind the English political thought of their era.

Whence came this "authority" which bulked so large in Winthrop's political theory? "It is yourselves," he tells the freemen in his speech, "who have called us to this office, and being called by you, we have our authority from God, in way of an ordinance, such as hath the image of God eminently stamped upon it, the contempt and violation whereof hath been vindicated with examples of divine vengeance." Note this conception of the divine origin of magistracy—of the sacrosanct character of the magistrate. "Iudges are Gods upon earthe," says Winthrop. "Whatsoever sentence the magistrate gives, according to these limittations, [internal only] the judgment is the Lords." Magistrates are the fathers of the commonwealth. To disobey them is to incur not merely the opprobrium of breaking a civil law, but to be guilty of defying the Fifth Commandment.

Does God bestow authority directly, or does he express his will through the voters? The evidence is fragmentary, but Winthrop probably meant that authority comes directly from God, and that the people merely choose the particular person to take office, without by their election conferring a divine right to rule. In the first place, he limits the sacrosanct character of the "powers that be" to the magistrates. If the people voting are the mouthpiece of God, every officer they elect should be considered as deriving his power from God, irrespective of his character or talents. Winthrop does not expressly deny that the deputies do so derive their power, but he comes very near such a denial in several places. He resents the fact that the deputies have been too often sitting as a court of justice; this is a function "to which they have no ordinary callinge . . . for our Saviour teaches us, that everye man that shall exercise power of Judgment over others, must be able to prove his callinge thereto." Again, "We should incurre Scandall, by undervaluing the gifts of God, and the Ordinance of magistracye, if the Judgment and Authoritye of any one of the Common ranke of the people, should beare equall weight, with that of the wisest and chiefest magistrate. . . ." The context makes it certain that the author included the deputies in the "Common ranke of the people."

The "gifts of God," the ability to prove a "callinge"—these are what give the magistrate his divine authority. Election without those gifts and that calling may give a certain circumscribed power to the deputies. It does not make the judgment of the deputy the judgment of God. This explains Winthrop's willingness to expand the powers of the magistrates by inferences often having no relation to the actual constitution of the colony. It explains his insistence that the powers of all others than the magistrates should be limited as far as possible. It is consistent with his repeated antithesis between "authority" and "liberty"—an antithesis that would have been patently absurd if he had believed that all authority came from the people.

If Winthrop held an exalted theory of the power of the magistrate, he held a no less lofty conception of the magistrate's duty. The magistrates must "square all their proceedings by the rule of Gods word, for the advancement of the gospell and the weale publick"; "In their Administrations, they are to holde forthe the wisdome and mercye of God, as well as his Iustice." "They are to be accountable to him for their miscarriages in the waye and order of this kingdome." If we can not prove that Winthrop read the following passage in the *Institutes* of Calvin, we can at least say that it is mirrored in many a sentence in his writings:

> For what an ardent pursuit of integrity, prudence, clemency, moderation, and innocence ought they to prescribe to themselves, who are conscious of having been constituted ministers of the Divine justice.

The magistrate, then, must answer to God. Must he answer to anyone else? What checks Winthrop was forced to accept from the royal charter and from circumstances, he accepted. The real bounds to the magistrate's power he thought should be self-imposed. He preached the doctrine of non-resistance repeatedly. "It was Luthers Counsell to the Anabaptists . . . that thoughe their magistrates did oppresse and iniure them, yet they should pray for them, and commend them, and seeke to winne them by gentlenesse." But the magistrate has no arbitrary power. He is limited by certain checks.

> The magistrates are members of the churches here, and, by that covenant, are regulated to direct all their wayes by the rule of the gospel, and if they

faile in anythinge, they are subject to the churches correction. 2dly. As they are freemen, they are regulated by oath, to direct their aymes to the wellfare of this civill body. 3dly. As they are magistrates, they are sworne to doe right to all, and regulated by their relation to the people, to seeke theire wellfare in all things.

The responsibility to the church amounted to little, as will appear when we come to Winthrop's ideas on church and state. The same assertion is true for the freeman's and the magistrate's oaths. Winthrop is careful to say nothing of what the people may do if these covenants are violated. Where officers are practising that soul-searching induced by Calvinism, constitutional checks conceivably would not have the force of the internal checks favored by Winthrop. We may wish that he had seen that such a system, like monarchy, relies too much on personal character. But he answers us neatly.

> What if the magistrates should growe corrupt etc? this is no more to be feared than of the deputies, and if of both, then of all the rest of the people, and if so, then it is past remedye.

To deny absolutely the truth of this reply we should have to forget much of what has happened since Winthrop lived.

One large power which Winthrop gave to the magistrate we have yet to discuss—that of fixing the penalty after conviction of a malefactor. This part of his theory is bound up with his views on the nature of law in general.

If we look for a developed body of thought concerning the fundamental bases of law in Winthrop's works, we shall be disappointed. He is even more scanty here than elsewhere. Busy leaders in a frontier community rarely compose treatises on the most abstruse of all political subjects. The law of nature, or the moral law—"created with and in man"—with God as its author, Winthrop, of course, recognized. Nor are we surprised to find him talking of the law of the Gospel, given to man in a state of regeneracy. But his treatment of these fundamental laws is brief and confused. In addition, Winthrop shared the view common to the Puritans in general, that "Moses his judicials" were valid law in modern societies. He was broader than some of his contemporaries, however, in allowing selection to be made from, and additions to, the Mosaic Code. Although God is the only lawgiver, "he hathe given power and giftes to men to interprett his Laws," Winthrop also had a strong sense of the legal force of custom. He opposed a definite written code for the colony because "such laws would be fittest for us, which should arise pro re nata upon occasions, etc., and so the laws of England and other states grew." It is pleasant to feel this cool breath of rationalism sweeping away momentarily the murk of Biblical citation, but we must not take it too literally. Other passages show that what Winthrop wished was a system of law based on the Mosaic Code, expanded by interpretation. The English common law had a rather different genesis! The fact is, the English lawyer and the devout Puritan clashed in Winthrop's nature, and he alternately speaks the language of each.

Winthrop recognized the validity of positive law, but insisted that it must conform to the law of God.

> We have no laws diametrically opposite to those of England, for then they must be contrary to the law of God and of right reason, which the learned in those laws have anciently and still do hold forth as the fundamental basis of their laws, and that if anything hath been otherwise established, it was an errour, and not a law.

We may compare this point of view with that of the "judicious" Hooker, but Winthrop may well have got these ideas from some other source, since they had been frequently expressed during and since medieval times.

The most important of the Governor's ideas on law was concerned with the advisability of fixed penalties. Should the penalty be determined in advance by law, or by the magistrate after conviction. He concludes that except in a few cases, penalties should not be prescribed. To have a fixed penalty is to sentence the offender before trial; to remove all need of wisdom in the judge, and to value the judgment of the magistrate less than that of ordinary jurymen, who are allowed to fix damages in civil cases. It is unjust to punish every man alike for the same offense. Even in England penalties are not fixed except for petty crimes. Most important, God has set few penalties, and we should follow his example.

Some of these reasons we should to-day regard as trivial, some fallacious. But the most significant fact about Winthrop's view is that he and his supporters were decidedly heterodox in their own generation. He was in error in saying that the laws of England had few fixed penalties. The belief that we are laying ourselves open to injustice if we do not have a known atonement for every crime has persisted, through Beccaria and Bentham, right down to our own day. Only in recent years has a school of penology appeared which favors the fitting of the punishment to the individual criminal. We are tempted to see Winthrop thinking in ultra-modern fashion on this question, but the analogy should not be pushed too far. His thought was Biblical, rather than rationalistic, idealistic rather than pragmatic, and he was thinking of punishment more than of reformation.

The penalty for crime should rarely be fixed, yet the judgment is not therefore arbitrary. The magistrate acts upon a rule, "which Rule is the Worde of God, and such conclusions and deductions, as are, or shalbe, regularly drawne from thence." So we come again to the one effective check which Winthrop puts upon the magistrate:—his duty, as a Christian called to office by divine authority, to be guided by the divine law. Who shall interpret that law? Is the magistrate subject to the control of those best fitted to expound it—to the control of the elders or the church?

As a matter of fact, the magistrates of Massachusetts Bay were subject to the control of both church and elders. In a society where every act is regarded as a moral debit or credit, every act becomes invested with religious meaning. Winthrop often called upon the church elders for advice upon matters not connected with religion. Charles Bourgeaud stated a more than approximate truth when he said that—

> By law the civil government was distinct from the ecclesiastical, but in fact it was strictly subordinate to it. Owing to their moral influence, the pastors and elders formed a sort of Council of Ephors; no important decision was arrived at without their consent.

But it was a settled belief of the Puritans that no elder could hold civil office. When the Boston church asked the churches of Salem and Plymouth their opinion on the question, both answered that no elder could at the same time be a magistrate. Winthrop, in a letter to Thomas Hooker in 1638, reproved the Connecticut people for having allowed the "managing of state business" to fall "upon some one or other of their ministers." Massachusetts, then, was not, in theory, a theocracy.

In practice, however, the advice of the elders was almost always followed. Probably the most extreme view of their power was stated by John Cotton. Winthrop narrates in his *Journal* that

> Mr Cotton preached . . . he laid down the nature or strength . . . of the magistracy, ministry, and people, viz.,—the strength of the magistracy to be their authority, of the people, their liberty; and of the ministry, their purity; and showed how all of these had a negative voice, etc.

This pronouncement, we are told, "gave great satisfaction to the company," but we ought not be sure that Winthrop shared in that satisfaction. We find him saying, at one time, that "the cause being of a civil nature, it belonged to the court, and not to the elders, to judge of the merit thereof." On the other hand, he often called upon the elders for their opinion in cases of a purely civil nature, and he was not ashamed to admit that "the ministers have great power with the people, whereby through the good correspondency between the magistrates and them, they are the more easyly governed."

Winthrop and the Massachusetts leaders seem to have made this distinction: the elders could hold no civil office, but as men gifted in the lore which was the great guide of life, they should be consulted upon all important questions. There was nothing new about this theory; it was held by almost all Puritans, both Disciplinarians and Separatists. On the question of the power of the church as a body over the magistrates, however, Winthrop differed from the belief of the earlier English Puritans.

The Puritans of the sixteenth century all agreed that even the highest magistrates were subject to church censure. Both Presbyterians and Separatists took this position. Robert Browne wrote, "who knoweth not, that though magistrates are to keep their civil power above all persons, yet they come under the censures of the Church if they be Christians." Barrow thought that the church "ought to have judgment ready against every transgression, without respect of persons." Thomas Cartwright had said that "civil magistrates must govern . . . according to the rules of God prescribed in his word, and that as they are nurses, so they be Servants unto the Church."

Winthrop dissented vigorously from these views.

> Magistrates as they are church members are accountable to the church for their failings, but that is when they are out of their calling; . . . If a magistrate shall, in a private way, take away a man's goods or his servants, etc., the church may call him to account for it; but if he doth this in pursuing a course of justice (though the thing be unjust) yet he is not accountable, etc. [The church has other weapons] wisdome, pietye, and meeknesse [to bind rulers] therefore no need to binde them by churche censures.

There is no doubt that Winthrop was here giving voice to the predominant sentiment of the leaders, elders as well as laymen. In 1636 a group of the ministers affirmed as their opinion "that no member of the court ought to be publicly questioned by a church for any speech in the court, without the license of the court."

What power ought the state to have over the church? The early Separatists regarded the two organizations as independent, denied to the civil power the right to establish the church by law or force, but nevertheless held that false and idolatrous forms of worship must be put down by the state. Winthrop and his associates seem to have kept close to this position. Defending the action of the Court in the Wheelwright case, Winthrop said:

> As for such as have taken offence, that the cause was not first referred to the Church, we desire them to consider these reasons. 1. This case was not matter of conscience, but of a civill nature, and therefore most proper for this Court to take cognizance of. . . . 2. In some cases of religious nature, as manifest heresie, notorious blasphemy, etc. the Civill power may proceed, *Ecclesia inconculta,* and that by the judgment of all the Ministers.

And then he makes the matter yet clearer:

> It is objected, that the Magistrates may not appoint a messenger of God, what hee should teach: admit so much, yet hee may limit him what hee may not teach, if hee forbid him to teach heresy or sedition, etc. hee incurres as well a contempt in teaching that which hee was forbidden, as sins in teaching that which is evil.

In theory, at least, this is all consistent with the ideas of Browne and the early Separatists. The civil power may not establish a church, or force any one to join it, but manifest heresy must be rooted out. But the fact departed from the theory. Any variation, however slight, from accepted doctrine was likely to be proved "manifest heresie" by the unfortunate practice of the Puritans in not resting content with what the suspected heretic had expressly said. At least one student, after reading the accounts of the years 1636-1638, has concluded that one who announced even mild dissent from established doctrine was almost certain to be proved a menace to the peace of the colony and a flagrant heretic simply by that dogged questioning and deduction of which the Puritans were so fond.

With one exception, Winthrop held no unusual ideas on the subject of the relation of church to state. Even in his declaration of magisterial immunity from church censure he was backed by the ministers. His theory embraced the idea of close coöperation between church and state, denying formal political power to the church and elders, giving large powers to the state over the church. It was the lingering voice of the doctrine which had remained uncontested before 1550, resisting the rising stream of thought which in the Old World, and lately in the New, had enunciated the theory of toleration and absolute separation of the two powers. It was a voice doomed to be smothered by the fact of religious diversity in the colonies, and the example of the mother nation. But dare we deny that it had great value in fostering a much-needed social unity?

. . . . .

We have now and then mentioned in passing a few sources of Winthrop's political theory. His position in the English social scale, his legal training, his tenure of office in Massachusetts Bay—these are the imponderables behind his thought, impossible to evaluate. The magazine from which he drew his ideas was almost filled by the Bible and Calvinism. These he tapped constantly. They form a root of his theory bulking so large that it might be thought futile to search for further sources.

We have seen Winthrop express a theory of law which may have come from Richard Hooker, and we have noted quotations from two classical authors, Cicero and Virgil. These are among the dozen (or fewer) citations to profane writers in all Winthrop's works. The excerpt from Isidore of Seville may well have been taken at second hand from some other writer; the *Etymologies* were very popular all through the Middle Ages. A very few of the two-score volumes which Winthrop presented to Harvard College might have furnished arguments or ideas on political questions. Besides the Bible and Calvin's *Institutes,* the *Decrees of the Council of Worms* and Gregory's *Decretals* were on the list. John Davenant's *Determinationes Questionum Quarundam Theologicarum* is an anti-papal work by a moderate Calvinist divine forced to conformity by Laud. The book listed as "Whittakeri praelectiones disputationes" was doubtless either that author's *Disputatio de Sacra Scriptura; Contra Huius Temporis Papistas, Inprimis, Robertum Bellarminum* (Canterbury, 1588), or his *Prælectiones in Controversiam de Romano Pontifice* (1608); both titles indicate the character of the works. The item listed as "Jacobi Fabrii Opera" probably contained a paraphrase of Aristotle's *Politics.* To his "Arbitrary Government Described" Winthrop appended a long quotation from Thomas Aquinas, which his editor, Mr. R. C. Winthrop, unfortunately did not see fit to print. The manuscript has only recently been found.

Of the innumerable pamphlets printed in England in the 1640's, Winthrop mentions only William Prynne's *Treachery and Disloyalty of Papists,* and *An Answer to Dr. Ferne* asserting that Parliament could after the superstructive, not the fundamental laws of England.

This list includes almost every book of a political nature which Winthrop cited or is known to have possessed. But with a few exceptions he does not cite these books. His political theory is Biblical and Calvinistic, in so far as it is drawn from literary sources.

. . . . .

The divine origin of the authority of the magistrate; the ability and character required to prove his calling to office; the divine law by which he must square all his acts; the necessity of obeying him unquestioningly; these are the threads that run all through the political theory that we have examined. They form a pattern now bright, now dull, but always appearing either as *motif* or background in Winthrop's discussion of every phase of political action. These theories were not new. But in Winthrop's lack of novelty lies his importance. During his life, and for many years after, the aristocratic tradition of which he was the most luminous exponent in America dominated the life of Massachusetts. Until the old school was gone, the ultimate democratic effects of the Reformation and the American frontier had to bide their time.

### Edmund S. Morgan (essay date 1958)

SOURCE: "Seventeenth-Century Nihilism" and "The New England Way," in *The Puritan Dilemma: The Story of John Winthrop,* edited by Oscar Handlin, Little, Brown and Company, 1958, pp, 134-54, 155-73.

[*A respected American historian, Morgan is the author of such studies as* The Puritan Family *(1944),* The Birth of the Republic, 1763-89 *(1956), and* Roger Williams: The Church and State *(1967). In the following excerpt, from his monograph on Winthrop, Morgan gives an account of Winthrop's role in the trial of Anne Hutchinson and in the writing of the* Body of Liberties *document.*]

On September 18, 1634, two hundred passengers disembarked at Boston's bustling, cluttered landing place and picked their way through the dirty streets. The squalor of the place was enough to make them quail, but they reminded themselves that it was holy ground, where they might worship God without bishops or kings or Romanizing ritual. Among the arrivals who strengthened their resolution with this thought were William Hutchinson and his wife Anne.

Winthrop described Hutchinson as "a man of a very mild temper and weak parts, and wholly guided by his wife." But a man with a wife like Anne Hutchinson could scarcely not have been guided by her. All we know about Anne Hutchinson was written by other hands than hers, for the most part by writers whose main purpose was to discredit her. Yet the force of her intelligence and character penetrate the libels and leave us angry with the writers and not with their intended victim.

Winthrop, who was one of the libelers, tells us at the outset that she was "a woman of a ready wit and bold spirit." This was an absurd understatement. Though Winthrop, in common with his century, believed that women's minds could not stand the strain of profound theological speculation, Anne Hutchinson excelled him not only in nimbleness of wit but in the ability to extend a theological proposition into all its ramifications. And like so many of the men and women of this time—like Roger Williams, for example—she was ready to trust her mind and to follow in whatever path it might lead her. In 1634 the path had led to Boston.

She was not, by intention at least, a separatist; she had once been tempted in that direction but did not succumb. She had nevertheless determined that she must not attend a church where the minister failed to teach the doctrines of divine grace in their undiluted purity. Until 1633 she had listened to the sermons of the Reverend John Cotton at Boston in Lincolnshire and had known them for true preaching. She had also admired her brother-in-law, the Reverend John Wheelwright. But when Cotton and Wheelwright were silenced by the bishops, "there was none in England," she said, "that I durst heare." After Cotton departed for New England, she persuaded her husband to follow him.

In singling out John Cotton as her spiritual leader, Mrs. Hutchinson showed, by Puritan standards, excellent taste. Cotton had already won a reputation in England before he left, and the Boston church chose him as teacher shortly after his arrival in New England in September, 1633. Here his fame rose steadily. Indeed, his wisdom was so revered that Hugh Peter, who was later to be honored as Cromwell's chaplain, urged that Cotton be commissioned to "go through the Bible, and raise marginal notes upon all the knotty places of the scriptures." Nathaniel Ward, the testy pastor of Ipswich, held himself unworthy to wipe John Cotton's slippers. And Roger Williams observed that many people in Massachusetts "could hardly believe that God would suffer Mr. Cotton to err."

Winthrop himself was one of Cotton's admirers and frequently took occasion to record the minister's opinions with approval. He valued most in Cotton what Mrs. Hutchinson did—the man's evanglical preaching of God's free grace. All New England Puritans believed in this doctrine, which they usually described in terms of a covenant between God and man whereby God drew the soul to salvation. Strictly speaking, there was nothing a man could do to lay hold of this "covenant of grace." If God predestined him to salvation, God would endow him with faith and fulfill the covenant. But the doctrine could be applied in a variety of ways, and the New England ministers had been suggesting the need to "prepare" oneself so as to facilitate the operation of God's saving grace when and if it should come.

Under the spell of this suggestion it was easy to develop notions of the kind that good Puritans always denounced as "Arminian"—whenever they could recognize them. Though preachers always took care to state that human efforts counted for nothing in the scale of eternity, it was easy to draw the opposite (Arminian) conclusion from their insistence on "preparation," easy to slip into Arminian ways of thinking without realizing it. The history of New England theology for a

century and a half after the founding is the history of this steady tendency toward Arminianism, punctuated by periodic reassertions of the Calvinist dogma of divine omnipotence and human helplessness.

John Cotton was the first of a long line of preachers—among whom the most eminent was Jonathan Edwards—to make this reassertion. He did not make it in the unequivocal terms that Edwards did, and perhaps for that reason he did not end as Edwards did by being expelled from his church. Instead he pulled his congregation back from their Arminian wanderings and won their gratitude. Winthrop counted himself as one of those whom Cotton had rescued. He noted in January, 1637, that "the Doctrine of free justification lately taught here took me in as drowsy a condition, as I had been in (to my remembrance) these twenty yeares, and brought mee as low (in my owne apprehension) as if the whole work had been to begin anew. But when the voice of peace came I knew it to bee the same that I had been acquainted with before . . ." Probably most members of the Boston church reacted to Cotton's preaching as Winthrop did. It woke them from their Arminian napping and sharpened their sense of God's free grace, but it did not make them feel in the end that their previous religious experiences had been false.

But the evangelical preaching of divine omnipotence and human helplessness has always produced extravagant results, for these doctrines may too easily be translated into a denial of any connection whatever between this world and the next. Puritanism allowed only a tenuous connection at best; it allowed a man to look at his life here as evidence of his prospects in eternity, but it gave him no opportunity to affect his eternal condition. When John Cotton warned his listeners away from the specious comfort of preparation and re-emphasized the covenant of grace as something in which God acted alone and unassisted, a bold mind might believe that life in this world offered no evidence at all of eternal prospects. And Mrs. Hutchinson was nothing if not bold.

After her arrival in Boston her admission to the church was delayed for a time because one of her fellow passengers had been disturbed by some unorthodox opinions she had expressed on shipboard. But John Cotton evidently recognized her theological talents and her zeal, and within two years she was admitted and won the admiration of a large part of the congregation. It was not uncommon at this time for small groups to hold weekly meetings for religious discussions, in which the sermon of the previous Sunday furnished the starting point. Mrs. Hutchinson, who had gained a wide acquaintance in Boston by serving as a midwife, soon found herself the center of one of these meetings, held in her home. She would explain, to the best of her ability, what her beloved Mr. Cotton had said on Sunday and would then go on to expand some of his doctrines.

In these weekly meetings she carried the principles of divine omnipotence and human helplessness in a dangerous direction, toward the heresy known to theologians as Antinomianism. Since man was utterly helpless, she reasoned, when God acted to save him He placed the Holy Ghost directly within him, so that the man's life was thereafter directed by the Holy Ghost, and the man himself, in a sense, ceased to be. At the same time she concluded that human actions were no clue to the question of whether or not this transformation had taken place. The fact that a man behaved in a "sanctified" manner, breaking none of the laws of God, was no evidence that he was saved. In Puritan terminology this meant that "sanctification" was no evidence of "justification," that men's lives in this world offered no evidence of their prospects in the next. The orthodox Puritans never claimed that the correspondence was perfect: hypocrisy together with the thousand imperfections of human vision could deceive the most skillful examiner. But it was usually possible to recognize sanctification, and that sanctification resulted from justification was not to be doubted at all. Mrs. Hutchinson doubted and denied it. She was, it seemed, an Antinomian.

Winthrop first became alarmed by her teachings in October, 1636, a few months after the departure of Roger Williams. He noted her errors and began a list of the awful conclusions that must ensue from them, but stopped and left a large blank in his journal, overcome perhaps by the train of horrors he saw before him. Before they were through with Mrs. Hutchinson the guardians of New England orthodoxy enumerated nearly a hundred dangerous propositions that could be deduced from her views. It is not possible to tell which propositions she actually endorsed and which were simply attributed to her, but the list is a formidable one, and strikes at the heart of the Puritan experiment.

Mrs. Hutchinson's first principle, "that the person of the Holy Ghost dwells in a justified person," was dangerously close to a belief in immediate personal revelation. It threatened the fundamental conviction on which the Puritans built their state, their churches, and their daily lives, namely that God's will could be discovered only through the Bible. In combination with the belief that sanctification offered no evidence of justification, it undermined the whole basis for moral endeavor which Puritan theologians had constructed since the time of Calvin. What reason for a man to exert himself for the right if he may "stand still and waite for Christ to doe all for him"? What reason for a church of saints, if "no Minister can teach one that is anoynted by the Spirit of Christ, more than hee knowes already unlesse it be in some circumstances"? What reason for a state ruled by the laws of God, if "the Will of God in the Word, or directions thereof, are not the rule whereunto Christians are bound to conforme themselves"?

These views were not necessarily separatist. Rather they were a seventeenth-century version of nihilism. But to make matters worse, Mrs. Hutchinson and her friends developed a new and especially invidious form of separatism, too. Though she denied that sanctification could be evidence of justification, she did maintain that any justified person could discern, presumably at the direction of the Holy Ghost within him, whether or not another person was justified. On the basis of this almighty insight Mrs. Hutchinson and her followers confidently pronounced any person they encountered as "under a covenant of grace" (really saved) or "under a covenant of works" (deluded and damned because relying on good works instead of divine grace), so that "it began to be as common here," Winthrop says, "to distinguish between men, by being under a covenant of grace or a covenant of works, as in other countries between Protestants and Papists." The wholesale destructiveness that might result from Mrs. Hutchinson's self-assurance became apparent when she hinted to her admirers that all the ministers in Massachusetts, with the exception of her two old favorites, John Cotton and John Wheelwright, were under a covenant of works and therefore unfit to preach the gospel.

Winthrop saw trouble ahead when he first took notice of Anne Hutchinson's views in October, 1636. The weekly meetings at her house were steadily swelling, and the people who attended them walked the streets of Boston wearing the expression of devotees. Those rapt faces, Winthrop knew, carried a threat to the colony's commission. But there was no law against religious gatherings, and Mrs. Hutchinson was careful to state her heresies in equivocal language. It would be difficult to prove anything against her.

By the end of October, 1636, her followers felt strong enough to seek an official spokesman for their doctrines in the Boston church. Because Mrs. Hutchinson was a woman, no one would think of proposing her for a church office, but her brother-in-law would do as well. John Wheelwright had arrived in June, with a reputation as an able preacher and with the additional recommendation of having been silenced by the bishops in England. Mrs. Hutchinson, of course, endorsed him, and he endorsed her. At a church meeting on October 30 it was moved that he be made a teacher, though the congregation possessed two other ministers—John Cotton as teacher and John Wilson as pastor. Winthrop grasped the chance to act and immediately opposed the election of a third minister, particularly one "whose spirit they knew not, and one who seemed to dissent in judgment."

As a member of the church, Winthrop had the right to

a voice in its affairs, but no more than any other member, and he was up against a growing majority of the Boston church, which included the largest single concentration of freemen in the colony. He was also up against the popular young governor, Henry Vane, who was on his feet at once to say that Wheelwright's doctrines were no different from those of Cotton. Cotton himself neither admitted nor denied the similarity, but obviously was in sympathy with the majority.

More was at stake here than the welfare of the Boston church, and Winthrop, calling on his own reserve of popularity, was able to persuade the meeting not to elect Wheelwright. But the victory cost him many friends, even though he protested that he meant no personal slight to Wheelwright, and "did love that brother's person, and did honor the gifts and graces of God in him." In the weeks that followed, Wheelwright took himself off to the scattered settlement at Mount Wollaston, leaving behind a congregation that grew ever more resentful of Winthrop and his ally, the pastor John Wilson. Wilson, as pastor, had played second fiddle ever since John Cotton had arrived, but Mrs. Hutchinson's infectious contempt reduced his influence in the congregation to the vanishing point. He and Winthrop were left almost alone to console each other.

Winthrop as usual was sure that people would see things his way if they would only listen to reason, and as usual he set down in black and white the reason he hoped they would listen to. Fortunately, before presenting this document to his opponents he sent a copy to his friend Thomas Shepard, the pastor at Cambridge, who saw at once that Winthrop was no theologian. Though Winthrop knew better than his opponents the necessity of living in this world, he was no match for them in speculating about the next. His arguments, if one may judge from Shepard's criticisms (Winthrop's text is lost), were studded with expressions that smacked of Arminianism; "and so," Shepard warned him, "while you are about to convince them of errours, they will proclayme your selfe to hold foorth worse." Winthrop, who was no Arminian, probably destroyed his composition, and Boston remained deluded and defiant.

Though Winthrop could make no headway within his church, the rest of the colony was beginning to take alarm. The members of the Boston faction, like most religious fanatics, were not content to march quietly along their short cut to Heaven. They hoped to entice the rest of the colony along it and thought the best way was to visit other congregations and heckle the ministers. This method did not prove as effective as Mrs. Hutchinson's winning words. The General Court began to take notice of the problem, and Governor Henry Vane found his popularity ebbing outside Boston as rapidly as Winthrop's had inside. In a petulant fit of tears Vane offered to resign, and the General Court obligingly agreed to let him. This so alarmed his Bos-

ton adherents, who enjoyed having a champion in the governor's chair, that they coaxed him hard to stay, and he finally allowed himself to be persuaded.

By the beginning of 1637 the colony was divided into two hostile camps, the one centering in Boston, the other spread out around it, each constantly sniping at the other. In January the General Court ordered a fast, so that the people might mourn their dissensions. But empty bellies seldom beget brotherly love, and when John Wheelwright showed up at the afternoon lecture by Cotton, he rose up at its conclusion to launch a momentous sermon of his own against those enemies of the Lord who thought that sanctification was an evidence of justification. These holy-seeming men, he said, must be put aside. They were under a covenant of works, and "the more holy they are, the greater enemies they are to Christ." True believers must hew them down: "we must lay loade upon them, we must kille them with the worde of the Lorde."

Wheelwright was speaking figuratively and not actually proposing a blood bath, but he made it plain that he thought most of the existing ministers and probably most of the magistrates, too, could be dispensed with. Someone took down his words, and at the next meeting of the General Court, in spite of the protests of Vane and a few others, he was convicted of sedition. The sentence was deferred till the following session, which the court appointed to be in Cambridge, away from the immediate source of trouble.

This meeting, held the following May, was the regular time for election of officers. When it assembled, a petition from Boston was presented against the conviction of Wheelwright. Governor Vane wanted to deal with the petition before proceeding to election, but Winthrop and the other magistrates insisted on having the election first. When the votes were cast, it was found that Vane had not only failed of re-election but had been left out of the government altogether. The freemen had finally decided to recall the man who was best qualified to restore the peace. Winthrop was back in the governor's chair with Dudley once again as deputy governor. "There was great danger of a tumult that day," Winthrop noted, "and some laid hands on others," but seeing themselves outnumbered, the Bostonians finally decided that this was not the time to hew down the unholy holy and departed for home.

Winthrop now had the authority to crush the opposition, and it was certainly his inclination to bring the whole unhappy business to as speedy an end as possible. But to suppress or banish so large a segment of the population would be to effect the very separation he wished to avoid. His principal weapon must still be persuasion. Instead of dealing with Wheelwright at once, he again deferred sentence and arranged for a general day of humiliation and for a synod of ministers to be held in the late summer to discuss the points at issue and provide the court with a well-defined statement by which to judge the current heresies. Wheelwright was told that the court was still convinced of his guilt, "but if, upon the conference among the churches, the Lord should discover any further light to them than as yet they had seen, they should gladly embrace it." Nor did Winthrop deal with the opposition for their riotous behavior and insolent speeches on election day. Though there had been ample provocation for an indictment, the court hoped that by refraining from this and by deferring Wheelwright's sentence, "their moderation and desire of reconciliation might appear to all."

The ministers from the beginning had tried to win Cotton away from his heretical admirers, but he held firmly to the top of the fence. He did not endorse Mrs. Hutchinson's consignment of the other ministers to perdition, but he refused to believe that she and Wheelwright held the heresies imputed to them. At the same time he himself disapproved the current doctrine of preparation and maintained that more rigorous views had helped to effectuate a marked awakening of the spirit in Boston.

During the summer months Winthrop's dignity and patience were repeatedly taxed by the sulking saints of that town. Until shamed into it, Boston made no move to provide him with the sergeant halberdiers who customarily accompanied the governor to the first day of General Court and to Sunday meeting. Rather than press the point, he used his own servants and politely declined when at last the town left-handedly offered men but not sergeants. His comings and goings from Boston were also pointedly ignored, in marked contrast to the honor accorded him by other towns, which sent a guard to escort him into and out of their territory. And Henry Vane, until his departure for England on August 3, conducted himself with unabashed schoolboy discourtesy, refusing the invitation to sit in the magistrates' seats at the Boston church, though he had sat there ever since his arrival in the colony, refusing to attend a dinner party at Winthrop's home and instead carrying off the intended guest of honor, a visiting English nobleman, to dine on Noddle's Island with Samuel Maverick.

Although Winthrop set much store by his official dignity, he did not allow himself to be goaded into further recriminations. Once more he put his pen to work, and this time Thomas Shepard found little to criticize beyond the fact that he was too charitable to his opponents. But the charity was calculated. If he could not win over the leaders of the opposition, he might at least draw away their less extravagant followers.

At the same time he did not propose to allow them to increase their numbers by bringing over like-minded friends from England, where the Reverend Roger Brierly of Grindleton Chapel had recently been achieving notoriety by preaching doctrines similar to those of Mrs. Hutchinson. Winthrop feared that the Grindletonians, as Brierly's followers were called, would shortly be gravitating to Massachusetts, and he accordingly sponsored an order of court forbidding anyone to entertain strangers for more than three weeks without permission of the magistrates. This arbitrary restriction of immigration was denounced by Henry Vane as unchristian. Winthrop defended it but enforced it with his usual flexibility by granting the immigrant friends and relatives of Mrs. Hutchinson and Wheelwright four months in which to decide upon a location for settlement outside the colony.

On August 30 the ministers convened in a synod—all those of Massachusetts, including Wheelwright and Cotton, together with a delegation from Connecticut. For twenty-four days they defined to each other the dreadful doctrines that were polluting the air above Boston, and reached a remarkable unanimity. Even John Cotton, faced with a solid phalanx of his colleagues, squeezed his views into line. Wheelwright alone remained aloof. Close to a hundred heretical propositions were meticulously described and condemned, though the synod tactfully declined to attribute them to specific persons. The unanimous opinion of this body of experts must have given pause to many who had flirted with the new ideas, but a hard core of devotees in Boston continued a noisy defiance.

Winthrop could see no further avenue of persuasion and in November decided that it was time for action. Wheelwright was summoned again before the General Court and upon his refusal to give up teaching his heresies was banished. But Winthrop knew that Wheelwright was not the main source of the trouble. When the court had finished with him, they sent for his sister-in-law.

What followed was the least attractive episode in Winthrop's career. Anne Hutchinson was his intellectual superior in everything except political judgment, in everything except the sense of what was possible in this world. In nearly every exchange of words she defeated him, and the other members of the General Court with him. The record of her trial, if it is proper to dignify the procedure with that name, is one of the few documents in which her words have been recorded, and it reveals a proud, brilliant woman put down by men who had judged her in advance. The purpose of the trial was doubtless to make her conviction seem to follow due process of law, but it might have been better for the reputation of her judges if they had simply banished her unheard.

Mrs. Hutchinson confronted them at Cambridge, where magistrates and deputies crowded into the narrow benches of the meetinghouse, the only building of suitable size in the town. The ministers too were on hand, but only as witnesses, for this was a civil court, in which they had no authority. There was no jury, and no apparent procedure. The magistrates (and even some of the deputies) flung questions at the defendant, and exploded in blustering anger when the answers did not suit them. Even Winthrop was unable to maintain his usual poise in the face of Mrs. Hutchinson's clever answers to his loaded questions.

The court was somewhat handicapped, because Mrs. Hutchinson throughout the preceding months had played her hand so cleverly that only minor charges could be framed against her. The court was preparing to deal with all Wheelwright's supporters who had signed the petition in his favor. They would be disfranchised, disarmed, and in some cases banished. But Mrs. Hutchinson had signed nothing and so could be charged only with "countenancing and encouraging" those who did. To this was added the even weaker charge that she held in her home meetings of men and women which were not tolerable or comely in the sight of God or fitting for her sex. Following these was a last and more serious indictment, that she had traduced the faithful ministers of the colony.

The ground of the first charge was that in entertaining seditious persons she broke the Fifth Commandment: she dishonored the governors, who were the fathers of the commonwealth. This was not really a far-fetched interpretation, for the Puritans always justified subordination and subjection to the state on the basis of the Fifth Commandment. But Mrs. Hutchinson's "entertainment" of seditious persons could be considered seditious only by the most tenuous reasoning, and her nimble wit quickly devised a dilemma for the court. "Put the case, Sir," she said to Winthrop, "that I do fear the Lord and my parents, may not I entertain them that fear the Lord because my parents will not give me leave?"

Winthrop was unable to find his way around this logical impasse and took refuge in blind dogmatism: "We do not mean to discourse with those of your sex but only this; you do adhere unto them and do endeavor to set forward this faction and so you do dishonour us."

The court next called upon her to justify the weekly meetings at her house. In answer she quoted two passages of Scripture: Titus II, 3-5, which indicated that the elder women should instruct the younger, and Acts XVIII, 26, wherein Aquila and Priscilla "tooke upon them to instruct Apollo, more perfectly, yet he was a man of good parts, but they being better instructed might teach him."

There followed this interchange:

*Court:* See how your argument stands, Priscilla with her husband, tooke Apollo home to instruct him privately, therefore Mistris Hutchinson without her husband may teach sixty or eighty.

*Hutch:* I call them not, but if they come to me, I may instruct them.

*Court:* Yet you shew us not a rule.

*Hutch:* I have given you two places of Scripture.

*Court:* But neither of them will sute your practise.

To this assertion Mrs. Hutchinson returned her most withering sarcasm: "Must I shew my name written therein?"

Mrs. Hutchinson was having the best of the argument, but the members of the court were only antagonized by her wit. As they saw it, she was usurping the position of a minister without the authority that a minister possessed from his election by a congregation. Her meetings were a fountain of dissension and separatism for which the community was liable to punishment by the Lord. On this note the court closed the argument: "We see no rule of God for this, we see not that any should have authority to set up any other exercises besides what authority hath already set up and so what hurt comes of this you will be guilty of and we for suffering you."

The greater part of the audience doubtless breathed a silent "Amen," and the trial moved forward to the final accusation, that she had insulted the ministers. The basis of this charge was a conference held the preceding December between the ministers and Mrs. Hutchinson. In spite of the fact that the conference had been private, and they had encouraged her to speak freely, they did not hesitate now to testify that she had designated them all, with the exception of Cotton and Wheelwright, as laboring under a covenant of works. One minister after another was called forward, and when the court adjourned for the day, the evidence against her on this charge looked overwhelming.

That night she went over some notes taken at the December conference by her most determined opponent, John Wilson. Finding some discrepancy between his notes and the testimony offered in court, she demanded the next morning that the ministers be required to give their evidence under oath. This created a considerable stir, because if the ministers swore to their testimony and it was proved to be wrong, they would be guilty not merely of perjury but of blasphemy, of taking the name of the Lord in vain. After much hemming and hawing by the other ministers John Cotton was called upon for the first time to give his version of the conference. With the tact which had enabled him to retain the favor of both sides he soothed the injured pride of his fellow ministers and then brought his speech to a dramatic close by declaring, "I must say that I did not find her saying they were under a covenant of works, nor that she said they did preach a covenant of works." And though pressed by the other ministers, he stood his ground.

With this testimony the case against Mrs. Hutchinson was about to collapse. The first two specifications against her had been too weakly sustained to warrant more than a serious admonition, and now the revered Mr. Cotton had knocked out the props from under the only remaining charge. The triumph was too much. Hitherto Mrs. Hutchinson had been on guard and had dexterously parried every thrust against her. Had she been content to hold her tongue at this point, her judges might have felt obliged to dismiss her with a censure. But instead she now proceeded to justify herself by a torrent of divine revelations.

Winthrop tried to stop her, but the floodgates were opened—perhaps by hysteria. Suddenly he must have seen where this outpouring might lead and was silent. The minutes raced by as she described how one thing after another had been revealed to her through scriptural passages thrust into her mind by God. To the Puritans this was an acceptable form of revelation. But then, still to the accompaniment of Biblical citations, she came to the revelation that she would come into New England and there be persecuted, but need fear no more than Daniel in the lions' den. "And see!" she cried, "this scripture fulfilled this day in mine eyes, therefore take heed what yee goe about to doe unto me . . . for I know that for this you goe about to do to me, God will ruine you and your posterity, and this whole State."

Here was the naked challenge. Winthrop and his colleagues believed that the Lord would punish Massachusetts if they *did not* punish Mrs. Hutchinson. Obviously either she or they were deluded, and they asked her "How shee did know that it was God that did reveale these things to her, and not Satan." With a final scriptural flourish to justify what she was about to do and with confidence in the Lord's deliverance, Mrs. Hutchinson at last threw off the confining authority of the Bible and swept arrogantly on.

*Mrs. H*: How did Abraham know that it was God that bid him offer his son, being a breach of the sixth commandment?

*Court*: By an immediate voice.

*Mrs. H*: So to me by an immediate revelation.

*Court*: How! an immediate revelation?

*Mrs. H*: By the voice of his own spirit to my soul.

Here it was at last, an acknowledgment of the heresy so long suspected. The Lord had indeed disclosed who was deluded, but He had left it to the court to strike her down! Winthrop recorded that "the Court and all the rest of the Assembly (except those of her owne party) did observe a speciall providence of God, that . . . her owne mouth should deliver her into the power of the Court, as guilty of that which all suspected her for, but were not furnished with proofe sufficient to proceed against her. . . ." It required only the briefest deliberation for the court to agree that Mrs. Hutchinson's words were sufficient cause for banishment, and when she said, "I desire to know wherefore I am banished," Winthrop gave the shabby final word: "Say no more, the court knows wherefore and is satisfied."

The sentencing of Anne Hutchinson was followed by the disfranchising and disarming of her closest adherents, who might at any moment receive an immediate revelation directing them to kill her judges. Religious enthusiasm was known to produce such results. Fortunately, the number of unwavering Hutchinson disciples was small. Her heretical declaration at the trial had driven off many in disillusionment. Though badly shaken, the Boston church for a time kept dogged faith that the declaration had been the result of unfair pressure and chicanery by the court. But when they sought to satisfy their doubts at a church meeting, Mrs. Hutchinson offered some testimony so obviously contrary to her own previous statements that they could only reluctantly conclude to abandon her. In March, 1637, they voted to excommunicate her, and at the end of the month, her banishment having been deferred four months because of the winter and her pregnancy, she departed for Rhode Island, followed by the few faithful.

Winthrop's victory at the trial had been an unsavory triumph of arbitrary power, but happily it represented more than the mere crushing of a helpless woman. When she left, Massachusetts lost a brilliant mind, but God's commission was secured. Even the Boston church recovered from the troubles and was restored to unity. Only a little over a year later Winthrop looked back and congratulated himself on not having withdrawn from the church when every hand was turned against him. "By this time," he writes, "there appeared a great change in the church of Boston; for whereas, the year before, they were all (save five or six) so affected to Mr. Wheelright and Mrs. Hutchinson, and those new opinions, as they slighted the present governour and the pastor, looking at them as men under a covenant of works, and as their greatest enemies; but they bearing all patiently, and not withdrawing themselves, (as they were strongly solicited to have done,) but carrying themselves lovingly and helpfully upon all occasions, the Lord brought about the hearts of all the people to love and esteem them more than ever before, and all breaches were made up, and the church was saved from ruin beyond all expectation; which could hardly have been, (in human reason,) if those two had not been guided by the Lord to that moderation."

Thus the final lesson of the Hutchinson affair was the same lesson that Winthrop had been learning all his life, the importance of not separating.

. . . . .

Massachusetts, then, was not going to crumble into a hundred holy little bands, all looking for perfection in this world and finding it in their own exclusive sanctimoniousness. With the successive expulsions of Roger Williams and Anne Hutchinson, the freemen who had rebuked Winthrop in 1634 demonstrated that their mission in the wilderness was the same as his: to found a society where the perfection of God would find proper recognition among imperfect men. Those who looked for a private heaven on earth might now look in Rhode Island—and much joy to them. Those who cared not for heaven or hell could await damnation in the Old World. Massachusetts, saved from the zealots, would go about the business to which Winthrop had committed it. Here between the Merrimack and the Charles would be a new Israel, where men might worship as God commanded and only as He commanded, where they might obey His laws in peace and be punished when they disobeyed, where they could live in the world as God required but not lose sight of the eternity that lay beyond it.

The freemen had shown their dedication to the goal Winthrop set them, but they still had their own ideas about how to reach it. Though they called for his assistance against Anne Hutchinson, they had no intention of relinquishing the share of power they had won in 1634. There would be four meetings of the General Court every year, making laws to limit the discretion of the magistrates, and the freemen would be represented by their elected deputies. A benevolent despotism, they were convinced, was not the way to carry out God's commission.

Winthrop disagreed, and so did a number of his fellow magistrates. They could not escape the changes made in 1634, but the settlement of that year had left a great many details of the government untouched, and they hoped that in settling those details they might still retain the kind of paternalistic state in which they believed. Even while they fought for the life of their experiment against Roger Williams and Anne Hutchinson, Winthrop and the freemen wrestled with each other over this problem. It was, of course, the old struggle for power that goes on inside every society, but in Massachusetts the stakes were high. If the people of this colony were to lead the world in establishing the kind of community God demanded, then they could not afford to err. The role of the deputies, of the clergy, of the magistrates, and of the people must be as God would have it; the laws must be His laws; the government must be His government.

The most difficult problem, in Winthrop's view, was that of the deputies. Winthrop had enough political sense to know that they were there to stay, but he could not bring himself to look on them as genuine officers of government. They were, rather, the representatives of the people, and their only role was to keep the government in touch with public opinion. The magistrates, on the other hand, though elected by the same voters, represented not the people but God. Their authority came from Him and not from the men who put them in office.

Winthrop did not want a government entirely free from popular control. In 1630 he had voluntarily abandoned the oligarchy which the charter made possible, and in 1631 he had persuaded the other magistrates to allow popular election of the governor and deputy governor as well as assistants. In 1634 he had been willing to give the people a voice in matters of taxation and land distribution and in the revision of laws they felt unsatisfactory. But he wanted no blurring of the distinction between rulers and ruled. To confound the two would be to make mockery of the authority God gave to rulers. As John Cotton put it, "if the people be governors, who shall be governed?" Moreover, if the purpose of government was to curb human depravity, then it must be set apart from the people and enabled to act upon them with all the majesty of divine sanction. This could never be if the government were run by the people or their deputies, and subject to their every corrupt whim.

The deputies understandably took a higher view of their role and of their competence to fill it than did Winthrop. While he tried to reduce their part in the new government, they did their best to enlarge it. Winthrop began the dispute shortly after his ouster from the governor's chair by claiming for the magistrates (the governor, deputy governor, and assistants) a "negative voice" on all legislation. The freemen wanted laws. Very well, but no law, he said, could be made without the consent of a majority of the magistrates, through all the freemen or their deputies should be for it. The deputies outnumbered the magistrates in the General Court and if allowed to carry measures by a simple majority, they might frustrate the work of the government, that is, of the magistrates, who were the authorized vicegerents of God.

Winthrop assumed that the line between governors and governed ran between the magistrates and the deputies. But he did not rest his case simply on this assumption. The freemen had claimed the charter as the basis of government. To the charter he went, therefore, and came up with the provision that the authority of the General Court was to be exercised by the majority of the members present, "whereof the Governor or Deputie Governor and six of the Assistants, at the least [are] to be seven." This passage, according to Winthrop, was not merely a definition of the quorum necessary to transact business. Rather it was a requirement that every measure have the approval of the governor or deputy governor and six assistants. It meant, in effect, that no law could be valid unless it was accepted by a majority of the magistrates as well as by a majority of the freemen or their deputies.

Since the General Court was the supreme court as well as the supreme legislature of Massachusetts, the negative voice also meant that no final judicial decision could be rendered against the will of the magistrates. That the magistrates should exercise such control seemed desirable to Winthrop for several reasons, foremost of which was that they were admittedly elected as the best qualified men in the colony for wisdom, judgment, ability, and knowledge. It was to the interest of every freeman to choose well, for the magistrates' duties included sitting as judges in the local county courts and in the monthly Court of Assistants where appeals were heard.

The freemen recognized the scarcity of qualified men; they re-elected many of the same magistrates again and again. This lack of men with the education, legal training, and experience necessary to fit them to make judicial decisions—or legislative ones—was a constant concern to Winthrop. In 1634 he had tried to bar the freemen from power in the General Court for just this reason. "For the present," he had told them, "they were not furnished with a sufficient number of men for such a business." They had taken their powers anyhow and transferred them to deputies. But the deputies, as a group, were no better qualified than the freemen. These pious but unlearned men were called upon to act as a supreme judiciary without even taking an oath to judge according to the laws of God and of the land (because they were not regular judges). Through the place they occupied in the General Court they enjoyed a power in judicial matters equal to that of the wisest and most learned magistrates in the land. Only by the negative voice could the magistrates prevent them from committing the grossest errors.

Winthrop was not able to get the negative voice accepted without opposition, even though it would guarantee an equal power of veto to the deputies. But the matter was so important to him that he supported it with a vehemence he seldom displayed. When Israel Stoughton, a substantial and straightforward freeman from Dorchester, drew up a list of arguments against it, Winthrop rode him down as "a troubler of Israel" and demanded that the General Court burn his argu-

ments and disbar him from office for three years. Winthrop still had enough prestige to carry this point, but in his vindictiveness against Stoughton he overreached himself. Stoughton, who was an honest and able man, admitted privately that Winthrop was "a man of men," but added wisely, "He is but a man: and some say they have idolized him, and do now confesse their error."

This was in 1635, when the election again left Winthrop out of the governorship. But the troubles with Roger Williams and Anne Hutchinson were now approaching, and many freemen were ready to give the magistrates a stronger hand to deal with separatism. In 1636, after Williams had departed, the General Court confirmed the negative voice by a statute declaring "that noe lawe, order, or sentence shall passe as an act of the Court, without the consent of the greater parte of the magistrates on the one parte, and the greater number of the deputyes on the other parte."

This was not the end of the question. Whenever the magistrates exercised their veto, there was apt to be argument about it, but they clung to their position and in 1644 secured it by a formal division of the General Court into two houses.

Meanwhile Winthrop and those who agreed with him on the desirability of a strong magistracy took advantage of the uproar caused by the Williams episode to inaugurate another device for stabilizing their authority. The meeting of the General Court in March, 1636, made provision for the election, as occasion might demand, of "a certaine number of magistrates for the tearme of their lyves, as a standing counsaile, not to be removed but upon due conviction of crime, insufficiency, or for some other waightie cause; the Governor for the tyme being to be always president of this counsaile." It was intended that the council should be drawn principally from ex-governors, and accordingly Winthrop and Dudley were selected as the first members. The following month they were empowered to run the colony in the intervals between meetings of the General Court. This they proceeded to do with a very free hand, for the definition of the council's powers had been left comfortably vague and ambiguous.

Thus the government of Massachusetts still had some of the character Winthrop desired for it when he took office again as governor in 1637. After he succeeded in driving Anne Hutchinson and her followers to Rhode Island, a grateful country was content for some time to let him manage affairs in his own way, and the General Court rewarded his services with generous grants of land in the new plantation then beginning at Concord. Friends wrote from England, too, congratulating him on his great success in vanquishing the dangerous opinions which had troubled the colony, and Englishmen demonstrated their confidence by coming over in such numbers as had never been seen before, three thousand in the summer of 1638 alone. God manifested His approval in other ways, too. In the spring of 1637, while Winthrop was in the process of subduing Mrs. Hutchinson, the colony became involved in war with the Pequot Indians. Through the timely warnings of Roger Williams, who was corresponding regularly with Winthrop, and with the assistance of the settlers in Connecticut, who bore the brunt of the fighting, the Pequots were destroyed, virtually the whole tribe killed or captured.

The abundant evidence of divine favor served to confirm Winthrop in his commitment to a government with wide discretionary powers, dedicated to the enforcement of the laws of God, but not accountable to anyone but God. Whenever his actions as governor were questioned, he would carefully explain why he had done what he did, and might even modify his decisions to meet criticisms, but he never failed to rebuke the questioners. The freemen were for the moment so pleased with his combination of firmness and flexibility that in 1638 and again in 1639 they re-elected him in spite of an intention expressed in 1635 to have the office rotate.

But the forces which produced the revolution of 1634 were not extinct. Thomas Dudley still insisted on rigor; and among the freemen new leaders were arising to challenge Winthrop's paternalism. Israel Stoughton, as soon as his three-year disqualification expired, was elected an assistant. With him stood Richard Bellingham, one of the original members of the Bay Company, and Richard Saltonstall, the son of an original member.

Bellingham had been a lawyer in England and a member of Charles I's Parliament of 1628. After his arrival in Massachusetts in 1634 he served for a year in the General Court as deputy for Boston and then was made an assistant and treasurer of the colony. He was a mercurial individual, melancholic and impetuous, not Winthrop's idea of a proper magistrate at all. Bellingham had equal misgivings about Winthrop's high notions of governmental authority and, perhaps from his experience in Parliament, had gained high notions of his own about the authority of the people. He and Saltonstall, who was elevated to the magistracy in 1637, generally deserted their colleagues for the side of the deputies whenever there was a dispute.

In spite of these defections, Winthrop might have been able to continue the high-toned government he thought best if he had not met with opposition from another quarter—the clergy. Although no clergyman ever held civil office in seventeenth-century Massachusetts, clerical influence was conspicuous on more than one occasion in reducing the authority of the magistrates and magnifying the liberties of the freemen.

The relationship between church and state was one of the things that the Puritans knew they must get right. They were certain that God had prescribed the terms of it, and they had thought much about it before leaving England, where church and state were confounded at every level from parish to Crown. In Massachusetts the Puritans drew a firmer dividing line between the two than existed anywhere in Europe. The state was still responsible for supporting and protecting the church: as guardian of the divine commission the state must punish heresy like any other sin. And it did so, inflicting loss of civil and political rights as well as other penalties. But in prosecuting heresy it did not operate as the agent of the churches. It formed its own judgments with the aid of a jury or in the General Court, where the respresentatives of the people sat in judgment with the magistrates. The church had no authority in the government and the government was particularly careful not to allow the actions of any church to affect civil and political rights. In England excommunication carried heavy civil disabilities, in Massachusetts none. The right to vote and hold office was not revoked by loss of church membership.

Though the clergy had no political authority of any kind, they did enjoy a very powerful indirect influence. They were highly respected by their congregations, and when unpopular measures had to be adopted, the magistrates counted on their assistance in reconciling people to the necessity of obedience. When a difficult decision had to be made, the magistrates frequently consulted the ministers, who were learned men and wise in the laws of God. In this way, though they were barred from the exercise of authority, a back door was left open through which they could influence state policy.

Normally the magistrates accepted the advice of the clergy, but the magistrates were big enough men in their own right to maintain their independence—as long as the government remained entirely in their hands. The admission of the deputies to the government magnified clerical influence. Thereafter, whenever the deputies and the magistrates were at odds on any question, both sides were tempted to seek the support of the ministers, whose influence on their congregations might swing the balance of power. Had they been ambitious for temporal authority and had their beliefs not forbidden it, the clergy might have won a regular position in the government. They did not attempt to do so; but when they were consulted in disputes between deputies and magistrates, they did not hesitate to throw their weight on one side or the other.

Although for the most part they supported the magistrates, they agreed with the deputies on the need for specific legislation to reduce discretionary authority. Even John Cotton, one of the most consistent supporters of stability in government, one of the most outspoken enemies of "mere democracy," argued that the prerogatives of authority must be clearly limited. "They will be like a Tempest," he said, "if they be not limited: a Prince himselfe cannot tell where hee will confine himselfe, nor can the people tell: But if he have liberty to speak great things, then he will make and unmake, say and unsay, and undertake such things as are neither for his owne honour, nor for the safety of the State. It is therefore fit for every man to be studious of the bounds which the Lord hath set."

With the ministers preaching the limitation of authority and Winthrop insisting on the opposite, the freemen began once more to grow concerned. Everyone admitted that Winthrop was a great man and an excellent governor, but his pre-eminence made his views seem the more dangerous. Every year brought more Englishmen to Massachusetts, men who had suffered from the discretion of an absolute ruler. In spite of Winthrop's benevolence and wisdom, they felt uneasy for the future.

The ministers continued to worry the subject, and before the election of 1639, some of them tried to persuade the freemen that it was dangerous to keep on re-electing Winthrop to the governorship. Their arguments proceeded, Winthrop wrote, "not out of any dislike of him, (for they all loved and esteemed him,) but out of their fear lest it might make way for having a governour for life, which some had propounded as most agreeable to God's institution and the practice of all well ordered states." Those ministers most sensitive to the dangers of unlimited authority evidently detected that Winthrop himself would not have been averse to a life term. Such was his popularity that they could not prevent his re-election, but they argued the matter so heatedly that many freemen received the impression there was a plot afoot to install a governor for life. As a result, the deputies at the next meeting of the General Court took steps to clip the wings of the Council for Life, established three years before. In their capacity as councilmen Winthrop and his colleagues had been exercising powers that (according to the deputies) they were entitled to exercise only when they sat as magistrates in the General or Assistants Court. Though the General Court did not abolish the council, they did confine its jurisdiction to a few specifically stated functions: military affairs, the Indian trade, and the customs service.

Winthrop accepted this decision with obvious reluctance, thereby perhaps confirming the fears of the deputies and the clergy that he wanted too much power. Before the next election the ministers busied themselves again to effect his ouster, "fearing lest the long continuance of one man in the place should bring it to be for life, and, in time, hereditary." It took some doing to persuade the people to elect anyone else. "Many of the elders," Winthrop noted, "labored much in it,"

though without any hard feeling toward him. Meeting in Boston in order to concert their efforts, "they sent some of their company to acquaint the old governour with their desire, and the reasons moving them, clearing themselves of all dislike of his government, and seriously professing their sincere affections and respect toward him." He thanked them, assured them that he understood their motives, and expressed "his unfeigned desire of more freedom that he might a little intend his private occasions"; but he doubtless made plain that he would not refuse if the people chose to call him once again—God intended men to use the talents He gave them.

The man whom the elders had selected as the most likely candidate to beat Winthrop was his old friend and antagonist, Thomas Dudley. By a narrow margin Dudley was elected, and in the following year, 1641, through equally strenuous efforts, Richard Bellingham was chosen by a majority of six votes over Winthrop.

With Winthrop out of the way for two years, the deputies were able to press forward with the project which they had pursued ever since their admission to the government. At their first meeting in the General Court in 1634 they had secured the passage of one or two general laws; and at ensuing sessions they kept adding more. They wanted as soon as possible a full and explicit body of legislation to restrain the magistrates and to guarantee civil rights and liberties, but they recognized that laws must be carefully drawn, especially in Massachusetts, where every clause must conform to the word of God. As early as 1635 they saw that their own piecemeal efforts would never provide them with an adequate code, and appointed a committee to frame a complete body of laws "in resemblance to a Magna Charta."

The committee, consisting of John Haynes, Richard Bellingham, Thomas Dudley, and Winthrop, never brought in a report. Winthrop was against the whole idea and quarreled with the other members over the question of leniency. The next year the deputies tried again with a mixed committee of magistrates and ministers. This one did produce a code, the work of John Cotton, but the details of it were not altogether pleasing to the deputies. Though Cotton believed in explicit legislation to limit authority, he had as high notions as Winthrop about keeping government stable. He had argued in 1634 for the reelection of Winthrop, and he went a step further in his code by providing that all assistants be elected for life terms. Though the deputies had agreed to establish the Council for Life, this wholesale creation of life tenures was too much for them. Cotton's code was "taken into further consideration" and quietly put on the shelf.

In 1638, after Winthrop had been back as governor for a year, the deputies resumed their efforts. Gradually things began to move, but as slowly as Winthrop could make them, and when Dudley took over again in 1640, no code had been established. Winthrop explained candidly in his journal why he and some of the other magistrates were dragging their feet. It was not, he said, that they wanted no laws at all, but that they wanted the laws to arise out of judicial decisions rather than out of wholesale legislative enactments. Massachusetts was a new country and a new kind of society, dedicated as no other society had been to carrying out God's covenant. Though the terms of that covenant were set down clearly in the Bible, they could not be applied exactly as they had been in Israel. To agree in advance on positive applications would impose an impossible rigidity. God's will would be defeated in the very attempt to carry it out. Much better to leave the magistrates a free hand. Let them search the Scriptures for the proper rule in each case as it arose. The decisions would be recorded, and when a similar case arose in the future, the judges could hark back to it and be guided by it. Through just such precedents the common law of England had arisen. And did not every good Englishman acknowledge that the common law was more binding, more in accordance with God's will, than the statutes enacted by Parliament?

There was another reason, too, why Winthrop disliked legislation: the Massachusetts charter forbade legislation contrary to the laws of England, and the right legislation would have to depart from English law at many points. There was, however, no express limitation on judicial or executive action, and these might escape notice. For example, if Massachusetts simply followed the practice of having civil magistrates perform the marriage ceremony (as the Scriptures, to Puritan eyes, demanded), no one in England need be the wiser. But to pass a law forbidding any but magistrates to perform it would be to invite interference from England, and might lead to revocation of the charter.

Winthrop's arguments were not unreasonable, but they were no answer to the deputies. He spoke of making laws by judicial precedents, but that was exactly what they feared: how could they be sure the precedents would be the right ones? Precedents accumulating slowly, almost surreptitiously, not exposed to public deliberation might be chains to bind the people in slavery. Government existed to control human corruption; but governors were human, and there must be some way of controlling their corruption, too. A code, therefore, the deputies would have, and they finally found the right man to draw it up—Nathaniel Ward of Ipswich.

Ipswich, the second largest settlement in the colony, attracted men of character (including Winthrop's eldest son, John). Nathaniel Ward, like many Puritans and especially those of Ipswich, was an outspoken man. He was older than Winthrop and had behind him ten years of legal training and practice in London, ten years on the Continent, and ten years as rector of Stondon-Massey in Essex. He came to Ipswich at the age of fifty-five in 1634, served as pastor for a couple of years, and then resigned because of ill health but stayed on in the town.

He was no democrat and no demagogue. Before he died he returned to England and dared stand before the House of Commons and denounce it for its treatment of the King. "I see the spirits of people runne high," he observed disapprovingly to Winthrop in 1639, "and what they gett they hould." But the deputies did well in selecting him to draw their code. His legal experience was more extensive than Winthrop's and had probably been gained in the common-law courts, where lawyers learned to match laws against the discretion of the King, and where the people of England were gradually accumulating a heritage of civil liberties. Ward disapproved of giving the people a free hand in the government, but he was clear that "they may not be denied their proper and lawfull liberties."

These liberties, along with the liberties of magistrates, churches, animals, servants, children, and women, he sought to protect in the Body of Liberties, as the code he drafted came to be called. There were a hundred provisions, many of which would have been welcomed by most men in old England, whether Puritan or not—for example, number nine: that "no monopolies shall be granted or allowed amongst us, but of such new Inventions that are profitable to the Countrie, and that for a short time"; or number ten, forbidding feudal restrictions on land: "All our lands and heritages shall be free from all fines and licences upon Alienations, and from all hariotts, wardships, Liveries, Primerseisins, yeare day and wast, Escheates, and forfeitures, upon the deaths of parents or Ancestors, be they naturall, casuall or Juditiall." There would be no Court of Wards and Liveries in Massachusetts. Ward introduced other innovations, too, based on his legal experience, to make Massachusetts judicial procedures simpler than English ones. And he guarded the traditional liberties for which Englishmen were even then struggling in the mother country: trial by jury and due process of law.

But the code was not merely a bill of rights to protect the inhabitants of Massachusetts from arbitrary government. It was a blueprint of the whole Puritan experiment, an attempt to spell out the dimensions of the New England way. Trial by jury was part of that way (although the General Court, exercising supreme jurisdiction, operated without a jury) and so was freehold tenure of lands, but only because these practices seemed in accord with the laws of God; for the New England way must be the way God wanted his kingdom on earth to be run, and every law must be measured by His holy word. "No custom or prescription," said the Body of Liberties, "shall ever prevaile amongst us in any morall cause, our meaning is [that no custom or prescription shall] maintaine anythinge that can be proved to bee morallie sinfull by the word of God." And it enumerated all those crimes which the laws of God branded as deserving death: idolatry, witchcraft, blasphemy, murder, bestiality, sodomy, adultery, man-stealing, false witness, and treason. The list included several crimes which were more lightly punished in England, but the very brevity showed that God demanded lesser punishments for most offenses than the King of England did. In England the number of capital crimes amounted to about fifty during the seventeenth century and rose to well over a hundred in the eighteenth.

The Body of Liberties did not describe in detail the machinery of government that had been worked out for God's kingdom in Massachusetts during the preceding ten years. It did not, for example, define the relative authority of deputies and magistrates, which was still a matter of dispute. But it did lay down some general principles of fundamental importance: it reaffirmed the decision of 1634 in a provision stating the right of each town to choose deputies for the General Court; it guaranteed the right of freemen to elect all officers of government annually; and it defined the relationship of church and state in unmistakable terms. The state could establish Christ's religion in every church, and it could "deale with any Church member in a way of Civill Justice, notwithstanding any Church relation, office or interest." The church, or rather any particular church, could "deale with any magestrate, Deputie of Court or other officer what soe ever that is a member in a church way in case of apparent and just offence given in their places, so it be done with due observance and respect," but "no church censure shall degrad or depose any man from any Civill dignitie, office, or Authoritie he shall have in the Commonwealth." In other words, a church might censure or excommunicate a magistrate (who happened to be a member) for some improper magisterial action, but the excommunication would not affect his authority or the validity of what he did.

The code also stated some of the principles governing the special institution that the people of Massachusetts had developed to replace the parishes and boroughs and manors from which they had come. In these institutions of English local government, church and state were hopelessly entwined. In order to separate them and also do away with archaic forms of land tenure, it was necessary to construct an altogether new kind of unit, a unit which would be a parish without church officers, a borough without aldermen, a manor without a lord. The New England town was not built after any pre-existing pattern, nor were all towns alike. But in the course of a decade towns had somehow come into being, and some common features had emerged to which the Body of Liberties gave the sanction of law:

the freemen of every town should have power to make bylaws (not contrary to the laws of the colony) and could also "choose yearly or for lesse time out of themselves a convenient number of fitt men to order the planting or prudentiall occasions of that Town." These "select persons" should not exceed nine in number and were to do nothing contrary to written instructions given them by their constituents. A unique form of local government had been created.

After much discussion and revision the code of liberties was finally accepted by the General Court in December, 1641. Winthrop recorded the fact in his journal without comment. He would doubtless have been happier if its provisions had been left unexpressed, but he probably found little to quarrel with in the substance of them. They defined the New England way for all to see, and if this might bring trouble, it might also prompt the world to imitation.

The freemen, in any case, were pleased to have things written out. There was still, of course, a great deal left undecided. Nothing, for example, had been said about the education of children, and in the following year the General Court made it a law that all parents see that their children be taught to read. A later enactment provided for free public schools. Many more laws would be needed in the coming years; but with the Body of Liberties established, the freemen felt safe in summoning Winthrop back as their leader. In May, 1642, they returned him to the governorship and kept him there, in spite of occasional protests by clergymen, for most of the remainder of his life.

Meanwhile, during the time Nathaniel Ward was constructing the Massachusetts Magna Charta, things began to happen in the rest of the world that would alter the significance of everything Winthrop and his colony had done or could ever do.

### Daniel B. Shea, Jr. (essay date 1968)

SOURCE: "Traditional Patterns of Puritan Autobiography: John Winthrop's 'Christian Experience'," in *Spiritual Autobiography in Early America,* Princeton University Press, 1968, pp. 100-10.

[*In the essay below, Shea explores Winthrop's "Christian Experience" as an account of his spiritual progress.*]

Any Puritan autobiography exhibits its author's awareness of the traditional stages through which a man passed as God brought him to grace. But some narratives serve as paradigms in their adherence to textbook descriptions of the order of grace. Edward Taylor's "Spiritual Relation" is one of these. Another, the **"Christian Experience"** of John Winthrop was written more than forty years before Taylor's "Relation," and yet there is little substantial difference between them. Taylor's diagram of his experience can be applied to Winthrop's relation with little difficulty. Taylor divides the whole process of conversion into two parts, conviction and repentance. As it relates to the understanding, conviction is more precisely termed illumination, "but as it affects the Conscience whereby it turns its Checks upon the Will, and affections its properly called Conviction . . . and is a Singular Spur unto Repentance." In turn Repentance divides neatly into Aversion, "whereby the heart is broken of[f] from Sin," and Conversion, "whereby the Soule is carried to God in Christ." Conversion then flowers triply into Love, Hope, and Joy while Obedience works daily to carry on "the work of Repentance unto perfection."

John Winthrop dated the beginning of his progress in the Spirit from the time he came under the ministry of Ezekiel Culverwell, a prominent explicator of the ways of grace to non-separating English Puritans. Winthrop gives Culverwell's preaching as the means by which he moved, in Taylor's terms, from illumination to real conviction: "living there sometimes I first found the ministry of the word to come to my heart with power (for in all before I found only light). . . ." Thereafter the stages succeed one another so nearly according to ideal form that a modern historian of the Puritans can safely offer Winthrop's narrative as representative of "hundreds of others." The typicality of the Taylor and Winthrop narratives, then, provides a basis for discussing later developments in Puritan spiritual autobiography while indicating the pervasive uniformity of its structure and vocabulary in the seventeenth century.

It would be difficult, nevertheless, to find autobiographical compositions which are wholly barren of individuality. Taylor's definitive articulation of his spirit in another form is hinted at in some of the language of the "Relation" and in his closing affirmation of the significance of the meditative act. Winthrop's narrative, although it lacks the names and dates that make his *Journal* the indispensable primary record of the Massachusetts Bay Colony, shows the impact of events and controversies in which the writer found himself engaged as a public magistrate.

For Winthrop, the winter of 1636-1637, during which the **"Christian Experience"** was composed, was a period of reassessment. Although he would soon be governor again, resuming the leadership he had exercised over the Bay Colony from 1630 to 1634, he was now in the third year of his exile from power. As an assistant, and more recently as deputy governor, he commanded influence, but was still denied executive power. Although he had not sought office energetically, rather had "earnestly desired, at every election, to have been freed," he would nevertheless be driven to seek an explanation for his eclipse, alternatively in the "jealousy" of the freemen or in some shortcoming of his own. Immersion in the affairs of the colony had left little time for introspection. In England, Winthrop had kept a diary, his **"Experiencia,"** which contain several extended passages of self-analysis. Since arriving in New England, he had made no additional entries. Now, on January 12, 1636/37 he was beginning his fiftieth year of life and it was time for an accounting.

Impetus for autobiographical composition did not come from the calendar alone. In the previous October, Winthrop had received a letter from Roger Williams in Providence. Since Winthrop's timely and prudent suggestion that Williams might avoid deportation to England by setting his "course to Narragansett Bay and Indians, for many high and heavenly and public ends," there had developed a warm and mutually respectful correspondence between the two men. From his frontier outpost Williams was able to convey a good deal of useful information to Winthrop, especially concerning the movements and disposition of the Indians. A kind of dialogue developed between them, ranging over the issues on which Williams had been found to hold heretical opinions.

Assuming reciprocal understanding on Williams' side, despite his reputation for intransigence, Winthrop apparently felt no need to suppress the topics on which they were divided or to veil them in gentlemanly obscurities. In a letter whose contents are known only through Williams' reply of October 1636, Winthrop had posed six questions intended finally to wring an admission from Williams that he had caused a great stir over nothing. Williams' detailed reply argues that the dictates of conscience are unavoidable: "the stroke lies upon the very Judgment." Yet Winthrop had gone beyond frankness to call into question Williams' motives and spiritual estate. His sixth question implied that contentiousness as to doctrine was not the habit of the saints, that if Williams had grace he could not have set himself apart so easily from his fellow believers.

For the record, Williams repeated Winthrop's question to him: "You aske whether my former Condicion would not have stood with a gracious Heart etc.?" He then proceeded to emulate his own highest praise of Winthrop ("You beare with Fooles gladly because you are Wise") by drawing the most elementary of distinctions between reprobation and misjudgment. Surely Winthrop must be aware of the irony that he, and not Roger Williams, was espousing the perfectionism of the enthusiasts. "At this Quaerie Sir I wonder much because you know what Sinnes yea all manner of Sinnes (the Sinn unto Death excepted) a Child of God may lye in Instance I neede not." Too much the controversialist to forego examples, Williams then drove home his most telling point: "Instances I shall be bold to present you with: First doe you not hope Bishop Usher hath a

Gracious Heart? and 2ndly Doe you not judge that your owne Heart was gracious even when (with the poysoned shirt on your back) you etc.?"

In the breaking off of the last sentence one feels Williams' reticence to deal as sharp a blow as he had sustained. As a result the sense of the poisoned-shirt allusion is ambiguous, perhaps implying a comparison between Williams' position in the colony and Winthrop's as a Puritan in England, perhaps referring to the controversy over the Governor's authority that led to Winthrop's defeat in 1634. In either case, Winthrop would have to reply that he hoped his judgment had been right and his spirit gracious at the same time. Williams claimed no more for himself.

The Winthrop papers contain no reply to Williams' question unless it is the spiritual autobiography written three months later. Simultaneously, another question was taking shape, which Winthrop assumed responsibility for posing to himself before someone else could point out the necessity. The Antinomian controversy, an explosion into the horrified view of the Bay Colony Puritans of that enthusiasm which had always been implicit in their doctrine of election, claims John Winthrop as a leading though not decisive figure. At first he only observed, and recorded what he saw. He set down in his *Journal* such errors of the Church of Boston as "that the Holy Ghost dwelt in a believer as he is in heaven; that a man is justified before he believes; that faith was before justification, but it was only passive, an empty vessel, etc." Soon Winthrop attempted to enter the controversy directly by means of two compositions, a "Declaration" to demonstrate that faith preceded justification, and an irenic attempt at a "Pacification" between the parties. But in the review of his arguments which he requested from Thomas Shepard, Winthrop faced the charitably phrased question, "whether it will be most safe for you to enter into the conflict with your pen (though the Lord hath made you very able and fit for it)," followed by a systematic baring of the flaws in his amateur's arguments. This was in December of 1636. Five months later Winthrop would be elected Governor once again and have his chance eventually to sit in judgment of Anne Hutchinson.

Whatever his limitations in doctrinal controversy, Winthrop knew two things for certain: that Antinomians encouraged impiety when they preached the dangerous doctrine that conviction, repentance, and other preparatory stages of conversion had nothing to do with God's bestowal of free grace; and that the doctrine of free grace, as a cornerstone of Puritan piety, needed to be preached with all the rigor of a John Cotton. The very extremity of Anne Hutchinson's position made it necessary to reaffirm an undistorted yet untained version of free grace and to allow, autobiographically, that he had just been rescued from creeping Arminianism: "The Doctrine of free justification lately taught here, took mee in as drowsy a condition, as I had been in (to my remembrance) these twenty yeares, and brought me as low in my owne apprehension as if the whole work had been to begin anew." The **"Christian Experience"** of John Winthrop is evidence that the public figure who sternly judged heresy welcomed the therapeutic effect of the Antinomian controversy on his own spiritual condition. A perfectly ordinary Puritan statement of the author's private dealings with his spirit, it nevertheless implies everywhere an involvement in a complex outer world of issues and personalities.

The conventional features of Puritan autobiography appear early in the **"Christian Experience."** Winthrop's opening statement, "In my youth I was very lewdly disposed," could be transposed to any of hundreds of other narratives without notice and with no special discredit to its new owner. Puritan autobiographers also suffered chronically from an adolescent disease that masqueraded as true conviction until it disappeared and left good health and a heart more depraved than ever: "But so soon as I recovered my perfect health, and met with somewhat els to take pleasure in, I forgot my former acquaintance with God, and fell to former lusts, and grew worse then before." Given the constant recurrence of these conventional features, it is not too severe a judgment to say that many spiritual narratives of the period were not so much composed as recited. The luxury of reducing past experience to predictable ritual was denied Winthrop, however, by the impact of his present experience. The narrator of the **"Christian Experience"** has been stirred to validate in autobiography his conviction that faith precedes justification and is the free gift of God, even though man must reach out his hands to receive it; and in an implicit concession to Roger Williams, he comes to acknowledge that there are ways for the justified man to offend God which the natural man has not dreamed of.

To begin, Winthrop describes the limited contributions made toward grace by his natural abilities. In his youth he had simply extended the application of certain "logicall principles" with which he was acquainted, and had achieved a better "understanding in Divinity then many of my yeares." Those years, which for many were "wild" and "dissolute," were somewhat less shameful for Winthrop because of the restraint he had felt imposed upon him by "natural reason" and the "sad checks of my naturall Conscience." This much, it could be admitted to the Antinomians, the Spirit had no part in. But through the means of Mr. Culverwell's ministry, grace began to make itself felt, "so as there began to bee some change which I perceived in my self, and others took notice of." How did these "strong excersises of Conscience" differ from the natural workings of conscience he had already experienced? Paradoxically, they prove themselves the work of the Spirit by leading to defeat rather than victory. Winthrop's irony gradually undermines the triumph that had seemed to proceed from his penitential fever at age fourteen: "I betook my self to God whom I did believe to bee very good and mercifull, and would welcome any that would come to him, especially such a yongue soule, and so well qualifyed as I took my self to be." Rather, the soul that would take its life from the Spirit of God first had to suffer total defeat. It was a battle, Winthrop saw, which he could not have won, whatever the strength of his depravity: "hee left mee not till hee had overcome my heart to give up itself to him, and to bid farewell to all the world, and untill my heart could answer, Lord, what wilt thou have mee to doe?"

For a time, Winthrop remembers, his only solace in defeat was a measure of "peace and comfort"; then came a gradual onset of delight and zeal, but in unsettled patterns. Could the autobiographer identify justification at the basis of these feelings? Had he consulted Anne Hutchinson, Winthrop would not have been assured by her probable reply. Whereas most Puritan ministers would counsel that a tree is known by its fruits, Anne Hutchinson maintained that "no sanctification can help to evidence to us our justification," as Winthrop reported in his *Journal*. For Mrs. Hutchinson, the soul knew of its graciousness by an "immediate revelation" or not at all. The full cruelty of this position was only too clear to one who had experienced repeated "tremblings of heart" and "plunges," who had feared he "was not sound at the root" and so received the praise of others as "a dart through my liver." In its naked irrationality, Mrs. Hutchinson's thinking was fearlessly consistent with the essence of the Puritan attitude toward conversion and divine sovereignty. Yet it would have had nothing to offer the self-accused hypocrite Winthrop described: "It was like hell to mee to think of that in Hebr:6," Paul's promise of damnation for those who fall away from repentance. Before he had ever heard of Anne Hutchinson, Winthrop implies, he had rejected the import of her thinking. Whatever uncertainties were involved in distinguishing God's determinations in the impalpable, a man pondering the fate of his soul preferred to scrutinize such evidence under the tutelage of Mr. Culverwel rather than wait for a thunderclap and bolt of lightning that might never come.

Hence the theological ambivalence of the John Winthrop we see portrayed in the **"Christian Experience."** Within the range of emphases which comprised Puritan orthodoxy, he appears first near the border which separated the impious doctrine of works from the legitimate search for evidences of salvation; then he appears as a bright embodiment of the doctrine of free grace, to be distinguished from the irrational intensity and lurid illuminism of the Antinomian. Of the two positions, the latter is more consciously assumed, in response, as Winthrop notes, to recent controversy. Even as one grants that the emphases may well have been compatible in the sequence of Winthrop's experience, one feels the strain of incompatible terminologies. Reviewing a period when grace was highly dubious, Winthrop is inclined to describe himself as "looking to my evidence more narrowly." He recalls being alerted by one of Perkins' works to a "better assurance by the seale of the spirit," and looking within was ashamed that "in all this time" he had "attained no better evidence of salvation." Even when Winthrop makes a point for free grace, describing a period of fruitless bondage to mere duties, he uses the legalistic term "evidence" uncritically. "I was held long under great bondage to the Law . . . yet neither got strength to my Sanctification nor betterd my Evidence. . . ."

Only when Winthrop begins to shape his autobiography as argument is there a noticeable shift in terminology. The idiom in which the Antinomian controversy was conducted penetrates to Winthrop's description of "the time that the Lord would reveale Christ unto mee whom I had so long desired." In the **"Experiencia"** he had kept in England, Winthrop located the cause of spiritual depression in his too great attachment to the world, and had attributed his experiences of divine favor to rejection of "earthly pleasures"; but in the **"Christian Experience"** he restates the essential struggle of this period in specifically doctrinal terms. After he had realized that his "greatest want was fayth in Christ," Winthrop recalls, "it pleased the Lord in my family exercise to manifest unto mee the difference between the Covenant of grace, and the Covenant of workes. . . . This Covenant of grace began to take great impression in me. . . ." Now it was impossible to feel discontent "for want of strength or assurance" because "mine eyes were only upon his free mercy in Jesus Christ." This is scarcely an Arminian position, yet Winthrop is anxious to demonstrate its compatibility with the assumption protested against by Mrs. Hutchinson, that a process of sanctification helps to reveal prior justification: "And the more I grew thus acquainted with the spirit of God the more were my corruptions mortifyed, and the new man quickened". In a closing paragraph describing how he learned to value both justification and sanctification, the amateur theologian has given way to an autobiographer who is the sole authority for his argument. Shaped to the uses of the present, experience gave the lie to both Antinomians and legalists.

### Wilson Carey McWilliams (essay date 1973)

SOURCE: "John Winthrop: The Statesman," in *The Idea of Fraternity in America,* University of California Press, 1973, pp. 133-49.

[*Here, McWilliams discusses Winthrop's political ideas*

*as a system of thought "guided by the fraternal imperative."*]

John Winthrop was a political man by vocation, a reflective man by nature and faith. None defended more strenuously the prerogatives of a specifically political wisdom distinct from that of the church. Yet Winthrop never conceived of a political understanding which did not depend on religious teaching; he relied on scriptural and religious authority rather more, and secular classical writings rather less, than did his clerical contemporaries.

His thought consists of a series of reflections on practical politics. It does no violence to Winthrop's ideas, however, to see in them an order and consistency amounting to systematic theory. In fact, Winthrop merits the supreme accolade which can be given a theorist: his diagnosis of his own times is relevant to others. He is a permanent contemporary.

Man, for Winthrop, was above all a social animal. The "paradise" of his spirit was love, which could be found only where there was likeness. Akin to his fellows both in the flesh and in the image of God common to all men, man found his delight in their company. Love, however, was no longer easy for men. Adam's fall had destroyed the instinctive sense of likeness which God had granted him. Men were now left with a darkened understanding which made them feel separate from God and different from their fellows.

Although his emotions now barricade him from others, man may be led by nearness, familiarity, and affection to acknowledge likeness for some of his fellows. The soul may then be enabled to grasp a partial love, imperfect because it is distorted and incomplete. Only Christ's redemption can make possible a sense of likeness without contact and intercourse. Among men in general, distance causes a slow attrition of affection. Memory causes a momentary awareness of the weakness of human will; prayer may cause a miraculous revival of affection and concern. Both memory and prayer, however, offer fleeting exceptions to the rules which testify to the nature of man.

Natural law indicated, Winthrop argued, that all men should be regarded as friends. Race, ethnicity, and nationality had no status in nature. The earth was given to men in common, belonging to no man to the exclusion of others. The increase of men and their flocks, however, produced scarcity in the natural environment. Not all men could be helped in their need; some distinctions were necessary to determine priorities of aid.

---

**An excerpt from Winthrop's "Christian Experience" (1636):**

I was now about 30 yrs of age, & now was the time come that the Lord would reveale Christ unto mee, whom I had long desired, but not so earnestly as since I came to see more clearly into the covenant of free grace. First therefore hee laid a sore affliction upon me wherein he laid me lower in myne own eyes than at any time before, & showed mee the emptiness of all my guifts & parts; left mee neither power nor will, so as I became as a weaned child. I could now no more look at what I had been or what I had done, nor be discontented for want of strength or assurance, mine eyes were only upon his free mercy in Jesus Christ. I knew I was worthy of nothing, for I knew I could do nothing for him or for myself. I could only mourn, & weep to think of free mercy to such a vile wretch as I was. Though I had no power to apply it yet I felt comfort in it. I did not long continue in this estate, but the good spirit of the Lord breathed upon my soule, & said I should live. Then every promise I thought upon held forth Christ unto me, saying, I am thy salvation. Now could my soul close with Christ, & rest there with sweet content, so ravished with his love, as I desired nothing, nor feared anything, but was filled with joy unspeakable & glorious, & with a spirit of adoption. Not that I could pray with more fervency or more enlargement of heart than sometimes before, but I could now cry, My Father, with more confidence. Meethought this condition & that frame of heart which I had after, was in respect of the former like the reign of Solomon, free, peaceable, prosperous, & glorious, the other, more like that of Ahaz, full of troubles, fears & abasements. And the more I grew thus acquainted with the spirit of God, the more were my corruptions mortified & the new man quickened. The world, the flesh, & Satan, were for a time silent, I heard not of them: but they would not leave mee so. This Estate lasted a good time, (divers months,) but not always alike, but if my comfort & joy slackened awhile, yet my peace continued, & it would returne with advantage. I was now growne familiar with the Lord Jesus Christ, he would oft tell mee he loved mee. I did not doubt to believe him. If I went abroad, he went with me, when I returned, he came home with mee. I talked with him upon the way, he lay down with me, & usually I did awake with him. Now I could go into any company & not lose him: &, so sweet was his love to me, as I desired nothing but him in Heaven or Earth.

*John Winthrop, in* Life and Letters of John Winthrop, Vol. II, *by Robert C. Winthrop, Little, Brown, and Company, 1869.*

---

Hence, the Covenant of Nature: men formed an implicit agreement to divide the world and to establish barriers, rights of property, special obligations due to some men and not to others. All this derived from a rule of natural justice: that man should aid his fellow to the limit of his own necessity. When all men cannot be aided, Winthrop argued, man acts "by way of commerce," lending where repayment is possible, giving up to that point which endangers his own needs and survival.

The sinful nature of man, however, dominated by corrupted passions, evades the constraint of reasoned natural law. Fallen nature in man, dominated by self-love and the desire for security, is "worse than beasts." Realizing that the goods of the world are perishing and scarce, men are not content with satisfying their needs. They feel driven to "lay up treasures" against some future calamity, and demand more than they need. Scarcity makes the fraternity of nature imperfect; the anxiety of fallen man magnifies the imperfection, making men rivals more than nature requires.

Nonetheless, the rule of natural justice remains the law. All men are to be considered friends and brothers where possible; the expansion of fraternity is a standard of ethics and an aim of civil policy. All relations of natural men require an element of prudence; no perfect trust or fraternity is possible. The existence of evil demands precautions, and scarcity requires that a man look to his own needs. It is still essential, Winthrop argued, that we treat men as worthy of trust until there is a probability that they are unworthy. Mere possibility is not enough; to this extent, the burden of proof lies with the accuser. To adopt suspicion as a first principle is to poison the relations of all men. Even men in nature owe one another an obligation to distrust only as a last resort, and a duty of assistance until their own needs are certainly or probably endangered.

Natural justice, being based on the nature of man, contains no rules for enemies. By nature, men are not enemies, and given the fall, an established enemy is outside the law: natural man owes no obligations toward his foe. Christian man is "set apart" from other men by the existence of a law which regulates his dealing with enemies. The Christian law, however, frees the Christian from the excuse of natural necessity and prudence. It commands him to give even when his survival is endangered, requires him to love his enemies and to show them charity. It orders him, in other words, to be more perfect than nature. To natural men, these duties will seem burdensome; only to the Elect will they seem privileges. Nonetheless, to the extent that the "exclusive" standards of the Elect can be made applicable to human affairs, they consist only in a more intense obligation to establish fraternity among men.

### Citizens and Magistrates

Politics must be guided by the fraternal imperative, subject only to the limitation that institutions, though they can instruct man, cannot be "effectual" in changing man's nature. Ends and means tend to overlap in Winthrop's analysis; the good city becomes a series of interlocking fraternities, binding magistrate and magis-

trate, magistrate and minister, and magistrate and citizen.

The central role of magistracy is hardly accidental, given Winthrop's view of the nature of his profession. Economic management, which demanded the knowledge of man's material needs and the means to fulfill them, was clearly lower than statecraft—which, because it was concerned with man's humanity, must know man's whole nature, including his spirit.

The church shared that concern, but the church's concern with the temporal world is less demanding than that of the magistrate. Unlike the minister and his congregation, the magistrate cannot select his "members"; he must take men as he finds them. Moreover, while the church need make no promise of material rewards, the magistrate is charged with caring for the public good.

Politics, in other words, demands both a knowledge of the good and a knowledge of the means of attaining it, both good intention and successful action. Thus, to perform his task, the magistrate needs the knowledge and the power of God. The demands on him are more exalted, the certainty of failure clearer, than for any other "natural man." Indeed, the obligations of the magistrate are greater than those of the Elect, while his ability to fulfill them is less. Magistrates, then, have a special need for encouragement and reproof from others in their position who can be expected to feel and understand the burdens of office. The Elect enjoy a special fraternity; the magistrate calls out to his fellow governors from the depth of his personal need.

Minister and magistrate also shared a fraternal bond; despite their distinct skills, their aims were identical. The magistrate should seek the counsel of the clergy in matters of faith and morals (his concern for worldly success made the magistrate especially prone to errors of moral judgment). The clergy, in turn, should accept a part of the burden for the inevitable failures of magistracy in its impossible task. Each, too, owed the other the duty of encouragement and support.

Against the "check and balance" theory of many of his contemporaries, Winthrop asserted the necessity of "friendship and affection" among those charged with the governing and the guiding of men. The fear of friendship among governors, he noted, is a counsel of division and not of love, and is based on a Machiavellian and not a Christian theory of politics. It violates the natural law, elevating suspicion over trust, and if enforced will inevitably wreak havoc with the community by raising distrust to the highest level of civil relations.

Moreover, such a counsel and policy violates the responsibility which the citizen owes the magistrate. That responsibility is greater than that which the Visible Christian owes his minister. Since politics has fewer givens than the church, the citizen should allow the magistrate a greater latitude in choice of means and a greater indulgence in failure than he grants to the minister.

Legal and formal restrictions of magisterial power are simply foolish. There is no point in seeking to eliminate the temptation to evil; men should avoid the prideful effort to be "more severe than God." The temptation to tyranny will exist whatever legal devices men create. Yet such rules, though they do not eliminate the danger of tyranny, may make it impossible for the magistrate to perform his functions. Seeking to prevent merely possible evils, Winthrop argued, is folly if it requires a cost to present good (an excellent rebuke to many "tests" of permissible speech later adopted by the United States Supreme Court). It is as much as men can do, Winthrop pointed out, to render tyranny improbable.

Many commentators intent, like Parrington [in *Main Currents in American Thought,* 1954], on seeing Winthrop as an autocrat, have neglected the specific restraints he advocated and the powers he conceded to the people at large. First, he argued that the community may limit the magistrate by statements of purpose and by general rules, for the right of the people in "giving or withholding their covenant" is not to be abridged. This constituent power did not exhaust the sphere of public liberty. At least in Massachusetts, Winthrop conceded the right of annual election of magistrates, and himself expanded the suffrage beyond that implied by the original charter. Finally, the people had a right to offer "counsel" on all laws and taxes, "counsel" having the expanded meaning often associated with premodern usage: no law or tax might be levied without the consent of the public or its representatives.

The people, exercising the power of God "mediately" in civil affairs, create commonwealths, elect governors, and judge their performance. Winthrop insisted only that those who hold divine power show some minimal approximation of divine charity toward those they elect. In modern terms, Winthrop's "autocracy" consisted of no more than a modern executive expects as a matter of course: the right to apply general policy to particular cases fairly free from restraint. His arguments did not presume a naive faith in magistrates; they were directed against a naive faith in legislators.

Winthrop had a more fundamental reason for opposing extensive formal limitations of executive power. He realized that the effort to eliminate all the possible evils of government, especially at the cost of many of its possible goods, is an indication of a desire to retreat from civic responsibility. In the first place, such a course rejects any share of collective responsibility; it regards the people always as victims, and never as victimizers. Secondly, it seeks to protect private concerns from interference at a cost to public goods. Natural man is always prone to self-concern, always likely to forget that "particular estates cannot subsist in the ruin of the public." Some minimal risk of tyranny may be useful in inducing men to take some concern for the community. Moreover, the private interests of magistrates are more closely bound to the interests of the whole than are those of citizens engaged in private pursuits. "Mere democracy" tends to encourage privatism, faction, and disunity; some magisterial power is needed if the interest of the community is to be upheld—not because magistrates are radically different in nature from citizens (though hopefully of greater political ability), but because they are of the same nature. Both citizens and magistrates assume the burden of guilt that comes to the finite man who wields the power of the Infinite. They too owe one another the fraternal duties of encouragement and reproof, admonition and affection.

## Profession and Action

Like most Puritans, Winthrop emphasized the natural limitations which compel men toward association and covenant. His assertion of the interdependence of private and public estates is of this order. So too is his argument that God had created differences of talent so that "all men might have need of one another." Differences in special gifts force men to seek association, because no one man can be self-sufficient.

There were, however, two defects to natural scarcity: (1) unless all citizens have at least that abundance necessary to life, conflict between them is bound to occur, and (2) natural scarcity operates more strongly against the poor than the rich, against the weak than the strong. Differences of ability may compel men toward association, but the less able are subject to greater compulsion than their more fortunate fellows.

The remedy for these shortcomings of nature must be sought in law and political action. Nature is inadequate because nature does not recognize, as men must, that differences in special gifts reflect no differences of merit. Winthrop carried his fraternal principles into economic policy; the state must guarantee minimal sustenance to all, and curb the excesses of the wealthy.

There was no doubt that wealth was perilous. Affluence led man to a dangerous feeling of independence, tempting him to believe that injury to the public might benefit his private fortune. The state, in Winthrop's view, must always prevent "oppression," which included usury and excess profiteering. The rich in Germany, he observed, had ignored the plight of the poor, and in their subsequent ruin could be read the moral lesson that each is bound to all.

His economic analysis went further than moralism. The state of English affairs had always disturbed him. "The land grows weary of her inhabitants," he had written; depression, poverty, and unemployment seemed to lie over Britain like a decree of judgment. Winthrop perceived, however, that this was the result not of nature but of defective civil policy. An early form of the "revolution of rising expectations" was sweeping England. A "riot of intemperance" was sweeping the land; men demanded more than was necessary and desired "fripperies" and luxuries of all kinds. The old upper limits to ambition had been swept away, and men were forced to struggle merely to maintain their station. "No man's estate is enough to keep sail with his equals." Compelled to seek an expansion in wealth and revenue, the aristocrats laid an increasingly hard hand on the poor. Change had introduced anxiety and insecurity, and had reintroduced the rapacity of man in the state of Original Sin.

Not all the ramparts of the English conscience had been destroyed. Rather, Winthrop observed that when some men practice acquisitive ethics with impunity, all men are confronted with a choice between imitating the unrighteous or suffering from their greed and lack of scruple. The Elect might choose to lose sustenance rather than engage in evil; unredeemed man must defend his own needs. The task of the state, which the royal government had not performed, is to avoid the necessity of such choices by preventing the unrighteous from acting with impunity. Failure to act is encouragement of evil. The failure of the state also laid a burden on the Visible Christian, who must do his duty and seek to set his fellows an example, even at the cost of suffering. In a fine rebuke to Roger Williams' separatism, Winthrop wrote that most Englishmen were doubtless corrupt but

> whores and drunkards they are not. Weak Christians they are indeed, and the weaker for the want of that tender care that should be had of them, (1) by those that are set over them to feed them and, nextly, for that spiritual pride that Satan rooted into the hearts of their brethren, who when they are converted do not and will not strengthen them but also censure them to be none of God's people nor any Visible Christians.

Fortunately, men did not need to face the choice between unrighteous action and natural suffering. A continent lay open in which God had made it possible for man to enjoy the earth's fruits without despoiling his fellow. Moreover, the example of a fraternal community might stir the hearts of men in England. England, apparently, was hopeless. Puritans could not bear adequate witness to God's word, let alone to their social principles. The unredeemed must judge men by their works; the Visible Christian, limited by the natural law, could only guide himself by what was possible in the environment of acquisitiveness. Isolated in scattered communities and surrounded by hostility, the Puritan in England could not be expected to set a standard much beyond that of his fellows. At best, he could suffer with them; he could make little demonstration of the positive goods that might be men's. In America, Puritan political principles might receive an adequate test.

Martyrdom was not infrequent in England, but the cause of martyrdom itself illustrated the limitation of the English environment. Persecution was based not on Puritan action, but on Puritan profession. The church could not require its members—most of whom would not be of the Elect—to go much beyond a statement of intellectual conviction. Action lies in the sphere of physical nature; profession is the public statement of an intellectual creed. Being free from emotion's control, the Elect may be expected to act rightly in both respects. The merely Visible Christian has made a statement of his conviction, but he cannot be assumed to control his emotions and physical desires so long as he is isolated. Lonely man, without his brothers, Winthrop implies, is cowardly man, and while he is alone no more than profession can be expected of him. Profession itself, at best half a faith, becomes an "agony" and a virtue; those who fall away do no more than might be expected.

In New England, however, Winthrop argued that "cohabitation and consortship," the intimate, daily support of brethren, raise men above what is to be expected of the average Puritan in England. "What most do in their churches by profession only," he admonished his fellow colonists, "we must bring into familiar and daily practice"; surrounded by his fellows, the New Englander had less excuse than his persecuted brother at home for falling short in the practice of fraternity.

> We must entertain each other in brotherly affection; we must be willing to abridge ourselves of our superfluities for the supply of others' necessities; we must uphold a familiar commerce together in all meekness, gentleness, patience and liberality. We must delight in each other, make others' conditions our own, rejoice together, mourn together, labor and suffer together; always having before our eyes our commission and community in the work, our community as members of the same body.

Winthrop was to write Hooker that New Englanders were brothers in three senses: (1) in peril and envious observation, (2) in consocation, and (3) in the work of God. The three correspond to the humanly-possible covenants of Puritan theology: the Covenant of Nature for "mutual encouragement and succor" against peril; the Civic Covenant, made possible by delight in association; the Church Covenant, produced by an intellectual conviction of the truth of the Word.

In at least two senses, New England differed from other states. First, there was no necessary conflict between the higher and lower covenants. Second, although the pattern of narrowing exclusiveness would apply—not all would be citizens or churchmen—it would be much softened. New Englanders would be far more equal in dignity and obligation than most communities. We, Winthrop asserted, are part of a fraternity closer than that which bound Israel to Moses, for with us there are no intermediaries between us and the Lord.

Winthrop's standard for New England was based on the theory that the standards of the Church Covenant, the best of all human covenants, can be made applicable as a standard for political practice if there is no hostile political environment to be taken as a given. Winthrop added to the traditional covenant theology of Puritanism the belief that, in the best circumstances, the magistrates and citizens of a Christian community could be elevated to a plane of equality with the church covenant itself; the secular and sacred could be of equal dignity where profession became the standard for action.

### Promise and Peril

New England's opportunity partly depended on her peril, a situation which had led many to wonder whether the new continent had been meant for Christian men. The entire structure of covenant theology had been premised on natural scarcity and a hostile environment. Within the covenants, man learned to see his fellows as his chief support against the rigors and insecurities of the world. At the same time, the rigors were required to drive men into the covenants. Indeed, whatever obligations it imposes, a hostile environment can make the community a thing of joy. Lacking an adverse environment, the duties of community may appear an onerous burden to be avoided where possible. And the Puritans encountered such a situation in New England; after an initial period of hardship, the force of natural scarcity was drastically reduced.

Winthrop had rebuked his English critics, who saw migration as a pursuit of ease and comfort, by asserting that life in New England would be hard, and success unsure. Winthrop was right about the early stages, but he never believed that those early conditions would last long (hence his belief that men might enjoy the fruits of the earth without conflict in New England). Before the colonists landed, he stressed the danger that they might pursue "carnal intention" and "fall to embrace this present world, seeking great things for ourselves and our posterity."

Life in America may have been hard, but land abounded, which to a traditional people meant wealth. In America, unlike England, intensive cultivation was not necessary and cooperative agriculture added little to individual well-being. John Cotton, in a phrase that was to have echoes, later denounced those who sought "elbow room" to the detriment of the community. Winthrop felt that punishment was deserved by those who would "enlarge their ease and safety" by deserting their fellows. Yet Winthrop had no doubt that in the new world such a course of action was possible; in America nature no longer compelled men into the civic covenant.

Winthrop's use of the phrase "ourselves and our posterity" was also a portent. Even in America, the Covenant of Nature was necessary for the individual, and the family retained a positive meaning. In England, the Puritans had seen the family as more exalted than the state, the arena where social reformation might begin. That emphasis, however, was only negative; since a corrupt state prevented action in the political sphere, the Puritan must make do with what he had by seeking to reconstitute the family in terms of the higher covenants. In America, the traditional Puritan emphasis on the family could serve to justify a different belief: that the family is more exalted than the state—or, however muted, than the church. The temptation to raise the status of the family arose from the primary temptation to remain a member of the Covenant of Nature alone.

The political community and the church could, of course, force the individual into membership in default of natural scarcity. Yet Puritan theorists understood fairly well that force applied by the community might constrain the individual from yielding to the temptations of nature, but it could not create the sense of political obligation. His consent, freely given, was always necessary. If the community were a burden and not a joy, a man's allegiance would lie with the Covenant of Nature, even if his body were compelled to serve the Civic Covenant.

Winthrop never slighted that understanding. His sterner colleagues always found him lenient. His generosity was partly due to his realization that in America, nature is unreliable; since it does not compel men into the political community, they must be induced to enter it. He feared harshness for the same reason he feared a "mere democracy." To transfer rule to the many is to give scope to their desire to reduce obligations; to treat the many harshly is to increase their resentment and thus heighten their desires to be rid of political obligation.

Most of the institutions of Puritanism were framed on the expectation of persecution by (or at least, alienation from) a surrounding political community. Congregational organization and class distinction argued for conflict as soon as the Puritan lost a sense of the salience of the factors which, uniting him to his fellows, set him apart from others. The Puritan institutions were designed to maximize intensity among a people already set apart from their kindred-in-blood and their kindred-in-politics, to provide support against the older ties and the threats of persecution which might lead a man to betray his own convictions. Winthrop did not always realize the significance of the change in political context which New England confronted, but its dissolutive tendency only emphasizes his thesis.

Winthrop understood that where neither the negative forces of nature nor a hostile community exist, the force of cohesion must be sought in positive moral obligations. The conscience of the individual must compel where man and nature do not. From the beginning, Winthrop defined the peculiar covenant of New England in terms which by the standards of Puritanism made it virtually impossible to fulfill. He demanded that New England produce the best possible human state, the best possible men, the most perfect of human fraternities.

His phrases were not the result of confident self-righteousness. In part, Winthrop's anxiety about the result explains his eagerness to pursue the "errors" of Roger Williams or Anne Hutchinson out of the Commonwealth. To many of his admirers, such as Morgan [in *The Puritan Dilemma,* 1958], Winthrop's conduct in the Hutchinson trial is the weakest moment of his career. Yet Mrs. Hutchinson, like Williams, taught a doctrine whose implications led directly to individualism. Against the positive moral obligations and the negative force of guilt which Winthrop hoped to inculcate as supports for man and for fraternity in New England, both Williams and Hutchinson appealed to a private moral insight which could justify men in their desire to remain in the Covenant of Nature. . . .

Winthrop feared Williams' teachings because they might encourage what was base in New England, might cause her to lose her glorious opportunity and become no better than the human average.

The permanent legacy of Winthrop to American thought is his realization of the American promise and the conditions under which Americans labor in seeking its fulfillment. . . . Heretofore, he might have said, all fraternity save that of the Elect (and to a small degree, the church) has been based on the effort to escape from the mastery of nature and of men. America, freed from such mastery, must now essay a giant stride, must seek to be mastered by a higher vision. Struggle against fathers in the flesh must yield to duty to the Father in the spirit of men,

> but if our hearts will not obey but shall be seduced and worship other gods, our pleasures and profits, and serve them, . . . we shall surely perish out of the good land whither we pass over this vast sea. . . .

That prescription was not one in which the Puritan, by his psychological or political theory, could maintain much hope. It was an intellectual last resort, almost a counsel of despair. Winthrop's own forebodings found confirmation in practice, and his influence, like the religious tradition in general, lies in its effects on the ideas and guilts of Americans more than the conduct of American life. Yet symbols have their power. The duty to establish the best city, short of which no failure is adequate or excusable: is that not the definition of the American dream?

## Richard S. Dunn (essay date 1984)

SOURCE; "John Winthrop Writes His Journal," in *The William and Mary Quarterly,* third series, Vol. XLI, No. 2, April, 1984, pp. 185-212.

[*In the following essay, Dunn examines the style, structure, and content of the journal Winthrop kept between 1630 and 1649.*]

Stored in the manuscript vault of the Massachusetts Historical Society within a locked case of handsome Victorian design are two fragile vellum-covered notebooks in the distinctive and devilishly difficult handwriting of John Winthrop, first governor of Massachusetts. These are the first and third manuscript volumes of Winthrop's journal, the prime source for the history of the Bay Colony from 1630 to 1649. In the first of these notebooks, measuring 7 1/4" x 5 3/4" and containing 188 pages, Winthrop made 169 pages of entries, starting on March 29, 1630, and running to September 14, 1636. There was once a second notebook with 358 pages of entries running from October 1636 to December 8, 1644; this volume was accidentally destroyed in 1825. The third notebook, measuring 10" x 6 3/8" and containing 186 pages, was only two-thirds filled when Winthrop died; he made 128 pages of entries in it, running from September 17, 1644, to January 11, 1649. This set of texts is surely the most baffling of all major early American documents to decipher or to edit. The handwriting in the two surviving volumes is notoriously hard to read, the ink is faded, the paper is often stained, worn, or torn, and the text is studded with marginalia, insertions, cancellations, and underscorings. Since the middle volume (containing 52 percent of Winthrop's text) is lost, the reader has to use a modernized transcription for this section, published by James Savage in 1825-1826, that obliterates many of the nuances in the original manuscript. It is safe to say that no one will ever publish a satisfactory edition of this remarkable document.

Problems start with the title. The work is alternatively known as ***The Journal of John Winthrop*** or as ***The***

*History of New England*. Winthrop himself did not call it a *journal*, at least directly, but he did call it a *history* and also an *annals*. When he began writing in his first notebook, he supplied no title but plunged directly into the opening entry:

>       Anno domini 1630: march 29: mundaye.
> Easter mundaye:
>
> Rydinge at the *Cowes* nearest the Ile of wight in the *Arbella*, a Shippe of 350: tunes whereof Captaine Peter Milborne was master. . . .

As Winthrop moved to his second notebook he wrote at the top of the opening page, "A Continuation of the History of N: England," and when he reached the third notebook he wrote on the outside cover, "3: vol booke of the Annalls of N: England," and inside on the opening page, "A continuation of the Historye of N: England." The dictionary definitions of these terms overlap, but the essential feature of a journal is that it is a daily or regular record of events noted down as they occur, whereas a history is a more formal narrative of events arranged systematically and usually after the fact and an annals has the added characteristic of being written year by year or arranged in yearly sequence. The trouble with Winthrop, as we shall see, is that he began by keeping a daily journal in 1630 and then recorded entries less frequently and regularly and wrote them up at greater length, so that by the 1640s he had converted his work into a form of history.

Over the years many people have endeavored to read, transcribe, and edit Winthrop's notebooks. For 150 years after the governor died in 1649 no one attempted publication, but such worthies as William Hubbard, Cotton Mather, Thomas Prince, Ezra Stiles, Jonathan Trumbull, and Jeremy Belknap borrowed the manuscript volumes from the Winthrop family for extended periods. From about 1755 to 1816 the third volume disappeared among Thomas Prince's books in the tower of Old South Church. Thus when Ezra Stiles copied from the manuscript in 1771 and Governor Trumbull and his secretary John Porter transcribed it in the 1780s and Noah Webster finally published it in 1790, these four gentlemen had only the first two volumes to work with. Webster's edition was entitled *A Journal Of the Transactions and Occurrences in the settlement of Massachusetts and the other New-England Colonies, from the year 1630 to 1644: written by John Winthrop, Esq. First Governor of Massachusetts: And now first published from a correct copy of the original Manuscript*. Webster had not read Winthrop's manuscript. He printed a transcription of the first two volumes by Porter, who was a much more exact transcriber than Stiles but whose copy was not as "correct" as Webster claimed, for it was marred by many hundred misreadings and omissions. The first two notebooks were given to the Massachusetts Historical Society in 1803 by the Winthrops, and the third in 1816 after it was discovered in Prince's library. When the task of transcribing this third book for publication "seemed to appall several of the most competent members" of the Society, James Savage (the librarian of the organization) undertook the job. He soon decided to prepare a new edition of the entire work, which he published in 1825-1826 under the title *The History of New England from 1630 to 1649. By John Winthrop, Esq. First Governour of the Colony of the Massachusetts Bay. From his Original Manuscripts*. In 1853 Savage reissued his edition with the same title and text but expanded annotations. He was a very painstaking, dogged, and shrewd judge of Winthrop's hand, and his reading of the text was a vast improvement over Porter's. But Savage did not make a complete transcription, for he ignored many of Winthrop's marginalia, memoranda, and cancellations as unimportant. He took liberties with Winthrop's language, and unhappily he also took the liberty of borrowing Winthrop's manuscript from the Society in order to work on it in his office, where on November 10, 1825, a fire destroyed the second volume. Thus Savage was both the first and the last editor to study all three of Winthrop's notebooks.

In 1908 James Kendall Hosmer published what was in effect a streamlined version of Savage's edition under the hybrid title *Winthrop's Journal, "History of New England," 1630-1649*. Hosmer made no effort to re-read the two surviving notebooks, but he reproduced Savage's text in larger print, with simpler annotations and a better index. He divided the narrative into chapters, one per year, which Winthrop had not done, and he expurgated a few passages that he considered "repulsive," such as Anne Hutchinson's monstrous birth, or too sexually explicit, such as William Hatchet's copulation with a cow. In 1931 the Committee of Publication of the Massachusetts Historical Society took a quite different approach. These editors decided, like Hosmer, to publish *The Journal of John Winthrop* (as they called it) in chapters or annual installments, but they intended to intersperse these installments among the governor's correspondence and other writings in the *Winthrop Papers* series and to reproduce the author's language as literally as possible. Only the first installment of this edition appeared: Winthrop's journal for 1630 in the *Winthrop Papers,* Volume II. Now, more than half a century later, Laetitia Yeandle and I have prepared a fifth edition of Winthrop's magnum opus. Drawing heavily upon the cumulative labors of our predecessors, we have devised a compromise text in which the opening and closing sections follow the original manuscript more closely than the middle section in Savage's modernized style; our edition will be published under the title *The Journal of John Winthrop, 1630-1649*.

Living closely with Winthrop's text, as I have been

*Title page of the second (1644) edition of Winthrop's* A Short Story
. . . of New England.

forced to do, has convinced me that the governor's notebooks offer an exceptional opportunity to study a seventeenth-century author at work. This opportunity is especially rewarding in the case of Winthrop, since he was both chief actor and chief recorder in Massachusetts for two crucial decades. He did more than any of the other Puritan founders to shape events and also to shape the historical perception of those events. One could doubtless learn a good deal more about Winthrop as a writer if the middle volume of his manuscript had not been burned. But it is possible, through examination of the two surviving volumes and related manuscripts at the Massachusetts Historical Society, to discover quite a bit about the governor's method of composition, to trace how he changed his method over time, and to demonstrate that these changes considerably affected the content and style of his narrative.

In March 1630, when Winthrop boarded the *Arbella* and opened his journal, he was a forty-two-year-old landed gentleman who had never participated in overseas colonization and whose interest in New England was extremely recent, but he brought to his task extensive expertise as a country squire, a city lawyer, and a

Puritan activist. Born on January 12, 1588, in Edwardston, Suffolk, he attended Trinity College, Cambridge, studied the law at Gray's Inn, served as attorney at the Court of Wards and Liveries in London and as justice of the peace in Suffolk, and inherited his father's position as lord of Groton manor. In his youth Winthrop became a dedicated convert to Puritanism, and over the years he formed a wide network of alliance with fellow Puritans. By 1630 he had a considerable family to provide for: he was married to his third wife, Margaret, and had seven living sons and one daughter. Groton manor contained some 515 acres and produced about £430 in annual income, placing Winthrop among the few thousand wealthiest men in England. But he had fallen into debt in the late 1620s, and was disgusted by the corruption (as he saw it) of English life and by Charles I's religious and political policies. When the king broke completely with his Puritan critics in Parliament in March 1629, Winthrop decided to emigrate to America. He joined the Massachusetts Bay Company, which had just received a royal charter granting broad powers of self-government. On August 26, 1629, he signed the Cambridge Agreement in which he pledged with eleven other Puritan gentlemen to move with his family to Massachusetts if the company government and charter were also transferred to America. The company shareholders accepted this plan, and on October 20, 1629, they chose Winthrop as their new governor. In the winter of 1629-1630 he organized a migration of about a thousand persons who would sail to Massachusetts in seventeen ships during the following spring and summer:

Winthrop had published no books or pamphlets when he started his journal, but he was a very experienced writer. His surviving papers from the 1620s, which are manifestly incomplete, include letters, diaries, treatises, and notebooks in a wide range of styles. To his wife, his children, and his dearest friends Winthrop could write rapturous and intimate letters in biblical cadences of love, reverence, and exaltation, but he was extremely careful never to employ such language in his journal. At intervals between 1607 and 1637 he also kept a private spiritual diary, which he called **"Experiencia,"** written partly in cypher, with many pages torn out and others obliterated. This notebook was his confessional, and it also was antithetical in style and content to the public journal he began in 1630. For example, in **"Experiencia"** he recorded in wrenching detail his deathbed parting with his second wife, Thomasine, in 1616, whereas in his journal he permitted himself only a succinct marginal memorial in 1647 to his beloved third wife, Margaret: "14 (4) In this sicknesse the Gouernors wife daughter of Sir Jo Tindale knight left this world for a better, beinge about 56. yeares of age: a woman of singuler vertue, prudence, modesty, and piety: and specially beloued and honored of all the Contry." But if Winthrop's **"Experiencia"** and his letters of love provided no models for the journal, other kinds of writing he pursued in the 1620s were more pertinent. As an attorney at the Court of Wards and Liveries from 1627 to 1629, Winthrop kept a docket of court cases in which he made summary digests of legal briefs—good training for the precise, terse, and sober expository style he aimed for in the journal. In 1627-1628 he compiled a notebook full of abstracts of sermons he had listened to, in which he reduced the preachers' lengthy expositions to lucid summaries—good training for the compact presentation of religious and political ideas and arguments in the journal. And in 1629, when he was trying to recruit emigrants to New England, he wrote a series of treatises designed to circulate in manuscript among fellow Puritans, in which he presented reasons for colonization, raised objections to these reasons, and answered the objections—good training for the gambit he adopted throughout the journal of stating both sides of an argument and then winding up emphatically in favor of the "correct" position.

Around October 1629, when Winthrop was elected governor of the Massachusetts Bay Company, he started to make entries in a new notebook, jotting down twelve pages of miscellaneous data concerning preparations for his trip to America. Among other things he noted the company's purchase of the *Arbella* for £750 and its contracts with a baker and a butcher in November 1629 to provide biscuit and salt meat for the voyage; he listed some of the people who were emigrating with him to Masscahusetts; and he drew a chart of the Massachusetts coastline from Gloucester to Salem (which he probably traced from a map supplied by Capt. Thomas Beecher, who had sailed to Massachusetts in the summer of 1629) to aid the last stage of the *Arbella*'s navigation to the company's American headquarters at Salem. Although none of these entries is dated, they all appear to have been made between late October 1629 and early March 1630. Winthrop arrived at Southampton by March 14, 1630, boarded the *Arbella* about March 20, and sailed across the Solent to anchor at Cowes, a port on the Isle of Wight, by March 22. One week later, on March 29, he flipped over the notebook he had been using and started his journal from the other end, so that his miscellaneous entries of 1629-1630 are now found upside down in reverse order at the back of the book.

Why did he start his journal on Easter Monday? Back in 1962 when I first commented on Winthrop's journal, I supposed that he chose this date as symbolic of the new life he was entering in moving from corrupt old England to a convenanted community in New England. But I now believe that Winthrop had a more prosaic reason: he supposed that his fleet would sail the morning. In fact, because of contrary winds the *Arbella* did not sail until April 8. The larger question, of course, is why Winthrop decided to keep a journal at all, and here I believe that his initial purpose was

simply to record the daily experience of what he knew would be a long and terrifying ocean voyage for the information of family and friends still in England who would be sailing in 1631 or after to join him in America. The year before, on April 25, 1629, Francis Higginson had started just such a sea journal when he crossed the Atlantic to join the Massachusetts Bay Company's advance settlement at Salem; Higginson finished this "True Relacion of the last Voyage to New England" (as he called it) on July 24, 1629, when he reached his destination, and sent it back to the company officers in London. Higginson's narrative made quite an impression on Winthrop. In October 1629, shortly before he was elected governor of the company, Winthrop sent from London to Suffolk a "booke" that can be identified from his description as Higginson's sea journal for his wife and children to read, and he asked his son Forth to copy part of it for distribution among neighbors "that haue a minde to N:E:" Between October 1629 and March 1630 Winthrop had been frantically busy with preparations for the trip. But now that he was on shipboard and could look forward to some enforced leisure during the voyage, he was in a position to perform the same service as Higginson.

The opening twenty-four manuscript pages in Winthrop's first notebook constitute his sea journal, which runs from March 29 to June 14, 1630, and systematically reports the events of every single day of the seventy-eight until the *Arbella* anchored at Salem. By inspecting the manuscript, noting the color of the ink, the thickness of the pen nib, the size of Winthrop's writing, and the slant of his hand, one can tell that he composed this sea journal directly as events occurred. He wrote the entries for fifty-seven days at fifty-seven sittings, and he wrote up the remaining twenty-one entries two or three days at a time. On April 15 Winthrop encountered his first Atlantic storm, and his notebook bears mute witness to this rough weather. The governor's hand danced about the page as he wrote: "About 10: at night the winde grew so highe and rayne withall, that we were forced to take in our toppsayle, and havinge lowed our maine saile and foresayle the strome was so greate, as it splitt our foresayle, and tore it in peeces; and a knott of the sea washed our tubbe overbord wherein our fishe was a wateringe." In narrating this sea journal Winthrop adopted the first person plural, a practice he generally followed thereafter. He referred to himself as "the governor" only twice and to himself as the author only four times, and he focused fat more on the actions of Capt. Peter Milborne, the commander of the *Arbella*. Winthrop's account contains much more concrete information than Higginson's journal of 1629 but offers fewer touches of drama or romance. His essential purpose was to record weather conditions and the ship's position, and he was so circumstantial that the *Arbella*'s route in 1630 can be traced with considerable accuracy. When he finally sighted the Maine coast on June 8, he expressed his joy in characteristic style: "we had nowe faire sunneshine weather, and so pleasant a sweet ethere, as did much refreshe vs, and there came a smell off the shore like the smell of a garden."

On reaching Massachusetts, Winthrop again followed Higginson's example and composed an account of the Atlantic crossing that he sent back to England. He reported to his son John on July 23, 1630, "for the Course of our voyage, and other occurentes you shall vnderstande them by a iournall which I sende with my letters to your vncle D"—that is, to Winthrop's brother-in-law Emmanuel Downing in London. In other letters Winthrop described this account as "a iournall and relation" and a "larger discourse of all thinges." He also sent home a chart of the *Arbella*'s route, prepared by Captain Milborne, and he directed that copies of his "iournall" be distributed to members of the family and friends. Since this "iournall" no longer survives, one can only speculate whether Winthrop copied it directly from his notebook sea journal. He cannot have added much new material, for he told his son John on August 14 that he had no time on first arrival to "make any perfect relation," and that he was still far too busy, so "I must referre you and all my freindes to my former reporte as it is."

Distracted though he was by the problems of settlement, Winthrop made the crucial decision to continue keeping a journal after he landed in Massachusetts. He never discussed his reasons for doing this in surviving correspondence, but he was clearly taking notes on events of public interest so that when he had the leisure he could write an account of the founding of the colony to be circulated like his sea journal. Winthrop had a fully developed conceptual framework within which to work. During the voyage he had composed **"A Modell of Christian Charity,"** his most celebrated and frequently quoted treatise, in which he explained to his fellow passengers their divine mission to create "a Citty vpon a Hill." He took it for granted that in Massachusetts, as in all societies, the leading men (such as himself) were endowed by God with riches, power, and dignity, while the followers would be poor, mean, and in subjection. But Massachusetts was also a community of Christians in collective covenant with God, so that the colonists had a special vocation to love and support one another and to obey the Lord's commandments. Should they serve the Lord faithfully, He would bless their efforts; should they deal falsely, He would destroy their plantation. Thus Winthrop's object in his journal was to chart the colonists' progress on their divine mission and to collect evidences of God's mercy and wrath.

However grand Winthrop's purpose, his entries during the first months in Massachusetts are maddeningly brief and irregular. Between June 17 and October 25, 1630, he recorded only two manuscript pages of entries, and

he was not much fuller in November and December 1630. In skeletal form he noted some of the basic events: the arrival of thirteen ships, the first meeting of the Court of Assistants, the formation of Boston church, the imprisonment of Thomas Morton of Merrymount, the deaths of several leading planters. On July 2 he also recorded a bitter personal blow: "my sone H[enry] W[inthrop] was drowned at Salem." He jotted a few entries once or twice a month, to judge by his handwriting and the color of the ink, and he left blank spaces for additions that he never filled in. Winthrop by no means conveyed the full gravity of the colonists' predicament in 1630. He never mentioned it in his journal, but he found on arrival that the servants sent ahead by the company in 1628-1629 had done almost nothing to prepare for the thousand new arrivals of 1630; they had not even raised enough crops to feed themselves. Winthrop was forced to release these servants from their indentures because he had brought no supplies to support them. The passengers on the Winthrop fleet were likewise short of food, the growing season for 1630 was well advanced, most of the livestock transported from England had died in transit, and shortly after landing the new settlers began to die of dysentery and scurvy. Amid these problems Winthrop supervised the settlement of six towns ringing Boston harbor, set up the colony government, traded with the Indians for corn and fish, and dispatched a ship back to England for emergency provisions. Massachusetts might well have collapsed completely had the governor been less resourceful and courageous.

Winthrop's meager entries are particularly regrettable because other accounts of the formation of the Massachusetts system of towns and churches in 1630 are also extremely skimpy. Had he had more leisure, he might have explained why the incoming colonists created so many towns instead of all living together, why each town had its own gathered church of self-nominated saints, and why Winthrop himself as governor chose first to settle at Charlestown and then moved to Boston. But even if he had had the leisure, he would never have described the physical process of settlement—the way in which the colonists built houses and started farms in the widerness—for he always excluded such mundane matters from his personal correspondence and his journal. And he had his reasons for silence on many other issues. The journal was a semi-public statement by the leader of the colony, and in the crisis months of 1630 he reported nothing that might get him in trouble with his fellow colonists or with the company at home or with Charles I's government. Winthrop probably privately blamed John Endecott for mismanaging the advance settlement at Salem, but he said nothing about it. Naturally he did not care to advertise that some 200 settlers died within the first year and that another 200 left in dismay. He probably also purposely omitted mention of the chief political event of 1630, the General Court of October 19. There

Winthrop and his fellow magistrates pushed through new company rules whereby the magistrates' powers were expanded and the freemen's powers were restricted.

By the winter of 1630-1631 Winthrop was finding a little more time and inclination to make entries. He remarked with surprise on the bitterly cold weather and composed his first extended anecdote, which was about the harrowing mishaps of six Bostonians shipwrecked on Cape Cod, four of whom froze to death. In February 1631 he reported jubilantly on the return of the *Lyon* from England with the supplies he had ordered and twenty new colonists; he did not report that the *Lyon* carried more than eighty disgruntled old colonists back to England on her return voyage. Winthrop must now have felt confident that the survival crisis was ending. At the height of the crisis he had insisted in private letters to his wife that he did not repent coming, for he saw the sickness and mortality as God's mode of testing the colonists' corrupt hearts. Now he spoke openly on this subject in his journal. "It hather been allwayes observed here," he noted in February 1631, "that suche as fell into discontente and lingered after their former Conditions in Englande, fell into the skirvye, and died." From 1631 onward, a persistent theme running through Winthrop's narrative is that any colonist who deserts Massachusetts or who dares to quarrel with the colony government will be punished by God for his wickedness.

During 1631 Winthrop settled into a new form of record keeping, in which he took up his notebook two or three times a month, composed several entries at a time, and wrote at greater length than in June-October 1630. As he continued to work on the journal in 1632 and later years, he cut down on the number of dated entries but inserted more undated ones and said more each time he wrote, so that by the mid-1630s he was averaging nearly a full page each time he put pen to paper. The changes year by year in his mode of composition as he worked through his first notebook are summarized in the following tabulation:

| Period | MS pages | Dated entries | Apparent writing sessions |
|---|---|---|---|
| Mar. 29-<br>June 14<br>1630 | 24 | 78 | 66 |
| June 17-<br>Dec. 26<br>1630 | 4 | 26 | 11 |
| Jan.-<br>Dec. 8<br>1631 | 11 | 52 | 32 |
| Jan. 27-<br>Dec. 5<br>1632 | 20 | 44 | 28 |
| Jan. 1-<br>Dec. 27<br>1633 | 22 | 30 | 29 |
| Jan. 21-<br>Dec. 22<br>1634 | 32 | 44 | 45 |
| Jan. 13-<br>Dec. 10<br>1635 | 29 | 37 | 37 |
| Jan.-<br>Sept. 14<br>1636 | 27 | 34 | 6 |

Obviously, Winthrop never resumed the daily reports of his sea journal but decided instead to focus on three or four events per month, which he often wrote up at considerable length. There is almost no evidence in his first volume that he wrote retrospectively. At most, he discussed incidents a month or two after they occurred. Hence throughout this section of the journal we are introduced to events as witnessed firsthand, without benefit of hindsight. Furthermore, Winthrop seldom tinkered with his text after he set it down. He made many small stylistic revisions as he shaped his presentation, and he inserted occasional new material in the margin or in the text to complete a story or to make a cross reference, but only rarely did he introduce substantive changes in interpretation.

Did Winthrop have a historiographical model for his narrative? Clearly, he was little influenced by the pagan historians of classical antiquity or by such secular English chroniclers as Holinshed, Hakluyt, or Capt. John Smith. In the 1640s he cited Sir Walter Raleigh's *History of the World* (1614) approvingly, but Raleigh's all-embracing epic was no model for him. Doubtless he admired John Foxe's Book of Martyrs (1563), a longtime favorite among Puritan readers, but this work too was of little help, for Foxe memorialized the sufferings of individual Protestant heroes whereas Winthrop was describing an organic community in action. His design was much closer to William Bradford's *Of Plymouth Plantation,* and Winthrop very likely consulted with his Pilgrim neighbor as he wrote. The two men met in December 1631 and visited each other thereafter. Bradford tells us that he started to compose his history "about the year 1630," and he kept working on it at intervals until about 1647, two years before Winthrop's death. But Winthrop had a more obvious and powerful model than Bradford: the Bible. In the historical books of the Old Testament, most particularly Exodus, Deuteronomy, and Judges, he could find a story exactly to his purpose, recounting amid plentiful evidences of human backsliding and divine wrath how God's chosen people escaped from captivity and came to the promised land.

As he composed his first notebook Winthrop gradually changed his perception of his own role as author-actor. In large part he responded to changing circumstances. From March to June 1630, on board the *Arbella,* Captain Milborne was in command and the journalist kept himself in the background. Then for nearly four years, from June 1630 to his electoral defeat in May 1634, Winthrop was governor of the colony and very much the central figure in his own story. From May 1634 to his electoral victory in May 1637 (which occurred after the completion of the first notebook), he was demoted to magistrate or assistant for two two years and deputy governor for one year; he was no longer in charge nor always in agreement with governmental policy. The changes of june 1630 and May 1634 required adjustments in his presentation. Once he landed in Massachusetts, the governor could no longer stay in the background and had to determine how to write up his own public actions and attitudes, and how much attention to give to his personal experiences and private thoughts. When he was demoted in May 1634, he had to decide whether to continue to report as an insider and how much to distance himself from the new colony leaders.

As we have seen, on arrival in Massachusetts Winthrop was both brief and evasive. As he resumed reporting at greater length in 1631 and 1632 he wrote at first more freely about his personal experiences than about his public actions. He reported the adventurous night he spent lost in the woods near Mystic (October 11, 1631), his joyous reunion with his wife and children when they arrived from England (November 2-11, 1631), his explorations into the back country beyond Watertown and Medford (January 27 and February 7, 1632), and the birth of a son (August 20, 1632); however, he made no mention of the General Court's key decision of May 1631 to bar non-church members from becoming freemen or exercising any voice in the government of the colony. Gradually Winthrop stopped saying much about his private affairs and focused more on public policy, and he soon was reporting controversial matters that are not mentioned in the official records of the General Court or the Court of Assistants. Only through the journal do we learn that on April 12, 1631, the magistrates reprimanded Salem church for choosing Roger Williams as their minister, or that between April and September 1632 Winthrop had a series of ugly confrontations with the deputy governor, Thomas Dudley. Winthrop is especially frank and explicit in describing his quarrel with Dudley. On May 1, 1632, he criticized the deputy governor for resigning from office ("desertinge his place" was Winthrop's phrase) and accused him face to face of greed and ostentation in his personal habits. On August 3, 1632, Dudley

counterattacked with a barrage of charges that Winthrop was exceeding his authority and misgoverning the colony. At one point "the deputye rose vp in great furye and passion and the Governor grewe verye hott allso, so as they bothe fell into bitternesse." Winthrop devoted more than five pages to a recital of Dudley's complaints and his responses, thereby disclosing a number of administrative actions not previously reported in the journal or the colony records.

Why did Winthrop write so candidly and fully on these sensitive issues? Obviously, Dudley's charges touched a raw nerve, and he wanted to dispose of them as systematically as possible. By talking the issues out he could hope to win over the reader even if he could not convince Dudley, and he could also display his integrity as a reporter. Furthermore, by exposing Dudley's faults and demonstrating the triviality of his complaints, Winthrop was making the point that the deputy governor was much his inferior as a statesman. The two men became lovingly reconciled, according to Winthrop, and indeed the record shows that they were usually allies after 1632. But the portrait that Winthrop sketched of Dudley as a jealous, irascible colleague is bound to linger in the consciousness of any reader. It is the first of a long series of unflattering vignettes in the journal. Winthrop was not a real portraitist; he never described people in three-dimensional detail. But like Benjamin Franklin in his *Autobiography,* he had the trick of thrusting a few barbs into most of the personages who figure prominently in his story. Naturally, he found little good to say about such outright adversaries as Thomas Morton, Sir Christopher Gardiner, John Mason, Sir Ferdinando Gorges, Roger Williams, John Wheelwright, Anne Hutchinson, Mary Dyer, John Underhill, Samuel Gorton, Peter Hobart, and Robert Child. But he was seldom unequivocally positive about his fellow magistrates. John Endecott was rash and blundering, Roger Ludlow was intemperate, John Haynes was too rich, Henry Vane was a spoiled youth, Israel Stoughton and Richard Saltonstall were dangerous incendiaries, John Humfrey was a deserter, Richard Bellingham was dishonest. Likewise among the clergy, John Cotton was unsound, John Eliot was naïve, Thomas Hooker was aggressive, the Rogers brothers were quarrelsome, Hugh Peter and Nathaniel Ward were meddlesome. To be sure, Winthrop seldom dwelt on these criticisms; he had much more praise than blame for most of his colleagues and he freely admitted his own defects on occasion. Yet the reader who accepts his presentation will certainly conclude that the author of the journal was much the best and wisest public man in early Massachusetts.

By 1632, one of Winthrop's chief purposes in the journal was to explain and defend his administration, and as he pursued his critics his interpretation became increasingly one-sided. For example, on February 17, 1632, he described his victory over the people of

Watertown who had refused to pay taxes levied by the magistrates because they had no representatives at the General Court. According to Winthrop, these people were finally convinced of their error, "so their submission was accepted, and their offence pardoned. But actually the Watertowners were the winners in this dispute. The May 1632 General Court voted that two representatives from every town should advise the magistrates on taxation, and in the court records the two spokesmen for Watertown were listed first, ahead of the representatives from the seven other towns. This modest concession satisfied the freemen for two years, but in the spring of 1634 they agitated for a larger share of power. Winthrop is our chief source on what happened next. On April 1 the representatives from the several towns asked to see the company charter and, when they read it, discovered that the freemen were authorized to meet four times a year to make laws. Winthrop tells how he explained to the representatives that this procedure could not work because the freemen were too numerous and were not properly qualified to choose "a select Companye" (that is, deputies from each town), to legislate; furthermore, such a legislative assembly would consume too much time. When he wrote this entry Winthrop mistakenly supposed that he had settled the matter. But on May 14, 1634, the General Court voted to give the freemen appreciably more power and the magistrates less. It was agreed that the General Court had the sole power to legislate and tax, that this body was to meet four times a year rather than annually, and that the freemen in each town were to choose deputies to represent them in these meetings. Those freemen who attended the May 1634 court of election voted by secret ballot for the first time, and they chose Thomas Dudley as governor and Roger Ludlow as deputy governor. There was apparently a move to drop Winthrop from the board of magistrates, but John Cotton preached an election sermon against this, and Winthrop was kept on.

The General Court of May 1634 was Winthrop's worst defeat. The constitutional change was a greater blow than the electoral change, because Winthrop could not accept the new deputies from the towns as in any way equal to the magistrates; for the rest of his life he fought to restore the magistrates' independence and supremacy. But at the moment of defeat he concealed his feelings. One week after this court session he wrote a very positive description of life in Massachusetts for an English correspondent, explaining that "Our Civill Government is mixt," with power divided among the magistrates, deputies, and freemen. He seems to have wavered a bit before deciding just what to report in his journal. First he made two entries about minor proceedings in the May court, leaving two large blank spaces that he never filled in. Then he turned the page and wrote out a full account of Cotton's sermon, the election results, and the constitutional change. "Manye good orders were made this Court," he concluded; "it

helde 3: dayes and all things were Carried verye peaceably: notwithstanding that some of the Assistantes were questioned by the freemen for some errores in their government and some fines imposed, but remitted again before the Court brake vp: the Court was kept in the meetingehowse at Boston," It would be interesting to know whether Winthrop was among those questioned and fined, and why he canceled his concluding testimonial of harmony. Perhaps he found it too self-seeking. Certainly, one of the "good orders" of the May court was very irritating to him: a directive that ex-governor Winthrop make an account of all public monies and goods he had received and paid out during his administration. Winthrop does not say so in the journal, but he entered a statement into the court records in which he pointed out testily that he had disbursed over £1,700 for public use and received less than £400 in compensation.

The next three years of the journal, from May 1634 to May 1637, composed when the author was out of power, constitute the most interesting section of the entire narrative. Winthrop now wrote at somewhat greater length than before and concentrated on political events, and perhaps because he was no longer defending his own record he supplied more inside information about the controversial issues of the day. These were difficult years for the Bay Colony. In England, Archbishop William Laud's new Commission for Regulating Plantations served a writ of quo warranto against the Massachusetts Bay Company, and the Court of King's Bench ordered the company's franchise seized into the king's hands. In America many of the Massachusetts colonists joined Thomas Hooker and John Haynes in an exodus to Connecticut, Roger Williams was banished and fled to Narragansett Bay, the Massachusetts government plunged into a bloody war against the Pequot Indians, and in October 1636 the Antinomian controversy exploded in Boston. Modern commentators have questioned whether these events would have taken place, or would have been so disruptive, had Winthrop remained in charge. The journal encourages such sentiments by hinting (and sometimes openly stating) that matters in 1634-1637 could have been much better handled.

Yet Winthrop was neither as full nor as frank a writer as he later became. For example, his series of thirteen succinct entries on Roger Williams's stormy career, from the day that Winthrop welcomed this "godly minister" in February 1631 to the news of his mysterious disappearance from Salem in January 1636, raises doubts about what really happened and why. Winthrop presented Williams's rebellion against the Massachusetts church-state system as the work of a rigid and isolated fanatic who enjoyed no support outside Salem. In January 1636 Winthrop seemed quite as eager as any of his fellow magistrates to ship the banished man back to England. And yet Williams later claimed that Winthrop "privately wrote to me to steer my course to Narragansett Bay and Indians, for many high and heavenly and public ends, encouraging me, from the freeness of the place from any English claims or patents." The letters that Williams sent to Winthrop in 1636-1637, just after he came to Narragansett Bay, do read as though he regarded the ex-governor as his benefactor and friend. And was it just coincidence that the leading Bay magistrates and clergy convened a private meeting on January 18, 1636, a week or so after Williams's flight, and roundly criticized Winthrop for his "ouer muche lenytye and remissenesse"? Did they suspect him of giving covert aid to Williams?

On another sensitive topic, the exodus from Massachusetts to Connecticut in 1635-1636, Winthrop by no means "told all" in his journal. It is clear from his report of a week-long debate in the September 1634 General Court on whether Thomas Hooker and his followers in Newtown (Cambridge) should be allowed to go to Connecticut that feelings ran high on this subject and that Winthrop strongly opposed the move. The court records are silent about this debate, but Winthrop reported that the Newtowners finally bowed to the magistrates' opposition, "so the feare of their removall to Conectecott was removed." Unfortunately, he never explained when or why this decision was reversed. In the summer of 1635, as the migration began, Winthrop wrote cheerfully to an English correspondent, "we are putt to rayse new Colonys about 100 miles to the west of vs, upon a very fine river and a most fruitfull place"; he added that Hooker was going next year, but certainly *not* because of any quarrel he had with John Cotton. Winthrop's truer feelings emerged as he made a series of dolorous journal entries between October 1635 and November 1636 about the misadventures of the Connecticut pioneers, who nearly froze and starved in their new milieu and lost all their cattle. Clearly, neither the Lord nor John Winthrop was pleased with this migration.

The journal reaches its most dramatic point in 1636-1637 with the Pequot War and the Antinomian controversy. Winthrop narrated both crises as they developed, without knowing how either of them would turn out. In July 1636 he learned that a trader named John Oldham had been murdered by Indians from Block Island, and he quickly filled the closing pages of his first notebook with entries on the Bay government's efforts to track down the murderers and on Endecott's expedition of August 24—September 14 against the Block Island and Pequot Indians. Taking up another notebook, the lost second volume of the journal, Winthrop continued his story in the four opening entries of the new book, dated in October 1636, which describe the expansion of the war in Connecticut. Then in late October he made his first report on "One Mrs. Hutchinson," and it soon became evident to him that this "woman of a ready wit and bold spirit" was an even more dangerous adversary than the Pequots. During the next months he focused primarily on the Antinomians but supplied periodic progress reports on the Indian war until the Pequots were vanquished in August 1637 and he could concentrate full measure on Mrs. Hutchinson and her followers. Much was at stake for Winthrop in this contest. Anne Hutchinson's stronghold was Winthrop's own Boston church, and her supporters initially included John Cotton as well as John Wheelwright and Governor Vane. She and her followers were zealously bent on driving such pharisees as Winthrop out of office, if not out of the colony. According to the journal, Winthrop was the chief opponent of the Antinomians: in the Boston church he alone defended the beleaguered pastor, John Wilson, and blocked the appointment of Wheelwright as an additional minister of the church. At the magistrates' meetings he stood up to Vane. Winthrop reported that he also stood up to John Cotton, and he seems to have supplied much of the pressure that persuaded Cotton to switch sides. At the May 1637 General Court, Winthrop scored the most satisfying triumph of his career when the freemen in a tense and stormy meeting elected him governor and dropped Vane and two other Antinomain magistrates from office. In November 1637 the General Court consolidated this victory by banishing Hutchinson and Wheelwright and disarming or disenfranchising seventy-five of their supporters. In March 1638 the Boston church was finally persuaded to excommunicate Hutchinson.

Once restored to power, Winthrop used his journal more aggressively than in the early 1630s to defend his record and denounce his opponents. In January 1638 he made a list of the "foul errors" and "secret opinions" of the Antinomians. In March 1638 he discovered that Mary Dyer, one of Hutchinson's supporters, had been delivered of a deformed stillborn fetus, and in September 1638 he heard that Hutchinson herself had a somewhat similar stillbirth after she was exiled to Rhode Island, whereupon Winthrop examined witnesses, had the corpse of Dyer's child exhumed, and entered full descriptions of both "monstrous births" into his journal as proof positive that God had turned against the Antinomians. However, even at this time of passionate controversy, when he was pursuing through the pages of his journal a woman whom he detested, Winthrop kept his language sober and controlled. The fiercest denunciation of Hutchinson is found, not in the journal, but in a separate account of the Antinomian controversy that Winthrop assembled and sent to England in the spring of 1638; this account was eventually published anonymously under the title *A Short Story of the Rise, reign, and ruine of the Antinomians, Familists & Libertines, that infected the Churches of New-England* (London, 1644). Winthrop's *Short Story* is a patchwork compilation of documents enumerating the theological errors of the Antinomians and elaborating his journal account of how and why the Massachusetts government and clergy passed sentence against them. Whoever found Winthrop's manuscript in London in 1644, and published it six years out-of-date, certainly garbled parts of the text and possibly inserted the most vituperative passages in order to enliven the piece. However that may be, Anne Hutchinson in the *Short Story* became an "American Jesabel," "a woman of a haughty and fierce carriage" who was "more bold than a man," a "great imposter" who gloried in her excommunication, and an "instrument of Satan" who poisoned the churches of New England. Winthrop was certainly capable of this language, but he was careful to avoid such polemical terms in the journal when reporting on Anne Hutchinson or any of his other adversaries.

Winthrop's manuscript journal for this particular period can no longer be examined, because he entered the section from October 1636 to December 1644 in the lost second notebook. We know from descriptions by Ezra Stiles (who read it in 1771) and by James Savage (who worked with it from 1816 to 1825) that this book was a substantial volume, about double the size of the first, with 366 pages of text and end notes. Winthrop appears to have used it for other purposes before he began making journal entries in it. At one end of the book, starting in May 1636 (immediately after his election as deputy governor in tandem with Vane), he kept notes on some of the executive decisions made by the governor and magistrates, and he continued to keep this informal record until April 1638. At the other end he started a list of "Gifts bestowed upon this Colony from 1634," and he seems to have recorded the first several of these gifts in 1635-1636. But he did not need a thick book for this list, and so he turned over a few blank leaves and took up his journal. As we have seen, he supplied a title for his work: "A Continuation of the History of N: England." At the outset of the second volume he still organized his text in the format he had been using since 1632, with three or four dated entries per month. But as he kept working, this format gradually changed. By 1639 he had only two dated entries per month, and in 1641 only one per month. He never abandoned dated entries altogether, and throughout the 1640s he kept inserting one or two dates per month; but the majority of entries were now undated, and increasingly he wrote for several consecutive pages on the same topic, so that his narrative became less segmented and more continuous: in short, more of a history.

It must be remembered that Winthrop was the governor of his colony for twelve of the nineteen years he kept the journal, and that he was continually a magistrate; he was in charge in 1630-1634, 1637-1640, 1642-1644, and 1646-1649. By the late 1630s he was clearly drafting the official history of his administration, and as he continued this task he became bothered by three problems that have agitated many historians: how to

praise the virtues of living men, how to discuss human errors without prejudicing the reputations of those involved, and whether to reveal "secret hid things which may be prouoking"—in particular, Massachusetts's policy of evading and rejecting orders from the home government. In January 1640 he asked Thomas Shepard's advice on these points, and Shepard urged him to be candid "in the compiling of the History" and to leave tricky points for possible revision before publication. Basically, Winthrop followed Shepard's advice. As far as one can tell from Savage's transcript of the second notebook, the governor deleted or queried only a few critical remarks about Vane, Hooker, Bellingham, and the French Acadian commander Charles de La Tour, together with a few references to himself that could be construed as too personal and prideful. Reporting on the General Court of December 1641 "(for history must tell the whole truth)," he devoted several pages to Bellingham's misconduct as governor of the colony. To balance things he also blamed himself (but more briefly) for plunging into an alliance with La Tour in July 1643. While he was writing, Winthrop made occasional notes to himself on where to add further documentation. For example, on September 21, 1638, he reported that Charles I's Committee for Regulating Plantations had ordered the colony to send home the royal charter, and that the General Court sent a humble petition instead. "These instruments are all among the governour's papers," Winthrop noted, "and the effect of them would be here inserted." At the back of his notebook he filed two documents that he may have planned to insert in his narrative: a set of sixteen questions posed to Cotton in 1637 and a letter from Dudley in 1638. By the time he reached 1643 and 1644 Winthrop was copying into his text verbatim transcripts of such important documents as the Articles of Confederation among Massachusetts, Plymouth, Connecticut, and New Haven in May 1643, the submission of two Narragansett sachems in June 1643, and Massachusetts's treaty of October 1644 with the French commander Charles d'Aulnay. Two comments should be made about these transcripts. First, whenever they can be checked against the originals or against contemporary copies they prove to be remarkably accurate. Second, Winthrop was surprisingly catholic in his choice: a verbatim copy of his own speech rejecting Goody Sherman's charges that the rich merchant Robert Keayne stole her sow is no surprise, but why did he transcribe Parliament's letter of safe conduct for Roger Williams, with its praise for Williams and its stinging rebuke to the Bay government for persecuting fellow Puritans? One can only regret that he had not started this practice much earlier.

Winthrop changed his method of composition in another, more fundamental way during the course of his second notebook. He began to write lengthy sections of his narrative at a sitting, some time after the events described had taken place. This point cannot be proved incontrovertibly, since the original manuscript is destroyed, but close examination of Winthrop's wording discloses solid evidence of a change from frequent writing sessions and contemporaneous reporting in 1636-1637 to irregular writing sessions and retrospective reporting by 1643-1644. The opening forty or fifty pages of the second notebook, running from October 1636 through November 1637, read as though the author was continuing his practice in the first notebook: he was making frequent entries as things happened or very soon after. He jumped back and forth between the Antinomian and Pequot crises in tune with the latest developments, he changed his mind several times about whether the Antinomian crisis was dying down or heating up, and he altered his portrayal of several characters as his story line changed course. In November 1636 Governor Vane was a "wise and godly gentleman," in December he became a petulant child who burst into tears and flew into rages, and as he quarreled more and more openly with Winthrop he went from bad to worse. John Cotton was evasive in October 1636, belligerent from December 1636 to April 1637, cautious in May, and reconciled to the other clergy in August, at which point Winthrop wrote: "this sudden change was much observed by some." Finally, the Lord Ley "showed much wisdom and moderation" on first arrival in June 1637, but within a month turned into a confederate of Vane's.

When we move ahead four years and examine Winthrop's text from September 2, 1641, to May 18, 1642, it appears that this entire section of about twenty manuscript pages was composed in May 1642 or after, since it contains repeated references to the General Court of that date. And when Winthrop reached the summer of 1643, he abandoned strict chronology. He discussed his diplomatic negotiations with La Tour (June 12—July 14, 1643) before taking up the Goody Sherman sow case (October 1642—May 1643) or the debate over the magistrates' "negative voice" or veto power in legislative proceedings (October 14, 1642—June 5, 1643). I believe that the long interlocking section of Winthrop's text from May 10, 1643, to October 12, 1643, which must have filled nearly fifty pages, was all composed at about the same time, probably in late 1643. Looking back over the complicated developments of the previous months, Winthrop evidently decided to explain his support for La Tour and his opposition to Goody Sherman as fully and systematically as possible because he had been roundly attacked for mishandling both situations. At this stage, I think he was still writing fairly close to the events described. When he narrated the Massachusetts government's invasion of Rhode Island in October 1643 to seize the radical Puritan Samuel Gorton, he did not yet know that Gorton would be released from imprisonment in March 1644. However, sometime between October 1643 and September 1644 Winthrop seems to have stopped working on his notebook for a long period. When he

came to reporting on the imprisonment of another enemy, Thomas Morton, in September 1644, he also reported Morton's release in 1645 and his death "within two years after," or about 1647, all in the same paragraph. Unless he inserted this paragraph later (a possibility not mentioned by Stiles or Savage), he composed the closing pages of his second notebook in 1647 or 1648.

My argument that Winthrop changed his method of composition during the course of the second notebook is admittedly conjectural, but I reach firmer ground with the third notebook, which carries the narrative from September 1644 to January 1649. Inspection of Winthrop's manuscript indicates that he wrote 129 pages of entries in only about fifteen sessions; he seems to have set down 20 pages at one stretch, and 15 pages on three other occasions. Obviously, he was working very fast, and in consequence he made more slips and errors than previously. He wrote up ten entries twice over, deleted seven of these repetitions, but did not notice the others. Sometimes he got his dates wrong, especially toward the beginning where he placed three incidents in 1645 that actually occurred in 1644, and he similarly mixed up several events in 1647 and 1648. He filled up much space with verbatim transcripts of important documents; the twelve documents copied into the third book account for one-quarter of the text. Winthrop's style betrays haste; he has lost the compact precision, immediacy, and variety of expression characteristic of the entries from the 1630s. He may have felt that he had no time to lose, because he appears to have composed most or all of this notebook during the last few months of his life. He cannot have started it immediately after completing the second, because his initial page on the arrival of Madame de La Tour, dated September 17, 1644, repeats an episode already described in the closing pages of the second book. He cannot have started the third book in 1644 or 1645 because he misdated too many of the opening entries: And in three places he looked well ahead to future events. On the twelfth page of this volume, under the date July 3, 1645 (actually July 3, 1644), when discussing the erection of free schools, he made reference to a General Court order of November 11, 1647. Under the date July 1, 1645, when discussing the Cambridge synod, he made a reference to May 1648. And under the date November 5, 1645, when discussing Henry Greene's ordination, he noted Greene's death in October 1648. None of these references was inserted later. Thus Winthrop not merely abandoned his former habit of day-by-day or month-by-month record keeping; he started the third volume three or four years after the events described, and he composed nearly two-thirds of it between mid-October 1648 and early March 1649, when he became fatally ill and too weak to write any more.

Fortunately, there is a further clue to Winthrop's method of composition in the late 1640s. When Ezra Stiles read the second notebook in 1771 he found several loose papers tucked into the book, including a "single sheet" that contained "sundry Entries in the Governor's Hand continuing the Memoirs to 1648," and he copied several of these entries. Jeremy Belknap, who had possession of the second notebook in the 1780s and 1790s, removed the loose papers so that these documents escaped destruction in 1825 and are now among the Belknap Manuscripts in the Massachusetts Historical Society. The "single sheet" of "Memoirs to 1648" is a large piece of paper folded twice to make eight pages, on which Winthrop jotted notes. The first four pages list eighty-five incidents that Winthrop apparently intended to discuss in his narrative, arranged chronologically from July 1643 to May 15, 1648. The remaining four pages contain his reflections on sacred and profane history. Winthrop seems to have jotted down his list of eighty-five items at various times, to judge by his handwriting, and he crossed off the ones that he incorporated into his text. I believe that he began keeping these notes when he laid aside his journal/history so as to jog his memory when he went back to work. Although the first two items date from 1643, the list starts in a systematic way in June 1644; this supports my contention that Winthrop stopped work on his second notebook temporarily at about that date. There is a note on the burial of George Phillips, July 2, 1644, worded almost exactly the same as Winthrop's entry on Phillips in his second notebook; when the governor took up his narrative again he evidently transferred this note directly into his text. Seven other items from the "Memoirs" list are incorporated into the closing pages of the second notebook. But the chief value of this little list was that it provided a skeletal outline for the third volume. The last item on the list dates from May 1648, supporting my contention that Winthrop wrote most or all of the third volume after that date. Certainly, he made heavy use of the "Memoirs" list; he incorporated sixty-three of these items into the third volume, sometimes copying them verbatim. The "Memoirs" page of notes for 1647 and 1648 is headed "not yet entered," but actually Winthrop did incorporate eleven of the fifteen incidents listed on this page. Altogether, he omitted only fourteen items from the "Memoirs" list.

Winthrop's four pages of reflections on sacred and profane history in the "Memoirs" are also very interesting because they help to elucidate his purpose in writing the journal/history. He scornfully denounces "heathen storyes (which are of so greate esteeme amonge men)" because the principal function of these secular histories is to narrate the reign and exploits of Satan, "where nothinge is to be seene but the boysterous and ambitious spirittes of Princes, the salvery and foole hard[i]nesse of their Captains and soldiers wherby millions of men are destroyed, and sent to hell before their tyme." The wars and battles celebrated by "hea-

then" historians are unnatural as well as vicious in Winthrop's eyes, because nature teaches all creatures to avoid destroying their own kind. Only Satan could have inspired the princes and captains to commit such carnage and imperil the human race. For Winthrop the truly glorious human actors are the saints who serve the King of Kings: their deeds, sufferings, and triumphs are the true stuff of history. The only "good use" of profane history is when it sets forth the wisdom, power, justice, and clemency of God and discovers the malicious practices of Satan.

Winthrop certainly believed that he was recording a chapter in the endless contest between God and Satan, and he certainly supposed that his purpose was to document God's design in bringing His people to New England while testing them with many challenges. But when he began his journal he rarely discussed teleology. One of the few times he did so was in July 1632, when he reported "a great combate between a mouse and a snake" at Watertown in which the victorious mouse symbolized "a poore contemptible people which God had brought hither," and the dead snake was the Devil. Winthrop knew, of course, that the Devil would not stay dead, and in his second volume he recorded many evidences of Satan's efforts to destroy Christ's kingdom in New England through such agents as the Pequot Indians, the Antinomians, and the Gortonists. God and Satan figure even more actively in the third volume. Winthrop saw the mutiny of the town of Hingham against the magistrates in 1645 as "the workinges of Sathan, to ruine the Colonies and Churches of Christ in New England"; he rejoiced in God's displeasure with Dr. Robert Child and the Remonstrants, who had dared to petition Parliament against the colony government in 1646; he reported that a clergyman attending the Cambridge synod of 1648 killed another snake that invaded the meeting house; and he punctuated his manuscript with examples of providential deliverances and punishments. His final entry, dated January 11, 1649, told about five persons who had recently drowned by "the righteous hande of God."

Winthrop, in common with the heathen story tellers he scorned, devoted much attention in his second and third volumes to sexual scandal—to cases of rape, fornication, adultery, sodomy, and buggery—but of course his purpose was hardly the same as theirs. When he reported that William Plain of Guilford was executed for masturbating or that George Spencer of New Haven was executed for siring a piglet with human resemblances, he was exhibiting these specimens of human depravity as proof that even in godly New England the Devil was continually at work. He dwelt as much on the penitential scaffold scenes as on the crimes, for God always searched out these sex offenders and punished them justly. Winthrop also reported on the punishments that God meted out to the political and religious rebels who rejected the Massachusetts church-state system. Anne Hutchinson, the greatest rebel, received the harshest judgment; first her monstrous birth in 1638 and then her murder by Indians in 1643. John Humfrey, who deserted Massachusetts for the West Indies in 1641 and took many other colonists with him, was also severely punished: a barn fire destroyed his hay and corn to the value of £160, and three child molesters repeatedly raped his little daughter. Dr. Child, the chief of the Remonstrants in 1646, was publicly humiliated on the streets of London, "and besides God had so blested his estate, as he was quite broken." Ironically, Winthrop's own estate had been blasted a few years before this; in 1639 his bailiff, James Luxford, contracted debts in his name totaling £2,500, and Winthrop was forced to sell much of his property. The Massachusetts freemen dropped him from the governorship for two years after this happened, and one of the deputies tried in 1641 to have him dropped from office altogether because he was "grown poor." But Winthrop barely mentioned his financial troubles, and then mainly to grumble that the colonists only raised £500 in a voluntary contribution to help him, for he refused to accept his property loss as a providential sign.

The final volume was definitely more a history than a journal. On the cover and the first page of this volume, as we have noted, Winthrop supplied two variant titles for his work: *The Annals of New England* and *The History of New England*. The first is a misnomer. Winthrop never wrote up the events of a given year as a separate unit or chapter, the way a proper annalist like Bradford organized *Of Plymouth Plantation,* and in the third volume it is not always clear which year he is talking about. One can also quarrel with his second title, since Winthrop viewed developments beyond the borders of Massachusetts with deep suspicion. His news bulletins from Maine, New Hampshire, Plymouth, Rhode Island, Connecticut, and New Haven were mainly reports of crimes and disorders. Winthrop's prime topic in his second and third volumes was Massachusetts politics, and on this subject he was particularly concerned to answer each and every challenge to his administration. The two great set pieces in his third volume are the Hingham mutiny of 1645 and the Remonstrants' protest of 1646. Winthrop deliberately magnified both events. He was furious at the Hingham petitioners for bringing charges against him at the General Court, and he was furious at the deputies for entertaining these charges, so he wrote up his impeachment trial as a humiliating personal ordeal. He described very particularly how he sat through the trial as an accused criminal, below the magistrates' bench and with his hat off. He described how the magistrates eventually persuaded the deputies to exonerate him and fine the petitioners (this decision was less clear-cut than Winthrop reported), and he described how he resumed his magistrate's seat and lectured the court after the trial. Indeed, he inserted into his narrative the whole text of this masterful "little speech" on the liberty of the people and the authority of the magistrates.

In discussing the Hingham case, Winthrop criticized Peter Hobart and the other town leaders with particular sharpness. Perhaps he was thinking of Hobart when he wrote the following in his "Memoirs" statement on sacred and profane history:

> If the Author sometymes mention the faylings of magistrates and Elders by name, he is not to be blamed 1: because the Historyes of the Scripture doe it frequently. 2: they were public, and therefore could not be concealed: 3: he mentions his owne faylings as well as others. 4: It is for edification to knowe that all godly men in all places and tymes have their infirmytyes. 5: this wilbe a meanes to cleare them from more and greater evills which have been charged vpon them by malignant toungues. 6: this will helpe to cleare the truethe of their profession, when thoughe they have had their errors etc. yet they have not approved allowed themselues to continue in them, or to Iustife them.

When he came to deal with the Remonstrants, Winthrop had no compunctions about disclosing the failings of Child and his six colleagues, because these people were outsiders who were trying to subvert the colony government and place it under parliamentary supervision. In 1646 the Remonstrants' petition to the General Court posed a serious threat, because Parliament had already intervened on behalf of Roger Williams and Samuel Gorton and might well do so for Child. But Winthrop did not write up the Remonstrants' protest until late 1648 or early 1649, and by this time he knew that Parliament had rejected Child's appeal. Yet he filled twenty-two pages of his third notebook with a blow-by-blow account of the General Court's proceedings in order to justify and explain the court's actions. Perhaps he thought that these actions looked a little severe. The Remonstrants had been held in jail for months in order to delay their appeal to Parliament, and they were collectively fined nearly £1,000, which was more than the colony's annual revenue.

As Winthrop changed from a journalist into a historian he wrote more voluminously: his treatment of the years 1643-1646 is over twice the length of his treatment of the years 1633-1636. He focused more on political developments and narrated them in greater detail, perhaps because he had more victories and fewer defeats to report in the 1640s. Winthrop's electoral defeat in May 1634 had been at least as important, both to him and to the colony, as his victory over the Hingham petitioners in 1645, but he wrote up the 1634 episode in two pages and the 1645 episode in seventeen. In the early 1630s he had been silent or evasive on controversial issues, but by the late 1640s he pursued such topics with special zest. One of the great features of the journal/history, especially in the second and third volumes, is that the author reveals so many of the friction points in his society; yet of course he was not trying to establish objectivity but to prove the correctness of his own position. For as Winthrop engaged in one political battle after another, and as he grew more candid in discussing the issues at stake, he also became increasingly doctrinaire, not to say self-righteous, in his prosecution of the men and women he silenced or banished. Thanks to his narrative, it is very easy to recognize the lasting significance of events in early Massachusetts and very difficult to remain neutral on the subject of Winthrop's own leadership. For some, he is one of the great figures in American history. For others, he is the kind of man you love to hate.

**Douglas Anderson (essay date 1990)**

SOURCE: "'This Great Household upon the Earth'," in *A House Divided: Domesticity and Community in American Literature,* Cambridge University Press, 1990, pp. 8-39.

[*In the following excerpt, Anderson traces Winthrop's idea of community as evidenced in his writings and compares it with those of Anne Bradstreet and Edward Taylor.*]

The Book of Deuteronomy, particularly its closing chapters, had an irresistible appeal for the first generation of New England Puritans because of the parallels they recognized between their own situation and that of the Children of Israel, poised upon the borders of the Promised Land. All of the Old Testament had typological significance, of course, and the New Testament was the source that the leaders of the emigrants would consult for guidance in shaping their communal institutions. But it was to Deuteronomy that John Winthrop turned when he sought a forceful conclusion for the discourse on Christian charity that he delivered at sea as the *Arbella* and her consort ships sailed west toward Massachusetts Bay.

The passage Winthrop chose partly to quote and partly to paraphrase was from Moses' "last farewell" to his people, after he had at length restored their laws and was preparing to die. This wonderfully dramatic moment was deservedly familiar to readers, playgoers, and congregations long before Winthrop singled it out. The medieval compilers of the *Gesta Romanorum* were influenced by Moses' words of farewell as they assembled their popular collection of monastic and chivalric tales. The same passage that Winthrop chose, and the chapter or two immediately following it, served as the source for some of the dialogue in the Exodus plays of the English *Corpus Christi* cycle, and William Shakespeare, drawing perhaps on all these sources, had incorporated elements of Moses' farewell into several scenes from *The Merchant of Venice*—most notably into Por-

tia's memorable lines on the quality of mercy. But Winthrop's treatment of his text is much more direct and, in its way, momentous than that of these literary predecessors. He uses it to capture in the form of a single choice the challenge facing the new colonists:

> And to shutt upp this discourse with that exhortation of Moses that faithfull servant of the Lord in his last farewell to Israell Deut. 30. Beloved there is now sett before us life, and good, deathe and evill in that wee are Commaunded this day to love the Lord our God, and to love one another to walke in his wayes and to keepe his Commaundements and his Ordinance, and his lawes, and the Articles of our Covenant with him that wee may live and be multiplyed, and that the Lord our God may blesse us in the land whether wee goe to possesse it: But if our heartes shall turne away soe that wee will not obey, but shall be seduced and worshipp other Gods our pleasures, and proffitts, and serve them; it is propounded unto us this day, wee shall surely perishe out of the good Land whether wee passe over this vast Sea to possesse it:

> Therefore lett us choose life,
> that wee, and our Seede,
> may live; by obeyeing his
> voyce, and cleaveing to him,
> for hee is our life, and
> our prosperity.

The images of a city on a hill and of a "speciall Commission" or covenant are the traditional metaphors that modern scholarship has focused on as the heart of Winthrop's speech, but the emphases of Winthrop's text itself suggest that this Mosaic choice was a central part of his message, the condensation of what he believed the Puritan errand signified. The idea of a special covenant was vital to the emigrants' sense of density, but in **"A Modell of Christian Charity"** Winthrop devotes only a paragraph to the implications of this contract, subordinating it (as he does in the passage above) as just one metaphor among others. Even the vision of a "Citty upon a Hill" is, in many respects, only a kind of conspicuous predicament in which, according to Winthrop, the emigrants simply find themselves. "[T]he eies of all people are upon us," he observes in an interesting modification of the Sermon on the Mount, implying that New England will be exposed to considerable scrutiny, like it or not. The choice between life and death, however, is at the center of what it means to be a deliberate participant in this dangerous enterprise. This is the master "modell" of Winthrop's title, and he set out in his discourse to identify the Puritan errand as closely as he could with the powerful appeal of life.

It may seem especially curious, then, that Winthrop chose to begin what he considered to be the "preface" of his speech with an explanation of the reasons why

God had ordained that "in all times some must be rich some poore, some highe and eminent in power and dignitie; others meane and in subjection". Where, one wonders, is the charity in this? Winthrop undertakes at the outset to explain to us nothing less than the reasons why such social divisions should exist. Perry Miller [in *Errand into the Wilderness*, 1956] mistakenly identified this apparently complacent—and from Winthrop's point of view wholly traditional—acceptance of social stratification as Winthrop's main text and thought it called for "incessant brooding" on the part of all students of American history. For Winthrop, however, these opening comments are not so much a bulwark for the rights of property, or a rehearsal of familiar aristocratic platitudes, but the beginnings of an assault upon ordinary notions of worldly ownership and worldly duty. His antagonist, in conformity with a rich tradition of Puritan thought, was the self, and he began **"A Modell of Christian Charity"** by boldly addressing the chief incitement to selfishness among his economically vulnerable listeners.

God, quite simply, reserves all earthly property to himself. Its uneven distribution among men is no more than another manifestation of the familiar renaissance concept of plenitude. God multiplies his "Stewards counting himself more honored in dispenceing his guifts to man by man, than if hee did it by his owne immediate hand". Winthrop reinforces the implications of this idea by examining the two primary rules that are to guide the lives of the emigrants, justice and mercy, and the two kinds of law to which they are subject, that of nature and that of grace. The import of these principles and laws is that "community of perills calls for extraordinary liberallity". It was quite clear to Winthrop's audience—even before Winthrop himself explicitly confirmed it—that the voyagers in the *Arbella* stood to one another as in a community of perils and that, regardless of the objections of prudent self-interest (with which instinct Winthrop holds a small debate in the text of his speech), they must all conduct their affairs "with more enlargement towardes others and lesse respect towards ourselves".

With Levitican scrupulousness, Winthrop is careful to discuss the various contingencies involved in lending, giving outright, and forgiving debts, but it is clear that he does not have in mind as the guiding virtue of his new community simply ordinary generosity:

> It is to be observed that both in Scriptures and latter stories of the Churches that such as have beene most bountifull to the poore Saintes especially in these extraordinary times and occasions god hath left them highly Commended to posterity . . . observe againe that the scripture gives noe causion to restraine any from being over liberall this way; but to all men to the liberall and cherefull practise hereof by the sweetest promises as to instance one for many, Isaiah 58.6: Is not this the fast that I have chosen

to loose the bonds of wickednes, to take off the heavy burdens to lett the oppressed goe free and to breake every Yoake, to deale thy bread to the hungry and to bring the poore that wander into thy house, when thou seest the naked to cover them etc. then shall thy light breake forthe as the morneing, and thy healthe shall growe speedily, thy righteousnes shall goe before thee, and the glory of the lord shall embrace thee, then thou shalt call and the lord shall Answer thee.

**"A Modell of Christian Charity"** in fact moves steadily toward a vision of communal unity that is founded upon two "patterns," as Winthrop would have called them, taken not from covenant legality but from apocalyptic vision and private life: the body and marriage. Both are traditional images, but that is precisely why Winthrop adopts them. He can draw upon the familiar associations of the body of Christ and the marriage of Christ with his church to enhance the authority of his appeal for community and his argument against the self.

For though he was in fact making a kind of argument, Winthrop knew (as Shakespeare's Portia came to recognize) that people could not be argued into "workes of mercy" toward one another. Mercy had to emerge from within, and that emergence required a psychological and spiritual transformation on the part of those who would found a new community upon a spiritually regenerate basis. Winthrop concluded that the "first mover or maine wheele" of mercy and justice in human life was love, the "bond or ligament" that knits together human beings as firmly as the parts of a single body are knit together in mutual dependence. In conformity with the taste of his age, Winthrop was prepared to extend this bodily conceit just as far as it could go in the service of his point, delving into some of the particulars of digestion, for example, in order to show that just as the mouth may "mince the food" for the whole body and yet receive "a due proporcion" of nourishment in return, so affection is always perfectly reciprocal in the kind of society he envisions for America. This conceit, however, unlike those in the more strictly secular verse of Winthrop's contemporaries, does not succed or fail purely on poetic grounds. Winthrop derives its authority from passages in I Corinthians, Galatians, Romans, and John. Nor is such a literal and spiritual view of their social "constitution" simply one desirable alternative among many. Winthrop is not discussing possible social options but necessities. The extraordinary nature of the colonizing enterprise demanded that "wee must not content our selves with usual ordinary meanes":

> Whatsoever wee did or ought to have done when wee lived in England, the same must wee doe and more allsoe where wee goe: That which the most in theire Churches maineteine as a truthe in profession

onely, wee must bring into familiar and constant practise, and in this duty of love wee must love brotherly without dissimulation, wee must love one another with a pure hearte fervently wee must beare one anothers burthens, wee must not looke onely on our owne things, but allsoe on the things of our brethren, neither must wee think that the lord will beare with such faileings at our hands as hee dothe from those among whome we have lived.

In its rhythmic sequence of binding exhortations ("wee must love . . . wee must beare . . .") this passage anticipates by a few paragraphs the culminating vision of Winthrop's speech, toward which he is building with both musical and argumentative care. The nature of Winthrop's message requires such orchestration, for in opposition to the stubborn claims of the self, Winthrop pits a social ideal more demanding and more rewarding (he suggests) than marriage. Yet it is to marriage, and to its extension in family, that he appeals as a model for how this binding love operates upon the inward lives of those who choose to "exercise" it.

The loyalty of David and Jonathan is the second of the instructive instances of social beauty upon which Winthrop calls to give his ideal a dramatic life, but his chief example of the self-effacing power of human affection is Eve. And just as Milton has Eve recite the most beautiful hymn to human love in *Paradise Lost* (4, 635-56), so Winthrop elects to describe the psychological impact of love solely through an elaborate characterization of its effects on her. Strikingly—and it would certainly have seemed striking to Winthrop's biblically sophisticated listeners—he departs from scriptural authority and assigns to Eve the "fleshe of my fleshe" acknowledgment that Genesis attributes to Adam:

> Now when the soule which is of a sociable nature finds any thing like to it selfe, it is like Adam when Eve was brought to him, shee must have it one with herselfe this is fleshe of my fleshe (saith shee) and bone of my bone shee conceives a great delightc in it, therefore shee desires nearenes and familiarity with it: shee hath a greate propensity to doe it good and receives such content in it, as feareing the miscarriage of her beloved shee bestowes it in the inmost closett of her heart, shee will not endure that it shall want any good which shee can give it, if by occasion shee be withdrawne from the Company of it, shee is still lookeing towards the place where shee left her beloved, if shee heare it groane shee is with it presently, if shee finde it sadd and disconsolate shee sighes and mournes with it, shee hath noe such joy, as to see her beloved merry and thrivcing, if shee see it wronged, shee cannot beare it without passion, shee setts noe boundes of her affecttions, nor hath any thought of reward, shee findes recompence enoughe in the exercise of her love towards it.

It is no simple matter to describe the uses to which Winthrop has put gender in this extraordinary passage. Despite the neuter pronouns with which he has referred to the "soule" in his opening sentence, it is possible to treat the insistent use of "shee" thereafter as a conventional gesture on the part of any properly educated English gentleman who wished his usage to conform to the gender of the Latin *anima* for soul. Even two centuries later Emerson will continue to treat the mind, the intellect, and the Reason as feminine, all the while insisting that living by the light of Reason is "manly." Such a reassuringly traditional reading of Winthrop's usage, however, does not square comfortably with the abruptness with which Eve's appearance in his initial main clause immediately transforms the pronouns. Nor can it account for the intensely sexual nature of the soul's commitment, the conception of delight, the fear of miscarriage, the maternal devotion to her "merry and thriveing" beloved. Winthrop's purposes in fact seem quite complex: He undertakes both to feminize Adam and to exalt Eve as the primary example of everyone who seeks the well-being of others above that of themselves. Eve is his model citizen, not his model wife, and she represents for Winthrop the conflation of the ideas of election and good citizenship that Amy Lang has identified [in *Prophetic Woman*] as one of the critical accomplishments of **"A Modell of Christian Charity."**

Part of the reason for Winthrop's uncharacteristic freedom with the language of Genesis in this instance may well be his desire to impress even more vividly upon his audience the revolutionary nature of their undertaking. If the demands of the self must yield to the force of communal love, then the demands of sexual primacy cannot be entirely inviolable. If we must maintain as a truth what others merely profess, then our domestic as well as our political relations call for careful examination. Eve's devotion in Winthrop's passage, after all, is both an acknowledgment of her exemplary power and a celebration of its domestic singlemindedness. At the same time Winthrop is drawing on an old exegetical tradition that identifies the figure of Eve both with her typological successor, Mary, and with the church. Adam's typological associations are with the inward process of election itself and with Christ, the Second Adam, whose apocalyptic return to earth marks the climactic "marriage" of Christian history but who is not readily available as a social presence in human life until the end of time. The typological network of Eve, Mary, and the church are, as Winthrop recognizes, "of a sociable nature," available in a way that Adam is not as a model for the operations of the human "church" understood both exclusively and inclusively. The Eve of Winthrop's passage is not occupied in distinguishing between the regenerate and the unregenerate in the objects of her affection; she is in pursuit of a "beloved" whose status seems to fluctuate between the confident joy of election and the disconsolate sorrow of doubt. She is capable of uniting the complete community of Massachusetts Bay, not simply (as Stephen Foster has suggested) those who "commune," in a network of affection that challenges the power of selfishness with a dramatic model of human, and female, generosity. This extraordinary capacity in Eve and in the typological network she embodies forms the connecting link between Milton's epics of the lost and regained Paradise. And . . . the range of Eve's appeal gave Emily Dickinson a model of female heroism upon which to shape the monologues of some of her boldest poems. This important modification of the hierarchal tradition is at the heart of Winthrop's model for the American community. The abrupt shift in focus from Adam to Eve with which his passage begins is only a condensed form of the shift in social focus that Winthrop proposes throughout **"A Modell of Christian Charity"**: the shift from self to self-lessness, the shift from death to life.

It is, moreover, not only Eve's marital devotion but also her maternal zeal that Winthrop presents as images of the larger social union of community. She is simultaneously both terms in her typological identity, both Eve and Mary, spouse and mother. The neutral pronouns of the passage that celebrate her impassioned devotion generalize her self-lessness and blur the distinction between spousal and parental love. The "beloved" over whom she solicitously hovers in Winthrop's description might as readily be her "merry and thriving" child as her husband. The result of this fusion of images is a far more complex and powerful presentation of the sociable nature, for Winthrop has not only employed his biblical figures in traditional typological ways, he has compressed the typological relationship into an extraordinarily rich and suggestive network of familial affection.

Winthrop's personal sense of the potency of the marital bond is perhaps one index of the meaning with which he, and no doubt many of his audience, invested the analogy between community and marriage. He was separated from his wife on the *Arbella*'s momentous voyage. She remained in England and planned to follow on a later ship. Winthrop's letters to her as he prepared to sail are a lively mixture of the latest news on his sailing arrangements, pious consolations for their separation, and domestic tenderness. "Mine owne, mine onely, my best beloved," he addresses her on March 10, 1630, and on March 28 writes in part to remind her of the pact that they had apparently made (in cheerful ignorance of the effect of distance upon time) to "meet in spiritt" on Mondays and Fridays "at 5: of the clocke at night" until they would be able to meet again in fact. For Winthrop, then, it meant a great deal to describe the emigrants' relationship to one another and their relationship to God as a "more neare bond of marriage".

The closing allusion in **"A Modell of Christian Charity"** to Moses and the choice of life emerges naturally from this discussion of the communal marriage and the communal body. If the bonds of contract alone were involved in the sanctifying of Massachusetts Bay, then it would be difficult to understand, except perhaps in a technical sense, why Winthrop and his companions found their enterprise so urgent and so moving. It would be particularly difficult to see how Winthrop intended to appeal to the always significant percentage of the emigrant population who were not literally covenanted, or contracted, to church membership. A sense of "contract" is deeply embedded in the origins of Puritan colonization, but even in the case of Winthrop's colleagues in the business-like Agreement at Cambridge, it was not contractual sanctity but a vision of life that urged them forward.

Like the Agreement at Cambridge, the Mayflower Compact, shaped by practical necessity though it was, shows evidence of the appeal of a similar visionary union. Its signers bound themselves into a "civil body politic" the very nature of which they had yet to agree upon and the laws of which they had yet to frame, even as they engaged themselves in advance to obey them. Such confidence looks more than a little imprudent from a modern standpoint, until we recall the sorts of implications that Winthrop would later draw from the traditional metaphor of the body as applied to human communities. Indeed, perhaps even more deeply than did Winthrop, William Bradford identified the founding of Plymouth and the trials of the separatists with the plight of a family. Bradford expressed the anguish of their original escape to Leyden by emphasizing the suffering of the husbands who were hurried away to sea by their Dutch captain as they watched their wives and children taken into custody on shore by a "great company, both horse and foot, with bills and guns and other weapons." The separatists' determination to leave Holland for America was motivated in some measure by their desire "for the propagating and advancing of the Gospel," but the reasons that seemed to carry the greatest weight with them—and that prompted the most moving prose from Bradford—were the strains of European exile upon their families: "As necessity was a taskmaster over them, so they were forced to be such, not only to their servants but in a sort to their dearest children, the which as it did not a little wound the tender hearts of many a loving father and mother, so it produced likewise sundry sad and sorrowful effects."

The escape from this sadness and sorrow brought with it the terrible conditions of their first New England winter. But even in the grimmest circumstances, Bradford identified the devoted nursing of Miles Standish and William Brewster as a dramatic instance of the sort of selfless tenderness that Winthrop was to invoke on behalf of his own community ten years later.

Standish and Brewster, among others, "spared no pains night nor day" in their devotion to the sick.

> but with abundance of toil and hazard of their own health, fetched them wood, made them fires, dressed them meat, made their beds, washed their loathsome clothes, clothed and unclothed them. In a word, did all the homely and necessary offices for them which dainty and queasy stomachs cannot endure to hear named; and all this willingly and cheerfully, without any grudging in the least, showing herein their true love unto their friends and brethren; a rare example and worthy to be remembered . . . And what I have said of these I may say of many others who died in this general visitation, and others yet living; that whilst they had health, yea, or any strength continuing, they were not wanting to any that had need of them. And I doubt not but their recompense is with the Lord.

Some of the same fluidity of gender and sensitivity to typology that Winthrop skillfully employs in **"A Modell of Christian Charity"** is present in the example of these maternal Pilgrim Fathers. Bradford had begun writing *Of Plymouth Plantation* just at the moment when the larger and better-financed expedition to Massachusetts Bay was about to supersede Plymouth in colonial history. But the shift in center of gravity from Plymouth to Boston involved virtually no charge at all in the relation that leaders in both colonies hoped to maintain between the claims of the self and the claims of the community. Winthrop gave that relation its definitive expression in the closing sentences of **"A Modell of Christian Charity,"** drawing on the commanding image of the body and on the verbal complexity of his portrait of Eve's restless devotion in order to suggest the kind of vitality that he felt in his social ideal:

> For this end, wee must be knitt together in this worke as one man, wee must entertaine each other in brotherly Affection, wee must be willing to abridge our selves of our superfluities, for the supply of others necessities, wee must uphold a familiar Commerce together in all meekenes, gentlenes, patience and liberality, wee must delight in eache other, make others Condicions our owne rejoyce together, mourne together, labour, and suffer together, allwayes haveing before our eyes our Commission and Community in the worke, our Community as members of the same body, soe shall wee keepe the unitie of the spirit in the bond of peace, the Lord wil be our God and delight to dwell among us, as his owne people and will commaund a blessing upon us in all our wayes, soe that wee shall see much more of his wisdome power goodness and truthe then formerly wee have beene acquainted with, wee shall finde that the God of Israell is among us, when tenn of us shall be able to resist a thousand of our enemies, when hee shall make us a prayse and glory, that men shall say of succeeding plantacions; the lord make it like that of New England.

Within a moment or two of this ringing forecast, Winthrop is quoting Moses on the choice of life. To his listeners it must have seemed a completely appropriate text with which to close, on metaphorical as well as on typological grounds.

Winthrop's accomplishment in **"A Modell of Christian Charity"** is the extraordinary degree of concentration with which he was able to express a wide range of hopes and fears shared by his colleagues. Perry Miller was among the first to recognize this representative property of Winthrop's discourse and to employ the speech in *The New England Mind: From Colony To Province* as a fixed point of reference from which to measure the dissolution of the Puritan errand as the eighteenth century progressed. Miller's influential treatment, however, has tended to obscure the degree to which Winthrop's initial vision of the emigrants' plight not only anticipated decline but absorbed the pattern of great promise and great peril—a pattern inherited from the Puritan vision of the plight of the individual soul and from their reading of the cyclical history of the people of Israel—and accepted it not as a unique and temporary predicament but as the ongoing condition of life. The Mosaic choice that Winthrop describes seems resonant with finality, but in fact, as he makes clear, it renews its terms constantly in the private, daily labor of life, in the intimate bonds of marriage, in the obligations of a parent and a neighbor.

The heroic, public work of Joshua or even of Nehemiah, the wall builder, with whom Cotton Mather was much later to identify Winthrop, is not the sphere of activity that Winthrop himself evokes as central to his new, American experience. He evokes instead a deeply domestic and familal set of values, and he offers a wonderfully assertive and commanding vision of Eve as the most comprehensive embodiment of those qualities necessary to avoid the figurative shipwreck that was all too vividly present to the imaginations of his seaborne listeners.

The image of Moses and the choice of life with which Winthrop closes is grand enough in its own right, but it has its roots in, and draws its authority from, unusually modest sources in human experience. Nor is it by any means clear that Winthrop saw this authority as the exclusive property of one sex. Indeed, though **"A Modell of Christian Charity"** begins in an apparent justification of the traditional structures of authority within the English community, that justification proves to be the preamble to a description of communal authority that is both more and less stable than the familiar three-way alliance of wealth, place, and masculinity. The comforting implications of the concept of divine plenitude give way to the necessity that people comfort one another, nurture one another, and delight in one another. Those are the values of the household, not of the Great Chain of Being, and authority is grounded in them much as the stature of Eve is grounded both in her typological identities and her power of affection, or that of William Brewster and Miles Standish is grounded in their nurturing strength during the first winter at Plymouth.

These are the central features, then, of the vision of life that Winthrop presents: the sense of the ongoing predicament of choice, the domestic center of meaning within which that choice takes place, the necessary identification of communal authority—of power—with the bonds and obligations of the family. It does not follow from the presence of these features in Winthrop's speech that he was binding himself always to act under their guidance. They simply represent his best description of those professed truths that the residents of Massachusetts Bay must strive to put into action in daily life. Like any good Puritan, Winthrop must have expected a great measure of failure on his own part as well as on that of others. The twin perceptions of impending failure and exhilarating opportunity are the definitive properties of Moses' choice, and these along with the other critical elements of Winthrop's discourse provide the context for the poetic achievements of Anne Bradstreet and Edward Taylor.

Anne Bradstreet—newly married and sailing to New England with a father and a husband each of whom would in turn succeed to Winthrop's position as governor—was among the listeners whom Winthrop addressed on the *Arbella* in 1630. Under the circumstances it would have been next to impossible for her to avoid feeling the pertinence of Winthrop's appeal to the models of the body and the family. Indeed her domestic life was so intimately involved with the political life of the colony that she comes quite close to being a historical equivalent to the figure of Eve that Winthrop uses in his speech: the wife whose marital devotion is indistinguishable from a political act, and whose love transforms the remote relationships of power.

It is scarcely an exaggeration to trace the character of Bradstreet's work to the social vision that **"A Modell of Christian Charity"** embodies. Her loving, verse letters to her absent husband, for example, present themselves as expressions of a private affection that is peripheral to the serious masculine business of the state. In the context of Winthrop's model, however, Bradstreet's private affections and her celebration of them have public stature. Her own family appeared to recognize this fact and treat her poetry much like a public resource. Bradstreet does, to be sure, complain in "The Prologue" to *The Tenth Muse* that men are prone to patronize her work, but men were also prone to conspire to publish it without the author's consent, and Nathaniel Ward wrote some cheerful introductory verses to Bradstreet's book in which he mocks the myopic incompetence of a sexist Apollo, "the old Don":

Good sooth quoth the old Don, tell ye me so,
I muse whither at length these girls will go;
It half revives my chill frost-bitten blood,
To see a woman once do ought that's good;
And shod by Chaucer's boots, and Homer's
   furs,
Let men look to't, lest women wear the spurs.

Bradstreet apparently engaged in poetic exchanges with her father that Emily Dickinson would have found marvelous, and Simon Bradstreet, her son, wished particularly that his mother would leave him some written record from which he could continue to take counsel after her death.

Like Emily Dickinson, Bradstreet assembled private books of her poetry, but unlike Dickinson, she had clearly in mind an ultimate purpose for them, as she indicates in the six lines with which she prefaced the brief spiritual autobiography that she wrote for her children:

This book by any yet unread,
I leave for you when I am dead,
That being gone, here you may find
What was your living mother's mind.
Make use of what I leave in love,
And God shall bless you from above.

These are characteristically simple couplets. Bradstreet obviously had no poetic aspirations for them. But even so they capture the sense of affectionate seriousness that she brought to her work. She leaves this book in "love," but she makes sure her children know that she does not intend it for reverent neglect. There is just enough of the benevolent, maternal taskmaster in her admonitory "make use" to leave the unmistakable impression of an authoritative, parental voice. Much of Bradstreet's most memorable poetry is tied, directly or indirectly, to this sense of her domestic role and to the events of domestic life. She and those around her, however, would not have considered this fact as evidence of a purely personal or limited sensibility.

The extraordinary stature that Bradstreet was willing to claim for her domestic posture is generally couched in language that is, at least apparently, self-effacing. But this is much the same kind of self-effacement that Winthrop understands to be the central achievement of Christian charity. It does not happen in us naturally but must be actively sought and struggled for. As often as not, in Bradstreet's case, the struggle seldom achieves even a temporary resolution. Nor is the reader always perfectly certain of the relative merits of the antagonists. This sense of struggle is present even in a poem like "The Author to Her Book," which seems merely conventional in its modesty and resignation. Bradstreet adopts in these dedicatory lines the stance of a mother embrassed by the flaws in her poetic child. She does her best to correct her offspring's "blemishes," but her own lack of skill and her child's stubborn imperfections defeat her best intentions. She finally dismisses her hobbling "work" with some cautious advice about avoiding critics and pleading the lowliness of one's parentage.

There seems, at first, little struggle here. Bradstreet solicits a bit of tenderness for her "rambling brat" and concocts one or two clever (if disturbing) puns on printing "rags" and on her offspring's crippled "feet," but only in the closing lines does she suggest the striking model for her creative zeal:

> In this array, 'mongst vulgars mayst thou
>     roam;
> In critics' hands, beware thou dost not come.
> And take thy way where yet thou art not
>     known.
> If for thy father asked, say thou hadst none;
> And for thy mother—she, alas, is poor,
> Which caused her thus to send thee out of
>     door.

These poems, Bradstreet claims, are perhaps imperfect, but they are also unfathered, created out of nothing but the author's "feeble brain," harshly judged for their failings yet forgiven by a mother whose nurturing hand seems at once affectionate and heavy with nearly an excess of formative power:

> I cast thee by as one unfit for light,
> Thy visage was so irksome in my sight;
> Yet being mine own, at length affection would
> Thy blemishes amend, if so I could:
> I washed thy face, but more defects I saw,
> And rubbing off a spot, still made a flaw.

Bradstreet is both a chagrined parent and an analogue for God in these seemingly modest lines. She is apologizing for her artistic inadequacies and asserting an extraordinary potency all at once—a potency that both evokes and dismisses the figure of the absent father. At the same time, Bradstreet's omnipotent motherhood is marked by the typological network that Winthrop exploited in his portrait of an equally affectionate and powerful Eve. Like Eve, Bradstreet the author is implicated in the "defects" of her crippled verse. She, after all, has made it. But she is also a mother strangely independent of earthly fathers—like Eve's typological descendant—and prophetically sensitive to the fate she envisions her child will suffer once it falls into the hands of critics. The fusion of the tradition of authorial modesty with typological ambition in these lines is both unsettling and invigorating. It represents the "willed resignation" that Robert Daly has described [in *God's Altar,* 1978] as the characteristic mark of Bradstreet's best verse, and at the same time asserts the kind of communal authority that Winthrop identified

with his sociable and selfless Eve.

Bradstreet was capable of evoking Winthrop's metaphors quite directly, often in contexts that strike a modern reader as almost inconceivably unsophisticated. "In Reference to Her Children, 23 June 1659" is a fine example of such an exaltation of the domestic posture, working out of conditions that are less poetically promising than the witty conceits of "The Author to Her Book." Like most of Bradstreet's work, "In Reference to Her Children" is metaphorically and structurally straightforward, ninety-four lines in more or less regular couplets, built on the commonplace fiction of a mother bird reminiscing about her chicks: "I had eight birds hatched in one nest," the poem begins, "Four cocks there were, and hens the rest." The earthy savor of such language would have seemed quite familiar to contemporary readers. John Cotton had preached a farewell sermon to some of the earliest emigrants to Massachusetts Bay in which he urged his listeners to "forget not the wombe that bore you and the breasts that gave you sucke. Even ducklings hatched under an henne, though they take the water, yet will still have recourse to the wing that hatched them: how much more should chickens of the same feather, and yolke?" Cotton's purpose was to encourage his listeners to remember England and it did not strike him as unseemly to do so in this simple way.

Bradstreet's metaphor is equally simple and traditional. She comments on each of her hatchlings in turn, from the eldest, who has now flown to "regions far," to the three youngest, who "still with me nest" but whose flight she already anticipates. The departure of her "brood" fills her with fear both because of the dangers of the world—fowlers, hawks, and untoward boys—and because her children are in want of wisdom. "O to your safety have an eye," she urges them, and after describing how she intends to pass her old age, singing "my weak lays" in a shady wood, she offers them her last piece of advice:

> When each of you shall in your nest
> Among your young ones take your rest,
> In chirping language, oft them tell,
> You had a dam that loved you well,
> That did what could be done for young,
> And nursed you up till you were strong,
> And 'fore she once would let you fly,
> She showed you joy and misery;
> Taught what was good, and what was ill,
> What would save life, and what would kill.
> Thus gone, amongst you I may live,
> And dead, yet speak, and counsel give:
> Farewell, my birds, farewell adieu,
> I happy am, if well with you.

What is most interesting, and most characteristic, about these concluding lines is the way in which Bradstreet is able to infuse her almost insistently naive conceit with a surprising, and moving, degree of seriousness. The change is anything but heavy-handed, but if we are alert, then the three pairs of antonyms—joy and misery, good and ill, life and "kill"—seem unmistakably to echo the structure of Moses' farewell injunctions on "life and good, death and evil" to which Winthrop had attached such significance nearly thirty years earlier. Bradstreet certainly does not force the association upon us, but there is a great deal of difference between the distressed mother bird who had cried "O to your safety have an eye" just a few lines earlier and the quality of calm and stately wisdom that suddenly settles upon the poem's close. The shift in tone that occurs in these final lines suggests Bradstreet's desire to entice us along into a delightful and striking contrast. But even without such a formal hint, it is clear that one of the chief advantages of Bradstreet's childlike conceit of birds, chicks, and nests is what we might call its inherent poetic humility.

As the rich fusion of tones in "The Author to Her Book" suggests, Bradstreet is engaged in a more or less steady struggle with the self. "The finest bread hath the least bran," she wrote in "Meditation 6," "the purest honey the least wax, and the sincerest Christian the least self-love". The vocation of a poet, however, is almost inevitably an assertion of the individual sensibility, particularly as Bradstreet practiced it. She was the family elegist and spiritual counselor, the family solicitor with God in many of her verse prayers. Unless we are devoted antiquarians, we know very little indeed about those "public employments" for which Bradstreet's husband was so often absent, but Bradstreet's amorous verse letters to him are familiar to many modern readers. At some level she sensed the potential incitement to egotism that such power over feelings and over human memory could represent. Taking counsel with the chastened peacock of her "Meditation 5," she appears to have focused her own literary efforts not on the dramatic display of poetical "gay feathers," but rather upon a considered exposure of those embarrassing black feet: "So he that glories in his gifts and adornings should look upon his corruptions, and that will damp his high thoughts". Bradstreet took some care to damp her own.

It is equally clear that accompanying this conventional, or corrective, humility of Bradstreet's is a genuinely religious sense of unworthiness, expressed most directly in the private verse laments that she left to her children, in which a succession of fainting fits, sicknesses, and periods of bodily weakness all conspire to remind her of her utter dependence upon God:

> My thankful heart with glorying tongue
> Shall celebrate Thy name,
> Who hath restored, redeemed, recured
> From Sickness, death, and pain.

> I cried, Thou seem'st to make some stay,
> I sought more earnestly
> And in due time Thou succor'st me
> And sent'st me help from high.

> Lord, whilst my fleeting time shall last,
> Thy goodness let me tell,
> And new experience I have gained
> My future doubts repel.

> An humble, faithful life, O Lord,
> Forever let me walk;
> Let my obedience testify
> My praise lies not in talk.

> Accept, O Lord, my simple mite,
> For more I cannot give.
> What Thou bestow'st I shall restore,
> For of thine alms I live.

When Bradstreet's powers are fully engaged, her poetry manages to sustain an unusually effective balance between the genuine humility of these private laments and the kind of forthright self-confidence ("My praise lies not in talk") that conventional humility disguises. Even in these lines from a "thankful heart," Bradstreet cannot resist reminding God that his succor was something less than prompt, and she does indeed expect to encounter future doubts. Her gratitude and obedience are not inconsistent with an essential, human assertiveness, just as her authorial modesty is not inconsistent with a willingness to hint at her own, God-like powers of composition—of judgment and amendment. For Bradstreet (as Robert Daly has again noted) man's relation to God was "familial," but that relation implied a degree of antagonism as well as intimacy that Bradstreet's own domestic roles permitted her to appreciate and dramatize.

The brief dedicatory verses to her father that appeared in the posthumous, 1678 edition of her poems clearly overstate her modesty in the conventional manner when she characterizes her offered work as "this crumb." But other elements of the poem—the allusion to the parable of the talents, in particular, and to the necessity for "forgiving" debts that Winthrop emphasizes in parts of **"A Modell of Christian Charity"**—establish just as clearly both a sense of dependence and a sense of Bradstreet's own personal adequacy. Both the indebtedness and the stubbornness are deeply felt:

> Most truly honoured, and as truly dear,
> If worth in me or ought I do appear,
> Who can of right better demand the same
> Than may your worthy self from whom it
> came?
> The principal might yield a greater sum,
> Yet handled ill, amounts but to this crumb;
> My stock's so small I know not how to pay,

My bond remains in force unto this day;
Yet for part payment take this simple mite,
Where nothing's to be had, kings loose their
     right.
Such is my debt I may not say forgive,
But as I can, I'll pay it while I live;
Such is my bond, none can discharge but I,
Yet paying is not paid until I die.

The similarity between the language of Bradstreet's private lament (also a "simple mite") and this more public poem is another index of the complex interplay in her work between genuine and conventional selflessness, between self-effacement and self-confidence. "In Reference to Her Children" is built around a similar balance, offering at the same instant two versions of Bradstreet's maternal solicitude: one the implicitly patronizing view of the fretful mother bird, the other quite boldly identifying her parental concern with that of Moses for his people.

Bradstreet's apparently simple "Meditation 6" on self-love is in some measure a general admission of this characteristic mixture of boldness and modesty: "The finest bread hath the least bran, the purest honey the least wax, and the sincerest Christian the least self-love." The best bread may well have the least bran, but at the same time Bradstreet implies that all bread has some. Bees' wax may be an unwelcome intruder in one's honey, but its presence there is anything but unnatural. Accordingly, though the best Christian may have the least self-love, Bradstreet is more than prepared to take a forgiving attitude toward that residue of egotism, provided that it does not try to assert itself too openly. Like many of her best meditations, the analogies in this one have a benevolently corrective effect upon its dogmatic basis. Just as Winthrop recognized in his closing exhortations to **"A Modell of Christian Charity,"** it is clearly desirable to struggle against the self, but it is entirely natural that the struggle should be at least a partial failure. "In Reference to Her Children" virtually enacts this struggle and dramatizes its fortunate failure. Without some sense of self there would, of course, be no poem at all. Without some potent restraint upon the self, the nature of the poem would change. The delicate allusion to Moses might harden into an unacceptably self-aggrandizing view of the speaker's role. Bradstreet intends that the emphasis fall where the title suggests: upon her children, not upon herself. She hopes simultaneously to enjoin "life" upon them and to embody the meaning of that injunction in her carefully balanced manner of giving it.

Not even the convention of poetic humility or a calculated simplicity, however, could disguise Bradstreet's immense satisfaction in her domestic roles. The images from "In Reference to Her Children," for example, are in one sense unsophisticated, but in the context of

the whole poem—its seriousness of purpose as well as its simplicity of means—they are fondly playful. The innocence of its primary metaphor does not trivialize the emotions expressed but serves instead as a constant, gentle reminder of a parent's vulnerability through her children:

O would my young, ye saw my breast,
And knew what thoughts there sadly rest,
Great was my pain when I you bred,
Great was my care when I you fed,
Long did I keep you soft and warm,
And with my wings kept off all harm,
My cares are more and fears than ever,
My throbs such now as 'fore were never.
Alas, my birds, you wisdom want,
Of perils you are ignorant;
Oft times in grass, on trees, in flight,
Sore accidents on you may light.
O to your safety have an eye,
So happy may you live and die.

These lines are solicitous and at the same time surprisingly blunt. Much as in the case of the typologically double identity of the speaker in "The Author to Her Book," Bradstreet assumes the role of a fussing mother bird, but she is also a demanding judge of her children's insufficient wisdom. It is clear that her sense of a mother's role (and voice) is anything but stereotypically simple. This same sort of complexity is present as well in the poems that reflect her status as wife.

The verse letters to her husband are among the most memorable of Brandstreet's poems, not only because of the enthusiasm with which they celebrate married love, but because of the nature of the love that they celebrate. Bradstreet always writes from the perspective of the homebound wife who wants her busy partner to return; yet just as the vulnerability of "In Reference to Her Children" is mutual, so the dependence between husband and wife is mutual in Bradstreet's love poems. "I have a loving peer," she writes in one verse letter, making rather skillful use of the two meanings of "peer" to establish the double assertion: I have a loving lord, and I have a loving equal. Bradstreet's love poems take what appears to be unrestrained delight in acknowledging her dependence upon her husband, but the terms in which she expresses that delight almost always affirm, directly or indirectly, that the dependence is mutual—the perfect model for the mutual dependence of society at large that Winthrop envisioned for America.

Bradstreet's reference to her "loving peer," for example, comes in the midst of a poem that seems particularly extravagant in its images of wifely dependence:

As loving hind that (hartless) wants her deer,
Scuds through the woods and fern with

hark'ning ear,
Perplext, in every bush and nook doth pry,
Her dearest deer, might answer ear or eye;
So doth my anxious soul, which now doth
    miss
A dearer dear (far dearer heart) than this.

Bradstreet goes on to compare herself to a "pensive dove" mourning the absence of her "turtle true," and to "the loving mullet, that true fish" that leaps onto the bank to die with "her captive husband" rather than lead a lonely life. The poem draws to a close by heaping up these three identities in a way that draws attention to their hyperbolic nature but also discloses in the parallelism of the first two lines of the following passage the differences among them:

Return my dear, my joy, my only love,
Unto thy hind, thy mullet, and thy dove,
Who neither joys in pasture, house, nor
    streams,
The substance gone, O me, these are but
    dreams.

Of these three images of wifely desolation, only one is stereotypically passive and helpless: the dove, with whose "uncouth" moanings for "my only love" even Bradstreet herself is a bit impatient earlier in the poem. The loving hind is a restless, energetic searcher, as nimble as the puns that characterize her, and the mullet is "true" with a nearly fierce joy in self-sacrifice. It is a chivalric rather than a "feminine" loyalty, and it produces exhilaration rather than despair. The love in this poem is a complex passion that asserts its power as much as it laments its incompleteness.

"A Letter to Her Husband, Absent Upon Public Employment" explores the same kind of complexity. It is a scolding, witty, erotic poem, that may also acknowledge an indirect debt to the memorable portrait of Eve in **"A Modell of Christian Charity."** Bradstreet closes her "letter" with an allusion to Genesis that is a bit truer to the biblical text than Winthrop's but which is nevertheless a stern reminder that the bonds of marriage are not dependent upon metaphysical conceits for their power and ought not to be subjected to strain for routine causes:

But when thou northward to me shall return,
I wish my Sun may never set, but burn
Within the Cancer of my glowing breast,
The welcome house of him my dearest guest.
Where ever, ever stay, and go not thence,
Till nature's sad decree shall call thee hence;
Flesh of thy flesh, bone of thy bone,
I here, thou there, yet both but one.

There is nothing merely "public" about Bradstreet's claim upon her husband. She openly reminds him, as

Winthrop's Eve served to remind his listeners, of the relationship between marital devotion and the kind of apocalyptic imagery that these lines evoke: a loving "sun" united with his bride and forming a single being.

"To My Dear and Loving Husband" brings this same, sobering force to bear even more directly, for though the title seems to express Bradstreet's confidence in her husband's affections, the text of the poem itself is more tentative in its claims of confidence and at the same time more emphatic about the momentous consequences of domestic loyalty:

If ever two were one, then surely we.
If ever man were loved by wife, then thee;
If ever wife was happy in a man,
Compare with me, ye women, if you can.
I prize thy love more than whole mines of
    gold
Or all the riches that the East doth hold.
My love is such that rivers cannot quench,
Nor ought but love from thee, give
    recompense.
Thy love is such I can no way repay,
The heavens reward thee manifold, I pray.
Then while we live, in love let's so persevere
That when we live no more, we may live
    ever.

Bradstreet is "happy" in her husband and prizes his love, but these assertions fall ever so slightly short of confirming that his love equals the resistless force of hers, and her direct address to the community of wives establishes that masculine affection is in general less satisfactory than it might be. The poem is a celebration of the Bradstreets' particular relationship and at the same time a plea for recompense and a reminder that earthly love and loyalty are the critical symbols of "covenanted" love, the basis upon which John Winthrop had established the Puritan community. They exert a momentous claim upon human attention. These messages are potentially so antagonistic to one another that their mixture in thirteen lines of poetry is an unusual achievement. Bradstreet's sense of the psychological richness and import of domestic life called for both extraordinarily exuberant and extraordinarily politic expression.

She is similarly politic and tender with her children. The "Meditations" that she prepared for her son Simon are, as we have seen, both reflections of sound doctrine and ameliorations of that doctrine to accommodate Bradstreet's sense of human limitation. Indeed, some of the most beautiful of these "Meditations" cast God in the role of a "prudent mother" who has a fund of good sense to draw upon in rearing her children. "Meditation 39" is the finest example of this domestic analogy. No wise mother, Bradstreet observes, will give her little child "a long and cumbersome garment," for that would only result in falls, bruises, or worse. Similarly, God recognizes that generous earthly endowments are likely to prove too cumbersome for weak Christians: "Therefore God cuts their garments short to keep them in such a trim that they might run the ways of His Commandment". The message of this meditation is both reassuring and discouraging. We might have preferred that God be more generous with earthly wealth and honor and let us take our chances with stumbling. But Bradstreet's understanding of maternal solicitude is not sentimental. Her sense of the role has a priestly quality to it that is both fond and stern. Her dedication of the "Meditations," for example, displays at once her care for Simon's well-being, her desire to respond to his request for something in writing by which to remember her, and her gently expressed suspicion that he might, after all, need just this sort of guidance and spiritual support. "I could think of nothing more fit for you nor of more ease to myself," writes Bradstreet, than these incitements to spiritual thinking. That motherly observation itself might well serve as Simon's first topic of meditation.

The prose memorial that she left to her children is similarly solicitous and stern. Bradstreet wished to share with her children a generous record of her own struggle with doubt and of her own assurance of God's ultimate provision for "this great household upon the earth". At the same time she casts these reflections as a deathbed speech—not unlike Moses' last farewell—which she hopes will "sink deepest" and give useful guidance: "I have not studied in this you read to show my skill, but to declare the truth, not to set forth myself, but the glory of God". This document is personal—Bradstreet meant it to remain private—but its voice is also public and, in its way, remote:

> I knowing by experience that the exhortations of parents take most effect when the speakers leave to speak, and those especially sink deepest which are spoken latest, and being ignorant whether on my death bed I shall have opportunity to speak to any of you, much less to all, thought it the best, whilst I was able, to compose some short matters (for what else to call them I know not) and bequeath to you, that when I am no more with you, yet I may be daily in your remembrance (although that is the least in my aim in what I now do), but that you may gain some spiritual advantage by my experience. I have not studied in this you read to show my skill, but to declare the truth, not to set forth myself, but the glory of God. If I had minded the former, it had been perhaps better pleasing to you, but seeing the last is the best, let it be best pleasing to you.

The same mixture of maternal solicitude and power that gave such richness to the texture of "The Author to Her Book" is responsible for the interplay of confidence and doubt, authority and affection in this striking paragraph. It is probably inadvisable to place too much emphasis upon the artful significance of seventeenth-century syntax. But Bradstreet's long first sentence in this passage—twice interrupted by dramatically contrasting asides—captures in a single unit of expression the complexity and importance of the domestic role as Bradstreet understood it. She captures as well the characteristic alternation between security and insecurity that Winthrop identified so deeply with the predicament of the *Arbella* emigrants. "Downy beds make drowsy persons," Bradstreet wrote in "Meditation 8," "but hard lodging keeps the eyes open; a prosperous state makes a secure Christian, but adversity makes him consider" (273). It was precisely to foster such considered living in her children that Bradstreet took on her authoritative role, but it was an authority that she naturally derived from the roles linking her to Winthrop's emblematic Eve and to the potent, mediating figure of Mary, whose sorrows Bradstreet also took up in the elegies she wrote for three of her grandchildren and for a daughter-in-law who died in childbirth.

Bradstreet's power as an elegist consists in her ability to dramatize what Robert Daly names the "weaning" process by which a Puritan learns to be resigned to the loss of earthly beauty. But in the best of these poems it is not entirely as an earthly speaker that Bradstreet presents herself anymore than she presents herself in the memorial to her children as an earthly presence or defends her poetic children in "The Author to Her Book" as an earthly creator. Her command over the powers of consolation does not really seem to derived from the traditional, natural metaphors of which the poems are composed. These, in fact, are curiously out of harmony with the deaths of children, as Bradstreet quietly shows us in "In Memory of My Dear Grandchild Elizabeth":

> Farewell dear babe, my heart's too much
>      content,
> Farewell sweet babe, the pleasure of mine eye,
> Farewell fair flower that for a space was lent,
> Then ta'en away unto eternity.
> Blest babe, why should I once bewail thy fate,
> Or sigh thy days so soon were terminate,
> Sith thou art settled in an everlasting state.
>
>                      2
>
> By nature trees do rot when they are grown,
> And plums and apples thoroughly ripe do fall,
> And corn and grass are in their season mown,
> And time brings down what is both strong and
>      tall.
> But plants new set to be eradicate,
> And buds new blown to have so short a date,
> Is by His hand alone that guides nature and
>      fate.

The first stanza begins with three formulaic laments

that the poet seems able to put aside, in the fifth line, with a serenity that makes even one lament seem superfluous. The child is "blest," and Bradstreet does not require the consolatory metaphor of fair flowers to reach her state of inward peace, as "settled" apparently as that of the infant's soul itself. Nor does the second stanza make more use of its more elaborate, natural parables of mutability. The child was neither grown nor ripe, not strong and tall. The lessons of nature simply encumber a relationship to the divine will that is direct and confident—that of a mother who recognizes that she had received her child directly from the same hand that now claims it. This is a posture that is not easy to credit in a human speaker, but neither is it easy to credit the complex posture that Bradstreet adopts in "The Author to Her Book" until one recognizes that Bradstreet is speaking (as a Puritan might put it) "typically" as well as humanly, face to face with God in a relation that Emerson would later recognize and envy as the mark of his Puritan ancestors.

In perhaps the finest of her poems envisioning her own death, Bradstreet made it clear just how deeply her imagination responded to the network of associations and images that Winthrop summoned up in his vision of Eve as the redemptive model for life in Massachusetts Bay. "As Weary Pilgrim" offers the reader a description of two figures, one the poet in a state of perplexity and glorious anticipation, the other a hypothetical traveler through life to whom the poet compares herself in the simile that the title suggests. This first pilgrim, however, is disturbingly content to die. He "hugs with delight his silent nest" in a selfish parody of Winthrop's vision of social delight, and "blesses himself" to think that his earthly trials are over and the grave's "safety" awaits. Bradstreet's own earthly pilgrimage is quite different, marked by the domestic temperament, by the vitality of the image of marriage, and by the thirst for life. Her "clay house" decays, but it is an existence "among the blest" that she counts upon after death and not a self-indulgent and isolated escape. The grave is a place of preparation, of urgency, leading to an apocalyptic marriage with Christ and the replacement of human weakness and dishonor with human power:

> What though my flesh shall there consume,
>     It is the bed Christ did perfume,
> And when a few years shall be gone,
>     This mortal shall be clothed upon.
> A corrupt carcass down it lays,
>     A glorious body it shall rise.
> In weakness and dishonour sown,
>     In power 'tis raised by Christ alone.
> Then soul and body shall unite
>     And of their Maker have the sight.
> Such lasting joys shall there behold
>     As ear ne'er heard nor tongue e'er told.
> Lord make me ready for that day,

Then come, dear Bridegroom, come away.

Bradstreet clearly chooses "life" in this poem, whereas the first weary (and, not incidentally, male) pilgrim chooses death. Her last two lines are characteristically retiring and bold, insecure about her personal worthiness and at the same time startlingly confident in her own powers of appeal. Christ too is an absent spouse, with whom Anne Bradstreet is willing to assert her erotic claims. "As Weary Pilgrim" progresses, then, from a depiction of the Old Adam of selfish contentment to an embodiment of an ecstatic and visionary Eve who is, at the same time, the community as Bride, the Church welcoming her "Bridegroom." Bradstreet's poetic exploration of Winthrop's typological triad from **"A Modell of Christian Charity"** is in its way the artistic midpoint between Winthrop's purposeful prose of 1630 and Edward Taylor's ecstatic meditations on the Eucharist and on Canticles, in which he celebrates at the outset of the eighteenth century the same communal and individual marriage.

The relationship between Edward Taylor's proliferation of images and the handful of metaphors assembled in **"A Modell of Christian Charity"** is both more and less direct than Anne Bradstreet's relationship to that same, fruitful speech. Nowhere does Taylor echo Winthrop as closely as Bradstreet does, for example, in the final lines of "In Reference to Her Children." Nor does he identify as closely as Bradstreet does with the fabric of domestic metaphor that links private with public life. It would be surprising if he did so, for Taylor is nearly two generations removed from the founders of Massachusetts Bay, arriving at Boston in his early twenties almost forty years after the *Arbella* and almost certainly with no access to the text of Winthrop's discourse.

At the same time, however, Taylor's poetry is dominated, to a far greater extent than is Bradstreet's, by the overriding subject of the soul's journey from death to life. Taylor has dozens of ways of describing the journey and of voicing the soul's aspiration toward God. He exhorts his Maker repeatedly to blow on the coal of his smoldering faith, to feed his spirit on heavenly food, to root up his "henbain," chokewort, and ragwort and plant him with honeysuckle, sage, and savory, to dress him in the bright garments of grace, to "screw" him up, to oil his rusty lock, to sharpen his dull pencil or brighten his dim ink, to fill his earthly bottle with heavenly liquor, to redecorate the "Flesh and Blood bag" of his soul and make it a shining temple. Extravagantly conceived and extravagantly mixed metaphors are the characteristic (and traditional) expressions of Taylor's pious zeal and spiritual exuberance, but they all focus on the contrast between what he called the "lifeless Life" or "Living Death" of sin and the spiritual life of grace.

To some degree, it is a disservice to Taylor to single out only one set of images from his lively multitude, since the experience of reading him is so decisively marked by the pleasure of tumbling along a stream of figurative language. But as Karl Keller has observed [in *The Example of Edward Taylor,* 1975], the significance of this inventive and eclectic richness for Taylor himself was its intensively focused interest in the great Puritan drama: the soul's preparation for grace, the exchanging of death for life. In a single stanza, Taylor is quite capable of touching on four or five distinct, and to some degree competing, metaphors, all of which converge toward the central subject of life, even though that critical word itself may be present only implicitly in one or two modifiers, or in the contrast between withered and "frim" (or flourishing) fruits:

> Lord, make my Faith thy golden Quill
>     wherethrough
>         I vitall Spirits from thy blood may suck.
> Make Faith my Grinders, thy Choice Flesh to
>     chew,
>         My Witherd Stock shall with frim Fruits
>     be Stuck.
> My Soule shall then in Lively Notes forth ring
>         Upon her Virginalls, praise for this thing.

As in Winthrop's image of the mouth that minces food for all the body, Taylor's "grinders" very nearly carry the idea of a conceit too far. Like Thoreau, however, Taylor himself seems to have feared only that he would not be extravagant enough. That such metaphorical diversity could tend to such spiritual unity is an underlying subject in most of Taylor's work, particularly in the "Preparatory Meditations," which are by their very nature diverse poetic approaches to a single spiritual goal: the sacrament of communion.

From what we might call a doctrinal standpoint, then, Taylor's application of the scriptural contrast between life and death is more explicit than Bradstreet's even as his figurative language is more lavish and more daring. In many ways they scarcely seem comparable except as extreme instances of opposite tendencies within the tradition of Puritan poetry. But Bradstreet and Taylor share a number of assumptions, in addition to the devotion to spiritual "life," that govern their work, the most important and most obvious of which is the context of familial discourse within which they understood their verse to be operating:

> My Lord I fain would Praise thee Well but
>     finde
>         Impossibilities blocke up my pass.
> My tongue Wants Words to tell my thoughts,
>     my Minde
>         Wants thoughts to Comprehend thy Worth,
>     alas!
> Thy Glory far Surmounts my thoughts, my
>     thoughts
>         Surmount my Words: Hence little Praise is
>     brought.
>
> But seing Non-Sense very Pleasant is
>     To Parents, flowing from the Lisping
>     Child,
> I Conjue to thee, hoping thou in this
>     Will finde some hearty Praise of mine
>         Enfoild,
>         But though my pen drop'd golden Words,
>     yet would
>         Thy Glory far out shine my Praise in
>     Gold.

In recent years the most acute and thorough of Taylor's readers have tended to agree that the self-deprecation expressed in stanzas such as these fairly mild ones (by Taylor's standards) reflects a genuine contempt on Taylor's part for his own poetic efforts. Anne Bradstreet's gentle dismissals of her verse seem almost vain by comparison to the depths of spiritual and artistic self-loathing to which Taylor repeatedly seems to sink, but even the most strongly stated of these depictions of human corruption - sometimes in their very extravagance—evoke the innocence of the lisping child and the image of parental solicitude that sustains the lines above. Taylor may well envision himself as a leper "all o're clag'd" with running sores and scabs, with "Stinking Breath," corrupted lungs, and a "Scurfy Skale" encrusting his entire body like the "Elephantik Mange," but the extremity of the description itself calls attention to its own conventional nature in a way that prevents the reader from taking such descriptions very seriously. The more highly wrought they get, the more childlike they seem, and the more plausible and more tender, in turn, seems the Lord's careful "springeing" and "besprinkling" that cures the leper's malady with His blood.

The personal usefulness of the "Preparatory Meditations" was, after all, to prepare and not to incapacitate. Taylor employed these poems as a means of readying himself for what he perceived as the momentous role he played administering and receiving the sacrament. The biblical quotations accompanying all but one of the meditations are the texts upon which he had chosen to preach on each communion Sunday, and all the meditations except the first one are dated. These poems are rooted just as deeply in Taylor's life as Bradstreet's domestic poems are rooted in hers, and their repetitive nature (like that of Bradstreet's laments) was from Taylor's perspective their primary meditative asset. They were meant to transform the mere repetitions of life into exalted occasions, all of the same fundamental kind to be sure but as diverse as the most heterogeneous natural imagery could make them. Collectively these poems also provide an extraordinary portrait of the ongoing interplay between security and insecurity in the Puritan imagination. William Scheick is only partly right when he states [in *The Will and the Word,* 1974] that the meditations nowhere depict "any sense of comfort on the poet's part." In fact the strategy of virtually every one of the poems is to enact the recovery of a degree of personal assurance sufficient to make the ceremony of communion possible both for Taylor as the priestly celebrant and for the reader. They are, as Scheick elsewhere perceptively notes, acts of preservation, however inadequate their language may have been to Taylor's vision and however incomplete the process of reassurance might remain. No orthodox Congregational sacramentalist—as Taylor was—would have felt comfortable laying claim to an absolute certainty of personal election. But the church as a social entity had to accommodate itself to irresolvable metaphysical uncertainty, and in one sense that act of accommodation is what the meditations perform, much as the figure of Eve accommodated the strict demands of election to the social necessities of Massachusetts Bay in **"A Modell of Christian Charity."**

The particular ways in which Taylor sought to make his poetry useful confirm his participation in the tradition of the believing self's inadequacy and at the same time suggest his own peculiar softening of that tradition. The "Preparatory Meditations" repeatedly assert the unaided soul's incapacity properly to praise or to serve God, but they do so in a remarkably homely, very nearly forgiving, fashion. One cannot escape the implication throughout Taylor's diction that even at their worst man's sins are not so serious after all. The cajoling attitude of the "Crumb of Dust" with which Taylor opens the "Prologue" to his meditational series represents the consistent tone of his poetic persona:

> Lord, Can a Crumb of Dust the Earth
>    outweigh,
>       Outmatch all mountains, nay the
>       Chrystall Sky?
> Imbosom in't designs that shall Display
>       And trace into the Boundless Deity?
>       Yea hand a Pen whose moysture doth
>       guild ore
>       Eternall Glory with a glorious glore. . . .
>
> I am this Crumb of Dust which is design'd
>       To make my Pen unto thy Praise
>       alone,
> And my dull Phancy I would gladly grinde
>       Unto an Edge on Zions Pretious Stone.
>       And Write in Liquid Gold upon thy
>       Name
>       My Letters till thy glory forth doth
>       flame.
>
> Let not th'attempts breake down my Dust I
>    pray
>       Nor laugh thou them to scorn but

> pardon give.
> Inspire this Crumb of Dust till it display
>       Thy Glory through't: and then thy dust
>       shall live.
>       Its failings then thou'lt overlook I
>       trust,
>       They being Slips slipt from thy Crumb
>       of Dust.

Taylor's posture throughout the poems that follow reflects both the humility and the assertiveness of these prefatory lines. These are clearly the words of a fallen speaker, aware of his diminished status in the universe, but aware as well of the larger typological design that makes a measure of bemusement at his own "Slips" something other than a gesture of theological impertinence. On occasion, to be sure, Taylor will revile man's corrupt condition, but it is nevertheless clear that he is prone to exercise a kind of poetic "grace" upon his human sinners, alleviating their afflictions in a way that anticipates, and to some extent symbolizes, the operations of genuine grace upon the genuinely corrupted spirit.

At times, in his joy at God's care for His erring and undeserving creatures, Taylor can approach a sort of elation in his lines that suggests both stark surprise and a kind of durable innocence on the part of the awe-struck speaker:

> Oh! Good, Good, Good, my Lord What more
>    Love yet!
>       Thou dy for mee! What am I dead in
>       thee;
> What, did Deaths arrow shot at me thee hit?
>       Didst slip between that flying shaft and
>       mee?
>       Didst make thyselfe Deaths marke shot
>       at for me?
>       So that her Shaft shall fly no far than
>       thee? . . .
>
> Oh!, Thou, my Lord, thou king of Saints, here
>    mak'st
>       A royall Banquet, thine to entertain
> With rich and royall fare, Celestiall Cates,
>       And sittest at the Table rich of fame.
>       Am I bid to this Feast? Sure Angells
>       stare,
>       Such rugged looks, and Ragged robes I
>       ware. . . .
>
> Who is the Object of this Love? and in
>       Whose mouth doth fall the Apple of this
>       tree?
> Is Man? A Sinner? Such a Wormhole thing?
>       Oh! matchless Love, laid out on such as
>       Hee!
>       Should Gold wed Dung, Should Stars

wooe Lobster Claws,
It would no wonder, like this Wonder,
   cause. . . .

Stanzas like these are not particularly unusual in Taylor's work, ingenuous as they are, and it would be a mistake to ascribe their peculiar charm either to the author's lack of poetic sophistication or (as Robert Daly suggests) to an extremely sophisticated suspicion of all metaphoric speech. One indirect way of asserting the inadequacies of the self—as we noted in Bradstreet's verse—is to make certain that one's imagery reflects the "inadequacy" of human vision in general. That, in part, is the purpose of Taylor's nearly comic pursuit of preposterous images. At the same time, in Taylor's work such language has the effect of convincing us that unregenerate man is not really a very great redemptive challenge. Taylor's generic sinner does not fall into the glorious metric apostasy of Milton's Satan, but into a kind of childish "naughtiness" in which the value of human life remains very much apparent despite its temporary state of degradation:

A Bran, a Chaff, a very Barly yawn,
   An Husk, a Shell, a Nothing, nay, yet
      worse:
A Thistle, Bryer prickle, pricking Thorn,
   A Lump of Lewdeness, Pouch of Sin, a
      purse
   Of Naughtiness I am, yea, what not,
      Lord?
   And wilt thou be mine Altar? and my
      Lord?

Mine Heart's a Park or Chase of sins: Mine
   Head
   'S a Bowling Alley: sins play Ninchole
      here.
Phansy's a Green: sin Barly-breaks in't led.
   Judgment's a pingle; Blindeman's Bluff's
      plaid there.
   Sin playes at Coursey-park within my
      Minde;
   My Will's a Walke in which it aires
      what's blind.

In her recent treatment of Taylor's typological poetics, Karen Rowe [in *Saint and Singer,* 1986] finds in these lines a "scathing self-denunciation" of the "sin-riddled soul's empty frivolities," a point of view that seems, at best, unjustifiably sober. Barley-breaks and Coursey-park are, like Blindman's Bluff, innocent games. A state of sin that can be characterized in this manner is already well on the way toward being forgiven.

Taylor wrote, of course, from the perspective of one of the elect. In the opening poem of "God's Determinations," he makes it clear that even in the full panic of their sense of sin, such elected souls resemble a "Child that fears the Poker Clapp," who falls to earth and "lies still for fear least hee—Should by his breathing lowd discover'd bee". The errors of such children invite gentle treatment and that is precisely the sort of treatment that they receive both in the drama of "God's Determinations" and in the lines of the "Preparatory Meditations." Presumably a cycle of poems and meditations describing the inner life of the damned would be considerably more grim, but Taylor's interest in their fate is quite perfunctory, and his portrait of the elect has sufficient variety in it to allow almost any reader to identify with the saved souls rather than with the lost ones. Ezra Stiles, Taylor's grandson and a temporary custodian of his papers, once occupied himself in calculating quite seriously the numbers of resurrected souls involved at Judgment Day. How crowded would Christ's courtroom be and how might the verdicts go in proportion of saved to lost souls? Stiles estimated that about 120 billion souls would be involved altogether, of which 90 billion would be saved and 30 billion damned. These are, by strict Calvinist standards, rather good odds. More importantly, perhaps, they seem consistent with Edward Taylor's own tendency to weight the human predicament in favor of election and then to focus his imagination upon the benevolence of that process of salvation.

Taylor's depiction of the anxieties of the insecure human soul is detailed and sincere; he is by no means complacent in his vision of the operations of grace. Even the saved are filled with a sense that they "have long ago deserv'de Hells flame," that God's "abused Mercy" could only "burn and scald" them, that Justice and Vengeance "Run hotly after us our blood to spill". Such accounts of the genuine terror of human life, however, are almost always followed by descriptions of our mortal plight that subtly, but decisively, relieve the strain and imply our ultimate rescue:

Who'le with a Leaking, old Crack't Hulk
   assay
To brave the raging Waves of Adria?
Or who can Cross the Main Pacifick o're?
Without a Vessell Wade from shore to shore?
What! wade the mighty main from brim to
   brim,
As if it would not reach above the Chin?
But oh! poor wee, must wade from brinck to
   brinck
With such a weight as would bright Angells
   sink.
Or venture angry Adria, or drown
When Vengeance's sea doth break the
   floodgates down.
If Stay, or Go to sea, we drown. Then see
In what a wofull Pickle, Lord, we bee.

To be saved from hell's flames and from an aroused, bloodthirsty Justice seems scarcely possible. But even a deeply shaken believer might reasonably expect to escape from a "wofull Pickle." In the dialogue poems from "God's Determinations" that prepare the soul to resist Satan's temptations and to achieve church fellowship, the "Saint" assures the "Soul" that God dispenses grace to human beings only gradually, for good psychological reasons:

> You think you might have more: you shall
>   have so,
> But if you'd all at once, you could not grow.
> And if you could not grow, you'd grieving
>   fall:
> All would not then Content you, had you all.
> Should Graces Floodgate thus at once breake
>   down,
> You most would lose, or else it you would
>   drown.
> He'l fill you but by drops, that so he may
> Not drown you in't, nor cast a Drop away.

Equipped with this kind of reassurance, even the most reluctant of Taylor's elect souls, the second and third "rancks" that originally had fled God's presence and held their breath waiting for the poker-clap, are filled with "holy Raptures" and able to capture the entire heavenly strategy in a single couplet:

> Sin sincks the Soul to Hell: but here is Love
> Sincks Sin to Hell: and soars the Soul above.

The sense of great peril and great promise that marks Winthrop's description of the American plight is present to Taylor's imagination in this sense of a carefully nurturing God, releasing His grace with all the cautious circumspection of a mother watching over her child's slow but steady growth. Taylor never explicitly manipulates God's gender, as Bradstreet is willing to do in her "Meditation 39," for example. He takes his images from emblem books and from the Bible, with very little of the kind of provocative modification that Winthrop himself was willing to employ in his treatment of the figure of Eve. But it is equally clear that Taylor is firmly grounded in the imaginative heritage of Winthrop's "modell," and in the preeminence that model had given to domestic settings and domestic instincts.

What finally gives Taylor's work its distinctive, infectious energy is the earnestness with which he takes to heart his own poetic version of this tradition, operating in the experience of election: Even in our degraded state, we are still children; even in his inconceivable majesty, God is still our parent and takes a parent's interest in us. The household metaphor that was so formative for Anne Bradstreet is critical to the sense of intimacy that Taylor feels with his attentive and forgiving Maker. It is possible to tease, to cajole, to "tweedle" praise, to fill one's address to God with the most

---

**An excerpt from Percival Lowell's elegy on John Winthrop (1649):**

> You English *Mattachusians* all
>
>     Forbear sometime from [s]leeping,
> Let every one both great and small
>     Prepare themselves for weeping.
> For he is gone that was our friend,
> This Tyrant Death hath wrought his end.
> Who was the very Chief among
>     The chiefest of our Peers
> Who hath in peace maintain'd us long
>     The space of nineteen years,
> And now hee's breathless, lifeless, dead,
> Cold earth is now become his bed.
> The Jews did for their *Moses* weep
>     Who was their Gubernator,
> Let us for *Winthrope* do the like,
>     Who was our Conservator
> With Lines of gold in Marble [s]tone
>     With pens of steel engrave his name
> O let the Mufes every one
>     In prose and Verse extol his Fame,
> Exceeding far those ancient Sages
> That ruled *Greeks* in former Ages.
> O [s]pightfull Death and also cruel
> Thou hast quite flain *New Englands* Jewel:
> Shew us vile *Tyrant* if thou can
> Tel where to find out such a man?
> Methinks I hear a spirit breathe
> *Non est inventus* here beneath.
> He was (we furely may fay this)
> *Rara avis in terris . . .*
>
> Therefore let us give him his due,
>     To him is due this [s]tile,
> He was an *Israelite* full true
>     Without all fraud or guile.
> Let *Winthrops* name [s]till famous be,
> With us and our Posterity.

> *Percival Lowell, in* Life and Letters of John Winthrop, Vol. II, *by Robert C. Winthrop, Little, Brown, and Company,* 1869.

---

humdrum domestic metaphors, to offer Him "wagon loads" of love and glory, to dedicate one's services as a spinning wheel, an organ pipe, a liquor bottle, a writer. The fullness and to some degree the very unevenness of Taylor's poetic discourse is a substantial part of its meaning. One does not attempt to polish or revise for God's benefit, any more than the compilers of the *Bay Psalm Book* would have attempted to polish God's altar. One simply opens one's humanity to God, and to the greatest extent possible one celebrates it. Taylor's confidence in God's closeness is at least as critical to the shape his poetry takes as is his awe at God's power. In this sense he is in perfect agreement with Milton, whose God is strikingly at ease in Paradise and much more at home there than among His marshaled ranks of militarized angels. Taylor's own wonderfully comfortable relations with God are by no means paradisal. He remained a crumb of dust, a bag of botches, a purse of naughtiness. But in this colloquial vocabulary of degradation, the intimacy of the family thrives.

## James G. Moseley (essay date 1990)

SOURCE: "Winthrop's *Journal:* Religion, Politics, and Narrative in Early America," in *Religion and the Life of the Nation: American Recoveries,* edited by Rowland A. Sherrill, University of Illinois Press, 1990, pp. 235-58.

[*Here, Moseley discusses the ways in which the tone of Winthrop's journal changes from a mere recording of historical fact to a personal, self-conscious narrative.*]

John Winthrop has often been portrayed as a self-righteous martinet, a Puritan dictator whose love for power was matched only by his unthinking Calvinist orthodoxy. Yet reading his three-volume **Journal** enables us to recover a more credible, if more complicated, image of the foremost founder of the Massachusetts Bay Colony. Several years ago historian Edmund Morgan wisely eschewed the authoritarian caricature and, instead, cast Winthrop [in *The Puritan Dilemma,* 1958] as representative of "the Puritan dilemma," that characteristic tension between the transcendent exuberance of an awakened spiritual life and the mundane requirements of living responsibly in a fallen world. Because Morgan pictured Winthrop as quite thoroughly molded by his spiritual experiences as a young man in England, he tended to read Winthrop's **Journal** as a straightforward chronicle of how Puritan religious convictions were translated into political realities in early New England. Yet Winthrop did not simply reach his religious conclusions in England and then embark prepared to govern accordingly in the New World. Reading the **Journal** with an ear for changes in Winthrop's narrative voice reveals that his character, attitudes, and beliefs were not so thoroughly formed by the time of migration as Morgan implied. Indeed, Winthrop's thinking underwent significant transformations in New England, and writing the **Journal** became his way of making sense of these revisions.

Winthrop's **Journal** is thus of more than historiographical interest, for it discloses the development of a prototypically American sensibility. Insofar as it represents a more complex Winthrop than previously known, then, the **Journal** allows us to reclaim one kind of integral response to American experience in religious and political terms which, it can be argued, is present-ly in danger of being lost to rigid, codified, and inflexible sentiments. Regaining imaginatively the compound of openness and integrity that Winthrop achieved in his **Journal** thus presents a possibility of recovery from the ambivalence that suspends contemporary American life between grandiose delusions and austere self-denial.

The current malaise is described well in the recipe for "the minimal self" outlined in Christopher Lasch's recent book [*The Minimal Self,* 1984] about "psychic survival in troubled times," when "selfhood becomes a kind of luxury." Since "emotional equilibrium [now] demands a minimal self, not the imperial self of yesteryear," this leading cultural critic is definitely expressing "no indignant outcry against contemporary 'hedonism,' self-seeking, egoism, indifference to the general good—traits commonly associated with 'narcissism.'" Lasch naturally wishes his contemporaries could do more than merely "survive." Yet he knows that the kind of selfhood that "implies a personal history, family, friends, a sense of place" requires "the critical awareness of man's divided nature," and, short of reading Freud, he can recommend no workable access to this crucial resource. He would like to revise the values of his readers, but he distrusts new visions and despairs of renewing the old. In this predicament, which Lasch describes with uncomfortable accuracy, how can recovery begin? Is there an alternative to "the minimal self"?

Winthrop's **Journal** shows that the impetus for revision, recovery, and renewal comes not merely in these late bad times but in the beginnings of the national story. It is true that many Europeans came to America seeking a new way of life. But this novelty was not, as it were, *de novo.* The New World was from its discovery a place of revisioning, a place where the problems of life in the Old World could be corrected or avoided. The ideal of the new was thus consciously or unconsciously formulated in reference to the problems of the old. Few Europeans succeeded in stamping the New World indelibly with the impress of the ideal they brought from the Old, as new geographic and social conditions meant that originating designs had to be recast. Nevertheless, without reference to such ideals novelty overwhelmed, experience became mere flux. Revision, then, was not a static pattern but a living process; revisioning thus integrates action and interpretation into the story of America. Without revisioning, the story disintegrates into wanton dynamism, lifeless traditionalism, or gross self-deceit. While much great American literature has examined the difficulty of integrating the driving energy of the new with the wisdom of respect for the past, the hypothesis here is that in at least one exemplary instance—the **Journal** of Puritan Governor John Winthrop—revisioning began early and worked well. Indeed, Winthrop's **Journal** invites revised thinking about the subsequent revisioning of America.

In the early parts of the *Journal* Winthrop records, as one might in a public diary, the facts and sundry impressions of the transatlantic crossing and the struggle to found a colony in Massachusetts Bay. The reader, then and now, knows Winthrop as a reporter and trusts the factuality of his voice. Within a few years, as Winthrop faces the challenge of chronicling events of greater complexity and duration, the entries are less frequently made and tend to lengthen into stories in which the narrator attempts to re-create mixed motives and to trace the processes of conflicts that defined the terms of life in the Bay Colony. As the *Journal* progresses, Winthrop begins to leave blanks in the text, spaces to which he can return to add more facts or to ponder the significance of the events he records. Likewise, he begins to refer to previous and subsequent entries, to employ obvious authorial rhetoric, to cover longer spans of time in some entries, and to group events according to their significance rather than to strict chronology. At one point, when dealing with Anne Hutchinson in the retrospection of his prose, Winthrop first attempts to record the events leading to and surrounding her expulsion from the colony; later, he writes a **"Short Story of the Rise, Reign, and Ruin of the Antinomians, and Libertines that Infected the Churches of New England."** The shift in narrative approach does not necessarily betray a change of mind on Winthrop's part about "this American Jesabel." But it does indicate an awareness that her story, and his involvement with it, requires a new way of recounting the experience.

Such changes are at least as significant, if not more so, than a more superficial change of ideas, for the alteration of narrative forms reveals Winthrop's nascent apprehension that life in America will require new structures of understanding and will repay novel interpretations. By the beginning of what was in his own text the third and final volume of the *Journal,* Winthrop is more consistently and more fully engaged as the historian of early America, composing a reflective narrative in which it is plain that events are being remembered and reviewed in terms of what the experiences themselves express—instead of simply what they may be construed to mirror in terms of the purposes of a transcendent God. Yet because Winthrop was not a highly self-conscious modern author, it is not surprising to find a mixture of narrative styles in the second and third sections of his *Journal*. With that caveat in mind, one can begin to see what the patterns of its telling suggest about the meaning of Winthrop's story of New England.

The Puritans went—or, from a contemporary perspective, came—to America with the explicit purpose of revising the practice of religion in England. Their reforming vision was articulated by John Winthrop in a lay sermon, **"A Modell of Christian Charity,"** delivered on board the *Arbella* in 1630. The basic model was clear: "GOD ALMIGHTIE in his most holy and wise providence hath soe disposed on the Condicion of mankinde, as in all times some must be rich some poore, some highe and eminent in power and dignitie; others meane and in subieccion." No one in England would have argued with that! The "reasons" behind the model suggest the distinctive mission of the Puritans. As "a Company professing our selues fellow members of Christ" they come "to seeke out a place of Cohabitation and Consorteship vnder a due forme of Government both ciuill and ecclesiasticall." This work will require "extraordinary" means; thus unlike "When we liued in England," now "that which the most in theire Churches maineteine as a truth in profession onely, we must bring into familiar and constant practice." Far from being a project designed and performed by men, Winthrop reminds his fellows that "Thus stands the cause betweene God and vs, wee are entered into Covenant with him for this worke." The covenant means that if God hears our prayers and brings us in peace to our desired place, then he has ratified the agreement and "will expect a strickt performance of the Articles contained in it." In order to muster the requisite love, justice, and humility, "wee must be knitt together in this worke as one man," and then "the God of Israell . . . shall make vs a prayse and glory, that men shall say of succeeding plantacions: the lord make it like that of New England: for we must Consider that wee shall be as a Citty vpon a Hill" with "the eies of all people . . . upon us." Faithfulness to this originating vision, therefore, would spur revision of religion and politics in England and throughout the civilized world.

Much has been written about the Puritans and their "errand into the wilderness," but the purpose here is to look not so much at what "really happened" as into how John Winthrop interpreted the early history of the project he led. It is not that he initially thought the project would require interpretation—far from it. He was so sure of the "modell" and of his own ability to govern that he began a journal simply to keep a record of the way the Puritan plan unfolded. He was ever in the thick of things, usually as governor, always as the recognized leader of the colony. But an interesting thing happened on the way to reforming England and the world. Not only did England have her own revolution and hence need little advice from Massachusetts but also some American Puritans, as the development of Winthrop's *Journal* reveals, were becoming more committed to revisioning as a process than they were to the society and institutions they set out initially to revise. To be sure, not everyone made this transition. Most were caught up too thoroughly in the rude exigencies of daily life, and those who had visions were generally overpowered by them. As his journal-keeping became an increasingly self-conscious literary project, Winthrop mapped out a "middle landscape," poised precariously between the rampant spirituality and the land-hungry expansionism of his companions. His literary enterprise afforded Winthrop a crucial angle of revision, which if not wholly yet still significantly enabled him to succeed where so many of his contemporaries failed. For Winthrop's writing began to give him a double or combined consciousness of himself both as an active participant in and as an interpretive observer of Puritan life. In the process Winthrop's narrative becomes considerably more than a quotidian chronicle, and the religious and political developments at the heart of his story need to be understood in relation to the changing nature of the narrative itself.

In the first and perhaps most obvious place, in the course of the years covered in his *Journal* Winthrop moved from a commitment to reform and renew the Church of England toward an affirmation of a new, more characteristically American religiousness. Tension between the old and the new is evident very early on. Thus on 27 July 1630, about a month after landing in Massachusetts, Winthrop observes: "We of the congregation kept a fast, and chose Mr. Wilson our teacher, and Mr. Nowell an elder, and Mr. Gager and Mr. Aspinwall, deacons. We used imposition of hands, but with this protestation by all, that it was only as a sign of election and confirmation, not of any intent that Mr. Wilson should renounce his ministry he received in England." Despite their protestations, such balancing became increasingly difficult.

The original idea was that, while the corrupt Anglicans required purifying, the separatists, such as those at nearby Plymouth, had severed their bonds with the communion of the saints. The Bay Colony was to chart a middle course, and Winthrop and the others were prepared to be welcomed back by a mother country awakened by New England's shining example. But William Bradford visited Boston in 1631, and on 25 October 1632 Winthrop records that when he and John Wilson and two Puritan captains visited the Pilgrims:

> The governour of Plimouth, Mr. William Bradford, (a very discreet and grave man,) with Mr. Brewster, the elder, and some others, came forth and met them without the town, and conducted them to the governour's house, where they were very kindly entertained, and feasted every day at several houses. On the Lord's day there was a sacrament, which they did partake in; and, in the afternoon, Mr. Roger Williams (according to their custom) propounded a question, to which the pastor, Mr. Smith, spake briefly; then Mr. Williams prophesied; and after the governour of Plimouth spake to the question; after him the elder; then some two or three more of the congregation. Then the elder desired the governour of Massachusetts and Mr. Wilson to speak to it, which they did. When this ended, the deacon, Mr. Fuller, put the congregation in mind of their duty of contribution; whereupon the governour and all the rest went down to the deacon's seat, and put into

the box, and then returned.

Winthrop soon saw the Pilgrims as allies and even spiritual brothers, and he did not return "home" when the Puritans came to power in England. New World associations had replaced ties from the Old.

Then, too, it was useful to convene elders from the various churches for specific causes and occasions, and in such meetings new steps were taken. In November of 1633, for example, Winthrop notes:

> The ministers in the bay and Sagus did meet, once a fortnight, at one of their houses by course, where some question of moment was debated. Mr. Skelton, the pastor of Salem, and Mr. Williams, who was removed from Plimouth thither, (but not in any office, though he exercised by way of prophecy,) took some exception against it, as fearing it might grow in time to a presbytery or superintendency, to the prejudice of the churches' liberties. But this fear was without cause; for they were all clear in that point, that no church or person can have power over another church; neither did they in their meetings excercise any such jurisdiction.

By denying so fervently the dangerous extreme of Presbyterianism, they abandoned the middle ground and forthrightly espoused radical congregationalism. There were indeed no bishops in New England!

The planting of new churches in new settlements seemed natural; nevertheless, in practice, such new developments required monitoring. As Winthrop explains on 1 April 1636, there were good reasons for keeping a close eye even on people led by a man of "bright learning and high piety" such as Richard Mather:

> Mr. Mather and others, of Dorchester, intending to begin a new church there, (a great part of the old one being gone to Connecticut,) desired the approbation of the other churches and of the magistrates; and, accordingly, they assembled this day, and, after some of them had given proof of their gifts, they made confession of their faith, which was approved of; but proceeding to manifest the work of God's grace in themselves, the churches, by their elders, and the magistrates, &c. thought them not meet, at present, to be the foundation of a church; and thereupon they were content to forbear to join till further consideration. The reason was, for that most of them (Mr. Mather and one more excepted) had builded their comfort of salvation upon unsound grounds, viz. some upon dreams and ravishes of spirit by fits; others upon the reformation of their lives; other upon duties and performances, &c; wherein they discovered three special errours: 1. That they had not come to hate sin, because it was filthy, but only left it, because it was hurtful. 2. That, by reason of this, they had never truly closed with Christ, (or rather Christ with them,) but had

made use of him only to help the imperfection of their sanctification and duties, and not made him their sanctification, wisdom, &c. 3. They expected to believe by some power of their own, and not only and wholly from Christ.

Evidently such guidance was effective, for four months later "a new church was gathered at Dorchester, with approprobation of the magistrates and elders." Thus some new form of church order appeared to be in line with God's purposes in New England. Although the full flowering was many years away, some of the seeds of denominationalism—America's distinctive contribution to ecclesiastical organization—found native soil in the early towns of New England.

In religious matters Winthrop entered arguments and made his own beliefs clear but finally moved against only those whose beliefs appeared to threaten the public order. No doubt he was heavy-handed and crude in the ways he orchestrated the removal of Anne Hutchinson and her followers from Massachusetts, but there is also no doubt that he acted in response to what he perceived as the clear and present danger her antinomian teachings involved. She was "a woman of a ready wit and bold spirit," he observed on 21 October 1636, who "brought over with her two dangerous errours: 1. That the person of the Holy Ghost dwells in a justified person. 2. That no sanctification can help us to evidence our justification." Winthrop knew instinctively that "From these two grew many branches," which would sprout beyond the bounds of decent communal order.

If they could not be pruned by the elders, the antinomians would have to be removed "root and branch" by the magistrates. As Winthrop saw it, Mrs. Hutchinson did more than sow dissent; she encouraged people to believe that since they were actually one with the Holy Spirit, they could live entirely as they pleased, without need for religious instruction and moral constraint. By December, John Wilson laid the blame for the growing and "inevitable danger of separation" squarely "upon these new opinions risen up amongst us, which all the magistrates, except the governour and two others, did confirm, and all the ministers but two." Winthrop defended Wilson in the church and in writing to the fence-sitting John Cotton, but to no avail. Given the spreading disturbances, it is not surprising that Winthrop's party applied increasingly unseemly pressure until Mrs. Hutchinson finally broke down in court, rapturously affirmed her erroneous beliefs, and was banished. Recalling the tenacity of the mainline's counterattack, one has to remember the overwhelming importance of spiritual affairs in Puritan life in order to understand—not to say excuse—Winthrop's treatment of these "familists."

In the heat of the controversy, when the future of the

Bay Colony as a coherent religious community seemed most in doubt, one of Winthrop's observations on 17 May 1637 reveals the more constant side of his character: "The intent of the court in deferring the sentence was, that, being thus provoked by their tumultuous course, and divers insolent speeches, which some of that party had uttered in the court, and having now power enough to have crushed them, their moderation and desire of reconciliation might appear to all." Such ambivalent sentiments were not simply for the sake of noble public appearance. In fact, Winthrop's characteristic tendency was toward leniency, as can be seen in his relations with Roger Williams and in Thomas Morton's personification of Winthrop as "Joshua Temperwell." In the entry for 29 October 1645 he points out that "sure the rule of hospitality to strangers, and of seeking to pluck out of the fire such as there may be hope of to be reduced out of error and the snare of the devil, do seem to require more moderation and indulgence of human infirmity where there appears not obstinacy against the clear truth." Thus he was at odds with spiritually adolescent hotheads such as Henry Vane and pedestrian precisionists such as Thomas Dudley. In the heat of the moment, the passionate found Winthrop's temperance objectionable; over the course of his life, though, the people often preferred Winthrop's spiritual moderation to Hutchinson's abandon or Dudley's authoritarianism.

While he could not abide Anne Hutchinson's bold antinomianism, Winthrop was no certain enemy of Roger Williams, who came to consider the governor a wise and trusted adviser. The "inner light," in Winthrop's eyes, needed the focus of orthodox doctrine to produce useful insight, and spiritual heat required the regulation of social sanction to fuel "a Citty vpon a Hill." Thus in late August of 1637 "the synod, called the assembly, of all the teaching elders" met to consider "about eighty opinions, some blasphemous, others erroneous, all unsafe, condemned by the whole assembly; whereto near all the elders, and others sent by the churches, subscribed their names; but some few liked not the subscription, though they consented to the condemning of them."

If theological opinions without critical consideration by the elders might have consequences that were unsafe for the community, outright immorality without clear punishment was at least equally pernicious. On 12 November 1641 Winthrop enables his readers to witness the fate of one Hackett, a young servant in Salem who "was found in buggery with a cow, upon the Lord's day." Even upon the ladder prepared to be hanged, full repentance had not come; "but the cow (with which he had committed that abomination) being brought forth and slain before him, he brake out into a loud and doleful complaint against himself" and was led in prayer by John Wilson and the other attendant elders. Winthrop's observation upon the lad's execution is noteworthy: "There is no doubt to be made but the Lord hath received his soul to his mercy; and he was pleased to lift up the light of his countenance so far towards him, as to keep him from despair, and to hold him close to his grace in a seeking condition; but he was not pleased to afford him that measure of peace and comfort as he might be able to hold out to others, lest sinful men, in the love of their lusts, should set mercy and repentance at too low a rate, and so miss of it when they vainly expect it." With such precise moral calibration, the Bay Colony would be no "burned-over district."

True piety required the guidance of a learned clergy. The weird misbeliefs and violence fostered by Samuel Gorton and his cohorts sprang from the fact, as Winthrop notes on 13 October 1643, that "they were all illiterate men, the ablest of them could not write true English, no not common words, yet they would take upon them the interpretation of the most difficult places of scripture, and wrest them any way to serve their own turns." Nevertheless, Winthrop's goal was not to douse the flame of religious enthusiasm but to sustain it within a steady range. Charismatic spirituality might lead either to disregard for moral regulations or to compulsive moralism. Winthrop wanted to keep true religion alive by avoiding both extremes, and he often found himself needing to protect the unwary from their neighbors' ire. While it certainly had its limits, Winthrop's lenity in such matters did more than get him in trouble with the inflexible among the saints. It also nurtured resources that could be tapped a century later by Jonathan Edwards in the Great Awakening. And the development of these spiritual resources can best be seen in the increasing creativity of the narrative voice in Winthrop's *Journal*. Looking at Puritan religious life through the changes in the *Journal*, then, suggests crucial relations between institutional and imaginative expressions of American spirituality.

Because of its overriding religious purposes, the Bay Colony's political life was supposed to be different from what its people had known in the old country. Unlike the factionalism that "hath been usual in the council of England and other states, who walk by politic principles only," asserted Winthrop on 30 October 1644, in Massachusetts:

> these gentlemen were such as feared God, and endeavored to walk to the rules of his word in all their proceedings, so as it might be conceived in charity, that they walked according to their judgments and conscience, and where they went aside, it was merely for want of light, or their eyes were held through some temptation for a time, that they could not make use of the light they had, for in all these differences and agitations about them, they continued in brotherly love, and in the exercise of all friendly offices each to other, as occasion required.

But, try as he might to see Puritan politics in terms of religion, Winthrop, as his friends in the ministry had on occasion to remind him, was no theologian; he was a leader of men and manager of worldly affairs, and so it is, in the second place, in the realm of politics itself that one looks for an understanding of the man. Indeed, much of the *Journal* is taken up with observing the hero's political reasoning and tact in the face of his opponents' passion and contrariness. Just as his style of religion changes, so too in politics the *Journal* reveals Winthrop's transformation (incomplete but undeniable) from being governor as ruler to being governor as first citizen. The architect of **"A Modell of Christian Charity,"** who sees power rightly held by the governor and dispensed through his wisdom on behalf of the governed, becomes in the press of founding, sustaining, and directing a successful colony the engineer of an increasingly political structure, who writes **"A Discourse on Arbitrary Gouerment."**

While remaining the elected governor more often than not throughout his life in the New World, Winthrop is continually in the process of giving away political power. In 1631 the people of Watertown agreed to pay their assessment for new fortifications after admitting their misunderstanding of the nature of the Bay Colony's government. "The ground of their errour," Winthrop notes on 17 February, was that

> they took this government to be no other but as of a major and aldermen, who have not power to make laws or raise taxations without the people; but understanding that this government was rather in the nature of a parliament, and that no assistant could be chosen but by the freemen, who had power likewise to remove the assistants and put in others, and therefore at every general court (which was to be held once every year) they had free liberty to consider and propound any thing concerning the same, and to declare their grievances, without being subject to question, or, &c. they were fully satisfied; and so their submission was accepted, and their offence pardoned.

This right of the freemen to elect their leaders was important—to Winthrop, to the freemen, and to others within the colony. Virtually from the outset, and then steadily, Winthrop oversaw the expansion of the franchise. During a private meeting of the assistants on 1 May 1632, "after dinner, the governour told them, that he had heard, that the people intended, at the next general court, to desire, that the assistants might be chosen anew every year and that the governour might be chosen by the whole court, and not by the assistants only." The news distressed at least one of the others, but his objections were "answered and cleared in the judgment of the rest," and Winthrop's information proved accurate. A week later, when the general court met in Boston, the change was made: "Whereas it was (at our first coming) agreed, that the freemen should choose the assistants, and they the governour, the whole court agreed now, that the governour and assistants should all be new chosen every year by the general court, (the governour to be always chosen out of the assistants;) and accordingly the old governour, John Winthrop, was chosen; accordingly all the rest as before, and Mr. Humfrey and Mr. Coddington also, because they were daily expected." For the moment, a more general electoral process was simply a better way of choosing the same leaders. Within a few years, however, religious unrest fueled political passions; new men were elected, and offices rotated among the old guard. By 1644 there was a move to grant the freemen's privileges to non-churchmen, and in May of 1646 the rights of freemen were given to non-freemen as well. Until his death in 1649, Winthrop remained the one most often elected. The people usually trusted his leadership, always respected his judgment, and approved of his judicious broadening of the franchise.

Likewise, Winthrop worked steadily to balance the power of the generally elected "assistants" and the locally representative "deputies," never yielding enough to satisfy the more "democratical" deputies, nevertheless leading toward a form of legislative power that was fully bicameral by 1644. Then, too, while seeking to retain an arena for judicial discretion, he oversaw the formulation of a general body of laws for adjudication within the colony—never minutely specific enough to satisfy the precisionists but nevertheless far from the arbitrariness of autocracy.

In politics as in religion, Winthrop was characteristically ambivalent. On the one hand, as a good Calvinist, he agreed with the elders who affirmed on 18 October 1642 that "in a commonwealth, rightly and religiously constituted, there is no power, office, administration, or authority, but such as are commanded and ordained by God" and that the political institutions of such a commonwealth "ought not to be by them either changed or altered, but upon such grounds, for such ends, in that manner, and only so far as the mind of God may be manifested therein." Yet on the other hand, compassion for others led him on 18 January 1635 to profess "that it was his judgment, that, in the infancy of plantations, justice should be administered with more lenity than in a settled state, because people were then more apt to transgress, partly of ignorance of new laws and orders, partly through oppression of business and other straits." Given the ongoing tug-of-war between antinomians and precisionists, Winthrop's ambivalence embroiled him in—and saw the colony through—many controversies. In all he sought balance: in "a little speech" in 1645 Winthrop reminded the people, as he notes on 14 May, "so shall your liberties be preserved, in upholding the honor and power of authority amongst you." And he welcomed the development in 1643 of an intercolonial government called the United Colonies, with its own commissioners—

elected by all freemen by May of 1645—to resolve disputes between the several colonies of New England and to coordinate their common defense. On the one hand, yielding power seemed to increase Winthrop's authority; on the other, in all these ways he was preparing the colony for orderly continuity following the passage of his personal charisma.

Caught in a tug-of-war between enemies in England who wanted to install a "general governor" over all the colonies of New England and the deputies from the several towns who wanted more democratic decision-making, Winthrop moved from advocating aristocracy to supporting a mixed government, or "buffered democracy," at its heart much like the concept developed a century and a half later by the more conservative among the founders of the American republic. On the one hand, Winthrop suggested the expansion of the franchise, the development of a bicameral legislature, the formulation of a general body of laws, and the constitution of an intercolonial government. Yet he did not go as far in any of these matters as their proponents wished. For, on the other hand, he believed that an excess of democracy would lead to instability. He agreed with those who spoke for the rights of the minority in a church dispute in September of 1646 "that it was not to be expected, that the major party should complain of their own act, and if the minor party, or the party grieved, should not be heard, then God should have left no means of redress in such a case, which could not be." This particular case had a Winthropian happy ending, for "some failing was found in both parties, the woman had not given so full satisfaction as she ought to have done, and the major party of the church had proceeded too hastily against a considerable party of the dissenting brethren, whereupon the woman who had offended was convinced of her failing, and bewailed it with many tears, the major party also acknowledged their errour, and gave the elders thanks for their care and pains." Thus it seems possible that Winthrop's changing attitudes toward governance may provide a clue for interpreting relations between the federal theology of the Puritans and the federalism of such "revolutionaries" as John Adams and Alexander Hamilton. In the later stages of his *Journal* Winthrop moves from reporting events to telling stories that let the experiences of various characters speak increasingly for themselves. This move reflects his growing willingness to give the people and their deputies a voice in government, and so it is through the *Journal* that one begins to observe connections between the political, religious, and imaginative forms of the American story.

Winthrop's sense of vocation evolves in several stages. While still in England, when the altogether prepared but somewhat skeptical and unwilling Winthrop is recruited, he joins the Puritan project with a plan for action. As the chief actor, formed for heroic leadership, he has a design, or "modell," with which he informs and charges the group's sense of common purpose. Then, in the New World, he guides his model into action, usually playing the hero but sometimes forced into a supporting role—a new stance which, by making him from time to time an observer, heightens his powers of perception and gives him a crucial angle of interpretation through which to view the development of his design. Thus in December of 1636, in the midst of the antinomian turmoil, while Winthrop is out of office he has time to write a long entry describing Henry Vane's petulant attempt to resign as governor and relating his own and John Wilson's wise probity during the turbulence surrounding Anne Hutchinson.

As Winthrop begins to see himself as both interpreter and actor, he examines the people whose actions he records with increasing attention to their unique circumstances and personal complexities. Winthrop's entry for 9 November 1641 begins with "Query, whether the following be fit to be published," indicating an increasingly discriminating awareness of his role as a writer, and then proceeds to recount how Governor Bellingham stole the affections of a young woman residing in his own house and induced her to marry him instead of the man to whom she was betrothed. The relation of this compromising incident, which led perhaps to Winthrop's becoming governor again at the next election, is followed three days later by another tale of infidelity:

> Mr. Stephen Batchellor, the pastor of the church at Hampton, who had suffered much at the hands of the bishops of England, being about 80 years of age, and having a lusty comely woman to his wife, did solicit the chastity of his neighbour's wife, who acquainted her husband therewith; whereupon he was dealt with, but denied it, as he had told the woman he would do, and complained to the magistrates against the woman and her husband for slandering him. The church likewise dealing with him, he stiffly denied it, but soon after, when the Lord's supper was to be administered, he did voluntarily confess the attempt, and that he did intend to have defiled her, if she would have consented. The church, being moved with his free confession and tears, silently forgave him, and communicated with him: but after, finding how scandalous it was, they took advice of other elders, and after long debate and much pleading and standing upon the church's forgiving and being reconciled to him in communicating with him after he had confessed it, they proceeded to cast him out.

Winthrop notes that "after this he went on in a variable course" and finally nearly two years later "he was released of his excommunication, but not received to his pastor's office." In this narrative, told primarily for the sake of its own interest, though perhaps in some measure also to document the scandals occurring during Bellingham's administration, Winthrop uses adjec-

tives deftly to delineate a memorable character, and he compresses events of two years' duration into a coherent short story.

This little story within a story is followed by a four-page tale of "a very foul sin, committed by three persons" involving the debauchery of a young girl who was abused "many times, so as she was grown capable of man's fellowship, and took pleasure in it." Then, following an authorial observation that "as people increased, so sin abounded, and especially the sin of uncleanness, and still the providence of God found them out," Winthrop tells the story of poor Hackett and the cow, and various other tales of disorder before this long entry is completed. By this time Winthrop is more than governor; he is working consciously as the author of early New England. By 1642 the form of his work is no longer that of journal entries; Winthrop begins simply to intersperse dates in the text of a flowing narrative. In 1643 a single entry covers two months, looking back in time in order to show present events in their proper light. And the entries themselves lengthen, with those of May 1645 and November 1646 surpassing twenty pages each. Thus in terms of particular literary devices, such as characterization, retrospective narration, and the avoidance of authorial intrusion, as well as in terms of the increasing flow and continuity of the narrative as a whole, Winthrop's text ceases to be a matter of recordkeeping and becomes a matter of history as literature.

More nuanced characterization of others and more awareness of their roles in the drama of the Bay Colony as a whole provide Winthrop an increasingly distanced perspective on his own motives and actions as a character in the story he tells. The decency and sympathy with which he treats the characters in his *Journal* is perhaps related to his characteristic leniency toward those in trouble and his urge to understand their motivations—tendencies which sometimes cost him his office when public passions ran high but which also made him a better writer. While in roughly equal measure hero and narrator, Winthrop develops a literary form that can embrace confrontations and hence a narrative vision that sustains and includes challenges in ways beyond his capacities as one of the actors in the drama of the Bay Colony. On 12 June 1643 Winthrop records his apology for the style of one of his writings in which he had made "appeal to the judgment of religion and reason, but, as I there carried it, I did arrogate too much to myself and ascribe too little to others." A few months later, on 14 July, he notes in his *Journal* one of his failings as governor: "this fault hath been many times found in the governour to be oversudden in his resolutions, for although the course were both warrantable and safe, yet it had beseemed men of wisdom and gravity to have proceeded with more deliberation and further advice." Thus sometimes directly in power and sometimes not, Winthrop emerges more as narrator than as actor, freer to tell the history of early America in its own terms, still bearing witness to the motivating power of his original model but more intrigued now with discovering what the model has engendered than with forcing the New World's light through the prism of his initial design. As he observes on 12 November 1641, "God hath not confined all wisdom etc. to any one generation, that they should set rules for others to walk by."

Winthrop's opponents seem to have been people of single visions. As a man of action and of observation, however, Winthrop learned that the spiritual power of a vision lives only in the ongoing revisioning it engenders. When visions are codified and institutionalized, they begin to die as authority degenerates into control. Models imposed on experience stifle vitality and become relics, whether venerated or despised. In some crucial ways a moderate from the outset, Winthrop discovered in writing his *Journal* that interpretation, through reference to a past ideal of the future, yields a kind of authority that need not violate the experience of the present. The ideal is reshaped as experience is represented. As a writer, Winthrop was able to respect the integrity of the present without losing sight of the ideal and without using the ideal to disfigure the vitality of the present. Like his movements in religion and politics, in his *Journal* Winthrop moves toward freedom even while he gains authority. It is in the product of his double vision, the text itself, that all the people of single vision continue to live for us. Their descendants made the jeremiad the literary form most characteristic of second—and third-generation Puritans. For them, as Sacvan Bercovitch says [in *The Puritan Origins of the American Self,* 1975], "every crisis called forth a reassertion of the design." In contrast, Winthrop kept the design alive by remaining open to the unexpected. Vision endures in revision; as he said on 12 November 1641, "for history must tell the whole truth."

The whole truth can be neither wholly expressed in action nor fully relished in observation. As a certain kind of conscious and unconscious experience, Winthrop's changing engagement in and interpretation of life in the New World generated a new literary form. Hence we might see the *Journal* as the first example of what Sacvan Bercovitch calls "auto-American-biography," the telling of one's own and America's story in the same imaginative act. Or we might consider Winthrop's *Journal* to be something like the first American "novel," especially insofar as the meaning Winthrop articulates as narrator is generated from the alteration of his original governing design and therein initiates what David Minter [in *The Interpreted Design,* 1969] calls "the interpreted design as a structural principle in American prose." In any case, in Winthrop's *Journal* this is all rudimentary rather than full-blown. On the one hand, when we see Winthrop as an actor who begins with a design upon the world and ends as a narrator or historian, we are not yet dealing with the developed literary genius of Hawthorne, James, Fitzgerald, or Faulkner that Minter explicates. Yet on the other hand, there is in Winthrop's *Journal* something akin to the impulse that led Norman Mailer to call the major sections of *The Armies of the Night* [1968] "history as a novel" and "the novel as history." There are certainly few other than inverse personal comparisons to be drawn between Mailer and Winthrop, but Mailer's intuitions about America hark back to an ancestry that might surprise him. Mailer and other recent keepers of the American dream have, like Winthrop, discovered that politics, religion, and narrative are modes of power, ways not only of responding to experience but also ways of controlling life by shaping its manifold energies into tractable, intelligible, forms. Revisioning America involves charting their ebbs and flows.

Recovering a sense of Winthrop's compound of integrity and openness yields resources for recovery from the ambivalent malaise of contemporary American life. Because he charted a course between the whirlpools of spiritual exuberance and the stagnation of moral precisionism, Winthrop's project suggests a strategy for coping with the expansive religious and political visions of Anne Hutchinson's cultural descendants and with the self-centered programs of latter-day Thomas Dudleys. Neither the grandiose delusions of religious and political imperialism nor the cunning austerity of an individual and cultural style that is "taut, toned, and coming on strong" will suffice to sustain a sense of purpose commensurate with American promise. Christopher Lasch's recipe for "minimal selfhood," for example, is more puritanical than authentically Puritan; Lasch's work, like much neoconservative cultural criticism, follows the form of the jeremiad while lacking its theological substance. Winthrop's revisioning defines an alternative to Lasch's studied pessimism as well as to the wistfully Emersonian optimism in many dreams of a larger and better life. Winthrop knew the answer to Emerson's Transcendentalist query, "Why should not we also enjoy an original relation to the universe?" Such dreams for a larger and better life are inevitably fashioned from fallible, if not meretricious, materials. An original relation to the universe, like the Puritans' **"Modell of Christian Charity,"** is already unreachably in the past. Although it is a lesson remembered usually in—or just after—times of crisis, revisioning is the only real way of having America at all.

Pointing to "some strange resistance in itself," Robert Frost says [in "West-Running Brook"], "It is this backward motion toward the source, / Against the stream, that most we see ourselves in, / The tribute of the current to the source." Readers who recall the elegiac ending of *The Great Gatsby*—Nick Carraway's remembrance of "a fresh green breast of the new world" that "had once pandered in whispers to the last and greatest of all human dreams; for a transitory enchanted moment man must have held his breath in the presence of this continent, compelled into an aesthetic contemplation he neither understood nor desired, face to face for the last time in history with something commensurate to his capacity for wonder"—such readers will confront Winthrop's journal entry for Tuesday 8 June 1630 with a start of recognition:

> The wind still W. and by S. fair weather, but close and cold. We stood N.N.W. with a stiff gale, and, about three in the afternoon, we had sight of land to the N.W. about ten leagues, which we supposed was the Isles of Monhegan, but it proved Mount Mansell. Then we tacked and stood W.S.W. We now had fair sun-shine weather, and so pleasant a sweet air as did much refresh us, and there came a smell off the shore like the smell of a garden.

> There came a wild pigeon into our ship, and another small land bird.

The Puritan imagination was saturated with Old Testament images: the birds present an antitype of the end of the Flood, and days of rain and fog end when sight of land is coupled with new sunshine and the smell of a garden!

Winthrop began with a vision and discovered the value of revisioning. Revisioning is where Americans begin. While "we can believe only by interpreting," Paul Ricouer points out [in *The Symbolism of Evil,* 1967], that "it is by *interpreting* that we can *hear* again." Or as Nick Carraway concludes, "So we beat on, boats against the current, borne back ceaselessly into the past." Thus recovering Winthrop involves more than pointing to the Puritan foundation of the American cultural edifice. Winthrop's achievement, the commitment to revisioning that informs his *Journal,* is more model than monument. He kept in play certain contradictory attitudes—individualism and communalism, innocent optimism and studied pessimism, interpretation and action—that work as antinomies throughout subsequent American cultural history. Neither in politics nor in literature was his work complete: governance of the Bay Colony often lacked Winthrop's guiding moderation, and his *Journal* is unabashedly an unfinished text. What can be recovered by looking backward at this curious blend of authoritarianism and moderation, of involvement and detachment, is the knowledge that the return of possibilities comes in the process of revisioning.

However much Americans now may wish for a reappearance of leadership with Winthrop's balanced sense of purpose, such renaissances depend on complicated historical and psychological processes that scholarship can investigate but not generate. Historical scholars contribute best to cultural recovery by rethinking the kind of history they write. The world of recent historical inquiry has been divided, if not between spiritual visionaries and moral precisionists, then between "humanists" who love theory and interpretation and "social scientists" who thrive on statistics and facts. Clifford Geertz is right to celebrate the blurring of these genres, and one goal of the present essay is to suggest that to undertake such interdisciplinary analysis—blending together in this case thinking about religion, politics, and narrative—is simply to render scholarship apposite to the variegated stuff of historical experience. The inability ever completely to fulfill such complex hermeneutical goals is the unavoidable price of wanting to see whole; to attempt, and thereby to achieve, less is the greater failure.

Study of the past may be hampered by artificial boundaries between various areas of life, and attempts to see the past whole may disclose distinctions more important than those made between academic disciplines. There is an irony, for example, in seeking faultless political candidates and then castigating them when their deficiencies inevitably appear. As Lewis Lapham asks [in *Harper's,* Dec., 1985], "who could bear the thought of being governed by human beings, by people as confused and imperfect as oneself? If a politician confessed to an honest doubt or emotion, how would it be possible to grant him the authority of a god?" In contrast, after being acquitted in an invidious political trial, on 14 May 1645 Winthrop reminds his fellow citizens that "it is you yourselves who have called us to this office, and being called by you, we have our authority from God" and then entreated them "to consider, that when you choose magistrates, you take them from among yourselves, men subject to like passions as you are. Therefore when you see infirmities in us, you should reflect upon your own, and that would make you bear the more with us, and not be severe censurers of the failings of your magistrates, when you have continual experience of like infirmaties in yourselves and others." Winthrop does not distinguish between the people and their leaders in terms of moral quality. He draws the line elsewhere:

> The covenant between you and us is the oath you have taken of us, which is to this purpose, that we shall govern you and judge your causes by the rules of God's laws and our own, according to our best skill. When you agree with a workman to build you a ship or house &c. he undertakes as well for his skill as for his faithfulness, for it is his profession, and you pay him for both. But when you call one to be a magistrate, he doth not profess nor undertake to have sufficient skill for that office, nor can you furnish him with gifts &c. therefore you must run the hazard of his skill and ability. But if he fail in faithfulness, which by his oath he is bound unto, that he must answer for. If it fall out that the case be clear to common apprehension, and the rule clear

also, if he transgress here, the errour is not in the skill, but in the evil of the will: it must be required of him. But if the cause be doubtful, or the rule doubtful, to men of such understanding and parts as your magistrates are, if your magistrates should err here, yourselves must bear it.

Assessing leaders in Winthrop's way would require continual self-assessment, which is always difficult, and might improve the quality and realism of American political discourse.

If self-scrutiny is the price of revisioning America, some things have not changed. For, as Winthrop went on to say, "concerning liberty, I observe a great mistake in the country." American life is still bedeviled by this mistake, although most people may no longer—perhaps for good reasons—be able to acknowledge it. As a true son of the Reformation, Winthrop distinguished between two kinds of liberty. On the one hand, there is everyone's "natural" liberty "to do what he lists." Such freedom to "do your own thing" is one of the few values Americans today now hold in common, even while recognizing that this "is a liberty to evil as well as to good" and that "this liberty is incompatible and inconsistent with authority." Unlike Winthrop, however, Americans now reject authority that curtails freedom. Certainly no one wants to reinhabit the cramped moral space of early New England. Yet in taking a stand for freedom, Americans may have forgotten what Winthrop envisioned, on the other hand, as the true form of liberty:

> The other kind of liberty I call civil or federal, it may also be termed moral, in reference to the convenant between God and man, in the moral law, and the politic covenants and constitutions, amongst men themselves. This liberty is the proper end and object of authority, and cannot subsist without it; and it is a liberty to that only which is good, just and honest. This liberty you are to stand for, with the hazard (not only of your good, but) of your lives, if need be. Whatsoever crosseth this, is not authority, but a distemper thereof. This liberty is maintained and exercised in a way of subjection to authority; it is of the same kind of liberty wherewith Christ hath made us free.

Without something like "civil" or "federal" or "moral" liberty, as Winthrop wrote on 22 September 1642, the Puritan community could not endure:

> Others who went to other places, upon like grounds, succeeded no better. They fled for fear of want, and many of them fell into it, even to extremity, as if they had hastened into the misery which they feared and fled from, besides the depriving themselves of the ordinances and church fellowship, and those civil liberties which they enjoyed here; whereas, such as staid in their places, kept their peace and ease, and enjoyed still the blessing of the ordinances, and

never tasted of those troubles and miseries, which they heard to have befallen those who departed. Much disputation there was about liberty of removing for outward advantages, and all ways were sought for an open door to get out at; but it is to be feared many crept out at a broken wall. For such as come together into a wilderness, where are nothing but wild beasts and beastlike men, and there confederate together in civil and church estate, whereby they do, implicitly at least, bind themselves to support each other, and all of them that society, whether civil or sacred, whereof they are members, how they can break from this without free consent, is hard to find, so as may satisfy a tender or good conscience in time of trial. Ask thy conscience, if thou wouldst have plucked up thy stakes; and brought thy family 3000 miles, if thou hadst expected that all, or most, would have forsaken thee there. Ask again, what liberty thou hast towards others, which thou likest not to allow others towards theyself; for if one may go, another may, and so the greater part, and so church and commonwealth may be left destitute in a wilderness, exposed to misery and reproach, and all for thy ease and pleasure, whereas these all, being now thy brethren, as near to thee as the Israelites were to Moses, it were much safer for thee, after his example, to choose rather to suffer affliction with thy brethren, than to enlarge thy ease and pleasure by furthering the occasion of their ruin.

The notion that freedom means staying rather than moving on, accepting hardship and confinement rather than seeking openness and a better life, is an idea that Americans learned to admire but not to emulate, a sentiment that makes the seventeenth-century mind remote from modern sensibility. Winthrop's commitment to such ideas is what makes it inappropriate, finally, to read him as a proto-Romantic who found change exhilarating. However much he made way for novelty, Winthrop's steadfast Puritanism cannot be overlooked. In fact, to interpret him as more modern than he was would be to miss the ways his life and work calls ours into question.

It is only by honoring his irreducible otherness that we can appreciate his way of revisioning America. Without his originating beliefs, his revisions in religion, politics, and narrative make the wrong kind of sense. Revision for its own sake keeps little but criticism alive; in this sense it is still true that where there is no vision, the people perish. Hence if we lack a coherent sense of purpose as a people, we could do worse than hypothetically to adopt Winthrop's model of civil liberty. It is so different from our conventional ideas that it might force us to begin the process of revision. Winthrop's Puritan vision will not provide the answers we need, but by framing the right questions it might inaugurate our own revisioning. The will for that task, and a steady commitment to it, is what Winthrop's *Journal* has to offer. In undertaking it, we keep something alive that is more important, finally, than any particular origin.

In life as in scholarship, possibilities come into focus only when limitations are recognized; one never grasps them whole, yet one doesn't simply have to get by without them. If historian John P. Diggins is right about "the lost soul of American politics," Winthropian revisioning presents a real alternative to the apparent contemporary options of nostalgic communalism and narcissistic individualism. Our world is different from but not more difficult than that of the Puritans. Winthrop sold all that he had to come to America and lost most of what he acquired here. Our sacrifices are more subtle but no less uncomfortable. Revising America will cost more than we imagine and require resources beyond ourselves. There is no other way to keep the dream alive. History that tells the whole truth is a rock against the current as it runs away. Resistance is all. Revisioning is most us.

## James G. Moseley (essay date 1992)

SOURCE: "Ways of Making History in Early New England," in *John Winthrop's World: History as a Story, The Story as History,* The University of Wisconsin Press, 1992, pp. 130-47.

[*In the following excerpt, Moseley focuses on Winthrop's journal as a history, noting its exemplification of a Puritan point of view, and comparing it with other historical accounts.*]

Winthrop's Journal was not only about Puritans; it was a Puritan history. This quality, so quickly lost by those who wrote about the early Puritans, comes clearly into focus when Winthrop's history is compared with the other great history of first-generation New England. Like the Puritans' Winthrop, the Pilgrims' William Bradford was both governor and historian, and the two men interacted as leaders of communities as close as Boston and Plimouth. For all their day-to-day cooperation, though, the theological differences between the Puritans and Separatists had important consequences for the ways the two men understood and wrote history.

William Bradford's *Of Plimouth Plantation, 1620-1647* chronicles the endurance of a small group of English Protestants who shared many of the Puritans' beliefs about the degeneracy of their native land and its established church. Instead of hoping to reform the Church of England, though, Bradford's Pilgrims decided that purity of belief and practice could be achieved only through "removal to some other place." Believing that true Reformation required separation, they sought religious freedom first in Holland, where their relative ease of acceptance exposed the group, especially the

children, to the unforeseen danger of assimilation. So they separated again, this time going all the way to New England, a decade ahead of the Puritans, and settling in Plimouth.

Governor Bradford's history of the people he led is a year-by-year account of the ongoing tribulations they faced—from the sharp financial dealings of their backers, from the Indians, from starvation, from smallpox, and from tensions within their own community between those who were truly committed to the general undertaking and those whose primary motivations sprang from self-interest. The main theme of Separatist history is spelled out early and informs Bradford's entire account: the trials and temptations confronting this small band of believers were unrelenting, "but they knew they were pilgrims, and looked not much on those things, but lift up their eyes to the heavens, their dearest country, and quieted their spirits." If the Puritans tried to live in the world without being of the world, then the Pilgrims sought to avoid being of the world by living apart from it. Unlike the Antinomians, the Pilgrims did not seek to be free from the rules that guide the soldier of faith in combat with the world, yet neither were they so bold as to expect to triumph in this life. Hence Bradford's history has an elegaic tone. Instead of hope for progress, the lives of Pilgrim saints display the courage of perseverance.

Although he was not a perfectionist, Bradford tended to distinguish between good and bad people; Winthrop, conversely, characteristically saw a mixture of good and bad within everyone. An interesting point of comparison comes in the early 1640s, when both historians had to deal with outbreaks of what their communities considered immoral and unnatural sexual acts. Both were committed to relating such unpleasant events; as Winthrop put it on 12 November 1641, "history must tell the whole truth," or, in Bradford's words, "the truth of history requires it." Yet their different interpretations of similar events suggest a crucial distinction between the Puritan and Separatist views of human nature and, consequently, between their respective ways of making history.

In his journal entry for that same day in 1641, Winthrop enables his readers to witness the fate of William Hackett, a young servant in Salem who "was found in buggery with a cow, upon the Lord's day." Although "he was noted always to have been a very stupid, idle, and ill-disposed boy, and would never regard the means of instruction, either in the church or family," the Puritans worked with him, "labouring by the word of God to convince him of his sin, and the present danger of his soul," until finally "it pleased the Lord so to bless his own ordinances, that his hard heart melted." There was no question of escaping punishment, but his execution was postponed a week to allow more time for spiritual progress. Yet even upon the ladder prepared to be hanged, he had not fully repented: "But the cow (with which he had committed that abomination) being brought forth and slain before him, he brake out into a loud and doleful complaint against himself" and was led in prayer by John Wilson and the other elders in attendance. Winthrop's observation upon the lad's execution is noteworthy: "There is no doubt to be made but the Lord hath received his soul to his mercy; and he was pleased to lift up the light of his countenance so far towards him, as to keep him from despair, and to hold him close to his grace in a seeking condition; but he was not pleased to afford him that measure of peace and comfort as he might be able to hold out to others, lest sinful men, in the love of their lusts, should set mercy and repentance at too low a rate, and so miss of it when they vainly expect it." With their complex view of human nature, the Puritans were capable of applying to a single individual both aspects of Paul's New Testament claim, "For the wages of sin is death; but the gift of God is eternal life through Christ Jesus our Lord." Their neighbors in Plimouth, in contrast, were inclined to separate Paul's clauses between the sinners and the saints.

In 1642 "the truth of history" required William Bradford to record how Thomas Granger was "detected of buggery, and indicted for the same, with a mare, a cow, two goats, five sheep, two calves and a turkey." While careful to "forbear particulars" regarding the young servant's "lewd practice towards the mare," Bradford does point out that "whereas some of the sheep could not be so well known by his description of them, others with them were brought before him and he declared which were they and which were not." But there is no mention of concern for the boy's soul. Instead, Bradford simply notes that Granger freely confessed the facts: "And accordingly he was cast by the jury and condemned, and after executed about the 8th of September, 1642. A very sad spectacle it was. For first the mare and the rest of the lesser cattle were killed before his face, according to the law, Leviticus XX.15; and then he himself was executed. The cattle were all cast into a great and large pit that was digged of purpose for them, and no use made of any part of them." Pilgrim authorities determined that "the knowledge and practice of such wickedness" was acquired "in old England," and Bradford points to a cautionary moral: "By which it appears how one wicked person may infect many, and what care all ought to have what servants they bring into their families." If Winthrop's narrative about Hackett expresses the characteristic Puritan concern with the struggle between sin and grace in each individual's life, then Bradford's account of Granger's fate articulates a typical Separatist desire to weed out wicked people who may have crept into the community of the saints.

Beyond its immediate moral offensiveness, Granger's buggery raised important concerns about the meaning of history for Bradford, who worried that such incidents might lead future generations to question the integrity of their origins. Without doubting the propriety of the Pilgrim proceedings, Bradford faced the larger issue squarely: "But it may be demanded how it came to pass that so many wicked persons and profane people should so quickly come over into this land and mix themselves amongst them? Seeing it was religious men that began the work and they came for religion's sake? I confess this may be marveled at, at least in time to come, when the reasons thereof should not be known; and the more because here was so many hardships and wants met withal. I shall therefore endeavour to give some answer hereunto." Explanation outdistances narration for Bradford; the posterity he envisages will look to history for a source of inspiring moral examples rather than for the early chapters of a continuing story. Winthrop's story outgrows the framework of his original design, whereas Bradford's events are controlled by the meanings they illustrate and the questions they answer.

Bradford's answers are soundly Separatist. First, "it is ever to be remembered that where the Lord begins to sow good seed, there the envious man will endeavor to sow tares." Second, building and planting in a wilderness required so much work that the supply of good servants was exhausted; therefore, "many untoward servants" were brought over, served out their times of indenture, began their own families, and increased. Third, "and a main reason hereof," the traders who transported godly persons were simply good businessmen who "to make up their freight and advance their profit, cared not who the persons were, so they had money to pay them. And by this means the country became pestered with many unworthy persons who, being come over, crept into one place or other." And fourth, some good people in England were simply getting rid of their problems: "So also there were sent by their friends, some under hope that they would be made better, others that they might be eased of such burthens, and they kept from shame at home, that would necessarily follow their dissolute courses." Bradford's conclusion sounds a distinctly Separatist note of despair: "And thus, by one means or other, in 20 years' time it is a question whether the greater part be not grown the worser?" Because Bradford portrayed the conflict between good and evil by drawing a line between good people and bad people, rather than by examining the moral battleground within every human soul, the cards always seemed to be stacked against the Separatists, even in a relatively free and open new land.

Bradford's basic orientation did not change when he moved from explaining the wickedness of such an otherwise insignificant servant as Thomas Granger to expounding the lifelong goodness of a true servant of God such as the Reverend William Brewster, a faithful elder of "this poor persecuted church above 36 years in England, Holland and in this wilderness" and one of the eldest of the Pilgrim saints. Elder Brewster exemplifies perseverance, for "notwithstanding the many troubles and sorrows he passed through, the Lord upheld him to a great age." Before cataloguing Brewster's virtues, Bradford makes his meaning clear: "I would now demand of any, what he was the worse for any former sufferings? What do I say, worse? Nay, sure he was the better, and they now added to his honour." Separatist virtues seem to emerge not simply in response to large challenges but chiefly through suffering. Endurance, rather than triumph, is the Pilgrim's goal.

Elder Brewster's intelligence and learning, his honesty and discretion, and his humility and faith earned him trust and affection throughout his life, especially in his role as a teaching minister in Plimouth. Rather than any particular accomplishments, though, what Bradford finds most noteworthy about Brewster is his life's demonstration of the longevity of the Pilgrim Fathers: "I cannot but here take occasion not only to mention but greatly to admire the marvelous providence of God! That notwithstanding the many changes and hardships that these people went through, and the many enemies they had and difficulties they met withal, that so many of them should live to very old age! It was not only this reverend man's condition (for one swallow makes no summer as they say) but many more of them did the like, some dying about and before this time and many still living, who attained to sixty years of age, and to sixty-five, divers to seventy and above, and some near eighty as he did. It must needs be more than ordinary and above natural reason, that so it should be." Given the "crosses, troubles, fears, wants and sorrows" they experienced, Bradford asks rhetorically, "What was it then that upheld them? It was God's visitation that preserved their spirits." Whatever ability and courage might accomplish, Bradford believed, the strength of saintly endurance required more than even Brewster's admirable character and virtues.

Once again, instead of telling a story, Bradford draws the lesson from the life: "God, it seems, would have all men to behold and observe such mercies and works of His providence as these are towards His people, that they in like cases might be encouraged to depend upon God in their trials, and also to bless His name when they see His goodness towards others." The lesson is one, Bradford acknowledges, that everyone will not appreciate: "It is not by good and dainty fare, by peace and rest and heart's ease in enjoying the contentments and good things of this world only that preserves health and prolongs life; God in such examples would have the world see and behold that He can do it without them; and if the world will shut their eyes and take no notice thereof, yet He would have His people to see and consider it." In Bradford's view, lack of widespread recognition does not diminish the truth. Indeed, for the Separatist, spiritual power and worldly failure seem to go hand in hand.

By 1644 even many of the faithful were lured to richer farmland and better harbors than Plimouth afforded, so that the staying image of Bradford's history is elegaic: "And thus was this poor church left, like an ancient mother grown old and forsaken of her children, though not in their affections yet in regard of their bodily presence and personal helpfulness; her ancient members being most of them worn away by death, and these of later time being like children translated into other families, and she like a widow left only to trust in God. Thus, she that had made many rich became herself poor." After recounting the successful prevention of war with the Indians by the commissioners of the United Colonies, Bradford's history ends by bemoaning the loss of Separatist stalwart Edward Winslow, who upon returning to England to battle New England's adversaries had become involved in the Civil War that was bringing the Reformation back to life. William Bradford in Plimouth seemed to feel that the Pilgrim project had ended. If the Puritans had been on an errand and had transformed its meaning into an ongoing enterprise, the Pilgrims were already—and in a sense always—looking backward rather than ahead.

In 1650 William Bradford turned away from writing the history of Plimouth and began to study Hebrew, seeking a personal connection with more ancient origins:

Though I am growne aged, yet I have had
    a longing
desire to see, with my owne eyes, something
    of that most
ancient language, and holy tongue, in which
    the Law
    and Oracles of God were write; and in
        which God
    and angels spake to the holy patriarks of
        old
        time; and what names were given to
            things
        from the creation. And though I
            cannot
        attaine to much herein, yet I am
            refresh-
        ed to have seen some glimpse hereof;
        (as Moyses saw the land of Ca-
            nan a farr off). My aime and
        desire is, to see how the words
            and phrases lye in the
                holy texte; and to
            discerne somewhat
                of the same,
                for my owne
                    contente.

Unlike John Winthrop, whose involvement in the story he was writing continued until sickness took his life, William Bradford had finished his effort to guide his plantation by recalling its connection to an inspiring past. Bradford's decision suggests telling differences between the kinds of history that he and Winthrop wrote and between the ways they understood their work as historians, in keeping with their moral and religious points of view.

Contemporary historian Peter Gay suggests [in *A Loss of Mastery,* 1969] that English Protestants were heirs both of medieval and of Renaissance attitudes toward history: "Medieval historians, in sum, for all their biographies, all their chronicles, all their universal histories, were in their hearts unhistorical—Renaissance historians, whether they found in history a cyclical movement, or progress, or chaos, justified the course of history by, and within, the course of history." Their medieval Christian heritage held that human history was meaningful by virtue of its connection to divine history, whereas Renaissance humanism taught that human history was justified, to the extent that it had meaning at all, in and on its own terms. As forthright participants in the reformation, English Protestants balanced these contradictory views of history, with Puritans and Separatists agreeing that the Reformation in England was moving too slowly, if indeed at all, under the dead hand of an established church. An unstable mixture of medieval and Renaissance ideas about history was part of the cultural baggage on board the *Mayflower* and the *Arbella,* as Bradford and Winthrop led their people to New England for the sake of the Reformation.

Because the Puritans and Separatists believed they were advancing the Reformation by migrating to New England, they shared many spiritual concerns, social commitments, and political convictions. People who set out to further and possibly to perfect the Protestant movement believed that change was possible, that history did not simply repeat itself. But separatism and Puritanism represented antithetical strains within the broad heritage of the Reformation, and in the hands of Bradford and Winthrop these tendencies were developed into two views of history that have ever since been in conflict. While they often cooperated as governors, as historians Bradford and Winthrop were the first voices in an ongoing cultural debate that has been—and continues to be—profoundly important for American life. Two contradictory attitudes about the nature of American society and the purpose of American foreign policy are rooted in the Separatist and Puritan ways of making history in early New England.

Bradford justified the Pilgrim migration by looking back to the New Testament, the first years of Christianity, and the marytrs of the early Reformation for models to encourage the Separatist saints to endure the trials they faced. Inspired by the heroes of the faith chronicled in John Foxe's influential *Book of Martyrs,* the Pilgrims sought to redeem the present by reclaiming the true Christian past. Worried about his people's fortitude, suspicious of conspiracies against them, and looking backward for models, Bradford wrote a history that is nostalgic in tone, as fearful of the Pilgrims' declension as it is full of belief in the rightness of their cause. A sense of history was important for Bradford because it linked the temptations of the present to the age-old ceaseless struggle of the saints. He did not expect his people to tame the wilderness or to transform the Church of England. He wanted them, more simply, to live as witnesses to the true faith.

If assimilation had threatened their cause in Holland, the isolation of Plimouth was more promising. For the Pilgrim community to succeed, it had to remain separate from the wickedness of the wider world. Hence as his people dispersed for richer farmland and better commerce, as their need for a common defense drew Plimouth into cooperative agreements with other colonies in New England, and as the English Civil War pulled good men like Winslow into new conflicts across the seas, Bradford lost the sense of involvement in a meaningful historical process. He wrote more about the longevity of the original Pilgrim saints than about new energies and future challenges. The purpose of writing history, for Bradford, was to illumine a darkening world by testifying to the purity and courage of saints who struggled valiantly against the world, even in defeat.

Conversely, Winthrop wrote of Puritans who struggled for meaning within, rather than against, the world. Because they believed so strongly in a God beyond history, the Puritans threw themselves passionately into history, in order to bring this world into conformity with the next. Although Winthrop clearly set forth his design for the Puritan project in his **"Modell of Christian Charity"** sermon on board the *Arbella,* his history of New England tells the story of events as they happened, rather than attempting to organize Puritan experience along the lines of a predetermined plan. As they worked to establish themselves and to build a society in accordance with their various, often conflicting interests, Winthrop's characters, himself included, were not pure saints. Indeed, the security of their community was actually threatened less by external enemies, though they had plenty, than by insiders who believed that their personal union with the Holy Spirit freed them from obeying the rules of moral behavior. These Antinomians were the people the Puritans wanted to keep out of the Bay Colony, because Anne Hutchinson and her sort of people did not understand the necessity of moral rules. People need religious authority, social order, and moral laws, the Puritans believed, not so much to separate the bad people from the good people as, more fundamentally, to enable people, all of whom are mixtures of good and bad, to make some spiritual progress while living together. Winthrop's sense of the meaning of history as it is lived and written reflects these Puritan differences from the Separatists.

In contrast to Bradford, who looked backward for models to use in his effort to render the present significant, Winthrop observed present experience in order to record the events of an ongoing story. The Puritan mind was full of biblical models, to be sure, but instead of the Pilgrims' adoption of Christian martyrs, the heroes of "God's New Israel" were the patriarchs of the Old Testament who led a chosen people into the promised land. In his work as governor, Winthrop defended the order that he believed a continuing community required, bowing to the pressure for some changes and leading the way in others. His political balance sustained the Puritan project as a whole, helping to keep a sense of movement alive. Unlike the Pilgrims, who bore witness to the truth of the gospel in a seemingly solitary, almost antihistorical way, Winthrop's Puritans were laying the foundations of a new society. Their New England would chart its own course when a civil war in their homeland halted immigration, disrupted trade, and made it clear that the eyes of the world were not riveted on their "Citty vpon a hill." Winthrop kept writing history not so much for an English audience as for whoever would want to know about the early years of New England.

The justification of Puritan history was coming to be within history itself. The history of New England itself began to assume some of the religious import for the sake of which it had originally begun. Given their realistic assessment of human nature, the Puritans knew that ongoing reform—of themselves and their society and thereby of the world—would be required if their project was to fulfill its promise. They learned to use the precariousness of their undertaking—whether the challenge came from Antinomians or Indians, marauding Frenchmen or adversaries in England—as a way of affirming the rightness of their enterprise, as their descendants would learn to use moral declension as a rhetoric of confirmation. If Bradford wrote history to help himself and his readers understand and endure the present through reference to the past, then Winthrop wrote in order to record the continuing reformation of the present into the future. Frequently in conflict with each other, Separatist and Puritan views of history long outlived Bradford and Winthrop to influence succeeding generations of Americans and their historians. In their own distinctive ways, both views charged history with religious importance. The way these alternatives focused the debate about America's role in history became one of New England's foremost contributions, for good or ill, to the history of American civilization.

As the more "medieval" of the two, the Separatist historian tends to interpret events by way of reference to particular moments in the past when exemplary acts revealed connections between the human and the divine. Likewise, Bradford's work as a historian is justified insofar as it remains true to God's plan. The honesty of his calling therefore requires him to say when the events he is recording fail to sustain the significance which the great models from the past have embodied. The Separatist's inherent dualism, seen in his desire to draw a firm line between good people and wicked people, inclines him toward a historyless cast of mind and makes him a foe of tradition as such. Everyone who responds to ambiguity and confusion by wanting to isolate the few good people from the mass of bad people and to find a place uncorrupted by the vicissitudes of history knows something of the Separatist dream. Yet even such an adventure, as Bradford discovered, begins to have its own history, from which there is finally no escape. The Separatist may then respond stoically, as Bradford did, resigning himself to events beyond his control and preserving a personal sense of meaning by abandoning history in favor of meditation upon those great moments from the past—in Bradford's case, at the very beginning of history itself—when truth was indeed said and done. Or with similar motivations, he may respond by trying to expell the bad people who have infiltrated the group, hoping to reclaim his people's original purity by securing borders that will prevent contact with a contaminated world.

When Pilgrim spirituality ebbed, the Separatist response to history remained. As the ultimate importance originally experienced through exemplary models from the past came to be invested instead in the identity of the present group, the Separatist view of history found cultural and political expression, often with religious overtones, in the ideology of American isolationism. Separatist political leaders have tried to protect America from involvement with an impure world, and Separatist historians have interpreted American history as a series of conflicts between darkness and light, in a myriad of forms. Separatist cultural criticism preserves Bradford's nostalgia, though often without recourse to the ancient models that sustained his religious faith. Whatever their professions, subsequent generations of Separatists have felt like Pilgrims, often without knowing exactly why. In contrast, Bradford's people "knew they were pilgrims." While salutary in some ways, the inevitable loss of a shared religious faith did not necessarily make American society more humane.

In keeping with the Renaissance humanism that Puritan leaders imbibed while acquiring university educations in divinity and law, the Puritan historian tends to find the meaning of events within his own history. Winthrop has a sense that history is the field in which a divine plan is being worked out. Rather than interpreting present experience in light of particular models in the past, the Puritan historian is alert for the ways current events, and the connections between them, may themselves have symbolic significance. The Puritan's belief that all people are mixtures of good and evil, seen in his insistence that even the justified saints need to pursue the hard path toward sanctification, inclines him to take history seriously. While there is no traditionless faith for the Puritan, he tends to believe that, human nature being what it is, even the English Protestant tradition can slip from its true purpose and will require occasional, perhaps continuing reformation and renewal. Everyone who, feeling surrounded by problems and failures, decides to stay on board and to work for change from within the system, convinced that some improvement is preferable to a fruitless search for perfection, experiences something of the Puritan temper. Yet even such a temperament, Winthrop learned, is apt to rise toward heedless enthusiasm or to fall into niggling precisionism. Since they take their own history so religiously, Puritans are always susceptible to flights of Antinomian fancy or to seizures of moralistic authoritarianism. The tendency of latter-day Puritans to move in one of these directions or the other recapitulates the tensions within the Bay Colony that Winthrop described.

Winthrop's commitment to writing history grew from his religious convictions about human nature, providing the governor a crucial additional perspective on his own involvement in history and strengthening his basic character, which historian Edmund S. Morgan has described so well: "John Winthrop, while trying to live as God required, learned that he must live *in* the world, face its temptations, and share its guilt; and Winthrop helped to prevent the government of Massachusetts from seeking a greater perfection in this world than God required or allowed. Winthrop had less control, and less understanding, of the church than the state. And the church, by any standards, had to be more pure than the state. . . . But the visible church, like the man himself, must remain *in* the world and must not only bring its members closer to God but must also help to redeem the rest of the world" [*Visible Saints,* 1963]. At his best, the Puritan historian applies Winthrop's sense of balance, self-criticism, and need for renewal not only to the people whose history he records but also to his own work as a historian. At his worst, whether in an Antinomian or precisionist mode, he thoroughly identifies the Puritan thrust toward renewal with the life of his group itself and assumes that his righteous people are called to reform the rest of the world.

The Puritan view of history was not lost when Puritan piety waned. Although the children of the founders designed a "Half-Way Covenant" to permit their offspring to retain church membership, subsequent generations soon lost the sense of balance that kept the original Puritans moving forward within the verges of a common path. As the errand into the wilderness took on its own meaning, Winthrop's Puritan view of history turned into a less explicitly religious tradition of reform, sometimes of America itself and sometimes, through the new nation's intervention, of the world. While some Puritan political leaders have crusaded for a congeries of social reforms, others, seeing less need for internal improvement, have tried with varying success to enlist America in campaigns to reform the world, usually according to their own image of American purity. Puritan historians have read and written American history as consensual themes of renewal. Puritan cultural critics have bemoaned America's moral decline as a way of renewing the nation's commitment to improve itself and the world, though often without recourse to the religious faith that sustained Winthrop's vision of "a Citty vpon a hill." Countless Americans have supported reform platforms and voted for reform tickets, purchased and tried out an apparently endless variety of self-improvement programs, often stirred deeply by vague motivations. In contrast, Winthrop's Puritans examined themselves scrupulously, reasoning carefully about the covenant they owned with God. While few contemporary Americans would choose to live within the ruled confines of the Massachusetts Bay Colony, many continue to respond, for better or worse, to the call for reform that characterizes the Puritan view of history.

There's nothing like a war to sharpen the debate between latter-day Puritans and Separatists and to make one wise for leaders with Winthrop's balanced involvement in and understanding of history. A clear view of Winthrop, heightened by consideration of what he shared with and where he differed from his colleague Bradford, might clarify current debates, if only by reminding present-day Americans that the Puritan and Separatist views of history were present, already in tension, in the earliest years of one of the traditions that most influentially informs American culture. Yet it is difficult to hear Winthrop's voice, for subsequent interpreters of America muted his image as they transformed the early historians of Pilgrim and Puritan saints into saints themselves. The telling differences between Bradford and Winthrop were silenced, as they were enshrined foremost among the founding fathers of New England. The inaugural hagiography was composed in a virtually insurmountable fashion by a third-generation descendant of premier Puritans, the complicated genius Cotton Mather.

Since his name was derived from two eminent grandfathers, John Cotton and Richard Mather, it is not surprising that Increase Mather's firstborn son felt driven to rekindle the fading embers of the Puritan faith. The New England in which the boy grew up was moving socially, politically, and commercially away from its Puritan foundations, and Cotton Mather devoted himself to restoring the spiritual vitality and shared moral commitments without which, he believed, thoroughgoing degeneration would ensue. Mather poured his energy into this task with an obsession that warranted historian Vernon Parrington's characterization: "Intensely emotional, high-strung and nervous, he was oversexed and overwrought, subject to ecstatic exaltations and, especially during his celibate years, given to seeing visions" [Quoted in Cotton Mather, *Magnalia Christi Americana,* ed. Raymond J. Cunningham, 1970]. However one accounts for or copes with Mather's personal peculiarity, if indeed one can, it is clear that writing history was one of the chief weapons he fashioned in the struggle to revitalize an entire society and that the way Mather wrote history had lasting consequences. If Mather failed to revamp New England, by enshrining the early Puritans in an aura of perfection he articulated a sense of guilt sufficient to keep their memory alive. His audience was chastened rather than transformed; a slightly guilty conscience kept their noses to the grindstone of change. Subsequent historians shared Mather's praise for the founding fathers of New England. Without his freight of guilt, these early leaders were appealed to as the inspiring ancestors of a new civilization.

"I write the Wonders of the Christian Religion, flying from the depravations of Europe, to the American Strand," announced Mather at the outset of his great work, *Magnalia Christi Americana; or, The Ecclesiastical History of New England.* Because the churches of New England were patterned on the earliest years of Christianity, Mather asserts, they were heirs of an ongoing Reformation, with its greatest moments still ahead. His recipe for revitalization is simple: "In short, the *first* Age was the *golden* Age: to return unto *that,* will make a man a Protestant, and, I may add, a Puritan." But if Mather seems to be summoning his contemporaries actually to achieve what earlier generations had so heroically attempted, he quickly reveals that the future of the Reformation is less social than cultural. The full import of the Reformation, it turns out, is involved with Mather's own work as a historian, for "whether New-England may *live* any where else or no, it must *live* in our History!" Pages of self-congratulatory comparisons with ancient historians great and small, however, bring Mather finally to acknowledge that the greatness of his own work will inhere more in the elegance and insight of his writing than in its effect upon his readers.

Indeed, bearing witness to the Puritan founders may primarily provoke negative reactions: "All good men will not be satisfied with every thing that is here set before them. In my own country, besides a considerable number of loose and vain inhabitants risen up, to whom the Congregational Church-discipline, which cannot live well where the power of godliness dyes, is become distasteful for the purity of it; there is also a number of eminently godly persons, who are for a larger

way, and unto these my Church-History will give distate, by the things which it may hapen to utter in favour of that Church-discipline on some few occasions; and the discoveries which I may happen to make of my apprehensions, that *Scripture,* and *reason,* and *antiquity* is for it; and that it is not far from a glorious resurrection." As if that were not enough rejection to expect, "on the other side, there are some among us who very strictly profess the Congregational Church-discipline, but at the same time they have an unhappy narrowness of soul, by which they confine their value and kindness too much unto their own party: and unto those my Church-History will be offensive, because my regard unto our own declared principles does not hinder me from giving the right hand of fellowship unto the valuable servants of the Lord Jesus Christ, who find not our Church-discipline as yet agreeable unto their present understandings and illuminations. If it be thus in my own country, it cannot be otherwise in that whereto I send this account of my own." The Christian tradition had appropriated Isaiah's prophecy that the Suffering Servant would be "despised and rejected of men"; now Mather anticipated a similar response to his own calling. Mather wrote history to continue the Reformation, not expecting that reform would actually occur but in order to carve out an enduring place for himself as a true Puritan. His ambivalences were thoroughgoing and profound, for while undercutting the direct import of writing history, he invested the historian, himself, with immense significance.

By translating history into the biography of saints, Mather sanctified his own vocation. In the process, history became sermonic, more Separatist than Puritan in temper. Turned into icons, leaders such as Bradford and Winthrop might be venerated by the faithful or debunked by iconoclasts but would rarely be read as historians. Held up as "the shields of the churches," the governors and magistrates of New England were "perpetuated by the essay of Cotton Mather," with a pointed epigram:

> The glories of that elder age,
> Lustrous and pure, shall never wane,
> While hero, martyr, ruler, sage,
> Its living monuments remain.

Despite ceaseless allusions to classical writers regarding his role as historian, and more in keeping with the tradition he was attempting to reclaim, Mather cast Bradford and Winthrop as Old Testament patriarchs. On the one hand, it was not difficult to find the proper niche for Bradford: "The leader of a people in a wilderness had need be a Moses; and if a Moses had not led the people of Plymouth Colony, when this worthy person was their governour, the people had never with so much unanimity and importunity still called him to lead them." On the other hand, the Puritan governor elicited so many patriarchal allusions that Mather virtually constructed for Winthrop a chapel of his own.

Indeed, Winthrop's virtues surpassed those of leaders from the classical tradition that Mather quoted so fulsomely to dignify his own work as a historian:

> Let Greece boast of her patient Lycurgus, the lawgiver, by whom diligence, temperance, fortitude and wit were made the fashions of a therefore longlasting and renowned commonwealth: let Rome tell of her devout Numa, the lawgiver, by whom the most famous commonwealth saw peace triumphing over extinguished war and cruel plunders; and murders giving place to the more mollifying exercises of his religion. Our New-England shall tell and boast of her Winthrop, a lawgiver as patient as Lycurgus, but not admitting any of his criminal disorders; as devout as Numa, but not liable to any of *his* heathenish madnesses; a governour in whom the excellencies of Christianity made a most improving addition unto the virtues, wherein even without *those* he would have made a *parallel* for the great men of Greece, or of Rome, which the pen of a Plutarch has eternized.

Mather sustained his own image as the Plutarch of a new republic by Romanizing the combined Old Testament model and New World order that he took Winthrop to represent. As "Nehemias Americanus," Mather's Winthrop promised to lead Christianity, in its American Puritan version, beyond ancient glories to found a new civilization.

For Mather, the Winthrop family heritage made the governor's justice, wisdom, and courage "the more illustrious, by emblazoning them with the constant liberality and hospitality of a gentleman. This made him the *terror* of the wicked, and the *delight* of the sober, the *envy* of the many, but the *hope* of those who had any hopeful design in hand for the common good of the nation and the interests of religion." It was natural for such an eminent person to be "chosen for the Moses" of the Puritan undertaking, and "nothing but a *Mosaic spirit* could have carried him through the temptations, to which either his farewell to his own land, or his travel in a strange land, must needs expose a gentleman of his education." Moreover, since he not only led his people across the sea but also governed their settling in the new land, Winthrop was more than Moses to Mather.

Given the Puritans' desire to reform England by reconstituting the church according to its original, true design, Winthrop recalled the biblical Nehemiah, who led his people in rebuilding the walls of Jerusalem after a period of exile. Yet Winthrop's designation as "Americanus" is also significant, for Puritans did their rebuilding in a new place. Thus Mather's characterization of Winthrop as Nehemias Americanus aptly expresses the ambivalence of the Puritan undertaking as

a whole. In some ways, it was a looking backward to origins and a reformulation of ongoing institutions; simultaneously, in other ways, it was a new undertaking in a new land. Winthrop was a successful leader, Mather suggests, because the unique combination of his virtues was apposite to the complex demands of the Puritan project.

Like Nehemiah, Winthrop knew how to endure petty infighting between the discontented and the overzealous in his own party, and he also knew when to be liberal with his goods and generous in overlooking faults: "But whilst he thus did, as our New-English Nehemiah, the part of a *ruler* in managing the public affairs of our American Jerusalem, . . . he made himself still an exacter *parallel* unto that governour of Israel, by doing the part of a neighbor among the distressed people of the new plantation." Winthrop's combined ability to husband frugally and to dispense bountifully evoked another patriarch in Mather's biblical imagination: "Indeed, for a while the governour was the Joseph, unto whom the whole body of the people repaired when their corn failed them; and he continued relieving them with his open-handed bounties, as long as he had any stock to do it with." The story of the arrival of a ship loaded with provisions at the very moment when Winthrop was "distributing the last handful of the meal in the barrel unto a poor man distressed by the 'wolf at the door'" elicits a wordly-wise aphorism from Mather: "Yea, the governour sometimes made his own *private purse* to be the *publick*: not by *sucking* into it, but by *squeezing* out of it." The following parable, together with Mather's pointed commentary, illustrates Winthrop's saintly leadership:

> In an hard and long winter, when wood was very scarce at Boston, a man gave him a private information that a needy person in the neighbourhood stole wood sometimes from *his* pile; whereupon the governour in a seeming anger did reply, "Does he so? I'll take a course with him; go, call that man to me; I'll warrant you I'll cure him of stealing." When the man came, the governour considering that if he had stolen, it was more out of necessity than disposition, said unto him, "Friend, it is a severe winter, and I doubt you are but meanly provided for wood; wherefore I would have you supply your self at my wood-pile till this cold season be over." And he then merrily asked his friends, "Whether he had not effectually cured this man of stealing his wood?" One would have imagined that so good a man could have had no enemies, if we had not a daily and woful experience to convince us that goodness it self will make enemies.

Such vignettes kept Winthrop's memory alive in folktales as well as in the more "official" chronicle Mather composed.

In Mather's view, "there hardly ever was a more sensible *mixture* of those two things, *resolution* and *con-descention,* than in this good man," and "it was not long before a compensation was made for these things by the *doubled respects* which were from all parts paid unto him." Such a *"mixture* of distant qualities" produced exactly the kind of leader the complex Puritan adventure required, demonstrating the particular way in which the achievements of God's New Israel surpassed the greatest accomplishments of classical antiquity: "In fine, the victories of an Alexander, an Hannibal, or a Caesar over *other men,* were not so glorious as the victories of this great man over *himself,* which also at last proved victories over other men." Foremost among the founders of New England, Winthrop stands in a way for the renewed triumph of the entire Old Testament tradition, as Mather's eulogy declares: "*Such a governour, after he had been more than ten several times by the people chosen their governour, was New-England now to lose; who having, like Jacob, first left his council and blessing with his children gathered about his bed-side; and, like David, 'served his generation by the will of God,' he 'gave up the ghost,' and fell asleep on March 26, 1649. Having, like the dying Emperour Valentinian, this above all his other victories for his triumphs, His overcoming of himself.*" Cleverly affirming his own role as the historian of the true faith, Mather adapts "the words of Josephus about Nehemiah, the governour of Israel," for Winthrop's epitaph: "He was by nature a man, at once benevolent and just: most zealous for the honour of his countrymen; and to them he left an imperishable monument—the walls of New England." The irony is that in trying to write a history that would keep Winthrop alive as a model for future generations, Mather encapsulated the exemplary governor within the walls of history.

As Mather's hero becomes more saintly, at once more admirable and also more removed from common life, the power of the historian is irrevocably increased. Mather's heightened self-consciousness of his own role as historian overwhelmed his subjects, transforming flesh-and-blood men such as Bradford and Winthrop into exemplary figures in the service of Mather's vocation as the Josephus of the Puritan faith and the Plutarch of a New World civilization. Mather's eagerness to wear both hats coincides with the merging of religious and civic virtues in his iconography of early New England. Future interpreters of America would look back to the founders through Mather's eyes, responding to new cultural crises by invoking the memory of a time when piety and politics were at one.

Regardless of its historical accuracy and its author's unusual personality, Mather's *Magnalia Christi Americana* had monumental consequences for succeeding generations of historians and other keepers of the American dream. In probing the national ideal that informs *Uncle Tom's Cabin,* for example, literary historian and critic Edmund Wilson [in *Patriotic Gore,*

1966] cites a revealing passage from the autobiography of Harriet Beecher Stowe: "There was one of my father's books that proved a mine of wealth to me. It was a happy hour when he brought home and set up in his bookcase Cotton Mather's *Magnalia,* in a new edition of two volumes. What wonderful stories those! Stories, too, about my own country. Stories that made me feel the very ground I trod on to be consecrated by some special dealings of God's providence." As for countless other Americans, for Stowe such feelings were intertwined with her emotional response to a reading of the Declaration of Independence: "I was as ready as any of them to pledge my life, fortune, and sacred honor for such a cause. The heroic element was strong in men, having come down by ordinary generation from a long line of Puritan ancestry, and just now it made me long to do something, I knew not what: to fight for my country, or to make some declaration on my own account." To suggest how naturally Mather's inheritance provides religious roots for the ideology of the American Way of Life, Wilson cites an episode from Stowe's work *Poganuc People:*

> After the singing came Dr. Cushing's prayer—which was a recounting of God's mercies to New England from the beginning, and of her deliverances from her enemies, and of petitions for the glorious future of the United States of America—that they might be chosen vessels, commissioned to bear the light of liberty and religion through all the earth and to bring in the great millennial day, when wars should cease and the whole world, released from the thraldom of evil, should rejoice in the sight of the Lord. The millennium was ever the star of hope in the eyes of the New England clergy; their faces were set eastward, towards the dawn of that day, and the cheerfulness of those anticipations illuminated the hard tenets of their theology with a rosy glow. They were children of the morning.

Mather had turned Bradford and Winthrop into saints whose names resounded in the litany of cultural nationalism.

In keeping with Mather's intentions, the saints were invoked to recall a present generation from its forgetfulness in order to restore its confidence in the future. As American society became increasingly diverse, reference to the faith of the founders became less specific. Distinctions between Pilgrims and Puritans, once so important, were muted. If Mather looked to the past in order to reclaim the Puritan spirit, his cultural descendants did so on behalf of Protestantism more broadly, then for the sake of Christianity, and finally to revive religiousness in general, to bloster moral commitments, or simply to affirm some shared sense of civic purpose. Whether Bradford and Winthrop were praised as saints or, later, debunked as authoritarians, Mather's iconography was remarkably durable. For they were not read as men who wrote the histories in which their acts as governors were recorded. Consequently, the telling differences between Separatist and Puritan views of history were not remembered, and the critical perspectives each of the two men brought to bear upon history itself went unobserved. In the process, American history itself, read as the progress of American civilization, was invested with an authority that was for Bradford and Winthrop, in their respective ways, beyond history.

When later Americans clashed over essentially Separatist or Puritan versions of their past, present, and future, therefore, their arguments were the more dangerous insofar as their foundations, and the differences between them, were forgotten. Two related but distinct sorts of difficulties were engendered by this lack of awareness. On the one hand, subsequent generations of Americans experienced clashes between the Separatist desire for cultural and political isolation and the Puritan drive toward moral and political reform. The battle between isolation and reformation was played out between political parties in response to questions of American involvement in international conflicts, and a more personal struggle between Separatist and Puritan tendencies divided the hearts of individual citizens. On the other hand, since the distinctive histories of the two visions were forgotten, the ongoing dilemma was often superficially resolved. When the differences were glossed over, it could be asserted that American beginnings were actually as pristine as the Pilgrims had wished and also that Americans were impelled to press forward like Puritans to reform the world—in the image of their own deceptively innocent origins. Confusing the ideologies of these early voyagers to New England could become, in the political culture of a major world power, a recipe for domination and international disaster. Whether the outcome was experienced as a conflict between or as an amalgamation of Separatist and Puritan views of history, the consequences of forgetfulness might be benign or malicious, but they could not be understood and directed toward constructive ends. Without an appreciation of what they inherited from this part of their history, Americans were at its mercy.

As the civilization New England helped to inaugurate became increasingly complex, Mather's saints lost their voices. Without their contributions, the debate about the meaning of America and its role in the world became more strident and less profound. Given the inescapably international character of contemporary economic and political affairs, national problems and world events are inextricably interwined for the United States. Hence, despite its understandable allure in periods of crisis, the Separatist tendency, manifested in the rhetoric of isolationism, remains an illusion, indeed unreachably in the past. If Bradford's voice is essentially contrapuntal, however, Winthrop's vision of principled involvement in the world, informed by his Puritan

understanding of human nature and shaped by his commitment to history as an ongoing process, remains vitally important. For Winthrop's voice to be of better service in the future than his icon has been in the past, we must learn to read the history of his story as a significant episode in early New England and as part of the continuing Puritan strain in American culture.

## FURTHER READING

Baritz, Loren. "Political Theology: John Winthrop." In his *City on a Hill: A History of Ideas and Myths in America,* pp. 3-45. New York: John Wiley & Sons, 1964.
    Overview of Winthrop's life and work, with emphasis on his ideology.

Bercovitch, Sacvan. *The Puritan Origins of the American Self.* New Haven: Yale University Press, 1975, 250 p.
    Takes Cotton Mather's biographical essay on Winthrop as a representative text and a starting point for a discussion about the "Puritan view of the self," "the individual in history," and "the idea of national election."

Bozeman, Theodore Dwight. *To Live Ancient Lives: The Primitivist Dimension in Puritanism.* Chapel Hill: University of North Carolina Press, 1988, 413 p.
    Traces "the primitivist strands in English Puritan thought through the period of the Great Migration," with numerous refrences to Winthrop.

Dawson, Hugh J. "John Winthrop's Rite of Passage: The Origins of the 'Christian Charitie' Discourse." *Early American Literature* 26, No. 3 (1991): 219-31.
    Argues that Winthrop's famous sermon was most likely composed in England prior to his departure, not aboard the *Arabella,* as is commonly assumed.

Delbanco, Andrew. *The Puritan Ordeal.* Cambridge: Harvard University Press, 1989, 306 p.
    Discusses "the experience of becoming an American in the seventeenth century," with numerous references to Winthrop.

Dunn, Richard S. "Book One: John Winthrop." In his *Puritans and Yankees: The Winthrop Dynasty of New England 1630-1717,* pp. 3-58. Princeton: Princeton University Press, 1962.
    Asserts that Winthrop was the first American "to define liberty as riding easy in harness," and cites his importance in passing on the "Puritan code of disciplined self-government."

Michaelsen, Scott. "John Winthrop's 'Modell' Covenant and the Company Way." *Early American Literature* 27, No. 2 (1992): 85-100.
    Suggests that "Winthrop's sermon not only bears a

significant relation to newly emerging theories of contract law and interpretation, but it reveals a great deal about the actual legal conditions of the Puritan voyage to America."

Morgan, Edmund S. "Notes and Documents: John Winthrop's 'Modell of Christian Charity' in a Wider Context." *The Huntington Library Quarterly* 50, No. 2 (Spring, 1987): 145-51.

Compares Winthrop's sermon with other, similar shipboard addresses, concluding that "his special gift lay in bringing disagreements to a happy issue."

Morrison, Samuel Eliot. "John Winthrop, Esquire." In his *Builders of the Bay Colony,* pp. 51-104. Boston: Houghton Mifflin Co., 1930.

Historical account of Winthrop's role in the establishment of the Bay Colony. Morrison asserts that "From his fellows of the ruling class, strong and able men, he stands out as a superior man of noble character, with a single eye to the common weal."

Mosse, George L. "John Winthrop: Christian Statesman." In his *The Holy Pretence: A Study in Christianity and Reason of State from William Perkins to John Winthrop,* pp. 88-106. Oxford: Basil Blackwell, 1957.

Argues that "it is in the works of Winthrop. . . that the Covenant theology becomes the means of harmonizing the word of God with the idea of reason of state."

Power, M. Susan. "John Winthrop: 'A Model' and the 'Journal'," "John Winthrop: Arbitrary Government and the Rule of Law," "John Winthrop's 'Declaration' and Elisha Williams' 'Essential Rights' Compared and Contrasted." In her *Before the Convention: Religion and the Founders,* pp. 65-84, 85-106, 107-26. Lanham, Md.: University Press of America, 1984.

Detailed discussion of Winthrop's writings mentioned above.

Rutman, Darrett B. *Winthrop's Boston: Portrait of a Puritan Town 1630-1649.* Chapel Hill: The University of North Carolina Press, 1965, 324 p.

Describes Boston in Winthrop's time as a "dynamic community" that was not strictly ideological.

————. *John Winthrop's Decision for America: 1629.* Philadelphia: J. B. Lippincott Co., 1975, 105 p.

Examines factors that contributed to Winthrop's decision to come to America and includes documents relating to his decisionmaking process.

Winthrop, Robert C. *Life and Letters of John Winthrop.* Boston: Ticknor and Fields, 1864, 452 p.

Standard biography.

---

Additional coverage of Winthrop's life and career is contained in the following sources published by Gale Research: *Dictionary of Literary Biography,* **Vol. 24,** and *Dictionary of Literary Biography,* **Vol. 30.**

# Literature Criticism from 1400 to 1800

Cumulative Indexes

# How to Use This Index

## The main references

**list all author entries in the following Gale Literary Criticism series:**

*BLC* = *Black Literature Criticism*
*CLC* = *Contemporary Literary Criticism*
*CLR* = *Children's Literature Review*
*CMLC* = *Classical and Medieval Literature Criticism*
*DA* = *DISCovering Authors*
*DC* = *Drama Criticism*
*HLC* = *Hispanic Literature Criticism*
*LC* = *Literature Criticism from 1400 to 1800*
*NCLC* = *Nineteenth-Century Literature Criticism*
*PC* = *Poetry Criticism*
*SSC* = *Short Story Criticism*
*TCLC* = *Twentieth-Century Literary Criticism*
*WLC* = *World Literature Criticism, 1500 to the Present*

## The cross-references

**list all author entries in the following Gale biographical and literary sources:**

*AAYA* = *Authors & Artists for Young Adults*
*AITN* = *Authors in the News*
*BEST* = *Bestsellers*
*BW* = *Black Writers*
*CA* = *Contemporary Authors*
*CAAS* = *Contemporary Authors Autobiography Series*
*CABS* = *Contemporary Authors Bibliographical Series*
*CANR* = *Contemporary Authors New Revision Series*
*CAP* = *Contemporary Authors Permanent Series*
*CDALB* = *Concise Dictionary of American Literary Biography*
*CDBLB* = *Concise Dictionary of British Literary Biography*
*DLB* = *Dictionary of Literary Biography*
*DLBD* = *Dictionary of Literary Biography Documentary Series*
*DLBY* = *Dictionary of Literary Biography Yearbook*
*HW* = *Hispanic Writers*
*JRDA* = *Junior DISCovering Authors*
*MAICYA* = *Major Authors and Illustrators for Children and Young Adults*
*MTCW* = *Major 20th-Century Writers*
*NNAL* = *Native North American Literature*
*SAAS* = *Something about the Author Autobiography Series*
*SATA* = *Something about the Author*
*YABC* = *Yesterday's Authors of Books for Children*

# Literary Criticism Series
# Cumulative Author Index

Aldanov, Mark (Alexandrovich)
1886(?)-1957 .............. **TCLC 23**
See also CA 118

Aldington, Richard 1892-1962...... **CLC 49**
See also CA 85-88; CANR 45; DLB 20, 36,
100, 149

Aldiss, Brian W(ilson)
1925- ............... **CLC 5, 14, 40**
See also CA 5-8R; CAAS 2; CANR 5, 28;
DLB 14; MTCW; SATA 34

Alegria, Claribel 1924-............ **CLC 75**
See also CA 131; CAAS 15; DLB 145; HW

Alegria, Fernando 1918-.......... **CLC 57**
See also CA 9-12R; CANR 5, 32; HW

Aleichem, Sholom .............. **TCLC 1, 35**
See also Rabinovitch, Sholem

Aleixandre, Vicente 1898-1984 ... **CLC 9, 36**
See also CA 85-88; 114; CANR 26;
DLB 108; HW; MTCW

Alepoudelis, Odysseus
See Elytis, Odysseus

Aleshkovsky, Joseph 1929-
See Aleshkovsky, Yuz
See also CA 121; 128

Aleshkovsky, Yuz ................ **CLC 44**
See also Aleshkovsky, Joseph

Alexander, Lloyd (Chudley) 1924- .. **CLC 35**
See also AAYA 1; CA 1-4R; CANR 1, 24,
38; CLR 1, 5; DLB 52; JRDA; MAICYA;
MTCW; SAAS 19; SATA 3, 49, 81

Alfau, Felipe 1902-.............. **CLC 66**
See also CA 137

Alger, Horatio, Jr. 1832-1899..... **NCLC 8**
See also DLB 42; SATA 16

Algren, Nelson 1909-1981 .... **CLC 4, 10, 33**
See also CA 13-16R; 103; CANR 20;
CDALB 1941-1968; DLB 9; DLBY 81,
82; MTCW

Ali, Ahmed 1910- ............... **CLC 69**
See also CA 25-28R; CANR 15, 34

Alighieri, Dante 1265-1321 ....... **CMLC 3**

Allan, John B.
See Westlake, Donald E(dwin)

Allen, Edward 1948-.............. **CLC 59**

Allen, Paula Gunn 1939-.......... **CLC 84**
See also CA 112; 143; NNAL

Allen, Roland
See Ayckbourn, Alan

Allen, Sarah A.
See Hopkins, Pauline Elizabeth

Allen, Woody 1935-........... **CLC 16, 52**
See also AAYA 10; CA 33-36R; CANR 27,
38; DLB 44; MTCW

Allende, Isabel 1942-.... **CLC 39, 57; HLC**
See also CA 125; 130; DLB 145; HW;
MTCW

Alleyn, Ellen
See Rossetti, Christina (Georgina)

Allingham, Margery (Louise)
1904-1966 .................. **CLC 19**
See also CA 5-8R; 25-28R; CANR 4;
DLB 77; MTCW

Allingham, William 1824-1889 ... **NCLC 25**
See also DLB 35

Allison, Dorothy E. 1949-........ **CLC 78**
See also CA 140

Allston, Washington 1779-1843.... **NCLC 2**
See also DLB 1

Almedingen, E. M. ................ **CLC 12**
See also Almedingen, Martha Edith von
See also SATA 3

Almedingen, Martha Edith von 1898-1971
See Almedingen, E. M.
See also CA 1-4R; CANR 1

Almqvist, Carl Jonas Love
1793-1866 ................ **NCLC 42**

Alonso, Damaso 1898-1990 ....... **CLC 14**
See also CA 110; 131; 130; DLB 108; HW

Alov
See Gogol, Nikolai (Vasilyevich)

Alta 1942-..................... **CLC 19**
See also CA 57-60

Alter, Robert B(ernard) 1935-...... **CLC 34**
See also CA 49-52; CANR 1, 47

Alther, Lisa 1944-............. **CLC 7, 41**
See also CA 65-68; CANR 12, 30; MTCW

Altman, Robert 1925-............. **CLC 16**
See also CA 73-76; CANR 43

Alvarez, A(lfred) 1929-.......... **CLC 5, 13**
See also CA 1-4R; CANR 3, 33; DLB 14,
40

Alvarez, Alejandro Rodriguez 1903-1965
See Casona, Alejandro
See also CA 131; 93-96; HW

Alvaro, Corrado 1896-1956 ....... **TCLC 60**

Amado, Jorge 1912-..... **CLC 13, 40; HLC**
See also CA 77-80; CANR 35; DLB 113;
MTCW

Ambler, Eric 1909-............ **CLC 4, 6, 9**
See also CA 9-12R; CANR 7, 38; DLB 77;
MTCW

Amichai, Yehuda 1924- ...... **CLC 9, 22, 57**
See also CA 85-88; CANR 46; MTCW

Amiel, Henri Frederic 1821-1881 .. **NCLC 4**

Amis, Kingsley (William)
1922-...... **CLC 1, 2, 3, 5, 8, 13, 40, 44;**
**DA; DAB**
See also AITN 2; CA 9-12R; CANR 8, 28;
CDBLB 1945-1960; DLB 15, 27, 100, 139;
MTCW

Amis, Martin (Louis)
1949-............... **CLC 4, 9, 38, 62**
See also BEST 90:3; CA 65-68; CANR 8,
27; DLB 14

Ammons, A(rchie) R(andolph)
1926-........ **CLC 2, 3, 5, 8, 9, 25, 57**
See also AITN 1; CA 9-12R; CANR 6, 36;
DLB 5; MTCW

Amo, Tauraatua i
See Adams, Henry (Brooks)

Anand, Mulk Raj 1905-........... **CLC 23**
See also CA 65-68; CANR 32; MTCW

Anatol
See Schnitzler, Arthur

Anaya, Rudolfo A(lfonso)
1937- ................... **CLC 23; HLC**
See also CA 45-48; CAAS 4; CANR 1, 32;
DLB 82; HW 1; MTCW

Andersen, Hans Christian
1805-1875 ........ **NCLC 7; DA; DAB;**
**SSC 6; WLC**
See also CLR 6; MAICYA; YABC 1

Anderson, C. Farley
See Mencken, H(enry) L(ouis); Nathan,
George Jean

Anderson, Jessica (Margaret) Queale
.......................... **CLC 37**
See also CA 9-12R; CANR 4

Anderson, Jon (Victor) 1940- ....... **CLC 9**
See also CA 25-28R; CANR 20

Anderson, Lindsay (Gordon)
1923-1994 ................... **CLC 20**
See also CA 125; 128; 146

Anderson, Maxwell 1888-1959 ..... **TCLC 2**
See also CA 105; DLB 7

Anderson, Poul (William) 1926- .... **CLC 15**
See also AAYA 5; CA 1-4R; CAAS 2;
CANR 2, 15, 34; DLB 8; MTCW;
SATA-Brief 39

Anderson, Robert (Woodruff)
1917-..................... **CLC 23**
See also AITN 1; CA 21-24R; CANR 32;
DLB 7

Anderson, Sherwood
1876-1941 ....... **TCLC 1, 10, 24; DA;**
**DAB; SSC 1; WLC**
See also CA 104; 121; CDALB 1917-1929;
DLB 4, 9, 86; DLBD 1; MTCW

Andouard
See Giraudoux, (Hippolyte) Jean

Andrade, Carlos Drummond de ...... **CLC 18**
See also Drummond de Andrade, Carlos

Andrade, Mario de 1893-1945..... **TCLC 43**

Andreas-Salome, Lou 1861-1937... **TCLC 56**
See also DLB 66

Andrewes, Lancelot 1555-1626 ....... **LC 5**
See also DLB 151

Andrews, Cicily Fairfield
See West, Rebecca

Andrews, Elton V.
See Pohl, Frederik

Andreyev, Leonid (Nikolaevich)
1871-1919 ................... **TCLC 3**
See also CA 104

Andric, Ivo 1892-1975 ............. **CLC 8**
See also CA 81-84; 57-60; CANR 43;
DLB 147; MTCW

Angelique, Pierre
See Bataille, Georges

Angell, Roger 1920-.............. **CLC 26**
See also CA 57-60; CANR 13, 44

Angelou, Maya
1928- .... **CLC 12, 35, 64, 77; BLC; DA;**
**DAB**
See also AAYA 7; BW 2; CA 65-68;
CANR 19, 42; DLB 38; MTCW;
SATA 49

Annensky, Innokenty Fyodorovich
1856-1909 .................. **TCLC 14**
See also CA 110

Anon, Charles Robert
See Pessoa, Fernando (Antonio Nogueira)

**Anouilh, Jean (Marie Lucien Pierre)**
  1910-1987 ...... **CLC 1, 3, 8, 13, 40, 50**
  See also CA 17-20R; 123; CANR 32;
  MTCW

**Anthony, Florence**
  See Ai

**Anthony, John**
  See Ciardi, John (Anthony)

**Anthony, Peter**
  See Shaffer, Anthony (Joshua); Shaffer,
  Peter (Levin)

**Anthony, Piers** 1934- ............. **CLC 35**
  See also AAYA 11; CA 21-24R; CANR 28;
  DLB 8; MTCW

**Antoine, Marc**
  See Proust, (Valentin-Louis-George-Eugene-)
  Marcel

**Antoninus, Brother**
  See Everson, William (Oliver)

**Antonioni, Michelangelo** 1912- ..... **CLC 20**
  See also CA 73-76; CANR 45

**Antschel, Paul** 1920-1970
  See Celan, Paul
  See also CA 85-88; CANR 33; MTCW

**Anwar, Chairil** 1922-1949 ........ **TCLC 22**
  See also CA 121

**Apollinaire, Guillaume** .. **TCLC 3, 8, 51; PC 7**
  See also Kostrowitzki, Wilhelm Apollinaris
  de

**Appelfeld, Aharon** 1932- ....... **CLC 23, 47**
  See also CA 112; 133

**Apple, Max (Isaac)** 1941-........ **CLC 9, 33**
  See also CA 81-84; CANR 19; DLB 130

**Appleman, Philip (Dean)** 1926- ..... **CLC 51**
  See also CA 13-16R; CAAS 18; CANR 6,
  29

**Appleton, Lawrence**
  See Lovecraft, H(oward) P(hillips)

**Apteryx**
  See Eliot, T(homas) S(tearns)

**Apuleius, (Lucius Madaurensis)**
  125(?)-175(?) ............... **CMLC 1**

**Aquin, Hubert** 1929-1977......... **CLC 15**
  See also CA 105; DLB 53

**Aragon, Louis** 1897-1982........ **CLC 3, 22**
  See also CA 69-72; 108; CANR 28;
  DLB 72; MTCW

**Arany, Janos** 1817-1882........ **NCLC 34**

**Arbuthnot, John** 1667-1735.......... **LC 1**
  See also DLB 101

**Archer, Herbert Winslow**
  See Mencken, H(enry) L(ouis)

**Archer, Jeffrey (Howard)** 1940- .... **CLC 28**
  See also BEST 89:3; CA 77-80; CANR 22

**Archer, Jules** 1915- ............. **CLC 12**
  See also CA 9-12R; CANR 6; SAAS 5;
  SATA 4

**Archer, Lee**
  See Ellison, Harlan (Jay)

**Arden, John** 1930- ......... **CLC 6, 13, 15**
  See also CA 13-16R; CAAS 4; CANR 31;
  DLB 13; MTCW

**Arenas, Reinaldo**
  1943-1990 ............. **CLC 41; HLC**
  See also CA 124; 128; 133; DLB 145; HW

**Arendt, Hannah** 1906-1975 ........ **CLC 66**
  See also CA 17-20R; 61-64; CANR 26;
  MTCW

**Aretino, Pietro** 1492-1556 ......... **LC 12**

**Arghezi, Tudor**................... **CLC 80**
  See also Theodorescu, Ion N.

**Arguedas, Jose Maria**
  1911-1969 ............... **CLC 10, 18**
  See also CA 89-92; DLB 113; HW

**Argueta, Manlio** 1936-............ **CLC 31**
  See also CA 131; DLB 145; HW

**Ariosto, Ludovico** 1474-1533........ **LC 6**

**Aristides**
  See Epstein, Joseph

**Aristophanes**
  450B.C.-385B.C......... **CMLC 4; DA;
                                DAB; DC 2**

**Arlt, Roberto (Godofredo Christophersen)**
  1900-1942 ............ **TCLC 29; HLC**
  See also CA 123; 131; HW

**Armah, Ayi Kwei** 1939- .... **CLC 5, 33; BLC**
  See also BW 1; CA 61-64; CANR 21;
  DLB 117; MTCW

**Armatrading, Joan** 1950-.......... **CLC 17**
  See also CA 114

**Arnette, Robert**
  See Silverberg, Robert

**Arnim, Achim von (Ludwig Joachim von
  Arnim)** 1781-1831 .......... **NCLC 5**
  See also DLB 90

**Arnim, Bettina von** 1785-1859.... **NCLC 38**
  See also DLB 90

**Arnold, Matthew**
  1822-1888 ..... **NCLC 6, 29; DA; DAB;
                              PC 5; WLC**
  See also CDBLB 1832-1890; DLB 32, 57

**Arnold, Thomas** 1795-1842 ...... **NCLC 18**
  See also DLB 55

**Arnow, Harriette (Louisa) Simpson**
  1908-1986 ............... **CLC 2, 7, 18**
  See also CA 9-12R; 118; CANR 14; DLB 6;
  MTCW; SATA 42; SATA-Obit 47

**Arp, Hans**
  See Arp, Jean

**Arp, Jean** 1887-1966............... **CLC 5**
  See also CA 81-84; 25-28R; CANR 42

**Arrabal**
  See Arrabal, Fernando

**Arrabal, Fernando** 1932- ... **CLC 2, 9, 18, 58**
  See also CA 9-12R; CANR 15

**Arrick, Fran**.................... **CLC 30**
  See also Gaberman, Judie Angell

**Artaud, Antonin** 1896-1948 ..... **TCLC 3, 36**
  See also CA 104

**Arthur, Ruth M(abel)** 1905-1979.... **CLC 12**
  See also CA 9-12R; 85-88; CANR 4;
  SATA 7, 26

**Artsybashev, Mikhail (Petrovich)**
  1878-1927 ................. **TCLC 31**

**Arundel, Honor (Morfydd)**
  1919-1973 .................. **CLC 17**
  See also CA 21-22; 41-44R; CAP 2;
  CLR 35; SATA 4; SATA-Obit 24

**Asch, Sholem** 1880-1957 .......... **TCLC 3**
  See also CA 105

**Ash, Shalom**
  See Asch, Sholem

**Ashbery, John (Lawrence)**
  1927- ...... **CLC 2, 3, 4, 6, 9, 13, 15, 25,
                                41, 77**
  See also CA 5-8R; CANR 9, 37; DLB 5;
  DLBY 81; MTCW

**Ashdown, Clifford**
  See Freeman, R(ichard) Austin

**Ashe, Gordon**
  See Creasey, John

**Ashton-Warner, Sylvia (Constance)**
  1908-1984 .................. **CLC 19**
  See also CA 69-72; 112; CANR 29; MTCW

**Asimov, Isaac**
  1920-1992 ...... **CLC 1, 3, 9, 19, 26, 76**
  See also AAYA 13; BEST 90:2; CA 1-4R;
  137; CANR 2, 19, 36; CLR 12; DLB 8;
  DLBY 92; JRDA; MAICYA; MTCW;
  SATA 1, 26, 74

**Astley, Thea (Beatrice May)**
  1925- ...................... **CLC 41**
  See also CA 65-68; CANR 11, 43

**Aston, James**
  See White, T(erence) H(anbury)

**Asturias, Miguel Angel**
  1899-1974 ......... **CLC 3, 8, 13; HLC**
  See also CA 25-28; 49-52; CANR 32;
  CAP 2; DLB 113; HW; MTCW

**Atares, Carlos Saura**
  See Saura (Atares), Carlos

**Atheling, William**
  See Pound, Ezra (Weston Loomis)

**Atheling, William, Jr.**
  See Blish, James (Benjamin)

**Atherton, Gertrude (Franklin Horn)**
  1857-1948 ...................**TCLC 2**
  See also CA 104; DLB 9, 78

**Atherton, Lucius**
  See Masters, Edgar Lee

**Atkins, Jack**
  See Harris, Mark

**Atticus**
  See Fleming, Ian (Lancaster)

**Atwood, Margaret (Eleanor)**
  1939- ..... **CLC 2, 3, 4, 8, 13, 15, 25, 44,
                      84; DA; DAB; PC 8; SSC 2; WLC**
  See also AAYA 12; BEST 89:2; CA 49-52;
  CANR 3, 24, 33; DLB 53; MTCW;
  SATA 50

**Aubigny, Pierre d'**
  See Mencken, H(enry) L(ouis)

**Aubin, Penelope** 1685-1731(?)........ **LC 9**
  See also DLB 39

**Auchincloss, Louis (Stanton)**
  1917- ............. **CLC 4, 6, 9, 18, 45**
  See also CA 1-4R; CANR 6, 29; DLB 2;
  DLBY 80; MTCW

**Barbusse, Henri** 1873-1935 ....... TCLC 5
See also CA 105; DLB 65

**Barclay, Bill**
See Moorcock, Michael (John)

**Barclay, William Ewert**
See Moorcock, Michael (John)

**Barea, Arturo** 1897-1957 ........ TCLC 14
See also CA 111

**Barfoot, Joan** 1946- .............. CLC 18
See also CA 105

**Baring, Maurice** 1874-1945 ....... TCLC 8
See also CA 105; DLB 34

**Barker, Clive** 1952- ............. CLC 52
See also AAYA 10; BEST 90:3; CA 121;
129; MTCW

**Barker, George Granville**
1913-1991 ................ CLC 8, 48
See also CA 9-12R; 135; CANR 7, 38;
DLB 20; MTCW

**Barker, Harley Granville**
See Granville-Barker, Harley
See also DLB 10

**Barker, Howard** 1946- ........... CLC 37
See also CA 102; DLB 13

**Barker, Pat** 1943- ............... CLC 32
See also CA 117; 122

**Barlow, Joel** 1754-1812 ........ NCLC 23
See also DLB 37

**Barnard, Mary (Ethel)** 1909- ...... CLC 48
See also CA 21-22; CAP 2

**Barnes, Djuna**
1892-1982 ... CLC 3, 4, 8, 11, 29; SSC 3
See also CA 9-12R; 107; CANR 16; DLB 4,
9, 45; MTCW

**Barnes, Julian** 1946- ........ CLC 42; DAB
See also CA 102; CANR 19; DLBY 93

**Barnes, Peter** 1931- ............ CLC 5, 56
See also CA 65-68; CAAS 12; CANR 33,
34; DLB 13; MTCW

**Baroja (y Nessi), Pio**
1872-1956 ............. TCLC 8; HLC
See also CA 104

**Baron, David**
See Pinter, Harold

**Baron Corvo**
See Rolfe, Frederick (William Serafino
Austin Lewis Mary)

**Barondess, Sue K(aufman)**
1926-1977 ................... CLC 8
See also Kaufman, Sue
See also CA 1-4R; 69-72; CANR 1

**Baron de Teive**
See Pessoa, Fernando (Antonio Nogueira)

**Barres, Maurice** 1862-1923 ....... TCLC 47
See also DLB 123

**Barreto, Afonso Henrique de Lima**
See Lima Barreto, Afonso Henrique de

**Barrett, (Roger) Syd** 1946- ........ CLC 35

**Barrett, William (Christopher)**
1913-1992 ................. CLC 27
See also CA 13-16R; 139; CANR 11

**Barrie, J(ames) M(atthew)**
1860-1937 ............. TCLC 2; DAB
See also CA 104; 136; CDBLB 1890-1914;
CLR 16; DLB 10, 141, 156; MAICYA;
YABC 1

**Barrington, Michael**
See Moorcock, Michael (John)

**Barrol, Grady**
See Bograd, Larry

**Barry, Mike**
See Malzberg, Barry N(athaniel)

**Barry, Philip** 1896-1949 ......... TCLC 11
See also CA 109; DLB 7

**Bart, Andre Schwarz**
See Schwarz-Bart, Andre

**Barth, John (Simmons)**
1930- ...... CLC 1, 2, 3, 5, 7, 9, 10, 14,
27, 51, 89; SSC 10
See also AITN 1, 2; CA 1-4R; CABS 1;
CANR 5, 23, 49; DLB 2; MTCW

**Barthelme, Donald**
1931-1989 ...... CLC 1, 2, 3, 5, 6, 8, 13,
23, 46, 59; SSC 2
See also CA 21-24R; 129; CANR 20;
DLB 2; DLBY 80, 89; MTCW; SATA 7;
SATA-Obit 62

**Barthelme, Frederick** 1943- ........ CLC 36
See also CA 114; 122; DLBY 85

**Barthes, Roland (Gerard)**
1915-1980 ............... CLC 24, 83
See also CA 130; 97-100; MTCW

**Barzun, Jacques (Martin)** 1907- .... CLC 51
See also CA 61-64; CANR 22

**Bashevis, Isaac**
See Singer, Isaac Bashevis

**Bashkirtseff, Marie** 1859-1884 ... NCLC 27

**Basho**
See Matsuo Basho

**Bass, Kingsley B., Jr.**
See Bullins, Ed

**Bass, Rick** 1958- ................ CLC 79
See also CA 126

**Bassani, Giorgio** 1916- ............. CLC 9
See also CA 65-68; CANR 33; DLB 128;
MTCW

**Bastos, Augusto (Antonio) Roa**
See Roa Bastos, Augusto (Antonio)

**Bataille, Georges** 1897-1962 ....... CLC 29
See also CA 101; 89-92

**Bates, H(erbert) E(rnest)**
1905-1974 ...... CLC 46; DAB; SSC 10
See also CA 93-96; 45-48; CANR 34;
MTCW

**Bauchart**
See Camus, Albert

**Baudelaire, Charles**
1821-1867 ..... NCLC 6, 29; DA; DAB;
PC 1; SSC 18; WLC

**Baudrillard, Jean** 1929- ........... CLC 60

**Baum, L(yman) Frank** 1856-1919 ... TCLC 7
See also CA 108; 133; CLR 15; DLB 22;
JRDA; MAICYA; MTCW; SATA 18

**Baum, Louis F.**
See Baum, L(yman) Frank

**Baumbach, Jonathan** 1933- ...... CLC 6, 23
See also CA 13-16R; CAAS 5; CANR 12;
DLBY 80; MTCW

**Bausch, Richard (Carl)** 1945- ...... CLC 51
See also CA 101; CAAS 14; CANR 43;
DLB 130

**Baxter, Charles** 1947- .......... CLC 45, 78
See also CA 57-60; CANR 40; DLB 130

**Baxter, George Owen**
See Faust, Frederick (Schiller)

**Baxter, James K(eir)** 1926-1972 .... CLC 14
See also CA 77-80

**Baxter, John**
See Hunt, E(verette) Howard, (Jr.)

**Bayer, Sylvia**
See Glassco, John

**Baynton, Barbara** 1857-1929 ...... TCLC 57

**Beagle, Peter S(oyer)** 1939- ........ CLC 7
See also CA 9-12R; CANR 4; DLBY 80;
SATA 60

**Bean, Normal**
See Burroughs, Edgar Rice

**Beard, Charles A(ustin)**
1874-1948 ................ TCLC 15
See also CA 115; DLB 17; SATA 18

**Beardsley, Aubrey** 1872-1898 ..... NCLC 6

**Beattie, Ann**
1947- .... CLC 8, 13, 18, 40, 63; SSC 11
See also BEST 90:2; CA 81-84; DLBY 82;
MTCW

**Beattie, James** 1735-1803 ....... NCLC 25
See also DLB 109

**Beauchamp, Kathleen Mansfield** 1888-1923
See Mansfield, Katherine
See also CA 104; 134; DA

**Beaumarchais, Pierre-Augustin Caron de**
1732-1799 .................... DC 4

**Beauvoir, Simone (Lucie Ernestine Marie
Bertrand) de**
1908-1986 .... CLC 1, 2, 4, 8, 14, 31, 44,
50, 71; DA; DAB; WLC
See also CA 9-12R; 118; CANR 28;
DLB 72; DLBY 86; MTCW

**Becker, Jurek** 1937- ............ CLC 7, 19
See also CA 85-88; DLB 75

**Becker, Walter** 1950- ............. CLC 26

**Beckett, Samuel (Barclay)**
1906-1989 ...... CLC 1, 2, 3, 4, 6, 9, 10,
11, 14, 18, 29, 57, 59, 83; DA; DAB;
SSC 16; WLC
See also CA 5-8R; 130; CANR 33;
CDBLB 1945-1960; DLB 13, 15;
DLBY 90; MTCW

**Beckford, William** 1760-1844 .... NCLC 16
See also DLB 39

**Beckman, Gunnel** 1910- ........... CLC 26
See also CA 33-36R; CANR 15; CLR 25;
MAICYA; SAAS 9; SATA 6

**Becque, Henri** 1837-1899 ........ NCLC 3

**Beddoes, Thomas Lovell**
1803-1849 ................ NCLC 3
See also DLB 96

**Bedford, Donald F.**
See Fearing, Kenneth (Flexner)

Beecher, Catharine Esther
1800-1878 . . . . . . . . . . . . . . . . NCLC 30
See also DLB 1

Beecher, John  1904-1980 . . . . . . . . . . CLC 6
See also AITN 1; CA 5-8R; 105; CANR 8

Beer, Johann  1655-1700 . . . . . . . . . . . LC 5

Beer, Patricia  1924- . . . . . . . . . . . . . . CLC 58
See also CA 61-64; CANR 13, 46; DLB 40

Beerbohm, Henry Maximilian
1872-1956 . . . . . . . . . . . . . . . TCLC 1, 24
See also CA 104; DLB 34, 100

Beerbohm, Max
See Beerbohm, Henry Maximilian

Beer-Hofmann, Richard
1866-1945 . . . . . . . . . . . . . . . . TCLC 60
See also DLB 81

Begiebing, Robert J(ohn)  1946- . . . . . CLC 70
See also CA 122; CANR 40

Behan, Brendan
1923-1964 . . . . . . . CLC 1, 8, 11, 15, 79
See also CA 73-76; CANR 33;
CDBLB 1945-1960; DLB 13; MTCW

Behn, Aphra
1640(?)-1689 . . . . . . LC 1, 30; DA; DAB;
DC 4; PC 13; WLC
See also DLB 39, 80, 131

Behrman, S(amuel) N(athaniel)
1893-1973 . . . . . . . . . . . . . . . . . CLC 40
See also CA 13-16; 45-48; CAP 1; DLB 7,
44

Belasco, David  1853-1931 . . . . . . . . . TCLC 3
See also CA 104; DLB 7

Belcheva, Elisaveta  1893- . . . . . . . . . CLC 10
See also Bagryana, Elisaveta

Beldone, Phil "Cheech"
See Ellison, Harlan (Jay)

Beleno
See Azuela, Mariano

Belinski, Vissarion Grigoryevich
1811-1848 . . . . . . . . . . . . . . . . . NCLC 5

Belitt, Ben  1911- . . . . . . . . . . . . . . . . CLC 22
See also CA 13-16R; CAAS 4; CANR 7;
DLB 5

Bell, James Madison
1826-1902 . . . . . . . . . . . . TCLC 43; BLC
See also BW 1; CA 122; 124; DLB 50

Bell, Madison (Smartt)  1957- . . . . . . CLC 41
See also CA 111; CANR 28

Bell, Marvin (Hartley)  1937- . . . . . CLC 8, 31
See also CA 21-24R; CAAS 14; DLB 5;
MTCW

Bell, W. L. D.
See Mencken, H(enry) L(ouis)

Bellamy, Atwood C.
See Mencken, H(enry) L(ouis)

Bellamy, Edward  1850-1898 . . . . . . NCLC 4
See also DLB 12

Bellin, Edward J.
See Kuttner, Henry

Belloc, (Joseph) Hilaire (Pierre)
1870-1953 . . . . . . . . . . . . . . TCLC 7, 18
See also CA 106; DLB 19, 100, 141;
YABC 1

Belloc, Joseph Peter Rene Hilaire
See Belloc, (Joseph) Hilaire (Pierre)

Belloc, Joseph Pierre Hilaire
See Belloc, (Joseph) Hilaire (Pierre)

Belloc, M. A.
See Lowndes, Marie Adelaide (Belloc)

Bellow, Saul
1915- . . . . . . CLC 1, 2, 3, 6, 8, 10, 13, 15,
25, 33, 34, 63, 79; DA; DAB; SSC 14;
WLC
See also AITN 2; BEST 89:3; CA 5-8R;
CABS 1; CANR 29; CDALB 1941-1968;
DLB 2, 28; DLBD 3; DLBY 82; MTCW

Belser, Reimond Karel Maria de
See Ruyslinck, Ward

Bely, Andrey . . . . . . . . . . . . TCLC 7; PC 11
See also Bugayev, Boris Nikolayevich

Benary, Margot
See Benary-Isbert, Margot

Benary-Isbert, Margot  1889-1979 . . . CLC 12
See also CA 5-8R; 89-92; CANR 4;
CLR 12; MAICYA; SATA 2;
SATA-Obit 21

Benavente (y Martinez), Jacinto
1866-1954 . . . . . . . . . . . . . . . . . TCLC 3
See also CA 106; 131; HW; MTCW

Benchley, Peter (Bradford)
1940- . . . . . . . . . . . . . . . . . . . CLC 4, 8
See also AAYA 14; AITN 2; CA 17-20R;
CANR 12, 35; MTCW; SATA 3

Benchley, Robert (Charles)
1889-1945 . . . . . . . . . . . . . . TCLC 1, 55
See also CA 105; DLB 11

Benda, Julien  1867-1956 . . . . . . . . TCLC 60
See also CA 120

Benedict, Ruth  1887-1948 . . . . . . . TCLC 60

Benedikt, Michael  1935- . . . . . . . . CLC 4, 14
See also CA 13-16R; CANR 7; DLB 5

Benet, Juan  1927- . . . . . . . . . . . . . . . CLC 28
See also CA 143

Benet, Stephen Vincent
1898-1943 . . . . . . . . . . TCLC 7; SSC 10
See also CA 104; DLB 4, 48, 102; YABC 1

Benet, William Rose  1886-1950 . . . TCLC 28
See also CA 118; DLB 45

Benford, Gregory (Albert)  1941- . . . . CLC 52
See also CA 69-72; CANR 12, 24, 49;
DLBY 82

Bengtsson, Frans (Gunnar)
1894-1954 . . . . . . . . . . . . . . . . TCLC 48

Benjamin, David
See Slavitt, David R(ytman)

Benjamin, Lois
See Gould, Lois

Benjamin, Walter  1892-1940 . . . . . TCLC 39

Benn, Gottfried  1886-1956 . . . . . . . . TCLC 3
See also CA 106; DLB 56

Bennett, Alan  1934- . . . . . CLC 45, 77; DAB
See also CA 103; CANR 35; MTCW

Bennett, (Enoch) Arnold
1867-1931 . . . . . . . . . . . . . . TCLC 5, 20
See also CA 106; CDBLB 1890-1914;
DLB 10, 34, 98, 135

Bennett, Elizabeth
See Mitchell, Margaret (Munnerlyn)

Bennett, George Harold  1930-
See Bennett, Hal
See also BW 1; CA 97-100

Bennett, Hal . . . . . . . . . . . . . . . . . . . CLC 5
See also Bennett, George Harold
See also DLB 33

Bennett, Jay  1912- . . . . . . . . . . . . . . CLC 35
See also AAYA 10; CA 69-72; CANR 11,
42; JRDA; SAAS 4; SATA 41;
SATA-Brief 27

Bennett, Louise (Simone)
1919- . . . . . . . . . . . . . . . . . CLC 28; BLC
See also BW 2; DLB 117

Benson, E(dward) F(rederic)
1867-1940 . . . . . . . . . . . . . . . . TCLC 27
See also CA 114; DLB 135, 153

Benson, Jackson J.  1930- . . . . . . . . . CLC 34
See also CA 25-28R; DLB 111

Benson, Sally  1900-1972 . . . . . . . . . . CLC 17
See also CA 19-20; 37-40R; CAP 1;
SATA 1, 35; SATA-Obit 27

Benson, Stella  1892-1933 . . . . . . . . . TCLC 17
See also CA 117; DLB 36

Bentham, Jeremy  1748-1832 . . . . . NCLC 38
See also DLB 107

Bentley, E(dmund) C(lerihew)
1875-1956 . . . . . . . . . . . . . . . . . TCLC 12
See also CA 108; DLB 70

Bentley, Eric (Russell)  1916- . . . . . . . CLC 24
See also CA 5-8R; CANR 6

Beranger, Pierre Jean de
1780-1857 . . . . . . . . . . . . . . . . NCLC 34

Berendt, John (Lawrence)  1939- . . . . CLC 86
See also CA 146

Berger, Colonel
See Malraux, (Georges-)Andre

Berger, John (Peter)  1926- . . . . . . CLC 2, 19
See also CA 81-84; DLB 14

Berger, Melvin H.  1927- . . . . . . . . . . CLC 12
See also CA 5-8R; CANR 4; CLR 32;
SAAS 2; SATA 5

Berger, Thomas (Louis)
1924- . . . . . . . . . . CLC 3, 5, 8, 11, 18, 38
See also CA 1-4R; CANR 5, 28; DLB 2;
DLBY 80; MTCW

Bergman, (Ernst) Ingmar
1918- . . . . . . . . . . . . . . . . . . CLC 16, 72
See also CA 81-84; CANR 33

Bergson, Henri  1859-1941 . . . . . . . TCLC 32

Bergstein, Eleanor  1938- . . . . . . . . . . CLC 4
See also CA 53-56; CANR 5

Berkoff, Steven  1937- . . . . . . . . . . . . CLC 56
See also CA 104

Bermant, Chaim (Icyk)  1929- . . . . . . CLC 40
See also CA 57-60; CANR 6, 31

Bern, Victoria
See Fisher, M(ary) F(rances) K(ennedy)

Bernanos, (Paul Louis) Georges
1888-1948 . . . . . . . . . . . . . . . . . TCLC 3
See also CA 104; 130; DLB 72

Bernard, April  1956- . . . . . . . . . . . . . CLC 59
See also CA 131

**Berne, Victoria**
See Fisher, M(ary) F(rances) K(ennedy)

**Bernhard, Thomas**
1931-1989 .............. **CLC 3, 32, 61**
See also CA 85-88; 127; CANR 32;
DLB 85, 124; MTCW

**Berriault, Gina** 1926- ............. **CLC 54**
See also CA 116; 129; DLB 130

**Berrigan, Daniel** 1921- ............. **CLC 4**
See also CA 33-36R; CAAS 1; CANR 11,
43; DLB 5

**Berrigan, Edmund Joseph Michael, Jr.**
1934-1983
See Berrigan, Ted
See also CA 61-64; 110; CANR 14

**Berrigan, Ted.** .................... **CLC 37**
See also Berrigan, Edmund Joseph Michael,
Jr.
See also DLB 5

**Berry, Charles Edward Anderson** 1931-
See Berry, Chuck
See also CA 115

**Berry, Chuck** ..................... **CLC 17**
See also Berry, Charles Edward Anderson

**Berry, Jonas**
See Ashbery, John (Lawrence)

**Berry, Wendell (Erdman)**
1934- ............ **CLC 4, 6, 8, 27, 46**
See also AITN 1; CA 73-76; DLB 5, 6

**Berryman, John**
1914-1972 ..... **CLC 1, 2, 3, 4, 6, 8, 10,
13, 25, 62**
See also CA 13-16; 33-36R; CABS 2;
CANR 35; CAP 1; CDALB 1941-1968;
DLB 48; MTCW

**Bertolucci, Bernardo** 1940- ........ **CLC 16**
See also CA 106

**Bertrand, Aloysius** 1807-1841 .... **NCLC 31**

**Bertran de Born** c. 1140-1215 ..... **CMLC 5**

**Besant, Annie (Wood)** 1847-1933 ... **TCLC 9**
See also CA 105

**Bessie, Alvah** 1904-1985. .......... **CLC 23**
See also CA 5-8R; 116; CANR 2; DLB 26

**Bethlen, T. D.**
See Silverberg, Robert

**Beti, Mongo** ................ **CLC 27; BLC**
See also Biyidi, Alexandre

**Betjeman, John**
1906-1984 ... **CLC 2, 6, 10, 34, 43; DAB**
See also CA 9-12R; 112; CANR 33;
CDBLB 1945-1960; DLB 20; DLBY 84;
MTCW

**Bettelheim, Bruno** 1903-1990 ...... **CLC 79**
See also CA 81-84; 131; CANR 23; MTCW

**Betti, Ugo** 1892-1953 ............. **TCLC 5**
See also CA 104

**Betts, Doris (Waugh)** 1932-.... **CLC 3, 6, 28**
See also CA 13-16R; CANR 9; DLBY 82

**Bevan, Alistair**
See Roberts, Keith (John Kingston)

**Bialik, Chaim Nachman**
1873-1934 ................. **TCLC 25**

**Bickerstaff, Isaac**
See Swift, Jonathan

**Bidart, Frank** 1939- .............. **CLC 33**
See also CA 140

**Bienek, Horst** 1930- ............ **CLC 7, 11**
See also CA 73-76; DLB 75

**Bierce, Ambrose (Gwinett)**
1842-1914(?) ....... **TCLC 1, 7, 44; DA;
SSC 9; WLC**
See also CA 104; 139; CDALB 1865-1917;
DLB 11, 12, 23, 71, 74

**Billings, Josh**
See Shaw, Henry Wheeler

**Billington, (Lady) Rachel (Mary)**
1942- ...................... **CLC 43**
See also AITN 2; CA 33-36R; CANR 44

**Binyon, T(imothy) J(ohn)** 1936- .... **CLC 34**
See also CA 111; CANR 28

**Bioy Casares, Adolfo**
1914- ... **CLC 4, 8, 13, 88; HLC; SSC 17**
See also CA 29-32R; CANR 19, 43;
DLB 113; HW; MTCW

**Bird, Cordwainer**
See Ellison, Harlan (Jay)

**Bird, Robert Montgomery**
1806-1854 ................. **NCLC 1**

**Birney, (Alfred) Earle**
1904- ................. **CLC 1, 4, 6, 11**
See also CA 1-4R; CANR 5, 20; DLB 88;
MTCW

**Bishop, Elizabeth**
1911-1979 ...... **CLC 1, 4, 9, 13, 15, 32;
DA; PC 3**
See also CA 5-8R; 89-92; CABS 2;
CANR 26; CDALB 1968-1988; DLB 5;
MTCW; SATA-Obit 24

**Bishop, John** 1935- .............. **CLC 10**
See also CA 105

**Bissett, Bill** 1939- ............... **CLC 18**
See also CA 69-72; CAAS 19; CANR 15;
DLB 53; MTCW

**Bitov, Andrei (Georgievich)** 1937-... **CLC 57**
See also CA 142

**Biyidi, Alexandre** 1932-
See Beti, Mongo
See also BW 1; CA 114; 124; MTCW

**Bjarme, Brynjolf**
See Ibsen, Henrik (Johan)

**Bjornson, Bjornstjerne (Martinius)**
1832-1910 ............... **TCLC 7, 37**
See also CA 104

**Black, Robert**
See Holdstock, Robert P.

**Blackburn, Paul** 1926-1971 ...... **CLC 9, 43**
See also CA 81-84; 33-36R; CANR 34;
DLB 16; DLBY 81

**Black Elk** 1863-1950 ............ **TCLC 33**
See also CA 144; NNAL

**Black Hobart**
See Sanders, (James) Ed(ward)

**Blacklin, Malcolm**
See Chambers, Aidan

**Blackmore, R(ichard) D(oddridge)**
1825-1900 ................. **TCLC 27**
See also CA 120; DLB 18

**Blackmur, R(ichard) P(almer)**
1904-1965 ................ **CLC 2, 24**
See also CA 11-12; 25-28R; CAP 1; DLB 63

**Black Tarantula, The**
See Acker, Kathy

**Blackwood, Algernon (Henry)**
1869-1951 ................... **TCLC 5**
See also CA 105; DLB 153, 156

**Blackwood, Caroline** 1931- ....... **CLC 6, 9**
See also CA 85-88; CANR 32; DLB 14;
MTCW

**Blade, Alexander**
See Hamilton, Edmond; Silverberg, Robert

**Blaga, Lucian** 1895-1961 .......... **CLC 75**

**Blair, Eric (Arthur)** 1903-1950
See Orwell, George
See also CA 104; 132; DA; DAB; MTCW;
SATA 29

**Blais, Marie-Claire**
1939- ............. **CLC 2, 4, 6, 13, 22**
See also CA 21-24R; CAAS 4; CANR 38;
DLB 53; MTCW

**Blaise, Clark** 1940-.............. **CLC 29**
See also AITN 2; CA 53-56; CAAS 3;
CANR 5; DLB 53

**Blake, Nicholas**
See Day Lewis, C(ecil)
See also DLB 77

**Blake, William**
1757-1827 .... **NCLC 13, 37; DA; DAB;
PC 12; WLC**
See also CDBLB 1789-1832; DLB 93;
MAICYA; SATA 30

**Blake, William J(ames)** 1894-1969 ... **PC 12**
See also CA 5-8R; 25-28R

**Blasco Ibanez, Vicente**
1867-1928 ................. **TCLC 12**
See also CA 110; 131; HW; MTCW

**Blatty, William Peter** 1928-........ **CLC 2**
See also CA 5-8R; CANR 9

**Bleeck, Oliver**
See Thomas, Ross (Elmore)

**Blessing, Lee** 1949-.............. **CLC 54**

**Blish, James (Benjamin)**
1921-1975 ................... **CLC 14**
See also CA 1-4R; 57-60; CANR 3; DLB 8;
MTCW; SATA 66

**Bliss, Reginald**
See Wells, H(erbert) G(eorge)

**Blixen, Karen (Christentze Dinesen)**
1885-1962
See Dinesen, Isak
See also CA 25-28; CANR 22; CAP 2;
MTCW; SATA 44

**Bloch, Robert (Albert)** 1917-1994 ... **CLC 33**
See also CA 5-8R; 146; CAAS 20; CANR 5;
DLB 44; SATA 12; SATA-Obit 82

**Blok, Alexander (Alexandrovich)**
1880-1921 ................... **TCLC 5**
See also CA 104

**Blom, Jan**
See Breytenbach, Breyten

**Bloom, Harold** 1930- ............. **CLC 24**
See also CA 13-16R; CANR 39; DLB 67

**Bloomfield, Aurelius**
See Bourne, Randolph S(illiman)

**Blount, Roy (Alton), Jr.** 1941- ..... **CLC 38**
See also CA 53-56; CANR 10, 28; MTCW

**Bloy, Leon** 1846-1917............ **TCLC 22**
See also CA 121; DLB 123

**Blume, Judy (Sussman)** 1938- ... **CLC 12, 30**
See also AAYA 3; CA 29-32R; CANR 13,
37; CLR 2, 15; DLB 52; JRDA;
MAICYA; MTCW; SATA 2, 31, 79

**Blunden, Edmund (Charles)**
1896-1974 ................. **CLC 2, 56**
See also CA 17-18; 45-48; CAP 2; DLB 20,
100, 155; MTCW

**Bly, Robert (Elwood)**
1926- ........ **CLC 1, 2, 5, 10, 15, 38**
See also CA 5-8R; CANR 41; DLB 5;
MTCW

**Boas, Franz** 1858-1942........... **TCLC 56**
See also CA 115

**Bobette**
See Simenon, Georges (Jacques Christian)

**Boccaccio, Giovanni**
1313-1375 ......... **CMLC 13; SSC 10**

**Bochco, Steven** 1943-............. **CLC 35**
See also AAYA 11; CA 124; 138

**Bodenheim, Maxwell** 1892-1954 ... **TCLC 44**
See also CA 110; DLB 9, 45

**Bodker, Cecil** 1927- .............. **CLC 21**
See also CA 73-76; CANR 13, 44; CLR 23;
MAICYA; SATA 14

**Boell, Heinrich (Theodor)**
1917-1985 .... **CLC 2, 3, 6, 9, 11, 15, 27,
32, 72; DA; DAB; WLC**
See also CA 21-24R; 116; CANR 24;
DLB 69; DLBY 85; MTCW

**Boerne, Alfred**
See Doeblin, Alfred

**Boethius** 480(?)-524(?) .......... **CMLC 15**
See also DLB 115

**Bogan, Louise**
·1897-1970 ....... **CLC 4, 39, 46; PC 12**
See also CA 73-76; 25-28R; CANR 33;
DLB 45; MTCW

**Bogarde, Dirk** .................... **CLC 19**
See also Van Den Bogarde, Derek Jules
Gaspard Ulric Niven
See also DLB 14

**Bogosian, Eric** 1953- ............. **CLC 45**
See also CA 138

**Bograd, Larry** 1953-.............. **CLC 35**
See also CA 93-96; SATA 33

**Boiardo, Matteo Maria** 1441-1494 .... **LC 6**

**Boileau-Despreaux, Nicolas**
1636-1711 ..................... **LC 3**

**Boland, Eavan (Aisling)** 1944-... **CLC 40, 67**
See also CA 143; DLB 40

**Bolt, Lee**
See Faust, Frederick (Schiller)

**Bolt, Robert (Oxton)** 1924-1995 .... **CLC 14**
See also CA 17-20R; 147; CANR 35;
DLB 13; MTCW

**Bombet, Louis-Alexandre-Cesar**
See Stendhal

**Bomkauf**
See Kaufman, Bob (Garnell)

**Bonaventura**.................... **NCLC 35**
See also DLB 90

**Bond, Edward** 1934-....... **CLC 4, 6, 13, 23**
See also CA 25-28R; CANR 38; DLB 13;
MTCW

**Bonham, Frank** 1914-1989........ **CLC 12**
See also AAYA 1; CA 9-12R; CANR 4, 36;
JRDA; MAICYA; SAAS 3; SATA 1, 49;
SATA-Obit 62

**Bonnefoy, Yves** 1923-........ **CLC 9, 15, 58**
See also CA 85-88; CANR 33; MTCW

**Bontemps, Arna(ud Wendell)**
1902-1973 ............ **CLC 1, 18; BLC**
See also BW 1; CA 1-4R; 41-44R; CANR 4,
35; CLR 6; DLB 48, 51; JRDA;
MAICYA; MTCW; SATA 2, 44;
SATA-Obit 24

**Booth, Martin** 1944-.............. **CLC 13**
See also CA 93-96; CAAS 2

**Booth, Philip** 1925-............... **CLC 23**
See also CA 5-8R; CANR 5; DLBY 82

**Booth, Wayne C(layson)** 1921- ..... **CLC 24**
See also CA 1-4R; CAAS 5; CANR 3, 43;
DLB 67

**Borchert, Wolfgang** 1921-1947 ..... **TCLC 5**
See also CA 104; DLB 69, 124

**Borel, Petrus** 1809-1859........ **NCLC 41**

**Borges, Jorge Luis**
1899-1986 ... **CLC 1, 2, 3, 4, 6, 8, 9, 10,
13, 19, 44, 48, 83; DA; DAB; HLC;
SSC 4; WLC**
See also CA 21-24R; CANR 19, 33;
DLB 113; DLBY 86; HW; MTCW

**Borowski, Tadeusz** 1922-1951 ...... **TCLC 9**
See also CA 106

**Borrow, George (Henry)**
1803-1881 .................... **NCLC 9**
See also DLB 21, 55

**Bosman, Herman Charles**
1905-1951 ................. **TCLC 49**

**Bosschere, Jean de** 1878(?)-1953... **TCLC 19**
See also CA 115

**Boswell, James**
1740-1795 ...... **LC 4; DA; DAB; WLC**
See also CDBLB 1660-1789; DLB 104, 142

**Bottoms, David** 1949-............. **CLC 53**
See also CA 105; CANR 22; DLB 120;
DLBY 83

**Boucicault, Dion** 1820-1890...... **NCLC 41**

**Boucolon, Maryse** 1937-
See Conde, Maryse
See also CA 110; CANR 30

**Bourget, Paul (Charles Joseph)**
1852-1935 ................. **TCLC 12**
See also CA 107; DLB 123

**Bourjaily, Vance (Nye)** 1922- .... **CLC 8, 62**
See also CA 1-4R; CAAS 1; CANR 2;
DLB 2, 143

**Bourne, Randolph S(illiman)**
1886-1918 ................. **TCLC 16**
See also CA 117; DLB 63

**Bova, Ben(jamin William)** 1932-.... **CLC 45**
See also CA 5-8R; CAAS 18; CANR 11;
CLR 3; DLBY 81; MAICYA; MTCW;
SATA 6, 68

**Bowen, Elizabeth (Dorothea Cole)**
1899-1973 ...... **CLC 1, 3, 6, 11, 15, 22;
SSC 3**
See also CA 17-18; 41-44R; CANR 35;
CAP 2; CDBLB 1945-1960; DLB 15;
MTCW

**Bowering, George** 1935-........ **CLC 15, 47**
See also CA 21-24R; CAAS 16; CANR 10;
DLB 53

**Bowering, Marilyn R(uthe)** 1949-... **CLC 32**
See also CA 101; CANR 49

**Bowers, Edgar** 1924- .............. **CLC 9**
See also CA 5-8R; CANR 24; DLB 5

**Bowie, David** .................... **CLC 17**
See also Jones, David Robert

**Bowles, Jane (Sydney)**
1917-1973 ................. **CLC 3, 68**
See also CA 19-20; 41-44R; CAP 2

**Bowles, Paul (Frederick)**
1910- ......... **CLC 1, 2, 19, 53; SSC 3**
See also CA 1-4R; CAAS 1; CANR 1, 19;
DLB 5, 6; MTCW

**Box, Edgar**
See Vidal, Gore

**Boyd, Nancy**
See Millay, Edna St. Vincent

**Boyd, William** 1952-........ **CLC 28, 53, 70**
See also CA 114; 120

**Boyle, Kay**
1902-1992 ..... **CLC 1, 5, 19, 58; SSC 5**
See also CA 13-16R; 140; CAAS 1;
CANR 29; DLB 4, 9, 48, 86; DLBY 93;
MTCW

**Boyle, Mark**
See Kienzle, William X(avier)

**Boyle, Patrick** 1905-1982.......... **CLC 19**
See also CA 127

**Boyle, T. C.** 1948-
See Boyle, T(homas) Coraghessan

**Boyle, T(homas) Coraghessan**
1948- ......... **CLC 36, 55, 90; SSC 16**
See also BEST 90:4; CA 120; CANR 44;
DLBY 86

**Boz**
See Dickens, Charles (John Huffam)

**Brackenridge, Hugh Henry**
1748-1816 ................. **NCLC 7**
See also DLB 11, 37

**Bradbury, Edward P.**
See Moorcock, Michael (John)

**Bradbury, Malcolm (Stanley)**
1932- ................... **CLC 32, 61**
See also CA 1-4R; CANR 1, 33; DLB 14;
MTCW

**Bradbury, Ray (Douglas)**
1920- ....... **CLC 1, 3, 10, 15, 42; DA;
DAB; WLC**
See also AAYA 15; AITN 1, 2; CA 1-4R;
CANR 2, 30; CDALB 1968-1988; DLB 2,
8; MTCW; SATA 11, 64

**Brown, Charles Brockden**
1771-1810 . . . . . . . . . . . . . . . . **NCLC 22**
See also CDALB 1640-1865; DLB 37, 59, 73

**Brown, Christy** 1932-1981 . . . . . . . . **CLC 63**
See also CA 105; 104; DLB 14

**Brown, Claude** 1937- . . . . . . . . **CLC 30; BLC**
See also AAYA 7; BW 1; CA 73-76

**Brown, Dee (Alexander)** 1908- . . **CLC 18, 47**
See also CA 13-16R; CAAS 6; CANR 11, 45; DLBY 80; MTCW; SATA 5

**Brown, George**
See Wertmueller, Lina

**Brown, George Douglas**
1869-1902 . . . . . . . . . . . . . . . . . **TCLC 28**

**Brown, George Mackay** 1921- . . . . **CLC 5, 48**
See also CA 21-24R; CAAS 6; CANR 12, 37; DLB 14, 27, 139; MTCW; SATA 35

**Brown, (William) Larry** 1951- . . . . . . **CLC 73**
See also CA 130; 134

**Brown, Moses**
See Barrett, William (Christopher)

**Brown, Rita Mae** 1944- . . . . . **CLC 18, 43, 79**
See also CA 45-48; CANR 2, 11, 35; MTCW

**Brown, Roderick (Langmere) Haig-**
See Haig-Brown, Roderick (Langmere)

**Brown, Rosellen** 1939- . . . . . . . . . . . **CLC 32**
See also CA 77-80; CAAS 10; CANR 14, 44

**Brown, Sterling Allen**
1901-1989 . . . . . . . . **CLC 1, 23, 59; BLC**
See also BW 1; CA 85-88; 127; CANR 26; DLB 48, 51, 63; MTCW

**Brown, Will**
See Ainsworth, William Harrison

**Brown, William Wells**
1813-1884 . . . . . . . **NCLC 2; BLC; DC 1**
See also DLB 3, 50

**Browne, (Clyde) Jackson** 1948(?)- . . . **CLC 21**
See also CA 120

**Browning, Elizabeth Barrett**
1806-1861 . . . . . **NCLC 1, 16; DA; DAB; PC 6; WLC**
See also CDBLB 1832-1890; DLB 32

**Browning, Robert**
1812-1889 . . **NCLC 19; DA; DAB; PC 2**
See also CDBLB 1832-1890; DLB 32; YABC 1

**Browning, Tod** 1882-1962 . . . . . . . . . **CLC 16**
See also CA 141; 117

**Brownson, Orestes (Augustus)**
1803-1876 . . . . . . . . . . . . . . . . **NCLC 50**

**Bruccoli, Matthew J(oseph)** 1931- . . **CLC 34**
See also CA 9-12R; CANR 7; DLB 103

**Bruce, Lenny** . . . . . . . . . . . . . . . . . . **CLC 21**
See also Schneider, Leonard Alfred

**Bruin, John**
See Brutus, Dennis

**Brulard, Henri**
See Stendhal

**Brulls, Christian**
See Simenon, Georges (Jacques Christian)

**Brunner, John (Kilian Houston)**
1934- . . . . . . . . . . . . . . . . . . . **CLC 8, 10**
See also CA 1-4R; CAAS 8; CANR 2, 37; MTCW

**Bruno, Giordano** 1548-1600 . . . . . . . . **LC 27**

**Brutus, Dennis** 1924- . . . . . . . . **CLC 43; BLC**
See also BW 2; CA 49-52; CAAS 14; CANR 2, 27, 42; DLB 117

**Bryan, C(ourtlandt) D(ixon) B(arnes)**
1936- . . . . . . . . . . . . . . . . . . . . . **CLC 29**
See also CA 73-76; CANR 13

**Bryan, Michael**
See Moore, Brian

**Bryant, William Cullen**
1794-1878 . . . . . . **NCLC 6, 46; DA; DAB**
See also CDALB 1640-1865; DLB 3, 43, 59

**Bryusov, Valery Yakovlevich**
1873-1924 . . . . . . . . . . . . . . . . . **TCLC 10**
See also CA 107

**Buchan, John** 1875-1940 . . . **TCLC 41; DAB**
See also CA 108; 145; DLB 34, 70, 156; YABC 2

**Buchanan, George** 1506-1582 . . . . . . . **LC 4**

**Buchheim, Lothar-Guenther** 1918- . . . **CLC 6**
See also CA 85-88

**Buchner, (Karl) Georg**
1813-1837 . . . . . . . . . . . . . . . . **NCLC 26**

**Buchwald, Art(hur)** 1925- . . . . . . . . . . **CLC 33**
See also AITN 1; CA 5-8R; CANR 21; MTCW; SATA 10

**Buck, Pearl S(ydenstricker)**
1892-1973 . . . . **CLC 7, 11, 18; DA; DAB**
See also AITN 1; CA 1-4R; 41-44R; CANR 1, 34; DLB 9, 102; MTCW; SATA 1, 25

**Buckler, Ernest** 1908-1984 . . . . . . . . **CLC 13**
See also CA 11-12; 114; CAP 1; DLB 68; SATA 47

**Buckley, Vincent (Thomas)**
1925-1988 . . . . . . . . . . . . . . . . . . **CLC 57**
See also CA 101

**Buckley, William F(rank), Jr.**
1925- . . . . . . . . . . . . . . . . . **CLC 7, 18, 37**
See also AITN 1; CA 1-4R; CANR 1, 24; DLB 137; DLBY 80; MTCW

**Buechner, (Carl) Frederick**
1926- . . . . . . . . . . . . . . . . . **CLC 2, 4, 6, 9**
See also CA 13-16R; CANR 11, 39; DLBY 80; MTCW

**Buell, John (Edward)** 1927- . . . . . . . . **CLC 10**
See also CA 1-4R; DLB 53

**Buero Vallejo, Antonio** 1916- . . . **CLC 15, 46**
See also CA 106; CANR 24, 49; HW; MTCW

**Bufalino, Gesualdo** 1920(?)- . . . . . . . . **CLC 74**

**Bugayev, Boris Nikolayevich** 1880-1934
See Bely, Andrey
See also CA 104

**Bukowski, Charles**
1920-1994 . . . . . . . . **CLC 2, 5, 9, 41, 82**
See also CA 17-20R; 144; CANR 40; DLB 5, 130; MTCW

**Bulgakov, Mikhail (Afanas'evich)**
1891-1940 . . . . . . . . **TCLC 2, 16; SSC 18**
See also CA 105

**Bulgya, Alexander Alexandrovich**
1901-1956 . . . . . . . . . . . . . . . . . **TCLC 53**
See also Fadeyev, Alexander
See also CA 117

**Bullins, Ed** 1935- . . . . . . . . **CLC 1, 5, 7; BLC**
See also BW 2; CA 49-52; CAAS 16; CANR 24, 46; DLB 7, 38; MTCW

**Bulwer-Lytton, Edward (George Earle Lytton)**
1803-1873 . . . . . . . . . . . . . . . **NCLC 1, 45**
See also DLB 21

**Bunin, Ivan Alexeyevich**
1870-1953 . . . . . . . . . . . **TCLC 6; SSC 5**
See also CA 104

**Bunting, Basil** 1900-1985 . . . . **CLC 10, 39, 47**
See also CA 53-56; 115; CANR 7; DLB 20

**Bunuel, Luis** 1900-1983 . . **CLC 16, 80; HLC**
See also CA 101; 110; CANR 32; HW

**Bunyan, John**
1628-1688 . . . . . . **LC 4; DA; DAB; WLC**
See also CDBLB 1660-1789; DLB 39

**Burckhardt, Jacob (Christoph)**
1818-1897 . . . . . . . . . . . . . . . . **NCLC 49**

**Burford, Eleanor**
See Hibbert, Eleanor Alice Burford

**Burgess, Anthony**
**CLC 1, 2, 4, 5, 8, 10, 13, 15, 22, 40, 62, 81; DAB**
See also Wilson, John (Anthony) Burgess
See also AITN 1; CDBLB 1960 to Present; DLB 14

**Burke, Edmund**
1729(?)-1797 . . . . **LC 7; DA; DAB; WLC**
See also DLB 104

**Burke, Kenneth (Duva)**
1897-1993 . . . . . . . . . . . . . . . **CLC 2, 24**
See also CA 5-8R; 143; CANR 39; DLB 45, 63; MTCW

**Burke, Leda**
See Garnett, David

**Burke, Ralph**
See Silverberg, Robert

**Burney, Fanny** 1752-1840 . . . . . . . **NCLC 12**
See also DLB 39

**Burns, Robert** 1759-1796 . . . . . . . . . . . . **PC 6**
See also CDBLB 1789-1832; DA; DAB; DLB 109; WLC

**Burns, Tex**
See L'Amour, Louis (Dearborn)

**Burnshaw, Stanley** 1906- . . . . . **CLC 3, 13, 44**
See also CA 9-12R; DLB 48

**Burr, Anne** 1937- . . . . . . . . . . . . . . . . **CLC 6**
See also CA 25-28R

**Burroughs, Edgar Rice**
1875-1950 . . . . . . . . . . . . . . . **TCLC 2, 32**
See also AAYA 11; CA 104; 132; DLB 8; MTCW; SATA 41

**Burroughs, William S(eward)**
1914- . . . . . . . **CLC 1, 2, 5, 15, 22, 42, 75; DA; DAB; WLC**
See also AITN 2; CA 9-12R; CANR 20; DLB 2, 8, 16, 152; DLBY 81; MTCW

**Burton, Richard F.** 1821-1890 . . . . **NCLC 42**
See also DLB 55

**Busch, Frederick** 1941- . . . **CLC 7, 10, 18, 47**
See also CA 33-36R; CAAS 1; CANR 45;
DLB 6

**Bush, Ronald** 1946- . . . . . . . . . . . . **CLC 34**
See also CA 136

**Bustos, F(rancisco)**
See Borges, Jorge Luis

**Bustos Domecq, H(onorio)**
See Bioy Casares, Adolfo; Borges, Jorge
Luis

**Butler, Octavia E(stelle)** 1947- . . . . . **CLC 38**
See also BW 2; CA 73-76; CANR 12, 24,
38; DLB 33; MTCW

**Butler, Robert Olen (Jr.)** 1945- . . . . . **CLC 81**
See also CA 112

**Butler, Samuel** 1612-1680 . . . . . . . . . . **LC 16**
See also DLB 101, 126

**Butler, Samuel**
1835-1902 . . . . . **TCLC 1, 33; DA; DAB;**
**WLC**
See also CA 143; CDBLB 1890-1914;
DLB 18, 57

**Butler, Walter C.**
See Faust, Frederick (Schiller)

**Butor, Michel (Marie Francois)**
1926- . . . . . . . . . . . . **CLC 1, 3, 8, 11, 15**
See also CA 9-12R; CANR 33; DLB 83;
MTCW

**Buzo, Alexander (John)** 1944- . . . . . . **CLC 61**
See also CA 97-100; CANR 17, 39

**Buzzati, Dino** 1906-1972 . . . . . . . . . **CLC 36**
See also CA 33-36R

**Byars, Betsy (Cromer)** 1928- . . . . . . . **CLC 35**
See also CA 33-36R; CANR 18, 36; CLR 1,
16; DLB 52; JRDA; MAICYA; MTCW;
SAAS 1; SATA 4, 46, 80

**Byatt, A(ntonia) S(usan Drabble)**
1936- . . . . . . . . . . . . . . . . . . . . **CLC 19, 65**
See also CA 13-16R; CANR 13, 33;
DLB 14; MTCW

**Byrne, David** 1952- . . . . . . . . . . . . . . **CLC 26**
See also CA 127

**Byrne, John Keyes** 1926-
See Leonard, Hugh
See also CA 102

**Byron, George Gordon (Noel)**
1788-1824 . . . . . **NCLC 2, 12; DA; DAB;**
**WLC**
See also CDBLB 1789-1832; DLB 96, 110

**C. 3. 3.**
See Wilde, Oscar (Fingal O'Flahertie Wills)

**Caballero, Fernan** 1796-1877 . . . . . **NCLC 10**

**Cabell, James Branch** 1879-1958 . . . **TCLC 6**
See also CA 105; DLB 9, 78

**Cable, George Washington**
1844-1925 . . . . . . . . . . . **TCLC 4; SSC 4**
See also CA 104; DLB 12, 74

**Cabral de Melo Neto, Joao** 1920- . . . **CLC 76**

**Cabrera Infante, G(uillermo)**
1929- . . . . . . . . . . . **CLC 5, 25, 45; HLC**
See also CA 85-88; CANR 29; DLB 113;
HW; MTCW

**Cade, Toni**
See Bambara, Toni Cade

**Cadmus and Harmonia**
See Buchan, John

**Caedmon** fl. 658-680 . . . . . . . . . . . . **CMLC 7**
See also DLB 146

**Caeiro, Alberto**
See Pessoa, Fernando (Antonio Nogueira)

**Cage, John (Milton, Jr.)** 1912- . . . . . **CLC 41**
See also CA 13-16R; CANR 9

**Cain, G.**
See Cabrera Infante, G(uillermo)

**Cain, Guillermo**
See Cabrera Infante, G(uillermo)

**Cain, James M(allahan)**
1892-1977 . . . . . . . . . . . . . **CLC 3, 11, 28**
See also AITN 1; CA 17-20R; 73-76;
CANR 8, 34; MTCW

**Caine, Mark**
See Raphael, Frederic (Michael)

**Calasso, Roberto** 1941- . . . . . . . . . . **CLC 81**
See also CA 143

**Calderon de la Barca, Pedro**
1600-1681 . . . . . . . . . . . . . . **LC 23; DC 3**

**Caldwell, Erskine (Preston)**
1903-1987 . . . . . . . **CLC 1, 8, 14, 50, 60;**
**SSC 19**
See also AITN 1; CA 1-4R; 121; CAAS 1;
CANR 2, 33; DLB 9, 86; MTCW

**Caldwell, (Janet Miriam) Taylor (Holland)**
1900-1985 . . . . . . . . . . . . . **CLC 2, 28, 39**
See also CA 5-8R; 116; CANR 5

**Calhoun, John Caldwell**
1782-1850 . . . . . . . . . . . . . . . . . **NCLC 15**
See also DLB 3

**Calisher, Hortense**
1911- . . . . . . . . . **CLC 2, 4, 8, 38; SSC 15**
See also CA 1-4R; CANR 1, 22; DLB 2;
MTCW

**Callaghan, Morley Edward**
1903-1990 . . . . . . . . . . **CLC 3, 14, 41, 65**
See also CA 9-12R; 132; CANR 33;
DLB 68; MTCW

**Calvino, Italo**
1923-1985 . . . . . **CLC 5, 8, 11, 22, 33, 39,**
**73; SSC 3**
See also CA 85-88; 116; CANR 23; MTCW

**Cameron, Carey** 1952- . . . . . . . . . . . **CLC 59**
See also CA 135

**Cameron, Peter** 1959- . . . . . . . . . . . **CLC 44**
See also CA 125

**Campana, Dino** 1885-1932 . . . . . . . **TCLC 20**
See also CA 117; DLB 114

**Campbell, John W(ood, Jr.)**
1910-1971 . . . . . . . . . . . . . . . . . . **CLC 32**
See also CA 21-22; 29-32R; CANR 34;
CAP 2; DLB 8; MTCW

**Campbell, Joseph** 1904-1987 . . . . . . . **CLC 69**
See also AAYA 3; BEST 89:2; CA 1-4R;
124; CANR 3, 28; MTCW

**Campbell, Maria** 1940- . . . . . . . . . . . **CLC 85**
See also CA 102; NNAL

**Campbell, (John) Ramsey**
1946- . . . . . . . . . . . . . . **CLC 42; SSC 19**
See also CA 57-60; CANR 7

**Campbell, (Ignatius) Roy (Dunnachie)**
1901-1957 . . . . . . . . . . . . . . . . . . **TCLC 5**
See also CA 104; DLB 20

**Campbell, Thomas** 1777-1844 . . . . **NCLC 19**
See also DLB 93; 144

**Campbell, Wilfred** . . . . . . . . . . . . . . **TCLC 9**
See also Campbell, William

**Campbell, William** 1858(?)-1918
See Campbell, Wilfred
See also CA 106; DLB 92

**Campos, Alvaro de**
See Pessoa, Fernando (Antonio Nogueira)

**Camus, Albert**
1913-1960 . . . . **CLC 1, 2, 4, 9, 11, 14, 32,**
**63, 69; DA; DAB; DC 2; SSC 9; WLC**
See also CA 89-92; DLB 72; MTCW

**Canby, Vincent** 1924- . . . . . . . . . . . **CLC 13**
See also CA 81-84

**Cancale**
See Desnos, Robert

**Canetti, Elias**
1905-1994 . . . . . . **CLC 3, 14, 25, 75, 86**
See also CA 21-24R; 146; CANR 23;
DLB 85, 124; MTCW

**Canin, Ethan** 1960- . . . . . . . . . . . . . . **CLC 55**
See also CA 131; 135

**Cannon, Curt**
See Hunter, Evan

**Cape, Judith**
See Page, P(atricia) K(athleen)

**Capek, Karel**
1890-1938 . . . . . . **TCLC 6, 37; DA; DAB;**
**DC 1; WLC**
See also CA 104; 140

**Capote, Truman**
1924-1984 . . . . . . **CLC 1, 3, 8, 13, 19, 34,**
**38, 58; DA; DAB; SSC 2; WLC**
See also CA 5-8R; 113; CANR 18;
CDALB 1941-1968; DLB 2; DLBY 80,
84; MTCW

**Capra, Frank** 1897-1991 . . . . . . . . . . **CLC 16**
See also CA 61-64; 135

**Caputo, Philip** 1941- . . . . . . . . . . . . . **CLC 32**
See also CA 73-76; CANR 40

**Card, Orson Scott** 1951- . . . . **CLC 44, 47, 50**
See also AAYA 11; CA 102; CANR 27, 47;
MTCW; SATA 83

**Cardenal (Martinez), Ernesto**
1925- . . . . . . . . . . . . . . . . . **CLC 31; HLC**
See also CA 49-52; CANR 2, 32; HW;
MTCW

**Carducci, Giosue** 1835-1907 . . . . . . . **TCLC 32**

**Carew, Thomas** 1595(?)-1640 . . . . . . . **LC 13**
See also DLB 126

**Carey, Ernestine Gilbreth** 1908- . . . . **CLC 17**
See also CA 5-8R; SATA 2

**Carey, Peter** 1943- . . . . . . . . . . . **CLC 40, 55**
See also CA 123; 127; MTCW

**Carleton, William** 1794-1869 . . . . . . **NCLC 3**

**Carlisle, Henry (Coffin)** 1926- . . . . . . **CLC 33**
See also CA 13-16R; CANR 15

**Carlsen, Chris**
See Holdstock, Robert P.

**Chandler, Raymond (Thornton)**
1888-1959 . . . . . . . . . . . . . . . . **TCLC 1, 7**
See also CA 104; 129; CDALB 1929-1941;
DLBD 6; MTCW

**Chang, Jung** 1952- . . . . . . . . . . . . . . **CLC 71**
See also CA 142

**Channing, William Ellery**
1780-1842 . . . . . . . . . . . . . . . . **NCLC 17**
See also DLB 1, 59

**Chaplin, Charles Spencer**
1889-1977 . . . . . . . . . . . . . . . . . . **CLC 16**
See also Chaplin, Charlie
See also CA 81-84; 73-76

**Chaplin, Charlie**
See Chaplin, Charles Spencer
See also DLB 44

**Chapman, George** 1559(?)-1634 . . . . . . **LC 22**
See also DLB 62, 121

**Chapman, Graham** 1941-1989 . . . . . . **CLC 21**
See also Monty Python
See also CA 116; 129; CANR 35

**Chapman, John Jay** 1862-1933 . . . . . **TCLC 7**
See also CA 104

**Chapman, Walker**
See Silverberg, Robert

**Chappell, Fred (Davis)** 1936- . . . . **CLC 40, 78**
See also CA 5-8R; CAAS 4; CANR 8, 33;
DLB 6, 105

**Char, Rene(-Emile)**
1907-1988 . . . . . . . . . . **CLC 9, 11, 14, 55**
See also CA 13-16R; 124; CANR 32;
MTCW

**Charby, Jay**
See Ellison, Harlan (Jay)

**Chardin, Pierre Teilhard de**
See Teilhard de Chardin, (Marie Joseph)
Pierre

**Charles I** 1600-1649 . . . . . . . . . . . . . . **LC 13**

**Charyn, Jerome** 1937- . . . . . . . . **CLC 5, 8, 18**
See also CA 5-8R; CAAS 1; CANR 7;
DLBY 83; MTCW

**Chase, Mary (Coyle)** 1907-1981 . . . . . . **DC 1**
See also CA 77-80; 105; SATA 17;
SATA-Obit 29

**Chase, Mary Ellen** 1887-1973 . . . . . . . **CLC 2**
See also CA 13-16; 41-44R; CAP 1;
SATA 10

**Chase, Nicholas**
See Hyde, Anthony

**Chateaubriand, Francois Rene de**
1768-1848 . . . . . . . . . . . . . . . . . **NCLC 3**
See also DLB 119

**Chatterje, Sarat Chandra** 1876-1936(?)
See Chatterji, Saratchandra
See also CA 109

**Chatterji, Bankim Chandra**
1838-1894 . . . . . . . . . . . . . . . . **NCLC 19**

**Chatterji, Saratchandra** . . . . . . . . . . **TCLC 13**
See also Chatterje, Sarat Chandra

**Chatterton, Thomas** 1752-1770 . . . . . . . **LC 3**
See also DLB 109

**Chatwin, (Charles) Bruce**
1940-1989 . . . . . . . . . . . . **CLC 28, 57, 59**
See also AAYA 4; BEST 90:1; CA 85-88;
127

**Chaucer, Daniel**
See Ford, Ford Madox

**Chaucer, Geoffrey**
1340(?)-1400 . . . . . . . . **LC 17; DA; DAB**
See also CDBLB Before 1660; DLB 146

**Chaviaras, Strates** 1935-
See Haviaras, Stratis
See also CA 105

**Chayefsky, Paddy** . . . . . . . . . . . . . . . . **CLC 23**
See also Chayefsky, Sidney
See also DLB 7, 44; DLBY 81

**Chayefsky, Sidney** 1923-1981
See Chayefsky, Paddy
See also CA 9-12R; 104; CANR 18

**Chedid, Andree** 1920- . . . . . . . . . . . . **CLC 47**
See also CA 145

**Cheever, John**
1912-1982 . . . . . . **CLC 3, 7, 8, 11, 15, 25,
64; DA; DAB; SSC 1; WLC**
See also CA 5-8R; 106; CABS 1; CANR 5,
27; CDALB 1941-1968; DLB 2, 102;
DLBY 80, 82; MTCW

**Cheever, Susan** 1943- . . . . . . . . . . **CLC 18, 48**
See also CA 103; CANR 27; DLBY 82

**Chekhonte, Antosha**
See Chekhov, Anton (Pavlovich)

**Chekhov, Anton (Pavlovich)**
1860-1904 . . . . . **TCLC 3, 10, 31, 55; DA;
DAB; SSC 2; WLC**
See also CA 104; 124

**Chernyshevsky, Nikolay Gavrilovich**
1828-1889 . . . . . . . . . . . . . . . . . **NCLC 1**

**Cherry, Carolyn Janice** 1942-
See Cherryh, C. J.
See also CA 65-68; CANR 10

**Cherryh, C. J.** . . . . . . . . . . . . . . . . . . **CLC 35**
See also Cherry, Carolyn Janice
See also DLBY 80

**Chesnutt, Charles W(addell)**
1858-1932 . . . . **TCLC 5, 39; BLC; SSC 7**
See also BW 1; CA 106; 125; DLB 12, 50,
78; MTCW

**Chester, Alfred** 1929(?)-1971 . . . . . . . **CLC 49**
See also CA 33-36R; DLB 130

**Chesterton, G(ilbert) K(eith)**
1874-1936 . . . . . . . . . **TCLC 1, 6; SSC 1**
See also CA 104; 132; CDBLB 1914-1945;
DLB 10, 19, 34, 70, 98, 149; MTCW;
SATA 27

**Chiang Pin-chin** 1904-1986
See Ding Ling
See also CA 118

**Ch'ien Chung-shu** 1910- . . . . . . . . . . **CLC 22**
See also CA 130; MTCW

**Child, L. Maria**
See Child, Lydia Maria

**Child, Lydia Maria** 1802-1880 . . . . **NCLC 6**
See also DLB 1, 74; SATA 67

**Child, Mrs.**
See Child, Lydia Maria

**Child, Philip** 1898-1978 . . . . . . . . **CLC 19, 68**
See also CA 13-14; CAP 1; SATA 47

**Childress, Alice**
1920-1994 . . **CLC 12, 15, 86; BLC; DC 4**
See also AAYA 8; BW 2; CA 45-48; 146;
CANR 3, 27; CLR 14; DLB 7, 38; JRDA;
MAICYA; MTCW; SATA 7, 48, 81

**Chislett, (Margaret) Anne** 1943- . . . . **CLC 34**

**Chitty, Thomas Willes** 1926- . . . . . . . **CLC 11**
See also Hinde, Thomas
See also CA 5-8R

**Chivers, Thomas Holley**
1809-1858 . . . . . . . . . . . . . . . . **NCLC 49**
See also DLB 3

**Chomette, Rene Lucien** 1898-1981
See Clair, Rene
See also CA 103

**Chopin, Kate**
. . . . . . . . **TCLC 5, 14; DA; DAB; SSC 8**
See also Chopin, Katherine
See also CDALB 1865-1917; DLB 12, 78

**Chopin, Katherine** 1851-1904
See Chopin, Kate
See also CA 104; 122

**Chretien de Troyes**
c. 12th cent. - . . . . . . . . . . . . . . **CMLC 10**

**Christie**
See Ichikawa, Kon

**Christie, Agatha (Mary Clarissa)**
1890-1976 . . . . . . **CLC 1, 6, 8, 12, 39, 48;
DAB**
See also AAYA 9; AITN 1, 2; CA 17-20R;
61-64; CANR 10, 37; CDBLB 1914-1945;
DLB 13, 77; MTCW; SATA 36

**Christie, (Ann) Philippa**
See Pearce, Philippa
See also CA 5-8R; CANR 4

**Christine de Pizan** 1365(?)-1431(?) . . . . **LC 9**

**Chubb, Elmer**
See Masters, Edgar Lee

**Chulkov, Mikhail Dmitrievich**
1743-1792 . . . . . . . . . . . . . . . . . . . **LC 2**
See also DLB 150

**Churchill, Caryl** 1938- . . . **CLC 31, 55; DC 5**
See also CA 102; CANR 22, 46; DLB 13;
MTCW

**Churchill, Charles** 1731-1764 . . . . . . . . **LC 3**
See also DLB 109

**Chute, Carolyn** 1947- . . . . . . . . . . . . . **CLC 39**
See also CA 123

**Ciardi, John (Anthony)**
1916-1986 . . . . . . . . . . . . **CLC 10, 40, 44**
See also CA 5-8R; 118; CAAS 2; CANR 5,
33; CLR 19; DLB 5; DLBY 86;
MAICYA; MTCW; SATA 1, 65;
SATA-Obit 46

**Cicero, Marcus Tullius**
106B.C.-43B.C. . . . . . . . . . . . . . . **CMLC 3**

**Cimino, Michael** 1943- . . . . . . . . . . . . **CLC 16**
See also CA 105

**Cioran, E(mil) M.** 1911- . . . . . . . . . . . **CLC 64**
See also CA 25-28R

**Cisneros, Sandra** 1954- . . . . . . **CLC 69; HLC**
See also AAYA 9; CA 131; DLB 122, 152;
HW

**Clair, Rene** . . . . . . . . . . . . . . . . . . . . . **CLC 20**
See also Chomette, Rene Lucien

**Colwin, Laurie (E.)**
1944-1992 . . . . . . . . . . **CLC 5, 13, 23, 84**
See also CA 89-92; 139; CANR 20, 46;
DLBY 80; MTCW

**Comfort, Alex(ander)** 1920- . . . . . . . . **CLC 7**
See also CA 1-4R; CANR 1, 45

**Comfort, Montgomery**
See Campbell, (John) Ramsey

**Compton-Burnett, I(vy)**
1884(?)-1969 . . . . . . **CLC 1, 3, 10, 15, 34**
See also CA 1-4R; 25-28R; CANR 4;
DLB 36; MTCW

**Comstock, Anthony** 1844-1915 . . . . **TCLC 13**
See also CA 110

**Conan Doyle, Arthur**
See Doyle, Arthur Conan

**Conde, Maryse** 1937- . . . . . . . . . . . **CLC 52**
See also Boucolon, Maryse
See also BW 2

**Condillac, Etienne Bonnot de**
1714-1780 . . . . . . . . . . . . . . . . . . **LC 26**

**Condon, Richard (Thomas)**
1915- . . . . . . . . . . . . **CLC 4, 6, 8, 10, 45**
See also BEST 90:3; CA 1-4R; CAAS 1;
CANR 2, 23; MTCW

**Congreve, William**
1670-1729 . . . . . . . . **LC 5, 21; DA; DAB;
DC 2; WLC**
See also CDBLB 1660-1789; DLB 39, 84

**Connell, Evan S(helby), Jr.**
1924- . . . . . . . . . . . . . . . . . **CLC 4, 6, 45**
See also AAYA 7; CA 1-4R; CAAS 2;
CANR 2, 39; DLB 2; DLBY 81; MTCW

**Connelly, Marc(us Cook)**
1890-1980 . . . . . . . . . . . . . . . . . . **CLC 7**
See also CA 85-88; 102; CANR 30; DLB 7;
DLBY 80; SATA-Obit 25

**Connor, Ralph** . . . . . . . . . . . . . . . . **TCLC 31**
See also Gordon, Charles William
See also DLB 92

**Conrad, Joseph**
1857-1924 . . . . **TCLC 1, 6, 13, 25, 43, 57;
DA; DAB; SSC 9; WLC**
See also CA 104; 131; CDBLB 1890-1914;
DLB 10, 34, 98, 156; MTCW; SATA 27

**Conrad, Robert Arnold**
See Hart, Moss

**Conroy, Pat** 1945- . . . . . . . . . . . **CLC 30, 74**
See also AAYA 8; AITN 1; CA 85-88;
CANR 24; DLB 6; MTCW

**Constant (de Rebecque), (Henri) Benjamin**
1767-1830 . . . . . . . . . . . . . . . . . **NCLC 6**
See also DLB 119

**Conybeare, Charles Augustus**
See Eliot, T(homas) S(tearns)

**Cook, Michael** 1933- . . . . . . . . . . . . **CLC 58**
See also CA 93-96; DLB 53

**Cook, Robin** 1940- . . . . . . . . . . . . . **CLC 14**
See also BEST 90:2; CA 108; 111;
CANR 41

**Cook, Roy**
See Silverberg, Robert

**Cooke, Elizabeth** 1948- . . . . . . . . . . **CLC 55**
See also CA 129

**Cooke, John Esten** 1830-1886 . . . . . **NCLC 5**
See also DLB 3

**Cooke, John Estes**
See Baum, L(yman) Frank

**Cooke, M. E.**
See Creasey, John

**Cooke, Margaret**
See Creasey, John

**Cooney, Ray** . . . . . . . . . . . . . . . . . . **CLC 62**

**Cooper, Douglas** 1960- . . . . . . . . . . . **CLC 86**

**Cooper, Henry St. John**
See Creasey, John

**Cooper, J. California** . . . . . . . . . . . . **CLC 56**
See also AAYA 12; BW 1; CA 125

**Cooper, James Fenimore**
1789-1851 . . . . . . . . . . . . . . **NCLC 1, 27**
See also CDALB 1640-1865; DLB 3;
SATA 19

**Coover, Robert (Lowell)**
1932- . . **CLC 3, 7, 15, 32, 46, 87; SSC 15**
See also CA 45-48; CANR 3, 37; DLB 2;
DLBY 81; MTCW

**Copeland, Stewart (Armstrong)**
1952- . . . . . . . . . . . . . . . . . . . . . **CLC 26**

**Coppard, A(lfred) E(dgar)**
1878-1957 . . . . . . . . . . **TCLC 5; SSC 21**
See also CA 114; YABC 1

**Coppee, Francois** 1842-1908 . . . . . . **TCLC 25**

**Coppola, Francis Ford** 1939- . . . . . . . **CLC 16**
See also CA 77-80; CANR 40; DLB 44

**Corbiere, Tristan** 1845-1875 . . . . . **NCLC 43**

**Corcoran, Barbara** 1911- . . . . . . . . . **CLC 17**
See also AAYA 14; CA 21-24R; CAAS 2;
CANR 11, 28, 48; DLB 52; JRDA;
SAAS 20; SATA 3, 77

**Cordelier, Maurice**
See Giraudoux, (Hippolyte) Jean

**Corelli, Marie** 1855-1924 . . . . . . . . **TCLC 51**
See also Mackay, Mary
See also DLB 34, 156

**Corman, Cid** . . . . . . . . . . . . . . . . . . . **CLC 9**
See also Corman, Sidney
See also CAAS 2; DLB 5

**Corman, Sidney** 1924-
See Corman, Cid
See also CA 85-88; CANR 44

**Cormier, Robert (Edmund)**
1925- . . . . . . . . . . **CLC 12, 30; DA; DAB**
See also AAYA 3; CA 1-4R; CANR 5, 23;
CDALB 1968-1988; CLR 12; DLB 52;
JRDA; MAICYA; MTCW; SATA 10, 45,
83

**Corn, Alfred (DeWitt III)** 1943- . . . . **CLC 33**
See also CA 104; CANR 44; DLB 120;
DLBY 80

**Corneille, Pierre** 1606-1684 . . . . **LC 28; DAB**

**Cornwell, David (John Moore)**
1931- . . . . . . . . . . . . . . . . . . . **CLC 9, 15**
See also le Carre, John
See also CA 5-8R; CANR 13, 33; MTCW

**Corso, (Nunzio) Gregory** 1930- . . . **CLC 1, 11**
See also CA 5-8R; CANR 41; DLB 5, 16;
MTCW

**Cortazar, Julio**
1914-1984 . . . . . **CLC 2, 3, 5, 10, 13, 15,
33, 34; HLC; SSC 7**
See also CA 21-24R; CANR 12, 32;
DLB 113; HW; MTCW

**CORTES, HERNAN** 1484-1547 . . . . . **LC 31**

**Corwin, Cecil**
See Kornbluth, C(yril) M.

**Cosic, Dobrica** 1921- . . . . . . . . . . . . **CLC 14**
See also CA 122; 138

**Costain, Thomas B(ertram)**
1885-1965 . . . . . . . . . . . . . . . . . . **CLC 30**
See also CA 5-8R; 25-28R; DLB 9

**Costantini, Humberto**
1924(?)-1987 . . . . . . . . . . . . . . . . **CLC 49**
See also CA 131; 122; HW

**Costello, Elvis** 1955- . . . . . . . . . . . . . **CLC 21**

**Cotter, Joseph Seamon Sr.**
1861-1949 . . . . . . . . . . . . **TCLC 28; BLC**
See also BW 1; CA 124; DLB 50

**Couch, Arthur Thomas Quiller**
See Quiller-Couch, Arthur Thomas

**Coulton, James**
See Hansen, Joseph

**Couperus, Louis (Marie Anne)**
1863-1923 . . . . . . . . . . . . . . . . . **TCLC 15**
See also CA 115

**Coupland, Douglas** 1961- . . . . . . . . . **CLC 85**
See also CA 142

**Court, Wesli**
See Turco, Lewis (Putnam)

**Courtenay, Bryce** 1933- . . . . . . . . . . **CLC 59**
See also CA 138

**Courtney, Robert**
See Ellison, Harlan (Jay)

**Cousteau, Jacques-Yves** 1910- . . . . . . **CLC 30**
See also CA 65-68; CANR 15; MTCW;
SATA 38

**Coward, Noel (Peirce)**
1899-1973 . . . . . . . . . . . **CLC 1, 9, 29, 51**
See also AITN 1; CA 17-18; 41-44R;
CANR 35; CAP 2; CDBLB 1914-1945;
DLB 10; MTCW

**Cowley, Malcolm** 1898-1989 . . . . . . . **CLC 39**
See also CA 5-8R; 128; CANR 3; DLB 4,
48; DLBY 81, 89; MTCW

**Cowper, William** 1731-1800 . . . . . . . **NCLC 8**
See also DLB 104, 109

**Cox, William Trevor** 1928- . . . **CLC 9, 14, 71**
See also Trevor, William
See also CA 9-12R; CANR 4, 37; DLB 14;
MTCW

**Coyne, P. J.**
See Masters, Hilary

**Cozzens, James Gould**
1903-1978 . . . . . . . . . . . . . . **CLC 1, 4, 11**
See also CA 9-12R; 81-84; CANR 19;
CDALB 1941-1968; DLB 9; DLBD 2;
DLBY 84; MTCW

**Crabbe, George** 1754-1832 . . . . . . . **NCLC 26**
See also DLB 93

**Craig, A. A.**
See Anderson, Poul (William)

**D'Annunzio, Gabriele**
  1863-1938 ............... **TCLC 6, 40**
  See also CA 104

**d'Antibes, Germain**
  See Simenon, Georges (Jacques Christian)

**Danvers, Dennis** 1947- ........... **CLC 70**

**Danziger, Paula** 1944- ........... **CLC 21**
  See also AAYA 4; CA 112; 115; CANR 37;
  CLR 20; JRDA; MAICYA; SATA 36,
  63; SATA-Brief 30

**Da Ponte, Lorenzo** 1749-1838.... **NCLC 50**

**Dario, Ruben** 1867-1916 .... **TCLC 4; HLC**
  See also CA 131; HW; MTCW

**Darley, George** 1795-1846 ........ **NCLC 2**
  See also DLB 96

**Daryush, Elizabeth** 1887-1977.... **CLC 6, 19**
  See also CA 49-52; CANR 3; DLB 20

**Dashwood, Edmee Elizabeth Monica de la
    Pasture** 1890-1943
  See Delafield, E. M.
  See also CA 119

**Daudet, (Louis Marie) Alphonse**
  1840-1897 ................. **NCLC 1**
  See also DLB 123

**Daumal, Rene** 1908-1944 ........ **TCLC 14**
  See also CA 114

**Davenport, Guy (Mattison, Jr.)**
  1927- ......... **CLC 6, 14, 38; SSC 16**
  See also CA 33-36R; CANR 23; DLB 130

**Davidson, Avram** 1923-
  See Queen, Ellery
  See also CA 101; CANR 26; DLB 8

**Davidson, Donald (Grady)**
  1893-1968 ............. **CLC 2, 13, 19**
  See also CA 5-8R; 25-28R; CANR 4;
  DLB 45

**Davidson, Hugh**
  See Hamilton, Edmond

**Davidson, John** 1857-1909 ....... **TCLC 24**
  See also CA 118; DLB 19

**Davidson, Sara** 1943- ............. **CLC 9**
  See also CA 81-84; CANR 44

**Davie, Donald (Alfred)**
  1922- ............... **CLC 5, 8, 10, 31**
  See also CA 1-4R; CAAS 3; CANR 1, 44;
  DLB 27; MTCW

**Davies, Ray(mond Douglas)** 1944- .. **CLC 21**
  See also CA 116; 146

**Davies, Rhys** 1903-1978 .......... **CLC 23**
  See also CA 9-12R; 81-84; CANR 4;
  DLB 139

**Davies, (William) Robertson**
  1913- ..... **CLC 2, 7, 13, 25, 42, 75; DA;
              DAB; WLC**
  See also BEST 89:2; CA 33-36R; CANR 17,
  42; DLB 68; MTCW

**Davies, W(illiam) H(enry)**
  1871-1940 ................... **TCLC 5**
  See also CA 104; DLB 19

**Davies, Walter C.**
  See Kornbluth, C(yril) M.

**Davis, Angela (Yvonne)** 1944- ...... **CLC 77**
  See also BW 2; CA 57-60; CANR 10

**Davis, B. Lynch**
  See Bioy Casares, Adolfo; Borges, Jorge
  Luis

**Davis, Gordon**
  See Hunt, E(verette) Howard, (Jr.)

**Davis, Harold Lenoir** 1896-1960.... **CLC 49**
  See also CA 89-92; DLB 9

**Davis, Rebecca (Blaine) Harding**
  1831-1910 ................. **TCLC 6**
  See also CA 104; DLB 74

**Davis, Richard Harding**
  1864-1916 ................. **TCLC 24**
  See also CA 114; DLB 12, 23, 78, 79

**Davison, Frank Dalby** 1893-1970 ... **CLC 15**
  See also CA 116

**Davison, Lawrence H.**
  See Lawrence, D(avid) H(erbert Richards)

**Davison, Peter (Hubert)** 1928- ..... **CLC 28**
  See also CA 9-12R; CAAS 4; CANR 3, 43;
  DLB 5

**Davys, Mary** 1674-1732 ............ **LC 1**
  See also DLB 39

**Dawson, Fielding** 1930- ........... **CLC 6**
  See also CA 85-88; DLB 130

**Dawson, Peter**
  See Faust, Frederick (Schiller)

**Day, Clarence (Shepard, Jr.)**
  1874-1935 ................. **TCLC 25**
  See also CA 108; DLB 11

**Day, Thomas** 1748-1789 ............ **LC 1**
  See also DLB 39; YABC 1

**Day Lewis, C(ecil)**
  1904-1972 ....... **CLC 1, 6, 10; PC 11**
  See also Blake, Nicholas
  See also CA 13-16; 33-36R; CANR 34;
  CAP 1; DLB 15, 20; MTCW

**Dazai, Osamu** ................... **TCLC 11**
  See also Tsushima, Shuji

**de Andrade, Carlos Drummond**
  See Drummond de Andrade, Carlos

**Deane, Norman**
  See Creasey, John

**de Beauvoir, Simone (Lucie Ernestine Marie
    Bertrand)**
  See Beauvoir, Simone (Lucie Ernestine
  Marie Bertrand) de

**de Brissac, Malcolm**
  See Dickinson, Peter (Malcolm)

**de Chardin, Pierre Teilhard**
  See Teilhard de Chardin, (Marie Joseph)
  Pierre

**Dee, John** 1527-1608 .............. **LC 20**

**Deer, Sandra** 1940- ............... **CLC 45**

**De Ferrari, Gabriella** 1941- ........ **CLC 65**
  See also CA 146

**Defoe, Daniel**
  1660(?)-1731 .... **LC 1; DA; DAB; WLC**
  See also CDBLB 1660-1789; DLB 39, 95,
  101; JRDA; MAICYA; SATA 22

**de Gourmont, Remy**
  See Gourmont, Remy de

**de Hartog, Jan** 1914- ............. **CLC 19**
  See also CA 1-4R; CANR 1

**de Hostos, E. M.**
  See Hostos (y Bonilla), Eugenio Maria de

**de Hostos, Eugenio M.**
  See Hostos (y Bonilla), Eugenio Maria de

**Deighton, Len** ............. **CLC 4, 7, 22, 46**
  See also Deighton, Leonard Cyril
  See also AAYA 6; BEST 89:2;
  CDBLB 1960 to Present; DLB 87

**Deighton, Leonard Cyril** 1929-
  See Deighton, Len
  See also CA 9-12R; CANR 19, 33; MTCW

**Dekker, Thomas** 1572(?)-1632....... **LC 22**
  See also CDBLB Before 1660; DLB 62

**Delafield, E. M.** 1890-1943 ....... **TCLC 61**
  See also Dashwood, Edmee Elizabeth
  Monica de la Pasture
  See also DLB 34

**de la Mare, Walter (John)**
  1873-1956 ......... **TCLC 4, 53; DAB;
                     SSC 14; WLC**
  See also CDBLB 1914-1945; CLR 23;
  DLB 19, 153; SATA 16

**Delaney, Franey**
  See O'Hara, John (Henry)

**Delaney, Shelagh** 1939- ........... **CLC 29**
  See also CA 17-20R; CANR 30;
  CDBLB 1960 to Present; DLB 13;
  MTCW

**Delany, Mary (Granville Pendarves)**
  1700-1788 ................... **LC 12**

**Delany, Samuel R(ay, Jr.)**
  1942- ............. **CLC 8, 14, 38; BLC**
  See also BW 2; CA 81-84; CANR 27, 43;
  DLB 8, 33; MTCW

**De La Ramee, (Marie) Louise** 1839-1908
  See Ouida
  See also SATA 20

**de la Roche, Mazo** 1879-1961 ...... **CLC 14**
  See also CA 85-88; CANR 30; DLB 68;
  SATA 64

**Delbanco, Nicholas (Franklin)**
  1942- .................... **CLC 6, 13**
  See also CA 17-20R; CAAS 2; CANR 29;
  DLB 6

**del Castillo, Michel** 1933- ......... **CLC 38**
  See also CA 109

**Deledda, Grazia (Cosima)**
  1875(?)-1936 ............... **TCLC 23**
  See also CA 123

**Delibes, Miguel** ................. **CLC 8, 18**
  See also Delibes Setien, Miguel

**Delibes Setien, Miguel** 1920-
  See Delibes, Miguel
  See also CA 45-48; CANR 1, 32; HW;
  MTCW

**DeLillo, Don**
  1936- ..... **CLC 8, 10, 13, 27, 39, 54, 76**
  See also BEST 89:1; CA 81-84; CANR 21;
  DLB 6; MTCW

**de Lisser, H. G.**
  See De Lisser, Herbert George
  See also DLB 117

**De Lisser, Herbert George**
  1878-1944 ................. **TCLC 12**
  See also de Lisser, H. G.
  See also BW 2; CA 109

**Doerr, Harriet** 1910- . . . . . . . . . . . . **CLC 34**
See also CA 117; 122; CANR 47

**Domecq, H(onorio) Bustos**
See Bioy Casares, Adolfo; Borges, Jorge
Luis

**Domini, Rey**
See Lorde, Audre (Geraldine)

**Dominique**
See Proust, (Valentin-Louis-George-Eugene-)
Marcel

**Don, A**
See Stephen, Leslie

**Donaldson, Stephen R.** 1947- . . . . . . . **CLC 46**
See also CA 89-92; CANR 13

**Donleavy, J(ames) P(atrick)**
1926- . . . . . . . . . . . . **CLC 1, 4, 6, 10, 45**
See also AITN 2; CA 9-12R; CANR 24, 49;
DLB 6; MTCW

**Donne, John**
1572-1631 . . **LC 10, 24; DA; DAB; PC 1**
See also CDBLB Before 1660; DLB 121,
151

**Donnell, David** 1939(?)- . . . . . . . . . . **CLC 34**

**Donoghue, P. S.**
See Hunt, E(verette) Howard, (Jr.)

**Donoso (Yanez), Jose**
1924- . . . . . . . . . **CLC 4, 8, 11, 32; HLC**
See also CA 81-84; CANR 32; DLB 113;
HW; MTCW

**Donovan, John** 1928-1992 . . . . . . . . **CLC 35**
See also CA 97-100; 137; CLR 3;
MAICYA; SATA 72; SATA-Brief 29

**Don Roberto**
See Cunninghame Graham, R(obert)
B(ontine)

**Doolittle, Hilda**
1886-1961 . . . . . **CLC 3, 8, 14, 31, 34, 73;
DA; PC 5; WLC**
See also H. D.
See also CA 97-100; CANR 35; DLB 4, 45;
MTCW

**Dorfman, Ariel** 1942- . . . . **CLC 48, 77; HLC**
See also CA 124; 130; HW

**Dorn, Edward (Merton)** 1929- . . . **CLC 10, 18**
See also CA 93-96; CANR 42; DLB 5

**Dorsan, Luc**
See Simenon, Georges (Jacques Christian)

**Dorsange, Jean**
See Simenon, Georges (Jacques Christian)

**Dos Passos, John (Roderigo)**
1896-1970 . . . . . **CLC 1, 4, 8, 11, 15, 25,
34, 82; DA; DAB; WLC**
See also CA 1-4R; 29-32R; CANR 3;
CDALB 1929-1941; DLB 4, 9; DLBD 1;
MTCW

**Dossage, Jean**
See Simenon, Georges (Jacques Christian)

**Dostoevsky, Fedor Mikhailovich**
1821-1881 . . . . . . **NCLC 2, 7, 21, 33, 43;
DA; DAB; SSC 2; WLC**

**Doughty, Charles M(ontagu)**
1843-1926 . . . . . . . . . . . . . . . . . **TCLC 27**
See also CA 115; DLB 19, 57

**Douglas, Ellen** . . . . . . . . . . . . . . . . . . **CLC 73**
See also Haxton, Josephine Ayres;
Williamson, Ellen Douglas

**Douglas, Gavin** 1475(?)-1522 . . . . . . . . **LC 20**

**Douglas, Keith** 1920-1944 . . . . . . . . **TCLC 40**
See also DLB 27

**Douglas, Leonard**
See Bradbury, Ray (Douglas)

**Douglas, Michael**
See Crichton, (John) Michael

**Douglass, Frederick**
1817(?)-1895 . . . . . . . **NCLC 7; BLC; DA;
WLC**
See also CDALB 1640-1865; DLB 1, 43, 50,
79; SATA 29

**Dourado, (Waldomiro Freitas) Autran**
1926- . . . . . . . . . . . . . . . . . . . **CLC 23, 60**
See also CA 25-28R; CANR 34

**Dourado, Waldomiro Autran**
See Dourado, (Waldomiro Freitas) Autran

**Dove, Rita (Frances)**
1952- . . . . . . . . . . . . . **CLC 50, 81; PC 6**
See also BW 2; CA 109; CAAS 19;
CANR 27, 42; DLB 120

**Dowell, Coleman** 1925-1985 . . . . . . . **CLC 60**
See also CA 25-28R; 117; CANR 10;
DLB 130

**Dowson, Ernest Christopher**
1867-1900 . . . . . . . . . . . . . . . . . **TCLC 4**
See also CA 105; DLB 19, 135

**Doyle, A. Conan**
See Doyle, Arthur Conan

**Doyle, Arthur Conan**
1859-1930 . . . . . . . . **TCLC 7; DA; DAB;
SSC 12; WLC**
See also AAYA 14; CA 104; 122;
CDBLB 1890-1914; DLB 18, 70, 156;
MTCW; SATA 24

**Doyle, Conan**
See Doyle, Arthur Conan

**Doyle, John**
See Graves, Robert (von Ranke)

**Doyle, Roddy** 1958(?)- . . . . . . . . . . . **CLC 81**
See also AAYA 14; CA 143

**Doyle, Sir A. Conan**
See Doyle, Arthur Conan

**Doyle, Sir Arthur Conan**
See Doyle, Arthur Conan

**Dr. A**
See Asimov, Isaac; Silverstein, Alvin

**Drabble, Margaret**
1939- . . . **CLC 2, 3, 5, 8, 10, 22, 53; DAB**
See also CA 13-16R; CANR 18, 35;
CDBLB 1960 to Present; DLB 14, 155;
MTCW; SATA 48

**Drapier, M. B.**
See Swift, Jonathan

**Drayham, James**
See Mencken, H(enry) L(ouis)

**Drayton, Michael** 1563-1631 . . . . . . . . **LC 8**

**Dreadstone, Carl**
See Campbell, (John) Ramsey

**Dreiser, Theodore (Herman Albert)**
1871-1945 . . . . . . **TCLC 10, 18, 35; DA;
WLC**
See also CA 106; 132; CDALB 1865-1917;
DLB 9, 12, 102, 137; DLBD 1; MTCW

**Drexler, Rosalyn** 1926- . . . . . . . . . . **CLC 2, 6**
See also CA 81-84

**Dreyer, Carl Theodor** 1889-1968 . . . . **CLC 16**
See also CA 116

**Drieu la Rochelle, Pierre(-Eugene)**
1893-1945 . . . . . . . . . . . . . . . . **TCLC 21**
See also CA 117; DLB 72

**Drinkwater, John** 1882-1937 . . . . . . **TCLC 57**
See also CA 109; DLB 10, 19, 149

**Drop Shot**
See Cable, George Washington

**Droste-Hulshoff, Annette Freiin von**
1797-1848 . . . . . . . . . . . . . . . . . **NCLC 3**
See also DLB 133

**Drummond, Walter**
See Silverberg, Robert

**Drummond, William Henry**
1854-1907 . . . . . . . . . . . . . . . . **TCLC 25**
See also DLB 92

**Drummond de Andrade, Carlos**
1902-1987 . . . . . . . . . . . . . . . . . **CLC 18**
See also Andrade, Carlos Drummond de
See also CA 132; 123

**Drury, Allen (Stuart)** 1918- . . . . . . . **CLC 37**
See also CA 57-60; CANR 18

**Dryden, John**
1631-1700 . . . . . . . . **LC 3, 21; DA; DAB;
DC 3; WLC**
See also CDBLB 1660-1789; DLB 80, 101,
131

**Duberman, Martin** 1930- . . . . . . . . . . **CLC 8**
See also CA 1-4R; CANR 2

**Dubie, Norman (Evans)** 1945- . . . . . . **CLC 36**
See also CA 69-72; CANR 12; DLB 120

**Du Bois, W(illiam) E(dward) B(urghardt)**
1868-1963 . . . . . . **CLC 1, 2, 13, 64; BLC;
DA; WLC**
See also BW 1; CA 85-88; CANR 34;
CDALB 1865-1917; DLB 47, 50, 91;
MTCW; SATA 42

**Dubus, Andre** 1936- . . . **CLC 13, 36; SSC 15**
See also CA 21-24R; CANR 17; DLB 130

**Duca Minimo**
See D'Annunzio, Gabriele

**Ducharme, Rejean** 1941- . . . . . . . . . . **CLC 74**
See also DLB 60

**Duclos, Charles Pinot** 1704-1772 . . . . . **LC 1**

**Dudek, Louis** 1918- . . . . . . . . . . **CLC 11, 19**
See also CA 45-48; CAAS 14; CANR 1;
DLB 88

**Duerrenmatt, Friedrich**
1921-1990 . . . . . . **CLC 1, 4, 8, 11, 15, 43**
See also CA 17-20R; CANR 33; DLB 69,
124; MTCW

**Duffy, Bruce** (?)- . . . . . . . . . . . . . . . . **CLC 50**

**Duffy, Maureen** 1933- . . . . . . . . . . . . **CLC 37**
See also CA 25-28R; CANR 33; DLB 14;
MTCW

**Dugan, Alan** 1923- . . . . . . . . . . . . . **CLC 2, 6**
See also CA 81-84; DLB 5

Eiseley, Loren Corey 1907-1977 ..... **CLC 7**
See also AAYA 5; CA 1-4R; 73-76;
CANR 6

Eisenstadt, Jill 1963- ............. **CLC 50**
See also CA 140

Eisenstein, Sergei (Mikhailovich)
1898-1948 ................ **TCLC 57**
See also CA 114

Eisner, Simon
See Kornbluth, C(yril) M.

Ekeloef, (Bengt) Gunnar
1907-1968 ................. **CLC 27**
See also CA 123; 25-28R

Ekelof, (Bengt) Gunnar
See Ekeloef, (Bengt) Gunnar

Ekwensi, C. O. D.
See Ekwensi, Cyprian (Odiatu Duaka)

Ekwensi, Cyprian (Odiatu Duaka)
1921- .................. **CLC 4; BLC**
See also BW 2; CA 29-32R; CANR 18, 42;
DLB 117; MTCW; SATA 66

Elaine ........................ **TCLC 18**
See also Leverson, Ada

El Crummo
See Crumb, R(obert)

Elia
See Lamb, Charles

Eliade, Mircea 1907-1986 ......... **CLC 19**
See also CA 65-68; 119; CANR 30; MTCW

Eliot, A. D.
See Jewett, (Theodora) Sarah Orne

Eliot, Alice
See Jewett, (Theodora) Sarah Orne

Eliot, Dan
See Silverberg, Robert

Eliot, George
1819-1880 ..... **NCLC 4, 13, 23, 41, 49;
DA; DAB; WLC**
See also CDBLB 1832-1890; DLB 21, 35, 55

Eliot, John 1604-1690 ............. **LC 5**
See also DLB 24

Eliot, T(homas) S(tearns)
1888-1965 ..... **CLC 1, 2, 3, 6, 9, 10, 13,
15, 24, 34, 41, 55, 57; DA; DAB; PC 5;
WLC 2**
See also CA 5-8R; 25-28R; CANR 41;
CDALB 1929-1941; DLB 7, 10, 45, 63;
DLBY 88; MTCW

Elizabeth 1866-1941 ............ **TCLC 41**

Elkin, Stanley L(awrence)
1930-1995 ...... **CLC 4, 6, 9, 14, 27, 51;
SSC 12**
See also CA 9-12R; 148; CANR 8, 46;
DLB 2, 28; DLBY 80; MTCW

Elledge, Scott. .................. **CLC 34**

Elliott, Don
See Silverberg, Robert

Elliott, George P(aul) 1918-1980 ..... **CLC 2**
See also CA 1-4R; 97-100; CANR 2

Elliott, Janice 1931- .............. **CLC 47**
See also CA 13-16R; CANR 8, 29; DLB 14

Elliott, Sumner Locke 1917-1991 ... **CLC 38**
See also CA 5-8R; 134; CANR 2, 21

Elliott, William
See Bradbury, Ray (Douglas)

Ellis, A. E. ...................... **CLC 7**

Ellis, Alice Thomas ............... **CLC 40**
See also Haycraft, Anna

Ellis, Bret Easton 1964- ........ **CLC 39, 71**
See also AAYA 2; CA 118; 123

Ellis, (Henry) Havelock
1859-1939 ................ **TCLC 14**
See also CA 109

Ellis, Landon
See Ellison, Harlan (Jay)

Ellis, Trey 1962- ................ **CLC 55**
See also CA 146

Ellison, Harlan (Jay)
1934- ......... **CLC 1, 13, 42; SSC 14**
See also CA 5-8R; CANR 5, 46; DLB 8;
MTCW

Ellison, Ralph (Waldo)
1914-1994 ....... **CLC 1, 3, 11, 54, 86;
BLC; DA; DAB; WLC**
See also BW 1; CA 9-12R; 145; CANR 24;
CDALB 1941-1968; DLB 2, 76;
DLBY 94; MTCW

Ellmann, Lucy (Elizabeth) 1956- .... **CLC 61**
See also CA 128

Ellmann, Richard (David)
1918-1987 ................. **CLC 50**
See also BEST 89:2; CA 1-4R; 122;
CANR 2, 28; DLB 103; DLBY 87;
MTCW

Elman, Richard 1934- ............. **CLC 19**
See also CA 17-20R; CAAS 3; CANR 47

Elron
See Hubbard, L(afayette) Ron(ald)

Eluard, Paul. ................. **TCLC 7, 41**
See also Grindel, Eugene

Elyot, Sir Thomas 1490(?)-1546 ..... **LC 11**

Elytis, Odysseus 1911- ........ **CLC 15, 49**
See also CA 102; MTCW

Emecheta, (Florence Onye) Buchi
1944- ............... **CLC 14, 48; BLC**
See also BW 2; CA 81-84; CANR 27;
DLB 117; MTCW; SATA 66

Emerson, Ralph Waldo
1803-1882 ..... **NCLC 1, 38; DA; DAB;
WLC**
See also CDALB 1640-1865; DLB 1, 59, 73

Eminescu, Mihail 1850-1889 ..... **NCLC 33**

Empson, William
1906-1984 ....... **CLC 3, 8, 19, 33, 34**
See also CA 17-20R; 112; CANR 31;
DLB 20; MTCW

Enchi Fumiko (Ueda) 1905-1986 .... **CLC 31**
See also CA 129; 121

Ende, Michael (Andreas Helmuth)
1929- ..................... **CLC 31**
See also CA 118; 124; CANR 36; CLR 14;
DLB 75; MAICYA; SATA 61;
SATA-Brief 42

Endo, Shusaku 1923- ..... **CLC 7, 14, 19, 54**
See also CA 29-32R; CANR 21; MTCW

Engel, Marian 1933-1985 ......... **CLC 36**
See also CA 25-28R; CANR 12; DLB 53

Engelhardt, Frederick
See Hubbard, L(afayette) Ron(ald)

Enright, D(ennis) J(oseph)
1920- ................ **CLC 4, 8, 31**
See also CA 1-4R; CANR 1, 42; DLB 27;
SATA 25

Enzensberger, Hans Magnus
1929- ..................... **CLC 43**
See also CA 116; 119

Ephron, Nora 1941- ......... **CLC 17, 31**
See also AITN 2; CA 65-68; CANR 12, 39

Epsilon
See Betjeman, John

Epstein, Daniel Mark 1948- ........ **CLC 7**
See also CA 49-52; CANR 2

Epstein, Jacob 1956- ............. **CLC 19**
See also CA 114

Epstein, Joseph 1937- ............. **CLC 39**
See also CA 112; 119

Epstein, Leslie 1938- ............. **CLC 27**
See also CA 73-76; CAAS 12; CANR 23

Equiano, Olaudah
1745(?)-1797 ............. **LC 16; BLC**
See also DLB 37, 50

Erasmus, Desiderius 1469(?)-1536.... **LC 16**

Erdman, Paul E(mil) 1932- ........ **CLC 25**
See also AITN 1; CA 61-64; CANR 13, 43

Erdrich, Louise 1954- .......... **CLC 39, 54**
See also AAYA 10; BEST 89:1; CA 114;
CANR 41; DLB 152; MTCW; NNAL

Erenburg, Ilya (Grigoryevich)
See Ehrenburg, Ilya (Grigoryevich)

Erickson, Stephen Michael 1950-
See Erickson, Steve
See also CA 129

Erickson, Steve ................... **CLC 64**
See also Erickson, Stephen Michael

Ericson, Walter
See Fast, Howard (Melvin)

Eriksson, Buntel
See Bergman, (Ernst) Ingmar

Ernaux, Annie 1940- ............. **CLC 88**
See also CA 147

Eschenbach, Wolfram von
See Wolfram von Eschenbach

Eseki, Bruno
See Mphahlele, Ezekiel

Esenin, Sergei (Alexandrovich)
1895-1925 ................. **TCLC 4**
See also CA 104

Eshleman, Clayton 1935- ........... **CLC 7**
See also CA 33-36R; CAAS 6; DLB 5

Espriella, Don Manuel Alvarez
See Southey, Robert

Espriu, Salvador 1913-1985 ........ **CLC 9**
See also CA 115; DLB 134

Espronceda, Jose de 1808-1842... **NCLC 39**

Esse, James
See Stephens, James

Esterbrook, Tom
See Hubbard, L(afayette) Ron(ald)

Estleman, Loren D. 1952- ........ **CLC 48**
See also CA 85-88; CANR 27; MTCW

**Eugenides, Jeffrey** 1960(?)- ........ **CLC 81**
See also CA 144

**Euripides** c. 485B.C.-406B.C. ........ **DC 4**
See also DA; DAB

**Evan, Evin**
See Faust, Frederick (Schiller)

**Evans, Evan**
See Faust, Frederick (Schiller)

**Evans, Marian**
See Eliot, George

**Evans, Mary Ann**
See Eliot, George

**Evarts, Esther**
See Benson, Sally

**Everett, Percival L.** 1956- ........ **CLC 57**
See also BW 2; CA 129

**Everson, R(onald) G(ilmour)**
1903- ...................... **CLC 27**
See also CA 17-20R; DLB 88

**Everson, William (Oliver)**
1912-1994 .............. **CLC 1, 5, 14**
See also CA 9-12R; 145; CANR 20; DLB 5,
16; MTCW

**Evtushenko, Evgenii Aleksandrovich**
See Yevtushenko, Yevgeny (Alexandrovich)

**Ewart, Gavin (Buchanan)**
1916- ................... **CLC 13, 46**
See also CA 89-92; CANR 17, 46; DLB 40;
MTCW

**Ewers, Hanns Heinz** 1871-1943 ... **TCLC 12**
See also CA 109

**Ewing, Frederick R.**
See Sturgeon, Theodore (Hamilton)

**Exley, Frederick (Earl)**
1929-1992 ................ **CLC 6, 11**
See also AITN 2; CA 81-84; 138; DLB 143;
DLBY 81

**Eynhardt, Guillermo**
See Quiroga, Horacio (Sylvestre)

**Ezekiel, Nissim** 1924- ............. **CLC 61**
See also CA 61-64

**Ezekiel, Tish O'Dowd** 1943- ....... **CLC 34**
See also CA 129

**Fadeyev, A.**
See Bulgya, Alexander Alexandrovich

**Fadeyev, Alexander** .............. **TCLC 53**
See also Bulgya, Alexander Alexandrovich

**Fagen, Donald** 1948- ............. **CLC 26**

**Fainzilberg, Ilya Arnoldovich** 1897-1937
See Ilf, Ilya
See also CA 120

**Fair, Ronald L.** 1932- ............. **CLC 18**
See also BW 1; CA 69-72; CANR 25;
DLB 33

**Fairbairns, Zoe (Ann)** 1948- ....... **CLC 32**
See also CA 103; CANR 21

**Falco, Gian**
See Papini, Giovanni

**Falconer, James**
See Kirkup, James

**Falconer, Kenneth**
See Kornbluth, C(yril) M.

**Falkland, Samuel**
See Heijermans, Herman

**Fallaci, Oriana** 1930- ............. **CLC 11**
See also CA 77-80; CANR 15; MTCW

**Faludy, George** 1913- ............. **CLC 42**
See also CA 21-24R

**Faludy, Gyoergy**
See Faludy, George

**Fanon, Frantz** 1925-1961 ..... **CLC 74; BLC**
See also BW 1; CA 116; 89-92

**Fanshawe, Ann** 1625-1680 .......... **LC 11**

**Fante, John (Thomas)** 1911-1983 ... **CLC 60**
See also CA 69-72; 109; CANR 23;
DLB 130; DLBY 83

**Farah, Nuruddin** 1945- ....... **CLC 53; BLC**
See also BW 2; CA 106; DLB 125

**Fargue, Leon-Paul** 1876(?)-1947 ... **TCLC 11**
See also CA 109

**Farigoule, Louis**
See Romains, Jules

**Farina, Richard** 1936(?)-1966 ....... **CLC 9**
See also CA 81-84; 25-28R

**Farley, Walter (Lorimer)**
1915-1989 ................... **CLC 17**
See also CA 17-20R; CANR 8, 29; DLB 22;
JRDA; MAICYA; SATA 2, 43

**Farmer, Philip Jose** 1918- ....... **CLC 1, 19**
See also CA 1-4R; CANR 4, 35; DLB 8;
MTCW

**Farquhar, George** 1677-1707 ........ **LC 21**
See also DLB 84

**Farrell, J(ames) G(ordon)**
1935-1979 ................... **CLC 6**
See also CA 73-76; 89-92; CANR 36;
DLB 14; MTCW

**Farrell, James T(homas)**
1904-1979 ........ **CLC 1, 4, 8, 11, 66**
See also CA 5-8R; 89-92; CANR 9; DLB 4,
9, 86; DLBD 2; MTCW

**Farren, Richard J.**
See Betjeman, John

**Farren, Richard M.**
See Betjeman, John

**Fassbinder, Rainer Werner**
1946-1982 ................... **CLC 20**
See also CA 93-96; 106; CANR 31

**Fast, Howard (Melvin)** 1914- ...... **CLC 23**
See also CA 1-4R; CAAS 18; CANR 1, 33;
DLB 9; SATA 7

**Faulcon, Robert**
See Holdstock, Robert P.

**Faulkner, William (Cuthbert)**
1897-1962 ..... **CLC 1, 3, 6, 8, 9, 11, 14,
18, 28, 52, 68; DA; DAB; SSC 1; WLC**
See also AAYA 7; CA 81-84; CANR 33;
CDALB 1929-1941; DLB 9, 11, 44, 102;
DLBD 2; DLBY 86; MTCW

**Fauset, Jessie Redmon**
1884(?)-1961 ........ **CLC 19, 54; BLC**
See also BW 1; CA 109; DLB 51

**Faust, Frederick (Schiller)**
1892-1944(?) ............... **TCLC 49**
See also CA 108

**Faust, Irvin** 1924- ................ **CLC 8**
See also CA 33-36R; CANR 28; DLB 2, 28;
DLBY 80

**Fawkes, Guy**
See Benchley, Robert (Charles)

**Fearing, Kenneth (Flexner)**
1902-1961 ................... **CLC 51**
See also CA 93-96; DLB 9

**Fecamps, Elise**
See Creasey, John

**Federman, Raymond** 1928- ...... **CLC 6, 47**
See also CA 17-20R; CAAS 8; CANR 10,
43; DLBY 80

**Federspiel, J(uerg) F.** 1931- ........ **CLC 42**
See also CA 146

**Feiffer, Jules (Ralph)** 1929- .... **CLC 2, 8, 64**
See also AAYA 3; CA 17-20R; CANR 30;
DLB 7, 44; MTCW; SATA 8, 61

**Feige, Hermann Albert Otto Maximilian**
See Traven, B.

**Feinberg, David B.** 1956-1994 ...... **CLC 59**
See also CA 135; 147

**Feinstein, Elaine** 1930- ............. **CLC 36**
See also CA 69-72; CAAS 1; CANR 31;
DLB 14, 40; MTCW

**Feldman, Irving (Mordecai)** 1928- .... **CLC 7**
See also CA 1-4R; CANR 1

**Fellini, Federico** 1920-1993 ..... **CLC 16, 85**
See also CA 65-68; 143; CANR 33

**Felsen, Henry Gregor** 1916- ....... **CLC 17**
See also CA 1-4R; CANR 1; SAAS 2;
SATA 1

**Fenton, James Martin** 1949- ....... **CLC 32**
See also CA 102; DLB 40

**Ferber, Edna** 1887-1968 .......... **CLC 18**
See also AITN 1; CA 5-8R; 25-28R; DLB 9,
28, 86; MTCW; SATA 7

**Ferguson, Helen**
See Kavan, Anna

**Ferguson, Samuel** 1810-1886 ..... **NCLC 33**
See also DLB 32

**Fergusson, Robert** 1750-1774 ....... **LC 29**
See also DLB 109

**Ferling, Lawrence**
See Ferlinghetti, Lawrence (Monsanto)

**Ferlinghetti, Lawrence (Monsanto)**
1919(?)- ........ **CLC 2, 6, 10, 27; PC 1**
See also CA 5-8R; CANR 3, 41;
CDALB 1941-1968; DLB 5, 16; MTCW

**Fernandez, Vicente Garcia Huidobro**
See Huidobro Fernandez, Vicente Garcia

**Ferrer, Gabriel (Francisco Victor) Miro**
See Miro (Ferrer), Gabriel (Francisco
Victor)

**Ferrier, Susan (Edmonstone)**
1782-1854 ................... **NCLC 8**
See also DLB 116

**Ferrigno, Robert** 1948(?)- .......... **CLC 65**
See also CA 140

**Feuchtwanger, Lion** 1884-1958 ..... **TCLC 3**
See also CA 104; DLB 66

**Feuillet, Octave** 1821-1890 ...... **NCLC 45**

**Feydeau, Georges (Leon Jules Marie)**
1862-1921 ................. TCLC **22**
See also CA 113

**Ficino, Marsilio** 1433-1499 ........ LC **12**

**Fiedeler, Hans**
See Doeblin, Alfred

**Fiedler, Leslie A(aron)**
1917- ................. CLC **4, 13, 24**
See also CA 9-12R; CANR 7; DLB 28, 67;
MTCW

**Field, Andrew** 1938- .............. CLC **44**
See also CA 97-100; CANR 25

**Field, Eugene** 1850-1895 ......... NCLC **3**
See also DLB 23, 42, 140; MAICYA;
SATA 16

**Field, Gans T.**
See Wellman, Manly Wade

**Field, Michael** .................. TCLC **43**

**Field, Peter**
See Hobson, Laura Z(ametkin)

**Fielding, Henry**
1707-1754 ...... LC **1**; DA; DAB; WLC
See also CDBLB 1660-1789; DLB 39, 84,
101

**Fielding, Sarah** 1710-1768 .......... LC **1**
See also DLB 39

**Fierstein, Harvey (Forbes)** 1954- ... CLC **33**
See also CA 123; 129

**Figes, Eva** 1932- ................. CLC **31**
See also CA 53-56; CANR 4, 44; DLB 14

**Finch, Robert (Duer Claydon)**
1900- ..................... CLC **18**
See also CA 57-60; CANR 9, 24, 49;
DLB 88

**Findley, Timothy** 1930- .......... CLC **27**
See also CA 25-28R; CANR 12, 42;
DLB 53

**Fink, William**
See Mencken, H(enry) L(ouis)

**Firbank, Louis** 1942-
See Reed, Lou
See also CA 117

**Firbank, (Arthur Annesley) Ronald**
1886-1926 .................. TCLC **1**
See also CA 104; DLB 36

**Fisher, M(ary) F(rances) K(ennedy)**
1908-1992 ............... CLC **76, 87**
See also CA 77-80; 138; CANR 44

**Fisher, Roy** 1930- ................ CLC **25**
See also CA 81-84; CAAS 10; CANR 16;
DLB 40

**Fisher, Rudolph**
1897-1934 ............. TCLC **11**; BLC
See also BW 1; CA 107; 124; DLB 51, 102

**Fisher, Vardis (Alvero)** 1895-1968 .... CLC **7**
See also CA 5-8R; 25-28R; DLB 9

**Fiske, Tarleton**
See Bloch, Robert (Albert)

**Fitch, Clarke**
See Sinclair, Upton (Beall)

**Fitch, John IV**
See Cormier, Robert (Edmund)

**Fitzgerald, Captain Hugh**
See Baum, L(yman) Frank

**FitzGerald, Edward** 1809-1883 .... NCLC **9**
See also DLB 32

**Fitzgerald, F(rancis) Scott (Key)**
1896-1940 ...... TCLC **1, 6, 14, 28, 55**;
DA; DAB; SSC **6**; WLC
See also AITN 1; CA 110; 123;
CDALB 1917-1929; DLB 4, 9, 86;
DLBD 1; DLBY 81; MTCW

**Fitzgerald, Penelope** 1916- ... CLC **19, 51, 61**
See also CA 85-88; CAAS 10; DLB 14

**Fitzgerald, Robert (Stuart)**
1910-1985 ................... CLC **39**
See also CA 1-4R; 114; CANR 1; DLBY 80

**FitzGerald, Robert D(avid)**
1902-1987 ................... CLC **19**
See also CA 17-20R

**Fitzgerald, Zelda (Sayre)**
1900-1948 ................... TCLC **52**
See also CA 117; 126; DLBY 84

**Flanagan, Thomas (James Bonner)**
1923- ..................... CLC **25, 52**
See also CA 108; DLBY 80; MTCW

**Flaubert, Gustave**
1821-1880 ........ NCLC **2, 10, 19**; DA;
DAB; SSC **11**; WLC
See also DLB 119

**Flecker, (Herman) James Elroy**
1884-1915 .................. TCLC **43**
See also CA 109; DLB 10, 19

**Fleming, Ian (Lancaster)**
1908-1964 ................. CLC **3, 30**
See also CA 5-8R; CDBLB 1945-1960;
DLB 87; MTCW; SATA 9

**Fleming, Thomas (James)** 1927- .... CLC **37**
See also CA 5-8R; CANR 10; SATA 8

**Fletcher, John Gould** 1886-1950 ... TCLC **35**
See also CA 107; DLB 4, 45

**Fleur, Paul**
See Pohl, Frederik

**Flooglebuckle, Al**
See Spiegelman, Art

**Flying Officer X**
See Bates, H(erbert) E(rnest)

**Fo, Dario** 1926- .................. CLC **32**
See also CA 116; 128; MTCW

**Fogarty, Jonathan Titulescu Esq.**
See Farrell, James T(homas)

**Folke, Will**
See Bloch, Robert (Albert)

**Follett, Ken(neth Martin)** 1949- .... CLC **18**
See also AAYA 6; BEST 89:4; CA 81-84;
CANR 13, 33; DLB 87; DLBY 81;
MTCW

**Fontane, Theodor** 1819-1898 ..... NCLC **26**
See also DLB 129

**Foote, Horton** 1916- .............. CLC **51**
See also CA 73-76; CANR 34; DLB 26

**Foote, Shelby** 1916- .............. CLC **75**
See also CA 5-8R; CANR 3, 45; DLB 2, 17

**Forbes, Esther** 1891-1967 ......... CLC **12**
See also CA 13-14; 25-28R; CAP 1;
CLR 27; DLB 22; JRDA; MAICYA;
SATA 2

**Forche, Carolyn (Louise)**
1950- ......... CLC **25, 83, 86**; PC **10**
See also CA 109; 117; DLB 5

**Ford, Elbur**
See Hibbert, Eleanor Alice Burford

**Ford, Ford Madox**
1873-1939 ......... TCLC **1, 15, 39, 57**
See also CA 104; 132; CDBLB 1914-1945;
DLB 34, 98; MTCW

**Ford, John** 1895-1973 ............. CLC **16**
See also CA 45-48

**Ford, Richard** 1944- .............. CLC **46**
See also CA 69-72; CANR 11, 47

**Ford, Webster**
See Masters, Edgar Lee

**Foreman, Richard** 1937- .......... CLC **50**
See also CA 65-68; CANR 32

**Forester, C(ecil) S(cott)**
1899-1966 .................. CLC **35**
See also CA 73-76; 25-28R; SATA 13

**Forez**
See Mauriac, Francois (Charles)

**Forman, James Douglas** 1932- ...... CLC **21**
See also CA 9-12R; CANR 4, 19, 42;
JRDA; MAICYA; SATA 8, 70

**Fornes, Maria Irene** 1930- ...... CLC **39, 61**
See also CA 25-28R; CANR 28; DLB 7;
HW; MTCW

**Forrest, Leon** 1937- ............... CLC **4**
See also BW 2; CA 89-92; CAAS 7;
CANR 25; DLB 33

**Forster, E(dward) M(organ)**
1879-1970 ..... CLC **1, 2, 3, 4, 9, 10, 13,
15, 22, 45, 77**; DA; DAB; WLC
See also AAYA 2; CA 13-14; 25-28R;
CANR 45; CAP 1; CDBLB 1914-1945;
DLB 34, 98; DLBD 10; MTCW;
SATA 57

**Forster, John** 1812-1876 ........ NCLC **11**
See also DLB 144

**Forsyth, Frederick** 1938- ...... CLC **2, 5, 36**
See also BEST 89:4; CA 85-88; CANR 38;
DLB 87; MTCW

**Forten, Charlotte L.** ........ TCLC **16**; BLC
See also Grimke, Charlotte L(ottie) Forten
See also DLB 50

**Foscolo, Ugo** 1778-1827 .......... NCLC **8**

**Fosse, Bob** ..................... CLC **20**
See also Fosse, Robert Louis

**Fosse, Robert Louis** 1927-1987
See Fosse, Bob
See also CA 110; 123

**Foster, Stephen Collins**
1826-1864 ................. NCLC **26**

**Foucault, Michel**
1926-1984 ............. CLC **31, 34, 69**
See also CA 105; 113; CANR 34; MTCW

**Fouque, Friedrich (Heinrich Karl) de la Motte**
1777-1843 ................. NCLC **2**
See also DLB 90

**Fourier, Charles** 1772-1837 ...... NCLC **51**

**Fournier, Henri Alban** 1886-1914
See Alain-Fournier
See also CA 104

Fournier, Pierre 1916-............ CLC 11
See also Gascar, Pierre
See also CA 89-92; CANR 16, 40

Fowles, John
1926-...... CLC 1, 2, 3, 4, 6, 9, 10, 15,
33, 87; DAB
See also CA 5-8R; CANR 25; CDBLB 1960
to Present; DLB 14, 139; MTCW;
SATA 22

Fox, Paula 1923-................ CLC 2, 8
See also AAYA 3; CA 73-76; CANR 20,
36; CLR 1; DLB 52; JRDA; MAICYA;
MTCW; SATA 17, 60

Fox, William Price (Jr.) 1926- ..... CLC 22
See also CA 17-20R; CAAS 19; CANR 11;
DLB 2; DLBY 81

Foxe, John 1516(?)-1587 .......... LC 14

Frame, Janet .......... CLC 2, 3, 6, 22, 66
See also Clutha, Janet Paterson Frame

France, Anatole................... TCLC 9
See also Thibault, Jacques Anatole Francois
See also DLB 123

Francis, Claude 19(?)- ........... CLC 50

Francis, Dick 1920- ........ CLC 2, 22, 42
See also AAYA 5; BEST 89:3; CA 5-8R;
CANR 9, 42; CDBLB 1960 to Present;
DLB 87; MTCW

Francis, Robert (Churchill)
1901-1987 .................. CLC 15
See also CA 1-4R; 123; CANR 1

Frank, Anne(lies Marie)
1929-1945 .. TCLC 17; DA; DAB; WLC
See also AAYA 12; CA 113; 133; MTCW;
SATA-Brief 42

Frank, Elizabeth 1945-............ CLC 39
See also CA 121; 126

Franklin, Benjamin
See Hasek, Jaroslav (Matej Frantisek)

Franklin, Benjamin
1706-1790 .......... LC 25; DA; DAB
See also CDALB 1640-1865; DLB 24, 43,
73

Franklin, (Stella Maraia Sarah) Miles
1879-1954 ................... TCLC 7
See also CA 104

Fraser, (Lady) Antonia (Pakenham)
1932- ...................... CLC 32
See also CA 85-88; CANR 44; MTCW;
SATA-Brief 32

Fraser, George MacDonald 1925-.... CLC 7
See also CA 45-48; CANR 2, 48

Fraser, Sylvia 1935-.............. CLC 64
See also CA 45-48; CANR 1, 16

Frayn, Michael 1933-...... CLC 3, 7, 31, 47
See also CA 5-8R; CANR 30; DLB 13, 14;
MTCW

Fraze, Candida (Merrill) 1945- ..... CLC 50
See also CA 126

Frazer, J(ames) G(eorge)
1854-1941 ................... TCLC 32
See also CA 118

Frazer, Robert Caine
See Creasey, John

Frazer, Sir James George
See Frazer, J(ames) G(eorge)

Frazier, Ian 1951-............... CLC 46
See also CA 130

Frederic, Harold 1856-1898...... NCLC 10
See also DLB 12, 23

Frederick, John
See Faust, Frederick (Schiller)

Frederick the Great 1712-1786 ...... LC 14

Fredro, Aleksander 1793-1876..... NCLC 8

Freeling, Nicolas 1927- ........... CLC 38
See also CA 49-52; CAAS 12; CANR 1, 17;
DLB 87

Freeman, Douglas Southall
1886-1953 ................. TCLC 11
See also CA 109; DLB 17

Freeman, Judith 1946-............ CLC 55
See also CA 148

Freeman, Mary Eleanor Wilkins
1852-1930 ........... TCLC 9; SSC 1
See also CA 106; DLB 12, 78

Freeman, R(ichard) Austin
1862-1943 ................. TCLC 21
See also CA 113; DLB 70

French, Albert 1943- ............. CLC 86

French, Marilyn 1929-...... CLC 10, 18, 60
See also CA 69-72; CANR 3, 31; MTCW

French, Paul
See Asimov, Isaac

Freneau, Philip Morin 1752-1832.. NCLC 1
See also DLB 37, 43

Freud, Sigmund 1856-1939 ....... TCLC 52
See also CA 115; 133; MTCW

Friedan, Betty (Naomi) 1921-...... CLC 74
See also CA 65-68; CANR 18, 45; MTCW

Friedlaender, Saul 1932- .......... CLC 90
See also CA 117; 130

Friedman, B(ernard) H(arper)
1926-........................ CLC 7
See also CA 1-4R; CANR 3, 48

Friedman, Bruce Jay 1930-.... CLC 3, 5, 56
See also CA 9-12R; CANR 25; DLB 2, 28

Friel, Brian 1929-........... CLC 5, 42, 59
See also CA 21-24R; CANR 33; DLB 13;
MTCW

Friis-Baastad, Babbis Ellinor
1921-1970 .................. CLC 12
See also CA 17-20R; 134; SATA 7

Frisch, Max (Rudolf)
1911-1991 ..... CLC 3, 9, 14, 18, 32, 44
See also CA 85-88; 134; CANR 32;
DLB 69, 124; MTCW

Fromentin, Eugene (Samuel Auguste)
1820-1876 ................. NCLC 10
See also DLB 123

Frost, Frederick
See Faust, Frederick (Schiller)

Frost, Robert (Lee)
1874-1963 .... CLC 1, 3, 4, 9, 10, 13, 15,
26, 34, 44; DA; DAB; PC 1; WLC
See also CA 89-92; CANR 33;
CDALB 1917-1929; DLB 54; DLBD 7;
MTCW; SATA 14

Froude, James Anthony
1818-1894 ................. NCLC 43
See also DLB 18, 57, 144

Froy, Herald
See Waterhouse, Keith (Spencer)

Fry, Christopher 1907-....... CLC 2, 10, 14
See also CA 17-20R; CANR 9, 30; DLB 13;
MTCW; SATA 66

Frye, (Herman) Northrop
1912-1991 ............... CLC 24, 70
See also CA 5-8R; 133; CANR 8, 37;
DLB 67, 68; MTCW

Fuchs, Daniel 1909-1993 ........ CLC 8, 22
See also CA 81-84; 142; CAAS 5;
CANR 40; DLB 9, 26, 28; DLBY 93

Fuchs, Daniel 1934-.............. CLC 34
See also CA 37-40R; CANR 14, 48

Fuentes, Carlos
1928- ...... CLC 3, 8, 10, 13, 22, 41, 60;
DA; DAB; HLC; WLC
See also AAYA 4; AITN 2; CA 69-72;
CANR 10, 32; DLB 113; HW; MTCW

Fuentes, Gregorio Lopez y
See Lopez y Fuentes, Gregorio

Fugard, (Harold) Athol
1932-.... CLC 5, 9, 14, 25, 40, 80; DC 3
See also CA 85-88; CANR 32; MTCW

Fugard, Sheila 1932- ............. CLC 48
See also CA 125

Fuller, Charles (H., Jr.)
1939-............. CLC 25; BLC; DC 1
See also BW 2; CA 108; 112; DLB 38;
MTCW

Fuller, John (Leopold) 1937-....... CLC 62
See also CA 21-24R; CANR 9, 44; DLB 40

Fuller, Margaret .............. NCLC 5, 50
See also Ossoli, Sarah Margaret (Fuller
marchesa d')

Fuller, Roy (Broadbent)
1912-1991 ................. CLC 4, 28
See also CA 5-8R; 135; CAAS 10; DLB 15,
20

Fulton, Alice 1952-............... CLC 52
See also CA 116

Furphy, Joseph 1843-1912........ TCLC 25

Fussell, Paul 1924-............... CLC 74
See also BEST 90:1; CA 17-20R; CANR 8,
21, 35; MTCW

Futabatei, Shimei 1864-1909 ...... TCLC 44

Futrelle, Jacques 1875-1912 ...... TCLC 19
See also CA 113

Gaboriau, Emile 1835-1873...... NCLC 14

Gadda, Carlo Emilio 1893-1973 .... CLC 11
See also CA 89-92

Gaddis, William
1922- ..... CLC 1, 3, 6, 8, 10, 19, 43, 86
See also CA 17-20R; CANR 21, 48; DLB 2;
MTCW

Gaines, Ernest J(ames)
1933-.......... CLC 3, 11, 18, 86; BLC
See also AITN 1; BW 2; CA 9-12R;
CANR 6, 24, 42; CDALB 1968-1988;
DLB 2, 33, 152; DLBY 80; MTCW

Gaitskill, Mary 1954-............ CLC 69
See also CA 128

Galdos, Benito Perez
See Perez Galdos, Benito

**Gale, Zona** 1874-1938 ........... **TCLC 7**
See also CA 105; DLB 9, 78

**Galeano, Eduardo (Hughes)** 1940-... **CLC 72**
See also CA 29-32R; CANR 13, 32; HW

**Galiano, Juan Valera y Alcala**
See Valera y Alcala-Galiano, Juan

**Gallagher, Tess** 1943-.... **CLC 18, 63; PC 9**
See also CA 106; DLB 120

**Gallant, Mavis**
1922- ........... **CLC 7, 18, 38; SSC 5**
See also CA 69-72; CANR 29; DLB 53;
MTCW

**Gallant, Roy A(rthur)** 1924- ....... **CLC 17**
See also CA 5-8R; CANR 4, 29; CLR 30;
MAICYA; SATA 4, 68

**Gallico, Paul (William)** 1897-1976 ... **CLC 2**
See also AITN 1; CA 5-8R; 69-72;
CANR 23; DLB 9; MAICYA; SATA 13

**Gallup, Ralph**
See Whitemore, Hugh (John)

**Galsworthy, John**
1867-1933 ...... **TCLC 1, 45; DA; DAB;
WLC 2**
See also CA 104; 141; CDBLB 1890-1914;
DLB 10, 34, 98

**Galt, John** 1779-1839 ........... **NCLC 1**
See also DLB 99, 116

**Galvin, James** 1951-............. **CLC 38**
See also CA 108; CANR 26

**Gamboa, Federico** 1864-1939...... **TCLC 36**

**Gandhi, M. K.**
See Gandhi, Mohandas Karamchand

**Gandhi, Mahatma**
See Gandhi, Mohandas Karamchand

**Gandhi, Mohandas Karamchand**
1869-1948 .................. **TCLC 59**
See also CA 121; 132; MTCW

**Gann, Ernest Kellogg** 1910-1991.... **CLC 23**
See also AITN 1; CA 1-4R; 136; CANR 1

**Garcia, Cristina** 1958- ........... **CLC 76**
See also CA 141

**Garcia Lorca, Federico**
1898-1936 ... **TCLC 1, 7, 49; DA; DAB;
DC 2; HLC; PC 3; WLC**
See also CA 104; 131; DLB 108; HW;
MTCW

**Garcia Marquez, Gabriel (Jose)**
1928- .... **CLC 2, 3, 8, 10, 15, 27, 47, 55,
68; DA; DAB; HLC; SSC 8; WLC**
See also AAYA 3; BEST 89:1, 90:4;
CA 33-36R; CANR 10, 28; DLB 113;
HW; MTCW

**Gard, Janice**
See Latham, Jean Lee

**Gard, Roger Martin du**
See Martin du Gard, Roger

**Gardam, Jane** 1928-............. **CLC 43**
See also CA 49-52; CANR 2, 18, 33;
CLR 12; DLB 14; MAICYA; MTCW;
SAAS 9; SATA 39, 76; SATA-Brief 28

**Gardner, Herb**.................. **CLC 44**

**Gardner, John (Champlin), Jr.**
1933-1982 ..... **CLC 2, 3, 5, 7, 8, 10, 18,
28, 34; SSC 7**
See also AITN 1; CA 65-68; 107;
CANR 33; DLB 2; DLBY 82; MTCW;
SATA 40; SATA-Obit 31

**Gardner, John (Edmund)** 1926-..... **CLC 30**
See also CA 103; CANR 15; MTCW

**Gardner, Noel**
See Kuttner, Henry

**Gardons, S. S.**
See Snodgrass, W(illiam) D(e Witt)

**Garfield, Leon** 1921-............. **CLC 12**
See also AAYA 8; CA 17-20R; CANR 38,
41; CLR 21; JRDA; MAICYA; SATA 1,
32, 76

**Garland, (Hannibal) Hamlin**
1860-1940 .......... **TCLC 3; SSC 18**
See also CA 104; DLB 12, 71, 78

**Garneau, (Hector de) Saint-Denys**
1912-1943 ................. **TCLC 13**
See also CA 111; DLB 88

**Garner, Alan** 1934-......... **CLC 17; DAB**
See also CA 73-76; CANR 15; CLR 20;
MAICYA; MTCW; SATA 18, 69

**Garner, Hugh** 1913-1979 .......... **CLC 13**
See also CA 69-72; CANR 31; DLB 68

**Garnett, David** 1892-1981 .......... **CLC 3**
See also CA 5-8R; 103; CANR 17; DLB 34

**Garos, Stephanie**
See Katz, Steve

**Garrett, George (Palmer)**
1929- ................. **CLC 3, 11, 51**
See also CA 1-4R; CAAS 5; CANR 1, 42;
DLB 2, 5, 130, 152; DLBY 83

**Garrick, David** 1717-1779 ......... **LC 15**
See also DLB 84

**Garrigue, Jean** 1914-1972 ........ **CLC 2, 8**
See also CA 5-8R; 37-40R; CANR 20

**Garrison, Frederick**
See Sinclair, Upton (Beall)

**Garth, Will**
See Hamilton, Edmond; Kuttner, Henry

**Garvey, Marcus (Moziah, Jr.)**
1887-1940 ............ **TCLC 41; BLC**
See also BW 1; CA 120; 124

**Gary, Romain** ................... **CLC 25**
See also Kacew, Romain
See also DLB 83

**Gascar, Pierre** ................... **CLC 11**
See also Fournier, Pierre

**Gascoyne, David (Emery)** 1916- .... **CLC 45**
See also CA 65-68; CANR 10, 28; DLB 20;
MTCW

**Gaskell, Elizabeth Cleghorn**
1810-1865 ............. **NCLC 5; DAB**
See also CDBLB 1832-1890; DLB 21, 144

**Gass, William H(oward)**
1924- ... **CLC 1, 2, 8, 11, 15, 39; SSC 12**
See also CA 17-20R; CANR 30; DLB 2;
MTCW

**Gasset, Jose Ortega y**
See Ortega y Gasset, Jose

**Gates, Henry Louis, Jr.** 1950-...... **CLC 65**
See also BW 2; CA 109; CANR 25; DLB 67

**Gautier, Theophile**
1811-1872 .......... **NCLC 1; SSC 20**
See also DLB 119

**Gawsworth, John**
See Bates, H(erbert) E(rnest)

**Gaye, Marvin (Penze)** 1939-1984 ... **CLC 26**
See also CA 112

**Gebler, Carlo (Ernest)** 1954-....... **CLC 39**
See also CA 119; 133

**Gee, Maggie (Mary)** 1948-........ **CLC 57**
See also CA 130

**Gee, Maurice (Gough)** 1931-....... **CLC 29**
See also CA 97-100; SATA 46

**Gelbart, Larry (Simon)** 1923- ... **CLC 21, 61**
See also CA 73-76; CANR 45

**Gelber, Jack** 1932-........ **CLC 1, 6, 14, 79**
See also CA 1-4R; CANR 2; DLB 7

**Gellhorn, Martha (Ellis)** 1908-.. **CLC 14, 60**
See also CA 77-80; CANR 44; DLBY 82

**Genet, Jean**
1910-1986 ... **CLC 1, 2, 5, 10, 14, 44, 46**
See also CA 13-16R; CANR 18; DLB 72;
DLBY 86; MTCW

**Gent, Peter** 1942-................. **CLC 29**
See also AITN 1; CA 89-92; DLBY 82

**Gentlewoman in New England, A**
See Bradstreet, Anne

**Gentlewoman in Those Parts, A**
See Bradstreet, Anne

**George, Jean Craighead** 1919-...... **CLC 35**
See also AAYA 8; CA 5-8R; CANR 25;
CLR 1; DLB 52; JRDA; MAICYA;
SATA 2, 68

**George, Stefan (Anton)**
1868-1933 ............... **TCLC 2, 14**
See also CA 104

**Georges, Georges Martin**
See Simenon, Georges (Jacques Christian)

**Gerhardi, William Alexander**
See Gerhardie, William Alexander

**Gerhardie, William Alexander**
1895-1977 ................... **CLC 5**
See also CA 25-28R; 73-76; CANR 18;
DLB 36

**Gerstler, Amy** 1956-.............. **CLC 70**
See also CA 146

**Gertler, T.** ...................... **CLC 34**
See also CA 116; 121

**Ghalib** 1797-1869 .............. **NCLC 39**

**Ghelderode, Michel de**
1898-1962 ................. **CLC 6, 11**
See also CA 85-88; CANR 40

**Ghiselin, Brewster** 1903- .......... **CLC 23**
See also CA 13-16R; CAAS 10; CANR 13

**Ghose, Zulfikar** 1935-............. **CLC 42**
See also CA 65-68

**Ghosh, Amitav** 1956- ............. **CLC 44**
See also CA 147

**Giacosa, Giuseppe** 1847-1906 ...... **TCLC 7**
See also CA 104

**Gibb, Lee**
See Waterhouse, Keith (Spencer)

**Gordimer, Nadine**
  1923- .... **CLC 3, 5, 7, 10, 18, 33, 51, 70;**
                    **DA; DAB; SSC 17**
  See also CA 5-8R; CANR 3, 28; MTCW

**Gordon, Adam Lindsay**
  1833-1870 ............... **NCLC 21**

**Gordon, Caroline**
  1895-1981 ... **CLC 6, 13, 29, 83; SSC 15**
  See also CA 11-12; 103; CANR 36; CAP 1;
  DLB 4, 9, 102; DLBY 81; MTCW

**Gordon, Charles William** 1860-1937
  See Connor, Ralph
  See also CA 109

**Gordon, Mary (Catherine)**
  1949- .................... **CLC 13, 22**
  See also CA 102; CANR 44; DLB 6;
  DLBY 81; MTCW

**Gordon, Sol** 1923-............... **CLC 26**
  See also CA 53-56; CANR 4; SATA 11

**Gordone, Charles** 1925-.......... **CLC 1, 4**
  See also BW 1; CA 93-96; DLB 7; MTCW

**Gorenko, Anna Andreevna**
  See Akhmatova, Anna

**Gorky, Maxim** ........ **TCLC 8; DAB; WLC**
  See also Peshkov, Alexei Maximovich

**Goryan, Sirak**
  See Saroyan, William

**Gosse, Edmund (William)**
  1849-1928 ................. **TCLC 28**
  See also CA 117; DLB 57, 144

**Gotlieb, Phyllis Fay (Bloom)**
  1926- ...................... **CLC 18**
  See also CA 13-16R; CANR 7; DLB 88

**Gottesman, S. D.**
  See Kornbluth, C(yril) M.; Pohl, Frederik

**Gottfried von Strassburg**
  fl. c. 1210-................ **CMLC 10**
  See also DLB 138

**Gould, Lois** ................... **CLC 4, 10**
  See also CA 77-80; CANR 29; MTCW

**Gourmont, Remy de** 1858-1915.... **TCLC 17**
  See also CA 109

**Govier, Katherine** 1948-.......... **CLC 51**
  See also CA 101; CANR 18, 40

**Goyen, (Charles) William**
  1915-1983 ........... **CLC 5, 8, 14, 40**
  See also AITN 2; CA 5-8R; 110; CANR 6;
  DLB 2; DLBY 83

**Goytisolo, Juan**
  1931- ............. **CLC 5, 10, 23; HLC**
  See also CA 85-88; CANR 32; HW; MTCW

**Gozzano, Guido** 1883-1916 ........ **PC 10**
  See also DLB 114

**Gozzi, (Conte) Carlo** 1720-1806 .. **NCLC 23**

**Grabbe, Christian Dietrich**
  1801-1836 ................. **NCLC 2**
  See also DLB 133

**Grace, Patricia** 1937-............ **CLC 56**

**Gracian y Morales, Baltasar**
  1601-1658 ................. **LC 15**

**Gracq, Julien** ................. **CLC 11, 48**
  See also Poirier, Louis
  See also DLB 83

**Grade, Chaim** 1910-1982 ......... **CLC 10**
  See also CA 93-96; 107

**Graduate of Oxford, A**
  See Ruskin, John

**Graham, John**
  See Phillips, David Graham

**Graham, Jorie** 1951-............. **CLC 48**
  See also CA 111; DLB 120

**Graham, R(obert) B(ontine) Cunninghame**
  See Cunninghame Graham, R(obert)
  B(ontine)
  See also DLB 98, 135

**Graham, Robert**
  See Haldeman, Joe (William)

**Graham, Tom**
  See Lewis, (Harry) Sinclair

**Graham, W(illiam) S(ydney)**
  1918-1986 ................. **CLC 29**
  See also CA 73-76; 118; DLB 20

**Graham, Winston (Mawdsley)**
  1910- ..................... **CLC 23**
  See also CA 49-52; CANR 2, 22, 45;
  DLB 77

**Grant, Skeeter**
  See Spiegelman, Art

**Granville-Barker, Harley**
  1877-1946 .................. **TCLC 2**
  See also Barker, Harley Granville
  See also CA 104

**Grass, Guenter (Wilhelm)**
  1927- ..... **CLC 1, 2, 4, 6, 11, 15, 22, 32,**
              **49, 88; DA; DAB; WLC**
  See also CA 13-16R; CANR 20; DLB 75,
  124; MTCW

**Gratton, Thomas**
  See Hulme, T(homas) E(rnest)

**Grau, Shirley Ann**
  1929- .............. **CLC 4, 9; SSC 15**
  See also CA 89-92; CANR 22; DLB 2;
  MTCW

**Gravel, Fern**
  See Hall, James Norman

**Graver, Elizabeth** 1964-.......... **CLC 70**
  See also CA 135

**Graves, Richard Perceval** 1945- .... **CLC 44**
  See also CA 65-68; CANR 9, 26

**Graves, Robert (von Ranke)**
  1895-1985 ...... **CLC 1, 2, 6, 11, 39, 44,**
                    **45; DAB; PC 6**
  See also CA 5-8R; 117; CANR 5, 36;
  CDBLB 1914-1945; DLB 20, 100;
  DLBY 85; MTCW; SATA 45

**Gray, Alasdair (James)** 1934- ...... **CLC 41**
  See also CA 126; CANR 47; MTCW

**Gray, Amlin** 1946- ............... **CLC 29**
  See also CA 138

**Gray, Francine du Plessix** 1930-.... **CLC 22**
  See also BEST 90:3; CA 61-64; CAAS 2;
  CANR 11, 33; MTCW

**Gray, John (Henry)** 1866-1934 .... **TCLC 19**
  See also CA 119

**Gray, Simon (James Holliday)**
  1936- .................... **CLC 9, 14, 36**
  See also AITN 1; CA 21-24R; CAAS 3;
  CANR 32; DLB 13; MTCW

**Gray, Spalding** 1941-............. **CLC 49**
  See also CA 128

**Gray, Thomas**
  1716-1771 ...... **LC 4; DA; DAB; PC 2;**
                    **WLC**
  See also CDBLB 1660-1789; DLB 109

**Grayson, David**
  See Baker, Ray Stannard

**Grayson, Richard (A.)** 1951-....... **CLC 38**
  See also CA 85-88; CANR 14, 31

**Greeley, Andrew M(oran)** 1928-.... **CLC 28**
  See also CA 5-8R; CAAS 7; CANR 7, 43;
  MTCW

**Green, Brian**
  See Card, Orson Scott

**Green, Hannah**
  See Greenberg, Joanne (Goldenberg)

**Green, Hannah** .................... **CLC 3**
  See also CA 73-76

**Green, Henry** ................... **CLC 2, 13**
  See also Yorke, Henry Vincent
  See also DLB 15

**Green, Julian (Hartridge)** 1900-
  See Green, Julien
  See also CA 21-24R; CANR 33; DLB 4, 72;
  MTCW

**Green, Julien** ................ **CLC 3, 11, 77**
  See also Green, Julian (Hartridge)

**Green, Paul (Eliot)** 1894-1981...... **CLC 25**
  See also AITN 1; CA 5-8R; 103; CANR 3;
  DLB 7, 9; DLBY 81

**Greenberg, Ivan** 1908-1973
  See Rahv, Philip
  See also CA 85-88

**Greenberg, Joanne (Goldenberg)**
  1932- .................... **CLC 7, 30**
  See also AAYA 12; CA 5-8R; CANR 14,
  32; SATA 25

**Greenberg, Richard** 1959(?)- ....... **CLC 57**
  See also CA 138

**Greene, Bette** 1934-.............. **CLC 30**
  See also AAYA 7; CA 53-56; CANR 4;
  CLR 2; JRDA; MAICYA; SAAS 16;
  SATA 8

**Greene, Gael** ..................... **CLC 8**
  See also CA 13-16R; CANR 10

**Greene, Graham**
  1904-1991 .... **CLC 1, 3, 6, 9, 14, 18, 27,**
                    **37, 70, 72; DA; DAB; WLC**
  See also AITN 2; CA 13-16R; 133;
  CANR 35; CDBLB 1945-1960; DLB 13,
  15, 77, 100; DLBY 91; MTCW; SATA 20

**Greer, Richard**
  See Silverberg, Robert

**Gregor, Arthur** 1923-.............. **CLC 9**
  See also CA 25-28R; CAAS 10; CANR 11;
  SATA 36

**Gregor, Lee**
  See Pohl, Frederik

**Gregory, Isabella Augusta (Persse)**
  1852-1932 .................. **TCLC 1**
  See also CA 104; DLB 10

**Gregory, J. Dennis**
  See Williams, John A(lfred)

**Haley, Alex(ander Murray Palmer)**
1921-1992 .... **CLC 8, 12, 76; BLC; DA;**
**DAB**
See also BW 2; CA 77-80; 136; DLB 38;
MTCW

**Haliburton, Thomas Chandler**
1796-1865 ................. **NCLC 15**
See also DLB 11, 99

**Hall, Donald (Andrew, Jr.)**
1928- .............. **CLC 1, 13, 37, 59**
See also CA 5-8R; CAAS 7; CANR 2, 44;
DLB 5; SATA 23

**Hall, Frederic Sauser**
See Sauser-Hall, Frederic

**Hall, James**
See Kuttner, Henry

**Hall, James Norman**   1887-1951 ... **TCLC 23**
See also CA 123; SATA 21

**Hall, (Marguerite) Radclyffe**
1886(?)-1943 ................ **TCLC 12**
See also CA 110

**Hall, Rodney**   1935- .............. **CLC 51**
See also CA 109

**Halleck, Fitz-Greene**   1790-1867 .. **NCLC 47**
See also DLB 3

**Halliday, Michael**
See Creasey, John

**Halpern, Daniel**   1945- ........... **CLC 14**
See also CA 33-36R

**Hamburger, Michael (Peter Leopold)**
1924- .................... **CLC 5, 14**
See also CA 5-8R; CAAS 4; CANR 2, 47;
DLB 27

**Hamill, Pete**   1935- .............. **CLC 10**
See also CA 25-28R; CANR 18

**Hamilton, Alexander**
1755(?)-1804 .............. **NCLC 49**
See also DLB 37

**Hamilton, Clive**
See Lewis, C(live) S(taples)

**Hamilton, Edmond**   1904-1977 ...... **CLC 1**
See also CA 1-4R; CANR 3; DLB 8

**Hamilton, Eugene (Jacob) Lee**
See Lee-Hamilton, Eugene (Jacob)

**Hamilton, Franklin**
See Silverberg, Robert

**Hamilton, Gail**
See Corcoran, Barbara

**Hamilton, Mollie**
See Kaye, M(ary) M(argaret)

**Hamilton, (Anthony Walter) Patrick**
1904-1962 ................... **CLC 51**
See also CA 113; DLB 10

**Hamilton, Virginia**   1936- ......... **CLC 26**
See also AAYA 2; BW 2; CA 25-28R;
CANR 20, 37; CLR 1, 11; DLB 33, 52;
JRDA; MAICYA; MTCW; SATA 4, 56,
79

**Hammett, (Samuel) Dashiell**
1894-1961 ....... **CLC 3, 5, 10, 19, 47;**
**SSC 17**
See also AITN 1; CA 81-84; CANR 42;
CDALB 1929-1941; DLBD 6; MTCW

**Hammon, Jupiter**
1711(?)-1800(?) ........ **NCLC 5; BLC**
See also DLB 31, 50

**Hammond, Keith**
See Kuttner, Henry

**Hamner, Earl (Henry), Jr.**   1923- ... **CLC 12**
See also AITN 2; CA 73-76; DLB 6

**Hampton, Christopher (James)**
1946- ....................... **CLC 4**
See also CA 25-28R; DLB 13; MTCW

**Hamsun, Knut** ............. **TCLC 2, 14, 49**
See also Pedersen, Knut

**Handke, Peter**   1942- .. **CLC 5, 8, 10, 15, 38**
See also CA 77-80; CANR 33; DLB 85,
124; MTCW

**Hanley, James**   1901-1985 ... **CLC 3, 5, 8, 13**
See also CA 73-76; 117; CANR 36; MTCW

**Hannah, Barry**   1942- ....... **CLC 23, 38, 90**
See also CA 108; 110; CANR 43; DLB 6;
MTCW

**Hannon, Ezra**
See Hunter, Evan

**Hansberry, Lorraine (Vivian)**
1930-1965 ...... **CLC 17, 62; BLC; DA;**
**DAB; DC 2**
See also BW 1; CA 109; 25-28R; CABS 3;
CDALB 1941-1968; DLB 7, 38; MTCW

**Hansen, Joseph**   1923- ............ **CLC 38**
See also CA 29-32R; CAAS 17; CANR 16,
44

**Hansen, Martin A.**   1909-1955 ..... **TCLC 32**

**Hanson, Kenneth O(stlin)**   1922- .... **CLC 13**
See also CA 53-56; CANR 7

**Hardwick, Elizabeth**   1916- ........ **CLC 13**
See also CA 5-8R; CANR 3, 32; DLB 6;
MTCW

**Hardy, Thomas**
1840-1928 ...... **TCLC 4, 10, 18, 32, 48,**
**53; DA; DAB; PC 8; SSC 2; WLC**
See also CA 104; 123; CDBLB 1890-1914;
DLB 18, 19, 135; MTCW

**Hare, David**   1947- ............ **CLC 29, 58**
See also CA 97-100; CANR 39; DLB 13;
MTCW

**Harford, Henry**
See Hudson, W(illiam) H(enry)

**Hargrave, Leonie**
See Disch, Thomas M(ichael)

**Harjo, Joy**   1951- ................ **CLC 83**
See also CA 114; CANR 35; DLB 120;
NNAL

**Harlan, Louis R(udolph)**   1922- ..... **CLC 34**
See also CA 21-24R; CANR 25

**Harling, Robert**   1951(?)- .......... **CLC 53**
See also CA 147

**Harmon, William (Ruth)**   1938- ..... **CLC 38**
See also CA 33-36R; CANR 14, 32, 35;
SATA 65

**Harper, F. E. W.**
See Harper, Frances Ellen Watkins

**Harper, Frances E. W.**
See Harper, Frances Ellen Watkins

**Harper, Frances E. Watkins**
See Harper, Frances Ellen Watkins

**Harper, Frances Ellen**
See Harper, Frances Ellen Watkins

**Harper, Frances Ellen Watkins**
1825-1911 ............. **TCLC 14; BLC**
See also BW 1; CA 111; 125; DLB 50

**Harper, Michael S(teven)**   1938- .. **CLC 7, 22**
See also BW 1; CA 33-36R; CANR 24;
DLB 41

**Harper, Mrs. F. E. W.**
See Harper, Frances Ellen Watkins

**Harris, Christie (Lucy) Irwin**
1907- ....................... **CLC 12**
See also CA 5-8R; CANR 6; DLB 88;
JRDA; MAICYA; SAAS 10; SATA 6, 74

**Harris, Frank**   1856(?)-1931 ....... **TCLC 24**
See also CA 109; DLB 156

**Harris, George Washington**
1814-1869 ................. **NCLC 23**
See also DLB 3, 11

**Harris, Joel Chandler**
1848-1908 ........... **TCLC 2; SSC 19**
See also CA 104; 137; DLB 11, 23, 42, 78,
91; MAICYA; YABC 1

**Harris, John (Wyndham Parkes Lucas)**
**Beynon**   1903-1969
See Wyndham, John
See also CA 102; 89-92

**Harris, MacDonald** ................ **CLC 9**
See also Heiney, Donald (William)

**Harris, Mark**   1922- ............... **CLC 19**
See also CA 5-8R; CAAS 3; CANR 2;
DLB 2; DLBY 80

**Harris, (Theodore) Wilson**   1921-.... **CLC 25**
See also BW 2; CA 65-68; CAAS 16;
CANR 11, 27; DLB 117; MTCW

**Harrison, Elizabeth Cavanna**   1909-
See Cavanna, Betty
See also CA 9-12R; CANR 6, 27

**Harrison, Harry (Max)**   1925- ...... **CLC 42**
See also CA 1-4R; CANR 5, 21; DLB 8;
SATA 4

**Harrison, James (Thomas)**
1937- ....... **CLC 6, 14, 33, 66; SSC 19**
See also CA 13-16R; CANR 8; DLBY 82

**Harrison, Jim**
See Harrison, James (Thomas)

**Harrison, Kathryn**   1961- .......... **CLC 70**
See also CA 144

**Harrison, Tony**   1937- ............. **CLC 43**
See also CA 65-68; CANR 44; DLB 40;
MTCW

**Harriss, Will(ard Irvin)**   1922- ...... **CLC 34**
See also CA 111

**Harson, Sley**
See Ellison, Harlan (Jay)

**Hart, Ellis**
See Ellison, Harlan (Jay)

**Hart, Josephine**   1942(?)- .......... **CLC 70**
See also CA 138

**Hart, Moss**   1904-1961 ............ **CLC 66**
See also CA 109; 89-92; DLB 7

Henry, O......... **TCLC 1, 19; SSC 5; WLC**
See also Porter, William Sydney

Henry, Patrick 1736-1799......... **LC 25**

Henryson, Robert 1430(?)-1506(?).... **LC 20**
See also DLB 146

Henry VIII 1491-1547............ **LC 10**

Henschke, Alfred
See Klabund

Hentoff, Nat(han Irving) 1925-..... **CLC 26**
See also AAYA 4; CA 1-4R; CAAS 6;
CANR 5, 25; CLR 1; JRDA; MAICYA;
SATA 42, 69; SATA-Brief 27

Heppenstall, (John) Rayner
1911-1981 ................. **CLC 10**
See also CA 1-4R; 103; CANR 29

Herbert, Frank (Patrick)
1920-1986 ........ **CLC 12, 23, 35, 44, 85**
See also CA 53-56; 118; CANR 5, 43;
DLB 8; MTCW; SATA 9, 37;
SATA-Obit 47

Herbert, George
1593-1633 ........ **LC 24; DAB; PC 4**
See also CDBLB Before 1660; DLB 126

Herbert, Zbigniew 1924-........ **CLC 9, 43**
See also CA 89-92; CANR 36; MTCW

Herbst, Josephine (Frey)
1897-1969 ................... **CLC 34**
See also CA 5-8R; 25-28R; DLB 9

Hergesheimer, Joseph
1880-1954 ................. **TCLC 11**
See also CA 109; DLB 102, 9

Herlihy, James Leo 1927-1993 ...... **CLC 6**
See also CA 1-4R; 143; CANR 2

Hermogenes fl. c. 175-........... **CMLC 6**

Hernandez, Jose 1834-1886...... **NCLC 17**

Herrick, Robert
1591-1674 ..... **LC 13; DA; DAB; PC 9**
See also DLB 126

Herring, Guilles
See Somerville, Edith

Herriot, James 1916-1995......... **CLC 12**
See also Wight, James Alfred
See also AAYA 1; CA 148; CANR 40

Herrmann, Dorothy 1941-........ **CLC 44**
See also CA 107

Herrmann, Taffy
See Herrmann, Dorothy

Hersey, John (Richard)
1914-1993 ....... **CLC 1, 2, 7, 9, 40, 81**
See also CA 17-20R; 140; CANR 33;
DLB 6; MTCW; SATA 25;
SATA-Obit 76

Herzen, Aleksandr Ivanovich
1812-1870 ................. **NCLC 10**

Herzl, Theodor 1860-1904....... **TCLC 36**

Herzog, Werner 1942-............ **CLC 16**
See also CA 89-92

Hesiod c. 8th cent. B.C.-......... **CMLC 5**

Hesse, Hermann
1877-1962 .... **CLC 1, 2, 3, 6, 11, 17, 25,
69; DA; DAB; SSC 9; WLC**
See also CA 17-18; CAP 2; DLB 66;
MTCW; SATA 50

Hewes, Cady
See De Voto, Bernard (Augustine)

Heyen, William 1940- ......... **CLC 13, 18**
See also CA 33-36R; CAAS 9; DLB 5

Heyerdahl, Thor 1914-............ **CLC 26**
See also CA 5-8R; CANR 5, 22; MTCW;
SATA 2, 52

Heym, Georg (Theodor Franz Arthur)
1887-1912 .................. **TCLC 9**
See also CA 106

Heym, Stefan 1913- .............. **CLC 41**
See also CA 9-12R; CANR 4; DLB 69

Heyse, Paul (Johann Ludwig von)
1830-1914 .................. **TCLC 8**
See also CA 104; DLB 129

Heyward, (Edwin) DuBose
1885-1940 .................. **TCLC 59**
See also CA 108; DLB 7, 9, 45; SATA 21

Hibbert, Eleanor Alice Burford
1906-1993 ................... **CLC 7**
See also BEST 90:4; CA 17-20R; 140;
CANR 9, 28; SATA 2; SATA-Obit 74

Higgins, George V(incent)
1939- ...............**CLC 4, 7, 10, 18**
See also CA 77-80; CAAS 5; CANR 17;
DLB 2; DLBY 81; MTCW

Higginson, Thomas Wentworth
1823-1911 ................. **TCLC 36**
See also DLB 1, 64

Highet, Helen
See MacInnes, Helen (Clark)

Highsmith, (Mary) Patricia
1921-1995 ........... **CLC 2, 4, 14, 42**
See also CA 1-4R; 147; CANR 1, 20, 48;
MTCW

Highwater, Jamake (Mamake)
1942(?)-.................... **CLC 12**
See also AAYA 7; CA 65-68; CAAS 7;
CANR 10, 34; CLR 17; DLB 52;
DLBY 85; JRDA; MAICYA; SATA 32,
69; SATA-Brief 30

Higuchi, Ichiyo 1872-1896....... **NCLC 49**

Hijuelos, Oscar 1951- ...... **CLC 65; HLC**
See also BEST 90:1; CA 123; DLB 145; HW

Hikmet, Nazim 1902(?)-1963....... **CLC 40**
See also CA 141; 93-96

Hildesheimer, Wolfgang
1916-1991 ................... **CLC 49**
See also CA 101; 135; DLB 69, 124

Hill, Geoffrey (William)
1932-.................**CLC 5, 8, 18, 45**
See also CA 81-84; CANR 21;
CDBLB 1960 to Present; DLB 40;
MTCW

Hill, George Roy 1921-........... **CLC 26**
See also CA 110; 122

Hill, John
See Koontz, Dean R(ay)

Hill, Susan (Elizabeth)
1942-.................. **CLC 4; DAB**
See also CA 33-36R; CANR 29; DLB 14,
139; MTCW

Hillerman, Tony 1925-............ **CLC 62**
See also AAYA 6; BEST 89:1; CA 29-32R;
CANR 21, 42; SATA 6

Hillesum, Etty 1914-1943 ........ **TCLC 49**
See also CA 137

Hilliard, Noel (Harvey) 1929-...... **CLC 15**
See also CA 9-12R; CANR 7

Hillis, Rick 1956-............... **CLC 66**
See also CA 134

Hilton, James 1900-1954........ **TCLC 21**
See also CA 108; DLB 34, 77; SATA 34

Himes, Chester (Bomar)
1909-1984 .... **CLC 2, 4, 7, 18, 58; BLC**
See also BW 2; CA 25-28R; 114; CANR 22;
DLB 2, 76, 143; MTCW

Hinde, Thomas ................. **CLC 6, 11**
See also Chitty, Thomas Willes

Hindin, Nathan
See Bloch, Robert (Albert)

Hine, (William) Daryl 1936-....... **CLC 15**
See also CA 1-4R; CAAS 15; CANR 1, 20;
DLB 60

Hinkson, Katharine Tynan
See Tynan, Katharine

Hinton, S(usan) E(loise)
1950- ............. **CLC 30; DA; DAB**
See also AAYA 2; CA 81-84; CANR 32;
CLR 3, 23; JRDA; MAICYA; MTCW;
SATA 19, 58

Hippius, Zinaida ................. **TCLC 9**
See also Gippius, Zinaida (Nikolayevna)

Hiraoka, Kimitake 1925-1970
See Mishima, Yukio
See also CA 97-100; 29-32R; MTCW

Hirsch, E(ric) D(onald), Jr. 1928-... **CLC 79**
See also CA 25-28R; CANR 27; DLB 67;
MTCW

Hirsch, Edward 1950- ......... **CLC 31, 50**
See also CA 104; CANR 20, 42; DLB 120

Hitchcock, Alfred (Joseph)
1899-1980 .................. **CLC 16**
See also CA 97-100; SATA 27;
SATA-Obit 24

Hitler, Adolf 1889-1945.......... **TCLC 53**
See also CA 117; 147

Hoagland, Edward 1932-.......... **CLC 28**
See also CA 1-4R; CANR 2, 31; DLB 6;
SATA 51

Hoban, Russell (Conwell) 1925- .. **CLC 7, 25**
See also CA 5-8R; CANR 23, 37; CLR 3;
DLB 52; MAICYA; MTCW; SATA 1,
40, 78

Hobbs, Perry
See Blackmur, R(ichard) P(almer)

Hobson, Laura Z(ametkin)
1900-1986 ................. **CLC 7, 25**
See also CA 17-20R; 118; DLB 28;
SATA 52

Hochhuth, Rolf 1931-........ **CLC 4, 11, 18**
See also CA 5-8R; CANR 33; DLB 124;
MTCW

Hochman, Sandra 1936-.......... **CLC 3, 8**
See also CA 5-8R; DLB 5

Hochwaelder, Fritz 1911-1986...... **CLC 36**
See also CA 29-32R; 120; CANR 42;
MTCW

Hochwalder, Fritz
See Hochwaelder, Fritz

**Howes, Barbara** 1914- . . . . . . . . . . . **CLC 15**
See also CA 9-12R; CAAS 3; SATA 5

**Hrabal, Bohumil** 1914- . . . . . . . . **CLC 13, 67**
See also CA 106; CAAS 12

**Hsun, Lu**
See Lu Hsun

**Hubbard, L(afayette) Ron(ald)**
1911-1986 . . . . . . . . . . . . . . . . . . **CLC 43**
See also CA 77-80; 118; CANR 22

**Huch, Ricarda (Octavia)**
1864-1947 . . . . . . . . . . . . . . . . . **TCLC 13**
See also CA 111; DLB 66

**Huddle, David** 1942- . . . . . . . . . . . . **CLC 49**
See also CA 57-60; CAAS 20; DLB 130

**Hudson, Jeffrey**
See Crichton, (John) Michael

**Hudson, W(illiam) H(enry)**
1841-1922 . . . . . . . . . . . . . . . . . **TCLC 29**
See also CA 115; DLB 98, 153; SATA 35

**Hueffer, Ford Madox**
See Ford, Ford Madox

**Hughart, Barry** 1934- . . . . . . . . . . . . **CLC 39**
See also CA 137

**Hughes, Colin**
See Creasey, John

**Hughes, David (John)** 1930- . . . . . . . **CLC 48**
See also CA 116; 129; DLB 14

**Hughes, (James) Langston**
1902-1967 . . . . . **CLC 1, 5, 10, 15, 35, 44;**
**BLC; DA; DAB; DC 3; PC 1; SSC 6;**
**WLC**
See also AAYA 12; BW 1; CA 1-4R;
25-28R; CANR 1, 34; CDALB 1929-1941;
CLR 17; DLB 4, 7, 48, 51, 86; JRDA;
MAICYA; MTCW; SATA 4, 33

**Hughes, Richard (Arthur Warren)**
1900-1976 . . . . . . . . . . . . . . . **CLC 1, 11**
See also CA 5-8R; 65-68; CANR 4;
DLB 15; MTCW; SATA 8;
SATA-Obit 25

**Hughes, Ted**
1930- . . . **CLC 2, 4, 9, 14, 37; DAB; PC 7**
See also CA 1-4R; CANR 1, 33; CLR 3;
DLB 40; MAICYA; MTCW; SATA 49;
SATA-Brief 27

**Hugo, Richard F(ranklin)**
1923-1982 . . . . . . . . . . . . . . **CLC 6, 18, 32**
See also CA 49-52; 108; CANR 3; DLB 5

**Hugo, Victor (Marie)**
1802-1885 . . . . . . . . **NCLC 3, 10, 21; DA;**
**DAB; WLC**
See also DLB 119; SATA 47

**Huidobro, Vicente**
See Huidobro Fernandez, Vicente Garcia

**Huidobro Fernandez, Vicente Garcia**
1893-1948 . . . . . . . . . . . . . . . . . **TCLC 31**
See also CA 131; HW

**Hulme, Keri** 1947- . . . . . . . . . . . . . . **CLC 39**
See also CA 125

**Hulme, T(homas) E(rnest)**
1883-1917 . . . . . . . . . . . . . . . . . **TCLC 21**
See also CA 117; DLB 19

**Hume, David** 1711-1776 . . . . . . . . . . . . **LC 7**
See also DLB 104

**Humphrey, William** 1924- . . . . . . . . . **CLC 45**
See also CA 77-80; DLB 6

**Humphreys, Emyr Owen** 1919- . . . . . **CLC 47**
See also CA 5-8R; CANR 3, 24; DLB 15

**Humphreys, Josephine** 1945- . . . . **CLC 34, 57**
See also CA 121; 127

**Hungerford, Pixie**
See Brinsmead, H(esba) F(ay)

**Hunt, E(verette) Howard, (Jr.)**
1918- . . . . . . . . . . . . . . . . . . . . . . **CLC 3**
See also AITN 1; CA 45-48; CANR 2, 47

**Hunt, Kyle**
See Creasey, John

**Hunt, (James Henry) Leigh**
1784-1859 . . . . . . . . . . . . . . . . . . **NCLC 1**

**Hunt, Marsha** 1946- . . . . . . . . . . . . . **CLC 70**
See also BW 2; CA 143

**Hunt, Violet** 1866-1942 . . . . . . . . . **TCLC 53**

**Hunter, E. Waldo**
See Sturgeon, Theodore (Hamilton)

**Hunter, Evan** 1926- . . . . . . . . . . . **CLC 11, 31**
See also CA 5-8R; CANR 5, 38; DLBY 82;
MTCW; SATA 25

**Hunter, Kristin (Eggleston)** 1931- . . . **CLC 35**
See also AITN 1; BW 1; CA 13-16R;
CANR 13; CLR 3; DLB 33; MAICYA;
SAAS 10; SATA 12

**Hunter, Mollie** 1922- . . . . . . . . . . . . **CLC 21**
See also McIlwraith, Maureen Mollie
Hunter
See also AAYA 13; CANR 37; CLR 25;
JRDA; MAICYA; SAAS 7; SATA 54

**Hunter, Robert** (?)-1734 . . . . . . . . . . . . **LC 7**

**Hurston, Zora Neale**
1903-1960 . . . . **CLC 7, 30, 61; BLC; DA;**
**SSC 4**
See also AAYA 15; BW 1; CA 85-88;
DLB 51, 86; MTCW

**Huston, John (Marcellus)**
1906-1987 . . . . . . . . . . . . . . . . . . **CLC 20**
See also CA 73-76; 123; CANR 34; DLB 26

**Hustvedt, Siri** 1955- . . . . . . . . . . . . . **CLC 76**
See also CA 137

**Hutten, Ulrich von** 1488-1523 . . . . . . . **LC 16**

**Huxley, Aldous (Leonard)**
1894-1963 . . . . . **CLC 1, 3, 4, 5, 8, 11, 18,**
**35, 79; DA; DAB; WLC**
See also AAYA 11; CA 85-88; CANR 44;
CDBLB 1914-1945; DLB 36, 100;
MTCW; SATA 63

**Huysmans, Charles Marie Georges**
1848-1907
See Huysmans, Joris-Karl
See also CA 104

**Huysmans, Joris-Karl** . . . . . . . . . . . . . **TCLC 7**
See also Huysmans, Charles Marie Georges
See also DLB 123

**Hwang, David Henry**
1957- . . . . . . . . . . . . . . . . . **CLC 55; DC 4**
See also CA 127; 132

**Hyde, Anthony** 1946- . . . . . . . . . . . . **CLC 42**
See also CA 136

**Hyde, Margaret O(ldroyd)** 1917- . . . **CLC 21**
See also CA 1-4R; CANR 1, 36; CLR 23;
JRDA; MAICYA; SAAS 8; SATA 1, 42,
76

**Hynes, James** 1956(?)- . . . . . . . . . . . **CLC 65**

**Ian, Janis** 1951- . . . . . . . . . . . . . . . . **CLC 21**
See also CA 105

**Ibanez, Vicente Blasco**
See Blasco Ibanez, Vicente

**Ibarguengoitia, Jorge** 1928-1983 . . . . **CLC 37**
See also CA 124; 113; HW

**Ibsen, Henrik (Johan)**
1828-1906 . . . . . . . **TCLC 2, 8, 16, 37, 52;**
**DA; DAB; DC 2; WLC**
See also CA 104; 141

**Ibuse Masuji** 1898-1993 . . . . . . . . . . **CLC 22**
See also CA 127; 141

**Ichikawa, Kon** 1915- . . . . . . . . . . . . . **CLC 20**
See also CA 121

**Idle, Eric** 1943- . . . . . . . . . . . . . . . . . **CLC 21**
See also Monty Python
See also CA 116; CANR 35

**Ignatow, David** 1914- . . . . . . **CLC 4, 7, 14, 40**
See also CA 9-12R; CAAS 3; CANR 31;
DLB 5

**Ihimaera, Witi** 1944- . . . . . . . . . . . . . **CLC 46**
See also CA 77-80

**Ilf, Ilya** . . . . . . . . . . . . . . . . . . . . . . . **TCLC 21**
See also Fainzilberg, Ilya Arnoldovich

**Immermann, Karl (Lebrecht)**
1796-1840 . . . . . . . . . . . . . . . . . **NCLC 4, 49**
See also DLB 133

**Inclan, Ramon (Maria) del Valle**
See Valle-Inclan, Ramon (Maria) del

**Infante, G(uillermo) Cabrera**
See Cabrera Infante, G(uillermo)

**Ingalls, Rachel (Holmes)** 1940- . . . . . **CLC 42**
See also CA 123; 127

**Ingamells, Rex** 1913-1955 . . . . . . . . **TCLC 35**

**Inge, William Motter**
1913-1973 . . . . . . . . . . . . . . **CLC 1, 8, 19**
See also CA 9-12R; CDALB 1941-1968;
DLB 7; MTCW

**Ingelow, Jean** 1820-1897 . . . . . . . **NCLC 39**
See also DLB 35; SATA 33

**Ingram, Willis J.**
See Harris, Mark

**Innaurato, Albert (F.)** 1948(?)- . . **CLC 21, 60**
See also CA 115; 122

**Innes, Michael**
See Stewart, J(ohn) I(nnes) M(ackintosh)

**Ionesco, Eugene**
1909-1994 . . . . **CLC 1, 4, 6, 9, 11, 15, 41,**
**86; DA; DAB; WLC**
See also CA 9-12R; 144; MTCW; SATA 7;
SATA-Obit 79

**Iqbal, Muhammad** 1873-1938 . . . . . **TCLC 28**

**Ireland, Patrick**
See O'Doherty, Brian

**Iron, Ralph**
See Schreiner, Olive (Emilie Albertina)

**Johnson, B(ryan) S(tanley William)**
1933-1973 . . . . . . . . . . . . . . . . . **CLC 6, 9**
See also CA 9-12R; 53-56; CANR 9;
DLB 14, 40

**Johnson, Benj. F. of Boo**
See Riley, James Whitcomb

**Johnson, Benjamin F. of Boo**
See Riley, James Whitcomb

**Johnson, Charles (Richard)**
1948- . . . . . . . . . . . . . **CLC 7, 51, 65; BLC**
See also BW 2; CA 116; CAAS 18;
CANR 42; DLB 33

**Johnson, Denis** 1949- . . . . . . . . . . . . . **CLC 52**
See also CA 117; 121; DLB 120

**Johnson, Diane** 1934- . . . . . . . . **CLC 5, 13, 48**
See also CA 41-44R; CANR 17, 40;
DLBY 80; MTCW

**Johnson, Eyvind (Olof Verner)**
1900-1976 . . . . . . . . . . . . . . . . . **CLC 14**
See also CA 73-76; 69-72; CANR 34

**Johnson, J. R.**
See James, C(yril) L(ionel) R(obert)

**Johnson, James Weldon**
1871-1938 . . . . . . . . . **TCLC 3, 19; BLC**
See also BW 1; CA 104; 125;
CDALB 1917-1929; CLR 32; DLB 51;
MTCW; SATA 31

**Johnson, Joyce** 1935- . . . . . . . . . . . . **CLC 58**
See also CA 125; 129

**Johnson, Lionel (Pigot)**
1867-1902 . . . . . . . . . . . . . . . . . **TCLC 19**
See also CA 117; DLB 19

**Johnson, Mel**
See Malzberg, Barry N(athaniel)

**Johnson, Pamela Hansford**
1912-1981 . . . . . . . . . . . . . . **CLC 1, 7, 27**
See also CA 1-4R; 104; CANR 2, 28;
DLB 15; MTCW

**Johnson, Samuel**
1709-1784 . . . . . **LC 15; DA; DAB; WLC**
See also CDBLB 1660-1789; DLB 39, 95,
104, 142

**Johnson, Uwe**
1934-1984 . . . . . . . . . **CLC 5, 10, 15, 40**
See also CA 1-4R; 112; CANR 1, 39;
DLB 75; MTCW

**Johnston, George (Benson)** 1913- . . . **CLC 51**
See also CA 1-4R; CANR 5, 20; DLB 88

**Johnston, Jennifer** 1930- . . . . . . . . . . **CLC 7**
See also CA 85-88; DLB 14

**Jolley, (Monica) Elizabeth**
1923- . . . . . . . . . . . . . . **CLC 46; SSC 19**
See also CA 127; CAAS 13

**Jones, Arthur Llewellyn** 1863-1947
See Machen, Arthur
See also CA 104

**Jones, D(ouglas) G(ordon)** 1929- . . . . **CLC 10**
See also CA 29-32R; CANR 13; DLB 53

**Jones, David (Michael)**
1895-1974 . . . . . . . . **CLC 2, 4, 7, 13, 42**
See also CA 9-12R; 53-56; CANR 28;
CDBLB 1945-1960; DLB 20, 100; MTCW

**Jones, David Robert** 1947-
See Bowie, David
See also CA 103

**Jones, Diana Wynne** 1934- . . . . . . . . **CLC 26**
See also AAYA 12; CA 49-52; CANR 4,
26; CLR 23; JRDA; MAICYA; SAAS 7;
SATA 9, 70

**Jones, Edward P.** 1950- . . . . . . . . . . . **CLC 76**
See also BW 2; CA 142

**Jones, Gayl** 1949- . . . . . . . . . **CLC 6, 9; BLC**
See also BW 2; CA 77-80; CANR 27;
DLB 33; MTCW

**Jones, James** 1921-1977 . . . . **CLC 1, 3, 10, 39**
See also AITN 1, 2; CA 1-4R; 69-72;
CANR 6; DLB 2, 143; MTCW

**Jones, John J.**
See Lovecraft, H(oward) P(hillips)

**Jones, LeRoi** . . . . . . . . **CLC 1, 2, 3, 5, 10, 14**
See also Baraka, Amiri

**Jones, Louis B.** . . . . . . . . . . . . . . . . . **CLC 65**
See also CA 141

**Jones, Madison (Percy, Jr.)** 1925- . . . **CLC 4**
See also CA 13-16R; CAAS 11; CANR 7;
DLB 152

**Jones, Mervyn** 1922- . . . . . . . . . **CLC 10, 52**
See also CA 45-48; CAAS 5; CANR 1;
MTCW

**Jones, Mick** 1956(?)- . . . . . . . . . . . . **CLC 30**

**Jones, Nettie (Pearl)** 1941- . . . . . . . . **CLC 34**
See also BW 2; CA 137; CAAS 20

**Jones, Preston** 1936-1979 . . . . . . . . . **CLC 10**
See also CA 73-76; 89-92; DLB 7

**Jones, Robert F(rancis)** 1934- . . . . . . . **CLC 7**
See also CA 49-52; CANR 2

**Jones, Rod** 1953- . . . . . . . . . . . . . . **CLC 50**
See also CA 128

**Jones, Terence Graham Parry**
1942- . . . . . . . . . . . . . . . . . . . . . **CLC 21**
See also Jones, Terry; Monty Python
See also CA 112; 116; CANR 35

**Jones, Terry**
See Jones, Terence Graham Parry
See also SATA 67; SATA-Brief 51

**Jones, Thom** 1945(?)- . . . . . . . . . . . . **CLC 81**

**Jong, Erica** 1942- . . . . . . **CLC 4, 6, 8, 18, 83**
See also AITN 1; BEST 90:2; CA 73-76;
CANR 26; DLB 2, 5, 28, 152; MTCW

**Jonson, Ben(jamin)**
1572(?)-1637 . . . . **LC 6; DA; DAB; DC 4;
WLC**
See also CDBLB Before 1660; DLB 62, 121

**Jordan, June** 1936- . . . . . . . . . **CLC 5, 11, 23**
See also AAYA 2; BW 2; CA 33-36R;
CANR 25; CLR 10; DLB 38; MAICYA;
MTCW; SATA 4

**Jordan, Pat(rick M.)** 1941- . . . . . . . . **CLC 37**
See also CA 33-36R

**Jorgensen, Ivar**
See Ellison, Harlan (Jay)

**Jorgenson, Ivar**
See Silverberg, Robert

**Josephus, Flavius** c. 37-100 . . . . . . **CMLC 13**

**Josipovici, Gabriel** 1940- . . . . . . . . **CLC 6, 43**
See also CA 37-40R; CAAS 8; CANR 47;
DLB 14

**Joubert, Joseph** 1754-1824 . . . . . . . **NCLC 9**

**Jouve, Pierre Jean** 1887-1976 . . . . . . **CLC 47**
See also CA 65-68

**Joyce, James (Augustine Aloysius)**
1882-1941 . . . . . . . **TCLC 3, 8, 16, 35, 52;
DA; DAB; SSC 3; WLC**
See also CA 104; 126; CDBLB 1914-1945;
DLB 10, 19, 36; MTCW

**Jozsef, Attila** 1905-1937 . . . . . . . . . **TCLC 22**
See also CA 116

**Juana Ines de la Cruz** 1651(?)-1695 . . . **LC 5**

**Judd, Cyril**
See Kornbluth, C(yril) M.; Pohl, Frederik

**Julian of Norwich** 1342(?)-1416(?) . . . . **LC 6**
See also DLB 146

**Juniper, Alex**
See Hospital, Janette Turner

**Just, Ward (Swift)** 1935- . . . . . . . . **CLC 4, 27**
See also CA 25-28R; CANR 32

**Justice, Donald (Rodney)** 1925- . . **CLC 6, 19**
See also CA 5-8R; CANR 26; DLBY 83

**Juvenal** c. 55-c. 127 . . . . . . . . . . . . **CMLC 8**

**Juvenis**
See Bourne, Randolph S(illiman)

**Kacew, Romain** 1914-1980
See Gary, Romain
See also CA 108; 102

**Kadare, Ismail** 1936- . . . . . . . . . . . . **CLC 52**

**Kadohata, Cynthia** . . . . . . . . . . . . . . **CLC 59**
See also CA 140

**Kafka, Franz**
1883-1924 . . . . **TCLC 2, 6, 13, 29, 47, 53;
DA; DAB; SSC 5; WLC**
See also CA 105; 126; DLB 81; MTCW

**Kahanovitsch, Pinkhes**
See Der Nister

**Kahn, Roger** 1927- . . . . . . . . . . . . . . **CLC 30**
See also CA 25-28R; CANR 44; SATA 37

**Kain, Saul**
See Sassoon, Siegfried (Lorraine)

**Kaiser, Georg** 1878-1945 . . . . . . . . . . **TCLC 9**
See also CA 106; DLB 124

**Kaletski, Alexander** 1946- . . . . . . . . . **CLC 39**
See also CA 118; 143

**Kalidasa** fl. c. 400- . . . . . . . . . . . . . . **CMLC 9**

**Kallman, Chester (Simon)**
1921-1975 . . . . . . . . . . . . . . . . . . . **CLC 2**
See also CA 45-48; 53-56; CANR 3

**Kaminsky, Melvin** 1926-
See Brooks, Mel
See also CA 65-68; CANR 16

**Kaminsky, Stuart M(elvin)** 1934- . . . **CLC 59**
See also CA 73-76; CANR 29

**Kane, Paul**
See Simon, Paul

**Kane, Wilson**
See Bloch, Robert (Albert)

**Kanin, Garson** 1912- . . . . . . . . . . . . . **CLC 22**
See also AITN 1; CA 5-8R; CANR 7;
DLB 7

**Kaniuk, Yoram** 1930- . . . . . . . . . . . . **CLC 19**
See also CA 134

**Kant, Immanuel** 1724-1804 . . . . . . **NCLC 27**
See also DLB 94

Kantor, MacKinlay 1904-1977 . . . . . . CLC 7
See also CA 61-64; 73-76; DLB 9, 102

Kaplan, David Michael 1946- . . . . . . CLC 50

Kaplan, James 1951- . . . . . . . . . . . . CLC 59
See also CA 135

Karageorge, Michael
See Anderson, Poul (William)

Karamzin, Nikolai Mikhailovich
1766-1826 . . . . . . . . . . . . . . . . . NCLC 3
See also DLB 150

Karapanou, Margarita 1946- . . . . . . . CLC 13
See also CA 101

Karinthy, Frigyes 1887-1938 . . . . . . TCLC 47

Karl, Frederick R(obert) 1927- . . . . . CLC 34
See also CA 5-8R; CANR 3, 44

Kastel, Warren
See Silverberg, Robert

Kataev, Evgeny Petrovich 1903-1942
See Petrov, Evgeny
See also CA 120

Kataphusin
See Ruskin, John

Katz, Steve 1935- . . . . . . . . . . . . . . . CLC 47
See also CA 25-28R; CAAS 14; CANR 12;
DLBY 83

Kauffman, Janet 1945- . . . . . . . . . . . CLC 42
See also CA 117; CANR 43; DLBY 86

Kaufman, Bob (Garnell)
1925-1986 . . . . . . . . . . . . . . . . . CLC 49
See also BW 1; CA 41-44R; 118; CANR 22;
DLB 16, 41

Kaufman, George S. 1889-1961 . . . . . CLC 38
See also CA 108; 93-96; DLB 7

Kaufman, Sue . . . . . . . . . . . . . . . . . . CLC 3, 8
See also Barondess, Sue K(aufman)

Kavafis, Konstantinos Petrou 1863-1933
See Cavafy, C(onstantine) P(eter)
See also CA 104

Kavan, Anna 1901-1968 . . . . . . CLC 5, 13, 82
See also CA 5-8R; CANR 6; MTCW

Kavanagh, Dan
See Barnes, Julian

Kavanagh, Patrick (Joseph)
1904-1967 . . . . . . . . . . . . . . . . . CLC 22
See also CA 123; 25-28R; DLB 15, 20;
MTCW

Kawabata, Yasunari
1899-1972 . . . . . CLC 2, 5, 9, 18; SSC 17
See also CA 93-96; 33-36R

Kaye, M(ary) M(argaret) 1909- . . . . . CLC 28
See also CA 89-92; CANR 24; MTCW;
SATA 62

Kaye, Mollie
See Kaye, M(ary) M(argaret)

Kaye-Smith, Sheila 1887-1956 . . . . . TCLC 20
See also CA 118; DLB 36

Kaymor, Patrice Maguilene
See Senghor, Leopold Sedar

Kazan, Elia 1909- . . . . . . . . . . CLC 6, 16, 63
See also CA 21-24R; CANR 32

Kazantzakis, Nikos
1883(?)-1957 . . . . . . . . . . TCLC 2, 5, 33
See also CA 105; 132; MTCW

Kazin, Alfred 1915- . . . . . . . . . . CLC 34, 38
See also CA 1-4R; CAAS 7; CANR 1, 45;
DLB 67

Keane, Mary Nesta (Skrine) 1904-
See Keane, Molly
See also CA 108; 114

Keane, Molly . . . . . . . . . . . . . . . . . . . CLC 31
See also Keane, Mary Nesta (Skrine)

Keates, Jonathan 19(?)- . . . . . . . . . . . CLC 34

Keaton, Buster 1895-1966 . . . . . . . . . CLC 20

Keats, John
1795-1821 . . . . . . . . NCLC 8; DA; DAB;
PC 1; WLC
See also CDBLB 1789-1832; DLB 96, 110

Keene, Donald 1922- . . . . . . . . . . . . . CLC 34
See also CA 1-4R; CANR 5

Keillor, Garrison . . . . . . . . . . . . . . . . CLC 40
See also Keillor, Gary (Edward)
See also AAYA 2; BEST 89:3; DLBY 87;
SATA 58

Keillor, Gary (Edward) 1942-
See Keillor, Garrison
See also CA 111; 117; CANR 36; MTCW

Keith, Michael
See Hubbard, L(afayette) Ron(ald)

Keller, Gottfried 1819-1890 . . . . . . . NCLC 2
See also DLB 129

Kellerman, Jonathan 1949- . . . . . . . . CLC 44
See also BEST 90:1; CA 106; CANR 29

Kelley, William Melvin 1937- . . . . . . CLC 22
See also BW 1; CA 77-80; CANR 27;
DLB 33

Kellogg, Marjorie 1922- . . . . . . . . . . . CLC 2
See also CA 81-84

Kellow, Kathleen
See Hibbert, Eleanor Alice Burford

Kelly, M(ilton) T(erry) 1947- . . . . . . . CLC 55
See also CA 97-100; CAAS 22; CANR 19,
43

Kelman, James 1946- . . . . . . . . . . CLC 58, 86
See also CA 148

Kemal, Yashar 1923- . . . . . . . . . . CLC 14, 29
See also CA 89-92; CANR 44

Kemble, Fanny 1809-1893 . . . . . . . NCLC 18
See also DLB 32

Kemelman, Harry 1908- . . . . . . . . . . . CLC 2
See also AITN 1; CA 9-12R; CANR 6;
DLB 28

Kempe, Margery 1373(?)-1440(?) . . . . . LC 6
See also DLB 146

Kempis, Thomas a 1380-1471 . . . . . . LC 11

Kendall, Henry 1839-1882 . . . . . . . NCLC 12

Keneally, Thomas (Michael)
1935- . . . . . . CLC 5, 8, 10, 14, 19, 27, 43
See also CA 85-88; CANR 10; MTCW

Kennedy, Adrienne (Lita)
1931- . . . . . . . . . . . CLC 66; BLC; DC 5
See also BW 2; CA 103; CAAS 20; CABS 3;
CANR 26; DLB 38

Kennedy, John Pendleton
1795-1870 . . . . . . . . . . . . . . . . NCLC 2
See also DLB 3

Kennedy, Joseph Charles 1929-
See Kennedy, X. J.
See also CA 1-4R; CANR 4, 30, 40;
SATA 14

Kennedy, William 1928- . . . CLC 6, 28, 34, 53
See also AAYA 1; CA 85-88; CANR 14,
31; DLB 143; DLBY 85; MTCW;
SATA 57

Kennedy, X. J. . . . . . . . . . . . . . . . CLC 8, 42
See also Kennedy, Joseph Charles
See also CAAS 9; CLR 27; DLB 5

Kenny, Maurice (Francis) 1929- . . . . CLC 87
See also CA 144; CAAS 22; NNAL

Kent, Kelvin
See Kuttner, Henry

Kenton, Maxwell
See Southern, Terry

Kenyon, Robert O.
See Kuttner, Henry

Kerouac, Jack . . . . . CLC 1, 2, 3, 5, 14, 29, 61
See also Kerouac, Jean-Louis Lebris de
See also CDALB 1941-1968; DLB 2, 16;
DLBD 3

Kerouac, Jean-Louis Lebris de 1922-1969
See Kerouac, Jack
See also AITN 1; CA 5-8R; 25-28R;
CANR 26; DA; DAB; MTCW; WLC

Kerr, Jean 1923- . . . . . . . . . . . . . . . . CLC 22
See also CA 5-8R; CANR 7

Kerr, M. E. . . . . . . . . . . . . . . . . CLC 12, 35
See also Meaker, Marijane (Agnes)
See also AAYA 2; CLR 29; SAAS 1

Kerr, Robert . . . . . . . . . . . . . . . . . . . CLC 55

Kerrigan, (Thomas) Anthony
1918- . . . . . . . . . . . . . . . . . . . . CLC 4, 6
See also CA 49-52; CAAS 11; CANR 4

Kerry, Lois
See Duncan, Lois

Kesey, Ken (Elton)
1935- . . . . . . CLC 1, 3, 6, 11, 46, 64; DA;
DAB; WLC
See also CA 1-4R; CANR 22, 38;
CDALB 1968-1988; DLB 2, 16; MTCW;
SATA 66

Kesselring, Joseph (Otto)
1902-1967 . . . . . . . . . . . . . . . . . CLC 45

Kessler, Jascha (Frederick) 1929- . . . . CLC 4
See also CA 17-20R; CANR 8, 48

Kettelkamp, Larry (Dale) 1933- . . . . CLC 12
See also CA 29-32R; CANR 16; SAAS 3;
SATA 2

Keyber, Conny
See Fielding, Henry

Keyes, Daniel 1927- . . . . . . . . . . CLC 80; DA
See also CA 17-20R; CANR 10, 26;
SATA 37

Khanshendel, Chiron
See Rose, Wendy

Khayyam, Omar
1048-1131 . . . . . . . . . . . CMLC 11; PC 8

Kherdian, David 1931- . . . . . . . . . . CLC 6, 9
See also CA 21-24R; CAAS 2; CANR 39;
CLR 24; JRDA; MAICYA; SATA 16, 74

Khlebnikov, Velimir . . . . . . . . . . . . . TCLC 20
See also Khlebnikov, Viktor Vladimirovich

**Khlebnikov, Viktor Vladimirovich** 1885-1922
  See Khlebnikov, Velimir
  See also CA 117

**Khodasevich, Vladislav (Felitsianovich)**
  1886-1939 ................. **TCLC 15**
  See also CA 115

**Kielland, Alexander Lange**
  1849-1906 .................. **TCLC 5**
  See also CA 104

**Kiely, Benedict** 1919-......... **CLC 23, 43**
  See also CA 1-4R; CANR 2; DLB 15

**Kienzle, William X(avier)** 1928- .... **CLC 25**
  See also CA 93-96; CAAS 1; CANR 9, 31;
  MTCW

**Kierkegaard, Soren** 1813-1855.... **NCLC 34**

**Killens, John Oliver** 1916-1987..... **CLC 10**
  See also BW 2; CA 77-80; 123; CAAS 2;
  CANR 26; DLB 33

**Killigrew, Anne** 1660-1685.......... **LC 4**
  See also DLB 131

**Kim**
  See Simenon, Georges (Jacques Christian)

**Kincaid, Jamaica** 1949- ... **CLC 43, 68; BLC**
  See also AAYA 13; BW 2; CA 125;
  CANR 47

**King, Francis (Henry)** 1923- ..... **CLC 8, 53**
  See also CA 1-4R; CANR 1, 33; DLB 15,
  139; MTCW

**King, Martin Luther, Jr.**
  1929-1968 .... **CLC 83; BLC; DA; DAB**
  See also BW 2; CA 25-28; CANR 27, 44;
  CAP 2; MTCW; SATA 14

**King, Stephen (Edwin)**
  1947-...... **CLC 12, 26, 37, 61; SSC 17**
  See also AAYA 1; BEST 90:1; CA 61-64;
  CANR 1, 30; DLB 143; DLBY 80;
  JRDA; MTCW; SATA 9, 55

**King, Steve**
  See King, Stephen (Edwin)

**King, Thomas** 1943-.............. **CLC 89**
  See also CA 144; NNAL

**Kingman, Lee**..................... **CLC 17**
  See also Natti, (Mary) Lee
  See also SAAS 3; SATA 1, 67

**Kingsley, Charles** 1819-1875..... **NCLC 35**
  See also DLB 21, 32; YABC 2

**Kingsley, Sidney** 1906-1995....... **CLC 44**
  See also CA 85-88; 147; DLB 7

**Kingsolver, Barbara** 1955-...... **CLC 55, 81**
  See also AAYA 15; CA 129; 134

**Kingston, Maxine (Ting Ting) Hong**
  1940-................. **CLC 12, 19, 58**
  See also AAYA 8; CA 69-72; CANR 13,
  38; DLBY 80; MTCW; SATA 53

**Kinnell, Galway**
  1927-.......... **CLC 1, 2, 3, 5, 13, 29**
  See also CA 9-12R; CANR 10, 34; DLB 5;
  DLBY 87; MTCW

**Kinsella, Thomas** 1928- ........ **CLC 4, 19**
  See also CA 17-20R; CANR 15; DLB 27;
  MTCW

**Kinsella, W(illiam) P(atrick)**
  1935-................... **CLC 27, 43**
  See also AAYA 7; CA 97-100; CAAS 7;
  CANR 21, 35; MTCW

**Kipling, (Joseph) Rudyard**
  1865-1936 ...... **TCLC 8, 17; DA; DAB;**
              **PC 3; SSC 5; WLC**
  See also CA 105; 120; CANR 33;
  CDBLB 1890-1914; CLR 39; DLB 19, 34,
  141, 156; MAICYA; MTCW; YABC 2

**Kirkup, James** 1918- .............. **CLC 1**
  See also CA 1-4R; CAAS 4; CANR 2;
  DLB 27; SATA 12

**Kirkwood, James** 1930(?)-1989 ...... **CLC 9**
  See also AITN 2; CA 1-4R; 128; CANR 6,
  40

**Kirshner, Sidney**
  See Kingsley, Sidney

**Kis, Danilo** 1935-1989 ............ **CLC 57**
  See also CA 109; 118; 129; MTCW

**Kivi, Aleksis** 1834-1872 ........ **NCLC 30**

**Kizer, Carolyn (Ashley)**
  1925-................. **CLC 15, 39, 80**
  See also CA 65-68; CAAS 5; CANR 24;
  DLB 5

**Klabund** 1890-1928.............. **TCLC 44**
  See also DLB 66

**Klappert, Peter** 1942-............. **CLC 57**
  See also CA 33-36R; DLB 5

**Klein, A(braham) M(oses)**
  1909-1972 .............. **CLC 19; DAB**
  See also CA 101; 37-40R; DLB 68

**Klein, Norma** 1938-1989 .......... **CLC 30**
  See also AAYA 2; CA 41-44R; 128;
  CANR 15, 37; CLR 2, 19; JRDA;
  MAICYA; SAAS 1; SATA 7, 57

**Klein, T(heodore) E(ibon) D(onald)**
  1947-....................... **CLC 34**
  See also CA 119; CANR 44

**Kleist, Heinrich von**
  1777-1811 .............. **NCLC 2, 37**
  See also DLB 90

**Klima, Ivan** 1931-................ **CLC 56**
  See also CA 25-28R; CANR 17

**Klimentov, Andrei Platonovich** 1899-1951
  See Platonov, Andrei
  See also CA 108

**Klinger, Friedrich Maximilian von**
  1752-1831 ................. **NCLC 1**
  See also DLB 94

**Klopstock, Friedrich Gottlieb**
  1724-1803 ................. **NCLC 11**
  See also DLB 97

**Knebel, Fletcher** 1911-1993........ **CLC 14**
  See also AITN 1; CA 1-4R; 140; CAAS 3;
  CANR 1, 36; SATA 36; SATA-Obit 75

**Knickerbocker, Diedrich**
  See Irving, Washington

**Knight, Etheridge**
  1931-1991 .............. **CLC 40; BLC**
  See also BW 1; CA 21-24R; 133; CANR 23;
  DLB 41

**Knight, Sarah Kemble** 1666-1727 ..... **LC 7**
  See also DLB 24

**Knister, Raymond** 1899-1932...... **TCLC 56**
  See also DLB 68

**Knowles, John**
  1926- .......... **CLC 1, 4, 10, 26; DA**
  See also AAYA 10; CA 17-20R; CANR 40;
  CDALB 1968-1988; DLB 6; MTCW;
  SATA 8

**Knox, Calvin M.**
  See Silverberg, Robert

**Knye, Cassandra**
  See Disch, Thomas M(ichael)

**Koch, C(hristopher) J(ohn)** 1932- ... **CLC 42**
  See also CA 127

**Koch, Christopher**
  See Koch, C(hristopher) J(ohn)

**Koch, Kenneth** 1925- ......... **CLC 5, 8, 44**
  See also CA 1-4R; CANR 6, 36; DLB 5;
  SATA 65

**Kochanowski, Jan** 1530-1584........ **LC 10**

**Kock, Charles Paul de**
  1794-1871 ................ **NCLC 16**

**Koda Shigeyuki** 1867-1947
  See Rohan, Koda
  See also CA 121

**Koestler, Arthur**
  1905-1983 ....... **CLC 1, 3, 6, 8, 15, 33**
  See also CA 1-4R; 109; CANR 1, 33;
  CDBLB 1945-1960; DLBY 83; MTCW

**Kogawa, Joy Nozomi** 1935-........ **CLC 78**
  See also CA 101; CANR 19

**Kohout, Pavel** 1928-.............. **CLC 13**
  See also CA 45-48; CANR 3

**Koizumi, Yakumo**
  See Hearn, (Patricio) Lafcadio (Tessima
  Carlos)

**Kolmar, Gertrud** 1894-1943...... **TCLC 40**

**Komunyakaa, Yusef** 1947-......... **CLC 86**
  See also CA 147; DLB 120

**Konrad, George**
  See Konrad, Gyoergy

**Konrad, Gyoergy** 1933- ...... **CLC 4, 10, 73**
  See also CA 85-88

**Konwicki, Tadeusz** 1926-.... **CLC 8, 28, 54**
  See also CA 101; CAAS 9; CANR 39;
  MTCW

**Koontz, Dean R(ay)** 1945-......... **CLC 78**
  See also AAYA 9; BEST 89:3, 90:2;
  CA 108; CANR 19, 36; MTCW

**Kopit, Arthur (Lee)** 1937- .... **CLC 1, 18, 33**
  See also AITN 1; CA 81-84; CABS 3;
  DLB 7; MTCW

**Kops, Bernard** 1926-.............. **CLC 4**
  See also CA 5-8R; DLB 13

**Kornbluth, C(yril) M.** 1923-1958.... **TCLC 8**
  See also CA 105; DLB 8

**Korolenko, V. G.**
  See Korolenko, Vladimir Galaktionovich

**Korolenko, Vladimir**
  See Korolenko, Vladimir Galaktionovich

**Korolenko, Vladimir G.**
  See Korolenko, Vladimir Galaktionovich

**Korolenko, Vladimir Galaktionovich**
  1853-1921 ................. **TCLC 22**
  See also CA 121

**Korzybski, Alfred (Habdank Skarbek)**
1879-1950 . . . . . . . . . . . . . . . . . TCLC 61
See also CA 123

**Kosinski, Jerzy (Nikodem)**
1933-1991 . . . . CLC 1, 2, 3, 6, 10, 15, 53,
70
See also CA 17-20R; 134; CANR 9, 46;
DLB 2; DLBY 82; MTCW

**Kostelanetz, Richard (Cory)** 1940- . . CLC 28
See also CA 13-16R; CAAS 8; CANR 38

**Kostrowitzki, Wilhelm Apollinaris de**
1880-1918
See Apollinaire, Guillaume
See also CA 104

**Kotlowitz, Robert** 1924- . . . . . . . . . . . CLC 4
See also CA 33-36R; CANR 36

**Kotzebue, August (Friedrich Ferdinand) von**
1761-1819 . . . . . . . . . . . . . . . . . NCLC 25
See also DLB 94

**Kotzwinkle, William** 1938- . . . CLC 5, 14, 35
See also CA 45-48; CANR 3, 44; CLR 6;
MAICYA; SATA 24, 70

**Kozol, Jonathan** 1936- . . . . . . . . . . . . CLC 17
See also CA 61-64; CANR 16, 45

**Kozoll, Michael** 1940(?)- . . . . . . . . . . CLC 35

**Kramer, Kathryn** 19(?)- . . . . . . . . . . . CLC 34

**Kramer, Larry** 1935- . . . . . . . . . . . . . CLC 42
See also CA 124; 126

**Krasicki, Ignacy** 1735-1801 . . . . . . . NCLC 8

**Krasinski, Zygmunt** 1812-1859 . . . . NCLC 4

**Kraus, Karl** 1874-1936 . . . . . . . . . . . TCLC 5
See also CA 104; DLB 118

**Kreve (Mickevicius), Vincas**
1882-1954 . . . . . . . . . . . . . . . . . TCLC 27

**Kristeva, Julia** 1941- . . . . . . . . . . . . CLC 77

**Kristofferson, Kris** 1936- . . . . . . . . . CLC 26
See also CA 104

**Krizanc, John** 1956- . . . . . . . . . . . . . CLC 57

**Krleza, Miroslav** 1893-1981 . . . . . . . . CLC 8
See also CA 97-100; 105; DLB 147

**Kroetsch, Robert** 1927- . . . . . . CLC 5, 23, 57
See also CA 17-20R; CANR 8, 38; DLB 53;
MTCW

**Kroetz, Franz**
See Kroetz, Franz Xaver

**Kroetz, Franz Xaver** 1946- . . . . . . . . CLC 41
See also CA 130

**Kroker, Arthur** 1945- . . . . . . . . . . . . CLC 77

**Kropotkin, Peter (Aleksieevich)**
1842-1921 . . . . . . . . . . . . . . . . . TCLC 36
See also CA 119

**Krotkov, Yuri** 1917- . . . . . . . . . . . . . CLC 19
See also CA 102

**Krumb**
See Crumb, R(obert)

**Krumgold, Joseph (Quincy)**
1908-1980 . . . . . . . . . . . . . . . . . CLC 12
See also CA 9-12R; 101; CANR 7;
MAICYA; SATA 1, 48; SATA-Obit 23

**Krumwitz**
See Crumb, R(obert)

**Krutch, Joseph Wood** 1893-1970 . . . . CLC 24
See also CA 1-4R; 25-28R; CANR 4;
DLB 63

**Krutzch, Gus**
See Eliot, T(homas) S(tearns)

**Krylov, Ivan Andreevich**
1768(?)-1844 . . . . . . . . . . . . . . . NCLC 1
See also DLB 150

**Kubin, Alfred** 1877-1959 . . . . . . . . TCLC 23
See also CA 112; DLB 81

**Kubrick, Stanley** 1928- . . . . . . . . . . CLC 16
See also CA 81-84; CANR 33; DLB 26

**Kumin, Maxine (Winokur)**
1925- . . . . . . . . . . . . . . . . CLC 5, 13, 28
See also AITN 2; CA 1-4R; CAAS 8;
CANR 1, 21; DLB 5; MTCW; SATA 12

**Kundera, Milan**
1929- . . . . . . . . . . . CLC 4, 9, 19, 32, 68
See also AAYA 2; CA 85-88; CANR 19;
MTCW

**Kunene, Mazisi (Raymond)** 1930- . . . CLC 85
See also BW 1; CA 125; DLB 117

**Kunitz, Stanley (Jasspon)**
1905- . . . . . . . . . . . . . . . . CLC 6, 11, 14
See also CA 41-44R; CANR 26; DLB 48;
MTCW

**Kunze, Reiner** 1933- . . . . . . . . . . . . . CLC 10
See also CA 93-96; DLB 75

**Kuprin, Aleksandr Ivanovich**
1870-1938 . . . . . . . . . . . . . . . . . TCLC 5
See also CA 104

**Kureishi, Hanif** 1954(?)- . . . . . . . . . . CLC 64
See also CA 139

**Kurosawa, Akira** 1910- . . . . . . . . . . . CLC 16
See also AAYA 11; CA 101; CANR 46

**Kushner, Tony** 1957(?)- . . . . . . . . . . CLC 81
See also CA 144

**Kuttner, Henry** 1915-1958 . . . . . . . TCLC 10
See also CA 107; DLB 8

**Kuzma, Greg** 1944- . . . . . . . . . . . . . . CLC 7
See also CA 33-36R

**Kuzmin, Mikhail** 1872(?)-1936 . . . . TCLC 40

**Kyd, Thomas** 1558-1594 . . . . . . LC 22; DC 3
See also DLB 62

**Kyprianos, Iossif**
See Samarakis, Antonis

**La Bruyere, Jean de** 1645-1696 . . . . . . LC 17

**Lacan, Jacques (Marie Emile)**
1901-1981 . . . . . . . . . . . . . . . . . CLC 75
See also CA 121; 104

**Laclos, Pierre Ambroise Francois Choderlos
de** 1741-1803 . . . . . . . . . . . . . NCLC 4

**La Colere, Francois**
See Aragon, Louis

**Lacolere, Francois**
See Aragon, Louis

**La Deshabilleuse**
See Simenon, Georges (Jacques Christian)

**Lady Gregory**
See Gregory, Isabella Augusta (Persse)

**Lady of Quality, A**
See Bagnold, Enid

**La Fayette, Marie (Madelaine Pioche de la
Vergne Comtes** 1634-1693 . . . . . . LC 2

**Lafayette, Rene**
See Hubbard, L(afayette) Ron(ald)

**Laforgue, Jules**
1860-1887 . . . . . . . . . . NCLC 5; SSC 20

**Lagerkvist, Paer (Fabian)**
1891-1974 . . . . . . . . . . CLC 7, 10, 13, 54
See also Lagerkvist, Par
See also CA 85-88; 49-52; MTCW

**Lagerkvist, Par** . . . . . . . . . . . . . . . . . SSC 12
See also Lagerkvist, Paer (Fabian)

**Lagerloef, Selma (Ottiliana Lovisa)**
1858-1940 . . . . . . . . . . . . . TCLC 4, 36
See also Lagerlof, Selma (Ottiliana Lovisa)
See also CA 108; SATA 15

**Lagerlof, Selma (Ottiliana Lovisa)**
See Lagerloef, Selma (Ottiliana Lovisa)
See also CLR 7; SATA 15

**La Guma, (Justin) Alex(ander)**
1925-1985 . . . . . . . . . . . . . . . . . CLC 19
See also BW 1; CA 49-52; 118; CANR 25;
DLB 117; MTCW

**Laidlaw, A. K.**
See Grieve, C(hristopher) M(urray)

**Lainez, Manuel Mujica**
See Mujica Lainez, Manuel
See also HW

**Lamartine, Alphonse (Marie Louis Prat) de**
1790-1869 . . . . . . . . . . . . . . . . NCLC 11

**Lamb, Charles**
1775-1834 . . NCLC 10; DA; DAB; WLC
See also CDBLB 1789-1832; DLB 93, 107;
SATA 17

**Lamb, Lady Caroline** 1785-1828 . . NCLC 38
See also DLB 116

**Lamming, George (William)**
1927- . . . . . . . . . . . . . . CLC 2, 4, 66; BLC
See also BW 2; CA 85-88; CANR 26;
DLB 125; MTCW

**L'Amour, Louis (Dearborn)**
1908-1988 . . . . . . . . . . . . . . CLC 25, 55
See also AITN 2; BEST 89:2; CA 1-4R;
125; CANR 3, 25, 40; DLBY 80; MTCW

**Lampedusa, Giuseppe (Tomasi) di** . . . TCLC 13
See also Tomasi di Lampedusa, Giuseppe

**Lampman, Archibald** 1861-1899 . . NCLC 25
See also DLB 92

**Lancaster, Bruce** 1896-1963 . . . . . . . . CLC 36
See also CA 9-10; CAP 1; SATA 9

**Landau, Mark Alexandrovich**
See Aldanov, Mark (Alexandrovich)

**Landau-Aldanov, Mark Alexandrovich**
See Aldanov, Mark (Alexandrovich)

**Landis, John** 1950- . . . . . . . . . . . . . . CLC 26
See also CA 112; 122

**Landolfi, Tommaso** 1908-1979 . . . CLC 11, 49
See also CA 127; 117

**Landon, Letitia Elizabeth**
1802-1838 . . . . . . . . . . . . . . . . NCLC 15
See also DLB 96

**Landor, Walter Savage**
1775-1864 . . . . . . . . . . . . . . . . NCLC 14
See also DLB 93, 107

**Mirbeau, Octave** 1848-1917...... **TCLC 55**
See also DLB 123

**Miro (Ferrer), Gabriel (Francisco Victor)**
1879-1930 .................. **TCLC 5**
See also CA 104

**Mishima, Yukio**
....... **CLC 2, 4, 6, 9, 27; DC 1; SSC 4**
See also Hiraoka, Kimitake

**Mistral, Frederic** 1830-1914 ...... **TCLC 51**
See also CA 122

**Mistral, Gabriela**........... **TCLC 2; HLC**
See also Godoy Alcayaga, Lucila

**Mistry, Rohinton** 1952-........... **CLC 71**
See also CA 141

**Mitchell, Clyde**
See Ellison, Harlan (Jay); Silverberg, Robert

**Mitchell, James Leslie** 1901-1935
See Gibbon, Lewis Grassic
See also CA 104; DLB 15

**Mitchell, Joni** 1943-.............. **CLC 12**
See also CA 112

**Mitchell, Margaret (Munnerlyn)**
1900-1949 .................. **TCLC 11**
See also CA 109; 125; DLB 9; MTCW

**Mitchell, Peggy**
See Mitchell, Margaret (Munnerlyn)

**Mitchell, S(ilas) Weir** 1829-1914 .. **TCLC 36**

**Mitchell, W(illiam) O(rmond)**
1914-...................... **CLC 25**
See also CA 77-80; CANR 15, 43; DLB 88

**Mitford, Mary Russell** 1787-1855.. **NCLC 4**
See also DLB 110, 116

**Mitford, Nancy** 1904-1973........ **CLC 44**
See also CA 9-12R

**Miyamoto, Yuriko** 1899-1951 ..... **TCLC 37**

**Mo, Timothy (Peter)** 1950(?)-...... **CLC 46**
See also CA 117; MTCW

**Modarressi, Taghi (M.)** 1931-...... **CLC 44**
See also CA 121; 134

**Modiano, Patrick (Jean)** 1945-..... **CLC 18**
See also CA 85-88; CANR 17, 40; DLB 83

**Moerck, Paal**
See Roelvaag, O(le) E(dvart)

**Mofolo, Thomas (Mokopu)**
1875(?)-1948 ........... **TCLC 22; BLC**
See also CA 121

**Mohr, Nicholasa** 1935-...... **CLC 12; HLC**
See also AAYA 8; CA 49-52; CANR 1, 32;
CLR 22; DLB 145; HW; JRDA; SAAS 8;
SATA 8

**Mojtabai, A(nn) G(race)**
1938-............... **CLC 5, 9, 15, 29**
See also CA 85-88

**Moliere**
1622-1673 ..... **LC 28; DA; DAB; WLC**

**Molin, Charles**
See Mayne, William (James Carter)

**Molnar, Ferenc** 1878-1952........ **TCLC 20**
See also CA 109

**Momaday, N(avarre) Scott**
1934-........ **CLC 2, 19, 85; DA; DAB**
See also AAYA 11; CA 25-28R; CANR 14,
34; DLB 143; MTCW; NNAL; SATA 48;
SATA-Brief 30

**Monette, Paul** 1945-1995.......... **CLC 82**
See also CA 139; 147

**Monroe, Harriet** 1860-1936....... **TCLC 12**
See also CA 109; DLB 54, 91

**Monroe, Lyle**
See Heinlein, Robert A(nson)

**Montagu, Elizabeth** 1917-........ **NCLC 7**
See also CA 9-12R

**Montagu, Mary (Pierrepont) Wortley**
1689-1762 .................... **LC 9**
See also DLB 95, 101

**Montagu, W. H.**
See Coleridge, Samuel Taylor

**Montague, John (Patrick)**
1929-..................... **CLC 13, 46**
See also CA 9-12R; CANR 9; DLB 40;
MTCW

**Montaigne, Michel (Eyquem) de**
1533-1592 ..... **LC 8; DA; DAB; WLC**

**Montale, Eugenio**
1896-1981 ....... **CLC 7, 9, 18; PC 13**
See also CA 17-20R; 104; CANR 30;
DLB 114; MTCW

**Montesquieu, Charles-Louis de Secondat**
1689-1755 ..................... **LC 7**

**Montgomery, (Robert) Bruce** 1921-1978
See Crispin, Edmund
See also CA 104

**Montgomery, L(ucy) M(aud)**
1874-1942 ................... **TCLC 51**
See also AAYA 12; CA 108; 137; CLR 8;
DLB 92; JRDA; MAICYA; YABC 1

**Montgomery, Marion H., Jr.** 1925-.. **CLC 7**
See also AITN 1; CA 1-4R; CANR 3, 48;
DLB 6

**Montgomery, Max**
See Davenport, Guy (Mattison, Jr.)

**Montherlant, Henry (Milon) de**
1896-1972 ................. **CLC 8, 19**
See also CA 85-88; 37-40R; DLB 72;
MTCW

**Monty Python**
See Chapman, Graham; Cleese, John
(Marwood); Gilliam, Terry (Vance); Idle,
Eric; Jones, Terence Graham Parry; Palin,
Michael (Edward)
See also AAYA 7

**Moodie, Susanna (Strickland)**
1803-1885 ................. **NCLC 14**
See also DLB 99

**Mooney, Edward** 1951-
See Mooney, Ted
See also CA 130

**Mooney, Ted** .................... **CLC 25**
See also Mooney, Edward

**Moorcock, Michael (John)**
1939-................... **CLC 5, 27, 58**
See also CA 45-48; CAAS 5; CANR 2, 17,
38; DLB 14; MTCW

**Moore, Brian**
1921- ...... **CLC 1, 3, 5, 7, 8, 19, 32, 90;**
**DAB**
See also CA 1-4R; CANR 1, 25, 42; MTCW

**Moore, Edward**
See Muir, Edwin

**Moore, George Augustus**
1852-1933 .......... **TCLC 7; SSC 19**
See also CA 104; DLB 10, 18, 57, 135

**Moore, Lorrie** .............. **CLC 39, 45, 68**
See also Moore, Marie Lorena

**Moore, Marianne (Craig)**
1887-1972 .... **CLC 1, 2, 4, 8, 10, 13, 19,**
**47; DA; DAB; PC 4**
See also CA 1-4R; 33-36R; CANR 3;
CDALB 1929-1941; DLB 45; DLBD 7;
MTCW; SATA 20

**Moore, Marie Lorena** 1957-
See Moore, Lorrie
See also CA 116; CANR 39

**Moore, Thomas** 1779-1852....... **NCLC 6**
See also DLB 96, 144

**Morand, Paul** 1888-1976 ......... **CLC 41**
See also CA 69-72; DLB 65

**Morante, Elsa** 1918-1985........ **CLC 8, 47**
See also CA 85-88; 117; CANR 35; MTCW

**Moravia, Alberto**....... **CLC 2, 7, 11, 27, 46**
See also Pincherle, Alberto

**More, Hannah** 1745-1833 ....... **NCLC 27**
See also DLB 107, 109, 116

**More, Henry** 1614-1687............. **LC 9**
See also DLB 126

**More, Sir Thomas** 1478-1535 ....... **LC 10**

**Moreas, Jean**.................... **TCLC 18**
See also Papadiamantopoulos, Johannes

**Morgan, Berry** 1919-.............. **CLC 6**
See also CA 49-52; DLB 6

**Morgan, Claire**
See Highsmith, (Mary) Patricia

**Morgan, Edwin (George)** 1920-..... **CLC 31**
See also CA 5-8R; CANR 3, 43; DLB 27

**Morgan, (George) Frederick**
1922-..................... **CLC 23**
See also CA 17-20R; CANR 21

**Morgan, Harriet**
See Mencken, H(enry) L(ouis)

**Morgan, Jane**
See Cooper, James Fenimore

**Morgan, Janet** 1945- ............. **CLC 39**
See also CA 65-68

**Morgan, Lady** 1776(?)-1859...... **NCLC 29**
See also DLB 116

**Morgan, Robin** 1941-.............. **CLC 2**
See also CA 69-72; CANR 29; MTCW;
SATA 80

**Morgan, Scott**
See Kuttner, Henry

**Morgan, Seth** 1949(?)-1990 ........ **CLC 65**
See also CA 132

**Morgenstern, Christian**
1871-1914 ................... **TCLC 8**
See also CA 105

**Morgenstern, S.**
See Goldman, William (W.)

**Moricz, Zsigmond** 1879-1942 ..... **TCLC 33**

**Morike, Eduard (Friedrich)**
1804-1875 ................. **NCLC 10**
See also DLB 133

Orris
See Ingelow, Jean

Ortega y Gasset, Jose
    1883-1955 . . . . . . . . . . . . TCLC 9; HLC
    See also CA 106; 130; HW; MTCW

Ortese, Anna Maria   1914- . . . . . . . . CLC 89

Ortiz, Simon J(oseph)   1941- . . . . . . . CLC 45
    See also CA 134; DLB 120; NNAL

Orton, Joe . . . . . . . . . . . . CLC 4, 13, 43; DC 3
    See also Orton, John Kingsley
    See also CDBLB 1960 to Present; DLB 13

Orton, John Kingsley   1933-1967
    See Orton, Joe
    See also CA 85-88; CANR 35; MTCW

Orwell, George
    . . . . . TCLC 2, 6, 15, 31, 51; DAB; WLC
    See also Blair, Eric (Arthur)
    See also CDBLB 1945-1960; DLB 15, 98

Osborne, David
    See Silverberg, Robert

Osborne, George
    See Silverberg, Robert

Osborne, John (James)
    1929-1994 . . . . . CLC 1, 2, 5, 11, 45; DA;
                                                    DAB; WLC
    See also CA 13-16R; 147; CANR 21;
    CDBLB 1945-1960; DLB 13; MTCW

Osborne, Lawrence   1958- . . . . . . . . CLC 50

Oshima, Nagisa   1932- . . . . . . . . . . . CLC 20
    See also CA 116; 121

Oskison, John Milton
    1874-1947 . . . . . . . . . . . . . . . . TCLC 35
    See also CA 144; NNAL

Ossoli, Sarah Margaret (Fuller marchesa d')
    1810-1850
    See Fuller, Margaret
    See also SATA 25

Ostrovsky, Alexander
    1823-1886 . . . . . . . . . . . . . . . . NCLC 30

Otero, Blas de   1916-1979 . . . . . . . . . CLC 11
    See also CA 89-92; DLB 134

Otto, Whitney   1955- . . . . . . . . . . . . . CLC 70
    See also CA 140

Ouida . . . . . . . . . . . . . . . . . . . . . . TCLC 43
    See also De La Ramee, (Marie) Louise
    See also DLB 18, 156

Ousmane, Sembene   1923- . . . . CLC 66; BLC
    See also BW 1; CA 117; 125; MTCW

Ovid   43B.C.-18(?) . . . . . . . . . CMLC 7; PC 2

Owen, Hugh
    See Faust, Frederick (Schiller)

Owen, Wilfred (Edward Salter)
    1893-1918 . . . . . . TCLC 5, 27; DA; DAB;
                                                    WLC
    See also CA 104; 141; CDBLB 1914-1945;
    DLB 20

Owens, Rochelle   1936- . . . . . . . . . . . CLC 8
    See also CA 17-20R; CAAS 2; CANR 39

Oz, Amos   1939- . . . CLC 5, 8, 11, 27, 33, 54
    See also CA 53-56; CANR 27, 47; MTCW

Ozick, Cynthia
    1928- . . . . . . . . CLC 3, 7, 28, 62; SSC 15
    See also BEST 90:1; CA 17-20R; CANR 23;
    DLB 28, 152; DLBY 82; MTCW

Ozu, Yasujiro   1903-1963 . . . . . . . . . CLC 16
    See also CA 112

Pacheco, C.
    See Pessoa, Fernando (Antonio Nogueira)

Pa Chin . . . . . . . . . . . . . . . . . . . . . CLC 18
    See also Li Fei-kan

Pack, Robert   1929- . . . . . . . . . . . . . . CLC 13
    See also CA 1-4R; CANR 3, 44; DLB 5

Padgett, Lewis
    See Kuttner, Henry

Padilla (Lorenzo), Heberto   1932- . . . CLC 38
    See also AITN 1; CA 123; 131; HW

Page, Jimmy   1944- . . . . . . . . . . . . . . CLC 12

Page, Louise   1955- . . . . . . . . . . . . . . CLC 40
    See also CA 140

Page, P(atricia) K(athleen)
    1916- . . . . . . . . . . . . . CLC 7, 18; PC 12
    See also CA 53-56; CANR 4, 22; DLB 68;
    MTCW

Paget, Violet   1856-1935
    See Lee, Vernon
    See also CA 104

Paget-Lowe, Henry
    See Lovecraft, H(oward) P(hillips)

Paglia, Camille (Anna)   1947- . . . . . . . CLC 68
    See also CA 140

Paige, Richard
    See Koontz, Dean R(ay)

Pakenham, Antonia
    See Fraser, (Lady) Antonia (Pakenham)

Palamas, Kostes   1859-1943 . . . . . . . TCLC 5
    See also CA 105

Palazzeschi, Aldo   1885-1974 . . . . . . . CLC 11
    See also CA 89-92; 53-56; DLB 114

Paley, Grace   1922- . . . . CLC 4, 6, 37; SSC 8
    See also CA 25-28R; CANR 13, 46;
    DLB 28; MTCW

Palin, Michael (Edward)   1943- . . . . . CLC 21
    See also Monty Python
    See also CA 107; CANR 35; SATA 67

Palliser, Charles   1947- . . . . . . . . . . . CLC 65
    See also CA 136

Palma, Ricardo   1833-1919 . . . . . . . TCLC 29

Pancake, Breece Dexter   1952-1979
    See Pancake, Breece D'J
    See also CA 123; 109

Pancake, Breece D'J . . . . . . . . . . . . . CLC 29
    See also Pancake, Breece Dexter
    See also DLB 130

Panko, Rudy
    See Gogol, Nikolai (Vasilyevich)

Papadiamantis, Alexandros
    1851-1911 . . . . . . . . . . . . . . . . TCLC 29

Papadiamantopoulos, Johannes   1856-1910
    See Moreas, Jean
    See also CA 117

Papini, Giovanni   1881-1956 . . . . . . TCLC 22
    See also CA 121

Paracelsus   1493-1541 . . . . . . . . . . . . LC 14

Parasol, Peter
    See Stevens, Wallace

Parfenie, Maria
    See Codrescu, Andrei

Parini, Jay (Lee)   1948- . . . . . . . . . . . CLC 54
    See also CA 97-100; CAAS 16; CANR 32

Park, Jordan
    See Kornbluth, C(yril) M.; Pohl, Frederik

Parker, Bert
    See Ellison, Harlan (Jay)

Parker, Dorothy (Rothschild)
    1893-1967 . . . . . . . . CLC 15, 68; SSC 2
    See also CA 19-20; 25-28R; CAP 2;
    DLB 11, 45, 86; MTCW

Parker, Robert B(rown)   1932- . . . . . . CLC 27
    See also BEST 89:4; CA 49-52; CANR 1,
    26; MTCW

Parkin, Frank   1940- . . . . . . . . . . . . . CLC 43
    See also CA 147

Parkman, Francis, Jr.
    1823-1893 . . . . . . . . . . . . . . . NCLC 12
    See also DLB 1, 30

Parks, Gordon (Alexander Buchanan)
    1912- . . . . . . . . . . . . . . . CLC 1, 16; BLC
    See also AITN 2; BW 2; CA 41-44R;
    CANR 26; DLB 33; SATA 8

Parnell, Thomas   1679-1718 . . . . . . . . . LC 3
    See also DLB 94

Parra, Nicanor   1914- . . . . . . . . CLC 2; HLC
    See also CA 85-88; CANR 32; HW; MTCW

Parrish, Mary Frances
    See Fisher, M(ary) F(rances) K(ennedy)

Parson
    See Coleridge, Samuel Taylor

Parson Lot
    See Kingsley, Charles

Partridge, Anthony
    See Oppenheim, E(dward) Phillips

Pascoli, Giovanni   1855-1912 . . . . . . TCLC 45

Pasolini, Pier Paolo
    1922-1975 . . . . . . . . . . . . . CLC 20, 37
    See also CA 93-96; 61-64; DLB 128;
    MTCW

Pasquini
    See Silone, Ignazio

Pastan, Linda (Olenik)   1932- . . . . . . CLC 27
    See also CA 61-64; CANR 18, 40; DLB 5

Pasternak, Boris (Leonidovich)
    1890-1960 . . . . . . CLC 7, 10, 18, 63; DA;
                                                    DAB; PC 6; WLC
    See also CA 127; 116; MTCW

Patchen, Kenneth   1911-1972 . . . CLC 1, 2, 18
    See also CA 1-4R; 33-36R; CANR 3, 35;
    DLB 16, 48; MTCW

Pater, Walter (Horatio)
    1839-1894 . . . . . . . . . . . . . . . . NCLC 7
    See also CDBLB 1832-1890; DLB 57, 156

Paterson, A(ndrew) B(arton)
    1864-1941 . . . . . . . . . . . . . . . TCLC 32

Paterson, Katherine (Womeldorf)
    1932- . . . . . . . . . . . . . . . . CLC 12, 30
    See also AAYA 1; CA 21-24R; CANR 28;
    CLR 7; DLB 52; JRDA; MAICYA;
    MTCW; SATA 13, 53

Patmore, Coventry Kersey Dighton
    1823-1896 . . . . . . . . . . . . . . . . NCLC 9
    See also DLB 35, 98

**Paton, Alan (Stewart)**
1903-1988 . . . . . . **CLC 4, 10, 25, 55; DA;
DAB; WLC**
See also CA 13-16; 125; CANR 22; CAP 1;
MTCW; SATA 11; SATA-Obit 56

**Paton Walsh, Gillian** 1937-
See Walsh, Jill Paton
See also CANR 38; JRDA; MAICYA;
SAAS 3; SATA 4, 72

**Paulding, James Kirke** 1778-1860. . **NCLC 2**
See also DLB 3, 59, 74

**Paulin, Thomas Neilson** 1949-
See Paulin, Tom
See also CA 123; 128

**Paulin, Tom** . . . . . . . . . . . . . . . . . . . . **CLC 37**
See also Paulin, Thomas Neilson
See also DLB 40

**Paustovsky, Konstantin (Georgievich)**
1892-1968 . . . . . . . . . . . . . . . . . . **CLC 40**
See also CA 93-96; 25-28R

**Pavese, Cesare**
1908-1950 . . . . . **TCLC 3; PC 13; SSC 19**
See also CA 104; DLB 128

**Pavic, Milorad** 1929- . . . . . . . . . . . . **CLC 60**
See also CA 136

**Payne, Alan**
See Jakes, John (William)

**Paz, Gil**
See Lugones, Leopoldo

**Paz, Octavio**
1914- . . . . . . . **CLC 3, 4, 6, 10, 19, 51, 65;
DA; DAB; HLC; PC 1; WLC**
See also CA 73-76; CANR 32; DLBY 90;
HW; MTCW

**Peacock, Molly** 1947- . . . . . . . . . . . . . **CLC 60**
See also CA 103; CAAS 21; DLB 120

**Peacock, Thomas Love**
1785-1866 . . . . . . . . . . . . . . . . . **NCLC 22**
See also DLB 96, 116

**Peake, Mervyn** 1911-1968 . . . . . . . **CLC 7, 54**
See also CA 5-8R; 25-28R; CANR 3;
DLB 15; MTCW; SATA 23

**Pearce, Philippa** . . . . . . . . . . . . . . . . **CLC 21**
See also Christie, (Ann) Philippa
See also CLR 9; MAICYA; SATA 1, 67

**Pearl, Eric**
See Elman, Richard

**Pearson, T(homas) R(eid)** 1956- . . . . **CLC 39**
See also CA 120; 130

**Peck, Dale** 1967- . . . . . . . . . . . . . . . **CLC 81**
See also CA 146

**Peck, John** 1941- . . . . . . . . . . . . . . . . **CLC 3**
See also CA 49-52; CANR 3

**Peck, Richard (Wayne)** 1934- . . . . . . **CLC 21**
See also AAYA 1; CA 85-88; CANR 19,
38; CLR 15; JRDA; MAICYA; SAAS 2;
SATA 18, 55

**Peck, Robert Newton** 1928- . . . . **CLC 17; DA**
See also AAYA 3; CA 81-84; CANR 31;
JRDA; MAICYA; SAAS 1; SATA 21, 62

**Peckinpah, (David) Sam(uel)**
1925-1984 . . . . . . . . . . . . . . . . . . **CLC 20**
See also CA 109; 114

**Pedersen, Knut** 1859-1952
See Hamsun, Knut
See also CA 104; 119; MTCW

**Peeslake, Gaffer**
See Durrell, Lawrence (George)

**Peguy, Charles Pierre**
1873-1914 . . . . . . . . . . . . . . . . . **TCLC 10**
See also CA 107

**Pena, Ramon del Valle y**
See Valle-Inclan, Ramon (Maria) del

**Pendennis, Arthur Esquir**
See Thackeray, William Makepeace

**Penn, William** 1644-1718 . . . . . . . . . . **LC 25**
See also DLB 24

**Pepys, Samuel**
1633-1703 . . . . . **LC 11; DA; DAB; WLC**
See also CDBLB 1660-1789; DLB 101

**Percy, Walker**
1916-1990 . . . . **CLC 2, 3, 6, 8, 14, 18, 47,
65**
See also CA 1-4R; 131; CANR 1, 23;
DLB 2; DLBY 80, 90; MTCW

**Perec, Georges** 1936-1982 . . . . . . . . **CLC 56**
See also CA 141; DLB 83

**Pereda (y Sanchez de Porrua), Jose Maria de**
1833-1906 . . . . . . . . . . . . . . . . . **TCLC 16**
See also CA 117

**Pereda y Porrua, Jose Maria de**
See Pereda (y Sanchez de Porrua), Jose
Maria de

**Peregoy, George Weems**
See Mencken, H(enry) L(ouis)

**Perelman, S(idney) J(oseph)**
1904-1979 . . . **CLC 3, 5, 9, 15, 23, 44, 49**
See also AITN 1, 2; CA 73-76; 89-92;
CANR 18; DLB 11, 44; MTCW

**Peret, Benjamin** 1899-1959 . . . . . . . **TCLC 20**
See also CA 117

**Peretz, Isaac Loeb** 1851(?)-1915 . . . **TCLC 16**
See also CA 109

**Peretz, Yitzkhok Leibush**
See Peretz, Isaac Loeb

**Perez Galdos, Benito** 1843-1920 . . . **TCLC 27**
See also CA 125; HW

**Perrault, Charles** 1628-1703 . . . . . . . . . **LC 2**
See also MAICYA; SATA 25

**Perry, Brighton**
See Sherwood, Robert E(mmet)

**Perse, St.-John** . . . . . . . . . . . . . **CLC 4, 11, 46**
See also Leger, (Marie-Rene Auguste) Alexis
Saint-Leger

**Perutz, Leo** 1882-1957 . . . . . . . . . . . **TCLC 60**
See also DLB 81

**Peseenz, Tulio F.**
See Lopez y Fuentes, Gregorio

**Pesetsky, Bette** 1932- . . . . . . . . . . . . **CLC 28**
See also CA 133; DLB 130

**Peshkov, Alexei Maximovich** 1868-1936
See Gorky, Maxim
See also CA 105; 141; DA

**Pessoa, Fernando (Antonio Nogueira)**
1888-1935 . . . . . . . . . . . . **TCLC 27; HLC**
See also CA 125

**Peterkin, Julia Mood** 1880-1961. . . . **CLC 31**
See also CA 102; DLB 9

**Peters, Joan K.** 1945- . . . . . . . . . . . . . **CLC 39**

**Peters, Robert L(ouis)** 1924- . . . . . . . . **CLC 7**
See also CA 13-16R; CAAS 8; DLB 105

**Petofi, Sandor** 1823-1849 . . . . . . . . **NCLC 21**

**Petrakis, Harry Mark** 1923- . . . . . . . . **CLC 3**
See also CA 9-12R; CANR 4, 30

**Petrarch** 1304-1374. . . . . . . . . . . . . . . . . **PC 8**

**Petrov, Evgeny** . . . . . . . . . . . . . . . . **TCLC 21**
See also Kataev, Evgeny Petrovich

**Petry, Ann (Lane)** 1908- . . . . . . **CLC 1, 7, 18**
See also BW 1; CA 5-8R; CAAS 6;
CANR 4, 46; CLR 12; DLB 76; JRDA;
MAICYA; MTCW; SATA 5

**Petursson, Halligrimur** 1614-1674 . . . . **LC 8**

**Philips, Katherine** 1632-1664. . . . . . . **LC 30**
See also DLB 131

**Philipson, Morris H.** 1926- . . . . . . . . **CLC 53**
See also CA 1-4R; CANR 4

**Phillips, David Graham**
1867-1911 . . . . . . . . . . . . . . . . . **TCLC 44**
See also CA 108; DLB 9, 12

**Phillips, Jack**
See Sandburg, Carl (August)

**Phillips, Jayne Anne**
1952- . . . . . . . . . . . . **CLC 15, 33; SSC 16**
See also CA 101; CANR 24; DLBY 80;
MTCW

**Phillips, Richard**
See Dick, Philip K(indred)

**Phillips, Robert (Schaeffer)** 1938-. . . **CLC 28**
See also CA 17-20R; CAAS 13; CANR 8;
DLB 105

**Phillips, Ward**
See Lovecraft, H(oward) P(hillips)

**Piccolo, Lucio** 1901-1969. . . . . . . . . . **CLC 13**
See also CA 97-100; DLB 114

**Pickthall, Marjorie L(owry) C(hristie)**
1883-1922 . . . . . . . . . . . . . . . . . **TCLC 21**
See also CA 107; DLB 92

**Pico della Mirandola, Giovanni**
1463-1494 . . . . . . . . . . . . . . . . . . **LC 15**

**Piercy, Marge**
1936- . . . . . . . . . **CLC 3, 6, 14, 18, 27, 62**
See also CA 21-24R; CAAS 1; CANR 13,
43; DLB 120; MTCW

**Piers, Robert**
See Anthony, Piers

**Pieyre de Mandiargues, Andre** 1909-1991
See Mandiargues, Andre Pieyre de
See also CA 103; 136; CANR 22

**Pilnyak, Boris** . . . . . . . . . . . . . . . . . **TCLC 23**
See also Vogau, Boris Andreyevich

**Pincherle, Alberto** 1907-1990 . . . **CLC 11, 18**
See also Moravia, Alberto
See also CA 25-28R; 132; CANR 33;
MTCW

**Pinckney, Darryl** 1953- . . . . . . . . . . . **CLC 76**
See also BW 2; CA 143

**Pindar** 518B.C.-446B.C. . . . . . . . . . **CMLC 12**

**Pineda, Cecile** 1942- . . . . . . . . . . . . . **CLC 39**
See also CA 118

Rice, Anne 1941- . . . . . . . . . . . . . . CLC 41
  See also AAYA 9; BEST 89:2; CA 65-68;
    CANR 12, 36

Rice, Elmer (Leopold)
    1892-1967 . . . . . . . . . . . . . . . . . CLC 7, 49
  See also CA 21-22; 25-28R; CAP 2; DLB 4,
    7; MTCW

Rice, Tim(othy Miles Bindon)
    1944- . . . . . . . . . . . . . . . . . . . . . . CLC 21
  See also CA 103; CANR 46

Rich, Adrienne (Cecile)
    1929- . . . . CLC 3, 6, 7, 11, 18, 36, 73, 76;
                                PC 5
  See also CA 9-12R; CANR 20; DLB 5, 67;
    MTCW

Rich, Barbara
  See Graves, Robert (von Ranke)

Rich, Robert
  See Trumbo, Dalton

Richard, Keith. . . . . . . . . . . . . . . . . . . CLC 17
  See also Richards, Keith

Richards, David Adams 1950- . . . . . . CLC 59
  See also CA 93-96; DLB 53

Richards, I(vor) A(rmstrong)
    1893-1979 . . . . . . . . . . . . . . . CLC 14, 24
  See also CA 41-44R; 89-92; CANR 34;
    DLB 27

Richards, Keith 1943-
  See Richard, Keith
  See also CA 107

Richardson, Anne
  See Roiphe, Anne (Richardson)

Richardson, Dorothy Miller
    1873-1957 . . . . . . . . . . . . . . . . . . TCLC 3
  See also CA 104; DLB 36

Richardson, Ethel Florence (Lindesay)
    1870-1946
  See Richardson, Henry Handel
  See also CA 105

Richardson, Henry Handel. . . . . . . . . TCLC 4
  See also Richardson, Ethel Florence
    (Lindesay)

Richardson, Samuel
    1689-1761 . . . . . . LC 1; DA; DAB; WLC
  See also CDBLB 1660-1789; DLB 39

Richler, Mordecai
    1931- . . . . . . . CLC 3, 5, 9, 13, 18, 46, 70
  See also AITN 1; CA 65-68; CANR 31;
    CLR 17; DLB 53; MAICYA; MTCW;
    SATA 44; SATA-Brief 27

Richter, Conrad (Michael)
    1890-1968 . . . . . . . . . . . . . . . . . . CLC 30
  See also CA 5-8R; 25-28R; CANR 23;
    DLB 9; MTCW; SATA 3

Ricostranza, Tom
  See Ellis, Trey

Riddell, J. H. 1832-1906 . . . . . . . . TCLC 40

Riding, Laura. . . . . . . . . . . . . . . . . . . CLC 3, 7
  See also Jackson, Laura (Riding)

Riefenstahl, Berta Helene Amalia 1902-
  See Riefenstahl, Leni
  See also CA 108

Riefenstahl, Leni. . . . . . . . . . . . . . . . CLC 16
  See also Riefenstahl, Berta Helene Amalia

Riffe, Ernest
  See Bergman, (Ernst) Ingmar

Riggs, (Rolla) Lynn 1899-1954 . . . . TCLC 56
  See also CA 144; NNAL

Riley, James Whitcomb
    1849-1916 . . . . . . . . . . . . . . . . . TCLC 51
  See also CA 118; 137; MAICYA; SATA 17

Riley, Tex
  See Creasey, John

Rilke, Rainer Maria
    1875-1926 . . . . . . . . TCLC 1, 6, 19; PC 2
  See also CA 104; 132; DLB 81; MTCW

Rimbaud, (Jean Nicolas) Arthur
    1854-1891 . . . . . NCLC 4, 35; DA; DAB;
                            PC 3; WLC

Rinehart, Mary Roberts
    1876-1958 . . . . . . . . . . . . . . . . . TCLC 52
  See also CA 108

Ringmaster, The
  See Mencken, H(enry) L(ouis)

Ringwood, Gwen(dolyn Margaret) Pharis
    1910-1984 . . . . . . . . . . . . . . . . . . CLC 48
  See also CA 148; 112; DLB 88

Rio, Michel 19(?)- . . . . . . . . . . . . . . . CLC 43

Ritsos, Giannes
  See Ritsos, Yannis

Ritsos, Yannis 1909-1990. . . . . CLC 6, 13, 31
  See also CA 77-80; 133; CANR 39; MTCW

Ritter, Erika 1948(?)- . . . . . . . . . . . . CLC 52

Rivera, Jose Eustasio 1889-1928. . . TCLC 35
  See also HW

Rivers, Conrad Kent 1933-1968. . . . . . CLC 1
  See also BW 1; CA 85-88; DLB 41

Rivers, Elfrida
  See Bradley, Marion Zimmer

Riverside, John
  See Heinlein, Robert A(nson)

Rizal, Jose 1861-1896. . . . . . . . . . NCLC 27

Roa Bastos, Augusto (Antonio)
    1917- . . . . . . . . . . . . . . . . CLC 45; HLC
  See also CA 131; DLB 113; HW

Robbe-Grillet, Alain
    1922- . . . . . . CLC 1, 2, 4, 6, 8, 10, 14, 43
  See also CA 9-12R; CANR 33; DLB 83;
    MTCW

Robbins, Harold 1916- . . . . . . . . . . . . CLC 5
  See also CA 73-76; CANR 26; MTCW

Robbins, Thomas Eugene 1936-
  See Robbins, Tom
  See also CA 81-84; CANR 29; MTCW

Robbins, Tom. . . . . . . . . . . . . . CLC 9, 32, 64
  See also Robbins, Thomas Eugene
  See also BEST 90:3; DLBY 80

Robbins, Trina 1938- . . . . . . . . . . . . . CLC 21
  See also CA 128

Roberts, Charles G(eorge) D(ouglas)
    1860-1943 . . . . . . . . . . . . . . . . . . TCLC 8
  See also CA 105; CLR 33; DLB 92;
    SATA-Brief 29

Roberts, Kate 1891-1985 . . . . . . . . . CLC 15
  See also CA 107; 116

Roberts, Keith (John Kingston)
    1935- . . . . . . . . . . . . . . . . . . . . . CLC 14
  See also CA 25-28R; CANR 46

Roberts, Kenneth (Lewis)
    1885-1957 . . . . . . . . . . . . . . . . . TCLC 23
  See also CA 109; DLB 9

Roberts, Michele (B.) 1949- . . . . . . . CLC 48
  See also CA 115

Robertson, Ellis
  See Ellison, Harlan (Jay); Silverberg, Robert

Robertson, Thomas William
    1829-1871 . . . . . . . . . . . . . . . . . NCLC 35

Robinson, Edwin Arlington
    1869-1935 . . . . . . . . . TCLC 5; DA; PC 1
  See also CA 104; 133; CDALB 1865-1917;
    DLB 54; MTCW

Robinson, Henry Crabb
    1775-1867 . . . . . . . . . . . . . . . . . NCLC 15
  See also DLB 107

Robinson, Jill 1936- . . . . . . . . . . . . . . CLC 10
  See also CA 102

Robinson, Kim Stanley 1952- . . . . . . CLC 34
  See also CA 126

Robinson, Lloyd
  See Silverberg, Robert

Robinson, Marilynne 1944- . . . . . . . . CLC 25
  See also CA 116

Robinson, Smokey. . . . . . . . . . . . . . . . CLC 21
  See also Robinson, William, Jr.

Robinson, William, Jr. 1940-
  See Robinson, Smokey
  See also CA 116

Robison, Mary 1949- . . . . . . . . . . . . . CLC 42
  See also CA 113; 116; DLB 130

Rod, Edouard 1857-1910 . . . . . . . . TCLC 52

Roddenberry, Eugene Wesley 1921-1991
  See Roddenberry, Gene
  See also CA 110; 135; CANR 37; SATA 45;
    SATA-Obit 69

Roddenberry, Gene . . . . . . . . . . . . . . . CLC 17
  See also Roddenberry, Eugene Wesley
  See also AAYA 5; SATA-Obit 69

Rodgers, Mary 1931- . . . . . . . . . . . . . CLC 12
  See also CA 49-52; CANR 8; CLR 20;
    JRDA; MAICYA; SATA 8

Rodgers, W(illiam) R(obert)
    1909-1969 . . . . . . . . . . . . . . . . . . . CLC 7
  See also CA 85-88; DLB 20

Rodman, Eric
  See Silverberg, Robert

Rodman, Howard 1920(?)-1985 . . . . . CLC 65
  See also CA 118

Rodman, Maia
  See Wojciechowska, Maia (Teresa)

Rodriguez, Claudio 1934- . . . . . . . . . . CLC 10
  See also DLB 134

Roelvaag, O(le) E(dvart)
    1876-1931 . . . . . . . . . . . . . . . . . TCLC 17
  See also CA 117; DLB 9

Roethke, Theodore (Huebner)
    1908-1963 . . . . . . CLC 1, 3, 8, 11, 19, 46
  See also CA 81-84; CABS 2;
    CDALB 1941-1968; DLB 5; MTCW

Rogers, Thomas Hunton 1927- . . . . . CLC 57
  See also CA 89-92

Rogers, Will(iam Penn Adair)
    1879-1935 .................. TCLC 8
    See also CA 105; 144; DLB 11; NNAL

Rogin, Gilbert 1929- .............. CLC 18
    See also CA 65-68; CANR 15

Rohan, Koda ................... TCLC 22
    See also Koda Shigeyuki

Rohmer, Eric ..................... CLC 16
    See also Scherer, Jean-Marie Maurice

Rohmer, Sax ................... TCLC 28
    See also Ward, Arthur Henry Sarsfield
    See also DLB 70

Roiphe, Anne (Richardson)
    1935- ..................... CLC 3, 9
    See also CA 89-92; CANR 45; DLBY 80

Rojas, Fernando de 1465-1541 ...... LC 23

Rolfe, Frederick (William Serafino Austin
    Lewis Mary) 1860-1913 ...... TCLC 12
    See also CA 107; DLB 34, 156

Rolland, Romain 1866-1944 ....... TCLC 23
    See also CA 118; DLB 65

Rolvaag, O(le) E(dvart)
    See Roelvaag, O(le) E(dvart)

Romain Arnaud, Saint
    See Aragon, Louis

Romains, Jules 1885-1972 ......... CLC 7
    See also CA 85-88; CANR 34; DLB 65;
    MTCW

Romero, Jose Ruben 1890-1952 ... TCLC 14
    See also CA 114; 131; HW

Ronsard, Pierre de
    1524-1585 .............. LC 6; PC 11

Rooke, Leon 1934- ........... CLC 25, 34
    See also CA 25-28R; CANR 23

Roper, William 1498-1578 ......... LC 10

Roquelaure, A. N.
    See Rice, Anne

Rosa, Joao Guimaraes 1908-1967 ... CLC 23
    See also CA 89-92; DLB 113

Rose, Wendy 1948- ......... CLC 85; PC 13
    See also CA 53-56; CANR 5; NNAL;
    SATA 12

Rosen, Richard (Dean) 1949- ...... CLC 39
    See also CA 77-80

Rosenberg, Isaac 1890-1918 ....... TCLC 12
    See also CA 107; DLB 20

Rosenblatt, Joe ................... CLC 15
    See also Rosenblatt, Joseph

Rosenblatt, Joseph 1933-
    See Rosenblatt, Joe
    See also CA 89-92

Rosenfeld, Samuel 1896-1963
    See Tzara, Tristan
    See also CA 89-92

Rosenthal, M(acha) L(ouis) 1917- ... CLC 28
    See also CA 1-4R; CAAS 6; CANR 4;
    DLB 5; SATA 59

Ross, Barnaby
    See Dannay, Frederic

Ross, Bernard L.
    See Follett, Ken(neth Martin)

Ross, J. H.
    See Lawrence, T(homas) E(dward)

Ross, Martin
    See Martin, Violet Florence
    See also DLB 135

Ross, (James) Sinclair 1908- ....... CLC 13
    See also CA 73-76; DLB 88

Rossetti, Christina (Georgina)
    1830-1894 ..... NCLC 2, 50; DA; DAB;
                          PC 7; WLC
    See also DLB 35; MAICYA; SATA 20

Rossetti, Dante Gabriel
    1828-1882 ... NCLC 4; DA; DAB; WLC
    See also CDBLB 1832-1890; DLB 35

Rossner, Judith (Perelman)
    1935- ................... CLC 6, 9, 29
    See also AITN 2; BEST 90:3; CA 17-20R;
    CANR 18; DLB 6; MTCW

Rostand, Edmond (Eugene Alexis)
    1868-1918 ...... TCLC 6, 37; DA; DAB
    See also CA 104; 126; MTCW

Roth, Henry 1906- ........... CLC 2, 6, 11
    See also CA 11-12; CANR 38; CAP 1;
    DLB 28; MTCW

Roth, Joseph 1894-1939 ......... TCLC 33
    See also DLB 85

Roth, Philip (Milton)
    1933- ...... CLC 1, 2, 3, 4, 6, 9, 15, 22,
                  31, 47, 66, 86; DA; DAB; WLC
    See also BEST 90:3; CA 1-4R; CANR 1, 22,
    36; CDALB 1968-1988; DLB 2, 28;
    DLBY 82; MTCW

Rothenberg, Jerome 1931- ....... CLC 6, 57
    See also CA 45-48; CANR 1; DLB 5

Roumain, Jacques (Jean Baptiste)
    1907-1944 ............... TCLC 19; BLC
    See also BW 1; CA 117; 125

Rourke, Constance (Mayfield)
    1885-1941 ................ TCLC 12
    See also CA 107; YABC 1

Rousseau, Jean-Baptiste 1671-1741 ... LC 9

Rousseau, Jean-Jacques
    1712-1778 ..... LC 14; DA; DAB; WLC

Roussel, Raymond 1877-1933 ..... TCLC 20
    See also CA 117

Rovit, Earl (Herbert) 1927- ......... CLC 7
    See also CA 5-8R; CANR 12

Rowe, Nicholas 1674-1718 .......... LC 8
    See also DLB 84

Rowley, Ames Dorrance
    See Lovecraft, H(oward) P(hillips)

Rowson, Susanna Haswell
    1762(?)-1824 ............... NCLC 5
    See also DLB 37

Roy, Gabrielle
    1909-1983 ......... CLC 10, 14; DAB
    See also CA 53-56; 110; CANR 5; DLB 68;
    MTCW

Rozewicz, Tadeusz 1921- ....... CLC 9, 23
    See also CA 108; CANR 36; MTCW

Ruark, Gibbons 1941- ............. CLC 3
    See also CA 33-36R; CANR 14, 31;
    DLB 120

Rubens, Bernice (Ruth) 1923- ... CLC 19, 31
    See also CA 25-28R; CANR 33; DLB 14;
    MTCW

Rudkin, (James) David 1936- ...... CLC 14
    See also CA 89-92; DLB 13

Rudnik, Raphael 1933- ............ CLC 7
    See also CA 29-32R

Ruffian, M.
    See Hasek, Jaroslav (Matej Frantisek)

Ruiz, Jose Martinez .............. CLC 11
    See also Martinez Ruiz, Jose

Rukeyser, Muriel
    1913-1980 .... CLC 6, 10, 15, 27; PC 12
    See also CA 5-8R; 93-96; CANR 26;
    DLB 48; MTCW; SATA-Obit 22

Rule, Jane (Vance) 1931- .......... CLC 27
    See also CA 25-28R; CAAS 18; CANR 12;
    DLB 60

Rulfo, Juan 1918-1986 .... CLC 8, 80; HLC
    See also CA 85-88; 118; CANR 26;
    DLB 113; HW; MTCW

Runeberg, Johan 1804-1877 ...... NCLC 41

Runyon, (Alfred) Damon
    1884(?)-1946 ............... TCLC 10
    See also CA 107; DLB 11, 86

Rush, Norman 1933- ............. CLC 44
    See also CA 121; 126

Rushdie, (Ahmed) Salman
    1947- .......... CLC 23, 31, 55; DAB
    See also BEST 89:3; CA 108; 111;
    CANR 33; MTCW

Rushforth, Peter (Scott) 1945- ..... CLC 19
    See also CA 101

Ruskin, John 1819-1900 ......... TCLC 20
    See also CA 114; 129; CDBLB 1832-1890;
    DLB 55; SATA 24

Russ, Joanna 1937- .............. CLC 15
    See also CA 25-28R; CANR 11, 31; DLB 8;
    MTCW

Russell, George William 1867-1935
    See A. E.
    See also CA 104; CDBLB 1890-1914

Russell, (Henry) Ken(neth Alfred)
    1927- ................... CLC 16
    See also CA 105

Russell, Willy 1947- .............. CLC 60

Rutherford, Mark ............... TCLC 25
    See also White, William Hale
    See also DLB 18

Ruyslinck, Ward 1929- ............ CLC 14
    See also Belser, Reimond Karel Maria de

Ryan, Cornelius (John) 1920-1974 ... CLC 7
    See also CA 69-72; 53-56; CANR 38

Ryan, Michael 1946- ............. CLC 65
    See also CA 49-52; DLBY 82

Rybakov, Anatoli (Naumovich)
    1911- ................... CLC 23, 53
    See also CA 126; 135; SATA 79

Ryder, Jonathan
    See Ludlum, Robert

Ryga, George 1932-1987 .......... CLC 14
    See also CA 101; 124; CANR 43; DLB 60

S. S.
    See Sassoon, Siegfried (Lorraine)

Saba, Umberto 1883-1957 ........ TCLC 33
    See also CA 144; DLB 114

Sabatini, Rafael 1875-1950 ....... TCLC 47

Sabato, Ernesto (R.)
1911- . . . . . . . . . . . . . CLC 10, 23; HLC
See also CA 97-100; CANR 32; DLB 145;
HW; MTCW

Sacastru, Martin
See Bioy Casares, Adolfo

Sacher-Masoch, Leopold von
1836(?)-1895 . . . . . . . . . . . . . NCLC 31

Sachs, Marilyn (Stickle) 1927- . . . . . CLC 35
See also AAYA 2; CA 17-20R; CANR 13,
47; CLR 2; JRDA; MAICYA; SAAS 2;
SATA 3, 68

Sachs, Nelly 1891-1970 . . . . . . . . . . . CLC 14
See also CA 17-18; 25-28R; CAP 2

Sackler, Howard (Oliver)
1929-1982 . . . . . . . . . . . . . . . . . CLC 14
See also CA 61-64; 108; CANR 30; DLB 7

Sacks, Oliver (Wolf) 1933- . . . . . . . . CLC 67
See also CA 53-56; CANR 28; MTCW

Sade, Donatien Alphonse Francois Comte
1740-1814 . . . . . . . . . . . . . . . . NCLC 47

Sadoff, Ira 1945- . . . . . . . . . . . . . . . . CLC 9
See also CA 53-56; CANR 5, 21; DLB 120

Saetone
See Camus, Albert

Safire, William 1929- . . . . . . . . . . . . CLC 10
See also CA 17-20R; CANR 31

Sagan, Carl (Edward) 1934- . . . . . . . CLC 30
See also AAYA 2; CA 25-28R; CANR 11,
36; MTCW; SATA 58

Sagan, Francoise . . . . . . . CLC 3, 6, 9, 17, 36
See also Quoirez, Francoise
See also DLB 83

Sahgal, Nayantara (Pandit) 1927- . . . CLC 41
See also CA 9-12R; CANR 11

Saint, H(arry) F. 1941- . . . . . . . . . . CLC 50
See also CA 127

St. Aubin de Teran, Lisa 1953-
See Teran, Lisa St. Aubin de
See also CA 118; 126

Sainte-Beuve, Charles Augustin
1804-1869 . . . . . . . . . . . . . . . . . NCLC 5

Saint-Exupery, Antoine (Jean Baptiste Marie
Roger) de
1900-1944 . . . . . . . . . TCLC 2, 56; WLC
See also CA 108; 132; CLR 10; DLB 72;
MAICYA; MTCW; SATA 20

St. John, David
See Hunt, E(verette) Howard, (Jr.)

Saint-John Perse
See Leger, (Marie-Rene Auguste) Alexis
Saint-Leger

Saintsbury, George (Edward Bateman)
1845-1933 . . . . . . . . . . . . . . . . TCLC 31
See also DLB 57, 149

Sait Faik . . . . . . . . . . . . . . . . . . . TCLC 23
See also Abasiyanik, Sait Faik

Saki . . . . . . . . . . . . . . . . . TCLC 3; SSC 12
See also Munro, H(ector) H(ugh)

Sala, George Augustus . . . . . . . . . . NCLC 46

Salama, Hannu 1936- . . . . . . . . . . . . CLC 18

Salamanca, J(ack) R(ichard)
1922- . . . . . . . . . . . . . . . . . CLC 4, 15
See also CA 25-28R

Sale, J. Kirkpatrick
See Sale, Kirkpatrick

Sale, Kirkpatrick 1937- . . . . . . . . . . CLC 68
See also CA 13-16R; CANR 10

Salinas, Luis Omar 1937- . . . CLC 90; HLC
See also CA 131; DLB 82; HW

Salinas (y Serrano), Pedro
1891(?)-1951 . . . . . . . . . . . . . . TCLC 17
See also CA 117; DLB 134

Salinger, J(erome) D(avid)
1919- . . . . . . CLC 1, 3, 8, 12, 55, 56; DA;
DAB; SSC 2; WLC
See also AAYA 2; CA 5-8R; CANR 39;
CDALB 1941-1968; CLR 18; DLB 2, 102;
MAICYA; MTCW; SATA 67

Salisbury, John
See Caute, David

Salter, James 1925- . . . . . . . . . CLC 7, 52, 59
See also CA 73-76; DLB 130

Saltus, Edgar (Everton)
1855-1921 . . . . . . . . . . . . . . . . . TCLC 8
See also CA 105

Saltykov, Mikhail Evgrafovich
1826-1889 . . . . . . . . . . . . . . . . NCLC 16

Samarakis, Antonis 1919- . . . . . . . . . . CLC 5
See also CA 25-28R; CAAS 16; CANR 36

Sanchez, Florencio 1875-1910 . . . . . TCLC 37
See also HW

Sanchez, Luis Rafael 1936- . . . . . . . . CLC 23
See also CA 128; DLB 145; HW

Sanchez, Sonia 1934- . . . CLC 5; BLC; PC 9
See also BW 2; CA 33-36R; CANR 24, 49;
CLR 18; DLB 41; DLBD 8; MAICYA;
MTCW; SATA 22

Sand, George
1804-1876 . . . . . NCLC 2, 42; DA; DAB;
WLC
See also DLB 119

Sandburg, Carl (August)
1878-1967 . . . . CLC 1, 4, 10, 15, 35; DA;
DAB; PC 2; WLC
See also CA 5-8R; 25-28R; CANR 35;
CDALB 1865-1917; DLB 17, 54;
MAICYA; MTCW; SATA 8

Sandburg, Charles
See Sandburg, Carl (August)

Sandburg, Charles A.
See Sandburg, Carl (August)

Sanders, (James) Ed(ward) 1939- . . . CLC 53
See also CA 13-16R; CAAS 21; CANR 13,
44; DLB 16

Sanders, Lawrence 1920- . . . . . . . . . . CLC 41
See also BEST 89:4; CA 81-84; CANR 33;
MTCW

Sanders, Noah
See Blount, Roy (Alton), Jr.

Sanders, Winston P.
See Anderson, Poul (William)

Sandoz, Mari(e Susette)
1896-1966 . . . . . . . . . . . . . . . . . CLC 28
See also CA 1-4R; 25-28R; CANR 17;
DLB 9; MTCW; SATA 5

Saner, Reg(inald Anthony) 1931- . . . . CLC 9
See also CA 65-68

Sannazaro, Jacopo 1456(?)-1530 . . . . . . LC 8

Sansom, William
1912-1976 . . . . . . . . . CLC 2, 6; SSC 21
See also CA 5-8R; 65-68; CANR 42;
DLB 139; MTCW

Santayana, George 1863-1952 . . . . . TCLC 40
See also CA 115; DLB 54, 71

Santiago, Danny . . . . . . . . . . . . . . . . CLC 33
See also James, Daniel (Lewis)
See also DLB 122

Santmyer, Helen Hoover
1895-1986 . . . . . . . . . . . . . . . . . CLC 33
See also CA 1-4R; 118; CANR 15, 33;
DLBY 84; MTCW

Santos, Bienvenido N(uqui) 1911- . . . CLC 22
See also CA 101; CANR 19, 46

Sapper . . . . . . . . . . . . . . . . . . . . . TCLC 44
See also McNeile, Herman Cyril

Sappho fl. 6th cent. B.C.- . . CMLC 3; PC 5

Sarduy, Severo 1937-1993 . . . . . . . . . . CLC 6
See also CA 89-92; 142; DLB 113; HW

Sargeson, Frank 1903-1982 . . . . . . . . CLC 31
See also CA 25-28R; 106; CANR 38

Sarmiento, Felix Ruben Garcia
See Dario, Ruben

Saroyan, William
1908-1981 . . . . . CLC 1, 8, 10, 29, 34, 56;
DA; DAB; SSC 21; WLC
See also CA 5-8R; 103; CANR 30; DLB 7,
9, 86; DLBY 81; MTCW; SATA 23;
SATA-Obit 24

Sarraute, Nathalie
1900- . . . . . . . . CLC 1, 2, 4, 8, 10, 31, 80
See also CA 9-12R; CANR 23; DLB 83;
MTCW

Sarton, (Eleanor) May
1912- . . . . . . . . . . . . . . . . CLC 4, 14, 49
See also CA 1-4R; CANR 1, 34; DLB 48;
DLBY 81; MTCW; SATA 36

Sartre, Jean-Paul
1905-1980 . . . . CLC 1, 4, 7, 9, 13, 18, 24,
44, 50, 52; DA; DAB; DC 3; WLC
See also CA 9-12R; 97-100; CANR 21;
DLB 72; MTCW

Sassoon, Siegfried (Lorraine)
1886-1967 . . . . . . . CLC 36; DAB; PC 12
See also CA 104; 25-28R; CANR 36;
DLB 20; MTCW

Satterfield, Charles
See Pohl, Frederik

Saul, John (W. III) 1942- . . . . . . . . . CLC 46
See also AAYA 10; BEST 90:4; CA 81-84;
CANR 16, 40

Saunders, Caleb
See Heinlein, Robert A(nson)

Saura (Atares), Carlos 1932- . . . . . . . CLC 20
See also CA 114; 131; HW

Sauser-Hall, Frederic 1887-1961 . . . . CLC 18
See also Cendrars, Blaise
See also CA 102; 93-96; CANR 36; MTCW

Saussure, Ferdinand de
1857-1913 . . . . . . . . . . . . . . . . TCLC 49

Savage, Catharine
See Brosman, Catharine Savage

Savage, Thomas 1915- . . . . . . . . . . . . CLC 40
See also CA 126; 132; CAAS 15

Savan, Glenn   19(?)- . . . . . . . . . . . .   **CLC 50**

Sayers, Dorothy L(eigh)
1893-1957 . . . . . . . . . . . . . . .   **TCLC 2, 15**
See also CA 104; 119; CDBLB 1914-1945;
DLB 10, 36, 77, 100; MTCW

Sayers, Valerie   1952- . . . . . . . . . . . .   **CLC 50**
See also CA 134

Sayles, John (Thomas)
1950- . . . . . . . . . . . . . . . .   **CLC 7, 10, 14**
See also CA 57-60; CANR 41; DLB 44

Scammell, Michael . . . . . . . . . . . . . .   **CLC 34**

Scannell, Vernon   1922- . . . . . . . . . .   **CLC 49**
See also CA 5-8R; CANR 8, 24; DLB 27;
SATA 59

Scarlett, Susan
See Streatfeild, (Mary) Noel

Schaeffer, Susan Fromberg
1941- . . . . . . . . . . . . . . . .   **CLC 6, 11, 22**
See also CA 49-52; CANR 18; DLB 28;
MTCW; SATA 22

Schary, Jill
See Robinson, Jill

Schell, Jonathan   1943- . . . . . . . . . . . .   **CLC 35**
See also CA 73-76; CANR 12

Schelling, Friedrich Wilhelm Joseph von
1775-1854 . . . . . . . . . . . . . . .   **NCLC 30**
See also DLB 90

Schendel, Arthur van   1874-1946 . . .   **TCLC 56**

Scherer, Jean-Marie Maurice   1920-
See Rohmer, Eric
See also CA 110

Schevill, James (Erwin)   1920- . . . . . . .   **CLC 7**
See also CA 5-8R; CAAS 12

Schiller, Friedrich   1759-1805 . . . .   **NCLC 39**
See also DLB 94

Schisgal, Murray (Joseph)   1926- . . . . .   **CLC 6**
See also CA 21-24R; CANR 48

Schlee, Ann   1934- . . . . . . . . . . . . . .   **CLC 35**
See also CA 101; CANR 29; SATA 44;
SATA-Brief 36

Schlegel, August Wilhelm von
1767-1845 . . . . . . . . . . . . . . .   **NCLC 15**
See also DLB 94

Schlegel, Friedrich   1772-1829 . . . .   **NCLC 45**
See also DLB 90

Schlegel, Johann Elias (von)
1719(?)-1749 . . . . . . . . . . . . . . .   **LC 5**

Schlesinger, Arthur M(eier), Jr.
1917- . . . . . . . . . . . . . . . . . .   **CLC 84**
See also AITN 1; CA 1-4R; CANR 1, 28;
DLB 17; MTCW; SATA 61

Schmidt, Arno (Otto)   1914-1979 . . . .   **CLC 56**
See also CA 128; 109; DLB 69

Schmitz, Aron Hector   1861-1928
See Svevo, Italo
See also CA 104; 122; MTCW

Schnackenberg, Gjertrud   1953- . . . . .   **CLC 40**
See also CA 116; DLB 120

Schneider, Leonard Alfred   1925-1966
See Bruce, Lenny
See also CA 89-92

Schnitzler, Arthur
1862-1931 . . . . . . . . . .   **TCLC 4; SSC 15**
See also CA 104; DLB 81, 118

Schopenhauer, Arthur
1788-1860 . . . . . . . . . . . . . . .   **NCLC 51**
See also DLB 90

Schor, Sandra (M.)   1932(?)-1990 . . .   **CLC 65**
See also CA 132

Schorer, Mark   1908-1977 . . . . . . . . .   **CLC 9**
See also CA 5-8R; 73-76; CANR 7;
DLB 103

Schrader, Paul (Joseph)   1946- . . . . . .   **CLC 26**
See also CA 37-40R; CANR 41; DLB 44

Schreiner, Olive (Emilie Albertina)
1855-1920 . . . . . . . . . . . . . . . .   **TCLC 9**
See also CA 105; DLB 18, 156

Schulberg, Budd (Wilson)
1914- . . . . . . . . . . . . . . . . . .   **CLC 7, 48**
See also CA 25-28R; CANR 19; DLB 6, 26,
28; DLBY 81

Schulz, Bruno
1892-1942 . . . . . . .   **TCLC 5, 51; SSC 13**
See also CA 115; 123

Schulz, Charles M(onroe)   1922- . . . .   **CLC 12**
See also CA 9-12R; CANR 6; SATA 10

Schumacher, E(rnst) F(riedrich)
1911-1977 . . . . . . . . . . . . . . . .   **CLC 80**
See also CA 81-84; 73-76; CANR 34

Schuyler, James Marcus
1923-1991 . . . . . . . . . . . . . . .   **CLC 5, 23**
See also CA 101; 134; DLB 5

Schwartz, Delmore (David)
1913-1966 . . .   **CLC 2, 4, 10, 45, 87; PC 8**
See also CA 17-18; 25-28R; CANR 35;
CAP 2; DLB 28, 48; MTCW

Schwartz, Ernst
See Ozu, Yasujiro

Schwartz, John Burnham   1965- . . . .   **CLC 59**
See also CA 132

Schwartz, Lynne Sharon   1939- . . . . .   **CLC 31**
See also CA 103; CANR 44

Schwartz, Muriel A.
See Eliot, T(homas) S(tearns)

Schwarz-Bart, Andre   1928- . . . . . . .   **CLC 2, 4**
See also CA 89-92

Schwarz-Bart, Simone   1938- . . . . . . . .   **CLC 7**
See also BW 2; CA 97-100

Schwob, (Mayer Andre) Marcel
1867-1905 . . . . . . . . . . . . . . .   **TCLC 20**
See also CA 117; DLB 123

Sciascia, Leonardo
1921-1989 . . . . . . . . . . . . .   **CLC 8, 9, 41**
See also CA 85-88; 130; CANR 35; MTCW

Scoppettone, Sandra   1936- . . . . . . . .   **CLC 26**
See also AAYA 11; CA 5-8R; CANR 41;
SATA 9

Scorsese, Martin   1942- . . . . . . . .   **CLC 20, 89**
See also CA 110; 114; CANR 46

Scotland, Jay
See Jakes, John (William)

Scott, Duncan Campbell
1862-1947 . . . . . . . . . . . . . . . .   **TCLC 6**
See also CA 104; DLB 92

Scott, Evelyn   1893-1963 . . . . . . . . . .   **CLC 43**
See also CA 104; 112; DLB 9, 48

Scott, F(rancis) R(eginald)
1899-1985 . . . . . . . . . . . . . . .   **CLC 22**
See also CA 101; 114; DLB 88

Scott, Frank
See Scott, F(rancis) R(eginald)

Scott, Joanna   1960- . . . . . . . . . . . . .   **CLC 50**
See also CA 126

Scott, Paul (Mark)   1920-1978 . . . .   **CLC 9, 60**
See also CA 81-84; 77-80; CANR 33;
DLB 14; MTCW

Scott, Walter
1771-1832 . . . . . . .   **NCLC 15; DA; DAB;**
**PC 13; WLC**
See also CDBLB 1789-1832; DLB 93, 107,
116, 144; YABC 2

Scribe, (Augustin) Eugene
1791-1861 . . . . . . . . . . .   **NCLC 16; DC 5**

Scrum, R.
See Crumb, R(obert)

Scudery, Madeleine de   1607-1701 . . . . .   **LC 2**

Scum
See Crumb, R(obert)

Scumbag, Little Bobby
See Crumb, R(obert)

Seabrook, John
See Hubbard, L(afayette) Ron(ald)

Sealy, I. Allan   1951- . . . . . . . . . . . . .   **CLC 55**

Search, Alexander
See Pessoa, Fernando (Antonio Nogueira)

Sebastian, Lee
See Silverberg, Robert

Sebastian Owl
See Thompson, Hunter S(tockton)

Sebestyen, Ouida   1924- . . . . . . . . . . .   **CLC 30**
See also AAYA 8; CA 107; CANR 40;
CLR 17; JRDA; MAICYA; SAAS 10;
SATA 39

Secundus, H. Scriblerus
See Fielding, Henry

Sedges, John
See Buck, Pearl S(ydenstricker)

Sedgwick, Catharine Maria
1789-1867 . . . . . . . . . . . . . . .   **NCLC 19**
See also DLB 1, 74

Seelye, John   1931- . . . . . . . . . . . . . . .   **CLC 7**

Seferiades, Giorgos Stylianou   1900-1971
See Seferis, George
See also CA 5-8R; 33-36R; CANR 5, 36;
MTCW

Seferis, George . . . . . . . . . . . . . . .   **CLC 5, 11**
See also Seferiades, Giorgos Stylianou

Segal, Erich (Wolf)   1937- . . . . . . .   **CLC 3, 10**
See also BEST 89:1; CA 25-28R; CANR 20,
36; DLBY 86; MTCW

Seger, Bob   1945- . . . . . . . . . . . . . . .   **CLC 35**

Seghers, Anna . . . . . . . . . . . . . . . . . . .   **CLC 7**
See also Radvanyi, Netty
See also DLB 69

Seidel, Frederick (Lewis)   1936- . . . . .   **CLC 18**
See also CA 13-16R; CANR 8; DLBY 84

Seifert, Jaroslav   1901-1986 . . . . .   **CLC 34, 44**
See also CA 127; MTCW

Sei Shonagon   c. 966-1017(?) . . . . . .   **CMLC 6**

**Spencer, Elizabeth** 1921- . . . . . . . . . **CLC 22**
See also CA 13-16R; CANR 32; DLB 6;
MTCW; SATA 14

**Spencer, Leonard G.**
See Silverberg, Robert

**Spencer, Scott** 1945- . . . . . . . . . . . . . **CLC 30**
See also CA 113; DLBY 86

**Spender, Stephen (Harold)**
1909- . . . . . . . . . . . . **CLC 1, 2, 5, 10, 41**
See also CA 9-12R; CANR 31;
CDBLB 1945-1960; DLB 20; MTCW

**Spengler, Oswald (Arnold Gottfried)**
1880-1936 . . . . . . . . . . . . . . . . . **TCLC 25**
See also CA 118

**Spenser, Edmund**
1552(?)-1599 . . . . **LC 5; DA; DAB; PC 8;**
**WLC**
See also CDBLB Before 1660

**Spicer, Jack** 1925-1965 . . . . . . **CLC 8, 18, 72**
See also CA 85-88; DLB 5, 16

**Spiegelman, Art** 1948- . . . . . . . . . . . **CLC 76**
See also AAYA 10; CA 125; CANR 41

**Spielberg, Peter** 1929- . . . . . . . . . . . . **CLC 6**
See also CA 5-8R; CANR 4, 48; DLBY 81

**Spielberg, Steven** 1947- . . . . . . . . . . **CLC 20**
See also AAYA 8; CA 77-80; CANR 32;
SATA 32

**Spillane, Frank Morrison** 1918-
See Spillane, Mickey
See also CA 25-28R; CANR 28; MTCW;
SATA 66

**Spillane, Mickey** . . . . . . . . . . . . . . **CLC 3, 13**
See also Spillane, Frank Morrison

**Spinoza, Benedictus de** 1632-1677 . . . . **LC 9**

**Spinrad, Norman (Richard)** 1940- . . . **CLC 46**
See also CA 37-40R; CAAS 19; CANR 20;
DLB 8

**Spitteler, Carl (Friedrich Georg)**
1845-1924 . . . . . . . . . . . . . . . . . **TCLC 12**
See also CA 109; DLB 129

**Spivack, Kathleen (Romola Drucker)**
1938- . . . . . . . . . . . . . . . . . . . . . **CLC 6**
See also CA 49-52

**Spoto, Donald** 1941- . . . . . . . . . . . . . **CLC 39**
See also CA 65-68; CANR 11

**Springsteen, Bruce (F.)** 1949- . . . . . . **CLC 17**
See also CA 111

**Spurling, Hilary** 1940- . . . . . . . . . . . **CLC 34**
See also CA 104; CANR 25

**Spyker, John Howland**
See Elman, Richard

**Squires, (James) Radcliffe**
1917-1993 . . . . . . . . . . . . . . . . . **CLC 51**
See also CA 1-4R; 140; CANR 6, 21

**Srivastava, Dhanpat Rai** 1880(?)-1936
See Premchand
See also CA 118

**Stacy, Donald**
See Pohl, Frederik

**Stael, Germaine de**
See Stael-Holstein, Anne Louise Germaine
Necker Baronn
See also DLB 119

**Stael-Holstein, Anne Louise Germaine Necker**
**Baronn** 1766-1817 . . . . . . . . . . **NCLC 3**
See also Stael, Germaine de

**Stafford, Jean** 1915-1979 . . . **CLC 4, 7, 19, 68**
See also CA 1-4R; 85-88; CANR 3; DLB 2;
MTCW; SATA-Obit 22

**Stafford, William (Edgar)**
1914-1993 . . . . . . . . . . . . . . **CLC 4, 7, 29**
See also CA 5-8R; 142; CAAS 3; CANR 5,
22; DLB 5

**Staines, Trevor**
See Brunner, John (Kilian Houston)

**Stairs, Gordon**
See Austin, Mary (Hunter)

**Stannard, Martin** 1947- . . . . . . . . . . . **CLC 44**
See also CA 142; DLB 155

**Stanton, Maura** 1946- . . . . . . . . . . . . . **CLC 9**
See also CA 89-92; CANR 15; DLB 120

**Stanton, Schuyler**
See Baum, L(yman) Frank

**Stapledon, (William) Olaf**
1886-1950 . . . . . . . . . . . . . . . . . **TCLC 22**
See also CA 111; DLB 15

**Starbuck, George (Edwin)** 1931- . . . . **CLC 53**
See also CA 21-24R; CANR 23

**Stark, Richard**
See Westlake, Donald E(dwin)

**Staunton, Schuyler**
See Baum, L(yman) Frank

**Stead, Christina (Ellen)**
1902-1983 . . . . . . . . . **CLC 2, 5, 8, 32, 80**
See also CA 13-16R; 109; CANR 33, 40;
MTCW

**Stead, William Thomas**
1849-1912 . . . . . . . . . . . . . . . . . **TCLC 48**

**Steele, Richard** 1672-1729 . . . . . . . . . **LC 18**
See also CDBLB 1660-1789; DLB 84, 101

**Steele, Timothy (Reid)** 1948- . . . . . . . **CLC 45**
See also CA 93-96; CANR 16; DLB 120

**Steffens, (Joseph) Lincoln**
1866-1936 . . . . . . . . . . . . . . . . . **TCLC 20**
See also CA 117

**Stegner, Wallace (Earle)**
1909-1993 . . . . . . . . . . . . . **CLC 9, 49, 81**
See also AITN 1; BEST 90:3; CA 1-4R;
141; CAAS 9; CANR 1, 21, 46; DLB 9;
DLBY 93; MTCW

**Stein, Gertrude**
1874-1946 . . . . . **TCLC 1, 6, 28, 48; DA;**
**DAB; WLC**
See also CA 104; 132; CDALB 1917-1929;
DLB 4, 54, 86; MTCW

**Steinbeck, John (Ernst)**
1902-1968 . . . . . . **CLC 1, 5, 9, 13, 21, 34,**
**45, 75; DA; DAB; SSC 11; WLC**
See also AAYA 12; CA 1-4R; 25-28R;
CANR 1, 35; CDALB 1929-1941; DLB 7,
9; DLBD 2; MTCW; SATA 9

**Steinem, Gloria** 1934- . . . . . . . . . . . . **CLC 63**
See also CA 53-56; CANR 28; MTCW

**Steiner, George** 1929- . . . . . . . . . . . . **CLC 24**
See also CA 73-76; CANR 31; DLB 67;
MTCW; SATA 62

**Steiner, K. Leslie**
See Delany, Samuel R(ay, Jr.)

**Steiner, Rudolf** 1861-1925 . . . . . . . **TCLC 13**
See also CA 107

**Stendhal**
1783-1842 . . . . **NCLC 23, 46; DA; DAB;**
**WLC**
See also DLB 119

**Stephen, Leslie** 1832-1904 . . . . . . . . **TCLC 23**
See also CA 123; DLB 57, 144

**Stephen, Sir Leslie**
See Stephen, Leslie

**Stephen, Virginia**
See Woolf, (Adeline) Virginia

**Stephens, James** 1882(?)-1950 . . . . . . **TCLC 4**
See also CA 104; DLB 19, 153

**Stephens, Reed**
See Donaldson, Stephen R.

**Steptoe, Lydia**
See Barnes, Djuna

**Sterchi, Beat** 1949- . . . . . . . . . . . . . . **CLC 65**

**Sterling, Brett**
See Bradbury, Ray (Douglas); Hamilton,
Edmond

**Sterling, Bruce** 1954- . . . . . . . . . . . . . **CLC 72**
See also CA 119; CANR 44

**Sterling, George** 1869-1926 . . . . . . . **TCLC 20**
See also CA 117; DLB 54

**Stern, Gerald** 1925- . . . . . . . . . . . . . . **CLC 40**
See also CA 81-84; CANR 28; DLB 105

**Stern, Richard (Gustave)** 1928- . . . **CLC 4, 39**
See also CA 1-4R; CANR 1, 25; DLBY 87

**Sternberg, Josef von** 1894-1969 . . . . . **CLC 20**
See also CA 81-84

**Sterne, Laurence**
1713-1768 . . . . . . **LC 2; DA; DAB; WLC**
See also CDBLB 1660-1789; DLB 39

**Sternheim, (William Adolf) Carl**
1878-1942 . . . . . . . . . . . . . . . . . . **TCLC 8**
See also CA 105; DLB 56, 118

**Stevens, Mark** 1951- . . . . . . . . . . . . . **CLC 34**
See also CA 122

**Stevens, Wallace**
1879-1955 . . . . . . . . **TCLC 3, 12, 45; DA;**
**DAB; PC 6; WLC**
See also CA 104; 124; CDALB 1929-1941;
DLB 54; MTCW

**Stevenson, Anne (Katharine)**
1933- . . . . . . . . . . . . . . . . . . . . **CLC 7, 33**
See also CA 17-20R; CAAS 9; CANR 9, 33;
DLB 40; MTCW

**Stevenson, Robert Louis (Balfour)**
1850-1894 . . . . . **NCLC 5, 14; DA; DAB;**
**SSC 11; WLC**
See also CDBLB 1890-1914; CLR 10, 11;
DLB 18, 57, 141, 156; JRDA; MAICYA;
YABC 2

**Stewart, J(ohn) I(nnes) M(ackintosh)**
1906-1994 . . . . . . . . . . . . . **CLC 7, 14, 32**
See also CA 85-88; 147; CAAS 3;
CANR 47; MTCW

**Stewart, Mary (Florence Elinor)**
1916- . . . . . . . . . . . . . . . **CLC 7, 35; DAB**
See also CA 1-4R; CANR 1; SATA 12

**Stewart, Mary Rainbow**
See Stewart, Mary (Florence Elinor)

**Swenson, May**
1919-1989 .... **CLC 4, 14, 61; DA; DAB**
See also CA 5-8R; 130; CANR 36; DLB 5;
MTCW; SATA 15

**Swift, Augustus**
See Lovecraft, H(oward) P(hillips)

**Swift, Graham (Colin)** 1949- .... **CLC 41, 88**
See also CA 117; 122; CANR 46

**Swift, Jonathan**
1667-1745 ..... **LC 1; DA; DAB; PC 9;**
**WLC**
See also CDBLB 1660-1789; DLB 39, 95,
101; SATA 19

**Swinburne, Algernon Charles**
1837-1909 ..... **TCLC 8, 36; DA; DAB;**
**WLC**
See also CA 105; 140; CDBLB 1832-1890;
DLB 35, 57

**Swinfen, Ann** .................... **CLC 34**

**Swinnerton, Frank Arthur**
1884-1982 ................. **CLC 31**
See also CA 108; DLB 34

**Swithen, John**
See King, Stephen (Edwin)

**Sylvia**
See Ashton-Warner, Sylvia (Constance)

**Symmes, Robert Edward**
See Duncan, Robert (Edward)

**Symonds, John Addington**
1840-1893 ................. **NCLC 34**
See also DLB 57, 144

**Symons, Arthur** 1865-1945 ....... **TCLC 11**
See also CA 107; DLB 19, 57, 149

**Symons, Julian (Gustave)**
1912-1994 ............. **CLC 2, 14, 32**
See also CA 49-52; 147; CAAS 3; CANR 3,
33; DLB 87, 155; DLBY 92; MTCW

**Synge, (Edmund) J(ohn) M(illington)**
1871-1909 .......... **TCLC 6, 37; DC 2**
See also CA 104; 141; CDBLB 1890-1914;
DLB 10, 19

**Syruc, J.**
See Milosz, Czeslaw

**Szirtes, George** 1948- ............. **CLC 46**
See also CA 109; CANR 27

**Tabori, George** 1914- ............. **CLC 19**
See also CA 49-52; CANR 4

**Tagore, Rabindranath**
1861-1941 .......... **TCLC 3, 53; PC 8**
See also CA 104; 120; MTCW

**Taine, Hippolyte Adolphe**
1828-1893 ................. **NCLC 15**

**Talese, Gay** 1932- ................. **CLC 37**
See also AITN 1; CA 1-4R; CANR 9;
MTCW

**Tallent, Elizabeth (Ann)** 1954- ..... **CLC 45**
See also CA 117; DLB 130

**Tally, Ted** 1952- ................. **CLC 42**
See also CA 120; 124

**Tamayo y Baus, Manuel**
1829-1898 ................. **NCLC 1**

**Tammsaare, A(nton) H(ansen)**
1878-1940 ................. **TCLC 27**

**Tan, Amy** 1952- ................. **CLC 59**
See also AAYA 9; BEST 89:3; CA 136;
SATA 75

**Tandem, Felix**
See Spitteler, Carl (Friedrich Georg)

**Tanizaki, Jun'ichiro**
1886-1965 ...... **CLC 8, 14, 28; SSC 21**
See also CA 93-96; 25-28R

**Tanner, William**
See Amis, Kingsley (William)

**Tao Lao**
See Storni, Alfonsina

**Tarassoff, Lev**
See Troyat, Henri

**Tarbell, Ida M(inerva)**
1857-1944 ................. **TCLC 40**
See also CA 122; DLB 47

**Tarkington, (Newton) Booth**
1869-1946 ................. **TCLC 9**
See also CA 110; 143; DLB 9, 102;
SATA 17

**Tarkovsky, Andrei (Arsenyevich)**
1932-1986 ................. **CLC 75**
See also CA 127

**Tartt, Donna** 1964(?)- ............. **CLC 76**
See also CA 142

**Tasso, Torquato** 1544-1595 ......... **LC 5**

**Tate, (John Orley) Allen**
1899-1979 .... **CLC 2, 4, 6, 9, 11, 14, 24**
See also CA 5-8R; 85-88; CANR 32;
DLB 4, 45, 63; MTCW

**Tate, Ellalice**
See Hibbert, Eleanor Alice Burford

**Tate, James (Vincent)** 1943- ... **CLC 2, 6, 25**
See also CA 21-24R; CANR 29; DLB 5

**Tavel, Ronald** 1940- ................. **CLC 6**
See also CA 21-24R; CANR 33

**Taylor, C(ecil) P(hilip)** 1929-1981 ... **CLC 27**
See also CA 25-28R; 105; CANR 47

**Taylor, Edward**
1642(?)-1729 ........ **LC 11; DA; DAB**
See also DLB 24

**Taylor, Eleanor Ross** 1920- ........ **CLC 5**
See also CA 81-84

**Taylor, Elizabeth** 1912-1975 ... **CLC 2, 4, 29**
See also CA 13-16R; CANR 9; DLB 139;
MTCW; SATA 13

**Taylor, Henry (Splawn)** 1942- ...... **CLC 44**
See also CA 33-36R; CAAS 7; CANR 31;
DLB 5

**Taylor, Kamala (Purnaiya)** 1924-
See Markandaya, Kamala
See also CA 77-80

**Taylor, Mildred D.** ................ **CLC 21**
See also AAYA 10; BW 1; CA 85-88;
CANR 25; CLR 9; DLB 52; JRDA;
MAICYA; SAAS 5; SATA 15, 70

**Taylor, Peter (Hillsman)**
1917-1994 ..... **CLC 1, 4, 18, 37, 44, 50,**
**71; SSC 10**
See also CA 13-16R; 147; CANR 9;
DLBY 81, 94; MTCW

**Taylor, Robert Lewis** 1912- ........ **CLC 14**
See also CA 1-4R; CANR 3; SATA 10

**Tchekhov, Anton**
See Chekhov, Anton (Pavlovich)

**Teasdale, Sara** 1884-1933 ......... **TCLC 4**
See also CA 104; DLB 45; SATA 32

**Tegner, Esaias** 1782-1846 ........ **NCLC 2**

**Teilhard de Chardin, (Marie Joseph) Pierre**
1881-1955 ................. **TCLC 9**
See also CA 105

**Temple, Ann**
See Mortimer, Penelope (Ruth)

**Tennant, Emma (Christina)**
1937- ................... **CLC 13, 52**
See also CA 65-68; CAAS 9; CANR 10, 38;
DLB 14

**Tenneshaw, S. M.**
See Silverberg, Robert

**Tennyson, Alfred**
1809-1892 ....... **NCLC 30; DA; DAB;**
**PC 6; WLC**
See also CDBLB 1832-1890; DLB 32

**Teran, Lisa St. Aubin de** .......... **CLC 36**
See also St. Aubin de Teran, Lisa

**Terence** 195(?)B.C.-159B.C. ...... **CMLC 14**

**Teresa de Jesus, St.** 1515-1582 ...... **LC 18**

**Terkel, Louis** 1912-
See Terkel, Studs
See also CA 57-60; CANR 18, 45; MTCW

**Terkel, Studs** .................... **CLC 38**
See also Terkel, Louis
See also AITN 1

**Terry, C. V.**
See Slaughter, Frank G(ill)

**Terry, Megan** 1932- .............. **CLC 19**
See also CA 77-80; CABS 3; CANR 43;
DLB 7

**Tertz, Abram**
See Sinyavsky, Andrei (Donatevich)

**Tesich, Steve** 1943(?)- .......... **CLC 40, 69**
See also CA 105; DLBY 83

**Teternikov, Fyodor Kuzmich** 1863-1927
See Sologub, Fyodor
See also CA 104

**Tevis, Walter** 1928-1984 .......... **CLC 42**
See also CA 113

**Tey, Josephine** .................. **TCLC 14**
See also Mackintosh, Elizabeth
See also DLB 77

**Thackeray, William Makepeace**
1811-1863 .... **NCLC 5, 14, 22, 43; DA;**
**DAB; WLC**
See also CDBLB 1832-1890; DLB 21, 55;
SATA 23

**Thakura, Ravindranatha**
See Tagore, Rabindranath

**Tharoor, Shashi** 1956- ........... **CLC 70**
See also CA 141

**Thelwell, Michael Miles** 1939- ..... **CLC 22**
See also BW 2; CA 101

**Theobald, Lewis, Jr.**
See Lovecraft, H(oward) P(hillips)

**Theodorescu, Ion N.** 1880-1967
See Arghezi, Tudor
See also CA 116

467

**Theriault, Yves** 1915-1983 . . . . . . . . **CLC 79**
See also CA 102; DLB 88

**Theroux, Alexander (Louis)**
1939- . . . . . . . . . . . . . . . . . . . . **CLC 2, 25**
See also CA 85-88; CANR 20

**Theroux, Paul (Edward)**
1941- . . . . . . . . **CLC 5, 8, 11, 15, 28, 46**
See also BEST 89:4; CA 33-36R; CANR 20,
45; DLB 2; MTCW; SATA 44

**Thesen, Sharon** 1946- . . . . . . . . . . . **CLC 56**

**Thevenin, Denis**
See Duhamel, Georges

**Thibault, Jacques Anatole Francois**
1844-1924
See France, Anatole
See also CA 106; 127; MTCW

**Thiele, Colin (Milton)** 1920- . . . . . . . **CLC 17**
See also CA 29-32R; CANR 12, 28;
CLR 27; MAICYA; SAAS 2; SATA 14,
72

**Thomas, Audrey (Callahan)**
1935- . . . . . . . . . **CLC 7, 13, 37; SSC 20**
See also AITN 2; CA 21-24R; CAAS 19;
CANR 36; DLB 60; MTCW

**Thomas, D(onald) M(ichael)**
1935- . . . . . . . . . . . . . . . . **CLC 13, 22, 31**
See also CA 61-64; CAAS 11; CANR 17,
45; CDBLB 1960 to Present; DLB 40;
MTCW

**Thomas, Dylan (Marlais)**
1914-1953 . . . **TCLC 1, 8, 45; DA; DAB;
PC 2; SSC 3; WLC**
See also CA 104; 120; CDBLB 1945-1960;
DLB 13, 20, 139; MTCW; SATA 60

**Thomas, (Philip) Edward**
1878-1917 . . . . . . . . . . . . . . . . . . **TCLC 10**
See also CA 106; DLB 19

**Thomas, Joyce Carol** 1938- . . . . . . . . **CLC 35**
See also AAYA 12; BW 2; CA 113; 116;
CANR 48; CLR 19; DLB 33; JRDA;
MAICYA; MTCW; SAAS 7; SATA 40,
78

**Thomas, Lewis** 1913-1993 . . . . . . . . **CLC 35**
See also CA 85-88; 143; CANR 38; MTCW

**Thomas, Paul**
See Mann, (Paul) Thomas

**Thomas, Piri** 1928- . . . . . . . . . . . . . . **CLC 17**
See also CA 73-76; HW

**Thomas, R(onald) S(tuart)**
1913- . . . . . . . . . . . . **CLC 6, 13, 48; DAB**
See also CA 89-92; CAAS 4; CANR 30;
CDBLB 1960 to Present; DLB 27;
MTCW

**Thomas, Ross (Elmore)** 1926- . . . . . . **CLC 39**
See also CA 33-36R; CANR 22

**Thompson, Francis Clegg**
See Mencken, H(enry) L(ouis)

**Thompson, Francis Joseph**
1859-1907 . . . . . . . . . . . . . . . . . . **TCLC 4**
See also CA 104; CDBLB 1890-1914;
DLB 19

**Thompson, Hunter S(tockton)**
1939- . . . . . . . . . . . . . . **CLC 9, 17, 40**
See also BEST 89:1; CA 17-20R; CANR 23,
46; MTCW

**Thompson, James Myers**
See Thompson, Jim (Myers)

**Thompson, Jim (Myers)**
1906-1977(?) . . . . . . . . . . . . . . . **CLC 69**
See also CA 140

**Thompson, Judith** . . . . . . . . . . . . . . **CLC 39**

**Thomson, James** 1700-1748 . . . . . **LC 16, 29**
See also DLB 95

**Thomson, James** 1834-1882 . . . . . . **NCLC 18**
See also DLB 35

**Thoreau, Henry David**
1817-1862 . . . . . **NCLC 7, 21; DA; DAB;
WLC**
See also CDALB 1640-1865; DLB 1

**Thornton, Hall**
See Silverberg, Robert

**Thurber, James (Grover)**
1894-1961 . . . . **CLC 5, 11, 25; DA; DAB;
SSC 1**
See also CA 73-76; CANR 17, 39;
CDALB 1929-1941; DLB 4, 11, 22, 102;
MAICYA; MTCW; SATA 13

**Thurman, Wallace (Henry)**
1902-1934 . . . . . . . . . . . . . **TCLC 6; BLC**
See also BW 1; CA 104; 124; DLB 51

**Ticheburn, Cheviot**
See Ainsworth, William Harrison

**Tieck, (Johann) Ludwig**
1773-1853 . . . . . . . . . . . . . . **NCLC 5, 46**
See also DLB 90

**Tiger, Derry**
See Ellison, Harlan (Jay)

**Tilghman, Christopher** 1948(?)- . . . . . **CLC 65**

**Tillinghast, Richard (Williford)**
1940- . . . . . . . . . . . . . . . . . . . . . **CLC 29**
See also CA 29-32R; CANR 26

**Timrod, Henry** 1828-1867 . . . . . . . **NCLC 25**
See also DLB 3

**Tindall, Gillian** 1938- . . . . . . . . . . . . **CLC 7**
See also CA 21-24R; CANR 11

**Tiptree, James, Jr.** . . . . . . . . . . . . **CLC 48, 50**
See also Sheldon, Alice Hastings Bradley
See also DLB 8

**Titmarsh, Michael Angelo**
See Thackeray, William Makepeace

**Tocqueville, Alexis (Charles Henri Maurice
Clerel Comte)** 1805-1859 . . . . . **NCLC 7**

**Tolkien, J(ohn) R(onald) R(euel)**
1892-1973 . . . . . . **CLC 1, 2, 3, 8, 12, 38;
DA; DAB; WLC**
See also AAYA 10; AITN 1; CA 17-18;
45-48; CANR 36; CAP 2;
CDBLB 1914-1945; DLB 15; JRDA;
MAICYA; MTCW; SATA 2, 32;
SATA-Obit 24

**Toller, Ernst** 1893-1939 . . . . . . . . . **TCLC 10**
See also CA 107; DLB 124

**Tolson, M. B.**
See Tolson, Melvin B(eaunorus)

**Tolson, Melvin B(eaunorus)**
1898(?)-1966 . . . . . . . . . . . **CLC 36; BLC**
See also BW 1; CA 124; 89-92; DLB 48, 76

**Tolstoi, Aleksei Nikolaevich**
See Tolstoy, Alexey Nikolaevich

**Tolstoy, Alexey Nikolaevich**
1882-1945 . . . . . . . . . . . . . . . . . . **TCLC 18**
See also CA 107

**Tolstoy, Count Leo**
See Tolstoy, Leo (Nikolaevich)

**Tolstoy, Leo (Nikolaevich)**
1828-1910 . . . . . **TCLC 4, 11, 17, 28, 44;
DA; DAB; SSC 9; WLC**
See also CA 104; 123; SATA 26

**Tomasi di Lampedusa, Giuseppe** 1896-1957
See Lampedusa, Giuseppe (Tomasi) di
See also CA 111

**Tomlin, Lily** . . . . . . . . . . . . . . . . . . . **CLC 17**
See also Tomlin, Mary Jean

**Tomlin, Mary Jean** 1939(?)-
See Tomlin, Lily
See also CA 117

**Tomlinson, (Alfred) Charles**
1927- . . . . . . . . . . . . . **CLC 2, 4, 6, 13, 45**
See also CA 5-8R; CANR 33; DLB 40

**Tonson, Jacob**
See Bennett, (Enoch) Arnold

**Toole, John Kennedy**
1937-1969 . . . . . . . . . . . . . . . **CLC 19, 64**
See also CA 104; DLBY 81

**Toomer, Jean**
1894-1967 . . . . . . **CLC 1, 4, 13, 22; BLC;
PC 7; SSC 1**
See also BW 1; CA 85-88;
CDALB 1917-1929; DLB 45, 51; MTCW

**Torley, Luke**
See Blish, James (Benjamin)

**Tornimparte, Alessandra**
See Ginzburg, Natalia

**Torre, Raoul della**
See Mencken, H(enry) L(ouis)

**Torrey, E(dwin) Fuller** 1937- . . . . . . . **CLC 34**
See also CA 119

**Torsvan, Ben Traven**
See Traven, B.

**Torsvan, Benno Traven**
See Traven, B.

**Torsvan, Berick Traven**
See Traven, B.

**Torsvan, Berwick Traven**
See Traven, B.

**Torsvan, Bruno Traven**
See Traven, B.

**Torsvan, Traven**
See Traven, B.

**Tournier, Michel (Edouard)**
1924- . . . . . . . . . . . . . . . . **CLC 6, 23, 36**
See also CA 49-52; CANR 3, 36; DLB 83;
MTCW; SATA 23

**Tournimparte, Alessandra**
See Ginzburg, Natalia

**Towers, Ivar**
See Kornbluth, C(yril) M.

**Towne, Robert (Burton)** 1936(?)- . . . . **CLC 87**
See also CA 108; DLB 44

**Townsend, Sue** 1946- . . . . . . . . **CLC 61; DAB**
See also CA 119; 127; MTCW; SATA 55;
SATA-Brief 48

**Townshend, Peter (Dennis Blandford)**
1945- .................... **CLC 17, 42**
See also CA 107

**Tozzi, Federigo** 1883-1920........ **TCLC 31**

**Traill, Catharine Parr**
1802-1899 ................. **NCLC 31**
See also DLB 99

**Trakl, Georg** 1887-1914.......... **TCLC 5**
See also CA 104

**Transtroemer, Tomas (Goesta)**
1931- ................... **CLC 52, 65**
See also CA 117; 129; CAAS 17

**Transtromer, Tomas Gosta**
See Transtroemer, Tomas (Goesta)

**Traven, B.** (?)-1969............. **CLC 8, 11**
See also CA 19-20; 25-28R; CAP 2; DLB 9, 56; MTCW

**Treitel, Jonathan** 1959- .......... **CLC 70**

**Tremain, Rose** 1943-.............. **CLC 42**
See also CA 97-100; CANR 44; DLB 14

**Tremblay, Michel** 1942-.......... **CLC 29**
See also CA 116; 128; DLB 60; MTCW

**Trevanian**....................... **CLC 29**
See also Whitaker, Rod(ney)

**Trevor, Glen**
See Hilton, James

**Trevor, William**
1928- ..... **CLC 7, 9, 14, 25, 71; SSC 21**
See also Cox, William Trevor
See also DLB 14, 139

**Trifonov, Yuri (Valentinovich)**
1925-1981 ................... **CLC 45**
See also CA 126; 103; MTCW

**Trilling, Lionel** 1905-1975.... **CLC 9, 11, 24**
See also CA 9-12R; 61-64; CANR 10; DLB 28, 63; MTCW

**Trimball, W. H.**
See Mencken, H(enry) L(ouis)

**Tristan**
See Gomez de la Serna, Ramon

**Tristram**
See Housman, A(lfred) E(dward)

**Trogdon, William (Lewis)** 1939-
See Heat-Moon, William Least
See also CA 115; 119; CANR 47

**Trollope, Anthony**
1815-1882 ..... **NCLC 6, 33; DA; DAB; WLC**
See also CDBLB 1832-1890; DLB 21, 57; SATA 22

**Trollope, Frances** 1779-1863..... **NCLC 30**
See also DLB 21

**Trotsky, Leon** 1879-1940........ **TCLC 22**
See also CA 118

**Trotter (Cockburn), Catharine**
1679-1749 .................... **LC 8**
See also DLB 84

**Trout, Kilgore**
See Farmer, Philip Jose

**Trow, George W. S.** 1943-........ **CLC 52**
See also CA 126

**Troyat, Henri** 1911-.............. **CLC 23**
See also CA 45-48; CANR 2, 33; MTCW

**Trudeau, G(arretson) B(eekman)** 1948-
See Trudeau, Garry B.
See also CA 81-84; CANR 31; SATA 35

**Trudeau, Garry B.**................ **CLC 12**
See also Trudeau, G(arretson) B(eekman)
See also AAYA 10; AITN 2

**Truffaut, Francois** 1932-1984...... **CLC 20**
See also CA 81-84; 113; CANR 34

**Trumbo, Dalton** 1905-1976........ **CLC 19**
See also CA 21-24R; 69-72; CANR 10; DLB 26

**Trumbull, John** 1750-1831....... **NCLC 30**
See also DLB 31

**Trundlett, Helen B.**
See Eliot, T(homas) S(tearns)

**Tryon, Thomas** 1926-1991...... **CLC 3, 11**
See also AITN 1; CA 29-32R; 135; CANR 32; MTCW

**Tryon, Tom**
See Tryon, Thomas

**Ts'ao Hsueh-ch'in** 1715(?)-1763....... **LC 1**

**Tsushima, Shuji** 1909-1948
See Dazai, Osamu
See also CA 107

**Tsvetaeva (Efron), Marina (Ivanovna)**
1892-1941 ................ **TCLC 7, 35**
See also CA 104; 128; MTCW

**Tuck, Lily** 1938-................. **CLC 70**
See also CA 139

**Tu Fu** 712-770..................... **PC 9**

**Tunis, John R(oberts)** 1889-1975 ... **CLC 12**
See also CA 61-64; DLB 22; JRDA; MAICYA; SATA 37; SATA-Brief 30

**Tuohy, Frank**.................... **CLC 37**
See also Tuohy, John Francis
See also DLB 14, 139

**Tuohy, John Francis** 1925-
See Tuohy, Frank
See also CA 5-8R; CANR 3, 47

**Turco, Lewis (Putnam)** 1934- ... **CLC 11, 63**
See also CA 13-16R; CAAS 22; CANR 24; DLBY 84

**Turgenev, Ivan**
1818-1883 ....... **NCLC 21; DA; DAB; SSC 7; WLC**

**Turgot, Anne-Robert-Jacques**
1727-1781 .................... **LC 26**

**Turner, Frederick** 1943-.......... **CLC 48**
See also CA 73-76; CAAS 10; CANR 12, 30; DLB 40

**Tutu, Desmond M(pilo)**
1931- .................. **CLC 80; BLC**
See also BW 1; CA 125

**Tutuola, Amos** 1920- ... **CLC 5, 14, 29; BLC**
See also BW 2; CA 9-12R; CANR 27; DLB 125; MTCW

**Twain, Mark**
.... **TCLC 6, 12, 19, 36, 48, 59; SSC 6; WLC**
See also Clemens, Samuel Langhorne
See also DLB 11, 12, 23, 64, 74

**Tyler, Anne**
1941- ........ **CLC 7, 11, 18, 28, 44, 59**
See also BEST 89:1; CA 9-12R; CANR 11, 33; DLB 6, 143; DLBY 82; MTCW; SATA 7

**Tyler, Royall** 1757-1826......... **NCLC 3**
See also DLB 37

**Tynan, Katharine** 1861-1931....... **TCLC 3**
See also CA 104; DLB 153

**Tyutchev, Fyodor** 1803-1873..... **NCLC 34**

**Tzara, Tristan** ................... **CLC 47**
See also Rosenfeld, Samuel

**Uhry, Alfred** 1936-............... **CLC 55**
See also CA 127; 133

**Ulf, Haerved**
See Strindberg, (Johan) August

**Ulf, Harved**
See Strindberg, (Johan) August

**Ulibarri, Sabine R(eyes)** 1919- ..... **CLC 83**
See also CA 131; DLB 82; HW

**Unamuno (y Jugo), Miguel de**
1864-1936 .... **TCLC 2, 9; HLC; SSC 11**
See also CA 104; 131; DLB 108; HW; MTCW

**Undercliffe, Errol**
See Campbell, (John) Ramsey

**Underwood, Miles**
See Glassco, John

**Undset, Sigrid**
1882-1949 ... **TCLC 3; DA; DAB; WLC**
See also CA 104; 129; MTCW

**Ungaretti, Giuseppe**
1888-1970 .............. **CLC 7, 11, 15**
See also CA 19-20; 25-28R; CAP 2; DLB 114

**Unger, Douglas** 1952-............. **CLC 34**
See also CA 130

**Unsworth, Barry (Forster)** 1930-.... **CLC 76**
See also CA 25-28R; CANR 30

**Updike, John (Hoyer)**
1932- ...... **CLC 1, 2, 3, 5, 7, 9, 13, 15, 23, 34, 43, 70; DA; DAB; SSC 13; WLC**
See also CA 1-4R; CABS 1; CANR 4, 33; CDALB 1968-1988; DLB 2, 5, 143; DLBD 3; DLBY 80, 82; MTCW

**Upshaw, Margaret Mitchell**
See Mitchell, Margaret (Munnerlyn)

**Upton, Mark**
See Sanders, Lawrence

**Urdang, Constance (Henriette)**
1922-....................... **CLC 47**
See also CA 21-24R; CANR 9, 24

**Uriel, Henry**
See Faust, Frederick (Schiller)

**Uris, Leon (Marcus)** 1924-....... **CLC 7, 32**
See also AITN 1, 2; BEST 89:2; CA 1-4R; CANR 1, 40; MTCW; SATA 49

**Urmuz**
See Codrescu, Andrei

**Urquhart, Jane** 1949-............. **CLC 90**
See also CA 113; CANR 32

**Ustinov, Peter (Alexander)** 1921-.... **CLC 1**
See also AITN 1; CA 13-16R; CANR 25; DLB 13

**Voltaire**
      1694-1778 . . . . . . . . . LC 14; DA; DAB;
            SSC 12; WLC

**von Aue, Hartmann** 1170-1210 . . . CMLC 15

**von Daeniken, Erich** 1935- . . . . . . . . CLC 30
      See also AITN 1; CA 37-40R; CANR 17,
      44

**von Daniken, Erich**
      See von Daeniken, Erich

**von Heidenstam, (Carl Gustaf) Verner**
      See Heidenstam, (Carl Gustaf) Verner von

**von Heyse, Paul (Johann Ludwig)**
      See Heyse, Paul (Johann Ludwig von)

**von Hofmannsthal, Hugo**
      See Hofmannsthal, Hugo von

**von Horvath, Odon**
      See Horvath, Oedoen von

**von Horvath, Oedoen**
      See Horvath, Oedoen von

**von Liliencron, (Friedrich Adolf Axel) Detlev**
      See Liliencron, (Friedrich Adolf Axel)
            Detlev von

**Vonnegut, Kurt, Jr.**
      1922- . . . . . . CLC 1, 2, 3, 4, 5, 8, 12, 22,
            40, 60; DA; DAB; SSC 8; WLC
      See also AAYA 6; AITN 1; BEST 90:4;
      CA 1-4R; CANR 1, 25, 49;
      CDALB 1968-1988; DLB 2, 8, 152;
      DLBD 3; DLBY 80; MTCW

**Von Rachen, Kurt**
      See Hubbard, L(afayette) Ron(ald)

**von Rezzori (d'Arezzo), Gregor**
      See Rezzori (d'Arezzo), Gregor von

**von Sternberg, Josef**
      See Sternberg, Josef von

**Vorster, Gordon** 1924- . . . . . . . . . . . CLC 34
      See also CA 133

**Vosce, Trudie**
      See Ozick, Cynthia

**Voznesensky, Andrei (Andreievich)**
      1933- . . . . . . . . . . . . . . . . CLC 1, 15, 57
      See also CA 89-92; CANR 37; MTCW

**Waddington, Miriam** 1917- . . . . . . . . CLC 28
      See also CA 21-24R; CANR 12, 30;
      DLB 68

**Wagman, Fredrica** 1937- . . . . . . . . . . CLC 7
      See also CA 97-100

**Wagner, Richard** 1813-1883. . . . . . . NCLC 9
      See also DLB 129

**Wagner-Martin, Linda** 1936- . . . . . . . CLC 50

**Wagoner, David (Russell)**
      1926- . . . . . . . . . . . . . . . . . CLC 3, 5, 15
      See also CA 1-4R; CAAS 3; CANR 2;
      DLB 5; SATA 14

**Wah, Fred(erick James)** 1939- . . . . . . CLC 44
      See also CA 107; 141; DLB 60

**Wahloo, Per** 1926-1975 . . . . . . . . . . . CLC 7
      See also CA 61-64

**Wahloo, Peter**
      See Wahloo, Per

**Wain, John (Barrington)**
      1925-1994 . . . . . . . . . . CLC 2, 11, 15, 46
      See also CA 5-8R; 145; CAAS 4; CANR 23;
      CDBLB 1960 to Present; DLB 15, 27,
      139, 155; MTCW

**Wajda, Andrzej** 1926- . . . . . . . . . . . . CLC 16
      See also CA 102

**Wakefield, Dan** 1932- . . . . . . . . . . . . CLC 7
      See also CA 21-24R; CAAS 7

**Wakoski, Diane**
      1937- . . . . . . . . . . CLC 2, 4, 7, 9, 11, 40
      See also CA 13-16R; CAAS 1; CANR 9;
      DLB 5

**Wakoski-Sherbell, Diane**
      See Wakoski, Diane

**Walcott, Derek (Alton)**
      1930- . . . . CLC 2, 4, 9, 14, 25, 42, 67, 76;
            BLC; DAB
      See also BW 2; CA 89-92; CANR 26, 47;
      DLB 117; DLBY 81; MTCW

**Waldman, Anne** 1945- . . . . . . . . . . . . CLC 7
      See also CA 37-40R; CAAS 17; CANR 34;
      DLB 16

**Waldo, E. Hunter**
      See Sturgeon, Theodore (Hamilton)

**Waldo, Edward Hamilton**
      See Sturgeon, Theodore (Hamilton)

**Walker, Alice (Malsenior)**
      1944- . . . . . . . CLC 5, 6, 9, 19, 27, 46, 58;
            BLC; DA; DAB; SSC 5
      See also AAYA 3; BEST 89:4; BW 2;
      CA 37-40R; CANR 9, 27, 49;
      CDALB 1968-1988; DLB 6, 33, 143;
      MTCW; SATA 31

**Walker, David Harry** 1911-1992. . . . CLC 14
      See also CA 1-4R; 137; CANR 1; SATA 8;
      SATA-Obit 71

**Walker, Edward Joseph** 1934-
      See Walker, Ted
      See also CA 21-24R; CANR 12, 28

**Walker, George F.**
      1947- . . . . . . . . . . . . . CLC 44, 61; DAB
      See also CA 103; CANR 21, 43; DLB 60

**Walker, Joseph A.** 1935- . . . . . . . . . CLC 19
      See also BW 1; CA 89-92; CANR 26;
      DLB 38

**Walker, Margaret (Abigail)**
      1915- . . . . . . . . . . . . . . . . CLC 1, 6; BLC
      See also BW 2; CA 73-76; CANR 26;
      DLB 76, 152; MTCW

**Walker, Ted** . . . . . . . . . . . . . . . . . . . . CLC 13
      See also Walker, Edward Joseph
      See also DLB 40

**Wallace, David Foster** 1962- . . . . . . . CLC 50
      See also CA 132

**Wallace, Dexter**
      See Masters, Edgar Lee

**Wallace, (Richard Horatio) Edgar**
      1875-1932. . . . . . . . . . . . . . . . TCLC 57
      See also CA 115; DLB 70

**Wallace, Irving** 1916-1990. . . . . . CLC 7, 13
      See also AITN 1; CA 1-4R; 132; CAAS 1;
      CANR 1, 27; MTCW

**Wallant, Edward Lewis**
      1926-1962 . . . . . . . . . . . . . . . CLC 5, 10
      See also CA 1-4R; CANR 22; DLB 2, 28,
      143; MTCW

**Walley, Byron**
      See Card, Orson Scott

**Walpole, Horace** 1717-1797. . . . . . . . . LC 2
      See also DLB 39, 104

**Walpole, Hugh (Seymour)**
      1884-1941 . . . . . . . . . . . . . . . . . TCLC 5
      See also CA 104; DLB 34

**Walser, Martin** 1927- . . . . . . . . . . . . CLC 27
      See also CA 57-60; CANR 8, 46; DLB 75,
      124

**Walser, Robert**
      1878-1956 . . . . . . . . . TCLC 18; SSC 20
      See also CA 118; DLB 66

**Walsh, Jill Paton**. . . . . . . . . . . . . . . . CLC 35
      See also Paton Walsh, Gillian
      See also AAYA 11; CLR 2; SAAS 3

**Walter, Villiam Christian**
      See Andersen, Hans Christian

**Wambaugh, Joseph (Aloysius, Jr.)**
      1937- . . . . . . . . . . . . . . . . . . CLC 3, 18
      See also AITN 1; BEST 89:3; CA 33-36R;
      CANR 42; DLB 6; DLBY 83; MTCW

**Ward, Arthur Henry Sarsfield** 1883-1959
      See Rohmer, Sax
      See also CA 108

**Ward, Douglas Turner** 1930- . . . . . . . CLC 19
      See also BW 1; CA 81-84; CANR 27;
      DLB 7, 38

**Ward, Mary Augusta**
      See Ward, Mrs. Humphry

**Ward, Mrs. Humphry**
      1851-1920 . . . . . . . . . . . . . . . . TCLC 55
      See also DLB 18

**Ward, Peter**
      See Faust, Frederick (Schiller)

**Warhol, Andy** 1928(?)-1987. . . . . . . . CLC 20
      See also AAYA 12; BEST 89:4; CA 89-92;
      121; CANR 34

**Warner, Francis (Robert le Plastrier)**
      1937- . . . . . . . . . . . . . . . . . . . . CLC 14
      See also CA 53-56; CANR 11

**Warner, Marina** 1946- . . . . . . . . . . . . CLC 59
      See also CA 65-68; CANR 21

**Warner, Rex (Ernest)** 1905-1986. . . . CLC 45
      See also CA 89-92; 119; DLB 15

**Warner, Susan (Bogert)**
      1819-1885 . . . . . . . . . . . . . . . NCLC 31
      See also DLB 3, 42

**Warner, Sylvia (Constance) Ashton**
      See Ashton-Warner, Sylvia (Constance)

**Warner, Sylvia Townsend**
      1893-1978 . . . . . . . . . . . . . . . CLC 7, 19
      See also CA 61-64; 77-80; CANR 16;
      DLB 34, 139; MTCW

**Warren, Mercy Otis** 1728-1814. . . NCLC 13
      See also DLB 31

**Warren, Robert Penn**
1905-1989 .... **CLC 1, 4, 6, 8, 10, 13, 18, 39, 53, 59; DA; DAB; SSC 4; WLC**
See also AITN 1; CA 13-16R; 129; CANR 10, 47; CDALB 1968-1988; DLB 2, 48, 152; DLBY 80, 89; MTCW; SATA 46; SATA-Obit 63

**Warshofsky, Isaac**
See Singer, Isaac Bashevis

**Warton, Thomas** 1728-1790 ........ **LC 15**
See also DLB 104, 109

**Waruk, Kona**
See Harris, (Theodore) Wilson

**Warung, Price** 1855-1911 ........ **TCLC 45**

**Warwick, Jarvis**
See Garner, Hugh

**Washington, Alex**
See Harris, Mark

**Washington, Booker T(aliaferro)**
1856-1915 ............. **TCLC 10; BLC**
See also BW 1; CA 114; 125; SATA 28

**Washington, George** 1732-1799 ...... **LC 25**
See also DLB 31

**Wassermann, (Karl) Jakob**
1873-1934 ................. **TCLC 6**
See also CA 104; DLB 66

**Wasserstein, Wendy**
1950- .......... **CLC 32, 59, 90; DC 4**
See also CA 121; 129; CABS 3

**Waterhouse, Keith (Spencer)**
1929- ..................... **CLC 47**
See also CA 5-8R; CANR 38; DLB 13, 15; MTCW

**Waters, Frank (Joseph)** 1902- ...... **CLC 88**
See also CA 5-8R; CAAS 13; CANR 3, 18; DLBY 86

**Waters, Roger** 1944- ............. **CLC 35**

**Watkins, Frances Ellen**
See Harper, Frances Ellen Watkins

**Watkins, Gerrold**
See Malzberg, Barry N(athaniel)

**Watkins, Paul** 1964- ............. **CLC 55**
See also CA 132

**Watkins, Vernon Phillips**
1906-1967 ................. **CLC 43**
See also CA 9-10; 25-28R; CAP 1; DLB 20

**Watson, Irving S.**
See Mencken, H(enry) L(ouis)

**Watson, John H.**
See Farmer, Philip Jose

**Watson, Richard F.**
See Silverberg, Robert

**Waugh, Auberon (Alexander)** 1939- .. **CLC 7**
See also CA 45-48; CANR 6, 22; DLB 14

**Waugh, Evelyn (Arthur St. John)**
1903-1966 ...... **CLC 1, 3, 8, 13, 19, 27, 44; DA; DAB; WLC**
See also CA 85-88; 25-28R; CANR 22; CDBLB 1914-1945; DLB 15; MTCW

**Waugh, Harriet** 1944- ............. **CLC 6**
See also CA 85-88; CANR 22

**Ways, C. R.**
See Blount, Roy (Alton), Jr.

**Waystaff, Simon**
See Swift, Jonathan

**Webb, (Martha) Beatrice (Potter)**
1858-1943 ................. **TCLC 22**
See also Potter, Beatrice
See also CA 117

**Webb, Charles (Richard)** 1939- ...... **CLC 7**
See also CA 25-28R

**Webb, James H(enry), Jr.** 1946- .... **CLC 22**
See also CA 81-84

**Webb, Mary (Gladys Meredith)**
1881-1927 ................. **TCLC 24**
See also CA 123; DLB 34

**Webb, Mrs. Sidney**
See Webb, (Martha) Beatrice (Potter)

**Webb, Phyllis** 1927- ............. **CLC 18**
See also CA 104; CANR 23; DLB 53

**Webb, Sidney (James)**
1859-1947 ................. **TCLC 22**
See also CA 117

**Webber, Andrew Lloyd** ............. **CLC 21**
See also Lloyd Webber, Andrew

**Weber, Lenora Mattingly**
1895-1971 ................. **CLC 12**
See also CA 19-20; 29-32R; CAP 1; SATA 2; SATA-Obit 26

**Webster, John** 1579(?)-1634(?) ....... **DC 2**
See also CDBLB Before 1660; DA; DAB; DLB 58; WLC

**Webster, Noah** 1758-1843 ....... **NCLC 30**

**Wedekind, (Benjamin) Frank(lin)**
1864-1918 ................. **TCLC 7**
See also CA 104; DLB 118

**Weidman, Jerome** 1913- ............ **CLC 7**
See also AITN 2; CA 1-4R; CANR 1; DLB 28

**Weil, Simone (Adolphine)**
1909-1943 ................. **TCLC 23**
See also CA 117

**Weinstein, Nathan**
See West, Nathanael

**Weinstein, Nathan von Wallenstein**
See West, Nathanael

**Weir, Peter (Lindsay)** 1944- ....... **CLC 20**
See also CA 113; 123

**Weiss, Peter (Ulrich)**
1916-1982 .............. **CLC 3, 15, 51**
See also CA 45-48; 106; CANR 3; DLB 69, 124

**Weiss, Theodore (Russell)**
1916- .................... **CLC 3, 8, 14**
See also CA 9-12R; CAAS 2; CANR 46; DLB 5

**Welch, (Maurice) Denton**
1915-1948 ................. **TCLC 22**
See also CA 121; 148

**Welch, James** 1940- ........ **CLC 6, 14, 52**
See also CA 85-88; CANR 42; NNAL

**Weldon, Fay**
1933- ........ **CLC 6, 9, 11, 19, 36, 59**
See also CA 21-24R; CANR 16, 46; CDBLB 1960 to Present; DLB 14; MTCW

**Wellek, Rene** 1903- .............. **CLC 28**
See also CA 5-8R; CAAS 7; CANR 8; DLB 63

**Weller, Michael** 1942- ......... **CLC 10, 53**
See also CA 85-88

**Weller, Paul** 1958- .............. **CLC 26**

**Wellershoff, Dieter** 1925- .......... **CLC 46**
See also CA 89-92; CANR 16, 37

**Welles, (George) Orson**
1915-1985 .............. **CLC 20, 80**
See also CA 93-96; 117

**Wellman, Mac** 1945- ............. **CLC 65**

**Wellman, Manly Wade** 1903-1986 .. **CLC 49**
See also CA 1-4R; 118; CANR 6, 16, 44; SATA 6; SATA-Obit 47

**Wells, Carolyn** 1869(?)-1942 ...... **TCLC 35**
See also CA 113; DLB 11

**Wells, H(erbert) G(eorge)**
1866-1946 ........ **TCLC 6, 12, 19; DA; DAB; SSC 6; WLC**
See also CA 110; 121; CDBLB 1914-1945; DLB 34, 70, 156; MTCW; SATA 20

**Wells, Rosemary** 1943- ............ **CLC 12**
See also AAYA 13; CA 85-88; CANR 48; CLR 16; MAICYA; SAAS 1; SATA 18, 69

**Welty, Eudora**
1909- ...... **CLC 1, 2, 5, 14, 22, 33; DA; DAB; SSC 1; WLC**
See also CA 9-12R; CABS 1; CANR 32; CDALB 1941-1968; DLB 2, 102, 143; DLBD 12; DLBY 87; MTCW

**Wen I-to** 1899-1946 ............. **TCLC 28**

**Wentworth, Robert**
See Hamilton, Edmond

**Werfel, Franz (V.)** 1890-1945 ...... **TCLC 8**
See also CA 104; DLB 81, 124

**Wergeland, Henrik Arnold**
1808-1845 ................. **NCLC 5**

**Wersba, Barbara** 1932- ............ **CLC 30**
See also AAYA 2; CA 29-32R; CANR 16, 38; CLR 3; DLB 52; JRDA; MAICYA; SAAS 2; SATA 1, 58

**Wertmueller, Lina** 1928- .......... **CLC 16**
See also CA 97-100; CANR 39

**Wescott, Glenway** 1901-1987 ....... **CLC 13**
See also CA 13-16R; 121; CANR 23; DLB 4, 9, 102

**Wesker, Arnold** 1932- .. **CLC 3, 5, 42; DAB**
See also CA 1-4R; CAAS 7; CANR 1, 33; CDBLB 1960 to Present; DLB 13; MTCW

**Wesley, Richard (Errol)** 1945- ....... **CLC 7**
See also BW 1; CA 57-60; CANR 27; DLB 38

**Wessel, Johan Herman** 1742-1785 .... **LC 7**

**West, Anthony (Panther)**
1914-1987 ................. **CLC 50**
See also CA 45-48; 124; CANR 3, 19; DLB 15

**West, C. P.**
See Wodehouse, P(elham) G(renville)

West, (Mary) Jessamyn
1902-1984 . . . . . . . . . . . . . . . . CLC 7, 17
See also CA 9-12R; 112; CANR 27; DLB 6;
DLBY 84; MTCW; SATA-Obit 37

West, Morris L(anglo) 1916- . . . . . CLC 6, 33
See also CA 5-8R; CANR 24, 49; MTCW

West, Nathanael
1903-1940 . . . . . TCLC 1, 14, 44; SSC 16
See also CA 104; 125; CDALB 1929-1941;
DLB 4, 9, 28; MTCW

West, Owen
See Koontz, Dean R(ay)

West, Paul 1930- . . . . . . . . . . . . . CLC 7, 14
See also CA 13-16R; CAAS 7; CANR 22;
DLB 14

West, Rebecca 1892-1983 . . CLC 7, 9, 31, 50
See also CA 5-8R; 109; CANR 19; DLB 36;
DLBY 83; MTCW

Westall, Robert (Atkinson)
1929-1993 . . . . . . . . . . . . . . . . . CLC 17
See also AAYA 12; CA 69-72; 141;
CANR 18; CLR 13; JRDA; MAICYA;
SAAS 2; SATA 23, 69; SATA-Obit 75

Westlake, Donald E(dwin)
1933- . . . . . . . . . . . . . . . . . . . CLC 7, 33
See also CA 17-20R; CAAS 13; CANR 16,
44

Westmacott, Mary
See Christie, Agatha (Mary Clarissa)

Weston, Allen
See Norton, Andre

Wetcheek, J. L.
See Feuchtwanger, Lion

Wetering, Janwillem van de
See van de Wetering, Janwillem

Wetherell, Elizabeth
See Warner, Susan (Bogert)

Whalen, Philip 1923- . . . . . . . . . . CLC 6, 29
See also CA 9-12R; CANR 5, 39; DLB 16

Wharton, Edith (Newbold Jones)
1862-1937 . . . . . . TCLC 3, 9, 27, 53; DA;
DAB; SSC 6; WLC
See also CA 104; 132; CDALB 1865-1917;
DLB 4, 9, 12, 78; MTCW

Wharton, James
See Mencken, H(enry) L(ouis)

Wharton, William (a pseudonym)
. . . . . . . . . . . . . . . . . . . . . . . . CLC 18, 37
See also CA 93-96; DLBY 80

Wheatley (Peters), Phillis
1754(?)-1784 . . . . LC 3; BLC; DA; PC 3;
WLC
See also CDALB 1640-1865; DLB 31, 50

Wheelock, John Hall 1886-1978 . . . . CLC 14
See also CA 13-16R; 77-80; CANR 14;
DLB 45

White, E(lwyn) B(rooks)
1899-1985 . . . . . . . . . . . . . CLC 10, 34, 39
See also AITN 2; CA 13-16R; 116;
CANR 16, 37; CLR 1, 21; DLB 11, 22;
MAICYA; MTCW; SATA 2, 29;
SATA-Obit 44

White, Edmund (Valentine III)
1940- . . . . . . . . . . . . . . . . . . . . . CLC 27
See also AAYA 7; CA 45-48; CANR 3, 19,
36; MTCW

White, Patrick (Victor Martindale)
1912-1990 . . CLC 3, 4, 5, 7, 9, 18, 65, 69
See also CA 81-84; 132; CANR 43; MTCW

White, Phyllis Dorothy James 1920-
See James, P. D.
See also CA 21-24R; CANR 17, 43; MTCW

White, T(erence) H(anbury)
1906-1964 . . . . . . . . . . . . . . . . . CLC 30
See also CA 73-76; CANR 37; JRDA;
MAICYA; SATA 12

White, Terence de Vere
1912-1994 . . . . . . . . . . . . . . . . . CLC 49
See also CA 49-52; 145; CANR 3

White, Walter F(rancis)
1893-1955 . . . . . . . . . . . . . . . . TCLC 15
See also White, Walter
See also BW 1; CA 115; 124; DLB 51

White, William Hale 1831-1913
See Rutherford, Mark
See also CA 121

Whitehead, E(dward) A(nthony)
1933- . . . . . . . . . . . . . . . . . . . . . . CLC 5
See also CA 65-68

Whitemore, Hugh (John) 1936- . . . . . CLC 37
See also CA 132

Whitman, Sarah Helen (Power)
1803-1878 . . . . . . . . . . . . . . . . NCLC 19
See also DLB 1

Whitman, Walt(er)
1819-1892 . . . . . NCLC 4, 31; DA; DAB;
PC 3; WLC
See also CDALB 1640-1865; DLB 3, 64;
SATA 20

Whitney, Phyllis A(yame) 1903- . . . . CLC 42
See also AITN 2; BEST 90:3; CA 1-4R;
CANR 3, 25, 38; JRDA; MAICYA;
SATA 1, 30

Whittemore, (Edward) Reed (Jr.)
1919- . . . . . . . . . . . . . . . . . . . . . . CLC 4
See also CA 9-12R; CAAS 8; CANR 4;
DLB 5

Whittier, John Greenleaf
1807-1892 . . . . . . . . . . . . . . . . . NCLC 8
See also CDALB 1640-1865; DLB 1

Whittlebot, Hernia
See Coward, Noel (Peirce)

Wicker, Thomas Grey 1926-
See Wicker, Tom
See also CA 65-68; CANR 21, 46

Wicker, Tom . . . . . . . . . . . . . . . . . . . CLC 7
See also Wicker, Thomas Grey

Wideman, John Edgar
1941- . . . . . . . . CLC 5, 34, 36, 67; BLC
See also BW 2; CA 85-88; CANR 14, 42;
DLB 33, 143

Wiebe, Rudy (Henry) 1934- . . . CLC 6, 11, 14
See also CA 37-40R; CANR 42; DLB 60

Wieland, Christoph Martin
1733-1813 . . . . . . . . . . . . . . . . NCLC 17
See also DLB 97

Wiene, Robert 1881-1938 . . . . . . . . TCLC 56

Wieners, John 1934- . . . . . . . . . . . . . CLC 7
See also CA 13-16R; DLB 16

Wiesel, Elie(zer)
1928- . . . . . . CLC 3, 5, 11, 37; DA; DAB
See also AAYA 7; AITN 1; CA 5-8R;
CAAS 4; CANR 8, 40; DLB 83;
DLBY 87; MTCW; SATA 56

Wiggins, Marianne 1947- . . . . . . . . . CLC 57
See also BEST 89:3; CA 130

Wight, James Alfred 1916-
See Herriot, James
See also CA 77-80; SATA 55;
SATA-Brief 44

Wilbur, Richard (Purdy)
1921- . . . . CLC 3, 6, 9, 14, 53; DA; DAB
See also CA 1-4R; CABS 2; CANR 2, 29;
DLB 5; MTCW; SATA 9

Wild, Peter 1940- . . . . . . . . . . . . . . . CLC 14
See also CA 37-40R; DLB 5

Wilde, Oscar (Fingal O'Flahertie Wills)
1854(?)-1900 . . . . TCLC 1, 8, 23, 41; DA;
DAB; SSC 11; WLC
See also CA 104; 119; CDBLB 1890-1914;
DLB 10, 19, 34, 57, 141, 156; SATA 24

Wilder, Billy . . . . . . . . . . . . . . . . . . . CLC 20
See also Wilder, Samuel
See also DLB 26

Wilder, Samuel 1906-
See Wilder, Billy
See also CA 89-92

Wilder, Thornton (Niven)
1897-1975 . . . . . . CLC 1, 5, 6, 10, 15, 35,
82; DA; DAB; DC 1; WLC
See also AITN 2; CA 13-16R; 61-64;
CANR 40; DLB 4, 7, 9; MTCW

Wilding, Michael 1942- . . . . . . . . . . CLC 73
See also CA 104; CANR 24, 49

Wiley, Richard 1944- . . . . . . . . . . . . CLC 44
See also CA 121; 129

Wilhelm, Kate . . . . . . . . . . . . . . . . . . CLC 7
See also Wilhelm, Katie Gertrude
See also CAAS 5; DLB 8

Wilhelm, Katie Gertrude 1928-
See Wilhelm, Kate
See also CA 37-40R; CANR 17, 36; MTCW

Wilkins, Mary
See Freeman, Mary Eleanor Wilkins

Willard, Nancy 1936- . . . . . . . . . . . CLC 7, 37
See also CA 89-92; CANR 10, 39; CLR 5;
DLB 5, 52; MAICYA; MTCW;
SATA 37, 71; SATA-Brief 30

Williams, C(harles) K(enneth)
1936- . . . . . . . . . . . . . . . . . . . CLC 33, 56
See also CA 37-40R; DLB 5

Williams, Charles
See Collier, James L(incoln)

Williams, Charles (Walter Stansby)
1886-1945 . . . . . . . . . . . . . . . . TCLC 1, 11
See also CA 104; DLB 100, 153

Williams, (George) Emlyn
1905-1987 . . . . . . . . . . . . . . . . . . CLC 15
See also CA 104; 123; CANR 36; DLB 10,
77; MTCW

Williams, Hugo 1942- . . . . . . . . . . . . CLC 42
See also CA 17-20R; CANR 45; DLB 40

Williams, J. Walker
See Wodehouse, P(elham) G(renville)

# Literary Criticism Series
# Cumulative Topic Index

This index lists all topic entries in Gale's *Classical and Medieval Literature Criticism, Contemporary Literary Criticism, Literature Criticism from 1400 to 1800, Nineteenth-Century Literature Criticism,* and *Twentieth-Century Literary Criticism.*

Topic Index

*Topic Index*

# *LC* Cumulative Nationality Index

# *LC* Cumulative Title Index

Title Index

"The 21th: and last booke of the Ocean to Scinthia" (Raleigh) **31**:265, 271-80, 282-4, 286-8
"The 23rd Psalme" (Herbert) **24**:274-75
*XCVI Sermons* (Andrewes) **5**:19, 22-5, 28, 33, 41
"A Chaulieu" (Rousseau) **9**:344
"A Chretophle de Choiseul" (Ronsard) **6**:433
"A Courtin" (Rousseau) **9**:343-44
"A de Lannoy" (Rousseau) **9**:345
"A Denyse sorciere" (Ronsard) **6**:430
"A Gui Peccate Prieur de Sougé" (Ronsard) **6**:437
"A Guillaume Des Autels" (Ronsard) **6**:433
"A Janne impitoyable" (Ronsard) **6**:419
"A Jean de Morel" (Ronsard) **6**:433
"A la fontaine Bellerie" (Ronsard) **6**:419, 430
"A la paix" (Rousseau) **9**:344
"A la reine sur sa bien-venüe en France" (Malherbe)
  See "Ode à Marie de Médicis, sur sa Bienvenue en France"
"A la reyne mère sur les heureux succez de sa régence" (Malherbe)
  See "Ode pour la Reine Mère du Roy pendant sa Régence"
"A l'ambassadeur de Venise" (Rousseau) **9**:344
"A l'empereur, après la conclusion de la quadruple alliance" (Rousseau) **9**:344
"A l'impératrice Amélie" (Rousseau) **9**:343
"A M. de Grimani" (Rousseau) **9**:340
*A Mme Denis nièce de l'auteur, la vie de Paris et de Versailles* (Voltaire) **14**:390
"A Monseigneur le Duc de Bellegarde, grand escuyer de France" (Malherbe) **5**:184
"A Philippe de Vendôme" (Rousseau) **9**:344
"A Philomèle" (Rousseau) **9**:345
"A Pierre L'Escot" (Ronsard) **6**:433

"A Robert de La Haye, Conseiller du Roi en son Parlement à Paris" (Ronsard) **6**:433
"A sa Muse" (Ronsard) **6**:430
"A son ame" (Ronsard) **6**:436
"A son livre" (Ronsard) **6**:425-27, 433-34
"A' the Airts" (Burns)
  See "Of A' the Airts"
"A une jeune veuve" (Rousseau)
  See "A une veuve"
"A une veuve" ("A une jeune veuve") (Rousseau) **9**:340, 344
"A Zinzindorf" (Rousseau)
  See "Ode au comte de Sinzendorff"
"Aaron" (Herbert) **24**:237
"Abbatis Eurditae" (Erasmus) **16**:128
"Abbot and the Learned Lady" (Erasmus) **16**:123, 142, 193
*L'abbrégé de l'art poétique françois (Art Poétique)* (Ronsard) **6**:406, 419, 427
*L'A.B.C.* (Voltaire) **14**:405
*Abdelazer; or, The Moor's Revenge* (Behn) **1**:28, 33, 39; **30**:67, 70-1, 77, 81
*Abecedarium Naturae* (Bacon) **18**:187
"Abel's blood" (Vaughan) **27**:300, 377-79
*Der abenteuerliche Simplicissimus, Teutsch, das hist: Die Beschreibun dess Lebens eines seltzamen Vaganten, gennant Melchio Sternfels von Fuchsheim (Simplician Writings)* (Grimmelshausen) **6**:235-48, 252
*Der abentheuerliche, wunderbare und unerhörte Ritter Hopffen-sack (Hopffen-Sack)* (Beer) **5**:54-5
*Abhandlung von der Nachahmung (On Imitation)* (Schlegel) **5**:274, 282-83
*Abhandlung von der Unähnlichkeit in der Nachahmung* (Schlegel) **5**:274
*Abode of Spring* (Jami)
  See *Baháristán*

"Abra; or, The Georgian Sultana" (Collins) **4**:210
*Abridgements of the History of Rome and England* (Goldsmith) **2**:71
*Abridgment of English History* (Burke)
  See *An Essay towards an Abridgement of the English History*
*Absalom and Achitophel* (Dryden) **3**:180, 185, 187, 189-92, 199, 201, 205, 213, 216-22, 225, 228, 231, 234, 240-43, 246; **21**:51, 53-7, 64-5, 86-7, 90-1, 94, 101-03, 111-13
*Absalom's Hair* (Calderon de la Barca)
  See *Los cabellos de Absalón*
*Absalom's Locks* (Calderon de la Barca) **23**:64
"Absolute Retreat" (Winchilsea)
  See "The Petition for an Absolute Retreat"
*Acajou et Zirphile* (Duclos) **1**:185, 187
*An Accidence; or, The Path-Way to Experience (A Sea Grammar)* (Smith) **9**:381-82
*The Accomplish'd Rake; or, Modern Fine Gentleman* (Davys) **1**:99-100
*An Account of a Battel between the Ancient and Modern Books in St. James's Library* (Swift)
  See *A Tale of a Tub, Written for the Universal Improvement of Mankind, to Which is Added an Account of a Battel between the Ancient and Modern Books in St. James's Library*
*An Account of Corsica, The Journal of a Tour to that Island; and the Memoirs of Pascal Paoli (Memoirs of Pascal Paoli; Tour of Corsica)* (Boswell) **4**:16, 25, 31, 33, 60, 71, 77-8
"An Account of the English Poets" (Addison) **18**:6, 16, 38-9, 41, 61
"Account of the Ensuing Poem" (Dryden) **21**:90
*The Account of the Fish Pool* (Steele) **18**:354

485

Title Index

Title Index

Title Index

Title Index

Title Index

Title Index

Title Index

Title Index

Title Index

Title Index

Title Index

Title Index

557

ISBN 0-8103-9276-3

90000